HANDBOOK OF LANGUAGE AND LITERACY

CHALLENGES IN LANGUAGE AND LITERACY

Kenn Apel, Barbara J. Ehren, Elaine R. Silliman,
and C. Addison Stone, *Series Editors*

HANDBOOK OF LANGUAGE AND LITERACY

Development and Disorders

Edited by
C. ADDISON STONE
ELAINE R. SILLIMAN
BARBARA J. EHREN
KENN APEL

THE GUILFORD PRESS
New York   London

© 2004 The Guilford Press
A Division of Guilford Publications, Inc.
72 Spring Street, New York, NY 10012
www.guilford.com

Paperback edition 2006

Printed in the United States of America

This book is printed on acid-free paper.

Last digit is print number: 9 8 7 6 5 4 3

Library of Congress Cataloging-in-Publication Data available from the Publisher.

ISBN 1-59385-005-0 (hc)   ISBN 1-59385-286-X (pbk)

About the Editors

C. Addison Stone, PhD, is Professor and Chair of Educational Studies in the School of Education at the University of Michigan. Prior to joining the Michigan faculty, Dr. Stone was Professor and Head of the Learning Disabilities Program, Department of Communication Sciences and Disorders, at Northwestern University. He received his PhD in developmental psychology from the University of Chicago. Dr. Stone's research interests center on cognitive and language development in children with learning disabilities and specific language impairment and on the social context of atypical children's learning and development. His current research focuses on parent and teacher perceptions of children with learning problems and on the interplay between such perceptions and the quality of adult–child interactions. Dr. Stone has published more than 50 articles, chapters, and books on topics related to normal and atypical development. He recently completed a 6-year term as chair of the Research Committee for the Council of Exceptional Children's Division for Learning Disabilities. He has served as coeditor of *Learning Disabilities Research and Practice* and is on the editorial boards of several other journals in the field.

Elaine R. Silliman, PhD, CCC-SLP, is Professor of Communication Sciences and Disorders (CSD) and Cognitive and Neural Sciences at the University of South Florida, where she is also Director of the PhD program in CSD. She received her PhD in speech and hearing science, with an emphasis on developmental psychology, at the Graduate Center of the City University of New York. Dr. Silliman is a Fellow of the American Speech–Language–Hearing Association (ASHA) and the International Academy for Research on Learning Disabilities; a past editor of the ASHA journal, *Language, Speech, and Hearing Services in Schools;* a past coordinator of the ASHA special interest division, Language Learning and Education; and an initial member of the Specialty Board on Child Language. Her research interests and publications focus on oral language–literacy connections in monolingual English-speaking children with social dialect variations, bilingual (Spanish–English) children, and children with language learning disabilities. Dr. Silliman has published more than 30 articles, chapters, and books related to language learning disabilities and the language basis of literacy. She serves on the editorial boards of *Topics in Language Disorders* and *Language, Speech, and Hearing Services in Schools.*

Barbara J. Ehren, EdD, CCC-SLP, is a research associate at the University of Kansas Center for Research on Learning. Her research and development work focuses on adolescent literacy, with an emphasis on the integration of the Strategic Instruction Model at the school level and on the shared responsibility of a variety of professionals for content literacy. Dr. Ehren has spent half her career in the schools, serving in several capacities including speech–language pathologist, classroom teacher, and district administrator in both special and general education. She is a Fellow of the American Speech–Language–Hearing Association (ASHA) and currently serves on the steering committee for Language Learning and Education (ASHA Division 1). She is also on the editorial boards of *Language, Speech, and Hearing Services in Schools* and *Communication Disorders Quarterly* and was an editor of a recent volume of *Seminars in Speech and Language* on literacy intervention for speech–language pathologists.

Kenn Apel, PhD, CCC-SLP, is Professor in the Department of Communication Disorders at Florida State University and a Fellow of the American Speech–Language–Hearing Association. His research and teaching interests are in typical and atypical language–literacy development, with a specific focus on reading and spelling. Dr. Apel is a former associate editor of *Language, Speech, and Hearing Services in Schools* and has served as a guest editor for that journal and for *Topics in Language Disorders*. He has authored or coauthored numerous peer-reviewed articles, books, and book chapters, as well as software programs and the spelling instructional curriculum SPELL-Links to Reading and Writing.

Contributors

Kenn Apel, PhD, CCC-SLP, Department of Communication Disorders, Florida State University, Tallahassee, Florida

Laura L. Bailet, PhD, Division of Neurology, Nemours Children's Clinic, Jacksonville, Florida

Anthony S. Bashir, PhD, Disability Services Office, Emerson College, Boston, Massachusetts

Kathryn M. Bell, PhD, Department of Educational Theory and Practice, West Virginia University, Morgantown, West Virginia

Virginia W. Berninger, PhD, Department of Educational Psychology, University of Washington, Seattle, Washington

Maria R. Brea-Spahn, MS, Departments of Psychology and Communication Sciences and Disorders, University of South Florida, Tampa, Florida

Bonnie Brinton, PhD, Office of Graduate Studies, Brigham Young University, Provo, Utah

Robert C. Calfee, PhD, Graduate School of Education, University of California–Riverside, Riverside, California

Joanne F. Carlisle, PhD, Educational Studies Program, School of Education, University of Michigan, Ann Arbor, Michigan

Marie Cassar, PhD, Department of Psychology, Indiana University, Bloomington, Indiana

Nancy Clark-Chiarelli, PhD, Education Development Center, Newton, Massachusetts

David H. Cooper, PhD, Department of Special Education, University of Maryland, College Park, Maryland

Holly K. Craig, PhD, Center for the Development of Language and Learning, University of Michigan, Ann Arbor, Michigan

Donald D. Deshler, PhD, Center for Research on Learning, University of Kansas, Lawrence, Kansas

David K. Dickinson, EdD, Lynch School of Education, Boston College, Chestnut Hill, Massachusetts

Mavis L. Donahue, EdD, Department of Special Education, University of Illinois at Chicago, Chicago, Illinois

Judith Felson Duchan, PhD, Communicative Disorders and Sciences, State University of New York at Buffalo, Buffalo, New York

Nell K. Duke, EdD, College of Education, Michigan State University, East Lansing, Michigan

Barbara J. Ehren, EdD, CCC-SLP, Center for Research on Learning, University of Kansas, Lawrence, Kansas

Linnea C. Ehri, PhD, Program in Educational Psychology, Graduate Center of the City University of New York, New York, New York

Sharon K. Foster, MS, CCC-SLP, Department of Special Education, University of Illinois at Chicago, Chicago, Illinois

Martin Fujiki, PhD, School of Education, Brigham Young University, Provo, Utah

Jeffrey W. Gilger, PhD, Department of Child Development, California State University, Los Angeles, California

Jennifer S. Hendrickson, PhD, Wake County Public Schools, Raleigh, North Carolina

Arturo E. Hernandez, PhD, Department of Psychology, University of Houston, Houston, Texas

Katherine Hilden, BA, College of Education, Michigan State University, East Lansing, Michigan

Janette Klingner, PhD, College of Education, University of Colorado at Boulder, Boulder, Colorado

B. Keith Lenz, PhD, Center for Research on Learning, University of Kansas, Lawrence, Kansas

Julie J. Masterson, PhD, Department of Communication Sciences and Disorders, Southwest Missouri State University, Springfield, Missouri

Allyssa McCabe, PhD, Department of Psychology, University of Massachusetts, Lowell, Massachusetts

Karla K. McGregor, PhD, Communication Sciences and Disorders, Northwestern University, Evanston, Illinois

Gayane Meschyan, PhD, Department of Psychology, Carnegie Mellon University, Pittsburgh, Pennsylvania

Maria Mody, PhD, Department of Radiology, Massachusetts General Hospital and Harvard Medical School, Boston, Massachusetts

Nicole L. Niessen, PhD, South Kansas Allied Health Program, Wichita, Kansas

Rollanda E. O'Connor, PhD, Department of Instruction and Learning, University of Pittsburgh, Pittsburgh, Pennsylvania

Michael Pressley, PhD, College of Education, Michigan State University, East Lansing, Michigan

Melinda S. Rice, PhD, Department of Education, Elon University, Elon, North Carolina

Froma P. Roth, PhD, Department of Hearing and Speech Sciences, University of Maryland, College Park, Maryland

Cheryl M. Scott, PhD, Department of Communication Disorders and Sciences, Rush University Medical Center, Chicago, Illinois

Elaine R. Silliman, PhD, CCC-SLP, Department of Communication Sciences and Disorders, University of South Florida, Tampa, Florida

Bonnie D. Singer, PhD, Innovative Learning Partners, Boston, Massachusetts

Margaret J. Snowling, PhD (DipClinPsych), Department of Psychology, University of York, York, United Kingdom

Deborah L. Speece, PhD, Department of Special Education, University of Maryland, College Park, Maryland

C. Addison Stone, PhD, School of Education, University of Michigan, Ann Arbor, Michigan

Rebecca Treiman, PhD, Psychology Department, Washington University, St. Louis, Missouri

Gary A. Troia, PhD, College of Education, University of Washington, Seattle, Washington

Anne van Kleeck, PhD, Department of Communication Sciences and Disorders, University of Georgia, Athens, Georgia

Sharon Vaughn, PhD, Department of Special Education, University of Texas at Austin, Austin, Texas

Julie A. Washington, PhD, Center for the Development of Language and Literacy, University of Michigan, Ann Arbor, Michigan

Barbara Hanna Wasik, PhD, School of Education, University of North Carolina, Chapel Hill, North Carolina

Carol Westby, PhD, Center for Family and Community Partnerships, University of New Mexico, Albuquerque, New Mexico

Louise C. Wilkinson, EdD, School of Education, Syracuse University, Syracuse, New York

Kathleen M. Wilson, PhD, Department of Teaching, Learning, and Teacher Education, University of Nebraska, Lincoln, Nebraska

Susan E. Wise, PhD, Department of Communication Sciences and Disorders, Northwestern University, Evanston, Illinois

Bernice Y. L. Wong, EdD, PhD, Faculty of Education, Simon Fraser University, Burnaby, British Columbia, Canada

Liliana Barro Zecker, PhD, Department of Teacher Education, DePaul University, Chicago, Illinois

Preface

This handbook is one of the first volumes in the new Guilford series Challenges in Language and Literacy. In developing the *Handbook*, it was our hope that it would embody many of the themes of the series, which aims to integrate interdisciplinary perspectives on language and literacy with empirically based principles and procedures for promoting effective learning outcomes in diverse students. The series is based on the premise that oral and written language skills are functionally intertwined in individual development. Understanding the complexity of this relationship requires the collaborative contributions of scholars and practitioners from multiple disciplines. The series focuses on typical and atypical language and literacy development from the preschool years to young adulthood. The goal is to provide informative, timely resources for a broad audience, including practitioners, scholars, and students in the fields of language science and disorders, educational psychology, general education, special education, and learning disabilities.

In developing our plan for the *Handbook*, we had three purposes in mind. First, we wanted the content to provide researchers, professionals, and graduate students with state-of-the-art knowledge regarding theory and research focused on linkages between spoken language development and typical and atypical literacy development. The integration of language and literacy has become an increasing focus within both the field of education and the field of speech–language pathology. Despite this converging set of emphases, few resources are currently available that incorporate these issues into a single volume. We hope that this book helps to fill that gap.

Our second aim in developing the *Handbook* was to offer a comprehensive examination of the empirical evidence on the integration of language-related processes with literacy instruction and its outcomes. All too often, literacy instruction takes place in a manner suggestive, consciously or unconsciously, of the independence of the processes of language and reading/ writing. It is our conviction that such an approach misses rich opportunities to improve the effectiveness of educational efforts.

Our third aim was to emphasize the benefits of a multidisciplinary approach to the study of language and literacy. In designing the *Handbook*, we have assembled contributors with multiple perspectives from the disciplines of language science and disorders, special education, and cognitive and educational psychology, among others, to address the complex issues surrounding the dynamic interactions among language processes and typical and atypical literacy development. This combination embodies our joint conviction that progress cannot be made in our understanding of the complex issues related to fostering literacy development without taking a multidisciplinary and interdisciplinary perspective.

The *Handbook* contains four major sections. Part I provides a critical overview of major theoretical and methodological approaches to the study of language and literacy acquisition, with a particular emphasis on developmental variations and underlying neurobiological and genetic correlates of atypical development. In Part II, variations in the sociocultural and sociolinguistic contexts of language and literacy acquisition are explored, including normative development and developmental variation. Part III examines the multiple components of the linguistic/discourse system and their relationships to successful and unsuccessful literacy learning. Part IV is devoted to an examination of the language and literacy profiles that characterize children, adolescents, and young adults struggling with word recognition, reading comprehension, writing, and spelling, and reviews the research-based evidence for effective practices in assessment and instruction/intervention.

We trust that readers of this book, whether they are students, researchers, or practitioners in literacy, special education, or speech–language pathology, will find in it the rich food for thought that provokes the kind of breakthroughs in basic knowledge and effective practice that served as the impetus for the book. We hope it will also serve to stimulate more conversations across the disciplinary and subdisciplinary boundaries that have historically characterized the academic study of these issues, as well as the provision of educational and clinical services to those who need them.

Any project on the scale of this handbook could not come to fruition without the assistance of a number of people in addition to the main editors. We were fortunate in being able to work with a fine group of associates. We would especially like to express our thanks to Brian Shulman. Brian was a founding member of the editorial team for both the *Handbook* and the broader series of which it is a part. He was instrumental in the conceptualization of this volume and assisted with the review of several manuscripts. Unfortunately, his increasing administrative responsibilities forced him to step down from his editorial duties. Although he is no longer a member of our team, his hand is still evident in this volume. We would also like to express our warm gratitude to Rochelle Serwator, our editor at The Guilford Press. Rochelle has kept our group inspired and on track, and neither the *Handbook* nor the series would exist without her encouragement and guidance. One other person whose participation has been indispensable is Jeanne Federico. Jeanne was a meticulous and tireless reader of many of the manuscripts, and she saved us from numerous editorial glitches. Finally, we would like to thank the authors of the chapters in this volume for their dedication and scholarship, and for their openness to crafting their ideas into the format dictated by the *Handbook*'s structure. We hope that their work receives the attention it justly deserves.

C. Addison Stone
Elaine R. Silliman
Barbara J. Ehren
Kenn Apel

Contents

HANDBOOK OF LANGUAGE AND LITERACY

I

THEORETICAL AND METHODOLOGICAL ISSUES IN THE STUDY OF LANGUAGE AND LITERACY DISORDERS

INTRODUCTION

This section provides a critical overview of selected theoretical and methodological approaches to the study of language and literacy acquisition, with a particular emphasis on applications to developmental variation and disability. Because issues of social context are the focus of Part II, several of the chapters in Part I pay particular attention to theory and research related to cognitive and neurological processes. However, both the first and the last chapter of this section also include treatment of the sociocontextual perspective.

In Chapter 1, Addison Stone provides an analysis of the "theoretical landscape" populated by language and literacy scholars and professionals. Stone characterizes the field of language and literacy as consisting of two major traditions, the cognitive science and sociocultural perspectives. He analyses the basic assumptions and methodologies adopted by these perspectives, pointing out potential strengths and limitations of each. He then points to what he sees as unnecessarily divisive rhetoric in the realms of research, practice, and policy and makes an argument for the crucial need to integrate the insights of these perspectives into a unified vision for research and practice.

The next two chapters in Part I deal with basic issues related to the neurobiology of language and learning, with particular emphasis on atypical children. In Chapter 2, Jeffrey Gilger and Susan Wise discuss current research methods and the resulting evidence regarding the genetic basis of language and literacy disabilities. They conclude from their analysis that there is considerable evidence for a genetic contribution to such disabilities, although they stress the complex polygenic nature of that contribution. Another important contribution of the chapter is the authors' discussion of the subtleties involved in conceptualizing the interplay between the genetic substrate and the experiential contributions to the expression of that substrate in the development of language and literacy.

In Chapter 3, Maria Mody looks in detail at the evidence regarding the neurological substrate for language and literacy. She begins with an argument for the close connection between language and literacy processes and then provides an accessible but authoritative overview of neuroimaging technologies, stressing the differential utility of various techniques for highlighting particular phenomena. With these issues as a backdrop, Mody devotes careful attention to an analysis of how neuroimaging is shedding light on the basic auditory, linguistic, and visual processes involved in learning to read and write.

Chapter 4, written by Gayane Meschyan and Arturo Hernandez, continues the focus on cognitive/linguistic processes emphasized by Mody. However, the emphasis here shifts from methodology rooted in neurobiology to the behavioral methodology of the cognitive tradition. In addition, Meschyan and Hernandez focus primarily on the question of learning a second language rather than a native language. The authors review recent research on the role of phonological processing in language learning, with particular emphasis on the ease of establishing accurate phonological representations of novel language sounds. They present preliminary evidence pointing to the role of individual differences in "phonological ability" as a predictor of the ease of mastering a first or second language, whether oral and written.

As is apparent, we hope, in our descriptions of the preceding chapters, issues of research methodology are an important secondary theme in all the chapters. In Chapter 5, however, Deborah Speece and David Cooper focus more squarely on methodology. Their particular interest is in methods for the study of language and literacy variation in the preschool and early elementary years. In their discussion, they compare the relative merits of four alternative methods for identifying children who are at risk for language and literacy mastery. The authors emphasize the need to incorporate issues of context into research on language and literacy processes, as well as the need for multi-method research models. One interesting feature of their analysis is their parallel emphasis on technical issues of validity and the issue of the social/political consequences of using particular research designs. In the words of the authors, "Much can be inferred about investigators' *values* by the models they test and the domains of variables they choose to include and exclude" (p. 89).

As a whole, the chapters in this section raise a number of important issues regarding the relative benefits of alternative theoretical and methodological approaches to the study of typical and atypical development of language and literacy. As such, the chapters provide an important context for those that follow.

1

Contemporary Approaches to the Study of Language and Literacy Development

A Call for the Integration of Perspectives

C. Addison Stone

The study of language and literacy acquisition has not been without its periods of turmoil. Chomsky's (1959) challenge to the empiricist perspective on language learning is a classic example. The cyclically recurring debates about the virtues of phonics-based versus meaning-driven approaches to literacy instruction represent another salient example (Allington & Woodside-Jiron, 1999; Foorman, Fletcher, Francis, & Schatschneider, 2000; Mathes & Torgesen, 2000; Taylor, Anderson, Au, & Raphael, 2000). We seem at present to be in the midst of yet another turbulent period—a period in which cognitive-processing views of language and literacy are pitted against sociocultural views in the arenas of scholarship, practice, and policy. As with past debates, the current debate has become highly politicized. In the present-day United States, federal legislation and the accompanying regulations include specifications for sanctioned approaches to literacy research and instruction (Feuer, Towne, & Shavelson, 2002; No Child Left Behind Act of 2001; Shavelson & Towne, 2002). At the same time, the tenor of academic discussions regarding literacy instruction has been infused with sociopolitical critiques focused on issues such as class privilege or racism, as well as the proper arenas and approaches for fostering greater literacy (Delpit, 1995; Ogbu, 1999).

Of particular relevance to the current chapter is the fact that these discussions and policy recommendations are all too often couched in a binary or exclusionary rhetoric. Stakeholders are urged to "take sides" or to engage in practices consistent with one approach or the other. In such times, it is particularly important to stand back and gain some perspective on the underlying issues. A major purpose of this chapter is to provide an occasion for such perspective taking. In the discussion to follow, I summarize the fundamental assumptions underlying current approaches to the study of language and literacy, highlighting major points of concurrence and divergence. Following this discussion, I consider implications for how we may engage in fruitful research and practice, and I emphasize the importance of integrating perspectives, if we are to gain a full understanding of language and literacy competencies.

This chapter consists of three major sections. In the first section, I paint the theoretical landscape with a broad brush, making a case for the analysis of current debates in terms of the juxtaposition of two competing perspectives on language and literacy: the cognitive science and sociocultural perspectives. I characterize each of these perspectives in terms of its core metaphors and also highlight significant variations within each perspective. In the second section, I consider a number of central questions about the nature of language and literacy acquisition from the vantage points of these two perspectives. Included in the list are questions of definition ("What is literacy?" and "How do we conceptualize variation in literacy skills across individuals?"), questions of methodology ("What are promising approaches to research?"), and questions of practice ("How should we assess literacy?" and "What are fruitful approaches to prevention/intervention?"). As I consider these questions, I compare and contrast responses offered either explicitly or implicitly by adherents of the two broad perspectives.

In the third and final section, I return to a discussion of the current debates, and to possible reconciliations between the two perspectives on language and literacy. I argue in the context of that discussion that both perspectives have made significant contributions to our understanding of language and literacy, and that we cannot afford to ignore either perspective. Thus, I consider how we can combine theoretical and methodological resources to address pressing issues in the study of typical and atypical language and literacy development. As one possible avenue for an integration of perspectives, I consider recent advances in theory and research that either call explicitly for integration (e.g., dynamic systems theory; Thelen & Smith, 1998) or that embody such integration implicitly (e.g., the instructional research of Brown and Campione, 1994). I also point to an interesting example of the early theoretical work of Vygotsky (1993) and Luria (1973) regarding the interplay between cognitive process and sociocultural activity.

It is my hope that the chapter as a whole provides a useful context within which to consider the issues raised in the various chapters in this volume. In addition, I hope

to provide a challenge for the future, a challenge to researchers, practitioners, and policymakers, to explore ways in which an integration of perspectives can provide a richer and more productive approach to issues of language and literacy development and diversity.

THE THEORETICAL LANDSCAPE

Although my focus in this chapter is on language and literacy, it is important to recognize that approaches to the study of language and literacy rest squarely within a broader set of issues related to human learning and performance. Even if one believes, for example, that language learning is somehow special relative to other domains of learning (i.e., that language is a "natural" human capability), one still tends to talk about issues of learning and performing in other knowledge domains in ways that bear similarity to those used to address issues in the domain of language. A scholar who tends to emphasize the active, constructive role of the individual learner in mastering verb forms, for example, also tends to emphasize individual mastery when talking about, for example, the child's concept of gravity, even though perhaps acknowledging differential contributions from experience. Similarly, if one tends to emphasize participation in social practices when talking about the acquisition of adult patterns of verb usage, one also tends to emphasize social participation when talking about the child's emerging concept of gravity.[1]

Thus, even in a discussion focused specifically on language and literacy, if we are to understand current debates in the field, it is important to consider broader issues of theoretical perspectives, including the defining metaphors that inform and shape our thinking across multiple lines of inquiry. In this section, I contrast two broad perspectives that have played, and continue to play, central roles in the study of human learning and performance. I then look briefly at how these perspectives have been instantiated in the study of language and literacy. As I do so, I discuss the work of representative theorists and researchers to illustrate current manifestations of these perspectives, and I consider possible reasons for the all-too-common absence of productive communication across perspectives.

Two Perspectives on Human Learning and Performance

Over the course of the last decade, it has become increasingly common to distinguish between two broad perspectives on the conceptualization of human capabilities (see, e.g., Anderson, Greeno, Reder, & Simon, 2000; Sfard, 1998). These perspectives have been much discussed, and they have been variously labeled. In this discussion, I refer to them as the cognitive science and sociocultural perspectives. Although I focus in the following discussion for the most part on contemporary theories and research, it is important to emphasize that these two perspectives, in their various guises and labels, have a long history in the fields of education, linguistics, and psychology. Thus, I am discussing "contemporary" perspectives only in the sense that I am focused on the current manifestations of, and current labels for, these perspectives.

The distinction between these broad theoretical perspectives can be rhetorically useful for scholarly exposition. In addition, I hope to show that it can also be useful for an appreciation of the underlying dynamics of policy debates. However, such dichotomies are not without risks of oversimplification and distortion. As I indicate below, each perspective is actually a family of perspectives. Although "family members" share certain features, those features are only partially overlapping, and certain features are shared with members of other families. I try to highlight such complexity, but I also try to highlight the underlying within-perspective features that serve to explain, at least in part, the complex nature of current controversies and gaps in scholarship and policy regarding language and literacy.

The cognitive science and sociocultural perspectives each represent attempts to build a comprehensive and coherent account of human capabilities.[2] They differ, however, in how they conceptualize the fun-

damental nature of the processes involved. Both perspectives are concerned with what it means to know something, how one comes to know something, how best to teach something to someone, and how best to conceptualize specific manifestations of knowing something. As I hope to demonstrate, however, the two perspectives differ in how they respond to each of these challenges.

The vast majority of theorists working on issues related to language and literacy operate explicitly or implicitly within either the cognitive science or the sociocultural tradition; however, it is also important to emphasize two qualifications to this picture. First, there are actually significant variations within traditions; thus, in actuality each perspective represents a spectrum of "subtheories." These subtheories themselves often acquire labels that may at times obscure family relationships. Within the cognitive science tradition, for example, one can identify adherents of information processing, connectionism, or constructivism, among others. Within the sociocultural tradition, one can identify adherents of sociolinguistics, social constructivism, participation theory, or critical theory. Second, although I consider in the following paragraphs the central features characterizing the two traditions as they relate to conceptions of language and literacy, in summarizing these points I also acknowledge points of contact or overlap of these perspectives.

The Cognitive Science Perspective

Although the term "cognitive science" appears to have originated in the 1970s (Dawson, 1998; Gardner, 1985), the roots of the perspective (variously labeled) can be traced back to 19th-century studies of individual differences in perceptual skills.[3] Howard Gardner (1985) provided an early but still useful characterization of this perspective. Gardner defined cognitive science as "a contemporary, empirically based effort to answer long-standing epistemological questions—particularly those concerned with the nature of knowledge, its components, its sources, its development, and its deployment" (p. 6). He identified five main features of cognitive science, but the first three seem particularly central. The first feature is the assumption that mental representations are an important theoretical building block for a theory of human performance. The second feature involves the assumption that "the computer serves as the most viable model of how the human mind functions" (p. 6). Gardner's third defining feature of cognitive science was the assumption that an analysis of affect, historical and cultural factors, and the context in which particular actions or thoughts occur was of secondary importance in the development of a model of human knowledge.

Within the cognitive science tradition, four theoretical variations—information processing, connectionism, constructivism, and modularity—have played a prominent role in the study of language and literacy. All four variations share assumptions concerning the importance of the individual as a processor of input from the environment. They also share assumptions concerning system constraints on the nature and quantity of information that can be processed. They differ, however, in the importance they place on the role of abstract representations or rule systems in the learning of language, and in their assumptions concerning the relative importance of experience versus innate programming in language and literacy acquisition.

In their study of language and literacy, information-processing theorists emphasize capacity and/or timing constraints in comprehension and/or production. Emphasis is placed on the role of perceptual and memory processes in higher level activity, and on the importance of building higher level strategies to manage lower level information. Limitations of phonological processing, for example, are seen as significant determinants of developmental and individual differences in language comprehension and word-recognition skills (e.g., Leonard, 1998; Torgesen, 1999). Difficulties with higher level comprehension are seen as due to a restricted repertoire of strategies and to limitations in background knowledge. When information-processing theorists turn their attention to issues of instruction, they emphasize the need to build basic process-

ing skills through structured skill building and extensive practice for automaticity (e.g., Rayner, Foorman, Perfetti, Pesetsky, & Seidenberg, 2001). In addition, they often emphasize the need to teach conscious strategies for organizing lower level information (e.g., Swanson, 1993).

Like information-processing models, connectionist models emphasize constraints on the processing of information, and experience-driven reorganization of lower level behavior into more complex patterns. In contrast to information-processing models, however, connectionist theorists argue against the need to postulate abstract rule systems to explain emerging regularities in language use. Instead, they emphasize how qualitative change and higher level organization can emerge from the repatterning of lower level systems (Elman et al., 1996). Connectionists tend to stress the crucial difference between their "single-level" model of information processing and the dual-level models characteristic of traditional information processing; that is, connectionists tend to deemphasize the role of an "executive system" that regulates information processing. However, not all cognitive scientists agree that the differences between traditional information processing models and connectionist models are fundamental ones (e.g., Dawson, 1998; Plunkett, 1995). Dawson (1998), for example, argues that connectionist networks embody the very logical rules highlighted more explicitly in traditional information-processing models, and that a full account of a connectionist model requires specification of this network structure. Similarly, Elman et al. (1996) acknowledge that the so-called "hidden units" present in the majority of current connectionist models are, in essence, abstract representations.

Information-processing and connectionist theorists emphasize the role of experience in shaping learning, and they conceptualize development in terms of the reorganization and automatization of behavior patterns. As a result, they tend to treat learning and development as comparable processes. In contrast to these views, constructivists tend to emphasize a distinction between learning, conceived of as the reorganization of localized mastery, and development, conceived of as systematized hierarchies of knowledge. Constructivists also emphasize that the learner is an active explorer of the environment and a seeker of understanding, whereas information-processing and connectionist theorists tend to present a relatively passive view of the learner as an integrator of received information. For the former group of theorists, the learner seeks and even orchestrates experiences, which are then used to confirm or modify existing understandings; for the latter, experiences tend to be seen as impinging on the learner, whose cognitive apparatus registers them and, as a result, makes automatic adjustments in connections and certainty levels. When the constructivist model is applied to the study of language and literacy acquisition, the view that emerges is one of the child as actively organizing input and constructing generalized understandings about language structure and patterns of use (e.g., Nelson, 1996). Contrary to the sociocultural tradition, however, the emphasis here is primarily on a process of individual knowledge construction and abstract representations, rather than on socially mediated activity.

One feature common to the majority of cognitive science models discussed earlier is the assumption that relatively little higher level knowledge is innate. Instead, these models tend to emphasize how a set of lower level learning mechanisms leads to the emergence of higher level concepts and/or rule-governed behavior. This position is particularly characteristic of connectionism (Elman et al., 1996), but most proponents of constructivism and information processing share it as well. In contrast, modularity or constraint theorists tend to emphasize innate constraints on cognitive processing that are unique to specific knowledge or concept domains. Such views have often been applied to analyses of language acquisition (e.g., Pinker, 1994). A central feature of such views is the postulation of innate rules or representations needing only exposure to appropriate stimuli to trigger the emergence of domain-specific knowledge.

In summary, the cognitive science tradition represents a spectrum of theories that share an emphasis on a conception of hu-man capabilities in terms of the individual's real-time processing of information. These theories range from information processing, with its emphasis on processing constraints and multilevel integration of information, to connectionism, with its emphasis on parallel processing and the extraction of inherent regularities from environmental input. Cognitive science theories also vary from the strong nativist and representational assumptions of modularists to the emphasis of constructivists and connectionists on the emergence of knowledge from system–environment interactions. All of these theories share, nonetheless, a focus on the processes by which individuals process and integrate information.

The Sociocultural Perspective

The sociocultural perspective (variously labeled) dates back to representatives of American pragmatism, such as William James and John Dewey (Valsiner & van der Veer, 2000). Central to this view is the assertion that human knowledge is inextricably embedded in the social and physical context, and that it is therefore inadvisable to talk in terms of decontextualized abilities or actions. Jean Lave (1990) provides a representative example of this perspective in the following statement: "The encompassing, synthesizing intentions reflected in a theory of understanding-in-practice make it difficult to argue for the separation of cognition and the social world, the form and content of learning, or learning and its 'applications'" (p. 323). Implicit in Lave's statement is the assertion that human knowledge is inextricably embedded in the social and physical context, and that it is therefore inadvisable to talk in terms of decontextualized abilities or actions (see Rogoff, 1998, for a succinct statement of this argument).

Within the sociocultural tradition, two variations, social constructivism and participation/practice theory, have played a prominent role in the study of both language and literacy. In addition, functional/sociolinguistics has played a key role in the study of language, and critical theory has played a role in the study of literacy. All four of these theoretical variations share assumptions concerning the critical role of social experience in shaping language and literacy capabilities. They also share an emphasis on patterns of use, in contrast to the relatively decontextualized abilities emphasized by the cognitive science tradition. They differ, however, in their emphasis on the role of individual knowledge construction and mental representations.

Functional/sociolinguistic theorists were the first within the modern sociocultural tradition to treat the analysis of language in a concerted manner. This model is an outgrowth of general linguistic theory that is focused specifically on the social uses of language. As such, it is less general in its scope than the other sociocultural models discussed here. However, it has played an important role in the emerging sociocultural view of language and literacy. Theorists and researchers working within this model (e.g., Ochs & Schieffelin, 1995) emphasize the complex social norms governing occasions of use of specific language constructions. In talking about the development of language and literacy, they emphasize implicit and explicit socialization practices involved in the child's emerging capabilities. More emphasis is placed on patterns of performance than on generalized knowledge. Also, more emphasis is placed on the role of the adult in language socialization than on the role of the child.

"Social constructivism," as I use the term here,[4] refers to a theory that maintains relatively close allegiance to Vygotsky's early sociohistorical model of development (1978, 1987). In this model, the child's developing capabilities are seen as the result of internalization or appropriation of society's practices via the guidance of adults or knowledgeable peers (Wertsch, 1985). Through guided participation in desired activities, children are led to adopt the patterns of use of the cultural tools characteristic of a given society. Such "tools" include language devices, literacy practices, and social rituals, as well as more concrete tools such as mnemonics. As children take over greater responsibility for independent use of these tools, they are seen as developing a set of enhanced capabilities that are mediated

by the cultural tools to which they have been exposed. Like the constructivist model within the cognitive science tradition, social constructivism emphasizes the role of individual sense making and integration of experience. However, in contrast to constructivists' treatment of social experience as grist for individual knowledge construction, social constructivists emphasize the formative role of social experience and cultural tools in determining the nature of the child's emerging cognitive and linguistic capabilities.

Participation/practice theory can be viewed as a natural fusion of the functional/sociolinguistic and social constructivist models. The development of this model was heavily influenced by ethnographic studies of language and literacy practices (e.g., Cook-Gumperz, 1986; Heath, 1983). Proponents of this view emphasize the fact that all instances of any specific behavior take place in a specific social/cultural setting, and they argue that it is therefore impossible to separate human action from its context, either in practical or theoretical terms (Rogoff, 1998). Borrowing from anthropological models of enculturation, participation/practice theorists conceptualize the acquisition of language and literacy as a gradual process of adopting local cultural practices. Thus, these theorists eschew discussions of abstract knowledge or abilities and talk instead in terms of patterns of practice. Although the emphasis of such theorists is often on higher level discourse practices (e.g., O'Connor & Michaels, 1996), there are also discussions of grammatical development from researchers in this area (Ochs & Schieffelin, 1995).

Critical theory can be seen as a natural outgrowth of participation/practice theory. Like participation theorists, critical theorists think of language and literacy in terms of cultural practices. However, they tend also to emphasize the fact that theorists and practitioners themselves embody a specific sociocultural orientation by virtue of their own social networks and practices. Here, the term "critical" is roughly synonymous with "self-reflective." A second notion of "critical" comes from the emphasis of many critical theorists on the fact that language and literacy practices should be viewed in terms of differential opportunities of occurrence within a given society. For adherents of this view, culture is often heavily infused with issues of privilege and denial of access (Ogbu, 1999; Street, 1993). One central issue for such theorists, then, is that of supporting the cultural practices of nonmainstream segments of society. A more hotly debated issue concerns the extent to which educational institutions should accommodate or even foster nonmainstream practices, as opposed to providing access to mainstream practices (Delpit, 1995).

As in the case of the various cognitive science theories summarized in the preceding section, the four sociocultural theories sketched here represent a family of related but distinct frameworks. They all share the notion that the irreducible unit of analysis for studying human behavior and development is the socially situated individual. They differ, however, in terms of the specific nature of their focus on social/cultural analysis (interpersonal exchanges vs. broad cultural patterns vs. local sociopolitical power hierarchies).

Distinguishing the Perspectives

A clearer sense of the defining differences between the cognitive science and sociocultural perspectives requires a more direct comparison of key assumptions. Several distinguishing features are summarized in Table 1.1. These features are drawn in part from an informative series of exchanges regarding alternative conceptions of learning and transfer appearing in *Educational Researcher* (Anderson et al., 2000; Greeno, 1997; Sfard, 1998).

Perhaps the major difference between the two perspectives lies in their conceptions of what it means to know something. For the prototypical cognitive scientist, knowledge consists of internal embodiments of environmental regularities, variously described as concepts, schemas, or neural networks. For the prototypical socioculturalist, in contrast, knowledge is nothing more than fluid/fluent participation in social activity. Many adherents of the latter perspective (as well as some adherents of cognitive science) expressly disavow decontextualized representational knowledge, whether conscious or unconscious, emphasizing instead the implicit know-how characteristic of cultural routines. There is no need, from this perspective, for example, to invoke a memory store of linguistic rules or strategies for summarizing text. Rather, it is sufficient to talk in terms of fluent practice in context. Furthermore, cognitive scientists tend to view the process of knowing as rational and sequential. They emphasize logical relationships and analyze the process of knowing into components, often working implicitly, if not explicitly, with a computer metaphor. In contrast, sociocultural theorists emphasize the evaluative nature of knowing and view the process of knowing or coming to know as one of interpretation.

For the majority of theorists working within the cognitive science tradition, learning is therefore a process of acquiring new representations, usually involving a process of internalization. As a result, human capabilities are conceptualized as stable action patterns. In contrast, the sociocultural tradition views learning as a process of socialization, in which the novice gradually participates more centrally in organized activities.

TABLE 1.1. Defining Features of Two Alternative Perspectives on Human Capabilities

Cognitive science perspective	Sociocultural perspective
• Knowledge as representation	• Knowledge as performance
• Mind as rational	• Mind as evaluative
• Operations as computational	• Operations as interpretive
• Learning as acquisition/internalization	• Learning as participation/appropriation
• Capability as skill	• Capability as practice/activity
• Unit of analysis: the individual	• Unit of analysis: social participation-in-context
• Context as modifying	• Context as constitutive

From this perspective, learning is a process of engaging in cultural practices rather than a process of incorporating information. Thus, the conceptualization of any human capability is in terms of fluent practice, not isolable behaviors. The emphasis of socioculturalists on cultural practices and enculturation characterizes their orientation to the participation-in-context as the minimal unit for analysis; context is an essential defining feature of human capability. In contrast, although the cognitive scientist often views the (physical or social) environment as an important modifier of performance or learning, environmental context is not an integral component of that performance. Thus, the minimal unit for analysis is the individual learner or performer.

Some Caveats

The preceding discussion has provided only the barest sketch of a set of highly nuanced theories of human knowledge and performance. I hope, however, that it conveys a general characterization of the key assumptions defining the communalities and differences among the various models. It is important to note that each perspective actually contains a spectrum of views; however, there is also value in highlighting "family resemblances" within each spectrum. The participation/practice model, for example, has much more in common with critical theory than with connectionism, because of a shared focus on social/institutional opportunities and constraints. Similarly, connectionism has more in common with classical information processing than with participation/practice theory, because of a shared emphasis on internal mechanisms.

Despite the "family differences" between perspectives, it is important to keep in mind that there are indeed some commonalities between specific theories across perspectives. For example, the social constructivist model shares with the constructivist model a relative emphasis on the individual's active role in making sense of the world. Similarly, the participation/practice model and the connectionist model share a skepticism regarding abstract mental representations. Thus, the actual situation is one of criss-crossing patterns of similarities and differences. Despite this reality, an understanding of current tensions in the study of language and literacy may come from taking stock of the theoretical landscape as I have sketched it here, that is, as a world with two "camps." One value lies in the awareness one gains regarding the unexamined theoretical entailments that accompany talk about human behavior in certain terms. A related value lies in heightened awareness of what one *loses* by ignoring the insights of the "competing" perspective. These issues are the central focus of the final section of this chapter.

CONTRASTING VIEWS OF LANGUAGE AND LITERACY

Although I tried from time to time in the preceding presentation of the major traditions and models to illustrate points in terms of issues of language and literacy, a concrete sense of how these various theories address such issues can only be obtained from a more focused discussion of specific issues. In this section, I present such an analysis, which is facilitated by a set of key questions about language and literacy. A comparison of the kinds of answers to these questions provided by representatives of the two perspectives yields insights into their unique windows on the issues. The questions to be considered range from fundamental issues of definition to questions for practice. The intent here is not to be exhaustive, either in terms of the questions posed or of the range of opinions within each perspective. Instead, the purpose is to provide some insight into how representatives of the two perspectives address questions of theory, research, and practice related to language and literacy. Armed with that insight, it will then be possible to consider the dangers of working solely within a single perspective, as well as whether and how the perspectives can be integrated.

What Is Language, and How Is It Learned?

The cognitive science and sociocultural perspectives differ sharply in their orientation to the study of spoken language. These differences relate, in part, to contrasting assumptions regarding the nature and development of language processes and, in part, to more superficial (though important) issues of differential emphasis on specific aspects of language.

The difference in focus between cognitive scientists and socioculturalists is created primarily by the fact that the former group has a long tradition of interest in grammar, whereas members of the latter group have been primarily interested in meaning and pragmatics. However, as will become clear below, this distinction is not an absolute one; cognitive science has contributed much to theory and research regarding meaning, for example, and socioculturalists have had a lot to say about how grammatical usage varies across institutional and interpersonal settings. However, the differing focus is sufficiently prominent to produce discussions that emphasize very different issues. Cognitive scientists stress complex rule systems and cognitive constraints governing the development of specific grammatical constructions, for example. In contrast, socioculturalists stress the social dynamics of language use (e.g., the word choices or discourse patterns characteristic of speech registers). Lemke (2003) speaks clearly for this aspect of the sociocultural perspective:

> What linguistics calls "language" is not, taken in isolation, an appropriate unit of analysis for developmental research; such units need to be defined more functionally, out of the flow and patternings of communicative–interactive–motor behavior. . . . You cannot, neither materially nor physiologically nor culturally, make meaning *only* with the formal linguistic sign system; other modes of meaning-making are always functionally coupled with language use in real activity. Language in use is always language-within-activity: socially and culturally meaningful, directly observable behavior—equally social in its meanings whether interactional or solo in its production. (p. 72)

The differential emphases of the cognitive science and sociocultural views of language are often more complementary than contradictory. However, they have the pragmatic effect of creating quite distinct scholarly communities. Although these differing emphases are important in understanding the distinctions between them, it is perhaps more informative to consider the distinctions that emerge when representatives of the two perspectives address the same aspect of language. Two such examples of common focus are examined briefly, so that the differences in theoretical orientation can be highlighted.

Word Meaning

One such area of convergence is the study of word meanings. Cognitive scientists have traditionally analyzed meaning in a relatively decontextualized fashion. Meanings are analyzed in terms of component features (e.g., +animacy, +intentionality), with the acquisition of meanings then viewed in terms of which features have or have not been mastered. Alternatively, meanings might be analyzed in terms of which features are "privileged" by children's word-learning heuristics, such as a focus on an object's function rather than its appearance, in the absence of more explicit orientation (Gelman & Williams, 1998). Although issues of context are not ignored, they are backgrounded. Thus, for example, issues of current and past experience become questions of the facilitation of learning (e.g., Golinkoff, Mervis, & Hirsh-Pasek, 1994; see McGregor, Chapter 14, this volume, for discussion of these issues). In contrast, the sociocultural perspective emphasizes the defining nature of context in determining meaning, both in acquisition and in everyday use (Bloom, 1998; Domzalski & Gavelek, 1999). Thus, from this perspective, the dynamics of word learning must be analyzed in social context.

The differing views of word meaning can perhaps be clarified by an example. In analyzing a child's growing understanding of the word *hypothesis,* for example, the cognitive scientist would focus on the number of key semantic features of the word evident in the child's usage pattern (e.g., +mental state, +inanimate, +counterfactual; –affect). Socioculturalists, on the other hand, would focus on the extent to which the child's usage of the word across various contexts re-

flected sensitivity to social/situational dynamics (e.g., co-occurrence with a formal
speech register, such as the register characteristic of schooling).

Grammatical Forms

Perhaps even more telling regarding the
contrasts between the cognitive science and
sociocultural perspectives is the different
mode of explanation adopted by the two
perspectives when considering grammatical
acquisition and usage. As mentioned earlier,
the sociocultural perspective rarely considers issues of grammar, often conceding this
territory to the cognitive scientists (Gee,
2001). However, one prominent exception
to this pattern is the work of Eleanor Ochs
and Bambi Schieffelein (Ochs & Schieffelin,
1995), who have been interested for some
time in the sociocultural dynamics involved
in the acquisition and use of specific grammatical constructions. The essence of the
theory represented by Ochs and Schieffelin
is that specific grammatical constructions
have social–symbolic value; therefore, many
aspects of what we call grammar are actually created in subtle ways by the sociocultural context.

> A language socialization enriched model de-
> cries reductionistic visions that view the socio-
> cultural context as "input" to be quantified
> and correlated with children's grammatical
> patterns. . . . [Our] approach rests on the as-
> sumption that, in every community grammati-
> cal forms are inextricably tied to, and hence
> index, culturally organized situations of use
> and that the indexical meanings of grammati-
> cal forms influence children's production and
> understanding of these forms. . . . (Ochs &
> Schieffelin, 1995, pp. 73–74)

When they talk specifically about language learning, Ochs and Schiefflin (1995)
reveal even more telling assumptions regarding the sociocultural perspective on language. For these authors, the language environment is not just a source of data for the
individual's rule-construction mechanisms
and/or a potential facilitator of learning. Instead, the context is actually central to the
creation of both grammatical and functional language patterns.

That is, children are being socialized the world
over to draw on similar grammatical resources
to index thoughts, feelings, knowledge, identities, acts, and activities not only because of biological and cognitive patterning but also because of universal characteristics of culture as
a common artifact of humankind. (p. 75)

While conceding that "the achievement of
grammatical competence in itself cannot be
said to depend on any particular cultural
circumstances" (p. 84), Ochs and Schiefflin
emphasize that years of neglect of the sociocultural nexus of language acquisition leave
us ignorant of its potential formative role in
acquisition.

In contrast to the sociocultural perspective on the dynamics of grammatical development offered by Ochs and Schieffelin, adherents of the cognitive science perspective
often emphasize the universal, semiau-
tonomous nature of language acquisition
(Maratsos, 1998; Pinker, 1994). In his discussion of the acquisition of grammar, for
example, Maratsos (1998) emphasizes the
need to postulate a language faculty, or
module. He concedes that some aspects of
grammar (e.g., the agent–action–patient order of English sentences) are likely acquired
by means of a generic cognitive system.
However, for a large proportion of the
realm of grammar (e.g., case and agreement
markers; formal categories; restrictions on
wh-processes), he argues for innate, faculty-
specific, modularized mechanisms.

> For example, whatever the actual nature of
> the relevant boundary properties for wh-
> processes, the language-particular inductions
> required for them are probably not something
> the conscious mind would have intuitively pre-
> dicted young children would automatically be
> doing. Any reasonably objective observer
> should be impressed by the robustness and ef-
> ficiency of the acquisitional systems that deal
> with these complex grammatical problems. It
> seems likely that some rather idiosyncratic
> species-specific and probably some faculty-
> specific human characteristics are at work
> here. (Maratsos, 1998, p. 457)

Summary

In summary, the sociocultural and cognitive
science views of language and language

learning differ in terms of both relative foci and basic assumptions regarding the nature of language and the nature of language learning. These differences can be characterized as issues of individual versus social–contextual dynamics and as issues of specialized versus general mechanisms. For the cognitive scientist, language is a knowledge system that must be acquired, perhaps by means of a dedicated processing system. For the socioculturalist, language is a system of cultural practices into which the child is gradually socialized.

What Is Literacy, and How Is It Mastered?

In contrast to the case of oral language, in which there is debate regarding the extent to which the target capability is natural or cultural, in the case of literacy, there is general agreement that a "non-natural" cultural sign system is at issue. Virtually no one argues, for example, that humans have evolved a specialized neurocognitive faculty for reading or writing. Instead, there is a general assumption that, in becoming literate, we are "recruiting" preexisting capabilities for new purposes. Thus, at least on this dimension, the cognitive science and sociocultural perspectives share common ground: Literacy involves the mastery of a set of cultural artifacts. Despite this seeming convergence, however, there is still a good deal of room for divergence, both with respect to how literacy is conceptualized and to how it is mastered.

The major difference with respect to conceptions of literacy relates to the issue of contexualization. For cognitive scientists, literacy skills (by which they usually mean reading and writing) are relatively decontextualized skill systems, and it is possible, perhaps even desirable, at least initially, to study them in isolation from situations of use (Adams, 2001). Thus, mastery of word recognition skills, for example, is often analyzed under controlled conditions in the laboratory or on the computer. It is assumed that the acquisition of such skills proceeds in a fixed, arguably universal sequence (Ehri, 1994; see Ehri and Snowling, Chapter 20, this volume), and that, once acquired, such skills can be used in any relevant situa-

tion. In contrast, the sociocultural theorist is likely to stress the situational specificity of literacy practices (e.g., Au, 1998; Scribner & Cole, 1994). Specific literacy practice is grounded in sociocultural experiences and is bound to such experiences (Scribner & Cole, 1994). Given these premises, decontextualized word recognition activities would be deemphasized in favor of naturally contextualized oral reading as a means of social communication (e.g., the reading of signs or directions in context). Similarly, as Smagorinsky (2001) argued, the interpretation of text is seen as inextricably tied to patterns of use: "From this perspective, texts are composed of signs that themselves are inscribed and codified as cultural artifacts and are read by people whose ways of encoding are conditioned by participation in cultural practice" (p. 146).

Relationship between Oral and Written Discourse

One interesting corollary of these points is that representatives of the two perspectives view the relation between oral language and literacy differently. For the cognitive scientist, there is a relatively "transparent" relation between the two systems. Once the child has cracked the code, he or she can readily bring his or her oral language skills to bear in interpreting and creating written code. For the socioculturalist, however, oral language and literacy represent distinct sets of cultural practices or patterns of use. Thus, it is only in specific cultural contexts that foster a close convergence of practices (e.g., Western formal schooling) that there would be a close wedding of the two domains. Even in this context, the similarities go only so far, because oral and written discourse remain distinct in all but the most academic discussions.

Literacy versus Multiple Literacies

A second interesting corollary of this contrast relates to the question of whether literacy is a single entity. From the perspective of cognitive science, it is possible to talk in terms of reading (or writing) as a single set of skills. With respect to reading, for example, individuals make use of general, trans-situational strategies for attacking words or summarizing text. In contrast to this unitary view, from the sociocultural perspective, the existence of multiple cultural practices within a given society implies the existence of multiple literacies (e.g., Gee, 1992; Heath, 1983; Scribner & Cole, 1994). For example, there are differing expectations for the literal accuracy and prosodic patterning involved in reading aloud in class versus reading to one friend a note written by another friend. In many cases, any particular individual would master only one set of literacy practices. However, in cases of community–school "mismatch" or in complex social settings more generally, individuals are assumed to master multiple sets of practices (Gee, 2001). Speakers of nonstandard dialects of English, for example, must become bidialectal or biliterate to succeed in mainstream public school classrooms. Also, because cultural practices evolve, literacy practices evolve. As Heath (1982) noted, "The nature of oral and written language and the interplay between them is ever shifting, and these changes both respond to and create shifts in the individual and societal meanings of literacy" (p. 466).

One interesting corollary of the sociocultural conception of literacy as a set of social practices is that this view has led many theorists to adopt a much broader view of literacy (e.g., Gee, 2001; Heath, 1982). If literacy is a matter of learning a set of cultural practices for the use of text, and if cultures vary in where or how they use written texts, with some cultures using gesture or pictures when others would use words, then one might broaden the notion of literacy to incorporate all cultural patterns of encoding meaning. From the perspective of socioculturalists, similar dynamics are at issue in these instances (e.g., the embodiment of meaning in signs, the recognition of the social symbolic value of, and situational constraints in the use of, specific signs). In contrast, for the cognitive scientist, unique processes are at issue in mastering phonology and orthography versus interpreting gestures or pictures. Hence, the cognitive scientist is less open to a conception of "literacy" that cuts across written and nonwritten "texts."

Summary

It is important to note here that despite the contrasts between the cognitive science and sociocultural perspectives highlighted earlier, adherents of the cognitive science perspective do stress the key role of social experiences in fostering literacy (e.g., Vernon-Feagans, Hammer, Miccio, & Manlove, 2001). In contrast to the sociocultural perspective, however, the role of such experiences tends to be conceptualized in terms of facilitating or hindering a common acquisition process, rather than as playing a formative role in the literacy practices per se. Thus, the key difference in conceptions of literacy and literacy learning is not one of decontextualized learning mechanisms versus experience-dependent mastery. Rather, it is an issue of experience-driven skill mastery versus socialization into culturally defined patterns of use. Context and experience are crucial for explaining mastery of literacy for adherents of both perspectives. However, the role of context is different. Consistent with the contrast made earlier between these two broad conceptions of human capability, context/experience is formative for the socioculturalist, but it is merely stimulative or facilitative for the cognitive scientist, however necessary its role.

How Do We Conceptualize Variation in Language and Literacy Skills?

Adherents of both the cognitive science and sociocultural perspectives would agree that there is enormous variation among individuals in terms of mastery of language and literacy. Such variation is evident not only between cultural or subcultural groups, but also within groups (see also Chapter 8 by Wasik and Hendrickson and Chapter 9 by van Kleeck, this volume). However, the two perspectives tend to differ in the way they conceptualize such variation, and in how they think such variation should be addressed.

Variations in language and literacy skills among cultural subgroups tend to be viewed by socioculturalists as instances of partially overlapping systems of cultural or familial practices. Members of a given group are enculturated into their community's patterns of language and literacy use. Within a given geopolitical area, such a community presumably overlaps both physically and culturally with other communities, but each group will tend to develop a somewhat unique pattern of practices. Such differences in what are often called "communities of practice" can be viewed either as natural side effects of cultural patterning or as evidence of hegemony on the part of a more powerful cultural subgroup (Willinsky, 1990). In either case, however, the issue is one of differing patterns of cultural practice, and emphasis is placed on documenting the fit of each pattern to its ecological niche.

Although adherents of the cognitive science perspective recognize the systematic, rule-governed nature of a given subculture's language or literacy usage, they tend to focus more on exploring dimensions of difference between groups than on describing internal patterns. In addition, they are more likely to think about specific experiential patterns that might be linked causally to particular cultural differences. For example, subcultural differences in vocabulary knowledge would be discussed more in terms of frequency of exposure to specific words (e.g., Hart & Risley, 1995) than in terms of broader cultural differences in the encouragement of decontextualized language as a tool for referring to objects and experiences (e.g., as opposed to pointing or direct engagement; Domzalski & Gavelek, 1999; Rogoff, 1990).

When attention is turned to differences among individuals within a given cultural group or community, sociocultural theorists tend to maintain their focus on patterns of cultural practice. Thus, within-group variations are more likely to be discussed in terms of local variations in activity patterns than in terms of intrinsic characteristics of the individual. This focus has the effect of making many sociocultural theorists leery of discussing individuals in terms of language or literacy disabilities, an orientation that they often call the "deficit model" (Trent, Artiles, & Englert, 1998). In contrast, while not denying experiential variations within communities, adherents of the cognitive science perspective are more likely than socioculturalists to conceptualize individual differences within a given community in terms of random variation in intrinsic linguistic or cognitive processing efficiency or capacity. As a result, cognitive scientists tend to view atypical children in terms of quantitative variations in intrinsic processing skills, whereas socioculturalists tend to emphasize qualitative differences in activity patterns.

Of course, this issue is far from clear-cut. One can believe in the existence of neurocognitive deficits, for example, but choose to focus one's efforts on identifying and fostering the strengths of an individual rather than lamenting the weaknesses. In addition, it is possible to view some functional limitations of an individual as based in neurocognitive deficits, while other limitations are attributed to cultural variations. Thus, hybrid conceptualizations are possible (even desirable—see the final section). However, these qualifications do not negate the fundamental differences between the cognitive science and sociocultural conceptualizations of variations in language and literacy.

How Do We Engage Effectively in Assessment and Prevention/Intervention?

Given the differing orientations outlined in the preceding section, it should not be surprising that when educators turn their attention to issues of assessment and intervention, their differing orientations lead once again to contrasting approaches. These approaches play themselves out at the level of work with individual children, at the level of program assessment, and at the level of policy decisions.

Educators working within the cognitive science tradition tend to focus on discrete skills, to assess those skills in controlled task settings, and to use quantitative tools to judge the adequacy of the skills they observe. Reading comprehension might be evaluated, for example, by means of a series of multiple-choice questions or via a count of the number of key idea units included in a retelling. Such an assessment would take place at a specific point in time, often in a special location, and it might make use of controlled passages similar to, but distinct from, those used in routine educational activities.

In contrast to the preceding approach, practitioners working within a sociocultural perspective would tend to focus on wholistic patterns of activity rather than on discrete skills. They would conduct evaluations using qualitative methods, and they would tend to work within the context of the child's ongoing activities rather than in a separate task and/or setting. Emphasis would be placed on collecting samples of actual practice over an extended period of time rather than on a one-time assessment of a controlled and distinct task. To assess reading comprehension, for example, a socioculturally oriented practitioner would be inclined to look at children's everyday talk or writing about what they read, and to evaluate the nature of their comprehension in terms of the overall understanding and coherence displayed in the commentary. Issues of style and stance might take precedence over specific content.

If the results from an assessment suggested that a child, a classroom, or a community was not demonstrating desired performance, the cognitive science and sociocultural traditions would take different approaches to intervention. Historically, the cognitive science perspective has tended to target discrete skills, whereas the sociocultural perspective has emphasized the need to change patterns of engagement in communities of practice, not specific skills. Lave (1990) has argued, for example, that individuals will not truly master desired activities unless their exposure to those activities is embedded in actual practice:

> The more the teacher, the curriculum, the texts, and the lessons "own" the problems or decompose steps so as to push learners away from owning problems, the harder it may be for them to develop the practice. . . . On the other hand, learners who understand what they are learning in terms that increasingly approach the breadth and depth of understanding of a master practitioner are likely to understand themselves to be active agents in the appropriation of knowledge, and hence may act as active agents on their own behalf. (pp. 324–325)

The preceding brief sketches of how these perspectives approach issues of assessment and intervention suggest uniformity within difference. This presumption of uniformity is misleading, however. For example, although individual socioculturalists share many assumptions regarding these issues, there are important debates within the perspective. One such debate relates to the wisdom of fostering mainstream cultural practices among individuals from distinct subcultures. Here, the issue is not so much how to foster specific literacy practices, but rather *whether* to do so (see, e.g., Delpit, 1995; Willinsky, 1990). Similarly, within the cognitive science perspective there are debates about whether one should concentrate on building weak skills (e.g., through direct practice) versus building compensatory strategies.

Despite such internal debates, adherents of the cognitive science and sociocultural perspectives display clear differences in their approaches to assessment and intervention. These differences reflect the overarching differences in conceptions of language and literacy described in the preceding pages.

What Are Promising Approaches to Research?

As one might expect, the differing views of language and literacy sketched here play themselves out in differing views of where and how to conduct research on these issues. Because adherents of the sociocultural perspective emphasize embeddedness of practice and view learning as enculturation, they tend to conduct research in intact sociocultural settings. Heath's (1983) classic study of language and literacy practices in different racial/economic communities in North Carolina is a prototypical example of this approach. Heath used extensive ethnographic analysis to identify patterns of use of oral and literate discourse. Although she talked in general terms about the relative frequency of various activities and included occasional systematic counts of specific behaviors, her main focus was on qualitative patterns of activity rather than on issues of frequency. Her concern was to document how children were socialized into language and literacy practices in the home and community. In instances of superficially overlapping practices across communities (e.g., emphasis on print), she stressed the differing occurrences of use (e.g., word play vs. decontextualized alphabet work). As a result, she focused primarily on patterns of oracy, literacy, or preliteracy practices rather than on frequency of exposure to print or specific vocabulary.

When sociocultural researchers turn their attention to issues of schooling, they tend to view the school and the classroom as cultural settings (Tharp & Gallimore, 1988), and to consider issues of continuity or discontinuity between home and school literacy practices (Gallimore & Goldenberg, 1993; Moll, 1994). Thus, once again, the preferred research strategy involves detailed analysis of literacy practices. The emphasis is on ethnographic analyses of instructional activities. Socioculturalists analyze specific instructional activities in terms of their fit within broader goal structures. As a result, their interest in teacher questions would focus more on the pragmatic force of the questions than on frequency or form of the questions, for example. This type of research does not lend itself readily to formal statistical analysis. Instead, researchers emphasize qualitative analyses of activity patterns, inferred goals, and "telling examples" of student mastery (Englert, Berry, & Dunsmore, 2001; Gallimore, 1998).

In contrast to the approach of sociocultural researchers, researchers working within the cognitive science perspective tend to focus on analyses of specific influences on the rate and generality of skill mastery. Issues of cultural or social context are treated as independent variables, usually by quantifying specific dimensions of difference across contexts. Thus, for example, one might look at the role of the frequency of exposure to language models (Hart & Risley, 1995) or the degree of structuring or pace of instruction (Brophy & Good, 1986), rather than at patterns of cultural practices. The emphasis in such research is placed on objective measurement, on experimental or quasi-experimental research designs, and on quantitative analyses of the relationship between instructional variables and learning outcomes. (For an informative comparison of the cognitive science and sociocultural approaches to the analysis of classroom discourse, see Carlsen, 1991).

The contrasting research strategies sketched here have important implications for what gets studied and how it is studied. As such, the two traditions will continue to focus on slightly different issues as they pursue their studies of language and literacy. Thus, this contrast has important implications for the future direction of scholarship. Recently, however, the contrast has also taken on a political tone as policymakers have begun to debate what counts as legitimate evidence to consider in reviewing the status of a knowledge base. In his recent commentary on the report of the National Reading Panel (NRP; 2000) regarding how to teach children to read, for example, Pressley (2002) argued that the Panel's conception of "scientifically valid" reading instructional research was too narrow. In deciding to rule out research based on qualitative methods, Pressley argued, "The NRP chose to keep critically important scientific insights about excellent reading instruction from teachers and other educational decision makers who are struggling to incorporate scientifically sound practices into schools" (p. 179). A similar debate is taking place with respect to the U.S. Department of Education's new What Works Clearinghouse (WWC), a web-based resource established to aid practitioners and policymakers in identifying validated instructional practices. See, for example, the summary of commentaries regarding the WWC's draft standards for minimally acceptable research designs. Both the draft standards and the commentary are posted on the WWC website (What Works Clearinghouse, 2003).

Yet another indication of current public debates regarding appropriate approaches to research methodology can be seen in recent discussions of how we should evaluate student learning and school success (Dillon, 2003; Erickson & Gutierrez, 2002; Feuer et al., 2002; Linn, Baker, & Betebenner, 2002; St. Pierre, 2002). Thus, the issue of appropriate methodology is not simply an academic one; major policy decisions in our schools and in our federal research institutes are being, and will be, made on the basis of one conception of "good" literacy research. Hence, it is crucial that we inform ourselves about these issues, and that we make reasoned decisions. (See Valencia & Wixson, 2000, for a general discussion of these tensions within the literacy policy community.)

TOWARD A CONVERGENCE OF PERSPECTIVES

Partly for rhetorical purposes and partly out of pragmatic necessity, the preceding sections provide a somewhat simplistic picture of how our two perspectives view language and literacy. Numerous issues have been glossed over, and the inevitable result is something like a pair of strawmen. Although the actual state of affairs is indeed more nuanced, it is nonetheless the case that we have been confronted for many years by distinct sets of assumptions about what language is, what literacy involves, and how to approach each of these domains at both theoretical and practical levels. These differences have often been "gentlemanly"; however, they have also often resulted in heated debates—debates about what count as legitimate questions to ask, and what count as legitimate approaches to answering these questions.

As I mentioned at the beginning of this chapter and in the preceding section, these debates have now surfaced at the level of government policy. Federal education initiatives such as the No Child Left Behind (NCLB) Act of 2001 mandate certain approaches to assessment, prevention, and intervention. By one count, for example, the phrase "scientifically based research" appears in the NCLB Act a total of 111 times (Feuer et al., 2002). In addition, it is the case that successful responses to funding initiatives, certainly at the National Institute of Child Health and Human Development (NICHD) and increasingly at the Department of Education, require one particular set of approaches to research design. In November 2002, the Office of Educational Research and Innovation in the U.S. Department of Education was renamed the Institute of Education Sciences. On the De-

partment of Education website, the mission of the new institute is described as follows: "The Institute of Education Sciences reflects the intent of the President and Congress to advance the field of education research, making it more rigorous in support of evidence-based education" (Institute of Education Sciences, 2003). Recent grant application guidelines from the Department of Education encourage research designs involving random assignment of participants to conditions. All of these developments point to an institutionalization of one particular perspective on literacy.

Unfortunately, the issues highlighted here are not just about how to do research; they also have important implications for what goes on in classrooms around the country. Thus, they have important implications for who learns what, and when. Given this reality, we cannot afford to stop at a bemused level of scholarly analysis. We must think carefully not only about how we got ourselves into this situation but also about what we can and should do about it.

Competing or Complementary Perspectives?

As in the case of the convoluted history of pendulum swings related to how best to teach reading (McGill-Franzen, 2000), the current debate between the cognitive science and sociocultural perspectives on language and literacy is often couched in binary terms. Either we teach phonics through explicit drill and practice or we engage children in open-ended discussions of how they feel about natural texts. Either we evaluate instructional approaches, using random assignment of children to classrooms and classrooms to "treatments," or we engage in close observation of naturalistic teaching episodes. Seemingly, we cannot do both, because only one of these perspectives is supposed to have the answer. Over the last decade, both literacy scholars (Kamil, 1995; Stanovich, 1990) and philosophers of science (Hacking, 1999) have occasionally questioned this mind-set of incompatibility, or what is sometimes termed "incommensurability." Stanovich (1990) stated the point succinctly:

In short, paradigms yes, incommensurability no. The latter concept has the potential to do much damage in insecure behavioral and social sciences such as educational research in reading disability. In particular, it has been used to drive a wedge between research frameworks and methods that instead should be used to bolster, rather than to refute, each other. (p. 228)

Interestingly, in expanding on his argument for closer communication between frameworks, Stanovich quotes Karl Popper, one of the philosophers of science most often associated with emphasizing the differences between the "two worlds" of science and humanism. As Stanovich points out, Popper (1970) argues strongly for the importance of dialogue between perspectives as a source of scientific progress.

The motivations for insisting on the feasibility and desirability of "cross-framework" communication have both principled and pragmatic dimensions. Both Kamil and Stanovich argue for the importance of using what works; that is, they argue for a form of "methodological pragmatism." Other scholars have made similar points. Erickson and Gutierrez (2002) have argued, for example, that we need both quantitative and qualitative studies of instructional interventions:

> Unless considerable proportions of a research budget, even in a large-scale formal experiment, are devoted to documenting the treatment as delivered on the ground [using qualitative methods], the causal inferences drawn from inspection of outcome data will remain unwarranted, and they are likely to be partially misleading half truths. (p. 21)

Berliner (2002) echoes this call, concluding that "a single method is not what the government should be promoting for educational researchers" (p. 20).

In a different context, and at a more abstract level, Cobb (1994) makes a parallel argument for what he calls "theoretical pragmatism":

> In place of attempts to subjugate research to a single, overarching theoretical scheme that is posited a priori, we might . . . [consider] reflecting on and documenting our attempts to

coordinate perspectives as we attempt to cope with our specific problems. In doing so, we would give up the quest for an acontextual, one-size-fits-all perspective. Instead, we would acknowledge that we, like teachers, cast around for ways of making sense of things as we address the situated problems of our practice. (p. 19)

What is common to all of these discussions is the conviction that there is much to be gained from using the tools (theoretical or methodological) of both perspectives in the pursuit of knowledge and/or educational outcomes. Indeed, we already have in the literature a number of successful examples of such combinations. For example, the work of Brown and Campione (1994) combines the planful structuring of learning opportunities emphasized in a cognitive science approach to instruction with the collaborative, activity-based approach of the sociocultural tradition. Similiary, Gaskins (1994), in her work on the development of instructional programs that encourage mindful, strategic comprehension among children with a history of poor reading, combines elements of the direct, explicit instruction of the cognitive science tradition, with attention to the infusion of opportunities for encountering the virtues of strategic activity in the natural flow of the curriculum. As a final example, the intervention work of Englert, Tarrant, Mariage, and Oxer (1994) combines an orientation to the use of abstract representations of knowledge structures and activity patterns with the natural flow of dialogue taking place in peer collaboration and large-group discussions. Many other similar examples exist in the literature pertaining to both basic development and instructional issues in the areas of language and literacy.

Integrating the Perspectives: A Challenge for the Future

Arguments for theoretical and methodological pragmatism, as well as working examples of such pragmatism, represent compelling justification for reasoned use of the tools provided by both the cognitive science and sociocultural perspectives. However, it is possible, even desirable, to make a stronger argument—an argument for an integration of perspectives on principled grounds. Sfard (1998) has argued, for example, that it is crucial to work simultaneously within both perspectives (referred to in her discussion as the "acquisition" and "participation" metaphors, respectively). Sfard's argument is that remaining mindful of multiple perspectives encourages consciousness raising about the inadequacy or insufficiency of each framework.

Although she encouraged a close juxtaposition of perspectives, Sfard expressed skepticism about the possibility of creating a single, integrated perspective that incorporates principles from the two individual perspectives. Her argument is that the two perspectives, although complementary in a crucial manner and therefore, in her words, not "incompatible," are nonetheless "incommensurate," and, as such, she argues, they cannot be integrated in a principled manner.

Sfard (1998) raises important concerns about the eventual integration of the cognitive science and sociocultural perspectives, and her article is crucial reading for anyone striving for such integration. However, the issue is far from resolved, and it is important to explore how an integration of perspectives might be accomplished. The value of such integration lies in its explicit recognition of the need to address multiple phenomena, to work at multiple levels of causation, in accounting for any phenomenon.

Anderson et al. (2000) have expressed a similar position. In their discussion of what they term the "cognitive" and "situative" perspectives, they call for

> a more inclusive and unified view of human activity in which dichotomies such as individual versus social, thinking versus acting, and cognitive versus situative will cease to be terms of contention, and, instead, figure in coherent explanatory accounts of behavior and in useful design principles for resources and activities of productive learning. (p. 13)

Such a unified view may, indeed, be a tall order, but it is a goal worth pursuing.

There are precedents to consider when contemplating an integration of perspectives. In a recent argument for a new theoretical approach to language development,

for example, Hollich, Hirsh-Pasek, and Golinkoff (2000) call for an "emergentist coalition model" of word learning. The "coalition" they have in mind involves the "associationist" and "constraints/principles" models from the cognitive science perspective and the "social-pragmatist" orientation of the sociocultural perspective. In their words, "Just as a one-legged table is inherently unstable, scientific explanations of complex processes that force either/or decisions are not as powerful as those that embrace differing perspectives" (p. 14).

A second prominent effort to integrate perspectives comes from proponents of dynamic systems theory. In an overview of this perspective, Thelen and Smith (1998) argue that it represents a new framework for conceptualizing human development and learning, a framework that can integrate the common dichotomies afflicting current theoretical debates. Thelen and Smith use the metaphor of a mountain stream to emphasize the ways in which the internal dynamics of a given system (in this case, fluid dynamics) interact with the dynamics of the broader context (the changing terrain over which the stream flows). The result of this interaction is the emergent properties of the target phenomenon (the ever-changing path and flow characteristics of the stream). By analogy, they see the salient patterns of human behavior and development as a system of "softly assembled" dynamic systems. Such systems are determined jointly by the internal dynamics of the individual and by the structured dynamics of the environment. These systems vary in their stability and openness to change. Thelen and Smith describe applications of this framework to various competency domains, including word learning.

Both of these endeavors at integration represent promising starts. However, in their present forms, both lean more heavily on principles from the cognitive science perspective. Considerable emphasis is placed on the dynamics involved in the integration of information (i.e., perceptual cues to word meaning), but sociocultural factors are still limited to specific contextual cues (e.g., eye gaze or sequence of mention as cues to meaning). By emphasizing such social/contextual factors in word learning, these theorists make a significant move to incorporate aspects of the sociocultural perspective; however, much more theory building will be necessary to capture the rich dynamics of cultural practices central to sociocultural theories.

One interesting historical example of theoretical integration comes from the work of Luria (1973). In his concept of "functional systems," Luria introduced the idea that patterns of culturally mediated practice would result in the creation of new neurological patterns of activity, with important implications for future behavior. Luria's work was undoubtedly influenced by the earlier work of his former colleague, Vygotsky. In his work as the founding director of the Soviet Union's Institute for Defectology (i.e., Special Education), Vygotsky (1993) argued that altered patterns of social engagement associated with the presence of an intrinsic sensory, cognitive, or affective deficit could result in compensatory patterns of higher cognitive activity. Both of these positions amount to arguments for a dynamic interplay between "process" and "practice." Recent research focused on changes in patterns of brain activity following intensive instruction or practice (Temple et al., 2003) can be seen as consistent with this general argument, if such intervention is viewed as analogous to immersion in a new pattern of cultural activity. In such examples, we may indeed be viewing the interplay of process and activity.

Regardless of how an integration of perspectives is ultimately achieved, the need for such a move is clear. Individual and subcultural differences in language and literacy are best conceptualized from multiple perspectives. Not all challenges for children with language learning disabilities are structural/representational, for example, nor are they explained completely by a focus on differential patterns of familial literacy practices. Similarly, interventions in the area of language and literacy should target both processes and practices. The list could go on. Clearly, there is, at minimum, a need for scholars and practitioners from different perspectives to work conjointly on the same problems. Ideally, however, more individu-

als will accept the challenge to work toward the integration of perspectives. It is only when we have moved beyond the "turf wars" or exclusionary mind-set regarding the "correct" perspective on language and literacy capabilities that we will begin to achieve a unified understanding of the complex issues we confront. Such a unified understanding is essential for the creation of maximally effective instructional environments.

ACKNOWLEDGMENTS

I would like to thank Joanne Carlisle, Elaine Silliman, and Anne van Kleeck for their comments on earlier drafts of this chapter. They should not, however, be blamed for my characterizations of the two perspectives.

NOTES

1. Although such consistency is the norm, it is not a necessary pattern. Gee (2001), for example, appears to view basic language development (what he calls "core grammar") as the product of an individualistic, biologically based acquisition process, but his view of discourse and literacy acquisition is squarely within a sociocultural tradition.

2. In contrasting the two perspectives, it is necessary to use a "meta-language" to refer to specific issues accounted for in differing ways by the perspectives. In doing so, I have tried to adopt a "theory-neutral" set of terms. This is, unfortunately, ultimately impossible to do. Thus, if the reader is so inclined, he or she could read into my set of meta-terms implicit biases toward one perspective or the other. For example, the term "capabilities" is intended in my discussion to be a "perspective-neutral" way of referring to what it is that humans can do and actually do. However, it is perfectly possible to view the term as mentalistic or rational, and, thus, to accuse me of implicitly adopting the cognitive science perspective as my meta-language. I urge the reader to give me the benefit of the doubt with respect to this issue.

3. Both traditions can actually be traced further back into their roots in philosophical traditions. The focus here is on their early instantiations in the fields of education, linguistics, and psychology.

4. The term "social constructivism" has been used to refer to various alternative theoretical perspectives. O'Connor (1998) distinguished among three such perspectives, all viewed by her as variants of social constructivism: the sociology of knowledge, neo-Piagetian theory, and the sociocultural–historical theory of mind. In this discussion, I reserve the term "social constructivism" for O'Connor's second perspective and use the term "participation/practice theory" to refer to her third variant. O'Connor's first variant is not discussed here, because it has not been applied directly to the study of language and literacy, except, perhaps, in certain historical arguments regarding the impact of literacy on human culture and cognition (e.g., Ong, 1986; Goody & Watt, 1968).

REFERENCES

Adams, M. (2001). Alphabetic anxiety and explicit, systematic phonics instruction: A cognitive science perspective. In S. B. Neuman & D. K. Dickinson (Eds.), *Handbook of early literacy research* (pp. 66–80). New York: Guilford Press.

Allington, R. L., & Woodside-Jiron, H. (1999). The politics of literacy teaching: How "research" shaped educational policy. *Educational Researcher, 28*(8), 4–13.

Anderson, J. R., Greeno, J. G., Reder, L. M., & Simon, H. A. (2000). Perspectives on learning, thinking, and activity. *Educational Researcher, 29,* 11–13.

Au, K. H. (1998). Constructivist approaches, phonics, and the literacy learning of students of diverse backgrounds. In T. Shanahan & F. V. Rodriguez-Brown (Eds.), *Yearbook of the National Reading Conference* (Vol. 47, pp. 1–21). Chicago: National Reading Conference.

Berliner, D. C. (2002). Educational research: The hardest science of all. *Educational Researcher, 31*(8), 18–20.

Bloom, L. (1998). Language acquisition in its developmental context. In W. Damon, D. Kuhn, & R. S. Siegler (Eds.), *Handbook of child psychology*: Vol. 2. *Cognition, perception, and language* (5th ed., pp. 309–370). New York: Wiley.

Brophy, J., & Good, T. L. (1986). Teacher behavior and student achievement. In M. C. Wittrock (Ed.), *Handbook of research on teaching* (pp. 328–375). New York: Macmillan.

Brown, A. L., & Campione, J. L. (1994). Guided discovery in a community of learners. In K. McGilly (Ed.), *Classroom lessons: Integrating cognitive theory and classroom practice* (pp. 229–270). Cambridge, MA: MIT Press.

Carlsen, W. S. (1991). Questioning in classrooms: A sociolinguistic perspective. *Review of Educational Research, 61,* 157–178.

Chomsky, N. (1959). Review of B. F. Skinner: Verbal behavior. *Language, 35,* 26–58.

Cobb, P. (1994). Where is the mind?: Constructivist and sociocultural perspectives on mathematical development. *Educational Researcher, 23*(7), 13–20.

Cook-Gumperz, J. (Ed.). (1986). *The social construction of literacy.* New York: Cambridge University Press.

Dawson, M. R. W. (1998). *Understanding cognitive science.* Malden, MA: Blackwell.

Delpit, L. (1995). The politics of teaching literate discourse. In *Other people's children: Cultural conflict in the classroom* (pp. 152–166). New York: New Press.

Dillon S. (2003, February 16). Thousands of schools may run afoul of new law. *New York Times,* p. A33.

Domzalski, A., & Gavelek, J. (1999). The acquisition of word meaning: Sociogenesis as an alternative to the standard (cognitivist) perspective. In T. Shanahan & F. V. Rodriguez-Brown (Eds.), *Yearbook of the National Reading Conference* (Vol. 48, pp. 306–316). Chicago: National Reading Conference.

Ehri, L. C. (1994). Development of the ability to read words: Update. In R. B. Ruddell, M. R. Ruddell, & H. Singer (Eds.), *Theoretical models and processes of reading* (pp. 323–358). Newark, DE: International Reading Association.

Elman, J. L., Bates, E. A., Johnson, M. H., Karmiloff-Smith, A., Parisi, D., & Plunkett, K. (1996). *Rethinking innateness: A connectionist perspective on development.* Cambridge, MA: MIT Press.

Englert, C. S., Berry, R., & Dunsmore, K. (2001). A case study of the apprenticeship process: Another perspective on the apprentice and the scaffolding metaphor. *Journal of Learning Disabilities, 34,* 152–171.

Englert, C. S., Tarrant, K. L., Mariage, T. V., & Oxer, T. (1994). Lesson talk as the work of reading groups: The effectiveness of two interventions. *Journal of Learning Disabilities, 27,* 165–185.

Erickson, F., & Gutierrez, K. (2002). Culture, rigor, and science in educational research. *Educational Researcher, 31*(8), 21–24.

Feuer, M. J., Towne, L., & Shavelson, R. J. (2002). Scientific culture and educational research. *Educational Researcher, 31*(3), 4–14.

Foorman, B. R., Fletcher, J. M., Francis, D. J., & Schatschneider, C. (2000). Response: Misrepresentation of research by other researchers. *Educational Researcher, 29*(6), 27–37.

Gallimore, R. (1998). Classrooms are just another cultural acticity. In D. L. Speece & B. K. Keogh (Eds.), *Research on classroom ecologies: Implications for inclusion of children with learning disabilities* (pp. 229–250). Hillsdale, NJ: Erlbaum.

Gallimore, R., & Goldenberg, C. (1993). Activity settings of early literacy: Home and school factors in children's emergent literacy. In E. A. Forman, N. Minick, & C. A. Stone (Eds.), *Contexts for learning: Sociocultural dynamics in children's development* (pp. 315–335). New York: Oxford University Press.

Gardner, H. (1985). *The mind's new science: A history of the cognitive revolution.* New York: Basic Books.

Gaskins, I. W. (1994). Classroom applications of cognitive science: Teaching poor readers how to learn, think, and problem solve. In K. McGilly (Ed.), *Classroom lessons: Integrating cognitive theory and classroom practice* (pp. 129–154). Cambridge, MA: MIT Press.

Gee, J. (1992). What is literacy? *Journal of Education, 171,* 5–25.

Gee, J. P. (2001). A sociocultural perspective on early literacy development. In S. B. Neuman & D. K. Dickinson (Eds.), *Handbook of early literacy research* (pp. 30–42). New York: Guilford Press.

Gelman, R., & Williams, E. M. (1998). Enabling constraints for cognitive development and learning: Domain specificity and epigenesis. In W. Damon, D. Kuhn, & R. S. Siegler (Eds.), *Handbook of child psychology* (5th ed.): Vol. 2. *Cognition, perception, and language* (pp. 575–630). New York: Wiley.

Golinkoff, R. M., Mervis, C., & Hirsh-Pasek, K. (1994). Early object labels: The case for a developmental lexical principles framework. *Journal of Child Language, 21,* 125–155.

Goody, J., & Watt, I. (1968). The consequences of literacy. In *Literacy in transitional societies* (pp. 27–68). Cambridge, UK: Cambridge University Press.

Greeno, J. G. (1997). On claims that answer the wrong question. *Educational Researcher, 26*(1), 5–17.

Hacking, I. (1999). *The social construction of what?* Cambridge, MA: Harvard University Press.

Hart, B., & Risley, T. R. (1995). *Meaningful differences in the everyday experience of young American children.* Baltimore: Brookes.

Heath, S. B. (1982). Protean shapes in literacy events: Ever-shifting oral and literate traditions. In E. Cushman, E. R. Kintgen, B. M. Kroll, & M. Rose (Eds.), *Literacy: A critical sourcebook* (pp. 443–466). Boston: Bedford/ St. Martins.

Heath, S. B. (1983). *Ways with words.* New York: Cambridge University Press.

Hollich, G. J., Hirsh-Pasek, K., & Golinkoff, R. (2000). Breaking the language barrier: An emergentist coalition model for the origins of word learning. *Monographs of the Society for Research in Child Development, 65*(3, Serial No. 262).

Institute for Educational Sciences. (2003). *www. ed.gov/about/offices/list/ies/index.html.* Retrieved February 18, 2003.

Kamil, M. L. (1995). Some alternatives to paradigm wars in literacy research. *Journal of Reading Behavior, 27,* 243–261.

Lave, J. (1990). The culture of acquisition and the practice of understanding. In J. W. Stigler, R. A. Schweder, & G. Herdt (Eds.), *Cultural psychology: Essays on comparative human development* (pp. 309–327). Cambridge, UK: Cambridge University Press.

Lemke, J. L. (2003). Language development and identity: Multiple timescales in the social ecology of learning. In C. Kramsch (Ed.), *Language acquisitions and language socialization: Ecological perspectives* (pp. 68–87). New York: Continuum Press.

Leonard, L. (1998). *Children with specific language impairment.* Cambridge, MA: MIT Press.

Linn, R. L. Baker, E. L., & Betebenner, D. W. (2002). Accountability systems: Implications of requirements of the No Child Left Behind Act of 2001. *Educational Researcher, 31*(6), 3–16.

Luria, A. R. (1973). *The working brain: An introduction to neuropsychology.* New York: Basic Books.

Maratsos, M. (1998). The acquisition of grammar. In W. Damon, D. Kuhn, & R. S. Siegle (Eds.), *Handbook of child psychology* (5th ed.) Vol. 2. *Cognition, perception, and language* (pp. 421–466). New York: Wiley.

Mathes, P. G., & Torgesen, J. K. (2000). A call for equity in reading instruction for all students: A response to Allington and Woodside-Jiron. *Educational Researcher, 29*(6), 4–14.

McGill-Franzen, A. (2000). Policy and instruction: What is the relationship? In M. L. Kamil, P. B. Mosenthal, P. D. Pearson, & R. Barr (Eds.), *Handbook of reading research* (Vol. III, pp. 889–908). Mahwah, NJ: Erlbaum.

Moll, L. C. (1994). Literacy research in community and classrooms: A sociocultural approach. In R. B. Ruddell, M. R. Ruddell, & H. Singer (Eds.), *Theoretical models and processes of reading* (4th ed., pp. 179–207). Newark, DE: International Reading Association.

National Reading Panel. (2000). *Teaching children to read: An evidence-based assessment of the scientific research literature on reading and its implications for reading instruction.* Washington, DC: National Institute of Child Health and Human Development.

Nelson, K. M. (1996). *Language in cognitive development: Emergence of the mediated mind.* New York: Cambridge University Press.

No Child Left Behind Act of 2001, Pub. L. No. 107–110.

Ochs, E., & Schieffelin, B. (1995). The impact of language socialization on grammatical development. In P. Fletcher & B. MacWhinney (Eds.), *The handbook of child language* (pp. 73–94). Cambridge, MA: Blackwell.

O'Connor, M. C. (1998). Can we trace the efficacy of "social constructivism"? In P. D. Pearson & A. Iran-Nejad (Eds.), *Review of research in education* (Vol. 23, pp. 25–71). Washington, DC: American Educational Research Association.

O'Connor, M. C., & Michaels, S. (1996). Shifting participant frameworks: Orchestrating thinking practices in group discussion. In D. Hicks (Ed.), *Discourse, learning, and schooling* (pp. 63–103). New York: Cambridge University Press.

Ogbu, J. U. (1999). Beyond language: Ebonics, proper English, and identity in a Black-American speech community. *American Educational Research Journal, 36,* 147–184.

Ong, W. (1986). Writing is a technology that restructures thought. In G. Baumann (Ed.), *The written word: Literacy in transition* (pp. 23–50). New York: Oxford University Press.

Pinker, S. (1994). *The language instinct: How the mind creates language*. New York: Morrow.

Plunkett, K. (1995). Connectionist approaches to language acquisition. In P. Fletcher & B. MacWhinney (Eds.), *The handbook of child language* (pp. 36–72). Cambridge, MA: Blackwell.

Popper, K. (1970). Normal science and its dangers. In I. Lakatos & A. Musgrave (Eds.), *Criticism and the growth of knowledge* (pp. 51–58). Cambridge, UK: Cambridge University Press.

Pressley, M. (2002). Effective beginning reading instruction. *Journal of Literacy Research, 34,* 165–188.

Rayner, K., Foorman, B. R., Perfetti, C. A., Pesetsky, C., & Seidenberg, M. (2001). How psychological science informs the teaching of reading. *Psychological Science in the Public Interest, 2*(2), 31–74.

Rogoff, B. (1990). *Apprenticeship in thinking.* New York: Oxford University Press.

Rogoff, B. (1998). Cognition as a collaborative process. In W. Damon, D. Kuhn, & R. S. Siegler (Eds.), *Handbook of child psychology* (5th ed.): Vol. 2. Cognition, perception, and language (pp. 679–744). New York: Wiley.

Scribner, S., & Cole, M. (1994). Unpackaging literacy. In R. B. Ruddell, M. R. Ruddell, & H. Singer (Eds.), *Theoretical models and processes of reading* (pp. 123–137). Newark, DE: International Reading Association.

Sfard, A. (1998). On two metaphors for learning and the dangers of choosing just one. *Educational Researcher, 27*(2), 4–13.

Shavelson, R. J., & Towne, L. (Eds.). (2002). *Scientific research in education.* Washington, DC: National Academy Press.

Smagorinsky, P. (2001). If meaning is constructed, what's it made from?: Toward a cultural theory of reading. *Review of Educational Research, 71,* 133–169.

St. Pierre, E. A. (2002). "Science" rejects postmodernism. *Educational Researcher, 31*(8), 25–27.

Stanovich, D. E. (1990). A call for an end to the paradigm wars in reading research. *Journal of Reading Behavior, 22,* 221–231.

Street, B. (1993). Introduction: The new literacy studies. In B. Street (Ed.), *Cross-cultural approaches to literacy* (pp. 1–21). London: Cambridge University Press.

Swanson, H. L. (1993). Principles and procedures in strategy use. In L. J. Meltzer (Ed.), *Strategy assessment and instruction for students with learning disabilities* (pp. 61–92). Austin, TX: Pro-Ed.

Taylor, B. M., Anderson, R. C., Au, K. H., & Raphael, T. E. (2000). Discretion in the translation of re-search to policy: A case from beginning reading. *Educational Researcher, 29*(6), 16–26.

Temple, E., Deutsch, G. K., Poldrack, R. A., Miller, S. L., Tallal, P., Merzenich, M. M., et al. (2003). Neural deficits in children with dyslexia ameliorated by behavioral remediation: Evidence from functional MRI. *Proceedings of the National Academy of Sciences, USA, 100,* 2860–2865.

Tharp, R., & Gallimore, R. (1988). *Rousing minds to life.* New York: Cambridge University Press.

Thelen, E., & Smith, L. B. (1998). Dynamic systems theory. In W. Damon & R. M. Lerner (Eds.), *Handbook of child psychology: Vol 1. Theoretical models of human development* (pp. 563–634). New York: Wiley.

Torgesen, J. K. (1999). Reading disabilities. In R. Gallimore, L. P. Bernheimer, D. L. MacMillan, D. L. Speece, & S. Vaughn (Eds.), *Developmental perspectives on children with high-incidence disabilities* (pp. 157–181). Mahwah, NJ: Erlbaum.

Trent, S. C., Artiles, A. J., & Englert, C. A. (1998). From deficit thinking to social constructivism: A review of special education theory, research, and practice from a historical perspective. In P. D. Pearson & A. Iran-Nejad (Eds.), *Review of research in education* (Vol. 23, pp. 277–307). Washington, DC: American Educational Research Association.

Valencia, S. K., & Wixson, K. K. (2000). Policy-oriented research on literacy standards and assessment. In M. L. Kamil, P. B. Mosenthal, P. D. Pearson, & R. Barr (Eds.), *Handbook of reading research* (3rd ed., pp. 909–935). Mahwah, NJ: Erlbaum.

Valsiner, J., & van der Veer, R. (2000). *The social mind: Construction of the idea.* New York: Cambridge University Press.

Vernon-Feagans, L., Hammer, C. S., Miccio, A., & Manlove, E. (2001). Early language and literacy skills in low-income African American and Hispanic children. In S. B. Neuman & D. K. Dickinson (Eds.), *Handbook of early literacy research* (pp. 192–210). New York: Guilford Press.

Vygotsky, L. S. (1978). *Mind in society.* Cambridge, MA: Harvard University Press.

Vygotsky, L. S. (1987). *Thinking and speaking.* New York: Ablex.

Vygotsky, L. S. (1993). *Fundamentals of defectology (Abnormal psychology and learning disabilities).* New York: Ablex.

Wertsch, J. V. (1985). *Vygotsky and the social formation of mind.* Cambridge, MA: Harvard University Press.

What Works Clearinghouse. (2003). *www.w-w-c.org.* Retrieved February 5, 2003.

Willinsky, J. (1990). *The new literacy.* London: Routledge.

2

Genetic Correlates of Language and Literacy Impairments

JEFFREY W. GILGER
SUSAN E. WISE

This handbook covers a broad range of topics related to language and literacy acquisition and disorders. Some chapters focus on treatment issues; others, on the sociocultural contexts of development; and still others, on the cognitive processes that underlie typical and atypical skills in language and literacy. Although each of these areas is treated separately, common threads inextricably tie them together.

One of these threads is etiology. Our approach to understanding etiology and our theories about how language and literacy are acquired or expressed over the lifespan implicitly or explicitly drives much of what is considered in terms of treatment, descriptions, or diagnoses, and the theoretical framework for understanding relevant cognitive components. Thus, the study of etiology is often essential to the psychology of reading and language.

With this in mind, the current chapter addresses the role of genetics (and, by extension, environments) on the development of language and reading impairments. Other extensive reviews of the area are available (see Felsenfeld & Drayna, 2001; Smith, Gilger, & Pennington, 2002; Smith, Kelley,

& Brower, 1998; Stromswold, 1998; Williams & Stevenson, 2001). Indeed, the number of studies investigating the role of genetics in all sorts of complex human behaviors and phenotypes has literally exploded in the past two decades, and there is no longer any reasonable doubt that genes play a role in almost every behavior thus far studied (Gilger, 2000; Sherman et al., 1997).[1]

In this chapter we first describe how developmental language impairments and reading impairments are typically considered in genetic research, and we point to several complexities in how these disorders are defined. Clearly, our definitions of these disorders influence study results and, in some situations, seriously modify the conclusions we draw about the genetic loci of these disabilities, their biological substrates, and their essential "innate" elements (Wood & Grigorenko, 2001).

Second, we provide a few models that illustrate how genes potentially give rise to impairments in the various domains of written or spoken language. Because we have yet to determine exactly how genes affect the brain to create problems in the language areas, this section is largely hypothetical. Whichever model turns out to be supported by future work, we conclude here that it is likely that more than one gene affects the language system, and that interactions with other genes and the environment increase a person's risk for impairment (Gilger, Ho, Whipple, & Spitz, 2001; Grigorenko, 2001). This sort of model contrasts the early classic or simple single-gene models that postulated more direct effects on reading or language impairments (Gilger, Borecki, Smith, DeFries, & Pennington, 1996).

Third, we summarize the basic methodologies used in genetic studies and the results that have been obtained to date. Our review supports the proposition that these disorders have a genetic component that runs in families as a risk factor, but that does not ensure that an individual carrying these genes will manifest clinical impairments in reading and/or language.

Finally, we close this chapter with a discussion about future research, and we revisit several models that have been posited in the past regarding how genes act to cause literacy and reading impairments. On the horizon, there is great promise for discoveries about how the brain works and develops, and researchers and practitioners dealing with language-related traits will benefit as genetic work progresses.

DEFINITIONAL ISSUES IN THE STUDY OF DEVELOPMENTAL LANGUAGE AND LITERACY IMPAIRMENTS

The reader is probably aware of the long and sometimes divisive history regarding the manner in which the field has traditionally defined language impairment (LI) and reading impairment (RI). For the purposes of this chapter, we are unable to do full justice to these intricacies (see other chapters in this volume), but we want to highlight four points related to their definition.

First, this chapter deals with nonsyndromic or *developmental* LI and RI. These forms of learning disorders or disabilities (LDs) have been described by a number of terms, such as "specific language impairment," "developmental expressive language disorder," "reading disability," and "dyslexia," among others (Owens, 1995; Pennington, 1991). This chapter does not deal with what may appear to be similar impairments that are either acquired (e.g., through head injury) or that occur as part of a known genetic condition (e.g., Fragile X, Turner Syndrome; Plumridge, Bennett, Dinno, & Branson, 1993; Shprintzen & Goldberg, 1986).

Second, although we talk about the heritability of LI and RI, it is critical to recognize that we are really talking about the genes that control the structure and function of the brain areas responsible for variations in language and reading (Gilger et al., 2001; Grigorenko, 2001). There are no genes for LI and RI per se. Rather, there are genes that affect brain development to such an extent that affected individuals have trouble learning appropriately in these domains.

Third, our aim is to address how RI and LI travel in families, and how genes affect this process. While the research that we review in this area has important ramifications for theories about the innateness of language, it does not directly address how or whether humans have some special predisposition to acquire language (Pinker, 1994). Research designs that appropriately address whether there are innate modules or mechanisms for language acquisition are different than those we discuss here. Although we personally agree that there are innate, species-specific neurological mechanisms for language and thought in humans, the innateness-of-language question is not terribly relevant to the issue of the heritabilities of LI and RI, where the focus is on the basis of *individual* and *group differences* in abilities. Moreover, whereas language seems to be a naturally acquired skill given normal circumstances, reading is a skill that depends on human neurology and language systems but has evolved as a result of cultural demands. RI can therefore be thought of as a disorder "created" by culture that would not otherwise exist; that is, language is a natural process for humans, but reading is not.

Finally, in this handbook is a section that deals with the cognitive-processing approach to LI and RI. Whereas we often think of, for example, poor reading performance in terms of low performance on some global reading test, a cognitive-processing or cognitive components approach recognizes that these low test scores are caused by deficits in some or all of the basic reading processes in phonology, orthographic skills, decoding, memory, speed, synthesis, attention, and the like. An increasing number of studies examine the genetic aspects of these processes, and it is important to bear in mind that when we speak of genetics of reading and language impairments, we are probably speaking of the heritability of these specific processes alone or in combinations as they affect performance on measures of general reading and language function (Gayan & Olson, 2001; Willcutt, Pennington, & DeFries, 2000).

Language Impairment as a Phenotype

In most research, developmental LI is primarily defined by exclusionary rather than inclusionary criteria. Exclusionary criteria are used essentially to rule out unwanted causes for the disorder, whereas inclusionary criteria are thought to represent the underlying or basic linguistic problem giving rise to a diagnosis of LI (see other chapters in this handbook). A person with the disorder fails to develop normal receptive and/or expressive language skills, without any evidence of deficits in nonverbal IQ, neurological impairment, or environmental or emotional problems that could explain the language delays. The definition of the LI phenotype has sometimes included consideration of subtypes (Owens, 1995; Watkins & Rice, 1994). For example, children with LI vary in the severity and pervasiveness of the linguistic impairment they exhibit, in the range of linguistic subsystems involved (morphology or syntax, etc.), and in the language modality affected (i.e., expressive or receptive language, or both). However, there is no generally accepted subtype taxonomy (Aram & Nation, 1975; Johnston, 1988, 1991; Leonard, 1989, 1991; Owens, 1995; Tallal & Stark, 1981; Tallal, Stark, & Mellits, 1985; Watkins & Rice, 1994). In terms of genetic research, the majority has

focused on oral expressive conditions globally defined, and it is clear that LI and speech disorders (e.g., stuttering) should not be combined as a general speech–language phenotype, because they seem to be genetically independent (Ambrose, Yairi, & Cox, 1993; Felsenfeld & Drayna, 2001).

The rates of LI depend on the definition used, the sample age, and the stringency of the cutoff for diagnosis. For example, overly broad phenotypes artificially inflate prevalence rates (e.g., Tallal, Ross, & Curtiss, 1989). When diagnoses are made cautiously across a number of studies, the prevalence estimates range from 6 to 8% of school-age children (Williams & Stevenson, 2001). Slightly less than 50% of these children will continue to have problems as they get older, and approximately 80% of the children with such deficits have both expressive and receptive problems (Rice, 1997; Tomblin, 1996). Older estimates of the male–female sex ratio were as high as 3:1, but later, perhaps better controlled studies, are now showing lower sex ratios, often in the area of 1:3 to 2:0 (Leske, 1981; Tomblin, Smith, & Zhang, 1997).

READING IMPAIRMENT AS A PHENOTYPE

Developmental RI is an unexpected difficulty in learning to read and spell despite adequate intelligence and opportunity, and without demonstrable sensory, psychiatric, or neurological factors that could explain the disorder. This definition, like that for LI, is exclusionary in that other causes of reading problems must be ruled out (e.g., emotional problems or environmental deprivation). It is noteworthy that there is a push in the field to define both RI and LI in terms of inclusionary symptoms, although a finite or gold standard set of inclusionary criteria has yet to be accepted, and there are arguments to support the idea that at least some exclusionary criteria may always be needed. Thus, the diagnosis of RI usually requires a measured discrepancy between demonstrated reading and/or spelling ability and the expected level of these skills based on age or intelligence, yet there is no universally accepted degree of deficit or discrepancy that constitutes a disability.

With the assumption that RI is etiologically heterogeneous, a number of attempts have been made to define subtypes that might reflect pathogenic differences. However, subtype assignment may not be consistent within families or even within the same child over time, so subtype classifications appear, at best, to have more descriptive than etiologic value (Pennington, 1991; Snowling, 1991; Stein, 2001; Wolff, 1999).

In school-age children, the rate of RI ranges from 5 to 10%, affecting approximately 1.2–1.7 times as many boys as girls (Smith et al., 2002). Broader definitions of RI may yield estimates as high as 30%, but often these estimates reflect research methodologies that do not require a significant discrepancy between reading and nonreading abilities.

BRIEF COMMENT ON THE RELATIONSHIP BETWEEN LANGUAGE IMPAIRMENT AND READING IMPAIRMENT

An early LI is often correlated with a child's risk of subsequent problems in writing and reading. In general, children with LI have problems extracting regularities from the language around them, registering the different contexts for language, and constructing word–referent associations for lexical growth. Thus, the child often has trouble in vocabulary development, and in morphologic and phonologic rule formation and application.

Although the etiologic relationship between LI and RI is unclear, the two disorders may have a common neuropsychological basis, perhaps reflected in phonology-related deficits, and the neurology of oral and written language is known to have similarities (Eden & Zeffiro, 1998; Eden et al., 1996; Galaburda, 1992, 1993; Joseph, Noble, & Eden, 2001; Leonard, Puranik, Kuldau, & Lombardino, 1998). The possibility that LI and RI may have a common genetic basis is currently being studied, but for now, the type and degree of shared etiology is unspecified. At the phenotypic level, this notion is sup-

ported by the finding that roughly 50% of children with LI go on to develop RI (Catts, Fey, Zhang, & Tomblin, 1999). Criteria for clear differential diagnosis between early signs of developmental LI and RI must await further research, but it is apparent that many children with LI do not simply grow out of their language-based difficulties, and that the presence of language-based problems at a prereading stage is often a predictor of future problems in other areas of learning (see Catts et al., 1999; Molfese, Molfese, & Modgline, 2001; Pennington, 1991).

GENETICS OF LANGUAGE IMPAIRMENT AND READING IMPAIRMENT

Why might LI and RI have genetic (as well as environmental) components? The answer is simple: *All* cognitive traits have a genetic component, because *all* cognitive traits reflect the functioning of a biological organ—the brain (Gilger, 2000). This is true for any aspect of cognition, be it an action as simple as pulling one's finger away from a flame, identifying an object in one's visual field, or a more complex cognitive activity, such as answering mathematical questions, reading, or driving a car (see the Glossary for definitions of some terms used in this chapter).

It has long been recognized that people differ in how they perform cognitive tasks. It is also clear that people differ genetically. Because all cognitive functions have a genetic component, it is a logical possibility that individual and group differences in cognitive abilities are a reflection of these genetic differences across people. The implications of this simple statement have been borne out in data from many research projects, showing quite clearly that individual differences in a variety of cognitive traits are due, at least in part, to genetics (Gilger, 2000).

However, genes do not explain all individual or group differences in cognitive functioning. Without exception, research tells us that cognitive traits, such as language, reading, and IQ, among others, also reflect environmental effects. The reader is referred to the references cited throughout this chapter for a complete review of the gene versus environment debates and how certain myths about how genes work have helped to fuel these debates (Gilger, 1995; Plomin, DeFries, McClearn, & McGuffin, 2001; Rowe, 1994).

How, then, do genes and environments act together to produce, for example, average vocabulary development or disabilities in reading? The answer to this question is no doubt complicated and is not fully understood at this time. But we can provide a rough model of how genetic (G) and environmental (E) effects, globally defined, might work together to produce variations in brain function or development that in turn yield the range of reading or language phenotypes we see in the general population (also see Mody, Chapter 3, this volume).

The model in Figure 2.1, called the *Basic Model*, is a representation of the actions of genes and environments as a person develops. However, it is a very simple model and, as such, does not do complete justice to the complexity of the mechanisms by which G and E operate in human cognitive development.

In this model, genes are "donated" at conception, and they affect growth throughout the lifespan. For the most part, this is an accurate depiction of how genes work: The genetic complement that a person receives is a combination of his or her parents' genes, and this complement essentially does not change over the course of a lifetime. Essentially, what we receive at conception is our genetic constitution, and that is that. The genetic potentials coded for by these genes are, in a sense, set before birth in our DNA. However, genes are not destiny, and the Basic Model shows that from conception on, E effects can modify how a person develops, and these effects can cause some deviations in the genetic path that was "preset." These E effects may occur within the family, outside of the family, through culture, schools,

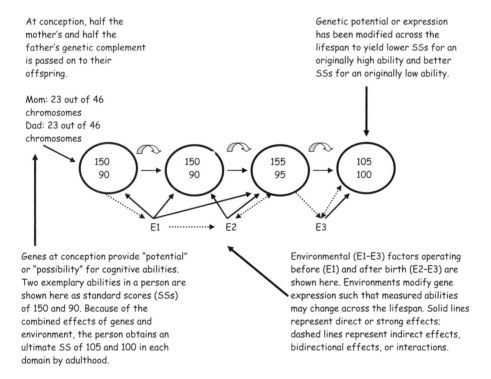

At conception, half the mother's and half the father's genetic complement is passed on to their offspring.

Genetic potential or expression has been modified across the lifespan to yield lower SSs for an originally high ability and better SSs for an originally low ability.

Mom: 23 out of 46 chromosomes
Dad: 23 out of 46 chromosomes

Genes at conception provide "potential" or "possibility" for cognitive abilities. Two exemplary abilities in a person are shown here as standard scores (SSs) of 150 and 90. Because of the combined effects of genes and environment, the person obtains an ultimate SS of 105 and 100 in each domain by adulthood.

Environmental (E1–E3) factors operating before (E1) and after birth (E2-E3) are shown here. Environments modify gene expression such that measured abilities may change across the lifespan. Solid lines represent direct or strong effects; dashed lines represent indirect effects, bidirectional effects, or interactions.

FIGURE 2.1. The Basic Model (solid lines) and the Expanded Model (dashed lines) of genetic and environmental effects on cognitive development from conception through adulthood.

unique accidents, and other chance occurrences (Gilger, 1995; Rowe, 1994). Thus, it could be said that no one actually achieves or becomes precisely what their genetic potential coded for—whether it coded for a person to become a criminal, a brilliant thinker, a gifted orator, or a disabled learner.

The hypothetical person represented in Figure 2.1 has a genetic code, such that if it were expressed in a vacuum, it would produce, say, high cognitive ability in one area and low cognitive ability in another.[2] These high and low abilities are depicted as standard scores of 150 and 90, respectively. Whereas at conception these cognitive ability potentialities may have been as described, as shown in Figure 2.1, environmental events across the lifespan can modify expression and, in this example, ultimately lower one ability and raise the other.

The general description of Figure 2.1 can be refined to portray better the complexities in the process by attending to the dashed and curved lines and arrows connecting G and E. This slight expansion of the Basic Model explicitly acknowledges the effects of genes on other genes (e.g., gene–gene interactions), as well as genetic changes that can take place after conception (somatic mutations, errors in decoding and transcribing, etc.). This refinement of Figure 2.1 also depicts the process whereby E and G can operate bidirectionally, and more complicated G–E relationships can occur during development.

The process of gene–gene interactions and postconception genetic changes is depicted by a → along the genetic pathway from conception to adulthood. For language and reading, the effect of genetic changes occurring after conception are likely to be minimal, if they exist at all at a population level. Still, it is important at least to note such effects in Figure 2.1. On the other hand, gene–gene interactions probably occur in significant ways to modify and affect reading and language abilities. These sorts of effects are better described in our later discussion of Figure 2.2.

Complicated G–E relationships, often called G × E interactions and G–E correlations (for a detailed discussion with regard to typical and atypical learning and development, see Gilger, 2000; Gilger et al., 2001; Plomin et al., 2001; Sherman et al., 1997), are shown by dashed lines and arrows. In brief, G × E interactions occur when a person's response to an environment is modified by his or her genetic complement, such that E does not always operate on all individuals in the same way—a person's genetic constitution can change the way E operates and/or change the way a person responds to E.

G–E correlations refer to another type of nonindependent, nondirect E effect, namely, G–E correlations (GECs), which exist when certain genotypes tend to be more often associated with certain environments. Thus, selective exposure to environments can be dependent on an individual's genotype. Three types of GECs have been described (Plomin, DeFries, & Loehlin, 1977; Scarr & McCartney, 1983): passive, evocative (or reactive), and active. For example, in the context of language ability, a passive GEC may occur when linguistically talented children inherit from their linguistically talented parents both genes and a family environment that enhances the development of language ability; that is, the children "passively" receive from their parents family environments that are correlated with their genetic propensities. Evocative GECs may occur when linguistically talented children are selected by teachers and are provided special opportunities, such as participation on debate teams, journalism or forensic clubs and activities; that is, the children "evoke" reactions from other individuals on the basis of their genetic propensities. Finally, active GECs might occur when linguistically talented children seek out or construct their own linguistically rich environments and select like peers; that is, the children "actively" select, construct, or reconstruct experiences correlated with their genetic propensities. Throughout the lifespan, the types of associations among genes and environments can cause increasing divergence between groups or individuals with differing genotypes, and, therefore, different environmental exposures as G and E build upon each other. The effect of GECs, or the amount of phenotypic variance accounted for by GECs, is probably even more pronounced for atypical, or learning disabled or disordered (LD) populations (Gilger et al., 2001).

In summary, the Basic Model expansion shows that, at any point in development, G and E operate in complex ways. The extent to which either G or E is more important depends on the trait in question, the person's age, and so on. It is also worth emphasizing yet again that when we speak of the G and E effects shown in Figure 2.1, we are really talking about G and E effects on the function and development of the brain.

RESEARCH ON THE GENETICS OF LANGUAGE IMPAIRMENT AND READING IMPAIRMENT

The field of genetics has had a long history of studying the basis of complex human traits. A variety of genetic methods are available, including family designs, twin studies, adoption studies, and linkage studies, among others. In the last 20 or so years, molecular genetics techniques have become increasingly popular, because they allow us to examine DNA for the specific genes that put individuals at risk for disorders such as LI and RI. Once these genes are identified, it is theoretically possible to characterize them and explain their biochemical properties and actions in neurodevelopment and cognitive functioning.

Overview of Language Impairment Genetics

There is evidence that LI is familial and heritable, but it is not yet clear whether there are single, major gene effects. Phenotypic and genotypic heterogeneity complicates the search for the key risk genes for LI.

Twin Studies

There are a number of twin methods, but essentially, twin designs look at monozygotic (MZ) and dizygotic (DZ) within-pair similarity for the trait in question (Plomin et al., 2001). Given certain assumptions, greater MZ than DZ within-pair similarity is suggestive of a genetic effect (Plomin et al., 2001). There are a number of twin studies of LI and related conditions (Bishop, 1994, 2001; Bishop, North, & Donlan, 1995; Dale et al., 1998; Howie, 1981; Lewis & Thompson, 1992; Tomblin & Buckwalter, 1998). It is also noteworthy that a number of studies exist concerning the etiology of the normal range of language; in general, these studies suggest mild to moderate heritability (h^2) for global language-related skills (e.g., expressive and receptive vocabulary) and significant shared family environmental effects, at least in preschool children (Hardy-Brown, 1983; Hardy-Brown & Plomin, 1985; Hay, Prior, Collett, & Williams, 1987; Hohnen & Stevenson, 1999; Locke & Mather, 1989; Matheny & Bruggermann, 1973; Mather & Black, 1984; Munsinger & Douglass, 1976; Osborne, Gregor, & Miele, 1968; Plomin, DeFries, & Fulker, 1988; Reznick, Corley, & Robinson, 1997; Scarr & Carter-Saltzman, 1983).

In a report of an ongoing twin study of LI, Tomblin and Buckwalter (1998) reported probandwise concordance rates of .96 and .69 for MZ and DZ twins, respectively, and a group heritability (h^2_g; DeFries & Fulker, 1988) estimate of .45, suggesting that about half of the deficits in the language of children with LI are due to genetic effects. Probandwise concordances and h^2_g estimates were also provided by Lewis and Thompson (1992) and Bishop et al. (1995). Specifically, Lewis and Thompson found MZ and DZ probandwise concordances of .86 and .48, respectively, and Bishop et al. found h^2_g estimates for several continuously measured indices of LI to range from .47 to .93.

A recent report (Dale et al., 1998) on data from a large sample of twins tested the relative roles of genes and environments in the serious language delays of 2-year-olds. The data supported the notion that both genetic and nongenetic factors are responsible for language acquisition. Additionally, they showed that the genetic and nongenetic factors operating during language development vary depending on the level of the child's skill at the time of assessment. Specifically, Dale et al. assessed the degree to which genetic influence on language delay in 2-year-olds differed from genetic influence in the typical range of language development. They attempted to partition the etiology of the hypothetical normal curve for the range of expressive vocabulary into two parts: the factors influencing the language abilities of individuals at the very low end of the curve versus the language abilities of individuals with the normal abilities. Having found that the heritability of language deficit significantly differs from the heritability of individual variation overall, Dale et al. concluded that children with seriously delayed expressive vocabulary were part of a distinct distribution, with a multifactorial etiology separate from that of more typically developing children. Furthermore, they predicted that specific genes may add to the risk for language delay, and that the majority of these genes would not be associated with language skills in the normal range.

These authors also found that shared environmental influences are more important for developmental differences in the normal range than in the etiology of developmental delays. This has ramifications for our understanding of the role of the early family environment (prenatal and postnatal) in the development of vocabulary skills. One conclusion that may be reached from these data is that the family plays a powerful role in the vocabulary skills of children with normal skills. However, faced with a child with seriously delayed growth in language, parents and professionals need look to biology more than to pre- and postnatal familial treatment for a causal mechanism.

Family Studies and Segregation Analysis

More family, segregation, and linkage studies of LI are needed, particularly projects that combine neuroimaging, quantitative, and molecular genetics. Nonetheless, the familial nature of LI has been noted in a number of studies (e.g., Lewis, 1992; Rice, 1997; Spitz, Tallal, Flax, & Benasich, 1997; Tallal et al., 1989; for reviews, see Stromswold, 1998; Williams & Stevenson, 2001), although some of the earlier works had sampling biases and tended to use overly broad phenotypes. In the Tallal et al. (1989) study, for example, 77% of the

probands with LI had a relative with a *language-related* disorder, including speech, language, or learning problems. However, they also found that 46% of the 50 control probands also had a similarly affected relative, suggesting that either the sample was biased or the phenotype was too broadly defined. Studies that are better controlled and use more stringent diagnostic criteria report, on average, that 17–43% of the first-degree relatives of probands with LI are also affected, representing a 2- to 7-fold increase over population base rate expectations for LI (Lewis, 1992; Tomblin, 1996).

There is probably etiologic and/or expressive heterogeneity for LI within families. For instance, Tomblin (1996) found that LI clustered more in some families than in others; out of 44 families with a proband with LI, 23 families had no other affected relatives. No phenotypic differences could be found between the familial and nonfamilial probands, however, so if these represented etiologic differences, they did not produce phenotypic differences, at least at the level of analysis in this study.

The percentage of people affected in families varies somewhat from study to study. For example, Spitz et al. (1997) found that approximately 50% of the children with a positive family history had language delays, whereas later work by Rice (1997) obtained lower results. Rates of LI also vary with differences in how the data are examined, such as combining the sexes, splitting the phenotypes, and/or analyzing generations separately (e.g., Rice, 1997). In one study of the families of 87 children with a preschool history of phonologic disorder, 26% of first-degree relatives had speech–language disorders by history, 5.8% had reading problems, and 5.6% had learning disabilities, all showing significant increases over the relatives of control probands (Lewis, 1992). When the frequencies of speech–language disorders were broken down by relationship to the proband, 42% of brothers, 22% of sisters, and about 18% of both mothers and fathers were affected. Relatives of female probands were found to be at higher risk than relatives of male probands, which is consistent with a multifactorial threshold trait. Significantly, this study also found that affected relatives clustered in families; 18 of the 87 families had no affected relatives, and these families were also less likely to have associated problems such as RI.

Lahey and Edwards (1995) supply further evidence for genetic heterogeneity with their finding that the proportion of affected family members was higher in children with expressive language deficits than in those with both expressive and receptive deficits. In contrast, Lewis and Freebairn (1997) did not find differences in the family histories of children with different subtypes of phonological disorder. However, they did observe that children with a positive family history tended to do more poorly on all of the tests, and that they had poorer oral motor coordination and production, which was also seen by Lahey and Edwards (1995).

Complex segregation analyses have been done by Lewis, Cox, and Byard (1993) and van der Lely and Stollwerck (1996). In both studies, the transmission of LI was clearly familial, but the mode of inheritance could not be well specified in the Lewis et al. (1993) work, where both multifactorial and single-gene inheritance were supported. The results of the van der Lely and Stollwerck (1996) study supported an autosomal dominant mode of inheritance. Reconciling the different results of these two studies requires recognition of their different methods, samples, and diagnostic criteria. For example, van der Ley and Stollwerck used a more limited definition of LI than did Lewis et al., and both studies may have had some difficulty in determining the presence of a disability in adult relatives.

Linkage and Molecular Work

Some families with apparent single-gene inheritance of language problems have been described. Gopnik (1990) reported a large family with multiple members who had grammatical defects, particularly in marking number and tense. It was hypothesized that this was due to an inability to construct language rules governing these properties. Because of the inheritance pattern, it was posited that this grammatical deficit was due to an autosomal dominant gene. In

1998, Fisher, Vargha-Khadem, Watkins, Monaco, and Pembrey reported that the phenotype in this family was significantly linked to chromosome 7 (7q31), with autosomal dominance and complete penetrance. The gene was tentatively titled SPCH1. However, more detailed studies of this family indicated that additional cognitive, linguistic, and praxic deficits beyond grammar were part of the familial phenotype (Vargha-Khadem, 1994; Vargha-Khadem, Watkins, Alcock, Fletcher, & Passingham, 1995). Thus, this family has relevance to our understanding of the developmental processes that lead to cognitive and linguistic traits; however, family members do not carry a "gene for language or grammar,'" as has been touted in the popular press (Hurst, Baraitser, Auger, Graham, & Norell, 1990).

Positron emission tomography (PET) scans in two of the family members demonstrated hypoactivation of left primary sensorimotor cortex, consistent with their oral apraxia, as well as increased activation in the left caudate nucleus and cortical regions around Broca's area. Magnetic resonance imaging (MRI) studies showed not only abnormalities in the amount of gray matter, namely, deficiencies in the caudate nuclei and regions of the left frontal cortex, but also demonstrated increased gray matter in the putamen, frontal operculum, and superior temporal cortex. Because abnormalities of the basal ganglia have been associated with aphasia and oral apraxia, the authors proposed that the SPCH1 gene may act on the basal ganglia and its cortical connections (Watkins, Gardian, & Vargha-Khadem, 1999).

It is interesting that an independent study of LI has also found tentative linkages to chromosome 7 (also see the genetic work on William's syndrome, which has been associated with loci on chromosome 7; Ewart et al., 1993). Tomblin et al. (1997) reported a linkage to the same general region of chromosome 7 as the Fisher et al. (1998) group reported using association analysis for a clearly defined group of children with LI. The phenotype of Tomblin et al. is more precise than that of Fisher et al., and these preliminary results hold promise. Moreover, the chromosome 7 area identified by Fisher et al. and Tomblin et al. is part of a region also linked to autism, a disorder that has as one of its hallmark symptoms severe problems with language (Bailey, Palferman, Heavey, & Le Couteur, 1998) It is important to recognize that these linkages are for areas of chromosomes where genes for LI risk may exist. As yet, no specific gene for LI has been identified among the 100 or more possible candidates in this chromosome area (Williams & Stevenson, 2001).

Overview of Reading Impairment Genetics

The familial nature of reading disability was noted around the turn of the century, and numerous reports of multiplex families followed (Hallgren, 1950; also see reviews by DeFries & Gillis, 1993; Smith & Goldgar, 1986). Subsequent systematic quantitative and molecular work has demonstrated clear genetic influence on the risk for RI.

Twin Studies

Many twin studies of reading disability have been reported, but at least some of these suffer from use of poor measurement tools, small sample sizes, and/or biases in the ascertainment of twins (Williams & Stevenson, 2001). Two well-designed, large twin studies are the Colorado Twin Study of Specific Reading Disability (CTS) and the London Twin Study (LTS). Both the CTS and the LTS report twin data supportive of moderate to strong genetic influence on RI and related conditions (Stevenson, 1991).

Using a specialized statistical technique, DeFries and colleagues (Defries & Alarcon, 1996; DeFries & Gillis, 1993) used the CTS data to ascertain whether the genetic factors operating in very poor readers were the same as those operating in readers with normal reading ability. This is the same "group heritability" approach used by Dale et al. (1998) and applied to LI. DeFries and colleagues reported an h_g^2 value of approximately .56, indicating that 56% of the deficit in reading in the RI sample is due to genetic effects. Similarly, Stevenson (1991), using similar techniques, reported a significant heritability for impaired spelling (62%); however, the LTS sample was ascer-

tained differently than the CTS sample. To date, analyses of the CTS have not found significant evidence that genes operate differently in poor readers than in readers with normal ability (Defries & Alarcon, 1996; DeFries & Gillis, 1993).

On a related issue, Pennington, Gilger, Olson, and DeFries (1992) demonstrated that there may not be an etiologic difference for the reading abilities–disabilities of "simply poor readers" versus "true dyslexics." In their study, age-discrepant-only and IQ-discrepant diagnostic phenotypes both appeared to detect the same heritable reading problem in these twins. Thus, the argument for an etiologic distinction between backward and "true" dyslexics may not be as tenable as was once proposed (Fletcher, 1992; Yule, Rutter, Berger, & Thompson, 1974).

Olson and colleagues (Gayan & Olson, 2001; Olson, Forsberg, & Wise, 1994) have also used this sample of twins to examine the heritabilities of orthographic and phonologic aspects of reading and spelling skills, as well as rapid automatic naming. They found that orthographic and phonological skills were equally heritable. The estimate of h_g^2 for orthographic coding was .56, which is quite comparable to .59 for phonologic coding. Using a bivariate analysis (selection of a proband based on the presence of a deficit in one skill, and assessing heritability based on measures of the other skill), they demonstrated that deficits in both skills were primarily influenced by the same genetic effects. Furthermore, both skills were related to phonological awareness, with $h_g^2 = .60$, which appeared to be the skill least influenced by shared family environment.

A recent article by Gayan and Olson (2001) also examined the heritabilities of orthographic and phonological variables (phonological decoding and awareness), and reading ability in terms of accuracy and speed. Again, individual and groups differences for these phenotypes could be attributed to genetics, as well as to environment. They also found a large degree of shared genetic variance among these traits, such that the genes influencing one phenotype overlapped significantly with the genes influencing another. However, each phenotype seemed to also have some unique or nonshared genetic variance. Thus, there may be genes that affect various pathways to reading simultaneously, and other genes that are more process-specific. Although Gayan and Olson (2001) point out that molecular genetics searches may discover process-specific genes, these genes may have very small effects relative to other genes that have larger effects across process domains.

Family Studies and Segregation Analysis

There have been many reports of families with histories of RI. Hallgren (1950) conducted the first large study of families loaded with dyslexia and noted the high degree of familial occurrence. Later studies that used more formalized assessment procedures (e.g., Finnuci, Guthrie, Childs, Abbey, & Childs, 1976; Hoien, Lundberg, Larsen, & Tonnessen, 1989) also found a positive family history of dyslexia.

The first formal segregation analysis of RI that based the diagnosis in first-degree relatives on actual testing was done by Lewitter, DeFries, and Elston (1980). When all the families were considered together, major gene inheritance could not be supported, but when the families of female probands were considered separately, autosomal recessive inheritance could not be rejected. Multifactorial inheritance was possible, but a multifactorial–threshold model (with a higher threshold in females) was rejected. Lewitter et al. concluded that genetic heterogeneity was likely in this population, which may have masked a major gene occurring within a subset of families.

Since that time, more sophisticated forms of segregation analysis have been developed that allow consideration of a combination of major gene and polygenic influences (i.e., "mixed models"). Pennington et al. (1991) used such analyses and examined four sets of families from studies based in Colorado, Washington State, and Iowa, as well as a Linkage kindred sample collected specifically for genetic linkage analysis. Evidence for a major dominant or additive gene was found for the Colorado, Washington State,

and the Linkage kindred samples. Segregation in the Iowa sample was more consistent with polygenic influence, and this may have been due to a decrease in the accuracy of the diagnosis in more remote relatives, resulting in lower rates of identified RI, which would mimic a polygenic model. For the dominant major gene model, penetrance in the heterozygote in the study with the most unbiased sample (Colorado) was 1.0 for males and 0.56 for females. The Washington sample was biased toward large multiplex families, and the Linkage kindred sample was selected for an autosomal dominant pattern; in those samples, the penetrance for males was still 1.0, but penetrance for females was 0.7–0.89. Estimates of the number of sporadic cases (i.e., cases of RI without the putative dominant allele) were low; penetrance for the homozygous unaffected genotype ranged from 0.001 to 0.039 in males and was consistently 0.000 in females.

In summary, penetrance estimates from the Pennington et al. study (1991) suggest that if males carry a gene for RI risk, they tend to express it in some fashion (mild or severe), whereas 11 to 44% of females can carry (and pass on) the risk gene(s) for RI and not demonstrate RI themselves. The sporadic or phenocopy rates in the study suggest that some small percentage of males may be diagnosed with RI for environmental reasons (i.e., they do not carry RI genes). females with RI, on the other hand, always appear to carry some genetic predisposition for the disorder.

Segregation analysis has also been performed on a quantitative measure of reading ability derived from standardized tests (Gilger et al., 1996). This analysis was based on the 125 control families (selected through normal reading probands) of the Colorado Family Reading Study (Lewitter et al., 1980). There was evidence for a fairly common major gene acting to produce normal reading variability, and it was estimated that this gene accounted for 54% of the reading variance in the sample. However, the authors cautioned that the analysis may have produced an overly simplistic picture. For instance, a combination of several "susceptibility" loci could mimic a single-gene pattern with greater effect. There may be a handful of genes that, in combination, push a person over the threshold and toward a diagnosis of RI (Gilger et al., 1996). As described elsewhere in this chapter, this conclusion seems to have been borne out by other twin, family, and molecular studies.

More recently, segregation analysis of five different phenotypes in nuclear families ascertained through a reading-disabled proband, found strong evidence for a major gene effect for two phenotypes: nonword memory and digit span. It was estimated that one to three loci were involved for both of these phenotypes. Weaker evidence for a major gene effect was found for spelling and nonword reading (Peterson et al., 1999). An adaptation of the twin method has also supported a major gene effect for RI (Alarcon, DeFries, & Fulker, 1995). Wijsman et al. (2000) examined the reading-related tasks of digit span and nonword repetition, and determined that major gene influence was present for nonword tasks, and that there was significant genetic influence on digit span. Moreover, their results indicate that more than one, but fewer than three genes, may contribute to the variance in these two abilities; although there appears to be shared genetic variance among these abilities, at least nonword reading seems to have its own unique genetic contributors.

Linkage and Molecular Work

Various methods of linkage analysis have been used in studies of RI, including the family study, lod (logarithm of odds) score approach (Morton, 1955), and studies of allele sharing between siblings, based on versions of the sib-pair analysis of Haseman and Elston (1972). In addition, definitions of phenotype have varied widely, from dichotomous affected–unaffected diagnoses to quantitative "summary" variables, to measures of phonological and orthographic phenotypes, among others. The majority of studies have focused on the first loci reported to show linkage, which were markers on chromosome 15 and chromosome 6. Subsequently, additional studies have suggested linkage for reading-related phenotypes on chromosomes 1, 2, 3, 7, and 18 (reviewed in Smith et al., 2002; Williams & Stevenson, 2001).

The first report of linkage with RI was to the centromeric region of chromosome 15 (Smith, Kimberling, Pennington, & Lubs, 1983), using extended families with apparent autosomal dominant transmission. This was not supported by subsequent analysis (e.g., Rabin et al., 1993), although suggestive evidence using two different means of analysis was found for linkage with markers farther down on chromosome 15q (Fulker et al., 1991; Smith, Kimberling & Pennington, 1991). Linkage to this region was also observed in one family studied by Grigorenko et al. (1997) and has been confirmed by association analysis in a sample from the United Kingdom (Morris et al., 1999). There have also been suggestive findings for markers on 1p36, in the region of the Rh gene (Grigorenko et al., 1998; Rabin et al., 1993). In a study of a large Norwegian family, positive linkage was found with markers on 2p (Fagerheim et al., 1999).

Genetic linkage with markers on chromosome area 6p21.3 was first noted by researchers using allele-sharing methods (Smith et al., 1991). These markers were in and around the human leukocyte antigen (HLA) region.[3] Additional markers in the region were examined in a sample of DZ twin pairs participating in the CTS, and linkage was found again (Smith et al., 1991). Subsequently, Cardon et al. (1994) utilized a regression analysis for two-loci and interval mapping, so that sharing of linked genes could be taken into account. Results of this analysis strongly suggested linkage in the DZ twin families for the region between two DNA markers within the HLA system. These findings were replicated by Fisher, Marlow, et al. (1999), Grigorenko et al. (1997), and Grigorenko, Wood, Meyer, and Pauls (2000), as well as another independent sample from the CTS (Gayan et al., 1999). However, Field and Kaplan (1998) did not replicate this linkage. One possible source of variation between the Field and Kaplan study and the studies by Cardon et al. (1994), Fisher et al. (1999), and Gayan et al. (1999) was the use of a dichotomous phenotype; however, further analysis of the data treating the phenotypes as quantitative traits still did not show linkage (Petryshen, Kaplan, Liu, & Field, 2000). Thus, the reasons for this difference are not clear, but they may reflect variations in ascertainment that resulted in genetic heterogeneity.

Interestingly, Cardon et al. (1994) and Gayan et al. (1999) found that the evidence for linkage to 6p21.3 markers increased as the population was selected for increasing severity, as determined by the phenotype scores. Thus, although evidence from quantitative genetic analyses indicate that the same genetic factors may influence reading ability in both normal and disabled readers (e.g., Defries & Alarcon, 1996; Defries & Gillis, 1993; Gilger et al., 1996), this preliminary analysis suggests that the gene(s) on 6 may act differently for people at the low end of the reading continuum.

Linkage studies have also addressed phenotypic issues by comparing different phenotypic measures to see if there were differences in the linkage results. Grigorenko et al. (1997) looked at phonologic and orthographic measures, as well as more global single-word reading measures. Linkage to chromosome 6p was most significant for a measure of phonemic awareness, although other phonologic measures were also significant. Conversely, linkage to chromosome 15q was significant for the single-word reading measure, leading these researchers to conclude that the two genes influenced different reading processes. Studies by Fisher et al. (1999) and Gayan et al. (1999) did not find similar results for the chromosome 6p linkage. While phonologic awareness measures were important, significant results were also found for the other phonologic measures, as well as orthographic coding measures, suggesting that the locus had a more general influence on reading ability. Subsequent analysis by Grigorenko et al. (2000) with a larger sample confirmed the linkage to 6p, but the phenotype was expanded to include other phonologic measures, as well as vocabulary. Thus, linkage to chromosome 6 does not support the assignment of a particular cognitive process to a specific gene, nor does it support dissociation between phonologic and orthographic abilities.

Although the most recent studies of chromosome 6 (Fisher et al., 1999; Gayan et al., 1999; Grigorenko et al., 2000) better localized the critical region carrying the putative gene, or genes, putting people at risk for RI, the responsible gene, or genes, have not been identified. Some candidate genes thought to be relevant to neurodevelopment and functioning in the region have been eliminated: Choi et al. (1998) rejected the gamma-aminobutyric acid (GABA) receptor GABBR1, and Smith et al. (2001) rejected myelin oligodendrocyte glycoprotein (MOG). Francks et al. (2002) have also attempted to narrow down a suspect region on chromosome 2. The candidate genes were SEMA4F and OTX1 (in the 2p12–16 area), and neither candidate was significantly associated with reading-related phenotypes. Others have identified what appears to be a promising candidate gene in the DYX1 area of 15, called DYX1C1 (Taipale et al., 2003). This gene forms protein that is regulated in the brain and that is 78% identical to the homologous protein in the mouse. Thus, the work on chromosomes 2, 15, 6, and 18 must proceed, perhaps a step at a time, toward identifying precisely which of the possibly hundreds of candidate genes contribute to the significant linkages found.

An important recent article by Fisher et al. (2002) reports on a genomewide scan for quantitative trait loci influencing risk for RI. Two primary samples, one from the United Kingdom and one from the United States, were used in the analyses. A region on chromosome 18 (18p11.2) turned out to be one of the most significant regions found for single-word reading ability in both samples. Measures of phonological coding and orthographic coding also showed linkages at this locus. A third U.K. sample was later tested and showed the strongest linkage in this region for phoneme awareness. These authors concluded that in this region of chromosome 18, a gene or genes affect several reading-related processes, serving as a general risk factor for developing RI. This is a highly important finding, and more research is needed on this area of chromosome 18.

In summary, the evidence so far supports the idea that both normal reading and RI are influenced by genetic factors. Classic multifactorial inheritance models were not supported by segregation analysis, and it is likely that a limited number of loci account for most of the tendency towards risk. Although the segregation analysis supports the hypothesis of a single dominant allele with decreased penetrance, it is also possible that the analysis cannot distinguish between the presence of one gene and very few key genes. These genes could be termed quantitative trait loci (QTLs), because they appear to influence the expression of reading ability along a continuum. At least one QTL appears to be around the HLA region of chromosome 6, and other QTLs may exist on chromosomes 18, 15, 3, 2, 1, and elsewhere (Nopula-Hemmi et al., 2001).

Conclusions on the Genetics of Language Impairment and Reading Impairment

The data reviewed here clearly indicate that LI and RI, as well as language and reading skills falling within the normal range, have a genetic component. It is also apparent that environmental factors contribute to the risk for LI and RI, and to variance in the normal ranges as well. Specifically, twin and other studies show that genetic effects account for much of the risk for LI and RI, but that a substantial portion remains unexplained by genetics alone. Many studies have in fact shown that the environment is a potent source of individual and group variation in language and reading-related abilities, and at the very least, people must be exposed to language and reading to acquire these skills (e.g., Bates, Bretherton, Beeghly-Smith, & McNew, 1982; Molfese et al., 2001; Pinker, 1994; Shore, 1995; Snow, 1996).

Because this chapter deals with the genetics of LI and RI, we do not describe or review in detail the research on environmental effects (Bates et al., 1982; Molfese, et al., 2001; Pinker, 1994; Shore, 1995; Snow, 1996; Tomblin, Hardy, & Hein, 1991). However, toward a better understanding of how genes operate in conjunction with environments, we want to briefly revisit the Basic Model presented in Figure 2.1 and elaborate further now that the genetic evidence has been summarized.

The expanded Basic Model of Figure 2.1 notes that genes and environments interact in complicated ways. However, in Figure 2.2, we add a few additional complexities. First, we describe a hypothetical oligogenic model in which four genes (G1–G4) and three environmental effects (E1–E3) represent the major factors influencing language and reading abilities in two different people (Person 1 and Person 2). Under certain circumstances, say, whether a person has the "good" or "bad" alleles of G1–G4, or whether the person experiences negative or positive types of E1–E3, RI and/or LI can result. Recall that every person in the population has G1–G4 but may have different forms of the genes (alleles) at these loci.

For the sake of illustration, we identify each of the four genes for the neurodevelopmental function they serve. These hypothetical genes are based on research that suggests that the brains of individuals with RI are anatomically different than the brains of normal readers (Grigorenko, 2001; Guttorm, Leppanen, & Richardson, 2001). Moreover, many of these observed brain differences may be due to cell migration, cell death, and differentiation errors, thus primarily arising *in utero* (Galaburda, Schrott, Sherman, Rosen, & Denenberg, 1996; Grigorenko, 2001). With this in mind, four illustrative genes are named: G1, a gene affecting cell connections; G2, a gene affecting cell growth and differentiation; G3, a gene affecting neuronal migration; and G4, an unidentified neurotransmitter. It is important to remember that these are hypothetical genes that represent general functions. The processes of neurodevelopment and function require the complex orchestration of many genes, and Figure 2.2 shows explicitly that G1–G4 exist and work in the context of other genes (Hartl & Jones, 2001; Pfaff, Berrentini, Joh, & Maxson, 2000). In fact, out of the 40,000–60,000 or so genes comprising the normal human genome, 30% or more are expressed in the brain and may be dedicated solely to brain development and/or function (Adams et al., 1991; Crowe, 1993).

E1–E3 are examples of environmental effects that can act differently at different points of development: E1 represents a viral infection; E2 is a linguistic stimulation vari-

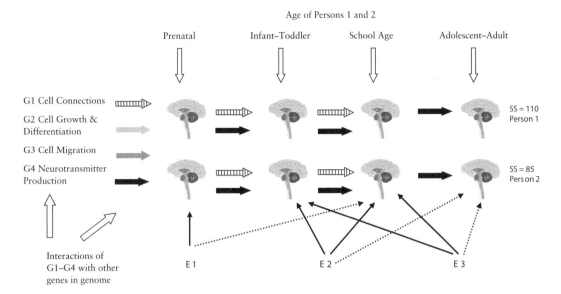

FIGURE 2.2. Oligogenic and lifespan model of genetic and environmental effects on brain and cognitive development. E1–E3 are environmental effects, where dashed lines indicate weaker or no effect relative to solid lines, where effects are stronger. G1–G4 represent a four-gene model, with each gene having unique effects on brain function or growth. Brain function is assessed by a surface phenotype: reading test standard score (SS). Note that genetic and environmental factors act differently at different points in time. See text for explanation.

able; and E3 is a nutritional variable. Again, as in the case of G1–G4, the precise nature of these environmental variables is unspecified. Nonetheless, it can be said that for developmental disorders, the environment may act in a manner that interferes or interacts with, helps or hinders, what would be the normal developmental pathway from gene to behavior. This is in contrast to the case of acquired disorders, in which the environment may actually damage an already existing structure or inhibit a previously normal function.

Figure 2.2 also shows that different genes are more important at different stages of development. For example, cell migration and differentiation are largely complete before birth, whereas cell connections continue to increase for years thereafter. Similarly, an environmental effect such as viral exposure (E1) may have a more significant negative effect on brain development if it occurs during a critical time *in utero*, when cells are rapidly migrating and differentiating, and it may have no effect on the brain if it occurs

later in life. E2 and E3, on the other hand, are important to the cell connectivity of the brain, particularly after birth. Also recall that the ultimate effects of E1–E3 depend to some extent on a person's genetic makeup, so that some people will be seriously affected, for example, by the operation of E1 *in utero,* whereas others may not (see discussion of Figure 2.1 and gene–environment interactions).

In the model, the joint actions of G1–G4 and E1–E3 are responsible for the variation of risk seen in the population for RI or LI. For example, let us assume that Person 1 in Figure 2.2 meets with a virus *in utero* but has an above average amount of linguistic stimulation and good nutrition early in life. This person, who also has the normal, or "good," alleles of G1 and G2, together with a nearly optimal postnatal environment, ends up with a well-functioning, typical brain and does not meet the criteria for RI or LI (as depicted by a reading standard score of 110 in Figure 2.2). Person 2 is different and ends up with below average reading ability (as depicted by a standard score of 85). Although G1 is normal, this person received the nonoptimal alleles of G2 and G3. This person also met with a virus *in utero* and experienced relatively impoverished linguistic environment as a young child. For these reasons, Person 2 experiences "atypical brain development" and manifests poor reading and/or language abilities (Gilger & Kaplan, 2001).

Depending on the circumstances, either all or a subset of the G and E factors can exert powerful effects. Indeed, research indicates that something like G1–G4 travels in families and occurs naturally in the general population, putting some people at risk for RI. Research also indicates that something like E1–E3 exists, although it may vary from person to person and family to family.

Furthermore, Figure 2.2 illustrates that key gene actions affecting reading and language may occur early or later in development. Some genes act *in utero*, then never work again (e.g., G2 and G3), whereas other genes continue to operate in the day-to-day activities of the brain (e.g., G4). In this way, when considering the genetics of RI or LI, we need to be aware that what we observe may be the distal effects of genes (i.e., effects that occurred early in development, such as those regulating neuronal migration and death, and that may or may not be operational throughout life) or the proximal and activational effects of genes that are expressed to some degree from conception on (i.e., those genes that regulate certain neurotransmitters needed for everyday cognitive functioning and the connections among neurons; see Gilger, 1995).

CONCLUSIONS AND FUTURE RESEARCH DIRECTIONS

In closing this chapter, we want to draw a bit from an article (Gilger & Kaplan, 2001) that advocates a view of LI and RI that fits well with the information we have reviewed thus far and explicitly acknowledges the following five points:

1. LI and RI are etiologically heterogeneous.

2. Neither LI or RI is due to single, major genes.
3. There is variation in the neurological/neuropsychological substrate leading to LI or RI in different people (although some commonalities exist).
4. LI and RI can reflect the operation of multiple cognitive and neuropsychological pathways.
5. LI and RI may reflect natural variation in the way the brain works for complicated cognitive skills.

As we have reviewed in this chapter, both genes and environments are responsible for the atypical developmental processes that can affect the brain and give rise to LI or RI. The currently available data also suggest that no single gene is responsible for the majority of cases or deficits of any particular form of developmental LI or RI. However, we are on our way to identifying tentative genes or "susceptibility alleles" as contributors to risk. There is increasing evidence that there are probably multiple and heterogeneous effects of the RI and LI risk genes that act alone or together to give rise to multiple cognitive or neuropsychological profiles of reading- and language-related skills, culminating at times in what looks like the same diagnosable disability on the surface, if all one does is assess, say, basic reading or expressive language vis-à-vis standard tests. Indeed, research on the genetics of RI and LI suggests that genes may influence multiple brain areas and functions simultaneously, and contribute to the variance in reading and language in a complex manner, rather than in a focused, singular, and direct manner, as predicted by single-gene and disease models. Different risk genes may operate on some or all of the subsystems or subabilities for reading or language and affect reading or language in their own way.

Other research in neurogenetics (not reviewed here) agrees that there are multiple genes involved in the development and function of the brain (Anderson, 1999; Crowe, 1993; Raff, 1996), and it is unlikely that a specific brain region or function is controlled solely by one gene (though certain genes may, theoretically, contribute a large effect in some areas of functioning). Furthermore, the complexities of the pathways, first from gene to gene product, and second, from gene product to behavior, provide additional opportunities for multiple genes to influence a behavior such as reading through various neurological and/or metabolic systems (e.g., multiple genes, along with environmental agents, may control cell migration or the manufacture of a functional neurotransmitter needed for a behavior; see Figures 2.1 and 2.2). Finally, the complicated and not fully understood operation of neurodevelopmental genes suggests that for traits as complex as learning in humans, a single genetic defect may yield multiple problems, especially if this defect is present in the earlier stages of development. For example, it is likely that a major gene that is important to cell migration or connection affects multiple brain areas to varying degrees and, thus, most often influences multiple skill areas. Moreover, even if a mutant gene's effects are highly localized and limited to specific brain areas early in development, these effects can be observed in other areas as the organism matures: Defects or variation in lower (or other) brain areas can influence the development and function of higher (or other) brain areas (Conn, 1992; Gerlai, 1996; Luria, 1973; Rondi-Reig, Caston, Delhaye-Bouchaud, & Mariani, 1999). In fact, the more that higher order brain functioning and cognition require integrative brain functions with demands on multiple areas, such as those involved in learning disorders, the less likely it is that even the most specific gene effect will yield a homogeneous and single-deficit phenotype.

Furthermore, even if the discrimination of subtypes of learning disabilities (e.g., RI vs. LI vs. attention-deficit/hyperactivity disorder [ADHD]) were a function of one or two distinct major genes influencing a different primary brain area for each disorder, the enormous comorbidity across these conditions would argue for the multifocal actions of each gene and/or the multifocal developmental effects of single genes that originally operated on more specific brain areas. If this is so, a "pure" form of RI, LI, or ADHD would be rare. Pure forms of any

developmental learning or behavior disorder are in fact difficult to find (reviewed in Gilger & Kaplan, 2001).

In summary, it is not likely that one common genetic or environmental factor alone will explain a significant majority of nonsyndromic developmental LI or RI cases in the population. Multiple factors, perhaps a couple of major genes, and a few environmental events interact to create a tendency toward or away from developmental LI or RI. These factors have variable effects on the neurology and neuropsychology responsible for LDs. Thus, people with LDs have "atypical brains," but not every LD brain is atypical in the same way. This fact is relevant to research and practice (Gilger & Kaplan, 2001).

It is important to acknowledge that the search for the genes that influence LI and RI is really a search for the genes that determine "atypical brain development" (Gilger & Kaplan, 2001). In other words, we are not really looking for genes that affect the surface phenotype of learning ability as measured by standardized tests; instead we are looking for genes that cause brain variation in the population, such that some people fare better than others when it comes to learning and intelligence. As such, future work in this area would do well to include multiple measures of brain function, including, but not limited to, tests of general reading, word recognition, math, processing speed, motoric processes, attention, visual–spatial abilities, and other direct and indirect measures of brain structure and processing, lest a limited phenotype miss much of the complexity of an individual's neurological status. For example, in genetic work, such an error may actually mislead researchers into believing they have found a susceptibility allele, say, for phonological processing in families with RI, when they have not even checked to see whether other neuropsychological phenotypes or cognitive components are also affected. A limited phenotypic focus may also lead researchers to conclude that their findings are null regarding a gene for RI or LI, when in fact they would have found genetic linkages had they assessed other possible phenotypic manifestations of an atypical brain in their sample (poor motor coordination, inattentiveness, oral apraxia, etc.). These cautionary statements about a limited phenotype are supported by some fine ongoing work (e.g., DeFries, Knopik, & Wadsworth, 1999; Fisher, Stein, & Monaco, 1999; Lyytinen, Leinonen, Nikula, Aro, & Leiwo, 1995; Pennington & Smith, 1997; Petryshen, Kaplan, Liu, & Field, 1999).

Current advances in imaging and genetics will make it possible to learn about how the brain develops to cause LDs, by going first from the brain and then to a phenotype, in contrast to the usual method of attempting to define a narrow or "gold standard" phenotype, then study it. For example, we could select groups of children with and without LD on the basis of some phenotype, as is typically done. However, we would use large-scale and broad-based imaging to examine multifocal abnormalities (if they exist). We in turn could use this broad scanning information to go back and conduct further phenotypic assessments, with the objective of clarifying how observable deviations from typical brain development or function are related to phenotypic abnormalities (or even superior skills; Gilger & Kaplan, 2001). This would require supplementing the standard tests with broader based assessments aimed at more fully describing each individual's neuropsychological strengths and weaknesses. With this approach, we would not be forcing a phenotype on what is believed to be a nonspecific neurological disorder; rather, we would be allowing the brain-based deviations to guide us. In other words, the brain could guide our exploration of phenotype. This type of brain-driven approach is currently underutilized in LD research, and it would be easy to add a molecular genetic or quantitative genetic component to these studies.

GLOSSARY

The following is a list of some terms and brief definitions used in this chapter. For more complete descriptions and examples of how these terms are used in the field, see Hartl and Jones (2001), Gilger (1995, 2000), Plomin et al. (2001), and King and Stansfield (1997).

Allele: One of the alternate forms of a gene with variation in the DNA sequence at a site (locus) on a chromosome. For example, some genes have recessive and dominant forms.

Autosomal dominant genes, traits, or disorders: Genes are represented as pairs in normal humans. Each member of a pair may interact in a dominant, recessive, or additive manner with the other. Dominance refers to the situation in which one gene of the pair is expressed over the other. Only one copy of a dominant gene is needed for the trait to be shown.

Autosomal recessive genes, traits, or disorders: Recessivity refers to the situation in which the effects of one gene are subordinate to those of another (*see* "Autosomal Dominant genes, traits, or disorders"). Two copies of the recessive genes are needed for the trait to be shown.

Chromosome: A thread-like structure composed primarily of chromatin, which contains DNA. These structures come in 23 pairs in normal humans and reside in the nuclei of cells.

Concordance: As used here, the extent to which members of twin pairs are alike for a phenotype. There are different types of concordance rates (e.g., probandwise) and the use of each depends on certain sampling methods and statistical assumptions.

Deoxyribonucleic acid (DNA): DNA is the essential molecule of chromosomes and, therefore, genes. Specific coding properties of DNA specify genes and gene products, and allow for the transmission of genetic information across generations.

Gene: *See* "Chromosome." A hereditary unit. There are different types of genes, but essentially a gene is a specific arrangement of chromosomal DNA that is required to produce a functional product (e.g., protein) necessary in development. The composition, regulation, synthesis, transcription, and other processes that concern genes can be quite complicated.

Genetic heterogeneity: The situation in which different and distinct genes can give rise to the same or similar behavior. Genetic heterogeneity is suspected for many complex traits, including dyslexia, specific language impairment, and psychiatric conditions.

Genotype: A person's genetic composition in general, or at a specific chromosome site.

Heritability (h^2): The standardized proportion of phenotypic variance or individual differences in a population due to genetic effects. The proportion of variance in a trait remaining once the contribution of environment to trait variance has been controlled, which ranges from 0 to 1.0. The heritability statistic does not apply to the individual, only to populations. Hence, if the h^2 estimate for IQ is .50, it does not mean that 50% of a person's IQ is due to genes. It does, however, reflect the extent to which differences in the IQs among people are due to genes.

Heritability, group form (h_g^2): Akin to regular h^2 but calculated differently, allowing for an assessment of the extent to which genes cause difference between, say, normal and abnormal groups of readers or speakers.

Heterozygote versus homozygote: Having two unalike alleles versus two alike alleles in a particular gene pair at a site (locus) on a chromosome.

Major gene or single gene models: Systems in which the phenotype is predominately determined by single genes with significant effects. Common in many genetic diseases.

Multifactorial-threshold models: In this context, a system in which a certain number of genetic and environmental factors add up to increase risk to a point that a threshold is met and the phenotype or disorder is expressed.

Nonshared and shared familial environmental effects: The literature often draws distinctions between "shared environmental effects" and "nonshared environmental effects." Suffice it to say here that shared effects tend to make family members alike, whereas nonshared effects make family members unalike. Both effects operate to add environmental variance to the population and are reflected in what is "left over" after heritability is calculated and the effects of genes are removed from the total variance in the population. For example, if heritability is .35, or 35% of the population variance is due to genetics, then the amount of variance explained by environment is .65.

Oligogenic trait or model: The situation in which each of a limited number of genes contribute significantly to trait variability. This is different from a classic polygenic model, in which it is assumed that many genes, each with small and relatively equal effects, add to the phenotypic variance in the population.

Penetrance: Also see "Variable expressivity." The likelihood that the effects of a gene will be expressed in a person with the gene. A gene is said to be fully penetrant if 100% of those carrying the gene show the gene effects. A gene is said to have incomplete penetrance if, say, only 60% of those with the gene manifest the trait.

Phenotype and phenotypic variance: Phenotype refers to the observable characteristics of gene expression. It can occur at the basic molecular level (e.g., proteins or blood type) or be more removed (e.g., language test scores or measures of brain structure). Phenotypic variance refers to individual differences in the population for a trait.

Proband: The family member through whom the family is ascertained. Probands typically have the trait or disorder of interest (e.g., a proband with dyslexia).

Quantitative-trait loci (QTLs): Variation in stretches of DNA, whether they represent specific genes or not, that are correlated with variations in a quantitatively measured trait. For example, variations in a stretch of DNA on chromosome 6 are significantly associated with variations in reading ability. Individuals with particular variations in this chromosomal region tend to have lower reading test scores than those with different variations (see text).

Susceptibility allele: An allele, that in combination with other alleles adds to the likelihood that a disorder will develop. *See* "Oligogenic trait or model; and "Quantitative trait loci (QTLs)."

Variable expressivity: The extent or manner in which a gene is expressed. If gene expressivity is variable, the trait may vary from mild to severe across people, from mild to severe within a person and across time, or as apparently different traits across people or across time.

NOTES

1. The Glossary briefly defines some of the terms used in this chapter.
2. As discussed in this chapter, genes never work in a vacuum. In fact, the normal expression and function of any particular gene most often depends on both the environment and other genetic influences. The term "vacuum," as used here, is a simple way of saying that, if a vacuum existed, the genetic code would be fully actualized as well as its imaginary potential, which of course, can never be known.
3. That genes for RI may be associated with a family of genes related to the human immune system is of more than passing interest. The immune system and neurodevelopment may indeed be tied together, and correlations between RI and immune system dysfunction have often been reported (see reviews in Bryden, MacManus, & Bulman-Fleming, 1994).

REFERENCES

Adams, M. D., Kelley, J. M., Gocayne, J. D., Dubnick, M., Polymeropoulos, M. H., Xiao, H., et al. (1991). Complementary DNA sequencing: Expressed sequence tags and human genome project. *Science, 252,* 1651–1656.

Alarcon, M., DeFries, J. C., & Fulker, D. W. (1995). Etiology of individual differences in reading performance: A test of sex limitation. *Behavior Genetics, 25,* 17–23.

Ambrose, N., Yairi, E., & Cox, N. (1993). Genetic aspects of early childhood stuttering. *Journal of Speech and Hearing Research, 36,* 701–706.

Anderson, S. A. (1999). Dlx genes, the striatal subventricular zone, and the development of neocortical interneurons. In D. D. Duane (Ed.), *Reading and attention disorders: Neurobiological correlates* (pp. 1–16). Timonium, MD: York Press.

Aram, D., & Nation, J. E. (1975). Patterns of language behavior in children with developmental language disorders. *Journal of Speech and Hearing Research, 18,* 229–241.

Bailey, A., Palferman, S., Heavey, L., & Le Couteur, A. (1998). Autism: The phenotype in relatives. *Journal of Autism and Developmental Disorders, 28,* 369–392.

Bates, E., Bretherton, I., Beeghly-Smith, M., & McNew, S. (1982). Social bases of language development: A reassessment. In H. Reese & L. Lipsett (Eds.), *Advances in child development and behavior* (Vol. 16, pp. 7–75). New York: Academic Press.

Bishop, D. V. (1994). Is specific language impairment a valid diagnostic category?: Genetic and psycholinguistic evidence. *Philosophical Transactions of the Royal Society of London, Series B, Biological Sciences, 346*(1315), 105–111.

Bishop, D. V. (2001). Genetic and environmental risks for specific language impairment in children. *Philosophical Transactions of the Royal Society of London, Series B, Biological Sciences, 356*(1407), 369–380.

Bishop, D. V., North, T., & Donlan, C. (1995). Genetic basis of specific language impairment: Evidence from a twin study. *Developmental Medicine and Child Neurology, 37,* 56–71.

Bryden, M. P., MacManus, I. C., & Bulman-Fleming, M. B. (1994). Evaluating the empirical support for the Geschwind–Behan–Galaburda model of cerebral lateralization. *Brain and Cognition, 26,* 103–167.

Cardon, L. R., Smith, S. D., Fulker, D. W., Kimberling, W. J., Pennington, B. F., & DeFries, J. C. (1994). Quantitative trait locus for reading disability on chromosome 6. *Science, 266,* 276–279.

Catts, H., Fey, M., Zhang, X., & Tomblin, J. B. (1999). Language basis of reading and reading disabilities: Evidence from a longitudinal investigation. *Scientific Studies of Reading, 3,* 331–361.

Conn, M. T. E. (1992). *Gene expression in neural tissue.* San Diego: Academic Press.

Crowe, R. R. (1993). Candidate genes in psychiatry: An epidemiological perspective. *American Journal of Medical Genetics, 48,* 74–77.

Dale, P. S., Simonoff, E., Bishop, D. V., Eley, T. C., Oliver, B., Price, T. S., et al. (1998). Genetic influence on language delay in two-year-old children. *Nature Neuroscience, 1,* 324–328.

DeFries, J., & Alarcon, M. (1996). Genetics of specific reading disability. *Mental Retardation and Developmental Disabilities Research Reviews, 2,* 39–47.

DeFries, J., & Fulker, D. (1988). Multiple regression analysis of twin data: Etiology of deviant scores versus individual differences. *Acta Geneticae Medicae et Gemellogiae, 37,* 205–216.

DeFries, J., & Gillis, J. J. (1993). Genetics of reading disability. In R. Plomin & G. E. McClearn (Eds.), *Nature, nurture, and psychology* (pp. 121–146). Washington, DC: American Psychological Association.

DeFries, J., Knopik, V., & Wadsworth, S. (1999). Colorado twin study of reading disability. In D. D. Duane (Ed.), *Reading and attention disorders: Neurobiological correlates* (pp. 17–42). Timonium, MD: York Press.

Eden, G., VanMeter, J. W., Rumsey, J. M., Maisog, J. M., Woods, R. P., & Zeffiro, T. A. (1996). Abnormal processing of visual motion in dyslexia revealed by functional brain imaging. *Nature, 382,* 66–69.

Eden, G., & Zeffiro, T. A. (1998). Neural systems affected in developmental dyslexia revealed by functional neuroimaging. *Neuron, 21,* 279–282.

Ewart, A. K., Morris, C. A., Atkinson, D., Ji, W., Sternes, K., Spallone, P., et al. (1993). Hemizygosity at the elastin locus in a developmental disorder, Williams syndrome. *Nature: Genetics, 5,* 11–16.

Fagerheim, T., Raeymaekers, P., Tonnessen, F. E., Pedersen, M., Tranebjaerg, L., & Lubs, H. A. (1999). A new gene (DYX3) for dyslexia is located on chromosome 2. *Journal of Medical Genetics, 36,* 664–669.

Felsenfeld, S., & Drayna, D. (2001). Stuttering and genetics: Our past and our future. In S. E. Gerber (Ed.), *The handbook of genetic communicative disorders* (pp. 152–177). San Diego: Academic Press.

Field, L. L., & Kaplan, B. J. (1998). Absence of linkage of phonological coding dyslexia to chromosome 6p23-p21.3 in a large family data set. *American Journal of Human Genetics, 63,* 1448–1456.

Finnuci, J. M., Guthrie, J. T., Childs, A. L., Abbey, H., & Childs, B. (1976). The genetics of specific reading disability. *Annual Reviews of Human Genetics, 40,* 1–23.

Fisher, S. E., Francks, C., Marlow, A. J., MacPhie, L., Newbury, D. F., Cardon, L., et al. (2001). Independent genome-wide scans identify a chromosome 18 quantitative-trait locus influencing dyslexia. *Nature: Genetics, 30,* 86–91.

Fisher, S. E., Marlow, A. J., Lamb, J., Maestrini, E., Williams, D. F., Richardson, et al. (1999). A quantitative-trait locus on chromosome 6p influences different aspects of developmental dyslexia. *American Journal of Human Genetics, 64,* 146–156.

Fisher, S. E., Stein, J. F., & Monaco, A. P. (1999). A genome-wide search strategy for identifying quantitative trait loci involved in reading and spelling disability (developmental dyslexia). *European Child and Adolescent Psychiatry, 8* (Suppl. 3), 47–51.

Fisher, S. E., Vargha-Khadem, F., Watkins, K. E., Monaco, A. P., & Pembrey, M. E. (1998). Localisation of a gene implicated in a severe speech and language disorder. *Nature: Genetics, 18,* 168–170.

Fletcher, J. M. (1992). The validity of distinguishing children with language and learning disabilities according to discrepancies with IQ: Introduction to the special series. *Journal of Learning Disabilities, 25,* 546–548.

Francks, C., Fisher, S. E., Olson, R. K., Pennington, B. F., Smith, S. D., DeFries, J. C., et al. (2002). Fine mapping of the chromosome 2p12–16 dyslexia susceptibility locus: Quantitative association analysis and positional candidate genes SEMA4F and OTX1. *Psychiatric Genetics, 12,* 35–41.

Fulker, D. W., Cardon, L. R., DeFries, J. C., Kimberling, W. J., Pennington, B. F., & Smith, S. D. (1991). Multiple regression analysis of sib-pair data on reading to detect quantitative trait loci. *Reading and Writing: An Interdisciplinary Journal, 3,* 299–313.

Galaburda, A., Schrott, L. M., Sherman, G. F., Rosen, G. D., & Denenberg, V. H. (1996). Animal models of developmental dyslexia. In C. H. Chase, G. D. Rosen, & G. F. Sherman (Eds.), *Developmental dyslexia: Neural, cognitive, and genetic mechanisms* (pp. 3–14). Baltimore: York Press.

Galaburda, A. M. (1992). Neurology of developmental dyslexia. *Current Opinion in Neurology and Neurosurgery, 5,* 71–76.

Galaburda, A. M. (1993). Neurology of developmental dyslexia. *Current Opinion in Neurobiology, 3,* 237–242.

Gayan, J., & Olson, R. K. (2001). Genetic and environmental influences on orthographic and phonological skills in children with reading disabilities. *Developmental Neuropsychology, 20,* 483–507.

Gayan, J., Smith, S. D., Cherny, S. S., Cardon, L. R., Fulker, D. W., Brower, A. M., et al. (1999). Quantitative-trait locus for specific language and reading deficits on chromosome 6p. *American Journal of Human Genetics, 64,* 157–164.

Gerlai, R. (1996). Gene-targeting studies of mammalian behavior: Is it the mutation or the background genotype? *Trends in Neuroscience, 19,* 177–181.

Gilger, J. (1995). Behavioral genetics: Concepts for research and practice in language development and disorders. *Journal of Speech and Hearing Research, 38,* 1126–1142.

Gilger, J. (2000). Contribution and promise of human behavioral genetics. *Human Biology, 72,* 229–255.

Gilger, J., Borecki, I. B., Smith, S. D., DeFries, J. C., & Pennington, B. F. (1996). The etiology of extreme scores for complex phenotypes: An illustration using reading performance. In C. H. Chase, G. D. Rosen, & G. F. Sherman (Eds.), *Developmental dyslexia:*

Neural, cognitive, and genetic mechanisms (pp. 63–85). Baltimore: York Press.

Gilger, J., Ho, H., Whipple, A., & Spitz, R. (2001). Genotype–environment correlations for language-related abilities: Implications for typical and atypical learners. *Journal of Learning Disabilities, 34,* 492–502.

Gilger, J., & Kaplan, B. J. (2001). The neuropsychology of dyslexia: The concept of atypical brain development. *Developmental Neuropsychology, 20,* 465–481.

Goei, V. L., Choi, J., Ahn, J., Bowlus, C. L., Raha-Chowdhury, R., & Gruen, J. R. (1998). Human gamma-aminobutyric acid B receptor gene: Complementary DNA cloning, expression, chromosomal location, and genomic organization. *Biological Psychiatry, 44,* 659–666.

Gopnik, M. (1990). Feature-blind grammar and dysphasia. *Nature, 344,* 715.

Grigorenko, E. L. (2001). Developmental dyslexia: An update on genes, brains, and environments. *Journal of Child Psychology and Psychiatry, 42,* 91–125.

Grigorenko, E. L., Wood, F. B., Meyer, M. S., Hart, L. A., Speed, W. C., Shuster, A., et al. (1997). Susceptibility loci for distinct components of developmental dyslexia on chromosomes 6 and 15. *American Journal of Human Genetics, 60,* 27–39.

Grigorenko, E. L., Wood, F. B., Meyer, M. S., & Pauls, D. L. (2000). Chromosome 6p influences on different dyslexia-related cognitive processes: Further confirmation. *American Journal of Human Genetics, 66,* 715–723.

Grigorenko, E. L., Wood, F. B., Meyer, M. S., Pauls, J. E., Hart, L. A., & Pauls, D. (1998, June 8–10). *Linkage studies suggest a possible locus for dyslexia near the Rh region on chromosome 1.* Paper Presented to the Annual Meeting of the Behavior Genetics Association, Stockholm, Sweden.

Guttorm, T., Leppanen, P., & Richardson, U. (2001). Event-related potentials and consonant differentiation in newborns with familial risk for dyslexia. *Journal of Learning Disabilities, 34,* 534–544.

Hallgren, H. (1950). Specific dyslexia ("Congenital word blindness"). *Acta Psychiatrica Scandinavica, 65* (Suppl.), 1287.

Hardy-Brown, K. (1983). Universals and individual differences: Disentangling two approaches to the study of language acquisition. *Developmental Psychology, 19,* 610–624.

Hardy-Brown, K., & Plomin, R. (1985). Infant communicative development: Evidence from adoptive and biological families for genetic and environmental influences on rate differences. *Developmental Psychology, 21,* 378–385.

Hartl, D., & Jones, E. W. (2001). *Genetics: Analysis of genes and genomes* (5th ed.). Sudbury, MA: Jones & Bartlett.

Haseman, J. K., & Elston, R. C. (1972). The investigation of linkage between a quantitative trait and a marker locus. *Behavior Genetics, 2,* 3–19.

Hay, D. A., Prior, M., Collett, S., & Williams, M.

(1987). Speech and language development in preschool twins. *Acta Geneticae Medicae et Gemellogiae (Roma)*, 36, 213–223.

Hohnen, B., & Stevenson, J. (1999). The structure of genetic influences on general cognitive, language, phonological, and reading abilities. *Developmental Psychology*, 25, 590–603.

Hoien, T., Lundberg, I., Larsen, P., & Tonnessen, F. E. (1989). Profiles of reading related skills in dyslexic families. *Reading and Writing: An Interdisciplinary Journal*, 1, 381–392.

Howie, P. (1981). Concordance for stuttering in monozygotic and dizygotic twin pairs. *Journal of Speech and Hearing Research*, 24, 317–321.

Hurst, J., Baraitser, M., Auger, E., Graham, F., & Norell, S. (1990). An extended family with a dominantly inherited speech disorder. *Developmental Medicine and Child Neurology*, 32, 347–355.

Johnston, J. R. (1988). Specific language disorders in the child. In N. Lass, L. McReynolds, J. Northern, & D. Yoder (Eds.), *Handbook of speech-language pathology and audiology* (pp. 685–715). Toronto: Decker.

Johnston, J. R. (1991). The continuing relevance of cause: A reply to Leonard's "Specific language impairment as a clinical category." *Language Speech and Hearing Services in Schools*, 22, 75–79.

Joseph, J., Noble, K., & Eden, G. (2001). The neurobiological basis of reading. *Journal of Learning Disabilities*, 34, 566–579.

King, R. C., & Stansfield, W. D. (1997). *A dictionary of genetics*. New York: Oxford University Press.

Lahey, M., & Edwards, J. (1995). Specific language impairment: Preliminary investigation of factors associated with family history and with patterns of language performance. *Journal of Speech and Hearing Research*, 38, 643–657.

Leonard, C. M., Puranik, C., Kuldau, J. M., & Lombardino, L. J. (1998). Normal variation in the frequency and location of human auditory cortex landmarks: Heschl's gyrus: Where is it? *Cerebral Cortex*, 8, 397–406.

Leonard, L. B. (1989). Language learnability and specific language impairment in children. *Applied Psycholinguistics*, 10, 179–202.

Leonard, L. B. (1991). Specific language impairment as a clinical category. *Language Speech and Hearing Services in Schools*, 22, 66–68.

Leske, M. C. (1981). Prevalence estimates of communicative disorders in the U. S. : Speech disorders. *Journal of the American Speech and Hearing Association*, 23, 217–225.

Lewis, B. (1992). Pedigree analysis of children with phonology disorders. *Journal of Learning Disabilities*, 25, 586–597.

Lewis, B. A., Cox, N. J., & Byard, P. J. (1993). Segregation analysis of speech and language disorders. *Behavior Genetics*, 23, 291–297.

Lewis, B. A., & Freebairn, L. (1997). Subgrouping children with familial phonologic disorders. *Journal of Communication Disorders*, 30, 385–401.

Lewis, B. A., & Thompson, L. A. (1992). A study of developmental speech and language disorders in twins. *Journal of Speech and Hearing Research*, 35, 1086–1094.

Lewitter, F. I., DeFries, J. C., & Elston, R. C. (1980). Genetic models of reading disability. *Behavior Genetics*, 10, 9–30.

Locke, J. L., & Mather, P. (1989). Genetic factors in the ontogeny of spoken language: Evidence from monozygotic and dizygotic twins. *Journal of Child Language*, 16, 553–559.

Luria, A. R. (1973). *The working brain*. Baltimore: Penguin.

Lyytinen, H., Leinonen, M., Nikula, M., Aro, M., & Leiwo, M. (1995). In search of the core features of dyslexia: Observations concering dyslexia in the highly orthographic regular Finnish language. In V. Berninger (Ed.), *The varieties of orthographic knowledge: II. Relationships to phonology, reading, and writing* (pp. 177–204). Dordrecht, the Netherlands: Kluwer Press.

Matheny, A., & Bruggerman, C. E. (1973). Children's speech: Heredity components and sex differences. *Folia Phoniatrica et Logopaedica (Basel)*, 25, 442–449.

Mather, P. L., & Black, K. N. (1984). Hereditary and environmental influences on preschool twins' language skills. *Developmental Psychology*, 20, 303–308.

Molfese, V., Molfese, D., & Modgline, A. (2001). Newborn and preschool predictors of second-grade reading scores: An evaluation of categorical and continuous scores. *Journal of Learning Disabilities*, 34, 545–554.

Morton, N. E. (1955). Sequential tests for the detection of linkage. *American Journal of Human Genetics*, 7, 277–328.

Munsinger, H., & Douglass, A. (1976). The syntactic abilities of identical twins, fraternal twins, and their siblings. *Child Development*, 47, 40–50.

Nopola-Hemmi, J., Myllyluoma, B., Haltia, T., Taipale, M., Ollikainen, V., Ahonen, T., et al. (2001). A dominant gene for developmental dyslexia on chromosome 3. *Journal of Medical Genetics*, 38, 658–664.

Olson, R., Forsberg, H., & Wise, B. (1994). Genes, environment and the development of orthographic skills. In V. Berninger (Ed.), *The varieties of orthographic knowledge: Vol. 1. Theoretical and developmental issues* (pp. 27–71). Dordrecht, the Netherlands: Kluwer Press.

Osborne, R. T., Gregor, A. J., & Miele, F. (1968). Heritability of factor V: Verbal comprehension. *Perceptual and Motor Skills*, 26, 191–202.

Owens, R. E. (1995). *Language disorders: A functional approach to assessment and intervention* (2nd ed.). Boston: Allyn & Bacon.

Pennington, B. F. (1991). *Diagnosing learning disorders: A neuropsychological framework*. New York: Guilford Press.

Pennington, B. F., Gilger, J. W., Olson, R. K., & DeFries, J. C. (1992). The external validity of age- versus IQ-discrepancy definitions of reading disability:

Lessons from a twin study. *Journal of Learning Disabilities, 25,* 562–573.

Pennington, B. F., Gilger, J. W., Pauls, D. L., Smith, S. A., Smith, S. D., & DeFries, J. C. (1991). Evidence for major gene transmission of developmental dyslexia. *Journal of the American Medical Association, 266,* 1527–1534.

Pennington, B. F., & Smith, S. D. (1997). Genetic analysis of dyslexia and other complex behavioral phenotypes. *Current Opinion in Pediatrics, 9,* 636–641.

Petryshen, T. L., Kaplan, B. J., Liu, M. F., & Field, L. L. (1999). Evidence for a susceptibility locus for phonological coding dyslexia on chromosome 6q13-q16. 2. *American Journal of Human Genetics, 65,* A32.

Petryshen, T. L., Kaplan, B. J., Liu, M. F., & Field, L. L. (2000). Absence of significant linkage between phonological coding dyslexia and chromosome 6p23-21. 3, as determined by use of quantitative-trait methods: Confirmation of qualitative analyses. *American Journal of Human Genetics, 66,* 708–714.

Pfaff, D. W., Berrentini, W. H., Joh, T. H. & Maxson, S. C. (2000). *Genetic influences on neural and behavioral functions.* Boca Raton, FL: CRC Press.

Pinker, S. (1994). *The language instinct: How the mind creates language.* New York: Morrow.

Plomin, R., Defries, J., & Fulker, D. (1988). *Nature and nurture during infancy and early childhood.* New York: Cambridge University Press.

Plomin, R., DeFries, J. C., & Loehlin, J. C. (1977). Genotype–environment interaction and correlation in the analysis of human behavior. *Psychological Bulletin, 84,* 309–322.

Plomin, R., DeFries, J. C., McClearn, G. E., & McGuffin, P. (2001). *Behavioral genetics* (4th ed.). New York: Worth.

Plumridge, D., Bennett, R., Dinno, N., & Branson, C. (1993). *The student with a genetic disorder.* Springfield, IL: Thomas.

Rabin, M., Wen, X. L., Hepburn, M., Lubs, H. A., Feldman, E., & Duara, R. (1993). Suggestive linkage of developmental dyslexia to chromosome 1p34-p36. *Lancet, 342,* 178.

Raff, M. (1996). Neural development: Mysterious no more? *Science, 274,* 1063.

Reznick, J. S., Corley, R., & Robinson, J. (1997). A longitudinal twin study of intelligence in the second year. *Monographs of the Society for Research in Child Development, 62,* (i–vi), 1–15.

Rice, M. (1997). Specific language impairments: In search of diagnostic markers and genetic contributions. *Mental Retardation and Developmental Disabilities Research Reviews, 3,* 350–357.

Rondi-Reig, L., Caston, J., Delhaye-Bouchaud, N., & Mariani, J. (1999). Cerebellar functions: A behavioral neurogenetic perspective. In B. Jones & P. Mormede (Eds.), *Neurobehavioral genetics: Methods and applications* (pp. 201–216). Boca Raton, FL: CRC Press.

Rowe, D. C. (1994). *The limits of family influence: Genes, experience, and behavior.* New York: Guilford Press.

Scarr, S., & Carter-Saltzman, L. (1983). Genetics and intelligence. In J. L. Fuller & E. C. Simmel (Eds.), *Behavior genetics: Principles and applications* (pp. 217–336). Hillsdale, NJ: Erlbaum.

Scarr, S., & McCartney, K. (1983). How people make their own environments: A theory of genotype→environment effects. *Child Development, 54,* 424–435.

Sherman, S. L., Defries, J., Gottesman, I. I., Loehlin, J. C., Meyere, J. C., Pelias, J. M., et al. (1997). ASHG Statement: Recent developments in human behavior genetics: Past accomplishments and future directions. *American Journal of Human Genetics, 60,* 1265–1275.

Shore, C. M. (1995). *Individual differences in language development* (Vol. 7). Thousand Oaks, CA: Sage.

Shprintzen, R. J., & Goldberg, R. B. (1986). Multiple anomaly syndromes and learning disabilities. In S. D. Smith (Ed.), *Genetics and learning disabilities* (pp. 153–176). San Diego: College Hill Press.

Smith, S. D., Gilger, J. W., & Pennington, B. F. (2002). Dyslexia and other language/learning disorders. In D. L. Connor & R. E. Pyeritz (Eds.), *Emory and Rimoin's principles and practices in medical genetics* (pp. 2827–2865). New York, NY: Churchill Livingstone.

Smith, S. D., & Goldgar, D. E. (1986). Single gene analyses and their application to learning disabilities. In S. D. Smith (Ed.), *Genetics of learning disabilities* (pp. 47–65). San Diego: College Hill Press.

Smith, S. D., Kelley, P., Askew, J., Hoover, D., Deffenbacher, K., Gayan, J., et al. (2001). Reading disability and chromosome 6p21. 3: Evaluation of MOG as a candidate gene. *Journal Of Learning Disabilities, 34*(6), 512–519.

Smith, S. D., Kelley, P. M., & Brower, A. M. (1998). Molecular approaches to the genetic analysis of specific reading disability. *Human Biology, 70,* 239–256.

Smith, S. D., Kimberling, W. J., & Pennington, B. F. (1991). Screening for multiple genes influencing dyslexia. *Reading and Writing: An Interdisciplinary Journal, 3,* 285–298.

Smith, S. D., Kimberling, W. J., Pennington, B. F., & Lubs, H. A. (1983). Specific reading disability: Identification of an inherited form through linkage analysis. *Science, 219,* 1345–1347.

Snow, C. E. (1996). Towards a rational empiricism: Why interactionism isn't behaviorism any more than biology is genetics. In M. Rice (Ed.), *Towards a genetics of language* (pp. 375–396). Hillsdale, NJ: Erlbaum.

Snowling, M. J. (1991). Developmental reading disorders. *Journal of Child Psychology and Psychiatry, 32,* 49–77.

Spitz, R. V., Tallal, P., Flax, J., & Benasich, A. A. (1997). Look who's talking: A prospective study of familial transmission of language impairments. *Journal of Speech Language and Hearing Research, 40,* 990–1001.

Stein, J. (2001). The magnocellular theory of developmental dyslexia. *Dyslexia, 7,* 12–36.

Stevenson, J. (1991). Which aspects of processing text

mediate genetic effects? *Reading and Writing: An Interdisciplinary Journal, 3*, 249–269.

Stromswold, K. (1998). Genetics of spoken language disorders. *Human Biology, 70*, 297–324.

Taipale, M., Kaminen, N., Nopola-Hemmi, J., Haitia, T., Myllyluoma, B., Lyytinen, H., et al. (2003). A candidate gene for developmental dyslexia encodes a nuclear teratricopeptide repeat domain protein dynamically regulated in brain. *Proceedings of the National Academy of Science, 100*, 11553–11558.

Tallal, P., Ross, R., & Curtiss, S. (1989). Familial aggregation in specific language impairment. *Journal of Speech and Hearing Disorders, 54*, 167–173.

Tallal, P., & Stark, R. E. (1981). Speech acoustic-cue discrimination abilities of normally developing and language impaired children. *Journal of the Acoustical Society of America, 69*, 568–574.

Tallal, P., Stark, R. E., & Mellitis, E. D. (1985). The relationship between auditory temporal analysis and receptive language development: Evidence from studies of developmental language disorder. *Neuropsychologia, 23*, 527–534.

Tomblin, B. (1996). Genetic and environmental contributions to the risk for specific language impairment. In M. Rice (Ed.), *Towards a genetics of language* (pp. 190–210). Mahwah, NJ: Erlbaum.

Tomblin, J. B., & Buckwalter, P. R. (1998). Heritability of poor language achievement among twins. *Journal of Speech, Language, and Hearing Research, 41*, 188–199.

Tomblin, J. B., Hardy, J. C., & Hein, H. (1991). Predicting poor communication status in preschool children using risk factors present at birth. *Journal of Speech and Hearing Research, 34*, 1096–1105.

Tomblin, J. B., Smith, E., & Zhang, X. (1997). Epidemiology of specific language impairment: Prenatal and perinatal risk factors. *Journal of Communication Disorders, 30*, 325–343.

Turic, D., Robinson, L., Duke, M., Morris, D. W., Webb, V., Hamshere, M., et al. (2003). Linkage disequilibrium mapping provides further evidence of a gene for reading disability on chromosome 6p21. 3–22. *Molecular Psychiatry, 8*, 176–185.

van der Lely, H., & Stollwerck, L. (1996). A grammatical specific language impairment in children: An autosomal dominant inheritance. *Brain and Language, 52*, 484–504.

Vargha-Khadem, F., Watkins, K., Alcock, K., Fletcher, P., & Passingham, R. (1995). Praxic and nonverbal cognitive deficits in a large family with a genetically transmitted speech and language disorder. *Proceedings of the National Academy of Science USA, 92*, 930–933.

Watkins, K., Gardian, D. G., & Vargha-Khadem, F. (1999). Functional and structural brain abnormalities associated with a genetic disorder of speech and language. *American Journal of Human Genetics, 65*, 1215–1221.

Watkins, K., & Rice, M. (1994). *Language impairments in children*. Baltimore: Brookes.

Wijsman, E. M., Peterson, D., Leutenegger, A., Thomson, J. B., Goddard, K. A., Hsu, L., et al. (2000). Segregation analysis of phenotypic components of learning disabilities: I. Nonword memory and digit span. *American Journal of Medical Genetics, 67*, 631–646.

Willcutt, E. G., Pennington, B. F., & DeFries, J. C. (2000). Twin study of the etiology of comorbidity between reading disability and attention-deficit/hyperactivity disorder. *American Journal of Medical Genetics, 96*, 293–301.

Williams, J., & Stevenson, J. (2001). Genetic language disorders. In S. E. Gerber (Ed.), *The handbook of genetic communicative disorders* (pp. 113–128). San Diego: Academic Press.

Wolff, P. H. (1999). A candidate phenotype for familial dyslexia. *European Child and Adolescent Psychiatry, 8* (Suppl.), 21–27.

Wood, F. B., & Grigorenko, E. L. (2001). Emerging issues in the genetics of dyslexia: A methodological preview. *Journal of Learning Disabilities, 34*, 503–511.

Yule, W., Rutter, M., Berger, M., & Thompson, J. (1974). Over and under achievement in reading: Distribution in the general population. *British Journal of Educational Psychology, 44*, 1–12.

3

Neurobiological Correlates of Language and Reading Impairments

MARIA MODY

Early auditory linguistic experience plays an important role in the acquisition of literacy skills. This accounts, at least in part, for the tremendous difficulties deaf children have in learning to read (Furth, 1966; Trybus & Karchmer, 1977). Additionally, reading requires awareness that speech is made up of smaller sounds called syllables and phonemes. In fact, phonological awareness is the single best predictor of reading success (Bradley & Bryant, 1983; Liberman, Shankweiler & Liberman, 1989; Shankweiler, Liberman, Mark, Fowler, & Fischer, 1979). Whereas children learn to speak without being specifically trained, for reading, a child must be given explicit instruction. This is why speaking and listening are easy, but reading is hard (Liberman, 1999). Our natural capacity for oral language must be adapted in the service of written language through exposure to and explicit practice with the sound–symbol correspondence rules specific to one's language. Such functional adaptations must necessarily be accompanied by changes in the corresponding neural circuitry underlying linguistic behavior.

To date, lesion and positron emission tomography (PET) studies have proven to be a rich source of information about the functional specialization of the brain. However, the advent of functional magnetic resonance imaging (fMRI) in the last 10 years has provided us with a powerful noninvasive means to explore the workings of the human brain. This chapter presents a description of some of the more popular neuroimaging techniques (electroencephalography [EEG], magnetoencephalography [MEG], and fMRI), their use in studies of cognitive function, and applications to disorders of language and reading. First, however, a brief overview of the processes of reading and language seems appropriate.

LEARNING TO READ

Phonological Translation Processes

Reading is a complex process consisting of different skills. Learning to read requires awareness that spoken words are made up of discrete units called "phonemes." At the outset, reading entails basic visuospatial processing abilities. When we read, it is visuo-orthographic information that comes first, and reading depends on visual letter recognition (Adams, 1990).

A beginning reader must learn to map letters onto phonemes. Mastery of the grapheme-to-phoneme correspondence patterns helps the novice reader associate a printed word with its spoken form, paving the way for written comprehension. The speed and effortlessness with which good readers appear to recognize and comprehend written words at a glance may erroneously suggest a direct visual route to meaning, one that bypasses phonology (Coltheart, 1978). In reality, skilled readers typically translate spellings to sounds as they read (Barron, 1981). However, as children gain experience with reading, sequences of letters (i.e., the more frequent words) become learned and overlearned, both visually and phonologically. Thus, for the skilled reader, visually familiar words make for speedier automatic phonological translation. In short, efficient word recognition does not occur at the cost of phonological coding; rather, it is mediated by a more automatic phonological translation. To the extent that syllables are normally represented by frequently encountered spelling patterns, good readers, who have an automatic tendency to break up familiar and unfamiliar words into syllables, become efficient at reading even unfamiliar words. Poor readers, on the other hand, struggle with long, polysyllabic words, using a letter-by-letter sounding-out strategy.

Good readers' automatic phonological translation of words in text also facilitates higher order comprehension processes. In order to extract meaning from a sentence, a reader has to phonologically decode, string together, and hold in memory its component parts. Superior phonological coding abilities make for more efficient comprehension. Thus, a skilled reader depends on efficient and complete processing both within and between orthographic, phonological, and semantic processors in the course of word recognition (Adams, 1990).

Learning to read, however, can be a struggle for some children. Of particular interest here is the child with dyslexia (also referred to as specific reading disability, SRD), who despite normal intelligence, adequate learning opportunities, and the absence of neurological and psychological problems, has tremendous difficulty learning to read. Such children frequently have an early history of language deficits, which raises interesting questions about the relationship between language and reading impairments.

Language and Reading

As mentioned earlier, a normally developing child has little difficulty learning to speak. The vegetative coos and grunts that predominate in an infant's early sound repertoire give way to more structured "canonical" babbling forms by 8–10 months of age (Oller, 1980). With the arrival of the first word, the utterances that follow over the next 1–2 years serve as evidence, in both form and function, of the phonological, semantic, and syntactic developments of the child. Studies have shown strong correlations between these early linguistic developments and later reading achievement (Catts, Fey, Zhang, & Tomblin, 1999; Scarborough, 1990, 1991).

Of the many models that attempt to explain dyslexia, there appears to be strong support for a phonological account (Bradley & Bryant, 1983; Lundberg, Olofsson, & Wall, 1980; Wagner & Torgesen, 1987). Other models, however, have linked dyslexia to a wider range of language dysfunctions extending beyond the phonological domain. These include syntactic analysis, semantic integration, and lexical retrieval (Bishop & Adams, 1990; Kamhi & Catts, 1989; Scarborough, 1991). Whereas such models treat written-language impairments as a consequence of deficits in early spoken language (Aram & Nation, 1980; Catts, 1991; Hall & Tomblin, 1978), it is not uncommon to find children with severe dyslexia who have normal to superior spoken language skills. It appears, then, that specific language impairment (SLI; i.e., a language disorder despite normal IQ and the absence of neurological or sensory impairments) and SRD (dyslexia) may dissociate rather freely (Locke et al., 1997). However, follow-up studies of children with SLI have shown them to be especially at risk for deficits in reading (Scarborough, 1990, 1991). These results raise questions as to whether children with specific reading difficulties may have had oral language problems in their early years, and whether these deficits persist—maybe in subtle form—in later school-age years (see also Gilger and Wise, Chapter 2, this volume).

Catts and colleagues (1999) found that 70% of their poor readers in second grade had a history of language and phonological processing problems in kindergarten. Insofar as regression analyses found that each of these abilities accounted for a unique variance in reading achievement, the authors stress the importance of targeting both phonological processing and oral language abilities in early intervention for reading disabilities. Prospective studies by Scarborough (1990, 1991) show that children's reading difficulties in later years may be quite reliably predicted from their syntactic performance at 2.6 and 4.0 years. In fact, 75% of the participants in her studies were correctly classified as reading impaired or normal readers based on these syntactic measures. It is, therefore, essential to monitor children's linguistic progress in their early years, especially if there is a family history of speech and language difficulties (Tomblin, 1989). Note, however, that not all children with early language deficits go on to have reading deficits. It appears that only those children whose spoken language problems persist are likely to have reading problems (Bishop & Adams, 1990; Catts, Fey, Tomblin, & Zhang, 2002).

According to Catts (1993), different aspects of reading may be predicted by different sets of variables. Performance on printed-word recognition is found to correlate highly with scores on phonological awareness and rapid naming, whereas reading comprehension is best predicted by oral language comprehension. This finding suggests that children with language impairments may present with various reading disability profiles. The classic phonologic dyslexic with difficulties in nonword reading and word recognition but intact comprehension appears to represent a distinct clinical phenomenon. Support for this latter view comes from the work of Leonard and colleagues (2001), who provide neuroanatomic evidence for a reading disability phenotype characterized by phonological deficits in the presence of normal oral and written comprehension.

In summary, some children outgrow their early language impairments, whereas others develop reading deficits in their school-age years. Those who persist with their spoken-language deficits often develop reading problems as well. The lack of consensus across different studies, to some extent, may be explained by differences in individual researchers' choice of standardized test measures and cutoff criteria. Nevertheless, insofar as children with oral-language deficits frequently have reading deficits, but specific reading disability may occur in the absence of oral language disorders, the relationship between spoken and written language remains unclear.

Recent advances in functional neuroimaging methods are helping to elucidate this relationship by comparing the brain activity evoked by linguistic stimuli, presented auditorily and visually, in good and poor readers. Electrophysiological recordings show differences between the two groups in timing and magnitude of cortical responses to these stimuli. Further evidence from fMRI studies appears to suggest that these differences may be traced to a core deficit in phonological processing in poor readers.

FUNCTIONAL NEUROIMAGING METHODS

Over a century ago, the pioneering work of neurologists Paul Broca (1824–1880) and Carl Wernicke (1848–1904) with patients with lesions showed the left hemisphere's superiority for language (Broca, 1861; Wernicke, 1874). Today, neuroimaging technology provides us with noninvasive means to probe the normal intact brain to understand its structure and function. Methods such as PET and fMRI help to identify the brain regions involved in a task, whereas EEG and MEG in addition to localizing the source of the electromagnetic signals, delineate the time course of the neural activity associated with a stimulus event. Taken together, these methods provide information about where and when in the brain task-related processing has occurred. What follows is a brief description of these methods.

Electrophysiological Techniques

Electroencephalography

EEG records continuous electrical activity in the brain at several different scalp sites; hence, it is capable of tracking electrical changes to online cognitive processing. Event-related potentials (ERPs) reflect these changes in electrical signals produced by cortical activity in response to a stimulus. They are time-locked to stimulus events and typically consist of averaged responses to many presentations of the stimulus.

In ERPs, one is usually interested in the differences between the waveforms for different types of stimuli (e.g., a word vs. a nonword, or nouns vs. verbs). These differences can take the form of latency, amplitude, and morphology of the waveform in millisecond time windows. Time point-by-time point comparisons allow one to determine when the waveforms start diverging relative to the onset of a stimulus event, and where in the scalp distributions these differences are maximal, by examining each electrode site. As with all neuroimaging methods, the aim is to uncover a neural activation pattern, which, in EEG, takes the form of a scalp signature that serves as an index of the type of stimulus being processed.

Recording of EEG from the surface of the head is not without difficulty. The signal from each electrode is small, partly due to differences in the relative resistance of the brain tissue, skull, and scalp (Vaughan, 1974). The low conductivity of the skull distorts the electric potentials, resulting in the EEG signal being spatially smeared at the scalp; this makes precise localization of the source currents difficult (Gevins & Remond, 1987). Some of these problems are partially overcome in magnetoencephalography.

Magnetoencephalography

MEG is used to make extracranial measurements of the weak magnetic fields generated by electrical activity within the brain (Cohen, 1999; Hämäläinen, Hari, Ilmoniemi, Knuutila, & Lounasmaa, 1993). MEG systems may consist of as many as 300 or more superconducting quantum interference device (SQUID) sensors covering the subject's head. Changes in electrical activity due to stimulus presentation result in changes in the magnetic fields and are picked up by these sensors. The same type of activity (mainly postsynaptic currents in cortical pyramidal cells) generates both EEG and MEG signals. However, compared with EEG, magnetic signals are not as affected by the structures surrounding the brain tissues; hence, identification of source areas and interpretation of the signals are often more straightforward than with conventional ERPs.

MEG is mainly sensitive to source currents that are tangential to the skull, typically those generated in sulci. Radial sources produce almost no magnetic field outside the head. MEG is also less sensitive to deep, subcortical source currents. On the basis of the spatial distribution of EEG and MEG signals, the location of the underlying activity can be estimated. Whereas EEG represents a broader sweep of the electrical activity in the brain, MEG helps to constrain the possible sources by looking at a smaller subset of the source currents. It is through combining these two complementary methods that one may obtain the best picture of the underlying activity (Wood, Cohen, Cuffin, Yarita, & Allison, 1985).

fMRI and PET

Unlike EEG and MEG, neuroimaging techniques such as fMRI and PET provide indirect measures of changes in neural activity to stimulus manipulations by measuring blood flow–related changes while subjects perform a task (Belliveau et al., 1991; Fox & Raichle, 1986). fMRI and PET paradigms typically involve comparison between two tasks that differ by one mental process. A subtraction of the activation for one from that for the other is assumed to identify regions sensitive to the dimension on which the two tasks differ. Task-related neural activity results in local increases in blood flow and oxygenated hemoglobin. The latter produces changes in the intensity of the signals measured by MRI, indicating activation areas in the MR images (Kwong et al., 1992; Ogawa et al., 1992).

The noninvasive nature of fMRI has made the blood–oxygenation level-dependent (i.e., BOLD) response a popular measure of brain activity. PET, on the other hand, requires injection of radioactive tracers and, hence, limits the number of stimuli that can be presented, as well as the frequency of subject participation in such studies. Although the number of fMRI facilities has grown rapidly in the last few years, the technique still remains fairly expensive. Additionally, the high spatial resolution of the method makes it very sensitive to motion artifacts: Even the smallest of subject movements can have an adverse affect on localization efforts. Fortunately, computational methods for realigning such images have come a long way. A more important consideration in fMRI analysis is the differences in the sizes and shapes of subjects' brains, making intersubject averaging a challenge. This has led to the development of techniques that provide ways of normalizing different brains to a standard space (Fischl, Sereno, & Dale, 1999; Friston, Frith, Liddle, & Frackowiak, 1991; Talairach & Tournoux, 1988).

In summary, electrophysiological techniques such as ERPs and MEG have excellent temporal resolution (in milliseconds), but only moderate spatial resolution (approximately a centimeter). Hemodynamic techniques, on the other hand, such as PET and fMRI, have superior spatial resolution (measurable in millimeters) but coarse temporal resolution (in seconds). Though noninvasive, fMRI is prone to motion artifacts, which makes it difficult to use with children. Similarly, the noise generated by the MRI scanners poses a problem for auditory stimulation, although manipulating imaging sequence parameters can help in this regard. The use of event-related fMRI has made it possible to identify brain activity associated with different cognitive processes. Recent development of a network analysis approach has allowed the examination of how different brain regions interact during cognitive

performance, thereby delineating the functional connectivity between these regions (McIntosh, 2000). Despite the expense related to doing functional imaging, the last decade has witnessed an explosion in the field of cognitive neuroscience research.

COGNITIVE NEUROIMAGING: MAPPING LANGUAGE AND READING IN THE BRAIN

The complex nature of the interactions between orthography, phonology, semantics, and syntax poses a challenge to the study of these individual processes in language and reading. Brain imaging tools provide the means to temporally and spatially segregate these component processes. In contrast, behavioral studies only provide reaction time and error measurements of these processes. Reaction time (RT) measures tend not to work as well in young children as they do in adults due to maturational issues. Additionally, behavioral studies typically use a yes–no answer format with children. Such answers, when used across a variety of tasks, can be open to multiple interpretations, because different processes might underlie the same answer depending on the task context in which it is elicited.

Behavioral measures are also relatively static and superficial descriptors given the dynamic nature of language processing. Their ability to capture the interplay between the various subprocesses in language is limited. Regardless of the method used, there is no substitute for well-designed, tightly controlled experiments to tease apart these processes. In this section, we look at how neuroimaging methods have been used in spatiotemporal mapping of language and reading in adults.

fMRI/PET Studies

Language and Reading

In its simplest sense, reading is speech at the level of print. Spoken and written language engage common linguistic processes and converge on phonology through use of articulatory speech patterns or orthographic symbols to convey meaning. Using PET and fMRI, researchers have been able to delineate these processes, and the interactions between them, in language and reading.

ORTHOGRAPHIC PROCESSING

This refers to the visual encoding of the characters that make up a written language. The presentation of these characters activates the primary visual cortex (also known as striate cortex or V1; see Figure 3.1, medial view), as well as several extrastriate visual areas. To the extent that orthographic awareness constitutes a linguistic ability, one can expect it to be localized in the left hemisphere when a stimulus consists of a linguistically acceptable letter string, as in real words or legal pseudowords. In fact, studies have shown that both words and legal pseudowords activate medial extrastriate regions in the left hemisphere (Petersen, Fox, Posner, Mintun, & Raichle, 1988; Petersen, Fox, Snyder, & Raichle, 1990), whereas illegal pseudowords or false-font strings do not (Price, Wise, & Frackowiak, 1996). However, other researchers argue that, rather than an orthographic pattern, it may be the lexical status of a visual word form that determines how a letter string will be processed in this area.

Pugh and colleagues (1996) found preferential activation for real words in medial extrastriate areas, but no difference in brain activity for pseudowords versus case judgment for consonant strings.

PHONOLOGICAL PROCESSING

Patient lesion studies, along with brain imaging research, have localized phonological processing in temporal and frontal brain regions (see Figure 3.1). Lesions to Broca's area in the left opercular frontal cortex can lead to expressive aphasia, because this area is implicated in motor speech planning and phonological perception (Blumstein, Baker, & Goodglass, 1977). This region is found to be most active on tasks requiring a detailed phonetic analysis. Tasks used have included phonological monitoring with syllables relative to passive listening (Zatorre, Evans, Meyer, & Gjedde, 1992; Zatorre, Meyer, Gjedde, & Evans, 1996), phoneme monitoring in auditorily presented nonwords relative to sequence monitoring in tone triplets (Demonet et al., 1992; Demonet, Price, Wise, & Frackowiak, 1994), syllable counting relative to semantic judgments (Price, Moore, Humphrey, & Wise, 1997), rhyme judgment versus orthographic case

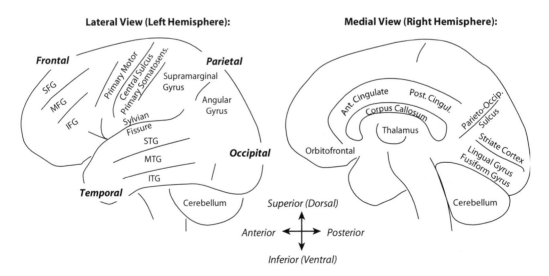

FIGURE 3.1. Lateral and medial views of the human brain, showing important areas for language and reading. SFG, superior frontal gyrus; STG; superior temporal gyrus; MFG, middle frontal gyrus; MTG, middle temporal gyrus; IFG, inferior frontal gyrus; ITG, inferior temporal gyrus.

judgment (Shaywitz et al., 1998), and reading of different word types—regular, irregular, and nonwords (Herbster, Mintun, Nebes, & Becker, 1997).

Lesions to Wernicke's area in the posterior superior temporal gyrus (STG) lead to receptive aphasia (see Figure 3.1). Here, it is language comprehension that appears to be disturbed (Damasio, 1992). Price, Warburton, et al. (1996) found activation in this area in response to real words compared to reversed speech. Similarly, Schlosser, Aoyage, Fulbright, Gore, and McCarthy (1998) found greater activation in this region for English speakers listening to English sentences than to Turkish sentences.

The STG activates bilaterally to passive listening of language stimuli, reflecting its role in perceptual analysis of speech signals (Binder et al., 1994; Petersen et al., 1988); however, it is the posterior region of the left STG that is specifically involved in auditory language comprehension (Petersen et al., 1988; Zatorre et al., 1996). The posterior STG is not active when processing simple tones (Demonet et al., 1992; Lauter, Herschovitch, Formby, & Raichle, 1985). Increasingly, studies have shown a functional dichotomy in the structure of the temporal lobe. Comparisons of speech to white noise and signal-correlated noise have yielded a nonspecific activation of the dorsal aspect of the STG to both speech and nonspeech, whereas ventral STG and superior temporal sulcus activity were more closely related to speech alone (Binder et al., 2000; Zatorre et al., 1992).

SEMANTIC PROCESSING

Many neuroimaging findings support those from lesion studies in implicating posterior brain regions in semantic processing (Bookheimer, Zeffiro, Fiflozzi, Gaillard, & Theodore, 1995; Herbster et al., 1997; Howard et al., 1992). However, recent evidence appears to indicate the involvement of the left inferior prefrontal cortex (LIPC) in semantic tasks. Early studies used a verb generation paradigm to probe semantic processing. Subjects had to generate verbs in response to presented nouns (e.g., *throw* when presented with *ball*). The control condition was a noun repetition task in which subjects just read out the presented noun. Both tasks required that the stimuli be read and the responses be produced aloud, but the verb generation task also necessitated semantic analysis, thereby generating the expected left prefrontal activation pattern (Petersen et al., 1988). Similar activation patterns were obtained on semantic monitoring in comparison to a tone-monitoring task (Kapur et al., 1994). In keeping with these PET findings, recent fMRI studies also showed greater left inferior prefrontal activity on semantic processing when subjects were asked to judge whether words were abstract or concrete, or similar in meaning (Demb et al., 1995; Gabrieli et al., 1996; Poldrack et al., 1999).

Fiez (1997) points out that both phonological and semantic interpretations of inferior prefrontal activation may be compatible. An analysis of the evidence from different studies suggests that the LIPC may contain functionally distinct subregions. The anterior portion within the ventral prefrontal cortex appears to be engaged in semantic processing, whereas a posterior dorsal area within the triangular and opercular portions of the inferior frontal gyrus is activated under phonological processing demands. A more recent finding appears to modify this view further, suggesting that the anterior LIPC and the anterior portion of the posterior LIPC are involved in both phonological and semantic decision making; it is the posterior region activation patterns that are dissociable along semantic and phonological lines (Gold & Buckner, 2002).

SYNTACTIC PROCESSING

Studies of syntax that use fMRI are few in number. Most converge on the finding that activation of the pars opercularis in the left third frontal convolution (i.e. in and around Broca's area) is associated with syntactic processing (Caplan, Alpert, & Waters, 1998; Ni et al., 2000; Stromswold, Caplan, Alpert, & Rausch, 1996). The results indicate that parts of Broca's area increase their activity with an increase in syntactic complexity. More recently, however, the role of Broca's area in syntactic processing has been challenged. According to Kaan and Swaab (2002), a closer look at neuroimaging findings suggests that "syntactic processing recruits not one brain region but multiple areas that are not each uniquely involved in syntactic tasks" (p. 355). The authors propose that different parts of the brain may be recruited for different aspects of syntactic processing, such as encoding, storage, and lexical processing (Kaan & Stowe, 2002; Keller, Carpenter, & Just, 2001; Stromswold et al., 1996).

Electrophysiological Studies

EEG/MEG Studies of Language

There exists a substantial body of literature pertaining to the use of electrophysiology and MEG in investigations of language and reading. In contrast to the high spatial resolution and accuracy of PET and fMRI, the strength of EEG and MEG lies in the time domain: They tell us, with millisecond precision, when a stimulus has been processed in the brain. The latencies and amplitudes of selected peaks that characterize the waveform data are thought to be associated with specific mental operations, and sometimes it is possible to determine the source generators of these signals in the brain (see Table 3.1). Common ERP components include N100, mismatch negativity (MMN), N200/P300, and N400 (see Figure 3.2).

AUDITORY N100

The electrical component N100, also referred to as N1, and its magnetic counterpart M100 (or N100m) are believed to reflect acoustic processing. This response, which peaks approximately 100 msec after stimulus onset, is elicited by an auditory stimulus and can be reliably measured in individual subjects (Figure 3.2). The N100 complex is known to vary as a function of stimulus intensity, presentation rate, and attention (Näätänen & Picton, 1987). The auditory N100 is thought to be generated in the auditory cortex. The N100/N100m, because of its robust nature, holds tremendous potential for studying the physiology of the auditory cortex in normal and clinical populations. Insofar as alterations in the latency and amplitude of the N100 may reflect encoding of stimulus attributes, the N100/M100 provides us with a means to examine sensory processing in various clinical populations, such as those with schizophrenia (Jacobson, 1994) and Alzheimer's disease (Pekkonen et al., 1996).

Interestingly, the N100/M100 also appears to be sensitive to higher-level cognitive influences. Kuriki and Murase (1989) showed that the M100 response to pure tones is localized bilaterally in the primary auditory cortices, whereas consonant–vowel syllable stimuli appear to engage language-specific processes in the left temporal lobe. The M100 response to phoneme discrimination also appears to be larger over the left hemisphere (Poeppel et al., 1996), reflecting a linguistic influence. However, it remains to be established whether the M100 reflects any speech-specific processes, because the data with vowels, to some extent, may be explained in terms of their spectral differences (Roberts, Ferrari, Stufflebeam, & Poeppel, 2000).

MMN

The MMN (the magnetic counterpart is called the mismatch field, MMF) is a preat-

TABLE 3.1. Some Common ERP Components Used in Language Studies

ERP component	Source	Function
N1	Auditory cortex	Sensory processing
MMN	Auditory cortex	Acoustic–phonetic discrimination
N2/P3	Temporal, parietal, frontal cortices	Orienting/voluntary detection response
N400	Left temporal cortex	Semantic analysis and integration of meaning

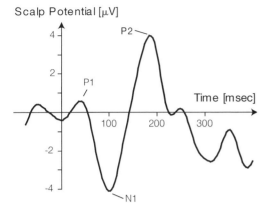

FIGURE 3.2. Waveform showing some common event-related potential (ERP) components. (The typical ERP components associated with sensory processing are shown. Cognitive ERPs such as MMN, N2, P3, and N4 are task-dependent and, hence, do not appear in the same waveform.)

tentive index of the brain's capacity to discriminate between two stimuli (Näätänen, 1995). It is obtained by subtracting the response to a standard stimulus (e.g., /ba/) from that to a deviant stimulus (e.g., /da/) presented in an oddball paradigm (i.e., a train of repeated stimuli interrupted by a different stimulus; e.g., /ba/ /ba/ /ba/ /da/ /ba/ /da/). The difference is maximum at frontocentral scalp sites and occurs 150–250 msec poststimulus. Source modeling of the magnetic MMN has placed its generators in the supratemporal auditory cortex.

The MMN response, like the M100, can be affected by native language influences (Cheour et al., 1998; Dehaene-Lambertz, 1997; Näätänen et al., 1997). In separate studies, these authors showed that the mismatch response to a stimulus was greater in those subjects for whom the standard and deviant stimuli were not only acoustically (i.e., physically) different but also contrasted in meaning; that is, they were phonologically contrastive. So, for example, the stimuli /ra/ and /la/, although differing in their physical properties, signal a meaningful contrast for English speakers but not for Japanese speakers; the latter group treats them as a single phoneme.

In a related experiment designed to test the sensitivity of the MMN responses to

acoustic versus phonetic distinctions, Phillips and colleagues (2000) used stimuli from within the same category (e.g., either /da/ or /ta/) and between categories (e.g., /da/ and /ta/) of a da/ta voice onset time continuum as standards and deviants. Voice onset time (VOT) refers to the time between the release of the oral occlusion in the production of a stop consonant and the onset of vocal fold vibration. Note that the points along a continuum representing this temporal distinction between /da/ and /ta/ tend to cluster perceptually into two categories, /da/ and /ta/, with the phoneme boundary falling roughly at the midpoint on this continuum. The authors were interested in finding out whether the auditory cortex had access to categorical representations relevant to speech sound processing. They confirmed that MMF could be generated based solely on a phonological feature distinction between standards and deviants. The MMF also yielded a left–right asymmetry, with a consonant category–based distinction seen in the left hemisphere and not the right (Phillips et al., 2000). The finding that perceptual processing is categorical early on in the auditory system has important implications for our understanding of speech perception deficits in children with reading and language impairments.

N200–P300

This complex of waves, also referred to as N2 and P3, is another ERP response used in studies of developmental language disorders (Figure 3.2). N200 is typically largest at the electrode site Cz (central location on the scalp) for auditory stimuli. It reflects activity in or near the auditory cortex and represents an active discrimination response. P300, on the other hand, is associated with an orienting response, as well as voluntary detection of target stimuli. It is largest at the electrode site Pz (over the parietal lobe, along the midline). Like MMN, N200 is a measure of the degree of stimulus contrast: The greater the difference, the shorter the latency and the larger the amplitude of N200 (Lawson & Gaillard, 1981). In the context of speech studies, it reflects the category membership of a standard–deviant pair; that is, N200 differs for a stimulus pair that is between-category, but not for a within-category phonetic contrast (Maiste, Weins, Hunt, Scherg, & Picton, 1995).

N400

First identified by Kutas and Hillyard (1980, 1983), the N400 ERP component (or the N4, as it is commonly known) is a negative scalp potential peaking at about 300–500 msec after the onset of a semantically incongruous word at the end of a sentence. For example, in the sentence "He ate an ice cream and a bicycle," the word *bicycle* would elicit an N400 response. For word pairs, the N400 response is smaller for a word that is semantically related to a preceding word than to one that is semantically unrelated. It is also smaller for a repeated than for a novel word (Rugg, 1985). The robustness of the response increases with the degree of unexpectedness of the eliciting word and the difficulty of integrating a word into the context. The N400 is broadly distributed bilaterally over posterior brain regions, is likely to arise from many generators, and has been identified both auditorily (Connolly & Phillips, 1994; Holcombe, Coffey, & Neville, 1992) and visually (Nigam, Hoffman, & Simons, 1992).

EEG/MEG Studies of Reading

As with spoken language, reading engages similar perceptual and cognitive processes. Visual features must be extracted to form letters, which in turn must be combined to perceive words. Phonological decoding of words facilitated by orthographic pattern recognition provides access to lexical entries and, hence, to the meaning of these words in isolation and through sentence context. The exquisite time resolution of EEG and MEG has made it possible to trace the progression of the neural activity associated with the full range of processes involved in any reading-related task.

EEG and MEG studies of word and pseudoword reading show initial activation occurring about 80–130 msec after stimulus onset, originating bilaterally in the occipital lobe. The amplitude of the response in this area varies with stimulus attributes, such as luminance contrast and the number of visual elements, reflecting a low-level processing associated with any visual stimulus (Helenius, Salmelin, Service, & Connolly, 1998; Tarkiainen, Helenius, Hansen, Cornellisen, & Samelin, 1999). This is followed by activity in occipitotemporal areas, predominantly in the left hemisphere, and thought to be sensitive specifically to letter-string processing. Lesion studies have implicated this area in alexia (Damasio & Damasio, 1983), leading some researchers to hypothesize a role for the occipitotemporal cortex in fluent reading (Pugh et al., 2000; Tarkiainen et al., 1999). Lexical access, in contrast, appears to involve both phonological and semantic processing, typically engaging posterior temporal and inferior parietal areas, and occasionally frontal areas, as well as mesial temporal regions (Simos et al., 2002). Similar results were obtained by Dale and colleagues (2000) in a combined fMRI and MEG study of semantic processing of visually presented words. In this study, the authors obtained an initial wave of activity, which spread rapidly to temporal, parietal and frontal areas within 185 msec; there was a high degree of temporal overlap between the different areas activated. Helenius and colleagues (1998), in an MEG study using sentence-final words that varied in their semantic appropriateness to the sentence context, identified cortical areas sensitive to word meaning, including the left superior and middle temporal gyri, in keeping with the results obtained by Simos et al. (2002) using magnetic source imaging.

In conclusion, ERPs and MEG allow us to investigate processes ranging from low-level perception of physical attributes of a linguistic stimulus (e.g., frequency, intensity, luminance) to higher level processes such as phoneme identification, discrimination, lexical analysis, and syntactic integration in spoken and written language. More importantly, these methods have highlighted the dynamic nature of language processing by revealing cortical interactions between phonological, semantic, and syntactic processes. Although the source local-ization of electrical and magnetic signals is often a challenge, the combination of the two methods has the potential to improve greatly the accuracy of the localization process.

Over the years, ERPs and MEG, along with fMRI, have been used to study deficits in sensory processing. Their more recent ap-plications to higher order cognitive func-tions have provided an impetus to the search for new clinical applications.

LANGUAGE AND READING IMPAIRMENTS: BRAIN–BEHAVIOR RELATIONSHIPS

As we have seen, neuroimaging can be used to study the functional organization of the brain. Techniques such as EEG, MEG, PET, and fMRI have allowed researchers to probe the brain to reveal differences in the pattern of functional disruption associated with different clinical populations. Subtle differences in brain structure and function of individuals with language-learning dis-abilities revealed through neuroimaging are helping to delineate the neurobiological bases of reading and language disorders. This can have a far-reaching impact given that 5–7% of the population is believed to have reading and/or language impairments (Leonard, 1998; Shaywitz, Shaywitz, Fletch-er, & Escobar, 1990; Tomblin, 1996; Yule & Rutter, 1976).

No neurobiological account of language and reading disorders may be considered complete without a look at the behavioral evidence. Unfortunately, despite a wealth of behavioral data, there remains the challeng-ing question of whether the deficit in read-ing and language is specifically linguistic in nature or a more general one in auditory processing. The mixed behavioral findings have also made it difficult to interpret the functional significance of the neuroanatomi-cal differences found among subjects with reading and language impairment. In the next section, we present neuroanatomical, behavioral, and functional imaging studies relevant to a more complete understanding of reading and language disorders.

Neuroanatomical Studies

Cerebral Asymmetry in Language and Reading Disorders

Early efforts to link differences in brain morphology with functional organization have their origin in the work of Geschwind and Levitsky (1968). These authors, in a postmortem study of 100 adult brains, found that over 65% of the brains had a left-greater-than-right asymmetry of the planum temporale (PT) and extended peri-sylvian area. (The PT is located in the upper portion of the temporal lobe inside the Syl-vian fissure and is found in both hemi-spheres.) In 1994, Foundas and colleagues confirmed the relationship between leftward asymmetry of the PT and language lateral-ization using the Wada test in combination with MRI scans (Foundas, Leonard, Gilmore, Fennel, & Heilman, 1994). The Wada test determines whether vital brain functions, such as speech and language, originate in a person's left or right hemi-sphere by testing these behaviors following an anesthetic injection that suspends activi-ty in one half of the brain. However, the work of Galaburda provided the major im-petus for research linking structural irregu-larities in the brain with language deficits (Galaburda, Sherman, Rosen, Aboitiz, & Geschwind, 1985). In a postmortem exami-nation of the brains of three individuals with dyslexia, 14–32 years of age, the au-thors found symmetrical PTs, which sug-gested that symmetry or reversed asymme-try of the PT was linked to dyslexia.

Volumetric MRI studies, however, have not found PT symmetry in children with dyslexia (Filipek, 1995; Rumsey, Donahue, et al., 1997; Schultz et al., 1994). Further-more, irregularities in the PT structure have also been observed in children with SLI (Plante, Swisher, & Vance, 1989; Plante, Swisher, Vance, & Rapcsak, 1991). Gauger, Lombardino, and Leonard (1997), using volumetric MRI, found differences between subjects with SLI and normal controls in an-terior and posterior brain structures. The subjects with SLI had a significantly smaller left pars triangularis and a rightward asym-metry of the whole planum. This larger than usual right perisylvian area is not necessarily restricted to persons with SLI, or dyslexia. Unaffected parents and siblings in some of these studies appear to share this atypical structural configuration, suggesting a possible role for genetic factors (Plante et al., 1989). Finally, not all reading or language-impaired children show this pattern (Leonard et al., 1993; Rumsey et al., 1986; Schultz et al., 1994). Consequently, the exact relationship of a right–left asymmetry to reading and language impairments remains uncertain.

Relating Cerebral Asymmetry to Language and Reading Measures

Attempts to correlate structural anomalies to reading behavior have yielded mixed results. In one study of the PT, Leonard et al. (1996) found that greater PT asymmetry correlated with phonemic awareness ability. However, this was inconsistent with their earlier finding, in which participants with developmental dyslexia showed an increased leftward asymmetry despite their deficits in phonological processing (Leonard et al., 1993).

Brain morphometric studies of individuals with dyslexia have not been very conclusive. The use of volumetric MRI techniques compared to conventional clinical MRI scans has greatly improved the accuracy of morphometric measurements (the former involves rapid acquisition of thinner and contiguous slice images, making it possible to obtain a three-dimensional view of the full brain). However, differences in population characteristics and measurement methodology across studies have made it difficult to interpret some of the results. Despite these conflicting findings, a difference in the magnitude, but not the direction, of the planar asymmetry does appear to be representative of a left-hemisphere dominance for language in both left- and right-handed individuals (Foundas, 2001). Interestingly, the asymmetry in cortical language areas includes the pars triangularis portion of Broca's area and was found to correlate closely with the left lateralization of language results with Wada testing (Foundas, Leonard, Gilmore, Fennell, & Heilman, 1996). Applications of these findings to larger samples of well-defined clinical populations hold tremendous promise for a better understanding of neuroanatomical differences and structure–function relationships in the brain.

In a more recent study, Leonard and her colleagues (2001), using volumetric MRI, identified four anatomical variables in phonological dyslexia (PD), which, when taken together, appear to predict long- and short-term memory: (1) marked rightward cerebral asymmetry, (2) marked leftward asymmetry of the anterior lobe of the cerebellum, (3) combined leftward asymmetry of the PT and posterior ascending ramus of the Sylvian fissure, and (4) a large duplication of Heschl's gyrus on the left. Spoken and written comprehension, by contrast, were predicted by a different anatomical variable, namely, low cerebral volume. The authors concluded that "the neuroanatomical correlates and prognoses of phonological and comprehension deficits are qualitatively and not just quantitatively different" (p. 154).

These results should be interpreted with some caution given the post hoc nature of the analyses: Subjects with PD ($n = 9$) were distinguished from subjects with unspecified reading deficits (URD; $n = 4$) only after extreme anatomical measures were found to cluster in subjects with poor phonological decoding skills. Additionally, the small number of subjects with URD makes it difficult to evaluate the robustness of the implied dissociation between phonological decoding and comprehension mechanisms. Nevertheless, if verified by future prospective studies as valid risk factors of a PD phenotype, these combined anatomical variables will have important consequences for diagnosis and intervention. At a weaker level, these findings may be taken as evidence against a common etiology for all reading and language disorders.

Behavioral Studies

Nature of Deficit in Language and Reading Impairments

Studies have shown that individuals with reading and or language impairments frequently have problems in domains other than phonology. In fact, 40% of children with reading disabilities may have an independent, co-occurring attention deficit disorder (Shaywitz, Fletcher, & Shaywitz, 1995). Many of these children also exhibit difficulties in auditory judgment tasks (De Weirdt, 1988; Kraus et al., 1996; Lowe & Campbell, 1965; McCroskey & Kidder, 1980; Tallal, 1980; Tallal & Piercy, 1973, 1974; Wright et al., 1997). The nature of the underlying deficit in reading and language disorders has been a controversy for over 25 years (Mody, Studdert-Kennedy, & Brady, 1997).

Proponents of an auditory account claim that the difficulties of children with reading and language impairments stem from a deficit in auditory temporal processing: These children are unable to process brief and/or rapid acoustic changes, such as those that occur in formant transitions at the onset of stop consonant–vowel syllables such as /ba/ and /da/ (Tallal, 1980; Tallal & Piercy, 1973, 1974, 1975). According to an alternative phonological account, children with reading and language impairment have intact auditory abilities; their difficulties lie in the encoding of phonetic distinctions in working memory (Brady, Shankweiler, & Mann, 1981; Shankweiler et al., 1979). As such, poor readers have weak or underspecified phonological representations, which would account for their difficulties in identification and discrimination of speech sounds, lexical retrieval, semantic processing, and even syntactic comprehension.

Evidence for an Auditory Temporal Processing Deficit Hypothesis

In a series of studies, Tallal and Piercy (1973, 1974, 1975) demonstrated that children with language impairments had deficits in both speech (phonetic) and nonspeech (auditory) discrimination. In a follow-up study, Tallal and Newcombe (1978) found that adult aphasics with focal brain lesions of the left hemisphere improved significantly in their perception of stop consonants when the stimuli incorporated extended formant transitions. From this, the authors concluded that the "left hemisphere must play a primary role in the analysis of specific rapidly changing acoustic cues, verbal and nonverbal, and such analysis is critically involved in the development and

maintenance of language" (p. 19). This conclusion is surprising, because it runs contrary to an earlier conclusion that "it is the brevity and not the transitional character" of the formant transitions that underlies the difficulty of dysphasic children (Tallal & Piercy, 1975, p. 73). The conflation of perceiving temporal properties of acoustic events with perceiving brief events rapidly has led to confusing terminology in the field, with theoretical and clinical consequences (Studdert-Kennedy & Mody, 1995). After all, the precise nature of a perceptual deficit bears directly on the underlying neural mechanism.

In a separate study, Schwartz and Tallal (1980) demonstrated a reduction in the magnitude of a right-ear advantage (REA) for synthetic stop consonant–vowel syllables when the initial transition was lengthened from 40 to 80 msec. The authors interpreted this finding as further evidence for a left-hemisphere dominance for processing rapidly changing acoustic events. However, it is important to note that an REA can vary as a function of hemispheric specialization and degree of access from the contralateral versus the ipsilateral ear. Whereas the former may be considered stable, ear access to a hemisphere can be manipulated by varying the characteristics of the signal. This leaves open the possibility that the reduced ear advantage obtained by Schwartz and Tallal (1980) may have arisen from an increased salience of the signal from the ipsilateral ear (Shankweiler & Studdert-Kennedy, 1967; Studdert-Kennedy & Shankweiler, 1970; see also Meschyan and Hernandez, Chapter 11, this volume, for further discussion).

Challenges to an Auditory Temporal Processing Deficit Hypothesis

Attempts to test various aspects of the auditory hypothesis have not been very successful (Bishop, Carlyon, Deeks, & Bishop, 1999; Bradlow et al., 1999; McNally, Hansen, Cornelissen, & Stein, 1997; Nittrouer, 1999). The notion of a left-hemisphere specialization (and, therefore, right-ear advantage) for rapid auditory processing has been challenged by a recent finding from a cross-linguistic study. Best and Avery (1999) found a right-ear advantage for stimuli incorporating rapid acoustic changes only in those subjects for whom these stimuli were linguistically relevant; the remaining subjects showed no ear preference for the stimuli. The results suggest that the processing of a cue, rapidly changing or otherwise, seems to depend on its phonological status in the language of the listener.

Aram and Ekelman (1988) failed to show differences between children with left- and right-hemisphere lesions on Tallal's tone temporal order judgment (TOJ) and discrimination tasks. This was contrary to their expectations based on findings by Tallal and Newcombe (1978), who showed that adults with left-hemisphere lesions did significantly worse than those with right-hemisphere lesions on the same tasks. Similarly, a direct test of the auditory basis for the speech perception deficits sometimes found in poor readers also failed to support the temporal processing deficit hypothesis. Good and poor readers selected to differ on Tallal's /ba/–/da/ TOJ at short interstimulus intervals were tested with nonspeech analogues that mimicked the acoustic trajectories of the second and third formant transitions that differentiate /ba/ from /da/. No significant differences were found between the groups with the nonspeech stimuli (Mody et al., 1997).

In a series of intervention studies, Tallal and colleagues (1996) found that the performance of a group of children with language impairments did improve significantly on a number of reading and language tests after intensive auditory training with acoustically modified speech, in which duration and amplitude were manipulated (Merzenich et al., 1996; Tallal et al., 1996). However, no attempts were made to separate the effects of adaptive training in temporal processing from the effects of stimulus intensity in the training. Nor did the authors investigate the effects of increasing the overall duration of the speech utterance relative to the effects of differentially slowing and amplifying the "problematic" transitional elements per se. Thus, Tallal and colleagues (1996) did not control for the different variables that were manipulated, and which may have contributed to the changes after the training. Consequently, their findings are ambiguous and open to interpretation (Brady, Scarbor-

ough, & Shankweiler, 1999; Hook, Macaruso, & Jones, 2001; Studdert-Kennedy, 2002).

How, then, does one explain the nonspeech deficits frequently reported in some children with reading and language impairments? An examination of the evidence to date suggests that the relation between phonological processing abilities and performance on tone discrimination and TOJ tasks is, at best, a correlational one, pointing to two independent and co-occurring deficits whose functional significance remains questionable (Rosen, 2003). More importantly, whereas phonological deficits are present in virtually every poor reader, auditory deficits, in contrast, are far from being consistent. The mixed results have led some researchers to turn to neuroimaging in search of a neural basis for the observed differences.

Functional Neuroimaging Studies

As mentioned earlier, neuroimaging studies of cognitive function have looked to lesion studies for confirmation of the functional organization of the brain. The advances in neuroimaging methods provide us with a powerful, noninvasive means to examine the nature of the functional disruption in reading and language impairments. In the next section, we present an overview of some of the applications of ERPs, MEG, and fMRI to disorders of reading and language.

Electrophysiology

ERP AND MEG STUDIES OF AUDITORY LANGUAGE PROCESSING IN INDIVIDUALS WITH READING AND LANGUAGE IMPAIRMENTS

Studies using ERPs have shown differences in neural activation patterns between children with and without language-based learning disabilities. The general consensus that phonological difficulties are central to reading and language impairments has led many neuroimaging researchers to focus on the neural substrates of phonological processing in dyslexia.

Molfese (2000) found auditory ERPs

(namely, N100, N200, P200) recorded at birth to speech and nonspeech stimuli correctly classified 81% of the 48 subjects in his study as normal, poor, or dyslexic readers at 8 years of age. Similarly, MMN recordings in very young infants show that language-specific memory traces develop by 1 year of age (Cheour et al., 1998). Kraus and her colleagues (1996) found a close correspondence between speech perception performance and related MMN responses in a group of children with learning and/or attention deficits. The authors concluded that electrophysiological responses (such as MMN) may be applicable clinically to "separate individuals who have auditory-system based deficits from individuals who have deficits originating later in the perceptual process" (p. 973). They went on to state that these results provide strong evidence that these discrimination deficits occur before higher level conscious perception. Some caution, however, is warranted here with regard to this interpretation of MMN results.

Studies using MMN have shown that very early on in the auditory pathways, the brain has access to phonological categories (Phillips et al., 2000; Schulte-Körne, Deimel, Bartling, & Remschmidt, 1998). Hence, a poor mismatch response in children with language and/or reading problems may well reflect their poor neurophysiological encoding of phonological distinctions, and not merely difficulties with auditory processing. Furthermore, despite its extensive use in normal adults and children, MMN shows considerable individual variability (Kurtzberg, Vaughan, Kreuzer, & Fleigler, 1995; Pekkonen, Rinne, & Näätänen, 1995). This is particularly true in children, whose auditory systems take several years to fully develop (Ponton, Eggermont, Kwong, & Don, 2000). Considerable work remains to be done before MMN can be used as a clinical tool (Cheour, Leppänen, & Kraus, 2000; Mody, Rivera, & Kurtzberg, 2001).

In one study, a group of children with learning problems failed to show improvements in their discrimination of a /da/–/ga/ stop consonant–vowel contrast, despite lengthening of the duration of the critical third formant transition cue (Bradlow et al., 1999). However, the group's MMN responses improved, resembling those of the normal children. The lengthened formant transition enhanced neural encoding at a preattentive level, without a corresponding improvement in behavioral performance. The results question the importance of the duration of formant transitions in the perceptual discrimination difficulties of children with learning problems. The application of MMN to investigate disorders of speech perception in children remains questionable.

Some ERP studies have also found a prolonged latency and reduced amplitude of the N100 component in children and adults with language impairments (Klein et al., 1995; Neville, Coffey, Holcomb, & Tallal, 1993). This early abnormal cortical activity pattern in N100, found in the PT and other fields within the superior temporal plane, has important implications for the study of dyslexia in view of the noted structural differences in this brain region between subjects with and without dyslexia.

ERP AND MEG STUDIES OF WRITTEN LANGUAGE PROCESSING IN INDIVIDUALS WITH READING AND LANGUAGE IMPAIRMENTS

Research suggests that persons with dyslexia may have a disruption in a mechanism that serves as an interface between visual and language domains, and that this mechanism may underlie the development of reading fluency. Using MEG, Salmelin and colleagues found that good readers showed a strong response to reading words relative to nonwords, 150–200 msec poststimulus onset, at occipitotemporal sites; the children with reading disabilities did not display this early response (Salmelin, Service, Kiesilä, Uutela, & Salonen, 1996). Thus, subjects with dyslexia appeared to have delayed visual word recognition, compared with fluent readers, when reading isolated words. They also showed enhanced activity, relative to the good readers, in the inferior frontal gyrus, suggestive of the former's difficulties with phonological decoding.

In a recent study, Wimmer, Hutzler, and Weiner (2002) found that poor readers exhibited reduced N1 amplitude to reading pseudowords, but not words, at central-parietal sites in the right hemisphere. Insofar as N1 is responsive to attentional demands (Luck, Fan, & Hillyard, 1993), and pseudowords may be considered attentionally more demanding than familiar words, the authors viewed their results as partially consistent with a sluggish attention shift hypothesis proposed by Hari and Renvall (2001). According to this hypothesis, individuals with dyslexia take longer than normal controls to disengage their attention from a previous target, a deficit associated with right parietal lobe dysfunction. Wimmer and colleagues (2002) also found a reduced N1 in left frontal sites relative to reading both words and pseudowords. Given the location of the N1 amplitude reduction, a site associated with phonological processing, the authors concluded that this reduction may reflect a deficit in the activation of phonological codes.

Individuals with developmental dyslexia have been found to display smaller and/or delayed P300 responses (Taylor & Keenan, 1990). A few researchers have also reported a reduced N400 response to deviant sentence endings in poor readers (Brandeis, Vetacco, & Steinhauser, 1994; Stelmack, Saxe, Noldy-Cullum, Campbell, & Amitage, 1988) and in children with language impairments (Neville et al., 1993). In a study of semantic cortical activation with dyslexic adults and matched controls, Helenius, Salmelin, Service, and Connolly (1999) found no significant difference between the groups in the spatial distribution of the subjects' MEG and N400 responses to deviant sentence endings in a reading task; however, the subjects with dyslexia had longer latencies. In general, the results with N400 in populations with reading and language impairment have not been very consistent.

Functional Imaging

FMRI STUDIES OF VISUAL PROCESSING IN DYSLEXIA

fMRI studies of children with reading and language impairments have primarily focused on their phonological abilities. However, visual deficits observed in some readers with dyslexia have led researchers to propose a possible role for visual processing deficits

in reading disability. Studies have shown that children with dyslexia process visual information more slowly than do normal controls. Findings include lower contrast sensitivity, longer visual persistence at low spatial frequencies, and slower flicker fusion rates (Lovegrove, 1993; Martin & Lovegrove, 1984, 1988). Taken together, these findings implicate the transient or magnocellular system, a theory supported by electrophysiological and anatomical studies (Livingstone, Rosen, Drislane, & Galaburda, 1991) that have shown evidence of an alteration of the magnocellular component of visual pathways in subjects with dyslexia. The magnocellular system, a subsystem of the visual pathways in the brain, is sensitive to low spatial and high temporal frequencies of visual motion stimuli with low luminance contrast.

Subjects with dyslexia also failed to show activation in area MT/V5 in the brain, in response to presentation of moving stimuli (Eden et al., 1996). Insofar as the MT/V5 complex receives a significant amount of input from the magnocellular stream (Maunsell & Newsome, 1987), these findings provide further support of a magnocellular deficit in dyslexia. Nevertheless, despite the evidence, problems in visual motion detection tend to be quite subtle in children with reading impairments. The co-occurrence of visual system abnormalities and reading disorders in dyslexia may be a consequence of damage to common neural systems. Any causal relationship between visual processing deficits and reading problems remains a speculative one (Eden & Zeffiro, 1998; see also Meschyan and Hernandez, Chapter 11, this volume).

FMRI STUDIES OF PHONOLOGICAL PROCESSING IN DYSLEXIA

Neuroimaging studies have implicated a number of foci of activation during word and pseudoword reading. These typically make up a left posterior circuit consisting of an occipitotemporal area, including the lateral extrastriate, and a temporoparietal circuit, which includes the angular gyrus, supramarginal gyrus, and posterior STG (Wernicke's area; see Figure 3.1). Both the occipitotemporal and temporoparietal circuits appear to be affected in reading disability (Horwitz, Rumsey, & Donahue, 1998; Rumsey, Horwitz, et al., 1997b; Salmelin et al., 1996; Shaywitz et al., 1998) and show reduced activation in children and adults with reading impairments. Some studies have also found that poor readers show increased activity in an anterior circuit in or near Broca's area (inferior frontal gyrus, IFG). This is believed to reflect a covert articulation strategy adopted by dyslexic readers, under conditions of effortful decoding (Pugh et al., 2000). The anterior activation pattern seen in some individuals with dyslexia may be viewed as compensatory activity due to a failure to develop the normal posterior circuitry for reading.

In one study, subjects were required to make judgments about line orientation, case, rhyme, and semantic category (Shaywitz et al., 1998). The authors found that good readers exhibited a systematic increase in activation in posterior brain areas implicated in reading as a function of increasing phonological demand across the tasks. Poor readers, in contrast, showed no such modulation of posterior activation but, rather, an increasing activation in anterior areas, such as the IFG (Broca's area), across the same tasks. This anterior–posterior dissociation in the activation patterns of good versus poor readers, under increasing phonological demand, is thought to represent a neurobiological marker for dyslexia (Shaywitz et al., 1998). The results resemble those obtained by Salmelin and colleagues (1996) using MEG. Interestingly, activity in the different brain areas engaged in reading also appears to be more highly correlated in normal readers compared to individuals with dyslexia (Horwitz et al., 1998). This finding suggests a disruption in poor readers' functional connectivity among components of the neural circuitry for reading.

INTEGRATING NEUROIMAGING RESULTS INTO A PHONOLOGICAL ACCOUNT OF READING DISABILITY

Findings from neuroimaging studies suggest that poor readers' reduced activation of the posterior neural circuitry for reading may be explained in terms of the relative contributions of the constituent temporoparietal and occipitotemporal circuits to the reading process. Frackowiak, Friston, Frith, Dolan, and Mazziota (1992) found greater activation of the temporoparietal circuit to pseudowords and low-frequency words than to familiar, high-frequency words, whereas the reverse held true for the occipitotemporal circuit. In keeping with these findings, Pugh and his colleagues (2000) have proposed that the development of the occipitotemporal circuit, which constitutes a memory-based word identification system supporting fluent word recognition, is dependent on the integrity of the temporoparietal circuit, which is responsible for basic decoding and analytical processing. This may explain why poor readers who have difficulties with phonological decoding, typically fail to achieve reading fluency: Their temporoparietal and occipitotemporal circuits, which are involved in phonological analysis and fluent word recognition, respectively, appear to be affected and, hence, show reduced activation.

According to Pugh and his colleagues (2000), the increased anterior activation sometimes observed in poor readers may be explained by the sensitivity of this region to grapheme–phoneme correspondences (Herbster et al., 1997). Poor readers' difficulties with mastering sound–symbol rules may necessitate the use of an articulatory recoding strategy under phonologically demanding conditions. This may account for the increased activity around Broca's area in poor readers compared to good readers. Although these are important findings, additional studies with children who have reading and/or language disorders will be needed to determine the specificity and sensitivity of this neurobiological marker.

CONCLUSIONS AND FUTURE RESEARCH DIRECTIONS

Reading and language are complex processes. Whereas there is a general consensus that phonological deficits are central to reading disability, there is mounting evidence that some children with reading and language impairments have deficits in other domains as well. However, the functional significance of the auditory, visual, and attention problems frequently observed in some children with reading and language impairments, and their relationship to the core deficit in phonology, remains unclear. The evidence to date suggests that these may be independent, co-occurring deficits (see also Gilger and Wise, Chapter 2, this volume). By delineating the pattern of functional disruption in children with language and reading problems, neuroimaging methods provide us with a means for examining the relationship between these various processes and their role in disorders of language and reading. As in any new and rapidly developing field, a systematic approach that combines behavioral and neuroimaging methods will help to answer some of these questions.

Efforts are currently under way across various institutions in the country to create a database of information about child and adult brains. One of the aims is to develop guidelines for determining what constitutes normal variations in brain morphometry across the lifespan. This can have large-scale implications for early identification of structural anomalies in the brain. Similarly, the development of a common set of age-appropriate oral and printed language tasks for use in neuroimaging could prove very useful. Performance on these tasks could be used to track corresponding changes in brain activation patterns as they relate to the development of reading and language abilities. The resulting functional markers will open the way to earlier and more specific diagnosis and intervention of reading disorders.

ACKNOWLEDGMENTS

This work was supported by a National Institute on Deafness and Other Communication Disorders award to Maria Mody. I am grateful to Seppo Ahlfors for helpful comments.

REFERENCES

Adams, M. J. (1990). Beginning to read: Thinking and learning about print. Cambridge, MA: MIT Press.

Aram, D., & Ekelman, B. L. (1988). Auditory temporal perception of children with left- or right-brain lesions. Neuropsychologia, 26, 931–935.

Aram, D., & Nation, J. (1980). Preschool language disorders and subsequent language and academic difficulties. Journal of Communication Disorders, 13, 229–241.

Barron, R. W. (1981). Development of visual word recognition: A review. In G. E. McKinnon & T. J. Waller (Eds.), Reading research: Advances in theory and practice (pp. 119–158). New York: Academic Press.

Belliveau, J. W., Kennedy, D. N., McKinstry, R. C., Buchbinder, B. R., Weisskoff, R. M., Cohen, M. S., et al. (1991). Functional mapping of the human visual cortex by magnetic resonance imaging. Science, 254, 716–719.

Best, C. T., & Avery, R. A. (1999). Left hemisphere advantage for click consonants is determined by linguistic significance and experience. Psychological Science, 10, 65–70.

Binder, J. R., Frost, J. A., Hammeke, T. A., Bellgowan, P. S. F., Springer, J. A., Kaufman, J. N., et al. (2000). Human temporal lobe activation by speech and nonspeech sounds. Cerebral Cortex, 10, 512–528.

Binder, J. R., Rao, S. M., Hammeke, T. A., Yetkin, F. Z., Jesmanowicz, A., Bandettini, P. A., et al. (1994). Functional magnetic resonance imaging of human auditory cortex. Annals of Neurology, 35, 662–672.

Bishop, D. V. M., & Adams, C. (1990). A prospective study of the relationship between specific language impairment, phonological disorders and reading retardation. Journal of Child Psychology and Child Psychiatry, 31, 1027–1050.

Bishop, D. V. M., Carlyon, R. P., Deeks, J. M., & Bishop, S. J. (1999). Auditory temporal processing impairment: Neither necessary nor sufficient for causing language impairment in children. Journal of Speech Language and Hearing Research, 42, 1295–1310.

Blumstein, S. E., Baker, E., & Goodglass, H. (1977). Phonological factors in auditory comprehension in aphasia. Neuropsychologia, 15, 19–30.

Bookheimer, S. Y., Zeffiro, T. A., Fiflozzi, C. M., Gaillard, W. D., & Theodore, W. H. (1995). Regional cerebral flow during object naming and word reading. Human Brain Mapping, 3, 93–106.

Bradley, L., & Bryant, P. (1983). Categorizing sounds and learning to read—a causal connection. Nature, 301, 419–421.

Bradlow, A. R., Kraus, N., Nichol, T. G., McGee, T. J., Cunningham, J., Zecker, S. G., et al. (1999). Effects of lengthened formant transition duration on discrimination and neural representation of synthetic CV syllables by normal and learning-disabled children. Journal of the Acoustical Society of America, 106, 2086–2096.

Brady, S. A., Scarborough, H., & Shankweiler, D. (1999). A perspective on two recent research reports. Perspectives: Proceedings of the Orton Dyslexia Society, 22, 5–8.

Brady, S. A., Shankweiler, D. P., & Mann, V. (1981). Speech perception and memory coding in relation to reading ability. Journal of Experimental Child Psychology, 35, 345–367.

Brandeis, D., Vetacco, D., & Steinhauser, H. C.

(1994). Mapping of brain electric micro-states in dyslexic children during reading. *Acta Paedopsychiatrica, 56,* 239–249.

Broca, P. (1861). A new case of loss of speech produced by a lesion of the posterior part of the second and third left frontal convolutions. *Bulletin de la Société Anatomique, 36,* 398–407.

Caplan, D., Alpert, N., & Waters, G. (1998). Effects of syntactic structure and prepositional number on patterns of regional cerebral blood flow. *Journal of Cognitive Neuroscience, 10,* 541–552.

Catts, H. W. (1991). Early identification of dyslexia: Evidence from a follow-up study of speech–language impaired children. *Annals of Dyslexia, 41,* 163–177.

Catts, H. W. (1993). The relationship between speech and language impairments and reading disabilities. *Journal of Speech and Hearing Research, 36,* 948–958.

Catts, H. W., Fey, M. E., Tomblin, J. B., & Zhang, X. (2002). A longitudinal investigation of reading outcomes in children with language impairments. *Journal of Speech, Language and Hearing Research, 45,* 1142–1157.

Catts, H. W., Fey, M. E., Zhang, X., & Tomblin, J. B. (1999). Language basis of reading disabilities: Evidence from a longitudinal investigation. *Scientific Studies of Reading, 3,* 331–361.

Cheour, M., Ceponiene, R., Lehtokoski, A., Luuk A., Allik, J., Alho, K., et al. (1998). Development of language-specific phoneme representation in the infant brain. *Nature Neuroscience, 1,* 351–353.

Cheour, M., Leppänen, P. H. T., & Kraus, N. (2000). Mismatch negativity (MMN) as a tool for investigating auditory discrimination and sensory memory in infants and children. *Clinical Neurophysiology, 111,* 4–16.

Cohen, D. (1999). Magnetoencephalography (neuromagnetism). In G. Adelman & B. H. Smith (Eds.), *Encyclopedia of neuroscience* (pp. 1079–1083). Amsterdam: Elsevier.

Coltheart, M. (1978). Lexical access in simple reading tasks. In G. Underwood (Ed.), *Strategies of information processing* (pp. 151–216). London: Academic Press.

Connolly, J. F., & Phillips, N. A. (1994). ERP components reflect phonological and semantic processing of the terminal word of spoken sentences. *Journal of Cognitive Neuroscience, 6,* 256–266.

Dehaene-Lambertz, G. (1997). Electrophysiological correlates of categorical phoneme perception in adults. *NeuroReport, 8,* 919–924.

Dale, A. M., Liu, A. K., Fischl, B., Buckner, R. L., Belliveau, J. W,. Lewine, J., et al. (2000). Dynamic statistical parametric mapping: Combining fMRI and MEG for high-resolution imaging of cortical activity. *Neuron, 26,* 55–67.

Damasio, A. R. (1992). Aphasia. *New England Journal of Medicine, 326,* 531–539.

Damasio, A. R., & Damasio, H. (1983). The anatomic basis of pure alexia. *Neurology, 33,* 1573–1583.

Demb, J. B., Desmond, J. E., Wagner, A. D., Vaidya, C. J., Glover, G. H., & Gabrieli, J. D. E. (1995). Se-

mantic encoding and retrieval in the left inferior prefrontal cortex: A functional MRI study of task difficulty and process specificity. *Journal of Neuroscience, 15,* 5870–5878.

Demonet, J.-F., Chollet, F., Ramsay, S., Cardebat, D., Nespoulous, J. L., Wise, R., et al. (1992). The anatomy of phonological and semantic processing in normal subjects. *Brain, 115,* 1753–1768.

Demonet, J.-F., Price, C., Wise, R., & Frackowiak, R. S. J. (1994). A PET study of cognitive strategies in normal subjects during language tasks: Influence of phonetic ambiguity and sequence processing on phoneme monitoring. *Brain, 17,* 671–682.

De Weirdt, W. (1988). Speech perception and frequency discrimination in good and poor readers. *Applied Psycholinguistics, 16,* 163–183.

Eden, G. F., van Meter, J. W., Rumsey, J. W., Maisog, J. M., Woods, R. P., & Zeffiro, T. (1996). Abnormal processing of visual motion in dyslexia revealed by functional brain imaging. *Nature, 382,* 66–69.

Eden, G. F., & Zeffiro, T. A. (1998). Neural systems affected in developmental dyslexia revealed by functional neuroimaging. *Neuron, 21,* 279–282.

Fiez, J. A. (1997). Phonology, semantics and the role of the left inferior prefrontal cortex. *Human Brain Mapping, 5,* 79–83.

Filipek, P. (1995). Neurobiological correlates of developmental dyslexia: How do dyslexic brains differ from those of normal readers? *Journal of Child Neurology, 10,* 62–69.

Fischl, B., Sereno, M. I., & Dale, A. M. (1999). Cortical surface-based analysis II: Inflation, flattening, a surface-based coordination system. *NeuroImage, 9,* 195–207.

Foundas, A. L. (2001). The anatomical basis of language. *Topics in Language Disorders, 21,* 1–19.

Foundas, A. L., Leonard, C. M., Gilmore, R., Fennell, E., & Heilman, K. M. (1994). Planum temporale asymmetry and language dominance. *Neuropsychologia, 32,* 1225–1231.

Foundas, A. L., Leonard, C. M., Gilmore, R. L., Fennell, E. B., & Heilman, K. L. (1996). Pars triangularis asymmetry and language dominance. *Proceedings of the National Academy of Sciences (USA), 93,* 719–722.

Fox, P. T., & Raichle, M. E. (1986). Focal physiological uncoupling of cerebral blood flow and oxidative metabolism during somatosensory stimulation in human subjects. *Proceedings of the National Academy of Sciences (USA), 83,* 1140–1144.

Frackowiak, R., Friston, K., Frith, C., Dolan, R., & Mazziota, B. (1992). *Human brain function.* New York: Academic Press.

Friston, K. J., Frith, C. D., Liddle, P. F., & Frackowiak, R. S. J. (1991). Plastic transformation of PET images. *Journal of Computer Assisted Tomography, 15,* 634–639.

Furth, H. (1966). A comparison of reading test norms for deaf and hearing children. *American Annals of the Deaf, 111,* 461–462.

Gabrieli, J. D. E., Desmond, J. E., Demb, J. E., Wagner, A. D., Stone, M. V., Vaidya, C. J., et al. (1996).

Functional magnetic resonance imaging of semantic memory processes in the frontal lobes. *Psychological Science, 7,* 278–283.

Galaburda, A., Sherman, G., Rosen, G., Aboitiz, F., & Geschwind, N. (1985). Developmental dyslexia: Four consecutive patients with cortical anomalies. *Annals of Neurology, 18,* 222–233.

Gauger, L. M., Lombardino, L. J., & Leonard, C. M. (1997). Brain morphology in children with specific language impairment. *Journal of Speech, Language and Hearing Research, 40,* 1272–1284.

Geschwind, N., & Levistsky, W. (1968). Human brain: Asymmetries in temporal speech region. *Science, 161,* 186–187.

Gevins, A. S., & Remond, A. (Eds.). (1987). *Methods of analysis of brain electrical and magnetic signal: EEG handbook I* (rev. ser.). Amsterdam: Elsevier.

Gold, B. J., & Buckner, R. L. (2002). Common prefrontal regions coactivate with dissociable posterior regions during controlled semantic and phonological tasks. *Neuron, 35,* 803–812.

Hall, P., & Tomblin, J. B. (1978). A follow-up study of children with articulation and language disorders. *Journal of Speech and Hearing Disorders, 43,* 227–241.

Hämäläinen, M. S., Hari, R., Ilmoniemi, R. J., Knuutila, J., & Lounasmaa, O. V. (1993). Magnetoencephalography—theory, instrumentation, and applications to non-invasive studies of the working human brain. *Review of Modern Physics, 65,* 413–497.

Hari, R., & Renvall, H. (2001). Impaired processing of rapid stimulus sequences in dyslexia. *Trends in Cognitive Neuroscience, 5,* 525–532.

Helenius, P., Salmelin, R., Service, E., & Connolly, J. (1998). Distinct time courses of word and context comprehension in the left temporal cortex. *Brain, 121,* 1133–1142.

Helenius, P., Salmelin, R., Service, E., & Connolly, J. (1999). Semantic cortical activation in dyslexic readers. *Journal of Cognitive Neuroscience, 11,* 535–550.

Herbster, A. N, Mintun, M. A., Nebes, R. D., & Becker, J. T. (1997). Regional cerebral blood flow during word and nonword reading. *Human Brain Mapping, 5,* 84–92.

Holcombe, P. J., Coffey, S. A., & Neville, H. J. (1992). Visual and auditory sentence processing: A developmental analysis using event-related brain potentials. *Developmental Neuropsychology, 8,* 203–241.

Hook, P. E., Macaruso, P., & Jones, S. (2001). Efficacy of Fast ForWord training on facilitating acquisition of reading skills by children with reading disabilities—a longitudinal study. *Annals of Dyslexia, 51,* 75–96.

Horwitz, B., Rumsey, J. M., & Donahue, K. (1998). Functional connectivity of the angular gyrus in normal reading and dyslexia. *Proceedings of the National Academy of Sciences (USA), 95,* 8939–8944.

Howard, D., Patterson, K., Wise, R., Brown, D., Friston, K., Weller, C., et al. (1992). The cortical localizations of the lexicons: Positron emission tomography evidence. *Brain, 115,* 1769–1782.

Jacobson, G. P. (1994). Magnetoencephalographic studies of auditory system function. *Journal of Clinical Neurophysiology, 11,* 343–364.

Kaan, E., & Stowe, L. A. (2002). Storage and computation in the brain: A neuroimaging perspective. In S. Nooteboom, F. Weerman, & F. Wijnen (Eds.), *Storage and computation in the language faculty* (pp. 257–298). Dordrecht, the Netherlands: Kluwer.

Kaan, E., & Swaab, T. Y. (2002). The brain circuitry of syntactic comprehension. *Trends in Cognitive Sciences, 6,* 350–356.

Kamhi, A. G., & Catts, H. W. (Eds.). (1989). *Reading disabilities: A developmental language perspective.* Boston: Allyn & Bacon.

Kapur, S., Rose, R., Liddle, P. F., Zipursky, R. B., Brown, G. M., Stuss, D., et al. (1994). The role of the left prefrontal cortex in verbal processing: Semantic processing or willed action? *NeuroReport, 5,* 2193–2196.

Keller, T. A., Carpenter, P. A., & Just, M. A. (2001). The neural bases of sentence comprehension: An fMRI examination of syntactic and lexical processing. *Cerebral Cortex, 11,* 223–237.

Klein, S. K., Kurtzberg, D. K., Brattson, A., Kreuzer, J., Stapells, D. R., Dunn, M., et al. (1995). Electrophysiological manifestations of impaired temporal lobe auditory processing in verbal auditory agnosia. *Brain and Language, 51,* 383–405.

Kraus, N., McGee, T., Carrell, T. J, Zecker, S. G., Trent, N., & Koch, D. (1996). Auditory neurophysiologic responses and discrimination deficits in children with learning problems. *Science, 273,* 971–973.

Kuriki, S., & Murase, M. (1989). Neuromagnetic study of the auditory response in left and right hemisphere of the human brain evoked by pure tones and speech sounds. *Experimental Brain Research, 77,* 127–134.

Kurtzberg, D., Vaughan, H. G., Kreuzer, J., & Fleigler, K. Z. (1995). Developmental studies and clinical applications of mismatch negativity: Problems and prospects. *Ear and Hearing, 16,* 117–129.

Kutas, M., & Hillyard, S. A. (1980). Reading senseless sentences: Brain potentials reflect semantic incongruity. *Science, 207,* 203–205.

Kutas, M., & Hillyard, S. A. (1983). Event-related brain potentials to grammatical errors and semantic anomalies. *Memory and Cognition, 11,* 539–550.

Kwong, K. K., Belliveau, J. W., Chesler, D. A., Goldberg, I. E., Weisskoff, R. M., Poncelet, B. P., et al. (1992). Dynamic magnetic resonance imaging of human brain activity during primary sensory stimulation. *Proceedings of the National Academy of Sciences (USA), 89,* 5675–5679.

Lauter, J. L., Herschovitch, C., Formby, C., & Raichle, M. E. (1985). Tonotopic organization in the human auditory cortex revealed by positron emission tomography. *Hearing Research, 20,* 199–205.

Lawson, E. A., & Gaillard, A. W. K. (1981). Mismatch negativity in a phonetic discrimination task. *Biological Psychology, 13,* 281–288.

Leonard, C. M., Eckert, M. A., Lomabardino, L. J., Oakland, T., Kranzler, J., Mohr, C. M., et al.

(2001). Anatomical risk factors for phonological dyslexia. *Cerebral Cortex, 11,* 148–157.

Leonard, C. M., Lomabardino, L. J., Mercado, L. R., Browd, S. R., Breier, J. R., & Agee, O. F. (1996). Cerebral asymmetry and cognitive development in children: A magnetic resonance imaging study. *Psychological Science, 7,* 89–95.

Leonard, C. M., Voeller, K. S., Lombardino, L., Morris, M. K., Alexander, A., Andersen, H., et al. (1993). Anomalous cerebral structure in dyslexia revealed with magnetic resonance imaging. *Archives of Neurology, 50,* 461–469.

Leonard, L. B. (1998). *Children with specific language impairment.* Cambridge, MA: MIT Press.

Liberman, A. M. (1999). The reading researcher and the reading teacher need the right theory of speech. *Scientific Studies of Reading, 3,* 95–111.

Liberman, I. Y., Shankweiler, D., & Liberman, A. M. (1989). The alphabetic principle and learning to read. In D. Shankweiler & I. Y. Liberman (Eds.), *Phonology and reading disability: Solving the reading puzzle* (International Academy for Research in Learning Disabilities Monograph Series, No. 6; pp. 1–33). Ann Arbor, Michigan: University of MI Press.

Livingstone, M. S., Rosen, G. D., Drislane, F. W., & Galaburda, A. M. (1991). Physiological and anatomical evidence for a magnocellular deficit in developmental dyslexia. *Proceedings of the National Academy of Sciences (USA), 88,* 7943–7947.

Locke, J. L., Hodgson, J., Macaruso, P., Roberts, J., Lambrecht-Smith, S., & Guttentag, C. (1997). The development of developmental dyslexia. In C. Hulme & M. Snowling (Eds.), *Dyslexia: Biology, cognition and intervention* (pp. 72–96). London: Whurr.

Lovegrove, W. (1993). Weakness in the transient visual system: A causal factor in dyslexia? *Annals of the New York Academy of Sciences, 682,* 57–96.

Lowe, A., & Campbell, R. (1965). Temporal discrimination in aphasoid and normal children. *Journal of Speech and Hearing Research, 8,* 313–314.

Luck, S. J., Fan, S., & Hillyard, S. A. (1993). Attention-related modulation of sensory-evoked brain activity in a visual search task. *Journal of Cognitive Neuroscience, 5,* 188–195.

Lundberg, I., Olofsson, A., & Wall, S. (1980). Reading and spelling skills in the first school years predicted from phonemic awareness skills in kindergarten. *Scandanavian Journal of Psychology, 21,* 159–173.

Maiste, A., Weins, A. S., Hunt, M. J., Scherg, M., & Picton, T. W. (1995). Event-related potentials and the categorical perception of speech sounds. *Ear and Hearing, 16,* 68–90.

Martin, F., & Lovegrove, W. (1984). The effect of field size and luminance on contrast sensitivity differences between specifically reading-disabled and normal children. *Neuropsychologia, 22,* 72–77.

Martin, F., & Lovegrove, W. (1988). Uniform and field flicker in control and specifically-disabled readers. *Perception, 17,* 203–214.

Maunsell, J. H. R., & Newsome, W. T. (1987). Visual processing in monkey extrastriate cortex. *Annual Review of Neuroscience, 10,* 363–401.

McCroskey, R., & Kidder, H. (1980). Auditory fusion among learning disabled, reading disabled and normal children. *Journal of Learning Disabilities, 13,* 18–25.

McIntosh, A. R. (2000). Towards a network theory of cognition. *Neural Networks, 13,* 861–870.

McNally, K. I., Hansen, P. C., Cornelissen, P. L., & Stein, J. F. (1997). Effect of time and frequency manipulation on syllable perception in developmental dyslexics. *Journal of Speech, Language and Hearing Research, 40,* 912–924.

Merzenich, M. M., Jenkins, W. M., Johnston, P., Schreiner, C., Miller, S., & Tallal, P. (1996). Temporal processing deficits of language-learning impaired children ameliorated by training. *Science, 271,* 77–81.

Mody, M., Rivera, M., & Kurtzberg, D. K. (2001, November). *Mismatch negativity: A clinical dilemma.* Poster presented at Annual Meeting of the American Speech–Language–Hearing Association, New Orleans, LA.

Mody, M., Studdert-Kennedy, M., & Brady, S. (1997). Speech perception deficits in poor readers: Auditory processing or phonological coding? *Journal of Experimental Child Psychology, 64,* 199–231.

Molfese, D. L. (2000). Predicting dyslexia at 8 years of age using neonatal brain responses. *Brain and Language, 72,* 238–245.

Näätänen, R. (1995). The mismatch negativity: A powerful tool for cognitive neuroscience. *Ear and Hearing, 16,* 6–18.

Näätänen, R., Lehtokoski, A., Lennes, M., Cheour, M., Huotilainen, M., Iivonen, M., et al. (1997). Language-specific phoneme representations revealed by electric and magnetic brain responses. *Nature, 385,* 432–434.

Näätänen, R., & Picton, T. (1987). The N1 wave of the human electric and magnetic response to sound: A review and analysis of the component structure. *Psychophysiology, 24,* 375–425.

Neville, H., Coffey, S. A., Holcomb, P. J., & Tallal, P. (1993). The neurobiology of sensory and language processing in language-impaired children. *Journal of Cognitive Neuroscience, 5,* 235–253.

Ni, W., Constable, R. T., Mencl, W. E., Pugh, K. R., Fulbright, R. K., Shaywitz, S. E., et al. (2000). An event-related neuroimaging study distinguishing form and content in sentence processing. *Journal of Cognitive Neuroscience, 12,* 120–133.

Nigam, A., Hoffman, J. E., & Simons, R. F. (1992). N400 to semantically anomalous pictures and words. *Journal of Cognitive Neuroscience, 4,* 15–22.

Nittrouer, S. (1999). Do temporal processing deficits cause phonological processing problems? *Journal of Speech, Language and Hearing Research, 42,* 925–942.

Ogawa, S., Tank, D. W., Menon, R., Ellermann, J. M., Kim, S., Merkle, H., et al. (1992). Intrinsic signal changes accompanying sensory stimulation: Functional brain mapping with magnetic resonance imaging. *Proceedings of the National Academy of Sciences (USA), 89,* 5951–5955.

Oller, D. K. (1980). The emergence of the sounds of speech in infancy. In G. Yeni-Komshian, J. F. Kavanaugh, & C. A. Ferguson (Eds.), *Child phonology: Production* (Vol. 1, pp. 93–112). New York: Academic Press.

Pekkonen, E., Huotilainen, M., Virtanen, J., Näätänen, R., Ilmoniemi, R. J., & Erkinjuntti, T. (1996). Alzheimer's disease affects parallel processing between the auditory cortices. *NeuroReport, 7,* 1365–1368.

Pekkonen, E., Rinne, T., & Näätänen, R. (1995). Variability and replicability of mismatch negativity. *Electroencephalography and Clinical Neurophysiology, 87,* 321–325.

Petersen, S. E., Fox, P. T., Posner, M. I., Mintun, M., & Raichle, M. E. (1988). Positron emission tomographic studies of the cortical anatomy of single-word processing. *Nature, 33,* 585–589.

Petersen, S. E., Fox, P. T., Snyder, A. Z., & Raichle, M. E. (1990). Activation of extrastriate and frontal cortical areas by visual words and word-like stimuli. *Science, 249,* 1041–1044.

Phillips, C., Pellathy, T., Marantz, A., Yellin, E., Wexler, K. Poeppel, D., et al. (2000). Auditory cortex accesses phonological categories: An MEG study mismatch study. *Journal of Cognitive Neuroscience, 12,* 1038–1055.

Plante, E., Swisher, L., & Vance, R. (1989). Anatomical correlates of normal and impaired language in a set of dizygotic twins. *Brain and Language, 37,* 643–655.

Plante, E., Swisher, L., Vance, R., & Rapcsak, S. (1991). MRI findings in boys with specific language impairment. *Brain and Language, 41,* 52–66.

Poeppel, D., Yellin, E., Phillips, C., Roberts, T. P. L., Rowley, H. A., Wexler, K., et al. (1996). Task-induced asymmetry of the auditory evoked M100 neuromagnetic field elicited by speech sounds. *Cognitive Brain Research, 4,* 231–242.

Poldrack, R. A., Wagner, A. D., Prull, M., Desmond, J. E., Glover, G. H., & Gabrieli, J. D. E. (1999). Functional specialization for semantic and phonological processing in the left inferior prefrontal cortex. *NeuroImage, 10,* 15–35.

Ponton, C. W., Eggermont, J. J., Kwong, B., & Don, M. (2000). Maturation of human central auditory system activity: Evidence from multi-channel evoked potentials. *Journal of Clinical Neurophysiology, 111,* 220–236.

Price, C. J., Moore, C. J., Humphrey, G. W., & Wise, R. J. S. (1997). Segregating semantic from phonological processes during reading. *Journal of Cognitive Neuroscience, 9,* 727–733.

Price, C. J., Warburton, E. A., Moore, C. J., Howard, D., Patterson, K., Frackowiak, R. S. J., et al. (1996). Hearing and saying: The functional anatomy of auditory word processing. *Brain, 119,* 919–931.

Price, C. J., Wise, R. J., & Frackowiak, R. S. (1996). Demonstrating the implicit processing of visually presented words and pseudowords. *Cerebral Cortex, 6,* 62–70.

Pugh, K. R., Mencl, W. E., Jenner, A. R., Katz, L., Frost, S., Lee, J. R., et al. (2000). Functional neuroimaging studies of reading and reading disability (developmental dyslexia). *Mental Retardation and Developmental Disabilities Reviews, 6,* 207–213.

Pugh, K. R., Shaywitz, B. A., Shaywitz, S. E., Constable, R. T., Skudlarski, P., Fulbright, R. K., et al. (1996). Cerebral organization of component processes in reading. *Brain, 119,* 1221–1238.

Roberts, T. P., Ferrari, P., Stufflebeam, S. M., & Poeppel, D. (2000). Latency of the auditory evoked neuromagnetic field components: Stimulus dependence and insights towards perception. *Journal of Clinical Neuropsychology, 17,* 114–129.

Rosen, S. (2003). Auditory processing in dyslexia and specific language impairment: Is there a deficit? What is its nature? Does it explain anything? *Journal of Phonetics, 31,* 509–527.

Rugg, M. (1985). The effects of semantic priming and word repetition on event-related potentials. *Psychophysiology, 22,* 642–647.

Rumsey, J., Donahue, B., Brady, D., Nace, K., Giedd, J., & Andreasen, P. (1997). Magnetic resonance imaging study of planum temporale asymmetry in men with developmental dyslexia. *Archives of Neurology, 54,* 1481–1489.

Rumsey, J., Dowart, R., Vermess, M., Denckla, M. B., Kreuss, M. J. P., & Rapoport, J. L. (1986). Magnetic resonance imaging of brain anatomy in severe developmental dyslexia. *Annals of Neurology, 43,* 1045–1046.

Rumsey, J. M., Horwitz, B., Donahue, K., Nace, K., Maisog, J. M., & Andreasen, P. (1997). Phonologic and orthographic components of word recognition: A PET-rCBF study. *Brain, 120,* 739–759.

Salmelin, R., Service, E., Kiesilä, P., Uutela, K., & Salonen, O. (1996). Impaired visual word processing in dyslexia revealed with magnetoencephalography. *Annals of Neurology, 40,* 157–162.

Scarborough, H. (1990). Very early language deficits in dyslexic children. *Child Development, 61,* 1728–1743.

Scarborough, H. (1991). Early syntactic development of dyslexic children. *Annals of Dyslexia, 41,* 207–220.

Schlosser, M. J., Aoyage, N., Fulbright, R. K., Gore, J. C., & McCarthy, G. (1998). Functional MRI studies of auditory comprehension. *Human Brain Mapping, 6,* 1–13.

Schulte-Körne, G., Deimel, W., Bartling, J., & Remschmidt, H. (1998). Auditory processing and dyslexia: Evidence for a specific speech processing deficit. *NeuroReport, 9,* 337–340.

Schultz, R., Cho, N., Staib, L., Kier, L., Fletcher, J., Shaywitz, S., et al. (1994). Brain morphology in normal and dyslexic children: The influence of sex and age. *Annals of Neurology, 35,* 732–742.

Schwartz, J., & Tallal, P. (1980). Rate of acoustic change may underlie hemispheric specialization for speech perception. *Science, 207,* 1380–1381.

Shankweiler, D. P., Liberman, I. Y., Mark, L. S., Fowler, C. A., & Fischer, F. W. (1979). The speech code and learning to read. *Journal of Experimental Psychology: Human Memory and Learning, 5,* 531–545.

Shankweiler, D. P., & Studdert-Kennedy, M. (1967). Identification of consonant and vowels presented to left and right ears. *Quarterly Journal of Experimental Psychology, 19,* 59–63.

Shaywitz, S. E., Fletcher, J. M., & Shaywitz, B. A. (1995). Defining and classifying learning disabilities and attention-deficit/hyperactivity disorder. *Journal of Child Neurology, 10*(Suppl. 1), S50–S57.

Shaywitz, S. E., Shaywitz, B. A., Fletcher, J. M., & Escobar, M. D. (1990). Prevalence of reading disability in boys and girls. *Journal of the American Medical Association, 264,* 998–1002.

Shaywitz, S. E., Shaywitz, B. A., Pugh, K. R., Fulbright, R. K., Constable, R. T., Mencl, W. E., et al. (1998). Functional disruption in the organization of the brain for reading in dyslexia. *Proceedings of the National Academy of Sciences (USA), 95,* 2636–2641.

Simos, P. G., Breir, J., Fletcher, J., Foorman, B., Castillo, E., & Papanicolaou, A. (2002). Brain mechanisms for reading words and pseudowords: An integrated approach. *Cerebral Cortex, 12,* 297–305.

Stelmack, R. M., Saxe, B. J., Noldy-Cullum, N., Campbell, K. B., & Amitage, R. (1988). Recognition memory for words and event-related potentials: A comparison of normal and disabled readers. *Journal of Clinical and Experimental Neuropsychology, 10,* 185–200.

Stromswold, K., Caplan, D., Alpert, N., & Rausch, S. (1996). Localization of syntactic comprehension by positron emission tomography. *Brain and Language, 52,* 452–473.

Studdert-Kennedy, M. (2002). Deficits in phonological awareness do not arise from a failure in rapid auditory processing. *Reading and Writing, 15,* 5–14.

Studdert-Kennedy, M., & Mody, M. (1995). Auditory temporal perception deficits in the reading impaired: A critical review of the evidence. *Psychonomic Bulletin and Review, 2,* 508–514.

Studdert-Kennedy, M., & Shankweiler, D. P. (1970). Hemispheric specialization for speech perception. *Journal of the Acoustical Society of America, 48,* 579–594.

Talairach, J., & Tournoux, P. (1988). *Co-planar stereotaxic atlas of the human brain.* New York: Thieme.

Tallal, P. (1980). Auditory temporal perception, phonics and reading abilities in children. *Brain and Language, 9,* 182–198.

Tallal, P., Miller, S., Bedi, G., Byma, G., Wang, X., Nagarajan, S. S., et al. (1996). Language comprehension in language-learning impaired children improved with acoustically-modified speech. *Science, 271,* 81–84.

Tallal, P., & Newcombe, F. (1978). Impairment of auditory perception and language comprehension in dysphasia. *Brain and Language, 5,* 13–24.

Tallal, P., & Piercy, M. (1973). Developmental aphasia: Impaired rate of non-verbal processing as a function of sensory modality. *Neuropsychologia, 11,* 389–398.

Tallal, P., & Piercy, M. (1974). Rate of auditory processing and selective impairment of consonant perception. *Neuropsychologia, 12,* 83–93.

Tallal, P., & Piercy, M. (1975). Developmental aphasia: The perception of brief vowels and extended stop consonants. *Neuropsychologia, 13,* 69–74.

Tarkiainen, A., Helenius, P., Hansen, P. C., Cornellisen, P. L., & Salmelin, R. (1999). Dynamics of letter string perception in the human occipito-temporal cortex. *Brain, 122,* 2119–2131.

Taylor, M. J., & Keenan, N. K. (1990). ERPs to visual and language stimuli in normal and dyslexic children. *Psychophysiology, 27,* 318–329.

Tomblin, J. B. (1989). Familial concentration of specific language impairment. *Journal of Speech and Hearing Disorders, 54,* 287–295.

Tomblin, J. B. (1996). *The big picture of SLI: Results of an epidemiological study of SLI among kindergarten children.* Paper presented at the ninth Symposium on Research in Child Language Disorders, University of Wisconsin, Madison.

Trybus, R., & Karchmer, M. (1977). School achievement scores of hearing-impaired children: National data on achievement status and growth patterns. *American Annals of the Deaf, 122,* 62–69.

Vaughan, H. G. (1974). The analysis of scalp-recorded potentials. In R. F. Thompson & M. M. Patterson (Eds.), *Bioelectric recording techniques: Part B. Electroencephalography and human brain potentials* (pp. 157–207). New York: Academic Press.

Wagner, R., & Torgesen, J. (1987). The nature of phonological processing and its causal role in the acquisition of reading skills. *Psychological Bulletin, 101,* 192–212.

Wernicke, C. (1874). *The aphasia symptom complex: A psychological study on an anatomic basis.* Breslau: Kohn.

Wimmer, H., Hutzler, F., & Wiener, C. (2002). Children with dyslexia and right parietal lobe dysfunction: Event-related potentials in response to words and pseudowords. *Neuroscience Letters, 331,* 211–213.

Wood, C. C., Cohen, D., Cuffin, B. N., Yarita, T., & Allison, T. (1985). Electrical sources in human somatosensory cortex: Identification by combined magnetic and potential recordings. *Science, 227,* 1051–1053.

Wright, B. A., Lombardino, L. J., King, W. M., Puranik, C. S., Leonard, C. M., Merzenich, M. M. (1997). Deficits in auditory temporal and spectral processing in language-impaired children. *Nature, 387,* 176–178.

Yule, W., & Rutter, M. (1976). Epidemiological and social implications of specific reading retardation. In R. Knight & D. Bakker (Eds.), *The neuropsychology of learning disorders* (pp. 25–39). Baltimore: University Park Press.

Zatorre, R. J., Evans, A. C., Meyer, E., & Gjedde, A. (1992). Lateralization of phonetic and pitch dis-crimination in speech processing. *Nature, 256,* 846–849.

Zatorre, R. J., Meyer, E., Gjedde, A., & Evans, A. C. (1996). PET studies of phonetic processing of speech: Review, replication and re-analysis. *Cerebral Cortex, 6,* 21–30.

4

Cognitive Factors in Second-Language Acquisition and Literacy Learning

A Theoretical Proposal and Call for Research

GAYANE MESCHYAN
ARTURO E. HERNANDEZ

The question of which factors facilitate and expedite the acquisition of a second language (L2) is of both practical and theoretical importance. Individuals who attain a good command of oral skills (listening and speech production) and written skills (reading and writing) in an L2 are at an advantage. They can compete with native speakers more successfully at school and at work, thereby increasing their chances of securing a higher standard of living. As the number of public school students from non-English-speaking homes increases in the United States, the importance of understanding those factors that facilitate the learning of an L2 becomes paramount.

Our purpose in this chapter is to review selected cognitive factors that facilitate L2 learning. (For a complementary discussion of sociocultural and institutional factors, see Zecker, Chapter 12, this volume.) Identifying predictors of quality L2 acquisition enables us to understand how language is organized in general, and it provides testable hypotheses for how L2 acquisition may be improved. We view our chapter as a proposal for a new way to think about L2 acquisi-

tion issues, and we hope that it encourages new research in this domain.

This chapter addresses four main issues. First, we define a key concept, namely, phonological ability. Second, we discuss selected cognitive abilities that facilitate native-language and L2 acquisition. Third, we present data concerning the relationship between L2 learning and native language abilities. Finally, we conclude with a brief discussion of the presented behavioral evidence and propose future research directions that can further contribute to our knowledge of individual differences in L2 learning.

WHAT IS PHONOLOGICAL ABILITY?

Before presenting the literature on native- and L2 development, we first define a term that appears frequently throughout this chapter, namely, "phonological ability." We use the term to refer to an individual's ability to perceive accurately and represent novel speech sounds, such as L2 words and phrases. This includes being sensitive to where in the spoken L2 word stresses are placed so as to represent the unfamiliar word with the proper accent. Furthermore, it also includes possessing sensitivity to the individual sound units (phonemes) that comprise an unfamiliar spoken word. This latter sensitivity, which relates to Brady's (1997) notion of speech perception, can manifest itself in one's ability to detect accurately differences between similar-sounding phonemes, such as detecting the difference in the "ea" sound in the words *year* and *yearn*. Hence, by phonological ability, we refer to the ability not only to represent a word with the proper accent, but also to perceive accurately the individual sound units that comprise the unfamiliar spoken word.

Although it may be considered a controversial point, we expect that this sensitivity to novel speech sounds is partly what discriminates individuals who have an easy time learning an L2 from those who find this task arduous and unpleasant. Of course, other factors, such as the motivation to learn the L2, the attitude toward the L2 (Gardner, 1985), and the instructional design for learning or acquiring the L2 (Bus & van IJzendoorn, 1999) all make their own important contributions to the learning process (see Zecker, Chapter 12, this volume). However, this chapter focuses mainly on the cognitive factors implicated in L2 learning.

The phonological ability construct is related to two concepts that appear in the developmental literature, namely, phonological awareness and phonological working memory. The term "phonological awareness" appears in the reading development literature. It refers to one's awareness that spoken words comprise individual sound units, and that these sound units can be manipulated. This awareness is thought to precede early reading abilities (Perfetti, Beck, Bell, & Hughes, 1987; Wagner & Torgesen, 1987).

The term "phonological working memory" is used in the native-language development literature and is derived from Baddeley's (1986) model of working memory. According to Baddeley's model, phonological working memory, specifically, the phonological loop component that comprises it, mediates language learning by providing temporary storage of unfamiliar sound forms until more permanent representations are constructed in long-term memory (Baddeley, Gathercole, & Papagno, 1998). The idea is that the ability to construct accurate and distinct short-term phonological representations of unfamiliar speech sounds predicts vocabulary learning.

Although the term "phonological ability" does share similarity with "phonological awareness" and "phonological working memory," our purpose in this chapter is to emphasize the importance of forming accurate sound representations of unfamiliar words and phrases. This point does not receive sufficient emphasis in the research on phonological awareness and phonological working memory.

Phonological ability underlies both phonological awareness and phonological working memory, and it is an important component of these two constructs. However, phonological awareness and phonological working memory require that additional manipulations be performed on the accurate phonological representations that have been formed. These manipulations include the maintenance of phonological information through rehearsal (in phonological working memory) and segmenting, blending, and phoneme deletion (in phonological awareness). Given that the ability to carry out these latter processes (i.e., segmenting, blending, and phoneme deletion) requires the temporary maintenance of a target phonological representation in phonological working memory, it follows that phonological awareness and phonological working memory also relate to each other (for review, see Gathercole & Baddeley, 1993a).

Because the ability to form accurate phonological representations is an important component of phonological awareness and phonological working memory, we next present research that has used these two constructs. However, in reviewing these studies, we acknowledge that these constructs also involve additional processes. Nevertheless, we believe they possess sufficient overlap with phonological ability to warrant the review of studies that have employed them.

THE ROLE OF PHONOLOGICAL ABILITY IN NATIVE- AND SECOND-LANGUAGE DEVELOPMENT

In this section, we review literature that implicates accurate phonological representations in native-language and L2 development. The first two subsections present evidence to suggest that phonological ability plays an important predictive role in native-language vocabulary and reading comprehension development, respectively. The latter two subsections review the role of phonological ability in L2 vocabulary and reading comprehension development, respectively.

Accurate Phonological Representations in Native-Language Vocabulary Development

A number of research findings suggest that the ability to store accurate phonological representations of new words in phonological working memory plays a causal role in the development of native-language vocabulary. Gathercole, Willis, Emslie, and Baddeley (1992) used the pseudoword (pronounceable nonword) repetition task as a measure of phonological working memory, in which the participant is asked to repeat aloud accurately an auditorily presented pseudoword. These authors found that the ability of 4-year-old children to repeat pseudowords aloud accurately predicted their native-language vocabulary knowledge 1 year later, at age 5 years. However, vocabulary knowledge at age 4 years was not a significant predictor of pseudoword repetition accuracy at age 5. The authors reasoned that this pattern of correlations suggests that phonological working memory is a preceding condition that causally predicts quality of vocabulary development in the native language. Because they measured phonological working memory using the pseudoword repetition task, which is a good way to measure an individual's ability to represent novel speech sounds accurately, their findings suggest that individuals who are able to form accurate phonological representations of novel sound forms are advantaged in learning new words. Furthermore, work by Gathercole, Service, Hitch, Adams, and Martin (1999) indicates that children with good phonological ability differ from those with poor phonological ability in how accurately they represent verbal material in their phonological working memory; however, they do not differ in the accuracy of their articulation.

Gathercole and Baddeley (1990) provide further indirect evidence of the role of phonological ability in learning new words. They controlled for nonverbal intelligence and showed that children with high phonological working memory, as measured by the pseudoword repetition task, learned unfamiliar, made-up toy names (e.g., *Sommel* and *Piemas*) more rapidly than did children with poor phonological working memory abilities. Furthermore, children with high phonological working memory retained the novel toy names for a longer period of time than did the children with poor phonological working memory.

Additional research that is more experimental in nature has provided evidence that disrupting the quality of the temporary phonological representations stored in phonological working memory leads to impaired long-term learning of the sound forms of new words (for review, see Baddeley et al., 1998; Gathercole & Baddeley, 1993b). For example, Papagno, Valentine, and Baddeley (1991) showed that requiring healthy Italian adults to repeat aloud an irrelevant word during a paired-associate learning task disrupted the learning of novel foreign-language (Russian) words, but not of familiar, native-Italian words. The repetition of an irrelevant sound out loud, which is an articulatory suppression condition, is believed to prevent the rehearsal of the novel sound forms that are temporarily stored in phonological working memory. Hence, the item decays when its short-term phonological representation cannot be refreshed through rehearsal. The absence of accurate and distinct short-term phonological representations of unfamiliar L2 words thus prevents long-term learning.

Once children construct more long-term phonological and semantic representations, vocabulary knowledge itself begins to mediate the learning of new words. Gathercole et al. (1992) demonstrated that, over age 5 years, phonological working memory no longer predicted new vocabulary acquisition. Rather, they found that, by that age, existing vocabulary knowledge itself began to mediate the learning of new vocabulary. Similar conclusions have also been made by Gathercole (1995), Gathercole, Hitch, Service, and Martin (1997), and Cheung (1996).

These results suggest that good phonological abilities precede and causally facilitate vocabulary development in one's native language. Once sufficient vocabulary knowledge has been developed, vocabulary size itself replaces phonological ability as the predictor of learning new words. (For further discussion on word learning, see McGregor, Chapter 14, this volume.)

Vocabulary knowledge will predict new-word learning as long as individuals possess sufficient long-term knowledge of their target language. However, when individuals have minimal knowledge of their target language (e.g., when beginning to learn an L2), we expect that phonological abilities will be more heavily taxed and, consequently, serve as a stronger predictor of language development.

In summary, we believe that good phonological ability predicts language competency (e.g., listening and reading comprehension, speech production) in a target language as a result of its direct effect on vocabulary development. Hence, there is ample evidence to suggest that vocabulary knowledge mediates the direct relationship between phonological ability and language competency.

Accurate Phonological Representations in Native-Language Reading Development

Individuals with good phonological awareness are more advantaged when developing early reading abilities, such as individual-word or pseudoword decoding (Durgunoğlu, Nagy, & Hancin-Bhatt, 1993; Durgunoğlu & Öney, 2002; Holopainen, Ahonen, Tolvanen, & Lyytinen, 2000; Perfetti et al., 1987). Decoding is the ability to convert a printed word or nonword accurately into sound. Individuals who are aware that spoken words are made up of smaller units of sound (phonemes) are more likely to understand that written words, too, are made up of smaller units (graphemes) that correspond to individual sounds. Hence, individuals who have an accurate phonological representation of words and can successfully manipulate (e.g., blend, segment) these representations are expected to have an easier time cracking the alphabetic code and reading individual words in an accurate manner.

For example, Perfetti et al. (1987) showed that the ability to blend individual sound units to form words or pseudowords plays a unidirectional, facilitating role in children's early reading development. Holopainen et al. (2000) also showed that a model emphasizing phonological awareness as a prerequisite for learning to read individual words fit their observed data better than did an alternative model that specified individual word-reading ability as a predictor of phonological awareness development.

Moreover, multiple regression analyses of longitudinal data have also shown a direct, predictive relationship between phonological awareness and reading comprehension ability in participants' native language. For example, Demont and Gombert (1996) showed that phonological awareness skills, such as syllable counting and final phoneme deletion, measured at the beginning of grade 1, explained 23% and 18%, respectively, of the variance in end-of-grade-2 reading comprehension, both before and after entering nonverbal intelligence and vocabulary knowledge into the regression equation. Furthermore, multiple regression analyses of longitudinal data (Juel, Griffith, & Gough, 1986) also revealed that, even when entered after IQ, vocabulary, and listening comprehension, phonological awareness still explained approximately 24% ($p < .01$) of the unique variance in grade-1 reading comprehension and 17% ($p < .01$) of the unique variance in grade-2 reading comprehension. Others (e.g., Gottardo, Stanovich, & Siegel, 1996; Torgesen, Wagner, Rashotte, Burgess, & Hecht, 1997) also found that phonological awareness still predicted native-language reading comprehension, albeit less strongly, when it was entered into the regression equation after other relevant variables. Finally, a longitudinal study by Gathercole and Baddeley

(1993a) showed that the ability to form ac- curate phonological representations of nov- el sound forms plays an important causal role in both vocabulary and reading devel- opment. Specifically, they showed that non- word repetition accuracy in children at age 4 years explained 10% of the variance in vocabulary knowledge and 9% of the vari- ance in reading comprehension 4 years later, when the children were 8 years old. Al- though the evidence is compelling, more caution in the interpretation of the results may be required because of the correlational nature of these findings (see also Scott, Chapter 16, and Donahue, Chapter 17, this volume, for other linguistic factors con- tributing to reading comprehension).

Accurate Phonological Representations in Second-Language Vocabulary Development

As indicated in the preceding section, the ability to repeat aloud unfamiliar sound forms (e.g., pronounceable nonwords) accu- rately has been consistently found to predict native language learning. Therefore, it is feasible that this ability can also play a pre- dictive role in L2 learning. In fact, several researchers have implicated good phonolog- ical or phonological–orthographic abilities in L2 learning success. For example, Service (1992) found that the ability of 9-year-old Finnish children to repeat aloud pronounce- able nonwords accurately in English (L2) predicted their English course grade, as well as their English reading and writing abili- ties. Service reasoned that many of the abili- ties that enable a student to perform well in an English (L2) course, such as listening and reading comprehension, are founded on good knowledge of English vocabulary. She concluded that the ability to represent accu- rately the sounds of the L2 must facilitate L2 vocabulary development, which is im- portant for higher level L2 cognitive abili- ties (e.g., L2 reading and listening compre- hension). In their later work, Service and Kohonen (1995) conducted fixed-order multiple regression analyses to show that English (L2) nonword repetition ability no longer predicted English proficiency when they controlled for English vocabulary

knowledge. These results again suggested that L2 vocabulary is necessary for higher level L2 cognitive abilities, and that once students have developed sufficient L2 vo- cabulary knowledge, phonological ability in the L2 loses its predictive ability.

Cheung (1996) showed that phonological ability is a good predictor of the speed of L2 (English) vocabulary learning in native-Chi- nese-speaking seventh graders. In addition, he also found that this predictive relation- ship existed only for students whose vocab- ulary knowledge in their L2 was below the group median. Hence, there is consistent ev- idence that long-term semantic and phono- logical information, as represented by vo- cabulary knowledge, interacts with the representations in short-term phonological memory to mediate language development.

More recent work by Sparks and col- leagues (Sparks & Ganschow, 1991, 1993; Sparks, Ganschow, & Javorsky, 1992; Sparks, Ganschow, & Pohlman, 1989) and Meschyan and Hernandez (2002) lends support to the relationship between accu- rate phonological representations and L2 learning. Sparks and colleagues found that high-school students with phonological de- ficiencies experienced difficulty during the early stages L2 learning. Meschyan and Hernandez (2002), working with English- speaking college students, also found that a measure of phonological–orthographic abil- ity (pseudoword decoding) predicted stu- dents' course grades in their L2 (Spanish) for the first quarter of L2 instruction, but not for the second or third quarter. They concluded that phonological–orthographic ability exerts its effect during the early stages of L2 learning, when minimal long- term knowledge of the L2 exists to mediate L2 learning.

When knowledge of L2 phonology is lim- ited, the ability to represent the speech sounds of the target language accurately is a preexisting ability that can facilitate and ex- pedite L2 acquisition. Good phonological ability is a facilitator of higher level L2 abil- ities, such as vocabulary knowledge and reading comprehension. Individuals with below-average phonological abilities are not prevented from learning an L2; however, their journey to L2 learning may be longer and more arduous, requiring more exposures to the novel language before long-term learning takes place (Cheung, 1996). As the process becomes more difficult, the danger of losing the motivation to learn the L2 increases. Hence, individuals with poor phonological abilities can become less invested in learning the L2 (Ganschow, Sparks, & Javorsky, 1998).

Accurate Phonological Representations in Second-Language Reading Development

In a recent study, Meschyan (2002) also investigated the nature of the direct relationship between phonological ability and reading comprehension, a relationship that has been consistently demonstrated in the native-language literature. However, Meschyan investigated this relationship in the L2 domain, with Spanish-speaking children in grades 4 and 5, who were learning English as an L2. Meschyan pitted two models against each other.

Model A hypothesized that the direct relationship between English (L2) phonological awareness and English (L2) reading comprehension was mediated by English decoding accuracy and English vocabulary knowledge. Good L2 phonological awareness was expected to predict good L2 decoding ability. Furthermore, good L2 decoding was hypothesized to predict good L2 reading comprehension directly and indirectly, by facilitating L2 vocabulary knowledge development (Meschyan & Hernandez, 2002). L2 vocabulary knowledge itself was, in turn, expected to predict L2 reading comprehension directly.

In contrast, Model B hypothesized that English (L2) vocabulary knowledge is the preceding ability that predicts L2 reading comprehension through its direct positive effects on L2 phonological awareness and L2 decoding accuracy. Hence, in Model B, L2 vocabulary knowledge served as the primary predictor of L2 reading comprehension, whereas L2 phonological awareness and L2 decoding were treated as the mediator variables.

The findings showed that Model A fit the observed data slightly better and more parsimoniously than the alternative Model B.

This suggests that possessing accurate phonological representations of L2 words, and the ability to manipulate these representations, is an ability that precedes and promotes higher level reading comprehension ability indirectly, through its direct and positive effects on L2 decoding accuracy. Accuracy in L2 decoding can then directly improve L2 reading comprehension. In addition, L2 decoding can also improve L2 reading comprehension indirectly by facilitating good L2 vocabulary knowledge. However, in light of the correlational nature of these results, some caution in their interpretation is warranted.

In summary, these studies suggest that the ability to form accurate phonological representations of unfamiliar L2 words may play a facilitating role in L2 vocabulary development and reading ability. An implication is that L2 learners who have below-average or even slight deficiencies in their L2 phonological or phonological–orthographic abilities can benefit from explicit instruction in the accurate representations of spoken or written L2 words.

Summary

In this section, we have presented evidence suggesting that the ability to form accurate phonological representations of unfamiliar words precedes and plays an important predictive role in native-language vocabulary and reading comprehension development. We have also presented evidence that suggests this ability also predicts vocabulary and reading comprehension abilities in an L2.

SECOND-LANGUAGE LEARNING AND NATIVE-LANGUAGE ABILITY: WHAT IS THE RELATIONSHIP?

Does L2 learning relate to native-language abilities, or does it develop relatively independently? In this section, we present selected findings on the relationship between L2 learning and native-language abilities. We conclude with a suggestion regarding what the presented evidence implies about the linguistic processes that subserve native- and

L2 phonological and phonological–orthographic abilities.

According to the linguistic coding differences hypothesis (LCDH; for review, see Sparks, 1995), L2 acquisition is founded on native-language abilities in the areas of phonological, syntactic, and semantic processing. However, of these three language codes, the one that is most consistently implicated in L2 learning problems is phonological or phonological–orthographic ability. Just as phonological processing deficiencies have been implicated in problems of reading development (Stanovich, 1988), poor phonological abilities have also been implicated in L2 learning. Our recent work with English-speaking college students (Meschyan & Hernandez, 2002) has provided strong and direct support for the LCDH. If poor native-language phonological–orthographic ability predicts poor L2 phonological–orthographic ability, then this would suggest that this ability is based on linguistic processes that are not specific to any particular language. Therefore, native language decoding ability should be a good indicator of L2 decoding ability. Furthermore, if the ability to convert printed words accurately into sound facilitates language development, as the LCDH suggests, then we would also expect that good phonological–orthographic ability in the native language would transfer to the L2 and facilitate L2 learning. In fact, this is what we found.

Meschyan and Hernandez (2002) showed that college students' native language (English) pseudoword decoding predicted their L2 (Spanish) learning by its direct effect on Spanish word-decoding ability. Individuals who were better at decoding pseudowords in English were also better at decoding words in their L2, Spanish. This good phonological–orthographic ability in participants' L2 in turn predicted three L2 learning measures: (1) Spanish vocabulary, (2) a test of Spanish competency, and (3) the course grade in Spanish 1. The latter two outcome variables included measures of vocabulary knowledge, as well as participants' knowledge of Spanish grammar (conjugations of verbs), and Spanish listening and reading comprehension abilities.

These findings suggest two things. First,

there appears to exist a common pool of linguistic processes that subserve both native-language (English) and L2 (Spanish) decoding abilities. Second, these results also implicate native-language and L2 phonological–orthographic abilities of college-age students as important predictors of later, higher order language abilities, such as vocabulary, syntax, and reading comprehension. These findings are consistent with the LCDH predictions that higher order language abilities are founded on lower order phonological–orthographic ability.

Studies with elementary-age children (e.g., Durgunoğlu et al., 1993; Gottardo, 2002; Quiroga, Lemos-Britton, Mostafapour, Abbott, & Berninger, 2002) have provided further corroboration of the LCDH (Sparks, 1995). The results showed a cross-language transfer of phonological ability (Gottardo, 2002; Quiroga et al., 2002) and word reading (Durgunoğlu et al., 1993; Quiroga et al., 2002). Children who were able to read words accurately in their native language (Spanish) were also better at reading words accurately in their L2 (English). Moreover, both Durgunoğlu et al. (1993) and Quiroga et al. (2002) showed that children's native language (Spanish) phonological awareness predicted their individual word-reading ability in English.

As further support for the LCDH, Comeau, Cormier, Grandmaison, and Lacroix (1999) found high correlations between children's native-language (English) and L2 (French) phonological awareness abilities ($r = .89$, $p < .001$). Furthermore, they also showed that native-language and L2 decoding abilities in these children were also highly correlated ($r = .87$, $p < .001$). Hence, the evidence we have reviewed thus far appears to suggest that both native-language and L2 phonological and phonological–orthographic (decoding) abilities are based on linguistic processes that are not specific to any given language.

CONCLUSIONS AND FUTURE RESEARCH DIRECTIONS

Our goal in this chapter has been to present behavioral evidence that the ability to form accurate phonological representations of novel words (or phonological ability) plays an important predictive role in L2 learning. The behavioral data we reviewed first showed that individual differences in this ability predicted native-language vocabulary and reading comprehension. We then presented evidence suggesting that phonological ability is also implicated in L2 vocabulary and reading comprehension abilities. Finally, we considered the relationship between native-language and L2 lower level phonological and phonological–orthographic abilities, and concluded that the linguistic processes that subserve these abilities in a native language are also recruited in an L2. However, whether the processes that subserve phonological and phonological–orthographic abilities are really linguistic in nature deserves consideration in future work.

In summary, there appears to be sufficient evidence to suggest that the ability to perceive and represent novel word forms accurately precedes and partly predicts higher-level language abilities, such as vocabulary and reading comprehension. Hence, individuals who demonstrate more ability in this area, either innately or through educational experiences, are likely to learn an L2 more easily and quickly than those who have less ability.

Although in this chapter we have focused exclusively on behavioral studies, we believe that neural imaging techniques (e.g., functional magnetic resonance imaging [fMRI]; diffusion tensor imaging [DTI]) can further illuminate the nature of individual differences in L2 learning. The behavioral evidence we have reviewed in this chapter and relevant fMRI experiments (e.g., Hasegawa, Carpenter, & Just, 2002; Kim, Relkin, Lee, & Hirsch, 1997) present corroborating evidence that first- and second-language processing rely on some of the same neural structures. We expect that natural variation in the microstructure of these regions will result in a strong correlation in first- and second-language ability. A corollary of this assumption is that this underlying ability is responsible for processing across many linguistic levels and may even predict the acquisition of syntax.

Newer research on the neural bases of reading and literacy promises to provide important insights into the neural bases of L2 learning. We predict, for example, that white matter density in temporoparietal areas will be shown to correlate with L2 learning, because the underlying phonological abilities necessary for processing an L2 rely on some of the same neural structures used in reading.

Currently, studies in these areas are lacking and need to delineate further the neural bases of L2 learning. We hope the ideas proposed in this chapter will encourage such research. The answers provided by these studies should help to characterize further the nature of L2 acquisition. By integrating studies at the behavioral and neural levels, we can begin to arrive at a more accurate and comprehensive theory of L2 learning and literacy development.

REFERENCES

Baddeley, A. D. (1986). *Working memory*. Oxford, UK: Oxford University Press.

Baddeley, A. D., Gathercole, S., & Papagno, C. (1998). The phonological loop as a language learning device. *Psychological Review, 105*, 158–173.

Brady, S. A. (1997). Ability to encode phonological representations: An underlying difficulty of poor readers. In B. Blachman (Ed.), *Foundations of reading acquisition and dyslexia* (pp. 21–47). Mahwah, NJ: Erlbaum.

Bus, A. G., & van IJzendoorn, M. H. (1999). Phonological awareness and early reading: A meta-analysis of experimental training studies. *Journal of Educational Psychology, 91*, 403–414.

Cheung, H. (1996). Nonword span as a unique predictor of second-language vocabulary language. *Developmental Psychology, 32*, 867–873.

Comeau, L., Cormier, P., Grandmaison, E., & Lacroix, D. (1999). A longitudinal study of phonological processing skills in children learning to read in a second language. *Journal of Educational Psychology, 91*, 29–43.

Demont, E., & Gombert, J. E. (1996). Phonological awareness as a predictor of recoding skills and syntactic awareness as a predictor of comprehension skills. *British Journal of Educational Psychology, 66*, 315–332.

Durgunoğlu, A. Y., Nagy, W. E., & Hancin-Bhatt, B. J. (1993). Cross-language transfer of phonological awareness. *Journal of Educational Psychology, 85*, 453–465.

Durgunoğlu, A. Y., & Öney, B. (2002). Phonological awareness in literacy acquisition: It's not only for children. *Scientific Studies of Reading, 6*, 245–266.

Ganschow, L., Sparks, R., & Javorsky, J. (1998). Foreign language learning difficulties: An historical perspective. *Journal of Learning Disabilities, 31,* 248–258.

Gardner, R. C. (1985). *Social psychology and second language learning: The role of attitudes and motivation.* London: Edward Arnold.

Gathercole, S. E. (1995). Is nonword repetition a test of phonological memory or long-term knowledge?: It all depends on the nonwords. *Memory and Cognition, 23,* 83–94.

Gathercole, S. E., & Baddeley, A. D. (1990). The role of phonological memory in vocabulary acquisition: A study of young children learning arbitrary names of toys. *British Journal of Psychology, 81,* 439–454.

Gathercole, S. E., & Baddeley, A. D. (1993a). Phonological working memory: A critical building block for reading development and vocabulary acquisition? *European Journal of Psychology of Education, 8,* 259–272.

Gathercole, S. E., & Baddeley, A. D. (1993b). *Working memory and language.* Hove, UK: Erlbaum.

Gathercole, S. E., Hitch, G. J., Service, E., & Martin, A. J. (1997). Phonological short-term memory and new word learning in children. *Developmental Psychology, 33,* 966–979.

Gathercole, S. E., Service, E., Hitch, G. J., Adams, A., & Martin, A. J. (1999). Phonological short-term memory and vocabulary development: Further evidence on the nature of the relationship. *Applied Cognitive Psychology, 13,* 65–77.

Gathercole, S. E., Willis, C. S., Emslie, H., & Baddeley, A. D. (1992). Phonological memory and vocabulary development during the early school years: A longitudinal study. *Developmental Psychology, 28,* 887–898.

Gottardo, A. (2002). The relationship between language and reading skills in bilingual Spanish–English speakers. *Topics in Language Disorders, 22,* 46–70.

Gottardo, A., Stanovich, K. E., & Siegel, L. S. (1996). The relationships between phonological sensitivity, syntactic processing, and verbal working memory in the reading performance of third-grade children. *Journal of Experimental Child Psychology, 63,* 563–582.

Hasegawa, M., Carpenter, P. A., & Just, M. A. (2002). An fMRI study of bilingual sentence comprehension and workload. *NeuroImage, 15,* 647–660.

Holopainen, L., Ahonen, T., Tolvanen, A., & Lyytinen, H. (2000). Two alternative ways to model the relation between reading accuracy and phonological awareness at preschool age. *Scientific Studies of Reading, 4,* 77–100.

Juel, C., Griffith, P. L., & Gough, P. B. (1986). Acquisition of literacy: A longitudinal study of children in first and second grade. *Journal of Educational Psychology, 78,* 243–255.

Kim, K. H., Relkin, N. R., Lee, K. M., & Hirsch, J. (1997). Distinct cortical areas associated with native and second languages. *Nature, 388,* 171–174.

Meschyan, G. (2002). *Role of phonological awareness and decoding skill in second language learning.* Manuscript in preparation.

Meschyan, G., & Hernandez, A. (2002). Is native language decoding skill related to second language learning? *Journal of Educational Psychology, 94,* 14–22.

Papagno, C., Valentine, T., & Baddeley, A. D. (1991). Phonological short-term memory and foreign-language vocabulary learning. *Journal of Memory and Language, 30,* 331–347.

Perfetti, C. A., Beck, I., Bell, L. C., & Hughes, C. (1987). Phonemic knowledge and learning to read are reciprocal: A longitudinal study of first grade children. *Merrill–Palmer Quarterly, 33,* 283–319.

Quiroga, T., Lemos-Britton, Z., Mostafapour, E., Abbott, R. D., & Berninger, V. W. (2002). Phonological awareness and beginning reading in Spanish-speaking ESL first graders: Research into practice. *Journal of School Psychology, 40,* 85–111.

Service, E. (1992). Phonology, working memory, and foreign-language learning. *Quarterly Journal of Experimental Psychology, 45A,* 21–50.

Service, E., & Kohonen, V. (1995). Is the relation between phonological memory and foreign language learning accounted for by vocabulary acquisition? *Applied Psycholinguistics, 16,* 155–172.

Sparks, R. (1995). Examining the linguistic coding differences hypothesis to explain individual differences in foreign language learning. *Annals of Dyslexia, 45,* 187–214.

Sparks, R., & Ganschow, L. (1991). Foreign language learning difficulties: Affective or native language aptitude differences? *Modern Language Journal, 75,* 3–16.

Sparks, R., & Ganschow, L. (1993). Searching for the cognitive locus of foreign language learning difficulties: Linking first and second language learning. *Modern Language Journal, 77,* 289–302.

Sparks, R., Ganschow, L., & Javorsky, J. (1992). Diagnosing and accommodating the foreign language learning difficulties of college students with learning disabilities. *Learning Disabilities Research and Practice, 7,* 150–160.

Sparks, R., Ganschow, L., & Pohlman, J. (1989). Linguistic coding deficits in foreign language learners. *Annals of Dyslexia, 39,* 179–195.

Stanovich, K. (1988). The right and wrong places to look for the cognitive locus of reading disability. *Annals of Dyslexia, 38,* 154–177.

Torgesen, J. K., Wagner, R. K., Rashotte, C. A., Burgess, S., & Hecht, S. (1997). Contributions of phonological awareness and rapid automatic naming ability to the growth of word-reading skills in second- to fifth-grade children. *Scientific Studies of Reading, 1,* 161–185.

Wagner, R. K., & Torgesen, J. K. (1987). The nature of phonological processing and its causal role in the acquisition of reading skills. *Psychological Bulletin, 101,* 192–212.

5

Methodological Issues in Research on Language and Early Literacy from the Perspective of Early Identification and Instruction

Deborah L. Speece
David H. Cooper

In this chapter, we review some of the primary methodological approaches to the study of the development of atypical language and literacy skills. To limit the scope of the review, we focus specifically on methods associated with early identification of later literacy problems. The developmental period of greatest interest to us is from preschool/kindergarten through early elementary school grades. It is during this time frame that questions linking oral language skills, emergent literacy skills, and conventional literacy skills are most often asked (Whitehurst & Lonigan, 1998). Because the goal of early identification has yet to be met (Jenkins & O'Connor, 2002; Scarborough, 1998), we review the prevailing methods with an eye toward identifying strengths and weaknesses of each approach.

Early identification is an appropriate point of reference for methodological considerations because of this volume's dual focus on language and literacy. Research in early identification is the necessary precursor to instructional efforts tied to a reduction in reading problems in the elementary school years. However, progress in realizing procedures that will accurately identify children is hampered, in part, by the methods used to address the problem. For example, there is a widely held presumption that oral language skills fuel later literacy accomplishments. With the exception of phonological awareness for which the evidence is unambiguous, there are studies that both support and refute this assumption as it pertains to other oral language skills. Methodological issues that cloud the relationship include, but are not limited to, univariate versus multivariate approaches, cross-sectional versus longitudinal designs, and statistical versus educational significance.

We review four designs that figure in many analyses of early identification: hit rate analysis, correlation/multiple regression analyses, subtype analysis, and treatment validity (see Table 5.1). Each design is described and illustrated with several research examples to provide a sense of strengths and weaknesses, and how the method addresses two fundamental questions: (1) How does the method address issues of classification and treatment? and (2) What counts as validation?

TABLE 5.1. Overview of Early Identification Designs

Design	Goals	Features	Strengths and limitations
Hit rate	Early identification for primary prevention	Univariate	Straightforward interpretation of indices
		Longitudinal	Requires large samples for low-incidence conditions
			Failure to account for history and protective factors
Correlation/multiple regression	Explanation of individual differences	Univariate and multivariate	Addresses shared variance
			Requires comprehensive theoretical model
			Potential for causal modeling (SEM)
Subtype analysis	Classification of participants into homogeneous groups	Multivariate	Emphasis on child's profiles of variables considered simultaneously
			Complex analysis and interpretation
			Requires comprehensive theoretical model
Treatment validity	Early identification	Univariate	Role of instruction emphasized
		Multiple assessments of responsiveness to instruction	Requires frequent progress monitoring
			Potential to identify effective interventions earlier
		Longitudinal	Labor-intensive

Usually, reviews of methodological issues would address experimental validity according to the tenets of internal and external validity. From the perspective of early identification, Messick's (1980, 1989, 1995) view of assessment validity is more pertinent. Messick (1995) proposed that validity should be judged on both scientific evidence and the consequences of test use. The evidential basis includes the traditional emphasis on content, criterion-related, and construct validity, as well as examination of relevance to an applied setting and utility. The consequential basis includes analysis of both social consequences and values implied when using the assessment in an applied setting. For example, consider the role of phonological awareness in the early identification of reading disabilities. The traditional validity evidence for this variable is positive given moderate to strong correlations with later reading (e.g., Wagner, Torgesen, Laughon, Simmons, & Rashotte, 1993). However, the utility of phonological awareness has been called into question, because young children who do not develop reading problems are too often identified as being at risk (e.g., Scarborough, 1998). Examination of the values and social consequences would suggest that too many children may be inaccurately labeled and receive unneeded but potentially expensive interventions, a classic problem of false positives. Thus, phonological awareness assessment would not appear to be valid as a univariate approach to early identification based on Messick's (1989; 1995) framework. In our discussion of each method of early identification, the status of the approach with respect to the evidential and consequential basis of validity is addressed.

HIT RATE ANALYSIS

Efforts to identify adverse conditions of development in as yet unaffected individuals gave rise to screening procedures in public health and were later adopted by the disciplines of developmental psychology and early childhood education. With primary prevention as the goal, screening techniques seek to classify children as "at risk" on the basis of easily detectable attributes that could be linked to later occurrence of deficits. Such linkages may be demonstrated statistically and/or proposed theoretically. In the classic design, children in relatively large numbers would be assessed by the most efficient (i.e., briefest) instrument, sorted into "at-risk" and "not-at-risk" groups, and retested later with proven diagnostic instruments. As a consequence of these diagnostic assessments, children are resorted into those with and without the adverse condition. Validity of the screening strategy is evaluated in terms of its accuracy of predicting group membership as determined by the diagnostic or "criterion" assessment. Concordance between prediction and criterion counts as a "hit" and can be quantified in a number of straightforward indices, including overall hit rate (the percentage of predictions supported by criterion testing), sensitivity (the percentage of adversely affected children who were correctly detected at screening), and specificity (the percentage of children unaffected by the condition who were correctly undetected by the screening). Errors of overprediction are indicated by the false-positive rate (percentage of those predicted to be affected who were ultimately not affected). Errors of underprediction are indicated by the false-negative rate (percentage of those predicted to be unaffected who, in fact, were affected adversely).

In recent years, the hit rate or "classificatory" approach (Scarborough, 1998) has grown in popularity as a method for evaluating the validity of procedures designed to detect reading/language disabilities. Investigators seek ever-increasing sensitivity, specificity, and overall hit rates, while attempting to shrink the inevitable errors in classification referred to as "false positives" (persons whom the screening test incorrectly identified as affected) and "false negatives" (adversely affected persons whom the screening procedure missed). Readers should be aware that other terminology is used. For example, Scarborough (1998) elects to report not the false-positive and -negative rates but rather their inverses: the positive and negative predictive powers. Readers familiar with the various indices will immediately do the math (subtracting the respective predictive powers from 1.0 to get the corresponding false-positive and -negative rates).

Two recent reviews of early identification studies (Jenkins & O'Connor, 2002; Scarborough, 1998) summarize the results in terms of correlational methods, as well as the hit rates and error rates derived from categorical methods. When children were classified as at risk for later reading disabilities on the basis of oral language measures, as well as additional measures such as task orientation behaviors and motor skills, the range of prediction errors reported by Jenkins and O'Connor was wide and, for the most part, substantial. Typical false-negative rates included 21% (Coleman & Dover, 1993), 35% (Torgesen, Burgess, Wagner, & Rashotte, 1996), 50% (Mantzicopoulos & Morrison, 1994), and an astounding 69% (Felton, 1992). False-positive rates varied as well, ranging from 47% (O'Connor & Jenkins, 1999) up to 67% (Uhry, 1993). Similar ranges of false-positive and false-negative rates are reported in Scarborough's (1998) review.

There seems to be some divergence of opinion as to the appropriate use of the hit rate strategy, including (1) the formula for calculation of the false-positive and false-negative rates, (2) interpretation of the importance of the overall hit rate, and (3) determination of exactly which indices are most important to report. For example, Mantzicopoulos and Morrison (1994) reported results of predicting reading skills in second grade ($N = 270$) from a battery of screening measures taken in kindergarten: "Although the false positive rate was relatively low (12.6%), the false negative rate was 50%" (p. 247). However, it can be seen from the data reported in their Table 1 (p. 247) that the actual false-positive rate (using the method of Fleiss, 1981) is 65% (30 average readers in second grade who had been erroneously predicted to be poor readers, divided by 46 children so predicted). Using the total N of their sample (270) as the denominator in their calculation produced the incorrect values.

A number of authors base assertions about the accuracy of predictions on the overall hit rate value. As we have argued elsewhere (Speece & Cooper, 1991), overall hit rates are deceptively high when the prevalence of the adverse outcome condition is low, as it almost always is in studies of developmental disabilities. The explanation for this can be reduced to the simple fact that correct predictions of the overwhelmingly large number of normal outcomes (true negatives) account for the bulk of the hits. For example, if we were to screen for a condition that occurs in 5% of subjects, *random* prediction would result in a 90% overall hit rate. The proof of this assertion follows (see Figure 5.1). Assume that a condition occurs in 5% of the general population (prevalence p = 5%). Draw a random sample of the population such that N = 10,000. Based on the knowledge that p = 5%, randomly assign 5% (N = 500) to the

positive screening result group and 95% (N = 9500) to the negative screening result group (see marginal values). The question now becomes, how accurate are these screening results? In other words, how many of these 500 screened positives are "hits"? Based on p = 5%, by chance alone, 5% (N = 25) of the 500 screened positives will also be positive for the condition when tested on the diagnostic criterion assessment (cell a of Figure 5.1). By the same logic, 95% (N = 475) will test negative on the diagnostic assessment (cell b).

Turning to the 9,500 subjects screened negative for the condition, and again, because p = 5%, by chance alone, 5% (N = 475) will have the condition and therefore test positive on the diagnostic assessment (cell c in Figure 5.1). Finally, 95% (N = 9025) of the screened negatives will also test negative for the condition on the diagnostic assessment (cell d).

According to convention, the overall hit rate for this random assignment procedure is $(a + d)/N$, which in this example equals 90.5%. This is also equivalent to $p^2 + q^2$, where q = $1 - p$. The explanation for large chance hit rates in low-prevalence conditions is due to a relatively large value of q.

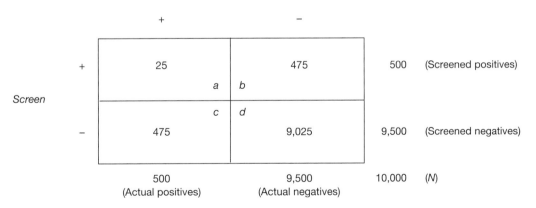

Diagnostic Criterion

		+	−		
Screen	+	25 _(a)_	475 _(b)_	500	(Screened positives)
	−	475 _(c)_	9,025 _(d)_	9,500	(Screened negatives)
		500 (Actual positives)	9,500 (Actual negatives)	10,000	(*N*)

"Chance" hit rate = 90.5% $(a + d)/N$

Assume:
        Prevalence p = 5%
Inverse of prevalence q = 95%

FIGURE 5.1. Chance hit rate example.

An overwhelmingly large number of true negatives will pass the screen, and therefore rack up a large number of hits.

Figure 5.2 contains actual data from Mantzicopolous and Morrison (1994). These authors state, "The hit rate resulting from this procedure reflects a relatively high (83%) proportion of children who were correctly classified" (p. 247). But chance alone, that is, a random assignment of children at screening to either at-risk or not-at-risk groups, would have resulted in a 79% overall hit rate. Thus, the data on which the authors base their conclusion do not represent an improvement over chance.

Authors tend to focus on the consequences of correct prediction in terms of their implications for validation of language–literacy theory, as well as targeted delivery of preventive intervention. However, it is the *errors* of prediction that require thoughtful attention. When viewed from the Messick perspective, errors (i.e., people classified incorrectly) serve to illustrate the values inherent in the assessment approach, as well as the social consequences of such assessments. In the present context of language-based predictions of deficiencies in the attainment of literacy, the consequences of both false-positive and false-negative prediction are significant (Scarborough, 1998). In the case of false positives, the practical consequences for individuals so affected are obvious: lowered expectations and unnecessary intervention. In the case of false negatives, the practical consequences are likewise obvious: delayed intervention and the accumulation of failure.

From the perspective of theory and efforts to demonstrate the mechanism(s) by which language develops from oral proficiency into skilled reading, the errors of prediction have less than obvious implications. High rates of false positives (and their companions, lowered specificity and overall hit rates) point in the direction of as yet unknown routes to literacy. How is it possible that a child fails an early oral language screening battery, yet goes on to acquire reading skills at a normal rate? In similar fashion, high rates of false negatives (and their companions, diminished sensitivity and overall hit rates) suggest as yet unidentified routes to disability. How is it possible to be proficient in oral language, yet fail to acquire basic literacy skills?

The answers to the questions raised by errors of prediction serve to highlight two in-

Diagnostic Criterion

		+	–		
Screen	+	16 *a*	30 *b*	45	(Screened positives)
	–	16 *c*	208 *d*	224	(Screened negatives)
		32 (Actual positives)	238 (Actual negatives)	270	(*N*)

Prevalence p = 12% $(a + c)/N$
Inverse of prevalence q = 88% $(1 - p)$
Hit rate = 83.0% $(a + d)/N$
"Chance" hit rate = 79.1% $(p^2 + q^2)$

FIGURE 5.2. Hit rate data from Mantzicopoulos and Morrison (1994).

herent and related consequences of using the hit rate method when it is applied to the validation of screening: (1) failure to account for the history that unfolds between screening and outcome, and (2) failure of the hit rate model to account for possible *protective* factors that may differentiate the noncases from the cases of reading disability. In the development of reading, the most obviously neglected history is that which involves instruction. In the studies cited earlier, as well as in others employing similar methods, researchers almost never accounted for variability in type and quality of instruction. Perhaps instructional data are just too difficult to document in large-scale longitudinal studies conducted in real classrooms. However, there are instances of efforts to account for instruction (e.g., Scanlon & Vellutino, 1996) that suggest further work along these lines may be warranted. O'Connor and Jenkins (1999) experimented with providing corrective feedback on letter knowledge and phonological tasks to kindergartners during the screening phase. These efforts were successful in reducing the rate of false-negative predictions to near zero, but at a cost of high-false-positive rates.

Summary

Hit rate designs have the advantage of being straightforward and involving ordinary mathematics in their interpretation. When low-incidence conditions are at issue, hit rate designs, not unlike other designs, require relatively large samples in order to net sufficient cases to provide stable indices. Thus, they prove useful in assessing the accuracy of early identification of a risk condition (evidential aspect of validity) but may, in their tendency to simplify relationships, fail to account for (1) history that may intervene between early screening and later diagnostic assessment, and (2) the effects of intervention (consequential validity). Finally, screening hit rate designs force investigators to confront the consequences of errors in prediction and to assign differential value to either errors of overprediction (false positives) or underprediction (false negatives).

CORRELATION/MULTIPLE REGRESSION

Correlational methods, including multiple regression, are useful from the perspective of explaining the individual differences observed among children as they develop early reading skills. In contrast to the hit rate approach described earlier, correlational methods avoid the classification of children according to various attributes, instead preserving for analysis the full range of knowledge and skills according to classic psychometric assessment. Variability in measured attributes, such as oral language, may then be tested for covariation with later observed abilities or deficits, with the resulting indices of association interpreted as "variance explained." The value of these approaches for classification of children lies in their potential to test theoretically important relationships among variables that may later be used to classify children into at-risk and not-at-risk groups for validation using hit rate methodology. In Messick's (1995) terms, we would view the contribution of correlational methods as evidential, not consequential; that is, the results may provide evidence of construct validity but not necessarily address the consequences for children that result from application of the method.

With respect to correlational results, the studies reviewed by Scarborough (1998) and Jenkins and O'Connor (2002) are widely divergent in their choice of variables, as well as the age ranges studied. There appears to be some consistency in findings that support the predictive power of phonological sensitivity and letter–name knowledge, whereas other oral language measures, such as oral vocabulary, verbal memory, and word retrieval, were less significant, yet potentially predictive depending on when reading outcomes were measured. A primer on correlational methods and multiple regression is not provided here; rather, we cite examples of language–literacy studies employing these methods and assess their contribution to the understanding of the theoretical linkages between oral language and reading, as well as their implications for the validity of early identification of language-based reading disabilities.

Share, Jorm, Maclean, and Matthews (1984) sought a battery of tests to administer in kindergarten that could successfully explain variation in first graders' reading achievement. They concluded that a battery of five tests consisting of letter copying, letter–name knowledge, sentence memory, phoneme segmentation, and gender was sufficient to explain 58% of the variance in a composite reading–spelling variable. From their results, it is evident that the phonological task was of primary importance, with other variables contributing small amounts to the overall explanation of reading variance. This robust finding has been reinforced repeatedly in the literature of the past two decades. The authors interpreted their findings as supportive of their specific two-factor theory of reading achievement.

Uhry (1993) adopted a combined approach using regression techniques, as well as hit-rate analysis. She distinguished between the two approaches' value, pointing out that the correlational approach contributed to understanding the stability of children's rank order on earlier and later assessments, whereas the classification approach was expected to be more useful in the identification of individual children at risk of failure. In her results, she reports that phonological and print decoding skills at the subword level in kindergarten were able to predict 39% of the variance in first-grade reading. This finding falls squarely in line with the predominant conclusions in the literature, and Uhry's discussion focuses on the theoretical importance of these results. Interestingly, her hit rate analysis of the same data, using cutoff scores to classify children as at-risk, resulted in a false-positive rate of 45%. This high false-positive rate demonstrates the limitations of adapting the correlational approach to early identification.

Spector (1992) employed a novel application of the correlational method, assessing the extent to which late-kindergarten word recognition scores could be predicted by a phonemic segmentation task assessed dynamically. In other words, would children's ability to *profit* from instruction in segmentation predict their reading ability more powerfully than a static measure of phonemic awareness, in addition to measures of vocabulary and invented spelling? The results supported the superiority of the dynamic assessment task when compared to static methods; a finding with practical applications for both early identification and early intervention. Spector was also able to show that the *gain* in children's performance from static to dynamic assessment was highly related to later reading performance: Gain scores explained an additional 21% of the reading variance after accounting for static assessment of phonemic awareness and oral vocabulary. An additional advantage of the dynamic assessment/regression approach was identified by Jenkins and O'Connor (2002), who pointed out that task difficulty, so often a limitation on early measurement of phonological skills, is controlled (and floor effects avoided) when children are given opportunities to demonstrate otherwise covert individual differences.

In an attempt to clarify further the changing and differential relationships between oral language and early reading development, Roth, Speece, and Cooper (2002) assembled a broad battery of oral language measures in three domains (metalinguistics, structural language, and narrative discourse) and followed 39 children from kindergarten through the end of second grade. Roth et al. devised a two-stage regression analysis strategy to identify parsimonious models that explained variance in early reading. First, variables were evaluated against other variables from the same language domain to identify the strongest predictors of reading from within each language domain. At the second stage of the analysis, the best predictors from the domain-specific analyses were pitted against one another to identify the set of variables from multiple domains that best predicted later reading. The main finding of the study was that semantic abilities (i.e., oral definitions and word retrieval) measured in kindergarten were the strongest unique predictors of second-grade reading *comprehension*. As expected, phonemic awareness skill in kindergarten was the strongest predictor of *single-word reading* at second-grade level. The finding that semantic skills, not phonemic awareness, predicted passage comprehension suggests that different oral language skills are important to different aspects of reading.

In addition to the correlation/regression approaches illustrated earlier, a variant, structural equation modeling (SEM), has been used to good effect by Whitehurst and Lonigan (1998) in the identification of causal relationships among early language skills and later reading. Although an extensive treatment of this design and analysis methodology is beyond the scope of this review, it is apparent that SEM has the potential to go beyond correlational models in explaining not only covariation in skills but also in allowing causal inferences to be made in support of specific and complex developmental theories of literacy. Whitehurst and Lonigan concluded that (1) phonological sensitivity, while independent of socioeconomic status, is a potent precursor of reading; (2) individual differences in children's language and literacy skills demonstrate impressive stability over the time span of the preschool through primary grades; and (3) causal relationships between language and literacy are not uniform across the primary grades, but change in theoretically important ways as the emphasis in reading evolves from decoding to comprehension.

Summary

Correlation/multiple regression designs are most useful when investigators are exploring the nature of individual differences in children's language and literacy skills measured at specific points in time. The concepts of shared and explained variance are familiar to most professionals in the field; thus, the evidential interpretation of results is generally straightforward. In order for the results to have validity beyond the evidential, investigators must specify elaborate models of complex and changing relationships among attributes, including the often-neglected effects of environment and instruction. Much can be inferred about investigators' *values* by the models they test

and the domains of variables they choose to include and exclude.

SUBTYPE ANALYSIS

Another multivariate approach, subtype analysis, identifies groups of children that exhibit similar profiles of strengths and weaknesses across the variables selected for study. Contrasted with multiple regression analyses, in which the goal is to explain variance in a sample, subtype analysis seeks to harness variance through the formation of classes, in which the members of each class are more similar to each other than to members of other classes. Subtyping is intuitively appealing, because the emphasis is on children and their profiles rather than variables; that is, subtypes represent the partitioning of a sample of actual children, which is more meaningful in many ways than knowing that several variables account for some specific proportion of variance in a criterion. Twenty years ago, the excitement about subtyping as a method was the potential to uncover subtype × treatment interactions (e.g., Lyon, 1985).

Subtypes may be based on clinical or empirical analyses. Clinical subtypes are obtained through visual analysis of the data, whereas empirical subtypes are obtained through statistical methods, such as cluster analysis. Clinical methods necessarily limit the number of variables that can be considered because of corresponding limitations to the clinician's cognitive capacity to consider simultaneously multiple variables (Morris, 1993). Empirical methods do not share this limitation but empirical solutions often produce many possible subtypes (e.g., 4–10), which restrict their usefulness for both practice and theory under the assumption that fewer subtypes are easier to interpret. In Messick's (1995) terms, as the number of subtypes increases, the relevance of the classification decreases.

Subtyping is not frequently used as an approach to early identification, but it may become more prevalent given recommendations to consider several variables simultaneously as potential markers of reading disability (Scarborough, 1998). The double-deficit model of reading disability, proposed by Wolf and Bowers (1999), is an example of clinical subtyping that may inform early identification efforts. They proposed that children who exhibit deficits on both phonological awareness and naming speed tasks will exhibit more severe problems learning to read than will children who exhibit just one of the deficits. There is descriptive evidence that supports (Wimmer, Mayringer, & Landerl, 2000) and refutes (Ackerman, Holloway, Youngdahl, & Dykman, 2001) predictions from this model.

Speece, Cooper, Roth, and De La Paz (1999) used empirical methods to subtype an unselected group of kindergarten children on a battery of oral language measures. They identified four subtypes, two representing strengths in either phonological awareness/high overall language skills or narrative skills, and two that represented low-average and low overall oral language skills. Some of the hypothesized differences between the subtypes were obtained both concurrently, in kindergarten, and predictively, when the children were in first grade. This validation evidence was obtained with an independent set of variables not used in the classification analysis (listening comprehension, reading, spelling). For example, in kindergarten, the high-narrative group had higher listening comprehension scores compared with the low overall language cluster. Also, the three subtypes with average or better profiles had higher early reading scores than the low overall cluster. In first grade, the most consistent evidence for validation was for the phonological awareness/high-average oral language subtype that received higher reading and spelling scores. Other examples of studies that used oral language variables for subtype analysis can be found in Feagans and Appelbaum (1986) and Morris et al. (1998).

Blashfield and Draguns (1976) noted that classification systems might promote either communication with practitioners or prediction, which is more central to scientific concerns. They further explained that these goals are in opposition, because communication requires simplicity and ease of implementation (e.g., double-deficit hypothesis, Wolf & Bowers, 1999), whereas prediction requires complexity and flexibility to examine theory (e.g., 10 subtypes identified by Morris et al., 1998). Ideally, these goals would not be mutually exclusive, and subtyping research would produce theoretically coherent and practically useful groupings of children to reflect Messick's (1980, 1989) unified view of validity. This is not the present state of affairs, due in part to the need for subtyping efforts to be derived from theory and to the almost exclusive view of validation as differences between subtypes (construct) rather than responsiveness to instruction (relevance and utility) (Skinner, 1981; Skinner & Blashfield, 1982; Speece, 2003).

Summary

The number of variables that can be reasonably considered limits clinical subtyping, and empirical subtyping is limited by the complexity associated with analysis and interpretation (see Speece, 2003, for a review of analysis strategies). More importantly, both approaches to classification need to be guided by a theoretical framework for variable selection and validation procedures. Subtype analysis can inform early identification efforts when the research is programmatic and tied to clinical concerns.

TREATMENT VALIDITY

Treatment validity is a newcomer to the literature on early identification. It was initially proposed as a method to identify children for special education services (Fuchs, 1995; Fuchs & Fuchs, 1998; Messick, 1984), but it also can serve as an early identification framework. Treatment validity operates on the principle that children who do not respond to well-crafted and implemented instruction (i.e., "treatments") may require more intensive efforts. The validity of the instruction is a function of the child's academic progress relative to the instruction received. If a child responds to an instructional modification in the general education classroom, then the decision to maintain the child in that environment, under those conditions, would be considered valid. If a child does not respond, then more intensive instructional effort (e.g., individual instruction with a special educator) may be required, with validity assessed in the same manner. In this way, treatment validity has something to offer to researchers interested in early identification and differs dramatically from "test now and later" paradigms represented by hit rate and correlational methods.

Two important differences between treatment validity paradigms and those that focus on assessment of individual differences are the role of instruction and the need for continuous measurement of progress. Instruction is central to the identification process, because it is the child's responsiveness to instruction that provides the basis for identification. Thus, some method of verifying that the instruction was delivered as intended should be in place. Frequent progress monitoring is necessary to gauge a child's response to instruction. The measurement problems associated with frequent measurement can be addressed by use of curriculum-based measurement (CBM) procedures (Fuchs & Fuchs, 1998). CBM provides a basis for generating multiple forms of basic skills assessments (reading, math, spelling, writing) that have strong psychometric characteristics (Deno, 1985; Shinn, 1989). In the treatment validity model proposed by Fuchs and Fuchs (1998), progress can be monitored weekly and interpreted after eight data points are collected.

Although conceptual models of the treatment validity paradigm have been proposed (e.g., Berninger & Abbott, 1994; Messick, 1984), there are few empirical analyses. "Layered" or "tiered" intervention strategies have been studied, in which instruction becomes increasingly intense for children who do not respond to the previous level of instruction (O'Connor, 2000). This approach is not typically conceptualized as early identification per se, but it could be viewed in that way. A primary difference between levels of instruction and treatment validity as a method of identification is the relative emphasis on frequent measurement.

Speece and Case (2001) incorporated features of the Fuchs and Fuchs (1998) model of treatment validity in a comparison of several definitions of reading disability among first- and second-grade children. One common feature was the assessment of responsiveness to instruction as defined by a child's dual discrepancy from classmates' performance on the basis of level of skills and slope of performance across time. In this case, the measure of interest was oral reading fluency. Children were considered dually discrepant readers if the number of words they could read in 1 minute (level) and the rate of progress (slope) were 1 standard deviation below the level and rate of classmates. Dual discrepancy calculations were based on a minimum of 10 data points collected across 5–6 months of a school year. Instruction was whatever procedures the general education teachers were using. Compared to children who met IQ reading achievement discrepancy and low-achievement definitions of reading disability, dually discrepant children were younger and more impaired on phonological processes. Furthermore, their teachers rated them lower on academic competence and social skills. Other relevant findings were that gender and ethnic ratios of the dually discrepant group reflected the population values, and that none of the reading or phonological measures administered in fall of the school year were sensitive to poor reader status in May. This study provided initial evidence that treatment validity approaches may identify a valid group of poor readers who require more intensive instruction than is available in general education classrooms. A follow-up study in which dually discrepant children did receive specially designed general education interventions showed that, across 3 years, children who consistently failed to respond to these interventions exhibited significantly lower phonological, reading, and behavioral skills than dually discrepant children who did respond. They also received more school-level attention, such as consideration for special education services, individual education plan (IEP) development, and additional reading instruction outside the general education classroom (Case, Speece, & Molloy, 2003).

Vellutino et al. (1996) classified a group of poor first-grade readers on the basis of their responsiveness to intensive, individual, daily tutoring that equaled 35–40 hours of instruction. The poor readers were those who received low ratings from their teachers regarding reading progress and scored below the 15th percentile on reading measures and 90 or above on an intelligence measure. Across six data points from kindergarten through second grade, slopes were inspected, and children were classified into one of four groups, ranging from very poor growth to very good growth. At the end of first grade, 67.1% of these poor readers scored in the average range (> 30th percentile). Of interest to early identification concerns, only three kindergarten measures distinguished the two most extreme responsiveness groups: letter identification, number identification, and counting by 1's. The poor sensitivity of some of these measures (Scarborough, 1998) highlights the potential for treatment-responsiveness validity paradigms. Although Vellutino et al. (1996) emphasized that initial intervention needs to be intensive, it is instructive to note that 59.5% of the poor readers who received small-group, school-based remediation instead of the researcher-delivered instruction improved to average-or-above reading performance by the end of first grade. This compares favorably with the 67.1% of the tutored group at average-or-above levels, and suggests that some schools may be able to reduce reading failure substantially with current resources.

Summary

The Speece and Case (2001) and Vellutino et al. (1996) studies differ on a number of dimensions, but both intertwine classification, treatment, and validation. Classification as being at risk or reading disabled is tied directly to responsiveness to treatment. From Messick's (1989, 1995) unified view of validity, treatment validity reflects construct validity (e.g., group differences on theoretically relevant variables), social consequential validity (e.g., proportionate representation of gender and ethnicity), and values (e.g., early identification) (Speece & Case, 2001). Although the approach may be viewed positively with respect to relevance (i.e., identification of children who require intensive instruction), its utility

(time required, costs) may be a negative factor. Frequent assessment and explicit small-group or individual instruction are time-intensive, expensive, difficult to organize, and require a major change in the way early identification is carried out in the schools (Simmons, Kuykendall, King, Cornichione, & Kameenui, 2000).

FINAL COMMENTS

Each method reviewed makes a contribution to the study of the early identification of later literacy problems, but none stands alone as the solution to the problem. A major stumbling block is the tension between the need for efficiency and the reality that classroom instruction plays a role in who develops academic problems. At this point, there are no efficient methods for characterizing instructional methods that can be used in conjunction with traditional child assessments to address this pressing educational need, although Scanlon and Vellutino (1996) made an important initial step in this direction. We are not convinced that it is possible to measure child characteristics only and develop a coherent system of early identification. Whitehurst and Lonigan (1998) stated the case well: "The developmental function for learning to read is cultural and exogenous, not biological and endogenous" (p. 866).

With this premise in mind, it seems most reasonable to view the methods as complementary and recommend a program of research that combines methods that take advantage of strengths and minimize weaknesses through the power of multiple methods. Several studies reviewed in this chapter combined multiple regression methods and hit rate analysis (e.g., Share et al., 1984; Uhry, 1993). Missing from these studies are both measurement of instruction and empirically validated classification. Subtyping studies may be one way to address the classification problem, whereas treatment validity studies may be one way to address the gap in measurement of instruction.

Another possibility not considered in this chapter is the use of qualitative methods to identify and refine contextual variables that may make a difference in a child's learning trajectory. Case et al. (2003) used a mixed methodology design to explore differences in instructional contextual factors between groups of at-risk children who differed in their responsiveness to instruction. Although the quantitative analysis did not yield statistically significant differences on contextual variables, the qualitative analyses yielded insights on differences in children's abilities to access learning. The most persistently nonresponsive children were not able to take advantage of their instructional contexts due to personal limitations, a nonresponsive classroom context, or both. The qualitative analysis provided a means to examine this phenomenon more closely than could be accomplished with quantitative methods.

It may also be necessary to broaden the measurement net to include variables that may not have direct theoretical relevance to literacy per se, but that are related to learning. For example, Torgesen et al. (1999) reported that teachers' ratings of classroom behavior had a unique effect on growth in word decoding skills from kindergarten to second grade. There is still a lot to be understood about the mechanisms that underlie this and other empirically demonstrated relationships, but these types of variables deserve further investigation in studies that illuminate the precise role of earlier appearing attributes in the ontogeny of reading–language learning disabilities.

REFERENCES

Ackerman, P. T., Holloway, C. A., Youngdahl, P. L., & Dykman, R. A. (2001). The double-deficit theory of reading disability does not fit at all. *Learning Disabilities Research and Practice, 16,* 144–152.

Berninger, V. W., & Abbott, R. D. (1994). Redefining learning disabilities: Moving beyond aptitude—achievement discrepancies to failure to respond to validated treatment protocols. In G. R. Lyon (Ed.), *Frames of reference for the assessment of learning disabilities* (pp. 163–183). Baltimore: Brookes.

Blashfield, R. K., & Draguns, J. G. (1976). Evaluative criterion for psychiatric classification. *Journal of Abnormal Psychology, 85,* 140–150.

Case, L. P., Speece, D. L., & Molloy, D. E. (2003). The validity of a response-to-instruction paradigm to identify reading disabilities: A longitudinal analysis of individual differences and contextual factors. *School Psychology Review, 32,* 557–582.

Coleman, J.M., & Dover, G. M. (1993). The RISK Screening Test: Using kindergarten teachers' ratings to predict future placement in resource classrooms. *Exceptional Children, 59,* 468–477.

Deno, S. L. (1985). Curriculum-based measurement: The emerging alternative. *Exceptional Children, 52,* 219–232.

Feagans, L., & Appelbaum, M. I. (1986). Validation of language subtypes of learning disabled children. *Journal of Educational Psychology, 78,* 358–364.

Felton, R. H. (1992). Early identification of children at risk for reading disabilities. *Topics in Early Childhood Special Education, 12,* 212–229.

Fleiss, J. L. (1981). *Statistical methods for rates and proportions.* New York: Wiley.

Fuchs, L. S. (1995, May). *Incorporating curriculum-based measurement into the eligibility decision-making process: A focus on treatment validity and student growth.* Paper presented at the Workshop on IQ Testing and Educational Decision Making, National Research Council, National Academy of Science, Washington, DC.

Fuchs, L. S., & Fuchs, D. (1998). Treatment validity: A unifying concept for reconceptualizing the identification of learning disabilities. *Learning Disabilities Research and Practice, 13,* 204–219.

Jenkins, J. R., & O'Connor, R. E. (2002). Early identification and intervention for young children with reading/learning disabilities. In R. Bradley, L. Danielson, & D. Hallahan (Eds.), *Identification of learning disabilities: Research to practice.* Mahwah, NJ: Erlbaum.

Lyon, G. R. (1985). Educational validation studies of learning disability subtypes. In B. P. Rourke (Ed.), *Neuropsychology of learning disabilities* (pp. 228–253). New York: Guilford Press.

Mantzicopoulos, P. Y., & Morrison, D. (1994). Early prediction of reading achievement: Exploring the relationship of cognitive and noncognitive measures to inaccurate classifications of at-risk status. *Remedial and Special Education, 15,* 244–251.

Messick, S. (1980). Test validity and the ethics of assessment. *American Psychologist, 35,* 1012–1027.

Messick, S. (1984). Assessment in context: Appraising student performance in relation to instructional quality. *Educational Researcher, 13*(3), 3–8.

Messick, S. (1989). Validity. In R. L. Linn (Ed.), *Educational measurement* (3rd ed., pp. 13–103). New York: Macmillan.

Messick, S. (1995). Validity of psychological assessment: Validation of inferences from persons' responses and performances as scientific inquiry into score meaning. *American Psychologist, 50,* 741–749.

Morris, R. D. (1993). Issues in empirical versus clinical subtyping. In G. R. Lyon, D. B. Gray, J. F. Kavanaugh, & N. A. Krasnegor (Eds.), *Better understanding learning disabilities: New views from research and their implications for education and public policy* (pp. 73–93). Baltimore: Brookes.

Morris, R. D., Stuebing, K. K., Fletcher, J. M., Shaywitz, S. E., Lyon, G. R., Shankweiler, D. P., et al. (1998). Subtypes of reading disability: Variability around a phonological core. *Journal of Educational Psychology, 90,* 347–373.

O'Connor, R. (2000). Increasing the intensity of interventions in kindergarten and first grade. *Learning Disabilities Research and Practice, 15,* 43–54.

O'Connor, R. E., & Jenkins, J. R. (1999). Prediction of reading disabilities in kindergarten and second grade. *Scientific Studies of Reading, 3,* 159–197.

Roth, F. P., Speece, D. L., & Cooper, D. H. (2002). A longitudinal analysis of the connection between oral language and early reading. *Journal of Educational Research, 95,* 259–272.

Scanlon, D. M., & Vellutino, F. R. (1996). Prerequisite skills, early instruction, and success in first-grade reading: Selected results from a longitudinal study. *Mental Retardation and Developmental Disabilities Research Reviews, 2,* 54–63.

Scarborough, H. S. (1998). Early identification of children at risk for reading disabilities: Phonological awareness and some other promising predictors. In B. K. Shapiro, P. J. Accardo, & A. J. Capute (Eds.), *Specific reading disability: A view of the spectrum* (pp. 75–107). Timonium, MD: York Press.

Share, D. L., Jorm, A. F., Maclean, R., & Matthews, R. (1984). Sources of individual differences in reading acquisition. *Journal of Educational Psychology, 76,* 1309–1324.

Shinn, M. R., (Ed.). (1989). *Curriculum-based measurement: Assessing special children.* New York: Guilford Press.

Simmons, D. C., Kuykendall, K., King, K., Cornichione, C., & Kameenui, E. J. (2000). Implementation of a schoolwide reading improvement model: "No one ever told us it would be this hard!" *Learning Disabilities Research and Practice, 15,* 92–100.

Skinner, H. A. (1981). Toward the integration of classification theory and methods. *Journal of Abnormal Psychology, 20,* 68–87.

Skinner, H. A., & Blashfield, R. K. (1982). Increasing the impact of cluster analysis research: The case of psychiatric classification. *Journal of Consulting and Clinical Psychology, 50,* 727–735.

Spector, J. E. (1992). Predicting progress in beginning reading: Dynamic assessment of phonemic awareness. *Journal of Educational Psychology, 84,* 353–363.

Speece, D. L. (2003). The methods of cluster analysis and the study of learning disabilities. In H. L. Swanson, K. R. Harris, & S. Graham (Eds.), *Handbook of learning disabilities.* New York: Guilford Press.

Speece, D. L., & Case, L. P. (2001). Classification in context: An alternative approach to identifying early reading disability. *Journal of Educational Psychology, 93,* 735–749.

Speece, D. L., & Cooper, D. H. (1991). Retreat, regroup, or advance: An agenda for empirical classification research in learning disabilities. In L. V. Feagans, E. J. Short, and L. J. Meltzer (Eds.), *Subtypes of learning disabilities* (pp. 33–52). Hillsdale, NJ: Erlbaum.

Speece, D. L., Cooper, D. H., Roth, F. P., & De La Paz, S. (1999). The relevance of oral language skills in early literacy: A multivariate analysis. *Applied Psycholinguistics, 20,* 167–190.

Torgesen, J. K., Burgess, S., Wagner, R. K., & Rashotte, C. (1996, April). *Predicting phonologically-based reading disabilities: What is gained by waiting a year?* Paper presented at the annual meeting of the Society for the Scientific Study of Reading, New York.

Torgesen, J. K., Wagner, R. K., Rashotte, C. A., Rose, E. R., Lindamood, P., Conway, T., et al. (1999). Preventing reading failure in young children with phonological processing disabilities: Group and individual responses to instruction. *Journal of Educational Psychology, 91,* 579–593.

Uhry, J. K. (1993). Predicting low reading from phonological awareness and classroom print. *Educational Assessment, 1,* 349–368.

Vellutino, F. R., Scanlon, D. M., Sipay, E. R., Small, S. G., Chen R., Pratt, A., et al. (1996). Cognitive profiles of difficult-to-remediate and readily remediated poor readers: Early intervention as a vehicle for distinguishing between cognitive and experiential deficits as basic causes of specific reading disability. *Journal of Educational Psychology, 88,* 601–638.

Wagner, R. K., Torgesen, J. K., Laughon, N. P., Simmons, K., & Rashotte, C. A. (1993). Development of young readers' phonological processing abilities. *Journal of Educational Psychology, 85,* 83–103.

Whitehurst, G. J., & Lonigan, C. J. (1998). Child development and emergent literacy. *Child Development, 69,* 848–872.

Wimmer, H., Mayringer, H., & Landerl, K. (2000). The double-deficit hypothesis and difficulties in learning to read a regular orthography. *Journal of Educational Psychology, 92,* 668–680.

Wolf, M., & Bowers, P. G. (1999). The double-deficit hypothesis for the developmental dyslexias. *Journal of Educational Psychology, 91,* 415–438.

II

THE POLITICAL AND SOCIAL CONTEXTS OF LANGUAGE AND LITERACY ACQUISITION

INTRODUCTION

This section provides a comprehensive discussion of the sociocultural context of language and literacy learning. The various chapters deal with the interplay between interpersonal, familial, and institutional contexts and the dynamics of language and literacy learning and instruction. Issues of normative development and developmental variation receive comparable treatment. The majority of the chapters focus on the preschool and early elementary years. However, the basic issues raised, as well many of the discussions of practice, pertain to older children as well.

In Chapter 6, Elaine Silliman, Louise Wilkinson, and Maria Brea-Spahn address the current sociopolitical context informing research, policy, and practice related to literacy instruction in the United States. They begin with a comprehensive overview of recent federally sponsored reports on the "reading crisis." Having sketched the evidence for the current push to improve reading instruction, they move to an analysis of recent federal legislation and regulations directed toward the improvement of literacy instruction. Throughout their analysis, the authors emphasize the need for current reform efforts to emphasize knowledge and practices related to the role of language development and variation in effective literacy instruction.

The next three chapters in this section address issues related to the family and community context for language and literacy acquisition. In Chapter 7, Bonnie Brinton and Martin Fujiki review research on the implications of atypical language/literacy development for family/peer interactions. They use a rich case study as a backdrop for a review of existing research on the social challenges of children with atypical language development. In the course of their analysis, they highlight the implications of the early and continuing challenges faced by these children for their success at literacy learning.

In Chapter 8, Barbara Wasik and Jennifer Hendrickson focus on family literacy and discuss the crucial role of family practices in the early literacy learning of young children. Based on their analysis of these issues, they stress the importance of interventions that focus on not just the child but rather on the family as a system. This orientation leads the authors to a review of recent research on the effectiveness of family literacy interventions and to a set of recommendations for future research and best practices in family literacy.

In Chapter 9, Anne van Kleeck looks in detail at one crucial aspect of family literacy practices—book-sharing interactions. She provides a comprehensive review of research on the features of book-sharing exchanges that are linked to successful literacy learning in young children. She also provides a thoughtful analysis of cultural differences in book-sharing practices and draws implications for how to proceed with research and best practices related to early literacy instruction.

In the final three chapters in this section, the focus is on slightly older children and on the wider world of the community and classroom. In Chapter 10, David Dickinson, Allyssa McCabe, and Nancy Clark-Chiarelli turn their attention to the potential role of the preschool in fostering language and literacy development. After building an argument for the powerful role that children's experiences in the preschool environment play in language and literacy development, they review evidence regarding current practices in preschool classrooms. In the course of this review, the authors identify a number of missed opportunities in current practice, and they present preliminary evidence for an alternative approach to instructional activities in the preschool, an approach that holds promise for fostering early language and literacy growth in at-risk children.

In Chapter 11, Holly Craig and Julie Washington focus on the question of how language variation impacts literacy acquisition, with particular attention to the case of African American English (AAE). In the initial part of their chapter, the authors provide an overview of our knowledge regarding the unique linguistic features of AAE. They then turn their attention to the issue of the black–white achievement gap, focusing particularly on literacy. After some consideration of the socioeconomic and cultural factors involved, Craig and Washington present an overview of recent research by themselves and others linking the specific linguistic features of AAE to reading and spelling performance. In the final sections of the chapter, they draw implications for both research and educational practice.

Liliana Zecker, in Chapter 12, addresses the issue of how to organize literacy instructional activities that are sensitive to linguistic/cultural variation and that foster biliteracy. In the initial part of her chapter, Zecker provides a thoughtful critique of past efforts to address this issue. She describes the experiences of children in a dual-language program, a bilingual-education pedagogical setting designed to support children's development as bilingual, biliterate, and multicultural individuals. Drawing on her analysis of past research and the promising findings from the dual-language program, Zecker then draws implications for future research and practice.

As a group, the chapters in Part II serve to highlight the many social, cultural, and institutional dynamics interacting with language and literacy development. Of equal importance is the sense one gains from reading these chapters that the research and practitioner community is poised to make significant advances in the coming years in the development of effective literacy instruction for at-risk children. Each author calls for further research, but each also makes persuasive arguments for the potential power of existing data-based practices that are both culturally sensitive and pedagogically sound.

6

Policy and Practice Imperatives for Language and Literacy Learning

Who Will Be Left Behind?

ELAINE R. SILLIMAN
LOUISE C. WILKINSON
MARIA R. BREA-SPAHN

One expectation about readers of this handbook is that wide variation exists in individual perspectives about the significance of educational policy for research and everyday practices. For example, literacy researchers and specialists in learning disabilities have a long-standing investment in the formulation of educational policy that affects regular or special education practices. In contrast, child language researchers who specialize in language disorders, and speech–language pathologists who provide language intervention services to children and adolescents, traditionally, have had less investment in the broader policy process. When attention is paid, it tends to be directed to the impact of specific aspects of policy implementation on local spheres of responsibility. In this chapter, we argue that all stakeholders in the education of children, irrespective of their personal areas of expertise or interest, must pay unequivocal attention to educational policy. A full understanding of the needs of children at risk for achieving necessary competencies in language and literacy learning requires appreciation of the larger policy framework that, today, is transforming how all children should be taught language and literacy

skills, and what they should be taught. The educational policy process can be conceptualized as how scientific knowledge is generated and translated socially into politically authorized interventions that then determine resource allocation (Lo Bianco, 2001). This policy environment and the social contexts of teaching and learning, in which the everyday realities of policy decisions are implemented in the classroom, are the focus of this chapter.

The first section describes educational events that have led to the new policy imperative for regular education, specifically, the legislative act, No Child Left Behind (NCLB; 2002), whose accountability provisions are also expected to impact on the reauthorization of the Individuals with Disabilities Education Act (IDEA). Anticipated consequences are discussed relating to the full implementation of the NCLB Act on teaching, learning, and the measurement of progress for all school-age children in the United States. A question emerges from these policy imperatives, which are intended to address the illiteracy crisis. How will the new fund of scientifically based research on language and literacy connections that is driving educational policy impact on both educational practice and the learning of students in regular and special education? The answer to this question, which is related, at least in part, to our social and scientific beliefs about what counts as literacy (Baynham & Prinsloo, 2001), is a critical one, because schools are being judged on how well they prepare all students to pass high-stakes tests in reading and writing. Therefore, the implementation of evidence-based curricula and practices is central to both the NCLB Act and the IDEA reauthorization.

The second part of the chapter addresses two disconnections between the legislated policy solutions and their instructional solutions in the classroom as currently driven by the implementation of the NCLB Act. One barrier for translating policy into effective practices at the classroom level is the knowledge gap that many educators have about the linguistic underpinnings of literacy learning. This disconnection must be dealt with, because the new policy environment requires highly qualified educators as the keystone for successful implementation. Current teacher education programs typically prepare elementary education teachers and related specialists as generalists. The curricula for teacher education have been described as "disjointed" (Bransford, Brown, & Cocking, 2000, p. 201), offering "different instructional options from which to select" (Berninger & Richards, 2002, p. 304), rather than a conceptual framework consistent with known factors that promote successful literacy outcomes for individual child profiles. Still others (e.g., Cummins, 2000; McCutchen & Berninger, 1999; Moats & Lyon, 1996; Strickland, Snow, Griffin, Burns, & McNamara, 2002; Wong Fillmore & Snow, 2000) argue that this conceptual framework should also include in-depth knowledge about what language is and how it works as the foundation of literacy, as well as a deep appreciation of relationships between theory and practice (Bransford et al., 2000; Gertsen, Chard, & Baker, 2000).

Moreover, according to a federally sponsored study (Carlson, Brauen, Klein, Schroll, & Westat, 2002), special education teachers and speech–language pathologists believed that they were insufficiently prepared in their professional degree programs to deal effectively with sociocultural and linguistic diversity. Therefore, another critical aspect of a conceptual storehouse for regular and special education teachers and speech–language pathologists concerns a broader understanding of student diversity, a concept that encompasses both sociocultural and linguistic diversity, and the biodiversity inherent to individual differences (Berninger & Richards, 2002). From a sociocultural perspective, students trapped in the illiteracy predicament are often described as those who come from low-income homes, where family socialization and practices in language and literacy may differ from the normative expectations and practices of schooling (e.g., Heath & Mangiola, 1991; for further discussion, see Wasik & Hendrickson, Chapter 8, Craig & Washington, Chapter 11, and Zecker, Chapter 12, this volume). From the perspective of biodiversity, a number of students struggling with literacy learning, such as those learning English as a second language (ESL), may also have a co-occurring language and learning disability (LLD), which further complicates the broader notion of student diversity. In reality, both facets of diversity coexist and reciprocally influence each other, both within and between individuals.

The final section addresses a second disconnection between policy and instruction. This divide is partially created by the inherent problem that exists when researchers must translate complex scientific evidence into meaningful and pragmatic classroom practices that work for individual children with diverse needs. As Stanovich (2003) cautions, "the difficulty of explaining these principles to the public and to teachers will not be aided by reducing them to bullet points" (p. 122). In practical terms, this translation gap plays out as a disconnection between the experimentally based evidentiary sources that researchers are concerned with and, as just mentioned, the beliefs held by many teachers and speech–language pathologists that research is not connected in any discernable way to classroom realities (Gersten & Dimino, 2001; Meline & Paradiso, 2003; National Research Council,

1999). For example, little is known about how educators, including speech–language clinicians, will actually confront the challenge of effectively tying together the multiple instructional components that comprise evidence-based practices, or how they will appropriately modify these components to engineer the learning potential of individual children (Berninger, Stage, Smith, & Hildebrand, 2001; Brown, 1992; Denton, Vaughn, & Fletcher, 2003). One proposed approach for bridging this disconnection between research and the implementation of evidence-based practices for beginning reading is response to instruction or the treatment validity model (see also Speece & Cooper, Chapter 5, this volume). The response to instruction approach is primarily premised on findings from the body of research implicating breakdowns in phonological processing as the core deficit characterizing the failure to read fluently (for a review of this research, see the chapter by Troia, Chapter 13, this volume). In packaging different instructional focuses, components, and strategies, this model has garnered some empirical support for either preventing or reducing the severity of reading failure or, alternatively, identifying who may have a real learning disability versus the appearance of a disability. The latter is speculated to be an outcome of inadequate reading instruction. The strengths and limitations of the response to instruction model are discussed in relation to its potential for meeting challenges of the new practice imperatives for students with language and literacy needs.

THE LANGUAGE–LITERACY LEARNING GAP IN THE 21ST CENTURY: POLICY IMPERATIVES

In 2002, the estimated public school enrollment for prekindergarten through grade 12 was 46.7 million. This number reflects a tripling of the immigrant population from 1970 to 2000 combined with the "baby boom" that peaked in 1990 (U.S. Department of Education, National Center for Education Statistics, 2003c). This sharp increase in enrollment coexists with a crisis of illiteracy in America, which is particularly regrettable given the changed sociodemographic characteristics of American classrooms. A growing achievement gap exists among (1) minority and nonminority students, (2) those from poorer versus richer families, (3) those whose native language is English, in contrast to those whose first language is not English, and (4) those identified for special education services versus those in regular education. In this section, we first draw on federal data sources to delineate the scope and nature of the achievement gap that begins in kindergarten, and we then describe the educational policy imperatives embodied in the NCLB Act that are intended to redress the illiteracy crisis.

Profiles of Achievement from Kindergarten to the End of Grade 1

The National Center for Education Statistics (NCES) of the U.S. Department of Education is responsible for data gathering on a variety of educational topics, including data related to the literacy achievement gap. However, interpretations of these large-scale indicator data on the achievement of American school-age students need to be made with caution. As Shadish, Cook, and Campbell (2002) warn, "Correlation does not prove causation . . . because we may not know which variable came first nor whether alternate explanations for the presumed effect exist" (p. 7), such as the hypothesized relationship between reading achievement and family socioeconomic status (SES). Given this cautionary statement, over the past several years, NCES sources have yielded a general profile of school readiness and subsequent academic achievement of groups of children at the beginning of the 21st century.

Kindergarten Readiness

The Early Childhood Longitudinal Study, Kindergarten Class of 1998–1999 (ECLS-K), a federally funded project, is following approximately 21,000 children from kindergarten entry through the spring 2004 school year, when this national sample completes the fifth grade (U.S. Department of

Education, National Center for Education Statistics, 2001a, 2003b). An individually administered standardized assessment was designed to evaluate proficiency levels in letter recognition, beginning sounds, ending sounds, sight words, and words in context, along with basic numeracy concepts. Children for whom school records indicated home languages other than English were administered an oral-language development scale, not further described, to determine whether they had "a certain level of (basic) English proficiency" (U.S. Department of Education, National Center for Education Statistics, 2001a, pp. 30–31). Approximately 68% of Hispanic children and 78% of Asian children met this standard in the fall and spring of the kindergarten year. However, direct assessment of oral language was not conducted for monolingual English-speaking children, based on the rationale that assessing a variety of reading skills over time yielded "powerful . . . estimates" (U.S. Department of Education, National Center for Education Statistics, 2003b, p. 3) of underlying oral-language knowledge. Also, children with disabilities who could not appropriately participate were excluded from assessment (U.S. Department of Education, National Center for Education Statistics, 2001a).

In regard to the beginnings of the achievement gap, the focus here is on what the "modal kindergartener" (U.S. Department of Education, National Center for Education Statistics, 2001a, p. 9) knows at kindergarten entry about emerging literacy. Approximately 66% could recognize letters, whether uppercase or lowercase. Only 29% knew beginning letter–sound names, and about 2% were capable of reading simple sight words. However, marked individual variations in knowledge levels that were apparent were attributed to a variety of factors, including age-related differences in when children entered kindergarten across the United States, the greater developmental lags that some males manifested in their communication abilities, and the critical finding that nearly 46% of the kindergarten sample came to school with one or more risk factors operating in their family backgrounds. Among these risk factors were (1)

a mother whose education was less than high school, (2) living in a single-parent household, (3) living in a family receiving welfare benefits, an index of family poverty, and (4) parents whose primary language was other than English. Regardless of whether children attended prekindergarten programs, such as Head Start, those who were more susceptible to multiple risk factors lived in an urban area with a population above 250,000 and/or were members of ethnic/linguistic minorities (specifically, African American or Hispanic children).[1] Trends indicated that the percentage of first-time kindergartners with two or more risk factors was five times greater for Hispanic children and four times greater for African American children than for their Caucasian peers (U.S. DOE, NCES, 2003a). However, the relative contributions of these individual risk factors to early school achievement are unknown. What is known is that multiple risk factors are not destiny. About 1 child in 100 from the high-risk group entered kindergarten advanced in reading or basic numeracy concepts (U.S. Department of Education, National Center for Education Statistics, 2001a).

End of Kindergarten and First-Grade Achievement in Reading

Using the same battery administered at kindergarten entry, the ECLS-K findings indicated that, at the end of kindergarten, 95% of children had letter recognition and 74% could now make initial letter–sound connections (54% could identify letter–sound links in the final position) (U.S. Department of Education, National Center for Education Statistics, 2002, 2003b). The battery in first grade was given only to the children who had been promoted on time from kindergarten (about 5% of the sample was not promoted). By the end of grade 1, letter identification reached 98%, whereas letter–sound understanding for beginning sounds increased to 94% (U.S. Department of Education, National Center for Education Statistics, 2002). Approximately three-quarters could read highly familiar sight words and about 4 children in 10 were capable of understanding words in context

(U.S. Department of Education, National Center for Education Statistics, 2003b), with a slight advantage for females in these two specific skills. Proficiency was greater for children from "nonpoor families," those who demonstrated more persistence in their approach to learning, and those who entered kindergarten from homes with greater literacy resources (U.S. Department of Education, National Center for Education Statistics, 2002, 2003b). Moreover, Caucasian and Asian children demonstrated greater proficiency in sight word and context reading, with Hispanic children more proficient than African American children in these domains (U.S. Department of Education, National Center for Education Statistics, 2002).

Thus, child and family characteristics, as well as variations in program structure and instructional practices, contributed to the profiles of proficiency or the lags in achievement that emerged by the end of grade 1. It should be acknowledged, however, that considerable heterogeneity exists among families, whether mainstream or less mainstream, in their literacy beliefs, values, and practices, which in turn affect the emerging literacy knowledge that children bring to school and how they learn to participate in literacy-related activities (Anderson, Anderson, Lynch, & Shapiro, 2003; for more discussion, see also Wasik & Hendrickson, Chapter 8, and van Kleeck, Chapter 9, this volume).

Reading between the Lines: Implications of the ECLS-K Profiles for Variations in Early Reading Profiles

Although results by the end of grade 1 are consistent with the overall proficiency expectations recognized in other national reports (e.g., Snow, Burns, & Griffin, 1998), these findings are somewhat ambiguous, because the content construction for the ECLS-K battery is unspecified. Given this qualification, the profile findings illuminate how individual differences in achieving letter knowledge, combined with variations in instructional practices, influence grade 1 outcomes.

In terms of individual differences, a significant question is the role of letter recognition as a predictor of word-recognition skill. The contribution of phonemic, or segmental, awareness is well established as a predictor of word recognition (for reviews, see the chapters in this volume by Ehri & Snowling, Chapter 20, Mody, Chapter 3, and Troia, Chapter 13, this volume). Letter–sound mapping is a necessary step for the development of segmental knowledge; however, less well determined is the association between letter recognition and initial word recognition, particularly for children who may be at risk due to language learning problems. Catts, Hogan, & Fey (2003) found that letter recognition was the strongest kindergarten predictor of outcomes in both word recognition and reading comprehension in grades 2 and 4 for many children, including those with an LLD, a finding that replicates Scarborough's (1998) meta-analysis of 24 research samples, as well as the work of Lonigan, Burgess, and Anthony (2000).

As Treiman, Tincoff, and Richmond-Welty (1997) speculate and others concur (e.g., Catts et al., 2003; Lonigan, Burgess, Anthony, & Barker, 1998), it may be that during the course of learning letter names, "children not only learn the names and visual forms of specific letters, but also increase their phonological sensitivity, learning about the phonological patterns that characterize the letter names" (p. 406). This learning is hypothesized to facilitate the acquisition of letter–sound correspondences, while simultaneously serving as the substrate for the development of the explicit phonemic awareness that is expected by the end of grade 1 (e.g., Snow et al., 1998; Torgesen & Mathes, 2000). Thus, it is reasonable to assume that preschool-age children who have minimal experiences with letter names either at home, in daycare, or in their therapeutic interactions due to a language-learning delay, are already at a distinct disadvantage when entering kindergarten, because they lack the "anchor for the entire reading 'system'" (van Kleeck, 2003, p. 301). This anchor, according to van Kleeck, is not necessarily promoted by storybook sharing, an activity in which caregivers tend to focus on meaning and not the forms of print. Thus, during the late preschool years, some children may need the facilitation offered by more explicit instruction (Lonigan et al., 1998).

The second issue surfacing from the ECLS-K study concerns effects of widespread variations in instructional practices that impact on the ease or difficulty with which children in kindergarten and grade 1 can map letters onto sounds (Treiman, Tincoff, Rodriguez, Mouzaki, & Francis, 1998). Unlike a letter- or sound-of-the-day approach, which is not grounded to the phonological properties of English (e.g., Burns, Griffin, & Snow, 1999), ease of learning is actually promoted when phonological considerations are optimal, that is, when (1) the letter has the phoneme in the letter name, (2) the position of a phoneme in a letter's name occurs in the beginning and not the end, and (3) there is more regularity in pronunciation, for example, /bi/, as opposed to multiple pronunciations as occurs with *c* and, most critically, with vowels.

At the current time, it is unknown how disparities in instructional practices may influence variability in children's learning of letter names and letter–sound names, particularly for children in multiple risk categories, including those who may have language-learning lags. The early identification of this group remains a challenge. Prior to age 4 years at a minimum, it may not be possible to distinguish reliably between children who have transient language problems that will resolve, and children who will go on to have persistent, albeit often subtle, problems in language learning that extend beyond the boundaries of normal language variation regardless of the language (e.g., Berninger & Hooper, in press; Dale, Price, Bishop, & Plomin, 2003; Thal & Katich, 1996) or dialect spoken (Silliman, Bahr, Wilkinson, & Turner, 2002). This consistent finding has significant consequences for the dependable identification of preschool-age children who have language-learning difficulties that extend beyond their sociocultural experiences with emerging literacy, the language or dialect they speak, and their poverty level, as well as for the nature of educational efforts at the preschool level that are directed toward preparing them for more formal reading instruction (Strickland, 2001). However,

it is known that kindergarten-age children who have identifiable problems with language learning are five to six times more likely than their peers without this profile to manifest reading difficulties by grade 2 (Catts, Fey, Zhang, & Tomblin, 1999).

Grade 4 Achievement and Beyond: The National Assessment of Educational Progress (NAEP)

As mandated by the U.S. Congress in 1969, the NAEP assesses and reports the educational achievement of American students on a cyclical basis, generally every 2 years. Until 2001, it had been a voluntary program, and many states did not participate. However, under the NCLB Act of 2001, the reading and mathematics assessments have become required measures.

The NAEP is distinctive in two ways (National Research Council, 2001): first, it is an expansive measure of program evaluation, because its assessment framework is broader than any local or state curriculum; second, the goal of assessment is "to reflect national consensus about what students should know and be able to do" (p. 40). Essentially, the NAEP functions as a basis for national benchmarking of state standards, assessments, and student achievement results. Most critically, the NAEP provides data to states, the national government, and the public to inform and to guide policymaking in education. The most recently available results on reading are from the 2000 and 2002 NAEP, both of which were administered to nationally representative samples. The 2000 assessment was given to 9,000 students in grade 4 only (U.S. Department of Education, National Center for Education Statistics, 2001b), whereas the 2002 assessment included approximately 270,000 students in grades 4, 8, and 12 (U.S. Department of Education, National Center for Education Statistics, 2003d).[2] Wide-scale state-level results were also reported for the first time in the 2002 assessment.

The reading situations and definition of achievement levels for the various NAEP assessments are similar, with some exceptions, such as the proportion of task items that vary with grade level (Loomis & Bourque,

2001). Students in grades 4, 8, and 12 are required to read two types of original texts that represent different reading purposes: reading for literary experience (narrative texts), and reading to gain information (expository or informational texts), whereas students in grades 8 and 12 engage in an additional reading situation—reading to perform a task (such as interpreting a U.S. income tax form). Three embedded achievement levels are defined (U.S. Department of Education, National Center for Education Statistics, 2001b, pp. 6, 14): (1) the basic level, which indexes partial mastery of the fundamental knowledge and skills required for understanding the overall meaning of what is read, and is prerequisite for proficiency; (2) the proficient level at which students demonstrate competency in their overall interpretative understanding of the text, offering both inferential and literal information; and (3) the advanced level, which is represented by a critical stance toward, and thoughtful reflection on, the materials read. The proficient level is the expected standard for all students relative to their grade levels. A criticism leveled at these three benchmarks is that they are confusing, because they are not clearly tied to changes in children's reading growth, and they lack functionality relative to everyday classroom practices (Denton et al., 2003).

The 2000 NAEP was administered to fourth-grade students prior to the enactment of the NCLB Act, whereas the results of the 2002 version may reflect some effects of a beginning shift to new instructional practices, particularly decoding practices, even prior to the NCLB law, at least for students in grade 4 who entered kindergarten in 1997. In addition, administration of the 2002 NAEP is the first time that accommodations were widely permitted for second language learners and those with disabilities (U.S. Department of Education, National Center for Education Statistics, 2003d). Because the reading assessment was first administered in 1992, the 2002 results allow for a decade of comparisons in reading performance. Three patterns have emerged.

1. The 2002 average scale score of 219 (of a maximum 500 scale score) for grade 4 has remained essentially unchanged since the 1992 NAEP. In contrast, the average of 264 for grade 8 has shown significant improvement since 1992. However, disturbingly, the average scaled score of 287 for grade 12 evidenced a significant decline from 1992, with 26% of students in their last year of high school unable to read at even the basic level. Moreover, this decline in performance in grade 12 was evident across the score distribution, including the 90th percentile. Combined with the percentages unable to read at a basic level at grades 4 and 8, 36% and 25%, respectively, the negative outcome is that significant numbers of students at all three grade levels, including those who were provided with accommodations, were not capable of engaging in the necessary inferential thinking that allows "the different sentences and ideas in a text to be connected in order to build up a fully integrated and coherent representation of the text" (Cain & Oakhill, 1998, p. 329). The result is breakdowns in reading comprehension (for a comprehensive discussion of social inferencing in the oral- and reading-comprehension domains, see Donahue & Foster, Chapter 17, this volume).

2. In grade 4, 75% of Caucasian students and 70% of Asian American students read at or above the basic level, contrasted with 44% of Hispanic students and 40% of African American students.

3. In terms of a widening achievement gap that is initially evident at kindergarten entry (U.S. Department of Education, National Center for Education Statistics, 2001a, 2002, 2003c), fourth-grade students reading below the basic level did not show an overall change from 1992 as the comparison point, although the average score in 2002 was higher than found in 2000. The reading performance for 60% of African American students, 56% of Hispanic American students, 30% of Asian American students, and 25% of Caucasian students fell below the basic level. Although the 30-point gap between fourth-grade Caucasian and African American students was smaller in 2002 than in 1994, average scores among fourth-grade Hispanic American students were 28 points below the scores of Cau-

casian students (a 28-point gap), showing a minimal change from 1992 (U.S. Department of Education, National Center for Education Statistics, 2003b, 2003d). One estimate is that 77% of second-language learners are concentrated in linguistically segregated schools, where most of the school population comes from low-income households (Edley, 2002). In fact, in the 100 largest school districts, which have school populations that range from at least 45,000 to over 1 million students, 68% of students are minority students, compared to 40% of total students (U.S. Department of Education, National Center for Education Statistics, 2001c). Thus, multiple risk factors, as defined by the ECLS-K study (U.S. Department of Education, National Center for Education Statistics, 2001a), do not appear to abate for many as they advance in school.

A final noteworthy point is that since 1992, females consistently have outperformed males in grades 4, 8, and 12 (U.S. Department of Education, National Center for Education Statistics, 2003d). On the 2002 NAEP, a 16-point gap in performance existed at grade 12 in favor of females, a larger disparity than in 1992. This "gender gap" first identified at the end of grade 1 in the ECLS-K project (U.S. Department of Education, National Center for Education Statistics, 2002) appears to have remained stable since the 1992 NAEP.

Concluding Comments

The vast collection of federal data reported in this section points to four conclusions: (1) A racial/ethnic and socioeconomic gap in emerging literacy knowledge is evident when young children enter kindergarten; (2) the gap is greater for children who enter school with a combination of multiple risk factors, such as mothers with less education, living in a single-parent family, whether the family receives welfare benefits, and whether the primary language spoken in the home is not English; (3) by grade 4, a significant discrepancy exists between the reading comprehension proficiency of Caucasian non-Hispanic students and their African American and Hispanic peers, and this dis-

crepancy continues through grade 12; and (4) these gaps generally have been stable for more than a decade.

These patterns, while distressing, are not a surprise; indeed, perhaps the most intractable problem in American education has been the achievement gaps among groups of children—by SES, first-language preference, and/or race and ethnicity. Other research has documented stable differences over time between kindergarten and seventh-grade (Tabors, Snow, & Dickinson, 2001), and between first grade and the end of high school (Cunningham & Stanovich, 1997); therefore, as time progresses, it becomes increasingly more difficult to undo the "failing to read" syndrome (Al Otaiba & Fuchs, 2002). The federal legislation, the NCLB Act of 2001, is the policy engine intended to remedy the seemingly intractable problem of the failure to read proficiently, as detailed in this section.

No Child Left Behind Act of 2001

Signed into law by President George W. Bush in January 2002, the NCLB Act is a major reform of the Elementary and Secondary Education Act (ESEA) initially passed in 1965. The NCLB legislation requires that all children must meet basic standards (set by states' core curricula) in mathematics and reading. In particular, the legislation requires states to guarantee that all children read proficiently by grade 3, and that all states must reach this goal within 12 years. The stakes are high for the states. If they fail to meet these goals, schools can lose federal funding provided under the Title I section of the ESEA, which totals approximately $25 billion. Importantly, the federal legislation requires that states report student achievement data by school, and that the data be disaggregated for students by poverty level, special education status, first language, and race/ethnicity. If any group of students fails to meet the bar, then schools could lose their share of Title I funding, which is allocated to 48% of all schools in the United States. There are four keystones of NCLB (U.S. Department of Education, 2002): increased accountability, increased choices for parents and students, putting reading first, and enhanced flexibility for states, school districts, and schools in their use of federal education funds. The last of these issues is not further discussed here.

Increased Accountability

A major aim of the NCLB Act is to strengthen Title I accountability by continuing the approach of the past decade on standards-based educational reform. States must set challenging academic standards for all students in each of the curricular content areas (initially, reading and mathematics), and annual tests and other assessment procedures must be designed to measure how well students in grades 3–8 are mastering the content and meeting the standards. Schools and school districts are held accountable for students' achievements in that continuous and adequate yearly progress (AYP) must be demonstrated, with serious consequences if students consistently fail to meet state-mandated standards. Under the AYP concept, "process is not enough; it's results that count" (Keegan, Orr, & Jones, 2002, p. 2). State accountability systems must define both the level of improvement by which AYP is operationalized at the district level and the rate at which all students will meet proficiency in 12 years. The achievement of consensus on what constitutes "proficient" or "adequate" remains one of the most challenging tasks in the implementation of NCLB (Keegan et al., 2002), as does the use of assessment for the dual purposes of accountability and instructional outcomes at the classroom level.

In addition to restructured state accountability systems, NCLB also mandates that the NAEP measures in reading and mathematics must be administered biannually in grades 4 and 8, and that, beginning with the 2002–2003 school year, states must assure in their state plan submitted to the U.S. DOE that they will participate in this component if they are to receive Title I funds (participation in other NAEP assessments is voluntary) (National Center for Education Statistics, 2003). A total of 44 states participated in the 2002 NAEP (U.S. Department of Education, National Center for Educa-

tion Statistics, 2003d). In essence, the NAEP will be used as a policy tool to verify state assessment results. Based on this broadened responsibility, the NAEP has established priorities for validity research (U.S. Department of Education, National Center for Education Statistics, 2003c). Because the original intent of the NAEP was to function as an independent yardstick of educational progress, not aligned with any one set of content standards, an essential validation priority is comparing the alignment of NAEP with state assessments and standards. This is a far from easy task for three reasons (Reckase, 2002): (1) the marked variation in the extent to which state assessment domains overlap with the NAEP, (2) the wide diversity of approaches in the 50 state assessments, and (3) the extent to which these state measures are adequately aligned with their own curricular and instructional goals in reading and mathematics. A high-to-essential validation priority is the scoring of accommodated performance for students with disabilities or those with limited English proficiency. The complex measurement issue to resolve is the empirical demonstration that "groups of accommodated and non-accommodated students with the same level of content proficiency obtain the same distribution of NAEP scores" (U.S. Department of Education, National Center for Education Statistics, 2003c, p. iv).

According to NCLB provisions, students with limited English proficiency are eligible for accommodations if they have attended school in the United States for fewer than 3 years (those enrolled in United States schools for 3 or more years must receive assessment of their reading and language arts skills in English) (National Research Council, 2002). For students with disabilities, the obligation resides with individual states to guarantee that appropriate accommodations are used, but states cannot limit the rights of the Individualized Education Plan (IEP) team to choose appropriate accommodations or alternate assessments when suitable accommodations cannot be offered. The tension between these two categories of accommodations is crystallized by the fact that "English language learners . . . do not have IEPs. Thus, there is no common basis for decision making about inclusion and accommodation for these students" (National Research Council, 2002, p. 16).

Accommodations for students' performance are an issue that states must address, in addition to reporting disaggregated test results. To ensure that schools are not masking the lack of progress for English-language learners and those with disabilities, states must report student achievement data by school and disaggregate results by poverty level, special education status, first-language status, and race/ethnicity. If any group of students fails to meet the bar established for proficiency, then the school could lose its share of monies allocated to Title I funding. Disaggregation is considered a necessary tool of accountability in order to provide parents and educators with a clearer picture of what is truly happening in their schools in relation to their children's academic progress (Keegan et al., 2002).

Increased Choices for Parents and Students

Beginning with the 2002–2003 school year, NCLB also contains other "big sticks" for parents of students attending Title I schools. Schools that failed to prepare their students according to the AYP level can be designated as "in need of improvement." According to the NCLB website,[3] approximately 7,000 schools nationwide met the criteria for this category in 2002–2003, with a large number of them in the second year improvement category under the former ESEA provisions; therefore, the remedy available to parents in this case is school choice. Parents can transfer their children to other public schools, including a public charter school within the school district, with the school district paying for transportation. It should be noted that public charter schools are subject to the same AYP requirements as are the regular public schools.

The next level of remedy for low-income parents becomes available when students attend "persistently failing schools (those that have failed to meet State standards for at least 3 of the preceding 4 years)" (U.S. Department of Education, 2002, p. 2). Students are now entitled to receive supplemental educational services, specifically, in reading, language arts, and mathematics, at the school district's expense from a state-approved list of public- or private-sector providers. These services can include tutoring, remediation, and academic intervention. They must also deliver high-quality instructional strategies that are research-based, take place outside the regular school day, and paid for at the school district's expense through Title I funds (for further information, see supplemental services on the NCLB website[3]). Specific academic goals must be agreed on with the district and the provider; the goals must be measurable and achieved within a certain deadline. Once a school makes AYP for 2 consecutive years, the fiscal obligation for payment of the supplemental services ends.

The ultimate solution for a persistently failing school is closing it entirely or, alternatively, restructuring it (U.S. Department of Education, 2002). This drastic action will be taken if a school fails to make AYP for 5 years.

Putting Reading First

Two additional and interrelated principles underlie NCLB Act. First, teachers, who should be "highly qualified," are central for successful implementation; and, second, instruction must be based on proven educational research, that is, evidence-based practice. There is a special focus on reading in this landmark legislation. NCLB puts reading first, known in this portion of the law as the Reading First Initiative, so that every child is able to read proficiently by grade 3. A basic assumption is that by requiring all students to master learning to read, there will be reduced identification of children for special education services (U.S. Department of Education, 2002), specifically, those identified with learning disabilities. Again, well-qualified teachers and related educational specialists are the key, both for early identification of students who are having difficulty with early reading requirements, and for tailoring the kind of reading instruction that will result in mastery and continued AYP.

Reflections on the Policy Imperative

At the beginning of the 21st century, there has been a significant societal and governmental response to this sustained illiteracy crisis through the passage of the NCLB Act. This is the first time since Sputnik, in the late 1950s, that such an extensive federal role is reaching into all of American education. It was sparked by the recognition that illiteracy can no longer be tolerated as an inevitable state for too many groups of American students, including those with language and learning disabilities. Because of this recognition, the NCLB Act also represents a radical departure from past national practice for parents with low income in the education of their children. Parents now have educational choices, including public charter schools, and depending on the AYP of their children's school, the choice of external supplemental services to be paid for from Title I funds—all as a result of the fact that schools are failing to provide an adequate education for their children. Never before has national legislation tied school failure so closely to parental choice. Ultimately, there is no shelter for failing schools, which will be "reorganized" out of existence after consistent failure. However, there are red flags being raised about the high stakes testing process, as well as concerns articulated about the scientific, theoretical, and empirical aspects of the NCLB Act.

Three Red Flags

One apprehension, expressed by the private sector, relates to the public's perception of failing schools. The Business Roundtable (2003), an association of chief executive officers of leading American corporations who advocate for public policies that promote strong economic growth nationally and globally, conducted an analysis of media reporting on failing schools. The concern focused on the social consequences that emerge when the media label a school as failing, rather than as "in need of improvement" (i.e., students, teachers, and the community are stigmatized, which then leads to their demoralization). In short, the analysis

indicated that news coverage did not accurately distinguish between different levels of progress that failing schools might be making, such as those showing some degree of positive change versus those that consistently failed to demonstrate any progress year after year.

However, another side to the degrees of improvement issue deals with substance rather than public perceptions. The manner in which states set cutoffs for determining when schools have improved may result in grade inflation, a second red flag. For example, a newspaper computer reanalysis of the reading scores by elementary schools from the Florida Comprehensive Assessment Test (FCAT; Waite, 2003) showed that nearly half of all Florida schools received an A grade in the spring 2003 assessment, a total higher than the combined total of schools graded B and C. This result was attributed to the grading system, which rewards equally both high-performing schools (the real A schools) and schools in which students were showing progress in reading; thus, an A grade can have two different meanings: in one case, a preponderance of students who score at or above grade level in a given school, and in other schools, a majority of students who score below grade level but nevertheless demonstrate improvement over the previous year's testing.

A third red flag, also related to score cutoffs, affects the performance of individual children rather than school performance: Large percentages of children may be failing some state reading assessments. Using Florida again as an example, in the spring 2003 reading assessment of the FCAT, 23% of children in grade 3 failed (i.e., they had little success with challenging content), the largest percentage of failures in the 3 years that the reading measure has been administered to third-grade students (Florida Department of Education, 2003). To reduce the number of retentions, new programs had to be initiated in the summer of 2003, such as summer reading camps, where alternate assessments (e.g., portfolios of classroom work or the passing of a nationally standardized test of reading) were employed to determine promotion to grade 4. This finding suggests that many children promoted to grade 4 will continue to need ongoing individualized instruction if they are to meet the increasingly more demanding reading standards for this grade.

These three red flags indicate trouble spots in the designs and outcomes of the high-stakes assessments that will need refinement to resolve validity issues, such as how cutoff scores are established for various levels of performance. Nevertheless, the conclusion drawn by Keegan et al. (2002) is still pertinent. What the NCLB Act sets forth for states is a "highly desirable accountability infrastructure that is stringent in and of itself—and presumably sufficient to produce desired results, when applied in tandem with improvements in instruction, curriculum, and high expectations" (p. 11). Arguably, the thorny challenge for the stringency criterion is the wide variation in how states go about meeting new educational standards.

Apart from the practical concerns about implementing new standards, another category of conflicting opinion exists about the new policy imperatives. This criticism does not center on the widespread consensus that improved instruction and curriculum in literacy learning, combined with high expectations for all learners, are essential to achieve for the current and future well-being of the country. Rather, critiques of the new educational policy are directed to basic theoretical and empirical assumptions underlying the NCLB Act for the real-life implementation of its accountability provisions.

Theoretical Differences in Assumptions about Individual Differences and the Process of Learning

A primary disagreement centers on the meaning of "individual differences." Berninger and Richards (2002) argue that erroneous scientific assumptions drive aspects of the NCLB Act. An implication of the phrase "no child left behind" is that the problem of diversity will be eliminated through instructional practices that will culminate in a world of homogeneous learners and result in high standards of achievement across the curriculum for all, a notion considered scientifically unrealistic for an obvious reason. Both biodiversity and sociocultural diversity are woven into our genetic makeup and social memberships and, therefore, cannot be homogenized by teaching efforts. Instead, these authors maintain that normal variation should be treated as an asset in building individual talents, although they acknowledge that research is lacking on how educators can effectively manage the wide range of variation inherent to every classroom.

A second dispute relates to assumptions about the meaning of "learning." Bransford et al. (2000) paint an educational vision for the first decades of the 21st century. As the primary outcome for all students, learning environments should be designed to foster their adaptive expertise or capacity to become expert problem solvers. Individuals with adaptive expertise are those who are "able to approach new situations flexibly and to learn throughout their lifetimes" (p. 48) in order to move beyond their current levels of expertise and advance their knowledge base. Clearly, to become an expert in any domain requires mastering reading (and writing) as the linguistic tools for discovering and solving problems. The federal and state governments are setting standards for appropriate reading outcomes based on the notion of scientifically validated practices; but less emphasized is a broader result that should evolve from the application of evidence-based practices. This critical outcome concerns how children are taught to do literacy, or how they are actually engaged in intentional learning processes (Bransford et al., 2000) and, therefore, enculturated as readers and writers through the discourse patterns of classroom literacy activities (Wilkinson & Silliman, 2000).

From a social constructivist perspective, unlike the implied cognitive constructivist framework of the Reading First Initiative (for further discussion of these two models, see Stone, Chapter 1, this volume; see also Stone, 1996), literacy learning does not exclusively consist of recruiting neurophysiological and cognitive events inside learners' heads. The process of literacy learning is also embedded in an array of sociocultural practices that privilege different ways of knowing and thinking about reality (Gee, 1999) and allow entry into the community of minds "where mental activities are salient, enabling new access to previously inaccessible sources of knowledge" (Nelson et al., 2003, p. 25). These enabling practices are patterned by the values and beliefs of social institutions, such as schools, and the ways in which power relations and subsequent social identities as competent (or less competent) learners are enacted through academic, or instructional, discourse, what Cazden and Beck (2003), following Gee (1999), refer to as the "socializing discourse of schooling." On the other hand, the functions of classroom discourse in the Cazden and Beck (2003) rendition are situated in sequences of talk that constitute lessons and, within lessons, variations in discourse patterns that craft social identities in doing literacy. How teachers and students jointly construct these social relationships govern who has access to literacy participation, when they can participate, and under what circumstances particular kinds of literacy participation are appropriate (see also Hall, 2002).

In theory, a critical, albeit implicit, aim of academic discourse transactions between the minds of teachers and the minds of students is to create a new social identity for students as members of a literacy community having shared purposes and understandings (Nelson et al., 2003); therefore, the dual function of the teaching role, as expressed through classroom discourse, is to scaffold the performance of social activities, such as learning to do literacy, in order to scaffold membership within the larger school literacy culture, including its ways of thinking, values, and beliefs (Gee, 1999). However, the contributions of the social constructivist tradition to illuminating actual classroom-based discourse practices that promote or hinder language and literacy learning, particularly in classrooms where children's bio- and sociocultural diversity (Berninger & Richards, 2002) is a prominent characteristic, have stood in the shadows of the more dominant cognitive constructivist paradigm. A reason for the seeming neglect of the social constructivist tradition in the Reading First Initiative may

be related to the current debate about what counts as scientific evidence.

Empirical Differences in What Counts as Scientific Evidence

A major criticism of the evidence-based foundation for the implementation of the NCLB Act is its narrowness in primarily drawing on educational intervention studies conducted in the experimental research tradition, while ignoring qualitative studies on literacy instruction conducted in actual classrooms (Pressley, 2001). As influenced by the work of Shadish et al. (2002), the bias toward experimental evidence is reflected in the development by the new Institute of Educational Sciences of the U. S. Department of Education on the development of a Study Design and Implementation Assessment Device (DIAD). This system will be employed to assess whether studies on educational interventions meet scientific (experimental) standards for generalizing causal effects (Valentine & Cooper, 2003). Shadish et al. (2002) do acknowledge that one purpose of qualitative research is to explore causal relationships and generate hypotheses. Moreover, qualitative designs may yield information that contradicts quantitative data. In their view, the major limitation of qualitative designs is that they "usually produce unclear knowledge about the counterfactual of greatest importance, how those who received treatment would have changed without treatment" (p. 501); thus, qualitative evidence has low power for explaining causal relationships. The conceptual stance taken for the DIAD follows this reasoning: "Because of our mission, our central focus, and the focus of the Study DIAD, is on research designs—such as (randomized) experiments, quasi-experiments and regression continuity designs—that have as their primary purpose uncovering causal relationships" (Valentine & Cooper, 2003, p. 2) in order to estimate the extent to which these causal relationships generalize (Shadish et al., 2002).

To summarize, the contentious question of what counts as scientific evidence is not a trivial one for the shaping of a scientific agenda by the federal government, and it will have influential consequences for the meaning of evidence-based practices. Among the seven priority topics selected by the DIAD for systematic review and subsequent reporting in 2004 (see the What Works Clearinghouse (2003) website),[4] two are of interest here. One topic concerns educational intervention studies meeting rigorous experimental standards that have been conducted in grades K–3 with students who are experiencing problems with beginning reading skills, including phonemic awareness, phonics, reading fluency, vocabulary development, and reading comprehension. A second priority topic pertains to a review of evidence for educational interventions that improve the language, literacy, and academic outcomes for elementary school students who are English-language learners (ELLs). While the experimental or quasi-experimental studies selected for inclusion in the database of the What Works Clearinghouse on these two topics may satisfy experimental definitions of construct validity (see Shadish et al., 2002), from an alternative perspective, they may not necessarily meet standards for consequential validity, or the social outcomes for which assessment data and interpretation are used in authentic contexts, such as schools (Johnston, 1998; Murphy, 1998; for further discussion on consequential validity, see Speece & Cooper, Chapter 5, this volume). These high-stakes social consequences include (1) teachers and schools who are being held publicly accountable, (2) students who may become depersonalized when viewed only in normative terms (Johnston, 1998), (3) the retention of students who do not pass state reading measures, (4) schools being assigned an A grade when the majority of students are still reading below grade level, and, importantly, (5) how reading is defined for assessment and instructional purposes.

In a larger frame, because "there is no absolute truth in concepts of reading (or concepts of bilingual proficiency)" (Murphy, 1998, p. 28), the validity of any evidence, and hence, the validity of the causal interpretations made, rests with the validity of the underlying theoretical constructs to which a researcher ascribes (Shadish et al., 2002). Answering the crucial question—

what counts as evidence of literacy, or what counts as evidence of bilingual or biliteracy proficiency across diverse children—requires a continuing and vigorous debate between the social constructivist and cognitive constructivist camps for the comprehensive understanding and implementation of evidence-based practices. We turn next to the world of teachers and classrooms to examine the new practice imperatives for teaching and instruction.

THE NEW PRACTICE IMPERATIVES FOR LANGUAGE AND LITERACY LEARNING IN THE 21ST CENTURY

The NCLB provisions mandate improved instruction and curriculum in tandem with high expectations for all children. Although the desired outcomes of the legislation cannot be disputed, the critical question is *how* to achieve these two outcomes for all students. The adjective *all* also refers to those who qualify for special education services, because most of these students spend considerable amounts of time in the regular education program and, in theory, are to benefit from the same administrative and support services as all other students (Chambers, Parrish, Esra, & Shkolnik, 2002). In this final section, we highlight two disconnections between the policy imperatives and their actual implementation as evidence-based practices, offering possible solutions to how positive outcomes might be better attained.

As previously noted, with the advent of the NCLB Act, states and school districts are under new pressure to guarantee a skilled teacher in every regular education classroom. The legislation requires that all teachers of core academic subjects (English, reading/language arts, math, science, foreign language, civics/government, economics, history, geography, arts, etc.) must be highly qualified (special education and related services are not defined in the NCLB statute as core academic subjects). This means that regular education teachers must hold a state license or certificate in teaching and demonstrate competency in the subject(s) they teach, and they must be able to demonstrate subject matter knowledge on the standardized tests that states select. At the heart of teacher competency is a basic question: What is an effective teacher? A general answer is that an effective teacher is one whose students learn. In particular, the effective teacher is an individual of high cognitive and verbal ability, with knowledge of subject matter taught and sufficient experience to be effectual with all students. The students of the effective teacher are those who achieve at the proficient, or competent, level on the state's high-stakes assessments. Test scores are one valued outcome in the NCLB framework, because the assumption is that students must have the knowledge to pass the tests. A second outcome is that all students will be prepared to achieve at each grade level, be ready to learn the curriculum at the next level, and, eventually, graduate from high school having completed the required curricula.

However, this general description of the effective teacher remains vague, because it does not recognize an existing disparity: the gap that needs to be traversed to improve the academic preparation and professional development of all school-based practitioners. (As used here, the term "practitioner" subsumes teachers and speech–language pathologists, among others.) The existing knowledge base of many practitioners appears disconnected from the conceptual storehouse necessary for promoting and maximizing successful educational outcomes for individual students, and even more so for ELLs. As Bransford et al. (2000) observe: "If teaching is conceived as constructing a bridge between the subject matter and the student, learner-centered teachers keep a constant eye on both ends of the bridge" (p. 136). One genuine issue for delineating who is the effective practitioner is how the foundations of the bridge are constructed through the scope and depth of educational preparation in linguistic systems. Linguistic systems collectively function as the conceptual engine for students' development of academic language proficiency and it is this kind of language proficiency that then permits entry into the oral and written registers of schooling (Cummins, 2000). The academic register, a situat-

ed variety of language use (see Conrad & Biber, 2001), is the discourse medium through which children engage with literacy concepts, processes, and content, and progressively become enculturated into a community of minds that Nelson et al. (2003) describe.

The second disconnection between policy and its implementation to be addressed concerns the complex problems intrinsic to the translation of scientifically based research into practices that practitioners can own on an everyday basis. Fundamental to this process of ownership and the subsequent delivery of quality instructional services is the practitioner's ability to construct, interconnect, and orchestrate multiple types of knowledge that, in turn, create responsive educational bridges (Bransford et al., 2000). These supports should also enable students to engage in the active and thoughtful discovery of language–literacy relationships. The conundrum to resolve is whether the various scientific and professional stakeholders will achieve consensus on new instructional models that have the potential to serve as educational bridges.

Highly Qualified Practitioners and the Challenges of the English-Language Learner

As an illustrative example of individual differences in the application of effective instructional practices for educational bridge building to academic language proficiency, we focus on Spanish-speaking children who are ELLs. At least four interrelated challenges motivate this focus.

The Challenges of Enrollment and Risk

One obvious challenge is the growing numbers of ELL students. According to the NCES (U.S. Department of Education, National Center for Education Statistics, 2003a), in 2000, Hispanic students constituted 17% of the K–12 enrollments, an 11% increase since 1972. A second reason is their risk status as a group. Approximately 71% of entering kindergartners from Hispanic (and African American) families have multiple risk indicators for negative educational outcomes, contrasted with 29% of entering kindergartners from Caucasian families (U.S. Department of Education, National Center for Education Statistics, 2003a).

The Instructional Challenge

A third challenge prompts the emphasis on ELL students. It stems from the activities of the What Works Clearinghouse (WWC; 2003). As mentioned earlier, a current WWC priority is a systematic review of evidence, based on DIAD standards, on replicable interventions, such as types of ESL and bilingual programs that increase oral English skills in addition to academic outcomes in reading and writing. However, only 7% of regular and special education teachers and 4% of school-based speech–language pathologists report themselves as Hispanic (Carlson et al., 2002). In addition, not all of these individuals are necessarily bilingual or biliterate. To implement evidence-based practices as an outcome of the WCC evaluations and to more effectively educate the rapidly growing population of ELL students, there will be increased demand for *both* bilingual and monolingual practitioners who have a multilayered understanding of the reciprocal relationships among everyday oral-language proficiency, academic language proficiency, bilingualism, and biliteracy. Following Hornberger and Skilton-Sylvester (2000), biliteracy is defined as "any and all instances in which communication occurs in two (or more) languages in or around writing" (pp. 97–98).

The Knowledge-Base Challenge

A final impetus for the concentration on ELL students follows from the first three challenges. The professional knowledge base of practitioners who teach Spanish-speaking ELL students, including those students having language-learning difficulties in Spanish, will require transformation, perhaps for unexpected reasons. One such reason is the "false negative" dilemma. The popular assumption is that ELL children are often misidentified and inappropriately placed in special education and related services, what is often referred to as the false positive problem. However, this assumption may not have external validity.

In the 23rd annual report submitted to Congress on the implementation of IDEA, the Office of Special Education Programs (OSEP) claimed that "disproportionately fewer [ELL] children receive special education compared to their enrollment in schools" (U.S. Department of Education, Office of Special Education Programs, 2002, p. II-36). Whereas that may be positive news, the 24th annual report further accentuates the complexity of unraveling the false-positives from the false negatives. From the vantage point of the false positive dilemma, of the 5.7 million students, ages 6–21 years, classified with disabilities under IDEA in 2000–2001, "among Hispanic students, the percentage receiving services for specific learning disabilities (60.3%) was higher than for all students with disabilities" (p. II-23).[5] On the other hand, other OSEP data (2002) documented that Hispanic students (not all of whom are necessarily ELLs) were also disproportionately *underrepresented* in the category of speech and language impairment. The implication of underrepresentation is that, irrespective of students' ethnic heritages, sociocultural memberships, or languages spoken, a subset of ELL children who have neurobiological disruptions to their language system are not being properly identified (they are the false negatives) and provided with access to appropriate educational programs. These outcomes place them even more in jeopardy for chronic educational failure than their ELL peers with intact language-processing systems, increasing the odds that they will be left behind and eventually drop out of school. Of consequence, Hispanic students born outside of the United States have the highest dropout rate (Dropout rates in the United States, 2001).

Because of the long-term social effects of the false-positive–false-negative predicament, the challenge for teachers and speech–language pathologists alike is to develop sufficient levels of metalinguistic awareness, for example, about contrastive features between the Spanish and English languages, in order to maximize the probability that more reliable professional judgments will be made about individual patterns of bilingual language use. The question is: What do practitioners explicitly learn about linguistic features as part of their professional preparation?

Selected sources from child language development and disorders offer contrastive linguistic analyses of Spanish and English for speech–language pathologists to apply in their assessment of children's oral-language status in both languages (e.g., Bedore, 1999; Brice, 2002; Kayser, 2002; Kohnert & Derr, in press). However, the extent to which this knowledge has been infused broadly into the graduate preparation of speech–language pathologists is debatable; furthermore, there has not yet been a concerted research effort to link this information to literacy learning.

In contrast, the psychoeducational literature on teachers' pedagogical knowledge in the ELL domain stresses the relevance of oral-language experiences for second-language learning. Seldom acknowledged, however, is the need for regular and special education teachers, whether bilingual or monolingual, to acquire specific cross-linguistic knowledge about differences (and similarities) in the phonologic, morphologic, and syntactic systems of Spanish versus English (e.g., Baker & Hornberger, 2001; Fletcher, Bos, & Johnson, 1999; Gersten & Baker, 2000; Ortiz, 2002; Schecter, Solomon, & Kittmer, 2003). These cross-linguistic contrasts may differentially interfere with the ability of certain children to decode and spell in English, which then creates an insurmountable barrier for many in achieving academic language proficiency. McCutchen and Berninger (1999) caution that just because a monolingual English-speaking teacher is literate does not mean that this person has accessible the explicit phonemic awareness necessary for the effective teaching of beginning reading (also see, Silliman, Bahr, Beasman, & Wilkinson, 2000, for a parallel conclusion). In a similar vein, whereas a bilingual teacher may have the requisite cultural knowledge about Spanish-speaking communities, and speak Spanish and English "fluently," it cannot be assumed that this same individual has explicit metalinguistic knowledge of critical linguistic contrasts between Spanish and English.

Building Sociocultural and Linguistic Bridges for English-Language Learners

The conceptual repertoire of the highly qualified practitioner is multifaceted and may be considered a dynamic process in two ways. First, knowledge chunks will shift, reorganize, and consolidate differentially *within* individual practitioners as they continuously develop new levels of adaptive expertise (Bransford et al., 2000). Second, this dynamic process is always filtered through individuals' transactions among their personal learning histories and styles, sociocultural beliefs, emotional attitudes, and interactional experiences (Yan & Fischer, 2002), in this case, with ELL students. The two key components of this multileveled, synergistic storehouse consists of a sociocultural knowledge base and a linguistic knowledge base. In Figure 6.1, we depict the general contents of the linguistic and sociocultural storehouse for the building of educational bridges through which both bilingual and monolingual practitioners can better enable ELL students to enter the community of minds (Nelson et al., 2003).

The Sociocultural Components

Three interrelated components of sociocultural knowledge transcend the type of educational program in which ELL students are commonly placed, such as English immersion, transitional, or two-way immersion (see Zecker, Chapter 12, this volume). How practitioners define bilingualism is critical for the design of instructional practices, including practices with children who may also have language development difficulties in Spanish. A general conception of bilingualism is that it refers to the use of two languages on a regular basis (Grosjean, 1992). This basic description is not the same as the common misconception that, for children to be considered bilingual, they must exhibit a similar range of abilities in their two languages; that is, children's abilities to speak, understand, read, and write across two languages must be "balanced"

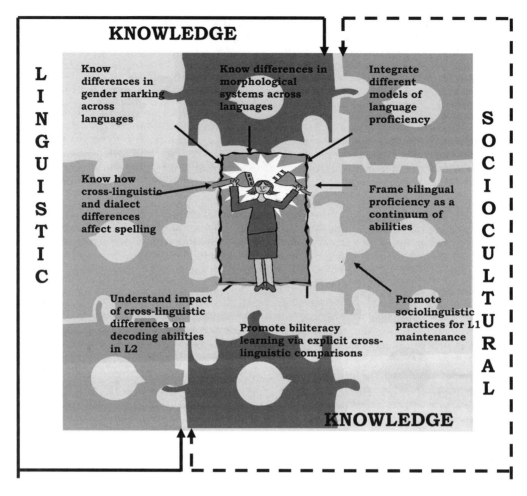

FIGURE 6.1. The linguistic and sociolinguistic storehouse needed for promoting the effective language and literacy learning of ELL children.

(Grosjean, 1982). Balanced bilingualism is a rare occurrence.

Two current models of bilingual proficiency, which are not mutually exclusive, are pertinent for inclusion in the conceptual storehouse. One is the *language activation model* (Grosjean, 1992, 1997), in which bilinguals activate their languages along a social continuum. The language mode selected and its degree of activation depend on such situationally specific factors as whether the conversational partners understand each other as monolingual or bilingual. The other framework is the *linguistic interdependence model* (Cummins, 1979, 2000), a two-way transfer model for those

educational contexts in which literacy in both languages (L1 and L2) is being facilitated. This model posits that a common underlying conceptual mechanism allows "linguistic and literacy-related knowledge and skills . . . learned in the L1 [to be] brought to bear on the learning of academic knowledge and skills in the L2" (Cummins, 2000, p. 190). In turn, the new L2 knowledge feeds back into the L1, depending on an individual's motivation and the opportunities afforded to develop biliteracy. Both the language activation and linguistic interdependence models stress that proficiency is neither an either–or phenomenon nor, at the other extreme, a balance of abilities across two languages (Bialystok, 2001; Cummins, 1979, 2000; Grosjean, 1982, 1997; Hornberger & Skilton-Sylvester, 2000). Instead, proficient bilingualism and biliteracy is both an individual and social resource (Cummins, 2000), and appears to exist on complex and intersecting continua influenced by a host of cognitive, linguistic, communicative, sociocultural, and instructional factors (Hornberger & Skilton-Sylvester, 2000). The towering obstacle that most ELL students encounter in becoming proficient in two spoken languages, much less two written languages, is the implied expectation that, upon entering school, they already have a degree of linguistic interdependence, as reflected in some level of academic discourse proficiency in Spanish, if not English.

Returning to Figure 6.1, the three components of sociocultural knowledge represent factors that influence variations in bilingual proficiency as articulated by the multiple and interconnected lenses of the language activation and linguistic interdependence models. Pivotal for designing effective educational practices for ELL students is understanding second-language and literacy learning as dynamic processes of continual adaptation mediated by complex interactions among neurobiological systems and sociocultural patterns of practice. Providing ELL students with equitable opportunities to develop their *own* language and literacy voices entails that practitioners, as well as policymakers, critically reflect on how school practices may act as a screen to mask power relationships that hinder language use (Hornberger & Skilton-Sylvester, 2000).

The Linguistic Components

As also shown in Figure 6.1, the conceptual storehouse of the highly qualified practitioner should also include explicit knowledge of contrastive educational linguistics (Wong Fillmore & Snow, 2000) in order to develop sensitivity to individual differences. The linguistic interdependence hypothesis accentuates how similarities in the linguistic features of two languages facilitate second-language learning. Less acknowledged are the ways in which distinctive differences

may interfere with the ease of second-language learning. Thus, the value of this knowledge is that practitioners are enabled to engage in cross-language comparisons to (1) discover the linguistic strengths of individual children for the support of language-transfer strategies and (2) discern sites of potential linguistic interference, which will vary for each child. Table 6.1 enumerates several specific differences in the oral and written discourse of Spanish and English. Each area is briefly summarized next, with examples included to highlight the importance of attending to patterns of individual variation in Spanish-speaking children who are struggling to develop English oral, word-recognition, and spelling skills.

Fusional Nature of Inflectional Morphology

Unlike English, Spanish morphology is fusional or agglutinating (Leonard, 1999), because features such as tense, person, and number can be multiply encoded onto a single grammatical morpheme. Fusional morphology, in turn, permits the omission of overt subjects and the utilization of more flexible syntactic organization in Spanish.

Consider Julio, a 9-year-old male from Puerto Rico, who is explaining to his mother why he missed the school bus: "*Salí talde de la ecuela*" (English version: "[I] left from school late"). In this utterance, Julio simultaneously encodes three grammatical notions into the inflectional suffix -*í*: (1) person ([I, omitted], *first* person), (2) number (*singular*), and (3) tense (*past* tense). Furthermore, because of the encoding of information in verbs, syntactic constructions in Spanish often omit overt subjects (Sebastián & Slobin, 1994); hence, Julio's elision of "I" in the example. In continuing with his explanation to his mother, Julio said: "*Etaba eperando que la profesora me dijera lo que tenía que hace*" (English translation: [I, omitted] was [V] waiting for the teacher to tell me what I had to do [NP]). This sentence exemplifies how fusional morphology adds flexibility to the syntactic organization of Spanish utterances.

Also, subject elision is not a feature in English, where explicit marking of the sub-

TABLE 6.1. Examples of Linguistic Contrasts between the Spanish and English Oral and Written Systems

Domain of language use	Spanish	English	Examples[a]
Oral language	1. Fusional inflectional morphology a. Subject ellipsis	1. Nonagglutinating morphology a. Explicit subjects required	a. **Spa.**—Salí talde de la ecuela. ([He or she] left late from school) **Eng.**—She (obligatory) went running outside.
	b. Flexible syntactic constructions	b. SVO order	b. **Spa.**—*Etaba* (V) *eperando que la profesora me dijera lo que tenia hace* (NP) ([I, omitted] was waiting for the teacher to tell me what I had to do) **Eng.**—I (S) want to go (V) outside (O)
	2. Morphological gender marking a. Articles + nouns	2. Morphological gender marking a. Gender unmarked	a. **Spa.**—*El* (masc.) *libro* (masc.) **Eng.**—The (neutral) bird
	b. Nouns + adjectives	b. Neutral articles and adjectives used	b. **Spa.**—*Mi mamá es linda.* (My mother is pretty) **Eng.**—The boy is nice.
Written language	1. Transparent orthography	1. Opaque orthography	**Spa.**—*gato* (cat), all consonants and vowels represented in pronunciation and spelling **Eng.**—night [nīt], five letters represent spelling, three phonemes
	2. Dialect influences on spellings	2. Dialect influences may affect spellings	**Spa.**—*etrellas* instead of *estrellas*/stars (aspiration of /s/ due to dialect) **Eng.**—*etudent* instead of *student*

[a]The examples contain pronunciation differences due to the dialects of the featured speaker; **Spa.**, Spanish; **Eng.**, English; SVO, subject–verb–object; NP, noun phrase.

ject is always obligatory; therefore, an ELL, like Julio, may experience difficulty in learning the obligatory nature of English pronouns and erroneously omit them in his spoken and written productions. For example, in explaining where he placed the books that he borrowed from the library, Julio said, "I put [them, omitted] in there." Similarly, the lack of rigidity in the ordering of syntactic elements in Spanish can often result in violations of English word order when children, like Julio, apply their knowledge of Spanish word-order regularities to spoken or written English (Gutierrez-

Clellen, 1998). These types of violations can lead to subsequent misevaluations that "something is wrong" with their language development.

As also noted in Table 6.1, in contrast to the neutral quality of the English language, in Spanish, feminine or masculine gender information is assigned to every noun (Bedore, 1999); therefore, Spanish speakers, like Teresa, a 7-year-old from Colombia, must attend to their process of language formulation to produce appropriate article–noun and noun–adjective gender agreement, as in her descriptive utterance: "*El libro viejo*" (the old book). The second-language learning implication is that ELLs, such as Teresa, may not be explicitly aware that English does not have gender marking. Again, in their talk or writing, they may apply knowledge of Spanish gender agreement to agents, as did Teresa when, in describing what she had learned in science class, she assigned gender to the subject, that is, "A butterfly grow. *She* turn into cocoon and fly away."

The highly qualified practitioner would be aware of these linguistic contrasts and their potential social impact on ELL children's development of interpersonal relationships. Perhaps even more essential is an understanding of how differences between Spanish and English affect the academic language development of these learners. Two features distinguish the Spanish and English written codes: consistencies and inconsistencies in grapheme–phoneme correspondences across the two languages due to the transparent–opaque distinction, and possible effects of dialectal differences on spelling. Because of space constraints, two other important aspects are not discussed here: differences in the alphabets of both languages, particularly for representations of the vowel system, and variations in the application of morphological forms to derive new word meanings (for a full discussion of English derivational morphology, see Carlisle, chapter 15, this volume).

Influence of Transparent versus Opaque Orthographies

Spanish orthography is classified as a transparent orthography due to the one-to-one correspondences between its phonemes and graphemes (Gutierrez-Clellen, 1999). For example, Alicia, a 10-year-old from Venezuela, readily spelled the Spanish word for *cat* exactly as she pronounced it: *gato*. When spelling in English, however, the opaque nature of English orthography interfered with her attempt. In trying to spell the word *night,* which contains five letters, of which only three are pronounced, Alicia spelled NIT.

There are also exceptions to the one-to-one concept in Spanish that may play a role in word-recognition and spelling activities in which phonemic segmentation and blending are a focus. For example, the Spanish word for cheese is pronounced as [*keso*] but spelled as *queso*. Similar to English, there are letters associated with more than one corresponding pronunciation, which, in turn, can create difficulty for children who are learning to spell. For example, if Alicia is to learn the conventional spelling of Spanish words containing the letter g, she must systematically learn about both of its pronunciations: [g] as in [g*ato*] (*gato,* cat), or [h] as in [*gente*] (*gente,* people).

Dialect Effects on Spelling

The one-to-one correspondences between pronunciation and spelling may also be impacted by the child's dialect. For example, an examination of Julio's spellings revealed common error patterns due to his Puerto Rican dialect: (1) omission or aspiration of the /s/ (e.g., *etrella* instead of *estrellas*/stars) and (2) substitution of /l/ for /r/ (e.g., [*bañal*] instead of [*bañar*]/take a shower). It is possible that the same spelling errors may also occur in Julio's English spellings of *children* (e.g., *etudent* instead of student). Research on this topic with ELL children is sorely needed in view of findings with monolingual English-speaking children that word-level recognition is facilitated best when interventions explicitly integrate sound–spelling connections as opposed to isolated instruction in either phonemic or orthographic awareness (e.g., Berninger et al., 1998).

In summary, the sociocultural and linguistic components just outlined, when incorporated and interconnected, sketch the conceptual knowledge base of the highly qualified practitioner. With such a storehouse of information, the practitioner will be better positioned to build educational bridges for second-language learners in their discovery of similarities and differences between Spanish and English, while simultaneously conveying that the native language is a valued asset. These bridges, in turn, should enrich the interdependence of children's linguistic repertoires in speaking, reading, spelling, and writing by increasing their opportunities for linguistic problem solving.

RESEARCH-TO-PRACTICE IMPLICATIONS FOR IMPLEMENTING EVIDENCE-BASED PRACTICES: THE CLASSROOM CHALLENGE

In this final section, we consider some reasons for the second disconnection between educational policy imperatives and the implementation of instructional practices in reading. We then examine briefly two variations in the response to instruction model that over the long term, as some argue, might decrease the gap by rendering the policy requirements of the Reading First Initiative into the scientifically valid practices that the initiative advocates. The question that arises from the possible implementation of one or both variations is who might still be left behind?

Reasons for the Research-to-Practice Divide

The Authenticity of Translation

A source of the disconnection between policy and practice resides in the belief held by many practitioners that research findings lack utility relative to the exigencies of daily classroom life. Most likely, the reasons for this persisting translation problem emanate from a complicated mixture of two factors. One is that the "path from research to practice is not direct" (Speece, MacDonald, Kilsheimer, & Krist, 1997, p. 186); the other is the erroneous belief held by many researchers that their peer-reviewed work on valid practices should result in relatively homogeneous applications across practitioners, students, and schools regardless of any individual differences (L. S. Fuchs & D. Fuchs, 1998).

The translation problem is also intertwined with the reality principle (Gersten & Brengelman, 1996; Gersten & Dimino, 2001). Practitioners want feasible, concretely defined procedures, not radically different methods, that then can be crafted to their specific situation in order to meet the particular needs of the students for whom they are responsible (Brown, 1992; Silliman, Ford, Beasman, & Evans, 1999; Speece et al., 1997; Stone, 1998). For example, actual mastery of new practices for instructional innovations may take much

longer to incorporate into everyday use than did the original research-based intervention. As a consequence, practitioners may simply give up or not maintain a high level of implementation, because the magnitude of effort does not justify their investment of time. The likelihood of sustaining new practices is significantly decreased when on-site mentoring by researchers, including the ongoing support afforded by professional networking and administrative leadership, is absent (Foorman et al., 2003; Gersten et al., 2000; Klingner, Ahwee, Pilonieta, & Menendez, 2003; Silliman et al., 1999). Even the National Research Council (1999) concedes that data on successful strategies are insufficient for translating research into instructional practices that are consistent with the reality principle, an obstacle that is due, in no small part, to a "cultural divide . . . [between] . . . the language of researchers and the language of practitioners" (p. 13).

The Alignment of the IDEA with the NCLB Act

In a broader context, the thrust to implement validated instructional approaches for beginning reading, in part, is linked with policy recommendations from the President's Commission on Excellence in Special Education (PCESE; 2002) to alter the underlying philosophy of special education services. IDEA, still in reauthorization at this writing, should be aligned with the core premises of the NCLB Act. At the most general level, this alignment probably will reflect two strategic principles: (1) Replace the long-standing "wait to fail" model of special education with a model of prevention through early identification and intervention using "scientifically based reading instruction," and (2) decrease the number of inappropriate referrals for IDEA services, particularly for the learning disabilities category, which increased 36% from 1992 to 2002 (PCESE, 2002). This will be accomplished by the substitution of testing as the primary criterion for decision making with a model that accentuates how students actually respond to early reading instruction.

Response to Instruction Model

The shift to the prevention of reading failure through early identification and intensive intervention has its origins in the long-standing concern over the sharp increase in the learning disability category. Overidentification is attributed to the misuse of the discrepancy concept (the gap between IQ and academic achievement), both as a definition of a learning disability and as a diagnostic method typically applied at one point in time to identify children (Case, Speece, & Molloy, 2003). Moreover, the discrepancy notion lacks empirical validity and offers minimal implications for curriculum and instruction (for reviews, see Fletcher et al., 1998; Fuchs, Mock, Morgan, & Young, 2003). As a result, research attention has shifted to the development of alternate assessments that (1) concentrate on the multi-component skills predictive of learning to read, (2) link more directly to curriculum and intervention, and (3) have the capability to identify individual differences in the response to intensive treatment. The response to instruction model represents this shift. Although there are conceptual and methodological variations, including the extent to which a variation is theory-driven (e.g., the functional language systems model of Berninger, Abbott, Abbott, Graham, & Richards, 2002; see also Vellutino & Scanlon, 2002), the general model derives from a cognitive constructivist framework grounded in construct and social consequential concepts of treatment validity.

The intent here is not to provide an exhaustive review of the response to instruction model and two of its variations, but to highlight some of its features, as well as potential strengths and limitations, in view of the likely effort to build this concept into the reauthorized IDEA. Of interest, response to instruction and dynamic assessment share common principles; both emphasize the assessment of learning potential tailored to a child's responsiveness to varying levels and intensity of intervention support (Abbott, Reed, Abbott, & Berninger, 1997; Bransford, Delclos, Vye, Burns, & Hasselbring, 1987). However, at least two qualifications warrant mention. First, on empirical grounds, although certain standards for the *efficacy* of the response to instruction model

may have been met (e.g., see the WWC DIAD, 6.0; 2003), the *effectiveness* of the model in restructuring everyday instructional practices has yet to be determined.[6]

Second, individual differences remain a perplexing problem across studies in terms of those children who do not respond favorably to intensive intervention. These children, who are variously referred to as nonresponders (Fuchs, 2003) or difficult to remediate (Vellutino & Scanlon, 2002), generate dissonance about certain premises underlying the two variations of the model, the remedial approach and the identification approach, which is based on the model of L. S. Fuchs and D. Fuchs (1998). For example, one inconsistency is that neither approach has yet examined at a more refined level of analysis how access to, or the ability to participate fully in, the language of the reading curriculum may contribute to certain children becoming less responsive to intervention, thereby increasing their odds of being left behind. Although both approaches overlap to some extent, they differ in their purposes for intervention, their implementation design, and the determination of nonresponsiveness to intervention (Al Otaiba & Fuchs, 2002; Fuchs, 2003).

Purposes of Intervention

Both approaches are treatment validity models (see the Speece & Cooper review of this model, Chapter 5, this volume). Both seek to reduce inequities in special education referral, especially for learning disabilities (L. S. Fuchs & D. Fuchs, 1998) but operate with different philosophies about the outcomes of instruction. The intent of the remedial method is twofold (Abbott et al., 1997; Berninger et al., 2003; Torgesen et al., 2001; Vellutino & Scanlon, 2002): (1) to prevent further academic failure by providing struggling readers in the general education classroom with the supplemental instruction that will allow them to achieve the necessary skills for learning to read, and (2) as described by Vellutino and Scanlon, to use intervention as a process for differentiating, at least in theory, between two groups of struggling readers, those who are *instructionally disabled* versus those who are *in-*

trinsically disabled. In framing a prevention perspective, the remedial approach seems to be asking who does not need special education. In this case, the most likely candidates are those children whose inability to achieve basic proficiency with the alphabetic code can be attributed to insufficient emerging literacy experiences, inadequate beginning reading instruction, or a combination of both factors.

The two goals of the identification model qualitatively diverge from the remedial approach: (1) to promote success with alphabetic reading for all students through intensive reading programs that teachers implement in their own general education classroom (Fuchs, 2003), and (2) to identify whether, after a phased process of ongoing, reading-related assessments, a child has a learning disability and, might therefore be eligible for a trial period of special education services. Hence, the primary question of interest in this approach radically differs from the remedial model. If teachers, administrators, parents, and researchers are to make informed and valid decisions on class- and schoolwide improvement rates over time under the Reading First Initiative, then the valid identification of children who may require at least a trial period of special education support can only be "judged situationally" (L. S. Fuchs & D. Fuchs, 1998, p. 211) from multiple sources of evidence obtained in the classroom.

Design and Implementation

Both the remedial and identification approaches seek to revamp the instructional environment, so that children struggling with the beginnings of formal literacy learning can achieve success. However, both approaches differ in their procedures for reengineering the learning situation.

DESIGN FORMAT

Most studies in the remedial framework have employed similar design formats. For example, they utilize a standard scripted protocol, or the "use of the same empirically validated treatment for all children with similar problems in a given domain" (Fuchs et al., 2003, p. 166) and make use of researcher-trained tutors, typically certified teachers, or doctoral students in educational or school psychology to provide individualized and intensive extra instruction. Hence, the remedial model is analogous to a traditional expert model in special education, in which specialists "pull-out" a student from the classroom for additional intervention. Of importance, balanced or integrated instruction has been built into several studies (e.g., Abbott et al., 1997; Berninger et al., 2003; Vellutino & Scanlon, 2002); that is, in each tutoring session, both word-level and text-processing strategies are facilitated, including multiple strategies for reading comprehension, spelling, and writing.

Unlike the longer empirical history of the remedial approach, the identification model has had limited application in relation to reading-related instruction. One adaptation of the Fuchs' (1998) classroom-based model is found in the work of Case et al. (2003), who utilized a partnership approach over 3 years to transform early reading practices into evidence-based practices, and to create effective and intensive reading programs for all students in the general education classroom. In other words, the operating assumption was that the redesign of the educational environment through extended professional development that stressed the relevance of phonological awareness, the alphabetic principle, and writing, would foster affirmative learning experiences for the majority of students. This premise about the redesign of practices appears well founded. A collaborative structure that includes *both* ongoing support from the research team and ongoing professional development, in which teachers can dialogue with one another about the realities of revising their instructional practices, is essential if teachers are to maintain high levels of implementation over time (Cutter, Palincsar, & Magnusson, 2002; Foorman et al., 2003).

In summary, in using a tutorial structure, the remedial method seeks comprehensive change in how children learn to read. By contrast, Case et al. (2003) relied on collaborative consultation to alter, support, and sustain teacher change in reading practices that would culminate in the narrower outcome of positive growth in children's level and rate of oral reading fluency.

INSTRUCTIONAL COMPONENTS

At least seven components of supplemental instruction are critical in the remedial approach for the systematic implementation of a literacy curriculum. The packaging of these components varies across studies depending on the definitions of instructional responsiveness in word-level recognition and fluency, reading comprehension, spelling, and writing. Variation also occurs within studies as related to the quality of procedures for monitoring implementation consistency across tutors. The seven components include the following:

- Extent to which reading and language arts activities are integrated (Foorman et al., 2003; Vellutino & Scanlon, 2002).
- Degree of flexibility allowed in selecting activities (Foorman et al., 2003; Vellutino & Scanlon, 2002), for example, whether curricular choices are highly scripted (or prescriptive) or allow more freedom of choice.
- Specific content taught; the scope, sequencing, and pacing of content; and the duration of activities in each session (Abbott et al., 1997; Berninger et al., 2003; Foorman et al., 2003; Vellutino & Scanlon, 2002).
- Types of dialogic strategies for guiding children in developing new literacy schemas, such as explicit cuing, teacher modeling of strategies for the segmenting of monosyllabic words, or the use of reflective questions, and so forth (Berninger et al., 2003).
- Nature and quality of feedback, for example, primarily corrective feedback of errors contrasted with encouraging children to apply problem-solving strategies to gain insight into connections between spelling and phonemic units (Berninger et al., 2003).
- Nature and quality of opportunities provided for authentic practice, as well as applications of newly acquired content and strategies to actual texts being read or written in the classroom.

- Methods of assessing the often-subtle advances in children's strategic responsiveness relative to expected outcomes.

The gold standard for determining progress in the remedial model is children's initial responses to remediation. This is typically evaluated with standardized measures of decoding and reading comprehension (Berninger et al., 2003; Vellutino & Scanlon, 2002) or a combination of standardized measures and within-session probes to determine growth in response accuracy from session to session (Abbott et al., 1997). A major advantage of this model, therefore, is that the consistency of implementing a multiply layered reading curriculum is better assured (Fuchs et al., 2003). It is far easier to train and monitor tutors in their accurate implementation of instructional components than to train and monitor the reliability with which diverse numbers of teachers implement a new reading program in their own classrooms.

Turning to the identification approach, comparable information has not been specified about the instructional components that teachers implemented for their whole classes, as well as modifications made for particular children. Instead, Case et al. (2003) concentrate on the methodology of using reading-related curriculum-based measurement (CBM) for three purposes: to inform instructional planning for all students, to monitor individual student progress continuously, and to gauge whether classrooms function as a facilitative educational setting. From a quantitative point of view, a facilitative educational setting is one in which the mean rate of growth in reading skills, or the general rate of responsiveness to instruction, is sufficiently high to merit shifting attention to individual students who actually need more differentiated instruction, which is the second phase in the Fuchs' (1998) model. A particular challenge for the second phase is the valid identification of those students who frequently evidence *dual discrepancies* (L. S. Fuchs & D. Fuchs, 1998; see also Speece & Case, 2001); that is, both their level and rate of performance in oral reading fluency consistently fall below the level and rate of their classmates, as opposed to those who are infrequently or never dually discrepant (Case et al., 2003; Speece, Case, & Malloy, 2003). In making these fine-grained distinctions, the choice and timing of CBM procedures are vital for defining the cutoffs and the magnitude of discrepancy that then lead to the decision that a child is less responsive, therefore requiring even more individualized intervention in the general education setting (the third phase in the Fuchs' model) prior to a special education referral (the last phase) (Fuchs, 2003; Speece et al., 2003).

On the other hand, unlike the remedial approach, Case et al. (2003) went beyond the technology of measurement to obtain qualitative information from interviews with teachers concerning how their beliefs about reading instruction, children at risk for reading problems, and their management styles might impact on interactions with individual children. In addition, field notes were collected during classroom observations that focused on a randomly selected child, with follow-up discussion then taking place with the teacher as one procedure for monitoring the consistency of interventions. The inclusion of qualitative data might illuminate how teachers' beliefs intertwine with their classroom discourse practices that then affect whether or not individual children learn to do literacy successfully. This insight has important ramifications for unpacking the meaning of nonresponsiveness to intervention.

Determining Who Is Difficult to Remediate

In the Vellutino and Scanlon (2002) remedial approach, students in grade 1 who showed significant improvement in word-level and text-processing skills in response to systematic, individualized, and intensive instruction delivered in a daily, 30-minute, one-to-one tutoring format for one school semester (approximately 70–80 sessions) were presumed to have normal learning potential because they were "more readily remediated" (p. 623); thus, based on the degree of improvement, these children appeared to meet criteria for a disability induced by their instructional experiences. In contrast to children who more readily responded to intervention, those who did not improve, despite the equivalent well-crafted and intensive instruction, qualified as "difficult to remediate." This less favorable outcome is attributed to an intrinsic disability primarily reflected in a core phonological processing deficit that then obstructs "all aspects of their reading development" (Vellutino & Scanlon, 2002, p. 623). The absence of improvement for this group led Vellutino and Scanlon to recommend that more long-term, intensive tutoring instruction may be necessary, a suggestion consistent with the treatment validity paradigm (see Speece & Cooper, Chapter 5, this volume). However, Vellutino and Scanlon concede that many of the children who were responsive to their comprehensive remedial program "lost ground" (p. 626) when, upon termination, they returned to classrooms that did not promote the consolidation of strategies and skills that would permit them to become more independent learners. This outcome might be anticipated when studies take place outside of actual classrooms and teachers are not partners in the process of change (Foorman et al., 2003).

In Case et al. (2003), the broad lens provided through teacher interviews and classroom observations that concentrated on individual children resulted in a different constellation of factors influencing responsiveness or nonresponsiveness. What counted most for individual child improvement were changes in children's social identity as competent learners, even if, by implication, children appeared to have a language-learning disability and/or were ELL. In other words, sociocultural practices regulating the orchestration of instructional dynamics, such as interactions between *teacher responsiveness* to child needs and the child's resulting access to learning, mattered more for identifying individual differences in the rate and quality of progress than did the static curriculum-based measures of oral reading fluency. Because the notion of "difficult to remediate" remains a fuzzy one, the Case et al. study demonstrates the significance of going beyond the traditional analysis of group differences in performance to examine the individual profiles of children for whom learning to read continues as a struggle (Abbott et al., 1997; Johnston, 2002).

Expanding the View of Language Contributions to Reading Failure and Success in Response to Instruction

Recall that the ECLS-K (U.S. Department of Education, National Center for Education Statistics, 2001a, 2003a) data showed that children who entered kindergarten with insufficient experience with letter names and letter–sound relationships were less able to profit from reading-focused instruction in kindergarten and grade 1, because the basic anchors for learning to read fluently had not been consolidated (van Kleeck, 2003; see also Vellutino & Scanlon, 2002). Early reading failure is not a trifling matter. Functional magnetic resonance imaging (fMRI) findings indicate that when these struggling readers mature into young adults, many still manifest persistently poor reading skills (Shaywitz et al., 2003). Shaywitz and colleagues attribute the roots of chronic reading failure to instructional practices in the early primary grades that fail children by not methodically exploiting the language-based phonological processing abilities related to fluent reading skill.

However, evidence is accumulating that the learning needs of children who are considered difficult to remediate may be more complicated than a phonological processing deficit for at least four reasons. First, data from a long-term study (Catts et al., 1999) show that, among poor readers identified in kindergarten as having a possible language-learning disability, by grade 2, only 14% had difficulties principally restricted to word-level recognition, what is commonly referred to as "dyslexia." The majority had continuing difficulties with a spectrum of oral-language skills or had combined problems with phonological processing and the academic language skills needed for success in school. Moreover, for some, it may not be until grade 3 that breakdowns in the language underpinnings of more advanced literacy learning become visible. Leach, Scarborough, and Rescorla (2003) found that, at grade 3, specific patterns emerged that

primarily involved comprehension difficulties in both the oral and reading domains, including problems with vocabulary learning and inferencing; still others at grade 3 may first demonstrate more widespread breakdowns. These findings justify appropriate caution in accepting a narrow phonological processing view as the sole engine for the design of either remedial or identification studies. Second, the phonological processing deficit view tends to ignore the functional interactions of domain-specific language systems (such as comprehension and production processes) with domain-general nonlanguage systems (e.g., working memory, attention, executive functions, etc.) (Berninger & Hooper, in press). Third, neither the remedial nor the identification model has been explicitly implemented with children who are ELL, a significant topic for future research, not only for the prevention of reading failure in English but also for the valid identification of oral-language barriers that encompass both first- and second-language learning. Without this dual emphasis, certain ELL children will continue to fall behind, with the likelihood that they will receive the "difficult to remediate" designation. Finally, a complex of both mental and social interactions will always influence whether individual children are responsive or less responsive to particular tasks, regardless of whether children are ELL or have inherent genetic and neural differences that are expressed in a constantly changing profile of language-learning disabilities.

In summary, even when good teaching characterizes the tutoring experience or literacy learning in the general education classroom, expert teaching is not enough when children have language and literacy learning problems that are broader than a phonological processing deficit and, often, not apparent. Indeed, to reduce the probability of these children continuing to be left behind, extensive educational restructuring targeted to the fiscal and structural integration of special education and related services with general education will be necessary, in combination with the implementation of true collaboration. Only then will the resources of language specialists, such as speech–language pathologists, be employed more appropriately to build the necessary educational bridges for supporting the varying language-based needs of struggling readers, regardless of who they are, through the application of evidence-based practices that are premised on two elements. These interdependent and fundamental elements combine a more holistic view of the dynamic transactions among language systems and processes with the social contexts of teaching and learning wherein children achieve a powerful new identity, that of being a proficient reader.

SOME CONCLUDING COMMENTS

As stated at the outset of the chapter, often researchers and practitioners with allegiance to speech–language pathology, as opposed to literacy education or learning disabilities, have not sufficiently valued the impact of educational policy imperatives on their assumptions about what counts as evidence of the language underpinnings of literacy, much less the assumptions motivating the practices engaged in to facilitate authentic language and literacy learning. We hope that this chapter's content contributes to a changed worldview.

A second anticipation is that our colleagues in literacy education, learning disabilities, and special education will begin to expand their conceptual storehouse about language-related processes in beginning reading beyond the realm of phonological processing. In real-life contexts, language operates as a synergetic system always in the service of communication; therefore, it is not possible to separate language and communication from its social and academic discourse functions.

Finally, we are hopeful that all readers, at a minimum, will reexamine their theoretical beliefs about the origins of literacy learning as a primarily "inside the head" mental phenomenon managed by processing software. Instead, we argue for a dynamic view that seeks to merge cognitive and social constructivism where interfaces are possible. In the words of Berninger and Richards (2002), "The Computing Brain is a social accomplishment in which multiple compo-

nents, both within the mental world and the external environment, learn to work together in a society of mind(s) . . ." (p. 278).

ACKNOWLEDGMENT

With deep gratitude, we acknowledge the insight, editorial assistance, and infinite patience that Addison Stone unhesitatingly provided to make this chapter a reality.

NOTES

1. For the purposes of this study, determination of race/ethnicity was based on parent report. Parents could select more than one race. Next, they had to identify whether the child was Hispanic and then select one or more races. In accord with the federal government categories, five composite race/ethnicity categories were then constructed from this information (U.S. Department of Education, National Center for Education Statistics, 2002, p. 33): white non-Hispanic, black non-Hispanic, Hispanic, Asian, and other (Pacific Islanders, American Indians, Alaska Natives, and multiracial). However, it is recognized that the meaning of "ethnicity," much less race, remains controversial. For example, Shonkoff and Phillips (2000) note that ethnicity can be a combination of national origin, minority status, language, and religion. Whether individuals define their ethnicity in terms of culture, identity, or minority status varies according to their social beliefs, values, and customs (see also van Kleeck, Chapter 9, this volume).

2. The 2002 NAEP reading assessment was administered to 140,000 students in grade 4 (in 5,500 schools), 115,000 students in grade 8 (in 4,700 schools), and 15,000 students in grade 12 (in approximately 700 schools). Assessment data were gathered from 48 states for grade 4, and 47 states for grade 8. The sample in grade 12 was a national sample only and, therefore, included fewer students and schools (U.S. Department of Education, National Center for Education Statistics, 2003d).

3. The No Child Left Behind website is *http://www.nochildleftbehind.gov*

4. The What Works Clearinghouse website is at *http://w-w-c.org*

5. In contrast, African American males are disproportionately classified as having mental retardation and emotional disturbance rela-

tive to their numbers in the estimated resident student population (U.S. Department of Education, National Center for Education Statistics, 2002). The President's Commission on Excellence in Special Education (2002) attributes this pattern of misidentification to the overall lack of teacher preparation in the behavioral management and instruction of those "with learning characteristics that make them 'at risk' in general education" (p. 26).

6. Efficacy is the "clinical trial" demonstration that a particular intervention approach delivers what it promises under *ideal* conditions, including the randomized assignment of children to treatment and control groups, and systematic attention to the fidelity of the intervention's implementation (Roby & Schultz, 1998; Shadish et al., 2002). Effectiveness, on the other hand, is a component of efficacy in that its realm is the translation of efficacy research into the *everyday, routine* conditions of classroom (or clinical) instruction; therefore, the efficacy of an intervention must be established first, before its use is warranted in the real-life classroom (Roby & Schultz, 1998).

REFERENCES

Abbott, S. P., Reed, E., Abbott, R. D., & Berninger, V. W. (1997). Year-long balanced reading/writing tutorial: A design experiment used for dynamic assessment. *Learning Disability Quarterly, 20,* 249–263.

Al Otaiba, S., & Fuchs, D. (2002). Characteristics of children who are unresponsive to early literacy intervention. *Remedial and Special Education, 23,* 300–316.

Anderson, J., Anderson, A., Lynch, J., & Shapiro, J. (2003). Storybook reading in a multicultural society: Critical perspectives. In A. van Kleeck, S. A. Stahl, & E. B. Bauer (Eds.), *On reading books to children: Parents and teachers* (pp. 203–230). Mahwah, NJ: Erlbaum.

Baker, C., & Hornberger, N. H. (Eds.). (2001). *An introductory reader to the writings of Jim Cummins.* Buffalo, NY: Multilingual Matters.

Baynham, M., & Prinsloo, M. (2001). New directions in literacy research. *Language and Education, 12*(2 & 3), 83–91.

Bedore, L. M. (1999). The acquisition of Spanish. In O. L. Taylor & L. B. Leonard (Eds.), *Language acquisition across North America: Cross-cultural and cross-linguistic perspectives* (pp. 157–207). San Diego: Singular.

Berninger, V. W., Abbott, R. D., Abbott, S. P., Graham, S., & Richards, T. (2002). Writing and reading: Connections between language by hand and language by eye. *Journal of Learning Disabilities, 35,* 39–56.

Berninger, V. W., & Hooper, S. (in press). A develop-

mental neuropsychological perspective on writing disabilities in children and youth. In D. Molfese & V. Molfese (Eds.), *Handbook of child neuropsychology.* Mahwah, NJ: Erlbaum.

Berninger, V. W., & Richards, T. L. (2002). *Brain literacy for educators and psychologists.* San Diego: Academic Press.

Berninger, V. W., Stage, S. A., Smith, D. R., & Hildebrand, D. (2001). Assessment for reading and writing intervention: A three-tier model for prevention and remediation. In J. J. W. Andrews, D. H. Saklofske, & H. L. Janzen (Eds.), *Handbook of Psychoeducational assessment: Ability, achievement, and behavior in children* (pp. 195–223). San Diego: Academic Press.

Berninger, V. W, Vaughn, K., Abbott, R. D., Brooks, A., Abbott, S. P., Rogan, L., et al. (1998). Early intervention for spelling problems: Teaching functional units of varying size with a multiple-connections framework. *Journal of Educational Psychology, 90,* 587–605.

Berninger, V. W., Vermeulen, K., Abbott, R. D., McCutchen, D., Cotton, S., Cude, J., et al. (2003). Comparison of three approaches to supplementary reading instruction for low-achieving second grade readers. *Language, Speech, and Hearing Services in Schools, 34,* 101–116.

Bialystok, E. (2001). *Bilingualism in development: Language, literacy, and cognition.* New York: Cambridge University Press.

Brice, A. E. (2002). *The Hispanic child: Speech, language, culture, and education.* Boston: Allyn & Bacon.

Bransford, J. D., Brown, A. L., & Cocking, R. R. (2000). *How people learn: Brain, mind, experience, and school.* Washington, DC: National Academy Press.

Bransford, J. D., Delclos, V. R., Vye, N. J., Burns, S., & Hasselbring, T. S. (1987). State of the art and future directions. In C. S. Lidz (Ed.), *Dynamic assessment: An interactional approach to evaluating learning potential* (pp. 479–496). New York: Guilford Press.

Brown, A. L. (1992). Design experiments: Theoretical and methodological challenges in creating complex interventions in classroom settings. *Journal of the Learning Sciences, 2,* 141–178.

Burns, M. S., Griffin, P., & Snow, C. E. (1999). *Starting out right: A guide to promoting children's reading success.* Washington, DC: National Academy Press.

Cain, K., & Oakhill, J, (1998). Comprehension skill and inference-making ability: Issues of causality. In C. Hulme & R. M. Joshi (Eds.), *Reading and spelling: Development and disorders* (pp. 329–342). Mahwah, NJ: Erlbaum.

Carlson, E., Brauen, M., Klein, S., Schroll, K., & Westat, S. W. (2002). *Study of personnel needs in special education: Key findings.* Washington, DC: U.S. Department of Education, Office of Special Education Programs. Retrieved May 2, 2003, from *http://www.ed.gov/offices/ OSERS/OSEP/*

Case, L. P., Speece, D. L., & Molloy, D. E. (2003). The validity of a response-to-instruction paradigm to identify reading disabilities: A longitudinal analysis of individual differences and contextual factors. *School Psychology Review, 32*, 557–582.

Catts, H. W., Fey, M. E., Zhang, X., & Tomblin, J. B. (1999). Language basis of reading and reading disabilities: Evidence from a longitudinal investigation. *Scientific Studies of Reading, 3*, 331–361.

Catts, H. W., Hogan, T. P., & Fey, M. C. (2003). Subgrouping poor readers on the basis of individual differences in reading-related abilities. *Journal of Learning Disabilities, 36*, 151–164.

Cazden, C. B., & Beck, S. W. (2003). Classroom discourse. In A. C. Graesser, M. A. Gernsbacher, & S. R. Goldman (Eds.), *Handbook of discourse processes* (pp. 165–197). Mahwah, NJ: Erlbaum.

Chambers, J. G., Parrish, T. B., Esra, P. E., & Shkolnik, J. L. (2002, November). *Special education expenditure project (SEEP): How does spending on special education students vary across districts?* (Report No. 2-02, U.S. Department of Education, Office of Special Education Programs). Retrieved June 28, 2003, from *http://www.ed.gov/offices/OSERS/OSEP*

Conrad, S., & Biber, D. (Eds.). (2001). *Variation in English: Multidimensional studies.* Harlow, UK: Pearson Education Limited.

Cummins, J. (1979). Cognitive/academic language proficiency, linguistic interdependence, the optimum age question and some other matters. *Working Papers in Bilingualism, 19*, 197–205.

Cummins, J. (2000). *Language, power, and pedagogy: Bilingual children in the crossfire.* Buffalo, NY: Multilingual Matters.

Cunningham, A. E., & Stanovich, K. E. (1997). Early reading development and its relation to reading exposure and ability 10 years later. *Developmental Psychology, 33*, 934–945.

Cutter, J., Palincsar, A. S., & Magnusson, S. J. (2002). Supporting inclusion through case-based vignette conversations. *Learning Disabilities Research and Practice, 17*, 186–200.

Dale, P. S., Price, T. S., Bishop, D. V. M., & Plomin, R. (2003). Outcomes of early language delay: I. Predicting persistent and transient language difficulties at 3 and 4 years. *Journal of Speech, Language, and Hearing Research, 46*, 544–560.

Denton, C. A., Vaughn, S., & Fletcher, J. M. (2003). Bringing research-based practice in reading intervention to scale. *Learning Disabilities Research and Practice, 18*, 201–211.

Dropout rates in the United States: 2000. (2001). *Education Statistics Quarterly, National Center for Education Statistics, 3*(4), 1–7. Retrieved May 13, 2002, from *http://nces.ed.gov/pubs2002/*

Edley, C., Jr. (2002). Education reform in context: Research, politics, and civil rights. In T. Ready, C. E. Edley, Jr., & C. E. Snow (Eds.), *Achieving high educational standards for all: A conference summary* (pp. 123–145). Washington, DC: National Academy Press.

Fletcher, J. M., Francis, D. J., Shaywitz, S. E., Lyon, G. R., Foorman, B. R., Stuebing, K. K., et al. (1998). Intelligent testing and the discrepancy model for children with learning disabilities. *Learning Disabilities Research and Practice, 13*, 186–203.

Fletcher, T. V., Bos, C. S., & Johnson, L. M. (1999). Accommodating English language learners with language and learning disabilities in bilingual education classrooms. *Learning Disabilities Research and Practice, 14*, 80–91.

Florida Department of Education. (2003, June). Reading and mathematics scores: Statewide comparison for 2001–2003. Retrieved July 5, 2003, from *http://www.firn.edu/doe/fcat/fcpress.htm*

Foorman, B. R., Chen, D., Carlson, C., Moats, L., Frances, D. J., & Fletcher, J. M. (2003). The necessity of the alphabetic principle to phonemic awareness instruction. *Reading and Writing: An Interdisciplinary Journal, 16*, 289–324.

Fuchs, D., & Fuchs, L. S. (1998). Researchers and teachers working together to adapt instruction for diverse learners. *Learning Disabilities Research and Practice, 13*, 126–137.

Fuchs, D., Mock, D., Morgan, P. L., & Young, C. L. (2003). Responsiveness-to-intervention: Definitions, evidence, and implications for the learning disabilities construct. *Learning Disabilities Research and Practice, 18*, 157–171.

Fuchs, L. S. (2003). Assessing intervention responsiveness: Conceptual and technical issues. *Learning Disabilities Research and Practice, 18*, 172–186.

Fuchs, L. S., & Fuchs, D. (1998). Treatment validity: A unifying concept for reconceptualizing the identification of learning disabilities. *Learning Disabilities Research and Practice, 13*, 204–219.

Gee, J. P. (1999). *An introduction to discourse analysis: Theory and method.* New York: Routledge.

Gersten, R., & Baker, S. (2000). The professional knowledge base on instructional practices that support cognitive growth for English-language learners. In R. Gersten, E. P. Schiller, & S. Vaughn (Eds.), *Contemporary special education research: Syntheses of the knowledge base on critical instructional issues* (pp. 31–79). Mahwah, NJ: Erlbaum.

Gersten, R., & Brengelman, S. U. (1996). The quest to translate research into classroom practice. *Remedial and Special Education, 17*, 67–74.

Gersten, R., Chard, D., & Baker, S. (2000). Factors enhancing sustained use of research-based instructional practices. *Journal of Learning Disabilities, 33*, 445–457.

Gersten, R., & Dimino, J. (2001). The realities of translating research into classroom practice. *Learning Disabilities Research and Practice, 16*, 120–130.

Grosjean, F. (1982). *Life with two languages: An introduction to bilingualism.* Cambridge, MA: Harvard University Press.

Grosjean, F. (1992). Another view of bilingualism. In R. Harris (Ed.), *Cognitive processing in bilinguals* (pp. 51–62). Amsterdam: North-Holland.

Grosjean, F. (1997). Processing mixed languages: Issues, findings, and models. In A. M. de Groot & J. F. Kroll (Eds.), *Tutorials in bilingualism: Psycholinguistic perspectives* (pp. 225–254). Mahwah, NJ: Erlbaum.

Gutierrez-Clellen, V. F. (1998). Syntactic skills of Spanish-speaking children with low school achievement. *Language, Speech, and Hearing Services in Schools, 29,* 207–215.

Gutierrez-Clellen, V. F. (1999). Language choice in intervention with bilingual children. *American Journal of Speech–Language Pathology, 8*(4), 291–302.

Hall, K. (2002). Co-constructing subjectivities and knowledge in literacy class: An ethnographic–sociocultural perspective. *Language and Education, 16,* 178–194.

Heath, S. B., & Mangiola, L. (1991). *Children of promise: Literate activity in linguistically and culturally diverse classrooms.* Washington, DC: National Education Association.

Hornberger, N. H., & Skilton-Sylvester, E. (2000). Revisiting the continua of biliteracy: International and critical perspectives. *Language and Education, 14,* 96–122.

Johnston, P. (1998). The consequences of the use of standardized tests. In S. Murphy, P. Shannon, P. Johnston, & J. Hansen (Eds.), *Fragile evidence: A critique of reading assessment* (pp. 89–101). Mahwah, NJ: Erlbaum.

Johnston, P. H. (2002). Commentary on "The interactive strategies approach to reading intervention." *Contemporary Educational Psychology, 27,* 636–647.

Kayser, H. R. (2002). Bilingual development and language disorders. In D. E. Battle (Ed.), *Communication disorders in multicultural populations* (3rd ed., pp. 205–232). Boston: Butterworth Heinemann.

Keegan, L. G., Orr, B. J., & Jones, B. J. (2002, February 13). *Adequate yearly progress: Results, not progress.* Paper presented at the 2002 conference, Will No Child Truly Be Left Behind?: The Challenges of Making the Law Work, sponsored by the Thomas B. Fordham Foundation. Retrieved May 9, 2003, from *http://www.edexcellence.net/nclbconference/nclbconferenceindex.html*

Klingner, J. K., Ahwee, S., Pilonieta, P., & Menendez, R. (2003). Barriers and facilitators in scaling up research-based practices. *Exceptional Children, 69,* 411–429.

Kohnert, K., & Derr, A. (in press). Language intervention with bilingual children. In B. Goldstein (Ed.), *Bilingual language development: A focus on Spanish–English speakers.* Baltimore: Brookes.

Leach, J. M., Scarborough, H. S., & Rescorla, L. (2003). Later-emerging reading disabilities. *Journal of Educational Psychology, 95,* 211–224.

Leonard, L. B. (1999). The study of language acquisition across languages. In O. Taylor & L. B. Leonard (Eds.), *Language acquisition across North America: Cross-cultural and cross-linguistic perspectives* (pp. 3–19). San Diego: Singular.

Loomis, S. C., & Bourque, M. L. (Eds.). (2001). *National Assessment of Educational Progress achievement levels, 1992–1998 for reading.* Retrieved June 20, 2003, from *http://www.nagb.org*

Lo Bianco, J. (2001). Policy literacy. *Language and Education, 15*(2 & 3), 212–227.

Lonigan, C. J., Burgess, S. R., & Anthony, J. L. (2000). Development of emergent literacy and early reading skills in preschool children: Evidence from a latent-variable longitudinal study. *Developmental Psychology, 36,* 596–613.

Lonigan, C. J., Burgess, S. R., Anthony, J. L., & Barker, T. A. (1998). Development of phonological sensitivity in 2-to 5-year-old children. *Journal of Educational Psychology, 90,* 294–311.

McCutchen, D., & Berninger, V. W. (1999). Those who *know,* teach well: Helping teachers master literacy-related subject-matter knowledge. *Learning Disabilities Research and Practice, 14,* 215–226.

Meline, T., & Paradiso, T. (2003). Evidence-based practices in schools: Evaluating research and reducing barriers. *Language, Speech, and Hearing Services in Schools, 34,* 273–283.

Moats, L. C., & Lyon, G. R. (1996). Wanted: Teachers with knowledge of language. *Topics in Language Disorders, 16*(2), 73–86.

Murphy, S. (1998). Evidence, validity, and assessment. In S. Murphy, P. Shannon, P. Johnston, & J. Hansen (Eds.), *Fragile evidence: A critique of reading assessment* (pp. 15–30). Mahwah, NJ: Erlbaum.

National Center for Education Statistics. (2003). *Important aspects of No Child Left Behind relevant to NAEP.* Retrieved May 30, 2003, from *http://nces.ed.gov/nationsreportcard/nclb.asp*

National Research Council. (1999). *Improving student learning: A strategic plan for educational research and its utilization.* Washington, DC: National Academy Press.

National Research Council. (2001). *Knowing what students know: The science and design of educational assessment.* Washington, DC: National Academy Press.

National Research Council. (2002). *Reporting test results for students with disabilities and English-language learners: Summary of a workshop.* Washington, DC: National Academy Press.

Nelson, K., Skwerer, D., Goldman, S., Henseler, S., Presler, N., & Walkenfeld, F. F. (2003). Entering a community of minds: An experiential approach to "theory of mind." *Human Development, 46,* 24–46.

No Child Left Behind Act of 2001, Pub. L. No. 107–110.

Ortiz, A. A. (2002). Prevention of school failure and early intervention for English language learners. In A. J. Artiles & A. A. Ortiz (Eds.), *English language learners with special education needs: Identification, assessment, and instruction* (pp. 31–48). McHenry, IL: Center for Applied Linguistics and Delta Systems Company.

President's Commission on Excellence in Special Education. (2002, July). *A new era: Revitalizing special education for children and their families.* Retrieved July 12, 2002 from, *http://www.ed.gov/inits/commissionsboards/whspecialeducation/index.html*

Pressley, M. (2001). *Effective beginning reading instruction.* Executive summary and paper commissioned by the National Reading Conference. Chicago: National Reading Conference. Retrieved February 16, 2003, from *http://nrc.oakland.edu*

Reckase, M. (2002, February 13). *Using NAEP to confirm state test results: An analysis of issues.* Paper presented at the 2002 conference Will No Child Truly Be Left Behind?: The Challenges of Making the Law Work, sponsored by the Thomas B. Fordham Foundation. Retrieved May 9, 2003, from *http://www.edexcellence.net/nclbconference/nclbconferenceindex.html*

Roby, R. R., & Schultz, M. C. (1998). A model for conducting clinical outcome research: An adaptation of the standard protocol for use in aphasiology. *Aphasiology, 12,* 787–810.

Scarborough, H. S. (1998). Early identification of children at risk for reading disabilities: Phonological awareness and some other promising predictors. In B. K. Shapiro, P. J. Accardo, & A. J. Capute (Eds.), *Specific reading disability: A view of the spectrum* (pp. 75–119). Timonium, MD: York Press.

Schecter, S. R., Solomon, P., & Kittmer, L. (2003). Integrating teacher education in a community-situated school agenda. In S. R. Schecter & J. Cummins (Eds.), *Multilingual education in practice: Using diversity as a resource* (pp. 81–96). Portsmouth, NH: Heinemann.

Sebastián, E. & Slobin, D. (1994). Development of linguistic forms: Spanish. In R. A. Berman & D. I. Slobin (Eds.), *Relating events in narrative: A crosslinguistic developmental study* (pp. 239–284). Hillsdale, NJ: Erlbaum.

Shadish, W. R., Cook, T. D., & Campbell, D. T. (2002). *Experimental and quasi-experimental designs for generalized causal inference.* Boston: Houghton Mifflin.

Shaywitz, S. E., Shaywitz, B. A., Fulbright, R. K., Skudlarski, P., Mencl, W. E., Constable, R. T., et al. (2003). Neural systems for compensation and persistence: Young adult outcome of childhood reading disability. *Biological Psychiatry, 54,* 25–33

Shonkoff, J. P., & Phillips, D. A. (2000). *From neurons to neighborhoods: The science of early childhood development.* Washington, DC: National Academy Press.

Silliman, E. R., Bahr, R. H., Beasman, J., & Wilkinson, L. C. (2000). Scaffolds for learning to read in an inclusion classroom. *Language, Speech, and Hearing Services in Schools, 31,* 265–279.

Silliman, E. R., Bahr, R. H., Wilkinson, L. C., & Turner, C. R. (2002). Language variation and struggling readers: Finding patterns in diversity. In K. G. Butler & E. R. Silliman (Eds.), *Speaking, reading, and writing in children with language learning disabilities* (pp. 109–148). Mahwah, NJ: Erlbaum.

Silliman, E. R., Ford, C. S., Beasman, J., & Evans, D. (1999). An inclusion model for children with language learning disabilities: Building classroom partnerships. *Topics in Language Disorders, 19*(3), 1–18.

Snow, C. E., Burns, M. S., & Griffin, P. (Eds.). (1998). *Preventing reading difficulties in young children.* Washington, DC: National Academy Press.

Speece, D. L., & Case, L. P. (2001). Classification in context: An alternate approach to identifying early reading disability. *Journal of Educational Psychology, 93,* 735–749.

Speece, D. L., Case, L. P., & Molloy, D. E. (2003). Responsiveness to general education instruction as the first gate to learning disabilities identification. *Learning Disabilities Research and Practice, 18,* 147–156.

Speece, D. L., MacDonald, V., Kilsheimer, L., & Krist, J. (1997). Research to practice: Preservice teachers reflect on reciprocal teaching. *Learning Disabilities Research and Practice, 12,* 177–187.

Stanovich, K. E. (2003). Understanding the styles of science in the study of reading. *Scientific Studies of Reading, 7,* 105–126.

Stone, C. A. (1996). Bridging the gap between qualitative and quantitative approaches to the analysis of instructional innovations for students with learning disabilities: A commentary on Gallimore and Lyon. In D. L. Speece & B. K. Keogh (Eds.), *Research on classroom ecologies: Implications for inclusion of children with learning disabilities* (pp. 251–260). Mahwah, NJ: Erlbaum.

Stone, C. A. (1998). Moving validated instructional practices into the classroom: Learning from examples about the rough road to success. *Learning Disabilities Research and Practice, 31,* 121–125.

Strickland, D. S. (2001). Early intervention for African American children considered to be at risk. In S. B. Neuman & D. K. Dickinson (Eds.), *Handbook of early literacy research* (pp. 322–347). New York: Guilford Press.

Strickland, D., Snow, C., Griffin, P., Burns, S. M., & McNamara, P. (2002). *Preparing our teachers: Opportunities for better reading instruction.* Washington, DC: Joseph Henry Press.

Tabors, P. O., Snow, C. E., & Dickinson, D. K. (2001). Home and schools together: Supporting language and literacy development. In D. K. Dickinson & P. O. Tabors (Eds.), *Beginning literacy with language* (pp. 313–334). Baltimore: Brookes.

Thal, D. J., & Katich, J. (1996). Predicaments in early identification of specific language impairment: Does the early bird always catch the worm? In K. N. Cole, P. S. Dale, & D. J. Thal (Eds.), *Assessment of communication and language* (vol. 6) (pp. 1–28). Baltimore, MD: Paul H. Brookes.

The Business Roundtable. (2003, July 2). *The Business Roundtable releases poll that reveals parents and voters support No Child Left Behind reporting requirements.* Retrieved July 3, 2002, from *http://www.brt.org*

Torgesen, J. K., Alexander, A. W., Wagner, R. K., Rashotte, C. A., Voeller, K. K. S., & Conway, T. (2001). Intensive remedial instruction for children with severe reading disabilities: Immediate and long-term outcomes from two instructional approaches. *Journal of Learning Disabilities, 34,* 33–58, 78.

Torgesen, J. K., & Mathes, P. G. (2000). *A basic guide to understanding, assessing, and teaching phonological awareness.* Austin, TX: Pro-Ed.

Treiman, R., Tincoff, R., & Richmond-Welty, E. D. (1997). Beyond zebra: Preschoolers' knowledge about letters. *Applied Psycholinguistics, 18,* 391–409.

Treiman, R., Tincoff, R., Rodriguez, K., Mouzaki, A., & Francis, D. J. (1998). The foundations of literacy: Learning the sounds of letters. *Child Development, 69,* 1524–1540.

U.S. Department of Education. (2002). *The No Child Left Behind Act of 2001: Executive summary.* Retrieved May 30, 2003, from *http://www.ed.gov/offices/oese/esea/exec-summ.html*

U.S. Department of Education, National Center for Education Statistics. (2001a). *Entering kindergarten: A portrait of American children when they begin school* (NCES 2001-035). Retrieved February 1, 2001, from *http://nces.ed.gov*

U.S. Department of Education, National Center for Education Statistics. (2001b). *The nation's report card: Fourth grade reading 2000* (NCES 2001–499). Retrieved April 3, 2001, from *http://nces.ed.gov*

U.S. Department of Education, National Center for Education Statistics. (2001c). *Characteristics of the 100 largest public elementary and secondary school districts in the United States: 1999–2000.* Retrieved May 15, 2003, from *http://nces.ed.gov*

U.S. Department of Education, National Center for Education Statistics. (2002). *Children's reading and mathematics achievement in kindergarten and first grade* (NCES, 2002–125). Retrieved May 13, 2002, from *http://nces.ed.gov*

U.S. Department of Education, National Center for Education Statistics. (2003a). *Status and trends in the education of Hispanics* (NCES 2003-008). Retrieved April 15, 2003, from *http://nces.ed.gov*

U.S. Department of Education, National Center for Education Statistics. (2003b). *The condition of education 2003* (NCES, 2003-067). Retrieved May 29, 2003, from *http://nces.ed.gov*

U.S. Department of Education, National Center for Education Statistics. (2003c). *An agenda for NAEP validity research* (NCES–2003-07). Retrieved May 29, 2003, from *http://nces.ed.gov*

U.S. Department of Education, National Center for Education Statistics. (2003d). *The nation's report card: Reading 2002* (NCES 2003–521). Retrieved June 20, 2003, from *http://nces.ed.gov*

U.S. Department of Education, Office of Special Education Programs. (2002, August). *Twenty-third annual report to Congress on the implementation of the Individuals with Disabilities Education Act.* Retrieved August 18, 2002, from *http://www.ed.gov/offices/osers/osep*

U.S. Department of Education, Office of Special Education Programs. (2003, September). *Twenty-fourth annual report to Congress on the implementation of the Individuals with Disabilities Act.* Retrieved September 25, 2003, from *http://www.ed.gov/about/reports/annual/osep/ 2002/index.html*

Valentine, J. C., & Cooper, H. (2003). *What Works Clearinghouse Design and Implementation Assessment Device* (version 0. 6). Washington, DC: US Department of Education. Retrieved May 13, 2003, from *http://w-w-c.org*

van Kleeck, A. (2003). Research on book sharing: Another critical look. In A. van Kleeck, S. A. Stahl, & E. B. Bauer (Eds.), *On reading books to children: Parents and teachers* (pp. 271–320). Mahwah, NJ: Erlbaum.

Vellutino, F. R., & Scanlon, D. M. (2002). The interactive strategies approach to reading intervention. *Contemporary Educational Psychology, 27,* 573–635.

Waite, M. (2003, July 6). All FCAT A's are not created equally. *St. Petersburg* [FL] *Times,* pp. 1A, 12A.

What Works Clearinghouse. (2003). *Evidence report topics—interventions for elementary school English language learners: Increasing English language acquisition and academic achievement.* Retrieved July 6, 2003, from *http://w-w-c.org/topic7.html*

Wilkinson, L. C., & Silliman, E. R. (2000). Classroom language and literacy learning. In M. L. Kamil, P. B. Mosenthal, P. D. Pearson, & R. Barr (Eds.), *Handbook of reading research* (Vol. III, pp. 337–360). Mahwah, NJ: Erlbaum.

Wong Fillmore, L., & Snow, C. E. (2000). *What teachers need to know about language* (ERIC Clearinghouse on Language and Linguistics). Retrieved May 9, 2003, from *http://www.cal.org/ericcll/teachers/teachers.pdf*

Yan, Z., & Fischer, K. (2002). Always under construction: Dynamic variations in adult cognitive microdevelopment. *Human Development, 45,* 141–160.

7

Social and Affective Factors in Children with Language Impairment

Implications for Literacy Learning

BONNIE BRINTON

MARTIN FUJIKI

Cody, a happy, outgoing, enthusiastic 4-year-old who enjoyed people, especially liked being with his family and playing with his three older brothers and baby sister. Many of his extended family members lived close by, and he frequently interacted with his grandparents, aunts, uncles, and cousins. Cody's mother nursed a growing concern about him, however. Cody had been slow to learn to talk, and he still did not express himself well. He spoke in short, simple sentences and often lacked the words to convey his thoughts. Although he was alert to visual information, he frequently did not seem to understand what his parents asked him to do. Cody's parents made it a point to immerse him in activities that were rich with language and print. They asked Cody questions about interesting things that went on around him. Cody usually did not respond appropriately to these questions, so his parents rephrased their questions again and again, into strings of requests that Cody seemed to avoid answering. The resulting interaction was strained and labored. Cody's mother tried to share books with him regularly, as she had done with her other boys. As she read the text, Cody became impa-

tient, turned the pages quickly, and squirmed to get away. Cody's mother felt that it was very important to read with him, and she was puzzled and worried that he disliked and avoided book-sharing activities. She made arrangements to have Cody evaluated at a center that specialized in neurodevelopmental disorders.

A team of specialists concurred that Cody had language impairment (LI)[1]. Team members explained that despite Cody's normal nonverbal IQ, his communication skill and academic performance would be jeopardized because of his impairment. Cody's parents pursued treatment immediately to provide support in these areas. As Cody matured, however, they found that his difficulty communicating and his struggles in school were only the beginning. Cody's impairment seemed to spread into other domains as well. Despite the fact that Cody was gregarious and enthusiastic, he had difficulty interacting with his peers, participating in cooperative play and work groups, and making friends. Each week seemed to bring a new academic or social problem. Cody's parents sometimes felt like they were playing an arcade game, where one smacks a monster with a mallet when it pops out of its hole. As soon as one monster is hit, others pop up in quick, unpredictable succession.

LANGUAGE IMPAIRMENT AND SOCIAL DIFFICULTY

If Cody's parents had picked up a textbook describing LI, they might have concluded that Cody's impairment would be isolated to realms directly influenced by his difficulty understanding and manipulating grammatical structures, and by the sluggish pace at which he acquired new words. They would have expected Cody's deficit with oral language to manifest itself in reading and writing as he began school. (In fact, they could already see Cody's LI manifest in his aversion to literacy activities.) From their reading, however, they would not have guessed that Cody's social difficulties would constitute a major factor influencing the way he experienced life at home, at school, and in his community.

Cody is not an unusual case. Recent research has demonstrated that children with LI are at risk for a variety of social problems. In one sense, an association between LI and social difficulties seems obvious. Language is most often used in social contexts, and most social interactions are carried out using oral or written language. Surely, impaired language ability could undermine social encounters. The relationship between LI and social competence cannot be characterized by a simple causal model, however. For one thing, LI does not always lead to social problems. Even though many children with LI demonstrate social difficulties, some of these individuals do well socially. In addition, children with LI frequently demonstrate social problems that are not easily attributed solely to their linguistic deficits (Bishop, 1997; Brinton, Fujiki, & Higbee, 1998; Farmer, 2000; Fujiki, Brinton, Morgan, & Hart, 1999). Many factors are associated with social difficulties. Some of these are intrinsic, such as LI. Others are extrinsic, such as the marital relationship of parents and parenting style (see Hart, Olsen, Robinson, & Mandleco, 1997, for review). It is difficult to explain

the interactional problems of children with LI, because we do not fully understand all of the factors that influence their social competence. It is evident, however, that language ability and social functioning are mutually influential entities that intertwine in complex ways early in development. For example, delays in language development and socialization are associated as early as age 2 (Paul, Looney, & Dahm, 1991). As Westby (1999) suggested, language and socioemotional problems "are so interactive that the cause and effect are not clear" (p. 181).

Managing the social aspects of LI may be as important as managing the linguistic deficits. The following discussion highlights some of the social factors that are particularly important in children with LI. We first focus on two aspects of social behavior that have been highlighted in the literature on these children: withdrawal and sociability. We then discuss some of the potential outcomes of negative social behavior, specifically examining friendship and peer acceptance. The studies cited that focus on the social skills of children with LI are summarized in Table 7.1 to provide extra detail, as well as to help the reader organize the work cited. We also consider how these social behaviors and outcomes are related to the acquisition of literacy. Particular attention is directed to how these factors may limit access to important literacy learning contexts and experiences, and how preferences and self-perceptions may restrict motivational processes and thus influence literacy. Finally, we return to Cody's case to illustrate how many of the issues that we have discussed have played out in his life. The discussion of Cody's case leads us to question traditional ideas about the nature of LI and to suggest directions for further research.

WITHDRAWAL AND LANGUAGE IMPAIRMENT

Withdrawal and aggression are the two most frequently discussed categories of problematic behavior in the child psychology literature. Although there are case study reports of aggressive behaviors in individual children with LI (e.g., Brinton, Fujiki, Mon-

TABLE 7.1. Summary of Cited Studies of the Social Competence of Children with Language Impairment

Researchers	Participants	What was done	Results
Paul, Looney, & Dahm (1991)	21 late talkers and 21 typically developing children, studied at ages 2 and then 3 years	Compared on the Vineland Adaptive Behavior Scales between the ages of 18 and 34 months and then again at about age 3	Initial evaluation showed that late talkers had significantly poorer scores on expressive language, receptive language, and socialization. Follow-up study revealed that about half of the late talkers still showed deficits in expressive language and socialization. One third remained delayed in receptive language.
Rice, Sell, & Hadley (1991)	26 preschoolers, ages 39–67 months: 9 typically developing, 6 language impaired (LI), 3 speech impaired (SI), 8 English as a Second Language (ESL); all children enrolled in the Language Acquisition Preschool (LAP)	Three rounds of observation in preschool setting, using the Social Interactive Coding System (SICS), an online coding system designed to capture conversational interactions	Typical children initiated interactions with each other, had a higher percentage of longer responses, preferred to address typical peers; children with limited communication abilities were more likely than their typical peers to initiate to adults and tended to shorten their responses or use nonverbal responses; ESL children were the least likely to initiate interactions and most likely to be avoided as a conversational partner.
Hadley & Rice (1991)	18 children enrolled in LAP: 4 LI, 4 SI; 4 marginal (previously classified as LI/SI but no longer qualified); 6 typical between ages 42 and 66 months	24 minutes of observational data (taken in 4-minute segments) during play time; data coded online (coding of responses to child's initiations)	Relative communication abilities influenced children's participation in social interactions. LI and SI children were ignored by peers and responded less often when peers initiated to them. Children with limited communication skills participated in fewer peer interactions than typical peers.
Craig & Washington (1993)	38 children ages 7–8: 5 with specific language impairment (SLI); 8 controls (4 age-matched, 4 language-matched to children with SLI); 25 children served as partners to the 13 participants (to form triads)	Described verbal and nonverbal attempts of children with SLI and their age- and language-matched peers to access ongoing interactions	Three children with SLI were unsuccessful in accessing the interaction. Two accessed the interaction, but without using typical linguistic forms. All typical children accessed the interactions.

TABLE 7.1. *Continued*

Researchers	Participants	What was done	Results
Grove, Conti-Ramsden, & Donlan (1993)	15 children with SLI, age 7; 15 same-age peers; 6 MLU-matched peers; all children interacted with another child from their class to form a dyad (SLI with SLI, etc.)	Interacting in dyads, children reviewed various toys and objects, and decided which ones their class would like, placing them in boxes labeled as happy, just OK, and sad; at the end of the session, the dyad chose a toy or object to play with	Dyads with children with SLI produced as many winning verbal moves as same-age peers, more than MLU peers. Dyads with SLI produced more non-verbal winning moves than same-age peers, but less than MLU peers (nonverbal winning moves were considered a less mature strategy than verbal moves).
Gertner, Rice, & Hadley (1994)	31 children in 3 groups: 9 typical (ND); 12 speech/language impaired (S/LI); 10 ESL	Two sociometric tasks to measure peer popularity: positive and negative nominations (children asked to select who they would/would not like to play with in a socio-dramatic play context)	ND group received most positive nominations; when nominations were combined to classify children as liked, disliked, low impact, or mixed, ND mostly in "liked," S/LI and ESL mostly in "disliked" or "low impact."
Stevens & Bliss (1995)	30 children with SLI and 30 typical children in grades 3–7	Two tasks: 1. Problem-solving activity in which an imaginary conflict scenario was presented and the child asked to give a solution 2. Role enactments of conflict situations	Children with SLI produced fewer strategies for problem-solving activity and used strategies at a lower developmental level in the hypothetical conflict task. Equal number of strategy types were used by both groups in role enactments.
Fujiki, Brinton, & Todd (1996)	19 children with SLI and 19 typical age-matched peers between 8 and 12 years of age	Compared groups on the Social Skills Rating System—Teacher Form, the Williams and Asher loneliness questionnaire, and an informal task estimating amount of peer interaction	Typical peers performed significantly below children with SLI on all three measures.
Guralnick, Connor, Hammond, Gottman, & Kinnish (1996)	36 typical, 36 boys with conduct disorder (CD), 4 to 5 years old, placed in 12 play groups, 6 boys per group	Peer sociometric ratings; videotaped recordings of each child analyzed for (1) global measures of social participation and cognitive play (Parten's [1932] index of social participation with some modifications), and (2) individual social behaviors (Individual Social Behavior Scale)	All children equally accepted on peer sociometric ratings, but children with CD were less socially integrated in play groups. Similar competencies between typical children and children with CD in ability to sustain group play, minimize conflict, join others in ongoing activities, and respond to social bids of others. Differences between groups on overall social activity: Group with CD engaged in fewer positive social interactions, conversed with peers less during nonplay activities, less successful with social bids, less directive with peers. *(continued)*

TABLE 7.1. *Continued*

Researchers	Participants	What was done	Results
Fujiki, Brinton, Robinson, & Watson (1997)	6 children with SLI (ages 8 years, 10 months to 12 years, 5 months), 6 chronological-age-similar (CA) peers, 6 language-similar (LS) peers (mean age of LS group was 6 years, 7 months); 36 children used as "partners" to form triads with each of the 18 children in the groups listed above	Children participated in a group negotiation task in which they worked with 2 partners to select toys their class would like	Children with SLI talked less than their partners and were talked to less by their partners in triadic interactions. Similar differences were not observed in the triads involving the CA or LS peers.
Brinton, Fujiki, Spencer, & Robinson (1997)	6 children with SLI (ages 8 years, 10 months to 12 years, 5 months), 6 CA peers, 6 LS peers; 36 children used as partners to form triads with each of the 18 children in the groups listed above	Observed ability of children to access ongoing dyadic interactions. Observed interactions of triad if access was achieved	Two children with SLI did not access the dyadic interaction; 4 needed varying amounts of time to access. All typical children achieved access. Even after access had been achieved, children with SLI talked less, were talked to less, and collaborated less than others in the triad.
Brinton, Fujiki, & McKee (1998)	Target participants: 6 children with SLI (ages 8 years, 10 months to 12 years, 5 months), 6 age-matched peers, 6 language-matched peers; Partners: 36 children used to form triads with each of the 18 children in the groups listed above	Observed ability of children to participate in a negotiation task (selecting a treat for the triad to share) with 2 same-age peers	No difference in number of utterances produced by SLI or typical peers. Children with SLI produced smaller percentage of negotiation strategies produced by their triad than was observed in triads involving controls. Children with SLI used developmentally lower level strategies than typical peers.
Brinton, Fujiki, & Higbee (1998)	Target participants: 6 children with SLI (ages 8 years, 10 months to 12 years, 5 months), 6 age-matched peers, 6 language-matched peers; Partners: 36 children used to form triads with each of the 18 children in the groups listed above	Target subject worked with 2 partners (same age and gender) to build cardboard periscope in cooperative work groups. Verbal and nonverbal collaborative actions were analyzed	Children with SLI played very minor roles in collaborative work; verbal and nonverbal contributions were minimal; and they performed less specialized tasks than typical partners.
Redmond & Rice (1998)	17 children with SLI and 20 typical age-matched peers, studied at ages 6 and 7 years	Administered the Child Behavior Checklist (CBCL) and Teacher's Report Form (TRF) to parents and teachers for children at ages 6 and 7 years	Teachers, but not parents, rated children with SLI as having more social and internalizing behavioral problems than typical peers.

TABLE 7.1. *Continued*

Researchers	Participants	What was done	Results
Fujiki, Brinton, Hart, & Fitzgerald (1999)	8 children with SLI, ages 6–10 years	Children in classes containing a child with SLI were asked to rate how much they liked to play with each child in the class; also asked to list their 3 best friends in the class	Although results were somewhat variable, children with SLI tended to be rated lower than peers in both friendship and acceptance.
Fujiki, Brinton, Morgan, & Hart (1999)	41 children with LI, 41 typical age- and gender-matched peers	Administered Teacher Behavior Rating Scale (TBRS) to assess subtypes of withdrawn and sociable behavior	Children with LI were rated as significantly more reticent than peers by teachers. Boys with LI were rated as demonstrating more solitary–active withdrawal. Children with LI rated significantly below typical peers on both subtypes of sociable behavior.
Farmer (2000)	4 groups, 8 children per group, ages 10–11 years: children with SLI at a special school; children with SLI in a language unit at mainstream school; typical CA matches; typical language–age matches	Administered several language tests and measures of social cognition	Children with SLI in the special school setting performed more poorly than typical children and children with SLI in the mainstream setting on several of the social cognitive tasks.
Tomblin, Zhang, Buckwalter, & Catts (2000)	581 second graders (164 children with LI)	Language, reading, and behavior measured with a variety of tests	Children with LI at greater risk for reading and behavior problems than peers; risk for reading problems greater than risk for behavior problems; risk for behavior problems appeared dependent on reading ability of the child with LI.
Brinton, Fujiki, Montague & Hanton (2000)	6 children with LI; 48 typical age-matched peers	Children with LI participated in 4 different cooperative work groups, with 2 typical peers in each group. Evaluated children's ability to participate and work with the group. Social profiles for children with LI obtained using the TBRS	The social profile of the children with LI was a good predictor of the children's ability to interact with typical peers.
Fujiki, Brinton, Isaacson, & Summers (2001)	8 children with LI; 8 typical age-matched peers	Participants videotaped on playground over time for a total of 1 hour. Playground behavior coded in 5-second segments	Typical children spent more time interacting with peers than LI children. LI children showed more withdrawn behaviors than typical peers.

(continued)

TABLE 7.1. *Continued*

Researchers	Participants	What was done	Results
Redmond & Rice (2002)	12 children with SLI; 17 typical children (8-year-olds); children originally recruited for longitudinal study at age 5	Parents and teachers filled out the Child Behavior Checklist (CBCL) and Teacher Report Form (TRF); compared with earlier reports on same children	Teacher and parent reports drew nearer to reaching consensus over time (with the exception of subcategory of Social Problems). Teachers reported fewer behavior problems over early elementary period.
Jerome, Fujiki, Brinton, & James (2002)	Young group: 23 children with SLI, ages 6–9; 23 typical age-matched. Older group: 17 children with SLI, ages 10–13; 17 typical, age-matched	Self-esteem measured using the Pictorial Scale of Perceived Competence and Social Acceptance for Young Children with the younger group, and the Self-Perception Profile for Children with the older group	Differences were not found in the way younger children with and without SLI perceived themselves. In the older groups, differences were found in scholastic competence, social acceptance, and behavioral conduct. In each comparison, children with SLI perceived themselves more negatively.

tague, & Hanton, 2000), group studies of the social behavior of children with LI have generally not identified high levels of aggression in comparison to typically developing peers (one exception is the Tomblin, Zhang, Buckwalter, and Catts [2000] study, showing that parents rated second graders with LI as demonstrating externalizing behavior, which may include aggressive behaviors). Withdrawal, however, is a different story. The results of a number of recent investigations suggest that children identified with LI show patterns of withdrawn behavior in school contexts. To understand what the results of these studies mean, it is important to consider the nature and consequences of withdrawn behavior.

Withdrawal Defined

"Withdrawal" is defined in many ways, but it is most useful to consider withdrawal as solitude or "the act of being alone" (Rubin & Asendorpf, 1993, p. 11). Withdrawal can thus be distinguished from peer neglect, rejection, or isolation (Rubin & Asendorpf, 1993). Several subtypes of solitude result in different social consequences (Coplan & Rubin, 1998; Coplan, Rubin, Fox, Calkins, & Stewart, 1994; Harrist, Zaia, Bates, Dodge,

& Pettit, 1997; Rubin, 1982). For example, one subtype of withdrawal is referred to as solitary–passive withdrawal (Coplan & Rubin, 1998), passive withdrawal (Rubin & Asendorpf, 1993), or unsociable behavior (Harrist, et al., 1997). Solitary–passive withdrawal is characterized by playing or working alone in constructive activities. In early and middle childhood, peers may view solitary–passive withdrawal negatively (Younger & Daniels, 1992), but teachers and parents may not be particularly concerned if children prefer playing alone.

Although solitary–passive withdrawal seems relatively benign, solitary–active withdrawal tends to appear more bizarre and is associated with active exclusion by peers (Harrist et al., 1997). Solitary–active withdrawal is "characterized by repeated sensorimotor action with or without objects and/or . . . solitary dramatizing" (Coplan et al., 1994, p. 130). For example, a group of children might dramatize cleaning the house and acting out several activities together. A child might demonstrate solitary–active withdrawal by enacting a vacuuming scenario in the midst of, but not with, the other children. Solitary–active withdrawal does not occur often in free play, but when it does, it is highly noticeable and invites peer rejection (Coplan et al., 1994). In addition, solitary–active withdrawal is associated with impulsivity and aggression (Rubin, 1982; Rubin & Mills, 1988).

A third type of withdrawal, reticence (Asendorpf, 1991; Coplan & Rubin, 1998), or passive–anxious withdrawal (Harrist et al., 1997), occurs when children would like to interact with others but are fearful of doing so. Reticent behavior may occur when a child would like both to approach and to avoid a play group (Asendorpf, 1991). Reticent children tend to spend time watching other children play or wandering about doing nothing. They are wary of new social situations (Rubin & Asendorpf, 1993).

Rating Scale Measures of Withdrawn Behavior

General probes using behavioral rating scales have suggested that children with LI demonstrate more withdrawn behavior at school than do their typically developing peers. For example, Redmond and Rice (1998) investigated a number of socioemotional behaviors in children with specific language impairment (SLI) and typically developing children, using the Child Behavior Checklist (CBCL; Achenbach, 1991a) and the Teacher Report Form (TRF; Achenbach, 1991b) to produce parent and teacher ratings, respectively. Ratings were obtained when the children were 6 and 7 years old. Redmond and Rice (1998) found that teachers reported higher levels of several clinical behaviors, including withdrawal. Parents did not report the same observations, however, suggesting that either the teachers and parents had different expectations for the children in comparison to their typically developing peers or the children's withdrawn behavior was limited to the school setting. It should be noted that although the children with SLI were rated differently than were their typically developing peers, they were not always rated low enough to fall within the clinical range established for the measures. This may stem from the fact that the CBCL and the TRF are designed to identify children with marked psychiatric problems. As such, they are less sensitive to milder manifestations of socioemotional or behav-

ioral difficulties (Merrell, 1999). It might also be noted that children with LI who produce scores low enough to fall into the clinical range would most likely wear a label of behavior disorder and be excluded from the subject pool.

Although global measures of withdrawn behavior are valuable, they do not provide information on specific types of withdrawn behavior. It is possible that children with LI might prefer solitude but spend that time positively engaged. In order to further clarify the nature of withdrawn behavior in children with LI, Fujiki, Brinton, Morgan, et al. (1999) administered the Teacher Behavioral Rating Scale (TBRS; Hart & Robinson, 1996) to the teachers of elementary school-children with LI and their typical peers. The TBRS is an informal measure designed to describe subtypes of withdrawn behavior, including solitary–active withdrawal, reticence, and solitary–passive withdrawal. Fujiki, Brinton, Morgan, et al. (1999) found that boys demonstrated more solitary–passive behavior than did girls, but LI was not a distinguishing factor; that is, teachers reported that boys (with or without LI) engaged in constructive, solitary activity more often than did girls. This difference had little to do with LI, but could probably be attributed to the less affiliative nature of boys in general (Grusec & Lytton, 1988).

When Fujiki, Brinton, Morgan, et al. (1999) considered solitary–active withdrawal and reticence, a very different profile emerged. Teachers reported that boys with LI demonstrated significantly more solitary–active withdrawal than did girls with LI, or typically developing boys or girls. Ten of the 23 boys with LI reportedly demonstrated solitary–active withdrawal. Considering that solitary–active withdrawal is a fairly rare behavior in children (Coplan et al., 1994), its occurrence in so many of the boys with LI was remarkable. Teachers also reported significantly more reticence in children with LI in comparison to their peers. Differences between children with LI and typically developing children were quite dramatic, because teachers reported that most of the children with LI wanted to interact with their peers but were often too anxious or fearful to do so.

Observational Measures of Withdrawal

Teacher reports are efficient and practical measures, but they also have obvious drawbacks, including potential bias. For this reason, Fujiki, Brinton, Isaacson, and Summers (2001) observed 8 children with LI and their typically developing peers as they interacted on the playground at recess. The results were reminiscent of the studies using teacher reports. Children with LI demonstrated withdrawn behaviors during 42% of their recess time compared to 17% for typically developing children. In addition, children with LI were distinguished from their peers on the basis of reticence and solitary–active withdrawal, but not solitary–passive withdrawal. In other words, the children with LI did not retreat to play constructive solitary games. Rather, they wandered from play group to play group, watching the interactions but not entering in. Typical children rarely engaged in solitary–active withdrawal, but 6 of the 8 children with LI did. These behaviors were highly noticeable and socially penalizing.

Summary

In summary, general measures have indicated that children with LI demonstrate more withdrawn behaviors than do their typically developing peers, at least in school settings. More specific probes indicate that it is not the case that children with LI prefer playing or working alone at constructive activities. Rather, these children are reticent, anxious to interact with their peers but afraid to do so. In addition, some children with LI, particularly boys, may engage in solitary–active withdrawn behaviors that call negative attention to themselves and invite rejection from their peers. Situations designed to allow children to enjoy spontaneous play, such as recess, may be isolating experiences for children with LI.

SOCIABLE BEHAVIOR, INTERACTIONAL SKILL, AND LANGUAGE IMPAIRMENT

It is possible that children who spend a good deal of time alone might interact skillfully when they do associate with peers. Strong social-language skills could mediate the effects of withdrawal. On the other hand, children who spend a lot of time in solitary activity might interact ineptly when they mix with peers. In this case, withdrawn behavior would cause greater concern. Given that the impact of withdrawal on a child's social world may be tempered or exacerbated by other behaviors, patterns of withdrawn behavior are best studied in conjunction with more positive social characteristics, such as sociable behavior.

Sociable Behavior Defined

Sociable behavior (sometimes referred to as "sociability") is a dimension that encompasses a wide variety of positive, outgoing behaviors, such as sharing, cooperating, and offering comfort to others (Hart, Robinson, McNeilly, Nelson, & Olsen, 1995). Many, if not most, of the behaviors we tend to think of as social-language skills manifest sociability. Sociable behavior is particularly important because of its close association with positive peer relationships. Children who are well liked by their peers consistently demonstrate better sociability skills than do children who are not well liked (Coie, Dodge, & Kupersmidt, 1990; Ladd & Price, 1987).

There are various aspects of sociable behavior, but subtypes have not been as clearly defined as those for withdrawal. For purposes of our discussion, we first consider studies using teacher questionnaires to produce overall ratings of sociability. We then focus on studies in which children have been observed demonstrating sociability skills such as entering ongoing interactions, negotiating with others, and cooperating in group projects.

Rating Scale Measures of Sociable Behavior

Fujiki, Brinton, and Todd (1996) administered the Social Skills Rating System—Teacher Form (Gresham & Elliott, 1990) to 8- to 12-year-old children with SLI. These children were rated as having significantly poorer scores on the social skills domain than their typical peers. This domain included three subscales evaluating cooperating, assertion, and self-control. Many, but not all, of the specific questions making up this domain focused on sociable behaviors, such as making friends.

In a study described previously, Redmond and Rice (1998) administered the CBCL and the TRF to the parents and teachers, respectively, of children with SLI and their typically developing peers. Teachers rated the children with SLI as displaying higher levels of social problems than their typical peers. Parents did not rate the groups differently on any of the targeted behaviors. In a follow-up study, Redmond and Rice (2002) retested 12 of 37 of the children with SLI at age 8 years (previous testing took place at ages 6 and 7). In contrast with some of the other behaviors studied, social problem ratings remained relatively stable. Teachers continued to rate children with SLI significantly lower than the typical group. Parent ratings were also stable and continued to show little difference between groups.

Fujiki, Brinton, Morgan, et al. (1999) used the TBRS to probe two general aspects of sociable behavior, labeled as (1) prosocial and (2) impulse control/likability, in children with LI and their typically developing peers. The prosocial subscale included items examining whether children helped peers with problems, comforted others, and shared food or other items. The impulse control/likability scale focused on children's ability to control anger, receive criticism well, and cooperate in rough-and-tumble play. Teachers rated the children with LI significantly lower than typical peers on both subscales.

In a replication of this study, Hart, Fujiki, Brinton, & Hart (in press) asked a second group of teachers to rate children with LI and their typical peers. It was again found that children with LI were rated as having significantly poorer sociable skills than their typical peers. Furthermore, children with more severe receptive language problems appeared to have greater problems with sociability than did children with less severe receptive problems.

Observational Studies of Sociable Behavior

Group studies using teacher report measures have proven useful in providing an overview of the sociable behavior of children with LI. Generally, it can be concluded that teachers do not perceive that these children have strong enough sociable skills to compensate for their withdrawn behavior when they have the opportunity to engage their peers. Report measures have their limits, however, and are therefore not a substitute for observation of naturalistic behavior. Fortunately, there are a few studies in which investigators observed children with LI directly as they worked or played with their peers. These types of studies are cumbersome and laborious to conduct, because they can involve recording children in work or play scenarios, transcribing hours of taped interaction, and devising reliable analysis systems. It is not surprising that these investigations usually involve small numbers of participants. Nevertheless, the results across studies show a fair amount of consistency. Some of the specific sociable behaviors tapped include entering ongoing interactions, participating in group decision making, cooperating in group projects, and negotiating.

In order to become a part of ongoing play and work groups, children first need to be able to enter or gain access to those groups. As anyone who has ever entered a room full of strangers at a social gathering can attest, this can be a fairly daunting task. There is little doubt, however, that gaining access is an important skill for children to master in social development (Corsaro, 1981; Dodge, Schlundt, Schocken, & Delugach, 1983).

Getting into the Play

Craig and Washington (1993) observed children with SLI, typically developing children of the same age (CA), and typically developing children with similar language levels (LS) as they tried to join two other children who were playing with toys. Children in both the CA and LS groups gained access to the play easily, and most did so quickly. The children with SLI had much more difficulty. Three of the five children with SLI studied never gained access to the play during the 20-minute observation period. The two children with SLI who did enter the play used nonverbal contributions to do so.

Craig and Washington noted that the children who could not enter play in these relatively simple contexts would be even more likely to fail in complex situations, such as the classroom or the playground.

Brinton, Fujiki, Spencer, and Robinson (1997) extended Craig and Washington's (1993) work by observing 8- to 12-year-old children with SLI and their typically developing CA and LS (language-similar) matched peers participating in an access task. As in the Craig and Washington study, all the typically developing children entered the play, and most did so quickly. Four of the six children with SLI studied entered the play eventually, but one of these children later left the interaction to wander about the room. Two children with SLI did not enter the interaction at all within the 20-minute time period. On a personal note, observing children perform this and other, similar social tasks makes one appreciate their social problems in a way that questionnaires and rating scales cannot. In reflecting on the data analysis from this study, we remember that it was almost painful to watch the tapes. It is difficult to fully grasp how long 20 minutes is for a child to hover, watch, or wander while other children are playing together.

Staying with the Play

Gaining initial access to a group is only the starting point. In the interaction that follows, children must carve a place for themselves within the work or play. Children with LI tend to exist on the outskirts of group activity, occasionally joining in, but rarely influencing the direction of the play. For example, Rice, Sell, and Hadley (1991) and Hadley and Rice (1991) observed children in the language acquisition preschool at the University of Kansas, where children with speech and language impairment were integrated with children learning English as a second language (ESL), and children with typically developing language skills. Rice et al. (1991) observed that children with speech and language impairment tended to talk with adults rather than with peers. Hadley and Rice (1991) noted that these children did not respond to conversational bids from their peers and were in turn often ignored by their peers.

Guralnick, Connor, Hammond, Gottman, and Kinnish (1996) found that 4- and 5-year-olds with communicative impairments were less integrated into play groups than were typically developing children. Brinton et al. (1997) and Fujiki, Brinton, Robinson, and Watson (1997) found that elementary school-age children with SLI who worked in triads with typically developing peers rarely became full participants. With few exceptions, they talked less and were talked to less than typically developing children.

There is also evidence that children with LI are at a disadvantage when groups need to resolve conflicts, make group decisions, or negotiate compromises. Stevens and Bliss (1995) found that children with SLI used fewer types of strategies than did typically developing children in a hypothetical conflict resolution task.

Grove, Conti-Ramsden, and Donlan (1993) found that dyads of children with SLI showed less mature joint decision making than did their age-matched peers. Brinton, Fujiki, and McKee (1998) observed children with SLI engaged with two other, typical children in a "high stakes" negotiation for candy. For the most part, children with SLI demonstrated sparse, immature negotiation strategies. Usually, a triad containing a child with SLI became a dyad in which two typical children negotiated a decision together, while the child with SLI supplied comments that were largely ignored.

Perhaps children with LI struggle so to become integrated with peers in work and play because their verbal communication is limited as a consequence of their impairment. We wondered what would happen if we could even the playing field somewhat for children with LI in terms of language demand. If children with LI could interact in a way that would not require so much language, could they find a place within group activity? Brinton, Fujiki, and Higbee (1998) observed 8- to 12-year-old children with SLI as they interacted with two typically developing peers in a cooperative work task. The task, building a periscope out of a shoebox, involved multiple subtasks, none of which was dependent on verbal interaction. Analysis focused on the verbal and nonverbal collaborative behavior of each child. The interaction of 6 children with SLI within their triads was considered in light of the interaction observed in triads containing only typically developing children. Triads consisting of typically developing children generally maintained a collaborative, balanced, interaction as the children worked together to build a periscope. In contrast, children with SLI were much less involved within their triads. Interestingly enough, they did better verbally than they did nonverbally. All of the children with SLI talked about the joint project, but 3 of the 6 children never contributed to the physical task of building the periscope at all. Two others did so only minimally. The children with SLI did not compensate for their language deficits by choosing nonverbal tasks. In fact, they tended to avoid them.

Realizing the possibility that "students who are perceived to be less skillful are ignored by other group members" (Slavin, 1995, p. 19), Brinton et al. (2000) decided to even the playing field a little more. We observed young elementary school-age children with LI as they interacted in four different triads completing four different cooperative tasks. Here, again, the tasks were highly visual, with many subtasks. In three of these four interactions, each child was assigned a specific role (e.g., a materials manager). This way, the child with LI in each triad would have something specific to do that would require little verbal skill. There was great variability in the triads. Some were quite collaborative, but most were not. Neither the assignment of roles nor the types of tasks assigned seemed to affect how well the children with LI collaborated with their peers. Rather, the social and behavioral profiles, as reported by their teachers, predicted performance. In other words, even when we tried to limit the effect of LI on the collaborative task, most of the children with LI either disrupted or withdrew from group work. Because the children with the lowest language test scores did not necessarily demonstrate the poorest social functioning, it seemed clear that LI was only part of the problem. Social abilities determined the nature of the group interactions.

Summary

Teacher reports and observational studies suggest that most children with LI show weak sociability skills in spontaneous and structured school activities. There is no reason to believe that the withdrawal prevalent in this population is mitigated by strong sociable behavior when children with LI do have the opportunity to interact with peers. One cannot help but wonder how these patterns of introverted behavior affect peer relationships, especially when they combine with poor communication skills. Speech–language pathologists and teachers who work with children with LI have long expressed concern about how these children fit in the social fabric of the classroom. One does not have to practice in a school setting long to hear peers label these children as "weird," "doofus," "boof," or whatever other epithet is currently fashionable. Many teachers have expressed concern that children with LI have few, if any, close friends. A few studies have investigated peer acceptance and friendship, and most have corroborated this clinical experience, as we see in the next section.

ACCEPTANCE AND FRIENDSHIP

Acceptance

Peer acceptance reflects a child's popularity with peers (Asher, Parker, & Walker, 1996; Doll, 1996). Acceptance reflects how peers view a child and how much they like to spend time with that child. A child's acceptance in a classroom is not dramatically altered by the changing opinion of one or two classmates, because it is a more general, group measure. Acceptance is influenced by a child's sociable behavior (Gottman, Gonso, & Rasmussen, 1975; Ladd, 1981) and by a variety of personal attributes, including personality and attractiveness (Young & Cooper, 1944). Acceptance, then, provides a general barometer of how peers feel about a child. It is often measured by asking classmates how much they like to interact with each of their peers. Gertner, Rice, and Hadley (1994) used a task in which children named classmates with whom they would like to interact and class-mates with whom they would not like to interact in sociodramatic play. They found that typically developing children were named as desired playmates most often. Children with LI, or with limited English ability, tended to elicit neutral or negative judgments from their peers. Gertner et al. felt that peer acceptance was directly related to communication skill.

Fujiki, Brinton, Hart, and Fitzgerald (1999) probed peer acceptance in the classrooms of 8 children with LI. They found that 3 of the 8 children were rated more than 1 standard deviation below the mean for children in their classes. This is a lower rate of acceptance than we would expect to see in a group of 8 children, but there was considerable variability in the peer ratings. One child was highly rejected by her peers; another was one of the most popular girls in her class. Here, again, acceptance was not directly related to severity of language impairment.

Friendship

Friendship offers a child something more than acceptance and contributes substantially to a child's sense of well-being at school (Doll, 1996). It is a reciprocal proposition that requires mutual commitment (Asher & Gazelle, 1999; Asher et al., 1996). Friendship involves equality, cooperation, closeness, companionship, and support (Asher et al., 1996). Preliminary evidence suggests that children with LI have difficulty establishing and maintaining friendships. Fujiki, Brinton, Hart, et al. (1999) found that 5 of the 8 children with LI they studied were not named as a reciprocal friend by anyone in their classes. In contrast, typically developing children were almost always named as a friend by someone in their class. It caused us particular concern to note that, in some instances, children with LI named as friends classmates who did not even like to play with them. In other words, they did not have a friend, and they did not always realize that peers they considered to be their friends did not like them.

Difficulty in making friends at school may impoverish the social experience of children with LI. Fujiki et al. (1996) found that 8- to 12-year-old children with SLI reported more loneliness in school and fewer peers to "hang out" with outside of school than did typically developing children. It seems likely that these children, who could very much benefit from a supportive friend, are often unable to establish a reciprocal relationship. What is more, as they mature, they may become painfully aware of their social status (Jerome, Fujiki, Brinton, & James, 2002).

In summary, acceptance and friendship reflect different aspects of a child's relationships with peers. Acceptance offers a child a measure of popularity, but friendship provides closeness, support, and camaraderie that can buffer the ups and downs of school life. Children with LI may or may not be well accepted by peers. Even those children who are accepted may have difficulty establishing and maintaining reciprocal friendships, however. The lack of supportive friendships can lead to isolation, loneliness, and exclusion from classroom activities.

LANGUAGE IMPAIRMENT, SOCIAL DIFFICULTIES, AND LITERACY PROBLEMS: BEDFELLOWS

Children with LI come to school with a different set of tools and experiences than do their typically developing peers. Obviously, their language deficits undermine their ability to perform many literacy tasks (Catts & Kamhi, 1999). Less apparent, but just as real, are the more subtle roadblocks to literacy associated with the social aspects of LI. Morrison and Cooney (2002) noted that there are "several pathways simultaneously influencing the growth of literacy skills in children" (p. 155). They explained that social skills such as cooperation and self-regulation form one path that shapes academic achievement in early childhood. In the following sections, we discuss some possible directions this path might take. For example, social difficulties associated with LI may limit access to many contexts in which literacy is most readily learned. In addition, preferences and self-perceptions associated with LI may restrict the motivational processes that help children persevere in the face of challenging literacy tasks.

"The Poor Get Poorer"

Literacy emerges within social contexts and transactions. There are many domains in which meaning is shared via print, including daily living, entertainment, religious, and schoolwork activities (Anderson & Stokes, 1984). Anything that interferes with a child's inclusion in the literacy activities and events within these domains may shift that child's place in the literate community. Children with LI may not enjoy traditional literacy events, however, and they may have a difficult time making sense of them. Because their language problems complicate literacy acquisition, children with LI need careful, repeated immersion in literacy activities that connect them with a wider literate community. Even though they need more exposure and experience in literacy activities than do most children, they are likely to get less. Over time, they may become further distanced from the literate community around them. Stanovich (1986) used the term "Matthew effects" to describe a negative spiral in which the educational environment encourages "the poor to get poorer."

There is evidence to suggest that children with disabilities are less involved in activities and contexts that are rich with literacy, even before they begin school. Parents report that many children with LI do not respond well to book sharing and other literacy activities. For example, Marvin and Wright (1997) surveyed the literacy practices of parents of over 300 children with special needs, including a subgroup of children with SLI. Parents of children with SLI watched television with their children (commenting on the program), told oral stories to their children, recited rhymes with their children, or engaged their children in finger plays, songs, or rhymes less frequently than did parents of children with other disabilities.

Schneider and Hecht (1995) observed mothers of children with disabilities and concluded that these mothers attempted to involve their children in book sharing by gearing their input to the level of their children's responsiveness. Still, mothers took on more responsibility for book sharing, devoting more effort to orienting their children, and less time to asking for input when their children were less engaged. Schneider and Hecht felt that the mothers made the most of their children's attention to the book-sharing activity. They also suggested, however, that the emergent literacy skills of children who were not easily engaged could be undermined by the nature of their experiences in book-sharing interactions. These studies imply that parents may make special efforts to provide literacy experiences for their children with LI, but too often these experiences do not seem natural or pleasant. As a result, these literacy activities may not teach children that print can be entertaining and connect them with their families and communities. This occurs even in families that are committed to providing print activities for their children. The problem may be compounded in culturally diverse families that may not stress literacy in the traditional sense.

When children with LI enter school, their access to literacy activities may be influenced by their social functioning. In preschool, effective literacy instruction is often embedded within social interactions. For example, Rowe (1989) observed a preschool classroom over an 8-month period and described the nature of social interaction in literacy acquisition. She found that "social interaction was an integral part of literacy events in this classroom and that it played an important role in children's literacy learning" (p. 343). Rowe concluded that social interaction provided the means through which children expressed their comprehension of text meaning, learned to appreciate another's perspective, and adjusted their understanding according to input from others.

A number of the factors discussed previously could deny access to children with LI to group conversations that facilitate important literacy processes. For example, consider Hadley and Rice's (1991) finding that preschool children with LI did not respond well to their peers' conversational bids and were ignored by their peers in conversation. Likewise, consider the finding that young children with LI were not well integrated into play groups (Guralnick et al., 1996), and that peers did not often designate children with LI as desirable playmates in sociodramatic play (Gertner et al., 1994). If these findings can be generalized to a wider population of preschoolers with LI, it is safe to assume that these children may not be full participants in play and work groups that constitute important literacy-learning contexts. They may not be able to join peers in acting out story events, talking about story characters, discussing classroom scripts, or working at writing centers. Here, again, these children with LI, who need the most immersion in literacy events, may get the least. Once again, the poor get poorer.

As children proceed through elementary school, they continue to construct literate communities within their classrooms. The nature of these communities varies according to a number of factors, including teachers' educational philosophies, instructional styles, and classroom procedures. Many teachers adopt cooperative learning models for their classrooms and encourage children to collaborate in reading and writing activities. For instance, Guice (1995) observed a sixth-grade classroom and reported that children interacted with, and sought advice from, their peers in myriad literacy activities. Despite classroom rules prohibiting most spontaneous conversations, the children were greatly influenced by their peer networks in the way that they evaluated and interpreted text. Some classrooms may be almost entirely organized around collaborative structures and tasks. Depending on their literacy skill level and social competence, children with LI may not attain full citizenship within the literate community of the classroom. Rather, they may exist as squatters or aliens (Kliewer, 1998), relegated to remedial groups where little is expected. In some cases, efforts to address LI with a pullout service delivery model may inadvertently distance a child from the literate community within the classroom. For example, in leaving the classroom for special services, a child with LI might miss out on activities in which children read together, select books, or discuss texts in structured or spontaneous contexts. Involving children with LI in full participation in the social-literacy fabric of the classroom may demand specific interventions (Brinton et al., 2000). As Nelson (1998) explained, "Simply placing children together in social contexts will not ensure that they will interact" (p. 170).

"All Right, but It'll Be Borrrring"

One child with LI approached every language and literacy task we introduced with a sigh, saying, "All right, but it'll be borrrring." As a first grader, he already anticipated that these tasks would be tedious, and he did not expect to be successful. Although compliant, he did not yet see the value of intervention tasks, beyond the possibility of earning some praise and a sticker. This child illustrates another way in which social competence might influence literacy acquisition—motivation. As noted by Wigfield and Guthrie (1997), motivation has received considerable attention in the recent literature as an important factor in literacy acquisition. Motivation both precedes and facilitates literacy, and may stem from extrinsic (grades, rewards, praise) or intrinsic (reading for the sake of reading) sources. Children who are intrinsically motivated read more extensively and more broadly than do children who rely on extrinsic motivators (Wigfield & Guthrie, 1997).

Wigfield (1997) explained that motivation includes several constructs that can be related to the following questions: "Can I succeed?" and "Do I want to succeed and why?" (pp. 16–17). Factors related most closely to the issue of "Can I succeed?" include beliefs about one's ability or self-efficacy in performing literacy tasks. Schunk and Zimmerman (1997) noted that "self efficacy predicts students' motivation for learning as well as their use of self-regulatory processes" (p. 34). Wigfield (1997) noted that children who feel they can succeed at reading perform better on reading measures than those who do not anticipate success. For children with LI, self-efficacy may be an important issue in literacy acquisition. Children with LI who have difficulty learning to read may acquire a negative view of their potential as readers. In turn, children with LI who have negative views of their potential may see little point in persisting in challenging activities and tasks designed to enhance their reading ability. There is limited research describing self-efficacy in children with LI, partly because self-reflections can be difficult to probe in young children who do not express themselves well. In addition, young children may not be able to evaluate their performance on academic tasks in relation to external expectations.

Harter (1999) explained that very young children view themselves in terms of their abilities, behaviors and preferences, but they cannot yet compare their abilities with those of others in a meaningful way. They think of themselves in terms of absolutes, as "all good" or "all bad." Fortunately, most children tend to think of themselves very positively, and they may overestimate their abilities and skill levels (Harter, 1999). Negative life experiences may emphasize negative attributes, however, to the extent that young children may view themselves in a totally negative manner. Difficulty with language or academics may result in negative experiences. Harter (1999) described a first-grade child with reading problems, who described herself as "all dumb," even though she had strengths in other areas. Jerome et al. (2002) probed self-perceptions in children with LI and in their typically developing peers. They found that 6- to 9-year-old children with LI, as a group, viewed themselves in a fairly undifferentiated manner, very much like their typically developing peers viewed themselves. Three children (out of 23) with LI, however, and 1 typically developing child (out of 23) rated themselves well below the mean across several domains. These 4 children expressed a pervasive, negative view of their abilities and attributes that could be expected to subvert their self-efficacy in the classroom.

As children mature, they no longer think of themselves in terms of absolutes. They begin to compare their performance with that of others, they generalize feedback from others, and their self-perceptions become more differentiated (Harter, 1999). It is at this point that the perceptions of self-efficacy of children with LI may be at risk. Jerome et al. (2002) also considered 10- to 13-year-old children with SLI and their typically developing peers. These older children demonstrated a more differentiated view of their abilities, and their negative self-perceptions were focused on areas influenced by

LI. For example, 8 of 17 children with SLI rated themselves significantly low in scholastic competence, but no typically developing child did so. As a group, children with SLI also perceived their social acceptance and behavioral conduct more negatively than did their typically developing peers. Their most negative self-perceptions, however, focused on their academic achievement. Although the Jerome et al. (2002) study probed self-perceptions of academic competence rather than literacy specifically, it can be assumed that literacy formed an important component of the larger domain of academics. If the results from this study can be generalized, many older children with LI may be particularly aware of their academic problems. If children with LI come to view their ability to read and write negatively as they proceed through elementary school, they are not likely to answer the question "Can I succeed?" positively.

Factors related to the question "Do I want to succeed and why?" include the perceived value of tasks, and intrinsic and extrinsic sources of motivation (Guthrie & Wigfield, 1999; Wigfield, 1997). The societal and cultural influences on perceptions of the value of literacy have been well documented. There is strong evidence, for example, that children with different experiences with literacy may view the value of reading very differently (e.g., Heath, 1983).

With respect to children with LI, anecdotal evidence suggests that some young children with LI dislike print- and book-sharing activities. In addition, we have rarely known older children with LI who considered reading and writing as recreational activities that they would choose to do on their own. Additional research is needed to describe how children with LI view the value and utility of various types of print.

CODY'S CASE: SOCIAL AND AFFECTIVE FACTORS IN LANGUAGE IMPAIRMENT AND LITERACY LEARNING

As with most clinical populations, the variability among children identified as having LI is so great that it is difficult to make sweeping generalizations. Each child with LI presents a unique profile of linguistic, academic, and social strengths and challenges. Despite the variability in children with LI, our research and clinical experience suggest that most of these children manifest social difficulties that will affect their ability to interact with their peers. In addition, these social difficulties may also undermine important aspects of literacy learning, such as access to literate communities, self-efficacy, and motivation. For children with LI, social factors that affect literacy learning combine with linguistic deficits that already impede the process. To illustrate the way that social factors are intertwined with more traditional language deficits, we began this chapter by introducing a single child, Cody. We now return to Cody's case to discuss the complex relationship between LI and social competence.

Cody at Age 4

When Cody was initially identified, he fit the "textbook" definition of LI; that is, his nonverbal IQ was well within the normal range, and there was a 36 point discrepancy between his verbal and nonverbal IQ scores. Hearing loss, neurological disorders, and psychopathology were ruled out. Cody's formal receptive and expressive language test scores were at least 1 standard deviation below the mean (most were 2 standard deviations below the mean). Analysis of his spontaneous language samples confirmed significant delays in syntax and vocabulary. No factors in Cody's history could explain his language problems. Cody came from a supportive family and rich language environment, and he was naturally affiliative, gregarious, and enthusiastic in temperament. We anticipated that Cody would have communication and academic difficulties secondary to his LI, but we felt that social competence would be his strong suit. As indicated earlier, it turned out that the social difficulties associated with Cody's LI represented a significant stumbling block to his ability to thrive within his academic and social world.

Cody entered language intervention in our clinic just before his fifth birthday. In-

tervention goals focused on Cody's structural language deficits as they manifest themselves in oral language and emerging literacy skills. At the same time, we focused on Cody's social interaction with his family members. We followed a similar treatment model for the next 11 years; that is, we worked on traditional structural language targets at the level of conversation and literacy events. At the same time, we also targeted social language skills to enhance Cody's ability to establish and maintain relationships. Cody's mother took on the role of his case manager, clearing the way for our clinic to coordinate with Cody's teachers and special service providers at school to support academics. Cody was consistently a diligent, focused, compliant student. He struggled with language and literacy tasks, but he made consistent progress with support from his teachers, special service providers, and family. We do not detail the more traditional aspects of Cody's treatment and development; instead, we concentrate on social parameters.

Initially, we worked with Cody's parents and preschool teachers to facilitate a more "Cody-centered" style of exchange in which adults slowed their speech rate, provided contextual support for topics, expanded on Cody's utterances, highlighted targeted elements, and avoided excessive questioning. Cody's parents reported that their interactions with him were much more satisfying than they had been previously.

We considered Cody's early aversion to print to be a serious concern because of its effect on both his future motivation to read and his engagement with his parents. Accordingly, another thrust of treatment was to show Cody that print could be useful, entertaining, and could connect him with his family. Cody dictated journal entries describing his activities, which he later used to convey information to family members. For Cody, sharing print about *himself* was compelling. It also seemed to motivate an interest in sharing print about others. Subsequently, we facilitated Cody's understanding of basic story grammar, and he began to enjoy making up imaginative stories about other characters. Although he continued to struggle with many aspects of literacy, his difficulties did not prevent his becoming an enthusiastic reader and writer.

Cody in Elementary School

Cody's relationship with his parents and siblings was strong. His parents and older brothers were accommodating and inclusive. He enjoyed interacting with children in the neighborhood and in the special preschool he attended. Cody's parents soon noticed, however, that Cody interacted best with children who were accommodating to him.

In first and second grade, it became apparent that Cody had difficulty reading the social cues of others and drawing social inferences. For instance, he was not always a reliable judge of who was his "friend" at school, and he sometimes reported a mutual relationship with a child with whom he had little in common. Cody's parents, in consultation with his teachers, began to select playmates to invite to their home, based on how these children were likely to interact with Cody.

Throughout the early elementary grades, Cody enjoyed unstructured outdoor activities with playmates, but he withdrew from structured (rule-based) outdoor games and indoor activities. For example, in third grade, his class regularly played a game at recess called "babies." One played "babies" by crawling around a sandbox, pretending to be a baby. Cody regularly gained access to this game and was a welcome and active participant. He was often excluded from more organized games and activities in his neighborhood, however.

Cody interacted best with accepting children who were interested in sociodramatic fantasy play with toys or objects. Cody's parents worked with school administrators and teachers to place him in classrooms with at least one or two boys who were good candidates for friends. Cody was usually well accepted by peers in his elementary school classrooms. His peers appreciated his enthusiasm and his entertaining stories. But Cody did not easily establish mutual friendships within his classes or his neighborhood. In fact, it was the exception rather than the rule. For example, when a friend

moved away, Cody could not establish a new relationship easily. Although his mother felt that this friendship had not been as close as Cody perceived it to be, Cody mourned the loss of this relationship for years.

As Cody progressed to the upper elementary grades, social difficulties became more prominent and more difficult to manage. He had difficulty working in cooperative groups with other children at school, and this limited his access to many literacy activities. He struggled to negotiate with his peers, and he was sometimes distressed if a work or play group did not adopt his ideas. Cody was often excluded from neighborhood activities. He tended to stay inside, and his parents had to encourage him to try to join in the neighborhood play. Starting in the fifth grade, he indicated, "I'm like a broken toy. I just get passed from one person to another. Nobody wants to play with a broken toy" (Brinton & Fujiki, 1999, p. 49). Although Cody had never been aggressive in any way with family or peers, he experienced a few isolated incidents in which he became so frustrated that he lashed out at peers verbally and physically. These incidents were remarkable because they were so atypical.

We monitored Cody's academic and social development carefully throughout his elementary school years. We were puzzled by the nature of his social difficulties and wondered if his social problems were secondary to his continued difficulty with language. Was it the case that he could not understand his peers' language, and could not formulate his own contributions effectively and efficiently? Observation confirmed that this was part of the problem. As Cody grew older, it became harder and harder for him to follow the fast-paced conversations of peer groups. This was not the sole cause of Cody's difficulties, however. Cody still could not read nonverbal social cues effectively. He could not consistently interpret the intentions of others correctly, nor could he accurately judge his listeners' reactions to his input. For example, Cody often had difficulty initiating and entering interactions. When he had the conversational floor, he was reluctant to give it up. He would talk on and on, seemingly oblivious to his partner's gradual loss of attention. For instance, once we observed Cody talking with a peer at the back of the room. Cody kept on talking as the peer lost interest and walked away.

On a rare occasion when Cody lashed out at some peers, he did not understand that the peers were offended by his words and actions. He evidently could not read their frowns or their cold behavior. We pursued treatment targets encouraging Cody to attend to the verbal and nonverbal messages of his conversational partners, and to gear his contributions in conversation to his listeners' needs.

Cody in Middle School

Cody's school district was structured so that sixth and seventh graders attended a large middle school. This was a particularly difficult transition for Cody. He did not establish close mutual friendships, he had no cohort to eat lunch with or "hang out" with in transitions from class to class, and he tended to withdraw from peers. He continued to have difficulty reading his peers' intentions and distinguishing between good-natured teasing and aggressive behavior. Although Cody's individual teachers were concerned and supportive, the school structure and administration tolerated a high level of student hostility within the school. Even though Cody was relatively large in stature, he was verbally and physically harassed regularly by his peers. The school administration trivialized his parents' complaints, until a school secretary observed another student hitting Cody's head against a wall. Cody's parents were in constant negotiation with the school administration to carry out accommodations written in the individualized educational program (IEP) to ensure his safety. In his neighborhood, Cody continued to be excluded by his peers, and he sometimes had a difficult time in community activities such as scouting. In treatment, Cody's speech–language pathologist teamed with a counseling psychologist to devise strategies to help Cody become less vulnerable to peer harassment. The counseling psychologist taught Cody several strategies to

handle aggressive overtures from peers, but he had difficulty determining when to employ these strategies. We concentrated on helping him understand the difference between friendly teasing behavior, annoying behavior, and bullying behavior.

Cody in Junior High School

Cody attended a large junior high school within his district for grades 8 and 9. His difficulty establishing friendships continued, and he was often alone at school. The administration of this school acted quickly and effectively to prevent Cody from being victimized by his peers, however, and school became a safer place for him. Nevertheless, Cody continued to struggle socially, and he did not establish friendships at school. He was sometimes included in neighborhood activities, but he was not an integral member of the neighborhood social group. As the eighth- and ninth-grade school years progressed, Cody was hard pressed to keep up in his classes, and his academic performance deteriorated in the second semester of each year. Cody's parents met with his teachers to provide adjustments and supports to help Cody compensate for unsatisfactory assignments and exams. This was not necessary for all assignments. Cody handled straightforward texts adequately and performed fairly well on subsequent exams on those texts. He struggled when he was asked to make inferences about text or draw conclusions involving abstract concepts. Assignments that required him to take the perspective of others were particularly troublesome. For example, his English teacher asked students to write a short paper reflecting on the events in *To Kill a Mockingbird* from the perspective of a character other than the protagonist. Cody simply could not grasp the nature of this assignment despite considerable time and help from his parents. His teacher agreed to adjust the assignment to a fabricated interview between Cody and one of the characters in the novel. Cody's interview was not sophisticated, but his teacher accepted it in lieu of the original assignment.

Cody's loneliness and the demands of keeping up with his academic work weighed heavily on him during junior high. He had periodically demonstrated some anxious behaviors for several years (e.g., strict time limits on assignments or being tardy for class were upsetting for him). By the end of the ninth grade, he was manifesting more pronounced symptoms of anxiety, and we referred him to a counseling psychologist who had experience with adolescents with language-learning impairments. She subsequently referred him to a psychiatrist. We collaborated with the psychologist and the psychiatrist to ensure that Cody's expressive and receptive language difficulties were accounted for in the evaluation. Cody began a trial period of medication for anxiety. Additional behavioral management techniques were also recommended.

On a brighter note, in our clinical intervention, Cody seemed, for the first time, to come to a realization that conversations are balanced between participants, and that each participant has a responsibility to include other speakers. Just as importantly, he was able to learn some strategies to gear his contributions to others. Cody was encouraged by the effectiveness of his new strategies in conversations in a clinical setting, and he chose to generalize them to conversations with his peers. Both Cody and his parents were pleased with the results as he became a full participant in some peer interactions. By relying on these strategies, Cody established some relationships with peers that had the potential to develop into more solid friendships. His mother noted that he did not use the strategies consistently, however, and that when he did not, he reverted back to old patterns, with the same old consequences.

To High School and Beyond

As of this writing, Cody is 16 years old and is making the transition to high school. He and his parents have selected his classes and arranged for special services to support his academic performance. For example, Cody's English and history courses are designed to provide extra support for students, and to allow students to accomplish all homework and assignments within the class time. In addition, Cody attends one class period a day within a resource setting, where he gets help completing homework for other classes. He enjoys reading fantasy and adventure novels even though his comprehension is restricted by his difficulty in drawing social inferences. He writes stories as well, but they all involve a simple plot structure in which villains and heroes engage in action-based conflicts. Cody is accustomed to putting in long hours studying to pass his classes, and at this point, he is taking a regular, if somewhat restricted, academic load. Cody and his parents feel that, with careful management, proper support services, and continued hard work, he will handle the basic requirements of the high school curriculum and graduate with a regular diploma. As they think about their past experience and look forward to Cody's reaching adulthood, their primary concerns center around his ability to function socially. Cody enjoys only minimal peer acceptance and maintains that he has never had "a true friend." His mother explains, "Academically, we can get by, but that isn't life. Conversation and relationships are more the essence of what life is."

CONCLUSIONS

Cody's story illustrates the complex and dynamic relationship between LI and social competence. His language and social challenges intertwined to limit his full participation in most peer interactions and many classroom activities. This, in turn, affected his literacy and academic development, as well as his ability to establish and maintain peer relationships. Some of Cody's difficulties in social conversation could be linked to his linguistic impairment, but others could not. For example, his difficulty keeping up in peer group conversations reflected his impaired language comprehension and formulation. At the same time, his inability to read the nonverbal and social cues of his listeners, and his difficulty making inferences based on social information, could not be attributed to his receptive and expressive language problems. Rather, his difficulty suggested a wider deficit that included aspects of social and emotional competence.

He was unable to appreciate the perspectives and emotions of others. This affected his interpretation of written text, as well as his ability to gear his contributions in interaction to his listeners' needs. These difficulties have traditionally been associated with diagnostic classifications such as autism spectrum disorder and have more recently been reported in children with fetal alcohol syndrome (Coggins, Olswang, Carmichael Olson, & Timler, 2003). These problems may be more prominent in children with LI than previously thought. A number of studies have suggested that this is the case (Boucher, Lewis, & Collis, 2000; Farmer, 2000; Ford & Milosky, 2003; Fujiki, Brinton, & Clarke, 2001). For example, Boucher et al. (2000) found that children with SLI had greater difficulty than children with autism on a task requiring them to label vocally expressed emotions then match the emotions to pictures of facial expressions.

Future research is essential to learn more about how problems in specific aspects of social and emotional competence are related to the social problems of children diagnosed with LI. This type of research will have intriguing theoretical implications in terms of the way that we understand and define LI. It may be necessary to rethink some of the boundaries that we have established to delineate categories of impairment. Traditional definitions of, and interventions for, LI certainly proved too narrow for Cody, despite the "textbook" profile of SLI he presented as a child.

Future research should address important clinical questions that push us to expand the scope of our intervention targets and strategies for children with LI. Our initial assessment of Cody predicted many problems, but it only hinted at the significance of the social–emotional component of his impairment. Initially, it was difficult to appreciate the extent of Cody's involvement. We did not realize how aspects of social and emotional competence intertwined with his language problem to limit his ability to understand and communicate within a social context. Cody certainly needed treatment to help him understand and formulate spoken and written language, but just as importantly, he needed intervention to guide his interpretation of the social and emotional context in which language occurred. For Cody, the most critical point of intervention seemed to be the integration of linguistic, social, and emotional information. Treatment activities taxed his capacity to simultaneously process language, comprehend social cues, and appreciate the perspectives and emotional states of others. He did not respond optimally to treatment approaches focused on more discrete linguistic, literacy, or social targets.

How well does Cody's case represent the experience of the wider population of children with LI? Cross-sectional studies and clinical experience indicate that Cody is not unusual. The children with LI sampled in many studies have demonstrated a high incidence of withdrawal, poor sociability, and limited peer relationships. Each of these children probably presents a unique profile, in which difficulties in language, social, and emotional functioning are intertwined. Careful longitudinal studies are needed to trace the course of this intertwined development. We look to future research to describe the relationship of social, emotional, and linguistic components of LI. We must also investigate how these components interact with myriad other factors, such as individual temperament, parenting styles, and cultural expectations. Just as we needed to broaden our scope of treatment for Cody over the years, we also need to broaden our research foci to capture the many facets of development in children with LI. Designing effective treatment programs depends on our ability to understand the underlying explanations for the behaviors we observe. For children like Cody, the explanations cannot come too soon.

NOTE

1. Throughout this chapter, the term "language impairment" is used to refer to children whose language difficulties do not stem from mental retardation, sensory deficits, or diagnosed emotional disturbance. In most cases, the term is used synonymously with "specific language impairment." When citing research studies, we have tried to use the designation used by the authors.

REFERENCES

Achenbach, T. M. (1991a). *Manual for the Child Behavior Checklist 4–18*. Burlington: University of Vermont Press.

Achenbach, T. M. (1991b). *Manual for the Teacher Report Form*. Burlington: University of Vermont Press.

Anderson, A. B., & Stokes, S. (1984). Social and institutional influences on the development and practice of literacy. In H. Goelman, A. Oberg, & F. Smith, (Eds.), *Awakening to literacy* (pp. 24–37). Exeter, NH: Heinemann.

Asendorpf, J. (1991). Development of inhibited children's coping and unfamiliarity. *Child Development, 62,* 1460–1474.

Asher, S. R., & Gazelle, H. (1999). Loneliness, peer relations, and language disorder in childhood. *Topics in Language Disorders, 19*(2), 16–33.

Asher, S. R., Parker, J. G., & Walker, D. L. (1996). Distinguishing friendship from acceptance: Implications for intervention and assessment. In W. M. Bukowski, A. F. Newcomb, & W. W. Hartup (Eds.), *The company they keep: Friendship in childhood and adolescence* (pp. 366–405). New York: Cambridge University Press.

Bishop, D. V. M. (1997). *Uncommon understanding: Development and disorders of language comprehension in children*. Hove, UK: Taylor & Francis.

Boucher, J., Lewis, V., & Collis, G. M. (2000). Voice processing abilities in children with autism, children with specific language impairments, and young typically developing children. *Journal of Child Psychology and Psychiatry, 41,* 847–857.

Brinton, B., & Fujiki, M. (1999). Social interactional behaviors of children with specific language impairment. *Topics in Language Disorders, 19*(2), 49–69.

Brinton, B., Fujiki, M., & Higbee, L. (1998). Participation in cooperative learning activities by children with specific language impairment. *Journal of Speech, Language, and Hearing Research, 41,* 1193–1206.

Brinton, B., Fujiki, M., & McKee, L. (1998). The negotiation skills of children with specific language impairment. *Journal of Speech, Language, and Hearing Research, 41,* 927–940.

Brinton, B., Fujiki, M., Montague, E. C., & Hanton, J. L. (2000). Children with language impairment in cooperative work groups: A pilot study. *Language, Speech, and Hearing Services in Schools, 31,* 252–264.

Brinton, B., Fujiki, M., Spencer, J. C., & Robinson, L. A. (1997). The ability of children with specific language impairment to access and participate in an ongoing interaction. *Journal of Speech, Language, and Hearing Research, 40,* 1011–1025.

Catts, H. W., & Kamhi, A. G. (1999). Language and reading disabilities. Needham Heights, MA: Allyn & Bacon.

Coie, J. D., Dodge, K. A., & Kupersmidt, J. B. (1990). Peer group behavior and social status. In S. R. Asher & J. D. Coie (Eds.), *Peer rejection in childhood* (pp. 17–59). New York: Cambridge University Press.

Coggins, T. E., Olswang, L. B., Carmichael Olson, H., & Timler, G. R. (2003). On becoming socially competent communicators: The challenge for children with fetal alcohol exposure. In L. Abbeduto (Ed.), *International Review of Research in Mental Retardation, Vol. 27: Language and communication in mental retardation* (pp. 121–150). Oxford, UK: Elsevier.

Coplan, R. J., & Rubin, K. H. (1998). Exploring and assessing nonsocial play in the preschool: The development and validation of the preschool play behavior scale. *Social Development, 7,* 72–91.

Coplan, R. J., Rubin, K. H., Fox, N. A., Calkins, S. D., & Stewart, S. L. (1994). Being alone, playing alone, and acting alone: Distinguishing among reticence, and passive and active-solitude in young children. *Child Development, 65,* 129–137.

Corsaro, W. A. (1981). Friendship in the nursery school: Social organization in a peer environment. In S. R. Asher & J. M. Gottman (Eds.), *The development of children's friendships* (pp. 207–241). Cambridge, UK: Cambridge University Press.

Craig, H. K., & Washington, J. A. (1993). The access behaviors of children with specific language impairment. *Journal of Speech and Hearing Research, 36,* 322–336.

Dodge, K. A., Schlundt, D. C., Schocken, I., & Delugach, J. D. (1983). Social competence and children's sociometric status: The role of peer group entry strategies. *Merrill–Palmer Quarterly, 29,* 309–336.

Doll, B. (1996). Children without friends: Implications for practice and policy. *School Psychology Review, 25,* 165–183.

Farmer, M. (2000). Language and social cognition in children with specific language impairment. *Journal of Child Psychology and Psychiatry and Allied Disciplines, 41,* 627–636.

Ford, J., & Milosky, L. M., (2003). Inferring emotional reactions in social situations: Differences in children with language impairment. *Journal of Speech, Language, and Hearing Research, 46,* 21–30.

Fujiki, M., Brinton, B., & Clarke, D. (2002). Emotion regulation in children with specific language impairment. *Language, Speech, and Hearing Services in Schools, 33,* 102–111.

Fujiki, M., Brinton, B., Hart, C. H., & Fitzgerald, A. (1999). Peer acceptance and friendship in children with specific language impairment. *Topics in Language Disorders, 19*(2), 34–48.

Fujiki, M., Brinton, B., Isaacson, T., & Summers, C. (2001). Social behaviors of children with language impairment on the playground: A pilot study. *Language, Speech, and Hearing Services in Schools, 32,* 101–113.

Fujiki, M., Brinton, B., Morgan, M., & Hart, C. H. (1999). Withdrawn and sociable behavior of children with specific language impairment. *Language, Speech, and Hearing Services in Schools, 30,* 183–195.

Fujiki, M., Brinton, B., Robinson, L., & Watson, V. (1997). The ability of children with specific language impairment to participate in a group decision task. *Journal of Children's Communication Development, 18*, 1–10.

Fujiki, M., Brinton, B., & Todd, C. M. (1996). Social skills of children with specific language impairment. *Language, Speech, and Hearing Services in Schools, 27*, 195–202.

Gertner, B. L., Rice, M. L., & Hadley, P. A. (1994). Influence of communicative competence on peer preferences in a preschool classroom. *Journal of Speech and Hearing Research, 37*, 913–923.

Gresham, F. M., & Elliott, S. N. (1990). *Social Skills Rating System—Teacher Form.* Circle Pines, MN: American Guidance Service.

Gottman, J., Gonso, J., & Rasmussen, B. (1975). Social interaction, social competence, and friendship in children. *Child Development, 46*, 709–718.

Grove, J., Conti-Ramsden, G., & Donlan, C. (1993). Conversational interaction and decision-making in children with specific language impairment. *European Journal of Disorders of Communication, 28*, 141–152.

Grusec, J. E., & Lytton, H. (1988). *Social development: History, theory and research.* New York: Springer-Verlag.

Guice, S. L. (1995). Creating communities of readers: A study of children's information networks as multiple contexts for responding to texts. *Journal of Reading Behavior, 27*, 379–397.

Guralnick, M. J., Connor, R. T., Hammond, M. A., Gottman, J. M., & Kinnish, K. (1996). The peer relations of preschool children with communication disorders. *Child Development, 67*, 471–489.

Guthrie, J. T., & Wigfield, A. (1999). How motivation fits into a science of reading. *Scientific Studies of Reading, 3*, 199–205.

Hadley, P. A., & Rice, M. L. (1991). Conversational responsiveness of speech- and language-impaired preschoolers. *Journal of Speech and Hearing Research, 34*, 1308–1317.

Harrist, A. W., Zaia, A. F., Bates, J. E., Dodge, K. A., & Pettit, G. S. (1997). Subtypes of social withdrawal in early childhood: Sociometric status and social-cognitive differences across four years. *Child Development, 68*, 278–294.

Hart, C. H., Olsen, S. F., Robinson, C. C., & Mandleco, B. L. (1997). The development of social and communicative competence in childhood: Review and a model of personal, familial, and extrafamilial processes. In B. R. Burleson (Ed.), *Communication yearbook 20* (pp. 305–373). Thousand Oaks, CA: Sage.

Hart, C. H., & Robinson, C. C. (1996). *Teacher Behavior Rating Scale.* Unpublished teacher questionnaire, Brigham Young University, Provo, UT.

Hart, C. H., Robinson, C. C., McNeilly, M. K., Nelson, L., & Olsen, S. (1995). *Multiple sources of data on preschooler's playground behavior.* Unpublished manuscript, Brigham Young University, Provo, UT.

Hart, K. I., Fujiki, M., Brinton, B., & Hart, C. H. (in press). The relationship between social behavior and severity of language impairment. *Journal of Speech, Language, and Hearing Research.*

Harter, S. (1999). *The construction of the self.* New York: Guilford Press.

Heath, S. B. (1983). *Ways with words: Language, life, and work in communities and classrooms.* Cambridge, UK: Cambridge University Press.

Jerome, A., Fujiki, M., Brinton, B., & James, S. (2002). Self-esteem in children with specific language impairment. *Journal of Speech, Language, and Hearing Research, 45*, 700–714.

Kliewer, C. (1998). Citizenship in the literate community: An enthnography of children with Down syndrome and the written word. *Exceptional Children, 64*, 167–180.

Ladd, G. W. (1981). Effectiveness of a social learning method for enhancing children's social interaction and peer acceptance. *Child Development, 52*, 171–178.

Ladd, G. W., & Price, J. M. (1987). Predicting children's social and school adjustment following the transition from preschool to kindergarten. *Child Development, 58*, 1168–1189.

Marvin, C. A., & Wright, D. (1997). Literacy socialization in the homes of preschool children. *Language, Speech, and Hearing Services in Schools, 28*, 154–163.

Merrell, K. W. (1999). *Behavioral, social, and emotional assessment of children and adolescents.* Mahwah, NJ: Erlbaum.

Morrison, F. J., & Cooney, R. R. (2002). Parenting and academic achievement: Multiple paths to early literacy. In J. G. Borkowski, S. L. Ramey, & M. Bristol-Power (Eds.), *Parenting and the child's world: Influence on academic intellectual, and social-emotional development* (pp. 141–160). Mahwah, NJ: Erlbaum.

Nelson, N. W. (1998). *Childhood language disorders in context: Infancy through adolescence* (2nd ed.). Needham Heights, MA: Allyn & Bacon.

Parten, M. B. (1932). Social participation among preschool children. *Journal of Abnormal Social Psychology, 27*, 243–269.

Paul, R., Looney, S. S., & Dahm, P. S. (1991). Communication and socialization skills at ages 2 and 3 in late-talking young children. *Journal of Speech and Hearing Research, 34*, 858–865.

Redmond, S. M., & Rice, M. L. (1998). The socioemotional behaviors of children with SLI: Social adaptation or social deviance? *Journal of Speech, Language, and Hearing Research, 41*, 688–700.

Redmond, S. M., & Rice, M. L. (2002). Stability of behavioral ratings of children with SLI. *Journal of Speech, Language, and Hearing Research, 45*, 190–201.

Rice, M. L., Sell, M. A., & Hadley, P. A. (1991). Social interactions of speech- and language-impaired children. *Journal of Speech and Hearing Research, 34*, 1299–1307.

Rowe, D. W. (1989). Author/audience interaction in the preschool: The role of social interaction in literacy learning. *Journal of Reading Behavior, 21*, 311–349.

Rubin, K. H. (1982). Non-social play in preschoolers: Necessary evil? *Child Development, 53*, 651–657.

Rubin, K. H., & Asendorpf, J. B. (1993). Social with-drawal, inhibition, and shyness in childhood: Conceptual and definitional issues. In *Social withdrawal, inhibition, and shyness in childhood* (pp. 3–17). Hillsdale, NJ: Erlbaum.

Rubin, K. H., & Mills, R. S. L. (1988). The many faces of social isolation in childhood. *Journal of Consulting and Clinical Psychology, 56,* 916–924.

Schneider, P., & Hecht, B. F. (1995). Interaction between children with developmental delays and their mothers during a book-sharing activity. *International Journal of Disability, 42,* 41–56.

Schunk, D. H., & Zimmerman, B. J. (1997) Developing self-efficacious readers and writers: The role of social and self-regulatory processes. In J. T. Guthrie & A. Wigfield (Eds.), *Reading engagement: Motivating readers through integrated instruction* (pp. 34–50). Newark, DE: International Reading Association.

Slavin, R. E. (1995). *Cooperative learning* (2nd ed.). Boston: Allyn & Bacon.

Stanovich, K. E. (1986). Matthew effects in reading: Some consequences of individual differences in the acquisition of literacy. *Reading Research Quarterly, 86,* 360– 406.

Stevens, L. J., & Bliss, L. S. (1995). Conflict resolution abilities of children with specific language impairment and children with normal language. *Journal of Speech and Hearing Research, 38,* 599–611.

Tomblin, J. B., Zhang, Z., Buckwalter, P., & Catts, H. (2000). The association of reading disability, behavioral disorders, and language impairment among second-grade children. *Journal of Child Psychology and Psychiatry, 41,* 473–482.

Westby, C. (1999). Assessment of pragmatic competence in children with psychiatric disorders. In D. L. Rogers-Adkinson & P. L. Griffith (Eds.), *Communication disorders and children with psychiatric and behavioral disorders* (pp. 177–258). San Diego: Singular.

Wigfield, A. (1997). Children's motivations for reading and reading engagement. In J. T. Guthrie & A. Wigfield (Eds.), *Reading engagement motivating readers through integrated instruction* (pp. 14–33). Newark, DE: International Reading Association.

Wigfield, A., & Guthrie, J. T. (1997). Relations of children's motivation for reading to the amount and breadth of their reading. *Journal of Educational Psychology, 89,* 420–432.

Young, L. L., & Cooper, D. H. (1944). Factors associated with popularity. *Journal of Educational Psychology, 35,* 513–535.

Younger, A. J., & Daniels, T. M. (1992). Children's reasons for nominating their peers as withdrawn: Passive withdrawal versus active isolation. *Developmental Psychology, 28,* 955–960.

8

Family Literacy Practices

BARBARA HANNA WASIK
JENNIFER S. HENDRICKSON

Family practices have received considerable
attention from those seeking to understand
how information, rules, routines, and beliefs
pass from one generation to another; and
how families promote social and emotional
competence. Interest in the family and home
life as determinants of children's literacy development and school success has a long history (see Cook, 1980; Goelman, Oberg, &
Smith, 1984; Purcell-Gates, 1995). Early researchers zeroed in on issues that are equally
relevant today: parental characteristics
(Della-Piana & Martin, 1976), parent–child
relationships (Freeberg & Berliner, 1967),
culture (Hess & Shipman, 1965), and the
home environment (Leichter, 1984; Teale,
1978). During the past 20 years, interest in
family literacy practices has dramatically increased, beginning with a seminal publication that appeared in the early 1980s (Taylor, 1983).

Our purpose here is to examine family literacy practices, including theoretical shifts
in how literacy is conceptualized, with a
view toward child outcomes and interventions designed for families. We first discuss
four factors: (1) social and cultural, (2) re-

search, (3) political, and (4) programmatic
influences, as well as developmental and educational theories that have contributed to
the increased attention to family literacy
practices. We propose a model for the variables that affect children's literacy and
language development. Key components include parental characteristics, child characteristics, the home environment, and
parent–child relationships. We then examine connections between family literacy
practices and school-related skills. Finally,
we assess the outcomes of family literacy interventions.

INCREASED INTEREST IN FAMILY LITERACY PRACTICES

The first factor that has strongly influenced
interest in family literacy practices is concern with social and cultural phenomena
(Auerbach, 1989; Gadsden, 1994, 2001).
Research documents that literacy practices
in families are rich and complex, and that
they vary as a function of culture (i.e., Delgado-Gaitan, 1990; Purcell-Gates, 1995;

Tabors & Snow, 2001; Taylor, 1983; Vernon-Feagans, Hammer, Miccio, & Manlove, 2001; Voss, 1996). Successful parent–child interventions focused on promoting literacy often incorporate participants' cultural perspectives (Emberton, 2004; Gadsden, 2001).

In the United States, attitudes toward speaking another language and toward other cultures are changing, and this also influences the study of family literacy practices. Since the late 1800s, many educational reform strategies have been developed for immigrant populations. But in the past, the emphasis was not on helping children maintain their home language or on including their culture in formal learning experiences. Today, public educators more often appreciate and understand other languages and cultures. As a result, they have turned their attention to gaining an understanding of second-language acquisition by adults, the role of parents with limited English proficiency in children's English literacy development, how best to teach literacy to children whose first language is not English, and changes in family dynamics that occur when children learn a language not spoken in the home (e.g., Rodriguez, Diaz, Duran, & Espinosa, 1995; Strucker, Snow, & Pan, 2004; Tabors & Snow, 2001).

A second factor that has increased interest in family literacy practices is the strong, cumulative empirical evidence demonstrating the home literacy environment's effect on later school performance. In particular, researchers have studied the low school performance of children from minority backgrounds, low-income families, or families with low educational levels (Snow, Burns, & Griffin, 1998; Vernon-Feagans, 1996; White, 1982; Whitehurst, 1996). Not only do children's home experiences correlate to early school performance, but findings have demonstrated strong relations between early school performance and performance in the later elementary grades (Juel, 1988) and between performance in first and 11th grade (Cunningham & Stanovich, 1998). This chain of influence further shows the need to examine preschool children's literacy environment.

The political *zeitgeist,* a third factor in promoting interest in family literacy, is seen as one of the major categories of interventions in the literacy arena. Considerable national attention has led to an increase in family literacy partnerships among educational services such as Head Start, state prekindergarten programs, and the adult education community. Federal legislation over the past few years has included a common definition of family literacy interventions that calls for adult education, parenting education, early childhood education, and parent and child literacy interactions (Wasik & Herrmann, 2004). Furthermore, federal legislation, illustrated by the No Child Left Behind initiative, with its emphasis on accountability through testing, shows the federal government's serious commitment to the development of reading proficiency in young children.

A fourth factor is the growing interest in interventions focused on enhancing the literacy skills of one or more members of the family. These intervention programs have prompted questions about literacy development and the contributions of home practices and early childhood educational experiences to children's literacy development—questions about not only the most appropriate way of helping families but also the match between program goals and family expectations (Gadsden, 1994, 2001; Taylor, 1997).

Although we have discussed these four factors separately, they continually interact to promote interest in family literacy practices. Research findings and concerns about culturally appropriate practice may each influence federal policies; federal policies, in turn, may prompt research on families with different cultural backgrounds.

In the next section, we expand on relatively recent shifts in theory about literacy development in young children and describe findings from several seminal studies that have influenced this shift.

THEORETICAL SHIFTS IN CONCEPTUALIZING LITERACY

Two sets of theories have influenced interest in family literacy practices. Theories and beliefs about family dynamics, including transactional theories, ecological theories, and family systems theories, make up the first set. The second set encompasses theories of language and literacy development (Wasik, Dobbins, & Herrmann, 2001; see also van Kleeck, Chapter 9, this volume).

Theories about Family Dynamics

During the first half of the 20th century, the prevailing theoretical view was that children's development is governed by maturation (Gesell, 1925). Following from this early view was the belief that teaching children to read before they were *ready* could be detrimental to their development. By mid-century, a competing theory was becoming more accepted, namely, a behavioral view that children's development is determined by environmental influences. As a result, the role of parents was seen as more significant, and early childhood intervention became more accepted as a means to help children at risk for school failure.

Problems existed, however, relative to both the maturational and behavioral views; consequently, newer theories recognized both biological and experiential factors as part of children's development (Bronfenbrenner, 1979, 1986; Sameroff & Chandler, 1975). These theories included transactional models, ecological models, and systems models.

Reviewing the influence of the transactional model on early childhood intervention, Meisels and Shonkoff (2000) encourage the acceptance of reciprocal influences between biological factors and environmental/social factors. To illustrate reciprocal influences, they note that "biological insults can be modified by environmental factors and that developmental vulnerabilities could have social and environmental etiologies" (p. 11).

Another highly influential theory, proposed by Bronfenbrenner (1979, 1986), conceptualized children's development as occurring within a set of nested environments. Bronfenbrenner's developmental ecological model (1995) has helped to underscore the importance of the home literacy environment for children's learning

about language and literacy. He believed that successful interventions treat "children as individuals situated within a family rather than as isolated experimental subjects or narrowly defined targets of nativist or nurturist theories" (Meisels & Shonkoff, 2000, p. 12).

Family systems theory, developed initially to provide a framework for understanding and providing services to families (Minuchin, 1974), also provides a framework for considering reciprocal influences in the family. Family systems theory views a family as a system in which changes in one member can bring about changes in another. Early work examining the role of families on children's school success supported a relation between family functioning and children's reading (Peck & Stackhouse, 1973).

The theories identified here are particularly relevant with regard to the informal literacy practices that take place within the home, in contrast to more formal literacy practices within education settings. Furthermore, their increasing acceptance among practitioners and researchers involved in early childhood education has provided a supportive theoretical foundation for examining families' literacy practices and their influence on children. In the next section, we examine theories related to children's literacy and how these have influenced the shift toward recognizing the importance of literacy development within the family.

Theories of Early Literacy Development

For many years, children's literacy was thought to develop in formal settings, and much of our study of children's literacy took place in the classroom (Scarborough, 2001; Wasik et al., 2001). One major event bringing increased attention to family literacy practices is a paradigm shift in views of children's literacy development to a reconceptualizaton known as "emergent literacy." The term "emergent" is derived from Clay's (1993) observational study of children's emerging reading behaviors. Rather than seeing schools as the first or sole setting for children's literacy development, scholars recognized that literacy skills develop over the preschool years, influenced by both the home literacy environment and parent–child interactions. Clay and other early scholars promoted awareness that literacy development begins in infancy and the preschool years within the informal settings of family, home, and community. More recently, the term "early literacy" has been used to describe the same phenomenon (Neuman & Dickinson, 2001).

Our current understanding of children's literacy development—which recognizes home and community as important settings for development prior to formal education—has received increasing support. Throughout the 1980s, a number of researchers studied the family's influence on children's language and literacy. Their work supported the idea that literacy development is an ongoing phenomenon of family life, and gave less support to the readiness theories identified earlier. Among these studies are the ethnographic works of Goodman, (1980), Heath (1983), Taylor (1983), Taylor and Strickland (1986), Taylor and Dorsey-Gaines (1988), Teale (1986), and Snow, Barnes, Chandler, Goodman, and Hemphill (1991).

Collectively, these ethnographers not only contributed to the shift toward emphasizing early literacy development, they also provided a foundation on which to conduct further research. Their work has raised awareness of the many literacy practices that take place in homes, how these practices differ considerably from one family to another, how strongly they relate to literacy and language development, and their prevalence outside formal settings. In the following sections, we explore some of these practices in more depth.

VARIATIONS IN LITERACY PRACTICES AMONG FAMILIES

In considering literacy's role in the life of the family, we find that children are prepared for educational settings through both the direct and the indirect, or unintentional, teaching of literacy. The indirect teaching of literacy occurs frequently in most families in numerous daily routines from the time an infant is born.

Parents and others engage the infant during caregiving activities by smiling, talking, and encouraging the child in play. Through these naturally occurring events, children learn language and early literacy skills. As children become older, opportunities for engaging them in more complex literacy activities increase considerably. Some families use fewer of these opportunities, and their children are frequently disadvantaged when they enter more formal learning settings.

Families engage in informal literacy practices in numerous ways: reading the newspaper, writing notes to family members, reading religious materials, writing letters, preparing grocery lists, reading recipes and food packaging, giving or receiving holiday cards, and reading books, road signs, and text on the television. As Taylor and Dorsey-Gaines (1988) note in their study of diverse groups of families, such literacy practices differ among and within families of different cultures, educational levels, and income.

Families also engage in more direct and intentional activities to teach literacy skills, including storybook reading, teaching children the alphabet song or helping them learn to identify alphabet letters, and encouraging them to make the scribbles of *pretend writing*. Each of these more formal activities can enhance the development of language and literacy in young children (Bus, 2001). Shared book reading, for example, has been found to influence vocabulary development in preschool children (Sénéchal, LeFevre, Hudson, & Lawson, 1996; Sénéchal, Thomas, & Monker, 1995; see also van Kleeck, Chapter 9, this volume).

From a review of the increasingly extensive literature on family literacy practices, we have developed a model to organize an analysis of major variables in family literacy practices. This model includes the following: (1) parental characteristics, (2) child characteristics, (3) the home environment, and (4) parent–child relationships. Earlier writers have identified similar variables, especially the home environment and parent–child relationships (Britto & Brooks-Gunn, 2001; Leichter, 1984), but for our purposes here, we have also distinguished parental and child characteristics in order to examine their unique influence. Though the variables in this model are seen as predictors of child literacy and language outcomes, each variable is also inextricably linked with the others in myriad ways to influence child outcomes.

Parental Characteristics

At least three kinds of parental characteristics can affect language and literacy learning: culture and ethnicity, parental beliefs, and socioeconomic status.

Culture and Ethnicity

Different cultures have different ways of integrating "talking, listening, writing, reading, acting, interacting, believing, valuing, and feeling" (Gee, 2001, p. 35). Any serious study of literacy development must include an examination of family culture and beliefs. As our society becomes increasingly diverse, considering culture's role in the development of literacy becomes even more essential (Auerbach, 1989; Gadsden, 1994, 2001). Summarizing findings from a number of studies with white, middle-class mothers and children, Vernon-Feagans et al. (2001) noted that parents (1) set up routines, (2) ask a lot of questions (see Anderson-Yockel & Haynes, 1994), (3) change their teaching strategies as the child becomes more proficient, and (4) produce more abstract utterances and questions as the child becomes older (see also Pelligrini, Perlmutter, Galda, & Brody, 1990). These patterns, however, are not consistent across other ethnic and income groups.

A number of studies investigating family cultures have found both similarities and differences among various cultural groups. For example, Yarosz and Barnett (2001) used the results of the National Household Survey to examine the question of who reads to young children. They found that the frequency of reading to children varied according to a number of factors, including ethnicity and the primary language spoken in the home. Differences among ethnic groups in the rates of reading to young children remained even when factors such as income, family size, and education were controlled. Viewing the amount of storybook reading across cultures, the Federal Interagency Forum on Child and Family Statistics (1999) reported that 44% of African American and 39% of Hispanic families read to their preschool children daily, in contrast to 64% of white families.

The quality of language and literacy activities also varies across cultures. Both Heath (1983) and Vernon-Feagans (1996) found a rich storytelling tradition among low-income African American families. The adults in these families gave children experiences with stories and encouraged them to tell oral narratives (Heath, 1983); in these families, children of different ages and skills often jointly created stories (Vernon-Feagans, 1996).

Although both black and white families expand on the text during book reading, white mothers were found to produce significantly more questions than black mothers (Anderson-Yockel & Haynes, 1994). Parental differences are most likely not the result of conscious choices, and if parents knew the advantages of particular activities for their children, they might engage in these activities (Edwards, 1995). Family intervention programs have demonstrated that most parents are very interested in learning ways to facilitate their children's later reading and writing.

Hispanic families in the United States must typically deal with bilingual issues, in addition to all other child-rearing activities. Many children from bilingual homes have been found to be at a disadvantage in regard to school success. Often, such families have received mixed messages about the best way to help their children. For example, some have been told to speak only English to their children, a practice that reduces the likelihood that the child will learn the native language and use it frequently in the home. Learning only English may also create disadvantages for these children as they grow up in the increasingly multicultural environment.

As one might expect, family practices also differ within cultures. Teale (1986) studied in-home literacy activities of preschoolers from low-income families and found within-culture differences. Differences within cultures have also been reported for Mexican American families, for whom a range of parental activities was observed across families, from encouraging the child to storybook reading (Delgado-Gaitan, 1990).

Family language patterns among Hispanic families in the United States can be very complex. As children move through the public schools, they typically begin to speak English much more often at school. Their parents, on the other hand, may not know English as well, and may frequently communicate in Spanish with family and community members who do not speak English. Who lives in the family, the language of the immediate community, and whether children attend bilingual schools are also important influences on the practices of bilingual families. Furthermore, children, even very young ones, can take on the role of language translator for their parents. Such roles clearly affect practices within a family, occasionally shifting traditional roles and responsibilities of the family members.

Many bilingual families have enrolled in family literacy programs. Indeed, the percentage of bilingual families, especially Spanish-speaking families, in the Even Start Family Literacy Program has increased dramatically over the past decade (Strucker et al., 2001), reflecting the interest of many Hispanic families in learning to speak and read English. Such interventions will also have a strong influence on the literacy practices of these families and their expectations for their children.

Parental Beliefs

A family's educational beliefs may significantly influence the literacy learning potential of the home (Britto & Brooks-Gunn, 2001; Bus, 2001; Johnson & Martin, 1985; McGillicuddy-DeLisi, 1985; Sénéchal & LeFevre, 2001). Some families view the education of children as primarily the work of the schools; others see a more active role for themselves in contributing to their children's learning. Children whose parents view reading as a source of entertainment, and who read for pleasure, tend to have a more positive attitude toward reading and better reading skills than do the children of

parents who tend to engage in more direct skills instruction in literacy interactions with their children (Baker, Scher, & Mackler, 1997; Britto & Brooks-Gunn, 2001).

However, parents across income levels hold common beliefs about the importance of becoming literate (Fitzgerald, Spiegel, & Cunningham, 1991; Gadsden, 1993; Heath, 1983; Wasik, Mamak, & Kingsley, 2002). Fitzgerald et al. (1991) interviewed families in both high- and low-literacy homes to obtain information about perceptions of early literacy learning. Importantly, their findings showed that all the parents believed literacy learning could begin before school. A significant difference, however, was found when parents described what they saw as being important in literacy activities. Parents with lower literacy skills considered skills development to be more important, whereas more highly literate parents saw literacy as a cultural activity and emphasized modeling literate behaviors for their children.

In a study of teenage mothers in an African American community, Neuman, Hagedorn, Celano, and Daly (1995) explored the mothers' beliefs about their children's literacy and learning in a family literacy program. They found a variety of parental beliefs about literacy, learning, and schooling, and they cautioned others not to view ethnic or cultural groups as homogeneous. On the other hand, they found that parents had a number of shared goals concerning their children's education. One study found common beliefs about the importance of education in the children's lives across low-income African American, Caucasian, and Hispanic parents, though certain practices differed among the groups, such as when parents begin reading to their children (Wasik et al., 2002).

Family beliefs affect the interactions that adults have with children relative to literacy, the materials that are available in the home, and the concepts and understandings that children develop. Parents' views of education and literacy may be strongly influenced by their own educational background and experience (Bus, 2001). If parents' own educational experience was negative and characterized by failure and frustration, then it is likely to limit their interactions with their children relative to education and literacy. Such parents may want to avoid literacy activities or may feel inadequate to provide help to a child. Thus, parents' own preference for reading and personal reading practices may mediate how they engage their children in literacy activities (Britto & Brooks-Gunn, 2001; Bus, 2001; Haden, Reese, & Fivush, 1996; Pellegrini, Galda, Jones, & Perlmutter, 1995).

Though families of various incomes and cultures value literacy, family practices do differ across income and social status levels. Such differences exist in part because some families have fewer resources to provide a literacy-rich environment, and because some families' sociocultural belief systems support one type of home environment over another (Vernon-Feagans et al., 2001). In the next section, we describe some of the differences documented across sociocultural and income status.

Socioeconomic Status

The relationship of socioeconomic status (SES) and family literacy practices has concerned many investigators (Adams, 1990; Hammer, 1999; Hart & Risley, 1995; Heath, 1983; Purcell-Gates, 1995; Storch & Whitehurst, 2001; Taylor & Dorsey-Gaines, 1988). Differences in social class have been found to predict strongly children's school performance. Considerable evidence indicates that children in low-SES families are at greater risk than children from high-SES families for poor development of language and literacy competencies, and for school failure as a function of the literacy practices in their homes (Adams, 1990; Anderson & Stokes, 1984; Carlson, 1998; Storch & Whitehurst, 2001; Vernon-Feagans et al., 2001).

In low-SES home environments, parent–child literacy interactions are more likely to be characterized by *practical* literacy, such as reading job applications and coupons (Pellegrini, 2001). In high-SES homes, by contrast, interactions aimed at teaching children literacy, such as reading storybooks and engaging in games based on language, are more common. Carlson (1998) found that high-SES parents reported creating

more literacy-rich home environments than did parents with lower social status. Zady and Portes (2001) examined the influence of SES on parents' ability to help their children with school projects. They found that low-SES, low-literacy parents sometimes cannot help their children as much with school projects, because of their own educational limitations.

Many factors, including a lack of financial resources, family support, educational background, and available time, influence low-SES parents' ability to provide children with the language and literacy environments that middle-income families can provide (Vernon-Feagans et al., 2001). Storch and Whitehurst (2001) have argued that very large differences exist among social classes in children's exposure to experiences that facilitate development of literacy skills, including enriching cultural experiences, educational toys and materials, and one-on-one reading opportunities. Other researchers have also documented differences in rates of book ownership, and the quality and frequency of shared book reading (Adams, 1990; Anderson & Stokes, 1984). The combined effects of these differences are striking. Adams (1990) estimated that a typical middle-class child enters first grade with 1,000–1,700 hours of one-on-one picture-book reading time. In contrast, a typical child from a low-income family has only 25 hours of one-on-one reading time by the time he or she enters first grade (Adams, 1990).

In a study of children from working-class and middle-class families, Stuart, Dixon, Masterson, and Quinlan (1998) found that middle-class children knew significantly more letter–sound correspondences than did working-class children. Although parental reports of teaching children letter names and sounds did not differ significantly, middle-class parents reported spending more time reading to their children, as well as using a wider range of teaching materials, than did working-class parents.

In one of the most significant studies of the home environment's impact on children's language and literacy, Hart and Risley (1995) observed children from infancy to age 3 in three income levels. They found a strong association between children's oral language and literacy and the family's socioeconomic class, with higher skills strongly associated with higher status. Children who had more words directed toward them had significantly larger vocabularies. The magnitude of these differences was considerable: Children from the low-income families entered kindergarten with a listening vocabulary of 3,000 words, whereas children from middle-income families entered with a listening vocabulary of 20,000 words. Other meaningful distinctions were also observed among income levels, such as the number of positive words addressed to the child, a situation that could be associated with the quality of the parent–child relationship. Yet regardless of parents' income levels, the quality of parent–child verbal interactions was a significant predictor of children's language skills.

Child Characteristics

Child characteristics—including engagement, language proficiency, cognitive and developmental levels, social behavior, motivation, and health conditions—can clearly influence literacy practices in the family. Children's level of engagement is significantly related to child outcomes (Sénéchal et al., 1995). Children who only listened to stories scored lower on comprehension and on production of new words than did children who actively point or label during reading.

With the shift toward understanding children's early literacy, research has increasingly focused on children's abilities in infancy and preschool in relation to later literacy and language. In a longitudinal study of children with expressive language delays, Rescorla and her colleagues consistently documented deficits in language and reading outcomes (Rescorla, 2000). Though these children were found to be within the average range on broad language and reading measures at ages 8 and 9 years (Manhardt & Rescorla, 2002; Rescorla, 2002) and at age 13 years (Rescorla, 2000), they demonstrated significantly lower scores on a number of specific language and academic measures when compared to typically devel-

oping children. Summarizing the literature on links between early language and later reading, Scarborough observed that "virtually" every study of preschoolers (e.g., Aram & Hall, 1989; Bishop & Adams, 1990) who were diagnosed at speech–language clinics "confirmed that preschoolers with language impairments are indeed at considerable risk for developing reading disabilities (as well as for continued oral language difficulties) at older ages" (Scarborough, 2001, p. 100). Summarizing across numerous studies related to early disabilities and later literacy development, Scarborough concludes that there is considerable continuity between early developmental differences and later performance (Scarborough, 1998, 2001).

Scarborough's research has also shown that children of parents with reading problems are at higher risk for difficulty in learning to read. These children scored lower on language instruments at age 30 months compared to similar peers whose parents did not have reading disabilities (Scarborough, 1989, 1990, 1991a, 1991b). This research, as well as that of others (e.g., Gallagher, Frith, & Snowling, 1999, cited in Scarborough, 2001), illustrates the close relation between parent–child characteristics and child outcomes.

Other child characteristics that have been studied in relation to literacy and language outcomes include children's health, in particular, the role of otitis media (Roberts & Burchinal, 2001). Otitis media with effusion (OME), or middle-ear infection, is one of the most prevalent medical conditions of childhood (Stool et al., 1994). An occurrence of OME can produce anything from no loss of hearing to a moderate loss that can linger for months. A child with frequent otitis media may find it difficult to hear verbal conversation. It is assumed that such a loss in the ability to hear conversation can create "a disadvantage for learning rules of language, affecting the developing of speech sounds, vocabulary, grammar, and use of language" (Roberts & Burchinal, 2001, p. 233). Consequently, investigators have explored many correlates of otitis media. In their recent summary of this literature, Roberts and Burchinal noted a lack of consensus about whether a relation exists between otitis media and later language or literacy difficulties. These authors concluded that looking for simple relations is not sufficient; rather, one must examine otitis media within a systems perspective, recognizing that home and childcare environments interact with child characteristics in determining child literacy and language outcomes.

Children's attention abilities have also been linked to reading ability. In one of the few studies to examine reading disability and attention-deficit/hyperactivity disorder (ADHD), Lonigan and his colleagues (1999) found that reading problems were substantially and uniquely associated with emergent literacy skills in children from both middle- and low-income families. Their findings also showed that the association between reading skills and ADHD is evident in preschool children (for an alternative perspective, see Westby, Chapter 19, this volume).

Other researchers have explored the relationship between home literacy activities and children's motivation or reading attitude (Purcell-Gates, 2000). In Durkin's (1966) study of early readers (cited in Purcell-Gates, 2000), early readers had both a rich home literacy environment and high interest in learning to read and write. Research also suggests that parents read more to children with high interest levels than to those with low interest levels (Morrow, 1983).

From this review, it is clear that one cannot study children's literacy outcomes in isolation from child characteristics. Children's cognitive, social, and behavioral characteristics are inextricably linked with their mastery of literacy and language.

Home Literacy Environment

Shared book reading, reading aloud to children, making print materials available, and promoting a positive attitude toward literacy are a few of the ways in which the home environment affects children's literacy learning. The home literacy environment has been well documented as a strong influence on children's literacy development, not only in early descriptive studies but also in more recent empirically based studies (Clark, 1984; Cochran-Smith, 1984; Morrow, 2001; Teale, 1984).

Storybook Reading

Studies have shown that children whose parents begin to read books to them at an early age display a greater interest in reading than children who lack this experience (Bus, 2001; Bus & van IJzendoorn, 1997, Bus, van IJzendoorn, & Pellegrini, 1995). Evidence also suggests that these children will continue to outperform peers whose home literacy environments are less enriching (Evans, Shaw, & Bell, 2000; Frijters, Barron, & Brunello, 2000; Leseman & de Long, 2000; Mantzicopoulos, 1997; Weinberger, 1996).

The occurrence of storybook reading as a family routine across income levels and cultures is striking, though significant differences exist in its prevalence, as we note in this chapter (for further discussion, see Craig & Washington, Chapter 11, and van Kleeck, Chapter 9, this volume). Storybook reading provides a variety of benefits for both parents and children, according to Taylor and Strickland (1986), including (1) bringing together members of the family, regardless of family size and their lifestyles; (2) providing opportunities for parents and children to learn about themselves and gain a deeper understanding of one another; (3) giving parents and children an opportunity to explore commonplace events and exceptional happenings; and (4) providing children with the opportunity to develop language, and literacy skills and values, in ways that are meaningful to them.

The home environment is complex, multilayered, and multidimensional, involving both physical and interpersonal features. Because of this complexity, Roskos and Twardosz (2004) suggest that, within the home, processes should be distinguished from resources in order to examine this environment's influence on family literacy practices. Noting that proximal processes have been found to support literacy and language development, they observe that researchers have given relatively little thought to the resources of the home environment with regard to the most frequently studied parent–child literacy activity, namely, storybook reading. In an intensive review of research on such reading, they find little attention to variables such as space for reading, time or people available to read to children, or routines that facilitate or hinder book reading. Yet these resources can dramatically influence the family's actions. It is clear that our knowledge of the home literacy environment must expand considerably if we are to understand how family resources support family literacy practices.

Cultural practices in the home can have a pronounced effect on children's language and literacy development. Ample evidence indicates that performance of children from Hispanic families is below that of non-Hispanic children during preschool and grade school (Strucker et al., 2004; Vernon-Feagans et al., 2001). Ezell, Gonzales, and Randolph (2000) examined the emergent literacy skills of a group of Mexican American preschoolers whose parents were migrant workers and who participated in Head Start. They found that the home literacy environment had a greater influence on children's emergent literacy skills than a number of other home and school factors, including home–school relationship, family composition, and family movement history.

Studies showing the importance of the home literacy environment for children in the United States (Clark, 1984; Cochran-Smith, 1984; Morrow, 1995, 2001; Teale, 1984) are corroborated by research abroad. Li and Rao (2000), for example, conducted a study of Chinese preschoolers in Beijing, Hong Kong, and Singapore. They found that home literacy education significantly predicted literacy attainment. In particular, parent–child literacy interactions, parental patterns of reading, and availability of reading materials in the home were especially good predictors of literacy attainment.

Parent–Child Relationships

When we consider the literacy practices occurring in the home, we tend to focus on *literacy-related* activities and outcomes, often to the exclusion of other, equally important relationships and outcomes, in particular, the social–emotional sequelae of family literacy practices (Baker, Afflerbach, & Reinking, 1996; Edwards & Pleasants, 1997). Yet the acquisition of literacy skills, like that of other skills, is heavily influenced by interpersonal interactions. Bloom (1998), for example, notes, "Children acquire language in the context of their psychological development and, in particular, developments in thinking, emotionality, and social interaction" (p. 309).

Children learn early language and literacy skills by interacting with others in the home. The quality of a child's relationship with parents or caregivers is critical to this learning process. Children with insecure attachment engage in less reading with their parents (Bus, 2001; Bus & van IJzendoorn, 1997, Bus et al., 1995). Nurturing caretakers and secure home environments provide children with a setting in which language and literacy can flourish. For example, Berlin, Brooks-Gunn, Spiker, and Zaslow (1995) report that parental support and warmth are associated with children's language ability. Edwards and Pleasants (1997) report that warmth and support in the parent–child relationship may modulate children's experiences with literacy.

Nurturing relationships are associated with enhanced literacy skills for children, including greater letter and number knowledge and understanding sound–symbol relations (Foster, 1997; Leichter, 1984). In a study by Sénéchal et al. (1996), parent–child interactions during shared storybook reading time had a significant influence on children's development of language skills, particularly the size of their vocabularies and the quality of their receptive language skills.

The quality of the parent–child relationship correlates with numerous outcomes for children, including behavioral, social–emotional, and educational outcomes. Many studies have investigated the association between the parent–child relationship and child academic outcomes. In a study of mother–child relationships, Pianta, Nimetz, and Bennett (1997) found that strong relationships correlate positively to children's performance on an assessment of basic school concepts. Similarly, Pianta and Harbers (1996) reported that mother–child interaction competence at school entry correlated significantly with academic achievement in grades 2, 3, and 4, as measured by the Iowa Test of Basic Skills (Hoover, Dunbar, & Frisbie, 2001). In a study of early predictors of referral for special education services, Pianta, Erickson, Wagner, Kreutzer, and Egeland (1990) found significant differences in mother–child interaction ratings for referred and nonreferred children. In particular, more positive interactions characterized the relationships between nonreferred children and their mothers compared to those of referred children.

Thus, positive parent–child interactions appear to be a significant factor in the development of children's literacy. However, positive parent–child interactions are not only a precursor to children's emergent literacy but can also be a consequence. By engaging in literacy activities together, parents and children have the opportunity to forge stronger, more positive relationships (Bus, 2001; Bus & van IJzendoorn, 1997; Bus et al., 1995; Taylor & Strickland, 1986). These relationships frequently have been linked to children's school success.

Other researchers have studied social and emotional support by examining the social climate in the home. Bus and van IJzendoorn (1997), for example, found that the social–emotional climate and warmth of the home are associated with children's school readiness skills. In a recent study of family literacy environments and children's emerging literacy skills among low-income, African American preschoolers and young school-age children, Britto and Brooks-Gunn (2001) found an important association between family literacy practices and social–emotional qualities of the parent–child relationship. Specifically, they found that encouragement and warmth in the home are positively correlated with children's emergent literacy.

It is clear, then, that a myriad of factors influence literacy development, especially the processes and resources in the home. But the child's characteristics also contribute significantly to this mix of variables. Consequently, researchers need to attend to multiple family literacy beliefs and practices in examining children's literacy outcomes.

LINKAGES BETWEEN FAMILY LITERACY PRACTICES AND SCHOOL-RELATED SKILLS

The relationship between family practices and children's performance in school has received considerable attention. Britto and Brooks-Gunn (2001) show that family practices are related to children's vocabulary and early reading, as well as their school readiness. Pellegrini (2001) observes that "the degree of similarity between home and school literacy events predicts success in school-based literacy" (p. 55). Furthermore, greater similarity exists between home literacy activities of high-SES families and actual school-based literacy activities than between activities in low-SES families and school practices (Pellegrini, 2001). Similarly, Heath (1983) reported that ways of using print vary between working-class and middle-class homes, with middle-class homes being more similar to school environments. Others also support the assertion that literacy practices in some homes are very different from what children encounter when they attend school (Auerbach, 1989; Taylor & Dorsey-Gaines, 1988). As Hannon (1998) observes: "Although almost all parents attempt to assist literacy development in some way, they do not all do it in the same way, to the same extent, with the same concept of literacy, or with the same resources" (p. 122).

To illustrate the possible impact of family and home influences on school activities, we have selected three school-related variables that are frequently addressed in the literature for illustrative purposes: oral language and letter–sound knowledge, reading comprehension, and written language and spelling.

Oral Language and Letter-Sound Knowledge

The home environment has been frequently studied as a basis of support for children's oral language development. Both direct and indirect teaching activities in the home influence children's growth in these areas. Even with the very young, parental practices can affect oral language. Studying the daily speech of 24-month-old children, Wells (1985) found that about 5% of their daily speech occurred during story time. Similarly, mothers' labeling of objects for children was most likely to occur during storybook reading (Ninio & Bruner, 1978).

Others have found that storybook reading is related to children's oral language skills (Sénéchal, LeFevre, Thomas, & Daley, 1998; Sénéchal et al., 1995). Frequency of library visits has been found to positively affect children's vocabulary (Sénéchal et al., 1996). Crain-Thoreson and Dale (1992) found that storybook reading at age 2 years is a significant predictor of vocabulary and syntax knowledge at 30 months. In their studies of parent–child conversations during mealtime, Dickinson and Tabors (1991) found that the proportion of narrative and explanatory talk contributed to children's decontextualized language skills.

Payne, Whitehurst, and Angell (1994) investigated the relation between activities in the home environment and children's language skills, finding that the home literacy environment was a significant predictor of language skills, accounting for 18% of the variance in children's scores on a measure of language development. The specific activities that contributed most to this finding included (1) frequency of shared picture-book reading, (2) age of onset of picture-book reading, (3) duration of shared picture-book reading at one sitting, (4) number of picture books in the home, (5) frequency of the child's requests to engage in shared reading activities, (6) frequency of shared trips to the library, (7) frequency of the caregiver's private reading, and (8) the caregiver's enjoyment of private reading.

One of the most often-cited mechanisms by which the home literacy environment influences children's development of language and literacy concepts is the teaching and learning of letters, sounds, and letter–sound correspondence. Evans, Shaw, and Bell (2000) examined the home literacy activities of kindergarten students and found that home activities involving letters contributed

significantly to the variance in children's letter–name and letter–sound knowledge in kindergarten. Furthermore, they found that when children were tested again in second grade, kindergarten letter–name and –sound knowledge accounted significantly for differences among children in reading comprehension and spelling achievement. In another study of family literacy practices in the homes of kindergarten students, Frijters, Barron, and Brunello (2000) found that home literacy activities (such as parent–child reading interactions, availability of print materials, and parental reading practices) and children's literacy interest accounted for 21% of the variance in children's oral vocabulary.

Phonological awareness, the appreciation of speech sounds without regard for their meaning, affects all aspects of literacy and "is critical to discovering the alphabetic principle (the idea that letters generally represent the small speech segments called phonemes)" (Snow et al., 1998, p. 248). Strong phonological skills have been linked to greater achievement in reading, written language, oral language, spelling, and vocabulary development. The direct teaching of letter–sound correspondence is a common family literacy practice in many homes, and several recent studies have underscored the significance of this direct teaching for children's ultimate literacy outcomes.

In another study of phonological sensitivity in 4- and 5-year-old children, Burgess (1999) examined factors including speech perception, oral language ability, early knowledge about print, and the home literacy environment as they related to growth in phonological sensitivity. He found that the home-literacy environment was the only factor that made a unique contribution to predicting phonological sensitivity.

Reading Comprehension

Strong associations have been documented between the literacy practices of the home and children's achievement in the area of reading comprehension. Leseman and de Long (2000) conducted a longitudinal study of the effects of family literacy practices on the development of reading comprehension in 4- to 9-year-old children. They found that the home literacy environment, including the availability of reading materials, parental support for reading, and the amount of shared book-reading time, had long-term effects on reading comprehension.

Written Language and Spelling

Home activities also affect children's literacy *output* in terms of written language. Frijters et al. (2000) report that the home literacy environment, coupled with children's interest in literacy activities, accounts for 18% of the variance in kindergarteners' early written language skills. Other studies support this finding. Examining direct teaching of writing skills by the parents of kindergarten and first-grade children, Sénéchal et al. (1998) found that the amount of direct teaching was significantly related to children's enhanced written language skills.

Teale (1986) studied the relationship between home background and young children's literacy development by making systematic observations of preschool children from low-income, ethnically diverse backgrounds. He noted that a range of literacy activities occurs in the home that preschoolers could engage in or observe, such as shopping or paying bills, reading, or parents' work-related reading. When adults engage in literacy activities, Teale concluded, their children receive opportunities to develop more literacy skills.

By contrast, Purcell-Gates (2001) suggests that, for children to learn written language, they need specific opportunities and interactions around print. She notes that the family practices necessary to develop written language knowledge are different from those needed for oral language. She believes that experiences such as storybook reading are essential for children to develop written language knowledge. Though the research base supporting this premise is small, data from three studies involving children from low-income families (Dahl & Freppon, 1995; Purcell-Gates, 1996; Purcell-Gates & Dahl, 1991) have shown that written register knowledge at the beginning of kindergarten for these children is almost nonexistent

compared with their peers who have been read to frequently (Purcell-Gates, 2001).

Further support for the effects of instruction on knowledge of written language comes from an early study by Hess, Holloway, Price, and Dickson (1982), who found that parental instruction in letter naming resulted in higher scores on letter recognition tests. In a study of linguistically precocious children, Crain-Thoreson and Dale (1992) found that the amount of experience with home and school instruction in letter names and sounds is a significant predictor of children's knowledge of print concepts and invented spelling.

Practices occurring in the home affect children's educational progress and outcomes through a number of mechanisms. Qualities of the parent–child relationship, in particular, are especially salient in terms of children's school outcomes, as well as specific activities, such as storybook reading, and direct and indirect teaching. In summary, home literacy practices clearly influence a number of areas of children's early school performance.

FAMILY LITERACY INTERVENTIONS

Family literacy interventions have become increasingly prevalent since the 1980s, though there are many examples of interest in such interventions prior to that time (Wasik & Herrmann, 2004; Wasik et al., 2001). When broadly defined, "family literacy programs" include a wide range of educational services designed to help parents, their children, or both parents and children enhance their literacy skills. This broad definition can involve an adult education program with a parenting component, early childhood education with a parenting component, or other parenting-only programs. Lately, the term has been associated with the recent federal definition of family literacy services, calling for adult education, parent education, parent and child literacy activities, and early childhood education (St. Pierre & Ricciuti, 2001; St. Pierre, Ricciuti, & Creps, 1999).

Both the Parent and Child Education (PACE) program in Kentucky and the comprehensive family literacy model of the National Center for Family Literacy (often referred to as the Kenan model) influenced the government's adoption of this comprehensive model, first for the Even Start Family Literacy Program, and later for other family literacy efforts. These early programs provided a model of multigenerational services involving both parents and their children engaged in learning literacy skills. Other large-scale family literacy interventions, such as the Parents as Teachers program (PAT) (Winter & McDonald, 1997) and the Home Instruction for Parents of Preschool Youngsters (HIPPY; Baker, Piotrkowski, & Brooks-Gunn, 1999), focus directly on parents, based on the premise that parental practices can enhance children's development.

A number of studies have shown that parenting interventions result in positive changes in child behavior. In this section, we review some of this research. First, however, it is important to note that there are conflicting beliefs about family literacy interventions (Auerbach, 1989; Taylor, 1997). Because a considerable body of data suggests that low-literacy families do not engage in practices linked with positive school outcomes that are common in families with higher literacy skills, interventions have often focused on helping parents with low literacy skills to learn new ways of interacting with their children. We have referred to this direct teaching method as the "coaching approach" (Wasik et al., 2001), which emphasizes the possibility of teaching effective strategies, including didactic teaching. We describe several examples of this approach in the next section.

Coaching Approach

Changes in the parent–child relationship and in the learning environment at home through participation in Head Start have been associated with children's gains in school readiness skills, including letter and number knowledge (Parker, Boak, Griffin, Ripple, & Peay, 1999). In one study, parents were taught to engage their children in the reading activity by asking questions and by prompting comments and questions from the children. This parental intervention produced improvements in the quality of children's interactive book reading (Taverne & Sheridan, 1995). Also, pretest–posttest measures that used the Peabody Picture Vocabulary Test—Revised (PPVT; Dunn & Dunn, 1997) indicated gains in children's vocabulary knowledge.

Whitehurst and Lonigan, and their colleagues, have examined the effects of a shared reading program, called "dialogic reading," on preschool children's language skills. The dialogic reading program calls for a shift in roles: instead of the parent reading and the child listening, the child learns to become the storyteller. The adult is taught to be an active listener who asks questions, adds information, and prompts the child to expand the sophistication of descriptions of picture books. Children from middle-income families who engaged in dialogic reading have shown positive outcomes. They outperformed their middle- and upper-income peers who engaged in a typical picture-book reading (Arnold, Lonigan, Whitehurst, & Epstein, 1994). Also, both teachers and low-income parents have successfully used dialogic reading intervention to produce significant changes in children's language skills (Lonigan & Whitehurst, 1998; Valdez-Menchaca & Whitehurst, 1992).

Dialogic reading has been found to affect significantly preschool children's expressive language, including mean length of utterance, writing, linguistic awareness, and print concepts (Whitehurst, Epstein, et al., 1994). Dialogic reading intervention has been found to have a greater effect on children's language when both teachers and parents actively use the technique (Whitehurst, Arnold, et al., 1994; Whitehurst, Epstein, et al., 1994).

Primavera (2000) describes a number of positive outcomes for low-income families of preschoolers in which parents learned to engage in literacy activities with their children at home. Improvements occurred in family literacy activities related to increased parent–child interaction time; increased time spent reading to the child; and improved family relationships, communication, and feelings of togetherness. Children, in particular, experienced enhanced language skills and interest in learning, whereas parents improved their understanding of child development and enhanced their own feelings of self-esteem and self-confidence.

Research by Neuman and her colleagues also supports coaching parents with their children. In a study with 6 teenage mothers, each mother was coached to use the strategies of labeling, scaffolding, and contingent responsiveness during play with her child. After coaching, all of the mothers used the strategies more often (Neuman & Gallagher, 1994). Though the coached behaviors decreased during follow-up, they did not return to precoaching levels. Edwards (1991, 1994), who developed the Parents as Partners in Reading program, acknowledged that questions are sometimes raised about the cultural appropriateness of coaching or direct instruction as methods to enhance children's literacy, but she also observed that many low-income and low-literacy parents are seeking explicit instruction on ways to enhance their children's literacy development. In her intervention program, parents receive knowledge and skills, as well as opportunities for modeling and practice.

Sociocultural Approach

In discussing a sociocontextual approach to family literacy, Auerbach (1989) proposed an approach to family literacy interventions that incorporates family, culture, and community, rather than attempting to transmit school literacy practices to the home. This approach is a social activity in which learners derive meaning from text and incorporate their own life experiences (Ada, 1988; Delgado-Gaitan, 1994; Neuman, 1996). Others have also supported valuing and building on the family's culture and strengths as opposed to *deficit* perspectives that emphasize transmission of literacy skills from the school to the family (Kerka, 1991; Taylor, 1997; Tett & St. Clair, 1997). This view has been called an "empowerment model," or a "strengths model" (Kerka, 1992). With multilingual families, in particular, researchers have documented the importance of building on family strengths,

emphasizing collaboration, and acknowledging the native culture (Rodriguez-Brown & Mulhern, 1993; Weinstein-Shr, 1992).

Examples of interventions that use the sociocultural theory include instructor facilitation, demonstration, interaction, and reciprocal teaching (Ada, 1988; Delgado-Gaitan, 1994; Handel & Goldsmith, 1994; Neuman, 1996). One example of engaging parents in the learning process is the Family Reading Program (Handel & Goldsmith, 1994). Geared toward poor readers, this project built on learner strengths in parent workshops using the following framework: (1) introduction activities, (2) presentation of a book, (3) demonstration of strategy, (4) practice in pairs, (5) group discussion, (6) preparation for reading at home, and (7) optional adult reading. Most participants used interactive strategies and had positive experiences with the program.

Following a model set forth by Ada (1988), Delgado-Gaitan (1994) worked with Spanish-speaking parents whose elementary-age children were identified as poor readers. Parents participated in discussion groups in which they were introduced to four categories of effective questions. Then, they were encouraged to create questions about the storybooks that reflected their own personal experience and knowledge. Results showed that increases in parents' self-perception and efficacy were related to positive child outcomes.

Neuman (1996) extended Ada's (1988) and Delgado-Gaitan's (1994) work. She introduced an intervention that included hour-long, weekly book clubs that lasted for 12 weeks. A parent leader and a bilingual teacher from the community facilitated the book clubs. Parents participated in group discussions and derived strategies for reading based on their experiences. After practicing with other parents, these parents then read to their children in the classroom.

The two approaches for working with parents illustrated here—the coaching model and the sociocultural model—are based on different beliefs about the role and purpose of intervention procedures. Although debates continue, we need to involve families in planning interventions and examine how interventions change family practices.

We also need to find ways to provide interventions that are both acceptable to parents and beneficial to their children's literacy development. Interventions, though criticized at times, may be welcome by families seeking new opportunities and possibilities for themselves and their children.

CONCLUSIONS

Family literacy practices are complex and dynamic, and they vary along many dimensions. They vary from one family to another, from one culture to another, and within cultures. Despite these differences, literacy practices within the family have a strong and enduring effect on children's language and literacy skills. Children whose parents actively engage them in literacy activities, such as book reading, and who engage in direct teaching of other literacy skills, such as letter and word recognition or letter–sound activities, demonstrate higher scores on early literacy instruments and on school performance indices, such as achievement and reading. Family characteristics, cultural values and beliefs, financial resources, and parents' educational levels affect literacy practices within the home. Furthermore, within the home, both activities and resources likely interact to influence children's language and literacy in ways we do yet understand. We are recognizing that parent and child relationships also influence children's learning; positive and supportive relationships lead to better child outcomes, including positive literacy outcomes.

Interventions to enhance family literacy must incorporate information on family values, culture, and beliefs, as well as build on the family's existing strengths and resources. Storybook reading, for instance, is consistent with the values and beliefs of almost every family and is a powerful process for encouraging the development of literacy in young children.

Over the past 20 years, we have gone from recognizing the critical influence of family literacy practices on family members to new and emerging theories of how literacy is transmitted across generations and an increasing empirical knowledge base about how family literacy practices affect young children's literacy development. During the next decade, we must continue to examine family literacy practices, with a special focus on how such information can be used in culturally responsive ways. Based on what we already know, however, practitioners concerned with children's literacy and language have a strong empirical base for encouraging active, positive parent participation to enhance child outcomes.

REFERENCES

Ada, A. F. (1988). The Parjaro Valley experiences. In T. Skutnabb-Kangas & J. Cummins (Eds.), *Minority education* (pp. 224–248). Cevedon, PA: Multilingual Matters.

Adams, M. (1990). *Beginning to read: Thinking and learning about print.* Cambridge, MA: MIT Press.

Anderson, A. B., & Stokes, S. J. (1984). Social and institutional influences on the development and practice of literacy. In H. Goelman, A. Oberg, & F. Smith (Eds.), *Awakening to literacy* (pp. 24–37). Portsmouth, NH: Heinemann.

Anderson-Yockel, J., & Haynes, W. (1994). Joint picture-book reading strategies in working-class African American and white mother–toddlers dyads. *Journal of Speech, Language, and Hearing Research, 37,* 583–593.

Aram, D. M., & Hall, N. E. (1989). Longitudinal follow-up of children with preschool communication disorders: Treatment implications. *School Psychology Review, 18,* 487–501.

Arnold, D. H., Lonigan, C. J., Whitehurst, G. J., & Epstein, J. N. (1994). Accelerating language development through picture book reading: Replication and extension to a videotape training format. *Journal of Educational Psychology, 86,* 235–243.

Auerbach, E. R. (1989). Toward a socio-contextual approach to family literacy. *Harvard Educational Review, 59,* 165–181.

Baker, A. J., Piotrkowski, C. S., & Brooks-Gunn, J. B. (1999). Home instruction program for preschool youngsters. *The Future of Children, 9*(1), 116–133.

Baker, L., Afflerbach, P., & Reinking, D. (1996). *Developing engaged readers in school and home communities.* Mahwah, NJ: Erlbaum.

Baker, L., Scher, D., & Mackler, K. (1997). Home and family influences on motivations for reading. *Educational Psychologist, 32,* 69–82.

Berlin, L. J., Brooks-Gunn, J., Spiker, D., & Zaslow, M. J. (1995). Examining observational measures of emotional support and cognitive stimulation in black and white mothers of preschoolers. *Journal of Family Issues, 16,* 664–686.

Bishop, D. V. M., & Adams, C. (1990). A prospective study of the relationship between specific language impairment, phonological disorders, and reading retardation. *Journal of Child Psychology and Psychiatry, 31,* 1027–1050.

Bloom, L. (1998). Language acquisition in its developmental context. In W. Damon, (Editor-in-Chief), D. Kuhn, & R. S. Siegler (Vol. Eds.), *Handbook of child psychology* (5th ed., Vol. 2, pp. 309–370). New York: Wiley.

Britto, P. R., & Brooks-Gunn, J. (2001). Beyond shared book reading: Dimensions of home literacy and low-income African American preschoolers' skills. In P. Britto & J. Brooks-Gunn (Eds.), *The role of family literacy environments in promoting young children's emerging literacy skills* (pp. 73–90). San Francisco: Jossey-Bass.

Bronfenbrenner, U. (1979). *The ecology of human development: Experiments by nature and design.* Cambridge, MA: Harvard University Press.

Bronfenbrenner, U. (1986). Ecology of the family as a context for human development: Research perspectives. *Developmental Psychology, 22,* 723–742.

Bronfenbrenner, U. (1995). Developmental ecology through space and time: A future perspective. In P. Moen, G. H. Elder, & K. Lushen (Eds.), *Examining lives in context* (pp. 619–647). Washington, DC: American Psychological Association.

Burgess, S. (1999). The influence of speech perception, oral language ability, the home literacy environment, and prereading knowledge on the growth of phonological sensitivity: A 1-year longitudinal study. *Reading Research Quarterly, 34,* 400–402.

Bus, A. G. (2001). Joint caregiver–child storybook reading: A route to literacy development. In S. B. Neuman & D. K. Dickinson (Eds.), *Handbook of early literacy research* (pp 179–191). New York: Guilford Press.

Bus, A. G., & van IJzendoorn, M. H. (1997). Affective dimension of mother–infant picture book reading. *Journal of School Psychology, 35,* 47–60.

Bus, A. G., van IJzendoorn, M. H., & Pellegrini, A. D. (1995). Joint book reading makes for success in learning to read: A meta-analysis on intergenerational transmission of literacy. *Review of Educational Research, 65,* 1–21.

Carlson, C. D. (1998). Socioeconomic status and reading achievement: The mediating role of home processes and pre-reading skills (No. AAM9835726). *Dissertation Abstracts International, 59*(5-A), 1509.

Clark, M. M. (1984). Literacy at home and at school: Insights from a study of young fluent readers. In H. Goelman, A. Oberg, & F. Smith (Eds.), *Awakening to literacy* (pp. 122–130). Portsmouth, NH: Heinemann.

Clay, M. M. (1993). *An observation study of early literacy achievement.* Portsmouth, NH: Heinemann.

Cochran-Smith, M. (1984). *The making of a reader.* Norwood, NJ: Ablex.

Cook, V. (1980). The influence of home and family on the development of literacy in children. *School Psychology Review, 9,* 369–373.

Crain-Thoreson, C., & Dale, P. S. (1992). Do early talkers become early readers?: Linguistic precocity, preschool language, and emergent literacy. *Developmental Psychology, 28,* 421–429.

Cunningham, A. E., & Stanovich, K. E. (1998). Early reading acquisition and its relationto reading experience and ability 10 years later. *Developmental Psychology, 33,* 934–945.

Dahl, K., & Freppon, P. A. (1995). A comparison of inner-city children's interpretation of reading and writing instruction in the early grades in skills-based and whole language classrooms. *Reading Research Quarterly, 1,* 50–74.

Delgado-Gaitan, C. (1990). *Literacy for empowerment: The role of parents in children's education.* London: Palmer Press.

Delgado-Gaitan, C. (1994). Sociocultural change through literacy: Towards empowerment of families. In B. Ferdman, R. M. Weber, & A. Ramirex (Eds.), *Literacy across languages and cultures* (pp. 143–170). Albany: State University of New York Press.

Della-Piana, G., & Martin, H. (1976). Reading achievement and maternal behavior. *Reading Teacher, 20,* 225–230.

Dickinson, D. K., & Tabors, P. O. (1991). Early literacy: Linkages between home, school, and literacy achievement at age five. *Journal of Research in Childhood Education, 6,* 30–46.

Dunn, L., & Dunn, L. (1997). *The Peabody Picture Vocabulary Test—Third Edition.* Circle Pines, MN: American Guidance Service.

Durkin, D. (1966). *Children who read early.* New York: Teachers College Press.

Edwards, P. A. (1991). Fostering literacy through parent coaching. In E. H. Hiebert (Ed.), *Literacy for a diverse society: Perspectives, practices, and policies* (pp. 199–214). New York: Teachers College Press.

Edwards, P. A. (1994). Responses of teachers and African-American mothers to a book-reading intervention program. In D. I. Dickinson (Ed.), *Bridges to literacy: Children, families, and schools* (pp. 199–214). New York: Teachers College Press.

Edwards, P. A. (1995). Combining parents' and teachers' thoughts about storybook reading at home and school. In L. M. Morrow (Ed.), *Family literacy: Connections in schools and communities* (pp 54–69). New Brunswick, NJ: International Reading Association.

Edwards, P. A., & Pleasants, H. M. (1997). Unclosseting home literacy environment: Issues raised through telling of parent stories. *Early Child Development and Care, 127–128,* 27–46.

Emberton, S. (2004). Family and Child Education (FACE): Family and literacy services for American Indians. In B. H. Wasik (Ed.), *Handbook of family literacy* (pp. 483–500). Mahwah, NJ: Erlbaum.

Evans, M. A., Shaw, D., & Bell, M. (2000). Home literacy activities and their influence on early literacy skills. *Canadian Journal of Experimental Psychology, 54*(2), 65–75.

Ezell, H. K., Gonzales, M. D., & Randolph, E. (2000). Emergent literacy skills of migrant Mexican American preschoolers. *Communication Disorders Quarterly, 21*(3), 147–153.

Federal Interagency Forum on Child and Family Statistics. (1999). America's children: Key national indicators of well-being. Washington, DC: U.S. Government Printing Office.

Fitzgerald, J., Spiegel, D. L., & Cunningham, J. W. (1991). The relationship between parental literacy level and perception of emergent literacy. *Journal of Reading Behavior, 23,* 191–213.

Foster, M. (1997). Family literacy: Questioning conventional wisdom. In D. Taylor (Ed.), *Many families, many literacies: An international declaration of principles* Portsmouth, NH: Heinemann.

Freeberg, N. E. & Berliner, D. C. (1967). Dimensions of parental practice concerned with cognitive development in the preschool children. *Journal of Genetic Psychology, 111,* 245–261.

Frijters, J. C., Barron, R. W., & Brunello, M. (2000). Direct and mediated influences of home literacy and literacy interest on prereaders' oral vocabulary and early written language skill. *Journal of Educational Psychology, 92,* 466–477.

Gadsden, V. L. (1993). Literacy, education, and identity among African Americans: The communal nature of learning. *Urban Education, 27,* 352–369.

Gadsden, V. (1994). Understanding family literacy: Conceptual issues. *Teachers College Record, 6,* 58–86.

Gadsden, V. L. (2004). Family literacy and culture. In B. H. Wasik (Ed.), *Handbook of family literacy* (pp. 401–425). Mahwah, NJ: Erlbaum.

Gee, J. P. (2001). A sociocultural perspective on early literacy development. In S. B. Neuman & David K. Dickinson (Eds.), *Handbook of early literacy research* (pp. 30–42). New York: Guilford Press.

Gesell, A. L. (1925). *The mental growth of the preschool child.* New York: Macmillan.

Goelman, H., Oberg, A. A., & Smith, A. (Eds.). (1984). *Awakening to literacy.* Portsmouth, NH: Heinemann.

Goodman, Y. M. (1980). The roots of literacy. In M. P. Douglas (Ed.), *Forty-fourth yearbook of the Claremont Reading Conference* (pp. 1–12). Claremont, CA: Claremont Reading Conference.

Haden, C. A., Reese, E., & Fivush, R. (1996). Mothers' extratextual comments during storybook reading: Stylistic differences over time and across texts. *Discourse Processes, 21,* 135–169.

Hammer, C. S. (1999). Guiding language development: How African American mothers and their infants structure play. *Journal of Speech and Hearing Research, 42,* 1219–1233.

Handel, R. D., & Goldsmith, E. (1994). Family reading—still got it: Adults as learners, literacy resources, and actors in the world. In D. K. Dickinson (Ed.), *Bridges to literacy: Children, families and schools* (pp. 150–174). Cambridge, MA: Blackwell.

Hannon, P. (1998). How can we foster children's early literacy development through parent involvement? In S. B. Neuman & K. A. Roskos (Eds.), *Children achieving: Best practices in early literacy* (pp.

121–143). Newark, DE: International Reading Association.

Hart, B., & Risley, T. R. (1995). *Meaningful differences in the everyday experience of young American children.* Baltimore: Brookes.

Heath, S. B. (1983). *Ways with words.* Cambridge, MA: Cambridge University Press.

Hess, R. D., Holloway, S., Price, G. G., & Dickson, W. P. (1982). Family environments and acquisition of reading skills: Towards a more precise analysis. In L. M. Laosa & I. Sigel (Eds.), *Families as learning environments for children* (pp. 87–113). New York: Plenum.

Hess, R. D., & Shipman, V. C. (1965). Early experience and the socialization of cognitive modes in children. *Child Development, 36,* 869–886.

Hoover, H., Dunbar, S., & Frisbie, D. (2001). *Iowa Test of Basic Skills.* Itasca, IL: Riverside.

Johnson, J. E., & Martin, C. (1985). Parents' beliefs and home learning environments: Effects on cognitive development. In I. E. Sigel (Ed.), *Parental belief systems* (pp. 25–50). Hillsdale, NJ: Erlbaum.

Juel, C. (1988). Learning to read and write: A longitudinal study of 54 children from first through fourth grades. *Journal of Educational Psychology, 78,* 243–255.

Kerka, S. (1991). *Family and intergenerational literacy* (ERIC Digest No. 111). Columbus, OH: ERIC Clearinghouse on Adult, Career, and Vocational Education (ERIC Document Reproduction Service No. 334 467)

Kerka, S. (1992). *Family literacy programs and practices: Practice application brief.* Columbus, OH: Eric Clearinghouse on Adult, Career, and Vocational Education (ERIC Document Reproduction Service No. 347 328)

Leichter, H. J. (1984). Families as environments for literacy. In H. Goelman, A. A. Oberg, & F. Smith (Eds.), *Awakening to literacy* (pp. 38–50). Portsmouth, NH: Heinemann.

Leichter, H. J. (1997). Some perspectives on the family. In D. Taylor (Ed.), *Many families, many literacies: An international declaration of principles.* Portsmouth, NH: Heinemann.

Leseman, P. P. M., & de Long, P. F. (2000). Development of reading skill: The impact of home literacy. *Pedagogische Studien, 77*(5–6), 290–306.

Li, H., & Rao, N. (2000). Parental influences on Chinese literacy development: A comparison of preschoolers in Beijing, Hong Kong and Singapore. *International Journal of Behavioral Development, 24,* 82–90.

Lonigan, C. J., Bloomfield, B. G., Anthony, J. L., Bacon, K. D., Phillips, B. M., & Samwel, C. S. (1999). Relations between emergent literacy skills, behavioral problems, and social competence in preschool children: A comparison of at-risk and typically developing children. *Topics in Early Childhood Special Education, 17,* 40–53.

Lonigan, C. J., & Whitehurst, G. J. (1998). Examination of the relative efficacy of parent and teacher involvement in a shared-reading intervention for preschool children from low-income backgrounds.

Early Childhood Research Quarterly, 17, 265–292.

Manhardt, J., & Rescorla, L. (2002). Oral narrative skills of late talkers at ages 8 and 9. *Applied Psycholinguistics, 23,* 1–21.

Mantzicopoulos, P. Y. (1997). The relationship of family variables to Head Start children's preacademic competence. *Early Education and Development, 8,* 357–375.

McGillicuddy-DeLisi, A. V. (1985). The relationship between parental beliefs and children's cognitive level. In I. E. Sigel (Ed.), *Parental belief systems: The psychological consequences for children* (pp. 7–24). Hillsdale, NJ: Erlbaum.

Meisels, S. J., & Shonkoff, J. P. (2000). Early childhood intervention: A continuing evolution. In J. P. Shonkoff & S. J. Meisels (Eds.), *Handbook of early childhood intervention* (2nd ed., pp. 3–31). Cambridge, UK: Cambridge University Press.

Minuchin, S. (1974). *Families and family therapy.* Cambridge, MA: Harvard University Press.

Morrow, L. M. (1983). Home and school correlates of early interest in literature. *Journal of Educational Research, 76,* 221–230.

Morrow, L. M. (Ed.). (1995). *Family literacy: Connections in schools and communities.* New Brunswick, NJ: International Reading Association.

Morrow, L. M. (2001). *Literacy development in the early years: Helping children read and write* (4th ed.). Boston: Allyn & Bacon.

Neuman, S. B. (1996). Children engaging in storybook reading: The influence of access to print resources, opportunity, and parental interaction. *Early Childhood Research Quarterly, 11,* 495–513.

Neuman, S. B., & Dickinson, D. K. (2001). Introduction. In *Handbook of early literacy development* (pp. 3–29). NY: Guilford Press.

Neuman, S. B., & Gallagher, P. (1994). Joining together in literacy learning: Teenage mothers and children. *Reading Research Quarterly, 29,* 382–401.

Neuman, S. B., Hagedorn, T., Celano, D., & Daly, P. (1995). Toward a collaborative approach to parent involvement in early education: A study of teenage mothers in an African-American community. *American Educational Research Journal, 32,* 801–827.

Ninio, A., & Bruner, J. S. (1978). The achievement and antecedents of labeling. *Journal of Child Language, 5,* 1–15.

Parker, F. L., Boak, A. Y., Griffin, K. W., Ripple, C., & Peay, L. (1999). Parent–child relationship, home learning environment, and school readiness. *School Psychology Review, 28,* 413–425.

Payne, A. C., Whitehurst, G. J., & Angell, A. L. (1994). The role of home literacy environment in the development of language ability in preschool children from low-income families. *Early Childhood Research Quarterly, 9*(3–4), 427–440.

Peck, B. B., & Stackhouse, T. W. (1973). Reading problems and family dynamics. *Journal of Learning Disabilities, 6,* 506–511.

Pellegrini, A. D. (2001). Some theoretical and methodological considerations in studying literacy in social context. In S. B. Neuman & D. K. Dickinson (Eds.), *Handbook of early literacy research* (pp. 54–65). New York: Guilford Press.

Pellegrini, A. D., Galda, L., Jones, I., & Perlmutter, J. (1995). Joint reading between mothers and their Head-Start children: Vocabulary development in two text formats. *Discourse Processes, 19,* 441–463.

Pellegrini, A., Perlmutter, J., Galda, L., & Brody, G. (1990). Joint reading between black Head Start children and their mothers. *Child Development, 61,* 443–453.

Pianta, R. C., Erickson, M. F., Wagner, N., Kreutzer, T., & Egeland, B. (1990). Early predictors of referrals for special services: Child-based measures vs. mother–child interactions. *School Psychology Review, 19,* 240–250.

Pianta, R. C., & Harbers, K. (1996). Observing mother and child behavior in a problem-solving situation at school entry: Relations with academic achievement. *Journal of School Psychology, 34,* 307–322.

Pianta, R. C., Nimetz, S. L., & Bennett, E. (1997). Mother–child relationships, teacher–child relationships and adjustment in preschool and kindergarten. *Early Childhood Research Quarterly, 12,* 263–280.

Primavera, J. (2000). Enhancing family competence through literacy activities. *Journal of Prevention and Intervention in the Community, 20*(1–2), 85–101.

Purcell-Gates, V. (1995). *Other people's words: The cycle of low literacy.* Cambridge, MA: Harvard University Press.

Purcell-Gates, V. (1996). Stories, coupons, and the *TV Guide*: Relationships between home literacy experiences and emergent literacy knowledge. *Reading Research Quarterly, 31,* 406–428.

Purcell-Gates, V. (2000). Family literacy. In M. L. Kamil, P. B. Mosenthal, P. D. Pearson, & R. Barr (Eds.), *Handbook of reading research* (pp. 853–870). Mahwah: NJ: Erlbaum.

Purcell-Gates, V. (2001). Emergent literacy is emerging knowledge of written, not oral, language. In P. R. Britto & J. Brooks-Gunn (Eds.), *The role of family literacy environments in promoting young children's emerging literacy skills* (pp. 7–22). San Francisco: Jossey-Bass.

Purcell-Gates, V., & Dahl, K. L. (1991). Low-SES children's success and failures at early literacy learning in skills-based classrooms. *Journal of Reading Behavior, 23,* 1–34.

Rescorla, L. (2000). Do late-talking toddlers turn out to have reading difficulties a decade later? *Annals of Dyslexia, 50,* 87–102.

Rescorla, L. (2002). Language and reading outcomes to age 9 in late-talking toddlers. *Journal of Speech, Language, and Hearing Research, 45,* 360–371.

Roberts, J. E., & Burchinal, M. R. (2001). The complex interplay between biology and environment: Otitis media and mediating effects on early literacy development. In S. B. Neuman & D. K. Dickinson (Eds.), *Handbook of early literacy research* (pp. 232–241). New York: Guilford Press.

Rodriguez-Brown, F. V., & Mulhern, M. M. (1993). Fostering critical literacy through family literacy: A

study of families in a Mexican-immigrant community. *Bilingual Research Journal, 17*, 1–16.

Rodriguez, J., Diaz, R., Duran, D., & Espinosa, L.
(1995). The impact of bilingual preschool education
on the language development of Spanish-speaking
children. *Early Childhood Research Quarterly, 10*,
475–490.

Roskos, K. A., & Twardosz, S. (2004). Resources,
family literacy, and children learning to read. In B.
H. Wasik (Ed.), *Handbook of family literacy* (pp.
287–303). Mahwah, NJ: Erlbaum.

Sameroff, A., & Chandler, J. (1975). Reproductive risk
and the continuum of caretaking casualty. *Review of
Child Development Research, 14*, 187–244.

Scarborough, H. S. (1989). Prediction of reading disability from familial and individual differences.
Journal of Educational Psychology, 81, 101–108.

Scarborough, H. S. (1990). Very early language deficits
in dyslexic children. *Child Development, 61*,
1728–1734.

Scarborough, H. S. (1991a). Early syntactic development of dyslexic children. *Annual of Dyslexia, 41*,
207–220.

Scarborough, H. S. (1991b). Antecedents to reading
disability: Preschool language development and literacy experiences for children from dyslexic families. *Reading and Writing, 3*, 219–233.

Scarborough, H. S. (1998). Early identification of children at risk for reading disabilities: Phonological
awareness and some other promising predictors. In
B. K. Shapiro, P. J. Accardo, & A. J. Capute (Eds.),
Specific reading disability: A view of the spectrum
(pp. 74–119). Timonium, MD: York Press.

Scarborough, H. S. (2001). Connecting early language
and literacy to later reading (dis)abilities: Evidence,
theory, and practice. In S. B. Neuman & D. K. Dickinson (Eds.), *Handbook of early literacy research*
(pp. 97–110). New York: Guilford Press.

Sénéchal, M., & LeFevre, J. (2001). Storybook reading
and parent teaching: Links to language and literacy
development. In P. Britto & J. Brooks-Gunn (Eds.),
*The role of family literacy environments in promot-
ing young children's emerging literacy skills* (pp.
39–52). San Francisco: Jossey-Bass.

Sénéchal, M., LeFevre, J., Hudson, E., & Lawson, E. P.
(1996). Knowledge of storybooks as a predictor of
young children's vocabulary. *Journal of Educational
Psychology, 88*, 520–536.

Sénéchal, M., LeFevre, J. A., Thomas, E. M., & Daley,
K. E. (1998). Differential effects of home literacy
experiences on the development of oral and written
language. *Reading Research Quarterly, 33*, 96–
116.

Sénéchal, M., Thomas, E. H., & Monker, J. A. (1995).
Individual differences in 4-year-old children's acquisition of vocabulary during storybook reading. *Journal of Educational Psychology, 87*, 218–299.

Snow, C. E., Barnes, W. S., Chandler, J., Goodman, J.
F., & Hemphill, L. (1991). *Unfulfilled expectations:
Home and school influences on literacy.* Cambridge,
MA: Harvard University Press.

Snow, C., Burns, M., & Griffin, P. (1998). *Preventing

reading difficulties in young children.* Washington,
DC: National Academy Press.

St. Pierre, R., Ricciuti, A., & Creps, C. (1999). *Synthesis of state and local Even Start evaluations.* Prepared for the U.S. Department of Education, Planning and Evaluation Service. Cambridge, MA: Abt
Associates.

St. Pierre, R., Ricciuti, A., & Tao, F. (2004). Continuous improvement in family literacy programs. In B.
H. Wasik (Ed.), *Handbook of family literacy* (pp.
587–600). Mahwah, NJ: Erlbaum.

Stool, S. E., Berg, A. O., Berman, S., Carney, C. J.,
Cooley, J. R., Culpepper, L., et al. (1994). *Managing
otitis media with effusion in young children: Quick
reference guide for clinicians* (AHCPR Publication
94-0623). Rockville, MD: Agency for Health Care
Policy and Research, Public Health Service, U.S. Department of Health and Human Services.

Storch, S. A., & Whitehurst, G. J. (2001). The role of
family and home in the literacy development of children from low-income backgrounds. In P. Britto &
J. Brooks-Gunn (Eds.), *The role of family literacy
environments in promoting young children's emerging literacy skills* (pp. 39–52). San Francisco: Jossey-
Bass.

Strucker, J., Snow, C., & Pan, B. A. (2004). Family literacy for ESOL families: Challenges and design principles. In B. H. Wasik (Ed.), *Handbook on family
literacy* (pp. 467–481). Mahwah, NJ: Erlbaum.

Stuart, M., Dixon, M., Masterson, J., & Quinlan, P.
(1998). Learning to read at home and at school.
British Journal of Educational Psychology, 68,
3–14.

Tabors. P. O., & Snow, C. E. (2001). Young bilingual
children and early literacy development. In S. B.
Neuman & D. K. Dickinson (Eds.), *Handbook of
early literacy research* (pp. 159–178). New York:
Guilford Press.

Taverne, A., & Sheridan, S. M. (1995). Parent training
in interactive book reading: An investigation of its
effects with families at risk. *School Psychology
Quarterly, 10*, 41–64.

Taylor, D. (1983). *Family literacy: Young children
learning to read and write.* Portsmouth, NH: Heinemann.

Taylor, D. (1997). *Many families, many literacies: An
international declaration of principles.* Portsmouth,
NH: Heinemann.

Taylor, D., & Dorsey-Gaines, C. (1988). *Growing up
literate: Learning from inner-city families.*
Portsmouth, NH: Heinemann.

Taylor, D., & Strickland, D. S. (1986). *Family storybook reading.* Portsmouth, NH: Heinemann.

Teale, W. H. (1978). Positive environments for learning to read: What studies of early readers tell us.
Language Arts, 55, 922–932.

Teale, W. H. (1984). Reading to young children: Its
significance for literacy development. In H. Goelman, A. Oberg, & F. Smith (Eds.), *Awakening to literacy* (pp. 110–121). Portsmouth, NH: Heinemann.

Teale, W. H. (1986). Home background and young
children's literacy development. In W. H. Teale & E.

Sulzby (Eds.), *Emergent literacy: Writing and reading* (pp. 173–203). Norwood, NJ: Ablex.

Tett, L., & St. Clair, R. (1997). Family literacy in the educational marketplace: A cultural perspective. *International Journal of Lifelong Education, 16*(2), 109–120.

Valdez-Menchaca, M. C., & Whitehurst, G. J. (1992). Accelerating language development through picture book reading: A systematic extension to Mexican day-care. *Developmental Psychology, 28,* 1106–1114.

Vernon-Feagans, L. (1996). *Children's talk in communities and classrooms.* Cambridge, MA: Blackwell.

Vernon-Feagans, L., Hammer, C. S., Miccio, A., & Manlove, E. (2001). Early language and literacy skills in low-income African American and Hispanic children. In S. B. Neuman & D. K. Dickinson (Eds.), *Handbook of early literacy research* (pp. 192–210). New York: Guilford Press.

Voss, M. M. (1996). *Hidden literacies: Children learning at home and at school.* Portsmounth, NH: Heinemann.

Wasik, B. H., Dobbins, D. R., & Herrmann, S. (2001). Intergenerational family literacy: Concepts, research, and practice. In S. B. Neuman & D. K. Dickinson (Eds.), *Handbook of early literacy research* (pp. 444–458). New York: Guilford Press.

Wasik, B. H., & Herrmann, S. (2004). Family literacy: History, concepts, services. In B. H. Wasik (Ed.), *Handbook of family literacy* (pp. 3–22). Mahwah, NJ: Erlbaum.

Wasik, B. H., Mamak, E., & Kingsley, D. (2002). *Beliefs and practices of African American, Caucasian, and Hispanic mothers.* Unpublished manuscript, University of North Carolina at Chapel Hill.

Weinberger, J. (1996). A longitudinal study of children's early literacy experiences at home and later literacy development at home and school. *Journal of Research in Reading, 19,* 14–24.

Weinstein-Shr, G. (1992). *Family and intergenerational literacy in multilingual families* (ERIC Q&A). Washington, DC: Center for Applied Linguistics, National Clearinghouse on Literacy Education (ERIC Document Reproduction Service No. ED378848)

Wells, G. (1985). Preschool literacy-related activities and success in school. In D. R. Olson, N. Torrence, & A. Hilyard (Eds.), *Literacy, language, and learning* (pp. 229–255). New York: Cambridge University Press.

White, K. (1982). The relation between socioeconomoic status and academic achievement. *Psychological Bulletin, 91,* 461–481.

Whitehurst, G. J. (1996). Language processes in context: Language learning in children reared in poverty. In L. B. Adamson & M. A. Romski (Eds.), *Research on communication and language disorders: Contributions to theories of language development* (pp. 233–266). Baltimore: Brookes.

Whitehurst, G. J., Arnold, D. H., Epstein, J. N., Angell, A. L., Smith, M., & Fischel, J. E. (1994). A picture book reading intervention in daycare and home for children from low-income families. *Developmental Psychology, 30,* 679–689.

Whitehurst, G. J., Epstein, J. N., Angell, A. L., Payne, A. C., Crone, D. A., & Fischel, J. E. (1994). Outcomes of an emergent literacy intervention in Head Start. *Journal of Educational Psychology, 86,* 542–555.

Winter, M., & McDonald, D. (1997). Parents as teachers: Investing in good beginnings for children. In G. Albee & T. Gullotta (Eds.), *Primary prevention works* (pp.119–145). Thousand Oaks, CA: Sage.

Yarosz, D. J., & Barnett, W. S. (2001). Who reads to young children?: Identifying predictors of family reading activities. *Reading Psychology, 22*(1), 67–81.

Zady, M. F., & Portes, P. R. (2001). When low-SES parents cannot assist their children in solving science problems. *Journal of Education for Students Placed at Risk, 6*(3), 215–229.

9

Fostering Preliteracy Development via Storybook-Sharing Interactions

The Cultural Context of Mainstream Family Practices

ANNE VAN KLEECK

Book sharing with preschoolers has become a major research focus among scholars in a wide variety of disciplines. Given the wide range of language and preliteracy skills potentially fostered by book sharing, and the impact these skills have on later literacy achievement, there are widespread efforts to develop interventions to teach both parents and preschool teachers "effective" book-sharing interactions. Book sharing, however, is a culturally based practice, reflecting cultural beliefs and attitudes. Although this is widely known and stated, there has been no effort to explore systematically the underlying cultural context that shapes mainstream book-sharing practices that would also serve to illuminate underlying reasons for different practices among different sociocultural or socioeconomic groups.

The term "preliteracy" used in this chapter is preferred to alternative terms that have been used for this same general period of development, including "emergent" (or "emerging") or "early" literacy. The phrase "emergent (or emerging) literacy" is generally used to refer to the same array of attitudes and beliefs, but to a narrower set of skills than I intend with the use of the term

"preliteracy." In particular, for most scholars using the term, "emergent literacy" does not encompass the development of phonological awareness and alphabet knowledge; indeed, there is often a philosophical orientation toward excluding such code-related skills (however, for an exception, see Whitehurst & Lonigan, 1998, 2001). The term "early literacy" is easily confused with, and sometimes used interchangeably with, "beginning reading," whereas "preliteracy" refers to development up to the juncture of beginning reading.

"Preliteracy" is intended in very much the same vein as that used by scholars when they refer to a prelinguistic stage of oral language development. In the prelinguistic stage, babies are learning about the form, content, and use of language, but they have not yet fully integrated these three dimensions of language simultaneously to produce conventional words (or approximations of conventional words) (Bloom & Lahey, 1978). Likewise, preliterate children may be learning about the form, content, and use of literacy, but they have not yet integrated these burgeoning areas of knowledge into conventional reading and writing skills.

This chapter has two interrelated goals. In Section I, I discuss the cultural factors that influence book-sharing interactions in mainstream-culture families and the ways in which other groups might differ relative to these factors. In Section II, I consider the kinds of intuitive (rather than intentional) general teaching strategies and the specific language interactional strategies that mainstream-culture parents might use during book sharing with their preschoolers. Here again, where such information is available, consideration is given to how other groups may differ relative to these practices. This is not intended to place mainstream-culture practices as the implicit starting point for understanding other cultural practices. It is merely meant to highlight that mainstream practices are very much influenced, though not in a simple or direct fashion, by cultural factors that are by no means universal.

This chapter does not consider *what* children learn from book sharing, because research on the various domains of preliteracy knowledge that can be developed by preschoolers has been well synthesized elsewhere (see Scarborough 2001; van Kleeck, 1998, 2003; Whitehurst & Lonigan, 1998). We know, for example, that book sharing with young preliterate children can promote learning relative to various domains of language (vocabulary, syntax, narrative abilities, and abstract language) and print form (alphabet knowledge, phonological awareness, and print conventions), which in turn can influence a number of aspects of later reading development (van Kleeck, 1998, 2003). What has yet to be organized and synthesized is research regarding *how* such learning is fostered in mainstream-culture families; hence, the focus of the current chapter. In addressing how book sharing fosters learning, I explore well-established areas in the research and discuss some crucial areas that have received surprisingly little emphasis in the empirical work to date.

Consideration of the potential applications of book-sharing research with mainstream culture families also requires a careful consideration of issues of culture. The chapter begins, therefore, with a brief overview of the different ideological perspectives that have emerged regarding the application of this research to intervention programs designed for families from non-mainstream groups. The overall framework for the remainder of the chapter follows the topics shown in Figure 9.1, which include the various cultural influences that permeate mainstream-culture family practices in the areas of general teaching strategies and language interactions during book sharing.

IDEOLOGICAL PERSPECTIVES ON THE APPLICATION OF BOOK-SHARING RESEARCH

In the preface to a recent volume on book sharing, my colleague Steve Stahl and I noted, "Divides between different groups of scholars seem to be common in literacy scholarship. The research on book sharing—a seemingly innocuous practice—is no exception" (van Kleeck & Stahl, 2003, p. vii). Indeed, a large range of ideological perspectives can be found in the extensive body of research and scholarship on book sharing that is amassing from a number of different disciplines. This array of perspectives stems, in great measure, from different responses to the widespread tendency in child development research to treat mainstream-culture socialization practices as normative and preferred. The vast differences in these perspectives, as such, may be reflective of what Roopnarine and Carter (1992) have referred to in their discussion of the cultural context of socialization as "an intellectual crisis" (p. 250) in Western psychology.

From one perspective, mainstream-culture practices are taught in family and preschool teacher interventions, because they reflect school practices and the literate style of discourse associated with academic success (e.g., Valdez-Menchaca & Whitehurst, 1992; Whitehurst et al., 1994). Wasik, Dobbins, and Hermann (2001) refer to this as the coaching approach (see also Wasik & Hendrickson, Chapter 8, this volume). Parents and teachers are taught mainstream interaction styles, because children are "most successful in becoming literate when their socialization history is isomorphic to the socialization practices of school" (Pellegrini, 2001, p. 55).

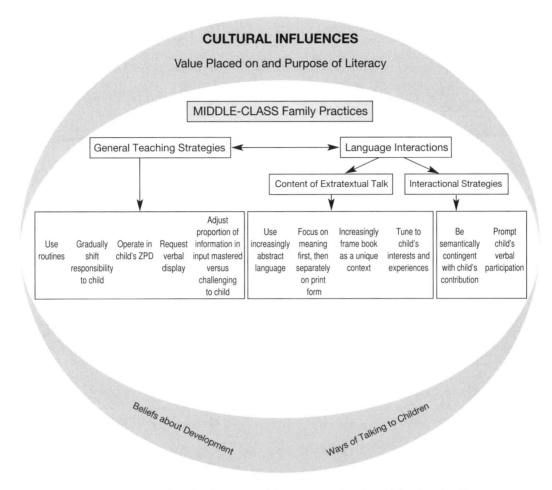

FIGURE 9.1. Cultural influences and literacy practices in middle-class families.

From a second perspective, Purcell-Gates (2000) points out the problem with this first approach, summarizing the view that "injecting academic, or school, literacy practices into homes in which they are viewed as 'foreign' and from outside the culture is inadvisable, patronizing, and will not 'work'" (p. 859). A more effective approach, sometimes called the sociocultural or facilitating approach (e.g., Wasik et al., 2001), is to develop, via collaborative efforts with families, interventions that respect the cultural practices of the community and the differing paths to literacy found in them (e.g., Bloome, Katz, Solsken, Willett, & Wilson-Keenan, 2000; Delgado-Gaitan, 1991; Neuman, 1996; New, 2001). This would allow devel-opment of new kinds of text activities that do not undermine core cultural values (Mc-Naughton, 2001). Indeed, many families in nonmainstream cultural groups do not engage in book sharing with their preschoolers at all. Only around 30% of Chinese American and Chinese Canadian families report reading to their children (Chao, 1994; Johnston & Wong, 2002). In the yearly statistics published by the Federal Interagency Forum on Child and Family Statistics (2002) the percentage of families that reported reading to their children every day in the last week included 64% of white, non-Hispanic families; 48% of black, non-Hispanic families; 42% of Hispanic families; and 48% of families living below the poverty level.

In a fashion related to the ideas put forth in the sociocultural perspective, it should be explicitly acknowledged that schools privilege some literacy practices, while dismissing or ignoring others (Anderson, Anderson, Lynch, & Shapiro, 2003). Hence, efforts should be made in classrooms, as well as in working directly with families, to build on cultural variations in literacy practices. Goldenberg (2001) cautions, however, that "there is very little evidence that cultural accommodation per se produces measured gains *in achievement*" (pp. 219–220).

A third ideological perspective that has been discussed regarding family literacy interventions is that they are simply inappropriate in some cultural groups (Anderson et al., 2003; Bus, Leseman, & Keultjes, 2000; Bus & Sulzby, 1996). Indeed, some families, particularly among minority groups, do not themselves see the value of preschool and early literacy activities (Fuller, Eggers-Pierola, Holloway, Liang, & Rambaud, 1996; Fuller, Holloway, & Liang, 1996; Garcia, 1997). Countering this stance, some scholars believe that low-income parents want to learn how to help their children and should not be denied access to practices that are known to be successful in helping them achieve literacy (Delpit, 1995; Edwards, 1994). As Anderson and his colleagues note (2003), children need to learn the kind of literate discourse that is fostered in book sharing if "they are to participate fully in Western-style educational, financial, and political institutions" (p. 223).

Luke and Luke (2001) provide an even stronger version of the third ideological perspective, which views family literacy intervention based on mainstream practices as inappropriate. These scholars consider programs of this nature to be completely misguided. They believe that such efforts only serve to divert funding and energy toward early childhood and literacy, and away from adolescence. They argue that "the current enthusiasm for early intervention programs is a 'rhetorical displacement' that attempts to solve the problems of unruly adolescence and the emergence of the 'techno-subject' through an 'inoculation' model dedicated to the restoration and preservation of print-based early childhood" (p. 91).

Regardless of these wide-ranging views on its application, family book sharing is a widely encouraged practice that is not likely to be abandoned by politicians, families, or educators in the near or distant future. It behooves us, then, to understand book-sharing practices within a cultural framework, perhaps especially because the practices of the mainstream culture exert such hegemonic influence.

SECTION I:
THE CULTURAL CONTEXT OF MAINSTREAM-CULTURE BOOK-SHARING PRACTICES

To understand the manner in which adults from mainstream culture tend to share books with young, preliterate children requires an understanding of the broader cultural issues that help to shape how these interactions unfold. The major cultural issues that impact literacy practices such as book sharing with young children, shown in Figure 9.1, include the value placed on and the purposes of literacy, family beliefs about child development (including language and literacy learning), and culturally determined ways of talking to children.

Katherine Au (1995) defines ethnicity as "groups with shared histories and cultural knowledge" (p. 85) and differentiates this category of diverse backgrounds from mainstream culture to include African Americans, Asian Americans, Hispanic Americans, or Native Americans who speak a primary language other than standard American English, and come from poor and working-class families. In addition to the diversity created by ethnicity, we might add families with children who have disabilities. Regardless of their socioeconomic or cultural background, these families face challenges in adapting to a child with special needs that can certainly create differences in their values, attitudes, beliefs, and practices.

Literacy practices of these and other non-mainstream families may differ from those of mainstream families, but it is critical to remember that cultural groups are by no means homogeneous, although there is a tendency to treat them as if they were

(Laosa, 1981). Doing so creates stereotypes and resulting insensitivity (for discussions, see van Kleeck, 1994; Weisner, Gallimore, & Jordon, 1988) that ignore research documenting rather vast differences within groups, including the well-studied mainstream middle class (e.g., Diaz, Neal, & Vachio, 1991; Hammett, van Kleeck, & Huberty, 2003; Neuman, Hagedorn, Celano, & Daly, 1995; Ninio, 1980; Norman-Jackson, 1982). It is important to keep this lack of homogeneity in mind, because most of the existing research reviewed in this section focuses on intergroup, and not intragroup, differences.

Value and Purposes of Literacy

Literacy is valued to the extent that it is deemed important to functioning in a particular society. As an extreme example, there is little need for literacy among members of a hunter–gatherer tribe. Even within a highly literate society, the importance of literacy may vary considerably among diverse groups. The value placed on literacy is reflected in and interacts with many of the other variables discussed in this chapter. For example, the value of literacy depends on the purposes it serves within a particular society, which in turn interact with and shape parental attitudes toward literacy, whether and how children are engaged in literate activities such as book sharing, and so forth.

The ways that adults in a child's environment use print have a well-documented effect on what children learn about print literacy before schooling (e.g., Heath, 1983; Purcell-Gates, 1995, 1996; Schieffelin & Cochran-Smith, 1984; Taylor & Dorsey-Gaines, 1988; Teale, 1986). The dramatic impact of the purposes for writing within a particular cultural group is illustrated by the example of the Cree-speaking people of northern Canada studied by Bennett and Berry (1991). A syllabic script for the Cree language was created and introduced by missionaries about 250 years ago, and spread rapidly and nearly universally to this (until recently) nomadic hunter society. "The Cree syllabic script was a breakthrough in ameliorating the isolation experienced in the bush" (p. 100) by allowing people to keep in touch via letter writing. With the introduction of the telephone, however, the use of the script began to wane as the Cree became "devoted," and even "addicted" (p. 101) users of the telephone to serve the interpersonal function previously served by the Cree script.

The Cree script, with its singular dominant purpose, was vulnerable because of the development of a more efficient technology. Written scripts in modern societies are far less vulnerable, because "almost no event of significance, ranging from declarations of war to simple birthday greetings, passes without appropriate written documentation" (Olson, 1994, p. 1). In mainstream American culture, both print and literate activity are ubiquitous, and children's exposure to a nearly constant deluge of literate activity very likely impacts on their perceptions of the necessity of becoming literate. Anderson and Stokes (1984) discuss several domains of literacy activities, including daily living, entertainment, school-related activity, religion, general information, work, and interpersonal communication (see van Kleeck, 1990, for an expansion and elaboration of these categories).

Baker, Scher, and Mackler (1997) discuss how middle-income families endorse literacy more as a source of entertainment than do low-income families. Other work has shown that parents' views of reading as a source of pleasure relate to similar views in their children, regardless of the family's income level (DeBaryshe, 1995; Scher & Baker, 1996). One suspects that a focus on entertainment relates to more storybook sharing and an emphasis on enjoyment within that context.

The oral and literate traditions within any cultural group, including cultural groups whose traditions may differ from those of the broader society in which they are embedded, are intimately tied to the functions that literacy serves for those groups. As Scribner and Cole (1981) noted, "Literacy is not simply knowing how to read and write a particular script but applying this knowledge for specific purposes in specific contexts of use. The nature of these practices . . . will determine the kinds of skills ("consequences") associated with literacy" (p. 236). Because literacy is not a monolithic achievement with general consequences, some scholars now talk about "multiple literacies" to capture the notion that many different social practices involve literacy, and that the learning associated with them is specific and contextually situated (e.g., Gee, 2001).

Watson (2001) discusses how the specific uses to which literacy is put, and not just the presence of literacy, serve to enhance or amplify ways of thinking that are also available to an extent in oral language. These ways of thinking include how we classify, reason, and remember, with literate thought being considered more abstract, analytical, logical, reflective, decontextualized, and complex (Olson & Torrance, 1991). Olson (1994) suggests that "literacy contributes in particular ways to the development of distinctive modes of thought that are conveyed through systematic education" (p. 17). Like Heath's (1983) notion of "taking meaning" from text, Olson's belief is that "ways of reading and ways of writing," or of interpreting and creating written texts, "yield a set of beliefs and assumptions, a 'logocentrism,' which pervades readers' understanding of language, the world, and themselves" (1994, p. 19).

Highly literate parents begin socializing their children into a literate mode of thought long before children begin their formal education and become print literate themselves. Although they use literate discourse with their children in a wide variety of contexts, one context that has been very widely studied is that of book sharing. Indeed, the vast and growing body of research on book sharing with preschoolers often focuses, implicitly or explicitly, on the ways in which adults socialize children into literate (or what Bruner, 1986, called "scientific cognitive") ways of taking meaning from and talking about texts.

With preschoolers, parents' literate discourse, whether used during book sharing or in other contexts, includes practices such as scaffolding the interaction, promoting increasingly abstract uses of language, and requesting that children verbally display knowledge they have already gained. These kinds of practices are discussed in the section of this chapter on book-sharing prac-

tices in mainstream families. What is important to understand at this juncture is how such practices are culturally determined and are not found, or are not found as frequently, in cultures that place more emphasis on oral discourse.

Beliefs about Child Development and Preliteracy Learning

Scholars have highlighted a wide range of general beliefs about children's development. Some examples include Heath's (1989) discussion of how mainstream adults in the United States often believe that children are "raised" or "trained," whereas other groups might believe children "grow up" largely apart from parental influences or intervention. Mainstream-culture parents tend to view children as being born very dependent and gradually growing through stages to become more independent (e.g., Harkness, Super, & Keefer, 1992), whereas working-class families might see the child as being born unsocialized and in need of discipline to become gradually more cooperative (Philipsen, 1975). From yet another perspective, Scollon and Scollon (1981) talk about how, in mainstream culture, children take the role of exhibitionist with skills they are learning, and are expected to show off their abilities, especially in school. In other groups, such as the Athabaskan culture studied by the Scollons, children are instead in the spectator role, and are expected to observe adults exhibiting skills to them.

All of these different perspectives can lead to distinct differences in interaction patterns with children, many of which are discussed later in a section entitled "Ways of Talking with Children." For example, if children are viewed as growing up with little adult intervention necessary, adults are much less likely to intervene verbally as events unfold with the child. If they are viewed as basically unsocialized, adults would tend to use much more directive, disciplinary talk. If children are expected to be spectators as events unfold, adults would not be requesting that they verbally display their knowledge.

The general belief that children "grow up," as opposed to requiring more active adult intervention in "raising" them, perhaps underlies the literacy practices of Hispanic families discussed by Madding (2002). These families did not believe that young children were ready for books until they were about 3 years old, believing they were too young to understand the material before that age. Madding reports that when book sharing and other practices are begun, Hispanic mothers seldom teach specific skills (e.g., letters, shapes) for this same reason: Preschool children are too young, and their teachers will take care of this when children reach school age and are old enough for the material. In contrast, book sharing often begins at 6 months of age in mainstream families (e.g., Heath, 1982; van Kleeck, Alexander, Vigil, & Templeton, 1996).

As is discussed later in this chapter, many other studies have found that nonmainstream parents tend to take a more analytical approach to interacting with print, training their preschooler to focus on the skills related to print form (e.g., letter recognition, writing drills), and not on the pleasurable aspects of reading for content and comprehension that middle-class parents tend to emphasize. In the nonmainstream cultures, this focus on analyzing the formal aspects of print appears to be related to several culturally ingrained attitudes and beliefs. These include respect for the authority of teachers and, hence, an attempt by parents to model the "teaching" of specific skills as they themselves may have been taught as a way of "bootstrapping" their children's opportunities for future success (Brice, 2002; Gadsden, 1993; Goldenberg, Reese, & Gallimore, 1992a).

Cultural groups sometimes differ in their perceptions about how learning is achieved during the preschool years. Chao (1996) found that many European American mothers "believed that parents need to foster the idea that learning is fun, interesting, exciting, and stimulating" (p. 416). They correspondingly believe that play is an important context for learning. Chinese American mothers in Chao's study instilled in their children the belief that learning "definitely involved hard work and effort" (p. 419), and that the outcome of learning was the mastery of specific skills. These perspectives are also reflected in views about homework. Chinese American mothers may correct their children's homework and have them redo it, and may even assign work beyond what the teacher has assigned (Chao, 1996).

Although the authors of the aforementioned studies have tied beliefs and corresponding practices to cultural or socioeconomic groups, it is critically important to remember that these findings represent central tendencies of groups and cannot be generalized to all members of a particular group, even within the samples studied. A study by Neuman and her colleagues (1995) underscores the fact that there is a great deal of diversity within these individual groups regarding beliefs and corresponding practices related to literacy. These researchers studied 19 African American mothers from low-income backgrounds via a series of peer-group discussions and found three sets of beliefs represented among them.

One belief system of almost half of the mothers focused on direct teaching, in adult-driven fashion, of discrete skills such as the alphabet, numbers, and colors. The children's role was to observe and/or to recite. Children were encouraged to be obedient and were discouraged from asking questions or displaying curiosity. Another group of mothers (also just under half) took a more maturational view in the belief that children would learn when they were ready, and no specific skills were taught. The adults' role was to provide a nurturing environment, and the children's role was essentially to teach themselves based on their own interests and needs. These mothers often believed, as did the Hispanic parents studied by Madding (1999), that their children were not ready for book sharing. A third, much smaller, group of mothers held the same beliefs usually attributed to mainstream, middle-class families, that children learned by adult guidance in contexts of conversation and play, in which adults follow the children's interests and encourage them to ask questions and to reason.

Families of children with disabilities, of course, come from a variety of backgrounds. Managing a child with a disability can certainly lead to different priorities and, hence, goals for learning during the preschool years. Light and Kelford Smith (1993) studied literacy practices in families of preschool children who used augmentative and assistive communication (AAC) systems, and found that the parental priorities were remarkably different from those of parents whose children were developing normally. Not unexpectedly, the parents of the AAC group identified their main concerns as relating to functional skills, such as communicating basic needs, feeding, and mobility. Skills specific to social interaction (i.e., making friends) and literacy (reading and writing) ranked lowest among the offered choices. The parents of preschoolers who were developing normally identified their priorities for their children as social, communicative, and literacy-related, with the functional skills being less important. These findings highlight the fact that a focus on literacy within a family may be a luxury that can only be afforded when more basic needs have been met.

Ways of Talking with Children

A literate style of discourse may be evident in even the very earliest ways in which members of any given culture socialize their children in the use of oral language (e.g., Heath, 1983). As Watson (2001) notes, "Oral language developed in literate cultural traditions is passed on to children in daily interaction" (p. 49). She further cites a number of scholars who have suggested that book sharing with preschoolers is a primary context for this cultural transmission (Bus & van IJzendoorn, 1988; Ninio & Bruner, 1978; Snow, 1983). Because of this, interventions designed to facilitate what is considered more effective book sharing between parents or teachers and preliterate children teach them how to engage in dialogue about the book. Indeed, the well-known intervention developed by Whitehurst and his colleagues (1988) is even called Dialogic Reading Training. The kinds of strategies taught in programs such as Dialogic Reading Training reflect numerous aspects of literate discourse and include asking open-ended questions, expanding children's sentences, and giving feedback when children attempt to communicate.

It is important, therefore, to be aware that the ways in which one engages in dialogue with children are very much culturally determined. In previous work, I integrated and summarized the culturally relative values, beliefs, and practices that underlie parent–child interaction (van Kleeck, 1994). Because book sharing is done in an interactive context, the different "ways of talking" discussed in the 1994 article are highly relevant to preliteracy development. I next update and relate to book sharing some of the key aspects of these differences discussed in that earlier article.

In mainstream American culture, adults are the primary caregivers to young children, and they typically interact with them in a dyadic, one-on-one, fashion. This is certainly typical of the interactions that occur in book sharing as well. In Hawaiian, Native American, African American, and Mexican American and other Hispanic cultures, siblings are often the primary caregivers, especially once the baby becomes mobile (Werner, 1984), and multiparty interactions may dominate, as Eisenberg (1982) discusses relative to the Mexican American families she studied.

In mainstream American culture, encouraging children to talk a great deal is valued, and reticence or shyness is viewed as a social "problem" (see Daly & McCroskey, 1984). Indeed, the techniques taught in book-sharing interventions are explicitly designed to increase the child's verbal participation in this particular literate activity. On the contrary, other cultures, such as the African American (Heath, 1983; Ward, 1971), Native American (Crago, 1990; Dumont, 1972; Freedman, 1979; John, 1972; Scollon & Scollon, 1981), Puerto-Rican American (Coles, 1977), Japanese (Clancy, 1986; Fischer, 1970), and other Asian/Pacific (see Cheng, 1989, for a review) groups that have been studied, value quietness in children and socialize their children accordingly. As Heath (1983) noted, parents in the African American working-class community she studied did not ask children questions in order to keep the conversation going, nor did they consider children to be appropriate conversational partners. As yet another example, Navajo mothers view talkativeness in children as discourteous, self-centered, and undisciplined (Freedman, 1979).

During an activity conducted with a young child in mainstream culture, adults frequently intervene to offer step-by-step verbal explanations, and children are encouraged to ask questions, after which they are often asked to recount the task verbally (Heath, 1989). Many accounts of adult support during book sharing in mainstream-culture families contain these same components. However, Hispanic parents do not tend to comment on ongoing events (Langdon, 1992). Among both Hispanic and Native American groups in the United States, nonverbal contextual cues are emphasized to convey information, and learning is accomplished primarily by observation (Kay-Raining Bird & Vetter, 1994; Langdon, 1992; Westby & Rouse, 1985; Wilson, 1994). Among the Louisiana African Americans studied by Ward (1971), children's information-seeking questions were often ignored, and the Inuit children studied by Crago (1990) were also discouraged from asking questions. In the book-sharing context, middle- and low-income African American mothers ask relatively few questions in comparison to white, middle-class mothers (Anderson-Yockel & Haynes, 1994; Hammer, 1999).

Both Scollon and Scollon (1981) and Heath (1989) discuss the notion of "display of knowledge," in which an adult asks a child to answer a question to which the adult already knows the answer, or simply asks the child to recite information verbally. Known-information or "test" questions abound in parent–child book-sharing routines in mainstream-culture families, particularly with infants and toddlers. This practice in effect socializes young children in the cultural rules for displaying knowledge, the most common participation structure they will later encounter in the classroom (e.g., Reid, 2000; Watson, 2001).

In nondominant cultural groups in the United States, verbal display of knowledge may not be part of children's socialization. African American children are rarely asked this type of question, and when they are, it is often to chastise them (Heath, 1983). In Ward's study of a rural Louisiana African American community, she noted that "children are not expected to exhibit any range of manners, skills or special knowledge" (1971, p. 53). Among Mexican Americans, such known information questions may be reserved for teasing children (Valdés, 1996). Native American children may be socialized not to respond to these known-information questions (Harris, 1998).

In mainstream culture, adults often follow a child's lead in a conversation by taking turns that are semantically contingent on the child's conversational contribution (e.g., Snow, 1979). Other American cultural groups do not believe that children should direct topics (e.g., the rural Louisiana African Americans studies by Ward, 1971). This may extend to a belief that it is the adult's role to issue directives and the child's role to obey them (Inuits studied by Crago, 1990; African Americans studied by Ward, 1971). In studies of infants, Chinese American mothers tended to direct their babies attention, whereas Anglo mothers followed it (Vigil, 1999; Wang, Goldin-Meadow, & Mylander, 1995).

A wide variety of accommodations in the speech directed to young children has been well documented in mainstream American and other middle-class industrialized cultures. This register, characterized by simplified, redundant, acoustically distinct speech, is often referred to as "motherese" (e.g., Newport, Gleitman, & Gleitman, 1977) or "child-directed talk" (van Kleeck & Carpenter, 1980). Heath (1983) did not find that this register typified the talk to young children among the African Americans in the working-class community she studied. Another way in which mainstream-culture adults accommodate to young children during interaction is by carrying the burden of understanding. When children are unintelligible or do not provide adequate information, adults ask clarification questions (e.g., Sachs, 1983). Their expansions of children's utterances may likewise serve as communication checks, in effect asking, "Is this what you mean?" (Brown, 1977), or they may serve to let others know what the child means (Wells, 1982). Here, again, we find clear differences in the interaction patterns of the rural African American community studied by Ward (1971). The mothers in her study did not imitate or expand their children's utterances, although they did repeat and expand their own speech.

Adults in mainstream culture interpret the behaviors and states of infants, and often verbalize them, thereby treating the infants as intentional beings and as conversational partners, even though it is a rather one-sided conversation in which burps, smiles, and so forth, constitute children's turns in the conversation (e.g., Lock, 1981; Ryan, 1974; Shotter, 1978; Snow, 1977). Book sharing in mainstream culture often begins when a baby is about 6 months of age. This early age is likely due to a combination of treating babies as intentional and the fact that infants are prepared to participate in meaning before they are able to give meaning independently. As Rogoff (1990) notes, even before their first words, infants display "impressive potential for shared meaning" (p. 82). Cultures vary regarding when adults begin treating children as intentional. In the northern New Mexico Hispanic community studied by Briggs (1984), and a Californian Hispanic community studied by Eisenberg (1982), a child is not treated as intentional until he or she is 1 year old. Ward (1971) likewise found that very little talk was directed at prelinguistic infants in the rural Louisiana African American community she studied. When infants are treated as conversational partners, the focus of the adult talk may differ. Japanese mothers use more affective talk, whereas mainstream-culture mothers use more referential talk (Minami, 1997; Toda, Fogel, & Kawai, 1990).

Different cultural groups may have different beliefs about how children learn language that affect interactions with young children. For the most part, parents in mainstream culture appear to believe that children learn to speak by being engaged in conversations from a young age. Direct teaching of language in this population tends to be limited to teaching children names of people, practicing politeness routines, and correcting mislabeling (Snow, 1977). Direct teaching, in which a caregiver explicitly tells a child what to say to someone else, is used far more frequently among other groups. Miller (1982) found it to be extensively used by the working-class Anglo families in Baltimore that she studied; Briggs (1984) and Eisenberg (1982) found it among the Hispanic communities they studied in New Mexico and California.

In Section I of this chapter, I discussed the broad cultural factors that influence book-sharing practices in mainstream-culture families, and the dimensions along which these values might differ from those held by families in nonmainstream cultures. These influences (the values and purposes of literacy, beliefs about development, and ways of talking to children) are included in the outermost part of Figure 9.1 to indicate that they exert influence on, and indeed encompass, the book-sharing practices listed in the central part of the figure. As such, the practices I discuss in the next section are a very logical extension of the cultural values, beliefs, and practices just discussed.

SECTION II: BOOK-SHARING PRACTICES IN MAINSTREAM-CULTURE FAMILIES

At the same time that scholars continue to understand better the culturally determined nature of book sharing and other literacy practices discussed in Section I of this chapter, book sharing with young preschoolers is becoming ever more ingrained as a recommended practice in the United States. A much cited document from the 1980s, *Becoming a Nation of Readers,* concluded that "the single most important activity for building the knowledge required for eventual success in reading is reading aloud to children" (Anderson, Hiebert, Scott, & Wilkinson, 1985, p. 23). Since that time, the recommendation to read books to young children has become entrenched in political rhetoric. Indeed, the federal government gathers and publishes data every 2 to 3 years on whether American families read books on a daily basis to young children 3–5 years of age (e.g., Federal Interagency Forum on Child and Family Statistics, 2002).

Although comprehensive analyses of the empirical research on book sharing have called into question the amount of impact that book sharing has on the language and literacy development important to school success (e.g., Bus, van IJzendoorn, & Pellegrini, 1995; Scarborough & Dobrich, 1994), as I discuss in this section, another line of research has begun to document that the amount of impact is related to *how* books are shared. Many of the book-sharing practices used by many mainstream-culture parents bode well for their children's later academic success. This is undoubtedly due in some measure to the isomorphism that many mainstream children experience between home and school in styles of interaction and uses of literacy (e.g., Heath & Branscombe, 1986; Panofsky, 1994; Pellegrini, 2001; Vernon-Feagans, Hammer, Miccio, & Manlove, 2001).

Mainstream book-sharing practices are both culturally determined and promote language and literacy skill development known to be important for school success. This calls for a two-pronged approach to developing literacy teaching methods and interventions. On the one hand, the information in this section provides specific teaching and interaction strategies that can be used to help children from different backgrounds to become *bicultural* in terms of literacy and literate practices. This solution may appear culturally insensitive, and without the second prong, discussed below, I believe it is. However, until all schools effectively accommodate children from all cultural and linguistic backgrounds at all levels in the educational system, we may be impeding children's potential for success by not consciously fostering the literacy skills and practices of the school/mainstream culture. It is better to do this with full awareness of the cultural differences that underlie many of these practices, which should help educators avoid giving messages that may subtly (or not so subtly) denigrate different practices. Indeed, understanding how preschool children can be socialized in mainstream practices known to promote their school success does not have to, and should not, imply that this is the only or the best set of practices. They are simply the practices that will help the child be successful in school, as school success is currently conceived and measured.

We often think that basic mainstream literacy practices, such as book sharing, are going on in educational settings. Such is not the case. Dickinson, McCabe, and Anastasopoulos (2003) reported on data from 133 preschool classrooms in the Boston area. In 166 observations, 66 classrooms did not engage in book reading at all. In the remaining 100 classrooms, the average time devoted to book sharing in a day was only around 10 minutes. On a composite score of several measures of the overall classroom environment, only 13% of the classrooms were rated as "strong" on supporting language, literacy, and the curriculum, whereas 44% were rated as "low quality." Even when book sharing does occur in preschool classrooms, Whitehurst and his colleagues have found that the quality of reading can be improved, with a resulting impact on children's subsequent language development (see Zevenbergen & Whitehurst, 2003, for a summary of several studies in Head Start settings).

The second prong of developing literacy teaching methods and interventions should consist of continuing attempts to adapt current school practices, so that they better fit the literacy practices that children from diverse backgrounds experience at home. If book sharing is not practiced in the home, for example, the teaching and interactional strategies discussed in this section can be used with other literacy activities that *are* practiced in the home, to help bridge the home and school cultures.

The teaching and interaction strategies discussed in this section also have potential applications to work with families. First of all, not all mainstream preschoolers receive the kind of socialization during book sharing that is associated with subsequent better print literacy achievement. In fact, variation in both the amount and type of book-sharing discussions among white, middle-class parents is enormous (e.g., Crain-Thoreson & Dale, 1992; Martin & Reutzel, 1999; Sigel & McGillcuddy-Delisi, 1984; van Kleeck, Gillam, Hamilton, & McGrath, 1997), and different styles found within the middle class are not all equally conducive to positive outcomes for children's language and literacy skills (e.g., Haden, Reese, & Fivush, 1996; Reese, Cox, Harte, & McAnally, 2003).

Second, many parents of children from nonmainstream cultural backgrounds do read to their children very regularly. For example, as mentioned earlier, data collected in 2001 indicated that 48% of black families and 42% of Hispanic families reported reading to their children every day in the past week (Federal Interagency Forum on Child and Family Statistics, 2002). Some of these families may be assuming, following the political sound bites, that simply reading to their children will reap later academic benefits for them. They may not be aware that how one shares and discusses books is of importance, and they may wish to have information about how to spend book-sharing time in ways that are known to be more effective for later academic success. Such information might be more consciously accepted or rejected by parents with different cultural values, and if accepted, more effectively applied, if they were aware of the cultural bases and hence biases of such practices discussed in Section I of this chapter. As such, although the two sections of this chapter may seem to be at odds with each other, I believe that they can effectively complement each other if they are used *together* in working with families and educators.

In reading Section II, remember that family influences on preliteracy in many mainstream-culture homes reflect literate discourse and the ways that it fosters the structure of teaching and talking to children. The family influences discussed in this section, shown in Figure 9.1, include the broad categories of general teaching strategies and language interactions. These two areas, of course, are interrelated. In light of the huge amount of variation in mainstream family practices, however, the strategies I discuss in this section are more prevalent in some mainstream culture families than in others.

General Teaching Strategies

The five general teaching strategies reviewed under this topic certainly apply to the lan-

guage interactions that go on during teaching, but they also go beyond the language aspects of interactions. As shown in Figure 9.1, they include having adults or more literate persons (1) use routines, (2) gradually shift responsibility to child, (3) operate in child's zone of proximal development (ZPD; Vygotsky, 1978), (4) request verbal display, and (5) adjust the proportion of information containing input already mastered versus information that is challenging to the child. All of these general teaching strategies are very much influenced by the cultural factors discussed in Section I of this chapter.

Use Routines

A routine event is any purposeful activity made up of smaller segments of activity and, like the notion of a script (Schank & Abelson, 1977), "it has strong temporally invariant structure, recurs frequently, and has goals, rules and props well understood by the participants" (Nelson, 1986, p. 14). For the young child, frequently occurring activities such as eating, dressing, bathing, feeding pets, grocery shopping, or doing laundry constitute such routine events. Bruner (1983) refers to highly restrained routine events as "formats," which he defines as having a sequential structure, clearly marked roles, and scripts for the accompanying communication. Bruner and his colleagues have focused their research on game formats such as peekaboo, build-and-bash, and object exchange (e.g., Ninio & Bruner, 1978).

Routines are considered helpful to young children's language learning because they provide a kind of "organizational prosthetic" (Constable, 1986) that serves to diminish the information-processing load (Shatz, 1983). Katherine Nelson and her colleagues (1986) discuss how children's knowledge of routine, everyday experiences constitutes the initial content of their mental representations and, hence, the original foundation for "thinking, talking, and acting" (1986, p. 3; see also Duchan, Chapter 18, this volume). Although this view is only one of many regarding the origins of mental representation (e.g., some view aspects of mental representation as innately given), the idea that routines foster learning by limiting the variation in input is far less controversial.

A child comes to understand a routine when he or she knows the invariant sequence of the events and the roles of the participants. As the child comes to know the routine and form a mental representation of it, he or she has to devote less mental energy or attention to the structure of the activity itself (Shatz, 1983). As such, correspondingly more attention can be devoted to the meaningful substance of the activity, and the language that accompanies the activity.

A number of researchers have found that during verbal routines with children in early stages of language development, children who are typically developing talk more (Conti-Ramsden & Friel-Patti, 1987; Snow, Perlmann, & Nathan, 1987), as do children with developmental delays (Yoder & Davies, 1992a). Two-year olds who are typically developing use more complex language during verbal routines (Conti-Ramsden & Friel-Patti, 1987). Children with developmental delays are also more intelligible during verbal routines (Yoder & Davies, 1992b). Furthermore, with children with developmental delays, intervention studies using verbal routines, or verbal routines combined with expansions of the children's utterances, have shown promising results for most of the children (Kim & Lombardino, 1991; Yoder, Spruytenburg, Edwards, & Davies, 1995).

In mainstream-culture families, book sharing is one of the common routines of particular relevance to preliteracy development. Jones (1996) refers to it as "a privileged discourse routine" (p. 34). In this routine, children come to know how books are shared (e.g., how they sit, pay attention, hold the book, turn the pages, generally respond to the adult's comments and questions) and can therefore be more attentive to the information conveyed by and about the particular book being shared. Children often let adults know that they enjoy routine events, not only by enjoying book sharing in general but also by often requesting that the very same book be read repeatedly (or, *ad nauseam,* the adult might say). Books are in many ways even more predictable than other routine events, in that they provide a very constrained context and topic, and have text language that does not vary at all from one reading to the next. Even the physical context of a book is usually quite constrained in one-on-one book sharing, because the child is often nestled next to the adult, with the book itself as the only salient object of attention for the two participants.

Gradually Shift Responsibility to Child

Theorists with a social constructivist orientation consider meaning to be socially created by "the joint intentional actions of minded creatures" (Harré, 1984, p. 8). This philosophical orientation is foundational to Vygotsky's approach to children's psychological development. Vygotsky claimed that "every function in the child's cultural development appears twice: first, on the social level, and later, on the individual level; first, between people (interpsychological), and then inside the child (intrapsychological)" (1978, p. 57).

From this perspective, children learn all higher level psychological functioning in social interaction with a more competent, experienced member of their culture, because most, if not all, aspects of literate thought are considered higher level thinking. That person provides a great deal of support to ensure the child's successful participation in an activity at whatever level the child is capable of participating. Over time, the adult gradually begins to relinquish control of the interaction to the child, with the goal that the child eventually perform the task independently. Vygotsky (1978) refers to this shift as movement from other-regulation to self-regulation, or as movement from interpsychological to intrapsychological functioning. This process eventually allows for independent action or problem solving by the child.

In the context of routine events, as children come to understand and mentally represent more about an event (e.g., the chronological sequence of activities within it, the roles of each participant in the event, the language that goes along with event), the adult gradually cedes more and more responsibility for the event's unfolding to the child. Eventually, the child is capable of performing the event independently, at which point the activity as a joint construction usually ceases to hold the child's attention (see van Kleeck, 1994, 2003, for a model depicting this gradual shift of responsibility to the child as the child's mental representation of an activity becomes more complete and flexible).

The notion of a gradual shift in responsibility is useful in thinking about the different roles an adult plays in interacting with a child based on where the child is in her or his learning (see Vigil & van Kleeck, 1996, for further discussion of this point). The adult does far more initially when the child knows very little, and far less as the child comes to know more and more. Correspondingly, the child does more over time. On a "micro" level of development, this is demonstrated nicely in book-sharing research that has focused on the role of the book's familiarity on the child's amount of participation in the discussion about the book. Most researchers have found that as specific books become more familiar, children talk more and the adult talks less during book sharing (e.g., De Temple & Snow, 1996; Goodsitt, Raitan, & Perlmutter, 1988; Robinson & Sulzby, 1984; but see Heath, 1982, for contrary findings). On a more "macro" level of development, we have evidence that adults do a great deal of discussion when sharing books with younger children, and that they gradually talk less and do more straight reading of the text as the child matures and develops through the preschool years (e.g., Goodsitt et al., 1988; van Kleeck & Beckley-McCall, 2002).

Operate in the Child's Zone of Proximal Development

Another concept in Vygotskyan theory germane to teaching is the notion of the zone of proximal development (ZPD). Vygotsky (1978) defines this zone as "the distance between the actual developmental level as determined by independent problem solving and the level of potential development as determined through problem solving under adult guidance or in collaboration with more capable peers" (p. 86). To operate effectively in a child's ZPD, the adult must tune to the child's linguistic and cognitive abilities to provide developmentally appropriate guidance. Bruner's term, "scaffolding" (1985, 1986), has often been used to refer to the same adult guidance during book sharing (e.g., Bus & van IJzendoorn, 1988; Edwards, 1989; Hockenberger, Goldstein, & Haas, 1999; Martin & Reutzel, 1999).

Similar to scaffolding is the notion of "mediation," which Mason (1992) defined as "a protective umbrella of explanations, interpretations, and clarifications . . . provided at the right moment by adults" (p. 216). In book sharing, the term "mediation" is often used to refer to the discussions about a book that go beyond the printed text (i.e., extratextual), that help the child understand the text (Altwerger, Diehl-Faxon, & Dockstader-Anderson, 1985; DeLoache & DeMendoza, 1987; Heath, 1982; Martin & Reutzel, 1999).

Within interactions as they unfold, adults often provide finely tuned support to children by structuring the task, pointing out significant items, and offering prompts and feedback to make the task manageable (Phillips & McNaughton, 1990). This online scaffolding is enhanced by a mother's "intimate knowledge of her child's linguistic ability, familiarity with text structure, and the child's background experiences" (Altwerger et al., 1985, p. 482). Adult mediation, or scaffolding, during book sharing has been described by Cochran-Smith (1984) as joint sense making, with the adult attempting to create a match between the child's knowledge and abilities, and the text. The child's reactions are monitored in order to repair any misunderstandings or "mismatches" that may occur. If a child signals that he or she is not understanding, the adult might modify the text (e.g., simplify words, summarize or restate, or omit information), explain inferences suggested by the text or illustrations, or provide additional explanations of concepts, words, or events occurring in the story.

Mainstream-culture adults appear to operate in the child's ZPD during book sharing by adjusting their interactions to the child's changing cognitive and linguistic abilities as the child develops (e.g., Altwerger et al., 1985; Bus & van IJzendoorn, 1988; DeLoache & DeMendoza, 1987; Dickinson, De Temple, Hirschler, & Smith, 1992; Murphy, 1978; Pellegrini, Brody, & Sigel, 1985; van Kleeck, 1998; van Kleeck & Beckley-McCall, 2002; van Kleeck et al., 1996). Ideally, the scaffolding or mediation process operates to keep the child successful, while over time also challenging him or her to develop new and higher level skills.

Another way in which book sharing is adjusted to a child's ZPD is by varying the difficulty of the books adults provide for children. As Rogoff (1990) notes, "Caregivers arrange the occurrence of children's activities and facilitate learning by regulating the difficulty of the task and by modeling mature performance during joint participation in activities" (p. 17). Parents and other family members might regulate the difficulty of book sharing in part by choosing books that have text they consider developmentally appropriate for their child.

In one study of 5 mothers reading to their two different-age preschoolers individually and simultaneously, van Kleeck and Beckley-McCall (2002) found that the mothers chose the linguistically simplest book (in terms of average number of words of text per page) for their younger child, the linguistically most complex book for their older child, and a book that (on average for all 5 mothers) fell in between these two levels of complexity when reading to both children at the same time. From another perspective, Martin and Reutzel (1999) found that when mothers shared the same book with children of different ages, they discussed it differently. With younger children (ages 1 year, 0 months —1 year, 6 months) they simplified concepts, and with older children (2 years, 0 months and 4 years, 0 months) they asked more questions to engage the children. Researchers have, in general, not considered book complexity as an aspect of how book-sharing interactions are tuned to children's developmental levels (see van Kleeck, 2003, for a discussion).

Request Verbal Display

As discussed earlier, adults in mainstream American culture socialize their children to display their knowledge verbally. Doing so requires that the adult be aware of not only the child's general linguistic and cognitive level of development but also of the child's specific knowledge base and attendant vocabulary. The notion of verbal display of knowledge is rarely addressed in book-sharing research or interventions, yet there is clear empirical evidence that it is a frequent part of the book-sharing routine.

DeLoache and DeMendoza (1987) looked at mothers interacting with 12-, 15-, and 18-month-old children, and examined the mothers' beliefs about their children's knowledge of words taken from the book that had just been shared. The mothers were asked to indicate whether the child could produce, comprehend only, or was unfamiliar with each word. The mothers were significantly more likely to skip over pictures when they thought their child did not know the label for that picture (asking for such labels only 8% of the time). They were also much more likely to ask the child for labels they thought the child could produce (49% of label requests) than for those that they believed the child could only comprehend (18% of label requests).

A study of mother–child interaction during spontaneous play also illustrates this phenomenon. Goodman, Larrivee, Roberts, Heller, and Fritz (2000) had mothers complete the MacArthur Communication Development Inventory (Fenson et al., 1993), a measurement tool that has parents indicate all the specific vocabulary items that their child knows. In comparing these maternal reports to the questions the mothers asked their 30-month-old children during play, it was found that the children already knew 94% of the words they were asked to supply in response to their mothers' questions. Goodman et al. (2000) concluded that the mothers' agenda appeared to be the maintenance of discourse with their children, and not the teaching of new vocabulary. Their position is also supported by Yoder and his colleagues (Yoder, Davies, & Bishop, 1994; Yoder, Davies, Bishop, & Munson, 1994). These data also support the idea that the mothers were socializing their children to display their knowledge verbally.

In an in-depth study of her own two children, Jones (1996) brought up other possibilities regarding the function of known-information questions. With infants, she suggested that adults talk and describe so much during book sharing to keep the child's attention and "to encourage the infant to locate, and then look at, a referent, and to do so for as long as possible. Sustained acts of visual and auditory attention in the infant are at the heart of all early reading activity, but such skills are not innate. They are achieved, and they are achieved via a judiciously managed process of adult intervention" (p. 48).

From another perspective, Jones (1996) notes that the items the adults return to most within the same book are those for which the infant has shown a special preference. As such, labeling the same object repeatedly within a book may be a manifestation of following the infant's interest and keeping the book-sharing routine child-centered. On yet another level, renaming the same or a similar character or item on different pages within a story may be teaching young children something about how stories work—"that referents return in similar if not identical form from one page to the next" (p. 45). Finally, Jones notes the possiblity that in labeling different tokens of items the child already "knows," the adult is expanding the child's category for that word by, in effect, saying, "and here is another instance of a cow." It may be that known-information questions function differently at different points in a young child's development, with some of the functions Jones discusses being important during infancy, and the ability to display knowledge verbally becoming more important later on.

Adjust the Proportion of Input Containing Information Already Mastered versus Information That Is Challenging to the Child

Although operating in the child's ZPD (Vygotsky, 1978) fosters new learning, quite the opposite is taking place when adults request verbal displays of knowledge—asking the child to display verbally what he or she has already mastered (or has at least begun to master). In a sense, then, there are two competing agendas in interactions with children—to teach new concepts and information, and to get children to display mastered concepts and information verbally. This leads to a question I have rarely ever seen addressed: What amount of input to a child should be challenging? In other words, what amount of input should be aimed at fostering development? I turn to a study on book sharing that I conducted with my colleagues and reinterpret findings from another book-sharing study in an attempt to answer this question.

Our own study (van Kleeck et al., 1997) was designed to look at the relationship between levels of concrete and abstract language in mothers' and fathers' book-sharing discussions when their preschoolers were between ages 3 years, 6 months and 4 years, 1 month, and their children's gains on a formal measure of abstract language knowledge 1 year later. There were significant correlations between the amount of book-sharing discussion at three of four different levels of abstraction (Levels I, II, and IV, with IV being the highest level of abstraction) and children's subsequent gains at the highest level of abstraction (Level IV). Although it made sense that the amount of parental discussion at the highest level of abstraction was related to the children's gains at that level, we wondered why the amount of input at the two lowest levels of abstraction (Levels I and II) was related to gains at the highest level only. To answer this, we turned to an idea forwarded without empirical support a quarter of a century ago by Blank, Rose, and Berlin (1978).

These authors had suggested that preschool teachers should aim about 30% of their discourse at a level of abstraction that would challenge the children, while keeping the other 70% at a level that children had already mastered, therefore allowing them to respond successfully. Our own findings, although with parents and not preschool teachers, mirrored this suggestion to a surprising extent. As a group, the 70 parents (35 mothers and 35 fathers) in our study provided an average of 37% of their book discussion at the two higher levels of abstraction (Levels III and IV) that were more challenging to the children, and 63% at the lower levels (Levels I and II) at which the children demonstrated much more skill on the pretest we had given them.

These percentages led us to conclude that perhaps abstract language skills in children are fostered simultaneously in two different, and seemingly opposite, ways. On the one hand, keeping most of the interaction at levels the child has already clearly mastered creates a climate in which the child feels competent and successful. The child can therefore better engage in the conversation and also learn to display verbally what he or she already knows. On the other hand, providing about one-third of interaction at levels that the child has not yet mastered (in the ZPD) creates challenges and opportunities for growth.

DeLoache and DeMendoza (1987) reported a similar finding with children who were younger than those in the van Kleeck et al. (1997) study. These authors reported two levels of complexity in the information provided by mothers during book sharing with children who were 12, 15, and 18 months old. They found that 74% of the information provided was simple (almost all labels), whereas the remainder was more complex (factual information, dramatizations, references to the child's experiences with related objects). They also noted, however, that the older children received significantly more complex input, with elaborations increasing from 12% to 23% to 42% across the three ages studied.

If the best learning environment has ample opportunity both for success and for challenge, it may be the case that this distinction is captured in online discourse by different illocutionary functions in adult book-sharing language. Questions may primarily socialize the child both to engage in the interaction and to display knowledge verbally, whereas comments may serve either to teach what the parent believes to be new information or to model higher levels of thinking about information presented in the book. Unfortunately, most book-sharing research cannot be reinterpreted to illuminate this possibility, because researchers often collapse the illocutionary functions of adults' book-sharing conversations. For example, several studies of the concrete-to-abstract dimension of adults' book-sharing language have not distinguished between questions and comments (e.g., DeTemple & Snow, 1996; Sigel & McGillicuddy-Delisi, 1984; van Kleeck et al., 1997).

A reinterpretation of a consistent finding in intervention studies conducted by Lonigan and his colleagues (i.e., Arnold, Lonigan, Whitehurst, & Epstein, 1994; Lonigan, 1991, 1993; Valdez-Menchaca & Whitehurst, 1992; Whitehurst et al., 1988) offers indirect support for the idea that children are learning both new information and to display mastered information in book-sharing interactions. Discussing several intervention studies conducted with his colleagues, Lonigan (1994) notes that "consistently larger and more enduring effects of the intervention have generally been found on measures of expressive language skills than on receptive language skills" (p. 307). Without using the lens of viewing adults as providing both challenging and already mastered input during book sharing, these findings do not make sense. If language knowledge is improved, one would expect an equal or greater impact on receptive language skills, because receptive skills are typically somewhat more advanced than expressive skills. However, it may be that these children are actually increasing their basic language knowledge (reflected in receptive language gains) but making even greater gains in their ability to display their language knowledge verbally (expressive language skill gains). Alternatively, it may be that measures of comprehension are simply far less reliable than measures of production, and that such findings are more an artifact of these measurement issues (P. Yoder, personal communication, December 6, 2002).

In this section, I have discussed general teaching strategies found in mainstream-culture families that can be applied to the book-sharing context. Of course, these strategies can also be used in other contexts. In the next section, I hone in on specific aspects of the language that adults can use in the book-sharing context and explore both the content of their language and specific interactional strategies they may employ.

Language Interactions

In mainstream-culture families, interaction during literate activities with preschoolers, and particularly during book sharing, tends to be fine-tuned to a child's language and cognitive level, interests and experience, knowledge, topic, and ability to respond. In the book-sharing context, the child can be gradually introduced to higher levels of literate discourse, to how books are constructed, and to the formal mechanisms of our alphabetic script. This section on language interactions that foster preliteracy and later literacy skills is organized around two dimensions of the talk that occurs during book sharing—the content and interactional strategies.

As can be seen in Figure 9.1 and in more detail in Figure 9.2, the discussion of the content of talk is subdivided into four suggestions: (1) Use increasingly abstract language; (2) focus on meaning first, then separately on print form; (3) increasingly frame the book as a unique context; and (4) tune to the child's interests and experiences. The

interactional strategies are divided into suggestions to (1) be semantically contingent with the child's contributions, and (2) prompt the child's verbal participation. Of course, how interactions are carried out interacts intimately with the teaching strategies just discussed, and with the social and cultural factors discussed earlier.

In interaction with young children, adults adjust in a somewhat global way to children's developmental level and interests. This influences the abstractness and the content of their talk. Adults also make adjustments to the child "online," so to speak, by following the child's conversational lead and encouraging his or her participation in the interaction.

Content of Extratextual Talk

The content of interactions during book sharing includes the general level of cognitive/semantic dimension, or the abstractness of the talk, that can occur with any topic, and the specific kinds of topics that typically get discussed. The topics include having adults (1) focus on meaning first, then separately on print form; (2) increasingly frame the book as a unique context; and (3) tune to the child's interests and experiences. Both

Content of Extratextual Talk				Interactional Strategies	
Use increasingly abstract language	Focus on meaning first, then separately on print form	Increasingly frame book as a unique context	Tune to child's interests and experiences	Be semantically contingent with child's contribution	Prompt child's verbal participation
1. Use concrete, immediate language / 2. Use more decontextualized, abstract language	1. Talk about pictures/story / 2. Talk about letters and print conventions; share rhyming books	1. Use book-related vocabulary / 2. Talk about authors, illustrators, etc.	Relate book to child's life	Use imitations and expansions / Use semantic extensions / Use clarification requests / Respond to child questions	Ask questions / Vertically scaffold / Hold child accountable / Provide praise and encouragement

FIGURE 9.2. The content and interactional strategies of language interactions used during book sharing in mainstream-culture families. 1, developmentally earlier; 2, developmentally later.

the abstractness and the topics of talk during book sharing tend to change developmentally over the preschool years.

USE INCREASINGLY ABSTRACT LANGUAGE

In talking to young children, one aspect of an adult's language concerns how directly it relates to the supportive perceptual context. The adult talk can be characterized as being embedded, or as increasingly disembedded, from the perceptual context. This dimension of talk forms a continuum that ranges from using concrete to using increasingly abstract language, a quality that has been referred to in a variety of ways in the literature. Some synonymous terms have included language that is "immediate" versus "nonimmediate" (Dickinson et al., 1992), "decontextualized" (e.g., Denny, 1991; Heath, 1982, 1983; Snow & Ninio, 1986), "distancing" (McGillicuddy-DeLisi, 1982; Sigel & McGilicuddy-Delisi, 1984), varying in "representational demand" it places on the child (Blank et al., 1978), and "disembedded" (e.g., Donaldson, 1978; Wells, 1985).

At the most concrete end of the continuum, adults might request or supply labels, or ask a child to locate an object pictured in a book. At the most abstract or cognitively challenging end of the continuum, they might request or supply predictions or explanations. Between these two extremes are linguistic activities such as naming attributes, recalling information, or making comparisons. Engaging children in more abstract discussions about book content has been shown to be related to children's subsequent abstract language development gains (van Kleeck et al., 1997) and to their later academic success (Heath, 1982, 1983; Wells, 1985). It is believed to help children deal in sophisticated ways with the information presented in books. Inferencing and reasoning are particularly helpful later on, when the school curriculum shifts from "learning to read" to "reading to learn," at around the third or fourth grade (e.g., Heath, 1982, 1983). Some scholars refer to this general kind of discussion as "literate language" and have argued that it is a ro-

bust predictor of early school-based literacy (e.g., Pellegrini, 2001; Pellegrini & Galda, 1998; Pellegrini, Galda, Bartini, & Charak, 1998).

Future research might further establish the importance of exposing preschoolers to decontextualized language during book sharing if direct links can be made to their later reading comprehension ability. The more decontextualized questions asked by the parents of preschoolers (e.g., those requiring inference, explanation, and prediction) directly correspond to the questions that mature readers spontaneously ask themselves to aid in their comprehension of written texts (e.g., Collins & Stevens, 1982; Garner & Alexander, 1982; see Chapter 14 by McGregor and Chapter 16 by Scott, this volume). Likewise, Hanmaker's (1986) review of research found that cognitively higher level questions were more effective than their lower level counterparts. Interventions aimed at enhancing text comprehension have also relied on strategies that include more abstract language. Palinscar and Brown (1984), for example, used summarizing, questioning oneself about the text content, clarifying, and predicting to improve children's text comprehension.

A far broader implication of abstract language comes from the work of a number of literacy theorists (e.g., Chafe & Danielwicz, 1987; Denny, 1991; Goody, 1977; Havelock, 1963; McLuhan, 1962; Ong, 1982). Denny (1991) summarized the position of these scholars, stating that "these authors correctly concentrate on decontextualization as the main style of thought encouraged by literacy" (1991, p. 81). This places decontextualized (or abstract) language in the realm of a culturally transmitted way of thinking. It aligns well with the Vygotskyan idea that higher levels of thought (or goal-directed behaviors of the individual) are mediated through language by the symbolic tools that have been internalized from the individual's interactions with others in his or her environment (Frawley, 1997; Vygotsky, 1978).

As children develop from infancy through the preschool years, parents from mainstream culture often place increasing cognitive demands on them during book-sharing routines by using more abstract language in their discussions, including their comments and questions about books being shared. In book-sharing research with longitudinal or cross-sectional designs, studies show that as young preliterate children mature, a larger percentage of adult talk about the text becomes more abstract or decontextualized, while a correspondingly lower percentage of the talk is at more concrete levels (e.g., Goodsitt et al., 1988; Heath, 1982, 1983; Ninio & Bruner, 1978; Snow & Ninio, 1986; van Kleeck & Beckley-McCall, 2002; van Kleeck, Gillam, & Breshears, 1998; van Kleeck, Vigil, & Beer, 1998; van Kleeck et al., 1996; Wheeler, 1983).

Some research has begun to suggest that middle-class parents vary among themselves in the amount of more decontextualized language they use during book sharing. Haden et al. (1996), for example, found that the use of abstract language was related to a stable style reflective of only 5 of the 19 mothers they studied. However, in a far larger study of the book-sharing styles of 96 middle-class parents with their preschoolers ages 3 years, 6 months–4 years, 1 month, Hammett and her colleagues (2003) found that although parents clustered into four different styles of interaction, in all of the clusters, they used fairly high proportions of abstract language with their children, even though the clusters varied considerably in the overall amount of input they provided. For three of the clusters ($n = 77$), between 40 and 47% of talk about the text was at higher, as opposed to lower, levels of abstraction, and for one cluster ($n = 19$), 28% of talk was at higher levels.

There is also evidence that the genre of the book makes a difference in how much adults use language at higher levels of abstraction. For example, Pellegrini, Perlmutter, Galda, and Brody (1990) found more higher level (i.e., more abstract) language used by African American mothers with their Head Start preschoolers when sharing an expository book as opposed to a storybook. In two of my own studies, more decontextualized language was used when sharing storybooks as opposed to alphabet books with children at ages 2, 3, and 4

years of age (van Kleeck, Gillam, et al., 1998; van Kleeck, Vigil, et al., 1998).

FOCUS ON MEANING AND ENJOYMENT OF PRINT FIRST, THEN ON PRINT FORM IN SIMPLER FORM–MEANING CONTEXTS

Convergent evidence from a number of studies suggests that in mainstream families, preliteracy development takes place in two discernable stages that differentially emphasize print form and print meaning. In the first stage, there is an almost exclusive focus on meaning when parents share books with their children (Phillips & McNaughton, 1990; Snow & Ninio, 1986; van Kleeck, 1998; Yaden, Smolkin, & Conlon, 1989). In this stage, even alphabet books are treated primarily as picture books, and parents will label the pictures but generally refrain from mentioning or discussing the letters associated with them (Bus & van IJzendoorn, 1988; van Kleeck, 1998; Yaden, Smolkin, & MacGillivray, 1993).

In the second stage of preliteracy development, older preschoolers are increasingly introduced to various aspects of the print form, which includes both alphabet knowledge and early stages of phonological awareness, such as rhyming. In this stage, the focus when sharing alphabet books shifts to discussing letters and the sounds they make (Bus & van IJzendoorn, 1988; van Kleeck, 1998). Print forms (sounds and letters) are usually attached to meaning, but to much smaller units of meaning. In other words, letters are attached to single words that start with them (*a* is for *apple*). In the second stage, in other contexts, and with other genres of books, meaning remains the paramount focus, and more abstract language is used to discuss books. The unit of meaning in these contexts consists of longer and longer texts as the child develops. By the end of this second stage, many parents may be sharing "chapter books" (books with separate chapters) with their children).

Similar stages have been suggested for early reading development. A first stage focuses on the function–meaning foundation for reading, whereas a second stage focuses on teaching the formal aspects of print (i.e., early decoding of print). A third stage integrates the previous two stages and focuses on reading comprehension (Chall, 1983; Downing, 1979; McCormick & Mason, 1986).

In work done on mothers' book-sharing discussions with their preschoolers, my colleagues and I found compelling evidence of an early meaning foundation and a later print form (i.e., alphabetic knowledge) introduction stage. In a longitudinal study, 14 mothers read three books (a storybook, a rhyming book, and an alphabet book) to their preschoolers when they were 2, 3, and 4 years of age. Utterances by the mothers that went beyond the text were coded as focusing on meaning, on form, or on other aspects of the mother–child interaction, such as getting the child's attention and controlling his or her behavior. Results showed that meaning was emphasized when the children were 2 years old (see van Kleeck, 1998, for a summary report of this data), even when the book being shared was an alphabet book. At ages 3 and 4, there was an increasing emphasis on discussing the letters in the alphabet book. However, the mothers continued to focus exclusively on meaning when sharing storybooks or rhyming books, even when their children were 3 and 4 years old.

The findings for the 4-year-olds in this longitudinal study were replicated in a second study in which 28 mothers read alphabet, rhyming, and storybooks to their children aged 3 years, 6 months to 4 years, 1 month (again, see van Kleeck, 1998). When sharing the rhyming or storybooks, neither letters nor their sounds were ever mentioned by the mothers. Alphabet knowledge was clearly emphasized, however, when they read the alphabet book. It was also clear from the transcripts of the alphabet book interactions that these mothers were making a conscious effort at times other than the videotaping to teach their children about letter names, shapes, and sounds. Nearly every transcript contained mothers' discussions about how the child should know a certain letter or the sound it made, because they had been working on learning it.

In some studies, book sharing does not appear to be related to children's development of phonological awareness (Baker, Fernandez-Fein, Scher, & Williams, 1998; Lonigan, Anthony, Dyer, & Collins, 1995; Raz & Bryant, 1990; Sénéchal, LeFevre, Thomas, & Daley, 1998; Whitehurst, Epstein, et al., 1994), whereas in other studies, a relationship has been found (Burgess, 1997; Dickinson, Bryant, Peisner-Feinberg, Lambert, & Wolf, 1999). These inconsistent findings are probably due at least in part to the fact that mainstream-culture parents most often read storybooks to their children, and most often focus on meaning while sharing them, and the genre of the book may be critical to whether phonological awareness is fostered. Indeed, Murray, Stahl, and Ivey (1996) found that reading alphabet books stressing letter sounds, as well as letter names, improved the phonological awareness skills of 4-year-olds. Or the inconsistencies may be due to indirect connections between book sharing and phonological awareness, in that some studies have begun to show that increases in vocabulary result in improvements in phonological awareness (for discussions, see Goswami, 2001; van Kleeck, 2003; Whitehurst & Lonigan, 2001), and there is ample evidence that vocabulary development is related to book sharing (see van Kleeck, 2003, for discussion).

Although previous research has demonstrated that preschool rhyming ability predicts beginning reading ability (e.g., Bradley & Bryant, 1983; Ellis & Large, 1987; Lundberg, Olofsson, & Wall, 1980), there have been no specific efforts to connect young children's rhyming abilities with their exposure to rhyming books. What has been noted, however, is a steady increase in mothers' choosing rhyming books as their preschoolers get older, a finding that fits well with the idea that print form should be emphasized later in the preschool years. Between 6 months and 3 years, 6 months of age, studies of middle- and low-income mothers found that they chose rhyming books only 8 to 10% of the time (De Temple & Snow, 1996; van Kleeck, 1995; van Kleeck et al., 1996). When their children were 4 years, 6 months old, low-income mothers chose rhyming books 21% of the time (De Temple & Snow, 1996).

Discussion of two stages of preliteracy development once again requires consideration of variation in family beliefs and practices. A number of studies have shown that in lower socioeconomic status (SES) families, parents tend to focus more on reading skills (drill and practice with letters, etc.) than on the meaning component of the book (Elliott & Hewison, 1994; Goldenberg, Reese, & Gallimore, 1992; Heath, 1983; McLane & McNamee, 1990; Sonnenschein, Brody, & Munsterman, 1996; Stipek, Milburn, Clements, & Daniels, 1992). Similarly, Goldenberg et al. (1992) found that Latino parents of kindergartners "constrained literacy events heavy with repetition and devoid of attention to meaning" (Goldenberg, 2001, p. 223). It may be that these parents were emphasizing skills they believe necessary in helping the child prepare for school (Delpit, 1988; Thompson, Mixon, & Serpell, 1996). These findings suggest that a first stage of preliteracy development, in which enjoyment and entertainment are paramount as parents focus on the meaning of the book, may not be part of the socialization process that all children receive. As always, though, what parents believe and, hence, do is more important than the SES (Spiegel, 1994; White, 1982), even though group data may show effects for SES.

INCREASINGLY FRAME BOOKS AS A UNIQUE CONTEXT

The book context is shaped in some respects by the specialized vocabulary relevant to books, including words such as *book, draw, write, read, page,* and *story,* that typically develops before the child can read. Jones (1996), in her account of how she and her husband read to their two children, talks about how the words *book* and *page* were "among the substantives which occur with the highest degree of frequency in adult speech at the 9-month sessions" (p. 28). Another way in which meaning is supported in the context of book sharing lies in gradually teaching children how books work. Snow and Ninio (1986) discussed the "rules" for interacting with books that young preschoolers are learning. These included ideas such as books are for reading, not manipulating; the book controls the topic; pictures are representations of things and

events, and are to be named; and book events occur outside of real time. Jones (1996) talks about infants learning that book sharing is an activity with clear boundaries that lasts for some time and, ideally, is not interrupted. In my own research, older preschoolers' mothers would mention things such as a book's author and illustrator. In some cases, I have even witnessed things such as copyright dates and ISBN numbers being explained to young prereaders. Interestingly, the children responded to these pieces of information by asking whether the copyright date was like the book's birthday, and the ISBN like its telephone number.

Tune to the Child's Interests and Experience

Many studies of book sharing have noted that, as part of the discussion when sharing books with their preschoolers, parents tie the content of the book to experiences they know their child has had (e.g., Cochran-Smith, 1984; Flood, 1977; Hayden & Fagan, 1987; Heath, 1982; Martinez & Roser, 1985; Shanahan & Hogan, 1983; van Kleeck et al., 1997; Wells, 1986). In one of my data sets of 35 middle-class mother–child dyads, the mothers related book information to their children's life experiences an average of four times while sharing an unfamiliar book, and a total of 28 of the mothers used this strategy (other analyses of this data, though not this particular one, are reported in van Kleeck et al., 1997). When parents do this during book sharing, they are modeling a strategy widely discussed as being one of the most important strategies used by fluent readers (e.g., Baker & Brown, 1984; Chapman, 1984; Harp, 1988; LaZansky, Spencer, & Johnston, 1987). An intervention study by Hockenberger et al. (1999) trained mothers of children with developmental disabilities and from low-SES backgrounds to use comments that related book content to experiences in their child's life. The mothers increased such comments, and their children increased both their own initiations and responses to their mothers.

Parents may accomodate children's interest in the book-sharing routine by allowing them to choose the book or books to be read. In a study of 10 families (Phillips and McNaughton, 1990), mothers reported that their children selected the titles 71.5% of the time. Martin and Reutzel (1999) reported on one mother who added a dog to a story that did not have a dog in it, because her child was fond of dogs. Jones (1996) discussed how both parents in her detailed study were highly influenced by their children's interests in terms of the pictures they discussed with them during book sharing. This child influence was captured in Jones's suggestion that children are "architects as well as apprentices" in the book-sharing context (p. 90).

Interactional Strategies

Although very specific interactional strategies are listed in Figure 9.2, research has rarely focused on this aspect of family book sharing as it occurs naturally in preschoolers homes. These strategies are, nonetheless, the exact kinds of things taught in book-sharing interventions. This has been true of interventions designed for preschoolers who are typically developing, though in some studies, they were nonetheless at risk for later reading and academic difficulties (e.g., Dale, Crain-Thoreson, Notari-Syverson, & Cole, 1996; Hockenberger et al., 1999; Lonigan & Whitehurst, 1998; Neuman & Gallagher, 1994). It has also been true for studies involving preschoolers with language delays (Crain-Thoreson & Dale, 1999; Dale et al., 1996; Hockenberger et al., 1999; McNeill & Fowler, 1999; Whitehurst & Lonigan, 1998). These studies have been able to demonstrate increases in child participation during book sharing, and in some cases, in children's language or preliteracy development.

It is important to note that the driving force behind all of the individual strategies listed in Figure 9.2 is to increase the child's verbal participation in the book-sharing activity. In book sharing, as in other kinds of conversations in many mainstream families, adults work to maintain the child's interest and participation in the conversation by following the child's lead in the interaction when he or she offers a verbal turn—what we call being semantically contingent—and

by prompting the child to interact when he or she has not initiated a verbal turn. However, as discussed earlier in the section, "Ways of Talking with Children," getting children to engage in high levels of participation in conversations with adults is in itself a cultural value that is not universally shared; indeed, the cultural relativity of many of these interactional strategies was also discussed.

From research on parent–child interaction in general (not just in the book-sharing context), we have learned that the amount of language input children receive at home is related either to a faster concurrent rate of language development or later, higher levels of development in a variety of domains (e.g., vocabulary, school achievement, reading ability, and cognition) (Feagans & Farran, 1982; Gottfried, 1984; Hart & Risley, 1992; 1995; Huttenlocher, Haight, Bryk, Seltzer, & Lyons, 1991; Walker, Greenwood, Hart, & Carta, 1994; Wells, 1985). Similarly, the amount of book sharing in the home has been shown to be related to children's language and literacy outcomes (see Scarborough & Dobrich, 1994, for a review). Other research has begun to demonstrate that the effect of the amount of adult input on children's development might be related to the amount of child participation: Children tend to match their parents amount of talk (Hart & Risley, 1999), and the more children talk, the faster their language develops (Hart & Risley, 1980, 1995, 1999; Nelson, 1973). The more children participate in interactions, the more practice they are getting in using their language skills, and the more their language develops. Also, the more children talk, the more adults can recast and expand their utterances, thereby fostering knowledge and language development, because children are more likely to process new information if the topic has already been established (Yoder, Davies, & Bishop, 1994; Yoder, Davies, Bishop, & Munson, 1994).

Importantly, the Hart and Risley (1999) landmark study indicates that adults set the stage for how much talk takes place in particular families. In this longitudinal study, the frequency of vocalization was similar for all 42 children during infancy. Over time, however, "the children's frequency of talking accelerated until their word and non-word utterances together matched their parents' frequency of talking to them" (p. 290). By the time the children in this study were 3 years old, their frequency of talk related closely to how much their parents had talked to them while they were learning to talk. Furthermore, the more the children talked, the greater their vocabulary by age 3 years. Moerk (1992) had similar findings in his microanalysis of one mother–child dyad followed longitudinally, and was even able to tie specific maternal language use to specific child language use. These findings indicate that children are socialized not only in how to use language but also in how much to use language. The more children use it, the more they benefit in terms of their language development.

Research in book sharing likewise indicates that not only reading to children but also engaging them in conversations about the text are most beneficial (De Temple & Snow, 1996; Sénéchal, Thomas, & Monker, 1995). Indeed, Flood (1977) demonstrated this a quarter of a century ago, when he found that children with higher response levels in parent–child book sharing had higher prereading skills than less actively involved children. We suspect, then, that the degree to which adults are able to engage children in participating in the book-sharing routine is an important variable in whether, and to what extent, language and preliteracy skills are fostered in this context. Flood's findings are supported by a recent study (Rush, 1999) of 39 mothers with children in Head Start programs; Rush found that the rate of children's language interaction and participation in literate activities related to their language and early literacy skills.

BE SEMANTICALLY CONTINGENT WITH THE CHILD'S CONTRIBUTION

As noted earlier in the discussion of culturally determined ways of talking with children, discussions during book sharing in mainstream-culture families serve as a prime context for transmitting a literate discourse style to young children. As such, the interactional strategies suggested for book sharing, and shown in Figure 9.2, are the same kinds of strategies discussed in that earlier section. Adults follow child initiations in a book-sharing conversation in a semantically contingent fashion by imitating, expanding, or semantically extending what the child has said; by seeking clarification when the child has not been understood; and by responding to questions posed by the child.

PROMPT THE CHILD'S VERBAL PARTICIPATION

Adults prompt the child to participate by asking questions and holding the child accountable for answering them, if he or she knows the child is capable of doing so, or by offering multiturn assistance (vertical scaffolding), if the child is not. Of course, these strategies certainly interact with each other, and also with other agendas, such as explaining information to the child. For example, an adult might vertically scaffold a child's comment to provide more explanation about a particular topic.

Children are also prompted to participate by general praise for their contributions to the book-sharing interaction. Different scholars have discussed how book sharing conducted in a positive fashion leads children to feel positive about reading (Arnold & Whitehurst, 1994; Bettelheim & Zelan, 1982; Daisey, 1991; Wigfield & Asher, 1984). Baker and her colleagues (1997) provide a review article on family influences on children's motivation for reading (see Wasik & Henrickson, Chapter 8, this volume). They argue that "the socioemotional context of early literacy experiences is particularly influential: children whose early encounters with literacy are enjoyable are more likely to develop a predisposition to read frequently and broadly in subsequent years" (p. 69).

Other than Bus and her colleagues, very few researchers have directly studied this dimension of book sharing (see Bus, 2003, for a review). The focus of this program of research has been on the influence of attachment on book sharing. In securely attached mother–child dyads, these interactions appear more positive, the children are more attentive and responsive, and the mothers use less controlling behavior and read to their children more often (Bus, Belsky, van

IJzendoorn, & Crnik, 1997; Bus & van IJzendoorn, 1988, 1992, 1995, 1997).

Most interventions include praising and encouraging the child as one of the techniques that is taught (e.g., see Zevenbergen & Whitehurst, 2003, for a review of dialogic reading studies). Nonetheless, as Anderson and his colleagues discuss (2003), some intervention studies suggest that importing book-sharing techniques to teach to non-mainstream groups may turn book sharing into a negative, tension-filled experience (Janes & Kermani, 2001; Twymon, 1990).

Intervention studies that increase children's participation in book sharing have used a combination of strategies simultaneously, making it impossible to know which specific strategies have been responsible for increased child participation. In one of our own studies, we attempted to look at specific strategies that are effective in increasing child participation by using sequential analysis techniques developed by Bakeman and Quera (1995) to determine what adult interactional behaviors elicit immediate participation by the child. In this study, 10 adult–child dyads were observed longitudinally during storybook sharing when the children were 2, 3, and 4 years of age (Ragan & van Kleeck, 2002).

Results indicated, first of all, that adult questions elicit more child responses than adult comments, a finding expected from research done with children in other contexts (Horgan, 1977; Olsen-Fulero & Conforti, 1983). Furthermore, children's responses were linguistically more complex (in terms of utterance length) following their mothers' *wh*-questions. The children's rate of response to these *wh*-questions increased developmentally from ages 2 to 3 years, then stabilized from ages 3 to 4 years. Other research has found that topic-continuing questions elicit more child responses than do topic-initiating questions (Yoder, Davies, Bishop, & Munson, 1994). It is important to consider that, although *wh*-questions are effective in eliciting children's responses, it may not be the case that "more is better." It remains an empirical question whether asking too many *wh*-questions may possibly have the opposite effect and cause the child to "shut down" conversationally.

Clearly, more research is needed to speci-fy the types of adult interactional strategies that are most effective in obtaining child participation. Furthermore, work is needed to determine what amount of interaction during book sharing is optimal for children's subsequent language and literacy development. The answer to this question may well vary depending on the developmental level of the child, the genre of book being shared, the specific skills one is hoping to foster, and a host of other variables.

CONCLUSIONS

If it is so culturally relative, why do we need to understand how literate discourse is socialized in the mainstream culture via practices such as book sharing? A rather simple answer might be that it reflects the practices of one cultural group, and educators should ideally be aware of all groups' literacy practices. But because literate discourse is a practice of the hegemonic culture, there are deeper reasons to be aware of it. As noted earlier, literate discourse permeates the belief systems and assumptions of its users and shapes their "understanding of language, the world, and themselves" (Olson, 1994, p. 19). Equally, if not more important for educators and speech–language pathologists, however, is the fact that it also shapes perceptions of others in a manner that, without awareness, can be quite insidious.

Teachers who engage in mainstream literate practices with their students (and not all do), may not be consciously aware of those practices. In these cases, teachers may harbor unquestioned beliefs about students in their classroom. For example, children may not tend to answer the ubiquitous known-information question posed by teachers in the classroom because of their socialization at home, not because they do not know the answers to these questions. Teachers, however, may assume that a child does not answer because he or she does not have the information. The teacher then comes to base his or her perceptions about the child's abilities on this faulty assumption, and treat the child accordingly, that is, challenge the "smart" child who knows the answers, but not the child who does not. Hence, the rich get richer, and the poor get poorer.

But it is not only the teacher's perceptions that may be shaped by faulty assumptions. Children are also shaping perceptions of themselves as learners. Early in their academic careers, they come to view themselves as either competent or incompetent learners (Delpit, 1995; Ogbu, 1990). Teachers who are not consciously aware of the cultural relativity of mainstream practices may view children from different backgrounds as less competent rather than as differently socialized learners, and thereby negatively shape children's perceptions of themselves.

Also, it may be that children from mainstream culture are susceptible to forming negative perceptions of themselves as learners as well. Although we often assume that mainstream practices are pervasive in mainstream homes, this is actually not the case. Although central tendencies found in group data might suggest that this is so, if one looks carefully at the rampant variability in these data, it becomes apparent that not all mainstream-culture families engage in extensive extratextual talk if they share books with their preschoolers (e.g., Hammett et al., 2003). Furthermore, book-sharing practices differ from those of the mainstream when the preschool child has a language delay (van Kleeck & Vander Woude, 2003). Intervention studies with high-SES families also indicate that the growth-fostering aspects of parents' book sharing can be improved within this group, and doing so impacts on their children's language development (Arnold et al., 1994; Whitehurst et al., 1988). If these interaction strategies can be improved, they must not have been optimal (using mainstream practices as the standard) in the first place. Nor can we assume, given the substantial variability in book-sharing practices in nonmainstream groups, that children from nonmainstream backgrounds are not receiving this kind of guidance during book sharing or other kinds of literate activities.

Another assumption we need to question is that children will encounter mainstream culture practices in educational settings, regardless of what their home experiences have been. Research on preschools by Dickinson and his colleagues (2003) discussed earlier, shows rather dramatically how untrue this assumption often is. Schools may privilege literate discourse practices, but it is not necessarily the case that they teach them to students (for further discussion, see Dickinson, McCabe, & Clark-Chiarelli, Chapter 10, this volume).

The goal of this chapter has been to consider *how* learning is fostered in the book-sharing context in mainstream-culture families to complement the numerous reviews of *what* skills children potentially learn in this context. Some children come to school without these skills; other may have them, but have not learned to display them. Neither group of children will be consciously guided to learn them by teachers or clinicians who are not consciously aware of how such learning can be fostered. Far worse, professionals who work with such children may develop faulty views of them as learners, and being only human, put their energy into the children with whom they can experience more visible success in teaching. Literate discourse practices may become part of the hidden agenda of the classroom, and children who have not been socialized in such literate discourse practices may be left to figure them out on their own. If they do not figure it out in an educational system that is insensitive to the different routes to literacy, the cost may be substantial. Indeed, they may be denied access to the educational, financial, and political institutions of the mainstream culture (Anderson et al., 2003). Teachers, clinicians, and other educators need to be aware of what they themselves do as a first step in becoming aware of alternative practices.

ACKNOWLEDGMENTS

My thanks to Bess Fjordbak for help in pulling together a few of the references on nonmainstream cultural groups, and to Colleen Cook for help with the reference list. My deep appreciation to Lisa Hammett, Ann Michael, Judy Vander Woude, Alice Vigil, and Paul Yoder for their perceptive and very helpful feedback on the information presented in this chapter.

REFERENCES

Altwerger, B., Diehl-Faxon, J., & Dockstader-Anderson, K. (1985). Read-aloud events as meaning construction. *Language Arts, 62,* 476–484.
Anderson, A. B., & Stokes, S. J. (1984). Social and insti-

tutional influences on the development and practice of literacy. In H. Goelman, A. Oberg, & F. Smith (Eds.), *Awakening to literacy* (pp. 24–37). Exeter, NH: Heinemann.

Anderson, J., Anderson, A., Lynch, J., & Shapiro, J. (2003). Storybook reading in a multicultural society: Critical perspectives. In A. van Kleeck, S. A. Stahl, & E. Bauer (Eds.), *On reading to children: Parents and teachers* (pp. 203–230). Mahwah, NJ: Erlbaum.

Anderson, R., Heibert, E., Scott, J., & Wilkinson, I. A. G. (1985). *Becoming a nation of readers: The report of the Commission on Reading.* Washington, DC: National Institute of Education.

Anderson-Yockel, J., & Haynes, W. O. (1994). Joint book-reading strategies in working-class African American and white mother–toddler dyads. *Journal of Speech and Hearing Research, 37,* 583–593.

Arnold, D. S., Lonigan, C. J., Whitehurst, G., & Epstein, J. (1994). Acclerating language development through picture-book reading: Replication and extension to a videotape training format. *Journal of Educational Psychology, 86,* 235–243.

Arnold, D. S., & Whitehurst, G. J. (1994). Accelerating language development through picture book reading: A summary of dialogic reading and its effects. In D. K. Dickinson (Ed.), *Bridges to literacy: Children, families, and schools* (pp. 103–128). Cambridge, MA: Blackwell.

Au, K. H. (1995). Multicultural perspectives on literacy research. *Journal of Reading Behavior, 27,* 85–100.

Bakeman, R., & Quera, V. (1995). *Analyzing interaction: Sequential analysis with SDIS and GSEQ.* New York: Cambridge University Press.

Baker, L., & Brown, A. L. (1984). Cognitive monitoring in reading. In J. Flood (Ed.), *Understanding reading comprehension* (pp. 21–44). Newark, DE: International Reading Association.

Baker, L., Fernandez-Fein, S., Scher, D., & Williams, H. (1998). Home experiences related to the development of word recognition. In D. L. Metsala & L. C. Ehri (Eds.), *Word recognition in beginning literacy* (pp. 263–287). Hillsdale, NJ: Erlbaum.

Baker, L., Scher, D., & Mackler, K. (1997). Home and family influences on motivations for reading. *Educational Psychologist, 32,* 69–82.

Bennett, J., & Berry, J. (1991). Cree literacy in the syllabic script. In D. Olson & N. Torrance (Eds.), *Literacy and orality* (pp. 90–104). Cambridge, UK: Cambridge University Press.

Bettelheim, B., & Zelan, K. (1982). *On learning to read.* New York: Knopf.

Blank, M., Rose, S. A., & Berlin, L. J. (1978). Test review: Preschool Language Assessment Instrument (PLAI). *Reading Teacher, 40,* 344–346.

Bloom, L., & Lahey, M. (1978). *Language development and language disorders.* New York: Wiley.

Bloome, D., Katz, L., Solsken, J., Willett, J., & Wilson-Keenan, J.-A. (2000). Interpolations of family/community and classroom literacy practices. *Journal of Educational Research, 93,* 155–164.

Bradley, L., & Bryant, P. (1983). Categorizing sounds and learning to read: A causal connection. *Nature, 30,* 419–421.

Brice, A. E. (2002). *The Hispanic child: Speech, language, culture and education.* Boston: Allyn & Bacon.

Briggs, C. (1984). Learning how to ask: Native metacommunicative competence and the incompetence of field workers. *Language in Society, 13,* 1–28.

Brown, R. (1977). Introduction. In C. Snow & C. Ferguson (Eds.), *Talking to children: Language input and acquisition* (pp. 1–27). Cambridge, UK: Cambridge University Press.

Bruner, J. (1985). Vygotsky: A historical and conceptual perspective. In J. Wertsch (Ed.), *Culture, communication, and cognition: Vygotskian perspectives* (pp. 21–34). Cambridge, UK: Cambridge University Press.

Bruner, J. (1983). *In search of mind: Essays in autobiography.* New York: Harper & Row.

Burgess, S. R. (1997). The role of shared reading in the development of phonological awareness: A longitudinal study of middle to upper class children. *Early Child Development and Care, 127–128,* 191–199.

Bus, A. G. (2003). Social-emotional requisites for learning to read. In A. van Kleeck, S. A. Stahl, & E. Bauer (Eds.), *On reading to children: Parents and teachers* (pp. 3–15). Mahwah, NJ: Erlbaum.

Bus, A. G., Belsky, J., van IJzendoorn, M. H., & Crnik, K. (1997). Attachment and book reading patterns: A study of mothers, fathers, and their toddlers. *Early Childhood Research Quarterly, 12,* 81–98.

Bus, A. G., Leseman, P. P., & Keultjes, P. (2000). Joint book reading across cultures: A comparison of Surinamese-Dutch, Turkish-Dutch, and Dutch parent–child dyads. *Journal of Language Research, 32,* 53–76.

Bus, A. G., & Sulzby, E. (1996). Becoming literate in a multicultural society. In J. Shimron (Ed.), *Literacy and education: Essays in memory of Dina Feitelson* (pp. 17–32). Cresskill, NJ: Hampton Press.

Bus, A. G., & van IJzendoorn, M. H. (1988). Mother–child interactions, attachment, and emergent literacy: A cross-sectional study. *Child Development, 59,* 1262–1272.

Bus, A. G., & van IJzendoorn, M. H. (1992). Patterns of attachment in frequently and infrequently reading dyads. *Journal of Genetic Psychology, 153,* 395–403.

Bus, A. G., & van IJzendoorn, M. H. (1995). Mothers reading to their three year olds: The role of mother–child attachment security in becoming literate. *Reading Research Quarterly, 40,* 998–1015.

Bus, A. G., & van IJzendoorn, M. H. (1997). Affective dimension of mother-infant picturebook reading. *Journal of School Psychology, 35,* 47–60.

Bus, A. G., van IJzendoorn, M.H., & Pellegrini, A.D. (1995). Joint book reading makes for success in learning to read: A meta-analysis on intergenerational transmission of literacy. *Review of Educational Research, 65*(1), 1–21.

Chall, J. (1983). *Stages of reading development.* New York: McGraw-Hill.

Chao, R. (1994). Beyond parental control and authoritarian parenting style: Understanding Chinese parenting through the cultural notion of training. *Child Development, 65,* 1111–1119.

Chao, R. (1996). Chinese and European American mothers' beliefs about the role of parenting in children's school success. *Journal of Cross-Cultural Psychology, 27,* 403–423.

Chapman, J. (1984). Comprehending and the teacher of reading. In J. Flood (Ed.), *Understanding reading comprehension* (pp. 261–272). Newark, DE: International Reading Association.

Cheng, L. (1989). Service delivery to Asian/Pacific LEP children: A cross-cultural framework. *Topics in Language Disorders, 9*(3), 1–14.

Clancy, P. (1986). The acquisition of communicative style in Japanese. In B. Schieffelin & E. Ochs (Eds.), *Language socialization across cultures* (pp. 213–250). Cambridge, UK: Cambridge University Press.

Cochran-Smith, M. (1984). *The making of a reader.* Norwood, NJ: Ablex.

Coles, R. (1977). *Eskimos, Chicanos, Indians.* Boston: Little, Brown.

Collins, A., & Stevens, A. (1982). Goals and strategies of inquiring teachers. In R. Glaser (Ed.), *Advances in instructional psychology* (Vol. 2, pp. 65–119). Hillsdale, NJ: Erlbaum.

Constable, C. M. (1986). The application of scripts in the organization of language intervention contexts. In K. Nelson (Ed.), *Event knowledge: Structure and function in development* (pp. 205–230). Hillsdale, NJ: Erlbaum.

Conti-Ramsden, G., & Friel-Patti, P. (1987). Situational variability in mother–child conversations. In K. Nelson & A. van Kleeck (Eds.), *Children's language* (Vol. 6, pp. 43–63). Hillsdale, NJ: Erlbaum.

Crago, M. (1990). Development of communicative competence in Inuit children. *Journal of Childhood Communication Disorders, 13,* 73–83.

Crain-Thoreson, C., & Dale, P. S. (1992). Do early talkers become early readers?: Linguistic precocity, preschool language, and early reading. *Developmental Psychology, 28,* 421–429.

Crain-Thoreson, C., & Dale, P. S. (1999). Enhancing linguistic performance: Parents and teachers as book reading partners for children with language delays. *Topics in Early Childhood Special Education, 19*(1), 28–39.

Daisey, P. (1991). Intergenerational literacy programs: Rationale, description and effectiveness. *Journal of Clinical Child Psychology, 20,* 11–17.

Dale, P. S., Crain-Thoreson, C., Notari-Syverson, A., & Cole, K. (1996). Parent–child book reading as an intervention technique for young children with language delays. *Topics in Early Childhood Special Education, 16*(2), 213–235.

Daly, J., & McCroskey, J. (1984). *Avoiding communication: Shyness, reticence, and communication apprehension.* Beverly Hills, CA: Sage.

De Temple, J., & Snow, C. E. (1996). Styles of parent–child book-reading as related to mothers' views of literacy and children's literacy outcomes. In J. Shimron (Ed.), *Literacy and education: Essays in honor of Dina Feitelson* (pp. 63–84). Cresskill, NJ: Hampton Press.

DeBaryshe, B. D. (1995). Maternal belief systems: Linchpin in the home reading process. *Journal of Applied Developmental Psychology, 16,* 1–20.

Delgado-Gaitan, C. (1991). Involving parents in the schools: A process of empowerment. *American Journal of Education, 100,* 20–47.

DeLoache, J. S., & DeMendoza, A. P. (1987). Joint picture book interactions of mothers and 1-year-old children. *British Journal of Developmental Psychology, 5,* 111–123.

Delpit, L. (1988). The silenced dialogue: Power and pedagogy in educating other people's children. *Harvard Educational Review, 58,* 280–298.

Delpit, L. (1995). *Other people's children: Cultural conflict in the classroom.* New York: New Press.

Denny, J. P. (1991). Rational thought in oral culture and literate decontextualization. In D. Olson & N. Torrance (Eds.), *Literacy and orality* (pp. 66–89). Cambridge, UK: Cambridge University Press.

Diaz, R., Neal, C., & Vachio, A. (1991). Maternal teaching in the zone of proximal development: A comparison of low- and high-risk dyads. *Merrill–Palmer Quarterly, 37,* 83–108.

Dickinson, D. K., Bryant, D., Peisner-Feinberg, E., Lambert, R., & Wolf, A. (1999, April). *Phonemic awareness in Head Start children: Relationship to language and literacy and parenting variables.* Paper presented at the meeting of the Society for Research in Child Development, Albuquerque, NM.

Dickinson, D. K., De Temple, J., Hirschler, J., & Smith, M. (1992). Book reading with preschoolers: Coconstruction of text at home and at school. *Early Childhood Research Quarterly, 7,* 323–346.

Dickinson, D. K., McCabe, A., & Anastasopoulos, L. (2003). A framework for examining book reading in early childhood classrooms. In A. van Kleeck, S. A. Stahl, & E. Bauer (Eds.), *On reading to children: Parents and teachers* (pp. 95–113). Mahwah, NJ: Erlbaum.

Donaldson, M. (1978). *Children's minds.* New York: Norton.

Downing, J. (1979). *Reading and reasoning.* New York: Springer-Verlag.

Dumont, R. (1972). Learning English and how to be silent: Studies in Sioux and Cherokee classrooms. In C. Cazden, D. Hymes, & V. John (Eds.), *Functions of language in the classroom* (pp. 334–369). New York: Teachers College Press.

Edwards, P. A. (1989). Supporting lower SES mothers' attempts to provide scaffolding for book reading. In J. Allen & J. Mason (Eds.), *Risk makers, risk takers, and risk breakers: Reducing the risk for young literacy learners* (pp. 225–250). Portsmouth, NH: Heinemann.

Edwards, P. A. (1994). Responses of teachers and African-American mothers to a book-reading intervention program. In D. K. Dickinson (Ed.), *Bridges to literacy: Children, families, and schools* (pp. 175–208). Cambridge, MA: Blackwell.

Eisenberg, A. (1982). *Language development in cultur-*

al perspective: Talk in three Mexican homes. Unpublished doctoral dissertation, University of California, Berkeley.

Elliott, J. A., & Hewison, J. (1994). Comprehension and interest in home reading. *British Journal of Educational Psychology, 64,* 203–220.

Ellis, N., & Large, B. (1987). The development of reading: As you seek so shall you find. *British Journal of Psychology, 78,* 1–28.

Feagans, L., & Farran, D. (1982). *The language of children reared in poverty: Implications for evaluation and intervention.* New York: Academic Press.

Federal Interagency Forum on Child and Family Statistics. (2002). *America's children: Key national indicators of well-being, 2002.* Retrieved February 10, 2003, from *http://www.childstats.gov/*

Fenson, L., Dale, P., Reznick, H., Thal, D., Bates, E., Hartung, J., et al. (1993). *MacArthur Communicative Development Inventories (CDI).* San Diego: Singular.

Fischer, J. (1970). Linguistic socialization: Japan and the United States. In R. Hill & R. Konig (Eds.), *Families in East and West* (pp. 107–119). The Hague: Mouton.

Flood, J. E. (1977). Parental styles in reading episodes with young children. *Reading Teacher, 30,* 864–867.

Frawley, W. B. (1997). *Vygotsky and cognitive science: Language and the unification of the social and computational mind.* Cambridge, MA: Harvard University Press.

Freedman, D. (1979, January). Ethnic differences in babies. *Human Nature Magazine,* pp. 36–43.

Fuller, B., Eggers-Pierola, C., Holloway, S., Liang, X., & Rambaud, M. (1996). Rich culture, poor markets: Why do Latino parents forgo preschooling? *Teachers College Record, 97,* 400–418.

Fuller, B., Holloway, S., & Liang, X. (1996). Family selection of child-care centers: The influence of household support, ethnicity, and parental practices. *Child Development, 67,* 3320–3337.

Gadsden, V. L. (1993). Literacy, education, and identity among African-Americans: The communal nature of learning. *Urban Education, 27,* 352–369.

Garcia, E. (1997). The education of Hispanics in early childhood: Of roots and wings. *Young Children, 52*(3), 5–14.

Garner, R., & Alexander, P. (1982). Strategic processing of text: An investigation of the effects on adults' question-answering performance. *Journal of Educational Research, 75,* 144–148.

Gee, J. P. (2001). A sociocultural perspective on early literacy development. In S. B. Neuman & D. K. Dickinson (Eds.), *Handbook of early literacy research* (pp. 30–42). New York: Guilford Press.

Goldenberg, C. (2001). Making schools work for low income families in the 21st century. In S. B. Neuman & D. K. Dickinson (Eds.), *Handbook of early literacy research* (pp. 211–231). New York: Guilford Press.

Goldenberg, C., Reese, L., & Gallimore, R. (1992). Effects of literacy materials from school on Latino children's home experiences and early reading achievement. *American Journal of Education, 100,* 497–536.

Goodman, J., Larrivee, L., Roberts, J., Heller, A., & Fritz, D. (2000, November). *Parental prompts by syntactic category and prompt type.* Paper presented at the meeting of American Speech–Language–Hearing Association, Washington, DC.

Goodsitt, J., Raitan, J. G., & Perlmutter, M. (1988). Interaction between mothers and preschool children when reading a novel and familiar book. *International Journal of Behavioral Development, 11,* 489–505.

Goody, J. (1977). *The domestication of the savage mind.* New York: Cambridge University Press.

Goswami, U. (2001). Early phonological development and the acquisition of literacy. In S. B. Neuman & D. K. Dickinson (Eds.), *Handbook of early literacy research* (pp. 111–125). New York: Guilford Press.

Gottfried, A. W. (1984). Home environment and early cognitive development: Integration, meta-analyses, and conclusions. In A. W. Gottfried (Ed.), *Home environment and early cognitive development: Longitudinal research* (pp. 329–342). San Diego: Academic Press.

Haden, C. A., Reese, E., & Fivush, R. (1996). Mother's extratextual comments during storybook reading: Stylistic differences over time and across texts. *Discourse Processes, 21,* 135–169.

Hammer, C. (1999). Guiding language development: How African-American mothers and their infants structure play. *Journal of Speech and Hearing Research, 42,* 1219–1233.

Hammett, L., van Kleeck, A., & Huberty, C. (2003). Clusters of parent interaction behaviors during book sharing with preschool children. *Reading Research Quarterly, 38,* 442–468.

Hanmaker, C. (1986). The effects of adjunct questions on prose learning. *Review of Educational Research, 56,* 212–242.

Harkness, S., Super, C., & Keefer, C. H. (1992). Learning to be an American parent: How cultural models gain directive force. In R. D'Andrade & C. Strauss (Eds.), *Human motives and cultural models* (pp. 163–178). Cambridge, UK: Cambridge University Press.

Harp, B. (1988). How are you helping your kids understand the reading process instead of just recalling information. *Reading Teacher, 42*(1), 74–75.

Harré, R. (1984). *Personal being.* Cambridge, MA: Harvard University Press.

Harris, G. (1998). American Indian cultures: A lesson in diversity. In D. Battle (Ed.), *Communication disorders in multicultural populations* (2nd ed., pp. 117–156). Stoneham, MA: Butterworth–Heinemann.

Hart, B., & Risley, T. R. (1980). *In vivo* language intervention: Unanticipated general effects. *Journal of Applied Behavioral Analysis, 13,* 407–432.

Hart, B., & Risley, T. R. (1992). American parenting of language-learning children: Persisting differences in family–child interactions observed in natural home environments. *Developmental Psychology, 28,* 1096– 1105.

Hart, B., & Risley, T. R. (1995). *Meaningful differences in the everyday experiences of young American children.* Baltimore: Brookes.

Hart, B., & Risley, T. R. (1999). *The social world of children learning to talk.* Baltimore: Brookes.

Havelock, E. (1963). *Preface to Plato.* Cambridge, MA: Harvard University Press.

Hayden, H. R., & Fagan, W. T. (1987). Keeping it in context: Strategies for enhancing literacy awareness. *First Language, 7,* 159–171.

Heath, S. B. (1982). What no bedtime story means: Narrative skills at home and school. *Language in Society, 11,* 49–76.

Heath, S. B. (1983). *Ways with words: Language, life, and work in communities and classrooms.* New York: Cambridge University Press.

Heath, S. B. (1989). The learner as cultural member. In M. Rice & R. Scheifelbusch (Eds.), *The teachability of language* (pp. 333–350). Baltimore: Brookes.

Heath, S. B., & Branscombe, A. (1986). The book as narrative prop in language acquisition. In B. Schieffelin & P. Gilmore (Eds.), *The acquisition of literacy: Ethnographic perspectives* (pp. 16–34). Norwood, NJ: Ablex.

Hockenberger, E. H., Goldstein, H., & Haas, L. S. (1999). Effects of commenting during joint book reading by mothers with low SES. *Topics in Early Childhood Special Education, 19*(1), 15–27.

Horgan, D. (1977). How to answer questions when you've got nothing to say. *Journal of Child Language, 5,* 159–165.

Huttenlocher, J., Haight, W., Bryk, A., Seltzer, M., & Lyons, T. (1991). Early vocabulary growth: Relation to language input and gender. *Developmental Psychology, 27,* 236–248.

Janes, H., & Kermani, H. (2001). Caregivers story reading to young children in family literacy programs: Pleasure of punishment. *Journal of Adolescent and Adult Literacy, 44,* 458–446.

John, V. (1972). Styles of learning-styles of teaching: Reflections on the education of Navajo children. In C. Cazden, D. Hymes, & V. John (Eds.), *Functions of language in the classroom* (pp. 331–345). New York: Teachers College Press.

Johnston, J., & Wong, M. Y. A. (2002). Cultural differences in beliefs and practices concerning talk to children. *Journal of Speech, Language, and Hearing Research, 45,* 916–926.

Jones, R. (1996). *Emerging patterns of literacy: A multidisciplinary perspective.* London: Routledge.

Kay-Raining Bird, E., & Vetter, R. S. (1994). Storytelling in Chippewa–Cree children. *Journal of Speech and Hearing Research, 37,* 1354–1368.

Kim, Y. T., & Lombardino, L. J. (1991). The efficacy of script contexts in language comprehension intervention with children who have mental retardation. *Journal of Speech and Hearing Research, 34,* 845–857.

Langdon, H. W. (1992). Language communication and sociocultural patterns in Hispanic families. In K. G. Butler (Ed.), *Hispanic children and adults with communication disorders: Assessment and intervention* (pp. 99–131). Gaithersburg, MD: Aspen.

Laosa, L. (1981). Maternal behavior: Sociocultural diversity in modes of family interaction. In R. W. Henderson (Ed.), *Parent–child interaction: Theory, research, and prospects* (Vol. 51, pp. 125–164). New York: Academic Press.

LaZansky, J., Spencer, F., & Johnston, M. (1987). Reading to learn: Setting students up. In R. J. Tierney, P. L. Anders, & J. N. Mitchell (Eds.), *Understanding readers' understanding: Theory and practice* (pp. 255–281). Hillsdale, NJ: Erlbaum.

Light, J., & Kelford Smith, A. (1993). The home literacy experiences of preschoolers who use AAC systems and of their nondisabled peers. *Augmentative and Alternative Communication, 9,* 10–25.

Lock, A. (1981). *The guided reinvention of language.* London: Academic Press.

Lonigan, C. J. (1991). *Environmental influences on language acquisition: An examination of the maternal-input hypothesis in the context of a picture book reading intervention.* Unpublished doctoral dissertation, State University of New York, Stony Brook.

Lonigan, C. J. (1993). Somebody read me a story: Evaluation of a shared reading program in low-income daycare. *Society for Research in Child Development Abstracts, 9,* 219.

Lonigan, C. J. (1994). Reading to preschoolers exposed: Is the emperor really naked? *Developmental Review, 14,* 303–323.

Lonigan, C. J., Anthony, J. L., Dyer, S. M., & Collins, K. (1995). Evaluation of a language enrichment program for pre-school aged children from low-income backgrounds. *Association for the Advancement of Behavior Therapy Abstracts, 2,* 365.

Lonigan, C. J., & Whitehurst, G. (1998). Relative efficacy of parent and teacher involvement in shared reading intervention for preschool children from low-income backgrounds. *Early Childhood Research Quarterly, 13,* 263–290.

Luke, A., & Luke, C. (2001). Adolescence lost/childhood regained: On early intervention and the emergence of the techno-subject. *Journal of Early Childhood Literacy, 1,* 91–120.

Lundberg, I., Olofsson, A., & Wall, S. (1980). Reading and spelling skills in the first school years predicted from phonemic awareness skills in kindergarten. *Scandinavian Journal of Psychology, 21,* 159–173.

Madding, C. C. (1999). Mamá é hijo: The Latino mother-infant dyad. *Multicultural Electronic Journal of Communication Disorders, 1*(2). Retrieved November 19, 2003, from *http://www.asha.ucf.edu/madding3.html*

Martin, L. E., & Reutzel, D. R. (1999). Sharing books: Examining how and why mothers deviate from the print. *Reading Research and Instruction, 39,* 39–70.

Martinez, M., & Roser, N. (1985). A case study of the effects of selected text factors on parent–child story time interactions. In J. A. Niles & R. V. Lalik (Eds.), *Issues in literacy: A research perspective*

(Vol. 34, pp. 168–174). Rochester, NY: National Reading Conference.

Mason, J. (1992). Reading stories to preliterate children: A proposed connection to reading. In P. B. Gough, L. C. Ehri, & R. Treiman (Eds.), *Reading acquisition* (pp. 215–243). Hillsdale, NJ: Erlbaum.

McCormick, C., & Mason, J. M. (1986). *Use of little books at home: A minimal intervention strategy that fosters early reading* (Technical Report No. 388). Champaign: University of Illinois at Urbana–Champaign, Center for the Study of Reading.

McGillicuddy-DeLisi, A. V. (1982). The relationship between parents' beliefs about development and family constellation, socioeconomic status, and parents' teaching strategies. In L. Laosa & I. Sigel (Eds.), *Familes as learning environments for children* (pp. 261–299). New York: Plenum Press.

McLane, J. B., & McNamee, G. D. (1990). *Early literacy*. Cambridge, MA: Harvard University Press.

McLuhan, M. (1962). *The Gutenberg galaxy*. Toronto: University of Toronto Press.

McNaughton, S. (2001). Co-constructing expertise: The development of parents' and teachers' ideas about literacy practices and the transition to school. *Journal of Early Childhood Literacy, 1,* 40–58.

McNeill, J. H., & Fowler, S. A. (1999). Let's talk: Encouraging mother–child conversations during story reading. *Journal of Early Intervention, 22,* 51–69.

Miller, P. (1982). *Amy, Wendy, and Beth: Learning language in South Baltimore*. Austin: University of Texas Press.

Minami, M. (1997). Cultural constructions of meaning: Cross-cultural comparisons of mother–child conversations about the past. In C. Mandell & A. McCabe (Eds.), *The problem of meaning: Behavioral and cognitive perspectives* (pp. 297–346). Amsterdam: Elsevier.

Moerk, E. (1992). *A first language taught and learned*. Baltimore: Brookes.

Murphy, C. M. (1978). Pointing in the context of a shared activity. *Child Development, 49,* 371–380.

Murray, B. A., Stahl, S. A., & Ivey, M. G. (1996). Developing phoneme awareness through alphabet books. *Reading and Writing: An Interdisciplinary Journal, 8,* 307–322.

Nelson, K. (1973). Structure and strategy in learning to talk. *Monographs of the Society for Research in Child Development, 38*(1–2, Serial No. 149).

Nelson, K. (1986). *Event knowledge: Structure and function in development*. Hillsdale, NJ: Erlbaum.

Neuman, S. B. (1996). Children engaging in storybook reading: The influence of access to print resources, opportunity, and parental interaction. *Early Childhood Research Quarterly, 11,* 495–513.

Neuman, S. B., & Gallagher, P. (1994). Joining together in literacy learning: Teenage mothers and children. *Reading Research Quarterly, 29,* 383–401.

Neuman, S. B., Hagedorn, T., Celano, D., & Daly, P. (1995). Toward a collaborative approach to parent involvement in early education: A study of teenage mothers in an African-American community. *American Educational Research Journal, 32,* 801–827.

New, R. S. (2001). Early literacy and developmentally appropriate practices: Rethinking the paradigm. In S. B. Neuman & D. K. Dickinson (Eds.), *Handbook of early literacy research* (pp. 245–262). New York: Guilford Press.

Newport, E., Gleitman, H., & Gleitman, L. (1977). Mother, I'd rather do it myself: Some effects and non-effects of maternal speech style. In C. Snow & C. Ferguson (Eds.), *Talking to children: Language input and acquisition* (pp. 109–149). Cambridge, UK: Cambridge University Press.

Ninio, A. (1980). Picture-book reading in mother–infant dyads belonging to two subgroups in Israel. *Child Development, 51,* 587–590.

Ninio, A., & Bruner, J. (1978). The achievement and antecedents of labelling. *Journal of Child Language, 5,* 1–15.

Norman-Jackson, J. (1982). Family interactions, language development, and primary reading achievement of black children in families of low-income. *Child Development, 53,* 349–358.

Ogbu, J. U. (1990). Minority status and literacy in comparative perspective. *Daedalus, 119,* 141–168.

Olsen-Fulero, L., & Conforti, J. (1983). Child responsiveness to mother questions of varying type and presentation. *Journal of Child Language, 10,* 495–520.

Olson, D. (1994). *The world on paper*. New York: Cambridge University Press.

Olson, D., & Torrance, N. (Eds.). (1991). *Literacy and orality*. Cambridge, UK: Cambridge University Press.

Ong, W. (1982). *Orality and literacy: The technologizing of the word*. London: Methuen.

Palinscar, A. S., & Brown, A. L. (1984). Reciprocal teaching of comprehension-fostering and comprehension-monitoring activities. *Cognition and Instruction, 1,* 117–175.

Panofsky, C. P. (1994). Developing the representational functions of language: The role of parent–child book-reading activity. In P. V. John-Steiner, C. Panofsky, & L. W. Smith (Eds.), *Sociocultural approaches to language and literacy* (pp. 223–242). Cambridge, UK: Cambridge University Press.

Pellegrini, A. D. (2001). Some theoretical and methodological considerations in studying literacy in social context. In S. B. Neuman & D. K. Dickinson (Eds.), *Handbook of early literacy research* (pp. 54–65). New York: Guilford Press.

Pellegrini, A. D., Brody, G. H., & Sigel, I. E. (1985). Parents' book reading habits with their children. *Journal of Educational Psychology, 77,* 332–340.

Pellegrini, A. D., & Galda, L. (1998). *The development of school-based literacy: A social ecological perspective*. London: Routledge.

Pellegrini, A. D., Galda, L., Bartini, M., & Charak, D. (1998). Oral language and literacy learning in context: The role of social relationships. *Merrill–Palmer Quarterly, 44,* 38–54.

Pellegrini, A. D., Perlmutter, J. C., Galda, L., & Brody, G. H. (1990). Joint reading between black Head Start children and their mothers. *Child Development, 61,* 443–453.

Philipsen, G. (1975). Speaking "like a man" in Teamsterville: Culture patterns of role enactment in an urban neighborhood. *Quarterly Journal of Speech, 61*, 26–39.

Phillips, G., & McNaughton, S. (1990). The practice of storybook reading to preschool children in mainstream New Zealand families. *Reading Research Quarterly, 25*, 196–212.

Purcell-Gates, V. (1995). *Other people's words: The cycle of low literacy.* Cambridge, MA: Harvard University Press.

Purcell-Gates, V. (1996). Stories, coupons, and the *TV Guide*: Relationships between home literacy experiences and emergent literacy knowledge. *Reading Research Quarterly, 31*, 406–428.

Purcell-Gates, V. (2000). Family literacy. In M. Kamil, P. Mosenthal, P. Pearson, & R. Barr (Eds.), *Handbook of reading research* (Vol. 3, pp. 853–870). Mahwah, NJ: Erlbaum.

Ragan, T. J., & van Kleeck, A. (2002, November). *Preschoolers' response during book sharing: A sequential analysis.* Paper presented at the annual meeting of the American Speech–Language–Hearing Association, Atlanta, GA.

Raz, I. S., & Bryant, P. E. (1990). Social background, phonological awareness, and children's reading. *British Journal of Developmental Psychology, 8*, 209–226.

Reese, E., Cox, A., Harte, D., & McAnally, H. (2003). Diversity in adults' styles of reading books to children. In A. van Kleeck, S. A. Stahl, & E. Bauer (Eds.), *On reading to children: Parents and teachers* (pp. 37–57). Mahwah, NJ: Erlbaum.

Reid, D. K. (2000). Discourse in classrooms. In K. Fahey & D. K. Reid (Eds.), *Language development, differences, and disorders* (pp. 3–38). Austin, TX: Pro-Ed.

Robinson, F., & Sulzby, E. (1984). Parents, children, and "favorite" books: An interview study. In F. Robinson & E. Sulzby (Eds.), *National Reading Conference yearbook* (Vol. 33, pp. 54–59). Rochester, NY: National Reading Conference.

Rogoff, B. (1990). *Apprenticeship in thinking: Cognitive development in social context.* Oxford, UK: Oxford University Press.

Roopnarine, J., & Carter, D. B. (1992). The cultural context of socialization: A much ignored issue. In J. Roopnarine & D. B. Carter (Eds.), *Parent–child socialization in diverse cultures* (pp. 245–251). Norwood, NJ: Ablex.

Rush, K. L. (1999). Caregiver–child interactions and early literacy development of preschool children from low-income environments. *Topics in Early Childhood Special Education, 19*(1), 3–14.

Ryan, J. (1974). Early language development: Toward a communicational analysis. In M. Richards (Ed.), *The integration of a child into a social world* (pp. 185–213). Cambridge, UK: Cambridge University Press.

Sachs, J. (1983). Talking about the there and then: The emergence of displaced reference in parent–child discourse. In K. Nelson (Ed.), *Children's language* (Vol. 4, pp. 1–28). Hillsdale, NJ: Erlbaum.

Scarborough, H., & Dobrich, W. (1994). On the efficacy of reading to preschoolers. *Developmental Review, 14*, 245–302.

Scarborough, H. S. (2001). Connecting early language and literacy to later reading (dis)abilities: Evidence, theory, and practice. In S. B. Neuman & D. K. Dickinson (Eds.), *Handbook of early literacy research* (pp. 97–110). New York: Guilford Press.

Schank, R., & Abelson, R. (1977). *Scripts, plans, goals, and understanding.* Hillsdale, NJ: Erlbaum.

Scher, D., & Baker, L. (1996, April). *Attitudes toward reading and children's home literacy environments.* Paper presented at the meeting of the American Educational Research Association, New York, NY.

Schieffelin, B. B., & Cochran-Smith, M. (1984). Learning to read culturally: Literacy before schooling. In H. Goelman, A. Oberg & F. Smith (Eds.), *Awakening to literacy* (pp. 3–23). Exeter, NH: Heinemann.

Scollon, R., & Scollon, S. (1981). *Narrative and face in inter-ethnic communication.* Norwood, NJ: Ablex.

Scribner, S., & Cole, M. (1981). *The psychology of literacy.* Cambridge, MA: Harvard University Press.

Sénéchal, M., Thomas E., & Monker, J. (1995). Individual differences in 4-year-old children's acquisition of vocabulary during storybook reading. *Journal of Educational Psychology, 87*(2), 218–229.

Shanahan, R., & Hogan, V. (1983). Parent reading style and children's print awareness. In J. Niles (Ed.), *Searches for meaning in reading/language processing and instruction* (pp. 212–217). Rochester, NY: National Reading Conference.

Shatz, M. (1983). Communication. In P. H. Mussen (Ed.), *Handbook of child psychology: Vol 3. Cognitive development* (pp. 841–889). New York: Wiley.

Shotter, J. (1978). Cultrual context of communication studies: Theoretical and methodological issues. In A. Lock (Ed.), *Action, gesture, and symbol* (pp. 43–78). London: Academic Press.

Sigel, I. E., & McGillicuddy-Delisi, A. V. (1984). Parents as teachers of their children: A distancing behavior model. In A. D. Pellegrini & T. D. Yawkey (Eds.), *The development of oral and written language in social contexts* (pp. 71–91). Norwood, NJ: Ablex.

Snow, C. E. (1977). The development of conversation between mothers and babies. *Journal of Child Language, 4*, 1–22.

Snow, C. E. (1979). The role of social interaction in language acquisition. In A. Collins (Ed.), *12th Minnesota Symposium on Child Psychology: Children's language and communication* (pp. 157–182). Hillsdale, NJ: Erlbaum.

Snow, C. E. (1983). Literacy and language: Relationships during the preschool years. *Harvard Educational Review, 53*, 165–189.

Snow, C. E., & Ninio, A. (1986). The contracts of literacy: What children learn from learning to read books. In W. H. Teale & E. Sulzby (Eds.), *Emergent literacy: Writing and reading* (pp. 116–137). Norwood, NJ: Ablex.

Snow, C. E., Perlmann, R., & Nathan, D. C. (1987). Why routines are different: Toward a multiple-factors model of the relation between input and language acquisition. In K. Nelson & A. van Kleeck (Eds.), *Children's language* (Vol. 6, pp. 65–97). Hillsdale, NJ: Erlbaum.

Sonnenschein, S., Brody, G., & Munsterman, K. (1996). The influence of family beliefs and practices on children's early reading development. In L. Baker, P. Afflerbach, & D. Reinking (Eds.), *Developing engaged readers in school and home communities* (pp. 1–20). Mahwah, NJ: Erlbaum.

Spiegel, D. L. (1994). A portrait of parents of successful readers. In E. H. Cramer & M. Castle (Eds.), *Fostering the love of reading: The affective domain in reading education* (pp. 74–87). Newark, DE: International Reading Association.

Stipek, D., Milburn, S., Clements, D., & Daniels, D. H. (1992). Parents' beliefs about appropriate education for young children. *Journal of Applied Developmental Psychology, 13,* 293–310.

Taylor, D., & Dorsey-Gaines, C. (1988). *Growing up literate: Learning from inner city families.* Portsmouth, NH: Heinemann.

Teale, W. (1986). Home background and young children's literacy development. In W. Teale & E. Sulzby (Eds.), *Emergent literacy: Writing and reading* (pp. 173–206). Norwood, NJ: Ablex.

Thompson, R., Mixon, G., & Serpell, R. (1996). Engaging minority students in reading: Focus on the urban learner. In L. Baker, P. Afflerbach, & D. Reinking (Eds.), *Developing engaged readers in school and home communities* (pp. 43–63). Mahwah, NJ: Erlbaum.

Toda, S., Fogel, A., & Kawai, M. (1990). Maternal speech to three-month-old infants in the United States and Japan. *Journal of Child Language, 17,* 279–294.

Twymon, S. (1990). *Early reading and writing instruction in the homes and school of three five-year-old children from black working class families.* Unpublished doctoral dissertation, University of Michigan, Ann Arbor.

Valdés, G. (1996). *Con respeto: Bridging the distances between culturally diverse families and schools.* New York: Teachers College Press.

Valdez-Menchaca, M. C., & Whitehurst, G. J. (1992). Accelerating language development through picturebook reading: A systematic extension to Mexican day care. *Developmental Psychology, 28,* 1106–1114.

van Kleeck, A. (1990). Emergent literacy: Learning about print before learning to read. *Topics in Language Disorders, 10*(2), 25–45.

van Kleeck, A. (1994). Metalinguistic development. In G. Wallach & K. Butler (Eds.), *Language learning disabilities in school-age children and adolescents: Some principles and applications* (pp. 53–98). New York: Macmillan.

van Kleeck, A. (1995). Emphasizing form and meaning separately in prereading and early reading instruction. *Topics in Language Disorders, 16*(1), 27–49.

van Kleeck, A. (1998). Preliteracy domains and stages: Laying the foundations for beginning reading. *Journal of Children's Communication Development, 20*(1), 33–51.

van Kleeck, A. (2003). Research on book sharing: An-

other critical look. In A. van Kleeck, S. A. Stahl, & E. Bauer (Eds.), *On reading to children: Parents and teachers* (pp. 271–320). Mahwah, NJ: Erlbaum.

van Kleeck, A., Alexander, E., Vigil, A., & Templeton, K. (1996). Modeling thinking for infants: Middle-class mothers' presentation of information structures during book sharing. *Journal of Research in Childhood Education, 10,* 101–113.

van Kleeck, A., & Beckley-McCall, A. (2002). A comparison of mothers' individual and simultaneous book sharing with preschool siblings: An exploratory study of five families. *American Journal of Speech-Language Pathology, 11,* 175–189.

van Kleeck, A., & Carpenter, R. (1980). Effects of children's language comprehension level on adults' child directed talk. *Journal of Speech and Hearing Research, 23,* 546–569.

van Kleeck, A., Gillam, R., & Breshears, K. D. (1998, November). *Effects of book genre on mother's emphasis on print meaning and form during book sharing.* Paper presented at the 1998 American Speech–Language–Hearing Association Annual Convention, San Antonio, TX.

van Kleeck, A., Gillam, R., Hamilton, L., & McGrath, C. (1997). The relationship between middle-class parents' book-sharing discussion and their preschoolers' abstract language development. *Journal of Speech–Language–Hearing Research, 40,* 1261–1271.

van Kleeck, A., & Stahl, S. A. (2003). Preface. In A. van Kleeck, S. A. Stahl, & E. Bauer (Eds.), *On reading to children: Parents and teachers* (pp. vii–xiii). Mahwah, NJ: Erlbaum.

van Kleeck, A., & Vander Woude, J. (2003). Book sharing with preschoolers with language delays. In A. van Kleeck, S. A. Stahl, & E. Bauer (Eds.), *On reading to children: Parents and teachers* (pp. 58–92). Mahwah, NJ: Erlbaum.

van Kleeck, A., Vigil, A., & Beer, N. (1998, November). *A longitudinal study of maternal book-sharing emphasis on print form and print meaning with preschoolers.* Paper presented at the 1998 American Speech–Language–Hearing Association Annual Convention, San Antonio, TX.

Vernon-Feagans, L., Hammer, C., Miccio, A., & Manlove, E. (2001). Early language literacy skills in low-income African American and Hispanic children. In S. B. Neuman & D. K. Dickinson (Eds.), *Handbook of early literacy research* (pp. 192–210). New York: Guilford Press.

Vigil, A., & van Kleeck, A. (1996). Clinical language teaching: Theories and principles to guide our responses when children miss our language targets. In M. Smith & J. Damico (Eds.), *Childhood language disorders* (pp. 64–96). New York: Thieme.

Vigil, D. (1999, November). *Joint attention in cultural context.* Paper presented at the American Speech–Language–Hearing Association, San Francisco, CA.

Vygotsky, L. S. (1978). Mind in society: The development of higher psychological processes. In M. Cole, J. Scribner, V. Steiner, & E. Souberman (Eds.), *Culture and thought: A psychological introduction.* Cambridge, MA: Harvard University Press.

Walker, D., Greenwood, C., Hart, B., & Carta, J. (1994). Prediction of school outcomes based on early language production and socioeconomic factors. *Child Development, 65,* 606–621.

Wang, X. L., Goldin-Meadow, S., & Mylander, C. (1995, March). *A comparative study of Chinese and American mothers interacting with their deaf and hearing children.* Paper presented at the meeting of the Society for Research in Child Development, Indianapolis, IN.

Ward, M. (1971). *Them children: A study in language learning.* Prospect Heights, IL: Waveland Press.

Wasik, B. H., Dobbins, D. R., & Hermann, S. (2001). Intergenerational family literacy: Concepts, research, and practice. In S. B. Neuman & D. K. Dickinson (Eds.), *Handbook of early literacy research* (pp. 444–458). New York: Guilford Press.

Watson, R. (2001). Literacy and oral language: Implications for early language acquisition. In S. B. Neuman & D. K. Dickinson (Eds.), *Handbook of early literacy research* (pp. 43–53). New York: Guilford Press.

Weisner, T., Gallimore, R., & Jordon, C. (1988). Unpackaging cultural effects on classroom learning: Native Hawaiian peer assistance and child-generated activity. *Anthropology and Education Quarterly, 19,* 327–353.

Wells, G. (1982). Influences of the home on language development. In A. Davies (Ed.), *Language and learning in home and school* (pp. 150–163). London: Heinemann.

Wells, G. (1985). Preschool literacy-related activities and success in school. In D. R. Olson, N. Torrance, & A. Hildyard (Eds.), *Literacy, language, and learning: The nature and consequences of reading and writing* (pp. 229–253). Cambridge, UK: Cambridge University Press.

Wells, G. (1986). *The meaning makers: Children learning language and using language to learn.* Portsmouth, NH: Heinemann.

Werner, E. (1984). *Child care: Kith, kin and hired hands.* Baltimore: University Park Press.

Westby, C., & Rouse, G. (1985). Culture in education and the instruction of language learning-disabled students. *Topics in Language Disorders, 5*(4), 15–28.

Wheeler, M. P. (1983). Context-related age changes in mothers' speech: Joint book reading. *Journal of Child Language, 10,* 259–263.

White, K. R. (1982). The relation between socioeconomic status and academic achievement. *Psychological Bulletin, 91,* 461–481.

Whitehurst, G. J., Arnold, D. S., Epstein, J. N., Angell, A. L., Smith, M., & Fischel, J. E. (1994). A picture book reading intervention in day care and home for children from low-income families. *Developmental Psychology, 30,* 679–689.

Whitehurst, G. J., Epstein, J. N., Angell, A. L., Payne, A. C., Crone, D. A., & Fischel, J. E. (1994). Outcomes of an emergent literacy intervention in Head Start. *Journal of Educational Psychology, 86*(4), 542–555.

Whitehurst, G. J., Falco, F. L., Lonigan, C. J., Fischel, J. E., DeBaryshe, B. D., Valdez-Menchaca, M. C., et al. (1988). Accelerating language development through picture book reading. *Developmental Psychology, 24,* 552–559.

Whitehurst, G. J., & Lonigan, C. J. (1998). Child development and emergent literacy. *Child Development, 69,* 848–872.

Whitehurst, G. J., & Lonigan, C. J. (2001). Emergent literacy: Development from prereaders to readers. In S. B. Neuman & D. K. Dickinson (Eds.), *Handbook of early literacy research* (pp. 11–29). New York: Guilford Press.

Wigfield, A., & Asher, S. R. (1984). Social and motivational influences on reading. In P. D. Pearson, R. Barr, M. L. Kamil & P. Mosenthal (Eds.), *Handbook of reading research* (pp. 423–452). New York: Longman.

Wilson, L. C. (1994, November). *Language development as perceived by reservation-based Navajo families.* Paper presented at the meeting of the American Speech–Language–Hearing Association, New Orleans, LA.

Yaden, D. B., Smolkin, L. B., & Conlon, A. (1989). Preschoolers' questions about pictures, print conventions, and story text during reading aloud at home. *Reading Research Quarterly, 24,* 188–214.

Yaden, D. B., Smolkin, L. B., & MacGillivray, L. (1993). A psychogenetic perspective on children's understanding about letter associations during alphabet book readings. *Journal of Reading Behavior, 25,* 43–68.

Yoder, P. J., & Davies, B. (1992a). Do children with developmental delays use more frequent and diverse language in verbal routines? *American Journal of Mental Retardation, 97,* 197–208.

Yoder, P. J., & Davies, B. (1992b). Greater intelligibility in verbal routines with young children with developmental delays. *Applied Psycholinguistics, 13,* 77–91.

Yoder, P. J., Davies, B., & Bishop, K. (1994). Reciprocal sequential relations in conversations between parents and children with developmental delays. *Journal of Early Intervention, 18,* 362–379.

Yoder, P. J., Davies, B., Bishop, K., & Munson, L. (1994). Effect of adult continuing *wh*-questions on conversational participation in children with developmental disabilities. *Journal of Speech and Hearing Research, 37,* 193–204.

Yoder, P. J., Spruytenburg, H., Edwards, A., & Davies, B. (1995). Effect of verbal routine contexts and expansions on gains in the mean length of utterance in children with developmental delays. *Language, Speech, and Hearing Services in Schools, 26,* 21–32.

Zevenbergen, A., & Whitehurst, G. (2003). Dialogic reading: A shared picture book reading intervention for preschoolers. In A. van Kleeck, S. A. Stahl, & E. Bauer (Eds.), *On reading to children: Parents and teachers* (pp. 177–200). Mahwah, NJ: Erlbaum.

10

Preschool-Based Prevention of Reading Disability

Realities versus Possibilities

DAVID K. DICKINSON
ALLYSSA MCCABE
NANCY CLARK-CHIARELLI

In this chapter, we address the topic of learning disabilities from a prevention perspective, highlighting the importance of early childhood classrooms as settings that have the potential to reduce the incidence of learning disabilities. This approach is consistent with that articulated by the National Research Council in *Preventing Reading Difficulties in Young Children* (Snow, Burns, & Griffin, 1998), which highlighted the centrality of high-quality early childhood programs in the prevention of reading difficulties. First, we set the stage by reviewing trends in the incidence of learning disabilities. We emphasize the centrality of language-related issues and the heavy overrepresentation of children from low-income and non-English-speaking homes among the learning disabled. Although some of these children no doubt suffer from significant biologically based impairments, we argue that, if provided strong support for language starting in the preschool years and continuing into the primary grades, many need never be identified as being learning disabled. Drawing on our own work, we discuss the

potential beneficial effects of preschool classrooms, but report data that point to the shortcomings in language support in far too many preschool classrooms. Such findings, we suggest, may help explain some of the current patterns of overrepresentation of children from low-income and non-English-speaking homes among the ranks of the learning disabled. We conclude with data that hold promise for the value of professional development as one means to enhance teachers' classroom support for language and early literacy.

THE PROBLEMATIC REALITY

Reading difficulties are numerous and increasing in frequency. Furthermore, much evidence suggests that they begin early in life and that many are preventable in theory. In the 1999–2000 school year, over half (50.5%) of the students receiving special education services in this country were categorized as having specific learning disabilities (U.S. Department of Education, 2002). This

209

translates into 2,871,966 students, an esti-mated 90% of whom are identified as hav-ing reading difficulties (Lyon, 1995). The etiology of many such cases is not due to hearing impairment, Down syndrome, autism, or any other known physical source, so many cases may well be pre-ventable. These large numbers fuel concerns that growing numbers of children are failing at one of life's most important tasks—learn-ing to read.

Whereas these estimates document the number of students *identified* as learning disabled, other sources suggest that as many as 20% of all children experience signifi-cant difficulty learning to read (Ameri-can Speech–Language–Hearing Association, 2002; Shaywitz, Escobar, Shaywitz, Fletch-er, & Makuch, 1992), and another 20% do not read fluently enough to read for plea-sure (Moats, 1999, 2000). Recent results from the 2000 National Assessment of Edu-cational Progress (NAEP) confirm that there is a problem, because more than one-third (37%) of fourth graders are considered to be below a basic level (National Center for Education Statistics, 2001). When these re-sults are examined relative to race/ethnicity, the picture becomes even more dismal. There is a vast discrepancy between the achievement of white, non-Hispanic stu-dents and their black and Hispanic peers. Whereas the 2000 data reveal that 40% of white students are at or above the proficient achievement level, only 12% of black stu-dents and 16% of Hispanic students are at these levels. Sadly, this gap in performance is not a new phenomenon, because this pro-file of differential performance levels has shown no change since 1992 (National Center for Education Statistics, 2001). In short, large numbers of children are not able to read at a level considered to be pro-ficient—a finding that has helped make lit-eracy a national priority.

These achievement gaps have early ori-gins in the type of language directed to chil-dren of different socioeconomic classes. Hart and Risley (1995) amply documented extremely large and stable differences in the amount and quality of oral language direct-ed to children of different social classes, as well as the long-term impact of such differ-ences. For example, children of professional families hear almost three times as many ut-terances per hour and over twice as many different words per hour as do children of parents on welfare. Moreover, whereas more than 80% of the feedback to 13- to 18-month-old children of professional fami-lies was positive, almost 80% of the feed-back to welfare peers was negative.

Particularly disheartening is the fact that impoverished early linguistic experience re-sults in limited early literacy skills, which in turn often translate into persistent deficits. Research has shown strong evidence of sta-bility in relative levels of reading perfor-mance between kindergarten and seventh grade (Tabors, Snow, & Dickinson, 2001), and between first grade and the end of high school (Cunningham & Stanovich, 1997). Children who are identified as being poor readers in the early grades remain poor readers throughout their school careers (Juel, 1988; Shaywitz et al., 1992; Torgesen, 1998). Moreover, once children fall behind, most of the compensatory education they receive has negligible results (McGill-Franzen & Allington, 1991). In fact, after children reach grade 3, reading difficulties are far less amenable to remediation (Good, Simmons, & Smith, 1998). Some have ar-gued that because the success rate of reme-diating reading difficulties is so low, identi-fication and intervention must start early (National Reading Panel, 2000).

RESPONDING TO THE CHALLENGES

Although research has identified a range of daunting problems, there is hope. Several strands of work suggest that the vast major-ity of children who show signs of early reading difficulty are capable of reading at grade-appropriate levels if they receive ef-fective early reading instruction (Clay, 1985; Iversen & Tunmer, 1993; Pinnell, 1989; Snow et al., 1998; Wasik & Slavin, 1993). These findings support the position suggested by Clay (1987), and by Vellutino and Scanlon (1998), among others, that de-ficiencies in instruction, rather than cogni-tion, may account for the prevalence of reading difficulties in our schools. In fact, recent estimates suggest that as few as 1.5–6% of children are not amenable to remediation in the early grades (Torgesen, 2000; Vellutino & Scanlon, 1998). This very small group of children displays marked differences in phonological-processing capacities (Foorman & Torgesen, 2001; McCardle, Scarborough, & Catts, 2001). These differences are assumed to be organic and inherently neurobiological in nature, and to require long-term intervention. One theory is that such children have a core deficit localized to phonological processing, and that this deficiency is modularized, so that skills in other language areas are not able to compensate (McCardle et al., 2001; Siegel, 1998; Stanovich, 1988; Stanovich & Siegel, 1994).

Restricting Our Focus

We do not focus on those children who have neurobiological deficiencies associated with phonological processing; rather, we are concerned with the far larger group of children who are experiencing literacy problems that reflect deficiencies in instruction and limitations in language experience. Our concern is for those children with more generalized limitations in language skills. Catts, Fey, Zhang, and Tomblin (1999) estimate that as many as 70% of struggling readers with phonological-processing difficulties also evidence deficits in higher level areas of language development, such as vocabulary, syntax, and narrative development. A substantial body of research clearly substantiates that multiple areas of language are also highly predictive of reading achievement: (1) *vocabulary* (e.g., Anderson & Freebody, 1981; Bishop & Adams, 1990; Dickinson & McCabe, 2001; Dickinson, McCabe, Anastasopoulos, Peisner-Feingerg, & Poe, 2003; Hart & Risley, 1995; Scarborough, 1989; Stahl & Fairbanks, 1986; Walker, Greenwood, Hart, & Carta, 1994; see Whitehurst & Lonigan, 2001, for review); (2) *syntax* (Dickinson, 1987; Scarborough, 1990, 1991; see Scarborough, 2001, for review); and (3) *discourse* (Beals, 2001; Bishop & Edmundson, 1987; Feagans & Applebaum, 1986; Fazio, Naremore, & Connell, 1996; Menyuk et al., 1991; see Vernon-

Feagans, Hammer, Miccio, & Manlove, 2001, for review).

The Case for the Importance of Strong Preschool Classrooms

A large body of accumulated research points to the conclusion that childcare experiences can have positive short- and long-term impact on children's development (Barnett, 1995, 2001). This conclusion is based on correlational and experimental research, and converging results suggest that the quality of teacher–child relationships and conversations can make particularly important contributions to children's growth.

Classroom Quality Is Important

Results of a number of correlational studies point to the importance of providing children high-quality preschool experiences. The ongoing National Institute of Child Health and Human Development (NICHD; 2000, 2002) study of the impact of childcare on children's development provides a powerful demonstration of the impact of variations in quality of care on children's language, cognitive, and emotional development. This study followed children from infancy to school entry and included 1,075 randomly selected children age 54 months. This study (2002) reported that, after taking into account family background factors, higher quality, center-based programs benefit children's language, cognitive, and social development at the end of preschool. The impact of variability in classroom quality on children's language and cognitive development was found to be reasonably large when compared to the effects of two well-established environmental factors that influence development, quality of parenting, and poverty (National Institute of Child Health and Human Development, 2002). Similarly, results from the Cost, Quality, and Outcomes Study also found beneficial effects on language, literacy, and mathematical achievement at the end of both preschool (Peisner-Feinberg & Burchinal, 1997; Peisner-Feinberg et al., 2001) and kindergarten. Similarly, Burchinal, Roberts, Hooper, and

Zeisel (2000) found a relationship between higher levels of childcare quality in the first 3 years of life and better performance on child outcomes (including cognitive, language, and communication measures).

The correlational evidence that points to the importance of the quality of preschool classrooms is bolstered by findings of two long-running experimental intervention studies. The Abecedarian project, a random-assignment, experimental intervention, provided intensive services to children throughout their preschool years and continued to provide some support for children in the elementary school years. Long-term follow-up evaluations of this intervention found evidence of beneficial effects of the preschool portion of this intervention as late as early adulthood (Campbell & Ramey, 1994, 1995). Long-term follow-up studies of the impact of the High/Scope Perry Preschool Study, another random-assignment intervention (Schweinhart, Barnes, Weikart, Barnett, & Epstein, 1993), also point to the potential long-term benefits of high-quality preschool on children's development.

Support for Language Is Key

Results from the NICHD and the Cost, Quality, and Outcomes Study suggest that high-quality teacher–child interactions may be important for improved outcomes for children, but these studies did not include a clear index of the quality of verbal interactions that children experienced. Several studies now provide converging evidence suggesting that the quality of teacher–child conversations may be of pivotal importance. One of the earliest major studies of the impact of preschool on children's language development, a large study carried out in Bermuda, examined a variety of features of classrooms, including measures of the nature of language that children experienced. A finding of particular importance to us is that children's language growth was significantly associated with the amount of time they spent talking with and listening to adults rather than children (McCartney, 1984). The most beneficial type of adult talk, called "representational" talk, commu-

nicated information and was not used to control children's behavior.

Further reason to believe that teacher–child interaction may be of considerable importance in supporting the language growth of preschool-age children comes from Huttenlocher, Vasilyeva, Cymerman, and Levine (2002), who examine the growth of 4-year-old children's syntactic skills over the course of 9 months. Huttenlocher et al. examined children's syntactic skills in the fall and spring, and also gathered information about the nature of the language children experienced in their preschool classrooms. In the fall, they found positive correlations between maternal language use and children's syntactic development, with these differences reflecting the social class background of the mothers (i.e., children from more advantaged homes displayed stronger skills). However, in their spring analyses of factors that predicted children's growth in syntactic skills, Huttenlocher et al. first examined the impact of the complexity of mothers' language use on children's syntactic development and found a positive association. Once the impact of teacher input was taken into consideration, it strongly predicted the fall-to-spring growth in syntax. Thus, classroom input can do much to bolster the syntactic skills of children most in need of support.

Myriad early interventions have been developed to improve language and literacy input to preschool and kindergarten children. One approach instructs teachers in techniques of reading interactively one-on-one and with small groups of children (Whitehurst et al., 1994). Some programs emphasize training in phonological awareness particularly (Stahl, 2001). Others focus on the use of high-quality children's literature in preschool, kindergarten, and early elementary school classrooms (Morrow & Gambrell, 2001). One widely used approach based on research on invented and developmental spelling involves having teachers engage in numerous word study activities, that are game-like in format but substantive in content (Bear, Invernizzi, Templeton, & Johnston, 1996). Numerous pullout programs have been implemented, with specific components dovetailed to meet each child's needs (e.g., Vellutino & Scanlon, 2001).

These myriad programs are by no means unrelated to each other. For example, phonological awareness is a key aspect of word study (Bear et al., 1996), and most such programs would be receptive to the use of good children's literature. All such emergent literacy programs involve the incorporation of large amounts of nurturant teacher verbal interaction with children, so our focus is on this common component.

Home–School Study of Language and Literacy Development

Our own work provides additional documentation of the potential contributions of classrooms to the long-term literacy development of young children from low-income homes (Dickinson & Tabors, 2001, 2002). During the preschool years, researchers visited children in their homes and classrooms, interviewed parents and teachers, and audiotaped conversations. In both homes and classrooms, mealtimes and book reading were taped, and in classrooms, teachers and children were recorded throughout the day. In the spring, kindergarten children's language and literacy skills were assessed (see Dickinson & Tabors, 2001, for details). They continued to assess children's reading and language abilities throughout the elementary grades and into middle school, and found very strong correlations between assessments of children's skills in kindergarten and end-of-seventh-grade assessments, with seventh-grade reading comprehension correlating with kindergarten receptive vocabulary ($r = .71$; $p < .001$) and storytelling ability ($r = .45$, $p < .01$). These findings add to existing reports of the long-term stability of literacy skills (Baydar, Brooks-Gunn, & Furstenberg, 1993; Hanson, & Farrell, 1995; Sameroff, Seifer, Baldwin, & Baldwin, 1993; Whitehurst & Lonigan, 2001). For example, Cunningham and Stanovich (1997), found that first-grade reading ability was a strong predictor of a variety of 11th grade measures of reading ability, even when measures of cognitive ability were taken into account.

When the children in this study were 4

years old, they and the lead teacher in their classroom were audiotaped for a day. These tapes were transcribed and coded in various ways. One analysis examined the impact of the quality of conversations during book reading on children in the first cohort of 4-year-olds in this study. Dickinson and Smith (1994) found that during book readings, the frequency of conversations that were analytic in nature (i.e., children discussed characters' motivations, the reasons for events, and the meanings of words) helped to predict children's vocabulary scores at the end of kindergarten, after they controlled for home factors and some classroom variables. These results were replicated in analyses that included the second cohort of children (Dickinson, 2001a).

In addition to book reading, conversations during meal-, free-play, and large-group times were transcribed and coded. Two composite measures of the quality of teacher–child discourse were created from empirically and conceptually related variables. One measure examined the quality of extended discourse and included variables such as the extent to which teachers remained engaged in extended conversations with children during free play, teachers' provision of information during group times, and the frequency with which they engaged children in analytic conversations about books. A second measure included the variety of rare words used throughout the day. These measures were included in regression analyses to predict children's end-of-kindergarten levels of receptive vocabulary and early literacy. After controlling for home background variables, Dickinson (2001b) found evidence of sizable effects of classroom experiences on the end-of-kindergarten measures. The most powerful classroom predictor was the frequency and content of extended conversations between teachers and children throughout the day. The extended teacher discourse variable included teachers' efforts to engage children in analytic thinking about stories while reading books, conversations that provided new information during group times, and efforts to extend one-to-one conversations during choice time (Dickinson, 2001b). Other important variables included use of varied vocabulary throughout the day (mealtimes, choice time, book reading, group times), evidence of a curriculum that encouraged writing, and efforts to provide new information and activities continually throughout the year. These classroom variables, in combination with home controls, accounted for 49% of the variance in children's end-of-kindergarten receptive vocabulary scores. Furthermore, the variance in children's kindergarten levels of performance at the beginning of their schooling experiences accounted for significant variance in growth trajectories at the end of fourth grade (Roach & Snow, 2000).

We conclude that children's literacy success in the early years plays a major role in determining their long-term literacy development. More importantly, the quality of preschool experiences can play an important role in helping children from less advantaged backgrounds enter school in a position to move forward successfully with literacy learning.

Typical Levels of Support for Development in Preschool Classrooms

Given that preschool classrooms have the potential to support later development, we are led to ask whether classrooms typically provide the type of support found to be beneficial to children. We address this question by examining several prior studies and by discussing new data of our own. Most indications are that far too few children receive the type of support for language and literacy development that is associated with optimal growth.

Considerable evidence points to deficiencies in the quality of support for language in many preschool classrooms. Nearly two decades ago, Tizard and Hughes (1984) compared children's home and school language experiences in British infant schools, and found that schools often were less rich language environments for working-class children. Compared with the home, adult–child conversations in school settings tended to occur less often and to be shorter. In classrooms, children tended to be less curious and to engage in *less* complex, *less* cognitively demanding conversations than

they did at home. Add to this regrettable set of findings the fact that children have to share teacher input with other children, and that they spend far less time with teachers than with their parents, and it becomes clear that preschools have not always provided the kind of language stimulation children of poverty require.

A major descriptive study of 119 classrooms across the United States was carried out in the early 1990s (Layzer, Goodson, & Moss, 1993). For this study, researchers spent a week observing interactions. They found that lead teachers engaged in one-to-one or small-group interactions with children 26% of the time, slightly less than the time (28%) when they were coded as interacting with no children at all. The extent to which teachers attended to individual children varied by setting. When the researchers considered classroom life from the point of view of children, they found that children quite often had no opportunities for individual contact with a teacher. In 20% of the classrooms observed, half or more of the children had no opportunities for individual attention from an adult during a day (Layzer et al., 1993).

Another study that examined language practices carefully was carried out in university-affiliated preschool classrooms, a location in which one would anticipate finding particularly strong classroom support for children's development. These researchers noted the frequency of interactions between teachers and children when they were in close proximity (3 feet or less apart) and found that 81% of the time, teachers did not talk to children they were near (Wilcox-Hertzog & Kontos, 1998).

Similar descriptive data emerged from the Home–School Study of Language and Literacy development (Snow, Tabors, & Dickinson, 2001). Tapes that the children made as they went about their daily lives were coded and analyzed to determine the amount of time that children engaged in conversation with different partners. Consistent findings emerged when children were 3 and 4 years old, even though they were typically in different classrooms. The 52 three-year-olds who were observed during free-play in their classrooms, on average, spent 21% of their time interacting with a teacher. When they were age 4, the 75 children who were observed spent only 17% of their time interacting with a teacher (Dickinson, 2001c).

Snow et al. (2001) also examined the transcripts of teacher–child dialogue using an automated system that allowed them to determine how often teachers used different words. They then created a "filter" for these words by putting in a list of words generally known by children (Chall & Dale, 1995) and adding common proper nouns. This "filter" was then used to sort through all the words spoken by teachers and children, resulting in a set of what Snow et al. called "rare words." Rare words were not necessarily exotic, including items such as *actually, assure, chores, ignore, punishment, ramp,* and *wisdom.* Because some of these words were used more than once, we determined how many different rare words were used. When the children were age 3, the authors found that, on average, during the 15 minutes of transcribed and analyzed free play, teachers used 12 rare words and 8 different word types; during the 15 minutes of analyzed large-group times, teachers used 13 different rare words and 8 different word types. When these same children were age 4 and in different classrooms, during free play, their teachers used 14 rare words and 9 different word types, and during large-group times, 15 words and 8 different word types. Given the huge need for vocabulary learning among many children from low-income and non-English-speaking homes, such limited variety of vocabulary exposure is problematic.

In summary, the relatively few intensive analyses of teacher–child interactions during the preschool day yield converging evidence that, in many preschools, children have relatively little access to adults for personalized conversations, in spite of the fact that the quality of conversations between teachers and children in the preschool years may play an important role in supporting growth during a critical period of development. Available data also suggest that when teachers are able to engage individuals or small groups in conversations, these interactions tend to include a relatively low density of varied vocabulary. We next report addi-

tional data that reveal patterns of teacher–child interaction, examined in terms of characteristics that studies of parent–child interaction have found to be valuable. First, we briefly discuss some of the rich work on parent–child interaction, then we return to additional consideration of teacher–child interaction.

The Role and Nature of Input: Lessons from Studies of Parent–Child Conversations

Extensive research examining the impact of adult-directed speech on multiple aspects of children's language development has demonstrated the critical importance of adult input for children's linguistic growth. From this rich research, we highlight two strands: research that examines adult conversational styles, and the impact of settings on talk.

Adult Styles of Talk

In primarily middle-class samples, parents have repeatedly been demonstrated to display stable individual differences in the language they direct to their children (Olsen-Fulero, 1982). Some parents produce more *conversation-eliciting,* or *referential language,* which means that they frequently ask questions, describe objects, request and reinforce names for things, and affirm and incorporate children's responses. Other parents produce more of what has been termed *directive,* or *expressive language,* which includes fewer nouns, more social expressions ("Say please"), more references to people, more commands and directives of the child's behavior, and more frequent negations of the child's actions (Della Corte, Benedict, & Klein, 1983; Furrow & Nelson, 1984; Goldfield, 1987; Hampson & Nelson, 1993; Nelson, 1973; see also van Kleeck, Chapter 9, this volume).

Talk to very young children is focused on the here and now, regardless of whether that here and now involves objects (referential talk) or behavior (expressive talk). As children pass the age of 2 years, however, parents turn their talk at least some of the time to events in the past. Fivush and Fromhoff (1988) differentiated between *elaborative* (talkative) and *repetitive* (less talkative) parents. In a parallel investigation, McCabe and Peterson (1991) found that some parents extended topics of conversation about past events, whereas others switched topics more frequently; topic-extending input predicted more complex child narration at 3 years.

The Effect of Adult Conversational Styles on Children

The variability in how adults talk with young children has important implications for children's early language acquisition. Conversation-eliciting, referential talk is positively associated with measures of children's advanced early language acquisition (Barnes, Gutfreund, Satterly, & Wells, 1983; Furrow, Nelson, & Benedict, 1979; Hoff-Ginsberg, 1986; Nelson, 1981; Snow, Perlman, & Nathan, 1987; Tomasello & Farrar, 1986), whereas elaborative, topic-extending talk about the past predicts narrative prowess (McCabe & Peterson, 1991; Peterson, Jesso, & McCabe, 1999). Similarly, the directive style has been negatively associated with certain measures of children's early language learning (Barnes et al., 1983; Hampson & Nelson, 1993; Nelson, 1981; Newport, Gleitman, & Gleitman, 1977), whereas the topic-switching style of narration has been negatively correlated with children's narrative skill (McCabe & Peterson, 1991).

These adult styles of input to children can be changed, and children's language development may reflect parental adoption of new ways of conversing. For example, improved parental input about the past has been demonstrated to cause stronger child oral-language skills (Peterson et al., 1999). When parents were randomly assigned to an intervention group that was asked to engage in topic-extending talk about the past with their 3-year-olds for a year, their children showed significant vocabulary improvement right away and, a year later, overall improvement in narrative skill compared to children in a control group.

Setting Effects

Although there is considerable evidence that adults have distinctive styles of conversing with children, it also is apparent that set-

tings have an impact on adult conversational styles. Note that, by "setting," we refer to activities co-constructed by adult and child participants, in which there is a common organizing focus for activity. A given setting may differ considerably in external features as long as it retains the same core-organizing focus and similar roles for participants (e.g., adult–child book reading may be done at home in bed or on a bus, and may involve varied kinds of print, including fiction and nonfiction books, catalogues, and comic books). It is important to consider setting when examining discourse because of its demonstrated impact on conversations.

Haden and Fivush (1996) found no association between mothers' conversational behaviors exhibited in free play and in talking about the past with their children, suggesting differences as a function of setting. Similarly, although Hoff-Ginsberg (1991) found social-class differences in maternal conversational style, she also found setting effects that were strong and significant. Mothers' child-directed speech during reading had the greatest lexical diversity, the greatest syntactic complexity, and the highest rate of topic-continuing replies, as well as being one of the two highest settings in terms of the overall rate of maternal speech. Toy play, on the other hand, had the highest rate of directives and the lowest rate of conversation-eliciting utterances. Mealtime was lower than all other settings in the rate of maternal speech and highest, along with dressing, in the rate of conversation-eliciting utterances. Maternal speech during dressing had less lexical diversity than all other contexts.

Evidence of the impact of setting on parental conversations is important, because it points to the need to identify settings in which teachers should be helped to make special efforts to enhance the use of the type of extended cognitively rich talk that most benefits children's language and literacy development. For example, the fact that adults spontaneously tend to find mealtimes a setting that is conducive to eliciting information from children suggests that staff should make special efforts to ensure that children have adults available to converse with during mealtimes, and that adults recognize that it is their obligation to use such times as opportunities for extended conversations.

In summary, work on parents' interactions with children establishes that adults have different ways of talking to children, but that these approaches can vary by setting and are malleable. That variation in adults' conversational styles affects children's learning provides further reason to ensure that teachers provide children with high-quality conversational experiences throughout the day.

EXAMINING MULTIPLE DIMENSIONS OF CLASSROOM DISCOURSE

Prior studies of mother–child and classroom discourse suggest that a number of features of teacher–child discourse are likely to be beneficial to children. Children are likely to benefit when adults (1) build on and extend what they are saying, (2) engage children in talk about cognitively rich topics (e.g., nonpresent topics, hypothetical or explanatory talk, talk about language), (3) use varied vocabulary, and (4) sustain a conversation about a single topic. Furthermore, based on prior work (Dickinson, 1991, 1994, 2001b, 2001c) and the research on parents, it is apparent that conversations are influenced by features of the classroom setting.

Our Approach

In an effort to capture these multiple dimensions that affect conversations, a time-sampling tool, the Teacher-Child Verbal Interaction Profile (TCVI; Dickinson, Howard, & Haines, 1998) was developed.[1] Using this tool, researchers observed teachers for 30-second intervals and, in the following 30 seconds, coded that interaction. The dimensions they coded include the following:

1. *Teacher engagement:* Teacher is present and engaged or teacher is not engaged. A teacher was coded as being "engaged" if she interacted with one or more children either through verbal means or by indicating through eye gaze or body posture that she was listening or observing children. Teachers who were physically ab-

sent, talking with other adults, or emotionally or physically unavailable were coded as "not engaged."
2. *Physical position:* Teacher is sitting, standing, or moving.
3. *Content:* Nonpresent talk, control, ongoing activities, preferences and feelings, literacy and math, general knowledge.
4. *Vocabulary:* Talk about the meanings of words or intentional efforts to define words.
5. *Conversational balance:* Teacher dominates the conversation, or the conversation is balanced between teacher and children, and/or a child sets the topic.
6. *Amount of teacher talk:* Minimal talk (5 seconds or less per interval) or more talk.
7. *Topic development:* A topic is established and pursued in a manner that adds additional details or depth (e.g., teacher elicits follow-up information about a birthday party).
8. *Activity:* Art, sand/water, writing/dictation, dramatic play/puppets, manipulation of materials/puzzle solving, science activity, book reading, blocks, computer games.

Here, we sample selectively from this rich database to provide an additional portrait of the structure of conversations in preschool classrooms.

Our data come from observations of 61 lead teachers, nearly all of whom were working in Head Start classrooms, 71% of whom had less than a bachelor's degree. Ten of these teachers were observed two different times, yielding 71 observations. During each visit, we observed teachers for at least sixteen 30-second intervals in one of two settings: mealtime or free play. Coding began once the observer determined that the activity had officially started and continued until the activity ended, or until the requisite number of intervals was obtained. Reliability of coding TCVI was assessed separately for each dimension. When dichotomous decisions were involved, percent agreement was used to assess reliability, whereas when data were coded with a system with more than two classifications, Cohen's kappa was employed. Agreement about dichotomous codes was 83% or better, and Cohen's kappa scores were .85 or higher.

Because findings regarding conversation often differ by setting, we analyzed our data by setting: free play and mealtime. These settings are similar in that the teacher tends not to have a formal agenda for instruction, so that the kind of individual, conversational give and take known to aid children's language acquisition can occur.

Profile of Classroom Conversations in Preschools

The TCVI data provide a profile of multiple dimensions of conversations in preschools. In general, they suggest that along several dimensions, good teachers (defined for current purposes as the top quartile as defined by the TCVI measures) are effectively engaging children, but that the lowest quartile of teachers is much less effective.

Optimal Patterns of Teacher–Child Classroom Conversation

Ideally, teachers seek every possible opportunity to become *engaged* with individual children in their classroom. The top quartile of teachers in our sample did so; they were always engaged (see Table 10.1). Earlier, we noted that research on mother-child interaction has made eminently clear the fact that children benefit from engaging in *balanced,* back-and-forth conversations in which both partners have turns; that is, the teacher cannot dominate the talk. We coded conversations as being "balanced" if children had a significant role in the conversation.[2] The

top 25% of teachers engaged in such conversations the majority of the time, with mealtime showing special strength (67% balanced talk; see Table 10.2). In addition to having balanced, back-and-forth interactions, prior research indicates that it is most helpful for children to be engaged in conversations that stay on and *develop one topic.* Our observations reveal that sticking to and deepening a topic can be a more difficult task than one might expect, because the busy world of preschool occasions many interruptions; even the best teachers in our sample managed to do so only a little over 20% of the time (see Table 10.2).

Of course, it is not simply the structure of conversations that is important. Children also need to engage in conversations that are interesting and cognitively enriching. We coded the extent to which conversations dealt with intellectually rich content, for example, noting whether conversations involved talk about literacy, word meanings, and topics that deepened children's general world knowledge, and we called such conversations *decontextualized talk* (see Table 10.3). Decontextualized talk did not include talk designed to control children's behavior and talk that simply accompanied or described ongoing activities. Stronger teachers engaged in decontextualized talk in at least 36% of the free-play intervals and 50% of the mealtime intervals.

One value of talk about interesting, cognitively rich topics is that such conversations can include new information as teachers converse about topics connected to the classroom's curriculum. Topics of this nature were coded as "academic talk." Among the

TABLE 10.1. Teacher Engagement and Amount of Talk during 30-Second Intervals during Free Play and Meal Time in Preschool Classrooms

	Mean	SD	Maximum	75%ile	25%ile	Minimum
Teacher engaged						
Free play	93	09	100	100	91	55
Meal time	93	09	100	100	88	67
Minimal talk						
Free play	29	19	80	36	13	0
Meal time	42	25	88	60	20	0

TABLE 10.2. Conversational Structure during 30-Second Intervals in Two Classroom Settings

	Mean	SD	Maximum	75%ile	25%ile	Minimum
Teacher–child balance						
Free play	41	20	90	58	25	4
Meal time	49	22	100	67	33	8
Developed topic						
Free play	14	10	38	22	6	0
Meal time	19	17	63	29	0	0

Note. Entries are percent of time.

top quartile of teachers, such conversational topics were seen in 18% of the intervals coded during free play (see Table 10.3). Talk about past and future events (i.e., "nonpresent talk") and also examples of decontextualized talk were more common, especially during mealtimes, when they were found in 38% of the intervals of the top-quartile teachers. Such talk may lead to use of varied vocabulary and explicit talk about words and their meanings, but even among the teachers displaying the strongest support for language, we found that explicit discussion of vocabulary was rare (see Table 10.3).

The Biggest Challenge: Lowest Quartile Patterns of Classroom Conversation

Whereas teachers with the strongest conversational skills displayed a number of areas of strength, those in the bottom quartile, as indexed by the data for the TCVI, had weaknesses in many areas. Although they were coded as being "engaged" in 88% of the mealtime intervals observed, this engagement was coded as being "minimal" (i.e., less than 5 seconds in duration) in 20% of the intervals. Thus, they were *actively* engaged in interactions with children during only about two-thirds of the intervals. Typically, during such uninvolved intervals, teachers simply sat quietly and ate, giving no indication of being involved with the children sitting around them. During free play, the bottom-quartile teachers were actively engaged in verbal interactions during only about three-quarters of the intervals coded (see Table 10.1).

Furthermore, the bottom-quartile group showed discouraging patterns in the structure and content of their conversations. Teachers in the lowest quartile dominated

TABLE 10.3. Conversational Content during 30-Second Intervals in Two Settings

	Mean	SD	Maximum	75%ile	25%ile	Minimum
New vocabulary						
Free play	1	2	0.9	3	0	0
Meal time	0.9	3	13	0	0	0
Academic talk[a]						
Free play	12	9	40	18	5	0
Meal time	3	7	31	5	0	0
Nonpresent talk[b]						
Free play	14	11	45	20	6	0
Meal time	22	19	67	38	7	0
Decontextualized talk[c]						
Free play	27	16	66	36	18	0
Meal time	34	21	80	50	17	0

Note. Entries are percent of time.
[a]Includes talk about language, mathematics, and general knowledge.
[b]Includes talk about past and future events.
[c]Includes "academic talk," "nonpresent," pretending, and personal preferences and feelings.

the conversation three-quarters of the time during free play, and two-thirds of the time during mealtimes (see Table 10.2). Thirty seconds is a long time for a child to be a mute audience for a talkative teacher. The extent to which such interactions represent important missed opportunities is particularly evident if one considers how few opportunities a given child has to converse with a teacher in the course of a day. The bleak picture continues when we discover that, among this bottom quartile of teachers, conversations that extend a topic were found in 6–7% or less of the observed intervals and contained decontextualized talk 18% or less of the time (see Table 10.2).

Talk about Vocabulary

Across all teachers, there was almost no explicit talk about language. We found evidence that teachers were making intentional efforts to define or talk about the meanings of words in less than 1% of the free-play and mealtime intervals (see Table 10.3). When we looked across all of the observed intervals within a classroom, in only 8% of free-play conversations and 11% of mealtime conversations did we find even one intentional effort to talk about the meanings of words; that is, in about 90% of the classrooms, *intentional talk about words never occurred* during the time we observed a given setting. This limitation in teacher–child discourse is of concern because, as noted previously, research suggests that significant numbers of low-income children are exposed to relatively limited amounts of varied vocabulary in their homes (Hart & Risley, 1995; Tabors, Beals, & Weizman, 2001). Thus, a strong Head Start preschool program would be one in which teachers make frequent intentional efforts to expose children to new vocabulary at school.

Why Is There So Much Low-Quality Teacher–Child Classroom Discourse?

The lack of supportive conversations may reflect how various settings are organized (e.g., teachers circulate during mealtimes). Given earlier observations about the negative impact of teacher movement on conversations (Dickinson, 1991), we examined teacher positioning and found considerable variation among teachers. Prior studies have found that children's mealtime conversations are better when teachers are present and sitting (Cote, 2001; Dickinson, 1991); therefore, it is interesting to note that during mealtimes in the bottom quartile of classrooms, teachers were seated only slightly more than half of the time (56%; see Table 10.4). Some teachers also were moving (15%) or standing (50%), often during many free-play intervals. Such physical positioning reduces their availability to children. Where teachers are and how they position themselves reflect complex issues connected to staffing, and strategies used for group management and for the division

TABLE 10.4. Teacher Positioning Talk during 30-Second Intervals during Free Play and Meal Time in Preschool Classrooms

	Mean	SD	Maximum	75%ile	25%ile	Minimum
Teacher sitting						
Free play	55	22	97	75	38	9
Meal time	73***	23	100	91	56	11
Teacher standing						
Free play	35**	21	85	50	19	0
Meal time	22	20	89	36	0	0
Teacher moving						
Free play	10*	10	47	15	3	0
Meal time	5	10	40	8	0	0

Note. Entries are percent of time.
*$p < .05$; **$p < .001$; ***$p < .0001$.

of responsibilities among teachers.

Although our descriptive data merely indicate what is happening during these two settings, such data can provide a starting point for fruitful discussions among staff regarding what should be happening during mealtimes and other conversational settings. The patterns in conversations that we observed also likely reflect the fact that many teachers are not aware of the importance of engaging in sustained conversations (Dickinson, 1991, 1994). Lacking such knowledge or encouragement to make the needed effort to engage in effective conversations, their interactions with children tend to be driven by other powerful factors, such as fatigue, a personal preference to eat quietly, or concerns with socialization (e.g., teaching manners) or behavior management concerns. In addition, the low frequency of intellectually engaging talk also suggests that, in some classrooms, content learning is not a high priority; children and teachers are not consistently talking about topics that will expand children's knowledge of the world, while building their spoken language skills. The limited amount of explicit talk about vocabulary likely reflects, in part, the previously noted restriction in the richness of the content of conversations, again, due to a lack of awareness of the importance of conversation to children's development.

In summary, we know that preschool classrooms hold the potential to provide important stimulus to the language and early literacy development of children from low-income homes, and that such support might provide the boost that some children need to avoid falling into a cycle of academic struggle that could lead them to become classified among the large number of children with learning disabilities. Yet careful examination of patterns of teacher–child conversations continue to indicate that considerable numbers of low-income children are not receiving optimal support for language growth in preschool. We now turn to a brief discussion of possible hopeful avenues for those interested in turning preschool classrooms into truly effective settings for the prevention of later learning difficulties.

HOPEFUL DIRECTIONS

We consider possible directions for future efforts to provide children the kinds of early childhood classrooms that may reduce the incidence of learning disabilities in two ways. First, we consider some pragmatic, logistical features of classrooms that, if attended to, might help elevate the quality of conversations in preschools, as well as in kindergarten and primary grade classrooms. However, we know that there are no simple routes to improvement, and we firmly believe that strong professional development must play a role in any attempt to enhance classroom quality. We support this assertion with data from an intervention that we have helped develop and assess.

Pragmatic Classroom Considerations

The TCVI included codes that enabled us to examine the relationships between the kinds of conversations teachers have with children and the features of classrooms that teachers potentially can control. We assume that, although it is very hard to be aware of fine-grained details of conversations, teachers may be able to attend to issues such as where they position themselves in the classroom. In particular, based on earlier work, we expected that better conversations would occur when teachers were stationary and, preferably, seated (Dickinson, 1991). This speculation was supported, because we found a significant positive correlation between the percentage of time teachers spent sitting and topic development during mealtime ($r = .38$, $p < .05$). This finding is complemented by the equally strong but negative correlation between topic development and the percentage of time teachers spent standing during mealtime ($r = -.41$, $p < .01$).

The content of teachers' talk also was related to their physical position. We found that cognitively rich talk, as defined earlier, was significantly positively correlated with the percentage of time teachers spent sitting during free play ($r = .36$, $p < .01$) and mealtimes ($r = .38$, $p < .01$). In addition, it was significantly *negatively* correlated with percentage of time teachers spent standing during free play ($r = -.28$, $p < .05$) and mealtimes

($r = -.43$, $p < .001$). Thus, we propose that simply encouraging teachers to sit down and talk at length with children is congruent with classroom dynamics and will benefit children's development of discourse and vocabulary (Peterson et al., 1999).

Moreover, teachers developed a topic more often when they were engaged in talking about nonpresent subjects, notably, narratives about past events, pretend play, and future talk ($r = .55$ for nonpresent talk, $p < .0001$). Similarly, nonpresent talk correlated with developing a topic ($r = .53$, $p < .0003$). Simply encouraging teachers to elicit longer narratives when talking with children about past events or entering into (though not dominating) pretend play, or planning or hypothesizing about the future, will benefit children in need of linguistic stimulation.

Contrary to our expectations, we found little evidence of consistent relationships between our indicators of high-quality conversations and activity settings during free play. This null result suggests that what is most important is that teachers understand and make intentional efforts to engage in sustained, productive conversations. In order for this to become a priority, teachers need strong professional development and mentoring support as they strive to acquire new ways of interacting with children.

Professional Development

It is clear that despite the potential that early childhood settings hold for enhancing young children's language and literacy development, many classrooms are falling far short of providing optimal support for children. Our data suggest that a key variable is likely the teacher's awareness of what constitutes good conversations, and her energetic efforts to engage in such conversations regularly with all children. In an effort to help preschool teachers better support children's early literacy development, Dickinson and numerous colleagues at the Center for Children and Families at Education Development Center (EDC) developed an intervention called the Literacy Environment Enrichment Program (LEEP). Now given as an academic course that is taken by teams of teachers and supervisors, LEEP has been de-

livered to teachers throughout New England and in North Carolina. It introduces teachers and their supervisors to basic information about language and literacy development, and grounds this information in classroom practice. Teachers try out new strategies, and both teachers and supervisors are encouraged to reflect on classroom instruction. As teachers are learning to link theory to practice in their classrooms, supervisors are helped to adopt effective methods to coach teachers.

To determine the impact of LEEP, we employed a comparison-group design in which LEEP and comparison-group classrooms were observed before and after the LEEP training, and children in these classrooms were assessed with a battery of tools that evaluated their language and literacy skills. We now have analyzed the impact of LEEP when delivered in two ways: (1) through face-to-face, institute-style delivery (two 3-day sessions) and (2) using interactive television in combination with the support of a website. For the latter, technology-assisted version of LEEP (T-LEEP), there were 10 sessions, with the first and last sessions being extended days that were conducted primarily face-to-face, with eight 3-hour interim sessions. In both cases, a team that included a classroom teacher and her supervisor took the course.

Analysis of the Institute form of delivery included 40 LEEP teachers and 231 children in their classrooms, and 62 comparison-group teachers and 328 children in their classrooms. We conducted analyses of the impact of LEEP on classroom practices by controlling for the classroom's quality ratings in the fall prior to the intervention, and for information about the teacher (e.g., education, years of experience, racial background). We found strong evidence that teachers who participated in LEEP made sizable improvements in the quality of their support for language and literacy. We also examined our data for evidence of the impact of teacher participation in LEEP on the learning of children in their classrooms. After we controlled for variables, such as age, parental education, gender, and preintervention scores on our assessments, we found that, on average, children whose teachers had been in LEEP had better scores on assessments of vocabulary, phonological awareness, and early literacy. Analyses of the T-LEEP have recently been conducted with the use of hierarchical linear modelling (HLM) to take into account the variation among children that is not related to classroom factors. Using this approach, we found strong evidence of both significant effects of participation in T-LEEP on children's receptive vocabulary scores, and modest impact on their literacy and phonemic awareness skills (Clark-Chiarelli et al., 2002; Dickinson, Anastasopoulos, Miller, Caswell, & Peisner-Feinberg, 2002).

We have, of course, the most information on our own approach. However, we wish to emphasize that our approach incorporates many of the components on which other professional development approaches focus; that is, LEEP incorporates instruction in the importance of, and techniques for, interactive reading one-on-one and with small groups of children, which is the focus of Whitehurst and his colleagues (1994). LEEP also includes substantial training in ways that teachers can foster phonological awareness (see Stahl, 2001, for review). LEEP explicitly endorses the use of high-quality children's literature, which is advocated by such researchers as Morrow and Gambrell (2001). LEEP also instructs teachers about invented spelling and other aspects of emergent writing, which are the focus of the approach developed by Bear et al. (1996). As we said earlier, most emergent literacy approaches are aware of and incorporate aspects of other approaches.

CONCLUSIONS

We have presented an argument that has a mixture of encouraging and discouraging news. The bad news includes the fact that, in the United States at present, large numbers of children are being identified as having learning problems, most of which involve reading difficulties. This distressing information is partly counterbalanced by the realization that it may be possible to avoid such problems for many of these children if they receive strong classroom support, preferably beginning in the preschool years. However, when we look carefully at interactions in many classrooms that serve those children at risk for academic failure, we find that the kinds of beneficial language interactions are few and far between, especially in classrooms of less-skilled teachers.

We also have found that professional development can enhance classroom language and literacy practices, and bolster children's growth in these areas, but much work remains to be done. First and most importantly, we have far to go to achieve the required magnitude of instructional improvement to stimulate early language and literacy skills if we are truly to set children who are most at risk on a path to success. We have explored several ways of delivering professional development, though we have yet to know what is the most optimal format. Quite possibly, we will find that the optimal format differs depending on factors such as whether instruction occurs in urban or rural areas, or whether it is directed toward better or less well-trained teachers going into the program.

In addition to finding effective ways to deliver high-quality professional development, we believe that if we are to substantially elevate the performance levels of children, we also need to provide teachers with better curricular support. Based on our examination of the characteristics of conversations that have the most beneficial effects on children, we believe that by helping teachers engage in productive conversations throughout the day, the optimal curriculum would bolster skills central to language and literacy (e.g., letter knowledge, phonemic awareness), while also building children's knowledge of the world and greatly expanding their vocabularies and spoken language skills.

In summary, we believe that the approach to enabling teachers to provide children the support they need for optimal development must combine a strong curriculum that provides guidance and structure, yet allows teachers the time and flexibility they need to engage children in extended conversations. For teachers to make the most of any curriculum and to use "teachable moments" effectively, they also need professional development geared to helping them understand why such interactions are powerful. For over 30 years, language researchers have known that children acquire language best when adults supply them with names for whatever they are interested in exploring. What matters is the *size* of a child's vocabulary, not whether it contains words describing rocks or vehicles or dinosaurs. No single program can specifically anticipate what any particular child or group of children might be interested in discussing. Only a teacher can respond to his or her students' emerging curiosity by supplying words. Only responsive, lively teachers can prevent reading difficulties by building children's vocabularies, phonological awareness, and love of stories read and told.

ACKNOWLEDGMENTS

The research discussed in this chapter is drawn from studies supported by the Spencer Foundation, the Agency for Children and Families (Grant Nos. 90CD0827 and 90YD0017), and the Office for Educational Research and Improvement (Award No. R305T990312-00). Work on this chapter was supported by Grant No. 90YD0094 from ACF and Award No. REC-9979948 from the Interagency Educational Research Initiative (IERI).

NOTES

1. We thank Ann Wolfe for her work on the analyses of this complex data set.
2. This is defined as follows: "the child initiates the conversation or has a significant amount of participation in the interaction (i.e., speaks more than once; speaks for a significant proportion of the conversation). There should be some occasion when different speakers take turns. . . . It could apply when there is a series of several questions asked by the teacher and the teacher listens to the child's response attentively" (Dickinson et al., 1998, p. 6).

REFERENCES

American Speech–Language–Hearing Association. (2002). *Communication facts: Special populations: Literacy—2002 edition.* Retrieved February 14, 2003, from *http://professional.asha.org/resources/factsheets/literacy.cfm*

Anderson, R. C., & Freebody, P. (1981). Vocabulary knowledge. In J. Guthrie (Ed.), *Comprehension and teaching: Research reviews* (pp. 77–117). Newark, DE: International Reading Association.

Barnes, S., Gutfreund, M., Satterly, D., & Wells, G. (1983). Characteristics of adult speech which predict children's language development. *Journal of Child Language, 10,* 6–84.

Barnett, W. S. (1995). Long-term effects of early childhood programs on cognitive and school outcomes. *The future of children: Long-term outcomes of early childhood programs, 5*(3), 25–50. Los Altos, CA: Center for the Future of Children, the David and Lucile Packard Foundation.

Barnett, W. S. (2001). Preschool education for economically disadvantaged children: Effects on reading achievement and related outcomes. In S. Neuman & D. K. Dickinson (Eds.), *Handbook of early literacy development* (pp. 421–443). New York: Guilford Press.

Baydar, N., Brooks-Gunn, J., & Furstenberg, F. F. (1993). Early warning signs of functional illiteracy: Predictors in childhood and adolescence. *Child Development, 64,* 815–829.

Beals, D. E. (2001). Eating and reading: Links between family conversations with preschoolers and later language and literacy. In D. K. Dickinson & P. O. Tabors (Eds.), *Beginning literacy with language* (pp. 75–92). Baltimore: Brookes.

Bear, D. R., Invernizzi, M., Templeton, S., & Johnston, F. (1996). *Words their way: Word study for phonics, vocabulary, and spelling.* Columbus, OH: Merrill.

Bishop, D. V. M., & Adams, C. (1990). A prospective study of the relationship between specific language impairment, phonological disorders and reading retardation. *Journal of Child Psychology and Psychiatry and Allied Disciplines, 31,* 1027–1050.

Bishop, D. V. M., & Edmundson, A. (1987). Language-impaired 4-year-olds: Distinguishing transient from persistent impairment. *Journal of Speech and Hearing Disorders, 52,* 156–173.

Burchinal, M. R., Roberts, J. E., Hooper, S., & Zeisel, S. A. (2000). Cumulative risk and early cognitive development: A comparison of statistical risk models. *Developmental Psychology, 36,* 793–807.

Campbell, F. A., & Ramey, C. T. (1994). Effects of early intervention on intellectual and academic achievement: A follow-up study of children from low-income families. *Child Development, 65,* 684–698.

Campbell, F. A., & Ramey, C. T. (1995). Cognitive and school outcomes for high-risk African-American student in middle adolescence: Positive effects of early intervention. *American Educational Research Journal, 32,* 743–772.

Catts, H. W., Fey, M. E., Zhang, X., & Tomblin, J. B. (1999). Language basis of reading and reading disabilities: Evidence from a longitudinal investigation. *Scientific Studies of Reading, 3,* 331–361.

Chall, J. & Dale, P. (1995). *Readability revisited: The new Dale–Chall readability formula.* Cambridge, MA: Brookline.

Clark-Chiarelli, N., Dickinson, D., Peisner-Feinberg, E., Anastasopoulos, L., Caswell, L., Sprague, K., et al. (2002, November). *The impact of the technology enhanced language environment enrichment program (T-LEEP): A collaboration among Education Development Center, Inc., Center for Applied Linguistics and Frank Porter Graham Child Development Center.* Poster session presented at the IERI Principal Investigator Conference, Alexandria, VA.

Clay, M. M. (1985). *The early detection of reading difficulties* (3rd ed.). Portsmouth, NH: Heinemann.

Clay, M. M. (1987). Learning to be learning disabled. *New Zealand Journal of Educational Studies, 22,* 155–173.

Cote, L. (2001). Language opportunities during mealtimes in preschool classrooms. In D. K. Dickinson & P. O. Tabors (Eds.), *Beginning language with literacy* (pp. 205–222). Baltimore: Brookes.

Cunningham, A. E., & Stanovich, K. E. (1997). Early reading acquisition and its relation to reading experience and ability 10 years later. *Developmental Psychology, 33,* 934–945.

Della Corte, M., Benedict, H., & Klein, D. (1983). The relationship of pragmatic dimensions of mothers' speech to the referential–expressive distinction. *Journal of Child Language, 10,* 35–44.

Dickinson, D. K. (1987). Oral language, literacy skills and response to literature. In J. Squire (Ed.), *The dynamics of language learning: Research in the language arts* (pp. 147–183). Urbana, IL: National Council of Teachers of English.

Dickinson, D. K. (1991). Teacher stance and setting: Constraints on conversation in preschools. In A. McCabe & C. Peterson (Eds.), *Developing narrative structure* (pp. 255–302). Hillsdale, NJ: Erlbaum.

Dickinson, D. K. (1994). Features of early childhood classrooms that support development of language and literacy. In J. Duchan, L. Hewitt, & R. Sonnenmeier (Eds.), *Pragmatics: From theory to practice* (pp. 185–201). Englewood Cliffs, NJ: Prentice-Hall.

Dickinson, D. K. (2001a). Book reading in preschool classrooms: Is recommended practice common? In D. K. Dickinson & P. O. Tabors (Eds.), *Beginning literacy with language: Young children learning at home and school* (pp. 175–203). Baltimore: Brookes.

Dickinson, D. K. (2001b). Putting the pieces together: The impact of preschool on children's language and literacy development in kindergarten. In D. K. Dickinson & P. O. Tabors (Eds.), *Beginning literacy with language: Young children learning at home and school* (pp. 257–287). Baltimore: Brookes.

Dickinson, D. K. (2001c). Large-group and free-play times: Conversational settings supporting language and literacy development. In D. K. Dickinson & P. O. Tabors (Eds.), *Beginning literacy with language: Young children learning at home and school* (pp. 223–255). Baltimore: Brookes Company.

Dickinson, D. K., Anastasopoulos, L., Miller, C., Caswell, L., & Peisner-Feinberg, E. (2002, April). *Enhancing preschool children's language, literacy and social development through an in-service professional development approach.* Paper presented at the annual conference of the American Educational Research Association, New Orleans, LA.

Dickinson, D. K., Howard, C., & Haines, R. (1998). *Teacher–Child Verbal Interaction Profile.* Unpublished coding manual. Newton, MA: Education Development Center.

Dickinson, D. K., & McCabe, A. (2001). Bringing it all together: The multiple origins, skills and environmental supports of early literacy. *Learning Disabilities Research and Practice, 16*(4), 186–202.

Dickinson, D. K., McCabe, A., Anastasopoulos, L., Peisner-Feinberg, E., & Poe, M. (2003). The comprehensive language approach to early literacy: The interrelationships among vocabulary, phonological sensitivity, and print knowledge among preschool-aged children. *Journal of Educational Psychology, 95,* 465–481.

Dickinson, D. K., & Smith, M. W. (1994). Long-term effects of preschool teachers' book readings on low-income children's vocabulary and story comprehension. *Reading Research Quarterly, 29,* 104–122.

Dickinson, D. K., & Tabors, P. O. (2001). *Beginning literacy with language: Young children learning at home and school.* Baltimore: Brookes.

Dickinson, D. K., & Tabors, P. O. (2002, March). Fostering language and literacy in classrooms and homes. *Young Children,* pp. 10–18.

Fazio, B. B., Naremore, R. C., & Connell, P. J. (1996). Tracking children from poverty at risk for specific language impairments: A 3-year longitudinal study. *Journal of Speech and Hearing Research, 39,* 611–624.

Feagans, L., & Appelbaum, M. I. (1986). Validation of language subtypes in learning disabled children. *Journal of Experimental Psychology, 78,* 358–364.

Fivush, R., & Fromhoff, F. A. (1988). Style and structure in mother–child conversations about the past. *Discourse Processes, 11,* 337–355.

Furrow, D., & Nelson, K. (1984). Environmental correlates of individual differences in language acquisition. *Journal of Child Language, 11,* 523–534.

Furrow, D., Nelson, K., & Benedict, H. (1979). Mothers' speech to children and syntactic development: Some simple relationships. *Journal of Child Language, 6,* 423–442.

Goldfield, B. A. (1987). The contributions of child and caregiver to referential and expressive language. *Applied Psycholinguistics, 8,* 267–280.

Good, R. III, Simmons, D. C., & Smith, S. (1998). Effective academic interventions in the United States: Evaluating and enhancing the acquisition of early reading skills. *School Psychology Review, 27,* 740–753.

Haden, C. A., & Fivush, R. (1996). Contextual variation in maternal conversational styles. *Merrill–Palmer Quarterly, 42,* 200–227.

Hampson, J., & Nelson, K. (1993). The relation of maternal language to variation in rate and style of language acquisition. *Journal of Child Language, 20,* 313–342.

Hanson, R. A., & Farrell, D. (1995). The long-term effects on high school seniors of learning to read in kindergarten. *Reading Research Quarterly, 30,* 908–933.

Hart, B., & Risley, T. (1995). *Meaningful differences in the everyday lives of American children.* Baltimore: Brookes.

Hoff-Ginsberg, E. (1986). Function and structure in maternal speech: Their relation to the child's development of syntax. *Developmental Psychology, 22,* 155–163.

Hoff-Ginsberg, E. (1991). Mother–child conversation in different social classes and communicative settings. *Child Development, 62,* 782–796.

Huttenlocher, J., Vasilyeva, M., Cymerman, E. & Levine, S. (2002). Language input and child syntax. *Cognitive Psychology, 45,* 337–374.

Iversen, S., & Tunmer, W. (1993). Phonological processing skills and the Reading Recovery program. *Journal of Educational Psychology, 85,* 112–126.

Juel, C. (1988). Learning to read and write: A longitudinal study of fifty-four children from first through fourth grade. *Journal of Educational Psychology, 80,* 437–447.

Layzer, J. I., Goodson, B. D., & Moss, M. (1993). *Life in preschool: Vol. 1. Final report to the U. S. Department of Education.* Cambridge, MA: Abt Associates, Inc.

Lyon, G. R. (1995). Research initiatives in learning disabilities: Contributions from scientists supported by the National Institute of Child Health and Development. *Journal of Child Neurology, 10*(Suppl. 1), S120–S126.

McCabe, A., & Peterson, C. (1991). Getting the story: A longitudinal study of parental styles in eliciting narratives and developing narrative skill. In A. McCabe & C. Peterson (Eds.), *Developing narrative structure* (pp. 217–254). Hillsdale, NJ: Erlbaum.

McCardle, P., Scarborough, H. S., & Catts, H. W. (2001). Predicting, explaining, and preventing children's reading difficulties. *Learning Disabilities Research and Practice, 16,* 230–239.

McCartney, K. (1984). Effect of quality of day care environment on children's language development. *Developmental Psychology, 20*(2), 244–260.

McGill-Franzen, A., & Allington, R. (1991). The gridlock of low reading achievement: Perspectives on practice and policy. *Remedial and Special Education, 12,* 20–30.

Menyuk, P., Chesnick, J., Liebergott, J. W., Korngold, B., D'Agostino, R., & Belanger, A. (1991). Predicting reading problems in at-risk children. *Journal of Speech and Hearing Research, 34,* 893–903.

Moats, L. (2000). *Speech to print: Language essentials for teachers.* Baltimore: Brookes.

Moats, L. C. (1999). *Teaching reading is rocket science: What expert teachers of reading should know and be able to do.* Washington, DC: American Federation of Teachers.

Morrow, L. M., & Gambrell, L. B. (2001). Literature-based instruction in the early years. In S. B. Neuman & D. K. Dickinson (Eds.), *Handbook of early literacy research* (pp. 348–360). New York: Guilford Press.

National Institute of Child Health and Human Development Early Child Care Research Network. (2000). The relation of child care to cognitive and language development. *Child Development, 71,* 960–980.

National Institute of Child Health and Human Development Early Child Care Research Network. (2002). Early child care and children's development prior to school entry: Results from the NICHD study of early child care. *American Educational Research Journal, 39*(1), 133–165.

National Center for Education Statistics. (2001). *The nation's report card: Fourth-grade reading 2000.* Jessup, MD: U.S. Department of Education.

National Reading Panel. (2000). Report of the National Reading Panel. Washington, DC: National Institute of Health and Development.

Nelson, K. (1973). Structure and strategy in learning to talk. *Monographs of the Society for Research in Child Development, 38*(Serial No. 149).

Nelson, K. (1981). Individual differences in language development: Implications for development and language. *Developmental Psychology, 17,* 170–187.

Newport, E. L., Gleitman, H., & Gleitman, L. R. (1977). Mother, I'd rather do it myself: Some effects and non-effects of maternal speech style. In C. E. Snow & C. Ferguson, (Eds.), *Talking to children: Language input and acquisition* (pp. 109–150). Cambridge, UK: Cambridge University Press.

Olsen-Fulero, L. (1982). Style and stability in mother conversational behavior: A study of individual differences. *Journal of Child Language, 9,* 543–564.

Peisner-Feinberg, E. S., & Burchinal, M. R. (1997). Relations between preschool children's child-care experiences and concurrent development: The Cost, Quality, and Outcomes Study. *Merrill–Palmer Quarterly, 43,* 451–477.

Peisner-Feinberg, E. S., Burchinal, M. R., Clifford, R. M., Culkin, M. L., Howes, C., Kagan, S. L., et al. (2001). The relation of preschool quality to children's cognitive and social developmental trajectories through second grade. *Child Development, 72,* 1534–1553.

Peterson, C., Jesso, B., & McCabe, A. (1999). Encouraging narratives in preschoolers: An intervention study. *Journal of Child Language, 26,* 49–67.

Pinnell, G. S. (1989). Reading recovery: Helping at risk children learn to read. *Elementary School Journal, 90,* 161–184.

Roach, K. A., & Snow, C. E. (2000, April). *What predicts 4th grade reading comprehension?* Paper presented at the annual conference of the American Education Research Association, New Orleans, LA.

Sameroff, A. J., Seifer, R., Baldwin, A., & Baldwin, C. (1993). Stability of intelligence from preschool to adolescence: The influence of social and family risk factors. *Child Development, 64,* 80–97.

Scarborough, H. (1989). Prediction of reading dysfunction from familial and individual differences. *Journal of Educational Psychology, 81,* 101–108.

Scarborough, H. (1990). Very early language deficits in dyslexic children. *Child Development, 61,* 1728–1734.

Scarborough, H. (1991). Early syntactic development of dyslexic children. *Annals of Dyslexia, 41,* 207–220.

Scarborough, H. (2001). Connecting early language and literacy to later reading (dis)abilities: Evidence, theory, and practice. In S. B. Neuman & D. K. Dickinson (Eds.), *Handbook of early literacy research* (pp. 97–110). New York: Guilford Press.

Schweinhart, L. J. Barnes, H. V., Weikart, D. P., Barnett, W. S., & Epstein, A. S. (1993). *Significant benefits: The High/Scope Perry Preschool Study through age 27* [Monographs of the High/Scope Educational Research Foundation, No. 10]. Ypsilanti, MI: High/Scope Press.

Shaywitz, S. E., Escobar, M. D., Shaywitz, B. A., Fletcher, J. M., & Makuch, R. W. (1992). Evidence that dyslexia may represent the lower tail of a normal distribution of reading ability. *New England Journal of Medicine, 326,* 145–150.

Siegel, L. S. (1998). Phonological processing deficits and reading disabilities. In J. L. Metsala & L. C. Ehri (Eds.), *Word recognition in beginning literacy* (pp. 141–161). Mahwah, NJ: Erlbaum.

Snow, C. E., Burns, S., & Griffin, P. (Eds.). (1998). *Preventing reading difficulties in young children.* Washington, DC: National Academy Press.

Snow, C. E., Perlman, R., & Nathan, D. (1987). Why routines are different: Toward a multiple-factors model of the relation between input and language acquisition. In K. Nelson & A. van Kleeck (Eds.), *Children's language* (Vol. 6, pp. 65–97). Hillsdale, NJ: Erlbaum.

Snow, C. E., Tabors, P. O., & Dickinson, D. K. (2001). Language development in the preschool years. In D. K. Dickinson & P. O. Tabors (Eds.), *Beginning literacy with language: Young children learning at home and school* (pp. 1–26). Baltimore: Brookes.

Stahl, S. A., & Fairbanks, M. (1986). The effects of vocabulary instruction: A model-based meta-analysis. *Review of Educational Research, 56,* 72–110.

Stahl, S. A. (2001). Teaching phonics and phonological awareness. In S. B. Neuman & D. K. Dickinson (Eds.), *Handbook of early literacy research* (pp. 333–347). New York: Guilford Press.

Stanovich, K. (1988). The right and wrong places to look for the locus of reading disabilities. *Annals of Dyslexia, 27,* 91–103.

Stanovich, K. E., & Siegel, L. S. (1994). Phenotypic performance profile of children with reading disabilities: A regression-based test of the phonological–core variable– difference model. *Journal of Educational Psychology, 86,* 24–53.

Tabors, P. O., Beals, D. & Weizman, Z. O. (2001). "You know what oxygen is?": Learning new words at home. In D. K. Dickinson & P. O. Tabors (Eds.), *Beginning literacy with language: Young children learning at home and school* (pp. 93–110). Baltimore: Brookes.

Tabors, P. O., Snow, C. E., & Dickinson, D. K. (2001). Homes and schools together: Supporting language and literacy development. In D. K. Dickinson & P. O. Tabors (Eds.), *Beginning literacy with language: Young children learning at home and school* (pp. 313–334). Baltimore: Brookes.

Tomasello, M., & Farrar, M. J. (1986). Joint attention and early language. *Child Development, 57,* 1454–1463.

Torgesen, J. K. (1998, Spring/Summer). Catch them before they fall. *American Educator,* pp. 32–41.

Torgesen, J. K. (2000). Individual differences in response to early intervention in reading: The lingering problem of treatment resisters. *Learning Disabilities Research and Practice, 15,* 55–64.

U.S. Department of Education. (2002). *Twenty-third annual report to Congress on the implementation of the Individuals with Disabilities Education Act.* Jessup, MD: Education Publications Center.

Vellutino, F. R., & Scanlon, D. M. (1998, April). *Research in the study of reading disability: What have we learned in the past four decades?* Paper presented at the annual conference of the American Educational Research Association, San Diego, CA.

Vellutino, F. R., & Scanlon, D. M. (2001). Emergent literacy skills, early instruction, and individual differences as determinants of difficulties in learning to read: The case for early intervention. In S. B. Neuman & D. K. Dickinson (Eds.), *Handbook of early literacy research* (pp. 295–321). New York: Guilford Press.

Vernon-Feagans, L., Hammer, C. S., Miccio, A., & Manlove, E. (2001). Early language and literacy skills in low-income African American and Hispanic children. In S. B. Neuman & D. K. Dickinson (Eds.), *Handbook of early literacy research* (pp. 192–210). New York: Guilford Press.

Walker, D., Greenwood, C., Hart, B., & Carta, J. (1994). Prediction of school outcomes based on early language production and socioeconomic factors. *Child Development, 65,* 606–621.

Wasik, B. A., & Slavin, R. E. (1993). Preventing early reading failure with one-to-one tutoring: A review of five programs. *Reading Research Quarterly, 28,* 178–200.

Whitehurst, G. J., Epstein, J. N., Angell, A. C., Payne, A. C., Crone, D. A., & Fischel, J. E. (1994). Outcomes of an emergent literacy intervention in Head Start. *Journal of Educational Psychology, 86,* 542–555.

Whitehurst, G. J., & Lonigan, C. J. (2001). Emergent literacy: Development from pre-readers to readers. In S. B. Neuman & D. K. Dickinson (Eds.), *Handbook of early literacy research* (pp. 11–29). New York: Guilford Press.

Wilcox-Herzog, A., & Kontos, S. (1998). The nature of teacher talk in early childhood classrooms and its relationship to children's play with objects and peers. *Journal of Genetic Psychology, 159*(1), 30–44.

11

Language Variation and Literacy Learning

HOLLY K. CRAIG
JULIE A. WASHINGTON

In this chapter, we discuss current understanding of the relationships between the literacy development of students and their linguistic status as speakers of African American English (AAE). AAE is a major type of language variation in the United States, and its relationship to literacy acquisition poses one of the most interesting and challenging issues facing educators today. Why aren't African American students reading better?

The focus of this chapter is on the difficulties confronting AAE-speaking students during literacy acquisition. These issues are not unique to this cultural linguistic community, however, but serve as a telling example of the relationships that can exist between linguistic variation, especially low-prestige differences from Standard American English (SAE), and a child's ability to read. In this chapter, we review important new findings that pertain to the language and literacy skills of African American students, discuss the difficulties that many African American children experience achieving basic literacy levels, and identify key issues for future research.

CHARACTERISTICS OF CHILD AAE

AAE is a systematic, rule-governed variation of English, spoken by descendants of former slaves in the United States (see Baugh, 2001, for a comprehensive discussion of the linguistic legacy of slavery). Not surprisingly, given the shared regional history between AAE and southern dialects of SAE, some features of AAE and SAE overlap. For many years, however, it has been clear that AAE and SAE are distinguishable (Fasold, 1981; Wolfram, 1974). The expansive set of features used by mature speakers of AAE evidences profound differences between AAE and SAE in terms of morphology, syntax, semantics, phonology, discourse, and prosody. As recently as 2001, LeMoine observed that "more often than not, African American language is viewed as slang, defective, or a corrupt form of English" (p. 171). Its status as a low-prestige dialect has important consequences. For example, teachers correct more dialectal miscues in reading than nondialectal ones (Cunningham, 1976–1977; Markham, 1984). Cecil (1988) found that teachers expected lower academic achievement, reading success, and intelligence from African American children who spoke AAE compared to a control group of African American peers who spoke SAE. Furthermore, teacher perceptions and expectations affect standardized achievement test data for African American students at a level much greater than that of their mainstream peers

228

(Entwisle & Alexander, 1988; Jussim, Eccles, & Madon, 1996).

Of foremost importance for educators and speech–language clinicians, most African American students are speakers of AAE and bring this heritage language to schooling. For example, using a continuous enrollment process from received consent forms in our research program at the University of Michigan, we found that every one of our one hundred 4- to 6-year-old African American students entering public schools in Metropolitan Detroit were speakers of AAE (Craig & Washington, 2002). Despite a large and rich literature undergirding our knowledge of adult AAE, until recently, very little was known about *child AAE*. The emerging literature that does characterize child AAE focuses primarily on the time of school entry and specifically on morpho-syntactic characteristics.

Morpho-Syntactic Characteristics of Child AAE

At school entry, preschool- and kindergarten-age African American students produce a variety of morpho-syntactic forms of AAE (Craig & Washington, 2002; Washington & Craig, 1994, 2002). They do not, however, use all of the forms that characterize adult AAE. Washington and Craig (2002) compared the morpho-syntactic types of AAE used by preschool, kindergarten, and first-grade students and their primary caregivers (most frequently, the biological mothers). The discourse of the children and their caregivers shared 23 morpho-syntactic forms of AAE, but these young children did not produce another three that were used by the adults. These three AAE forms were *completive done* ("I think we *done* ate enough"), *preterite had* ("You *had* got his toes stuck before"), and *resultative be done* ("We *be done* dropped these and broke them"). It is important to note that these forms require advanced knowledge of verb constituents, and it was not until the upper elementary grades that we observed the same forms produced by children. These findings underscore the need to examine the linguistic variations of children in their own right rather than assuming that adult and child forms will be the same, an insight that has been the cornerstone of the long-standing field of research in child language acquisition (Brown, 1973).

Table 11.1 lists the morpho-syntactic forms that one might expect to encounter in the discourse of school-age African American students, based on research over the last decade or so that has focused on the expressive language of children. Two forms of AAE occur most frequently, and this is the case for both children and their caregivers (Washington & Craig, 1994, 2002): *zero copula and auxiliary forms of the verb "to be"* ("Where __ the brush?") and *subject–verb agreement* ("Now she need_ some shoes").

Boys may be expected to produce significantly more AAE in their discourse than girls, almost twice the amount (Craig & Washington, 2002; Washington & Craig, 1998). Low socioeconomic status (LSES) appears related to greater levels of AAE for kindergartners (Washington & Craig, 1998). In addition, discourse genre influences the frequency of occurrence of AAE forms, such that genres that are more narrative or monologue-type tend to elicit more instances of child AAE (Washington, Craig, & Kushmaul, 1998). Increased levels of AAE can relate to increased levels of linguistic sophistication in young children. Craig and Washington (1994, 1995) found that preschoolers from low-income homes who were the heaviest dialect users compared to their peers, also used more complex syntactic and semantic forms during spontaneous discourse. This nascent line of research is a promising beginning, but many research questions remain. In particular, what additional extrinsic child variables influence morpho-syntactic variation in this population, and how do these forms change developmentally?

Phonological Characteristics of Child AAE

The empirical study of child AAE to date, focusing primarily on the morpho-syntactic characteristics of student discourse, remains quite incomplete. The phonological characteristics of child AAE must be understood as

TABLE 11.1. Morpho-Syntactic Types of Child AAE with Examples from African American Students in the Elementary Grades

Definition	Example
Ain't *Ain't* used as a negative auxiliary in *have + not, do + not, are + not,* and *is + not* constructions	"You <u>ain't</u> know that?"
Appositive pronoun Both a pronoun and a noun, or two pronouns, used to signify the same referent	"And the other people <u>they</u> wasn't."
Completive *done* *Done* used to emphasize a recently completed action	"<u>Done</u> set the fire."
Double marking Multiple agreement markers for regular nouns and verbs, and hypercorrection of irregulars	"He trie<u>s</u> to kill<u>s</u> him." "They are taking the poor <u>hitted</u> boy to a hospital"
Double copula/auxiliary/modal Two modal auxiliary forms used in a single clause	"You must <u>have didn't</u> know that."
Existential *it* *It* used in place of *there* to indicate the existence of a referent without adding meaning	"I think <u>it</u>'s a girl or a boy is yelling."
Fitna/sposeta/bouta Abbreviated forms coding imminent action	"He <u>fitna</u> be ten." "He <u>bouta</u> fall."
Preterite *had* *Had* appears before simple past verbs	"The car almost <u>had</u> broke his bike."
Indefinite article *A* used regardless of the vowel context	"He had <u>a</u> accident."
Invariant *be* Infinitival *be* coding habitual actions or states	"And they <u>be</u> cold."
Multiple negation Two or more negatives used in a clause	"It <u>not</u> raining <u>no</u> more."
Regularized reflexive pronoun *Hisself, theyself, theirselves* replace reflexive pronouns	"Bouta fall and trying to hold <u>hisself</u> back up."
Remote past *been* *Been* coding action in the remote past	"*I* <u>been</u> knew how to swim."
Subject–verb agreement Subjects and verbs differ in marking of number	"He feel_ cold."
Undifferentiated pronoun case Pronoun cases used interchangeably	"<u>Her</u> fell."
Zero article Articles variably included	"There was _ fire."

TABLE 11.1. *Continued*

Definition	Example
Zero copula/auxiliary Copula and auxiliary forms of the verb *to be* variably included	"He __ dead."
Zero *-ing* Present progressive *-ing* variably included	"The boy is scream___ help! help!"
Zero modal auxiliary *Will, can, do,* and *have* variably included as modal auxiliaries	"He might _____ been in the car."
Zero past tense *-ed* markers variably included on regular past verbs, and present forms of irregulars used	"They were taking him into the ambulance when he crash__ into the car."
Zero plural *-s* variably included to mark number	"And those saying something with the book_ in their hands."
Zero possessive Possession coded by word order so *-s* is deleted or the case of possessive pronouns is changed	"He left somebody__ books on the steps." "They got <u>they</u> two book."
Zero preposition Prepositions variably included	"They were playing _____ iceskates."
Zero *to* Infinitival *to* variably included	"That man right there getting ready _ slip on his one foot."

Note. Data from Craig et al. (in press); Washington and Craig (1994, 2002).

well. Characterizing child AAE in terms of its phonological features is challenging for a number of reasons. First, it is important to discern which linguistic variations represent phonological forms of child AAE and which are developmental sound production patterns. Seymour and Seymour (1981), in one of the few studies examining the phonological patterns of African American children, compared the consonant errors of AAE- and SAE-speaking 4- and 5-year-olds, and were unable to identify unique patterns by dialectal group. Both groups evidenced consonant production errors that were more likely developmental in nature, for example, simplification of consonant clusters (*and* /ænd/ changes to *an* /æn/). Only quantitative differences between groups were observed. Consistent with the results of Seymour and Seymour, Haynes and Moran (1989) found increased frequencies of final consonant deletions for AAE compared to SAE speakers. They examined responses to formal testing at each of grades preschool through third and convincingly demonstrated the importance of considering the context of maturational development when searching for AAE features. In particular, the mean number of final consonant deletions decreased from 8.02 at preschool to 3.36 at third grade.

Cluster reduction is a major phonological form of AAE for adults, and its identification in child AAE exemplifies the problem researchers and practitioners face in distinguishing developmental from dialectal patterns. For young children, the process of cluster reduction usually reflects the difficulties inherent in coordinating complex motor movements between different places (e.g., front /p/[1] from back /k/ sounds) and manners of articulation (e.g., stops /k/ from fricatives /h/). When comparing young AAE and SAE speakers, therefore, it is not surprising that Seymour and Seymour (1981), for example, found that both groups evidenced cluster reduction, and that this phonological process was not uniquely attributable to AAE.

A number of large-scale, phonologically based, prevention programs have shown significant improvements in later outcomes for children at risk for reading failure (Brown & Felton, 1990; Foorman, Francis, Fletcher, Schatschneider, & Mehta, 1998; Torgesen et al., 1999; Vellutino et al., 1996; Whitehurst et al., 1994). Appreciable numbers of African American students have participated in most of these investigations. African American students represented 50% of the participants in the Brown and Felton (1990), 52% of the participants in the Torgesen et al. (1999), and 45% of the participants in the Whitehurst et al. (1994) prevention studies. At the time of these studies, the programs were built on understandings of the phonological awareness of mainstream children.

Unfortunately, most reports of these programs do not separate performance outcomes for the African American students, so it is not clear how successful they have been for the African American cohort of the participant samples. On a national level, African American students are overrepresented in the lowest levels of literacy achievement (Grigg, Daane, Jin, & Campbell, 2003) and, accordingly, may be the children who cluster in the low tail of the performance distributions in these prevention programs as well. Consistent with this view, Foorman et al. (1998) did disaggregate the performances of the African American students participating in their program, and reported significantly lower expected scores for them than for the sample average in word reading after a year's enrollment. Perhaps instructional strategies for African American students need to be distinguished from those designed for SAE-speaking students.

In our own research program at the University of Michigan, African American elementary school children often produced cluster reductions while reading aloud; for example, students changed the word *find* to *fine* by reducing the /nd/ to /n/. However, the same students created phonological clusters by saying /ɪts/, the result of contracting *it is* into *it's*. Accordingly, it is a straightforward matter to assume that an African American student in the elementary grades who reduces clusters is using this AAE feature and not evidencing motor sequencing limitations, particularly when he or she also demonstrates the volitional motor control required to create phonological clusters that express morpho-syntactic relationships. It is probably inappropriate, however, to make the same assumption for young children who developmentally are still gaining motor control, even though consonant cluster reduction is a major feature of the dialect.

It is also important to distinguish phonological forms of child AAE from a student's vocabulary limitations. Labov, Baker, Bullock, Ross, and Brown (1998) attempted to classify the reading errors of 20 African American second and third graders from West Philadelphia. Although thought provoking, their results are difficult to interpret because phonology was considered in relative isolation from other aspects of oral language, particularly without consideration of the student's vocabulary knowledge. For example, they report that *globes* was produced as *globs* and *trout* as *throat,* and so forth. It is not clear that variations from print such as these are the result of phonological features of child AAE. They may better represent a failure to recognize the printed word during decoding, and the consequent search and substitution of a known word from the student's own lexicon. More work like that of Labov and colleagues for child AAE needs to be done, and research of this type would benefit from considering phonology in concert with other key components of the child's developing linguistic system.

THE BLACK–WHITE ACHIEVEMENT GAP AND ITS PRECURSORS

African American students are much more likely than their majority peers to fail to obtain basic levels of literacy. The prevalence of reading below basic levels is much greater for African American than for majority students, 60% compared to 25%, whereas majority students were much more likely than African American students to read at or above basic levels, 75% compared to 40% on the 2002 administration of the National Assessment of Educational Progress (NAEP) (Grigg et al., 2003). Good reading comprehension is foundational to learning across the academic content areas. It is not surprising, therefore, that African American students' performance is significantly lower than that of majority students in science, math, and geography (Grigg et al., 2003). Labeled the "black–white test score gap" (Jencks & Phillips, 1998), this disparity is measurable at school entry and continues through 12th grade (Phillips, Crouse, & Ralph, 1998). Moreover, recorded as early as 1910 (Fishback & Baskin, 1991), the black–white achievement gap has persistently spanned generations of U.S. stu-

dents. Lower levels of academic achievement for African American students translate into lower adult literacy levels, lower earnings, higher levels of unemployment, and higher rates of poverty (Sable, 1998). Current explanations for the gap have focused on a number of child external variables, particularly the role of poverty in low achievement and the nature of early literacy learning experiences for African American students.

The Role of Poverty

Poverty and the density of associated risk factors faced by many African American children have been implicated in the black–white achievement gap. Table 11.2 compares key indicators for the economic, social, and educational well-being of African American children to those of their Hispanic and white peers. Of note, African American children are more than three times as likely as their white peers to live in

TABLE 11.2. Selected Risk Factors by Population Segment

	Black, non-Hispanic	Hispanic	White, non-Hispanic
Population			
% of U.S. children	15	16	64
Family backgrounds and socioeconomic status			
% of children in two-parent home	38	65	77
% of children living in poverty	30	27	9
% of children with a parent working full time all year	65	73	84
% of mothers with a bachelor's-level education	8	8	20
% of fathers with a bachelor's-level education	5	9	23
% of low-birthweight infants	13.1	6.5	6.8
Rate of adolescent births per 1,000	45	53	14
Schools and educational readiness			
% of 3- to 5-year-olds read to every day	48	42	64
% of 3- and 4-year-olds identifying all colors	63	55	84
% of 3- and 4-year-olds recognizing all letters	16	9	21
% of 3- and 4-year-olds counting to 50 or higher	14	13	7
% of 3- and 4-year-olds writing first name	42	37	48
% of 3- and 4-year-olds holding pencil properly	94	91	90
% of 3- and 4-year-olds writing and drawing	67	55	65
% of children 5 years and older owning fewer than 10 books	27	31	3
% of children 5 years and older owning more than 50 books	13	19	47

Note. Data from the Federal Interagency Forum on Child and Family Statistics (2003); Nettles and Perna (1997).

poverty, and are more likely to live in families in which the levels of parental education are lower than for majority children. Poverty and low levels of literacy tend to co-occur, and without doubt, many African American students are impacted by these family socioeconomic characteristics.

Although widely implicated, poverty and its covariables are not a sufficient explanation for the reading failure experienced by so many African American students. Thompson (2003) examined the reading skills of fourth-grade, urban, African American students from Metropolitan Seattle and found that some students from both low (LSES)- and middle-socioeconomic-status (MSES) homes were performing at high levels, one standard deviation or more above the mean, on the Woodcock Reading Mastery Tests—Revised (Woodcock, 1987), a major standardized test of reading. Furthermore, both LSES and MSES African American students were members of the cohort scoring at the lowest levels on this test as well. These findings are consistent with an earlier report by Singham (1998), who found that reading performances of MSES African American students were more comparable to those of LSES students than to MSES white students. LSES no more predestines an African American child to reading failure than MSES guarantees positive reading outcomes. Accordingly, it will be important for the planning of prevention and intervention programs appropriate for African American students to disambiguate the effects of poverty and its covariables from other barriers specific to literacy learning.

Although poverty and its covariables can have profound adverse effects on a child's well-being, recent research indicates that formal public preschool experience may mitigate some of these effects for literacy learning. Craig, Connor, and Washington (2003) followed the reading comprehension growth of two cohorts of African American students observed at Time 1 as either preschoolers or kindergartners. The preschoolers were all LSES, enrolled in a state-funded public preschool for children at risk, whereas the kindergartners were all from MSES homes in the same communities, with no public

preschool experiences. At first grade, the Time 1 LSES preschoolers were performing as well as the Time 1 MSES kindergartners on the Reading Comprehension portion of the Metropolitan Achievement Tests (1993), and by second and third grades, the Time 1 LSES preschoolers were outperforming the Time 1 MSES kindergartners. By third grade, the Time 1 MSES kindergartners evidenced a 1-year lag in performance expectations on the MAT, whereas the Time 1 LSES preschoolers approximated grade-level expectations. Examination of the language skills of the preschoolers at the time of entry into public school education indicated that levels of complex syntax production and skills in abstract pattern-matching skills were positive predictors for the later outcomes in reading comprehension.

Storybook Reading

Home-based storybook reading, vocabulary, letter knowledge, and phonological awareness are four strong early predictors of later reading success. Each skill is fundamentally linguistic in nature. Students from diverse cultural backgrounds, who speak a different linguistic variety of English, therefore, may not begin formal schooling with the same skills on these predictors as their mainstream peers. Thus, students who speak a minority language such as AAE may be misunderstood if their potential for reading success is measured by one of these four linguistic predictor variables. Yet if these predictors index prerequisite or precursory skills, differences between minority language users and their mainstream peers may signify the potential for reading failure and must be understood.

Opportunities for home-based storybook reading in particular, and family literacy practices overall, predict later reading skills in the general population (Bus, van IJzendoorn, & Pelligrini, 1995; Scarborough & Dobrich, 1994). However, minority families may adopt a different style of literacy practices than the mainstream in part to preserve cultural identity (Heath, 1983; Ogbu, 1988). Indeed, home literacy practices differ in substantial ways between the families of most African American students and their mainstream peers. African American preschoolers are less likely to be read to on a daily basis and likely own fewer books (see Table 11.2). The reading of storybook texts is a common and early primary form of literacy exposure for mainstream children (DeTemple, 2001; Whitehurst & Lonigan, 2001). Alternatively, for many young African American children, environmental print (e.g., names on signs, trademarks, etc.) represents a first and important form of literacy experience. For example, we recently met a 4-year-old African American boy who, although not yet able to spell his name, recognized the Nike trademark symbol and readily spelled *Nike.*

Instead of joint storybook reading, storytelling in African American homes often takes the form of oral, collaborative, fictionalized narratives (Heath, 1983; Vernon-Feagans, 1996). For African American children, storytelling and book reading do not invite the question–response routines so characteristic of the parent–child joint storybook reading experienced by most young majority children (Anderson-Yockel & Haynes, 1994; Hammer, 1999; Pelligrini, Perlmutter, Galda, & Brody, 1990). Of course, interactive questioning and responding around storytelling also characterize early literacy exchanges in classrooms. All of these characteristics of African American home literacy practices, although acculturating, positive, and enjoyable, are not a close fit to the expectations that the typical African American child will face in classrooms (Feagans & Haskins, 1986). Vernon-Feagans, Hammer, Miccio, and Manlove (2001) suggest that "school systems meet parents halfway" (p. 201), because literacy practices are tied to cultural beliefs. As a nation, if we truly value cultural diversity, it is inappropriate and unrealistic to ask families to change the cultural practices of their homes in fundamental ways, especially in terms of those aspects that are self-defining. Are there bridges between home and school that might facilitate these literacy transitions?

In designing early school-based approaches to literacy instruction, it will be important to consider the ways in which environmental print conforms to or differs from print and spelling conventions in early texts. For example, Labov et al. (1998) observed that African American second and third graders do not adhere to the silent-e rule when reading. A robust vowel rule with few exceptions, the silent-e rule requires that [e] is not pronounced following consonant singletons in final word positions, and the vowel preceding the consonant is pronounced in its long-vowel form. For example, the word *bake* is read and pronounced with [e] silent, and [a] as /e/. If the silent-e rule were not applied, *back* and *bake* would be homophones. Labov et al. reported that for their second and third graders, 90% of the contexts in which the silent-e rule should have applied were in error. The silent-e rule has validity only in a printed medium, so children whose oral environments include names such as Kwame (pronounced /kwame/ or /kwami/) may experience final [e] in a first, a frequent, and indeed prototypical sense as a non-silent [e]. It is interesting to speculate that a child who can pronounce and spell *Nike,* and perhaps has an older sibling named Kwame may not sound out words such as *like* and *blame* the same way as their SAE-speaking peers. Furthermore, if the articulated nonsilent [e] is the typical form experienced within a child's environment, then in any practical sense, it is the "rule" and the silent-e rule will be the exception. Linguistically, most exceptions to general rules develop later than the more broadly generalized prototype (e.g., irregular verbs compared to the general rules governing regular verb forms) and may be acquired slowly over an extended period, and then one exemplar at a time. The silent-e rule may be especially problematic for African American students during literacy acquisition because it does not conform to their linguistic prototype, and as an irregular, is likely to be acquired over a protracted period of time and on a case-by-case basis for specific lexical items. It is possible that other printed regularities are experienced as exceptions by dialect speakers as well, and we need to improve our understanding of them.

Phonological Awareness

Successful readers must understand the relationship between spoken sounds and letters, so that they can sound out words and thereby associate their pronunciations with words in their vocabularies. Of early literacy skills, therefore, phonological awareness, letter knowledge, and vocabulary development are crucial component skills. These skills have their roots in home literacy, and in early preschool and kindergarten experiences.

Phonological awareness is a strong predictor of later reading achievement (Bus & van IJzendoorn, 1999; Bus et al., 1995; Hecht, Burgess, Torgesen, Wagner, & Rashotte, 2000; Torgesen, Wagner, Rashotte, Burgess, & Hecht, 1997). To begin to read, children must grasp that graphemes correspond to phonemes, and they must develop an awareness that language has a phonological structure (Adams, 1990). Only recently has a phonological feature scoring taxonomy been formalized for children (Craig, Thompson, Washington, & Potter, 2003). Investigation of the phonological awareness skills of African American students has awaited information on the child phonological AAE feature system. Unfortunately, therefore, at this time we know virtually nothing about the phonological awareness skills of African American students. In the absence of basic information about the phonological features of child AAE and their developmental course, the examination of phonological awareness skills will remain incomplete. Urban children in particular, with street and playground rhymes, contemporary rap, and hip-hop influences as part of their background knowledge, in principle should have the potential to perform successfully on traditional tasks designed to assess early phonological awareness skills, such as rhyming. However, without prompts that either mirror the phonological structure of child AAE or, alternatively, are noncontrastive with AAE, current approaches to assessing phonological awareness will fail with most African American students. For example, if a young African American child is asked to select the "rhyme" for a word like *stole* /stol/ from pictured stimulus prompts of *coal* /kol/ and *cold* /kold/, the choice would be unclear. When the prompt is spoken by an SAE-speaker and the child's

strategy is to say the words to him- or herself, because of cluster reduction, both choices would be noncontrastive and sound the same (/kol/ substitutes for both). The child's response then would likely be to say, "I don't know," or guess. What difficulties would an AAE-speaking student experience if enrolled in a reading program that required him or her to "say the sounds that are different" in SAE minimal word pairs that are dialect homophones and not different phonologically for most speakers of AAE?

Letter Knowledge

Letter knowledge appears to be the strongest single predictor of later reading achievement (Scarborough, 1998). Labov et al. (1998) found no evidence of limited letter knowledge in the performances of the second- and third-grade African American students participating in their oral reading tasks. Adams (1990) notes that better letter knowledge reflects increased knowledge of print and other types of literacy materials. For the African American student who has considerable knowledge of environmental print, limited letter knowledge may not be a contributing factor to his or her literacy acquisition in terms of recognizing letters and naming them. However, phonemes may not map onto graphemes for these same African American readers the way they do for mainstream children, if the sound and letter correspondences for the AAE speakers vary in significant ways. The students may be able to name the letters of the alphabet readily but connect the graphemes to phonemes in nonmainstream ways. For example, in our research program, we have found that many of our African American elementary grade students pronounce *frequently* (/frikɛntli/) as though the [qu] were a /k/. When names like Kwame are pronounced such that the [kw] is /kw/ and the [qu] in Dominique (/damInik/) and Quraun (/kɣan/) is pronounced as /k/, variations from text are easily explained and predictable. Others have emphasized the positive influence of lyrical, commemorative, kinship and African names, often spelled with non-SAE renderings, on African American students (Lieberson & Mikelson, 1995; Smith, 1996). It is the case (Federal Interagency Forum on Child and Family Statistics, 2003), that African American children differ only minimally from mainstream peers in their ability to write their name at the time of school entry (see Table 11.2). Perhaps the inherent importance of cultural–linguistic given names in a young African American child's environment make their spellings especially salient, and thereby impact the child's early approaches to decoding in systematic and nonstandard ways.

Vocabulary

Larger vocabularies relate positively to later reading success (Nation & Snowling, 1998; Snow, Burns, & Griffin, 1998). African American students evidence the same performance gaps on measures of vocabulary as they do in other areas of academic achievement (Bracken, Sabers, & Insko, 1987; Washington & Craig, 1992). Improved understanding of these vocabulary differences has been hindered by biased assessment instruments. For example, in an examination of the performances of young, at-risk African American preschoolers and kindergartners on the Peabody Picture Vocabulary Test—Revised (PPVT-R; Dunn & Dunn, 1981), Washington and Craig (1992) found that not only were the mean scores low but there was also very little statistical spread in student performances. Despite the application of a generous scoring adjustment in which 16 items missed by more than half of the children were given scoring credit, most students scored at least one standard deviation below the standard score mean of 100. Only 9% of the sample scored above the mean. We concluded that the revised version of this widely used test discriminated against children from differing cultural, linguistic, and economic backgrounds. Phillips, Brooks-Gunn, Duncan, Klebanov, and Crane (1998) reported a significant gap between African American and majority peers on the PPVT-R as well, and attributed the discrepancies to demographic differences in the student cohorts, in particular, family income, household size, and so on. Overall, very little is understood about the vocabu-

lary skills of African American students beyond knowing that the black–white achievement gap encompasses this aspect of linguistic achievement as it does others.

It is not surprising that many young African American children evidence differences in vocabulary from mainstream peers given that their preliteracy experiences are so different. If storybooks contribute to the breadth of a child's vocabulary (Whitehurst & Lonigan, 2001), then children with limited early exposure to stories will not share the vocabularies of those with greater exposure. This does not necessarily mean that the size of the vocabularies differ, but any assessment instrument built on assumptions around word exposure from texts will penalize the performance of students acquiring words in other domains, such as environmental print. Therefore, poor performances on standardized tests of vocabulary breadth may be assessing the currency of a child's vocabulary in the sense of its usefulness for academic purposes as much as its size. Furthermore, the role of poverty, lower educational attainment of caregivers, and limited literacy skills for important adult models in an African American child's life will all contribute to a child's limited word knowledge. Consistent with this view, Washington and Craig (1999) found that the children of caregivers with less than a high school graduation level had significantly lower vocabulary scores on the more culture-fair PPVT-III (Dunn & Dunn, 1997) compared to children whose primary caregiver was a high school or college graduate.

THE IMPACT OF AAE ON LITERACY ACQUISITION

Reading

The role of AAE in the literacy acquisition of African American students was the focus of considerable early inquiry. With rare exceptions (Bartel & Axelrod, 1973), the general consensus of these studies was that African American students produced AAE during oral reading tasks, but dialect was unrelated to reading comprehension. This finding was robust across studies for students as early as first grade and extending through ninth grade (e.g., Rystrom, 1973–1974; Steffensen, Reynolds, McClure, & Guthrie, 1982). Dialect appeared unrelated for studies focusing only on morphosyntactic features (Gemake, 1981; Simons & Johnson, 1973; Steffensen et al., 1982), only on phonological features (Hart, Guthrie, & Winfield, 1980; Melmed, 1973; Rystrom, 1973–1974; Seymour & Ralabate, 1985), or both (Goodman & Buck, 1973; Harber, 1977). Not surprisingly in the context of so much agreement and failure to find important relationships between AAE features and reading comprehension, little additional research has focused on the potential role of AAE in literacy acquisition since the mid-1980s.

This prior research was handicapped, however, by its dependence on adult AAE as a theoretical framework and source of information on specific features for examination. For the most part, these earlier studies adopted a feature-based approach to the search for AAE-reading linkages, examining in particular zero past, variations in the inclusion–exclusion of the third-person subject–verb agreement inflection, and consonant cluster reduction. Specific features were selected from extant information

about adult dialect usage, and children's reading comprehension was then examined for relationships to these selected features. Although the study of selected features continues (e.g., Green, 1995), it is likely that information of this type will contribute only to our linguistic understandings of the ways the features operate, and provide little insight into the ways that children acquire language and literacy skills as AAE speakers. We are in a better situation now to use child-centered information, and the importance of a potential AAE-reading linkage warrants revisiting these issues. Viewing child AAE as an expansive set of features may be more productive than probing features in isolation from each other.

Table 11.3 presents an example of an oral reading passage from the Gray Oral Reading Test—3rd Edition (GORT-3; Wiederholt, & Bryant, 1992) by a third-grade African American boy with good/average scores on language and cognitive tests. This student is from an LSES home in Metropolitan Detroit. Like many of the students in our research program, his reading of this passage includes AAE features. Indeed, of 64 second- through fifth-grade urban, African American students, 60 of them, representing 94% of the sample, read passages from the GORT-3

TABLE 11.3. The Oral Reading of Passage B-4 from the GORT-III, by a Typically Developing Third-Grade African American Boy

Story	AAE features
One bright summer day a young boy <u>and</u> his grandmother walked $\qquad$ /æn/ to a nearby pond to fish. The boy's grandmother showed him how	CCR
to put worms on the hook so they would not come off. For a long	
while they sat quietly waiting for the fish to bite. Suddenly the boy	
got a good bite. As he tried to land the fish, he became so excited	
that he <u>dropped</u> his pole into the water. The fish quickly swam $\qquad$ /drɑp/ away with it, and soon the pole had disappeared. The boy looked	CCR/ZPST
wide-eyed at his grandmother. <u>Then</u> they both had a good laugh. /waɪd-aɪzɛd/ $\qquad$ /dɛn/	STH

Note. AAE variations from print are <u>underlined</u>, and all spoken changes are indicated on the line below. CCR, consonant cluster reduction; ZPST, zero past tense; STH, substitution of [th].

aloud using AAE features at various points (Craig, Thompson, Washington, & Potter, in press). Table 11.3 shows that, for this child, three of the four variations from print reflect the operation of an AAE feature. Scoring this rendering in a strict manner, in other words considering each of the four variations as "deviations" from print, yields an accuracy score on the GORT-3 of 2 for this passage, a performance at the low end of the rate and accuracy continuum. However, scoring only the one variation that was not consistent with AAE as a "deviation" (*wide-eyed* said /waɪd-aɪzɛd/) yields an accuracy score of 4, a much improved performance. Consistent with the prior literature from the 1970s and 1980s, when one considers the large number of potential opportunities for the production of a morpho-syntactic or phonological feature of AAE within this passage, the effect of the dialect was limited. The effect was measurable, however, and underscores the need for test examiners to be sensitive to variations from print that may be dialect-driven rather than the result of a reading problem. Consistent with the prior literature from the 1970s and 1980s, despite use of dialectal features during oral reading, comprehension of the passages was acceptable in that three of this student's five responses were correct. Furthermore, there was no clear pattern of correct responding relative to question type; the student responded correctly to both the factual question and to half of the inferential questions. However, like many students participating in our research program, this student was a very slow reader. It took him 82 seconds to read this paragraph, a rate at the very low end of the expected time continuum. This student seems to have made a trade-off between achieving SAE accuracy as a dialect speaker and rate (Craig et al., in press). It will be important to understand, when children make an accuracy–rate trade-off, whether there are additional associated costs, especially relative to performances on standardized tests that often have time constraints.

Spelling

Most of the literature on the impact of AAE on literacy has focused on reading, and the complementary study of writing is scant. Although there is an increasing interest in oral narrative generation by African American students and its unique cultural–linguistic characteristics (see the review by Bloome, Champion, Katz, Morton, & Muldrow, 2001), the potentially more informative context for examining the specific impact of AAE is in written word generation skills, particularly spelling. Only a few studies have examined the written spelling of African American children, and again, these were early studies conducted in the 1970s. Major methodological problems make these studies difficult to interpret (see the review and critique by Scott & Rogers, 1996), with the exception of a study by Kligman and Cronnell (1974), which found that AAE-speaking second graders were likely to make dialect-related spelling errors. Focusing on six specific features, they found that the African American students made three times the number of spelling errors of the white students, and five times the number of errors on words that could take a dialect feature, most frequently changing the word to the dialectal form. They also found that the features were not equally likely to create a spelling variation for these students, such that final consonants were most affected, whereas deletion of the past tense was the least affected of the six features. Comparing spoken to written production of these features, Kligman and Cronnell also observed that oral productions did not directly relate to written productions of the same features. In particular, all clusters were candidates for deletion during speaking, but those functioning grammatically as the past tense were more likely to be deleted during writing (e.g., *crossed* was written as *cross*). DeStefano (1972) made a similar observation for fifth graders, finding differences in the distributions of AAE features between spoken and written language samples. AAE verb features were increased in speaking compared to writing, whereas noun features were more prevalent during writing. Although of limited number, these studies suggest that the role of dialect during writing warrants further study. The methodology of Windsor, Scott, and Street (2000) provides a potentially valuable model for within-child comparisons of oral and written contexts.

To illustrate these issues, Table 11.4 presents a sample of spontaneous writing by a third-grade African American boy with good/average scores on language and cognitive tests, in this case from an MSES home in Metropolitan Detroit, when asked to write a story. In this sample, of 18 variations from SAE orthography, 11 are likely attributable to AAE. In other words, even at third grade, approximately half of this student's nonstandard sentence structure and spellings reflected changes to AAE. Although most words were still produced consistent with SAE, the AAE variations are

highly salient, and the broader impact of these salient forms is unknown. Our understanding of child AAE and literacy achievement will remain critically incomplete in the absence of information about the impact of AAE in writing.

DIRECTIONS FOR FUTURE RESEARCH

Considered as a whole, the last three decades of research convincingly demonstrate that no single variable will likely explain the black–white achievement gap, particularly for literacy. As this chapter indicates, there is still much to be learned

TABLE 11.4. A Spontaneous Writing Sample by a Third-Grade Typically Developing African American Boy

Story

AAE features

1 = Zero possessive	7 = Subject–verb agreement
2 = Preterite *had*	8 = Consonant cluster movement
3 = Subject–verb agreement	9 = Consonant cluster movement or reduction
4 = /t/ for /θ/	10 = Zero possessive
5 = Double marking	11 = Subject–verb agreement
6 = Subject–verb agreement	

Note. All spelling variations from SAE orthography are underlined, and those consistent with AAE features are numbered and identified.

about child AAE, and about the ways in which this source of linguistic variation affects literacy acquisition. As we improve our understanding of child AAE, we may find that dialect influences literacy acquisition and is one of the variables requiring consideration. It is also likely, however, that the role of AAE will be different than previously conceptualized. Prior research demonstrating that individual AAE features were not causally related to reading comprehension does not preclude that being a speaker of AAE presents formidable challenges when acquiring SAE forms of literacy.

In this chapter, we have suggested that, based on past lessons, it is unlikely that future research will discover a direct link between isolated features and reading failure. Variables relating to home literacy practices and to the risk factors faced by significant numbers of African American students warrant further investigation. In addition, it may be the case that measures sensitive to being a speaker of AAE in a more global sense are better predictors of the likelihood that typically developing AAE speakers will readily acquire important literacy skills. In our research program, we have found it useful to determine the child's level of dialect use with a fairly global measure, designated the *dialect density measure* (DDM; Craig, Washington, & Thompson-Porter, 1998). DDM varies systematically with gender, SES, and discourse genre (Washington & Craig, 1998; Washington et al., 1998). DDM varies considerably among children even when the students are fairly homogeneous in terms of background characteristics (Washington & Craig, 1994). Of note, the children do not vary in the specific types of features they use, only in the frequencies with which the shared features are produced during discourse. It seems important to determine the relationship between dialect density and literacy acquisition. Are heavier dialect users having more difficulty matching their phonemes and morphemes to graphemes and vocabulary? Is the development of decoding skills and text comprehension complicated by more densely produced features in oral language? It will be important in framing these questions to look for positive relationships, and to recall that

African American students that at the time of school entry are the heaviest dialect users are the most linguistically sophisticated students overall (Craig & Washington, 1994, 1995).

Overall, our challenge is to think more broadly and comprehensively about the student who is an AAE speaker and the processes involved in literacy acquisition. Our approaches must address the multifaceted components of being raised as an AAE speaker in an AAE-speaking community. Vernon-Feagans et al. (2001) noted that most research with African American children from low-income homes has isolated a few variables for study rather than considering combinations of explanations and their interactions. Recalling the proposals of Rutter (1987) and Sameroff, Seifer, Barocas, Zax, and Greenspan (1987), Vernon-Feagans and colleagues (2001) suggest that it may be instructive to view the causes of low achievement from the perspective of a "cumulative risk model." Accordingly, a child faced with only one barrier to literacy acquisition may not be at risk for reading difficulties, whereas a child facing multiple barriers may be. An AAE-speaking African American child entering school from an LSES home, with limited exposure to literacy materials of any type, and faced with a teacher who has low expectations for him or her, is at high risk for reading failure compared to the child who faces only one of these barriers. Conceivably, these risk factors may "load" at different levels for different developmental stages and for various educational tasks.

As future research addresses these issues, informative heuristics must be identified to guide this work. The work of the great linguist Kenneth Pike (1967) offers one such analytical framework. Pike differentiated between two types of analytical units beneficial to the development of taxonomies of linguistic behavior. Etic units were those available in advance and emic units were those determined during analysis. Consideration of both levels of analysis has been invaluable when identifying and describing new ways to characterize child language behaviors in the past (Bloom & Lahey, 1978) and, more recently, when identifying the morpho-syntactic characteristics of child AAE (Washington & Craig, 1994, 2002). Essentially, the etic–emic approach can be conceptualized as describing child language behaviors initially in terms of a preexisting referent (the etic phase), often the mature adult form of the linguistic system of interest. Next, any behaviors not observed that were available a priori from the preexisting system are identified, and any behaviors unaccounted for are categorized as unique child features (the emic phase). The success of the etic–emic approach in providing comprehensive taxonomies recommends the approach to the study of child AAE at this time, when it is so critical to advance our understanding of more than the morpho-syntactic characteristics.

Recently, for example, we formalized a taxonomy for the phonological features produced by child AAE speakers. Essentially, we started with what we already know about the phonological characteristics of adult AAE and compared child productions using this etic approach. Fortunately, Stockman (1996) started this process, providing a comprehensive list of potential phoneme changes by AAE speakers, at the level of the phoneme, and based largely on the published descriptions of adult AAE speakers. Next, it was important to conceptualize the approximately 60 forms she identified into a manageable set, to determine which of these mature forms of AAE are apparent in child discourse and which are not, to probe for any forms that appear to be uniquely child-based, and to explore the course of their developmental changes. We examined the sound patterns of second- through fifth-grade African American students while reading aloud passages from the GORT-3. The etic portion of the process required identification of all variations from print, then determination of AAE features as identified in the work of others, primarily Stockman (1996). By examining the sound patterns of elementary-grade students, we avoided the potential confounds of motor immaturity faced by Seymour and Seymour (1981), and our use of text made the intended target unambiguous for interpretation of the children's responses. Table 11.5 lists the phonological child AAE forms we

found in our examinations of variations from print by elementary-grade African American students (Craig, Thompson, et al., 2003). The phonological variations have been conceptualized into a fairly manageable system of nine features, and examples are provided for the phonological features from the students' reading aloud of the GORT-3. This taxonomy has the potential to advance our understanding of child AAE but requires considerable future research to determine its utility. This is a daunting task, but it is of the highest priority if we are to improve our understanding of the reading challenges faced by AAE-speaking students and use this information to design appropriate prevention and intervention programs.

SUMMARY

Why aren't African American students reading better? As we discuss in this chapter, a number of potential factors may be involved. Future research must prioritize improving our understanding of child AAE. Whereas syntax, morphology, and phonology require the use of conventional but arbitrary symbols to exchange meaning, knowledge of these linguistic systems is foundational to all modes of expressing and receiving the meanings of others, including both oral and written exchanges. It is important, therefore, to understand the role of systematic variations in child AAE and their relationships to literacy acquisition. Future research would benefit from answers to the following questions:

1. What are the relationships between being a child speaker of AAE and the acquisition of production and comprehension skills in reading, writing, and spelling?
2. How can early prevention programs bridge a student's heritage language and cultural approaches to literacy, and the expectations of schools and the curriculum?

Although the focus of this chapter has been on the acquisition of language and lit-

TABLE 11.5. Phonological Types of Child AAE with Examples from African American Students in the Elementary Grades Reading Aloud

Definition	Example
Postvocalic consonant reduction Deletions of consonant singles following vowels	"mouth" /maʊ/ for /maʊθ/
"g" dropping Substitutions of /n/ for /ŋ/ in final word positions	"waiting" /wetɪn/ for /wetɪŋ/
Substitutions for /θ/ and /ð/ /t/ and /d/ substitute for /θ/ and /ð/ in prevocalic positions	"this" /dɪs/ for /ðɪs/
/f/ and /v/ substitute for /θ/ and /ð/ in intervocalic positions, and in postvocalic positions	"birthday" /bɤfde/ for /bɤθde/ "both" /bof/ for /boθ/
Devoicing final consonants Voiceless consonants substitute for voiced following the vowel	(none observed)
Consonant cluster reduction Deletion of phonemes from consonant clusters	"find" /faɪn/ for /faɪnd/
Consonant cluster movement Reversal of phonemes within a cluster, with or without consonant reduplication	"escape" /ɛkskep/ for /ɛskep/
Syllable deletion Reduction of an (unstressed) syllable in a multisyllabic word	"became" /kem/ for /bikem/
Syllable addition Addition of a syllable to a word, usually as a hypercorrection	"forests" /forɪstsɪz/ for /forɪsts/
Substitutions for /aʊ/ /ɑ/ for /aʊ/	"our" /ɑr/ for /aʊr/

Note. Data from Craig, Thompson, et al. (2003).

eracy by African American students, most of the challenges faced by African American students learning to read and write are echoed in the experiences of other minorities, most notably Hispanic students, who enter school with heritage languages and culture-specific literacy practices that differ from the mainstream. As the United States becomes more diverse and the demands for a literate citizenry increase, the need to en-sure the literacy acquisition of all students is on the forefront of educational imperatives, for example, in the priorities of the No Child Left Behind Act of 2001 (2002). Increasing our understanding of the nature and governing principles of these linguistic systems, and the ways that linguistic variation influences literacy acquisition, should greatly improve our ability to impact the educational achievement of all students.

ACKNOWLEDGMENTS

This work was supported by the Center for Improvement of Early Reading Achievement (CIERA) at the University of Michigan—U.S. Department of Education, Office of Educational Research and Improvement, Grant Nos. R305R70004 and R305T990368.

NOTE

1. Phonemes are indicated using / /, and graphemes with [ ].

REFERENCES

Adams, M. J. (1990). *Beginning to read: Thinking and learning about print*. Cambridge, MA: MIT Press.

Anderson-Yockel, J., & Haynes, W. (1994). Joint picture-book reading strategies in working-class African American and white mother–toddler dyads. *Journal of Speech, Language, and Hearing Research, 37*, 583–593.

Bartel, N. R., & Axelrod, J. (1973). Nonstandard English usage and reading ability in black junior high students. *Exceptional Children, 39*, 653–655.

Baugh, J. (2001). Coming full circle: Some circumstances pertaining to low literacy achievement among African Americans. In J. Harris, A. Kamhi, & K. Pollock (Eds.), *Literacy in African American communities* (pp. 277–288). Hillsdale, NJ: Erlbaum.

Bloom, L., & Lahey, M. (1978). *Language development and language disorders*. New York: Wiley.

Bloome, D., Champion, T., Katz, L., Morton, M. B., & Muldrow, R. (2001). Spoken and written narrative development: African American preschoolers as storytellers and storymakers. In J. Harris, A. Kamhi, & K. Pollock (Eds.), *Literacy in African American communities* (pp. 45–76). Hillsdale, NJ: Erlbaum.

Bracken, B. A., Sabers, D., & Insko, W. (1987). Performance of black and white children on the Bracken Basic Concept Scale. *Psychology in the Schools, 24*, 22–27.

Brown, I. S., & Felton, R. H. (1990). Effects of instruction on beginning reading skills in children at risk for reading disability. *Reading and Writing, 2*, 223–241.

Brown, R. (1973). *A first language: The early stages*. Cambridge, MA: Harvard University Press.

Bus, A. G., & van IJzendoorn, M. H. (1999). Phonological awareness and early reading: A meta-analysis of experimental training studies. *Journal of Educational Psychology, 91*, 403–414.

Bus, A. G., van IJzendoorn, M. H., & Pelligrini, A. D. (1995). Joint book reading makes for success in learning to read: A meta-analysis on intergenerational transmission of literacy. *Review of Educational Research, 65*, 1–21.

Cecil, N. L. (1988). Black dialect and academic success: A study of teacher expectations. *Reading Improvement, 25*, 34–38.

Craig, H. K., Connor, C. M., & Washington, J. A. (2003). Early positive predictors of later reading comprehension for African American students: A preliminary investigation. *Language, Speech, and Hearing Services in Schools, 34*, 31–43.

Craig, H. K., Thompson, C. A., Washington, J. A., & Potter, S. L. (2003). Phonological features of child African American English. *Journal of Speech, Language, and Hearing Research, 46*, 623–635.

Craig, H. K., Thompson, C. A., Washington, J. A., & Potter, S. L. (in press). Performances of elementary grade African American students on the Gray Oral Reading Tests. *Language, Speech, and Hearing Services in Schools*.

Craig, H. K., & Washington, J. A. (1994). The complex syntax skills of poor, urban, African-American preschoolers at school entry. *Language, Speech, and Hearing Services in Schools, 25*, 181–190.

Craig, H. K., & Washington, J. A. (1995). African-American English and linguistic complexity in preschool discourse: A second look. *Language, Speech, and Hearing Services in Schools, 26*, 87–93.

Craig, H. K., & Washington, J. A. (2002). Oral language expectations for African American preschoolers and kindergartners. *American Journal of Speech–Language Pathology, 11*, 59–70.

Craig, H. K., Washington, J. A., & Thompson-Porter, C. (1998). Average c-unit lengths in the discourse of African American children from low income, urban homes. *Journal of Speech, Language, and Hearing Research, 41*, 433–444.

Cunningham, P. M. (1976–1977). Teachers' correction responses to black-dialect miscues which are non-meaning-changing. *Reading Research Quarterly, 12*, 637–653.

DeStefano, J. (1972). Productive language differences in fifth-grade black students' syntactic forms. *Elementary English, 47*, 552–558.

DeTemple, J. M. (2001). Parents and children reading books together. In D. K. Dickinson & P. O. Tabors (Eds.), *Beginning literacy with children: Young children learning at home and school* (pp. 31–51). Baltimore: Brookes.

Dunn, L., & Dunn, L. (1997). *Peabody Picture Vocabulary Test* (3rd ed.). Circle Pines, MN: American Guidance Service.

Dunn, L., & Dunn, L. (1981). *Peabody Picture Vocabulary Test—Revised*. Circle Pines, MN: American Guidance Service.

Entwisle, D. R., & Alexander, K. L. (1988). Factors affecting achievement test scores and marks of black and white first graders. *Elementary School Journal, 88*, 449–472.

Fasold, R.W. (1981). The relation between black and white speech in the South. *American Speech, 61*, 163–189.

Feagans, L., & Haskins, R. (1986). Neighborhood dialogues of black and white 5-year-olds. *Journal of Applied Developmental Psychology, 7*, 181–200.

Federal Interagency Forum on Child and Family Statistics. (2003). *America's children: Key national indicators of well-being, 2003* (Federal Interagency Forum on Child and Family Statistics). Washington, DC: U.S. Government Printing Office.

Fishback, P. V., & Baskin, J. H. (1991). Narrowing the black–white gap in child literacy in 1910: The roles of school inputs and family inputs. *Review of Economics and Statistics, 73,* 725–728.

Foorman, B. R., Francis, D. J., Fletcher, J. M., Schatschneider, C., & Mehta, P. (1998). The role of instruction in learning to read: Preventing reading failure in at-risk children. *Journal of Educational Psychology, 90,* 37–55.

Gemake, J. S. (1981). Interference of certain dialect elements with reading comprehension for third graders. *Reading Improvement, 18,* 183–189.

Goodman, K. S., & Buck, C. (1973). Dialect barriers to reading comprehension revisited. *Reading Teacher, 27,* 6–12.

Green, L. (1995). Study of verb classes in African American English. *Linguistics and Education, 7,* 65–81.

Grigg, W. S., Daane, M. C., Jin, Y., & Campbell, J. R. (2003). *The nation's report card: Reading 2002* (NCES 2003-521). Washington, DC: U.S. Department of Education, Institute of Education Sciences, National Center for Education Statistics.

Hammer, C. S. (1999). Guiding language development: How African American mothers and their infants structure play. *Journal of Speech, Language, and Hearing Research, 42,* 1219–1233.

Harber, J. R. (1977). Influence of presentation dialect and orthographic form on reading performance of black, inner-city children. *Educational Research Quarterly, 2*(2), 9–16.

Hart, J. T., Guthrie, J. T., & Winfield, L. (1980). Black English phonology and learning to read. *Journal of Educational Psychology, 72,* 636–646.

Haynes, W. O., & Moran, M. J. (1989). A cross-sectional-developmental study of final consonant production in southern black children from preschool through third grade. *Language, Speech, and Hearing Services in Schools, 20,* 400–406.

Heath, S. B. (1983). *Ways with words.* Cambridge, UK: Cambridge University Press.

Hecht, S. A., Burgess, S. R., Torgesen, J. K., Wagner, R. K., & Rashotte, C. A. (2000). Explaining social class differences in growth of reading skills from beginning kindergarten through fourth-grade: The role of phonological awareness, rate of access, and print knowledge. *Reading and Writing, 12,* 99–127.

Jencks, C., & Phillips, M. (Eds.). (1998). *The black–white test score gap.* Washington, DC: Brookings Institution Press.

Jussim, L., Eccles, J., & Madon, S. (1996). Social perception, social stereotypes, and teacher expectations: Accuracy and the quest for the powerful self-fulfilling prophecy. *Advances in Experimental Social Psychology, 28,* 281–387.

Kligman, D., & Cronnell, B. (1974). *Black English and spelling* (Southwest Regional Laboratory for Educa-

tion Research and Development Technical Report No. 50). Washington, DC: U.S. Department of Health, Education and Welfare. (ERIC Document Reproduction Service ED108234)

Labov, W., Baker, B., Bullock, S., Ross, L., & Brown, M. (1998). *A graphemic–phonemic analysis of the reading errors of inner city children.* Unpublished manuscript. Retrieved June 6, 2001, from *http://www.ling.upenn.edu/~wlabov/Papers/GAREC/GAREC.html*

LeMoine, N. R. (2001). Language variation and literacy acquisition in African American students. In J. Harris, A. Kamhi, & K. Pollock (Eds.), *Literacy in African American communities* (pp. 169–194). Hillsdale, NJ: Erlbaum.

Lieberson, S., & Mikelson, K. S. (1995). Distinctive African American names: An experimental, historical, and linguistic analysis of innovation. *American Sociological Review, 60,* 928–946.

Markham, L. (1984). De dog and de cat: Assisting speakers of Black English as they begin to write. *Young Children, 39*(4), 15–24.

Melmed, P. J. (1973). Black English phonology: The question of reading interference. In J. L. Laffey & R. W. Shuy (Eds.), *Language differences: Do they interfere?* (pp. 70–85). Newark, DE: International Reading Association.

Metropolitan Achievement Tests (7th ed.). (1993). San Antonio, TX: Harcourt Brace.

Nation, K., & Snowling, M. J. (1998). Semantic processing and the development of word-recognition skills: Evidence from children with reading comprehension difficulties. *Journal of Memory and Language, 39,* 85–101.

Nettles, M., & Perna, L. (1997). *The African American education data book: Preschool through high school education* (Vol. II). Fairfax, VA: Frederick D. Patterson Research Institute of the College Fund.

No Child Left Behind Act of 2001, 20 U.S.C. § 6301 et seq. (2002).

Ogbu, J. (1988). Cultural diversity and human development. *New Directions for Child Development, 42,* 11–28.

Pellegrini, A., Perlmutter, J., Galda, L., & Brody, G. (1990). Joint reading between black Head Start children and their mothers. *Child Development, 61,* 443–453.

Phillips, M., Brooks-Gunn, J., Duncan, G. J., Klebanov, P., & Crane, J. (1998). Family background, parenting practices, and the black–white test score gap. In C. Jencks & M. Phillips (Eds.), *The black–white test score gap* (pp. 103–145). Washington, DC: Brookings Institution Press.

Phillips, M., Crouse, J., & Ralph, J. (1998). Does the black–white test score gap widen after children enter school? In C. Jencks & M. Phillips (Eds.), *The black–white test score gap* (pp. 229–272). Washington, DC: Brookings Institution Press.

Pike, K. (1967). *Language in relation to a unified theory of the structure of human behavior.* The Hague: Mouton.

Rutter, M. (1987). Psychosocial resilience and protective mechanisms. *American Journal of Orthopsychiatry, 57,* 316–331.

Rystrom, R. (1973–1974). Perceptions of vowel letter–sound relationships by first grade children. *Reading Research Quarterly, 2,* 170–185.

Sable, J. (1998). The educational progress of black students. In J. Wirt, T. Snyder, J. Sable, S. P. Choy, Y. Bae, J. Stennett, A. Gruner, & M. Perie (Eds.), *The condition of education 1998* (NCES 98-013, pp. 2–10). Washington, DC: U.S. Department of Education, National Center for Education Statistics. Retrieved August 14, 2002, from *http://nces.ed.gov/pubs98/98013.pdf*

Sameroff, A. J., Seifer, R., Barocas, R., Zax, M., & Greenspan, S. (1987). Intelligence quotient scores of 4-year-old children: Social environmental risk factors. *Pediatrics, 79,* 343–350.

Scarborough, H. S. (1998). Early identification of children at risk for reading disabilities: Phonological awareness and some other promising predictors. In B. K. Shapiro, P. J. Accardo, & A. J. Capute (Eds.), *Specific reading disability: A view of the spectrum* (pp. 75–120). Timonium, MD: York Press.

Scarborough, H. S., & Dobrich, W. (1994). On the efficacy of reading to preschoolers. *Developmental Review, 14,* 245–302.

Scott, C. M., & Rogers, L. M. (1996). Written language abilities of African American children and youth. In A. G. Kamhi, K. E. Pollock, & J. L. Harris (Eds.), *Communication development and disorders in African American children* (pp. 307–332). Baltimore: Brookes.

Seymour, H. N., & Ralabate, P. K. (1985). The acquisition of a phonologic feature of Black English. *Journal of Communication Disorders, 18,* 139–148.

Seymour, H. N., & Seymour, C. M. (1981). Black English and Standard American English contrasts in consonantal development of four and five-year old children. *Journal of Speech and Hearing Disorders, 46,* 274–280.

Simons, H. D., & Johnson, K. R. (1973). Black English syntax and reading interference. *Research in the Teaching of English, 8,* 339–358.

Singham, M. (1998). The canary in the mine: The achievement gap between black and white students. *Phi Delta Kappan, 80,* 8–15.

Smith, L. A. (1996). Unique names and naming practices among African American families. *Families in Society, 77,* 290–297.

Snow, C., Burns, S., & Griffin, M. (1998). *Preventing reading difficulties in young children.* Washington, DC: National Academy Press.

Steffensen, M. S., Reynolds, R. E., McClure, E., & Guthrie, L. F. (1982). Black English vernacular and reading comprehension: A cloze study of third, sixth, and ninth graders. *Journal of Reading Behavior, 14,* 285–298.

Stockman, I. J. (1996). Phonological development and disorders in African American children. In A. G. Kamhi, K. E. Pollock, & J. L. Harris (Eds.), *Communication development and disorders in African American children* (pp. 117–153). Baltimore: Brookes.

Thompson, C. A. (2003). *The oral vocabulary abilities of skilled and unskilled African American readers.* Unpublished doctoral dissertation, University of Michigan, Ann Arbor.

Torgesen, J. K., Wagner, R. K., Rashotte, C. A., Burgess, S., & Hecht, S. A. (1997). The contributions of phonological awareness and rapid automatic naming ability to the growth of word reading skills in second to fifth grade children. *Scientific Studies of Reading, 1,* 161–185.

Torgesen, J. K., Wagner, R. K., Rashotte, C. A., Rose, E., Lindamood, P., Conway, T., et al. (1999). Preventing reading failure in young children with phonological processing disabilities: Group and individual responses to instruction. *Journal of Educational Psychology, 91,* 579–593.

Vellutino, F. R., Scanlon, D. M., Sipay, E. R., Small, S. G., Pratt, A., Chen, R., et al. (1996). Cognitive profiles of difficult to remediate and readily remediated poor readers: Early intervention as a vehicle for distinguishing between cognitive and experiential deficits as basic causes of specific reading disability. *Journal of Educational Psychology, 88,* 601–638.

Vernon-Feagans, L. (1996). *Children's talk in communities and classrooms.* Cambridge, MA: Blackwell.

Vernon-Feagans, L., Hammer, C. S., Miccio, A., & Manlove, E. (2001). Early language and literacy skills in low-income African American and Hispanic children. In S. B. Neuman & D. K. Dickinson (Eds.), *Handbook of early literacy research* (pp. 192–210). New York: Guilford Press.

Washington, J. A., & Craig, H. K. (1992). Performances of low-income, African American preschool and kindergarten children on the Peabody Picture Vocabulary Tests—Revised. *Language, Speech, and Hearing Services in Schools, 23,* 329–333.

Washington, J. A., & Craig, H. K. (1994). Dialectal forms during discourse of urban, African American preschoolers living in poverty. *Journal of Speech and Hearing Research, 37,* 816–823.

Washington, J. A., & Craig, H. K. (1998). Socioeconomic status and gender influences on children's dialectal variations. *Journal of Speech, Language, Hearing, and Research, 41,* 618–626.

Washington, J. A., & Craig, H. K. (1999). Performances of at-risk, African American preschoolers on the Peabody Picture Vocabulary Test—III. *Language, Speech, and Hearing Services in Schools, 30,* 75–82.

Washington, J. A., & Craig, H. K. (2002). Morphosyntactic forms of African American English used by young children and their caregivers. *Applied Psycholinguistics, 23,* 209–231.

Washington, J., Craig, H., & Kushmaul, A. (1998). Variable use of African American English across two language sampling contexts. *Journal of Speech, Language, and Hearing Research, 41,* 1115–1124.

Whitehurst, G. J., Epstein, J. N., Angell, A. L., Payne, A. C., Crone, D. A., & Fischel, J. E. (1994). Outcomes of emergent literacy intervention in Head Start. *Journal of Educational Psychology, 86,* 542–555.

Whitehurst, G. J., & Lonigan, C. L. (2001). Emergent literacy: Development from prereaders to readers. In S. B. Neuman & D. K. Dickinson (Eds.), *Handbook of early literacy research* (pp. 11–29). New York: Guilford Press.

Wiederholt, J. L., & Bryant, B. R. (1992). *Gray Oral Reading Tests, third edition (GORT-3)*. Austin, TX: Pro-Ed.

Windsor, J., Scott, C.M., & Street, C.K. (2000). Verb and noun morphology in the spoken and written language of children with language learning disabilities. *Journal of Speech, Language, and Hearing Research, 43,* 1322–1336.

Wolfram, W. (1974). The relationship of white southern speech to vernacular black English. *Language, 50,* 498–527.

Woodcock, R. W. (1987). *Woodcock Reading Mastery Tests—Revised.* Circle Pines, MN: American Guidance Service.

12

Learning to Read and Write in Two Languages

The Development of Early Biliteracy Abilities

Liliana Barro Zecker

During the last two decades, numerous investigations have documented developmental patterns in early literacy learning among monolingual children from a variety of language and ethnic backgrounds, carefully describing growth in all areas of budding reading and writing knowledge (Ferreiro, 1997; Harris & Hatano, 1999; Pontecorvo, Orsolini, Burge, & Resnick, 1996; Teale & Sulzby, 1986). Adopting a theoretical framework that underscores learners' active construction of knowledge, investigations have left behind the notion of reading readiness in favor of a characterization of early literacy learning as *emergent literacy*, a developmental and constructivist process (Teale & Sulzby, 1986). There is now a well-founded understanding of how children discover, attempt to make sense of, and best learn about the diverse yet mutually influential facets of what Dyson (1985) termed the "written language kaleidoscope" (Yaden, Rowe, & MacGillivray, 2000). By describing a myriad of emergent literacy behaviors, from early types of storybook reading and invented spelling to intermediary forms of text composition, researchers in early literacy development have compiled a quite detailed picture of how young children learn to read and write (Dyson, 1989; 1993; Ferreiro, Pontecorvo, Ribeiro, & García Hidalgo, 1996; Ferreiro & Teberosky, 1979; Goswami, 1999; Lensmire, 1994; Newkirk, 1989; Sulzby, 1985a, 1985b; Zecker, 1996, 1999).

Drawing on the emergent literacy paradigm just described, I discuss developmental biliteracy, the simultaneous acquisition of reading and writing skills in two languages during the early elementary school years. Once neglected as an area of research despite its presence and importance, development in biliteracy is at the center of current research concerned with the academic abilities and future of the rapidly growing U.S. bilingual population. The ideas in this chapter describe recent paradigm shifts in the understanding of bilingualism and biliteracy, and the resulting reformulation of central concepts inherent to biliteracy learning and teaching among U.S. bilingual students. The new outlook questions the marked preoccupation with determining language dominance and points to the limitations of what traditionally has been a *sequential* (as opposed to *simultaneous*) stance toward first- and second-language learning (Moll & Dworin, 1996; Reyes & Halcón, 2000). Instead, drawing on socioconstructivist perspectives, more recent research offers a renewed perspective on bilingualism and biliteracy learning by proposing a more dynamic continuum framework. This continuum model helps researchers avoid limiting and static categories (such as first and second language). Instead, it highlights the multilayered, mutually influential nature of the different aspects of literate (and biliterate) knowledge that children develop as they become literate–biliterate people.

In the initial section, I provide a brief historical background on investigations of reading and writing abilities among bilingual youngsters. Following this brief background, I describe some of the reconceptualizations shaping current research on bilingualism and biliteracy learning and development. In the third section, I describe the experiences of children in a dual-language program, a bilingual education pedagogical setting designed to support children's development as bilingual, biliterate, and multicultural individuals. Finally, in the closing section, I summarize the main points and draw implications for future research and practice.

PAST RESEARCH IN BILITERACY

Research in the acquisition of biliteracy, the ability to read and write in two languages, has been plentiful. Most studies, however, have compared the acquisition of literacy skills in *adult* learners' first (L1) and second language (L2) within what is best described as a *sequential* framework—after L1 is well established—and from the standpoint of *cross-language transfer;* that is, given learners' well-mastered L1 abilities (orally and in writing), most studies of biliteracy have focused on which aspects of L1 knowledge can or do influence the acquisition of literacy skills in the L2, and how they contribute to the development of individuals' biliterate skills (Durgunoğlu, Mir, & Ariño-Martí, 2002; Durgunoğlu & Verhoeven, 1998).

On the other hand, research on the development of biliteracy skills among young children exposed to two languages *simultaneously* from early on in their language-learning experiences has been limited (Bialystok, 1995; García, 2001). A few longitudinal studies have addressed the acquisition of biliteracy among young children from a cognitive-linguistic developmental standpoint. For the most part, these are case study investigations generally reported by academic parent–researchers (Bauer, 2000; Fantini, 1985; Wodala, 1994). This case study–based research corpus, while informative, has had limited curricular and assessment implications for the diverse ethnolinguistic and socioeconomic reality of many U.S. elementary bilingual education classrooms.

In general, the unique characteristics of the U.S. sociocultural, sociopolitical, and sociolinguistic context restrict comparisons with investigations of biliteracy acquisition embedded in other countries' particular histories of immigration, schooling, and language–culture learning differences (Cummins, 2001; Moll & Dworin, 1996; Ogbu, 1987; Tolchinsky Landsman, 1991). Because Spanish-speaking students constitute 75% of the 10 million English-language learners in U.S. schools (National Center for Education Statistics, 2000), numerous investigators have studied the literacy achievement of English-language learners for whom Spanish is the native or heritage language (Ferdman, Weber, & Ramírez, 1994; García, 2000; Padilla & Benavídes, 1992; Pérez, 1998; Tinajero & Ada, 1993). There are, of course, also numerous studies reporting on early biliteracy skills among English-language learners with other L1 backgrounds that contribute to the overall understanding of biliteracy development among bilingual youngsters (Bauer, 2000; Bialystok, 1997; Geva, Wade-Wooley, & Shany, 1993; López, 2000).

For many years, the majority of the investigations that evaluated the achievement of students enrolled in a variety of U.S. bilingual programs, which mostly were transitional-bilingual in nature, measured the achievement levels of bilingual students in English. Few studies took into consideration programmatic differences and the varying lengths of time that characterized the bilingual education experiences of different students (García, 2000). It is important to note that most of the students participating in those investigations had received little or no instruction in native-language literacy, because native language maintenance and biliteracy development are not goals of the majority of bilingual programs in the United States (García, 2001; Moll & Dworin, 1996; Reyes, 2000). Nevertheless, when programmatic variation was taken into consideration by investigators, results indicated that those students who had experienced the most opportunity to develop their native language did better on English achievement measures (Collier & Thomas, 2001; García, 2000; Thomas & Collier, 1997).

Breaking with the predominant trends in bilingualism research at the time, Edelsky (1986) provided a pioneering and perhaps, to this date, most thorough discussion of the biliterate skills often observed in U.S. classrooms. Responding to what she deemed "not a trivial void" (p. 29) in knowledge about how bilingual children write in either or both of their two languages, Edelsky conducted a yearlong study of development in written language among Spanish-speaking first, second, and third graders enrolled in a bilingual program serving migrant workers in the southwestern United States. Her analyses compared children's writing in English and Spanish, and described students' use of code switching, stylistic devices, and structural features. Edelsky's work lay mostly dormant until recently. Her observations provided extremely thorough analyses of children's written products in English and Spanish. The findings indicated that bilingual students develop spontaneous biliteracy abilities even when the majority of U.S. bilingual education programs do not support literacy instruction in students' native language (the non-English language).

In spite of the undeniable presence of biliteracy in U.S. bilingual programs and its paramount consequences for the academic and cognitive lives of many students, the development of biliteracy skills among bilingual students remained, for the most part,

"neglected in the literature" (Moll & Dworin, 1996, p. 222). Only more recently have U.S. researchers of bilingualism and bilingual classroom contexts begun to study "developmental biliteracy"—defined as the simultaneous development of reading and writing abilities in two languages (Reyes & Halcón, 2000). Given the increasing numbers of English-language learners attending U.S. schools now and in the foreseeable future, the need for pedagogically relevant research on the development of biliteracy is long overdue (Cummins, 1993, 1994; García, 2001; Reyes & Halcón, 2000; Rueda & García, 1996; Wong-Fillmore, 1992).

RETHINKING BILITERACY

The puzzling research gap in the area of biliteracy acquisition among bilingual students in the United States is, at least in part, best explained by Hornberger's (1994) description of the challenge faced by investigators. She argues that "when one attends to both [literacy and bilingualism], already complex issues seem to become further muddled" (p. 105). Hornberger proposes a dynamic look at biliteracy learning, so that research can document the *development of interplaying factors* (as opposed to static results) by adopting an overarching continuum scheme to describe the mutually related yet individually multidimensional aspects of bilingualism and biliteracy. Hornberger argues that the distinct end points commonly used to depict biliterate development and biliterates' language use—such as monolingual versus bilingual individuals, oral versus literate practices, and first versus second languages—are limiting. A continuum perspective avoids such artificial polarizations that, Hornberger claims, exist only in theory. In reality, Hornberger argues, these opposite points (e.g., first and second language for a given individual, or oral versus literate nature of certain communicative exchanges) lie on a continuum of features that are not discrete when one looks at biliteracy and bilingualism *in action*. In other words, language dominance and an individual's level of bilingualism/biliteracy vary across sociolinguistic contexts (school or home) and the discursive practices that characterize them, as well as specific communicative situations (more or less oral- or literate-like discourse).

This more flexible framework, which takes into account the situated aspects of learning in general, and of language learning in particular, characterizes most recent studies of the development of biliterate skills among bilingual children in U.S. bilingual programs. It responds to current trends in sociocognitive and sociolinguistic research that follow a socioconstructivist perspective. Based on Vygotskian ideas, socioconstructivism conceptualizes learning (literacy and other types) as a meaning-making, socially and culturally situated process during which learners craft new knowledges via interactions among themselves and with more expert others (Moll, 1992; Padilla & Benavídes, 1992; Pérez, 1998).

A New Look at Developmental Biliteracy

Grounded on the theoretical principles outlined earlier, the latest studies on biliteracy learning take a more dynamic and contextualized approach. In general, they show diminished preoccupation, for example, with trying to determine students' dominant language or to define precisely levels of bilingualism. As Reyes (2000) and Moll and Dworin (1996) discuss, classifications such as *first-* and *second-language learners* become meaningless in many U.S. bilingual contexts in which children are simultaneously exposed to language and literacy learning in two languages. Like Hornberger (1994), many investigators accentuate the continual aspects of bilingualism and biliteracy learning, the multiple possible paths to the acquisition of biliteracy skills, and the unique characteristics of emerging into literate life from a *developmentally bilingual* language-learning experience (García, 2000, 2001; Moll & Dworin, 1996; Reyes & Halcón, 2000). In general, these more recent studies of biliteracy development among children growing up in U.S. bilingual school contexts microanalyze specific aspects of the process of early biliteracy learning and development (e.g., orthographic knowledge) within *specific literacy-task contexts* (e.g.,

journal writing), and they take into account *programmatic, curricular,* and individual *student* characteristics.

Noticeably, many of the investigations concerned with the development of biliteracy skills among young children emerging simultaneously into literacy in two languages describe in particular the development of writing skills (as opposed to reading). In fact, a review of available research indicates that it is mainly through the description of how children negotiate early writing abilities in two languages that investigators have *come to know* more about biliteracy development. Arguably, writing allows for a more transparent window into young bilinguals' early biliterate experiences and the ways in which they juggle, orchestrate, and deploy linguistic resources (Edelsky, 1986; Gutiérrez, Baquedano-López, & Alvarez, 2000; Moll & Dworin, 1996; Reyes, 2000). Reading processes, on the other hand, because of their more covert, intake-based nature, seem to yield a less obvious view into the developmental biliteracy puzzle and young children's hypothesis-testing strategies. This shift in focus, from reading to writing developmental processes, also marks a departure from previous investigations of literacy development among bilinguals, which, as mentioned before, mainly reported on the reading abilities of bilingual education students (Ramírez, 2000).

Emergent Biliteracy Knowledge: Juggling the Common and the Particular

Numerous studies of emergent biliteracy abilities have investigated the development of phonemic awareness and graphophonemic knowledge among young writers who are learning to write in language systems with varying degrees of orthographic transparency (i.e., regularity of letter–sound correspondence). For example, many investigations have looked at how young children juggle the different demands of English spelling (a not very transparent orthography) and Spanish spelling (a more transparent orthography) (Davis, Carlisle, & Beeman, 1999; Pérez, 1994a; Tolchinsky, 1998). Other studies have compared children's emergent reading and writing abilities in English and in languages that are not alphabetic (e.g., Hebrew, Chinese) (Bialystok, 1997), or bilingual children's early knowledge of concepts about print in their two languages (Bialystok, 1997; Pellicer, 2002). Some researchers have documented emergent patterns of invented spelling (Flores, 1990; Silva, 1998; Vernon, 1993), and budding knowledge of genre traits among bilingual children in kindergarten, first, and second grade (Carlisle, Beeman, & Zecker, 2001; Durgunoğlu et al., 2002; Flores, 1990; Kuhlman, 1993; Maguire & Graves, 2001; Quintero & Huerta-Macías, 1995).

Still other investigators have focused on more sociocognitive factors affecting the development of biliterate skills. Researchers have described, for instance, kindergartners' perceptions of biliteracy or the relationships between biliteracy development and the collaborative literacy interactions of family and peers (Ada, 1988; Battle, 1993; Delgado-Gaitán, 1990; Griego-Jones, 1994; Hornberger, 1992; Mulhern, 1994; Pérez, 1994b). Manyak (2000) describes teachers' construction of biliterate environments in a first-grade immersion class.

All of the studies cited earlier have contributed to a collage of insights on how children become biliterate. Because of the multilayered characteristics of biliteracy learning, a clean summary of research findings poses a challenge. The model proposed by Fitzgerald and Shanahan (2000) to describe the different kinds of knowledge involved in the development of reading–writing processes provides a heuristic to organize the major findings of developmental biliteracy research (Durgunoğlu et al., 2002). There are four major kinds of knowledge that writers and readers need to orchestrate as they develop literate skills (Fitzgerald & Shanahan, 2000):

1. *Meta-knowledge:* knowledge about the purposes and functions of literacy and the learner's ability to supervise her or his own meaning making.
2. *Prior knowledge:* domain-specific background knowledge, including, for example, topic-pertinent vocabulary.
3. *Text-attribute knowledge:* knowledge of (a) graphophonemic correspondences,

(b) syntax (including punctuation and grammar), and (c) text/genre traits (e.g., story grammar).
4. *Procedural knowledge:* knowledge about how to orchestrate information in 1, 2, and 3 above. This type of knowledge is considered by some investigators to be part of meta-knowledge and related to general metacognitive skills.

The results of most investigations of early biliteracy acquisition fall mainly into two of these knowledge areas, discussing (1) the meta-knowledge and (2) the text-attribute knowledge of biliterate students. Numerous studies report a certain *common knowledge* that appears to be at the basis of literacy learning and development, whether in the less or more dominant language, a kind of common literacy-competence resource fund that bilingual learners seem to apply across reading and writing situations regardless of particular language characteristics. Edelsky (1986) best summarized this when she concluded that the bilingual children she observed appeared to have available a "repertoire [of literacy skills] from which alternatives are selected" (p. 75). She hypothesized that "children were developing separate systems while making use of one system to fill in the holes in the other" (p. 77). Other investigators have observed the presence of this common literacy meta-knowledge that students seem to deploy across languages, regardless of the language in which they receive literacy instruction (Reyes & Halcón, 2000).

When studies of emergent biliteracy skills among young children address development in one or more specific aspects of knowledge of text attributes (orthography, syntax, text structure, etc.), conclusions seem to indicate that all aspects of text-attribute knowledge are correlated across the products of emergent biliterate students. Investigations of bilingual children's emergent graphophonemic knowledge (i.e., early spelling and word-decoding skills in alphabetic languages) conclude that the phonemic structure of the students' best-known language influences children's word reading and spelling abilities in the L2 (in most investigations, English) (Durgunoğlu et al.,

2002; Edelsky, 1986). The same conclusion applies to investigations of young bilingual children's writing when syntactic knowledge and their knowledge of text format and text structure characteristics are compared. All these aspects of early biliteracy knowledge seem to develop simultaneously, in a seamless way, rather than sequentially, and they appear to support each other as complementary cognitive–linguistic resources (Durgunoğlu et al., 2002).

New Pedagogical Frameworks

Results from the investigations cited earlier have begun to force the rethinking of biliteracy learning and instruction in the United States. There is clear evidence that many young bilingual children in U.S. classrooms move between two linguistic worlds in fluid ways, even when they do not receive instruction to support their development as bilingual and biliterate individuals (Reyes, 2000). Findings call for a reformulation in the goals and pedagogical practices of U.S. bilingual education programs, which until now have limited the potential of bilingual students to develop sound biliteracy skills (August & Hakuta, 1997; García, 2001; Gutiérrez et al., 2000; Moll & Dworin, 1996; Reyes, 2000). In general, instruction in reading and writing for language-minority children in U.S. schools relies heavily on the development of basic skills, postponing students' opportunities to engage in critical reasoning and the kinds of epistemic transactions with text that characterize true literate thinking (Cummins, 1994; Wells & Chang-Wells, 1992).

For the most part, literacy instruction in early elementary bilingual programs remains segregated by language, ignorant of the global aspects of cross-language transfer documented by investigations in L2 acquisition, and too timid (or reluctant?) to unleash students' bilingual/biliterate potential for fear of confusing them (Cummins, 2001; Gutiérrez, 2001; Reyes, 2000). More investigations are needed to document the development of biliteracy abilities in instructional environments that overtly support the development of bilingualism and biliteracy for all students. As García (2001) explains,

"The increasing number of dual-language immersion programs in the United States now provide the opportunity to investigate more systematically how well bilingual children respond to literacy instruction in two languages" (p. 232).

Two-way immersion (TWI), or dual-language, programs are fairly new and still rare within bilingual education options in the United States—approximately 260 nationwide at present (Christian, 1996; Lessow-Hurley, 2000). Detailed accounts of students' progress in literacy and biliteracy and/or of biliteracy curricula development across time in dual-language programs are sparse. Certain aspects of dual-language program development have been sketched, but only recently have researchers been able to report on dual-language students' progress in language and academic achievement over time (Arlington Public Schools and Center for Applied Linguistics, 1997; Barfield & Rhodes, 1993; Cazabon, Lambert, & Hall, 1993; Christian & Mahrer, 1992, 1993; Christian & Montone, 1994; Collier & Thomas, 2001; Freeman, 1996; Howard, 2002; Howard & Loeb, 1998; Lindholm, 1990, 1992; Lindholm-Leary, 2001; Lindholm & Molina, 1998).

Although questions have been raised about the sociocultural implications of some dual-language programs that serve Latino students (Amrein & Peña, 2000; Valdés, 1997), in general, dual-language programs are considered ideal, fertile grounds for true multicultural education that promotes high academic achievement and strong bilingual competence for *minority as well as majority students* (Cloud, Genesee, & Hamayan, 2000). Contrary to other bilingual education options, dual-language programs respect and maintain the native language of language- and ethnic-minority students, and challenge traditional notions about the language of power and intergroup relations (Cummins, 1994). In fact, recognizing the potential far-reaching impact of TWI programs for language-majority and language-minority students' academic achievement, the U.S. Department of Education recently stated its intent to increase the number of dual-language schools to 1,000 nationwide over the next 5 years (Riley, 2000).

Given the intricate interdependence between oral language and literacy learning within the sociocultural experience of everyday classroom life (Dyson, 1989), dual-language bilingual education contexts require *new ways of teaching* and *new thinking about how bilingualism/biliteracy is developed, learned, and taught*. The different aspects proposed by Hornberger (1994) as part of the continuum of biliteracy (context, individual, and discourse types) interact and interplay in unique ways within dual-language models. One of the biggest challenges for educational research is to document the crafting of these new ways of teaching and learning, so that accumulated experiences inform the building of new curricular and assessment practices that are more dynamic, process oriented, and ecologically valid (Lindholm-Leary, 2001). To date, very little is known about how the unique pedagogical characteristics of dual-language programs influence *growth in biliteracy,* the simultaneous learning of reading and writing in two languages, *from a developmental perspective that takes into account psycholinguistic and cognitive/psychosocial growth.*

EMERGENT LITERACY AND BILITERACY IN A DUAL-LANGUAGE PROGRAM

In an effort to document emergent patterns of biliteracy growth, the preliminary results reported in this section describe the development of early biliterate abilities among kindergartners enrolled in a bilingual education program framed within the TWI, or dual-language, model (Zecker, 2001).[1]

The Setting

Responding to a marked growth in the number of Spanish-speaking children of Mexican origin attending its schools, and to strong parental interest in bilingual education opportunities for monolingual English-speaking children, a new TWI program was initiated in a midwestern suburban public school district serving a racially and socioeconomically mixed population. In this district TWI model, monolingual native English- and

Spanish-dominant children receive 70% of instruction (including content area instruction) in the non-English language (Spanish in this case); English is used for 30% of the instructional time. Students receive language arts instruction in their dominant language following the district language arts curriculum, which can be described as a balanced approach that incorporates many of the Guided Reading Four Blocks program components (Cunningham, Hall, & Defee, 1998). This program consists of four instructional blocks (Working with Words, Guided Reading, Self-Selected Reading, and Writing). It provides teachers with an instructional structure that accommodates students' wide range of ability levels and attends to and scaffolds both basic skills and higher order literacy comprehension and expression abilities.

Two kindergarten classrooms, with 24 students each, comprised an almost equal number of English-dominant and Spanish-dominant speakers. Although teachers and administrators recognized the limitations of language dominance assessments, language dominance of the incoming kindergartners was determined in two ways: a home language survey and administration of a language assessment scale that measured Spanish and English oral abilities of Spanish-speaking applicants. Both kindergarten classes were balanced for race and gender according to school district guidelines and population (Zecker, 2001).

During weekly visits, the investigator observed daily literacy curricular routines; she attended specially planned literacy-related events as well (e.g., Parents' Night, Curriculum Night). Meetings with teachers took place formally, during planned assessment team meetings, and informally, after school and during breaks.

During quarterly individual interviews, students were asked to complete brief writing (e.g., "Write a story for me") and reading tasks (e.g., "Read this book for me"; "Read what you wrote here"). In the fall, students were asked to complete these tasks only in their dominant language, but some of the Spanish-dominant children spontaneously showed some knowledge of English. During the winter and spring data collections, students were asked to complete reading and writing tasks in both languages. The preliminary findings reported next describe students' emergent literacy and biliteracy development in kindergarten during the first year of implementation of this TWI program.

Emergent Reading and Writing in the Native Language

All students' writing and reading renditions were analyzed by using an adaptation of the Forms of Writing and Rereading developed by Sulzby, Barnhart, and Hieshima (1989). These checklists consist of descriptive categories of emergent reading and writing forms found to be typical of children's early literacy attempts.

Analyses of students' emergent reading and writing behaviors in their dominant language from October to April (summarized in Tables 12.1 and 12.2) indicated that they followed commonly observed patterns of emergent literacy development among young children (Ferreiro, 1997; Ferreiro & Teberosky, 1979; Sulzby, 1985a, 1985b). As the school year progressed, these kindergartners applied phonemic writing systems and demonstrated increasing familiarity with high-frequency words and typical orthographic patterns in English (for the English-dominant students) and Spanish (for the Spanish-dominant students). Similarly, end-of-the-year reading attempts were indicative of students' growing awareness of written discourse characteristics and increasing ability to apply and orchestrate a variety of word identification techniques and cueing systems for conventional reading.

TABLE 12.2. Emergent Reading Forms in Dominant Language

Reading forms	Assessment point		
	Fall	Winter	Spring
Labeling and describing	33%	14%	5%
Oral monologue	2%	0%	2%
Mixed oral–written monologue	9%	15%	6%
Written monologue	24%	36%	36%
Naming letters	7%	2%	2%
Aspectual/strategic reading	4%	15%	13%
Conventional	4%	6%	36%
Refusal	17%	14%	0%

Note. Entries are the percentage of students performing in each category.

Early Biliteracy

Preliminary analyses of students' emergent biliterate abilities also yielded interesting and pedagogically relevant results. The analyses focused on the type of reading and writing behaviors that exemplified their emergent biliteracy development, students' indications of their growing awareness and knowledge of distinctive features in both languages, and the time when students started displaying these biliterate abilities. In this investigation, as in other reports of emergent biliterate competencies, children's written products provided more obvious windows into their development into biliteracy than observations of their reading attempts.

It is widely recognized that all aspects of oral and written language development (listening, speaking, reading, and writing) are intimately linked, and that development in one area of language learning affects development in the others. With that in mind, accurate analyses of these students' growth in biliteracy cannot be divorced from students' oral language abilities in their less dominant language. Whereas most of the Spanish-

TABLE 12.1. Emergent Writing Systems Used in the Children's Dominant Language

Writing systems	Assessment point		
	Fall	Winter	Spring
Prephonemic (Drawing, scribble, letter-like shapes, letter strings)	87%	34%	2%
Phonemic (Invented spelling, conventional spelling, or a mix of both)	13%	66%	98%

Note. Entries are the percentage of students performing in each category.

dominant (SD) students arrived at the TWI kindergarten experience having been exposed to some English, either informally in everyday life experiences or formally in a nursery school situation, only 4 of the total 24 English-dominant (ED) students had comparable exposure to Spanish. All 4 had been exposed to Spanish in both home *and* nursery school settings. As might be expected, in general, many—although not all—of the SD kindergartners incorporated English into their oral and literacy experiences and interactions earlier and more frequently than many ED students incorporated Spanish. SD students were observed to display biliterate skills earlier and more fluidly than ED students. On the other hand, many ED students mastered the Spanish orthographic code faster, attaining *conventional* word decoding and word spelling abilities in Spanish quite readily, scoring high on district standardized measures administered in Spanish, even when they often did not know the meaning of the words they were decoding or spelling from dictation.

Early Biliterate Writing Forms

As mentioned before, during the fall individual interviews, students were not asked to write in their second language. However, it is noteworthy that some students, both ED and SD, started to incorporate words into the other language in their spontaneous compositions and/or journal writing as early as October, approximately 6 weeks after school started. Journal writing seemed one of the most fertile curricular routines for the display of biliterate skills. Many of the students' first attempts at writing in the nondominant language consisted of copying available environmental print, because both classrooms had numerous labels and thematically organized word lists on display:

A bruja was   [A witch was
plain wt mi   playing with me]
(Wally, ED, 10/24/00)

YO COMI MUCHO   [I ate much of
Mi PAvo I HaD   my turkey I had
fo.R THANSGiVNG   for Thanksgiving]
(Matt, ED, 11/27/00)

In the winter, during their individual interviews, many students balked at the request to "write a story" in the second language, but they were very proud to demonstrate their biliteracy skills by writing lists of words, usually well-known expressions, when asked to write "anything you want" in their nondominant language:

SNiLA AeDut [Cinderella is cute]
(Marissa, SD, 1/12/01)

HoYes [*Hoy es*]
(Derek, ED, 1/19/01)

The presence of biliterate behaviors was even more prevalent by the end of the school year, when many students wrote a list of words or everyday phrases connected to classroom routines and instruction in the content areas:

OLA [*hola*]   LOONO [*luna*]
QUDADOS [*cuadrados*]
BENOSDEAS [*buenos días*]   SOL [*sol*]
TYEPO [*tiempo*]
FELESKOMPLANYOS [*feliz cumpleaños*]
YOKYRO [*yo quiero*]
(Sal, ED, 4/25/01 writing all over his page)

HOI AS MARTS [*Hoy es martes*]
HOI AS NUVLADO [*Hoy está nublado*]
(Jamie, ED, 4/25/01)

LaLiPap [lollipop]   PaSiCOS [popsicle]
(Frank, SD, 4/26/01)

FALHASCAmeNDSeG [Flowers come out
                in the spring]
(Gastón, SD, 4/30/01)

Also during the spring, some ED students spontaneously chose to use Spanish, the language of instruction in the content areas, to complete science and social studies activities. Zinnia wrote, as part of a social studies unit on the home and family:

Le gusta mi   [I like my
casa porke   house because
mi mama y papa   my mom and dad]
(Zinnia, ED, 5/7/01)

Several students also attempted writing that went beyond listing common words and everyday expressions, venturing into writing that demanded composing of connected text:

my mama jn tu mexiqo   [My mother went to Mexico]

(Nanette, SD, 4/24/01)

a Y B a r o u a P i ñ a D a [I borrowed
e n o S t o r B i C a S   (bought) a *piñata*
M a i B r o d r s B   in a store because
u r D e i   (it was) my
                             brother's
                             birthday]

(Cecilia, SD, 4/30/01)

Me FAMiLiA POR   [My family by
LiZZY G.   Lizzy G.
Me FAMiLiA   My family
AMOR ME   loves me
Me FAMiLiA ES   My family is
PEKENYO   small
PORKe IY   because there are
4 PERSONES   4 people]

(Lizzy, ED, 4/24/01. She asked for the word "small" in Spanish. An adult provided the word—*pequeña*—orally.)

Table 12.3 shows that children applied their growing knowledge about writing in general to tackle the task of writing in their nondominant language. By spring, the refusals had decreased, and many of the students were able to write in the other language using phonetic or invented spellings. These observations indicated that students did not revert to less mature forms when writing in the less-dominant language; rather, they were able to apply growing literacy knowledge in a biliterate way.

Early Biliterate Reading Forms

When students were asked to read in the nondominant language, they were able to choose from among a group of books that were familiar to them, either because they were children's classics, well-known television- or movie-character-based books, or part of their classroom materials. Many students chose to read well-known books from the classroom. Table 12.4 summarizes these findings, indicating students' growing awareness of written language features even in their nondominant language. Noticeably, by the end of the school year, 23% of the students were reading the nondominant language conventionally even when, given their more limited command of that language, they did not have available some of the fundamental cueing systems (e.g., syntactic, semantic) that aid readers of all ages, but specially emergent readers, in the reading of less familiar text.

As has been observed in other investigations reporting on bilingual students' reading abilities, lack of vocabulary and syntax

TABLE 12.3. Emergent Writing Systems Used in Children's Less-Dominant Language

Writing systems	Assessment point	
	Winter	Spring
Prephonemic	23%	3%
Drawing, scribbled letter-like shapes, letter strings	4%	
Known labels	19%	
Phonemic (invented spelling, conventional spelling, or a mix of both)	38%	72%
Refusals	38%	23%

Note. Entries are the percentage of students performing in each category.

TABLE 12.4. Emergent Reading Forms in Less-Dominant Language

Reading forms	Assessment point	
	Winter	Spring
Labeling and describing	2%	2%
Oral monologue	6%	0%
Mixed oral–written monologue	13%	4%
Written monologue	21%	19%
Naming letters	2%	4%
Aspectual/strategic reading	9%	17%
Conventional	6%	23%
Refusal	38%	30%

Note. Entries are the percentage of students performing in each category.

knowledge in the less dominant language was a major factor affecting these students' abilities to complete reading tasks in the nondominant language (García, 2000). Many students, ED as well as SD, commented on their lack of understanding of what they were reading, even when they had deployed graphophonemic knowledge to the best of their abilities. Recently, the same ED students, now in 2nd grade, commented to their teacher, after taking a standardized reading test in Spanish, that they did "a lot of guessing" because they did not know "so many words" in Spanish.

When looking at these results, it is important to consider that many of the books the children chose to read during the individual interviews were highly familiar to them, and that memory of the text played a big role in their ability to read the text conventionally. In other words, these students were able to read conventionally familiar text, but it is doubtful that they would have shown similar levels of conventional command of the reading process with unfamiliar text.

General Reflections

Language-specific differences between English and Spanish—with Spanish orthography following a more regular or stable letter–sound correspondence than English orthography (Goswami, 1999)—seemed to play a role in the preliminary results on reading and writing just reported, perhaps especially inflating the number of ED students who were able to read and write Spanish "conventionally." As explained before, many ED students who had mastered all the phoneme–grapheme correspondences in Spanish, aided by the strong regularity of those correspondences in the language, appeared to be able to decode text readily, even when they were often uncertain about the meaning of what they were reading. Similarly, this command of phoneme–grapheme correspondences in Spanish allowed some ED students to complete Spanish developmental spelling assessments (writing a series of words from dictation) and other writing tasks quite accurately, even when they did not always know the meaning of the words they were writing. Spanish, with its simpler orthogra-

phy, seemed to allow these kindergartners, having conquered the alphabetic principle, to demonstrate their growing graphophonemic matching skills with ease.

Given the small number of students enrolled in the target TWI program, statistical comparisons should be made with caution. However, the results of the standardized, early literacy, district-mandated assessment taken by the kindergartners confirm and complement the preliminary observations reported earlier. These assessments consisted of letter identification, concepts about print, and developmental spelling tests, and were administered in both languages starting in the winter. The standardized assessments show that both ED and SD students made not only extensive but also, and more importantly, *comparable* gains in their emergent dominant-language literacy abilities, achieving at similar levels by the end of the school year. The district program evaluation report also showed that SD students enrolled in the TWI program performed dramatically better on early literacy achievement measures that were administered in Spanish than did kindergarten English-language learners enrolled in the district transitional bilingual education program. Similarly, TWI ED students also performed considerably better on English literacy achievement measures than did English speakers enrolled in what are termed general education (nonbilingual) classes.

The most telling observation on the powerful literacy and biliteracy learning yields of this TWI environment came from one of the TWI teachers in the program. Ms. A commented that in her considerably extensive experience teaching bilingual kindergartners, this was the first time that the scores on the district-mandated literacy assessments in the winter and spring did not identify children according to racial or native-language group (Ms. A, personal communication, winter 2001). In other words, the distribution of low and high scores no longer aligned with students' language backgrounds.

The Culture of the TWI Classrooms

The observation of these kindergartners throughout the school year yielded pedagogically relevant results in terms of their early growth in literate and biliterate abilities. However, there are also important implications to be drawn from the observation of the biliterate culture of the TWI classes that supported and scaffolded that development. As they describe successful biliteracy development among bilingual students, researchers all emphasize the importance of language-learning situations that foster the development of both languages in an unmarked, holistic manner (Manyak, 2000; Moll & Dworin, 1996; Reyes, 2000). Children seem to develop bilingual and biliterate abilities more spontaneously and successfully when they experience instructional environments that allow for the use of both languages for communicative purposes, and that celebrate bilingualism and biliteracy. On the contrary, learning environments in which languages are marked or reserved for specific use (e.g., English for academic use, Spanish for social use) do not seem to support the development of biliteracy as efficiently (Lindholm-Leary, 2001; Manyak, 2000).

The TWI culture, one in which the way of doing, thinking, and interacting was always *bilingual,* evolved with time and made many aspects of language learning and language contrast especially salient for these students. Literacy and, more importantly, biliteracy experiences permeated TWI classroom life. Students, through their immersion in a bilingual/biliterate classroom culture that engaged them in bilingual communicative acts, seemed to explore and construct their social identities as bilingual individuals. They, as speakers, "readers and writers, position[ed] one another in particular ways, drawing on conventions and resources provided by the culture" (Kern, 2000, p. 34).

An example of how some of these TWI kindergartners perceived language-group memberships and their developing persona as not only TWI students but also as individuals is best illustrated by the conversation cited below. Luke, an ED student of Anglo background, with limited exposure to Spanish before entering the TWI program, told his mother about a planned playdate with Santiago, a Latino student with barely emergent knowledge of English. When Luke's mother asked, "Is Santiago one of the Spanish-speaking children [in your class]?" Luke answered without hesitation, "No . . . he is bilingual, like me."

Although, according to plans, students received language arts instruction in their dominant language, reading and writing in both languages became the *way of doing things* in these classrooms. As the results reported here indicated, with time, students came to believe they could *do school* in both languages. Many visitors to the TWI classrooms commented on the boundless linguistic energy that seemed to characterize these classes. Parents, teachers, and administrators admired the children's high levels of involvement in conversation, regardless of the language used. The general feeling seemed to be "Of course we can do this, in English, in Spanish, and in both!"

During the first hour of his first day in kindergarten, Ray (ED) asked:

"Mr. U [his teacher], why are you talking to me in Spanish? I don't understand *a word* you are saying!"

(Ray, ED, first day of school)

But it took only another hour for the first example of *doing school in two languages* to crop up:

MR. U: ¡Atención! ¡Atención!

SHEILA (ED): Attention! Attention!

MR. U: ¡Sí muy bien, Sheila! *Atención y attention* suenan parecido. ¡Lo notaste tu!" [Yes, very good, Sheila! *Atención* and *attention* sound similar. You noticed it!]

(Sheila, ED, and Mr. U, first day of school)

Approximately 3 weeks later, during an English as a second language (ESL) lesson, when SD students received instruction in English, the teacher explained to the group members that they needed to sing a song a couple of times, adhering to original lyrics, because "some of our friends are learning some English words." Ray's comments now are different than those he made on the first day:

"Yeah, and we are learning a *lot* of Spanish!!"
(Ray, ED, 10/5/00)

Responding to the intense language-learning experience that was carefully planned and masterfully retooled by the teachers, students initiated queries, remarked on the differences between languages, and shared their linguistic insights freely and constantly. They actively participated in the unveiling of the intricacies of the bilingualism/biliteracy learning process from the beginning of the school year.

In this TWI program, certain curricular routines proved to be especially fertile grounds for biliteracy engagements. Teachers found that Morning Message and Calendar (conducted in Spanish) provided an ideal springboard into discussions about languages, their distinctive characteristics, and key, emergent literacy and biliteracy concepts (e.g., *martes* and *miércoles* start with the same letter; most days of the week have the same—*es*—ending) (Barbour & Zecker, 2002; Zecker, Barbour, Jones, & Puentes, 2002).

Children's comments and questions revealed thoughtful engagement in the language-learning process and evidenced the juggling of literate metaknowledge with language-specific knowledge discussed in previous sections. In fact, many questions about language differences and contrast were not posed by the teachers but, on the contrary, were initiated by the children, demonstrating the high levels of language and literacy awareness they were gaining:

Justine (ED) mentions that Spanish *i* has the same name as the English letter *e*.
(Justine, ED, 10/30/00)

During a read-aloud, Matt (ED) reads aloud the title of the book *El Otoño* before the teacher does. Wally (ED) then comments:

"I know it's in Spanish because the *n* has the little thing on top."
(Wally, ED, gesturing to represent the mark on top of the ñ, 10/19/00)

On a different day, Edgard (ED), trying to complete some journal writing in Spanish,

asked his teacher for help spelling *cuando* (when). Ms. R encouraged him to use phonemic cues, and the following dialogue ensued:

Ms. R: Dilo, a ver ¿Qué sonido escuchas? [Say it, what sound do you hear?]
EDGARD: C . . . u . . . u . . . u. . . Is it a *u* or a *w*?
Ms. R: ¿Qué te parece? [What do you think?]
EDGARD: (*talking to himself as he walks to his chair*) It's a *u* because they don't use many *w*'s.
(Edgard, ED, 2/15/02)

These preliminary results, although expected in terms of the developmental path followed by kindergartners, indicated strong and widespread progress in literacy skills for all the TWI students in these two classrooms, regardless of their language and ethnic background. They highlight the students' response to a literacy-rich environment that allowed them to grow as bilingual and biliterate individuals by emphasizing meaningful communicative practices. Perhaps more importantly, they highlight the undeniable nature and power of language and literacy as sociocultural practices, and the importance of classroom experiences in markedly scaffolding students' construction of selves as knowers.

Summary

In general, these kindergartners' development as biliterate readers and writers followed a pattern that did not replicate native-language literacy development step by step, as if the children were starting anew with the new language; rather, it was a side-by-side process. The fact that these kindergartners did not retrace emergent literacy developmental steps but seemed to resort to similar emergent forms of reading and writing, whether in the dominant or "other" language, supports the notion that developmental biliteracy learning is a *seamless* or *boundless* process, even in its early stages (Reyes, 2000). When attempting to read and write in their less dominant language, these students did not revert to less sophisticated emergent literacy behaviors. On the contrary, they approached reading and writing tasks by deploying known strategies, adjusting their performance to language differences and their limitations in the oral command of the less-known language, and demonstrating reliance on a fund of common language/literacy knowledge. These observations underscore children's language-learning flexibility and their responsiveness to rich, biliterate classroom environments that scaffold the development of biliteracy and bilingualism by building on children's language heritages.

In an era of indiscriminate bilingual education bashing, when the call is to introduce relevant and pedagogically responsible changes in literacy and biliteracy instruction for the bilingual children who populate U.S. schools, the experiences of dual-language students, like the kindergartners described in this chapter, deserve attention. Their kindergarten journey shows the promise of bilingual programs that tap into bilingual students' potential and seek language richness for all, programs that put an end to the notion of bilingualism-as-a-deficit and bilingual education as a missionary-like quest to save English-language-learning ethnic minorities (Gutiérrez, 2001).

CONCLUSIONS

In general, findings from studies of developmental biliteracy among young children emphasize the multilayered, dynamic nature of language-learning processes, and the complex interplay and balance between translanguage knowledge and attention to linguistic code particularities that developing bilingual readers and writers seem capable of juggling. These findings reiterate the importance of applying dynamic research frameworks to the study of language and literacy learning, investigative paradigms that take into account the sociocultural construction of language and knowledge, and the situated aspects of learning (Hornberger, 1994).

Recent research on developmental biliteracy has indicated that young bilingual learners developing early biliteracy skills simultaneously appear to cultivate a general reservoir of literacy meta-knowledge and

are not at risk of confusion. Young biliterates seem to draw on this reservoir when facing literacy tasks, regardless of language, and at the same time construct parallel stores of language-specific literacy knowledge. As reported in many of the studies reviewed in this chapter, there appears to be no need for young readers and writers to relearn (or, more importantly, be retaught) certain aspects of *being literate* as they explore literacy in their less dominant language (Pérez, 1998; Reyes, 1992). These ideas have important implications for the development of literacy curricula in bilingual education programs, many of which often disregard students' previous literacy-learning experiences, reiterate basic instruction, and focus on form rather than on communicative uses of language. Finally, but definitely not less importantly, the rethinking of biliteracy development and its implications for bilingual education reform in the United States are likely to have serious and fundamental repercussions for teacher education programs, stressing, one more time, the paramount need for the preparation of multilingual, multicultural professional educators.

NOTE

1. Readers are requested to contact the author for a copy of the Zecker (2001) Final Report to the Spencer Foundation prior to citing specific findings of this investigation.

REFERENCES

Ada, A. F. (1988). The Pájaro Valley experience: Working with Spanish-speaking parents to develop children's reading and writing skills in the home and through the use of children's literature. In T. Skutnab-Kangas & J. Cummins (Eds.), *Minority education: From shame to struggle* (pp. 223–238). Clevendon, UK: Multilingual Matters.

Amrein, A., & Peña, R. (2000). Asymmetry in dual language practice: Assessing imbalance in a program promoting equality. *Education Policy Analysis Archives*, 8. Available online at *http://epaa.asu.edu/epaa/v8n8.html*

Arlington Public Schools and Center for Applied Linguistics (1997). *Investigating alternative assessment in two-way bilingual immersion programs*. Final Report to the U.S. Deptartment of Education—OBEM-

LA. Arlington, VA: Arlington Public Schools Education Center.

August, D., & Hakuta, K. (1997). *Improving schools for language minority-children.* Washington, DC: National Academy Press.

Barbour, K., & Zecker, L. B. (2002). *Curricular routines in a dual language classroom: How to scaffold emergent biliteracy development.* Manuscript in preparation.

Barfield, S. C., & Rhodes, N. C. (1993). *Review of the seventh year of the partial immersion program at Key Elementary School.* Washington, DC: Center for Applied Linguistics.

Battle, J. (1993). Mexican-American bilingual kindergartners' collaborations in meaning making. In D. J.. Leu & C. K. Kinzer (Eds.), *Forty-second yearbook of the National Reading Conference: Examining central issues in literacy research, theory, and practice* (pp. 163–170). Chicago: National Reading Conference.

Bauer, E. B. (2000). Code-switching during shared and independent reading: Lessons learned from a preschooler. *Research in the Teaching of English, 35,* 101–131.

Bialystok, E. (Ed.). (1995). *Language processing by bilingual children.* Cambridge, UK: Cambridge University Press.

Bialystok, E. (1997). Effects of bilingualism and biliteracy on children's emerging concepts of print. *Developmental Psychology, 33,* 429–440.

Carlisle, J. F., Beeman, M., & Zecker, L. B. (2001). *Learning to write in two languages: More on the question of transfer.* Manuscript in preparation.

Cazabon, M., Lambert, W. E., & Hall, G. (1993). *Two-way bilingual education: A progress report on the Amigos program* (Research Report No. 7). Santa Cruz, CA and Washington, DC: National Center for Research on Cultural Diversity and Second Language Learning.

Christian, D. (1996). Two-way immersion education: Students learning through two languages. *Modern Languages Journal, 80*(1), 66–76.

Christian, D., & Mahrer, C. (1992). *Two-way bilingual programs in the United States, 1991–1992.* Santa Cruz, CA and Washington, DC: National Center for Research on Cultural Diversity and Second-Language Learning.

Christian, D., & Mahrer, C. (1993). *Two-way bilingual programs in the United States, 1992–1993.* Santa Cruz, CA and Washington, DC: National Center for Research on Cultural Diversity and Second-Language Learning.

Christian, D., & Montone, C. (1994). *Two-way bilingual programs in the United States, 1993–1994.* Santa Cruz, CA and Washington, DC: National Center for Research on Cultural Diversity and Second-Language Learning.

Cloud, N., Genesee, F., & Hamayan, E. (2000). *Dual language instruction.* Boston: Thomas Learning.

Collier, V., & Thomas, W. (2001). A national study of school effectiveness for language minority students' long-term academic achievement final report: Project 1.1. Available at: *http://www.crede.ucsc.edu/research/ llaa/1.1-final.html*

Cummins, J. (1993). Empowerment through biliteracy. In J. V. Tinajero & A. F. Ada (Eds.), *The power of two languages: Literacy and biliteracy for Spanish-speaking students* (pp. 9–25). New York: Macmillan.

Cummins, J. (1994). The socioacademic achievement model in the context of coercive and collaborative relations of power. In R. DeVillar, C. Faltis, & J. Cummins (Eds.), *Cultural diversity in schools* (pp. 363–390). Albany: State University of New York Press.

Cummins, J. (2001). *Negotiating identities: Education for empowerment in a diverse society* (2nd ed.). Los Angeles: California Association for Bilingual Education.

Cunningham, P., Hall, D., & Defee, M. (1998). Non-ability grouped, multi-level instruction: Eight years later. *Reading Teacher, 51,* 652–664.

Davis, L., Carlisle, J., & Beeman, M. (1999). Hispanic children's writing in English and Spanish when English is the language of instruction. In T. Shanahan & F. Rodriguez-Brown (Eds.), *Forty-eighth yearbook of the National Reading Conference* (pp. 238–248). Chicago: National Reading Conference.

Delgado-Gaitán, C. (1990). *Literacy for empowerment: The role of parents in children's education.* London: Falmer Press.

Durgunoğlu, A. Y., Mir, M., & Ariño-Martí, S. (2002). The relationship between bilingual children's reading and writing in their two languages. In S. Ransdell & M.L. Barbier (Eds.), *New directions for research in L2 writing* (pp. 81–100). Dordrecht, the Netherlands: Kluwer.

Durgunoğlu, A. Y., & Verhoeven, L. (1998). *Acquisition of literacy in a multilingual context: A cross-cultural perspective.* Mahwah, NJ: Erlbaum.

Dyson, A. H. (1985). Individual differences in emerging writing. In M. Farr (Ed.), *Advances in writing research: Children's early writing development* (pp. 59–125). Norwood, NJ: Ablex.

Dyson, A. H. (1989). *Multiple worlds of child writers: Friends learning to write.* New York: Teachers College Press.

Dyson, A. H. (1993). *Social worlds of children learning to write in an urban primary school.* New York: Teachers College Press.

Edelsky, C. (1986). *Writing in a bilingual program: Había una vez.* Norwood, NJ: Ablex.

Fantini, A. (1985). *Language acquisition of a bilingual child.* Clevedon, UK: Multilingual Matters.

Ferdman, B, Weber, R., & Ramírez, A. (Eds.). (1994). *Literacy across languages and cultures.* Albany: State University of New York Press.

Ferreiro, E. (1997). *Alfabetización: Teoría y práctica* [*Literacy: Theory and practice*]. Mexico City, Mexico: Siglo XXI.

Ferreiro, E., Pontecorvo, C., Ribeiro, N., & García Hidalgo, I. (1996). *Caperucita Roja aprende a escribir* [Little Red Riding Hood learns to write]. Barcelona: Editorial Gedisa.

Ferreiro, E., & Teberosky, A. (1979). *Los sistemas de escritura en el desarrollo del niño. [Literacy before schooling]*. Mexico: Siglo XXI.

Fitzgerald, J., & Shanahan, T. (2000). Reading and writing relations and their development. *Educational Psychologist, 35*, 39–50.

Flores, B. (1990). *Children's sociopsychogenesis of literacy and biliteracy*. Proceedings from the First Research Symposium on Limited English Proficiency Students Issues (OBELMA). Retrieved January, 2000, from *http://www.ncbe.gwu.edu/ncbepubs/symposia*

Freeman, R. D. (1996). Dual language planning at the Oyster Bilingual school: It is much more than language. *TESOL Quarterly, 30*(3), 557–582.

García, G. E. (2000). Bilingual children's reading. In M. L Kamil, P. B. Mosenthal, P. D. Pearson, & R. Barr (Eds.), *Handbook of reading research* (Vol. 3, pp. 813–834). Mahwah, NJ: Erlbaum.

García, G. E. (2001). A theoretical discussion of young bilingual children's reading (preschool-grade 3). In J. Hoffman, D. Schallert, C. Fairbanks, J. Worthy, & B. Maloch (Eds.). *50th yearbook of the National Reading Conference* (pp. 228–238). Chicago: National Reading Conference.

Geva, E., Wade-Wooley, L., & Shany, M. (1993). The concurrent development of spelling and decoding in two different orthographies. *Journal of Reading Behavior, 25*, 383–406.

Goswami, U. (1999). The relationship between phonological awareness and orthographic representation in different orthographies. In M. Harris & G. Hatano (Eds.), *Learning to read and write: A crosslinguistic perspective* (pp. 134–156). Cambridge, UK: Cambridge University Press.

Griego-Jones, T. (1994). Assessing students' perceptions of biliteracy in two-way bilingual classrooms. *Journal of Educational Issues of Language Minority Students, 13*, 79–93.

Gutiérrez, K. (2001). What's new in the English language arts: Challenging policies and practices, ¿y qué? *Language Arts, 78*(6), 564–569.

Gutiérrez, K., Baquedano-López, P., & Alvarez, H. (2000). Literacy as hybridity: Moving beyond bilingualism in urban classrooms. In M. de la Luz Reyes & J. Halcón (Eds.). *The best for our children: Critical perspectives on literacy for Latino students* (pp. 122–141). New York: Teachers College Press.

Harris, M., & Hatano, G. (Eds.). (1999). *Learning to read and write: A crosslinguistic perspective*. Cambridge, UK: Cambridge University Press.

Hornberger, N. H. (1992). Biliteracy contexts, continua and contrasts: Policy and curriculum for Cambodian and Puerto Rican students in Philadelphia. *Education and Urban Society, 24*, 196–211.

Hornberger, N. H. (1994). Continua of biliteracy. In B. Ferdman, R. Weber, & A. Ramírez (Eds.), *Literacy across languages and cultures* (pp. 103–140). Albany: State University of New York Press.

Howard, E. (2002). Two-way immersion: A key to global awareness. *Educational Leadership, 10*, 62–64.

Howard, E., & Loeb, M. (1998). *In their own words: Two-way immersion teachers talk about their professional experiences*. Washington, DC: Center for Applied Linguistics.

Kern, R. (2000). *Literacy and language teaching*. New York: Oxford University Press.

Kuhlman, N. (1993). *Emerging literacy in a two-way bilingual first grade classroom* (ERIC Document Reproduction Service No. ED360868).

Lensmire, T. (1994). *When children write*. New York: Teachers College Press.

Lessow-Hurley, J. (2000). *The foundations of dual language instruction*. New York: Addison Wesley-Longman.

Lindholm, K. J. (1990). Bilingual immersion education: Criteria for program development. In A. Padilla, H. Fairchild, & C. Valadez (Eds.), *Bilingual education: Issues and strategies* (pp. 91–105). Newbury Park, CA: Sage.

Lindholm, K. J. (1992). Two-way bilingual/immersion education: Theory, conceptual issues, and pedagogical implications. In R. V. Padilla & A. H. Benavides (Eds.), *Critical perspectives on bilingual education research* (pp. 195–220). Tempe, AZ: Bilingual Press/Editorial Bilingüe.

Lindholm, K. J., & Molina, R. (1998). Learning in dual language education classrooms in the U.S.: Implementation and evaluation outcomes. In J. Arnau & J. M. Artigal (Eds.), *Immersion programmes: A European perspective* (pp. 80–93). Barcelona: Universidad de Barcelona.

Lindholm-Leary, K. J. (2001). *Dual language education*. Clevendon, UK: Multilingual Matters.

López, M. G. (2000). The language situation of the Hmong, Khmer, and Loatian communities in the United States. In S. L. McKay & S. C. Wong (Eds.), *New immigrants in the United States* (pp. 232–262). Cambridge, UK: Cambridge University Press.

Maguire, M. H., & Graves, B. (2001). Speaking personalities in primary school children's L2 writing. *TESOL Quarterly, 35*, 561–593.

Manyak, P. (2000, December). *Negotiating life and literacy in a first-grade English immersion class*. Paper presented at the Annual Meeting of National Reading Conference, Scottsdale, AZ.

Moll, L. (1992). Literacy research in community and classrooms: A sociocultural approach. In R. Beach, J. L. Green, M. L. Kamil, & T. Shanahan (Eds.), *Multidisciplinary perspectives on literacy research* (pp. 211–244). Urbana, IL: National Council of the Teachers of English.

Moll, L., & Dworin, J. (1996). Biliteracy development in classrooms: Social dynamics and cultural possibilities. In D. Harris (Ed.), *Discourse: Learning and schooling* (pp. 221–246). Cambridge, UK: Cambridge University Press.

Mulhern, M. (1994). *Webs of meaning: The literate lives of three Mexican-American kindergartners*. Unpublished doctoral dissertation, University of Illinois, Chicago.

National Center for Educational Statistics. (2000). Retrieved February, 2001, from *http://nces.ed.gov*

Newkirk, T. (1989). *More than stories*. Portsmouth, NH: Heinemann.

Ogbu, J. (1987). Variability in minority responses to schooling: Nonimmigrants versus immigrants. In G. Spindler & L. Sindler (Eds.), *Interpretive ethnography in education: At home and abroad* (pp. 255–280). Hillsdale, NJ: Erlbaum.

Padilla, R. V., & Benavídes, A. H. (Eds.) (1992). *Critical perspectives on bilingual education research*. Tempe, AZ: Bilingual Press/Editorial Bilingüe.

Pellicer, A. (2002, July). *Children's role as translators: Metalinguistic awareness on the notion of the technical term "word."* Paper presented at the 8th International Conference of the European Association for Research on Learning and Instruction. Stafford, UK.

Pérez, B. (1994a). Spanish literacy development: A descriptive study of four bilingual whole-language classrooms. *Journal of Reading Behavior, 26,* 74–94.

Pérez, B. (1994b). Biliteracy development in Latino communities. In R. Rodríguez, N. J. Ramos, & J. Ruiz-Escalante (Eds.), *Compendium of readings in bilingual education: Issues and practices* (pp. 119–123). San Antonio: Texas Association for Bilingual Education.

Pérez, B. (1998). *Sociocultural context of language and literacy*. Mahwah, NJ: Erlbaum.

Pontecorvo, C., Orsolini, M., Burge, B., & Resnick, L. (1996). *Children's early text construction*. Mahwah, NJ: Erlbaum.

Quintero, E., & Huerta-Macías, A. (1995). Bilingual children's writing: Evidence of active learning in social context. *Journal of Research in Childhood Education, 9,* 157–165.

Ramírez, J. D. (2000). *Bilingualism and literacy: Problem or opportunity? A synthesis of a reading research on bilingual students*. Proceedings of research symposium on High Standards in Reading for Students from Diverse Language Groups: Research, Practice, and Policy. Washington, DC: U.S. Department of Education, OBLEMA. Available online at *www.ncla.gwu.edu/ias*

Reyes, M. de la Luz. (1992). Challenging venerable assumptions: Literacy instruction for linguistically different students. *Harvard Educational Review, 62,* 427–446.

Reyes, M. de la Luz. (2000). Unleashing possibilities: Biliteracy in the primary grades. In M. de la Luz Reyes & J. J. Halcón (Eds.), *Best for our children: Critical perspectives on literacy for Latino students* (pp. 96–121). New York: Teachers College Press.

Reyes, M. de la Luz, & Halcón, R. (Eds.) (2000). *The best for our children: Critical perspectives on literacy for Latino students*. New York: Teachers College Press.

Riley, R. (March, 2000). *Excelencia para todos—excellence for all: The progress of Hispanic education and the challenges of a new century*. Remarks as prepared for delivery by U.S. Secretary of Education, Bell Multicultural High School, Washington, DC.

Rueda, R., & García, E. (1996). Teachers' perspectives on literacy assessment and instruction with language-minority students: A comparative study. *Elementary School Journal, 96,* 311–332.

Silva, A. (1998). Emergent Spanish writing of a second grader in a whole language classroom. In B. Pérez (Ed.), *Sociocultural context of language and literacy* (pp. 223–248). Mahwah, NJ: Erlbaum.

Sulzby, E. (1985a). Children's emergent reading of favorite storybooks: A developmental study. *Reading Research Quarterly, 20,* 458–481.

Sulzby, E. (1985b). Kindergarteners as writers and readers. In M. Farr (Ed.), *Advances in writing research: Vol. 1. Children's writing development* (pp. 127–199). Norwood, NJ: Ablex.

Sulzby, E., Barnhart, J., & Hieshima, J. (1989). Forms of writing and rereading from writing: A preliminary report. In J. Mason (Ed.), *Reading–writing connections* (pp. 31–63). Boston: Allyn & Bacon.

Teale, W., & Sulzby, E. (Eds.). (1986). *Emergent literacy*. Norwood, NJ: Ablex.

Thomas, W., & Collier, V. P. (1997). *Bilingual and ESL classrooms: Teaching in multicultural contexts*. Boston: McGraw-Hill.

Tinajero, J. V.,& Ada, A. F. (Eds.). (1993). *The power of two languages: Literacy and biliteracy for Spanish-speaking students*. New York: Macmillan.

Tolchinsky, L. (1998). Early acquisition in Catalan and Israeli communities. In A. Y. Durgunoğlu & L. Verhoeven (Eds.), *Literacy development in multilingual contexts: Cross-cultural perspectives* (pp. 267–288). Mahwah, NJ: Erlbaum.

Tolchinsky Lansman, L. (Ed.). (1991). *Culture, schooling and psychological development*. Norwood, NJ: Ablex.

Valdés, G. (1997). Dual-language immersion programs: A cautionary note concerning the education of language-minority students. *Harvard Educational Review, 67,* 391–429.

Vernon, S. (1993). Initial sound/letter correspondences in children's early written productions. *Journal of Research in Childhood Education, 8,* 12–22.

Wells, G., & Chang-Wells, G. L. (1992). *Constructing knowledge together: Classrooms as centers of inquiry and literacy*. Portsmouth, NH: Heinemann.

Wodala, K. (1994). The development of initial reading in a bilingual child. In G. Extra & L. Verhoeven (Eds.), *The cross-linguistic study of bilingual development* (pp. 129–144). Amsterdam: Royal Netherlands Academy of Arts and Sciences.

Wong-Fillmore, L. (1992). Against our best interest: The attempt to sabotage bilingual education. In J. Crawford (Ed.). *Language loyalties: A source book on the official English controversy* (pp. 367–373). Chicago: University of Chicago Press.

Yaden, D., Rowe, D., & MacGillivray, L. (2000). Emergent literacy: A matter (polyphony) of perspectives. In M. Kamil, P. Mosenthal, P. D. Pearson, & R. Barr (Eds.), *Handbook of reading research* (Vol. III, pp. 425–454). Mahwah, NJ: Erlbaum.

Zecker, L. B. (1996). Early development in written language: Children's emergent knowledge of genre-specific characteristics. *Reading and Writing: An Interdisciplinary Journal, 8,* 5–25.

Zecker, L. B. (1999). Different texts, different emergent writing forms. *Language Arts, 76*(6), 483–490.

Zecker, L. B. (2001, August). *Emergent biliteracy*. Final Report to the Spencer Foundation Small Grants Program, Chicago, IL.

Zecker, L. B., Barbour, K., Jones, J., & Puentes, A. (2002, January). *Emergent biliteracy: The experiences of kindergartners in a two-way immersion bilingual education program.* Paper presented at the annual meeting of the Chicago Metropolitan Association for Education of Young Children, Chicago, IL.

III

LANGUAGE PROCESSES UNDERLYING ATYPICAL LITERACY LEARNING: COMPLEMENTARY PERSPECTIVES

INTRODUCTION

General consensus exists among language researchers that the multiple processing levels of the linguistic-discourse system continuously interact in a synergistic manner. A major issue for language research and its professional applications is how these interactions can be made more visible. Responding to these concerns, the contributors in Part III provide in-depth examinations of the various processes that constitute typical language development, the relationship of these processes to literacy learning, and how disruption of these processes affects literacy learning in critical and dynamic ways.

The first three chapters in this section collectively focus attention on children's orientation to the orthographic word as a phonemic and morphological unit, on processes of word learning, and on the effects of these processes on word reading and reading comprehension. In Chapter 13, Gary Troia provides an incisive discussion of phonological processing and its relationship to beginning reading, including the role of phonological processing in non-alphabetic languages, such as Chinese. He then asks what mechanism might be responsible for children's progressive ability to attend to the phoneme as an abstract linguistic unit, as well as their increasing aptitude in rapidly retrieving phonological codes from the lexicon in order to decode fluently. Troia argues that one process accounting for this shift in the linguistic knowledge base might be lexical restructuring, a word-specific process whereby children must eventually reorganize their lexicon from more holistic representations into segmental representations as they acquire new word meanings sharing similar phonological properties. The difficulties that many poor readers encounter with phonological processing are then dissected in terms of the evidence for two conflicting accounts: auditory temporal processing and speech perception. Troia links the speech-perception explanation to the notion of incomplete lexical restructuring. According to this view, a less dense lexicon may be the product of fuzzy phonological representations that then will impact all aspects of phonological processing. Troia also warns that many published studies of phonological processing have not sufficiently attended to the significance of children's other oral language abilities as contributors to their success with beginning reading.

In Chapter 14, Karla McGregor takes readers further into word learning by making an important distinction between the breadth and depth of vocabulary knowledge. She attributes breadth to the process of fast mapping, or the incidental learning of new word meanings. Fast mapping becomes discernible at around 16 to 19 months, when young children experience a rapid burst in their rate of word learning, and it continues through the school-age years, when reading and writing substantially influence the rate of incidental learning. McGregor accounts for the depth of lexical knowledge through a slow-mapping process, or the extended mapping of fast-mapped word meanings via the multiple exposures afforded through formal interactions with written texts. She points out that the greater a child's lexical depth and breadth, the more that child will have access to the conceptual resources for attaining proficient word recognition and reading comprehension. McGregor then makes the case for lexical deficits predating reading experience in children who ultimately struggle with word recognition and reading comprehension. She also argues that children with reading disability are likely to have less plentiful semantic networks due to their increasingly restricted opportunities to learn new meanings and enrich them through text interactions. The chapter concludes with implications for the support of vocabulary learning by teachers and speech–language pathologists.

From a complementary perspective, Joanne Carlisle in Chapter 15 approaches the slow mapping of meanings in terms of word-formation processes motivated by derivational morphology. She makes the argument that the comprehension and use of morphologically complex words evolves over a long period of language learning and demands the integrated processing of phonological, semantic, and syntactic knowledge, combined with an implicit sensitivity towards morphological structure. Carlisle's thorough review of factors influencing the development of morphological awareness is followed by a comprehensive discussion of various linguistic attributes that affect children's learning of derivations. Among these attributes are word frequency (word and affix familiarity) and the degree of transparency, or family resemblance, between a base word and its derivations. Carlisle than poses an important question about the connections among oral language knowledge of morphology, the ability to engage in morphological analysis, and proficiency in word reading and text-level comprehension. In the concluding section of the chapter, she outlines the need for explicit instruction in morphological analysis for students with reading and language learning disabilities.

Chapters 13–15 stress the relevance of children's progressive use of analogical reasoning in their discovery of relationships that guide new ways of thinking about units of form and meaning. In Chapters 16–18, readers are exposed to the broader levels of the linguistic/discourse system, in which inferential processes assume an even greater role in proficient reading and writing.

In Chapter 16, Cheryl Scott argues that federal and academic reports on the underlying causes of literacy difficulties have not paid "attention to sentence-level grammar as a significant contributor to the nation's literacy ills or as an instructional target" (p. 338). Scott finds this oversight striking, given the developmental psycholinguistic research on syntax as a core deficit in the diagnosis of a specific language impairment in children who typically are also at high risk for significant reading and writing problems. Scott details several syntactic and language modality factors that contribute to complexity in sentence processing in both reading and writing. These same factors may function as insurmountable obstacles for less linguistically proficient students. Drawing on models of sentence processing, she stresses the importance of parsing skill, or the accessibility of implicit and explicit knowledge of tree and phrase structure, for proficiency in reading and writing. Scott argues that parsing is particularly important beginning in grade 4, when children are increasingly confronted with sentence structures that differ significantly from their everyday conversational use. In addition, she carefully considers current methodological limitations for determining causal links between oral syntactic abilities and reading and writing impairments and suggests research avenues that might address these restrictions.

In Chapter 17, Mavis Donahue and Sharon Foster take readers into another less-explored domain of literary comprehension. These authors suggest that complex discourse knowledge and interpersonal reasoning is required for students to appreciate the social paradoxes in more intricate narrative texts, such as Jane Austin's *Emma*. Donahue and Foster argue that the ability to interpret the reasons fictitious people behave as they do in literary texts is premised on the ability to process text content through our social scripts, whose origins are found in oral discourse experiences. The implication is that identifying interactions among difficulties in social cognition and reading comprehension may illuminate why some readers strain to understand particular texts when their decoding ability, vocabulary, fluency levels, and awareness of text structures suggest that they should not be struggling. In the final section of their chapter, Donahue and Foster provide some suggestions for further research on interactions between social cognition and reading comprehension, and they offer guidelines for practitioners to consider in recruiting the social-problem-solving abilities of struggling readers.

Continuing with the analysis of larger systems that guide comprehension and inferencing in both the oral and written domains, Judith Duchan, in Chapter 18, presents a schema framework to fuse multiple perspectives on theory and practice in language and literacy learning. Duchan defines schemas as "abstract, complex, ever changing conceptual structure[s] [that] provide children with the conceptual apparatus for making sense of the world around them" (p. 378). She then indicates how the portrayal of schemas depends on researchers' theoretical interests and on the functions of the particular schema model in explaining a conceptual domain. Duchan attributes the growth of inferencing and meta-representations to schema knowledge, since, by their character, schemas "are based on going beyond the information provided to a more general understanding" (p. 386). She discusses four kinds of schemas in relation to their respective developmental pathways for various aspects of language and literacy learning in the intermediate and upper grades. For example, she argues that children must have consolidated the appropriate schemas for competent oral participation in a variety of complicated discourse genres, as well as for reading and writing. In the final part of her discussion, Duchan highlights gaps in our knowledge about schema development and effective instructional practices. Of critical import, Duchan asks that researchers and practitioners reflect on the paradigms that guide their decisions on what should be studied and what is relevant to teach.

The final chapter in Part III tackles a topic seldom regarded in the literature on potential linkages between language and literacy learning—the metalinguistic knowledge that intersects with executive functions and metacognition to promote self-regulation in reading comprehension. In this synthesizing chapter, Carol Westby first presents the role of metacognition and executive functioning in analyzing text critically and applying this information for problem-solving purposes. Next, she traces the neurobiological development of self-regulation, as well as the socialization practices that influence this outcome. Westby then describes the strategies that good readers employ for evaluating and promoting self-regulation in reading. In the final portion, Westby proposes a language intervention framework for thinking about deficits in executive functioning and their impact on reading comprehension.

As a group, the authors of the seven chapters in Part III meticulously address the complexities of the language processes that are implicated in literacy learning. At the same time, they clearly portray the theoretical and methodological challenges that must be unraveled beyond phonological processing if causal linkages are to emerge between other spoken-language domains and atypical literacy learning.

13

Phonological Processing and Its Influence on Literacy Learning

GARY A. TROIA

Phonological processing is one of the most well-researched phenomena in cognitive psychology, although it continues to offer scholars and educators much to scrutinize and debate. Phonological processing refers to cognitive operations that rely on the phonological structure of language for their execution, especially those associated with the recognition, comprehension, storage, retrieval, and production of linguistic codes. Phonological processing operations typically function automatically, such as during real-time speech perception, but skilled language users gradually develop the ability to consider purposefully and manipulate phonological information (Catts, Fey, Zhang, & Tomblin, 1999). Phonological processing is in its own right worthy of extensive investigation, but it is the relationship of phonological processing with the development and performance of literate acts, most notably reading and spelling, that confers its preeminence for those who study how children and adults use phonological information.

The primary goal of this chapter is to review the extant literature on phonological processing and its connections with English-language literacy. First, phonological processing operations that are closely associated with literacy are defined, and their linkages with each other and with reading and spelling are examined. Next, the implications of poor phonological processing for literacy acquisition and achievement are discussed, followed by a consideration of perceptual disorders as a root cause for observed impairments in phonological processing. The chapter concludes with implications for integrating research with practice.

PHONOLOGICAL PROCESSING OPERATIONS: DEFINITIONS AND TIES TO LITERACY

Overview of Phonological Processing

Phonological processing is critical for the development of proficient literacy skills, principally because alphabetic orthographies encode lexical entries more or less at the level of the phoneme, the smallest segment of a spoken language's phonological structure that cues meaningful differences between words. When attempting to identify a printed word, beginning readers of an alphabetic script rely mostly on phonological recoding, converting the letters and letter strings into their corresponding phonemes, then reassembling the sounds to pronounce the word (Torgesen, Wagner, & Rashotte, 1997; Torgesen et al., 2001). Phonological recoding is facilitated by graphophonemic knowledge and phonological awareness. Sufficient knowledge of letter–sound associations permits accurate and rapid mapping between phonemes and graphemes (Adams, 1990; Catts, 1989; Juel, 1988; Juel, Griffith, & Gough, 1986; Liberman & Shankweiler, 1985, 1991; Vellutino & Scanlon, 1991), but to take full advantage of an alphabetic orthography, readers also must possess explicit awareness of the segmental nature of speech—that speech comprises discrete sounds (Liberman & Shankweiler, 1991); otherwise, the association between letters and sounds holds little meaning. As would be expected, both graphophonemic knowledge and phonological awareness make substantial and unique contributions to growth in reading and spelling skills, especially word recognition (Adams, 1990; Burgess & Lonigan, 1998; Lonigan, Burgess, Anthony, & Barker, 1998).

In addition to letter–sound knowledge and phonological awareness, working memory and lexical retrieval also appear to play a prominent role in the development of proficient reading and spelling. As children read or spell a word, they retrieve orthographic and phonological information about the word from the lexicon and hold this information in working memory as they map the constituent sounds to their corresponding letters (Gathercole & Baddeley, 1993; Swank, 1994; Wagner, Torgesen, Laughon, Simmons, & Rashotte, 1993). Lexical retrieval and working memory predict additional variance in basic reading ability beyond that predicted by graphophonemic knowledge and phonological awareness (Manis, Doi, & Bhadha, 2000; Wolf & Bowers, 1999; see also Meschyan & Hernandez, Chapter 4, this volume).

Phonological awareness, retrieval of phonologically coded information from the lexicon, and phonological coding in working memory are considered to be the core

phonological processing operations important to literacy (Wagner & Torgesen, 1987). However, their relations to reading and spelling achievement, and to each other, are complex and influenced by age, task and stimulus attributes, and literacy experiences. Each of these core phonological processing operations and their relations are considered next in more detail. First, however, the relevance of phonological processing in alphabetic languages other than English and in nonalphabetic languages, such as Chinese, is briefly addressed. An understanding of how phonological processing is utilized in other written languages affords a more comprehensive view of the fundamental properties and complexities of this phenomenon.

Relevance of Phonological Processing in Other Languages

In the past decade, research has established that phonological processing is critical for literacy in other alphabetic languages, such as Spanish and German (e.g., Carrillo, 1994; Gonzales & Valle, 2000; Wimmer, 1993), perhaps more so than for literacy in English, because reading success in these relatively orthographically transparent languages depends more heavily on phonological recoding of print. For example, children learning to read Spanish, German, Italian, Greek, and Turkish are able to decode pseudowords (i.e., orthographic and phonological rimes) with greater accuracy and speed than are children learning to read English, presumably because these languages possess more regular spelling patterns and simply require a direct mapping of graphemes onto phonemes to recover the phonological structure of the printed stimulus (Cossu, Shankeiler, Liberman, & Gugliotta, 1995; Goswami, Gombert, & de Barrera, 1998; Goswami, Porpodas, & Wheelwright, 1997; Landerl, Wimmer, & Frith, 1997; Oney, Peter, & Katz, 1997; Wimmer & Goswami, 1994). It is important to note that whereas the relevance of phonological processing in languages with isomorphic symbol-to-sound correspondence is undisputed, the development and importance of certain phonological processing skills may differ substantially in some of these languages. In Spanish, for instance, awareness of onsets and rimes is not particularly relevant for learning to read (Jimenez, Alvarez, Estevez, & Hernandez-Valle, 2000).

On the surface, phonological processing might not appear to be central to literacy in nonalphabetic languages such as Chinese. After all, Chinese is presumably an ideographic script in which each symbol represents a concept or word. In actuality, Chinese is morphosyllabic—each character represents one morpheme and one syllable (Mattingly, 1992)—and a majority of the characters, close to 85%, are ideophonetic compounds in which a semantic component, or radical, cues word meaning, and a phonetic radical cues word pronunciation (Ho & Bryant, 1997a, 1997b, 1997c; Tan & Perfetti, 1998). However, the phonetic radical helps the reader predict a character's pronunciation only about 40% of the time (Zhou, 1978). Because of this limitation, Pin-Yin, a roman script that standardizes character pronunciation, was introduced in 1949 in most Chinese-speaking countries (except Hong Kong). Given that traditional Chinese characters contain partial phonetic information and most children learning to read Chinese are also taught Pin-Yin, it follows that phonological processing should play a crucial role in Chinese literacy.

Phonological awareness is, in fact, significantly correlated with concurrent and subsequent Chinese character recognition performance even after controlling for IQ, socioeconomic status, and initial reading level (Ho & Bryant, 1997a, 1997b, 1997c; Ho, Law, & Ng, 2000; Hu & Catts, 1998; Huang & Hanley, 1995), as are verbal memory (Hu & Catts, 1998; So & Siegel, 1997) and rapid naming (Hu & Catts, 1998). Ho and Bryant (1997a, 1997b) reported that first and second graders learning to read Chinese spontaneously used real phonetic radicals to recognize and pronounce pseudocharacters, but these findings should be interpreted cautiously, because the use of Pin-Yin probably yields an overestimate of the impact of phonological processing on Chinese character reading. To identify the precise role of phonological processing in reading traditional Chinese, Chan and Siegel (2001) assessed the recognition and recall of real and nonsense characters by poor and average readers in Hong Kong (recall that Pin-Yin is not taught there). They found that both older children with reading disabilities and average readers of all ages made more phonologically related pronunciation errors (errors were expected because of the low reliability of the phonetic radical in cueing pronunciation) than younger children with reading problems when reading real characters. Additionally, older poor readers and average readers of all ages performed better on the pseudocharacter recognition task and were more likely to confuse target characters with phonologically related foils during recall. Chan and Siegel argued that their results demonstrated the importance of phonological processing in Chinese reading. However, other studies suggest that phonological processing may be relevant when attempting to read compound characters (those containing both radicals) but not integrated ones (those containing neither radical), because phonological priming (using homophonous characters) effects are evident for the former but not the latter (Leck, Weekes, & Chen, 1995; Weekes, Chen, & Lin, 1998).

Cross-linguistic studies, such as those summarized here, indicate that the interdependence of phonological processing and reading is most likely universal, although the degree to which literacy achievement and phonological processing capabilities are related is, in part, a function of the phonetic regularity (or, as in the case of Chinese, the availability of phonetic cues) of a particular orthography. Additionally, some specific phonological processing skills (e.g., awareness of onsets and rimes) may be more or less important for literacy in languages that differ in their phonological structure. The importance of phonological processing in these diverse writing systems reinforces its theoretical and practical significance for all literacy learners, but we should be mindful of the fact that much of the research in this domain has been conducted with native English speakers learning to read and write English. When faced with studies that report the relative contributions of various phonological processing measures to variance in reading proficiency, for example, it is not possible to assume that the same relative contributions would be evident for children learning to read another script, alphabetic or otherwise. The remainder of this chapter deals with phonological processing in English, so the assumptions and interpretations presented are limited in scope.

Phonological Awareness

Development of Phonological Awareness

Phonological awareness in English unfolds over a protracted length of time, beginning in the early preschool years and continuing through the early elementary school years. It appears to emerge as an outcome of typically developing children's natural propensity for language and word play, early exposure to print and print-related concepts, and exemplary formal reading instruction (Ehri, 1987; Perfetti, Beck, Bell, & Hughes, 1987; Scarborough & Dobrich, 1994; Snow, Burns, & Griffith, 1998; Torgesen, Wagner, & Rashotte, 1994; Troia, Roth, & Graham, 1998; van Kleeck & Schuele, 1987). According to Gottardo, Stanovich, and Siegel (1996), children initially demonstrate sensitivity to shallower aspects of English phonological structure and then, later, to deeper aspects. Thus, young children find it easier to isolate and manipulate syllables than subsyllabic units of onsets and rimes, which they find easier to isolate and manipulate than individual sounds within the onset or rime portion of a word (Ball, 1993; Bruck & Treiman, 1990; Treiman & Zukowski, 1991, 1996).

Investigators also have reported that awareness of shallower aspects of phonological structure (e.g., rimes) is significantly correlated with subsequent development of sensitivity to deeper phonological structures (Bryant, MacLean, Bradley, & Crossland, 1990; Burgess, Lonigan, Anthony, & Barker, 1996; MacLean, Bryant, & Bradley, 1987). Deeper levels of phonological sensitivity presumably are difficult to attain, because smaller segments of speech are less perceptually salient than syllables (Gleitman & Rozin, 1977; Liberman, 1982; Liberman,

Shankweiler, Liberman, Fowler, & Fischer, 1977). However, even preschoolers can demonstrate sensitivity to subsyllabic segments. For example, children as young as 2 or 3 years can detect rhymes and alliteration (Chaney, 1992; Lonigan et al., 1998; MacLean et al., 1987; van Kleeck & Bryant, 1983; van Kleeck & Schuele, 1987). This does not necessarily mean that preschoolers exhibit conscious awareness of and the ability to manipulate onsets, rimes, and phonemes. To the contrary, when young children are asked to compare rimes or onsets for rhyming or alliteration tasks, they may simply use their implicit capacity to detect sound differences to perform these tasks. As such, these may tap epilinguistic abilities, or functional and relatively automated language skills, rather than metalinguistic abilities (Goswami, 1999, 2000).

Two lines of research evidence have converged to show that phonological sensitivity is related to success in literacy learning: correlational evidence and intervention evidence. First, a substantial amount of variance in concurrent and subsequent reading and spelling achievement is accounted for by performance on measures of phonological sensitivity, even when controlling for initial IQ, family income, vocabulary knowledge, and verbal memory (e.g., Blachman, 1984; Bryant et al., 1990; Felton & Wood, 1989; Goswami & Bryant, 1990; Juel et al., 1986; Mann, 1984, 1993; Swank, 1994; Torgesen et al., 1994; Treiman, 1991; Wagner & Torgesen, 1987; Wagner, Torgesen, & Rashotte, 1994). In fact, kindergartners' performance on phonological awareness tasks, particularly *phonemic* awareness tasks, is the single best predictor of their first- and second-grade reading achievement (Perfetti et al., 1987; Torgesen et al., 1994; Wagner & Torgesen, 1987). It has been demonstrated that this predictive relationship exists even before children begin school; individual differences in phonological sensitivity among preschoolers account for a large portion of variance in later reading achievement (Bryant et al., 1990; Burgess et al., 1996; Chaney, 1994; Lonigan et al., 1998). Second, teaching children (at least young children) how to manipulate speech sounds substantially improves literacy achievement. However, these gains are more robust and consistent when training in phonological sensitivity is coupled with instruction in graphophonemic knowledge (e.g., Ball & Blachman, 1988; Bradley & Bryant, 1983; Bus & van IJzendoorn, 1999; Byrne & Fielding-Barnsley, 1991; Hatcher, Hulme, & Ellis, 1994; Lundberg, Frost, & Peterson, 1988; Tangel & Blachman, 1992).

Influence of Reading and Spelling on Phonological Sensitivity

Although phonological sensitivity appears to have a causal role in the acquisition of basic literacy skills (Tunmer, Herriman, & Nesdale, 1988; Tunmer & Nesdale, 1985), there is evidence that advances in reading and spelling proficiency promote further development of phonological awareness (e.g., Ehri, 1987; Morais, Cary, Alegria, & Bertelson, 1979; Perfetti et al., 1987; Read, Zhang, Nie, & Ding, 1986; Torgesen et al., 1994; Wagner, 1988; Yopp, 1988; for further discussion, see Ehri & Snowling, Chapter 20, and Cassar & Treiman, Chapter 29, this volume). Not surprisingly, differences in performance on phonological awareness tasks between preschoolers from middle- and low-income families are attributable to their dissimilar experiences with printed material (Bowey, 1995; Lonigan et al., 1998). Thus, when preschoolers are exposed to storybooks or alphabet books that incorporate letter–sound information, significant improvements in phonological awareness are observed, but when these materials do not contain letter–sound information, phonological sensitivity is unaffected (Murray, Stahl, & Ivey, 1996). Furthermore, knowledge of the alphabet has been found to be significantly related to the development of deeper levels of phonological sensitivity (Bowey, 1994; Johnston, Anderson, & Holligan, 1996; Stahl & Murray, 1994; Wagner et al., 1994), though not necessarily shallower levels (Burgess & Lonigan, 1998; Naslund & Schneider, 1996). Burgess and Lonigan (1998), for instance, found that letter–*name* knowledge made a unique contribution to growth in deep phonological sensitivity (e.g., phonemic awareness) among 4- and 5-year-old children after controlling for age and oral language abilities, but letter–*sound* knowledge did not, possibly due to floor effects on the letter–sound measure at the beginning of their study (also see Wagner et al., 1994). It is quite possible that letter names, being more ubiquitous and fixed than letter sounds, help children penetrate the syllable boundary by providing a memorable label for individual sounds. Subsyllabic sensitivity, in turn, probably influences the progression of letter–name and letter–sound knowledge (Whitehurst & Lonigan, 1998). Finally, young readers may overgeneralize their acquired orthographic knowledge to perform demanding phonological awareness tasks, such as when a child reports that there are four sounds in the word *ship* (Ehri & Wilce, 1980, 1985).

Phonological Awareness Tasks

Phonological awareness tasks appear to load on two distinct but highly related factors—phonological analysis and phonological synthesis (Torgesen et al., 1994; Wagner et al., 1993). Analysis tasks require the segmentation of spoken stimuli into smaller units, whereas synthesis tasks require the blending of small units into larger segments. Analysis tasks appear to be more demanding than synthesis tasks, because the ability to segment develops later and is more difficult to train (Torgesen, Morgan, & Davis, 1992). Numerous analysis and synthesis tasks can be used to assess and teach phonological sensitivity, but their associated level of difficulty varies along five dimensions: (1) the level of depth of the phonological unit; (2) the position of the unit in the stimulus word; (3) the number of units in the stimulus word; (4) the stimulus word frequency; and (5) the type of task.

- The phonological units, in order of increasing depth and difficulty, are syllables, onsets/rimes, and phonemes (Bruck & Treiman, 1990; Fox & Routh, 1975; Liberman, Shankweiler, Fischer, & Carter, 1974; Treiman & Zukowski, 1991, 1996).
- These units tend to be easier to segment when they occur at the beginning of a

stimulus, but easier to blend when they are added to the end of a stimulus (Helfgott, 1976; Lewkowicz & Low, 1979; Stanovich, Cunningham, & Cramer, 1984).

- Analysis and synthesis tasks seem to be simpler for children when (1) the number of units to manipulate in the stimulus are few and (2) the stimulus is a relatively high-frequency word (Schreuder & van Bon, 1989; Torgesen et al., 1989; Troia, Roth, & Yeni-Komshian, 1996; Tunmer & Nesdale, 1982).
- The types of analysis and synthesis tasks include, in order of increasing difficulty, matching, oddity detection, same–different judgment, segment isolation, simple production (e.g., when asked to say a word that begins with the same sound as *door,* the child responds with *duck*), counting, and compound production (e.g., when asked to change the *f* in the word *fan* to *m* and the child responds with *man*; Lewkowicz, 1980; Troia et al., 1998; Yopp, 1988).

Regardless of the type of task used for assessment, individual differences in phonological sensitivity remain relatively stable from kindergarten onward (Byrne, Freebody, & Gates, 1992; Lonigan et al., 1998; MacLean et al., 1987; Torgesen & Burgess, 1998; Wagner et al., 1994).

Retrieval of Phonological Codes from the Lexicon

There is little doubt that information held in long-term memory is phonologically coded for rapid and efficient retrieval (Elbro, 1996; Fowler, 1991; Katz, 1986; Metsala, 1997a; Swank, 1994; Wolf, 1982). Two commonplace means of assessing the retrieval of phonological codes from the lexicon include confrontation naming and serial, or rapid, naming (Denckla & Rudel, 1976a, 1976b; German, 1982, 1984). In a confrontation naming task, an individual is shown (i.e., confronted with) a depiction of a familiar word and asked to name it as quickly as possible before progressing to the next naming trial. In a serial, or rapid, naming task, an individual is presented with a

series of familiar pictured stimuli that are randomly repeated and is asked to name the entire array as quickly as possible. Regardless of the naming task used, age and word frequency effects are generally observed; older children and adults name stimuli faster and more accurately than do younger children, and high-frequency stimuli are named faster and more accurately than low-frequency stimuli (Denckla & Rudel, 1976a; Troia et al., 1996; Wolf, 1982).

Lexical Restructuring and Retrieval

These findings most likely reflect a progressive restructuring of the lexicon as more and more words that share similar phonological properties are learned (Fowler, 1991; Metsala, 1997a; Metsala & Walley, 1998; Walley, 1993). Specifically, as more words that sound alike (e.g., words beginning with the same sound or that share the same phonological rime pattern) are added to the lexicon, there is greater pressure for segmental representation of those words to create an efficient storage and retrieval system. Words with shared segments are stored together in groups or lexical neighborhoods that vary in density, which is a product of the number of similar-sounding words, the degree of similarity, and the frequency of words in the neighborhood (Charles-Luce & Luce, 1990; Goldinger, Luce, & Pisoni, 1989). Older children and adults would be expected to have more segmentally structured lexicons than do younger children, and would thus be able to capitalize on this organization during naming tasks. When a word is retrieved from long-term memory, its entire lexical neighborhood is activated. According to Luce (1986), words in sparse neighborhoods have fewer competing neighbors and are consequently retrieved faster and more accurately, whereas words in dense neighborhoods have greater competition from other words with shared phonological properties and are retrieved more slowly and less accurately. Lexical restructuring is word-specific rather than lexicon-wide. High-frequency words located in either type of neighborhood (e.g., *chair* is a high-frequency word from a dense neighborhood, and *fence* is a high-frequency word from a sparse neighborhood) have a greater probability of being segmentally represented than do low-frequency words; therefore, more efficient retrieval of these high-frequency words would be expected. In addition to faster and more accurate naming performance (Damian & Martin, 1999), lexical restructuring leads to better speech discrimination (Jusczyk, 1986; Walley, 1993), more accurate articulation (Studdert-Kennedy, 1986), and further vocabulary growth (Lindblom, 1992).

Of the growing experimental evidence of lexical restructuring, the most direct evidence comes from studies that employ speech-gating tasks, in which the acoustical signal of a stimulus word is presented in small, sequential increments. After each "gate," the listener is asked to try to identify the target word. In comparison to adults, children require more acoustic input to identify a target word correctly, regardless of word length and familiarity (Elliott, Hammer, & Evan, 1987; Walley, 1988; Walley, Michela, & Wood, 1995). Metsala (1997a) reported that 7- to 9-year-old children needed the most input to recognize words from sparse neighborhoods successfully, but less input to identify low-frequency words from dense neighborhoods, and the least to identify high-frequency words from dense neighborhoods. Metsala interpreted these findings as evidence that dense lexical neighborhoods were more segmentally structured than sparse neighborhoods and that high-frequency words were represented segmentally to a greater degree than were low-frequency words.

In a different study, Metsala (1997b) found that the amount of acoustic input required for correct spoken-word identification contributed unique variance to single-word reading and pseudoword (i.e., nonword) decoding performance beyond that contributed by vocabulary and phonological awareness scores, at least in younger children. Moreover, children with reading disabilities, matched for vocabulary knowledge with average readers, required more acoustic input for correct spoken-word recognition than their peers. Quite possibly, poor readers have functional limitations in their lexical restructuring that may affect

the extent to which they can accurately and efficiently map orthographic and phonological segments (see Fowler, 1991). Collectively, these findings fit well with those obtained in naming studies and provide strong support for the relevance of phonological structure in long-term memory.

Lexical Restructuring and Phonological Awareness

Lexical restructuring also may play an important role in the development of phonological awareness. Significant correlations between oral vocabulary and phonological awareness have been observed even when shared variance attributable to age and nonword repetition accuracy is removed (Chaney, 1992, 1994; Metsala, 1999). Children with larger vocabularies tend to do better on phonological awareness tasks (Bowey & Francis, 1991; Metsala, 1999). In addition, preliminary evidence suggests that children perform better on some phonological awareness tasks when the stimulus words are from dense rather than sparse lexical neighborhoods (De Cara & Goswami, 2002; Metsala, 1999). The influence of word frequency on phonological awareness performance (see Troia et al., 1996) may be an artifact of lexical restructuring; that is, the phonological structure of high-frequency words may be easier to manipulate, because such words already have undergone segmental analysis for storage and retrieval purposes.

Retrieval and Phonological Awareness

It has long been known that a substantial portion of variance in reading achievement is explained by performance on measures of serial and confrontation naming, and that performance on such tasks separates average and poor readers (Blachman, 1984; Denckla & Rudel, 1976a, 1976b; German, 1979; Swank, 1994; Torgesen et al., 1994; Wolf, 1984, 1986). Given that rapid and accurate performance on naming tasks relies on the phonological integrity of words stored in long-term memory, there is reason to suppose that naming and phonological awareness share many of the same phonological processing resources. This supposition is contested among researchers, in part because correlations between phonological awareness and naming measures are found inconsistently (cf. Ackerman, Dykman, & Gardner, 1990; Blachman, 1984; Cornwall, 1992; Torgesen et al., 1994; Troia et al., 1996; Wagner & Torgesen, 1987), and because there is growing evidence that phonemic awareness and serial naming contribute unique variance to word recognition (Allor, 2002; Bowers, 1995; Cornwall, 1992; Felton & Brown, 1990; Manis, Seidenberg, & Doi, 1999; McBride-Chang & Manis, 1996; Torgesen, Wagner, Rashotte, Burgess, & Hecht, 1997).

Wolf and her colleagues (e.g., Bowers & Wolf, 1993; Wolf & Bowers, 1999; Wolf, Bowers, & Biddle, 2000) argue that these findings demonstrate that serial naming tasks primarily tap nonphonological processes important in word recognition, such as attention, visual recognition, and information processing speed. Furthermore, they argue that naming speed deficits may independently contribute to reading difficulties and, when present, may exacerbate reading problems that arise from limited phonemic awareness. Those children who demonstrate such a "double deficit" do, in fact, tend to be the worst readers and generally are more resistant to reading interventions (Allor, Fuchs, & Mathes, 2001; Bowers, 1995; Bowers & Wolf, 1993; Torgesen et al., 1994; Vellutino et al., 1996; Wolf & Bowers, 1999, 2000).

According to Manis et al. (2000), children with a double deficit are disadvantaged in both decoding (because they lack sufficient sensitivity to speech sounds to capitalize on an alphabetic script) and sight word recognition (because they are unable to process information rapidly enough to store and retrieve orthographic patterns efficiently). On the other hand, Schatschneider, Carlson, Francis, Foorman, and Fletcher (2002) contend that because serial naming and phonological awareness are positively correlated (at least in beginning normal readers and older poor readers), children who exhibit a double deficit are bound to demonstrate lower scores on phonemic awareness measures (and consequently on tests of word recognition) than children who exhibit only a deficit in phonemic awareness. In their view, this occurs because of the shared attributes of rapid naming and phonemic awareness (i.e., phonological processing) that are more profoundly impaired in these children, rather than as an independent contribution of slow naming speed.

In summary, chronological age and word frequency have strong effects on naming speed and accuracy. The process of lexical restructuring, by which individual words are progressively segmented in their lexical representation and grouped into neighborhoods with other words that share similar phonological features, may offer a productive means of explaining these effects. Measures of the degree to which lexical entries have been phonologically segmented also are associated with performance on phonological awareness, word recognition, and pseudoword decoding tasks, which lends credence to the supposition that lexical restructuring plays a key role in the gradual emergence of phonemic awareness. Although phonemic awareness and rapid serial naming appear to make independent contributions to word recognition, potentially because serial naming tasks rely heavily on nonphonological processes (e.g., orthographic pattern recognition) that are valuable in reading quickly and accurately, it is possible that they are, in fact, two sides of the same coin. If, indeed, phonemic awareness and rapid naming are related aspects of phonological processing, their interdependence may be grounded in how much the lexicon has undergone segmental restructuring.

Phonological Coding in Working Memory

Working memory can be conceptualized as a limited-capacity mental workspace for complex processing operations under the control of a central executive system. The central executive system allocates resources and manages the deployment of flexible strategies for information storage and retrieval (Just & Carpenter, 1992). These strategies are acquired over time, so the efficiency of working memory increases with age. The central executive system recruits and coordinates three subordinate systems to perform these functions—the phonological loop, the visuospatial sketch pad, and the episodic buffer (Baddeley & Hitch, 1974, 2000).

The phonological loop is a short-term store in which verbal information is coded via phonological characteristics and is subject to rapid decay unless rehearsal is employed (Baddeley, 1986; Gathercole & Adams, 1993; Gathercole & Hitch, 1993). The visuospatial sketch pad is another short-term store in which visual details and spatial relationships are encoded as a fleeting image. The episodic buffer temporarily holds information from the two other subordinate systems and from long-term memory, such that information from these different sources is bound together to form a single, coherent episode. Of the three subordinate systems, the phonological loop is most important for language and literacy learning. For example, the phonological loop is thought to play a prominent role in learning the pronunciation of new vocabulary (Baddeley, Gathercole, & Papagno, 1998; Gathercole & Baddeley, 1989) and in mediating the acquisition of syntax (Adams & Gathercole, 1995). Consequently, poor utilization of the phonological loop is associated with impairments in phonology and morphology (Gathercole & Baddeley, 1990; Montgomery, 1995). Furthermore, performance on working memory tasks is strongly related to reading achievement (Siegel, 1994; Swanson, 1994). This last finding is not surprising. The process of recovering phonological codes from print undoubtedly places significant demands on working memory in general and on the phonological loop in particular.

A number of researchers have reported a strong correlation between working memory and phonological awareness (Kamhi & Catts, 1986; Mann & Liberman, 1984; Snowling, Hulme, Smith, & Thomas, 1994; Torgesen et al., 1994; Wagner & Torgesen, 1987). In a study with 7- and 8-year-old children, Oakhill and Kyle (2000) administered two phonemic awareness tasks (sound categorization and sound deletion) and two memory tasks (word span, a short-term memory task, and sentence span, a working memory task in which children finished the last word in several sentences and recalled those words in order). After controlling for word recognition ability, they found the children's success with the sentence span task, but not the word span task, predicted their phonological awareness performance. A consistent association, however, between working memory and naming performance has not been found (cf. Ackerman et al., 1990; Cornwall, 1992; Torgesen, Wagner, Simmons, & Laughon, 1990). This may be due to dissimilarities among the naming tasks used by researchers; serial naming tasks seem to have a more stable relationship with working memory than confrontation naming tasks, presumably because in a serial naming task, preservation of stimuli in working memory is required as the same stimuli are repeatedly identified in an array (Stanovich, 1985; Stanovich, Feeman, & Cunningham, 1983; Stanovich, Nathan, & Vala-Rossi, 1986).

Phonological awareness, lexical retrieval, and phonological coding in verbal memory all have been found to predict literacy achievement in orthographically diverse alphabetic and nonalphabetic languages. The causal relationship between phonological awareness and literacy is historically the best researched and, perhaps, the most obvious among the three, because phonological awareness is directly amenable to intervention, with salutary effects on reading and spelling. Each of the three phonological processing operations has been found to be related to the others, depending on how and when they are measured. A progressive restructuring of words within the lexicon in response to the acquisition of an increasing number of phonologically similar words may hold the key to explaining how children develop (1) sensitivity to deeper levels of phonological structure, (2) faster and more accurate retrieval of known words, and (3) efficient use of the phonological loop for coding information in working memory. Whether or not one assumes that the phoneme constitutes an innate or an emergent unit of cognitive processing, the close ties between phonological processing and literacy presuppose that disruptions in any one or more of the three basic operations would have a deleterious impact on reading and spelling achievement. A brief summary of how phonological processing impairments affect literacy performance is presented next.

IMPLICATIONS OF IMPAIRED PHONOLOGICAL PROCESSING FOR LITERACY

The chief problem encountered by children identified with reading disabilities is slow and inaccurate decoding (Liberman & Shankweiler, 1985; Rack, Snowling, & Olson, 1992; Stanovich, 1988; Vellutino & Scanlon, 1987). It is generally assumed that these poor decoding skills are attributable to a core phonological processing deficit (Lyon, 1995; Share & Stanovich, 1995; Stanovich, 1988; Stanovich & Siegel, 1994). A consequence of this deficit is inferior performance, regardless of IQ, in one or more cognitive operations that utilize phonological information, including phonological awareness (e.g., Blachman, 1991; Metsala, 1999; Stanovich, 1986, 1991; Vellutino & Scanlon, 1987; Wagner & Torgesen, 1987), naming (e.g., Badian, 1993; Felton & Wood, 1989; Wolf & Bowers, 1999), and verbal memory (e.g., Rapala & Brady, 1990; Torgesen et al., 1994).

The phonological processing deficiencies of poor readers not only have a deleterious effect on these children's decoding and spelling abilities but also negatively impact their development of fluent reading and writing (Ball, 1993). Fluent reading is necessary for efficient text comprehension, because working memory, in which phonological representations of words are accumulated to form text propositions, has a limited capacity (Liberman & Shankweiler, 1991; Perfetti, 1986; Stanovich, 1986). When cognitive resources in working memory must be allocated to decoding rather than propositional analysis, comprehension deteriorates. Thus, impaired phonological processing indirectly compromises reading comprehension skills via its effects on decoding and fluent word recognition (Juel et al., 1986; Tunmer & Nesdale, 1985). These deficits in phonological processing continue

to plague most adults who struggle with reading (Bruck, 1990, 1992; Felton, Naylor, & Wood, 1990; Pennington, Van Orden, Smith, Green, & Haith, 1990; Snowling, Nation, Moxham, Gallagher, & Frith, 1997; Wilson & Lesaux, 2001).

Children with reading disabilities appear to be relatively more impaired in phonological processing than in orthographic processing (Olson, Wise, Connors, Rack, & Fulker, 1989; Pennington et al., 1986; Stanovich & Siegel, 1994; see also Cassar & Treiman, Chapter 29, this volume). Consequently, poor readers exhibit pseudoword decoding deficits in comparison to other children matched for reading level, a comparison that permits us to eliminate differences in reading exposure and orthographic awareness as proximal causes for these deficits (IJzendoorn & Bus, 1994; Rack et al., 1992). In average readers, a regularity effect is observed, meaning that orthographically regular words are read more accurately (and often faster) than irregular words, owing to the efficiency of phonological recoding. Regular words exhibit a high degree of grapheme–phoneme transparency, whereas irregular words do not, but it is important to note that many words typically considered orthographically irregular do, in fact, derive their spellings from fairly consistent morphological patterns. Although poor readers would be expected to demonstrate a diminished regularity effect as a result of their phonological processing deficits (Manis, Szeszulski, Holt, & Graves, 1990; Olson, Kliegel, Davidson, & Foltz, 1985), this is typically not the case (Bruck, 1990; Metsala, Stanovich, & Brown, 1998; Olson et al., 1985; Stanovich, Nathan, & Zolman, 1988).

However, this negative finding pertaining to a diminished regularity effect is anticipated in a connectionist model of reading processes (Seidenberg & McClelland, 1989). This model predicts that degraded representations of words in long-term memory are associated with relatively poor pseudoword and irregular word decoding, but relatively good recognition of orthographically transparent words (Brown, 1997; Elbro, 1998). More specifically, regular words are likely to have somewhat better lexical specification (e.g., phonological, orthographic, semantic, and syntactic information) than irregular words or pseudowords for poor readers, in part, owing to their more frequent successful encounters with regular words in text. This account fits well with the theoretical and empirical framework of lexical restructuring described earlier; some spoken vocabulary words known by poor readers fail to undergo complete segmental restructuring and consequently have underdeveloped lexical specification, but orthographically transparent words may have a greater probability of lexical restructuring due to more fruitful reading attempts.

POSSIBLE ORIGINS OF IMPAIRED PHONOLOGICAL PROCESSING

It is unclear just exactly why some children have phonological processing disorders, but impaired perceptual ability has been postulated as a plausible explanation. Specifically, poor perception of the temporal properties of acoustic (verbal or otherwise) and nonacoustic stimuli has been espoused to be a fundamental weakness in many children with language and reading disorders who exhibit phonological processing problems. This section presents arguments for and against this position. In support of a temporal processing disorder, studies are reviewed in which discrimination and serial judgment impairments have been found with the use of speech and nonspeech auditory stimuli, as well as visual and kinesthetic stimuli that are rapidly presented and/or characterized by transient features. Arguments against a temporal processing disorder include the conceptual and methodological weaknesses of the seminal research, failures to replicate key findings, and nonspecificity among children with disabilities (e.g., perceptual deficits are not constrained to the temporal dimension).

Evidence for a Temporal Processing Disorder

Speech Perception Weaknesses

Poor speech perception has been found to be associated with problems in word recognition and pseudoword decoding (De-Weirdt, 1988; Godfrey, Syrdal-Lasky, Millay, & Knox, 1981; Metsala, 1997b; Mody, Studdert-Kennedy, & Brady, 1997; Reed, 1989; Tallal, 1980; Werker & Tees, 1987). On the other hand, speech perception is not a unique predictor of reading performance beyond the first grade (McBride-Chang, 1996; Metsala, 1997b; Scarborough, 1998; Werker & Tees, 1987). Speech perception also contributes independently to variance in phonological awareness performance (Chiappe, Chiappe, & Siegel, 2001; Manis et al., 1997; McBride-Chang, 1995; Nittrouer, 1999). However, only a subset of poor readers who exhibit phonological awareness impairments also exhibit difficulties with speech perception (Manis et al., 1997). This subset likely comprises children with specific language impairments (SLIs), because problems in speech perception appear to hinder the acquisition of grammatical markers, and delayed morphological development is a prominent characteristic of SLI (Elliott & Hammer, 1988; Joanisse, Manis, Keating, & Seidenberg, 2000; Joanisse & Seidenberg, 1998; Leonard, McGregor, & Allen, 1992; Stark & Heinz, 1996).

McBride-Chang and her colleagues (McBride-Chang, 1996; McBride-Chang, Wagner, & Chang, 1997) believe that speech perception influences reading indirectly through its relationship with phonological awareness. For example, McBride-Chang et al. (1997) used a speech discrimination task with kindergartners in which the words *bath* and *path* were presented on a continuum of voice onset time, which is the acoustic property that differentiates these words. Discrimination performance was correlated with performance on phonemic awareness tasks administered at the same time and 15 months later. Children with the highest kindergarten speech discrimination scores eventually became the strongest readers in first grade, but when the variance explained by IQ, verbal memory, phonological awareness, and letter knowledge was statistically removed, speech perception did not make an independent contribution to growth in word recognition. However, speech discrimination made an independent contribution to growth in phonological awareness, as did IQ and memory (also see McBride-Chang, 1995).

Auditory Temporal Processing Deficits

The perceptual difficulties experienced by at least some children with reading problems may be specific to speech stimuli (Bishop, Carlyon, Deeks, & Bishop, 1999; Brady, Shankweiler, & Mann, 1983; Mody et al., 1997; for further discussion, see Mody, Chapter 3, this volume) or may be part of a general auditory perceptual disorder characterized by difficulties with rapidly occurring auditory input (Tallal, Merzenich, Miller, & Jenkins, 1998; Tallal, Miller, & Fitch, 1993; Wright, Bowen, & Zecker, 2000; Wright et al., 1997). Early research designed to investigate the specificity of auditory processing difficulties focused on children with SLI. As a group, these children display more errors than their nondisabled peers when asked to identify, discriminate, and serially order speech stimuli that rely on temporally cued information, such as brief formant transitions that cue place of articulation and rapidly occurring voice onset times that cue consonant voicing features (Elliott, 1986; Elliott & Hammer, 1988; Elliott, Hammer, & Scholl, 1989; Leonard et al., 1992; Tallal & Piercy, 1974, 1975).

Tallal and Piercy (1974), for example, found that children with SLI performed more poorly than their typically developing peers on discrimination and temporal order judgment tasks using pairs of synthesized consonant–vowel (CV) syllables in which the formant transitions of the stop consonants were 43 milliseconds (msec) in duration (the total duration of each syllable was 250 msec) and the syllables were separated by an interstimulus interval (ISI) of 95 msec or less. In contrast, the children with SLI performed just as well as the control participants on these tasks when pairs of synthesized steady-state vowels of the same total duration were used as stimuli, regardless of the ISI between the syllables. In a subsequent experiment using similar procedures with the same group of children, Tallal and Piercy (1975) presented two vowel–vowel syllables (/ɛɪ/ and /æɪ/) in which the first steady-state vowel of the syllable had a duration of 43 msec, and two CV syllables (/ba/ and /da/), in which the formant transitions were lengthened to 95 msec. The performance of the children with SLI on the discrimination and serial-ordering tasks, compared with that of the children without disabilities, was diminished for the vowel–vowel stimuli but not for the CV stimuli at shorter ISIs. These findings led the researchers to conclude that the duration of the acoustical cue (and not the formant transition itself) was critical to accurate perception.

Deficits in processing the temporal aspects of acoustic signals among children with SLI are not confined to speech, though. These children also perform more poorly than their age-matched peers without language disorders on discrimination and serial-ordering tasks when pairs of complex nonverbal tones that differ only in fundamental frequency are presented with a combination of brief ISIs and short tone durations (Tallal & Piercy, 1973a, 1973b). Complex nonverbal tones are tones composed of multiple frequencies similar to those found in the spectra of speech sounds. Deficits in perceiving rapidly changing acoustic information in speech and nonspeech stimuli also have been found in some children with reading disabilities (De Weirdt, 1988; Godfrey et al., 1981; Hurford & Sanders, 1990; Reed, 1989; Tallal, 1980; Thibodeau & Sussman, 1979; Werker & Tees, 1987), particularly those who have poor pseudoword reading skills presumably arising from phonological processing difficulties (Adlard & Hazan, 1998; Tallal, 1980; Tallal & Stark, 1981). For example, Reed (1989) presented complex nonverbal tones of 75-msec duration, vowels (/ɛ/ and /æ/) of 250-msec duration, and CV syllables (/ba/ and /da/) of 250-msec duration, separated by an ISI of 400, 300, 150, 50, or 10 msec to good and poor readers. Although the performance of the good readers on discrimination and temporal order judgment tasks was not substantially affected by decreasing ISIs, the performance of poor readers was affected. In other words, their accuracy decreased significantly with shorter ISIs for nonverbal tones (recall that these were of shorter duration than the other stimuli) and CV syllables (with brief formant transitions), but not steady-state vowels. Reed then identified the poor readers who performed worst on the perceptual tasks and compared them with their matched controls on a vowel serial-ordering task in which white noise was introduced. The increased difficulty of this task negatively affected the performance of both groups equally. Because the children with reading disabilities did not experience comparatively greater difficulty with processing the steady-state auditory cues in vowels under demanding conditions, a deficit in processing brief acoustical information appeared to be at the heart of the weaker performance of children with reading problems.

Temporal Processing Impairments in Other Modalities

Children with SLI and reading disabilites appear to have perceptual difficulties with rapidly presented acoustic stimuli that contain transient information. Similarly, they display more discrimination errors when presented with rapidly occurring visual patterns (e.g., flashes) than do their normal peers (e.g., Eden, Stein, Wood, & Wood, 1995; Lovegrove, 1993; Rose, Feldman, Jankowski, & Futterweit, 1999; Tallal, Stark, Kallman, & Mellits, 1981), and they are less adept at perceiving and producing sequential motor movements, especially ones that occur rapidly (Tallal, Stark, & Mellits, 1985; Wolf, 1991; Wolff, Cohen, & Drake, 1984). In conjunction with research findings from psychoacoustic studies such as those described earlier, these results imply that many children with language and learning disabilities have a perceptual disorder that may be related to pansensory deficits in temporal processing (for a review of this body of work, see Farmer & Klein, 1995; Klein & Farmer, 1995; Tallal, Miller, & Fitch, 1993). The auditory temporal processing deficit described by Tallal, Merzenich, and their colleagues to be at the core of at least some developmental disabilities (Tallal, 1984, 1990; Tallal, Miller, Jenkins, & Merzenich, 1997; Tallal et al., 1993) is

but one aspect of this fundamental disorder. Such a disorder may emerge as early as the first year of life, possibly serving as a biological marker of SLI (Benasich & Tallal, 1996), and continue to manifest itself throughout the lifespan as differences in perceptual behavior, linguistic competence, neurophysiological functioning, and brain morphology (e.g., Galaburda, Corsiglia, Rosen, & Sherman, 1987; Galaburda & Livingstone, 1993; Galaburda, Menard, & Rosen, 1994; Merzenich & Jenkins, 1995; Merzenich, Schreiner, Jenkins, & Wang, 1993; Nagarajan et al., 1999; Tallal et al., 1993).

Evidence against a Temporal Processing Disorder

Conceptual and Methodological Flaws

Although studies that support the existence of a general temporal processing disorder in some children with SLI and reading disabilities are persuasive, they have not gone unchallenged. Perhaps the most notable critics are Studdert-Kennedy and his colleagues (Mody et al., 1997; Studdert-Kennedy & Mody, 1995; Studdert-Kennedy et al., 1995), who contend that findings from the most influential studies (Reed, 1989; Tallal, 1980; Tallal & Piercy, 1973a, 1973b) are flawed both conceptually and methodologically for three reasons. First, they take issue with use of the term "temporal processing," because it has been applied rather indiscriminately to different phenomena. For example, temporal processing has been used to describe (1) perception of temporal aspects of the acoustic signal, including formant transition duration, voice onset time, and fricative-vowel gap time; (2) perception of acoustic events that are sequentially ordered; and (3) perception of brief acoustic events. Studdert-Kennedy and colleagues insist that there is a differentiation between rate of processing and processing of rate (see Mody, Chapter 3, this volume). In the former case, rapid perception of brief acoustic events is implied; in the latter, perception of the temporal characteristics (e.g., rapid changes in formant frequencies or voicing) of the stimuli is implied. In the studies conducted by Tallal and her col-leagues, this differentiation is not clearly made, although it appears that rate of pro-cessing is of concern (see Tallal, 1980).

Second, Studdert-Kennedy and others reason that independent deficits are likely responsible for the perceptual difficulties children with SLI and reading disabilities display on nonverbal and verbal auditory discrimination tasks, in that problems with the latter arise from a linguistic deficit rather than a general auditory perceptual disorder. Specifically, children with lan-guage impairments and reading problems perform poorly on perceptual tasks involv-ing speech stimuli because they are less ca-pable of forming phonological representa-tions for the stimuli (also see Sussman, 1993). A phonological processing disorder could result in poor discrimination of phonemes that differ in only one articulato-ry feature (i.e., place of articulation, manner of articulation, or voicing), as do /b/ and /d/ in the CV syllables used in much of Tallal's work.

Third, they argue that appropriate non-speech control stimuli have not been used in much of the research in speech discrimina-tion; consequently, difficulty with rapidly presented brief tones may relate to a differ-ent underlying deficit. Tones presented to children with SLI in Tallal and Piercy's (1974, 1975) studies did not share the same brief and rapidly changing onset frequencies as the CV syllables that were presented. If a temporal processing disorder were the root cause for the children's perceptual difficul-ties, then such nonverbal stimuli should elic-it the same pattern of diminished perfor-mance. Mody et al. (1997) set out to examine this hypothesis in a sample of skilled and less skilled second-grade readers. In their study, described below, the less skilled readers read at grade level and ex-hibited temporal order judgment difficul-ties, whereas the skilled readers read above grade level and did not display serial order judgment problems.

Mody et al. (1997) created two complex nonverbal tones of 250-msec duration with a 35-msec transition to serve as nonspeech control stimuli for synthetic CV syllables that differed on one articulatory feature (/ba/ and /da/). The two tones were com-posed of sine waves, with durations and fre-quency trajectories identical to those of the center frequencies of the second and third formants of /ba/ and /da/, respectively. Thus, tone discrimination depended on per-ceiving brief transitions in formant frequen-cies, but not on creating phonological repre-sentations. They also assessed the children's ability to discriminate between other pairs of CV syllables that differed on all three ar-ticulatory features (place, manner, voicing): /ba/–/sa/ and /da/–/ʃa/. They found that less skilled readers did not differ significantly from skilled readers at any ISI (ranging from 10 to 100 msec) on tone discrimina-tion (actually, the skilled readers performed more poorly than the less skilled readers at the shortest ISI). However, the less skilled readers did make significantly more dis-crimination errors when presented with /ba/ and /da/ at shorter ISIs. The skilled and less skilled readers performed comparably when discriminating between the two other CV-syllable contrast pairs. The researchers con-cluded that trouble with discriminating be-tween CV syllables could not be caused by a general deficit in processing rapid acoustic information, because such a deficit also would have affected the less skilled readers' ability to discriminate between nonverbal tones that were acoustically similar to their corresponding CV syllables. Moreover, be-cause the children who performed poorly on the /ba/–/da/ discrimination task did not ex-hibit similar deficiencies in discriminating less phonetically similar CV syllables, Mody et al. proposed that it was phonetic similari-ty between phonemes that created perceptu-al difficulties for some children. Support of this last point was provided in a study by Stark and Heinz (1996), who found that children with SLI had difficulty identifying steady-state vowels of both long and short duration that were phonetically similar (/ɛ/ and /æ/), but not vowels that were more contrastive.

Lack of Specificity and Replication

At least three other reasons suggest that the presence of an auditory temporal processing deficit in children (and adults) with disabilities should not be accepted at face value (e.g., Bishop et al., 1999; Chiappe, Stringer, Siegel, & Stanovich, 2002; Helzer, Champlin, & Gillam, 1996; Marshall, Snowling, & Bailey, 2001; Nittrouer, 1999; Sussman, 1993). First, children with SLI and reading problems perform poorly on discrimination tasks in which aspects of the acoustic signal other than duration or speed are manipulated, which indicates that temporal processing alone cannot explain these children's auditory perceptual deficits. For example, De Weirdt (1988) found that poor readers were disadvantaged in comparison to good readers on a pure-tone discrimination task in which the frequency of the tones was manipulated rather than formant transition duration or ISI. In this study, tones were presented at a constant duration of 130 msec and an ISI of 1 sec.

Second, replication of the Tallal findings (Tallal, 1980; Tallal & Piercy, 1973a, 1973b) has been difficult to achieve (e.g., Norrelgen, Lacerda, & Forssberg, 2002). When pairs of complex nonverbal tones differing in fundamental frequency were presented at 40-, 75-, and 250-msec duration with ISIs of 10, 50, 100, and 400 msec, respectively, to a large sample of children with and without learning difficulties, Waber et al. (2001) found no interaction between disability status and either stimulus duration or ISI. The children referred for learning problems consistently performed worse than their nonreferred peers, and the magnitude of this difference remained constant across ISIs and tone durations. Thus, impaired perception associated with briefer and faster stimuli, reported in Tallal's work, was not found among this group of children with academic weaknesses. In fact, Stark and Tallal (1988) reported that a group of children with SLI exhibited discrimination errors for CV syllables with formant transitions lasting 40 and 80 msec, which conflicted with their prior findings. However, in this experiment, only two formant frequencies were used to synthesize the stimuli rather than five. This raises the possibility that children with disabilities require more acoustic information, or greater redundancy in that acoustic information, to be able to perform discrimination tasks successfully.

Godfrey et al. (1981) reported that their children with and without reading disabilities had more trouble discriminating /da/–/ga/ pairs than /ba/–/da/ pairs, because the former differed only in their third formant, whereas the latter differed in both their second and third formants. Once again, the amount of acoustic information present appeared to affect children's relative discriminative abilities; when differences were cued by less information, discrimination became more difficult (also see Adlard & Hazan, 1998). This possibility is consistent with the position taken by Studdert-Kennedy and associates (Mody et al., 1997; Studdert-Kennedy & Mody, 1995; Studdert-Kennedy et al., 1995).

Finally, researchers have paid little attention to the role of attentional capacity in temporal processing and how attention influences performance on psychoacoustic tasks. Breier, Fletcher, Foorman, Klaas, and Gray (2003) examined this issue in a large-scale study with 150 children between the ages of 7 and 14 years who were identified as having either reading disabilities (but not SLI), attention-deficit/hyperactivity disorder (ADHD), reading disabilities plus ADHD, or normal development. Two findings stood out: (1) children with ADHD exhibited weaker performance across perceptual tasks, and (2) the groups with reading disabilities exhibited higher detection thresholds for tone onset time asynchrony but not tone gaps, which implied that these children may have been more sensitive to backward masking effects (these occur when a second signal is delivered in close temporal proximity to the first signal and would be expected to elevate thresholds). Such findings challenge the existence of a pervasive deficit in auditory temporal processing among children with reading disabilities, and suggest that attention is an important variable to consider.

RECOMMENDATIONS FOR THE INTEGRATION OF FUTURE RESEARCH WITH PRACTICE

Basic and applied research has revealed much about the way children learn to capitalize on the phonological structure of language to develop efficient means for processing verbal information in spoken and written form. There is little doubt that much more remains to be discovered about phonological processing and its association with literacy skills. Yet we should not assume that phonological processing is the most important contributor to these skills; literacy functions rely on multiple and integrated oral language abilities, including morphosyntactic, semantic, and pragmatic abilities, in addition to phonological processing abilities. These other oral language variables have been largely ignored in literacy research; consequently, we know little about how they interact and collectively influence reading and writing achievement. Our narrow focus has forged a two-edged sword: The breadth and depth of our knowledge about the role of phonology in literacy has been sharpened dramatically, while our understanding of the influence of other factors has remained relatively blunted. Likewise, much controversy surrounds the possible origins of phonological processing deficits, yet there has been a rush to devise interventions based on a potentially narrow view of how children perceive and interpret acoustic information. I discuss both of these issues in more detail below, with the goal of promoting an appreciation of how future research in the area of phonological processing can inform educational practice.

Beyond Phonology: The Importance of Other Oral Language Abilities in Literacy

Although phonological processing deficits seem to be a proximal cause of reading problems, there is strong evidence that impairments in other aspects of oral language (e.g., semantic and syntactic processing) have a detrimental effect on literacy. Oral language abilities in early childhood predict beginning literacy skills such as phonological awareness, letter knowledge, and concepts about print, as well as later reading achievement (Bishop & Adams, 1990; Chaney, 1992; Scarborough, 1990, 1991, 1998; Stothard, Snowling, Bishop, Chipchase, & Kaplan, 1998). In fact, this

relationship extends downward into infancy, because brain wave responses of babies to verbal stimuli predict later reading performance, although their responses to other sounds do not (Molfese, 1999). General oral language measures significantly improve how well we can predict reading ability, especially reading comprehension, even when the contribution of phonological awareness is removed (Catts, Fey, Zhang, & Tomblin, 2001; Catts et al., 1999; Roth, Speece, & Cooper, 2002; Scarborough, 1990).

Retrospective studies offer additional evidence of the importance of oral language skills in reading achievement. For example, Catts et al. (1999) identified the oral language and phonological processing profiles of good and poor second-grade readers when they were in kindergarten. The poor readers were three to four times more likely to have had phonological processing weaknesses and four to five times more likely to have had oral language problems. Overall, 73% of the poor readers had exhibited deficiencies in some aspect of phonological processing or oral language, with almost 40% having a combined deficit profile, almost 20% having primary oral language deficits, and less than 15% having primary phonological processing deficits. Almost all of the children who fell in the latter group exhibited somewhat depressed scores on tests of oral language competence. These findings were observed when poor reading was defined by word recognition or reading comprehension performance.

Investigators concerned with reading disabilities typically confine their study samples to children who possess average IQ or above (i.e., reading disability is defined using a discrepancy model), but this restricts the range of language ability represented in the research. In a longitudinal study conducted by Catts and his colleagues (1999), the percentage of children in kindergarten through fourth grade with pure dyslexia was relatively small in comparison to the percentage of children who had more generalized language impairments that extended beyond the phonological domain. Because so many children with a reading disability also have SLI, it is probable that many published studies of phonological processing have overlooked the importance of children's other oral language abilities (McCardle, Scarborough, & Catts, 2001). This may explain, for example, why up to 30% of children who receive phonological awareness training fail to make appreciable gains in either phonemic awareness or literacy (Foorman, Francis, Novy, & Liberman, 1991; Torgesen & Davis, 1996; Torgesen et al., 1992, 1994), and even when gains are realized, they may attenuate in as few as 18 months (Bus & van IJzendoorn, 1999). Language abilities beyond the phonological domain require more intensive scrutiny and thoughtful integration in research and practice, so that more children are able to benefit from phonological awareness instruction. Similarly, much of the current research on phonological awareness instruction has not systematically evaluated individual growth or group treatment response in relation to the five dimensions of task difficulty identified previously (depth of phonological unit, position of unit, number of units in word, word frequency, and type of task). Also, it is unclear to what degree lexical restructuring predicts how well children perform on phonological awareness tasks and respond to interventions.

Interventions for Temporal Processing Disorders: Too Much Too Soon?

The controversy surrounding the temporal processing disorder that is presumed to be the root cause, in at least some cases, for phonological processing difficulties and linguistic impairments in children with reading disabilities and SLI has yet to be resolved. Nevertheless, interventions based on this presumption have been developed and tested. According to Robey and Schultz (1998), establishing the efficacy of an intervention is a developmental process that includes a series of research stages, beginning with exploratory studies that document (1) the viability of the treatment, (2) the precise benefits of the treatment and how best to measure them, (3) the circumstances under which these benefits can be anticipated, (4) the durability of the treatment effects, and (5) the safety of the treatment. Exploratory

research typically employs case studies, single-subject experiments, and small-group quasi-experimental investigations, all of which do not include external controls for rival interpretations of the outcomes. Next, efficacy studies are conducted with large samples that are randomly assigned to experimental and control conditions, typically in laboratory settings at first, and then in more natural clinical settings with diverse populations. Investigations in real-world contexts help to determine how effective the intervention is under typical circumstances, its cost-effectiveness (e.g., compared to other interventions), and consumer satisfaction. In the case of interventions designed to remediate temporal processing difficulties, almost every study that has been performed to date has been exploratory.

Exploratory Studies

Hurford and Sanders (1990) were able to improve speech discrimination among second- and fourth-grade children with reading disabilities. The intervention was relatively brief; children participated in the training activities for 30–45 minutes per day for 3 or 4 days. One group of 13 children received the experimental treatment, in which their discrimination skills were progressively refined for decreasing ISIs, first using pairs of steady-state vowels, then CV syllables with liquid and nasal consonants (which are continuant sounds, much like vowels), and finally CV syllables with initial stop consonants. Another group of 11 children, matched for age, reading level, and pretest phoneme discrimination performance, completed the same activities, but the stimuli consisted of simple pure tones. Following training, the children in the experimental treatment group performed significantly better than did those in the control group on a measure of speech discrimination that used untrained consonant sounds in the test stimuli. Moreover, their posttreatment performance was similar to that of a group of children without reading problems. Hurford (1990) replicated this study with a group of 18 second- and third-grade poor readers who also exhibited weak phonemic awareness on a sound deletion task. Although another 18 children in the control group showed little improvement in phonemic awareness at the end of the study, those who were taught to discriminate pairs of syllables at faster presentation rates demonstrated significant improvement.

Habib et al. (1999) used acoustically modified speech in a rhyme detection task with 10- to 12-year-old French-speaking children with reading disabilities to improve their phonological awareness. The formant transitions were differentially amplified, and the entire speech signal was slowed by a constant factor, with a gradual reduction in degree of modification over the treatment period. The 6 children who completed the activities for 1 hour per day, 5 days per week, for 5 consecutive weeks with acoustically modified speech showed significantly greater improvement in phonological awareness than 6 children who completed the same activities with unmodified speech and did not display any significant improvement. The two groups were matched for pretest phonological awareness performance, "educational" level, and "cognitive" level. These results were observed again after 1 month had elapsed. In contrast, McAnally, Hansen, Cornelissen, and Stein (1997) found that neither compression nor expansion of syllable duration (the manipulation was uniform across the syllable rather than isolated to the formant transition) or consonant formant frequencies significantly improved the discrimination of consonant–vowel–consonant (CVC) syllables (all consonants were stops) in white noise over baseline performance (discrimination without acoustic modifications) of 15 adolescents with dyslexia and 15 adolescents with average reading skills.

These studies indicate that speech discrimination and phonological awareness (at least in younger students with reading problems) can be improved with discrimination training that incorporates acoustic signal modifications that affect the temporal envelope of the stimuli. However, all of these studies employed quasi-experimental designs and small samples; thus, they did not meet the criteria for efficacy research. Moreover, they investigated entirely different interventions and in no way replicated or extended findings for a single treatment approach. A number of recent studies have focused on one intervention approach, a computer-assisted instructional program called Fast ForWord Language™ (FFW), which uses intensive training in auditory perceptual and spoken language comprehension skills to improve the communicative competence and academic success of at-risk children and those identified with disabilities.

FFW uses seven interactive game-like exercises to provide practice in nonverbal and verbal sound discrimination, vocabulary recognition, and language comprehension. Children between the ages of 4 and 14 complete the exercises for 60–80 minutes each day during the first week of training, and for 100 minutes each day thereafter until they complete the program, usually within 4–8 weeks. Most importantly, according to the developers, the acoustic waveforms presented in the exercises are prolonged by using an algorithm that retains their spectral content and, in some cases, their transitional elements are amplified. As children progress through the exercises, signal duration and intensity are gradually normalized. These signal modifications are made to address the presumed auditory perceptual difficulties of at least some children with SLI and reading disabilities.

Exploratory studies of the FFW software have yielded promising results. In one study conducted by the developers (Merzenich et al., 1996), 7 children with language disorders and reading difficulties between the ages of 5 and 9 participated in activities that incorporated the acoustic modifications described earlier with gradual normalization for 3 hours per day, 5 days per week, for 4 weeks. The children played prototypes of two FFW game-like exercises and were provided individual instruction on eight other language processing tasks. In addition, they listened to acoustically modified, prerecorded stories at home for 1–2 hours each day. Five of the 7 participants' performance on the prototype exercises improved substantially over the treatment period, but performance on the other eight exercises was not reported. As a group, their performance on norm-referenced tests of speech discrimination and language comprehension improved significantly. Moreover, changes in presumed temporal processing (evaluated by performance on a nonverbal auditory sequential perception task) were highly correlated with posttest performance in language comprehension.

In a second exploratory study carried out by the developers (the results are summarized in Veale, 1999, and on the Scientific Learning Corporation website at *www. scilearn.com*), over 500 children between 4 and 14 years of age, with language comprehension deficits, received FFW training from 63 specially trained clinicians at 35 sites (primarily clinics and private practices) in the United States and Canada. The children varied in their diagnoses and severity of disability, but according to Tallal et al. (1997), approximately 90% of the participants achieved a gain of about one standard deviation on one or more norm-referenced tests of auditory perception and discrimination and oral language development.

An entire issue of the *American Journal of Speech–Language Pathology* (2001, Vol. 10) was devoted to a series of five independent exploratory studies (case studies and single-subject research studies) of FFW in school, clinic, and home settings. According to Gillam, Frome Loeb, and Friel-Patti (2001), all of the children who received FFW training in these studies made significant improvements (their posttest scores exceeded the 95% confidence interval of their pretest scores) on at least one standardized oral language measure (and, in a few cases, a formal reading measure). However, gains were evident for only a fraction of the measures given and were quite inconsistent across participants. Some of these gains were observed 3 months later. Increases in utterance length, but not utterance grammaticality, were observed for some of the participants. Interestingly, some scores declined from pretest to posttest, and several children were reluctant and even unyielding when asked to continue their participation in the FFW training.

Although the degree of success with the intervention exercises was expected to predict performance gains, there was little evidence of such a relationship. Additionally, there was a lack of progress in temporal

processing (measured by the difference between simultaneous and backward masking thresholds) associated with treatment outcomes in two of the studies. Finally, similar improvements in oral language performance were observed in one study in which FFW was evaluated against a bundle of computer exercises that did not incorporate acoustic signal modifications. These three findings did not support the contention that FFW improved auditory temporal processing.

Hook, Macaruso, and Jones (2001) also performed an independent exploratory study of FFW. Eleven children with reading disabilities, between the ages of 7 and 12 years, participated in the FFW intervention for approximately 2 months, while 9 other children with reading disabilities, matched for age, IQ, phonemic awareness ability, and reading level, participated in a comparison treatment in which the children completed activities from the Orton–Gillingham (OG) multisensory alphabetic training program. Another 11 poor readers, matched on the same criteria, served as a longitudinal no-contact control group. The students in the FFW group and the OG group made significant but equivalent gains in phonological awareness, but neither group demonstrated significant gains in word recognition, and the OG group achieved higher posttest scores in decoding than did the FFW group. These results were obtained despite the fact that the FFW group received more than double the amount of intervention time (56 hours) as that received by the OG group (25 hours). Both the FFW group and the no-contact control group showed gains in phonemic awareness and all aspects of reading (word recognition, decoding, and comprehension) over a 2-year period following the intervention, but those gains were similar between groups. Children who participated in FFW displayed immediate gains in oral language production, but not oral language comprehension, serial naming rate, or working memory; the gains in oral language were not maintained 2 years later. Finally, the completion rate of the FFW activities was not related to treatment outcomes.

Troia and Whitney (2003) examined FFW treatment outcomes for a group of elementary-school-age children referred for poor achievement. Twenty-five students between the ages of 6 and 12 years participated in the FFW program for about 2 months, while 12 other children, matched for grade, IQ, and special education eligibility, served as a no-contact control group. The children in the FFW group outperformed their peers on norm-referenced measures of verbal expression (i.e., vocabulary usage, expressive morphosyntactic competence, and use of figurative language, multiple meanings, and pragmatics), and when the weakest students in both groups were compared, in syllable and sound blending and reduction of problem behavior ratings. Thus, FFW had a substantial, albeit limited impact on children's oral language skills, academic performance, and social behaviors. Interestingly, Troia and Whitney did not find an aptitude–treatment interaction for their sample, possibly because the students performed well within the average range on most of the dependent measures before beginning the FFW program.

Overall, these exploratory studies support a cautious progression toward FFW efficacy research. Much still remains to be discovered about the nature of the treatment outcomes and how best to evaluate them. Because the FFW intervention is multifaceted, it is difficult to isolate the components of the treatment regimen (e.g., discrete learning trials, massed practice, immediate feedback and reinforcement, instruction in multiple language skills, progress monitoring and responsive adaptation, signal lengthening and amplification) that are most closely associated with observed improvements in auditory perceptual skills and language performance (Gillam, 1999; Studdert-Kennedy et al., 1995; Veale, 1999). We certainly require a better grasp of the nature of temporal processing and its relationships with the various cognitive and linguistic skills, including phonological processing, required for literacy achievement to make sense of the current findings.

The fact that studies conducted by the developers appear to yield stronger and more widespread positive effects may be due to compounded methodological limitations. For example, children in the Merzenich et

al. (1996) study were provided with individual language therapy and homework assignments, in addition to the computer exercises, which made it impossible to attribute the treatment results solely to the FFW exercises. In addition, intervention time in this study approximated 300 minutes per day, three times the 100 minutes per day required of FFW participants (Gillam, 1999). In both studies conducted by the developers of FFW, treatment gains may have been overestimated, because (1) some of the outcome measures were similar to the FFW exercises, (2) regression to the mean was not accommodated by applying confidence intervals, and (3) there was no control of Rosenthal effects—the examiners also delivered the intervention, which may have biased their administration and scoring (see Gillam, 1999; Studdert-Kennedy et al., 1995; Veale, 1999).

Efficacy Studies

Tallal et al. (1996) matched 22 children with language and reading impairments, between 5 and 10 years of age, for nonverbal intelligence, receptive language skills, and age, then assigned them to an experimental treatment condition in which the activities incorporated acoustically modified signals or to a comparison treatment condition in which the same activities were presented with unmodified acoustic waveforms (e.g., natural speech). The activities used in both conditions included revised and newly developed prototypes of the FFW games. Additional individual language instruction and homework were provided to both groups. Children in both treatment groups showed significant improvements in speech discrimination, memory, and receptive language skills after 4 weeks of daily training (improvements in exercise performance were evident for most, but not all, of the children), but those who completed the activities using acoustically modified signals demonstrated significantly greater gains (about 2 years growth) that were maintained 6 weeks later. In addition, children in the experimental treatment condition displayed significant gains in nonverbal auditory sequential perception, whereas those in the comparison treatment condition did not.

In a school pilot study (see Veale, 1999, and the corporation's website), 452 at-risk students in grades K–3 in 19 public schools, in 9 school districts across the country, participated in a stratified randomized group experiment. The majority (67%) of children who received FFW training over a period of about 40 school days demonstrated significantly greater progress (an average of 1.8 years growth) in language comprehension and phonological awareness in comparison to their peers who did not receive training. This and the Tallal et al. (1996) efficacy study have been criticized on many of the same grounds outlined for the developers' exploratory studies. Additionally, the Tallal et al. study technically does not meet the criteria for efficacy research because the sample size was small.

In a study with migrant, Spanish-speaking students in grades 1 through 6, Troia (in press) found that children in a FFW treatment group ($n = 99$) achieved a significantly greater gain than those in a no-contact control group ($n = 92$) on a measure of sight word recognition. Pretest to posttest changes in test scores were equivalent for the two groups on norm-referenced measures of English-language proficiency, oral language competence, phonological awareness, decoding and reading comprehension, and classroom behavior. However, when students who were least fluent in spoken English in each group were compared, the children in the treatment group demonstrated superior gains in expressive language, sight word recognition, and pseudoword decoding. FFW seemed to have a substantial but circumscribed impact on the oral language skills and reading performance of children in the study. It should be noted that almost 40% of the students never advanced to training levels at which the synthesized speech approximated normal rate and amplification characteristics; consequently, they may have not been able to achieve demonstrable improvements in oral and written language. In this study, random assignment was used for a majority of the participants (66%), so it only approximates a rigorous evaluation of treatment efficacy.

Nevertheless, the findings parallel those from the independent exploratory studies.

CONCLUSIONS

Phonological processing operations include phonological awareness, retrieval of phonological information from the lexicon, and phonological coding in working memory. All have well-established relevance in learning to read and write alphabetic and, to some extent, nonalphabetic languages. A core deficit in phonological processing appears to be at the heart of many literacy-learning problems, although it is likely not the sole deficit in many cases. Scientists are making headway into understanding how phonological information is perceived and used during these operations, and are using this knowledge to develop more sophisticated and effective interventions to ameliorate and perhaps even prevent poor literacy achievement. Efforts that incorporate comprehensive systems theories and analyses that account for numerous interactive variables will go far in advancing this agenda.

REFERENCES

Ackerman, P. T., Dykman, R. A., & Gardner, M. Y. (1990). Counting rate, naming rate, phonological sensitivity, and memory span: Major factors in dyslexia. *Journal of Learning Disabilities, 23,* 325–327.

Adams, A. M., & Gathercole, S. E. (1995). Phonological working memory and speech production in preschool children. *Journal of Speech and Hearing Research, 38,* 403–414.

Adams, M. J. (1990). *Beginning to read: Thinking and learning about print.* Cambridge, MA: MIT Press.

Adlard, A., & Hazan, V. (1998). Speech perception in children with specific reading disabilities (dyslexia). *Quarterly Journal of Experimental Psychology: Human Experimental Psychology, 51A,* 153–177.

Allor, J. H. (2002). The relationships of phonemic awareness and rapid naming to reading development. *Learning Disability Quarterly, 25,* 47–57.

Allor, J. H., Fuchs, D., & Mathes, P. G. (2001). Do students with and without lexical retrieval weaknesses respond differently to instruction? *Journal of Learning Disabilities, 34,* 264–275.

Baddeley, A. D. (1986). *Working memory.* Oxford, UK: Oxford University Press.

Baddeley, A. D., Gathercole, S. E., & Papagno, C.

(1998). The phonological loop as a language learning device. *Psychological Review, 105,* 158–173.

Baddeley, A. D., & Hitch, G. (1974). Working memory. In G. A. Bower (Ed.), *Recent advances in learning and motivation* (Vol. 8, pp. 47–90). New York: Academic Press.

Baddeley, A. D., & Hitch, G. (2000). Development of working memory: Should the Pascual-Leone and the Baddeley and Hitch models be merged? *Journal of Experimental Child Psychology, 77,* 128–137.

Badian, N. A. (1993). Phonemic awareness, naming, visual symbol processing, and reading. *Reading and Writing: An Interdisciplinary Journal, 5,* 87–100.

Ball, E. W. (1993). Phonological awareness: What's important and to whom? *Reading and Writing: An Interdisciplinary Journal, 5,* 141–159.

Ball, E. W., & Blachman, B. A. (1988). Phoneme segmentation training: Effects of reading readiness. *Annals of Dyslexia, 38,* 208–225.

Benasich, A. A., & Tallal, P. (1996). Auditory temporal processing thresholds, habituation, and recognition memory over the first year. *Infant Behavioral Development, 19,* 339–357.

Bishop, D. V., Carlyon, R. P., Deeks, J. M., & Bishop, S. J. (1999). Auditory temporal processing impairment: Neither necessary nor sufficient for causing language impairment in children. *Journal of Speech, Language, and Hearing Research, 42,* 1295–1310.

Bishop, D. V. M., & Adams, C. (1990). A prospective study of the relationship between specific language impairment, phonological disorders, and reading retardation. *Journal of Child Psychology and Psychiatry, 31,* 1027–1057.

Blachman, B. A. (1984). Relationship of rapid naming ability and language analysis skills to kindergarten and first-grade reading achievement. *Journal of Educational Psychology, 76,* 610–622.

Blachman, B. A. (1991). Early intervention for children's reading problems: Clinical applications of the research in phonological awareness. *Topics in Language Disorders, 12*(1), 51–65.

Bowers, P. G. (1995). Tracing symbol naming speed's unique contributions to reading disabilities over time. *Reading and Writing: An Interdisciplinary Journal, 7,* 189–216.

Bowers, P. G., & Wolf, M. (1993). Theoretical links among naming speed, precise timing mechanisms and orthographic skill in dyslexia. *Reading and Writing: An Interdisciplinary Journal, 5,* 69–85.

Bowey, J. A. (1994). Phonological sensitivity in novice readers and nonreaders. *Journal of Experimental Child Psychology, 58,* 134–159.

Bowey, J. A. (1995). Socioeconomic status differences in preschool phonological sensitivity and first-grade reading achievement. *Journal of Educational Psychology, 87,* 476–487.

Bowey, J. A., & Francis, J. (1991). Phonological analysis as a function of age and exposure to reading instruction. *Applied Psycholinguistics, 12,* 91–121.

Bradley, L., & Bryant, P. E. (1983). Categorizing sounds and learning to read: A causal connection. *Nature, 301,* 419–421.

Brady, S. A., Shankweiler, D., & Mann, V. (1983). Speech perception and memory coding in relation to reading ability. *Journal of Experimental Child Psychology, 35,* 345–367.

Breier, J. I., Fletcher, J. M., Foorman, B. R., Klaas, P., & Gray, L. C. (2003). Auditory temporal processing in children with specific reading disability with and without attention deficit/ hyperactivity disorder. *Journal of Speech, Language, and Hearing Research, 46,* 31–42.

Brown, G. D. A. (1997). Connectionism, phonology, reading and regularity in developmental dyslexia. *Brain and Language, 59,* 207–235.

Bruck, M. (1990). Word recognition skills of adults with childhood diagnoses of dyslexia. *Developmental Psychology, 26,* 439–454.

Bruck, M. (1992). Persistence of dyslexics' phonological awareness deficits. *Developmental Psychology, 28,* 874–886.

Bruck, M., & Treiman, R. (1990). Phonological awareness and spelling in normal children and dyslexics: The case of initial consonant clusters. *Journal of Experimental Child Psychology, 50,* 156–178.

Bryant, P. E., MacLean, M., Bradley, L. L., & Crossland, J. (1990). Rhyme and alliteration, phoneme detection, and learning to read. *Developmental Psychology, 26,* 429–438.

Burgess, S. R., & Lonigan, C. J. (1998). Bidirectional relations of phonological sensitivity and pre-reading abilities: Evidence from a preschool sample. *Journal of Experimental Child Psychology, 70,* 117–141.

Burgess, S. R., Lonigan, C. J., Anthony, J. L., & Barker, T. (1996, April). *Predictors of the development of emergent literacy skills in preschool-age children: Evidence from a longitudinal study.* Paper presented at the 4th annual meeting of Society for the Scientific Study of Reading, New York, NY.

Bus, A. G., & van IJzendoorn, M. H. (1999). Phonological awareness and early reading: A meta-analysis of experimental training studies. *Journal of Educational Psychology, 91,* 403–414.

Byrne, B., & Fielding-Barnsley, R. (1991). Evaluation of a program to teach phonemic awareness to young children. *Journal of Educational Psychology, 83,* 451–455.

Byrne, B., Freebody, P., & Gates, A. (1992). Longitudinal data on the relations of word-reading strategies to comprehension, reading time, and phonemic awareness. *Reading Research Quarterly, 27,* 141–151.

Carrillo, M. (1994). Development of phonological awareness and reading acquisition: A study in Spanish language. *Reading and Writing: An Interdisciplinary Journal, 6,* 279–298.

Catts, H. W. (1989). Phonological processing deficits and reading disabilities. In A. G. Kamhi & H. W. Catts (Eds.), *Reading disabilities: A developmental language perspective* (pp. 101–132). Boston: Allyn & Bacon.

Catts, H. W., Fey, M. E., Zhang, X., & Tomblin, J. B. (1999). Language basis of reading and reading disabilities: Evidence from a longitudinal investigation. *Scientific Studies of Reading, 3,* 331–361.

Catts, H. W., Fey, M. E., Zhang, X., & Tomblin, J. B. (2001). Estimating the risk of future reading difficulties in kindergarten children: A research-based model and its clinical implementation. *Language, Speech, and Hearing Services in Schools, 32,* 38–50.

Chan, C. K. K., & Siegel, L. S. (2001). Phonological processing in reading Chinese among normally achieving and poor readers. *Journal of Experimental Child Psychology, 80,* 23–43.

Chaney, C. (1992). Language development, metalinguistic skills, and print awareness in 3-year-old children. *Applied Psycholinguistics, 13,* 485–514.

Chaney, C. (1994). Language development, metalinguistic awareness, and emergent literacy skills of 3-year-old children in relation to social class. *Applied Psycholinguistics, 15,* 371–394.

Charles-Luce, J., & Luce, P. A. (1990). Similarity neighborhoods of words in young children's lexicon. *Journal of Child Language, 17,* 205–215.

Chiappe, P., Chiappe, D. L., & Siegel, L. S. (2001). Speech perception, lexicality, and reading skill. *Journal of Experimental Child Psychology, 80,* 58–74.

Chiappe, P., Stringer, R., Siegel, L. S., & Stanovich, K. E. (2002). Why the timing deficit hypothesis does not explain reading disability in adults. *Reading and Writing: An Interdisciplinary Journal, 15,* 73–107.

Cornwall, A. (1992). The relationship of phonological awareness, rapid naming, and verbal memory to severe reading and spelling disability. *Journal of Learning Disabilities, 25,* 532–538.

Cossu, G., Shankweiler, D., Liberman, I. Y., & Gugliotta, M. (1995). Visual and phonological determinants of misreadings in a transparent orthography. *Reading and Writing: An Interdisciplinary Journal, 7,* 237–256.

Damian, M. F., & Martin, R. C. (1999). Semantic and phonolgical codes interact in single word production. *Journal of Experimental Psychology: Learning, Memory, and Cognition, 25,* 345–361.

De Cara, B., & Goswami, U. (2002). Similarity relations among spoken words: The special status of rimes in English. *Behavior Research Methods: Instruments and Computers, 34,* 416–423.

Denckla, M. B., & Rudel, R. (1976a). Naming of object-drawings by dyslexic and other learning disabled children. *Brain and Language, 3,* 1–15.

Denckla, M. B., & Rudel, R. (1976b). Rapid "automatized" naming (RAN): Dyslexia differentiated from other learning disabilities. *Neuropsychologia, 14,* 471–479.

De Weirdt, W. (1988). Speech perception and frequency discrimination in good and poor readers. *Applied Psycholinguistics, 9,* 163–183.

Eden, G. F., Stein, J. F., Wood, H. M., & Wood, F. B. (1995). Temporal and spatial processing in reading disabled children. *Cortex, 31,* 451–468.

Ehri, L. C. (1987). Learning to read and spell words. *Journal of Reading Behavior, 19,* 5–31.

Ehri, L. C., & Wilce, L. S. (1980). The influence of orthography on readers' conceptualization of the phonemic structure of words. *Applied Psycholinguistics, 1,* 371–385.

Ehri, L. C., & Wilce, L. S. (1985). Movement into reading: Is the first stage of printed word learning visual or phonetic? *Reading Research Quarterly, 20,* 163–179.

Elbro, C. (1996). Early linguistic abilities and reading development: A review and a hypothesis. *Reading and Writing: An Interdisciplinary Journal, 8,* 453–485.

Elbro, C. (1998). When *reading* is "readn" or "somthn": Distinctness of phonological representations of lexical items in normal and disabled readers. *Scandinavian Journal of Psychology, 39,* 149–153.

Elliott, L. L. (1986). Discrimination and response bias for CV syllables differing in voice onset time among children and adults. *Journal of the Acoustical Society of America, 80,* 1250–1255.

Elliott, L. L., & Hammer, M. A. (1988). Longitudinal changes in auditory discrimination in normal children and children with language-learning problems. *Journal of Speech and Hearing Research, 53,* 467–474.

Elliott, L.L., Hammer, M. A., & Evan, K. E. (1987). Perception of gated, highly familiar spoken monosyllabic nouns by children, teenagers, and older adults. *Perception and Psychophysics, 42,* 150–157.

Elliott, L.L., Hammer, M. A., & Scholl, M. E. (1989). Fine-grained auditory discrimination in normal children and children with language-learning problems. *Journal of Speech and Hearing Research, 32,* 112–119.

Farmer, M. E., & Klein, R. M. (1995). The evidence for a temporal processing deficit linked to dyslexia: A review. *Psychonomic Bulletin and Review, 2,* 460–493.

Felton, R. H., & Brown, I. S. (1990). Phonological processes as predictors of specific reading skills in children at risk for reading failure. *Reading and Writing: An Interdisciplinary Journal, 2,* 39–59.

Felton, R. H., Naylor, C. E., & Wood, F. B. (1990). Neuropsychological profile of adult dyslexics. *Brain and Language, 39,* 485–497.

Felton, R. H., & Wood, F. B. (1989). Cognitive deficits in reading disability and attention deficit disorder. *Journal of Learning Disabilities, 22,* 3–13, 22.

Foorman, B. R., Francis, D. J., Novy, D. M., & Liberman, D. (1991). How letter–sound instruction mediates progress in first-grade reading and spelling. *Journal of Educational Psychology, 83,* 456–469.

Fowler, A. E. (1991). How early phonological development might set the stage for phonological awareness. In S. A. Brady & D. Shankweiler (Eds.), *Phonological processes in literacy: A tribute to Isabelle Y. Liberman* (pp. 97–117). Hillsdale, NJ: Erlbaum.

Fox, B., & Routh, D. K. (1975). Analyzing spoken language into words, syllables, and phonemes: A developmental study. *Journal of Psycholinguistic Research, 4,* 331–342.

Galaburda, A. M., Corsiglia, J., Rosen, G. D., & Sherman, G. F. (1987). Planum temporale asymmetry:

Reappraisal since Geschwind and Levitsky. *Neuropsychologia, 25,* 853–868.

Galaburda, A. M., & Livingstone, M. (1993). Evidence for a magnocellular defect in developmental dyslexia. In P. Tallal, A. M. Galaburda, R. Llinas, & C. von Euler (Eds.), *Temporal information processing in the nervous system: Special reference to dyslexia and dysphasia* (pp. 57–69). New York: New York Academy of Sciences.

Galaburda, A. M., Menard, M. T., & Rosen, G. D. (1994). Evidence for aberrant auditory anatomy in developmental dyslexia. *Proceedings of the National Academy of Sciences, 91,* 8010–8013.

Gathercole, S. E., & Adams, A. (1993). Phonological working memory in very young children. *Developmental Psychology, 29,* 770–778.

Gathercole, S. E., & Baddeley, A. D. (1989). Evaluation of the role of phonological STM in the development of vocabulary in children: A longitudinal study. *Journal of Memory and Language, 28,* 200–213.

Gathercole, S. E., & Baddeley, A. D. (1990). The role of phonological memory in vocabulary acquisition: A study of young children learning new names. *British Journal of Psychology, 81,* 439–454.

Gathercole, S. E., & Baddeley, A. D. (1993). *Working memory and language.* Hove, UK: Erlbaum.

Gathercole, S. E., & Hitch, G. J. (1993). Developmental changes in short-term memory: A revised working memory perspective. In A. Collins, S. E. Gathercole, M. A. Conway, & P. E. Morris (Eds.), *Theories of memory* (pp. 189–210). Hove, UK: Erlbaum.

German, D. (1979). Word-finding skills in children with learning disabilities. *Journal of Learning Disabilities, 12,* 43–48.

German, D. (1982). Word-finding substitutions in children with learning disabilities. *Language, Speech, and Hearing Services in Schools, 13,* 223–230.

German, D. (1984). Diagnosis of word-finding disorders in children with learning disabilities. *Journal of Learning Disabilities, 17,* 353–359.

Gillam, R. B. (1999). Computer-assisted language intervention using Fast ForWord®: Theoretical and empirical considerations for clinical decision-making. *Language, Speech, and Hearing Services in Schools, 30,* 363–370.

Gillam, R. B., Frome Loeb, D., & Friel-Patti, S. (2001). Looking back: A summary of five exploratory studies of Fast ForWord. *American Journal of Speech–Language Pathology, 10,* 269–273.

Gleitman, L. R., & Rozin, P. (1977). The structure and acquisition of reading I: Relations between orthographies and the structure of language. In A. S. Reber & D. L. Scarborough (Eds.), *Toward a psychology of reading: The proceedings of the CUNY conference* (pp. 1–53). Hillsdale, NJ: Erlbaum.

Godfrey, J. J., Syrdal-Lasky, A. K., Millay, K. K., & Knox, C. M. (1981). Performance of dyslexic children on speech perception tests. *Journal of Experimental Child Psychology, 32,* 401–424.

Goldinger, S. D., Luce, P. A., & Pisoni, D. B. (1989). Priming lexical neighbors of spoken words: Effects of competition and inhibition. *Journal of Memory and Language, 28,* 501–518.

Gonzales, J. E. J., & Valle, I. H. (2000). Word identification and reading disorders in the Spanish language. *Journal of Learning Disabilities, 33,* 44–60.

Goswami, U. (1999). Orthographic analogies and phonological priming: A comment on Bowey, Vaughan, and Hansen (1998). *Journal of Experimental Child Psychology, 72,* 210–219.

Goswami, U. (2000). Phonological representations, reading development and dyslexia: Towards a cross-linguistic theoretical framework. *Dyslexia, 6,* 133–151.

Goswami, U., & Bryant, P. E. (1990). *Phonological skills and learning to read.* Hillsdale, NJ: Erlbaum.

Goswami, U., Gombert, J. E., & de Barrera, L. F. (1998). Children's orthographic representations and linguistic transparency: Nonsense word reading in English, French, and Spanish. *Applied Psycholinguistics, 19,* 19–52.

Goswami, U., Porpodas, C., & Wheelwright, S. (1997). Children's orthographic representations in English and Greek. *European Journal of Psychology of Education, 12,* 273–292.

Gottardo, A., Stanovich, K. E., & Siegel, L. S. (1996). The relationships between phonological sensitivity, syntactic processing, and verbal working memory in the reading performance of third-grade children. *Journal of Experimental Child Psychology, 63,* 563–582.

Habib, M., Espresser, R., Rey, V., Giraud, K., Braus, P., & Gres, C. (1999). Training dyslexics with acoustically modified speech: Evidence of improved phonological performance. *Brain and Cognition, 40,* 143–146.

Hatcher, P. J., Hulme, C., & Ellis, A. W. (1994). Ameliorating early reading failure by integrating the teaching of reading and phonological skills: The phonological linkage hypothesis. *Child Development, 65,* 41–57.

Helfgott, J. A. (1976). Phonemic segmentation and blending skills of kindergarten children: Implications for beginning reading acquisition. *Contemporary Educational Psychology, 1,* 157–169.

Helzer, J. R., Champlin, C. A., & Gillam, R. B. (1996). Auditory temporal resolution in specifically language-impaired and age-matched children. *Perceptual and Motor Skills, 83,* 1171–1181.

Ho, C. S. H., & Bryant, P. E. (1997a). Development of phonological awareness of Chinese children in Hong Kong. *Journal of Psycholinguistic Research, 26,* 109–126.

Ho, C. S. H., & Bryant, P. E. (1997b). Learning to read beyond the logographic phase. *Reading Research Quarterly, 32,* 276–289.

Ho, C. S. H., & Bryant, P. E. (1997c). Phonological skills are important in learning to read Chinese. *Developmental Psychology, 33,* 946–951.

Ho, C. S. H., Law, T. P. S., & Ng, P. M. (2000). The phonological deficit hypothesis in Chinese developmental dyslexia. *Reading and Writing: An Interdisciplinary Journal, 13,* 57–79.

Hook, P. E., Macaruso, P., & Jones, S. (2001). Efficacy of Fast ForWord training on facilitating acquisition of reading skills by children with reading difficulties—a longitudinal study. *Annals of Dyslexia, 51,* 75–96.

Hu, C. F., & Catts, H. W. (1998). The role of phonological processing in early reading ability: What we can learn from Chinese. *Scientific Studies of Reading, 2,* 55–79.

Huang, H. S., & Hanley, J. R. (1995). Phonological awareness and visual skills in learning to read Chinese and English. *Cognition, 54,* 73–98.

Hurford, D. P. (1990). Assessment and remediation of a phonemic discrimination deficit in reading disabled second and fourth graders. *Journal of Experimental Child Psychology, 50,* 396–415.

Hurford, D. P., & Sanders, R. E. (1990). Training phonemic segmentation ability with a phonemic discrimination intervention in second- and third-grade children with reading disabilities. *Journal of Learning Disabilities, 23,* 564–569.

IJzendoorn, M. H., & Bus, A. G. (1994). Meta-analytic confirmation of the nonword reading deficit in developmental dyslexia. *Reading Research Quarterly, 29,* 266–275.

Jimenez, J., Alvarez, C., Estevez, A., & Hernandez-Valle, I. (2000). Onset-rime units in visual word recognition in Spanish normal readers and children with reading disabilities. *Learning Disabilities Research and Practice, 15,* 135–145.

Joanisse, M. F., Manis, F. R., Keating, P., & Seidenberg, M. S. (2000). Language deficits in dyslexic children: Speech perception, phonology, and morphology. *Journal of Experimental Child Psychology, 77,* 30–60.

Joanisse, M. F., & Seidenberg, M. S. (1998). Specific language impairment: A deficit in grammar or processing? *Trends in Cognitive Sciences, 2,* 240–247.

Johnston, R. S., Anderson, M., & Holligan, C. (1996). Knowledge of the alphabet and explicit awareness of phonemes in prereaders: The nature of the relationship. *Reading and Writing: An Interdisciplinary Journal, 8,* 217–234.

Juel, C. (1988). Learning to read and write: A longitudinal study of 54 children from first through fourth grades. *Journal of Educational Psychology, 80,* 437–447.

Juel, C., Griffith, P. L., & Gough, P. B. (1986). Acquisition of literacy: A longitudinal study of children in first and second grade. *Journal of Educational Psychology, 78,* 243–255.

Jusczyk, P. W. (1986). Toward a model of the development of speech perception. In J. S. Perkell & D. H. Klatt (Eds.), *Invariance and variability in speech processes* (pp. 1–33). Hillsdale, NJ: Erlbaum.

Just, M. A., & Carpenter, P. A. (1992). A capacity theory of comprehension: Individual differences in working memory. *Psychological Review, 99,* 122–149.

Kamhi, A. G., & Catts, H. W. (1986). Toward an understanding of developmental language and reading

disorders. *Journal of Speech and Hearing Disorders, 51,* 337–347.

Katz, R. (1986). Phonological deficiencies in children with reading disability: Evidence from an object-naming task. *Cognition, 22,* 225–257.

Klein, R. M., & Farmer, M. E. (1995). Dyslexia and a temporal processing deficit: A reply to the commentaries. *Psychonomic Bulletin and Review, 2,* 515–526.

Landerl, K., Wimmer, H., & Frith, U. (1997). The impact of orthographic consistency on dyslexia: A German–English comparison. *Cognition, 63,* 315–334.

Leck, K. J., Weekes, B. S., & Chen, M. J. (1995). Visual and phonological pathways to the lexicon: Evidence from Chinese readers. *Memory and Cognition, 23,* 468–476.

Leonard, L., McGregor, K., & Allen, G. (1992). Grammatical morphology and speech perception in children with specific language impairment. *Journal of Speech and Hearing Research, 35,* 1076–1085.

Lewkowicz, N. K. (1980). Phonemic awareness training: What to teach and how to teach it. *Journal of Educational Psychology, 72,* 686–700.

Lewkowicz, N. K., & Low, L. Y. (1979). Effects of visual aids and word structure on phonemic segmentation. *Contemporary Educational Psychology, 4,* 238–252.

Liberman, I. Y. (1982). A language-oriented view of reading and its disabilities. In H. Myklebust (Ed.), *Progress in learning disabilities* (Vol. 5, pp. 81–101). New York: Grune & Stratton.

Liberman, I. Y., & Shankweiler, D. (1985). Phonology and the problems of learning to read and write. *Remedial and Special Education, 6,* 8–17.

Liberman, I. Y., & Shankweiler, D. (1991). Phonology and beginning reading: A tutorial. In L. Rieben & C. A. Perfetti (Eds.), *Learning to read: Basic research and its implications* (pp. 3–17). Hillsdale, NJ: Erlbaum.

Liberman, I. Y., Shankweiler, D., Fischer, F. W., & Carter, B. (1974). Explicit syllable and phoneme segmentation in the young child. *Journal of Experimental Child Psychology, 18,* 201–212.

Liberman, I. Y., & Shankweiler, D., Liberman, A. M., Fowler, C., & Fischer, F. W. (1977). Phonetic segmentation and recoding in the beginning reader. In A. S. Reber & D. L. Scarborough (Eds.), *Toward a psychology of reading: The proceedings of the CUNY conference* (pp. 207–225). Hillsdale, NJ: Erlbaum.

Lindblom, B. (1992). Phonological units as adaptive emergents of lexical development. In C. A. Ferguson, L. Menn, & C. Stoel-Gammon (Eds.), *Phonological development: Models, research, implications* (pp. 131–163). Timonium, MD: York Press.

Lonigan, C., Burgess, S. R., Anthony, J. L., & Barker, T. A. (1998). Development of phonological sensitivity in 2- to 5-year-old children. *Journal of Educational Psychology, 90,* 294–311.

Lovegrove, W. (1993). Weakness in the transient visual system: A causal factor in dyslexia? In P. Tallal, A. M. Galaburda, R. Llinas, & C. von Euler (Eds.),

Temporal information processing in the nervous system: Special reference to dyslexia and dysphasia (pp. 57–69). New York: New York Academy of Sciences.

Luce, P. A. (1986). Neighborhoods of words in the mental lexicon. *Research on speech perception* (Technical Report No. 6). Bloomington: Indiana University, Department of Psychology, Speech Research Laboratory.

Lundberg, I., Frost, J., & Peterson, O. (1988). Effects of an extensive program for stimulating phonological awareness in pre-school children. *Reading Research Quarterly, 23,* 263–284.

Lyon, G. R. (1995). Toward a definition of dyslexia. *Annals of Dyslexia, 45,* 3–27.

MacLean, M., Bryant, P. E., & Bradley, L. L. (1987). Rhymes, nursery rhymes, and reading in early childhood. *Merrill–Palmer Quarterly, 33,* 255–282.

Manis, F. R., Doi, L. M., & Bhadha, B. (2000). Naming speed, phonological awareness, and orthographic knowledge in second graders. *Journal of Learning Disabilities, 33,* 325–333.

Manis, F. R., McBride-Chang, C., Seidenberg, M. S., Keating, P., Doi, L. M., & Petersen, A. (1997). Are speech perception deficits associated with developmental dyslexia? *Journal of Experimental Child Psychology, 66,* 211–235.

Manis, F. R., Seidenberg, M. S., & Doi, L. M. (1999). See Dick RAN: Rapid naming and the longitudinal prediction of reading subskills in first and second grades. *Scientific Studies of Reading, 3,* 129–157.

Manis, F. R., Szeszulski, P. A., Holt, L. K., & Graves, K. (1990). Variation in component word recognition and spelling skills among dyslexic children and normal readers. In T. H. Carr & B. A. Levy (Eds.), *Reading and its development: Component skills approaches* (pp. 207–259). New York: Academic Press.

Mann, V. A. (1984). Longitudinal prediction and prevention of early reading difficulty. *Annals of Dyslexia, 34,* 117–136.

Mann, V. A. (1993). Phoneme awareness and future reading ability. *Journal of Learning Disabilities, 26,* 259–269.

Mann, V. A., & Liberman, I. Y. (1984). Phonological awareness and verbal short-term memory. *Journal of Learning Disabilities, 17,* 592–599.

Marshall, C. M., Snowling, M. J., & Bailey, P. J. (2001). Rapid auditory processing and phonological ability in normal readers and readers with dyslexia. *Journal of Speech, Language, and Hearing Research, 44,* 925–940.

Mattingly, I. G. (1992). Linguistic awareness and orthographic form. In R. Frost & L. Katz (Eds.), *Orthography, phonology, morphology, and meaning* (pp. 11–26). Amsterdam, Elsevier.

McAnally, K. I., Hansen, P. C., Cornelissen, P. L., & Stein, J. F. (1997). Effect of time and frequency manipulation on syllable perception in developmental dyslexics. *Journal of Speech, Language, and Hearing Research, 40,* 912–924.

McBride-Chang, C. (1995). Phonological processing, speech perception, and reading disability: An integrative review. *Educational Psychologist, 30,* 109–121.

McBride-Chang, C. (1996). Models of speech perception and phonological processing in reading. *Child Development, 67,* 1836–1856.

McBride-Chang, C., & Manis, F. R. (1996). Structural invariance in the associations of naming speed, phonological awareness, and verbal reasoning in good and poor readers: A test of the double deficit hypothesis. *Reading and Writing: An Interdisciplinary Journal, 8,* 323–339.

McBride-Chang, C., Wagner, R. K., & Chang, L. (1997). Growth modeling of phonological awareness. *Journal of Educational Psychology, 89,* 621–630.

McCardle, P., Scarborough, H. S., & Catts, H. W. (2001). Predicting, explaining, and preventing children's reading difficulties. *Learning Disabilities Research and Practice, 16,* 230–239.

Merzenich, M. M., & Jenkins, W. M. (1995). Cortical plasticity and learning: Some basic principles. In B. Jules & I. Kovacs (Eds.), *Maturational windows and adult cortical plasticity* (Vol. 22, pp. 247–272). San Francisco: Addison-Wesley.

Merzenich, M. M., Jenkins, W. M., Johnston, P., Schreiner, C., Miller, S. L., & Tallal, P. (1996). Temporal processing deficits of language-learning impaired children ameliorated by training. *Science, 271,* 77–81.

Merzenich, M. M., Schreiner, C., Jenkins, W., & Wang, X. (1993). Neural mechanisms underlying temporal integration, segmentation, and input sequence representation: Some implications for the origin of learning disabilities. *Annals of the New York Academy of Sciences, 682,* 1–21.

Metsala, J. L. (1997a). An examination of word frequency and neighborhood density in the development of spoken-word recognition. *Memory and Cognition, 25,* 47–56.

Metsala, J. L. (1997b). Spoken word recognition in reading disabled children. *Journal of Educational Psychology, 89,* 159–169.

Metsala, J. L. (1999). Young children's phonological awareness and nonword repetition as a function of vocabulary development. *Journal of Educational Psychology, 91,* 3–19.

Metsala, J. L., Stanovich, K. E., & Brown, G. D. A. (1998). Regularity effects and the phonological deficit model of reading disabilities: A meta-analytic review. *Journal of Educational Psychology, 90,* 279–293.

Metsala, J. L., & Walley, A. C. (1998). Spoken vocabulary growth and the segmental restructuring of lexical representations: Precursors to phonemic awareness and early reading ability. In J. L. Metsala & L. C. Ehri (Eds.), *Word recognition in beginning literacy* (pp. 89–120). Mahwah, NJ: Erlbaum.

Mody, M., Studdert-Kennedy, M., & Brady, S. A. (1997). Speech perception deficits in poor readers: Auditory processing or phonological coding? *Journal of Experimental Child Psychology, 64,* 199–231.

Molfese, D. L. (1999, April). Predicting reading performance at eight years of age from auditory brain potentials recorded at birth. In V. J. Molfese (Chair), *Longitudinal studies of reading abilities: Biological and educational influences on development and persistence.* Symposium conducted at the annual meeting of the Society for Research in Child Development, Albuquerque, NM.

Montgomery, J. (1995). Examination of phonological working memory in specifically language-impaired children. *Applied Psycholinguistics, 16,* 355–378.

Morais, J., Cary, L., Alegria, J., & Bertelson, P. (1979). Does awareness of speech as a sequence of phones arise spontaneously? *Cognition, 7,* 323–331.

Murray, B. A., Stahl, S. A., & Ivey, M. G. (1996). Developing phoneme awareness through alphabet books. *Reading and Writing: An Interdisciplinary Journal, 8,* 307–322.

Nagarajan, S., Mahncke, H., Salz, T., Tallal, P., Roberts, T., & Merzenich, M. M. (1999). Cortical auditory signal processing in poor readers. *Proceedings of the National Academy of Science, 96,* 6483–6488.

Naslund, J. C., & Schneider, W. (1996). Kindergarten letter knowledge, phonological skills, and memory processes: Relative effects on early literacy. *Journal of Experimental Child Psychology, 62,* 30–59.

Nittrouer, S. (1999). Do temporal processing deficits cause phonological processing problems? *Journal of Speech, Language, and Hearing Research, 42,* 925–942.

Norrelgen, F., Lacerda, F., & Forssberg, H. (2002). Temporal resolution of auditory perception and verbal working memory in 15 children with language impairment. *Journal of Learning Disabilities, 35,* 539–545.

Oakhill, J., & Kyle, F. (2000). The relation between phonological awareness and working memory. *Journal of Experimental Child Psychology, 75,* 152–164.

Olson, R. K., Kliegel, R., Davidson, B. J., & Foltz, G. (1985). Individual differences and developmental differences in reading disability. In G. E. MacKinnon & T. G. Waller (Eds.), *Reading research: Advances in theory and practice* (Vol. 4, pp. 1–64). New York: Academic Press.

Olson, R. K., Wise, B., Connors, F., Rack, J., & Fulker, D. (1989). Specific deficits in component reading and language skills: Genetic and environmental influences. *Journal of Learning Disabilities, 22,* 339–348.

Oney, B., Peter, M., & Katz, L. (1997). Phonological processing in printed word recognition: Effects of age and writing system. *Scientific Studies of Reading, 1,* 65–83.

Pennington, B. F., McCabe, L. L., Smith, S. D., Lefly, D. L., Bookman, M. O., Kimberling, W. J., & Lubs, H. A. (1986). Spelling errors in adults with a form of familial dyslexia. *Child Development, 57,* 1001–1013.

Pennington, B. F., Van Orden, G. C., Smith, S. D., Green, P. A., & Haith, M. M. (1990). Phonological processing skills and deficits in adult dyslexics. *Child Development, 61,* 1753–1778.

Perfetti, C. A. (1986). Continuities in reading acquisition, reading skill, and reading disability. *Remedial and Special Education, 7*(1), 11–21.

Perfetti, C. A., Beck, I., Bell, L., & Hughes, C. (1987). Phonemic knowledge and learning to read are reciprocal: A longitudinal study. *Merrill–Palmer Quarterly, 33,* 283–319.

Rack, J. P., Snowling, M. J., & Olson, R. K. (1992). The nonword reading deficit in developmental dyslexia: A review. *Reading Research Quarterly, 27,* 29–53.

Rapala, M. M., & Brady, S. A. (1990). Reading ability and short-term memory: The role of phonological processing. *Reading and Writing: An Interdisciplinary Journal, 2,* 1–25.

Read, C., Zhang, Y., Nie, H., & Ding, B. (1986). The ability to manipulate speech sounds depends on knowing alphabetic writing. *Cognition, 24,* 31–44.

Reed, M. A. (1989). Speech perception and the discrimination of brief auditory cues in reading-disabled children. *Journal of Experimental Child Psychology, 48,* 270–292.

Robey, R. R., & Schultz, M. C. (1998). A model for conducting clinical-outcome research: An adaptation of the standard protocol for use in aphasiology. *Aphasiology, 12,* 787–810.

Rose, S. A., Feldman, J. F., Jankowski, J. J., & Futterweit, L. R. (1999). Visual and auditory temporal processing, cross-modal transfer, and reading. *Journal of Learning Disabilities, 32,* 256–266.

Roth, F. P., Speece, D. L., & Cooper, D. H. (2002). A longitudinal analysis of the connection between oral language and early reading. *Journal of Educational Research, 95,* 259–272.

Scarborough, H. S. (1990). Very early language deficits in dyslexic children. *Child Development, 61,* 1728–1734.

Scarborough, H. S. (1991). Antecedents to reading disability: Preschool language development and literacy experiences of children from dyslexic families. *Reading and Writing: An Interdisciplinary Journal, 3,* 219–233.

Scarborough, H. S. (1998). Early identification of children at risk for reading disabilities: Phonological awareness and some other promising predictors. In B. K. Shapiro, P. J. Accardo, & A. J. Capute (Eds.), *Specific reading disability: A view of the spectrum* (pp. 75–119). Baltimore: York Press.

Scarborough, H. S., & Dobrich, W. (1994). On the efficacy of reading to preschoolers. *Developmental Review, 14,* 245–302.

Schatschneider, C., Carlson, C. D., Francis, D. J., Foorman, B. R., & Fletcher, J. M. (2002). Relationship of rapid automatized naming and phonological awareness in early reading development: Implications for the double-deficit hypothesis. *Journal of Learning Disabilities, 35,* 245–256.

Schreuder, R., & van Bon, W. H. J. (1989). Phonemic analysis: Effects of word properties. *Journal of Research in Reading, 29,* 59–77.

Seidenberg, M. S., & McClelland, J. L. (1989). A distributed, developmental model of word recognition and naming. *Psychological Review, 96*, 523–568.

Share, D. L., & Stanovich, K. E. (1995). Cognitive processes in early reading development: Accommodating individual differences into a model of acquisition. *Issues in Education: Contributions from Educational Psychology, 1*, 1–57.

Siegel, L. S. (1994). Working memory and reading: A life-span perspective. *International Journal of Behavioural Development, 17*, 109–124.

Snow, C. E., Burns, S., & Griffith, P. (Eds.) (1998). *Preventing reading difficulties in young children.* Washington, DC: National Academy Press.

Snowling, M. J., Hulme, C., Smith, A., & Thomas, J. (1994). The effects of phonemic similarity and list length on children's sound categorisation performance. *Journal of Experimental Child Psychology, 58*, 160–180.

Snowling, M. J., Nation, K., Moxham, P., Gallagher, A., & Frith, U. (1997). Phonological processing skills of dyslexic students in higher education: A preliminary report. *Journal of Research in Reading, 20*, 31–41.

So, D., & Siegel, L. S. (1997). Learning to read Chinese: Semantic, syntactic, phonological and working memory skills in normally achieving and poor Chinese readers. *Reading and Writing: An Interdisciplinary Journal, 9*, 1–21.

Stahl, S. A., & Murray, B. A. (1994). Defining phonological awareness and its relationship to early reading. *Journal of Educational Psychology, 86*, 221–234.

Stanovich, K. E. (1985). Explaining the variance in reading ability in terms of psychological processes: What have we learned? *Annals of Dyslexia, 35*, 67–95.

Stanovich, K. E. (1986). Matthew effects in reading: Some consequences of individual differences in the acquisition of literacy. *Reading Research Quarterly, 21*, 360–407.

Stanovich, K. E. (1988). Explaining the difference between the dyslexic and the garden-variety poor reader: The phonological-core variable-difference model. *Journal of Learning Disabilities, 21*, 590–604.

Stanovich, K. E. (1991). Conceptual and empirical problems with discrepancy definitions of reading disability. *Learning Disability Quarterly, 14*, 269–280.

Stanovich, K. E., Cunningham, A. E., & Cramer, B. (1984). Assessing phonological awareness in kindergarten children: Issues of task comparability. *Journal of Experimental Child Psychology, 38*, 364–370.

Stanovich, K. E., Feeman, D. J., & Cunningham, A. E. (1983). The development of the relation between letter-naming speed and reading ability. *Bulletin of the Psychonomic Society, 21*, 199–202.

Stanovich, K. E., Nathan, R. G., & Vala-Rossi, M. (1986). Developmental changes in the cognitive correlates of reading ability and the developmental lag hypothesis. *Reading Research Quarterly, 21*, 267–283.

Stanovich, K. E., Nathan, R. G., & Zolman, J. E. (1988). The developmental lag hypothesis in reading: Longitudinal and matched reading-level comparisons. *Child Development, 59*, 71–86.

Stanovich, K. E., & Siegel, L. S. (1994). Phenotypic performance profiles of children with reading disabilities: A regression-based test of the phonological-core variable difference model. *Journal of Educational Psychology, 86*, 25–53.

Stark, R. E., & Heinz, J. M. (1996). Vowel perception in children with and without language impairment. *Journal of Speech and Hearing Research, 39*, 676–686.

Stark, R. E., & Tallal, P. (1988). *Language, speech, and reading disorders in children: Neuropsychological studies.* San Diego: College-Hill.

Stothard, S. E., Snowling, M. J., Bishop, D. V. M., Chipchase, B. B., & Kaplan, C. A. (1998). Language-impaired preschoolers: A follow-up into adolescence. *Journal of Speech, Language, and Hearing Research, 41*, 407–418.

Studdert-Kennedy, M. (1986). Sources of variability in early speech development. In J. S. Perkell & D. H. Klatt (Eds.), *Invariance and variability in speech processes* (pp. 58–76). Hillsdale, NJ: Erlbaum.

Studdert-Kennedy, M., Liberman, A. M., Brady, S. A., Fowler, A. E., Mody, M., & Shankweiler, D. P. (1995). Lengthened formant transitions are irrelevant to the improvement of speech and language impairments. *Haskins Laboratories Status Report on Speech Research, SR 119/120*, 35–38.

Studdert-Kennedy, M., & Mody, M. (1995). Auditory temporal perception deficits in the reading-impaired: A critical review of the evidence. *Psychonomic Bulletin and Review, 2*, 508–514.

Sussman, J. E. (1993). Perception of formant transition cues to place of articulation in children with language impairments. *Journal of Speech and Hearing Research, 36*, 1286–1299.

Swank, L. K. (1994). Phonological coding abilities: Identification of impairments related to phonologically based reading problems. *Topics in Language Disorder, 14*(2), 56–71.

Swanson, H. L. (1994). Short-term memory and working memory: Do both contribute to our understanding of academic achievement in children and adults with learning disabilities? *Journal of Learning Disabilities, 27*, 34–50.

Tallal, P. (1980). Auditory temporal perception, phonics, and reading disabilities in children. *Brain and Language, 9*, 182–198.

Tallal, P. (1984). Temporal or phonetic processing deficit in dyslexia?: That is the question. *Applied Psycholinguistics, 5*, 167–169.

Tallal, P. (1990). Fine-grained discrimination deficits in language-learning impaired children are specific neither to the auditory modality nor to speech perception. *Journal of Speech and Hearing Research, 33*, 616–617.

Tallal, P., Merzenich, M. M., Miller, S., & Jenkins, W. (1998). Language learning impairments: Integrating basic science, technology, and remediation. *Experimental Brain Research, 123*, 210–219.

Tallal, P., Miller, S. L., Bedi, G., Byma, G., Wang, X.,

Nagarajan, S. S., et al. (1996). Language comprehension in language-learning impaired children improved with acoustically modified speech. *Science, 271,* 81–84.

Tallal, P., Miller, S. L., & Fitch, R. H. (1993). Neurobiological basis of speech: A case for the preeminence of temporal processing. *Annals of the New York Academy of Sciences, 682,* 27–47.

Tallal, P., Miller, S. L., Jenkins, W. M., & Merzenich, M. M. (1997). The role of temporal processing in developmental language-based learning disorders: Research and clinical implications. In B. Blachman (Ed.), *Foundations of reading acquisition and dyslexia: Implications for early intervention* (pp. 49–66). Hillsdale, NJ: Erlbaum.

Tallal, P., & Piercy, M. (1973a). Defects of non-verbal auditory perception in children with developmental aphasia. *Nature, 241,* 468–469.

Tallal, P., & Piercy, M. (1973b). Developmental aphasia: Impaired rate of non-verbal processing as a function of sensory modality. *Neuropsychologia, 11,* 389–398.

Tallal, P., & Piercy, M. (1974). Developmental aphasia: Rate of auditory processing and selective impairment of consonant perception. *Neuropsychologia, 12,* 83–93.

Tallal, P., & Piercy, M. (1975). Developmental aphasia: The perception of brief vowels and extended stop consonants. *Neuropsychologia, 13,* 69–74.

Tallal, P., & Stark, R. E. (1981). Speech acoustic-cue discrimination abilities of normally developing and language-impaired children. *Journal of the Acoustical Society of America, 69,* 568–574.

Tallal, P., Stark, R. E., Kallman, C., & Mellits, E. D. (1981). A re-examination of some nonverbal perceptual abilities of language-impaired and normal children as a function of age and sensory modality. *Journal of Speech and Hearing Research, 24,* 351–357.

Tallal, P., Stark, R. E., & Mellits, E. D. (1985). Identification of language-impaired children on the basis of rapid perception and production skills. *Brain & Language, 25,* 314–322.

Tan, L. H., & Perfetti, C. A. (1998). Phonological codes as early sources of constraint in Chinese word identification: A review of current discoveries and theoretical accounts. *Reading and Writing: An Interdisciplinary Journal, 10,* 165–200.

Tangel, D. M., & Blachman, B. A. (1992). Effect of phoneme awareness instruction on kindergarten children's invented spelling. *Journal of Reading Behavior, 24,* 233–261.

Thibodeau, L., & Sussman, H. (1979). Performance on a test of categorical perception of speech in normal and communicatively disordered children. *Journal of Phonetics, 7,* 375–391.

Torgesen, J. K. Alexander, A. W., Wagner, R. K., Rashotte, C. A., Voeller, K. S., & Conway, T. (2001). Intensive remedial instruction for children with severe reading disabilities: Immediate and long-term outcomes from two instructional approaches. *Journal of Learning Disabilities, 34,* 33–58.

Torgesen, J. K., & Burgess, S. R. (1998). Consistency of reading related phonological processes throughout early childhood: Evidence from longitudinal–correlational and instructional studies. In J. L. Metsala & L. C. Ehri (Eds.), *Word recognition in beginning literacy* (pp. 161–188). Mahwah, NJ: Erlbaum.

Torgesen, J. K., & Davis, C. (1996). Individual difference variables that predict response to training in phonological awareness. *Journal of Experimental Child Psychology, 63,* 1–21.

Torgesen, J. K., Morgan, S., & Davis, C. (1992). The effects of two types of phonological awareness training on word learning in kindergarten children. *Journal of Educational Psychology, 84,* 364–370.

Torgesen, J. K., Wagner, R. K., Balthazar, M., Davis, C., Morgan, S., Simmons, K., et al. (1989). Developmental and individual differences in performance on phonological synthesis tasks. *Journal of Experimental Child Psychology, 47,* 491–505.

Torgesen, J. K., Wagner, R. K., & Rashotte, C. A. (1994). Longitudinal studies of phonological processing and reading. *Journal of Learning Disabilities, 27,* 276–286.

Torgesen, J. K., Wagner, R. K., & Rashotte, C. A. (1997). Prevention and remediation of severe reading disabilities: Keeping the end in mind. *Scientific Studies of Reading, 1,* 217–234.

Torgesen, J. K., Wagner, R. K., Rashotte, C. A., Burgess, S., & Hecht, S. (1997). Contributions of phonological awareness and rapid automatic naming ability to growth of word-reading skills in second- to fifth-grade children. *Scientific Studies of Reading, 1,* 161–185.

Torgesen, J. K., Wagner, R. K., Simmons, K., & Laughon, P. (1990). Identifying phonological coding problems in disabled readers: Naming, counting, or span measures? *Learning Disability Quarterly, 13,* 236–243.

Treiman, R. (1991). Children's spelling errors on syllable–initial consonant clusters. *Journal of Educational Psychology, 83,* 346–360.

Treiman, R., & Zukowski, A. (1991). Levels of phonological awareness. In S. A. Brady & D. P. Shankweiler (Eds.), *Phonological processes in literacy: A tribute to Isabelle Y. Liberman* (pp. 67–83). Hillsdale, NJ: Erlbaum.

Treiman, R., & Zukowski, A. (1996). Children's sensitivity to syllables, onsets, rimes, and phonemes. *Journal of Experimental Child Psychology, 61,* 193–215.

Troia, G. A. (in press). Migrant students with limited English proficiency: Can Fast ForWord Language™ make a difference in their language skills and academic achievement? *Remedial and Special Education.*

Troia, G. A., Roth, F. P., & Graham, S. (1998). An educator's guide to phonological awareness: Assessment measures and intervention activities for children. *Focus on Exceptional Children, 31*(3), 1–12.

Troia, G. A., Roth, F. P., & Yeni-Komshian, G. H. (1996). Word frequency and age effects in normally developing children's phonological processing. *Jour-*

nal of Speech and Hearing Research, 39, 1099–1108.

Troia, G. A., & Whitney, S. D. (2003). A close look at the efficacy of Fast ForWord Language™ for children with academic weaknesses. *Contemporary Educational Psychology, 28,* 465–494.

Tunmer, W. E., Herriman, M. L., & Nesdale, A. R. (1988). Metalinguistic abilities and beginning reading. *Reading Research Quarterly, 23,* 134–158.

Tunmer, W. E., & Nesdale, A. R. (1982). The effects of digraphs and pseudowords on phonemic segmentation in young children. *Applied Psycholinguistics, 3,* 299–311.

Tunmer, W. E., & Nesdale, A. R. (1985). Phonemic segmentation skill and beginning reading. *Journal of Educational Psychology, 77,* 417–427.

van Kleeck, A., & Bryant, D. (1983, October). *A diary study of very early emerging metalinguistic skills.* Paper presented at the Eighth Annual Boston University Conference on Language Development, Boston, MA.

van Kleeck, A., & Schuele, C. M. (1987). Precursors to literacy: Normal development. *Topics in Language Disorders, 7*(2), 13–31.

Veale, T. K. (1999). Targeting temporal processing deficits through Fast ForWord®: Language therapy with a new twist. *Language, Speech, and Hearing Services in Schools, 30,* 345–352.

Vellutino, F. R., & Scanlon, D. M. (1987). Phonological recoding, phonological awareness, and reading ability: Evidence from a longitudinal and experimental study. *Merrill–Palmer Quarterly, 33,* 321–363.

Vellutino, F. R., & Scanlon, D. M. (1991). The preeminence of phonologically based skills in learning to read. In S. A. Brady & D. P. Shankweiler (Eds.), *Phonological processes in literacy: A tribute to Isabelle Y. Liberman* (pp. 237–252). Hillsdale, NJ: Erlbaum.

Vellutino, F. R., Scanlon, D. M., Sipay, E. R., Small, S. G., Pratt, A., Chen, R., & Denckla, M. (1996). Cognitive profiles of difficult to remediate and readily remediated poor readers: Early intervention as a vehicle for distinguishing between cognitive and experiential deficits as basic causes of specific reading disability. *Journal of Educational Psychology, 88,* 601–638.

Waber, D. P., Weiler, M. D., Wolff, P. H., Bellinger, D., Marcus, D. J., Ariel, R., et al. (2001). Processing of rapid auditory stimuli in school-age children referred for evaluation of learning disorders. *Child Development, 72,* 37–49.

Wagner, R. K. (1988). Causal relations between the development of phonological processing abilities and the acquisition of reading skills: A meta-analysis. *Merrill–Palmer Quarterly, 34,* 261–279.

Wagner, R. K., & Torgesen, J. K. (1987). The nature of phonological processing and its causal role in the acquisition of reading skills. *Psychological Bulletin, 101,* 192–212.

Wagner, R. K., Torgesen, J. K., Laughon, P., Simmons, K., & Rashotte, C. A. (1993). Development of

young readers' phonological processing abilities. *Journal of Educational Psychology, 85,* 83–103.

Wagner, R. K., Torgesen, J. K., & Rashotte, C. A. (1994). The development of reading-related phonological processing abilities: New evidence of bidirectional causality from a latent variable longitudinal study. *Developmental Psychology, 30,* 73–78.

Walley, A. C. (1988). Spoken word recognition by young children and adults. *Cognitive Development, 3,* 137–165.

Walley, A. C. (1993). The role of vocabulary development in children's spoken word recognition and segmentation ability. *Developmental Review, 13,* 286–350.

Walley, A. C., Michela, V. L., & Wood, D. R. (1995). The gating paradigm: Effects of presentation format on spoken word recognition by children and adults. *Perception and Psychophysics, 57,* 343–351.

Weekes, B. S., Chen, M. J., & Lin, Y. B. (1998). Differential effects of phonological priming on Chinese character recognition. *Reading and Writing: An Interdisciplinary Journal, 10,* 201–222.

Werker, J. F., & Tees, R. C. (1987). Speech perception in severely disabled and average reading children. *Canadian Journal of Psychology, 41,* 48–61.

Whitehurst, G. J., & Lonigan, C. J. (1998). Child development and emergent literacy. *Child Development, 69,* 848–872.

Wilson, A. M., & Lesaux, N. K. (2001). Persistence of phonological processing deficits in college students with dyslexia who have age-appropriate reading skills. *Journal of Learning Disabilities, 34,* 394–400.

Wimmer, H. (1993). Characteristics of developmental dyslexia in a regular writing system. *Applied Psycholinguistics, 14,* 1–33.

Wimmer, H., & Goswami, U. (1994). The influence of orthographic consistency on reading development: Word recognition in English and German children. *Cognition, 51,* 91–103.

Wolf, M. (1982). The word retrieval process and reading in children and aphasics. In K. E. Nelson (Ed.), *Children's language* (Vol. 3, pp. 437–493). Hillsdale, NJ: Erlbaum.

Wolf, M. (1984). Naming, reading, and the dyslexias: A longitudinal overview. *Annals of Dyslexia, 34,* 87–115.

Wolf, M. (1986). Rapid alternating stimulus naming in the developmental dyslexias. *Brian and Language, 27,* 360–379.

Wolf, M. (1991). Naming speed and reading: The contribution of the cognitive neurosciences. *Reading Research Quarterly, 26,* 123–141.

Wolf, M., & Bowers, P. G. (1999). The double-deficit hypothesis for the developmental dyslexias. *Journal of Educational Psychology, 91,* 415–438.

Wolf, M., & Bowers, P. G. (2000). Naming speed deficits in developmental reading disabilities: An introduction to the special issue on the double-deficit hypothesis. *Journal of Learning Disabilities, 33,* 322–324.

Wolf, M., Bowers, P. G., & Biddle, K. (2000). Naming

speed processes, timing, and reading: A conceptual review. *Journal of Learning Disabilities, 33,* 387–407.

Wolff, P. H., Cohen, C., & Drake, C. (1984). Impaired motor timing control in specific reading retardation. *Neuropsychologia, 22,* 587–600.

Wright, B. A., Bowen, R. W., & Zecker, S. G. (2000). Nonlinguistic perceptual deficits associated with reading and language disorders. *Current Opinion in Neurobiology, 10,* 482–486.

Wright, B. A., Lombardino, L. J., King, W. M., Pu-

ranik, C. S., Leonard, C. M., & Merzenich, M. M. (1997). Deficits in auditory temporal and spectral resolution in language-impaired children. *Nature, 387,* 176–178.

Yopp, H. K. (1988). The validity and reliability of phonemic awareness tests. *Reading Research Quarterly, 23,* 159–177.

Zhou, Y. G. (1978). To what degree are the 'phonetic radicals' of present-day Chinese characters still phonetic radicals? *Chinese Language Journal, 146,* 172–177.

14

Developmental Dependencies between Lexical Semantics and Reading

KARLA K. McGREGOR

To read is to access the lexicon via print. Therefore, successful reading depends, in part, on a well-developed lexicon. My purpose in this chapter is to address the link between the semantic lexicon and reading in the child's developing linguistic system. The first section introduces two aspects of lexical learning, the processes of fast and slow mapping, and explores the child's active contributions as well as environmental support for word mapping in both younger and older word learners. The next two sections review evidence suggesting that lexical semantic knowledge and reading are interdependent, both in populations of normally developing children and in those with reading impairments. The final section highlights the practical implications of research on the lexicon–reading link.

TYPICAL LEXICAL DEVELOPMENT

Lexical acquisition begins as early as 5–7 months of age, as infants begin to parse recurrent words from the speech stream (Juscyk & Aslin, 1995; Saffran, Aslin, & Newport, 1996). At 8 months, children recognize about 15 words, and at 10–14 months, they typically speak their first words (Fenson et al., 1994).

Children's early lexicons are characterized by a large proportion of nominals (words for objects and people) (Gentner, 1982; Gentner & Boroditsky, 2001; Nelson, 1973). The proportion of nominals increases until the child has roughly 50–100 words in the lexicon. After this point, the proportion of verbs and other predicates increases (Bates, Bretherton, & Snyder, 1988). Exact proportions of nominals in the early vocabulary vary across both language communities (Choi & Gopnik, 1995; Kim, McGregor, & Thompson, 2000) and individuals within a given language community. Among English learners, some children are said to have a "referential," or object-oriented, learning style, whereas others are said to have an "expressive," or social, learning style. Compared to referential learners, expressive children have a higher proportion of formulaic phrases and words for social routines, and a lower proportion of nominals in their lexicons. Although both learning styles represent normal paths into the language system, referential learners demonstrate productive (as opposed to rote) knowledge of verbs and closed-class words, and generally larger and less context-bound semantic lexicons at an earlier age than do expressive learners (Bates et al., 1988).

Fast Mapping

The first mappings between words and referents emerge gradually, but many children show a burst in rate of word learning at 16–19 months, after they have approximately 50 words in their productive lexicons (Benedict, 1979; Goldfield & Reznick, 1990). Although the nature of this spurt is debated (see Bloom, 2000), from toddlerhood forward, children are quick to make inferences about the matching of a word to its referent. They can do so after only one or two exposures to a new word in context, a feat termed "fast mapping" (Carey, 1978). It is estimated that via fast mapping, children acquire, on average, 9 or 10 words a day, or as many as 5,000 words by age 6 years (Beck & McKeown, 1991).

During the school years, the rate of fast mapping remains high. Average growth in lexical breadth (size) is estimated at 3,000 words per year, or about 8–10 words per day, between ages 10 and 18 years (Nagy & Herman, 1987). Ten-year-olds know roughly 40,000 words (Anglin, 1993), and the recent high school graduate, 80,000 (Nagy & Herman, 1987). Incidental word learning improves between kindergarten and high school (Dickinson, 1984). In particular, there is a spurt in incidental learning of morphologically complex words (e.g., *discovery, undecided*) beginning at age 8 years (Anglin, 1993) and another spurt in the incidental learning of words from written texts beginning at 10–11 years (Werner & Kaplan, 1952).

Nagy, Anderson, and Herman (1987) measured the fast-mapping abilities of 352 third, fifth, and seventh graders 6 days after a single reading of two grade-level texts. The children who read a given text knew 3.3% more of the difficult words contained therein than those who did not read the text. Factors affecting the likelihood of learning from a single exposure were the de-

gree of conceptual difficulty of the words to be learned, the proportion of unfamiliar words per text that were conceptually difficult, and the average length of unfamiliar words. Passages with many long and conceptually difficult words decreased the likelihood of fast mapping.

Slow Mapping

Although initial maps of word meaning are made quickly, they are refined with multiple exposures to the word, exposures that may occur over a period of weeks, months, or years. This refinement, a process that Carey (1978) dubs "extended," or "slow mapping," involves increased accuracy of extensions, increased elaboration of meaning, and development of a semantic network. As Bloom (2000) notes, when it comes to slow mapping, it is not accurate to think of the child learning 10 new words per day but rather "one-hundredth of each of a thousand different words" (p. 25).

Category Extensions

One process accomplished during slow mapping is the adjustment of category extensions. Children's lexical-semantic boundaries are sometimes over-extended (e.g., *moon* for all round objects) or underextended (e.g., *bird* for only prototypically shaped birds). Not all extension errors are based in perceptual similarity; instead, common actions and functions (*up* for turning on a light), semantic associations (*nap* for blanket), or predicate statements (*doll* to label a chair where a doll had been placed) may serve as the source of these errors (Rescorla, 1980). Extension errors may be evident in both comprehension and production or in production alone. Underextensions (and context-bound usage in general) tend to occur when a word is first mapped; overextensions tend to occur later (Barrett, 1995; Dromi, 1987). For a given word, incorrect extensions may persist briefly or for a period of months (Clark, 1973). Extension continues to be a problem for older children, although most notably for words that capture complex concepts, including verbs (e.g., *ask, tell*), complex nouns (e.g., *brother, sis-*

ter), and relational terms (e.g., *more, less*) (Clark, 1973).

Nippold, Schwarz, and Undlin (1992) studied production and comprehension errors in use of one type of relational term, adverbial conjuncts (e.g., *similarly, nevertheless*), in 12-, 15-, 19-, and 23-year-olds. With increasing age, accuracy steadily improved. As is often the case in earlier lexical learning, comprehension led production at each age. Not even the young adults reached ceiling-level performance in their production of conjuncts. They continued to make some errors, such as the following: "Jason's mother did not think he was ready for a cross-country bicycling trip. *Moreover*, she gave permission for a river rafting trip" (Nippold et al., 1992, p. 111). Such errors demonstrate that long-term learning is required to fully map the extension of meanings in the lexicon.

Semantic Elaboration

During slow mapping, word meanings also become more elaborately represented in semantic memory. Whereas a toddler may know that dogs bark, a preschooler may also know that they are prone to fleas and that dogs enjoy chewing bones. Preschoolers' drawings and definitions reveal a continuum of semantic knowledge for familiar objects, with some meanings being more richly elaborated than others (McGregor, Friedman, Reilly, & Newman, 2002). Semantic naming errors produced by toddlers (Gershkoff-Stowe & Smith, 1997) and preschoolers (McGregor et al., 2002) are associated with missing or sparse semantic knowledge of target words.

Semantic elaboration in the school years also involves increasing decontextualization and flexibility of previously acquired word knowledge. Nonliteral and nondominant word meanings develop. For example, children's comprehension of metaphors (e.g., "drowning in work," "skin of silk") significantly improves between ages 8 and 12 years (Evans & Gamble, 1988). The likelihood that children in this age range will comprehend a metaphor depends on how fully they know the words within the metaphoric phrase (Baldwin, Luce, & Read-

ence, 1982; Evans & Gamble, 1988). In general, the learning of multiple word meanings proceeds from the more concrete (e.g., a person skipping) to the more abstract (e.g., a tape skipping), or from the physical meaning (e.g., a cold drink) to the psychological meaning (e.g., a cold heart). Children first view multiple meaning words as homonyms and gradually come to realize relationships between the multiple meanings (Asch & Nerlove, 1960; Nippold, Cuyler, & Braunbeck-Price, 1988).

Semantic Networks

Semantic networks, too, are further developed during the slow-mapping process. Children acquire basic level terms (e.g., *dog*) more readily than superordinates (e.g., *animal*) or subordinates (e.g., *collie*). Two types of relationships between basic-level terms, thematic and taxonomic, characterize the organization of the semantic lexicon from an early age (Aitchison, 1994). Thematic relations involve co-occurrence (e.g., *lion* and *roars; dog* and *leash*). The learning of thematic relations depends on the frequency and communicative saliency of these objects and relationships in the child's everyday life (Anglin, 1977; Nelson, 1985). Taxonomic relationships involve class membership (e.g., *lion* and *dog*). Children begin to build hierarchies of taxonomic relations, both at the superordinate and subordinate levels, at age 2 years (Clark, 1995). There are notable increases in taxonomic knowledge between ages 3 and 5 years (Anglin, 1977); however, even 3-year-olds can name superordinates and subordinates when pragmatic context obligates their use (Elbers, van Loon-Vervoorn, & van Helden-Lankhaar, 1992; Waxman & Hatch, 1992).

The semantic network continues to develop during the school years. One notable change is the syntagmatic–paradigmatic shift. At age 5 years, most children respond to word-association tasks by providing a word that follows in the syntax of a typical sentence (e.g., *car* might elicit *drives*), but by age 9, most children respond by providing a word that is of the same word class or paradigm (e.g., *car* might elicit *truck*) (Lippman, 1971). Although "syntagmatic" and "paradigmatic" refer to syntactic-level phenomena, they map with some consistency onto the semantic-conceptual relations "thematic" and "taxonomic," respectively. Therefore, in some respects, the syntagmatic–paradigmatic shift may reflect an adjustment in relative saliency of thematic (syntagmatic) and taxonomic (paradigmatic) relations in the semantic lexicon.

Children's definitions suggest that taxonomic relations do become increasingly salient over time. Whereas preschoolers' definitions include the functional and physical characteristics of the objects being defined (McGregor et al., 2002), it is not until age 10 years that children's definitions consistently include taxonomic-category labels (Benelli, Arcuri, & Marchesini, 1988). In addition, developmental changes in automatic semantic processing reveal the shift toward taxonomic organization. For example, kindergartners name a target picture such as *dog* more quickly (relative to a neutral baseline) after first naming a picture bearing a thematic relation to the target (e.g., *bone*), but not after naming a picture bearing a taxonomic relation to the target (e.g., *lion*). In contrast, second graders demonstrate quicker naming after either type of relation (McCauley, Weil, & Sperber, 1976).

Environmental Contributions

Children receive support for both fast and slow mapping from the people, objects, and events in their environment. To build a semantic lexicon, children must be exposed to words in meaningful contexts. All things being equal, words that occur frequently in input are learned more readily than those that occur infrequently (Schwartz & Terrell, 1983). Children who receive less frequent or less diverse input because of socioeconomic disadvantage have measurably smaller lexicons than their more advantaged peers (Hart & Risley, 1995). Whereas a child of poverty may present with no diminished capacity for word learning, the effects of reduced opportunities for learning established in the preschool years are long-lasting. The reading vocabulary of a third grader from a poor family averages 5,000 fewer words than that of a typical middle-class peer (White, Graves, & Slater, 1990). Children from impoverished environments exhibit several disadvantages when it comes to incidental learning. Compared to their high-vocabulary peers, they have more words to learn (fast map) and more words to elaborate (slow map) from any given passage and, given their limited lexical knowledge, they have less usable lexical context for bootstrapping (Shefelbine, 1990).

Word learning is facilitated by communicative interaction with adults. The language development of children who have been neglected lags behind that of children who have been abused (Culp et al., 1991). Presumably, interaction is key to this difference in outcome, because neglected children lack communicative interaction. Abused children experience communicative interactions, although they may be quite negative in nature. Interactions that are well tuned to the child may be particularly facilitative of lexical learning. For example, parents who label objects on which their children are focused tend to have children with large vocabularies (Adamson, 1995; Tomasello & Farrar, 1986).

The school years present new lexical learning environments. Formal schooling provides increased opportunities for ostensive (didactic) lexical learning. New words are taught in relation to topic knowledge of science, history, and math, among other curricular areas. Spelling lessons generally emphasize the meaning, as well as the forms, of new words.

Despite increased opportunities for ostensive learning, incidental learning continues to account for the majority of words acquired in the school years (Nagy, Herman, & Anderson, 1985). Written text is the primary source of incidental word learning for persons who read at or above the third-grade level (Nagy & Anderson, 1984). In the course of a single year of school, the average fifth grader is exposed to 500,000 words in text (Nagy & Herman, 1987). Roughly 10,000 of these will be unfamiliar (Nagy & Herman, 1987); that is, the child will have 10,000 opportunities to learn new word meanings and many times that number of opportunities to further slow mapping.

Within written texts, parsing new words is aided by the visual cue of spacing between words. Fast and slow mapping are made possible by the words themselves, and by the meaningful text around the words. Words provide cues to their meanings via their morphological forms. For example, a word ending in -ed likely refers to an action that occurred in the past, whereas a word beginning with re- likely refers to an action that recurs. The linguistic context surrounding an unfamiliar word provides both syntactic and semantic cues to drive inferences. Furthermore, the script of the topic that emerges from the text as a whole, as well as the reader's prior knowledge of the topic and the purpose for reading about the topic, all cue word meaning (Drum & Konopak, 1987). Each of these can serve to reduce the possible hypotheses that a reader will entertain about a new word, making word learning more effective and efficient.

Child Contributions

Children are actively engaged in learning the words in their environment, and they bring a variety of skills to bear on the task. To read environmental input, they apply perceptual skill, social cognition, and linguistic knowledge (Hollich et al., 2000). To interpret the input, they make hypotheses about word meanings and extensions (Fisher, Hall, Rakowitz, & Gleitman, 1994; Gopnik, Meltzoff, & Kuhl, 1999; Welder & Graham, 2001), and to learn from the input, they create and maintain representations in memory (Mandler, 1988). Each of these skills is present during infancy, and each further develops over the course of the preschool years. As a result, incidental word learning improves during the preschool years (Rice & Woodsmall, 1988).

Much research has focused on the child's astonishing ability to fast-map. According to a recent theory of word learning, the emergentist coalition model (Hollich et al., 2000), children accomplish this feat by paying attention to multiple cues in their environment and, by doing so, develop and refine heuristics to maximize the efficiency of word learning. Perceptual cues such as salience of the referent, prosodic characteristics of the new word, and temporal contiguity between spoken words and referents, drive early word learning. Children's use of the latter cue is evinced by their association of count noun syntax (e.g., a block) with solid objects and mass noun syntax (e.g., some sand) with nonsolid substances. Soja (1992) explored 2-year-olds' application of this associative cue. When presented with a solid object named with count noun syntax (e.g., a dax), 2-year-olds extended the new word to an object of the same shape; when given a nonsolid with mass noun syntax (e.g., some dax) they extended to a similar substance. Smith (2000) argues that such attentional biases grow out of the strength of associated word–object or word–substance pairings that the child has received in input.

After an initial period of word learning, increased social cognition and linguistic ability result in a shift from perceptual cues toward increased reliance on social context and eye gaze. Tomasello and Akhtar (1995) demonstrated that 2-year-olds monitor the eye gaze of their communicative partner to determine whether a new word refers to an unfamiliar object or an unfamiliar action. Importantly, toddlers do not learn new words when the partner's eyes—hence, his or her referential intention—are hidden (Baldwin et al., 1996).

Children not only use environmental cues but also develop heuristics (or perhaps, refine innate ones) to limit the problem space of word-to-referent matching. One well-documented heuristic is the whole-object constraint (Markman, 1989). Young word learners tend to assume that words map to whole objects, as opposed to their parts. For example, Mervis and Long (1987) exposed 2-year-olds to an unusual object with not only a characteristic shape but also a highly salient part. After naming the object with a novel word, the investigators asked the children to select another exemplar from a set of two new objects, one that matched the overall standard in every way except that it lacked the part, and the other that differed from the standard in every way except that it possessed the relevant part. The children preferred to extend the novel label to the object that matched the standard but lacked the part. Children are especially likely to extend words to whole objects that are similar in shape (Baldwin, 1989).

These are useful heuristics that guide the child to many correct inferences about the meanings of early nominal categories. For example, the word *bird* does indeed refer to a whole object and extends fairly accurately on the basis of shape to robins, sparrows, and finches. However, children's word-learning heuristics are not foolproof. For example, extension of whole-object labels is not always possible on the basis of shape (consider the atypical shape of the ostrich). Furthermore, languages do indeed include words for parts (e.g., *wing, beak*), not just wholes. As children become more sophisticated, they make use of other heuristics. For example, they come to extend object labels to like kinds, not just to things that look alike (see Golinkoff, Mervis, & Hirsh-Pasek, 1994, for a review). Some later heuristics, such as the conventionality bias (i.e., the desire to use words as they are typically used in the ambient environment), guide the child during the slow-mapping process toward refined, elaborated, and, eventually, adult-like meaning representations.

Compared to preschoolers, school-age children bring more sophisticated skills to the task of lexical semantic learning. They have in place a large lexicon and a well-developed syntactic system from which to infer new word meanings. Between ages 8 and 11 years, they become more adult-like in their inductive reasoning about semantic categories (Sloutsky, Lo, & Fisher, 2001). Their well-developed analogical reasoning, together with their increasing world knowledge, allow them to make sense of metaphorical words (Clark, 1995; Gentner, 1977). Their memorial skills, including memory for words, continue to increase. These increases are credited to improved knowledge of the world, use and awareness of retrieval cues, and inhibition of irrelevant information (see Haberlandt, 1999, for a review).

Finally, older children are sophisticated enough to seek and create their own environments for lexical learning. Those who are inquisitive enough to look up or ask about new words learn many words. Those who read well and enjoy reading provide themselves with a richer word-learning environment than those who do not. This aspect of lexical learning is discussed in more detail later.

Individual Differences

Delayed lexical acquisition is frequently associated with deficits in perceptual or cognitive processes such as attention, discrimination, hypothesis testing, and memory. Such co-occurrences suggest the critical importance of intact capacities to support the word-learning process. For example, one of the earliest behavioral manifestations of specific language impairment (SLI) is delayed onset of first words (Trauner, Wulfeck, Tallal, & Hesselink, 1995). Upon testing, these children are also found to have poor auditory perception (Wright et al., 1997), deficient working memory (Gathercole & Baddeley, 1990), and inadequate hypothesis testing when given syntactic cues to meaning (O'Hara & Johnston, 1997; van der Lely, 1994). Not surprisingly, these children map fewer words than their agemates under experimental word-learning conditions (Oetting, Rice, & Swank, 1995; Rice, Buhr, Nemeth, 1990; Rice, Buhr, & Oetting, 1992; Rice, Oetting, Marquis, Bode, & Pae, 1994).

Children with autism represent another interesting case population. These children are hypothesized to have a theory-of-mind deficit, such that they are unable to infer word meaning from social cues. For example, they do not check an adult's eye gaze as a cue for word-to-referent matching. This deficit in reading others' mental states and intentions has measurable effects on their lexical learning (Baron-Cohen, Baldwin, & Crowson, 1997).

In summary, building a semantic lexicon is a gradual process that begins in infancy and extends through adolescence and beyond. Although children are fast to hypothesize word-to-referent matches, they gradually refine these hypotheses until category extensions, semantic elaboration, and networks of semantically related items become adult-like. Studies of impaired populations suggest that optimal lexical learning occurs only when the child brings intact perceptual, social, cognitive, and memorial skills to bear on the task. Contexts that involve communicative interaction with an engaged adult are especially conducive to the lexical learning of toddlers and preschoolers. After children learn to read, the world of print becomes their primary input for word learning. The remainder of this chapter focuses on the lexicon–reading connection.

LEXICAL PROCESSES AND READING

For many years, scholars have noted that lexical knowledge and reading comprehension strongly correlate (Davis, 1944; 1968). Thorndike (1973) collected vocabulary and reading data from over 100,000 children representing 15 countries and three age groups: 10-, 14- and 17-year-olds. He found median correlations between lexical knowledge and reading comprehension of .66 to .75. In some respects, the correlation yields a simple message: Children who know more words understand texts better than those who know fewer words. Some of this correlation likely reflects the relationship of both lexical knowledge and reading ability to levels of general learning aptitude and cognitive ability (Anderson & Freebody, 1983; Gernsbacher, Varner, & Faust, 1990; Sternberg, 1987), and to levels of cultural exposure (Anderson & Freebody, 1983; Stahl, Hare, Sinatra, & Gregory, 1991). Nevertheless, there remain true relationships between lexical knowledge and reading, with important implications for development and intervention.

Reading comprehension depends heavily on the ability to comprehend words in spoken language (Rayner, Foorman, Perfetti, Pesetsky, & Seidenberg, 2001). The notion that people who have greater lexical depth and breadth are better able to interpret words within written texts is referred to as the "instrumentalist hypothesis" (Anderson & Freebody, 1983). Empirical evidence supports an instrumental role for lexical semantics in reading comprehension. Stahl and colleagues (1991) found that 10th graders' breadth of lexical knowledge significantly predicted the number of units they recalled

from a written text. Vocabulary scores accounted for roughly 15% of the variance in number of units recalled. This effect was independent of the subjects' overall world knowledge of the topic.

In addition, depth of lexical semantic knowledge, as manifested by well-established semantic networks, plays a role in reading.[1] During reading, word recognition is primed (facilitated) by meaningful linguistic contexts in both child and adult readers (Plaut & Booth, 2000; Schwantes, 1981; 1991; Stanovich, Nathan, West, & Vala-Rossi; 1985). For example, reading the word *coat* will speed recognition of the related word *glove*. Priming effects are thought to reflect the spreading activation between interconnections within an established semantic network (Stanovich et al., 1985). Noting that semantic priming effects on word recognition are larger for children than adults, Stanovich posits that children compensate for their deficient knowledge of spelling–sound correspondence by bringing semantic knowledge to bear (Stanovich et al., 1985; Stanovich, West, & Feeman, 1981). This explanation is supported by experiments demonstrating that, whereas semantic priming decreases with age and reading ability, phonological priming (e.g., *coat* to prime *cat*) increases (Booth, Perfetti, & MacWhinney, 1999). Interestingly, this developmental trade-off is language-specific. In languages with salient or regular grapheme-to-phoneme correspondence, such as Korean, phonological priming decreases with age, whereas semantic priming increases (Kang & Simpson, 1996). Therefore, the lexical semantic network plays a role in word recognition, but the extent of that role may vary with development, reading ability, and the language of the text to be read.

To this point, we have considered unidirectional relationships between the lexicon and reading. Breadth and depth of lexical semantic knowledge play a role in successful reading comprehension; however, the reverse is also true: Reading enhances lexical–semantic knowledge. The reciprocal nature of the lexicon–reading relationship has been explored most extensively under the rubric of "Matthew Effects" (Stanovich,

1986). Those who have good lexical skills come to the task of reading with an advantage over those with poor lexical skills, whether because of better lexical knowledge or some underlying skill, such as keen verbal aptitude. That advantage translates into earlier and more facile acquisition of reading skill. As better readers, these children are exposed to more opportunities for lexical learning. For example, during the fifth grade, the child whose reading ability is at the 90th percentile gets roughly 200 times more exposure to written text than the child whose reading ability is at the 10th percentile (Anderson, Wilson, & Fielding, 1986, cited in Nagy et al., 1987). Furthermore, better readers learn new words from context more efficiently than do poorer readers, even when differences in lexical knowledge base are controlled (Sternberg, 1985). The predicted net result is an upward spiral for children with strong vocabulary and reading skills and a downward spiral, relative to their stronger peers, for children with weak vocabulary and reading skills. Stanovich referred to a Bible verse in the Book of Matthew when he labeled this hypothesized "rich-get-richer" cycle as a Matthew Effect.

In support of the Matthew Effects hypothesis, Stanovich and his colleagues (Allen, Cipielewski, & Stanovich, 1992; Cipielewski & Stanovich, 1992; Cunningham & Stanovich, 1991; Stanovich & Cunningham, 1992) used a method of hierarchical regression to determine whether variance in lexical knowledge is associated with reading (as measured by amount of print exposure). To be conservative, these investigators first partialed out effects of general ability (e.g., age, IQ, comprehension skills, phonological decoding skills) before entering measures of print exposure into the equation. Consistently, they found that print exposure accounts for significant variance in lexical knowledge (see Stanovich, 1993, for a review). This is true for both children (Cunningham & Stanovich, 1991; Echols, Stanovich, West, & Zehr, 1996) and adults (Stanovich & Cunningham, 1992).

Studies from independent laboratories also yield support for Matthew Effects. Ewers and Brownson (1999) compared the ability of kindergartners with either high or low lexical knowledge to learn from a storybook that was read to them once. Those with higher lexical knowledge learned more new words than did those with lower lexical knowledge. Walsh, Rafferty, and Turner (1992) reported similar findings. Shefelbine (1990) examined individual differences in incidental word learning from written contexts. In a sample of sixth graders with either high or low vocabulary skills, he found that breadth of lexical knowledge (as measured by standardized vocabulary tests) and depth of lexical knowledge (as measured by definition and drawing tasks) positively predicted the amount of incidental word learning at posttest. Children in both low- and high-vocabulary groups learned incrementally. From pretest to posttest, some words changed from no knowledge to partial knowledge, others from partial knowledge to high knowledge, and still others from no knowledge to high knowledge. For the high-vocabulary group, the probability of learning an unknown word to a high degree was twice that of the low-vocabulary group.

Despite evidence that vocabulary and reading are developmentally related, longitudinal studies offer mixed support for one prediction of the Matthew Effects hypothesis, namely, increasing gaps between poor and good performers over time. In a study of 235 children over their first 3 years of school, Bast and Reitsma (1998) found no changes in the gap between children with poor or good reading comprehension and vocabulary, although increasing individual differences in word recognition were noted. Other investigators, studying more than 500 children from grades 1 through 6, reported that initially low performers on reading comprehension, vocabulary, and spelling showed *greater* rates of progress than their medium- and high-performing peers with all groups retaining their initial ranking (Aarnoutse, van Leeuwe, Voeten, & Oud, 2001). In contrast are the findings of Serviclaes, Sprenger-Charolles, Carre, and Demonet (2001), who followed 19 children with dyslexia and 19 normal readers from ages 5 to 13 years. At age 5, both groups demonstrated equivalent oral-vocabulary skills, but at age 13, the vocabulary of the children with dyslexia was significantly lower. It is not clear how to reconcile these conflicting results. One possibility is that Matthew Effects on vocabulary and reading development emerge over a number of years and are therefore apparent only in studies involving older cohorts of children. In addition, it would be helpful for investigators to describe the educational interventions provided for the children who participate in such studies, so that possible mediation of Matthew Effects can be discerned.

RECIPROCAL INFLUENCES OF IMPAIRED LEXICAL AND READING PROCESSES

Given possible reciprocal relations between lexical semantic knowledge and reading, one would predict children with impaired lexical processes to be at a disadvantage in learning to read. Studies demonstrating that lexical deficits predate reading experience in many children who become *poor comprehenders* or *garden variety poor readers* support this prediction (Scarborough, 1990; Stanovich et al., 1984). Furthermore, children with reading deficits would be predicted to develop or increase lexical weaknesses due to their limited access to print as a word-learning environment. This scenario is common to children diagnosed as *dyslexic*. Operational definitions of these three populations of impaired readers appear in Table 14.1. Empirical studies that illustrate relationships between impaired lexical and reading processes follow.

Weak Lexical Semantics as a Risk Factor for Reading Impairment

Clinicians and teachers have long noted that children with speech and language impairments frequently have difficulty learning to read. Two subgroups of affected children are particularly vulnerable: children who have difficulties with phonological awareness and rapid naming, and those whose primary weaknesses are in the semantic and syntactic domains (i.e., children with specific language impairment [SLI]) (Catts, 1993). Of interest here, the latter subgroup is

TABLE 14.1. Classification of Children with Reading Disabilities

Specific reading impairment. An unexpected difficulty learning to read despite adequate environmental input and cognitive processing. Although the scientific and clinical validity of discrepancy scores are currently debated (see Vellutino, Scanlon, & Lyon, 2000, for a discussion), specific reading impairment is typically identified by a discrepancy between reading scores (lower) and scores on other measures of cognitive processing (higher). Two subtypes are **dyslexia** and specific reading comprehension deficits (**poor comprehension**).

Dyslexia. A specific reading impairment in which the most prominent weakness is the inability to decode words via grapheme–phoneme correspondence rules (variously referred to as a nonlexical route deficit, a phonological dyslexia, or a phonological core deficit; Jackson & Coltheart, 2001). It is often identified by difficulty reading pseudowords that conform to regular spelling rules relative to both chronological and younger reading-matched peers. Rapid automatized naming (RAN) is slower than that of chronological agemates (Denckla & Rudel, 1976).

Poor comprehension. A specific reading impairment in which the most prominent weakness is difficulty using a semantic, or top–down approach to reading (variously referred to as a lexical route deficit or a surface dyslexia; Jackson & Coltheart, 2001). It is often identified by difficulty reading exception words relative to their chronological-age peers (Coltheart, Masterson, Byng, Prior, & Riddoch, 1983; Nation & Snowling, 1998). RAN deficits are closely linked to exception word–reading performance (Manis, Seidenberg, & Doi, 1999; Wolf & Bowers, 1999).

Garden variety poor reading. A nonspecific reading impairment characterized by low reading ability commensurate with overall delays in cognitive processing. Those affected present with deficits in both decoding and reading comprehension, as well as broad deficits in receptive and expressive oral language (Catts, Fey, Zhang, & Tomblin, 1999). RAN is significantly slower in garden-variety poor readers than in those with dyslexia (Catts et al., 1999).

prone to impairment in reading comprehension (Catts, 1993).

To illustrate, consider a longitudinal study by Bishop and colleagues. These investigators identified 88 children as having SLI at age 4.0 years, then followed the children's language and reading progress at ages 5.5, 8.0, and 15.0 years. Children who had resolved cases of SLI by age 5.5 years, had normal reading accuracy, reading comprehension, and spelling at age 8.0, but those with unresolved SLI at 5.5 years went on to have reading impairments at age 8.0. Twelve percent of the entire sample had reading comprehension scores at age 8.0 that were unexpectedly low given their performance IQ levels (Bishop & Adams, 1990). These children presented with clinical profiles that resembled those of poor comprehenders rather than those of dyslexics.

Alarmingly, when this same cohort was sampled at age 15.0, the percentage of affected members had grown to between 23% (for reading comprehension problems) and 43% (for reading accuracy problems) (Snowling, Bishop, & Stothard, 2000). Although the growing rate of reading impairment could be, in part, an artifact of the different tests used at the 8.0- and 15.0-year sampling, the reading profiles of the SLI group had also changed—not only reading comprehension but also word recognition was affected. Word-recognition deficits were particularly prominent in those children with SLI and performance IQs less than 100. Finally, Stothard, Snowling, Bishop, Chipchase, and Kaplan (1998), reporting on this same SLI cohort, found that, over time, those with the poorest reading outcomes demonstrated a widening gap in their vocabulary skills relative to their normal peers. Clearly, a preschooler with SLI is at increased risk for reading impairment. Worse still, the impact of that impairment is likely to broaden over time.

If children with poor lexical semantic skills become impaired readers, do impaired readers evince poor lexical semantic skills? The answer appears to be yes. Nation and Snowling (1998) compared 9-year-olds with poor reading comprehension and normal readers matched for decoding skill, age, and nonverbal ability on measures of lexical se-

mantic knowledge and processing. The poor comprehenders performed significantly more poorly than their agemates on a standardized measure of receptive and expressive vocabulary. Also, they were significantly slower and inaccurate in judging whether two words were synonymous (but not in judging whether two words rhymed). Finally, the poor comprehenders generated significantly fewer category exemplars than their normal peers, but they equaled their peers in rhyme fluency.

In 1999, Nation and Snowling investigated the automatic semantic processing of poor comprehenders using a priming paradigm. In the paradigm, 10-year-olds listened to real words and pseudowords, and made a lexical decision after each. Both poor comprehenders and their normal peers responded more quickly to given words presented after a functionally related word (e.g., *broom–floor*) than after an unrelated word (i.e., they demonstrated priming effects in response to thematic primes). However, the two groups differed in their response to taxonomic primes. The normal readers demonstrated priming to all taxonomic cues (e.g., *cat–dog, airplane–train*), but the poor comprehenders demonstrated priming only to taxonomic exemplars that were also thematically associated in everyday life (e.g., *cat–dog*, but not *airplane–train*). Nation and Snowling concluded that poor comprehenders are less sensitive to abstract semantic relationships than their peers. Like much younger children, these 10-year-old poor comprehenders demonstrated a weak taxonomic structure in their semantic lexicons. Because all of the tasks administered by Nation and Snowling required oral responses to oral stimuli, their results demonstrate that the problems of poor comprehenders are not limited to written texts. These children present with broad deficits in lexical semantic knowledge.

Impaired Reading as a Risk Factor for Weak Lexical Semantics

Thus far, we have established that, as a group, preschoolers with weak lexical semantic systems may develop reading impairments over time. Their profiles more closely resemble those of poor comprehenders than those of dyslexics. Furthermore, children who are poor comprehenders tend to present with broad deficits in lexical semantic knowledge and processing. In this section, the focus turns to the relationship between dyslexia and lexical semantics.

It is generally accepted that phonological processing is the core deficit in dyslexia. As such, affected children have great difficulty decoding words via phoneme-to-grapheme relationships. Although the phonological route into reading is impaired, the lexical semantic route is relatively preserved. In fact, given discrepancy criteria for identification of dyslexia (American Psychiatric Association, 1994), children with dyslexia will, by definition, have normal vocabulary and other oral-language abilities. Nevertheless, the relationship between reading and lexical semantics is still apparent in the dyslexic population. For example, Scarborough (1990) found that a group of children classified as dyslexic at age 8 had presented with significantly poorer vocabulary skills than their peers at age 3.

Even among those who bring intact lexical semantic systems to bear on the task of learning to read, the reading failures associated with dyslexia eventually reduce their opportunities to learn the meanings of new words and to enrich the meanings of old ones. Vellutino, Scanlon, and Tanzman (1988) present a case in point. The investigators compared the ability of children with dyslexia[2] and normal readers in the second and sixth grades to recall words from taxonomically organized lists. The children heard the lists read aloud (storage phase), then recalled as many of the words as possible (retrieval phase). Conditions of presentation and recall varied. In the first condition, storage was semantically cued (the category labels for groups of words on the lists were provided when the lists were read). In the second condition, retrieval was semantically cued (the category labels for groups of words on the lists were provided when the words were recalled). A third condition involved both storage and retrieval cues, and a fourth included neither cue. The second-grade children with dyslexia and their normal-reading peers differed least in the uncued storage condition. In contrast, the sixth grade dyslexic and normal readers differed most in this condition. These findings suggest Matthew Effects. Semantically organized storage was relatively intact in second graders with dyslexia, but by the sixth grade, deficiencies in this domain had emerged.

In summary, the lexicon–reading link is complex. Knowledge of individual word meanings and connections between related meanings contributes to successful reading. This knowledge is in some ways more critical for novice than for experienced readers, at least in English, because novices must compensate for their underdeveloped phonological route to reading. Once children become literate, reading experience contributes to further development of the semantic lexicon. Because of the reciprocal developmental relationship between the lexicon and reading, children with impairments in either domain are likely to demonstrate secondary impairments in the other.

RESEARCH TO PRACTICE IMPLICATIONS

Two themes in the literature reviewed here bear important research-to-practice implications. First, despite the current emphasis on phonological processes in reading, this literature suggests that vocabulary also plays an important role in reading. Adequate vocabulary knowledge is especially critical for reading comprehension. By implication, children with weak vocabularies are prime candidates for early language and reading intervention. Speech–language pathologists can readily diagnose delays in children's vocabulary development by age 2. Parent-report inventories provide valid estimates of receptive vocabulary size in children functioning below the 16-month level and expressive vocabulary size in children functioning below the 30-month level (Fenson et al., 1994; see also Rescorla, 1989). For older children, quantification of lexical semantic usage in discourse yields valid assessment information (Miller, 1996).

Interventionists should view the lexicon–literacy link as one more motivation to address early vocabulary delays. Children with vocabulary deficits need to be met "more than half way" as they face the word-learning task. Highly enriched environments, for example, homes, schools, and clinics where conversational exchange and exposure to print are abundant, may facilitate vocabulary development (Bast & Reitsma, 1998; Hart & Risley, 1995). In addition, direct instruction of word forms and meanings may be required for children who are not good incidental word learners (Nicholson & Whyte, 1992).

A second theme in the research reviewed here is that reading plays an important role in later vocabulary development. It follows that speech–language pathologists should carefully monitor vocabulary development of children with dyslexia and other reading limitations. Because the effects of limited reading on vocabulary growth are known to grow over time (Vellutino et al., 1988), such monitoring should continue even when no vocabulary deficits have been previously noted. Finally, the creative teacher, in collaboration with the speech–language pathologist and other educational personnel, can provide poor readers with opportunities for word learning that go beyond typical reading assignments, so as to prevent or reduce future vocabulary deficits. Such opportunities might include listening to an adult read a story aloud, while explaining unfamiliar words along the way (Walsh et al., 1992) or independent reading with the use of the dictionary (Nicholson & Whyte, 1992). Word-learning activities embedded in oral contexts such as song, dramatic play, role play, discussion, and conversation may also be beneficial.

The relationships between the lexicon and reading are ripe for exploration in the clinic, the classroom, and the research laboratory. Perhaps this review will motivate readers to begin exploring!

ACKNOWLEDGMENTS

I thank Addison Stone for this opportunity to learn more about the lexicon–reading connection. Thanks are also due to Henricke Blumenfeld, Kristy Grohne, Rita Kaushanskaya, Li Sheng, and Evar Strid. These students provided thoughtful critiques and discussion of the lexicon–reading connection during a doctoral seminar held at Northwestern University in the fall of 2001. Thanks also go to Kanika So for her assistance in retrieving published literature for this chapter. Finally, I gratefully acknowledge the support of Award No. R29 DC03698 from the National Institute on Deafness and Other Communication Disorders.

NOTES

1. Here, I view the semantic network as one aspect of depth of lexical knowledge. See Ruddell (1994) for a different perspective.
2. Selection criteria used in this study resulted in recruitment of children whose profiles were consistent with the designation of "dyslexic." However, this is not the designation used by the authors.

REFERENCES

Aarnoutse, C., van Leeuwe, J., Voeten, M., & Oud, H. (2001). Development of decoding, reading comprehension, vocabulary, and spelling during the elementary school years. *Reading and Writing: An Interdisciplinary Journal, 14,* 61–89.

Adamson, L. B. (1995). *Communication development during infancy.* Madison, WI: Brown & Benchmark.

Aitchison, J. (1994). *Words in the mind: An introduction to the mental lexicon.* Oxford, UK: Blackwell.

Allen, L., Cipielewski, J., & Stanovich, K. E. (1992). Multiple indicators of children's reading habits and attitudes: Construct validity and cognitive correlates. *Journal of Educational Psychology, 84,* 489–503.

American Psychiatric Association. (1994). *Diagnostic and statistical manual of mental disorders* (4th ed.). Washington, DC: Author.

Anderson, R. C., & Freebody, P. (1983). Reading comprehension and the assessment and acquisition of word knowledge. In B. Hutson (Ed.), *Advances in reading/language research: A research annual* (pp. 231–256). Greenwich, CT: JAI Press.

Anglin, J. M. (1977). *Word, object, and conceptual development.* Norton.

Anglin, J. M. (1993). Vocabulary development: A morphological analysis. *Monographs of the Society for Research in Child Development, 58*(10; Serial No. 238).

Asch, S. E., & Nerlove, H. (1960). The development of double-function terms in children: An exploratory investigation. In B. Kaplan & S. Wapner (Eds.), *Perspectives in psychological theory: Essays in honor of Heinz Werner* (pp. 47–60). New York: International Universities Press.

Baldwin, D. A. (1989). Priorities in children's expectations about object label reference: Form over color. *Child Development, 60,* 1289–1306.

Baldwin, D. A., Markman, E. M., Bill, B., Desjardins, N., Irwin, J. M. & Tidball, G. (1996). Infants' reliance on a social criterion for establishing word–object relations. *Child Development, 67,* 3135–3153.

Baldwin, R. S., Luce, T. S., & Readence, J. E. (1982). The impact of subschemata on metaphorical processing. *Reading Research Quarterly, 17,* 528–543.

Baron-Cohen, S., Baldwin, D. A., & Crowson, M. (1997). Do children with autism use the speaker's direction of gaze strategy to crack the code of language? *Child Development, 68,* 48–57.

Barrett, M. (1995). Early lexical development. In P. Fletcher & B. MacWhinney (Eds.), *The handbook of child language* (pp. 362–392). Cambridge, MA: Blackwell.

Bast, J., & Reitsma, P. (1998). Analyzing the development of individual differences in terms of Matthew effects in reading: Results from a Dutch longitudinal study. *Developmental Psychology, 34,* 1373–1399.

Bates, E., Bretherton, I., & Snyder, L. (1988). *From first words to grammar: Individual differences and dissociable mechanisms.* Cambridge, UK: Cambridge University Press.

Beck, I., & McKeown, M. (1991). Conditions of vocabulary acquisition. In R. Barr, M. L. Kamil, P. Mosenthal, & P. D. Pearson (Eds.), *Handbook of reading research* (Vol. 2, pp. 789–814). New York: Longman.

Benedict, H. (1979). Early lexical development: Comprehension and production. *Journal of Child Language, 6,* 183–200.

Benelli, B., Arcuri, L., & Marchesini, G. (1988). Cognitive and linguistic factors in the development of word definitions. *Journal of Child Language, 15,* 619–635.

Bishop, D. V. M., & Adams, C. (1990). A prospective study of the relationship between specific language impairment, phonological disorders and reading retardation. *Journal of Child Psychology and Psychiatry, 31,* 1027–1050.

Bloom, P. (2000). *How children learn the meanings of words.* Cambridge, MA: MIT Press.

Booth, J. R., Perfetti, C. A., & MacWhinney, B. (1999). Quick, automatic, and general activation of orthographic and phonological representations in young readers. *Developmental Psychology, 35,* 3–19.

Carey, S. (1978). The child as word learner. In M. Halle, J. Bresnan, & G. A. Miller (Eds.), *Linguistic theory and psychological reality* (pp. 264–293). Cambridge, MA: MIT Press.

Catts, H. W. (1993). The relationship between speech–language impairments and reading disabilities. *Journal of Speech and Hearing Research, 36,* 948–958.

Catts, H. W., Fey, M. E., Zhang, X., & Tomblin, J. B. (1999). Language basis of reading and reading disabilities: Evidence from a longitudinal investigation. *Scientific Studies of Reading, 3,* 331–362.

Choi, S., & Gopnik, A. (1995). Early acquisition of verbs in Korean: A cross-linguistic study. *Journal of Child Language, 22,* 497–529.

Cipielewski, J., & Stanovich, K. E. (1992). Predicting growth in reading ability from children's exposure to print. *Journal of Experimental Child Psychology, 54,* 74–89.

Clark, E. (1995). Later lexical development and word formation. In P. Fletcher & B. MacWhinney (Eds.), *The handbook of child language* (pp. 393–412). Cambridge, MA: Blackwell.

Clark, E. V. (1973). What's in a word?: On the child's acquisition of semantics in his first language. In T. E. Moore (Ed.), *Cognitive development and the acquisition of language* (pp. 65–110). New York: Academic Press.

Coltheart, M., Masterson, J., Byng, S., Prior, M., & Riddoch, M. J. (1983). Surface dyslexia. *Journal of Experimental Psychology: Human Experimental Psychology, 35,* 469–495.

Culp, R. E., Watkins, R. V., Lawrence, H., Letts, D., Kelly, D. J., & Rice, M. L. (1991). Maltreated children's language and speech development: Abused, neglected, and abused and neglected. First Language, 11, 377–389.

Cunningham, A. E., & Stanovich, K. E. (1991). Tracking the unique effects of print exposure in children: Associations with vocabulary, general knowledge, and spelling. *Journal of Educational Psychology, 83,* 264–274.

Davis, F. (1944). Fundamental factors of comprehension in reading. *Psychometrika, 9,* 185–197.

Davis, F. (1968). Research in comprehension in reading. *Reading Research Quarterly, 3,* 499–545.

Denckla, M. B., & Rudel, R. G. (1976). Rapid automatized naming (R. A. N.): Dyslexia differentiated from other learning disabilities. *Neuropsychologia, 14,* 471–479.

Dickinson, D. K. (1984). First impressions: Children's knowledge of words gained from a single exposure. *Applied Psycholinguistics, 5,* 359–374.

Dromi, E. (1987). *Early lexical development.* Cambridge, UK: Cambridge University Press.

Drum, P. A., & Konopak, B. C. (1987). Learning word meanings from written context. In M. G. McKeown & M. E. Curtis (Eds.), *The nature of vocabulary acquisition* (pp. 73–87). Hillsdale, NJ: Erlbaum.

Echols, L., Stanovich, K., West, R., & Zehr, K. (1996). Using children's literacy activities to predict growth in verbal cognitive skills: A longitudinal investigation. *Journal of Educational Psychology, 88,* 296–304.

Elbers, L., van Loon-Vervoorn, A., & van Helden-Lankhaar, M. (1992). Contrast and the development of lexical organization and innovation. *First Language, 12,* 343–344.

Evans, M. A., & Gamble, D. L. (1988). Attribute saliency and metaphor interpretation in school age children. *Journal of Child Language, 15,* 435–449.

Ewers, C. A., & Brownson, S. M. (1999). Kindergarteners' vocabulary acquisition as a function of active vs. passive storybook reading, prior vocabulary, and working memory. *Journal of Reading Psychology, 20*, 11–20.

Fenson, L., Dale, P., Reznick, S., Bates, E., Thai, D., & Pethick, S. (1994). Variability in early communicative development. *Monographs of the Society for Research in Child Development, 59*(5, Serial No. 242).

Fisher, C., Hall, D. G., Rakowitz, S., & Gleitman, L. R. (1994). When it is better to receive than to give: Structural and conceptual cues to verb meaning. *Lingua, 92*, 333–375.

Gathercole, S., & Baddeley, A. (1990). Phonological memory deficits in language disordered children: Is there a causal connection? *Journal of Memory and Language, 29*, 336–360.

Gentner, D. (1977). Children's performance on a spatial analogies task. *Child Development, 48*, 1034–1039.

Gentner, D. (1982). Why nouns are learned before verbs: Linguistic relativity versus natural partitioning. In S. A. Kuczaj (Ed.), *Language development: Vol. 2. Language, thought, and culture* (pp. 301–333). Hillsdale, NJ: Erlbaum.

Gentner, D., & Boroditsky, L. (2001). Individuation, relativity, and early word learning. In M. Bowerman & S. Levinson (Eds.), *Language acquisition and conceptual development* (pp. 215–256). New York: Cambridge University Press.

Gernsbacher, M. A., Varner, K. R., & Faust, M. E. (1990). Investigating differences in general comprehension skill. *Journal of Experimental Psychology, Learning, Memory, and Cognition, 16*, 430–445.

Gershkoff-Stowe, L., & Smith, L. B. (1997). A curvilinear trend in naming errors as a function of early vocabulary growth. *Cognitive Psychology, 34*, 37–71.

Goldfield, B. A., & Reznick, J. S. (1990). Early lexical acquisition: Rate, content, and the vocabulary spurt. *Journal of Child Language, 17*, 171–183.

Golinkoff, R. M., Mervis, C. B., & Hirsh-Pasek, K. (1994). Early object labels: The case for a developmental lexical principles framework. *Journal of Child Language, 21*, 125–155.

Gopnik, A., Meltzoff, A. N., & Kuhl, P. K. (1999). *The scientist in the crib: Minds, brains, and how children learn.* New York: Morrow.

Haberlandt, K. (1999). *Human memory.* Boston: Allyn & Bacon.

Hart, B. & Risley, T. R. (1995). *Meaningful differences in the everyday experience of young American children.* Baltimore: Brookes.

Hollich, G. J., Hirsh-Pasek, K., Golinkoff, R. M., Brand, R. J., Brown, E., Chung, H. L., et al. (2000). Breaking the language barrier: An emergentist coalition model for the origins of word learning. *Monographs of the Society for Research in Child Development, 65*. (3, Serial No. 262)

Jackson, N. E., & Coltheart, M. (2001). *Routes to reading success and failure.* New York: Taylor & Francis.

Jusczyk, P. W., & Aslin, R. M. (1995). Infants' detection of the sound patterns of words in fluent speech. *Cognitive Psychology, 29*, 1–23.

Kang, H., & Simpson, G. B. (1996). Development of semantic and phonological priming in a shallow orthography. *Developmental Psychology, 32*, 860–866.

Kim, M., McGregor, K. K., and Thompson, C. K. (2000). Early lexical development in English-and Korean-speaking children: Language-general and language-specific patterns. *Journal of Child Language, 27*, 225–254.

Lippman, M. Z. (1971). Correlates of contrast word associations: Developmental trends. *Journal of Verbal Learning and Verbal Behavior, 10*, 392–399.

Mandler, J. M. (1988). How to build a baby: On the development of an accessible representational system. *Cognitive Development, 3*, 113–136.

Manis, F. R., Seidenberg, M. S., & Doi, L. M. (1999). See Dick RAN: Rapid naming and the longitudinal prediction of reading subskills in first and second graders. *Scientific Studies of Reading, 3*, 129–157.

Markman, E. M. (1989). *Categorization and naming in children: Problems of induction.* Cambridge, MA: MIT Press.

McCauley, C., Weil, C. M., & Sperber, R. D. (1976). The development of memory structure as reflected by semantic-priming effects. *Journal of Experimental Child Psychology, 22*, 511–518.

McGregor, K. K., Friedman, R. M., Reilly, R. M., & Newman, R. M. (2002). Semantic representation and naming in young children. *Journal of Speech, Language, and Hearing Research, 45*, 332–346.

Mervis, C. B., & Long, L. M. (1987, April). *Words refer to whole objects: Young children's interpretation of the referent of a novel word.* Paper presented at the biennial meeting of the Society for Research in Child Development, Baltimore, MD.

Miller, J. F. (1996). The search for the phenotype of disordered language performance. In M. L. Rice (Ed.), *Toward a genetics of language* (pp. 297–314). Mahwah, NJ: Erlbaum.

Nagy, W. E., & Anderson, R. C. (1984). How many words are there in printed school English? *Reading Research Quarterly, 19*, 304–330.

Nagy, W. E., Anderson, R. C., & Herman, P. A. (1987). Learning word meanings from context during normal reading. *American Educational Research Journal, 24*, 237–270.

Nagy, W. E., & Herman, P. A. (1987). Breadth and depth of vocabulary knowledge; Implications for acquisition and instruction. In M. G. McKeown & M. E. Curtis (Eds.), *The nature of vocabulary acquisition* (pp. 19–35). Hillsdale, NJ: Erlbaum.

Nagy, W., Herman, P., & Anderson, R. (1985). Learning word meanings from context during normal reading. *American Education Research Journal, 20*, 233–253.

Nation, K., & Snowling, M. J. (1998). Semantic processing and the development of word recognition skills: Evidence from children with reading comprehension difficulties. *Journal of Memory and Language, 39*, 85–101.

Nation, K., & Snowling, M. J. (1999). Developmental differences in sensitivity to semantic relations among good and poor comprehenders: Evidence from semantic priming. *Cognition, 70,* B1–B13.

Nelson, K. (1973). Concept, word and sentence: Interrelations in acquisition and development. *Psychological Review, 81,* 267–295.

Nelson, K. (1985). *Making sense: The acquisition of shared meaning.* San Diego: Academic Press.

Nicholson, T., & Whyte, B. (1992). Matthew effects in learning new words while listening to stories. In D. J. Leu & C. K. Kinzer (Eds.), *Literacy research, theory, and practice: Views from many perspectives.* (pp. 499–503). Chicago: National Reading Conference.

Nippold, M. A., Cuyler, J. S., & Braunbeck-Price, R. (1988). Explanation of ambiguous advertisements: A developmental study with children and adolescents. *Journal of Speech and Hearing Research, 31,* 466–474.

Nippold, M. A., Schwarz, I. E., & Undlin, R. A. (1992). Use and understanding of adverbial conjuncts: A developmental study of adolescents and young adults. *Journal of Speech and Hearing Research, 35,* 108–118.

Oetting, J. B., Rice, M. L., & Swank, L. K. (1995). Quick incidental learning (QUIL) of words by school-age children with and without specific language impairment. *Journal of Speech and Hearing Research, 38,* 434–445.

O'Hara, M., & Johnston, J. (1997). Syntactic bootstrapping in children with specific language impairment. *European Journal of Disorders of Communication, 32,* 147–163.

Plaut, D. C., & Booth, J. R. (2000). Individual and developmental differences in semantic priming: Empirical and computational support for a single-mechanism account of lexical processing. *Psychological Review, 107,* 786–823.

Rayner, K., Foorman, B. R., Perfetti, C. A., Pesetsky, D., & Seidenberg, M. S. (2001). How psychological science informs the teaching of reading. *Psychological Science in the Public Interest, 2*(Suppl.), 31–74.

Rescorla, L. A. (1980). Overextension in early language development. *Journal of Child Language, 7,* 321–335.

Rescorla, L. A. (1989). The Language Development Survey: A screening tool for delayed language in toddlers. *Journal of Speech and Hearing Disorders, 54,* 587–599.

Rice, M. L., Buhr, J., & Oetting, J. B. (1992). Specific language-impaired children's quick incidental learning of words: The effect of a pause. *Journal of Speech and Hearing Research, 35,* 1040–1048.

Rice, M. L., Buhr, J., & Nemeth, M. (1990). Fast mapping word-learning abilities of language delayed preschoolers. *Journal of Speech and Hearing Disorders, 55,* 33–42.

Rice, M. L., Oetting, J. B., Marquis, J., Bode, J., & Pae, S. (1994). Frequency of input effects on word comprehension of children with specific language impairment. *Journal of Speech and Hearing Research, 37,* 106–122.

Rice, M. L., & Woodsmall, L. (1988). Lessons from television: Children's word learning when viewing. *Child Development, 59,* 420–429.

Ruddell, M. R. (1994). Vocabulary knowledge and comprehension: A comprehension–process view of complex literacy relationships. In R. B. Ruddell & M. R. Ruddell (Eds), *Theoretical models and processes of reading* (4th ed., pp. 414–447). Newark, DE: International Reading Association.

Saffran, J. R., Aslin, R. M., & Newport, E. L. (1996). Statistical learning by 8-month-old infants. *Science, 274,* 1926–1928.

Scarborough, H. S. (1990). Very early language deficits in dyslexic children. *Child Development, 61,* 1728–1743.

Schwantes, F. M. (1981). Locus of the context effect in children's word recognition. *Child Development, 52,* 895–903.

Schwantes, F. M. (1991). Children's use of semantic and syntactic information for word recognition and determination of sentence meaningfulness. *Journal of Reading Behavior, 23,* 335–350.

Schwartz, R., & Terrell, B. (1983). The role of input frequency in lexical acquisition. *Journal of Child Language, 10,* 57–64.

Serviclaes, W., Sprenger-Charolles, L., Carre, R., & Demonet, J. F. (2001). Perceptual discrimination of speech sounds in developmental dyslexia. *Journal of Speech, Language, and Hearing Research, 44,* 384–399.

Shefelbine, J. L. (1990). Student factors related to variability in learning word meanings from context. *Journal of Reading Behavior, 22,* 71–97.

Sloutsky, V. M., Lo, Y. F., & Fisher, A. V. (2001). How much does a shared named make things similar?: Linguistic labels, similarity, and the development of inductive inference. *Child Development, 72,* 1695–1709.

Smith, L. B. (2000). Learning how to learn words. In R. M. Golinkoff, K. Hirsh-Pasek, L. Bloom, L. B. Smith, A. L. Woodward, N. Akhtar, M. Tomasello, & G. Hollich (Eds.), *Becoming a word learner* (pp. 51–80). Oxford, UK: Oxford University Press.

Snowling, M., Bishop, D. V. M., & Stothard, S. E. (2000). Is preschool language impairment a risk factor for dyslexia in adolescence? *Journal of Child Psychology and Psychiatry, 41,* 587–600.

Soja, N. (1992). Inferences about the meanings of nouns: The relationship between perception and syntax. *Cognitive Development, 7,* 29–46.

Stahl, S. A., Hare, V. C., Sinatra, R., & Gregory, J. F. (1991). Defining the role of prior knowledge and vocabulary in reading comprehension: The retiring of number 41. *Journal of Reading Behavior, 23,* 487–508.

Stanovich, K. E. (1986). Matthew effects in reading: Some consequences of individual differences in the acquisition of literacy. *Reading Research Quarterly, 21,* 360–406.

Stanovich, K. E. (1993). Does reading make you

smarter?: Literacy and the development of verbal intelligence. *Advances in Child Development and Behavior, 24,* 133–180.

Stanovich, K. E., & Cunningham, A. E. (1992). Studying the consequences of literacy within a literate society: The cognitive correlates of print exposure. *Memory and Cognition, 20,* 51–68.

Stanovich, K. E., Cunningham, A. E., & Feeman, D. J. (1984). Intelligence, cognitive skills, and early reading progress. *Reading Research Quarterly, 19,* 278–303.

Stanovich, K. E., Nathan, R. G., West, R. F., & Vala-Rossi, M. (1985). Children's word recognition in context: Spreading activation, expectancy, and modularity. *Child Development, 56,* 1418–1428.

Stanovich, K. E., West, R. F., & Feeman, D. J. (1981). A longitudinal study of sentence context effects in second-grade children: Tests of an interactive–compensatory model. *Journal of Experimental Child Psychology, 32,* 185–199.

Sternberg, R. J. (1985). *Beyond IQ: A triarchic theory of human intelligence.* Cambridge, UK: Cambridge University Press.

Sternberg, R. J. (1987). Most vocabulary is learned from context. In M. G. McKeown and M. E. Curtis (Eds.), *The nature of vocabulary acquisition,* (pp. 89–105). Hillsdale, NJ: Erlbaum.

Stothard, S. E., Snowling, M. J., Bishop, D. V. M., Chipchase, B. B., & Kaplan, C. A. (1998). Language impaired preschoolers: A follow-up into adolescence. *Journal of Speech, Language, and Hearing Research, 41,* 407–418.

Thorndike, R. L. (1973). Reading as reasoning. *Reading Research Quarterly, 9,* 135–147.

Tomasello, M., & Akhtar, N. (1995). Two-year-olds use pragmatic cues to differentiate reference to objects and actions. *Cognitive Development, 10,* 201–224.

Tomasello, M., & Farrar, J. (1986). Joint attention and early language. *Child Development, 57,* 1454–1463.

Trauner, D., Wulfeck, B., Tallal, P., & Hesselink, J. (1995). Neurologic and MRI profiles of language impaired children. San Diego: Center for Research in Language, University of California at San Diego. (Publication No. CND-9513)

van der Lely, H. K. J. (1994). Canonical linking rules: Forward versus reverse linking in normally developing and specifically language-impaired children. *Cognition, 51,* 29–72.

Vellutino, F. R., Scanlon, D. M., & Tanzman, M. S. (1988). Lexical memory in poor and normal readers: Developmental differences in the use of category cues. *Canadian Journal of Psychology, 42,* 216–241.

Vellutino, F. R., Scanlon, D. M., & Lyon, G. R. (2000). Differentiating between difficult-to-remediate and readily remediated poor readers: More evidence against the IQ–achievement discrepancy definition of reading disability. *Journal of Learning Disabilities, 33,* 223–238.

Walsh, M., Rafferty, H., & Turner, I. (1992). Challenging the Matthew effects: Vocabulary acquisition for all? *Educational Psychology in Practice, 8,* 131–137.

Waxman, S. R., & Hatch, T. (1992). Beyond the basics: Preschool children label objects flexibly at multiple hierarchical levels. *Journal of Child Language, 19,* 153–166.

Welder, A. M., & Graham, S. A. (2001). The influence of shape similarity and shared labels on infants' inductive inferences about nonobvious object properties. *Child Development, 72,* 1653–1673.

Werner, H., & Kaplan, E. (1952). The acquisition of word meanings: A developmental study. *Monographs of the Society for Research in Child Development, 15*(Serial No. 51).

White, T. G., Graves, M. F., & Slater, W. H. (1990). Growth of reading vocabulary in diverse elementary schools: Decoding and word meaning. *Journal of Educational Psychology, 82,* 281–290.

Wolf, M., & Bowers, P. G. (1999). The double-deficit hypothesis for the developmental dyslexias. *Journal of Educational Psychology, 91,* 415–438.

Wright, B. A., Lombardino, L. J., King, W. M., Puranik, C. S., Leonard, C. M., & Merzenich, M. M. (1997). Deficits in auditory temporal and spectral resolution in language-impaired children. *Nature, 387,* 176–178.

15

Morphological Processes That Influence Learning to Read

JOANNE F. CARLISLE

Although it can be said that all aspects or components of language work together in linguistic acts of comprehension and expression, this statement may be more characteristic of morphological processing than of syntactic, semantic, or phonological processing alone. Morphology, which refers to the study of word structure, involves integrative linguistic processing that is centered around morphemes (the smallest units of meaning) and combinations of morphemes. Although researchers sometimes treat morphological processing as a special case of some other aspect of language processing (e.g., grammatical awareness, as noted by Bowey, 1994), this approach misrepresents the nature of language processing with regard to the role of morphology. Morphology is not just a matter of syntactic or grammatical processing, for instance. Inflections are not just grammatical "units." As Bybee (1995) has pointed out, evidence comes from the fact that inflections (i.e., base words with suffixes that serve as grammatical markers) can be stored and accessed as lexical units; this is not the case for true grammatical units (e.g., phrases).

In English, three types of morphologically complex words are recognized: inflections, derivations, and compounds. Linguists disagree about the extent to which inflections and derivations are discrete categories. The common explanation is that inflections involve the addition of one or more suffixes that change the grammatical role of a base word but do not change its word class or its meaning, whereas derivations involve the attachment of prefixes or suffixes that often results in changes in both meaning and word class. However, inflectional suffixes (such as the past tense markers on verbs or the plural marker) are semantically active. For example, the concept of plurality (i.e., "more than one") changes the word semantically perhaps even more than grammatically. English is rich in derivations and compounds, but there are relatively few inflectional markers; these are limited to verb tense markers, the plural and possessive forms, and the comparative and superlative forms of adjectives (e.g., *small, smaller, smallest*). Compounding and deriving word forms are productive processes in English. "New" words can be heard in everyday conversations and read in newspapers. Because English-language users are attuned to the productivity of word-formation processes, it is likely that they often do not notice the appearance of a "new" word on the evening news show. Nonetheless, as I argue here, comprehending and using complex word forms requires integrated processing of phonology, semantics, syntax, and, of course, morphology.

Perhaps because morphological processing requires the coordinated processing of form and meaning at lexical and sublexical levels, and involves complex linguistic relations, it is a prolonged aspect of language learning—one that starts in the preschool years but continues into adulthood. Nonetheless, children's awareness of the morphological composition of words, like other forms of linguistic awareness, contributes to their understanding of written texts. This chapter takes as its theme the complexities of morphological processing as they affect word reading and reading comprehension. One purpose is to consider what we know about factors that affect the processing and learning of morphologically complex words. The second purpose is to examine the extent to which (and how) morphological processing contributes to children's acquisition of reading skill, with a particular concern for children with language-learning disabilities.

MORPHOLOGICAL PROCESSING AND LANGUAGE LEARNING

Morphological processing provides a way to understand and use language by incorporating semantic and grammatical information at the word and subword levels. Of course, learning morphemes depends on learning the phonological representation of morphemes. For example, one of Clark's (1992) children (age 3 years, 5 months) said of a dinosaur he has just drawn, "It looks growly, doesn't it?" To be able to use the adjectival ending -y to form the novel word *growly* (i.e., *growl* + *y*), he must have learned from phonological analysis of numerous other words that -y attaches to nouns (e.g., *muddy, snowy, sticky*). In written language, the spelling of a word can also affect the salience of the morphemic

constituents. In the sentence, "Even the artist could not tell the *reproduction* from the original," the word *produce* is the base form and provides the core meaning (here, "to make"). The prefix *re-* carries the semantic comment of "again." The suffix *-tion* adds both semantic and grammatical information, roughly meaning "the state or condition of" and marking the word as a noun. This word is a member of the English word family that includes *product, productive, productivity,* and so on.

What happens when a young reader encounters this word in a passage and does not recognize or know the word? Not knowing the meaning of the base word *produce*, this reader is unlikely to initiate an analytic process that would result in figuring out the meaning of the whole word. Similarly, lack of awareness of *re-* functioning as a prefix, or *-tion* functioning as a suffix, might also lead the reader to treat the word as if it were one morpheme (Schreuder & Baayan, 1995). Finally, the shift in sound (and spelling) that accompanies the addition of the suffix (both the vowel and the consonant in the second syllable are affected) might also affect the reader's awareness that the word could be read and understood by analysis of its morphological composition. Although phonological and orthographic transparency (i.e., when the complex word form retains the sound and spelling of the base word) facilitates awareness of morphological structure, opaque relations tend to make morphological structure less obvious. So much for the problems.

What are the advantages to the reader, should he or she be able to parse the word into its constituent morphemes? Morphological analysis (whether consciously undertaken or not) is likely to yield a reasonable estimate of the correct pronunciation and meaning of the word. Both facility in accessing words in memory and assigning appropriate meanings in context are likely to help the reader construct meaning from the text in which this sentence is found.

Morphological Learning

Recognizing morphemes in words and learning word-formation processes begin in the preschool years, for most children about the time they start speaking in four-word utterances (on average) (Brown, 1973; Clark, 1982). Table 15.1 includes some of the many examples from Clark (1982) and Bowerman (1982), illustrating preschool children's novel uses of morphemes to convey their thoughts. Several important points can be made with reference to these examples. First, they show the children's basic grasp of combinatory principles. Second, word forms are manipulated to convey meanings and grammatical roles, and that is the basic purpose of combining morphemes. For example, "needled," in the first example, carries the central semantic concept in the word *needle* (turned into a verb) and is correctly marked for its grammatical role (i.e., "is needled" is a passive voice, present tense).

MacWhinney (1978) and Clark (1982, 1992) (among others) have concerned themselves with the process by which children learn principles of morphological composition; the debate has largely centered on learning by rule or by analogy. However, both systems may be operative. As Clark (1982) said,

> In deciding how to add word endings, children might well begin by comparing new instances to specific exemplars already in their repertoires. But later, after being exposed to a large number of forms in a coherent paradigm, they should have a plethora of exemplars to work from, and their use of an inflection might take on the form of a general rule. Or they might simultaneously use rules in some domains and analogy in others. (p. 397)

Novel uses of word forms, such as those in Table 15.1, reveal that children are learning formal properties, quite likely from observing patterns of form and meaning (i.e., from experience with language). However, they seem to treat these as open-ended possibilities for making new words to express particular meanings. Often, they combine morphemes in ruleful ways (as in the case with *needled* and *unopen* in Table 15.1). In other instances, they use a morpheme for its meaning, while violating a principle of usage (as in "I pulled it unstapled"). Preschool children have access to word-formation principles that are common and affixes that are productive. For example, agentive *-er* is highly productive, and preschool children understand its meaning and the word-formation principle that it obeys (adherence to a verb) (Clark, 1982). As it is used here, the term "productivity" refers to the extent to which a given affix (or suffixes) can be attached to different base words to convey appropriate meanings, while adhering to basic principles of morphemic combination. Preschool children use *-er* to describe agents and instruments, using familiar verbs and the *-er* to mark "one who" or "that which" (e.g., "winder" for an old-fashioned machine for making ice cream, or "storyer" for the role the father is asked to adopt—"You be the storyer."). In contrast, preschoolers are not likely to be familiar with other suffixes that are similar in meaning (e.g., *-ent* as in *student* or *correspondent*; or *-ist*, as in *pianist* or *guitarist*), presumably because these are less common and less productive.

Along with frequency (exposure to words) and productivity, phonological and semantic transparencies make the existence of morphological structure more salient to children. They learn not just the representation of the base form in a complex word (e.g., *run* in *running*) but also variants that

TABLE 15.1. Examples of Children's Novel Uses of Morphemes

Clark
Child age 3 years, 2 months (asking if the pants his mother is mending are ready): "Is it all needled?"
Clark
Child age 3 years, 11 months (putting crackers in her soup): "I'm crackering my soup."
Bowerman
Child age 4 years, 11 months (wants D to take lid off styrofoam cooler): "Will you unopen this?"
Bowerman
Child age 3 years, 8 months (after pulling stapled book apart): "I pulled it unstapled."

Note. From Clark (1982) and Bowerman (1982).

are systematic and often governed by phonotactics (i.e., ways that sounds at morpheme boundaries are adjusted by their neighbors). In the early elementary years, they are likely to learn regular phonological patterns, such as the vowel and consonantal shifts in *five* and *fifth*, *wife* and *wives* (MacWhinney, 1978). They also learn allomorphs of the past tense (as in *grabbed*, *packed*, and *batted*) and the plural (as in *dogs*, *cats*, and *bushes*).

Learning Inflections

By first grade, most children appropriately use morpho-phonological rules for the formation of inflections, as shown in Berko's (1958) classic study of children's oral production. For example, most of the children used the allomorph of the past tense that suited the final consonant of the base word (e.g., *spowed* with /d/, but *motted* with /ed/). However, Smith-Lock (1995) found that children with language impairments (ages 5–7) performed like children who are matched in language development (ages 3–4), and significantly worse than children who are the same age on tasks that required formation of inflections (real and nonsense words) to complete sentences, as well as the ability to judge and repair sentences with incorrect inflectional forms. In general, the results of this study suggest that language-impaired children's awareness of word forms and their ability to analyze, judge, and manipulate word forms are developmentally delayed.

Children with language-learning disabilities are often found to have significant problems learning inflectional morphemes. Researchers have offered a number of different explanations for this difficulty. One group of explanations is based on the view that such children have specific deficits with grammatical learning. Clahsen (1991), for example, suggested that such children have a selective impairment in understanding the way that agreement of number and tense is expressed by inflectional morphemes (e.g., lack of agreement of subject and verb). Rice and Oetting (1993) also suggested that deficits in grammatical learning account for the frequency with which children with language-learning disabilities make errors in verb tenses and in subject–verb agreement. Gopnik and her associates (e.g. Gopnik & Crago, 1991) suggested that some children have a familial or genetic basis for their difficulties in acquiring implicit rules that mark tense, number, and person.

A different group of explanations focuses on the possibility that children with language-learning disabilities have limited processing capacity. According to Leonard (1998), these limitations might affect working memory (the computational region of memory), time (the speed with which information is processed), or energy (the cognitive resources available for or devoted to completion of a task). All of these possible sources of problems have been linked to children's difficulties in comprehending and producing inflected word forms. For example, Leonard and his colleagues (e.g., Leonard, McGregor, & Allen, 1992) have suggested that limitations in general processing capacity affect children's perception of grammatical morphemes and, thus, their understanding of the functions of such inflections as past tense markers. The surface hypothesis, as it is called, takes into account the short duration and lack of phonetic salience of grammatical morphemes in English. For example, the past tense might be marked by a single consonant (e.g., /d/ in *grabbed*) or an unstressed syllable (e.g., *landed*). These characteristics make it hard for children with language-learning disabilities to learn morphological paradigms such as the proper formation of past tenses. Although adequate discussion of this and other alternatives is beyond the scope of this chapter, it is important to recognize that there are still many unanswered questions about why some children have particular difficulties learning grammatical morphology.

Learning Derivations

Whereas most children do learn most English inflections before they start formal schooling, this is not the case for derivations. Berko (1958) found that the preschool and first-grade children in her study did not show productive knowledge of derivational principles. For example, when shown a picture of a dog covered with irregular green spots, the child is told: "This is a dog with quirks on him. He is all covered with quirks. What kind of dog is he? He is a ____ dog." The preschoolers and first graders in Berko's study tended to provide the response *quirk dog,* using compounding instead of derivation to form the required word. (In contrast, adults consistently gave the response, *quirky* dog.) In other studies, preschoolers and first graders have been found to use -*y* adjectives in creating novel words (Clark, 1982) and have the ability to use -*y* adjectives in sentence contexts (Carlisle & Nomanbhoy, 1993). The differences in the results of these studies may reflect the task and language-processing requirements. Spontaneous production of novel forms may tap tacit knowledge of language, as might sentence-completion tasks, whereas production of a word form when the base is a nonsense word presumably requires more explicit knowledge of word-formation rules and an ability to manipulate words for different purposes.

In derivations, more so than in inflections, the complexity of morpho-phonological relations makes it hard for children to appreciate the morphological structure of many words. Jones (1991) asked first graders to imitate complex words, omit specific portions, and tell about the meanings of the resulting parts. Many of the items involved omission of segments that were repeated at the end of the first segment and the beginning of the second segment. For example, the children may have had trouble appreciating that *ear* and *ring* were found in *earring,* because they heard a single /r/ sound. They also had difficulty segmenting words in which the sound of the base word was not retained in the complex word form (e.g., *natural* or *pressure*). Thus, the tasks required the children to move beyond the surface-level phonological representation in order to delete and tell about one of the morphemes. First graders with delayed language development performed less well than their peers, but their performance on these tasks showed that they nevertheless formed morphophonemic segments. In the second experiment in this study, the children were

asked to omit the word ending (e.g., *plants* or *glands*). Adults' responses on this task had been consistent with the spelling of the words, but children with delayed language development often deleted segments inaccurately (e.g., all said *glan* instead of *gland*). Among other findings, the results showed the importance of word familiarity in making such judgments. According to Jones, the children performed best when both the base word(s) and affixes were common in child language.

Morphological Problem Solving

School-age children make rapid gains in their knowledge of morphologically complex words. This growth is evident from Anglin's (1993) study of vocabulary knowledge. He found marked growth in children's knowledge of compounds, inflections, and derivations between grades 3 and 5. Most noteworthy is the large number of derivations that children appear to learn between grades 3 and 5; this number far exceeds the number of base words (what Anglin calls "psychologically basic words") that are learned in the same period.

One factor that influences the estimate of morphologically complex words that children know is what Anglin calls "morphological problem solving." The older children in Anglin's study were able to demonstrate that they could figure out a likely meaning of an unfamiliar word by analysis of the parts. Thus, words that the children were not likely to have heard before the interview (e.g., *knotless* or *treelet*) were defined accurately by many third- and fifth-grade children. About *treelet,* for example, one fifth grader said that he knew that a riverlet was a little creek, so a treelet must be a "very small" tree (Anglin, 1993, p. 101). This child used analogical reasoning as a way to infer the meanings of unfamiliar, morphologically complex words. As with the Jones (1991) study, note that such reasoning depends on some basic familiarity with both the base form and the affix(es).

In using Anglin's task for a study of morphological learning, Carlisle and Fleming (2003) found that first graders seemed aware that *knotless* was made up of two morphemes, as was evident in their mention of the word *knot*. However, they seemed unable to decompose *treelet,* most often saying that they had never heard of this word before. This difference cannot be because of lack of familiarity with the base word *tree,* because *tree* is presumably more familiar to children than *knot*. A more likely explanation is that the first graders did not think of *tree* as a known base word (free morpheme), because of the unfamiliarity of the suffix *-let*. In general, in instances in which children do not know the word parts (base words or affixes), they are not likely to process a word morphologically.

Factors That Affect the Development of Morphological Awareness

Morphological awareness refers to children's sensitivity to the morphological structure of words. We can distinguish *tacit knowledge* about language structures that comes from experience listening to and using language, and *explicit knowledge,* often referred to as "linguistic awareness." Tacit knowledge is evident in tasks that require children to supply the correct word ending and may require little analytic thinking on their part. For example, children might be given a sentence such as, "Sally had a dress and Linda had a dress. Together they had two _____." The response "dresses" might be stimulated by the combined influence of "dress" and "two-," such that the child's language-processing mechanisms would generate the expectation of a plural noun to complete the sentence. On the other hand, some tasks require children to manipulate or define morphologically complex words that are not presented in sentence contexts. Such tasks might place greater requirements on children's language-analysis abilities, so they might require more explicit morphological awareness.

Morphological awareness is likely to become more explicit during the school-age years for most students as they are immersed in reading, writing, and thinking about language. Thus, as students progress from grade 1 to grade 5, they are more and more likely to use the kind of morphological problem solving described by Anglin

(1993). They are increasingly capable of analyzing the structure of derived words and compounds, and inferring the meaning from word parts.

For elementary school children, the particular challenge is learning to integrate two aspects of words—their form and their meaning. Carlisle and Fleming (2003) gave first and third graders an oral task that involved judging whether there was a small word in a longer word whose meaning was similar. Thus, for *robber,* the answer would be "yes" (the small word being rob), whereas for *dollar,* the answer would be "no." Word pairs were scored, so that only if a child responded to both robber and dollar correctly did he or she get credit. When scored in this way, first graders averaged 57% correct, whereas third graders averaged 72% correct. Further analysis of the children's responses indicated that the first graders tended to ignore dissimilarities of meaning—for example, responding "yes" to *dollar* and saying that *doll* was the small word. In short, there was a significant change from first to third grade in children's ability to make judgments that involved consideration of both form and meaning of words.

It is possible that comprehension of the task itself affected the children's performance, although they were given training items and feedback on these. Only one first grader seemed unable to understand the task, and her performance on this and other tasks was subsequently not included in the study. On the other hand, some of the young children appeared to forget to monitor both form and meaning while they were doing the task (i.e, when no further feedback was given). This in itself is evidence (albeit anecdotal) that it is difficult for first graders to analyze word form and meaning at the same time.

Word Frequency and Structural Transparency

In addition to the challenge of coordinating judgments of form and meaning, two factors play a role in the extent to which children will infer the morphological status of a word and use awareness of the morphological composition to read and understand words and sentences. First, as mentioned earlier, the frequency of a word and its constituent morphemes (along with other distributional characteristics) affects perceptions of its morphemic structure. This means that experience with language and, in particular, experience analyzing words for reading and writing, affect morphological processing. Frequency is associated with productivity, that is, the extent to which a given affix is attached to base words, including those that are "invented" spontaneously. The important role of language experience in morphological learning is a theme that runs throughout the discussion in this chapter.

Second, relational knowledge can be enhanced or obscured by the phonological structure, the orthographic structure, and the semantic content. This factor is one of "transparency." To the extent that a morphologically complex word lacks transparency in sound, spelling, and meaning, its morphological composition will go unnoticed by a large portion of the children who encounter it. Each of these forms of transparency deserves further discussion.

Phonological Transparency

Phonology plays an essential role in morphological learning. As discussed earlier, children become aware of morphemes as phonemes or strings of phonemes that co-occur in certain contexts. For example, -less is recognized as a phonological unit that speakers of the language attach to nouns. Gradually, the child comes to realize that the presence of -less after a noun changes it to mean "without" or "lacking". Repeated encounters with a particular phonological string in a particular position within a word give rise to the child's inference of a stable, predictable meaning and use of that morphemic element.

The child who is limited in the ability to learn morphemes by extracting regularities of phonological units in different contexts is likely to be language impaired in morphology, and possibly in other areas of language learning as well—for instance, vocabulary learning. Both in spoken- and written-language contexts, the morphemic structure of

a word is most noticeable when the sound of the base word is preserved in the complex word form. For example, *healing* is readily seen as a word form that has to do with *heal*, but not so with *health;* that is, phonologically transparent words are those for which the pronunciation of the base form is intact or "stable" in the derived form (e.g., *enjoy* in *enjoyment*), whereas in nontransparent ("opaque") words, the base form undergoes a shift in pronunciation in the derived form (e.g., *nature* in *natural*). Poor readers, whose underlying difficulties often stem from phonological processing problems, have considerable difficulties appreciating morphological relations that involve sound shifts between the base and derived form (Fowler & Liberman, 1995; Windsor, 2000). The children in Fowler and Liberman's (1995) study were grouped in age from 7 years, 5 months to 8 years, 5 months, and from 8 years, 5 months to 9 years, 8 months. Development trends were noted for the younger and older students, particularly when production of the complex form was needed to complete a sentence, but at both age levels, the children performed better on the phonologically transparent words (e.g., *fourth*) than on words with phonological shifts (e.g., *fifth*). The researchers interpreted the difficulties of the poor readers as a consequence of their phonological processing difficulties. However, because normally achieving readers in this study, and in others, also perform less well on phonologically opaque words, as compared to transparent words (e.g., Carlisle, 2000; Singson, Mahoney, & Mann, 2000), the effect of phonological processing difficulties appears to be a matter of degree rather than of kind.

The effects of phonological transparency are most evident when children need to produce complex word forms, as opposed to simply decomposing them to find the base form (Carlisle, 2000). Figure 15.1 illustrates the performance of third and fifth graders on an oral task that required either decomposing a derived word to finish a sentence (e.g., "Driver. Children are too young to _____.") or producing a derived form to finish a sentence (e.g., "Farm. My uncle is a _____."). Note that at both grade levels

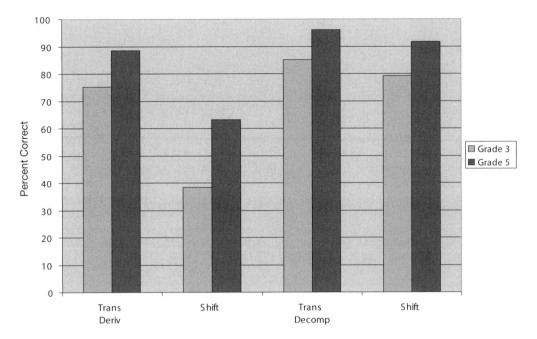

FIGURE 15.1. Third and fifth graders' performance on the Test of Morphological Structure. Deriv, derivation task; Decomp, decomposition task; Trans, transparent words.

and on both types of items (decomposition and derivation), the students performed better on transparent than on phonological shift forms.

With regard to students with language-learning disabilities (LLD), Windsor (2000) used two oral tasks to assess morphological awareness. One involved finding the base form within a derived word presented in a sentence context (supported by a video skit; e.g., "Luckily the accident was bloodless"), and the other involved picking the right ending for a word in an orally presented sentence with a video context (e.g., "Weakling. He felt like a weakling because he couldn't get the jar open. Weakling.") They then heard and saw three choices concerning the suffix—the correct ending (-*ling*), a reduced ending (-*ing*), or no suffix. The performance of students with LLD (between the ages of 10 to 12 years, 6 months) was compared to that of both chronological-age (CA) and language-age (LA) matched students. On these tasks, Windsor found that the students with LLD performed less well than their CA peers on the Base Production

task, but only when the derived form was not transparent (i.e., "opaque"). There were no differences among the groups on the transparent words. The CA group also performed better than LLD and LA groups on the Suffix Identification Task, again, with the LLD and LA children performing particularly poorly on the "opaque" words. Other studies, too, have reported that poor readers perform less well than their peers on morphological processing tasks when the test items are words that undergo shifts in phonological representation (Champion, 1997; Leong, 1989).

The impact of phonological changes on morphological processing may be particularly apparent when morphological awareness is assessed with oral tasks. Oral tasks necessarily place a heavy processing requirement on phonology, so we should not be surprised that phonological complexities affect children's performance. Researchers commonly compare performances on phonologically "opaque" and transparent derivational relations, the difference stemming from the intactness of the phonological representation of the base in the complex word. Generally, transparency is treated as a dichotomous variable, with words having or lacking transparency. Under these conditions, school-age children perform less well on words with phonological shifts (also called "opaque"; e.g., *heavily*) than on words that are phonologically transparent (e.g., *quickly;* e.g., (Carlisle, 1988, 1995, 2000; Fowler & Liberman, 1995; Singson et al., 2000). However, other factors may affect the processing of words as well. We have already seen that familiarity of the base word and suffix plays a role. Thus, if the child does not realize that the word ending is a suffix, morphological processing is not likely to be initiated. However, phonological complexities may combine with other aspects of word structure in such a way as to either highlight or obscure the morphemic composition; these aspects include orthographic and semantic transparency.

Orthographic Transparency

Along with phonology, the role of orthographic representation is important in the development of morphological awareness. Orthographic patterns consistently aligned with the phonological representation of morphologically complex words facilitate recognition and recall. Orthographic regularities are also believed to help students learn to recognize the relations of morphologically complex words that vary in phonological form; thus, silent letters or unstressed vowels can be identified (e.g., *muscle* and *muscular,* or *bomb* and *bombard*) (Chomsky, 1970). However, in word reading, morphological processing may be inhibited when the derived form retains relatively little of the orthographic gestalt of the base form (e.g., *retention* and *retain*) (Jarvella & Snodgrass, 1974). How different the base and derived forms can be before adults no long see a family resemblance is still not understood.

A study by Derwing, Smith, and Wiebe (1995) demonstrated that positive recognition of morpheme similarities in words might be based in part on orthographic similarity. Using a version of the "Comes From" task (Derwing & Baker, 1979; e.g.,

"Does dirty come from dirt?"), Derwing and his colleagues (1995) found that children and college students made use of spelling similarities in analyzing morphologically complex words. However, spelling commonalities did not necessarily lead to the perception of a morphological relationship, if the semantic connection lacked transparency. Still, for word pairs such as *necklace* and *lace,* spelling similarity might have made the subjects consider the possibility of a morphological relation. These authors concluded that spelling and other sources of information about words that children pick up in school are likely to influence their sense of the morphological relatedness of words.

For adults and for older students, there is considerable evidence of sensitivity to systematic relations in the orthography despite phonological variation (Jarvella & Snodgrass, 1974; Templeton & Scarborough-Franks, 1985). Templeton and Scarborough-Franks asked 6th and 10th graders to add a suffix to a nonsense word and then spell the words. In one condition, the students were given the test items in writing (nonsense base word and sentence), whereas in another condition, the students were given the nonsense base word and the sentence frame orally. The target responses required making phonological changes to produce the complex form, such as vowel laxing or vowel reduction. Test words were created by changing the spelling of word stems, so that, for example; *divine* and *divinity* were changed to *tivine* and *tivinity.* The student was shown the suffix *-ity* that was to be added and heard (or read): "Tivine, John was impressed with the __ of the boy." The results showed that the orthographic presentation yielded significantly better performance than the oral presentation at both grade levels. The researchers concluded that the stability of orthographic representations may help students learn complex patterns of phonological relations that characterize many derived forms. Derived forms of this type are relatively low in frequency, so that the derived forms (and often their base counterparts) are often not familiar to children until the middle school years or beyond (Templeton & Scarborough-Franks, 1985).

What happens when words are not completely transparent in the sense of having the spelling of the base form intact in the derived form (e.g., *helpless*)? Middle school and junior high students (including those with reading disabilities) have been found to perform less well on an oral task of decomposing or producing derived forms of words with both orthographic and phonological changes (e.g., *decide, decision*) than on words transparent in both phonology and orthography (e.g., *enjoy, enjoyment*) (Carlisle, 1988). The error rate on such words was greater than for words that underwent phonological changes only (e.g., *magic, magician*) or orthographic changes only (e.g., *day* and *daily*).

It is not entirely clear why orthographic transparency affects performance on oral morphological awareness tasks. One possibility is that much of the learning of morphological relations comes through exposure to words in written texts. Combined phonological or orthographic shifts may together obscure morphological relations.

Semantic Transparency

Semantics is the third area in which transparency (or relative lack thereof) affects perceptions of morphological relations and morphological learning. Although recognized as a crucial determinant of morphological learning, the role of semantic transparency in morphological learning has received relatively little systematic study. A young language-learner's awareness of semantic relations (which in turn affects perceptions of morphological relations) is affected by the complexities inherent in word meanings. Words can have various meanings. Sometimes the meanings of members of the word family build clearly on the meanings of the base words (e.g., *divide, divisible, indivisible*), whereas in other cases, they do not (e.g., *form, inform, formation*). In some cases, there seems to be no discernible semantic link. For example, none of the common meanings of *apply* (i.e., to bring into contact with something, to be pertinent, to make a request) seem related to today's common meaning of *appliance* (i.e., a device or instrument operated by electricity and designed for household use). In English, there are many derivations and compounds whose meanings are not at all evident from analysis of the parts. Compounds such as *red tape* (referring to impediments in the use of official forms and procedures) are very difficult for English-language learners to understand. Even native speakers of English effectively treat such compounds as monomorphemic words.

Several studies have looked at the extent to which semantic similarity affects students' judgments of morphological relations. Derwing and Baker (1979) asked children and adults to indicate whether they thought one word "came from" another. Word pairs varied on two dimensions—phonological similarity (PS) and semantic similarity (SS)—and included all combinations of such pairs, for example, *teacher* and *teach* (high on both SS and PS), *puppy* and *dog* (high on SS and low on PS), *eerie* and *ear* (high on PS but not SS), and *carpenter* and *wagon* (low on both SS and PS). The results showed that young, school-age children tended to think two words were related when they were phonologically similar. One factor that might have contributed particularly to this result was that some of the word pairs were likely to be unfamiliar to young students. Without prior knowledge of the meaning of words such as *eerie*, the children were left with similarities of sound and spelling as the only basis for making such judgments. The older students were more able to recognize morphological relations. They also tended to identify as "related" words whose relations were largely etymological and might be taught in school (e.g., *moon* and *month*). Mahoney (1994; Mahoney, Singson, & Mann, 2000) extended Derwing and Baker's findings by looking at the relation of performance on a "Comes From" task and reading. They found that for both school-age children and older students, relational knowledge of derived forms was significantly associated with word-reading skill.

Nagy and Anderson (1984) demonstrated that unfamiliar words that children encounter in texts (particularly those with phonological and orthographic similarity of base, and derived forms and known affixes) tend to be semantically transparent. Specifically, they estimated that there were 139,020 semantically transparent derived forms in texts read by children in grades 3–9. In contrast, there were only 49,080 derived words that were relatively opaque semantically. Semantically transparent words embrace the meaning of the base word in the meaning of the complex form, as in the case of *redness*. Semantically opaque words pairs (e.g., *groove* and *groovy*) may be phonologically and orthographically transparent, but there are no apparent semantic links. Among the opaque derived words, these researchers estimated that there are about 27,000 words whose component parts do contribute in some way to the meaning of the derived word.

> Even in these cases, then, knowledge of word formation processes will be helpful to the reader trying to figure out the meaning of words in context. On the other hand, the semantic opacity of these words is sufficient that many readers—especially poor readers—will not be able to figure out their meanings, and thus will have to learn them individually. (p. 314)

A characteristic of lexical items that affects perceptions of similarity in meaning is polysemy. When words have more than one meaning, a student may not know the particular meanings that are closely linked and give clues to a morphological relation. For example, *comic* and *comical* might seem to be close in meaning, unless a person's understanding of *comic* is a soft-covered book of serial cartoons. If so, that person might not see the relation of *comic* and *comical*. Another example is the word *pointless*, as in "Her argument was pointless." If, to the language user, *point* means the tip of something, as in "The point of the pencil broke right before the test began," then the meaning "has no tip" does not make sense in the sentence containing *pointless*. Problems involving semantic drift and polysemy are common and certainly lead to the impression that words that appear to be morphologically complex often are not. White, Power, and White (1989) studied common prefixes with the purpose of determining

how useful it would be to instruct fourth graders in word structure. They found that most uses of the most common prefixes (e.g., *re-, un-*) were on words that were "analyzable." However, whether instruction in word structure would help children learn the many words with less common prefixes, or words with suffixes instead of prefixes, is unknown.

Related to this area is the semantic content of suffixes that also carry grammatical information. Some suffixes have relatively concrete meanings. For example, *-ful* often can be seen to reflect the meaning "full of"—as in *hopeful* or *graceful*. However, other suffixes have meanings that are quite abstract. For example, *-able* and *-ous* change nouns or verbs to adjectives (e.g., *fame* to *famous*, or *work* to *workable*). They mean something like "of or pertaining to, having the characteristic of." Carlisle and Fleming (2003), using Anglin's (1993) word interview, found that children seldom provided definitions that clearly indicated the grammatical role and meaning of such suffixes. Instead, they tended to define the word by focusing on the meaning of the base word. Similarly, several studies, have shown that fourth graders tend to focus on the meaning of the derived words by attending to the base word only (Champion, 1997; Tyler & Nagy, 1989). By eighth grade, students showed a more complete understanding of the semantic and syntactic roles of the suffixes.

Windsor (1994) investigated school-age children's knowledge of the meanings of derivational suffixes (as compared to that of adults). She used a nonsense-word task that tested both comprehension and production of derivational suffixes. Both children and adults showed greatest accuracy in comprehension and production with the meaning "without X" (e.g., hopeless). In contrast, they showed low comprehension of a diminutive suffix (*-ette*) and the suffix *-ful* (meaning "character of X"). Low production was noted with the suffix "can be Xed" (e.g., *-able*). A follow-up study (Windsor & Hwang, 1997) showed that students with language-learning disabilities performed less well than their chronological-age peers, but similarly to their language-age peers, on these suffix comprehension and production tasks. There is no question that many suffixes are difficult for children to understand and explain, not only because of their abstract meanings and the varied semantic and syntactic roles they play, but also because children tend to focus predominantly on the meaning of the base word. The base word carries the primary semantic content. However, lack of understanding of the semantic and syntactic aspects of suffixes can lead to inaccurate or incomplete comprehension of language, oral or written.

MORPHOLOGICALLY COMPLEX WORDS IN TEXTS

Morphological processing is bound to play a significant role in the acquisition of reading skills for the simple reason that it is essential to language comprehension. In particular, however, readers who are unaware of morphological components of written words are at a particular disadvantage in decoding, vocabulary, and reading comprehension. Some researchers argue that awareness of morphological structure of words affects reading and spelling development for students after the elementary years, but not much before that (Henderson, 1985). However, a significant relationship between reading achievement and morphological processing has been reported for young readers (Brittain, 1970; Carlisle, 1995).

When we read natural texts (as opposed to words in isolation), morphological processing involves accessing the semantic, syntactic, and phonological characteristics of base words and their affixes, initially through the orthographic representation of morphemes and words. For adults, studies show that word recognition (i.e., lexical access) is sensitive to the morphological composition of words, including transparent and nontransparent words (Fowler, Napps, & Feldman, 1985; Napps, 1989; Stolz & Feldman, 1995). For young readers, morphological recognition may occur primarily when words are phonologically and orthographically transparent. As discussed earlier, in some instances, the spelling provides a stable representation of the base morpheme or affix, even when there is some shift in the phonology (e.g., *final* and *finality*). This is true of the past tense allomorphs, which are pronounced differently but spelled consistently (*-ed*), as in *grabbed, patted,* and *packed.*

Efficiency of processing and ease of recall are thought to be benefits of morphological awareness. Consistent spelling of morphemes leads to ease of recognition of base forms and affixes. Of course, there are degrees of orthographic transparency, ranging from intact representation of the base word and affix (e.g., *hopeless*) to only partial representation of the base word in the derived form (e.g., *crucial*, with its base word *crux*). How much of the base form needs to be retained in the complex form to preserve morphemic identity is not known. Still, all readers of English are dependent on representation of words on a morphemic as well as a phonemic basis. Imagine how difficult it would be to read English if the spelling of words represented phonemes without regard for morphemic identity! Taking inflections as a case in point, the plural marker would be spelled differently in different words (e.g., *cats, *dogz,* and *bushez*), as would the past tense marker (e.g., *grabd, *packt*).

Clearly, facility with morphological processing is a potential aid to a reader only if there are sufficient numbers of complex words in written texts for morphological processing to play a role. Thus, an important question is whether morphologically complex words are sufficiently common in children's texts to make it likely that morphological processing plays a role in reading. In an analysis of words that appear in children's texts (third through ninth grade), Nagy and Anderson (1984) found that affixed words outnumber base words by a factor of about four to one. They also found that high-frequency words (words occurring more than once in a million words) were often base words, but among low-frequency words, affixed words were more common. By fourth grade, it is the less frequent morphologically complex words that are a major component of children's vocabulary growth.

These results, which reflect the word characteristics in printed English, echo those of Anglin's study (1993) of vocabulary growth. Furthermore, as noted earlier, a large portion of the unfamiliar morphologically complex words that children encounter in texts are analyzable; that is, the meaning of the word can be inferred through analysis of the parts. According to White et al. (1989), 80% of the prefixed words in children's texts contain the most common prefixes (e.g., *re-*) and can be readily figured out by young readers. Furthermore, 80% of these words had suffixes; of these, about 90% were either inflectional suffixes or neutral derivational suffixes. Such suffixes also tend to be transparent in form and meaning. Nagy and Anderson (1984) noted that "while context is often not sufficient to determine the meaning of an unfamiliar word, it may provide enough information to permit a guess at the appropriate meaning of a word whose semantic content is partially determined by its morphology" (p. 327).

THE RELATION OF ORAL MORPHOLOGY AND READING ACHIEVEMENT

The next important question is whether, implicitly or explicitly, young readers of English benefit from awareness of morphological units when they are reading. One way to answer this question is to consider whether there is a relation between morphological awareness in oral language and reading (i.e., both word reading and reading comprehension). It should be pointed out that studies that focus on the relation of oral morphological awareness and the reading of words in isolation are asking whether the formal properties of morphology affect reading—that is, the ability to decompose morphologically complex words, to negotiate instances in which there is lack of phonological and orthographic transparency. For word reading, semantic and syntactic aspects of morphological processing may play a relatively small role. This is not the case when vocabulary and reading comprehension are the areas of reading with which

we are concerned. Here, students' understanding of the meanings of base morphemes and affixes, and the ability to infer meanings of words from structural analysis and context, are also of central concern.

Word Reading: Tapping Formal Knowledge

A number of studies have reported a significant association between morphological awareness and word reading (e.g., Carlisle, 1995, 2000; Carlisle & Stone, 2003; Champion, 1997; Elbro & Arnbak, 1996; Fowler & Liberman, 1995; Leong, 1989; Singson et al., 2000; Windsor, 2000). In the elementary school years, correlations are in the moderate range. In one study, the correlation between first graders' morphological production task and word reading was .46 ($p < .001$) (Carlisle & Nomanbhoy, 1993). In another study, for third through sixth graders, the correlation between morphological awareness task and word reading was .58 ($p < .001$) (Singson et al., 2000). Singson et al. carried out a path analysis to examine the contribution of morphological awareness, phoneme awareness, and vocabulary to word-reading on a standardized word identification test. They found that morphological awareness offered a separate contribution to word reading, over and above that made by vocabulary and phoneme awareness. In fact, morphological awareness was as good a predictor of word-reading skill as either phonemic awareness or vocabulary knowledge for the third through sixth graders in their study.

In many studies, the relationship of morphological awareness and word reading has been established by comparing performance on oral tasks of morphological awareness and word reading. It is possible, however, that to some degree, the reported relation of morphological awareness and reading reflects the impact of linguistic awareness on word reading generally (not specifically on morphological awareness); that is, performance on both the morphological awareness task and the word-reading task may reflect a general analytical approach toward language (e.g., Bowey, 1994; Bowey & Patel, 1988). There is some evidence to support this hypothesis. For example, Carlisle

(1995) found that morphological awareness and phonological awareness together accounted for 34% of the variance in second graders' reading comprehension. Three tasks were used—morphological production, which accounted for 10% of the variance; morphological judgment, which accounted for 3% of the variance; and phonological awareness, which accounted for 3% of the variance. Thus, a total of 16% of the variance was accounted for by unique contributions of the linguistic awareness tasks. The remaining variance (18%) was shared, and it is this shared variance that may represent a general analytic regard for language.

The argument that different forms of linguistic awareness work in concert with one another makes sense. For example, for the project described earlier, the second-grade reading passages did not contain many morphologically complex words, so it would be hard to argue that morphological awareness on an oral task was directly applied to the reading and understanding of the words in the passages of the reading test. The same sort of explanation may help us interpret the results of other studies. For example, other researchers (e.g., Fowler & Liberman, 1995; Singson et al., 2000) found a significant relationship between performance on an oral morphological awareness task and a standardized word-reading test. Because few of the words on these word-reading tests are morphologically complex, some part of this relationship is probably also attributable to an analytical approach to naming words in isolation.

Two studies that investigated the relation of oral morphological awareness and word reading have included a task of reading morphologically complex words. These also show a significant relation (Carlisle, 2000; Elbro & Arnback, 1996). Carlisle (2000) found that for third and fifth graders, awareness of derivational structure and reading-derived forms were significantly related (.36 and .39 respectively, both $p < .05$). Elbro and Arnbak (1996) asked Danish adolescents with dyslexia and younger students with normally developing reading skills to read a set of complex words that were semantically transparent and nontransparent; the word-reading task included compounds, as well as inflections and derivations. The students with dyslexia read morphologically complex words that were semantically transparent faster and more accurately than they read nontransparent words. These researchers suggested that morpho-semantic transparency is a compensatory mechanism in word decoding and comprehension for dyslexic adolescents, one that may be more important for students with dyslexia than for younger students with comparable reading skills.

In a study mentioned earlier, Carlisle (2000) found differences in reading phonologically transparent and nontransparent words for normally achieving third and fifth graders. The two types of words were matched for word length and frequency (base and surface forms). Both third and fifth graders read transparent words significantly more accurately than they read shift words. In another study that focused on reading derived words, Carlisle, Stone, and Katz (2001) compared poor- and average-achieving readers' reading of stable (e.g., *cultural*) and shift forms (e.g., *natural*). The two types of words were matched for frequency of the base and derived forms, and all of the words were transparent orthographically. (The students were not asked to read the base forms.) A significant interaction was found for group and word type on both speed and accuracy measures of word naming. Both good and poor readers read stable words better than shift words, but the advantage for stable words was much more pronounced for the poor readers. The results of this study support Elbro and Arnbak's (1996) argument that awareness of morphological units in transparent forms may particularly facilitate word reading for poor readers, providing an advantage not evident from their ability to read other types of words.

Phonological and orthographic transparency may be an advantage for word reading when compared to reading words that lack such transparency. However, we should also ask whether transparent morphological structure is an advantage when compared to reading monomorphemic words of equivalent length. Carlisle and Stone (2003) attempted to answer this question by comparing students' reading of phonologically and orthographically transparent derived words (e.g., *shady* or *robber*) with their reading of words that look like complex words but are not—pseudoderived forms such as *lady* or *corner*. If student performance was similar in terms of accuracy and speed of reading two word types, we might conclude that these two types of transparency offered no particular advantage in word reading. In this study, three groups of students were given the two word types (real and pseudoderived words) in random order to read aloud; the two types of words were matched for spelling and word frequency. The results showed that poor readers in fourth through sixth grade, a group of chronological-age matched readers (CA), and reading-age-matched (RA) readers read the real derived words more accurately than they read the pseudoderived words. In terms of speed, the RAs were faster on the real than pseudo-forms, whereas the poor readers and CAs read the real and pseudoderived forms with equivalent speed. These results suggest that with common words (selected to be so because the RA students were second and third graders), two morphemes present an advantage over one morpheme, when the words are of equivalent length and frequency. Recognition of the smaller linguistic/orthographic units (e.g., *rob* and *-er*) might therefore aid students' word reading. Furthermore, morphological units in such transparent words appear to offer a benefit for both normally achieving readers and children with reading difficulties.

It is likely that any morphological processing that was carried out as students read words such as *shady* on the computer was not at the level of conscious application of analytical strategies. We would expect this, because the words are so common, and therefore are probably accessed via lexical representations (Gordon, 1989; Perfetti, 1992). There is some evidence to support this idea, because the older, normally achieving readers, read the words in less than 1 second on average—a good indication of automaticity of word reading. However, reading unfamiliar words might trigger the use of more deliberate word analysis,

and in cases in which an unfamiliar derived word contains a familiar base morpheme, there might be some way in which noticing a familiar base word aids the reading of a more complex word form. This appears to be the case for older elementary/middle school students (fourth through sixth grade), but not second and third graders. In this study (Carlisle & Stone, 2003), these groups of children were asked to read very uncommon words that had familiar base words within them (e.g., *pailful* or *queendom*). For the children in both age groups, regression analyses were run to determine whether the base-word frequency and the number of syllables in the word contributed to accuracy and speed of reading. If the base-word frequency made a significant contribution, it would suggest that the more familiar the base word, the more likely it would aid in word reading. If the number of syllables made a significant contribution, it would suggest that longer words were harder to read (and/or took longer to read).

The results showed that for the younger children, the two variables accounted for 51% of the variance in word-reading speed, but only the number of syllables made a significant contribution. For accuracy, the two variables accounted for 55% of the variance, but here, too, only the number of syllables was a significant contributor. For the older students, however, number of syllables affected speed (accounting for 39% of the variance), whereas both the familiarity of the base morphemes and the number of syllables affected accuracy of word reading (together accounting for 59% of the variance). Thus, for the older students, noticing the base appears to have had a positive effect on word-reading accuracy. For the younger students, this advantage has not yet been realized, possibly because they are just learning word-identification strategies for multisyllabic words, and also because they have had less experience encountering unfamiliar derivations in written texts.

It may be important to point out that the response latencies for these children were quite long—on average 1½ seconds for the older students, and over 2½ seconds for the younger students. As a point of comparison, these same older students were able to read high-frequency derived words in less than 1 second, thus showing "automaticity" of word recognition. We might surmise, then, that some amount of analytical processing took place in their efforts to recognize the very unfamiliar words.

There is much that we still do not know about morphological structure and word reading. Studies of adults have indicated that morphological decomposition affects word recognition, and that the effects cannot be attributed to simple overlap of orthographic elements, phonological similarity, or semantic relatedness (Fowler et al., 1985; Napps, 1989; Stoltz & Feldman, 1995). Along the same lines, there is evidence that, for adults, speed of recognition of base words (e.g., *love*) is influenced by family frequency—that is, the sum of the frequencies of the members of the word family (e.g., *lovely, lover, loveliness*) (Nagy, Anderson, Schommer, Scott, & Stallman, 1989). These results suggest that parsing complex words during reading supports ease of recognition of the base word itself. Our minds retain common morphemes in sound and spelling as familiar units.

Reading Comprehension: Integrating Form and Meaning

Morphological awareness should be expected to contribute to reading comprehension for the simple reason that morphological processing contributes to language comprehension. What is true for spoken language, we would expect to be true also for written language, unless we have evidence to the contrary. In the act of comprehending natural texts, morphologically complex words contribute lexical, semantic, and syntactic information. It is true that word-reading abilities contribute significantly to comprehension, because it is hard to understand passages that contain words that are not familiar and cannot be named. However, the ability to read morphologically complex words is only one part of the contribution of morphological knowledge or awareness to reading comprehension. We would expect, then, that linking analyses of form and meaning would be a crucial aspect of morphological awareness as it relates to reading comprehension.

As early as second grade, morphological awareness may make a contribution to reading comprehension. This finding was evident from a longitudinal study described earlier (Carlisle, 1995), in which the phonological and morphological awareness of first graders was assessed in the beginning of the school year, before the children had acquired sufficient reading skill. In the spring of the second grade, phonological awareness and morphological awareness together accounted for a significant portion of the variance in reading comprehension. Performance on a production task of morphological awareness made a significant, unique contribution, greater than that made by phonological awareness. This stands to reason, because morphological processing requires analysis of the syntactic and semantic components of words and word parts, not just their sound structure.

One concern is whether students actually access the semantic and syntactic information in derived words as a way to build meaning during reading. Tyler and Nagy (1990) investigated this aspect of students' analysis of morphologically complex words by asking ninth- and 11th-grade students to select the version of a target sentence that best paraphrased a given sentence. Construction of the sentences was based on pairs of words that differed only in the derivational suffix (e.g., *deceptive* and *deception*). A sample item for a suffixed word is as follows:

Mary was afraid that a general indecision about the use of nuclear weapons might be a threat to national security.

  a. Mary feared that, if most people couldn't make up their minds about using atomic bombs, the country could be put in danger. (Correct)
  b. Mary feared that a military officer who couldn't make up his mind about using atomic bombs might put the country in danger. (Syntactic error)
  c. Mary feared that a public discussion about using atomic bombs might put the country in danger. (Lexical error)
  d. Mary feared that a military officer who openly discussed using atomic bombs might put the country in danger. (Double error)

Notice, for example, that if the student misread or misinterpreted the word *indecision* as *indecisive*, he or she would likely pick item b, making a syntactic error. This study, then, provided a way to assess the extent to which students accurately process the syntactic and semantic/lexical roles of suffixes and words with suffixes in reading sentences. One finding from this study was that students made fewer errors on suffixed words than on nonsuffixed words that were similar in overall word frequency. Here, again, is evidence that morphological awareness supports efficient word learning and sentence processing. On the other hand, the results also showed that there were more syntactic errors for suffixed than for nonsuffixed words, revealing the difficulty of understanding the roles of suffixes both grammatically and semantically. Finally, the results also showed that poorer readers made more syntactic errors than did better readers.

In a study of third and fifth graders, Carlisle (2000) examined the extent to which performance on three different morphological awareness tasks contributed to reading comprehension: an oral morphological awareness task that required either producing or decomposing a derived word, a task of defining morphologically complex words, and a task of reading derived words. For the third graders, the three tasks accounted for 43% of the variance in reading comprehension; of the three morphology tasks, only the word-reading task made a significant independent contribution. For the fifth graders, the three morphology tasks accounted for 55% of the variance in reading comprehension. Of the three tasks, only the oral morphological awareness task made a significant independent contribution. These results suggest developmental changes in the importance of different aspects of morphological awareness to comprehension. For the third graders, the ability to read derived words was the major influence on their access to the ideas and information in the passages, whereas for the fifth graders, awareness of the structure, meaning, and grammatical roles of words played a more important role than the ability to decode derived words.

As part of a previously mentioned study of morphological awareness and reading,

Windsor (2000) carried out regression analyses to determine the contribution of morphological awareness to reading performance (word reading and comprehension). First, performance on the two oral tasks was reorganized; the transparent and opaque items on each task were added together to yield a transparent score and an opaque score. The three subject groups (language-disabled, chronological-age-matched, and language-age matched groups) were combined for these analyses, and age and vocabulary were entered first in both analyses. For word identification, the transparent score and the opaque score both accounted for an additionally significant portion of the variance, but of the two, the opaque score was the stronger contributor. For reading comprehension, the transparent score did not contribute significantly, but the opaque score did. Windsor interpreted the results as indicating the strong link between awareness of the structure of opaque words and reading performance. She noted the similarity of her results and those of Fowler and Liberman (1995), because in both studies, 26–27% of the variance in word reading was attributable to combined oral performance on transparent and opaque derived forms.

Windsor's study may be best suited to assess the relation of morphological processing to word reading, as opposed to comprehension, because of the nature of the morphological awareness tasks. Because these tasks focused on students' ability to decompose derived words and to identify the correct suffix in a sentence context, students may not have needed to focus on word structure as it relates to meaning. Furthermore, the target words for these tasks were selected on the basis of semantic transparency. As informative as the results are, they leave open issues concerning the impact of the complexities of semantic processing of derived words on reading comprehension.

Other researchers, too, have downplayed the fact that morphemes are units of meaning. In some studies (e.g., Singson et al., 2000; Windsor, 2000), differences in vocabulary knowledge are statistically controlled, before the relation of morphological awareness and reading is determined. If morphological processing leads to vocabulary growth, and morphological learning is dependent on familiarity of base words and affixes, removing the effects of word knowledge is a problematic concept where reading comprehension is concerned. Future studies should certainly address this issue. Among the many unanswered questions is whether vocabulary knowledge differentially affects performance on transparent and opaque words. It does seem that removing the influence of semantics and syntax (both of which are likely to be represented by a vocabulary score from a standardized test) would seem to have the effect of heightening the influence of the phonological aspects of morphological processing.

Some researchers have focused on the potential of morphological problem solving (to use Anglin's phrase) for vocabulary development. The premise is that students who are sensitive to the morphemic constituents within words may use this awareness as the basis for efficient word learning (Nagy & Anderson, 1984). The building-block analogy offered earlier would apply here: It is presumably easier to use known morphemes to learn and remember an unknown word than to learn an entirely unfamiliar word as a new lexical item. Support for this idea comes from a study by Freyd and Baron (1982), in which eighth graders and superior fifth graders were given a vocabulary test on which they were to define simple words (e.g., *bachelor*) and derived words (e.g., *oceanic*). The able fifth graders showed an advantage in defining the derived words, presumably because of their stronger verbal abilities. A follow-up task that involved learning the meanings of pseudowords showed that the fifth graders did better on words that were morphologically related (e.g., *skaf* = steal, and *skaffist* = thief), whereas the eighth graders performed similarly on related and unrelated words. The researchers concluded that students, especially those with excellent language-learning capabilities, use morphological relations to learn new words.

Wysocki and Jenkins (1987) studied morphological generalization when derived words with suffixes (e.g., *sapient*) were taught to the fourth, sixth, and eighth graders. By comparing performance on "transfer" words (words related to the taught words, e.g., *sapience*) and "control" words (words not taught), the researchers were able to determine the extent to which the students learned to derive meanings of unfamiliar forms of words. They also compared the effect of sentence contexts on the students' ability to provide appropriate definitions for the transfer and control words. The researchers found that the sixth and eighth graders far surpassed the fourth graders in their ability to provide definitions of unfamiliar words that included both semantic information from the base form and an awareness of the grammatical role of the suffix. They also found that when the words were semantically transparent, the students did not need the information from sentence contexts, whereas with words whose definitions were less evident from their morphological components, context was helpful in deriving meaning. The older students made better use of combined morphological generation and information from sentence contexts than did the younger students. Another finding from this study is that students, particularly the younger ones, tended to define the complex words by giving a definition of the base word or the original stimulus word. For example, sapient and sapience were defined similarly, with *sapient* having been the stimulus word.

The studies of students' understanding of derived words indicate the importance of morphological analysis for the purpose of meaning making. Too often, morphology is considered a matter of word form only, and the central component of linking analyses of form and meaning is neglected. It seems clear that if morphological processing abilities are going to facilitate comprehension, the integration of the semantic and syntactic information embedded in word structures must play a central role—acknowledging still that awareness of phonological and orthographic relations, and familiarity with the composite morphemes are necessary as well.

IMPLICATIONS FOR EDUCATION

To summarize the discussion, morphological processing is an integral part of language processing and plays a role in oral and written language comprehension. Preschool children learn productive forms of morphological composition, but morphological learning is still developing in the late school-age years, because the complexities of processing many derived forms requires considerable exposure to both oral and written language. Inflections are generally learned by the early elementary school years, whereas derivations are learned from the preschool years through adulthood, for individuals who are immersed in a language-rich environment. The special focus on derivation in this chapter is because it is this aspect of morphology that appears to be most closely tied to achievement in reading. With derivation in mind, certain factors affect morphological learning from early childhood on. Two of these factors are word and morpheme frequency, and word transparency. Frequency involves familiarity not only with the base form but also with affixes. Transparency is often regarded as a matter of the preservation of the base-word phonology in the complex word form, but in fact, orthographic transparency and semantic transparency are factors that affect perceptions of morphological relations and morphological learning as well.

For school-age children (grade 2 and above), morphological awareness has been shown to be related to word reading, even when accounting for the effects of vocabulary and phonological awareness. Because of the nature of word-reading processes, it is not surprising that formal aspects of morphological processing are closely related. However, when reading comprehension is the outcome of interest, understanding of the syntactic and semantic roles of derivations becomes increasingly important. Students with language-learning disabilities, like their peers, may derive benefits from awareness of the morphological structure of transparent words for word reading, but they also appear to experience greater problems learning complex morphological relations, as they are used to understand written texts.

Relatively little work has been done to date to develop instructional programs that would help children with language-learning

disabilities acquire effective morphological processing—both strategies and knowledge of words. Two programs designed to assist students with learning disabilities in learning higher level decoding skills have been developed by Henry (1988, 1993) and Lovett, Lacerenza, and Borden (2000). Henry has placed particular emphasis on the value of teaching students about base morphemes and affixes that come from three etymological sources. She has recommended that Anglo-Saxon words and word-formation principles be taught first, followed by Latin, and then Greek. Lovett, on the other hand, has studied methods to teach poor readers a variety of decoding strategies, one of which involves removing prefixes and/or suffixes in order to read the base word first (e.g., *taste* within *distasteful*), then read the whole word. These strategies are taught one at a time and practiced until they are well learned and the students show competence in trying out the different strategies on difficult, unfamiliar words. Results of studies suggest that both types of instructional programs are beneficial to struggling readers.

In terms of a focus on the meanings and grammatical roles played by morphologically complex words, some vocabulary programs include structural analysis as one of a number of useful strategies (National Reading Panel, 2000; Nagy, Osborn, Winsor, & O'Flahavan, 1994; Templeton, 1989). At present, we need systematic studies of methods to help students improve their awareness of morphological structure, their knowledge of affixes, and their understanding of how to untangle complex words during reading. Such studies would ideally provide us with insights into the characteristics of instructional programs that work well with students who have reading problems, as well as those who have more general language-learning disabilities.

Until such instructional programs are available to teachers and accepted by the educational community as vital parts of a complete program of instruction in reading, students with reading and language-learning disabilities are likely to continue to struggle with reading and understanding complex words. This is not only because they lack insights into the benefits of morphological analysis but also because they have simply learned less from their experiences with language over the years. This language–experience gap, by its very nature, adversely affects their knowledge and awareness of morphology.

To summarize, much work remains to be done in terms of understanding students' learning of morphology, the relation of such learning to literacy acquisition, and, above all, the components of instructional programs that support the development of students' morphological awareness. An underlying theme in this chapter has been the integrated nature of language processing that naturally accompanies the development of morphological awareness. Comprehending and using complex word forms requires integrated processing of phonology, semantics, syntax, and, of course, morphology. Currently, the most common form of instruction that involves morphologically complex words involves the teaching of spelling rules that govern suffix addition. Further research is needed to study programs of instruction for students, with and without language-learning disabilities, that focus on the ways that word structure informs meaning. Awareness of phonological and orthographic relations, and familiarity with the composite morphemes, are necessary for students' developing word-reading skills. However, if morphological processing abilities are going to facilitate comprehension, the integration of the semantic and syntactic information embedded in word structures must play a central role as well.

REFERENCES

Anglin, J. M. (1993). Vocabulary development: A morphological analysis. *Monographs of the Society for Research in Child Development, 58*(Serial No. 238).

Berko, J. (1958). The child's learning of English morphology. *Word, 14*, 150–177.

Bowerman, M. (1982). Reorganizational processes in lexical and syntactic development. In E. Wanner & L. Gleitman (Eds.), *Language acquisition: The state of the art* (pp. 319–346). Cambridge, UK: Cambridge University Press.

Bowey, J. (1994). Grammatical awareness and learning to read: A critique. In E. Assink (Ed.), *Literacy acquisition and social context* (pp. 122–149). London: Harvester Wheatsheaf/Prentice-Hall.

Bowey, J. A., & Patel, R. K. (1988). Metalinguistic ability and early reading achievement. *Applied Psycholinguistics, 9*, 367–383.

Brittain, M. M. (1970). Inflectional performance and early reading achievement. *Reading Research Quarterly, 6*, 34–48.

Brown, R. (1973). *A first language: The early stages.* Cambridge, MA: Harvard University Press.

Bybee, J. (1985). *Morphology: A study of the relation between meaning and form.* Amsterdam: Benjamins.

Bybee, J. (1995). Diachronic and typological properties of morphology and their implications for representation. In L. B. Feldman (Ed.), *Morphological aspects of language processing* (pp. 225–246). Hillsdale, NJ: Erlbaum.

Carlisle, J. F. (1988). Knowledge of derivational morphology and spelling ability in fourth, sixth, and eighth graders. *Applied Psycholinguistics, 9*, 247–266.

Carlisle, J. F. (1995). Morphological awareness and early reading achievement. In L. B. Feldman (Ed.), *Morphological aspects of language processing* (pp. 189–209). Hillsdale, NJ: Erlbaum.

Carlisle, J. F. (2000). Awareness of the structure and meaning of morphologically complex words: Impact on reading. *Reading and Writing, 12*(3–4), 169–190.

Carlisle, J. F., & Fleming, J. (2003). Lexical processing of morphologically complex words in the elementary years. *Scientific Studies of Reading, 7*, 239–253.

Carlisle, J. F., & Nomanbhoy, D. (1993). Phonological and morphological development. *Applied Psycholinguistics, 14*, 177–195.

Carlisle, J. F., & Stone, C. A. (2003). The effects of morphological structure on children's reading of derived words. In E. Assink & D. Santa (Eds.), *Reading complex words: Cross-language studies* (pp. 27–52) New York: Kluwer Academic.

Carlisle, J. F., Stone, C. A., & Katz, L. A. (2001). The effects of phonological transparency on reading derived words. *Annals of Dyslexia, 51*, 249–274.

Champion, A. H. (1997). Knowledge of suffixed words in reading and oral language contexts: A comparison of reading disabled and normal readers. *Annals of Dyslexia, 47*, 29–55.

Chomsky, C. (1970). Reading, writing, and phonology. *Harvard Educational Review, 40*, 287–309.

Clahsen, H. (1991). *Child language and developmental dysphasia.* Amsterdam: Benjamin.

Clark, E. V. (1982). The young word maker: A case study of innovation in the child's lexicon. In E. Wanner & L. Gleitman (Eds.), *Language acquisition: The state of the art* (pp. 390–425). Cambridge, UK: Cambridge University Press.

Clark, E. V. (1992). Later lexical development and word formation. In P. Fletcher & B. MacWhinney (Eds.), *The handbook of child language* (pp. 393–412). Oxford, UK: Blackwell.

Derwing, B. L., & Baker, W. J. (1979). Morpheme recognition and the learning of rules for derivational morphology. *Canadian Journal of Linguistics, 21*, 38–66.

Derwing, B. B. L., Smith, M. L., & Wiebe, G. E. (1995). On the role of spelling in morpheme recognition: Experimental studies with children and adults. In L. B. Feldman (Ed.), *Morphological aspects of language processing* (pp. 3–27). Hillsdale, NJ: Erlbaum.

Elbro, C., & Arnbak, E. (1996). The role of morpheme recognition and morphological awareness in dyslexia. *Annals of Dyslexia, 46,* 209–240.

Fowler, A. E., & Liberman, I. Y. (1995). The role of phonology and orthography in morphological awareness. In L. B. Feldman (Ed.), *Morphological aspects of language processing* (pp. 157–188). Hillsdale, NJ: Erlbaum.

Fowler, C., Napps, S., & Feldman, L. B. (1985). Relations among regular and irregular morphologically related words in the lexicon as revealed by repetition priming. *Memory and Cognition, 13,* 241–255.

Freyd, P., & Baron, J. (1982). Individual differences in acquisition of derivational morphology. *Journal of Verbal Learning and Verbal Behavior, 21,* 282–295.

Gopnik, M., & Crago, M. (1991). Familial aggregation of a developmental language disorder. *Cognition, 39,* 1–50.

Gordon, P. (1989). Levels of affixation in the acquisition of English morphology. *Journal of Memory and Language, 28,* 519–530.

Henderson, E. (1985). *Teaching spelling.* Boston: Houghton Mifflin.

Henry, M. K. (1988). Beyond phonics: Integrated decoding and spelling instruction based on word origin and structure. *Annals of Dyslexia, 38,* 259–275.

Henry, M. K. (1993). Morphological structure: Latin and Greek roots and affixes as upper grade code strategies. *Reading and Writing: An Interdisciplinary Journal, 5,* 227–241.

Jarvella, R. J., & Snodgrass, J. G. (1974). Seeing ring in rang and retain in retention: On recognizing stem morphemes in printed words. *Journal of Verbal Learning and Verbal Behavior, 13,* 590–598.

Jones, N. K. (1991). Development of morphophonemic segments in children's mental representations of words. *Applied Psycholinguistics, 12,* 217–239.

Leonard, L. B. (1998). *Children with specific language impairment.* Cambridge, MA: MIT Press.

Leonard, L., McGregor, K., & Allen, G. (1992). Grammatical morphology and speech perception in children with specific language impairment. *Journal of Speech and Hearing Research, 35,* 1076–1085.

Leong, C. K. (1989). Productive knowledge of derivational rules in poor readers. *Annals of Dyslexia, 39,* 94–115.

Lovett, M., Lacerenza, L., & Borden, S. L. (2000). Putting struggling readers on the PHAST track: A program to integrate phonological and strategy-based remedial reading instruction and maximize outcomes. *Journal of Learning Disabilities, 33,* 458–476.

MacWhinney, B. (1978). The acquisition of morphophonology. *Monographs of the Society for Research in Child Development, 43*(1-2, Serial No. 174).

Mahoney, D. L. (1994). Using sensitivity to word structure to explain variance in high school and college level reading ability. *Reading and Writing: An Interdisciplinary Journal, 6,* 19–44.

Mahoney, D., Singson, M., & Mann, V. (2000). Reading ability and sensitivity to morphological relations. *Reading and Writing: An Interdisciplinary Journal, 12,* 191–218.

Nagy, W. E., & Anderson, R. C. (1984). How many words in printed school English? *Reading Research Quarterly, 19,* 304–330.

Nagy, W. E., Anderson, R., Schommer, M., Scott, J. A., & Stallman, A. C. (1989). Morphological families and word recognition. *Reading Research Quarterly, 24,* 262–282.

Nagy, W. E., Osborn, J., Winsor, P., & O'Flahavan, J. (1994). Structural analysis: Some guidelines for instruction. In F. Lehr & J. Osborn (Eds.), *Reading, language, and literacy: Instruction for the 21st century* (pp. 45–58). Hillsdale, NJ: Erlbaum.

Napps. S. E. (1989). Morphemic relationships in the lexicon: Are they distinct from formal and semantic relationships? *Memory and Cognition, 17,* 729–739.

National Reading Panel. (2000). *Teaching children to read: Reports of the subgroups.* Washington, DC: National Institute of Child Health and Human Development. Available online at *http://www.nichd.nih.gov/publications/nrp/report.htm*

Perfetti, C, (1992). The representation problem in reading acquisition. In P. Gough, L. Ehri, & R. Treiman (Eds.), *Reading acquisition* (pp. 107–143). Hillsdale, NJ: Erlbaum.

Rice, M., & Oetting, J. (1993). Morphological deficits in children with SLI: Evaluation of number marking and agreement. *Journal of Speech and Hearing Research, 36,* 1249–1257.

Schreuder, R., & Baayan, R. H. (1995). Modeling morphological processing. In L. B. Feldman (Ed.), *Morphological aspects of language processing* (pp. 131–154). Hillsdale, NJ: Erlbaum.

Singson, M., Mahoney, D., & Mann, V. (2000). The relation between reading ability and morphological skills: Evidence from derivational suffixes. *Reading and Writing: An Interdisciplinary Journal, 12,* 219–252.

Smith-Lock, K. M. (1995). Morphological usage and awareness in children with specific language impairment. *Annals of Dyslexia, 45,* 163–185.

Stoltz, J. A., & Feldman, L. B. (1995). The role of orthographic and semantic transparency of the base morpheme in morphological processing. In L. B. Feldman (Ed.), *Morphological aspects of language processing* (pp. 109–129). Hillsdale, NJ: Erlbaum.

Templeton, S. (1989). Tacit and explicit knowledge of derivational morphology: Foundations for a unified approach to spelling and vocabulary development in the intermediate grades and beyond. *Reading Psychology, 10,* 233–253.

Templeton, S., & Scarborough-Franks, L. (1985). The spelling's the thing: Knowledge of derivational morphology in orthography and phonology among older students. *Applied Psycholinguistics, 6,* 371–390.

Tyler, A., & Nagy, W. E. (1989). The acquisition of English derivational morphology. *Journal of Memory and Language, 28,* 649–667.

Tyler, A., & Nagy, W. E. (1990). Use of derivational morphology during reading. *Cognition, 36,* 17–34.

White, T. G., Power, M. A., & White, S. (1989). Morphological analysis: Implications for teaching and understanding vocabulary growth. *Reading Research Quarterly, 24,* 283–304.

Windsor, J. (1994). Children's comprehension and production of derivational suffixes. *Journal of Speech and Hearing Research, 37,* 408–417.

Windsor, J. (2000). The role of phonological opacity in reading achievement. *Journal of Speech, Language, and Hearing Research, 43,* 50–61.

Windsor, J., & Hwang, M. (1997). Knowledge of derivational suffixes in students with language-learning disabilities. *Annals of Dyslexia, 47,* 57–68.

Wysocki, J. K., & Jenkins, J. R. (1987). Deriving word meanings through morphological generalization. *Reading Research Quarterly, 22,* 66–81.

16

Syntactic Contributions to Literacy Learning

CHERYL M. SCOTT

There is increasing concern about the vast number of children and adults in the United States who struggle to read and write. Unfavorable literacy achievement comparisons with other developed nations led the National Academy of Sciences to convene a committee of reading experts to study the problem (Committee on the Prevention of Reading Difficulties in Young Children, 1998). Shortly thereafter, the U.S. Congress established a panel of experts to cull through research on reading instruction to determine whether a consensus of best instructional practices could be reached. The resulting report detailed recommendations in phonemic awareness, phonics, fluency, vocabulary, and text-comprehension instruction (Report of the National Reading Panel, 2000). Similarly, in the area of writing, national tests show that a significant number of U.S. students, even by the time they are twelfth graders, struggle to compose adequate informational and persuasive texts (Persky, Daane, & Jin, 2003). Reports such as these discuss the underlying causes of literacy difficulties at the level of individual sounds (e.g., segmenting words into component sounds), words (word recognition, weak lexical representation), and discourse (e.g., weak knowledge of text structure). The same reports devote little, if any, attention to sentence-level grammar as a significant contributor to the nation's literacy ills or as an instructional target.

The lack of attention to syntax in these national reports is curious for several reasons. Syntax, of course, is a fundamental component of language, and sentences are the "domain" of syntax, or grammar.[1] After Chomksy (1965) provided a theoretical template for the study of language acquisition, research into children's acquisition of grammar played a central role in the burgeoning field of developmental psycholinguistics. Syntax has always been viewed as a core deficit in children with the high-incidence diagnosis of specific language impairment (Leonard, 1998; Paul, 2001; Rice, 2000), and these same children are at high risk for reading and writing disorders (Catts, Fey, Zhang, & Tomblin, 1999; Scarborough, 1991). Why, then, has syntax seemingly taken a backseat in the agendas of developmental and instructional literacy research? Indeed, why devote an entire chapter to sentences in this handbook?

The answer, in part, is that sentences "do the work" of text. We all speak, listen, read, and write to communicate messages. These messages are usually conceived and remembered at a textual level; that is, we want to understand a story (not a sentence), or we want to persuade someone to agree with our point of view (not a sentence). However, one by one, sentences communicate the key propositions that eventually add up to a text with its associated "gist." In written form, sentence boundaries are unambiguously communicated with appropriate punctuation and spacing. Do some children have particular difficulty with the syntax of sentences and, if so, how does that affect their ability to read and write? These are the main questions addressed here.

This chapter is divided into three broad sections. The first establishes a framework for the topic by discussing the notion of syntactic complexity—those factors that make one sentence more difficult than another to comprehend or produce, as well as the different types of complexity in written, compared to spoken, language. Also covered in this section is a review of sentence comprehension and production models, with specific applications to reading and writing. In the second section, discussion turns to the relationship between syntax and reading disorders. The nature of this relationship is explored in research addressing two types of questions: (1) whether a child's facility with syntax in early development predicts later reading, and (2) whether good and poor readers perform differently on syntactic tasks. In the final section, the relationship between syntax and writing development and disorders is explored.

SYNTACTIC COMPLEXITY AND LITERACY

What Makes Sentences Complex?

Sentences vary considerably in the challenges they present to the user and, specifically of interest for this chapter, to the developing reader and writer. One morning recently, I picked up the morning newspaper and encountered the following lead-off sentence in an article on the front page:

As congressional leaders declared bluntly Sunday that they didn't believe former Enron Corp. chief executive Jeffrey Skilling's claims of ignorance about the tangled financial deals that brought his company down, Skilling's former boss, Kenneth Lay, said he would not testify before Congress this week.

To comprehend this 44-word sentence with five verbs (and clauses), at some level and in some manner I had to understand that the main subject and predicate would not be found until the 34th word of the sentence, and that the three preceding (left-branching) clauses (and the propositions they encoded) were subordinate to the matrix (main) clause. Fortunately, not all sentences are this long or this challenging, but they do exist along a continuum of complexity according to a variety of characteristics (Biber, 1988).

Stimulated by Chomsky's (1965) seminal generative grammar, there has been a great deal of theoretical and empirical work on what constitutes syntactic complexity in sentences. Some investigators have worked mainly at the theoretical (representational) level, working out the specifics of the abstract representations of sentences, while others have put these representations to the "test" in experiments that ask individuals to process sentences and act on them in some way. Work has been done on syntactic complexity as a determinant of both sentence comprehension (Gibson, 1998) and production (Thompson & Faroqi-Shaw, 2002).

At least three general factors contribute to the complexity of a sentence. First, sentences are more or less difficult to process depending on certain features of open-class words (nouns and verbs) and their relationships. For example, children have more difficulty comprehending reversible passive sentences ("The cat was chased by the dog") than nonreversible passives ("The apple was eaten by the boy") (Bever, 1970), where, in the nonreversible example, interpretation is aided by the fact that apples do not eat boys. Characteristics of verbs have syntactic relevance, namely, the argument structure complexity obligated by the verb,[2] as shown in studies of the production difficulties of individuals with aphasia (Thompson, 2003), and verb errors made by children with specific language impairment (Grela & Leonard, 2000).

Two additional contributors to complexity are the number and type of syntactic operations. The number of syntactic operations is usually reflected in sentence length. Indeed, average sentence length is probably the most commonly used metric of young children's overall level of expressive language development (Brown, 1973; Templin, 1957) precisely because, when children add grammatical structures to their repertoire (e.g., they add the auxiliary verb *is* to the verb *sleeping*), these operations add words. Likewise, sentence length is usually one of several key variables in text readability formulas (e.g., Fry, 1977).

The type of syntactic operation is also a contributor; some are harder than others. For example, sentences in which the subordinate adverbial clause precedes the main clause ("Until she had 500 signatures, she could not use the petition") are harder for elderly adults to process than those that follow the main clause ("She could not use the petition until she had 500 signatures") (Kemper, 1987). A great deal of work on relative clauses has shown that object-extracted relatives ("The mayor who the reporter scolded walked away") are harder to process than subject-extracted relatives ("The mayor who scolded the reporter walked away") (Gibson, 1998). The list of difficult structures is long, but many of these can be captured in several overarching principles, including the following:

- Sentences that do not conform to canonical word order (subject–verb–object [SVO] in English), such as passives or object-cleft sentences ("It was the teacher that the boy admired").
- Sentences with any type of long-distance dependency, in which a syntactic prediction "awaits" confirmation. This is the case in sentences in which the main subject and verb are interrupted by intervening clauses or phrases (e.g., sentences with center-embedded relative clauses), or in *wh-* questions in which the *wh-* pronoun "moves" from the word it indexes, leaving a gap (e.g., "What did the boy on the team take [missing object] to the game?").
- Sentences with local ambiguities that require a reanalysis to resolve (e.g., "After the fans applauded the players returned to the bullpen"; "The clown had frightened children at the party").
- Sentences in which reference must be resolved, either in cases of empty pronoun (PRO) subjects (e.g., "Sally patted Nancy before [PRO] turning out the light") or in cases where there are several potential referents (e.g., "Mary sees Jane is feeding herself"; "John noticed Bill is beating him").

Complexity and Language Development

The ability to comprehend and produce more complex sentences with age has been well researched in children with typical and atypical language development. Indexes of syntactic complexity have been built to capture early developmental periods (e.g., Crystal, Fletcher, & Garman, 1976; Scarborough, 1990a). A common experimental paradigm in comparing young children with and without language disorders is to observe their responses to sentences that are systematically varied for complexity (e.g., reversible vs. nonreversible passives in a recent study by Bishop, Bright, James, Bishop, & Van der Lely, 2000). Similarly, syntactic complexity is frequently treated as a dependent variable when studying spoken and written language production differences in school-age children with language and learning disabilities[3] (e.g., Gillam & Johnston, 1992; Scott & Windsor, 2000). The number of syntactic operations per sentence increases for both speaking and writing through the adolescent years as children produce longer sentences with elaborated phrase structure and combinations of clauses (see reviews in Nippold, 1998; Perera, 1984; Romaine, 1984; Scott, 1988a, 1988b). The relevance of the notion of syntactic complexity in the developmental literature on spoken language, and as a variable in language disorders, then, seems clear. As will be shown, the relative lack of interest in syntax (and sentences) as a contributor to literacy problems, and as a target of literacy instruction, is therefore puzzling.

Complexity and Language Modality

In a discussion about how children become competent at comprehending and producing written sentences, it is important to ask whether written sentences are more or less complex than spoken sentences. To continue with the examples of complexity cited thus far, are object-cleft sentences and center-embedded relative clauses more frequent in written language? This is a difficult question, because written–spoken sentence complexity variations could result from genre (a different type of language; e.g., chatting vs. academic prose) as well as modality (a different delivery system, via writing or speaking).

If we imagine written and spoken language activities during a typical school day of a fifth grader, it is reasonable to assume that this student is immersed in expository (informational) reading and writing. In terms of sentence-level structures, expository text favors different structures than are found in this child's conversations with peers, to be sure, but this type of language is also different from a fiction book (narrative) that the student might be reading. Structures more common in expository sentences include noun phrases with more extensive pre- and postmodification (*the eventual future of the Cherokee Nation in the Oklahoma Territory was difficult to predict*), passives, nonfinite forms of verbs (verbs not marked for tense or number, e.g., *failing to improve in the last quarter, the economy . . .*), phrasal coordination, and nominalizations (the nominal derivative of a verb, e.g., *adaptation*) (Biber, 1988). In adult written texts, informational sentences (those found in newspaper editorials, official documents, etc.) are on average considerably longer than narrative sentences (personal letters, novels) (Frances & Kucera, 1982). A partial answer to the question about how complexity differs in speaking and writing, then, can be answered by referring to genre differences. To the extent that informational language is more often delivered in written form, written language will be different from spoken language.

Another approach to the question is to ask whether there are differences attributable exclusively to modality, or the act of writing as opposed to speaking the language. Halliday (1985, 1987) has argued that written sentences are lexically dense (a

higher proportion of open-class, content words) and nominally embedded (a larger number of structures that pre- and postmodify head nouns of noun phrases, such as attributive adjectives, relative clauses, and prepositional phrases), a code he referred to as hierarchical. Speakers, however, proceed by stringing together clauses with coordinating and subordinating conjunctions (a linear code). Halliday (1987) illustrated the difference with the following comparison (p. 62):

- More "written": Every previous visit had left me with a sense of the risk to others in further attempts at action on my part.
- More "spoken": Whenever I'd visited there before I'd end up feeling that other people might get hurt if I tried to do anything more.

Halliday concluded from his studies that complex sentences occur in both spoken and written language, but certain kinds of complexity congregate in writing. Biber (2001), analyzing a variety of adult spoken and written texts for the co-occurrence of a set of sentence complexity features (e.g., types of dependent clauses, noun phrase integration features) concluded that the fundamental difference between speaking and writing complexity is one of variety. Whereas writing affords considerable freedom to draw on an elaborate array of complexity features as befits the particular text type, speaking, regardless of the register, restricts the kinds of features used. Both Biber (1988, 2001) and Halliday (1985) looked to processing differences inherent in the act of speaking and writing for explanation. Speaking, with online temporal constraints, favors a linear code. The speaker is under considerable pressure to be fluent, without too many revisions or pauses, particularly long ones. The writer can take more time to consider wording and structure carefully and can revise and edit as long as patience and time permit. With more time, embedding, a hierarchical process (as opposed to conjunction, a linear process), can flourish.

Another way to determine whether there are structural differences attributable to modality per se would require comparisons of spoken and written renditions of the same material. In fact, studies with adults (Beaman, 1984) and school-age children with and without language learning disabilities (Scott, 2002a; Scott & Klutsenbaker, 1989) support Halliday's (1987) characterization of spoken and written sentence form. Indirect evidence of modality differences can be found in studies that compare oral with literate forms of narratives (book retelling) in young preschool children (Sulzby, 1996). Even young children with language impairments retell book stories with literate features, albeit at a lower rate than age peers for certain forms (Kaderavek & Sulzby, 2000).

To summarize, not all sentences, spoken or written, are equally easy to process, whether one is a young child or an adult with a range of language abilities. In fact, the complexity "value" of sentences has been one of the most studied variables of language processing generally, and more specifically in language acquisition and disorders. In light of the well-established connection between spoken language abilities and literacy acquisition, it is pertinent to ask whether a child's facility with syntax is an important variable in reading and writing. The question is all the more interesting, because written sentences appear to be different from spoken forms when it comes to sentence complexity. The next portion of this section considers complexity further within theoretical models of sentence comprehension and production. Most models assume a tacit, implicit level of language processing. This section ends with a discussion of how, in addition to tacit processing, reading and writing at times most likely require more explicit, conscious levels of sentence processing and awareness.

Sentence Processing Models and Literacy

Whether listening, speaking, reading, or writing, language users must process the grammar of sentences. Most models of sentence processing[4] are found in the area of listening and reading, with some work in speaking, and very little in writing. Most of the empirical work is with adults. Sentence complexity is frequently a major variable

that is manipulated in experimental work on sentence processing. The importance of understanding how sentences are processed when individuals read and write seems obvious enough. As Rayner and Pollatsek (1994) point out, sentences correspond to "idea units," are universally marked in alphabetic writing systems (that must be read/comprehended or written/produced), and, unlike larger text units such as paragraphs, can be unambiguously identified as legal (grammatical) or not. As is the case for comparing the form of written and spoken sentences, we can ask if written sentence processing is different from spoken.

Reading Sentences

Sentence comprehension in reading draws on several types of information, including syntax itself, word meaning, and the meaning of word combinations. Rayner and Pollatsek (1994) distinguish three levels of sentence comprehension in reading. As Chomsky's famous *colorless green ideas sleep furiously,* or examples with nonsense words (e.g., *the prenacks chaded the fronkins*) illustrate, sentence grammar can be comprehended apart from sentence meaning on the basis of word order and morphosyntactic markers (*the,* past tense *-ed,* plural *-s* in the nonsense example). At a second level, sentences can be comprehended for their meaning (who does what to whom), which involves taking the meaning of individual words and putting these together to form sentence meaning. Just as sentences do not have to be semantically meaningful to convey grammatical meaning, they do not have to be perfectly grammatical to convey semantic meaning (e.g., "Yesterday I walk home from school"). Sentence pairs such as "Mary kissed John"/"John was kissed by Mary" and "John is easy to please"/"John is eager to please" remind us that syntactic and semantic contributions to sentence comprehension are usually operating in tandem. The fact that we easily understand these sentences in spite of their tricky surface structures is testimony to the fact that we know the underlying phrase structure representations of the sentences. A third level of sentence comprehension involves propositional interpretation and assessment of truth value. Because these analyses frequently draw on broader stretches of text, this level is not considered further here.

Phrase structure grammars are not intended as representations of how listeners/readers arrive at a syntactic analysis of a sentence in real time. Models of sentence processing in real time are known as theories of syntactic parsing. A problem for parsers is the fact that, as words "role out" in the sentence, they can be grammatically ambiguous, as in the following example from Rayner and Pollatsek (1994, p. 247).

(1) Since Jay always jogs a mile this seems like a short distance to him.
(2) Since Jay always jogs a mile seems like a short distance to him.

The analysis of the word *mile* as a complement of *jogs* works for the first sentence but not for the second. To account for sentences like these, Frazier and Rayner (1982) proposed a garden-path model of parsing in which readers go up a garden path, constructing "first-available" analyses that may have to be revised later on (as in the second sentence). Eye-movement measurements during reading confirm that readers are put off when they encounter the verb *seems* in the second sentence and are faced with recalculating their first analysis (Frazier, 1987; Frazier & Rayner, 1982). Longer fixation times in cases like this, and in other instances of syntactic stress, validate the view of a parser that responds in measurable ways to complexity factors during reading (Rayner, 1998).

The literature on sentence parsing in skilled (adult) readers is extensive, and a variety of alternatives and refinements to the garden path account have appeared (e.g., Holmes, 1987). Detailed processing accounts of specific types of structures, such as those involved in long distance (filler-gap) dependencies, are available (Frazier, 1987). There has been considerable work on the interface of memory and the stages of sentence comprehension (Waters, Caplan, & Hildebrandt, 1987). Questions about the relationship between purely syntactic processing (the first level of processing) and se-

mantic processing (the second level), and the relative independence and timing features of both, abound (Rayner, Carlson, & Frazier, 1983). Another question is the extent to which the results of a syntactic analysis are actually used (Flores d'Arcais, 1987). Finally, the continuing development of brain imaging holds promise for understanding the neural basis of syntactic processing and advancing theories even further (Caplan, 2002; see also Mody, Chapter 3, this volume, for a review of neuroimaging). All of these accounts require familiarity with post–1965 (Chomsky, 1965) accounts of generative grammar (for an overview, see Shapiro, 1997).

The Importance of Parsing In Reading: An Example of a Fourth-Grade Reader

The consequences of inaccurate sentence-by-sentence parsing in reading became clear to me several years ago in a clinical session on reading comprehension with John,[5] a 10-year-old with a language learning disability. We were working on reading comprehension strategies using a reciprocal teaching approach (Palincsar & Brown, 1984). The passage in question was from a typical fourth-grade social studies text; the topic was the settlement of territories west of the eastern seaboard. One of the strategies in the reciprocal teaching approach involves generating questions over material just read. John read the following passage (sentence numbers have been added):

(1) Thousands of pioneers went to live in the unsettled land between the Appalachian Mountains and the Mississippi River. (2) This land was then known as the West. (3) Land that was part of the United States but did not have enough people to be a state was called a territory. (4) The land to the west of the Appalachian Mountains was divided into two territories. (5) The Northwestern Territory was the land north of the Ohio River and east of the Mississippi.

Then it was his turn to make up a question, which is reproduced below:

Why was the apple ation mountains divided into two parts?

John's question provided a unique window into the normally unobserved parse of a single sentence during reading. It revealed that he understood sentence 4 to mean that the Appalachian Mountains (themselves) were divided into two territories. He had incorrectly attached the verb (*was divided*) to the immediately preceding noun (*Appalachian mountains*) rather than the true head noun (*land*) of the entire subject noun phrase that preceded the verb (*The land to the west of the Appalachian mountains*). John used a strategy commonly used by children much younger when they encounter sentences with this type of long distance dependency— when in doubt, attach the verb to the closest previous noun (Chomsky, 1969). John's question and what it revealed about his parsing ability provide a clear demonstration that the comprehension of individual sentences is central in the broader picture of text comprehension.

Producing Sentences

The sentence as a unit of language production has also received attention in recent years (Bock & Levelt, 1994; Levelt, 1989, 1999). In general, these models proceed serially from the intent to speak (the highest message level) "down" to a level at which major lexical concepts are chosen, down further to the arrangement of these lexical items in a grammatical framework, and finally to a level of programming and executing the articulatory gestures that result in intelligible speech. Thompson and Faroqi-Shaw (2002) summarized the grammatical encoding portions of the model to include the following:

- *Functional assignment:* Assigning roles such as agent, theme, and experiencer, which, in English, are signaled by word order. The verb is central at this level, because it carries information via its argument structure that obligates one or more functional roles (e.g., agent, experiencer).
- *Functional processing:* Ordering of items within phrases and ordering of phrases within a clause-size unit (constituent assembly), and generating number, tense, and aspect markers, along with auxiliary

verbs, determiners, and prepositions (morpheme retrieval).

Each of these processes has an ample literature exploring operational details and interactions. Speech error data have been a mainstay of this research, and the regularity of such errors underscores the rule-governed nature of the encoding process. Thompson and Faroqi-Shaw (2002) reviewed the past 25 years of research and concluded that distinct levels of processing and a basically modular organization, both basic tenets of Garrett's original framework (1975) of grammatical sentence encoding, remain in force.

Compared to the literature on sentence processing in listening, reading, and speaking, models of the process of generating written sentences are undeveloped. This is not surprising when the many varieties of writing, the time it takes to write (compared to much faster times for reading, listening, and speaking), and the two major ways to write (typing vs. handwriting) are considered. A skilled typist writing an e-mail to a friend, describing something that happened that day, may be able to produce language at a rate that approaches speaking, but this would be a very different situation than that of the writer struggling to compose an academic text.

Daiute (1984), however, chose to concentrate on the similarities of writing and speaking in her study of the first-draft writing (placement essays) of college freshmen and students in the 6th through 12th grades. Daiute noticed a similarity in the types of errors produced by speakers and writers, and proposed that the same short-term memory limitations affected sentence accuracy. As in speaking, a basic processing problem for the writer is to coordinate the grammar of the current sentence under production with that of the previous sentence. However, specific grammatical information from the previous sentence has already been lost due to short-term memory limitations (the sentence has been recoded for abstract propositional content). Even though the writer has access to the previous sentence, Daiute's (1984) analysis of first draft writing errors suggested that writers do not consult such sentences during the production of the following sentence. She illustrated what can happen when a writer forgets the specific grammar of the previous sentence with the following example: *Four years ago was the best time of my career which I wasn't in a position to know that then* (Daiute, 1984, p. 209). In this example, the underlined portion "overlaps" with two clauses. These types of errors occurred more frequently when memory was taxed—in longer sentences, at spots well "into" the sentence, and at the start of optional structures that add complexity (Daiute, 1984). Even though Daiute's work looked promising as an explanation of certain types of writing errors and for ties to the more frequently modeled process of speaking, there does not appear to be follow-up work along similar lines.

Additional, Unique, and Conscious Uses of Syntax in Reading and Writing

Level of Awareness

Models of sentence comprehension and production assume an automatic, unconscious, tacit level of processing. The models do not claim that sentence parsers (or producers) are consciously aware of phrase structures in the sense of being able to name parts of sentences and discuss how they work. The only claim is that they behave as if they have this knowledge (e.g., they could identify *Mary kissed John* and *John was kissed by Mary* as grammatical and synonymous).

When considering reading and writing, however, the distinction between an automatic and a more conscious level of processing becomes important. Both activities, particularly in developmental stages, are thought to require, at times, a more conscious level of language awareness that presumably would include some type of syntactic awareness. This awareness is unlikely to be dichotomous, either unconscious or conscious; it is more likely to vary along a continuum of conscious awareness and effort. At one end of the continuum, we might skim a written text without parsing any sentence in its entirety. Or, to pursue the e-mail

example, we could dash off an e-mail with hardly a second thought about sentences, style, or effect on the reader at the other end. But for many instances of more deliberate reading and writing, a more explicit, conscious type of encounter with syntax is required (Menyuk & Chesnick, 1997). A typical scenario in late elementary school and beyond is one in which students are reading to learn about a topic that is partially or entirely new, in a book that may use unknown or partially known words and, as outlined earlier, are encountering sentence structures quite different from casual conversation. Students must digest this information, and perhaps summarize this newly learned material in written form. Even harder, the student might be asked to integrate new material from several recently read sources into a cohesive written whole. As such, a student may need to be aware of sentences in a different way, at a metalinguistic level not required for casual speaking and listening. Of course, all text-level writing, by virtue of the fact that sentences are explicitly marked by punctuation, requires conscious decisions about sentences that are not necessary for listening, speaking, or even reading.

To the reader, the language on the written page comes without intonation, stress, rhythm, and pause—all cues that indicate how words are grouped together. Because spoken language comes with these prosodic cues, listeners, in essence, have the first round of syntactic processing done for them (Perera, 1984). Without such information, sentence parsing in reading is a harder task. Tying together the lack of prosody with the parsing challenges of complex written sentences, Perera (1984) hypothesized that sentences will be hard to parse in reading when (1) predictions are harder to make, (2) sentences do not divide into optimal units, and (3) when a heavy burden is imposed on working memory (p. 287). Several examples of each category are listed in Table 16.1. These are the types of sentences that might give a child or adolescent reader pause, and, hopefully, trigger rereading or another strategic maneuver.

Perera (1984) also reviewed research from a variety of studies on adolescent and

TABLE 16.1. Examples of Sentence Structures That Make Text Harder to Comprehend

Structures that are difficult to predict

These include a wide variety of sentence patterns that are less familiar because they occur less often in the language, are acquired late, or are found almost exclusively in written language, including:

Concealed negatives: *This type of parrot is rarely seen with its mate.*

Literary negatives: *Nowhere is this more evident than in the comparison of pre- and postwar economies.*

Long subject noun phrases: *Difference in water temperature, the abundance of food supplies and the availability of the right places to breed or spawn are the main reasons for the migration of aquatic animals.* (Perera, 1984, p. 292)

Nominalization: *The exploration and mapping of the Northwest Territories by Lewis and Clarke was of a scope never before seen.*

Ellipsis in coordinated sentences: *A camel is well equipped to survive in the desert, and a polar bear in the Artic* (Perera, 1984, p. 295)

Subject clauses introduced by a wh-word or (the fact) that: *What the readers want for their leisure reading is debatable.*

Non-finite clauses used as subjects: *Finding her views dismissed so easily led Joann to doubt her value to the organization.*

Structures that are difficult to segment

These include structures that complicate assignment of words/phrases to grammatical constituents, including:

Repeated words or word classes: *The costume that the child who performed disliked disappeared; The teacher she had had was given several awards.*

Optionally deleted function words: *The notorious judge decided [that] the case was without precedent; The teacher[that] the boy liked left for another position.*

Ambiguous function words: *The air is driven out as steam from the water fills the bottle.* (Perera, 1984, p. 310)

Words that belong to more than one grammatical class: *The old watch was auctioned off for a handsome sum; The faithful support the home team no matter what.*

Intrinsic structural ambiguity: *Animals who are uncontrolled frequently are impounded; Racing boats can be dangerous.*

Structures that tax working memory

These include any structures that require keeping a word or phrase in mind long enough to "complete" the constituent analysis, including:

Structures that interrupt main subjects and verbs (e.g., those with long postmodifying phrases or clauses that follow the head noun): *Harold, whose army had just marched across England after fighting an invading group of Norwegians back, was tired and sore. (Scott, 1988a)*

Ellipsis with long distances between the ellipsis and its referent: *John explained to Bill how to use the right club or the right conditions and circumstances but [   ] was not an effective teacher of actual technique.*

Note. The outline of structures and examples are adapted from Perera (1984). Additional examples and categories can be found there.

---

adult readers, pointing to an average span of 10 words for verbatim recall of read material. She suggests that for young and slow readers, syntactic predictions, ambiguities, and other processing anomalies that are not resolved within a 10-word space will tax the parser inordinately from the perspective of working memory.

Thus, while models of sentence comprehension and production generally presuppose that the language processor is a tacit mechanism, reading and writing is assumed to require, at times, a more explicit type of processing. Such times would include academic as opposed to social uses of language and forms of language that tax the processor (unknown words and long, syntactically complex sentences). To date, processing models have not included language awareness as a variable, and it would be difficult to do so without a more developed construct of what constitutes language awareness. Even so, we can assume that these models are applicable to reading and writing, but their exact fit is unknown.

Paraphrasing, Revising, and Other Literate Sentence-Level Activities

It is easy to imagine additional scenarios requiring a level of syntactic awareness that goes above and beyond anything required for casual spoken language, pleasurable reading, or casual writing. The student who is called upon to stand up before peers to argue a point will be effective at least in part because of style choices conveyed by syntax. This would seem to require the awareness that there is more than one way to say the same thing. Syntactic awareness is not the only skill needed to paraphrase, but it is an important one (Donahue & Pidek, 1993). Many a high school student practices paraphrasing sentences from original sources when writing term papers. Editing written work or monitoring spoken language requires that the language user be able to judge the grammaticality of sentences.

Spelling

Even in an unlikely endeavor such as spelling, syntax has a role. Young children are phonetic spellers whose major approach to the task is "spell it like it sounds." But this strategy causes problem for the child when spelling words such as *walked* and *fact,* whose endings sound alike. Eventually, the child's morphosyntactic awareness overrides phonetic strategies, enabling the child to spell correctly words such as *dressed, next, lost, cold,* and *filled* according to their nonverb, regular verb, or irregular verb status (Bryant, Nunes, & Bindman, 1997) as

well as phrases such as *oak trees* versus *tree's branches* (Bryant, Nunes, & Bindman, 2000). Particularly when editing for spelling errors, children with more advanced levels of syntactic awareness will have an advantage. I once worked with a child who could compose good written narrative summaries at the text and sentence levels. This fourth grader, however, was a terrible speller; furthermore, he lacked a level of morphosyntactic awareness that he could bring to the task of editing his spelling. In one narrative composition, not a single verb (of 32) that required the regular past tense ending *-ed* was spelled correctly. Intervention with this student consisted of teaching a self-questioning strategy ("Does this word function as a verb?") during editing, an activity designed to raise his level of morphosyntactic awareness.

This review of models of sentence processing and conditions of more conscious processing underscores the fact that the grammatical analysis of sentences is a critical component of text processing. Even though the process is imperfectly understood, models are becoming increasingly sophisticated in their ability to explain (1) what constitutes complexity for listeners, readers, and speakers, and (2) how these processes interrelate with lexical and other semantic components. It is important to approach the section that follows against this backdrop of the syntactic challenges posed by complex written language, as well as the more deliberate engagement with syntax required for literacy. It will be shown that the path from a preschool language impairment that includes difficulties with syntax, to literacy disorders in later school years, is a direct one for many children.

SYNTACTIC IMPAIRMENTS AND READING

Approaches to investigating the relationship between children's general syntactic ability and their success in reading divide into two categories. In the first approach, measures of prereading oral syntax are related to success in the early stages of learning to read. A second methodology is to compare groups of children with and without reading problems on syntactic tasks.

Syntax as a Predictor of Reading Impairment

A common paradigm for studying the relationship between prereading language and early reading has employed a multivariate design. The goal is to calculate the amount of variance in reading ability accounted for by several language domains including syntax (for discussion of the multivariate design, see Speece & Cooper, Chapter 5, this volume). For example, Catts et al. (1999) tested reading at second-grade level for a large group of children whose phonological processing and oral language skills had been assessed in kindergarten. As expected, phonological processing in kindergarten was a good predictor of grade 2 reading, but oral language skills also contributed substantial and unique variance. Oral language skills tested in kindergarten included grammar, vocabulary, and narrative tasks. DeJong and van der Leij (2002) tested language factors and reading at the end of grade 1, and reading at the end of grade 3 in Dutch children. They found that phonological processing was related to word decoding in grade 1 but had no additional effects 2 years later. In contrast, for reading comprehension, earlier word decoding and oral vocabulary skills, as well as listening comprehension, exerted additional influence at grade 3. Results highlighted the importance of separating out the two major components of reading (word decoding and comprehension) because of the possibility of different underlying determinants. In these investigations, grammatical abilities are not easily separable from a broader oral language or listening comprehension domain, with the result that sytactic determinants cannot be isolated. Nevertheless, it is a safe assumption that syntax plays a significant role in the types of oral language tasks found in prospective longitudinal research (e.g., a sentence repetition task in Catts et al., 1999).

Another approach in studying the relationship of early language skills and reading outcomes is to do follow-up testing of young children in at-risk groups (Rescorla, 2002; Scarborough, 1990b), or of children with identified language impairments (e.g., Bishop & Adams, 1990; Catts, 1993; Stothard, Snowling, Bishop, Chipchase, & Kaplan, 1998). Consistently, research has shown that children with spoken language impairments are likely to become reading impaired children in their later school years. Additionally, studies in this camp have shown that oral language skills, including semantics and syntax, are strong precursors of later literacy (Gallagher, Frith, & Snowling, 2000). However, beyond establishing an association, these studies are not particularly helpful in isolating the specific contribution of early syntax to later reading. By design, these studies use groups of children who have met general selection criteria; it is very likely that the children are heterogeneous with regard to their language profiles, even if syntactic impairment is a prominent feature.[6]

Because reading is seen as a long-term developmental process, the nature and strength of the association with syntax could change over time (Goulandris, Snowling, & Walker, 2000). Rescorla's (2002) work with late talkers, for example, showed a stronger association with reading when the children were 8–9 years old than when they were 6–7 years old. As Scarborough (1991) suggested, the measured contribution of a particular language variable will be strongest during a period of rapid change for that variable. Scarborough's (1990b) study, frequently cited as evidence of a strong relationship between early syntax and reading, employed a detailed structural analysis of 2-hour language samples with 2-½-year-old toddlers and was undertaken at a time of rapid developmental change. Scarborough and Dobrich (1990) followed a small cohort of children with early language delays between the ages of 2 and 8 years, and compared syntax measures with typically developing children over the same age range. Although children in the two groups started out with very different syntactic abilities, by age 60 months, the children with language delays "caught up" to their age peers on measures of production syntax. The authors labeled the recovery as illusory, because it overlapped with a developmental plateau shown for the typically developing children, and because the children with language delay (3 of 4) went on to have significant reading impairments as second graders. Interestingly, the same recovery was not apparent for skills measured by a sentence-level receptive syntax task. The point of interest is that a unitary syntax "ability," one that behaves with equanimity over time and tasks, has eluded researchers interested in the connection between syntax and reading.

Catts and Hogan (2002) recently reported on a longitudinal study of a large group of children given a battery of reading and language tests in the second and fourth grades. Persistent poor readers (children with reading comprehension scores at least one standard deviation below the mean in second and fourth grades) had the lowest scores in word recognition and fluency, and in oral language (as measured by standardized tests of vocabulary, grammar, and text comprehension) in both grades. Early poor readers (children whose reading problems dissipated by the fourth grade) were children whose second-grade word recognition and fluency were poor, but whose oral language scores were within –0.5 standard deviation, and were slightly higher in the fourth grade. A third group of children read within normal limits in the second grade, but their reading had deteriorated in the fourth grade (late poor readers, representing 19.5% of all fourth-grade poor readers). These children had normal word recognition and fluency scores in both grades, but oral language scores that were slightly below the mean in second grade had decreased further in the fourth grade, particularly in the area of text comprehension. These results point to the importance of taking a long-term, developmental perspective on the question of associations between oral language skills and reading (including sentence- and text-level comprehension).

To summarize, associations between children's syntactic abilities and reading have been demonstrated in longitudinal designs tying early oral language skills to later reading. The associations remain somewhat opaque, however, because it is difficult to isolate the syntactic "piece" of broader language tasks used to establish oral language impairments, and because the nature of the association might change over a broad developmental period. Future researchers could highlight syntactic contributions at different developmental periods more clearly by designing a better match between predictive syntax tasks and the literacy outcomes they are attempting to explain. For example, a picture-pointing sentence comprehension task could be given to 5-year-olds that contained some of the same structures known to increase sentence parsing difficulties at an early age. Later, these same structures could be manipulated within a text to increase the likelihood of degraded comprehension.

Finally, as several language–reading researchers have pointed out, answers to the question of causation require a level of evidence beyond correlations (Bryant et al., 1997; McCardle, Scarborough, & Catts, 2001). Experimental training studies aimed at improving children's syntactic abilities and measures of the consequences for reading, as has been done for phonemic awareness, are the next step. To date, syntax has been understudied as a variable in training studies with children who have reading impairments (Bowey, 1994).

Syntactic Ability in Reading Impairment

A second approach in the study of syntactic contributions to reading has been to study syntactic abilities in children who are already reading. The largest group of studies in this category has dealt with children's awareness of grammar. The reasoning was that reading may require some heightened awareness of grammar beyond that necessary for listening. Interest in children's grammatical awareness came under the umbrella of a more general interest in the development of metalinguistic awareness in the mid-1970s (e.g., Hakes, 1980).[7]

Researchers using a variety of tasks across a broad age range have provided strong evidence of a link between grammatical awareness and reading in children. Most commonly, the link is thought to be with reading comprehension (Bowey, 1994), but several researchers have also indicated that grammatical awareness could enhance word recognition via the use of context (Gaux & Gombert, 1999; Tunmer, Nesdale, & Wright, 1987). Studies have used cross-sectional designs of good and poor readers matched for age and also longitudinal (predictive) designs. The prototypical syntactic awareness task is grammatical judgement and correction, but other tasks such as oral cloze and sentence assembly have also been used.

Methodological Considerations

Not surprisingly, questions of methodology and interpretation have surfaced. Methodological questions have centered on syntactic tasks used, and subject selection and matching criteria. Arguments about task include whether the tasks are truly explicit (vs. implicit), whether they tap semantic and general working memory processes in addition to syntactic processes, and whether stimuli used are so difficult that they are de facto measures of syntactic development rather than awareness. Questions of interpretation include the extent to which associations between grammatical awareness and reading are mediated by differences in verbal working memory and in decoding ability, and whether syntactic awareness fosters reading or the reverse (see Bowey, 1994, for an analysis of all of these issues). Unfortunately, with few exceptions, linguistic (representational) accounts of syntactic complexity have seldom been used by researchers when choosing syntactic structures or tasks (but see the following discussion of research by Waltzman & Cairns, 2000).

Research Designed to Address Methodological Issues

Researchers have dealt with these questions in a variety of ways. In an experiment designed to untangle syntax and working memory, Bentin, Deutsch, and Liberman (1990) compared fourth-grade good readers and those with learning disorders on the purely auditory task of identifying words masked by white noise in the context of short grammatical and ungrammatical sentences. The researchers reasoned that the short sentences would not tax working memory, but that their degraded state would require the children to draw actively on their syntactic abilities. They reasoned further that readers with learning disorders would not use syntactic information as efficiently and, therefore, would not be "thrown off" by the incorrect sentences, resulting in a smaller effect for the incongruous sentences. Their predictions were supported. Furthermore, when subjects failed to repeat words verbatim, the good readers' "errors" were actual grammatical corrections, whereas those of the readers with learning disorders were more often random. The good readers also outperformed the poor readers on a follow-up grammatical judgement and correction task.

In a second experiment using a similar paradigm, the same researchers (Bentin et al., 1990) controlled for the effects of decoding on reading comprehension by matching good readers with children who were poor readers overall on standard tests, but were matched in basic decoding ability (i.e., a reading-level design). Bentin and colleagues reasoned that the relatively poor reading performance in the latter group would reflect inefficient use of sentence context, a necessity for reading Hebrew, which uses an unvoweled orthography.[8] The syntactically incorrect, degraded sentences had the same effect on both groups; however, the poor readers made fewer corrections in their repetitions. Likewise, the groups performed similarly on the judgement task, but the poor readers were unable to correct as many sentences. The researchers concluded that the inability to correct the sentences could not be attributed to general cognitive issues, and that the poor readers were uniquely impaired in the ability to use their syntactic knowledge productively. In their interpretation, Bentin et al. claimed that the conscious level of syntactic processing was problematic. Because of their careful design, these experiments may have come closer than others in uncovering a direct link between syntax and poor reading, one that cannot be explained by working memory or by phonological processing difficulties.

Several later studies using a reading-level design lend further support to the strength

of the association between syntactic awareness and reading comprehension. Nation
and Snowling (2000) compared poor comprehenders and normal readers' performance on a word order correction task that
manipulated voice (active–passive) and re-
versibility. The children were matched in
age and nonword reading. Poor comprehenders' were worse at correcting word order
generally, but all children found passives,
and particularly reversible passives, to be
harder. The findings were interpreted to
mean that poor comprehenders have a generalized, persistent delay in language processing that encompasses semantic as well
as syntactic processes. On the issue of
whether verbal working memory accounts
for the observed differences, Nation and
Snowling contended that "the difficulties
poor comprehenders have with verbal
working memory will be a consequence of
the same language processing limitations
that contribute to their difficulties with syntactic awareness" (p. 237). Tunmer et al.
(1987) also used a reading-level design to
compare poor fourth-grade readers and
good second-grade readers on oral cloze
and oral correction tasks. As a group, the
fourth graders did worse, but within each
grade, syntactic awareness was associated
with reading comprehension scores. The
two findings together strengthen, but do not
seal, a causal relationship between syntactic
awareness and reading comprehension.

Syntactic awareness and reading have
also been investigated in older poor readers,
both preadolescents and adults. With older
individuals, tasks used with younger children show ceiling effects, so different syntactic awareness measures must be devised.
Cupples and Holmes (1992) showed that
adult average and good comprehenders differed in their ability to judge whether words
belonged to the same form class (a syntactic
judgement) but were similar in judging semantic relatedness. With preadolescent
good and poor readers, Gaux and Gombert
(1999) looked at links between (1) seven
syntactic and morphosyntactic tasks that
varied along an implicit–explicit dimension:
repetition, judgement, correction, localization, explanation, replication, and identification of function; (2) two types of agram-

maticality: morphosyntax and syntax; and
(3) two types of reading measures: recoding
and comprehension. Results indicated different contributions depending on all three
variables and the degree of reading impairment. The results of this study underscore
the difficulty of uncovering the exact nature
of the relationship between syntactic awareness and reading,

Connections between syntax and reading
have also been explored in studies using
tasks that are not as clearly grammatical
awareness tasks, or in studies using a combination of awareness and other tasks. Several investigations have cast a broad net and
measured syntax in many different ways.
For example, Vogel (1975) compared children with dyslexia and normal second-
grade readers on nine measures of oral syntax that included detecting intonational
variations, recognition of grammaticality,
comprehension of syntax, knowledge of
morphology (two different cloze tasks), sentence closure (two cloze tasks in which
function words were deleted), sentence repetition, and use of grammatical forms in
spontaneous speech. With two exceptions,
the normal readers scored significantly
higher than the children with dyslexia. On
two tasks (the syntax comprehension task
and the grammaticality task), both groups
had difficulty.

As mentioned previously, only a few investigators of the syntax–reading connection have used linguistic theory (representational accounts of grammar) directly in the
study design. An investigation by Waltzman
and Cairns (2000) employed theoretical accounts of syntactic control and binding to
generate stimulus sentences for parsing by
third-grade children with and without reading impairments. The principle of control
assigns a referent to a "silent" pronominal
element in a sentence (e.g., *Horse kicks cow
before PRO eating grass*), with the result
that the right subject (agent) can be assigned
to a verb (in this case, the horse rather than
the cow). The principle of binding assigns
reflexive and personal pronoun reference
within sentences. Perhaps due to floor effects (all children had difficulty with certain
sentences), only one linguistic contrast differentiated the groups. Waltzman and

Cairns have drawn on contemporary linguistic theory in this study on connections between syntactic abilities and reading, but this type of methdology is, unfortunately, rare. By asking readers to manipulate sentences containing complexity features understood at a more theoretical level (as is the case for control and binding features), researchers could test hypotheses about sentence parsing–reading connections more directly. For example, children's performance on sentence-level tasks (e.g., pointing to a picture that demonstrates correct parsing of a particular type of grammatical structure) could be compared with their ability to derive meaning from written passages in which crucial distinctions are signaled with the same structure.

Research summarized in this section demonstrates that it is relatively easy to establish an association between syntactic ability and reading. By way of contrast, it is exceedingly difficult to understand the true nature of this relationship. Syntax-as-knowledge is difficult to isolate from syntax-as-process, and any one syntactic structure or task that might be chosen for study is a small slice of the entire syntactic faculty. Nevertheless, research designed to address some of the methodological issues raised in this section lends credence to the notion that poor readers have some unique difficulties with syntax that set them apart from age- and even decoding-matched peers. Although all children (good and poor readers) tend to have difficulty with the same types of syntactic structures, children with reading problems have inordinate problems under more stressful conditions (e.g., correcting as opposed to just detecting an error). Moreover, these difficulties are evident even when working-memory constraints and decoding abilities are experimentally controlled (Bentin et al., 1990).

SYNTACTIC IMPAIRMENT AND WRITING

Children write poorly for many reasons. They might not have anything they want to communicate. They may want to communicate but have inadequate information about a topic. They might struggle so much with spelling that they cannot "see the forest for the trees." Or they may want to communicate, and may have the requisite information, but because of poor language skills in general, they cannot use words well, construct sentences that are grammatically correct and well-suited to the type of writing, or organize their information into a well-formed text. The problem could also be a combination of any of these factors at various levels of intensity.

Attempts to discover syntactic contributions to writing impairment are even more difficult than is the case for reading impairment. As discussed in the first section, theoretical accounts of the process of writing sentences are undeveloped. The previous section on syntactic impairments and reading summarized findings in two research domains: (1) longitudinal studies of children whose early oral language skills and later reading skills were both measured, and (2) studies of syntactic abilities of children identified on the basis of their reading difficulties. Neither type of design has been prominent in the literature on writing impairment in children.

Nevertheless, there is ample reason to believe that syntactic difficulties contribute significantly to the writing difficulties of many children and adolescents. In part, this is because written sentences, compared to spoken ones, pose special problems, as shown in the preceding discussion of modality differences in syntactic complexity. To reiterate, writing requires a wider repertoire of complex sentence structures (Biber, 2001), and many of these structures are, by nature, difficult to process (they are longer, they deviate from canonical word order, they set up long distance dependencies, etc.). Structures that are difficult to process are found more often in informational varieties of text that children are expected to write in upper-elementary school grades and beyond. Moreover, structures found more frequently in writing are among those that are late-developing in children (Nippold, 1998; Perera, 1984; Scott, 1988a, 1988b).

Other evidence comes from observing the course of writing development over time. It takes a considerable amount of time after children start writing at the text level before their sentences match spoken sentences in terms of grammatical complexity, and more time still before they begin to use the modality-specific syntax characteristic of writing (Kroll, 1981; Reppen, 2001; Scott, 1994, 1999, 2002a). An indirect source of evidence of a syntax–writing connection in children with literacy impairments comes from the fact that poor readers, in whom the association with syntax is more direct, are frequently poor writers (Juel, 1988).

One advantage that the study of writing affords over reading is the fact that the products of syntactic processing can be directly observed on paper. By way of contrast, syntactic parsing as the culprit in a reading comprehension failure is not directly observable and can be difficult to isolate from lexical or text-level difficulties (an exception is the occasional and direct, if serendipitous, example of sentence parsing difficulty in the example of John on page 345 in this chapter). Thus, syntax in children's writing has been measured and described in various groups of children and adolescents with identified writing impairments, or in children who are at high risk for writing difficulties based on a broader diagnosis of learning disability or language learning disorder. It is not surprising then, that the major source of information about syntax and writing impairments is descriptive in nature.

Descriptions of Syntax in Poor Writers

A number of studies have used a group design to compare the writing of children or adolescents with low achievement, learning, and/or language difficulties with that of age-matched peers. One commonly used measure of overall syntactic complexity is average sentence length in words.[9] Studies that have examined sentence length in narrative writing have sometimes failed to find differences (e.g., Houck & Billingsley, 1989; Morris & Crump, 1982), but those looking at a wider variety of school-based writing samples found sentences to be less complex, as indicated by average sentence length (see Hunt, 1970, and Loban, 1976, for comparisons of low-achieving and normal-achieving children and adolescents). Using another

global measure of syntactic complexity, the average number of clauses per sentence, Hunt (1970) and Loban (1976) again demonstrated differences between low- and normal-achieving students.

Several studies have conducted group comparisons of the use of particular types of syntactic structures. Structures indicative of higher level written text found to occur less often in the writing of problem writers include adverbial clauses of concession (e.g., *unless, although*; Loban, 1976), a more limited range of conjunctions (Anderson, 1982; Hunt, 1970), and fewer nonfinite verbs (Loban, 1976). Grammatical errors more characteristic of problem writers include noun–verb agreement (Morris & Stick, 1985), problems with noun-phrase premodification (Anderson, 1982), and morphosyntactic errors, including omissions of obligatory tense, person, and number inflections, and auxiliary/copula forms of *be* (Windsor, Scott, & Street, 2000). A review of much of the earlier research in syntactic complexity and grammatical errors for both narrative and expository writing can be found in Newcomer and Barenbaum (1991).

Comparisons of Spoken and Written Syntax in Poor Writers

Another research strategy has been to compare spoken and written syntax of children and adolescents with language learning disorders. Two studies are noteworthy in that the methodology controlled for genre; that is, children were asked to speak and write the same types of texts. In this way, as noted previously, group differences, if found, could be attributed solely to modality. If differences are found in the way groups respond to a writing task *compared to* a speaking task, then the researcher has made a stronger case that the unique syntactic requirements of writing are differentially problematic for certain children. This was the conclusion of Gillam and Johnston (1992), who compared narrative spoken and written samples in four groups of children, ages 9–12 years. Children with language impairments were compared to children with reading impairments, as well as age- and language-matched peers on a variety of sentence and text-level measures. Children with language and reading impairments produced fewer complex sentences when writing compared to speaking, whereas the opposite was true for the typically developing children. The types of sentences that most distinguished the groups were those that contained several different types of subordination (e.g., *The boy didn't go because he was afraid of the bats that lived in caves* contains an adverbial clause and a relative clause). The writing of children with language and reading impairments contained fewer of these types of sentences. Not only did grammatical errors increase substantially in the writing of the children with language impairments, but also errors were at their highest when the written sentence was complex (i.e., contained two or more clauses).

Scott and Windsor (2000) also compared 11-year-old children with language learning disabilities (LLD) with age-matched peers, and with language-matched peers who were, on average, 2 years younger. The children both spoke and wrote summaries of narrative and expository films. Although modality did not affect overall syntactic complexity, indexed by either average sentence length or average number of clauses per sentence, modality did have a significant impact on grammatical error, and differentially so, for children with LLD. A subsequent, more detailed account of the nature of these grammatical errors revealed that verb morphosyntax and, specifically, omission of regular past tense endings, accounted for more errors than any other category (Windsor et al., 2000). To emphasize the fact that grammatical error in writing was a significant feature of these children's language profile, it was notable that error rate was the only one of 10 general language-performance measures that differentiated children with LLD from both age- and language-matched peers.

Using the same data set from Scott and Windsor (2000), Scott (2002a) recently reported results from a detailed comparison of spoken and written grammar. The premise was that the writing of typically developing 11-year-old children should reflect some degree of syntactic adjustment attrib-

utable to modality. Modality differences were discussed in the first section of this chapter, with reference to the work of Biber (1988, 2001) and Halliday (1985, 1987). This type of adjustment would characterize Kroll's (1981) differentiation stage of speaking–writing development. Scott directly compared spoken and written utterances only if they contained the same content, which was operationally defined as at least one common idea unit (an idea unit is typically expressed as a clause). For example, one typically developing child said, *And once cactuses die animals move into the cactus to live,* but wrote *Animals make homes out of dead plants.* Restricting the analysis to this select subset of data, group comparisons revealed significant differences in the frequency rate of written forms in favor of the typically developing children. Children with LLD produced such structures (e.g., nominalization, passive voice) at only half the rate of their age-matched peers; however, they did not differ from language-matched peers who were a full 2 years younger.

To summarize, research has uncovered higher rates of grammatical error, lower overall measures of complexity, and lower rates of written modality variations in the writing of school-age children and adolescents with LLD. Of what importance are these findings? Regarding error, from midelementary grades onward in a student's education, there is no tolerance for any grammatical error in final-draft writing, or in any professional or job-related writing thereafter. For complexity and modality variation, the answer depends on the importance one attaches to the ability to vary one's language form in accordance with modality and genre. In a recent model of linguistic literacy and its development, Ravid and Tolchinksy (2002) placed such an ability at the core of their definition of linguistic literacy. They wrote, "Our view of linguistic literacy thus consists of one defining feature: control over linguistic variation; of one concomitant process: metalanguage; and of one condition: familiarity with writing and written language" (p. 420). This ability emerges in early adolescence and continues to develop through formal schooling in the course of continued and protracted experience with reading and writing academic language. The ability to vary one's language requires a level of cognitive control over language (metalinguistic awareness) associated with writing, which offers the user a permanent record to be revised and edited (Ravid & Tolchinksy, 2002).

CONCLUSIONS AND FUTURE DIRECTIONS

This chapter has shown how sentences, particularly the long and complex sentences of written text, can be challenging for language users when reading and writing. Because sentences are not "over" from a processing perspective until the final word, a 27-word sentence will be harder to process than a 10-word sentence, and written expository text, the language of school, has the longest sentences of all (Francis & Kucera, 1982). Theoretical and experimental work on sentences in the last 25 years have increased our understanding of the grammatical factors that contribute to complexity. Length and complexity frequently, but not always, go hand in hand.

Children and adolescents with language learning disabilities, by definition, have a more difficult time comprehending and/or producing complex language at an implicit level, and when explicit processing is also required, as it is for reading and writing, additional complications arise. They may use a more immature parsing strategy or have difficulty paraphrasing text. Consequently, reading comprehension problems may persist even after word recognition difficulties have abated, or may become apparent for the first time as sentences in texts become more difficult (Catts & Hogan, 2002; Snowling, 2000). Problems recognizing agrammatical sentences, applying syntactic knowledge to spelling, and accessing and controlling modality and genre variations in form may be reflected in students' writing.

This chapter, in the second and third sections, has reviewed investigations in three areas that establish a definite association between syntactic abilities and literacy acqui-

sition. These include longitudinal studies that link early prereading language abilities with early reading achievement, research comparing syntactic awareness abilities of good and poor readers, and descriptive studies of the writing of children and adolescents with and without language learning disorders. Some investigators have come closer than others to establishing a direct causal link between syntax and reading or writing, but by and large, the evidence is still associative in nature. The task ahead for researchers interested in moving beyond association to explanation is formidable.

Reading and writing (as well as speaking and listening) are basically text-level activities concerned with comprehending and generating ideas that are conceived and remembered in "gist" form. As a result, the contributions of components of text, such as sentence-level grammar, are difficult to isolate (albeit more observable for the activity of writing, as pointed out). The same situation poses a challenge for language testing in general, not just for reading and writing. The clinician or researcher who wants to determine a child's syntactic ability must first isolate exactly what part(s) of grammar should be targeted developmentally, then choose from an array of possible methodologies for eliciting representative behaviors. These challenges hold whether normative or criterion-referenced testing is the area of interest, or whether implicit or more explicit language processing is targeted (Gaux & Gombert, 1999). Difficulties stemming from the inherent complexity of syntax, as well as problems isolating syntax, have contributed to the preponderance of associative rather than direct evidence, and have made it difficult to compare studies directly.

The inherent heterogeneity of children and adolescents who struggle with literacy is yet another barrier in pinpointing the contribution of syntax. The necessity to group subjects in studies according to one or even a few scores or characteristics obscures individual differences in syntactic ability and/or in reading and writing typology membership (Scott, 2002b). Thus, two children may score quite differently on a syntax-dependent subtest of a general language test but obtain the same overall score used as criterion for inclusion in the study. Researchers have rarely had either the requisite numbers of subjects or the inclination to go back to these types of differences when interpreting results.

One approach for future researchers' consideration is to employ more sophisticated, syntax-specific instruments, those based on theoretically motivated basic research in the acquisition of syntax, as criterion measures in group designs. Examples of tests and protocols within this framework are increasing (e.g., Rice & Wexler, 2002; Seymour, 2000). This tactic would benefit research designs by decreasing the heterogeneity within a group of poor readers or writers, and by affording a stronger match between qualifying subject characteristics and dependent measures. For example, a group of children known to have difficulty on auditory parsing tasks with certain types of complex grammatical forms could be given reading comprehension passages that manipulate those same forms in various ways. Scott (2002b) recently suggested possible demarcations of poor writers based on syntactic profiles and history.

Although it is unlikely that syntactic difficulties are the only contributor to poor reading comprehension, a better understanding of the contribution of syntax requires being very clear about what syntax entails or, more specifically, what a theory of syntax entails (see Shapiro, 1997). A recent example of research built on a syntactic theory is the work of Bishop et al. (2000). Reading ability was not measured (by design), but the study is cited here because it illustrates the use of syntactic theory in delineating the nature of language impairment. These researchers were interested in the validity of a grammatically based subtype of children with language impairment. Starting with a theory of specific language impairment (SLI) as a representational deficit for dependent syntactic relationships (RDDR), several tests/tasks were chosen because they required the children to calculate such dependent relationships (e.g., active–passive, pronominal reference) in order to respond correctly. Whereas the theoretical construct held generally (i.e., syntactic dependencies were problematic for

children with SLI), few children showed a pattern of impairment predicted by the hypothesis across all measures used. It would have been enlightening to see the relationship between reading comprehension and the children's oral data, particularly for the children who showed a "purer" RDDR pattern.

Other approaches might isolate syntactic contributions to reading comprehension problems by developing online checks of sentence-level parsing. Direct questioning of the "who did what to whom" type, requests to paraphrase, and requests to generate questions would all be helpful in checking sentence-level comprehension, when inserted strategically in a text. This approach could be even more focused in a text that was strategically constructed to include sentences with specific grammatical forms of interest (e.g., those listed in Table 16.1).

Finally, as others have argued (McCardle et al., 2001), one of the ultimate designs that strengthens the explanatory power of a variable is found in intervention studies. If children given intensive instruction in phonemic awareness and phonics make major gains in reading, then phonological processing as a cause of reading impairment is given credence (Report of the National Reading Panel, 2000). Instruction in grammar as an remedy for reading comprehension problems is largely untested, but there is a fledgling literature on syntax instruction in expressive language disorders and writing. Some have argued for focused efforts that build awareness of higher level structures specific to writing and informational language (e.g., Scott, 1995), and that take advantage of what is known about typical writing errors of students (e.g., Daiute, 1984). The theoretical framework of structural priming has been exploited in an attempt to increase the frequency of complex syntax in conversations of school-age children (Johnson, Marinellie, Cetin, Marassa, & Correll, 1999). In general education, there is a long debate about the effects of grammar instruction on writing. In a review of this literature, Noguchi (1991) concludes that there is a place for such instruction, but it must be more selective and efficient (see also Weaver, 1996). Sentence combining, a "staple" of the grammatical component of a writing curriculum (Daiker, Kerek, & Morenberg, 1985), continues to have its proponents (Scott, 1995). The material reviewed in this chapter gives credence to the argument that basic and applied researchers continue the search for more direct links between syntax and literacy, as well as instructional paradigms that build on such research.

NOTES

1. In this chapter, the terms "syntax" and "grammar" are used interchangeably.
2. The verb *sleep* requires only one argument (an agent, someone who sleeps), but the verb put requires an agent, a theme (something put), and a location.
3. A variety of terms are used as descriptors for children who have difficulty learning and using spoken and written language (e.g., specific language impairment, language learning disabilities/disorder, language disorder, language impairment, learning disability). The strategy followed here is to preserve terminology used by authors whose work is cited.
4. The term "sentence processing" is used in a general sense to cover both sentence decoding (comprehension) and encoding (production).
5. John is a pseudonym.
6. Researchers continue to debate whether there is a homogeneous grammatical subtype of specific language impairment (see Bishop et al., 2000).
7. In terms of sheer volume of research effort, however, the study of the conscious awareness of grammar has always been the poor sister to research in phonological awareness (Bowey, 1994).
8. In Hebrew orthography, letters represent consonants, and vowels are signaled by diacritics, which are frequently omitted. The result is that Hebrew has a large number of homographs, and context plays an important role in disambiguating meaning.
9. T-units (terminable units, after Hunt, 1965) are the preferred unit of measure in most studies. A T-unit is defined as one main clause and all attached dependent clauses. In most cases, a T-unit is synonymous with a sentence, except in some cases of coordinated clauses.

REFERENCES

Anderson, P. (1982). A preliminary study of syntax in the written expression of learning disabled and nor-

mal children. *Journal of Learning Disabilities, 15,* 359–362.

Beaman, K. (1984). Coordination and subordination revisited: Syntactic complexity in spoken and written narrative discourse. In D. Tannen (Ed.), *Coherence in spoken and written discourse* (pp. 48–81). Norwood, NJ: Ablex.

Bentin, S, Deutsch, A., & Liberman, I. (1990). Syntactic competence and reading ability in children. *Journal of Experimental Child Psychology, 48,* 147–172.

Bever, T. G. (1970). The cognitive basis for linguistic structure. In J. R. Hayes (Ed.), *Cognition and the development of language* (pp. 279–362). New York: Wiley.

Biber, D. (1988). *Variation across speech and writing.* Cambridge, UK: Cambridge University Press.

Biber, D. (2001). On the complexity of discourse complexity: A multi-dimensional analysis. In S. Conrad & D. Biber (Eds.), *Variation in English: Multi-dimensional studies* (pp. 215–240). London: Longman.

Bishop, D. V. M., & Adams, C. (1990). A prospective study of the relationship between specific language impairment, phonological disorders, and reading retardation. *Journal of Child Psychology and Psychiatry, 21,* 1027–1050.

Bishop, D. V. M., Bright, P., James, C., Bishop, S. J., & Van der Lely, H. K. J. (2000). Grammatical SLI: A distinct subtype of developmental language impairment? *Applied Psycholinguistics, 21,* 159–181.

Bock, K., & Levelt, W. (1994). Language production: Grammatical encoding. In M. Gernsbacher (Ed.), *Handbook of psycholinguistics* (pp. 945–984). San Diego: Academic Press.

Bowey, J. (1994). Grammatical awareness and learning to read: A critique. In E. Assink (Ed.), *Literacy acquisition and social context* (pp. 122–149). New York: Harvester Wheatsheaf.

Brown, R. (1973). *A first language: The early stages.* Cambridge, MA: Harvard University Press:

Bryant, P., Nunes, T., & Bindman, M. (1997). Children's understanding of the connection between grammar and spelling. In B. Blachman (Ed.), *Foundations of reading acquisition and dyslexia* (pp. 219–240). Mahwah, NJ: Erlbaum.

Bryant, P., Nunes, T., & Bindman, M. (2000). The relations between children's linguistic awareness and spelling: The case of the apostrophe. *Reading and Writing: An Interdisciplinary Journal, 12,* 253–276.

Caplan, D. (2002). The neural basis of syntactic processing: A critical look. In A. B., Hillis (Ed.), *Handbook of adult language disorders: Integrating cognitive neuropsychology, neurology, and rehabilitation* (pp. 331–350). Philadelphia: Psychology Press.

Catts, H. (1993). The relationship between speech–language impairments and reading disabilities. *Journal of Speech and Hearing Research, 36,* 948–958.

Catts, H., Fey, M. E., Zhang, X., & Tomblin, J. B. (1999). Language basis of reading disabilities: Evidence from a longitudinal investigation. *Scientific Studies of Reading, 3,* 331–361.

Catts, H., & Hogan, T. (2002, June). *The fourth grade slump: Late emerging poor readers.* Paper presented at the annual meeting of the Society for the Scientific Study of Reading, Chicago, IL.

Chomsky, C. (1969). *The acquisition of syntax in children from 5 to 10.* Cambridge, MA: MIT Press.

Chomsky, N. (1965). *Aspects of a theory of syntax.* Cambridge, MA: MIT Press.

Committee on the Prevention of Reading Difficulties in Young Children. (1998). *Preventing reading difficulties in young children.* Washington, DC: National Academy Press.

Crystal, D., Fletcher, P., & Garman, M. (1976). *The grammatical analysis of language disability: A procedure for assessment and remediation.* London: Arnold.

Cupples, L., & Holmes, V. M. (1992). Evidence for a difference in syntactic knowledge between skilled and less skilled adult readers. *Journal of Psycholinguistic Research, 21*(4), 249–274.

Daiker, D. A., Kerek, A., & Morenberg, M. (1985). *Sentence combining: A rhetorical perspective.* Carbondale: Southern Illinois University Press.

Daiute, C. (1984). Performance limits on writers. In R. Beach & L. S. Bridwell (Eds.), *New directions in composition research* (pp. 205–224). New York: Guilford Press.

DeJong, P. F., & van der Leij, A. (2002). Effects of phonological abilities and linguistic comprehension on the development of reading. *Scientific Studies of Reading, 6*(1), 51–77.

Donahue, M. L., & Pidek, C. M. (1993). Listening comprehension and paraphrasing in content-area classrooms. *Journal of Childhood Communication Disorders, 15*(2), 35–42.

Flores d'Arcais, G. (1987). Syntactic processing during reading for comprehension. In M. Coltheart (Ed.), *The psychology of reading* (pp. 619–633). Hillsdale, NJ: Erlbaum.

Frances, W. N., & Kucera. H. (1982). *Frequency analysis of English usage: Lexicon and grammar.* Boston: Hughton Mifflin.

Frazier, L. (1987). Sentence processing: A tutorial review. In M. Coltheart (Ed.), *Attention and performance XII: The psychology of reading* (pp. 559–587). Hillsdale, NJ: Erlbaum.

Frazier, L., & Rayner, K. (1982). Making and correcting errors during sentence comprehension: Eye movements in the analysis of structurally ambiguous sentences. *Cognitive Psychology, 14,* 178–210.

Fry, E. (1977). Fry's readability graph: Clarifications, validity, and extension to level 17. *Journal of Reading, 21,* 242–252.

Gallagher, A., Frith, U., & Snowling, M. (2000). Precursors of literacy delay among children at genetic risk of dyslexia. *Journal of Child Psychology and Psychiatry, 41,* 203–213.

Garrett, M. F. (1975). The analysis of sentence production. In G. Bower (Ed.), *Psychology of learning and motivation* (Vol 9, pp. 133–177). New York: Academic Press.

Gaux, C., & Gombert, J. E. (1999). Implicit and explicit syntactic knowledge and reading in pre-adoles-

cents. *British Journal of Developmental Psychology, 17,* 169–188.

Gibson, E. (1998). Linguistic complexity: Locality of syntactic dependencies. *Cognition, 68,* 1–76.

Gillam, R., & Johnston, J. (1992). Spoken and written language relationships in language/learning impaired and normally achieving school-age children. *Journal of Speech and Hearing Research, 35,* 1303–1315.

Goulandris, N. K., Snowling, M. J., & Walker, I. (2000). Is dyslexia a form of specific language impairment?: A comparison of dyslexic and language impaired children as adolescents. *Annals of Dyslexia, 50,* 103–120.

Grela, B., & Leonard, L. (2000). The influence of argument–structure complexity on the use of auxiliary verbs by children with SLI. *Journal of Speech, Language, and Hearing Research, 43,* 1115–1125.

Hakes, D. (1980). *The development of metalinguistic abilities in children.* New York: Springer-Verlag.

Halliday, M. A. K. (1985). *Spoken and written language.* Oxford, UK: Oxford University Press.

Halliday, M. A. K. (1987). Spoken and written modes of meaning. In R. Horowitz & S. J. Samuels (Eds.), *Comprehending oral and written language* (pp. 55–82). San Diego: Academic Press.

Holmes, V. M. (1987). Syntactic parsing: In search of the garden path. In M. Coltheart (Ed.), *Attention and performance XII: The psychology of reading* (pp. 587–599). Hillsdale, NJ: Erlbaum.

Houck, C., & Billingsley, B. (1989). Written expression of students with and without learning disabilities. *Journal of Learning Disabilities, 22,* 561–568.

Hunt, K. (1965). *Grammatical structures written at three grade levels.* Champaign, IL: National Council of Teachers of English.

Hunt, K. (1970). Syntactic maturity in school children and adults. *Monographs of the Society for Research in Child Development, 35* (Serial No. 134, No. 1).

Johnson, C., Marinellie, S., Cetin, P., Marassa, L., & Correll, K. (1999, November). *Facilitating a child's syntactic style during conversational language intervention.* Paper presented at the annual convention of the American Speech–Language–Hearing Association, San Francisco, CA.

Juel, C. (1988). Learning to read and write: A longitudinal study of 54 children from first through fourth grades. *Journal of Educational Psychology, 80,* 437–447.

Kaderavek, J., & Sulzby, E. (2000). Narrative production by children with and without specific language impairment: Oral narratives and emergent readings. *Journal of Speech, Language, and Hearing Research, 43,* 34–49.

Kemper, S. (1987). Syntactic complexity and elderly adults' prose recall. *Experimental Aging Research, 13,* 47–52.

Kroll, B. (1981). Developmental relationships between speaking and writing. In B. Kroll & R. Vann (Eds.), *Exploring speaking–writing relationships: Connections and contrasts* (pp. 32–54). Urbana, IL: National Council of Teachers of English.

Leonard, L. (1998). *Children with specific language impairment*. Cambridge, MA: MIT Press.

Levelt, W. (1989). *Speaking: From intention to articulation*. Cambridge, MA: MIT Press.

Levelt, W. (1999). Producing spoken language: A blueprint for the speaker. In C. M. Brown & P. Hagoort (Eds.), *The neurocognition of language* (pp. 83–122). New York: Oxford University Press.

Loban, W. (1976). *Language development: Kindergarten through grade twelve* (Research Report No. 18). Champaign, IL: National Council of Teachers of English.

McCardle, P., Scarborough, H., & Catts, H. (2001). Predicting, explaining, and preventing children's reading difficulties. *Learning Disabilities Research and Practice, 16*, 230–239.

Menyuk, P., & Chesnick, M. (1997). Metalinguistic skills, oral language knowledge, and reading. *Topics in Language Disorders, 17*(3), 75–89.

Morris, N., & Crump, D. (1982). Syntactic and vocabulary development in the written language of learning disabled and non-learning disabled students at four age levels. *Learning Disability Quarterly, 5*, 163–172.

Morris, N., & Stick, S. (1985, November). *Oral/written language analysis of learning disabled and normal high schoolers*. Paper presented at the annual meeting of the American Speech–Language–Hearing Association, Washington, DC.

Nation, K., & Snowling, M. (2000). Factors influencing syntactic awareness skills in normal readers and poor comprehenders. *Applied Linguistics, 21*, 229–241.

Newcomer, P., & Barenbaum, E. (1991). The writing composing ability of children with learning disabilities. *Journal of Learning Disabilities, 24*, 578–593.

Nippold, M. (1998). *Later language development* (2nd ed.). Austin, TX: Pro-Ed.

Noguchi, R. (1991). *Grammar and the teaching of writing* (Stock No. 18747-3020). Urbana, IL: National Council of Teachers of English.

Palincsar, A. S., & Brown, A. L. (1984). Reciprocal teaching of comprehension fostering and comprehension-monitoring activities. *Cognition and Instruction, 1*(2), 117–175.

Paul, R. (2001). *Language disorders from infancy through adolescence: Assessment and intervention* (2nd ed.). St. Louis: Mosby.

Perera, K. (1984). *Children's writing and reading: Analyzing classroom reading*. London: Blackwell.

Persky, H., Daane, H., & Jin, Y. (2003). *The nation's report card: Writing 2002*. Washington, DC: U.S. Department of Education.

Ravid, D., & Tolchinksky, L. (2002). Developing linguistic literacy: A comprehensive model. *Journal of Child Language, 29*, 417–447.

Rayner, K. (1998). Eye movements in reading and information processing: 20 years of research. *Psychological Bulletin, 124*(3), 372–422.

Rayner, K., Carlson, M., & Frazier, L. (1983). The interaction of sysntax and semantics during sentence processing: Eye movements in the analysis of semantically biased sentences. *Journal of Verbal Learning and Verbal Behavior, 22*, 358–374.

Rayner, K., & Pollatsek, A. (1994). *The psychology of reading*. Hillsdale, NJ: Erlbaum.

Report of the National Reading Panel. (2000). National Institute of Child Health and Human Development. *Teaching children to read: Reports of the subgroups* (NIH Pub. No. 00-4754).

Reppen, R. (2001). Register variation in student and adult speech and writing. In S. Conrad & D. Biber (Eds.), *Variation in English: Multi-dimensional studies* (pp. 187–199). London: Longman.

Rescorla, L. (2002). Language and reading outcomes to age 9 in late-talking toddlers. *Journal of Speech, Language, and Hearing Research, 45*, 360–371.

Rice, M. L. (2000). Grammatical symptoms of specific language impairment. In D. V. M. Bishop & L. B. Leonard (Eds.), *Speech and language impairments in children* (pp. 17–34). Philadelphia: Taylor & Francis.

Rice, M. L., & Wexler, K. (2002). *Test of early grammatical impairment*. San Antonio, TX: Psychological Corporation.

Romaine, S. (1984). *The language of children and adolescents*. Oxford, UK: Blackwell.

Scarborough, H. (1990a). Index of productive syntax. *Applied Psycholinguistics, 11*, 1–22.

Scarborough, H. (1990b). Very early language deficits in dyslexic children. *Child Development, 61*, 1728–1743.

Scarborough, H. (1991). Early syntactic development of dyslexic children. *Annals of Dyslexia, 41*, 207–220.

Scarborough, H. S., & Dobrich, W. (1990). Development of children with early language delay. *Journal of Speech and Hearing Research, 33*, 70–83.

Scott, C. (1988a). Producing complex sentences. *Topics in Language Disorders, 8*(2), 44–66.

Scott, C. (1988b). Spoken and written syntax. In M. Nippold (Ed.), *Later language development: Ages 9 through 19* (pp. 45–95). San Diego: College Hill Press.

Scott, C. (1994). A discourse continuum for school-age students: Impact of modality and genre. In G. Wallach & K. Butler (Eds.), *Language learning disabilities in school-age children and adolescents: Some underlying principles and applications* (2nd ed., pp. 219–252). Columbus, OH: Macmillan/Merrill.

Scott, C. (1995). Syntax for school children: A discourse approach. In M. Fey, S. Warren, & J. Windsor (Eds.), *Language intervention in the early school years* (pp. 107–143). Baltimore: Brookes.

Scott, C. (1999). Learning to write. In H. Catts & A. Kamhi (Eds.), *The language basis of reading disabilities* (pp. 224–258). Boston: Allyn & Bacon.

Scott, C. (2002a, June). *Speaking and writing the same texts: Comparisons of school children with and without language learning disabilities*. Paper presented at the annual meeting of the Society for Text and Discourse. Chicago, IL.

Scott, C. (2002b). A fork in the road less traveled:

Writing intervention based on language profile. In E. Silliman & K. Butler (Eds.), *Speaking, reading, and writing in children with language learning disabilities: New paradigms in research and practice* (pp. 219–238). Mahwah, NJ: Erlbaum.

Scott, C., & Klutzenbaker, K. (1989, November). *Comparing spoken and written summaries: Text structure and surface form.* Paper presented at the Annual Convention of the American Speech–Language–Hearing Association, St. Louis, MO.

Scott, C., & Windsor, J. (2000). General language performance measures in spoken and written narrative and expository discourse in school-age children with language learning disabilities. *Journal of Speech, Language, and Hearing Research, 43,* 324–339.

Seymour, H. (2000, June). *The development of a dialect sensitive language test.* Paper presented at the Symposium for Research in Child Language Disorders, Madison, WI.

Shapiro, L. (1997). Tutorial: An introduction to syntax. *Journal of Speech, Language, and Hearing Research, 40,* 254–272.

Snowling, M. J. (2000). Literacy and literacy skills: Who is at risk and why? In D. V. M. Bishop, & L. B. Leonard (Eds.), *Speech and language impairments in children* (pp. 245–259). Philadelphia: Taylor & Francis.

Stothard, S., Snowling, M., Bishop, D. V. M., Chipchase, B., & Kaplan, C. (1998). Language impaired preschoolers: A follow-up into adolescence. *Journal of Speech, Language, and Hearing Research, 41,* 407–418.

Sulzby, E. (1996). Roles of oral and written language as children approach conventional literacy. In C.

Pontecrovo, M. Orsollini, B. Burge, & L. Resnick (Eds.). *Early text construction in children* (pp. 25–46). Hillsdale, NJ: Erlbaum.

Templin, M. (1957). *Certain language skills in children.* Minneapolis: University of Minnesota Press.

Thompson, C. (2003). Unaccusative verb production in agrammatic aphasia: The argument structure complexity hyothesis. *Journal of Neurolinguistics 16,* 151–167.

Thompson, C., & Faroqi-Shaw, Y. (2002). Models of sentence production. In A. B. Hillis (Ed.), *Handbook of adult language disorders: Integrating cognitive neuropsychology, neurology, and rehabilitation* (pp. 311–330). Philadelphia: Psychology Press.

Tunmer, W., Nesdale, A., & Wright, D. (1987). Syntactic awareness and reading acquisition. *British Journal of Developmental Psychology, 5,* 25–34.

Vogel, S. A. (1975). *Syntactic abilities in normal and dyslexic children.* Baltomore: University Park Press.

Waltzman, D. E., & Cairns, H. S. (2000). Grammatical knowledge of third grade good and poor readers. *Applied Psycholinguistics, 21,* 263–284.

Waters, G., Caplan, D., & Hildebrandt, N. (1987). Working memory and written sentence comprehension. In M. Coltheart (Ed.), *Attention and performance XII: The psychology of reading* (pp. 531–555). Hillsdale, NJ: Erlbaum.

Weaver, C. (1996). *Teaching grammar in context.* Portsmouth, NH: Heinemann.

Windsor, J., Scott, C., & Street, C. (2000). Verb and noun morphology in the spoken and written language of children with language learning disabilities. *Journal of Speech, Language, and Hearing Research, 43,* 1322–1336.

17

Social Cognition, Conversation, and Reading Comprehension

How to Read a Comedy of Manners

MAVIS L. DONAHUE
SHARON K. FOSTER

"There is only one thing to do with a person as impossible as she. I must have
a party for her. Otherwise, everyone will feel at once how much I dislike her!"
JANE AUSTEN (1816), *Emma*

In the metacognitive *tour de force* of a book review titled "How to Read a How-to-Read Book," Shulevitz (2002) claimed, "Reading, as an act, is always solitary but never lonely" (p. 27). Most readers would agree that the most satisfying reading resembles a lively imaginary conversation. Perhaps the best example is reading a Jane Austen novel, an experience deserving of overlapping and gossipy internal dialogues with the text. Noting the incongruity of the second sentence of Emma's remarks in the preceding quotation, the reader may immediately question the author's intent, the character's reasoning and relationship with the "impossible person," and the social context that would make the linking of the first two sentences plausible. The answers are provided in the third sentence, which in turn triggers the reader's recognition of social customs that differ from his or her own expectations.

This interpretive process seems remarkably similar to descriptions of social cognition, or what Shantz (1982) has called

"thinking about people thinking about people"; she defines social cognition as "conceptions and reasoning about people, the self, relations between people, social groups, roles and rules, and the relation of such conceptions to social behavior" (p. 376). Yet theories about relations between language and literacy development rarely explicate how understanding written text may recruit the same social cognitive processes that underlie oral discourse. Given that many students with learning disabilities have difficulties in both social cognition and reading comprehension, identifying interactions among aspects of these two domains may help to explain why some readers struggle to comprehend certain texts that are well within their decoding, vocabulary, and fluency abilities.

Our purpose in this chapter is to describe and integrate some conceptual frameworks that converge on the social discourse knowledge that oral and written language comprehension may share. Research on how individuals make sense of socially complex

363

discourse is organized in three phases of information processing for both oral and written texts: perception and interpretation of social cues; clarification of goals; and constructing and evaluating social responses. This framework is used to highlight the convergences in research questions and findings across two typically separate domains of research: social cognition and reading comprehension. As we reveal recurrent themes across these bodies of research and theories, we explore implications for current and future research on students who have difficulties in reading comprehension and social discourse.

READING COMPREHENSION AS "THINKING ABOUT PEOPLE THINKING ABOUT PEOPLE"

Shulevitz's (2002) claim that reading is "never lonely" is at once mundane and paradigm shattering. The notion that reading comprehension invokes the reader's social knowledge is certainly not new (Dewey, 1906). Yet no current theory of reading comprehension is sufficiently complex, detailed, and interactive to explain how readers make sense of text that calls for high levels of social inferencing. To illustrate this challenge, consider that any compelling theory must explain how readers mobilize their social-cognitive resources for two literacy activities that seem to be at opposite ends of a continuum of "loneliness," namely, participating in an instant-messaging conversation and reading a 19th-century comedy of manners.

Instant Messaging and Conversation

One new literacy activity makes the conversational nature of reading comprehension impossible to ignore, namely, the use of instant messaging on the Internet. More than half of adolescents between the ages of 12 and 17 years use instant messaging (IM) and chat rooms, and one-fourth of those students report that they often present themselves as different people to their readers (Lenhart, Rainie, & Lewis, 2001, cited by Alvermann, 2001). As a context in which

the identity and agenda of the author and the reader are often unknown or ambiguous, IM gives new urgency to the need for readers to approach text from a questioning stance. IM is also an apt metaphor for the social and interactive nature of reading in "the old-fashioned way," as well as for oral discourse processes.

Armed with the essentials of IM print conventions, emoticons (the punctuation-based graphics that convey authors' feelings about their messages), and "netiquette," IM readers make sense of their partners' text based on their own prior knowledge and expectations, formulate a response, then receive feedback. Using typical strategies to organize the text (e.g., recruiting genre knowledge to predict text structure, summarizing), they constantly monitor their own comprehension processes. Ideas that contradict their knowledge base or expectations about the author can be immediately queried and clarified. However, superimposed on these social cognitive processes is the realization that a chat room author may be "posing," so questions about the author's identity, purpose, and credibility can never be far from the reader's mind. Evaluations of the author's choice of words, topics, and attitudes filter the reader's simultaneous construction and interpretation of meaning.

In some ways, then, IM represents a "hybrid," or intermediate step, between comprehending an oral versus a written text. Like talking, the give-and-take of IM provides opportunities for immediate feedback and constant readjustments of the participants' original hypotheses. Similarly, the conversational partner (author) is a tangible presence whose perspective and agenda are easy to consider. However, like reading, the text remains visible, allowing for rereading and confirming interpretations. And the pace of exchanging conversational turns is dramatically slower than the milliseconds that regulate face-to-face social interaction, offering time for reflection, rebuttal, and even reinventing one's identity. Some have suggested that these Internet-based literacy features may enhance traditional reading comprehension, especially awareness of the author (Leu, 2000). It seems equally possible that a transitional literacy event such as IM may help to highlight the subtleties of oral conversation.

The complex nature of the social-cognitive processing needed for this hybrid literacy activity is compellingly illustrated in the Lewis and Fabos (2000) case study of the IM practices of two 13-year-old girls. In addition to maintaining their "best friends" bond by sharing news and feelings, they each negotiate and manipulate other peer relationships through careful attention to the style and content of IM messages. They are well aware that they adjust the form and vocabulary of their messages to match the styles of their correspondents, especially those whose social networks are desirable. For example, the girls pay more attention to their spelling if their partner is considered to be "smart." Favorite topics of popular boys are monitored closely. At the same time, the girls can stay up-to-date with the social news and gossip that is the currency of junior high school relationships. This juggling of multiple social goals and partners is particularly impressive given that each girl may be swapping narratives with dozens of partners at any one time, each in a separate window.

Turn taking and timing are perhaps the most telling indicators of the manipulation of social relationships. When a popular peer comes online, the girls may wait to see whether that individual will initiate conversation first, so as not to appear overly eager. Similarly, it is important not to respond too quickly to an initiation, because it suggests that you are a "loser," with few friends online. From the reader's perspective, a long wait time is therefore not an insult, but instead is a signal of the honor of dialoguing with a popular IM partner. On the other hand, as narratives evolve over short, disjointed conversational turns, the girls will actually send back-channel messages or emoticons that suggest, "Go on—I'm still listening."

Perhaps because of the intense nature of these social analyses, both girls believed that IM can be preferable to face-to-face conversations (e.g., they felt less awkward and pressured to respond with "quick comebacks," especially with boys). In fact, they

found boys to be more open and talkative, because "it's a different medium and they can test themselves a bit more" (Lewis & Fabos, 2000, p. 466). Interestingly, their beliefs echoed some recent findings (Baker, 2002) that individuals who meet online may actually develop stronger relationships than those who date in the traditional way.

If Jane Austen Had Instant Messaging

The social knowledge needed to navigate this literacy subculture seems remarkably sophisticated. However, we suggest that it may be no more demanding than the comprehension of other written texts involving complex interpersonal relationships. In fact, these girls' social reasoning and strategies shown in IM are highly reminiscent of another genre that even young readers are expected to understand, namely, a comedy of manners. Typically a witty narrative that satirizes the customs of a particular social class or group, the comedy of manners genre has entertained audiences as long as there have been social in-groups and outgroups. Although novels by Jane Austen are regarded as the quintessential example of the genre, many children's classics share the characteristic literary devices needed to poke fun at rigid social rules (e.g., "fish out of water" characters who highlight the arrogance of the group, misunderstandings, mistaken identities, social climbing, and deception). A few obvious examples are *Tacky the Penguin* (Lester, 1988), *Amelia Bedelia* (Parish, 1985), *Martha Speaks* (Meddaugh, 1992), and *Matilda* (Dahl, 1988).

Jane Austen's *Emma*, published in 1816, is a particularly fertile site for analyzing the social inferences needed to understand a comedy of manners. In fact, the main character would have undoubtedly excelled at the social machinations underlying IM. A young woman from an upper-class British family in the early 1800s, Emma is at once a snobbish busybody and a kindhearted friend. At the pinnacle of her social hierarchy, she perceives herself to be the "last word" on the complicated social relationships and customs of her society. She therefore considers it part of her *noblesse oblige* to find eligible bachelors for marriageable maidens. Unfortunately, she is not very talented at these intrigues, which leads to an amusing series of miscommunications and social blunders.

One episode illustrates the depth of social sophistication and perspective taking needed for understanding this text. With the best of intentions, Emma decides to arrange a marriage between the handsome vicar in her village, Mr. Elton, and her friend Harriet, a charming but gullible young woman whose social status is a bit questionable. Emma's scheme to bring her two friends together seems to be going smoothly for several weeks, until Mr. Elton corners Emma in a carriage, passionately declares his love for her, and begs her to marry him! Emma is astounded and horror-struck. Mr. Elton is equally appalled when Emma insists that it is Harriet who should be his bride.

This poses a major dilemma for the reader. How could each of these characters have come to such faulty conclusions? How is Emma at the same time so socially knowledgeable, yet so naive in her matchmaking episodes? Solving these conundrums is not only the task of the characters but also the key challenge for the reader of this novel and, in fact, any comedy of manners. One technique is to read the same text from a perspective other than Emma's worldview, which may unearth clues that she blithely ignores. In fact, when her brother-in-law John Knightly points out that Mr. Elton seems to be in love with Emma, and that she seems to be encouraging him, she haughtily responds:

> "I assure you, you are quite mistaken, Mr. Elton and I are very good friends, and nothing more," and she walked on, amusing herself in the consideration of the blunders which often arise from a partial knowledge of circumstances, of the mistakes which people of high pretensions to judgment are for ever falling into; and not very well pleased with her brother for imagining her blind and ignorant, and in want of counsel. (Austen, 1816, p. 104)

To Jane Austen fans, of course, this passage is filled with delightful and multilayered ironies and contradictions. To appreciate the satire, the reader must engage in some sophisticated discourse processing along the way. Invoking Hymes's time-honored definition of "communicative competence," understanding these scenes depends on characters' and readers' knowledge of "when to speak, when not, and as to what to talk about with whom, when, where, in what manner" (1971, p. 277), as well as the essence of intersubjectivity, i.e. ("Who else knows what they know?"). Although this level of interpersonal complexity may escape some readers, it is likely that seventh-grade girls who are expert in IM can effortlessly work out these social intricacies.

CROSSING DISCIPLINARY BOUNDARIES TO FIND THE READER IN READING COMPREHENSION

Unfortunately, no model for reading comprehension can replicate the social-discourse processing of a typical seventh-grade girl. However, several disciplinary frameworks may be useful to explore how meaning is constructed through relationships among a reader, an author, and a text. Current constructivist models agree that meaning does not reside in the author, the text, or the reader, but in the "transaction" between the words in the text and the cognitive processes that the reader enlists to make sense of them (e.g., Anderson & Pearson, 1984; Marshall, 2000; Rosenblatt, 1995). Although Rosenblatt's transactional model broke new theoretical ground in the 1930s, its impact on reading and literary theory showed a kind of "sleeper" effect, resurfacing four decades later to fuel interest in reader-response frameworks (e.g., Fish, 1980). The active contribution of the reader to creating meaning has become increasingly salient, as the authority of the text and the author has lost theoretical ground. Given that every author/speaker has presuppositions that are not made explicit, every text (oral or written) has gaps. The reader's task is to fill in those gaps to construct ideas that make personal sense, using prior knowledge and text structure.

How does the reader go about this inferential task? It is telling that some reading theorists (e.g., Williams, 1984) invoke the linguistic philosopher Grice (1975) and his "cooperative conversationalist" principle to explain this process. Attempting to explain "the logic of conversation," Grice proposed that conversational partners are able to accomplish an effective exchange of information through the mutual adherence to four simple maxims: Speakers (and presumably authors) make an effort to be informative (Maxim of Quantity), truthful (Maxim of Quality), relevant (Maxim of Relation), and clear (Maxim of Manner); in turn, listeners (and readers) interpret their utterances and draw inferences by assuming that speakers have indeed followed these maxims. Yet certain conditions call for the suspension of these maxims (e.g., when irony, sarcasm, or politeness are the speaker's overriding goals). When speakers violate these maxims, listeners are cued to seek inferences about the indirect meaning, a process that Grice termed "conversational implicature." The second sentence in Emma's statement at the beginning of this chapter provides an example: The proposal to host a party for an extremely annoying person seems so irrelevant that a listener/reader may first infer that the speaker deliberately flouted the Maxim of Relation in order to show humor or sarcasm. (Of course, the third sentence clarifies how the party proposal is indeed relevant and, in fact, is critical to Emma's social goals.)

Another promising crossing of disciplinary boundaries is to integrate the perspectives of those who study constructive models of reading comprehension, and those who study the social knowledge that underlies children's interactions with others (e.g., Crick & Dodge, 1994). Although these theorists rarely cite the other discipline's work, they seem to be grappling with similar questions, methodologies, and interpretations. An attempt to integrate these two bodies of knowledge may help reframe the puzzling finding that many students struggle with reading comprehension even after typical decoding, vocabulary, and fluency skills are mastered. In a nutshell, to what extent do these reading comprehension profiles reflect the well-documented social information-processing problems of many students with

learning disabilities (Wong & Donahue, 2002)?

Are Struggling Comprehenders "Inactive" or "Freely Associating" in Recruiting Their Social Database?

A Paradox

The research base on reading comprehension in students with learning disabilities (LD) is small. Studies of "higher order" or "inferential" comprehension are even more rare. This is not surprising given that most students with LD face significant hurdles in phonological processing, word decoding, fluency, and vocabulary knowledge. A limited-capacity information-processing paradigm suggests that readers whose word recognition is not automatic must allocate more attention toward decoding, which then reduces the focus on integrating semantic and text structure cues, and monitoring meaning. Given considerable research support for this "bottleneck" explanation (Perfetti, 1994), it seems reasonable to hypothesize that improvement in decoding and fluency will automatically remove obstacles to comprehension.

Nevertheless, there is increasing evidence that many students struggle with reading comprehension despite fundamental word-recognition, vocabulary, and fluency skills (e.g., Nation & Snowling, 1998; Oakhill & Yuill, 1996). In fact, an eminent panel of researchers was convened by the U.S. Department of Education to write a comprehensive review of the literature on effective interventions for reading comprehension for students with disabilities (Gersten et al., 1998). In generating possible sources of reading comprehension deficits that persist even when lower order skills have been mastered, this review "rounds up the usual suspects" in the low performance of students with LD in most academic domains. Most are metacognitive deficiencies or inefficiencies: in knowledge base, relevant background knowledge, knowledge of story and expository structures, and strategic processing.

However, this review proposes two other frameworks that appear to be contradictory. Students with LD have been characterized as "inactive readers," in that they often fail to apply the knowledge base and text strategies that they in fact possess. In particular, they have difficulty on tasks that require inferencing, or "going beyond the text" to integrate information (e.g., Laing & Kamhi, 2002; McCormick, 1992; Oakhill & Yuill, 1996). On the other hand, these students have also been portrayed as "freely associating readers," who depend *too much* on their own knowledge base, therefore missing the gist of the text. This overreliance on background knowledge may reflect earlier tendencies to depend on context to compensate for word-recognition difficulties (Nation & Snowling, 1998). (It is interesting to note that reader response frameworks are not mentioned in the Gersten et al. [1998] review.)

Interpreting the Paradox

How can this apparent paradox be resolved? Although not all inferential tasks require social knowledge, it is likely that most tap some aspect of interpersonal reasoning, at least in narrative and persuasive texts. One comprehensive model developed to understand the complex factors underlying social interaction (Crick & Dodge, 1994) may elucidate this question. Based on dozens of studies of children's social development, the model hypothesizes that children approach any social situation with a database of memories of past social experiences, as well as acquired social rules and schemas (parallel to reading theorists' notion of "prior knowledge"), and then receive a particular set of social cues as input. Before making a social response, the child processes these cues in five interactive phases: (1) encoding, through attending to and perceiving social cues; (2) representing and interpreting the cues; (3) selecting a goal; (4) retrieving possible responses from long-term memory; and (5) evaluating and choosing a response. A key feature is that feedback loops connect all previous steps, filtered through the database of social experiences.

Most studies examine these five phases in isolated ways. However, one comprehensive study (Tur-Kaspa & Bryan, 1994) of all phases of social information processing in

one sample of students can serve as an "advance organizer" for the following research: Students in grades 3, 4, 7, and 8 listened to brief, audiotaped conflict narratives (without resolutions) about children interacting with peers, teachers, or siblings. For example, "One free period, Bill has nothing to do. He walks outside and sees two of his classmates playing a game. Bill really wants to play with them. He walks up to them but they just keep playing." Students were then asked to retell the story and state the problem (encoding and interpretation), suggest possible solutions, evaluate other solutions, choose a solution, and then enact it, through roleplaying.

In general, compared to average-achieving peers in both the younger and older age groups, students with LD performed more poorly in all phases of social information processing. When compared to low-achieving peers who had not been identified as having disabilities, the students with LD demonstrated greater difficulty in two phases: encoding social cues, and selecting competent social solutions. Looking more closely, however, these findings of Tur-Kaspa and Bryan (1994) foreshadow evidence for both characterizations of struggling readers as "inactive" or "freely associating" in their processing of social cues.

First, even for this simple narrative, the retellings of students with LD included not only fewer key ideas but also more "insertions," ideas not provided by the text. This finding could be interpreted in a positive way, as evidence that the students activated prior knowledge in a "transaction" with the text, or in a negative way, as evidence that they added idiosyncratic details in a "freely associative" way. Evidence for an "inactive" approach comes from the pattern that students with LD generated the same repertoire of social solutions for the protagonist as did the other groups. However, when asked, "Which of these solutions would *you* choose?", students with LD selected less effective social solutions. Again, this could be interpreted in opposite ways: These students failed to activate their social knowledge base at the appropriate time; or, based on their own database of peer difficulties, they reasoned that their marginal social status may call for solutions different from those that work for other classmates (Wong & Donahue, 2002). These dilemmas are echoed in many of the studies reviewed in the next section.

CONVERGING QUESTIONS ACROSS STUDIES OF SOCIAL COGNITION AND READING COMPREHENSION

In the following section, the convergences in research questions and findings are highlighted across two typically separate domains of research: social cognition and reading comprehension. Studies are organized according to their focus on three phases of social information processing: perceiving and interpreting social cues; clarifying social goals; and constructing and evaluating social responses.

Perception and Interpretation of Social Cues

Social Cognition Studies

Although social cognition studies are not substitutes for reading comprehension research, they may provide insights about the perceptions that students bring to a reading task, allowing inferences to be drawn between comprehension of real-life situations and comprehension of written text. The scenarios used to assess social problem solving in these studies may lack the shifts across time and place, cast of secondary characters, and subplots that enrich literature selections, but they can follow a story grammar format familiar to written text, which includes setting and character, introduction of a problem or conflict, attempts to resolve the conflict, and a resolution or outcome. (However, many studies use brief narrative "stems" that introduce the setting and conflict, then invite the listener to predict possible outcomes.) Audio and verbal presentations have been supplemented with written texts to support students' listening comprehension, without requiring them to complete a reading task.

Given that early characterizations of LD focused on problems in perceptual process-

ing, it is no surprise that the perception and interpretation of interpersonal cues are two of the most frequently studied domains. Using narrative texts presented orally, and sometimes with accompanying written scripts, students have been asked to recall and interpret characters' nonverbal behavior, words, and actions, and to predict consequences. Whether scenes were enacted on videotape or read aloud with accompanying written scripts, students with LD typically generated less sophisticated and less accurate interpretations of the social scenarios before them. For example, in a study of African American boys with learning and behavioral concerns, Weiss (1984) presented a series of social scenarios, either verbally or via videotape. The scenarios depicted boys engaged in neutral, friendly, cooperative, teasing, horseplay, fighting, or angry interactions. Results indicated that the groups with LD rated scenes as less friendly than did the groups of typical achievers. In addition, students with LD related more inaccurate pieces of information when retelling scenarios that had been presented verbally.

One particularly challenging task for students with LD seems to be the identification of characters' deception, an important literary device. For example, students were read narratives about peer interactions in which one person lied to another. Students with LD were able to recognize that the statements were inaccurate, but they were less likely than peers to realize that the character was deliberately lying, and they generally failed to question the character's motives (Pearl, Bryan, Fallon, & Herzog, 1991). Similarly, when asked to predict how a peer might urge them to participate in misconduct, adolescents with LD were more likely than typical classmates to anticipate direct invitations (e.g., "Let's sneak out this video") rather than indirect and persuasive requests (e.g., "This video isn't worth much so no one will even care if we sneak it out") (Pearl, Bryan, & Herzog, 1990; Pearl & Bryan, 1992).

These findings are similar to other explanations that students with LD give their conversational partners the benefit of the doubt, reflecting their overreliance on the

Gricean assumptions (Donahue, 2000). From a social cognitive perspective, Pearl et al. (1991) suggest that these students may not be able to imagine why someone would lie or manipulate. Therefore, given their difficulty in disregarding their own perspective when making an inference about another person's intentions, they "might adhere to their scripted knowledge more rigidly than other students and thus fail to recognize significant deviations (p. 15)." Again, this illustrates the "freely associating" explanation, in that an overreliance on one's social database may actually obscure textual cues.

Reading Comprehension Studies

Research on reading comprehension has found considerable individual variation in readers' willingness or ability to mobilize their social databases. Readers' encoding and interpretation of textual cues about social interaction differ according to their social-cognitive abilities, attitudes, and even personalities. In a unique study that directly sought to identify the social-cognitive processes that readers tap in order to comprehend written text, Hynds (1985) asked 83 typically achieving 11th-grade readers to write about a liked and disliked peer, then a favorite and least favorite character in a short story. Students whose descriptions of peers were rich and multidimensional were more likely to offer complex portrayals of fictional characters. This higher level of social-cognitive ability was especially evident among students who reported reading extensively beyond the curricular demands placed upon them. Students with high and low levels of social-cognitive ability, as assessed through the peer writing task, demonstrated no differences in their response to factual questions about the story. However, social-cognitive ability did predict scores on inferential questions. Those students who expressed insights about their peers were more likely to form successful inferences about the narrative text.

Hynds also examined these students' awareness of critical narrative elements. From a list of 20 questions, students were asked to choose the 5 questions that were most important to understanding the story.

Those with higher levels of social-cognitive ability were more likely to select questions that reflected interest in others. In other words, their choices reflected awareness of the actions and motivations of not only the characters but also the author (e.g., "How can we explain the way people behave in the story?"; "What is the writer's attitude toward people in the story?") Other question choices demonstrated links between characters in the text and people familiar to the readers themselves (e.g., "Are any of the characters in the story like people I know?"). In contrast, students with less social-cognitive ability seemed to focus on their own level of engagement, choosing questions such as "Does the story succeed in getting me involved in the situation?" For these students, a plot revolving around topics of personal interest or familiar experience may prove to be more enticing.

Another study of adolescent readers pointed out the difficulty that many face in perceiving characters' emotions, especially in complex narratives about social situations (Curran, Kintsch, & Hedberg, 1996). Even typical readers in grades 8 and 9 failed to recall all of the details needed to understand the characters' interactions, although they were able to access the information when directly probed. Students with LD not only recalled less character information than did typical readers but also their interpretations did not benefit from the probes. This pattern echoes the findings of Tur-Kaspa and Bryan (1994) and Weiss (1984) that many students find it challenging to encode and recall social interaction cues in even brief narratives, whether presented in auditory, video, or written form. This pattern may reflect general memory limitations, or the "inactive reader" explanation that students did not apply their own social schemas to organize the information in the text.

The perception and encoding of social cues in text have also been found to be influenced by readers' emotional ties to characters (e.g., Campbell & Williams, 2000; Gaskins, 1996; Hynds, 1989). In one clever research design, Gaskins (1996) selected avid, eighth-grade basketball fans from Boston and Philadelphia to read and retell a passage about a game. Only readers who were self-proclaimed fanatic supporters of their hometown teams were selected. The text described a fight during a game between a Boston team (presumably the Celtics) and a Philadelphia team (presumably the 76ers). Although the text itself was neutral in terms of the validity of the referees' calls and which team started the fight, the readers' descriptions and interpretations of the text were directly biased by their emotional involvement in the teams. This was dramatically illustrated by the comparison of readers' responses to a control passage of the same story with fictional teams. This finding portrays both groups as "freely associating readers," in that their expectations induced them to elaborate on ideas that did not appear in the text, although resulting in opposite interpretations.

Clarification of Goals

Social Cognition Studies

The notion that variations in social information processing may reflect differences in social goals is a relatively new one; earlier versions of social information processing did not even include this component. However, it is likely to be a powerful factor in explaining the social strategies of students with LD (see also the chapter by Brinton & Fujiki, Chapter 7, this volume). One study found that, in response to narratives about conflict, boys without LD were more likely to have the goal of compromise, whereas the boys with LD preferred the goals of acquiescence, avoidance, or following rules (Carlson, 1987).

In order to examine the social goals and strategies that children with LD chose in four hypothetical situations involving making and keeping friends, Oliva and La Greca (1988) conducted interviews consisting of both open-ended and multiple-choice questions. Participants were 60 boys divided into an older group, ages 11–13 years, and a younger group, ages 8–9 years. On open-ended questions, students without LD expressed more friendly and sophisticated, or specific, goals than did those with LD. Older students generated friendlier strategies and goals than did younger children. Over-

all, the responses of older students with LD were most like those of younger students without LD. Interestingly, when given a set of choices in a multiple-choice format, however, students with LD were not significantly different from their peers without LD, providing some evidence for the "inactive reader" profile. Students in both groups chose friendlier strategies and more sophisticated goals when questions were presented in a multiple-choice format than when they were open-ended, suggesting that some written formats may support and facilitate comprehension.

Reading Comprehension Studies

Although readers' social goals for characters have not been directly studied in reading comprehension research, much has been written about differences in the individual's own goals as a reader. In particular, one critical theme discussed by Rosenblatt (1995) has been recently reintroduced and reframed (i.e., her distinction between *efferent* and *aesthetic* purposes for reading). She argued that the reader's "stance," or purpose, for reading may vary, and that the same reader may take away different meanings from the same text at different times. For example, if we read *The Great Gatsby* (Fitzgerald, 1925) to find out facts about the history of bootlegging in the 1920s, we are taking an efferent stance, the "reading for information" goal often associated with traditional schooling. If we select *The Great Gatsby* for an emotional journey that symbolizes lost dreams, we are taking an aesthetic stance.

Vipond, Hunt, Jewett, and Reither (1990) suggest that the aesthetic stance can be further broken down into two goals or modes: story-driven reading and dialogic reading. Pleasure readers who immerse themselves in text to "find out what happens next" in a world of characters and plots are operating in a story-driven mode. Readers who see the interpretation of text as an active conversation between themselves and the author are engaged in dialogic, or "point-driven" reading (i.e., as if they are frequently querying, "So what's your point?"). They begin the reading task as an opportunity to question and evaluate the author's ideas, and continue to seek answers to their questions as they proceed through the text.

Of course, expert readers move flexibly in and out of efferent, aesthetic, story-driven, and dialogic modes, depending on their own characteristics, the nature of the text, and the task and setting demands. In studies that attempted to account for the wide range of reader responses to short stories, Vipond et al. (1990) tested these reader, text, and task variables. In fact, their studies of "think-alouds" suggest that readers can be rather easily induced to change modes, depending on differences among texts and the kinds of questions asked by the experimenters.

For our purposes, perhaps the most interesting question is, "What triggers a dialogic response?" Some readers seemed to bring a characteristic stance, based on their personalities and interests in the topic. Reading ability was also a factor. In fact, some expert readers (e.g., professionals reading in their fields) create assumptions about the author and context before they even begin to read (Geisler, 1990). Similarly, Vipond et al. (1990) reported that college professors are more dialogic than undergraduate students. For all readers, however, dialogic reading may be motivated when they encounter ideas that are discrepant from their expectations (especially if in an information-driven mode), or unresolved issues in the plot (especially if in a story-driven mode). This has important implications for understanding why struggling readers often do not actively question authors' ideas, given the evidence that these students are "inactive" in monitoring and identifying incongruous or confusing segments of both oral and written discourse.

Constructing and Evaluating Social Responses

Social Cognition Studies

Students' generation and evaluation of ways to respond to social dilemmas are obviously greatly influenced by how they perceive the interaction, and their goals for themselves or the characters, filtered through their social scripts. However, a number of studies

suggest that this phase of the social information processing remains particularly challenging for students with LD, even when their perceptions and goals are similar to those of other students.

In one early study that used both an auditory and written format, Silver and Young (1985) presented to eighth-grade boys a series of social problem-solving tasks, all of which were read aloud while students followed along on a written script. Both open-ended and multiple-choice questions were used to assess students' ability to predict outcomes, to identify the means that would lead to a desired goal, and to identify consequences. In both formats, students with LD generated fewer appropriate outcomes and consequences for problem situations than did their nondisabled peers. Students with LD also identified less often than their typically achieving peers the means that would lead to a specific goal. These findings have been replicated across different age groups, types of social problems, and methodologies. For example, when asked about how a child might join in an activity with others or resolve a situation involving conflict, students with LD have been found to generate fewer alternative responses (Carlson, 1987; Hartas & Donahue, 1997; Toro, Weissberg, Guare, & Liebenstein, 1990; Tur-Kaspa & Bryan, 1994) and to prefer less competent strategies (Bryan, Sonnefeld, & Greenberg, 1981; Carlson, 1987; Tur-Kaspa & Bryan, 1994) than their classmates.

Reading Comprehension Studies

Several studies of reading comprehension by Joanna Williams and her colleagues (Campbell & Williams, 2000; Williams, 1991, 1993; Williams & Ellsworth, 1990) have assessed students' knowledge of solutions to comparable social-interaction dilemmas in written texts. In fact, because most of these studies provide both an auditory and a written version of the scenarios to control for decoding problems, the procedures are almost identical to those of the social cognition studies. However, these studies offer richer explanations for why it appears that students with LD appear to have less access to appropriate social responses. The dilemmas of how to interpret students' under- or overuse of their prior knowledge to understand narratives are especially apparent in these studies.

For example, adolescents with and without LD were asked to read along with an audiotape of short texts about a character's personal/social problem, to retell the problem, then to predict how the main character would solve the problem (Williams, 1991). Students whose retellings included elaborations that were not literally in the text, but typically were based on their own prior knowledge or beliefs, made less accurate predictions. This pattern held true for all students, but students with LD were more likely than typical readers to "import information from sources other than the text" (Williams, 1993, p. 633) and, consequently, generated less effective problem solutions.

Two intriguing studies explored the comprehension of text that may violate readers' social values. Williams (1991) and Campbell and Williams (2000) examined adolescents' predictions of a character's decision about a social dilemma (e.g., deciding to go to a movie with a friend vs. fulfilling his promise to his mother to wash recycled bottles). The final sentence in each vignette stated the character's priority, strongly suggesting his probable choice (e.g., "Larry would rather see the movie, though, even if it means making his mother mad"). Adolescents with LD (Williams, 1991) and typical adolescents (Campbell & Williams, 2000) attended to the final statement on control paragraphs in which the two choices were neutral in terms of social values. However, all readers were more likely to ignore the final statement in paragraphs in which the character seemed likely to violate a social norm (selfishness vs. helpfulness), and instead tended to predict that the character would select a more conscientious response. This response pattern was significantly more likely for students with LD (Williams, 1991). This is analogous to the Pearl et al. (1991) study showing that students with LD were more reluctant to believe that a character was lying, perhaps because this violated their social scripts.

In a closer look at the effects of readers' attitudes toward social norms on their comprehension, Campbell and Williams (2000) first collected data on adolescents' "social desirability," a personality measure of the need to present oneself in a favorable light, often correlated with the need for social approval. For example, many "true" responses on statements such as "I never say anything that would make a person feel bad" would be typical of an individual with high social desirability. After reading the kinds of vignettes described earlier, students with higher social desirability attitudes were more likely to predict that the character would select the response that conformed to social norms, apparently disregarding the final priority statement. In fact, social desirability scores predicted reading comprehension independent of reading levels. The authors suggest that readers with high social desirability needs, who typically are stricter in their expectations of themselves and others, may have had difficulty feeling empathy for characters who were planning to behave selfishly. One hypothesis is that readers' emotional responses to this dissonance may actually distract attention from text-based ideas, or lead readers to resolve their conflict with the characters by casting about for other possible explanations. Interestingly, readers justified their incorrect predictions by invoking their "real-world social knowledge" (i.e., ideas not represented in the text but based on students' prior experiences). For example, one reader reported, "Larry will wash those bottles because he will get punished if he does not do what his mother says."

In one of the few studies that used an authentic literary text, Williams (1993) assessed children's ability to identify story themes. In two experiments, students with LD (approximately 14 years old) were compared with two groups of typical readers, an age-matched group and a younger group (approximately 10 years old), matched on reading comprehension scores. Students were asked to read along with an audiotape of condensed versions of two short stories. One focused on an adolescent girl's efforts to become popular with her classmates, even at the cost of changing her usual social identity; the second dealt with a girl's experiences living with her grieving grandfather after her grandmother's death. At two mid-points in the story, readers were asked to summarize and then predict what would happen next. At the end of the story, readers summarized, stated the theme of the story, and then justified their theme. The three groups did not differ on the number of acceptable predictions, or on the abstractness of their themes. Nondisabled age-matched readers outperformed both of the other groups on the number of idea units in the summaries, and the number of acceptable theme statements. However, generating a theme judged acceptable by adult readers was a difficult task for both the LD readers and the younger group: Only 10% of these students produced a theme statement for the first story (21% for the second story) compared with 100% (64% for the second story) of the nondisabled readers.

In a more sensitive measure of "theme awareness," however, students' verbal protocols were coded for phrases that suggested emerging recognition of themes. Surprisingly, for both stories, students with LD showed significantly less theme awareness than even their younger reading-matched controls, who in turn showed less theme awareness than the older non-LD readers. In an effort to explore this finding, verbal protocols were also examined for "idiosyncratic responses," defined as ideas based on personal feelings or experiences rather than on information from the text. For example, one girl with LD justified her prediction about the main character's actions with the comment, "Because I used to be like that—when I was a little kid—too shy." Although these "intrusions" were not frequent (only 50 were produced by 70 students during open-ended discussions of two stories), they seemed to be related to theme representation. Students who verbalized more idiosyncratic ideas were also less likely to show theme awareness. The two groups of nondisabled readers were not found to differ in the use of idiosyncratic ideas, despite a 4-year age difference. However, students with LD mentioned more idiosyncratic ideas than either group of nondisabled readers.

As the author points out, these findings are based on small samples of students in private schools, so replication is important. Of course, this pattern supports other evidence that students with LD have difficulty "getting the point." However, the ideas considered "idiosyncratic" or "intrusions" in students' summaries might be reframed as "activating prior knowledge" or "making intertextual links" in reader response models. It is possible that what appear to be reading comprehension "errors" or misinterpretations of text may in fact reflect differences in the ways readers process social-cognitive cues. Reader-based variables, including affective domains such as attitudes, personality traits, and emotional involvement, seem to influence not only the encoding and interpretation of social cues but also the goals readers set for themselves and the characters in their texts.

In case studies of 4 typical adolescent readers, Hynds (1989) illustrates the variation across readers in their ability or willingness to bring their prior knowledge about social domains to understanding text. Although all 4 students showed age-appropriate social-cognitive abilities, they differed in the degree to which they applied their understandings about people to reading comprehension. Both motivational and classroom factors seemed to play a role. One reader did not realize that his own social experiences were even applicable to literary texts. Two students were likely to disengage if the text was discrepant from their social scripts. Another student, an avid reader outside the classroom, showed sophisticated links between her social cognitive knowledge and understanding of story characters, but this skill emerged only in written work, not during oral discourse. These patterns suggest that engaging social-cognitive processes in text comprehension is not automatic for all students, and that this ability seems to be unrelated to typical measures of school achievement. Another critical dimension seems to be the social context in which the text is read, discussed, and transformed (e.g., Beach, 2000; Lewis, 1998; Moller & Allen, 2000).

Despite the difficulty of constructing abstract themes, three recent studies found that students with LD (grades 5–8) and even young typical and disabled readers (in grades 2 and 3) in high poverty schools (Wilder & Williams, 2001; Williams, Brown, Silverstein, & deCani, 1994; Williams et al., 2002) can be taught to identify story themes. After a multicomponent intervention program that included structured lessons, strategy training, and discussion, students were able to identify instructed themes in unfamiliar stories. Ironically, the discussion component of instruction encouraged students to map themes to their own life experiences, cognitive activities that were considered to be "idiosyncratic responses" in previous studies. Nevertheless, recognizing themes that had not been included in the instruction continued to be difficult for many students.

HOW TO READ A COMEDY OF MANNERS

So what do we now know about how to understand the characters' social interactions in a comedy of manners novel? For example, how could Emma and Mr. Elton have had such a communication breakdown? To discern and appreciate the ironies, we must engage and apply our own social-cognitive processes by getting inside the heads of our characters.

According to her database of social memories and scripts, Emma is not only at the pinnacle of social status, but she also has quite a high opinion of herself and of her matchmaking skills. She also proclaims that she has no interest in marriage for herself, an unusual position to take in that era. In light of these beliefs, it does not occur to her that Mr. Elton might have illusions of being a suitable match for her. For example, in one episode, Emma decides to draw a portrait of Harriet. Mr. Elton pleads to be allowed to attend every sitting, commenting on every line drawn, waxing eloquent about how lovely Harriet is, and how perfect the drawing is. He even gallantly volunteers to travel to London himself to have the drawing framed.

Emma eagerly encourages these attentions, perceiving them as unmistakable signals of Mr. Elton's love for Harriet. In other words, this lens filtered her perceptions of Mr. Elton's interest in the drawing of her friend as showing a love for Harriet, not for the one who drew the portrait. Her success as a matchmaker is verified, and she continues her matchmaking goals, which include persuading the doubtful Harriet that Mr. Elton really is wooing her.

What social-cognitive processes do we need to make sense of Mr. Elton's behavior? According to his own database and social status, Mr. Elton does not consider himself to be of high enough social status to court Emma. Yet Harriet is definitely out of the question as a mate; as a poor vicar, he knows he must marry a wealthy woman, and he no doubt assumes that Emma understands that need. Although he is probably startled at Emma's sudden interest and attentions, his snobbery and avarice preclude the realization that it is *Harriet* that Emma has in mind for him. So he perceives and interprets Emma's behavior as clear evidence that she is interested in him. Selecting a goal of convincing Emma to be his wife, and accessing the response to pursue her through flattery, gallant behavior, and praise for the beauty of her friend Harriet, he evaluates and confirms his response through Emma's apparent delight in his attentions. Finally, he arranges to be alone with her and declares his undying devotion, enacting his social response. Emma's unambiguous response is "I have seen you only as the admirer of my friend. In no other light could you have been more to me than a common acquaintance!"

Of course, this analysis may illuminate the social-cognitive processes of Emma and Mr. Elton, but it is incomplete without your response as the reader. What is your database on social mores of the early 19th-century British upper class? How do your database, interests, and attitudes filter the details of the text as you perceive and interpret the characters' goals and actions? What is your goal in reading the novel? To what degree are you reading to find out what happens next? As you engage in dialogue with the author, do you find personal meaning in the text related to your own matchmaking efforts, or interactions with snobs, or complicated love life? As you anticipate the next social moves and reactions of the characters, are you gathering enough momentum to form a coherent story?

FINAL THOUGHTS

Explaining the development of both oral and written language comprehension is obviously a thorny and multifactored phenomenon (cf. Bishop, 1997). Persistent difficulties in phonological awareness, decoding, fluency, vocabulary knowledge, and text structure awareness loom large in assessment and intervention approaches to comprehension problems. However, converging evidence across several disciplines suggests that an analysis of the reader's social-cognitive processing may also shed light on the reading comprehension profiles of many students, especially those with social-cognitive difficulties, and especially in texts that pose social dilemmas. The apparently "freely associative" or "off-the-wall" interpretations that some students derive from socially complex texts may in fact be reasonable conclusions, in light of the ways in which readers' database of social experiences filters their perception and interpretation of textual cues, their selection of interpersonal and reading goals, and their predictions and evaluation of characters' social responses (Donahue & Foster, in press). Conversely, so-called "inactive readers" may be unwilling or unable to apply their knowledge about people to reading comprehension, especially if the text is discrepant from their social schemas.

Of course, research is needed to assess directly interactions among social-cognitive processes and reading comprehension, especially to identify individual differences among readers and their responses to particular kinds of texts and text genres. Also, more conceptual work is needed to clarify the contributions of the readers' social database to comprehension. Based on current models, reader interpretations that elaborate on the literal meaning of the text may be perceived as either "a failure to suppress irrelevant information" (Bishop, 1997) or as active construction of meaning through the creation of intertextual links. A teacher hearing a reader's comment that goes be-

yond the text must make an instantaneous decision about whether to discourage and correct the "intrusion" or to scaffold the reader's attempt to connect the idea to the text (Hynds & Appleman, 1997). Complicating the decision, the teacher may recognize that a child with LD may have fewer expressive language resources to make clear how his or her personal insight is relevant to the text. A discourse analysis of these comments may reveal that they form a very broad category, and that some are more "idiosyncratic" than others. Determining the discourse features that establish a comment's relevance will be a dynamic process, of course, depending on the nature of the text and the reader's goals.

Research on interventions that recruit these social cognition and reading comprehension relationships may be especially promising. Williams and Ellsworth (1990) suggest the reciprocal effectiveness of teaching social problem solving within the context of written narrative instruction. Similarly, encouraging students to map text themes to their own interpersonal experiences proved to be helpful in teaching students to identify themes in unfamiliar stories (Wilder & Williams, 2001; Williams et al., 1994, 2002). This approach is entirely consistent with current constructivist models of literature-based instruction that focus on individual reader responses and dialogue about text (e.g., Donahue, Szymanski, & Flores, 1999; Raphael & Au, 1998).

At the least, however, these converging findings suggest that we must be alert to those features of texts that require complex social inferences. Creating a measure of "social readability" or "interpersonal considerateness" of text may be useful for selecting literature for individual students, especially because typical readability measures do not appear to predict the degree to which readers must "think about people thinking about people." For example, well-known short stories such as *Charles* and *The Lottery* by Shirley Jackson (1948) rarely exceed the fourth-grade readability level, yet their social inferencing demands often stump high school students. In fact, popular literature choices for preschool through adolescent students include many themes that occur in the comedy of manners genre. Consider the degree to which readers must "get inside the heads of characters" to appreciate stories with themes such as "fish out of water" (e.g., *Tacky the Penguin* [Lester, 1988], *Harry Potter and the Sorcerer's Stone* [Rowling, 1998], *Freak the Mighty* [Philbrick, 1993], *A Wrinkle in Time* [L'Engle, 1962]); communication breakdowns (e.g., any book in the *Amelia Bedelia* series [Parish, 1985], Shakespeare's *Romeo and Juliet*); deception (trickster tales and detective stories, including the first-grade reading-level series *Nate the Great* [Sharmat, 1977]); mistaken identities (e.g., *The True Confessions of Charlotte Doyle* [Avi, 1992], *The Prince and the Pauper* [Twain, 1909]); and a clash of cultures (e.g., *Sign of the Beaver* [George, 1983], *Things Fall Apart* [Achebe, 1958], *The Indian in the Cupboard* [Banks, 1980]).

In an analysis of children's responses to multicultural literature, Galda (1998) offers the metaphor that certain texts may act as mirrors or windows. For children who can link an experience in their database with a text theme, a book allows them to see themselves in the story. For children who cannot identify with a character or situation, a book may act as a window, a vicarious look into another culture or experience. Ultimately, however, Galda describes reading in this way: "Rather than a mirror of ourselves, or a window into the lives of others, reading can be like looking through a slowly darkening window. Initially we see through the window in the lives of others, but as we come to know the characters the light slowly dims and their image is replaced by our own" (Galda, 1998, p. 8). Presumably, the reverse is also true; children who approach text as a mirror may also come to see through their own social dilemmas to a window on other worlds.

REFERENCES

Achebe, C. (1958). *Things fall apart*. London: Heinemann.

Alvermann, D. E. (2001). *Effective literacy instruction for adolescents*. Executive Summary and Paper Commissioned by the National Reading Conference. Chicago, IL: National Reading Conference.

Anderson, R., & Pearson, P. D. (1984). A schema-theoretic view of basic processes in reading comprehension. In P. D. Pearson (Ed.), *Handbook of reading research* (pp. 255–292). New York: Longman.

Austen, J. (1816). *Emma*. New York: Bantam Classics.

Avi, M. (1992). *The true confessions of Charlotte Doyle*. New York: HarperCollins.

Baker, A. (2002). What makes an online relationship successful? Clues from couples who met in cyberspace. *Cyberpsychology and Behavior, 5,* 363–375.

Banks, L. R. (1980). *The Indian in the cupboard.* Garden City, NJ: Doubleday.

Beach, R. (2000). Reading and responding to literature at the level of activity. *Journal of Literacy Research, 32,* 237–251.

Bishop, D. (1997). *Uncommon understanding: Development and disorders of language comprehension in children.* Hove, UK: Psychology Press.

Bryan, J. H., Sonnefeld, L. J., & Greenberg, F. Z. (1981). Ingratiation preferences of learning disabled children. *Learning Disability Quarterly, 4,* 170–179.

Campbell, K., & Williams, J. (2000). Readers' social desirability and text that violates social values: Evidence of an interaction. *Journal of Educational Psychology, 92,* 515–523.

Carlson, C. I. (1987). Social interaction goals and strategies of children with learning disabilities. *Journal of Learning Disabilities, 20,* 306–311.

Crick, N. R., & Dodge, K. A. (1994). A review and reformulation of social information-processing mechanisms in children's social adjustment. *Psychological Bulletin, 115,* 74–101.

Curran, C., Kintsch, E., & Hedberg, N. (1996). Learning-disabled adolescents' comprehension of naturalistic narratives. *Journal of Educational Psychology, 88,* 494–507.

Dahl, R. (1988). *Matilda.* New York: Penguin.

Dewey, J. (1906). *The child and the curriculum.* Chicago: University of Chicago Press.

Donahue, M. (2000). Influences of school-age children's beliefs and goals on their elicited pragmatic performance: Lessons learned from kissing the Blarney Stone. In L. Menn & N. Bernstein-Ratner (Eds.), *Methods for studying language production* (pp. 353–368). Mahwah, NJ: Erlbaum.

Donahue, M., & Foster, S. (in press). Integration of language and discourse components with reading comprehension: It's all about relationships. In E. R. Silliman & L. C. Wilkinson (Eds.), *Language and literacy learning.* New York: Guilford Press.

Donahue, M., Szymanski, C., & Flores, C. (1999). "When Emily Dickinson met Steven Spielberg": Assessing social information processing in literacy contexts. *Language, Speech, and Hearing Services in Schools, 30,* 274–284.

Fish, S. (1980). *Is there a text in this classroom?* Cambridge, MA: Harvard University Press.

Fitzgerald, F. S. (1925). *The great Gatsby.* New York: Simon & Schuster.

Galda, L. (1998). Mirrors and windows: Reading as transformation. In T. E. Raphael & K. H. Au (Eds.), *Literature-based instruction: Reshaping the curriculum* (pp. 1–11). Norwood, MA: Christopher-Gordon.

Gaskins, R. W. (1996). "That's just how it was": The effect of issue-related emotional involvement on reading comprehension. *Reading Research Quarterly, 31,* 386–405.

Geisler, C. (1990). The artful conversation: Characterizing the development of advanced literacy. In R. Beach & S. Hynds (Eds.), *Developing discourse practices in adolescence and adulthood* (pp. 93–109). Norwood, NJ: Ablex.

George, E. G. (1983). *The sign of the beaver.* Boston: Houghton Mifflin.

Gersten, R., Williams, J., Fuchs, L., Baker, S., Koppenhaver, D., Spadorcia, S., et al. (1998). *Improving reading comprehension for children with disabilities: A review of research.* Washington, DC: Special Education Programs (ED/OSERS).

Grice, H. P. (1975). Logic and conversation. In P. Cole & J. Morgan (Eds.), *Syntax and semantics: Vol. 3. Speech acts* (pp. 41–58). New York: Academic Press.

Hartas, D., & Donahue, M. (1997). Conversational and social problem-solving skills in adolescents with learning disabilities. *Learning Disabilities Research and Practice, 12,* 213–220.

Hymes, D. (1971). On communicative competence. In J. Pride & J. Holmes (Eds.), *Sociolinguistics* (pp. 269–285). Baltimore: Penguin.

Hynds, S. (1985). Interpersonal cognitive complexity and the literary response processes of adolescent readers. *Research in the Teaching of English, 19,* 386–404.

Hynds, S. (1989). Bringing life to literature and literature to life: Social constructs and contexts of four adolescent readers. *Research in the Teaching of English, 23,* 30–61.

Hynds, S., & Appleman, D. (1997, December). Walking our talk: Between response and responsibility in the literature classroom. *English Education,* pp. 272–294.

Jackson, S. (1948). *The lottery and other stories.* New York: Farrar, Straus & Giroux.

Laing, S., & Kamhi, A. (2002). The use of think-aloud protocols to compare inferencing abilities in average and below average readers. *Journal of Learning Disabilities, 35,* 436–447.

L'Engle, M. (1962). *A wrinkle in time.* New York: Bantam/Doubleday/Dell.

Lenhart, A., Rainie, L, & Lewis, O. (2001, June 20). *Teenage life online: The rise of the instant-message generation and the Internet's impact on friendships and family relationships.* Retrieved November 20, 2003, from *http://www.pewinternet.org/reports/toc.asp?report=36)*

Lester, H. (1988). *Tacky the penguin.* New York: Houghton Mifflin.

Leu, D. J., Jr. (2000). Literacy and technology: Deictic consequences for literacy education in an information age. In M. L. Kamil, P. B. Mosenthal, P. D. Pearson, & R. Barr (Eds.), *Handbook of reading research* (Vol. 3, pp. 743–770). Mahwah, NJ: Erl-

baum.

Lewis, C. (1998). Literary interpretation as a social act. *Journal of Adolescent and Adult Literacy, 42,* 168–177.

Lewis, C., & Fabos, B. (2000). But will it work in the heartland?: A response and illustration. *Journal of Adolescent and Adult Literacy, 43,* 462–469.

Marshall, J. (2000). Research on response to literature. In M. Kamil, P. Mosenthal, P. D. Pearson, & R. Barr (Eds.), *Handbook of reading research* (pp. 381–402). Mahwah, NJ: Erlbaum.

McCormick, S. (1992). Disabled readers' erroneous response to inferential comprehension questions: Description and analysis. *Reading Research Quarterly, 27,* 54–77.

Meddaugh, S. (1992). *Martha speaks.* New York: Houghton Mifflin.

Moller, K., & Allen, J. (2000). Connecting, resisting and searching for safer places: Students respond to Mildred Taylor's *The Friendship. Journal of Literacy Research, 32,* 145–186.

Nation, K., & Snowling, M. (1998). Individual differences in contextual facilitation: Evidence from dyslexia and poor reading comprehension. *Child Development, 69,* 996–1011.

Oakhill, J., & Yuill, N. (1996). Higher order factors in comprehension disability: Processes and remediation. In C. Cornoldi & J. Oakhill (Eds.), *Reading comprehension difficulties: Processes and intervention* (pp. 69–92). Hillsdale, NJ: Erlbaum.

Oliva, A., & La Greca, A. (1988). Children with learning disabilities. Social goals and strategies. *Journal of Learning Disabilities, 21,* 301–305.

Parish, P. (1985). *Amelia Bedelia goes camping.* New York: Avon.

Pearl, R., & Bryan, T. (1992). Students' expectations about peer pressure to engage in misconduct. *Journal of Learning Disabilities, 25,* 582–585, 597.

Pearl, R., Bryan, T., Fallon, P., & Herzog, A. (1991). Learning disabled students' detection of deception. *Learning Disabilities Research and Practice, 6,* 12–16.

Pearl, R., Bryan, T., & Herzog, A. (1990). Resisting or acquiescing to peer pressure to engage in misconduct: Adolescents' expectations of probable consequences. *Journal of Youth and Adolescence, 19,* 43–55.

Perfetti, C. (1994). Psycholinguistics and reading ability. In M. A. Gernsbacher (Ed.), *Handbook of psycholinguistics* (pp. 849–894). San Diego: Academic Press.

Philbrick, R. (1993). *Freak the mighty.* New York: Scholastic.

Raphael, T. E., & Au, K. H. (1998). *Literature-based instruction: Reshaping the curriculum.* Norwood, MA: Christopher-Gordon.

Rosenblatt, L. (1995). *The reader, the text, the poem: The transactional theory of the literary work.* Carbondale: Southern Illinois Press.

Rowling, J. K. (1998). *Harry Potter and the sorcerer's stone.* New York: Scholastic.

Shantz, C. U. (1982). Thinking about people thinking

about people. *Contemporary Psychology, 27,* 376–377.

Sharmat, M. W. (1977). *Nate the great.* New York: Bantam/Doubleday/Dell.

Shulevitz, J. (2002, January 27). How to read a how-to-read book. *New York Times Book Review,* p. 27.

Silver, D., & Young, R. (1985). Interpersonal problem-solving abilities, peer status, and behavioral adjustment in learning disabled and non-learning disabled adolescents. *Advances in Learning and Behavioral Disabilities, 4,* 201–223.

Toro, P. A., Weissberg, R. P., Guare, J., & Liebenstein, N. L. (1990). A comparison of children with and without learning disabilities on social problem-solving skill, school behavior, and family background. *Journal of Learning Disabilities, 23,* 115–120.

Tur-Kaspa, H., & Bryan, T. (1994). Social-information processing skills of students with learning disabilities. *Learning Disabilities Research and Practice, 9,* 12–23.

Twain, M. (1909). *The prince and the pauper: A tale for young people of all ages.* New York: Harper.

Vipond, D., Hunt, R., Jewett, J., & Reither, J. (1990). Making sense of reading. In R. Beach & S. Hynds (Eds.), *Developing discourse practices in adolescence and adulthood* (pp. 110–135). Norwood, NJ: Ablex.

Weiss, E. (1984). Learning disabled children's understanding of social interactions of peers. *Journal of Learning Disabilities, 17,* 612–615.

Wilder, A., & Williams, J. (2001). Students with severe learning disabilities can learn higher order comprehension skills. *Journal of Educational Psychology, 93,* 268–278.

Williams, J. (1984). Categorization, macrostructure, and finding the main idea. *Journal of Educational Psychology, 76,* 874–879.

Williams, J. (1991). Comprehension by learning-disabled and nondisabled adolescents of personal/social problems presented in text. *American Journal of Psychology, 104,* 563–586.

Williams, J. (1993). Comprehension of students with or without learning disabilities: Identification of narrative themes and idiosyncratic text representations. *Journal of Educational Psychology, 85*(4), 631–641.

Williams, J., Brown, L., Silverstein, A., & deCani, J. (1994). An instructional program in comprehension of narrative themes for adolescents with learning disabilities. *Learning Disability Quarterly, 17,* 205–221.

Williams, J., & Ellsworth, N. (1990). Teaching learning disabled adolescents to think critically using a problem-solving schema. *Exceptionality, 1,* 135–147.

Williams, J., Lauer, K., Hall, K., Lord, K., Gugga, S., Bak, S., et al. (2002). Teaching elementary school students to identify story themes. *Journal of Educational Psychology, 94,* 235–248.

Wong, B. Y. L., & Donahue, M. (Eds.). (2002). *Social dimensions of learning disabilities: Essays in honor of Tanis Bryan.* Mahwah, NJ: Erlbaum.

18

The Foundational Role of Schemas in Children's Language and Literacy Learning

JUDITH FELSON DUCHAN

Teachers and speech–language therapists have many frameworks to choose from as they go about their everyday business. In this chapter I argue that those who provide services to children must understand and work within different available frameworks, one of which is schema theory. They need to see how and why frameworks underlying their practices can lead them to dichotomous thinking involving heroes and villains, and how they can avoid this way of thinking. They need to arrive at a broader and deeper way of thinking about approaches to teaching—thinking that is in allows for multiple, viable perspectives. In so doing, they will be better able to provide support for all children, including those with language and learning disabilities.

THE SCHEMA VIEW OF CHILDREN'S LEARNING

A schema is an abstract, complex, ever-changing conceptual structure. It is a coherent representation of all or part of an existing or imagined reality. Yet, at the same time, it provides a means for creating new

realities based on the existing ones. Schemas thereby provide children with the conceptual apparatus for making sense of the world around them. They have been called "the building blocks of cognition" (Rumelhart, 1980, p. 33).

A schema-based rendering of oral and written communication prompts questions about what schemas children need to learn in order to make sense of the language they hear and see. This view leads clinicians and teachers to assess children's schema knowledge and to provide them with the schemas that are necessary for speaking, understanding, reading, and writing.

Theoreticians have postulated different types of schemas to explain different aspects of children's language and literacy learning. Nelson (1986; Nelson & Gruendel, 1981), studied children's development and use of generalized event representations (referred to as GERs), a type of schema that provides children with a way to understand, remember, engage in, and talk about everyday activities. Bruner (1975; Bruner & Sherwood, 1976) has studied children's acquisition of one type of event representation, a joint-action routine, and has postulated a process of parental scaffolding by which children come to acquire this sort of schema understanding. Stein and Glenn (1979) have shown the influence of story grammar, a type of schema related to story organization, that they see as aiding a child in understanding and retelling simple stories. Finally, Lakoff and Johnson have studied the schemas that constitute metaphorical thinking (Johnson, 1987; Lakoff, 1987; Lakoff & Johnson, 1980, 1999). In so doing, they have shown how complex metaphors can structure one's thinking. For example, they have described how a conduit metaphor is often used to conceptualize acts of communication as the sending and receiving of information through an invisible conduit (Lakoff & Johnson 1980; see also Reddy, 1979).

Schema theory has also been helpful in accounting for ways that children conceive of the sound and alphabetic systems of their native languages (Kuhl, 1991). Theorists have, for example, postulated phonological schemas to account for children's ability to classify speech sounds into phonemes, such as different productions of the letter [p] into the phoneme /p/. A form of schema theory, while not called that, has also been developed to account for the patterned regularities in children's invented spellings (Read, 1971, Reece & Treiman, 2001).

The picture of how schemas actually work in these different conceptual domains has been painted differently depending on the interests of the theorists, the type of schema being studied, and the use to which the schema is put. This chapter details the similarities and differences among different versions of schema theory, the course of their development in children, and their usefulness for educational and clinical practices. In the final section, some problems raised by schema theory are outlined, along with some suggestions for how to go about solving them.

SCHEMAS: HOW THEY WORK

Schemas come in many sizes and shapes, and are used by children to accomplish a variety of functions. What is common to all schemas is that they are abstract forms or structures that become concrete when put to use. Some scholars liken this abstract-to-concrete transformation of information to a slot-filling activity, with the abstract schema containing slots to be filled with specific details of a particular experience (e.g., Mandler, 1979, p. 263). For example, an abstract action schema, such as a grasp, when activated by a rattle, accommodates to the specific shape of the rattle. This results in the child grasping the rattle in ways that differ from how he or she might grasp a bottle or a piece of cloth. Similarly, an abstract story schema, with separate slots for different story components, provides a child with a way to understand the contribution of various parts of a particular story. Little Red Riding Hood's slot for a setting has her at home with her mother, making preparations to visit her grandmother.

This ability of schemas to translate the general to the specific, the known to the new, serves children in a variety of ways. One function is to provide the conceptual basis for children to recognize and understand parts of things as whole entities. Another function is to offer children a means for interpreting parts of things in relation to other parts, and in relation to the whole. In so doing, schemas help children interpret and remember experiences, and allow them to predict what will happen on new occasions.

Prototypes

One kind of schema, a prototype (Rosch, 1978, 1981; Rosch & Mervis, 1975), is a mental structure that allows children to classify particular entities into like groups. Dogs are animals; my collie is a type of dog, as well as a type of animal. Prototype theory, like other theories of concept acquisition, render general categories as being made up of identifying attributes (or features, or components). But unlike other theories, prototype theory does not require that particular features be present in order for an object to qualify for classification. For other theories of classification, in order for an animal to be classified as a dog, it needs to bark, to have four legs, ears, and so on (e.g., Oshershon & Smith, 1981).

In prototype theory, the attributes are not criterial. A animal does not have to a have bark in order to qualify as a dog. Rather, objects have core and peripheral attributes or features that qualify different dogs as good or less good members of the class of dogs. They thereby fall somewhere along a gradient from most to least typical. Some dogs, such as a chihuahua (with little hair, small size, a peculiar bark), are less dog-like than others, such as a collie, which has more "typical" or "core" features. The dog prototype is the dog that has the most core features. Robins and sparrows are prototypical birds; apples and oranges are prototypical fruits; hammers and saws are prototypical tools. Ostriches, kiwis, and wrenches, on the other hand, are outliers, located in the periphery of their respective categories, and are therefore atypical (i.e., less prototypical) (see Figure 18.1).

Particular speech sounds, when treated from within prototype theory, have been found to have prototypical and peripheral exemplars (Grieser & Kuhl, 1989; Kuhl, 1991; Samuel, 1982; Sussman & Gekas, 1997). A prototypical /p/ sound has distinctive aspiration and a specified onset and voicing. A /p/ sound that is more peripheral or less prototypical has too little or too much aspiration, or no aspiration at all. Phonological prototypes are presumed to allow children to recognize, remember, and produce sounds and letters as they read, write, listen, and speak.

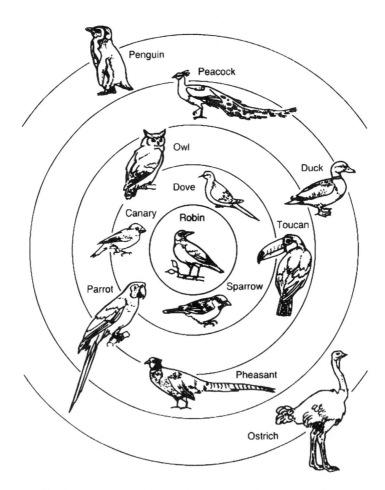

FIGURE 18.1. A robin has more core features than an ostrich. From Aitchison (1987, p. 54). Copyright 1987 by Blackwell Publishing, Inc. Reprinted by permission.

Generalized Event Representations

Nelson (1986; Nelson & Gruendel, 1981) has studied schemas that children use to represent familiar events, adopting the ideas from the notion of script first forwarded by the cognitive scientists, Schank and Abelson (1977). Nelson's generalized event representations (GERs), like Schank and Abelson's scripts, are made up of subevents. A birthday party GER involves opening presents, as well as blowing out birthday candles on a birthday cake.

Nested schemas in a GER contain information about who should do what, the temporal and causal relationships between the elements of the event (one gives presents before opening them), what props are needed to carry out the schema, and how the schema parts fit meaningfully together into a whole. For a schema about a restaurant, the participants are waiters, waitresses, and customers; the actions involve ordering, eating, and paying for food; and props include menus and food.

Children use GERs to understand, recall, describe, and participate in events. GERs play a key role in their understanding and production of meanings as they go about reading, writing, listening or speaking.

Narrative Schemas

Narrative schemas represent the underlying structure of a particular type of discourse, one that is found in classic stories told to children. Different versions of story schemas represent stories in different ways, the most popular of which has been the story grammar schema forwarded by Stein and Glenn (1979). These authors analyzed stories written for children, such as Aesop's fables, and found the stories to have the following components:

- *Setting:* Introduction of main characters, as well as the time and place for the story action. (Once upon a time there were three bears: the momma bear, the papa bear and the baby bear. They all lived in a tiny house in a great big forest.)
- *Initiating event:* An action or happening that sets up a problem or dilemma for the story. (One day a little girl named Goldilocks came by.)
- *Internal response:* The protagonist's reactions to the initiating event. (She was surprised to see the house and noticed it was empty.)
- *Attempt:* An action or plan of the protagonist to solve the problem. (She went inside to find the three bears, and she ate the baby bear's soup, broke the baby bear's chair, and fell asleep in the baby bear's bed.)
- *Consequence:* The result of the protagonist's actions. (The bears return to find things eaten and broken, and to find Goldilocks in the baby's bed.)
- *Reaction:* A response by the protagonist to the consequence. (Goldilocks ran away.)

The elements of a story grammar schema are usually portrayed as strung together in a given order, making up an episode. In multiple-episode stories, the elements are recycled, maintaining the prescribed order. In this sense, the grammar provides a schematic template for recognizing, organizing, and predicting specific information in particular stories. The story grammar schema thereby provides children with a means for understanding and predicting the structure and function of story parts in relation to the overall structure of the story. In so doing, it allows children to follow the flow of a story they are reading or listening to, and provides them with an organizational structure for creating their own oral or written stories.

The story grammar of Stein and Glenn (1979) emphasizes the plot structure of stories. Other schemas have been proposed as a way to account for other aspects of stories, such as children's understanding of suspense (high point schema of Labov & Waletsky, 1967); their understanding of how elements are strung together (Applebee, 1978; Westby, 1988); their ability to track shifts in the locale, time, and character perspectives that are being played out in the story (Duchan, Bruder, & Hewitt, 1995; Peterson, 1990); and their ability to identify a story's main theme (Williams, 2002). Stanzas have also been proposed as a schematic way that children handle rhythm and timing in the stories they create (Gee, 1999; Minami & McCabe, 1991, Sutton-Smith, 1981).

Metaphors

Lakoff and his colleagues have outlined a type of schema that works like a metaphor (Lakoff, 1987; Lakoff & Johnson, 1980; Reddy, 1979). These authors hypothesize that one complex conceptual structure (an idealized cognitive model, or ICM) serves as a source or vehicle for thinking about a set of related experiences, referred to as the target (Lakoff, 1987, Ch. 4). The target is conceptualized in terms of the meanings and experiences associated with the source. People's lives (target) become conceptualized as journeys (source), their communication (target) as message passing (source), and their anger (target) as the heating of fluid in a container (source) (Lakoff, 1987).

These metaphorical structures, or ICMs, have been found to be pervasive in the thinking of adults, assisting them in the perceptions and understanding of reality, and offering them an inferential structure for reasoning about different aspects of reality. For example, a common adult view of communication that has strongly affected educational and clinical practices is based on a target domain made up of a blend of conduit and container metaphors. The container metaphor of communication treats information as being "stored" and "retrieved" from the mind of a sender, and sent to and "stored" in the mind of the receiver. The transfer is based on a more general conduit metaphor that depicts the information as being "sent" over an invisible "conduit" from sender to receiver. The container and conduit metaphors are also present in the thinking about written language: Information contained in the text becomes transferred to the mind of the reader. Information in the mind of a writer becomes transferred, through writing, into a text.

In summary, schema theorists see schemas as serving a central role in children's language and literacy development and performance. The particular domains selected here are those that have had the clearest association with schema theory and that are closely related to language and literacy. The trends described in the literatures reviewed include the following:

- The development of prototypes provides children with a means for classifying sounds and letters, and a way to understand the differential role of attributes in a hierarchical classification system.
- The acquisition of event representations provides children with fundamental understanding and structuring of familiar events.
- The growth of narrative schemas offers a way to conceptualize story plots and character roles.
- Idealized cognitive models, such as metaphors, provide a means for transferring understandings from one domain to another.

Although proponents of the various types of schemas proposed them for specific conceptual domains, their applications can be more flexible than that. Event schemas are useful when creating and understanding narratives (Seidman, Nelson, & Gruendel, 1986), and prototypes are useful, and are indeed required, when building metaphorical parallels (Lakoff & Johnson, 1980). These types of schemas are interrelated in real-life situations, as children go about their daily lives.

SCHEMAS: HOW THEY GROW

Children's schema learning has been depicted a number of different ways. The developmental picture, like the rendering of the schemas themselves, depends on what schema theorists take to be relevant about the schemas they are depicting.

Prototypes for Reading

Phonological prototypes are known at birth. Infants who are just born display abilities to distinguish universal phonemes—sounds that are from different prototypes for all human languages (Aslin, Jusczyk, & Pisoni, 1997). The boundaries of these distinctions shift by the time a child is 6 months old, in accord with the phonemic structure of the language the child hears (Kuhl, 1991). This shift toward the native language continues, resulting in a disappearance of the prototype boundaries that children find irrelevant in their native language (Jusczyk, 1997).

Phonological prototypes for particular languages are usually worked out by the time children are 5 years old. Also, by this time, many children have developed knowledge, some in the form of schemas, about the nature of print. They may be reading signs around them, and they know about the nature of books; they probably enjoy playing a bit with the subcomponents of words, and they may be recognizing some letters of the alphabet and calling them by name. Children bring these emergent literacy skills to the task of learning the alphabetic principle: that spoken words are made up of sounds, and that these sounds correspond to letters in the alphabet (Clay, 1978, 1982; Erickson, 2000; Teale & Sulzby, 1986).

Prototypes for Spelling

Children in kindergarten and first grade are also taught to use letters of the alphabet to create their own texts. To do this, they need to develop an understanding of how their oral version of words translates into written counterparts. In so doing, they invent spellings that reflect their ideas of how to segment words. Many studies have traced patterns and stages in children's conceptions of spelling. Among the earliest and best-known of these was the study by Read (1971). He found that children as young as age 4 were able to draw from their ideas of phonemes and letters to create logical but incorrect spellings, for example, by representing the fricative prototype created by the transition between /t/ and /r/ cluster with a *chr* (e.g., spelling the word *try* as *chrie*) (p. 13). An interesting example provided by Read is children's frequent spelling substitutions of tense (long *e*) for lax vowels (short *e*) (FESH/*fish*; EGLU/*igloo*). Although Read relied on patterns of phonological feature substitutions to explain children's errors, he might just as well have

hypothesized a single category for tense and lax vowel pairs, with the tense vowel being the prototypical, preferred one and the lax one being more peripheral.

Studies of children's spelling development have revealed spelling strategies other than those based on awareness of phonemes and their combinations. Children have been found to apply a letter-naming strategy in which they use the letter name when creating their words (e.g., Reece & Treiman, 2001; Treiman, 1994; Treiman & Bourassa, 2000). For example, they may spell *light* as LIT, using the pronunciation of the vowel name *I* (*eye*). Children also insert a vowel in each syllable of a word, in order to show that the letters together make up a syllable. This occurs at a stage in which they have not yet learned the various sound–letter correspondences of vowels, so they use whatever vowels are available (MES for *miss*). Finally, some children use a rule of inserting letters such as an *i* after an *e*, following their observation that sometimes letters are not pronounced (silent). These three strategies have been portrayed as being used by children at three different stages in their development: the semiphonetic, phonetic, and transitional stages of invented spelling (Gentry, 1978). Gentry has offered the following growth in the invented spelling of the word *type* to illustrate the stages and strategies just discussed: TP (letter naming, semiphonetic), TIP (vowel insertion plus letter naming, phonetic), TIPE (silent-letter insertion, transitional).

The stages of spelling development are usually treated as linguistic rules that apply to words in a uniform way. But some recent evidence suggests that these strategies vary depending on the phonological structures of the target words. Reece and Treiman (2001) have found, for example, that the letter-naming strategy applies differently to words containing the syllabic /r/ and the /u/ vowel, and Varnhagen, McCallum, Burstow, Pawlik, and Poon (1997) have found that there is more letter naming for the vowel /e/ than for /ai/ and /o/. These exceptions in the linguistic strategy portrayal of spelling development have not been examined in a schema theoretical way, but there are lessons to be learned from classifying sounds and their combinations into core and peripheral categories that will predict how they be spelled by inventive spellers. This rendition, if it works like the prototype approach for phoneme acquisition, can offer a more detailed and predictive representation for the spelling inventions of particular children, or groups of children.

In summary, children who are learning to read and write draw from a set of well-established ideas about sounds, letters, and words, and how they all go together to make meaning. The typical way of rendering this learning is as linguistic rules or srategies. Some of these complex processes may involve prototypes, although they have not been talked about or studied from a schema theoretical point of view (but see Richgels, 2001; Read, 1971; and Reece & Treiman, 2001, for an approximation).

Generalized Event Representations

Nelson, when studying children's learning of GERs, focused on when children begin to conceptualize events and how their conceptualizations are used to describe, recall, and engage in familiar, everyday happenings. Nelson found evidence of the effects of such event knowledge on tasks measuring children's memory, language, discourse, and categorization abilities (Nelson, 1986). Event knowledge was shown to be a conceptual precursor to children's understanding of objects ("this bottle"), object classifications ("That animal is a dog"), social relationships and roles (mother, sister), language symbols (names for people, actions, events) and narratives (Nelson, 1986).

Nelson did a number of studies to trace the development of GERs in normally developing children ages 3–8 years or so (e.g., Nelson, 1986). Nelson and Gruendel (1981) found a developmental progression from GERs of familiar episodes to less familiar episodes, and from more linear, temporally organized representations of a few subevents to a more hierarchical, nested representation of entire events. For example, a 3-year-old described making cookies: "Well, you bake them and eat them," whereas a 6½-year-old described making cookies in a hierarchical way, using sub-

events within subevents: "Add three cups of butter . . . two cups of sugar, one cup of flour. Mix it up . . . knead it. Get it in a pan, put it in the oven. Bake it . . . set it up to 30. Take it out and it'll be cookies" (Nelson & Gruendel, 1981, p. 135).

The descriptions of the 3-year-olds were generalized, in that they involved a general "you" and a tenseless, habitual verb (e.g., *eat, bake*). The descriptions of older children included specific subparts of the activity (putting in ingredients) as well as naming "the main act" (bake it) (Slackman, Hudson, & Fivush, 1986). Children in Nelson's studies were also found to progress from a stage in which they needed scaffolding (perceptual or verbal cuing) to participate in events or to talk about them, to a stage in which they could conjure up the GERs on their own.

GERs have been found to be central in children's ability to respond to comprehension questions about what they have heard or read. Bishop and Adams (1992) found that children diagnosed with specific language impairment (SLI) had difficulty answering both literal and inferential questions about an event in a story depicted in pictures and presented orally. The authors explain the children's difficulty using the schema theoretical framework of Gernsbacher (1990), called a "structure building framework." The model postulates that a mental model is built from the information given and serves to suppress irrelevant information. Bishop (1997) uses this schema based theoretical framework to account for the difficulty that children with SLI have in suppressing less relevant content, shown by their difficulty in answering questions such as those in Table 18.1.

Narratives

Some of children's earliest words have been treated as stories (Paley, 2001). Vivian Paley, and her colleague, Lillian Tully, a preschool teacher, observed children as young as age 2 telling and acting out stories for one another. A child named Alex, when asked for a story, said, "Mama." Mrs. Tully later read Alex's story to other children as they acted it out by moving in time with her

TABLE 18.1. A Selection of the Literal and Inferential Questions in Bishop and Adams (1992)

Story that was read to children

Andrew was skating on the ice, wrapped up in his woolly hat, gloves, and scarf. He skated to the middle of the pond, where the ice was thin. Andrew cried out when the ice gave way under his weight and he crashed through it. A man rushed quickly to rescue him, pulling him out by both arms. When he got home, Andrew wrapped in on a blanket and sat down by the fire, holding a hot cup of tea.

Literal questions

1. What was Andrew doing at the start of the story?
2. What was he wearing on his head?
3. Did he skate to the middle of the pond or to the edge?

Inferential questions

1. Why was Andrew all wrapped up when he went skating?
2. Why wasn't he wearing ordinary shoes?
3. Did Andrew know that the ice was thin?

stretched-out version of the word. When asked whether children's stories are often about their mothers, Mrs. Tully responded: "Mostly, yes. Seems like the best reason to tell a story, when you are two, is to keep Mama in mind. And to get everyone to do something with you on your terms. Maybe you're not so lonely then" (Paley, 2001, p. 6).

Although Mrs. Tully does not say it, her depiction of the meaning of Alex's story is schema-based. She sees Alex's story as evolving from a rich conceptual structure having to do with feelings of safety, as embodied in his mother. The story schema that Mrs. Tully proposes differs from Stein and Glenn's (1979) story grammar schema. In so doing, Mrs. Tully opens the door to thinking of stories as being built from structures such as prototypes or GERs—structures that apply to the acting out activities carried out in the classrooms of Lillian Tully and Vivian Paley.

Children's later narratives contain various elements of the story grammar. By the time

they are 5 years old, children can tell entertaining stories, with settings, episodes, and endings (Applebee, 1978; Westby, 1988). It is not until children reach age 6, after they have entered school, that they learn to tell stories describing the subjective or inner life of the characters, an aspect of storytelling that is reflected in the "internal response" constituent of the story grammar schema (Botvin & Sutton-Smith, 1977; Roth & Spekman, 1986).

Narrative structures, when first acquired, are not directly accessible to the child. Rather, like linguistic rules and motor learnings, they are part of implicit knowledge, what some have called "part of the subconscious." Later, after children have developed a basic knowledge of stories and are using that knowledge in their story creations and interpretations, they come to a stage at which they can explicitly reflect on their story knowledge, or draw from their story knowledge to reflect on other matters.

Metaphors

People who are around very young children are charmed by the metaphors they create, such as calling a centipede a "comb," or commenting that a dripping faucet is "drooling." Also evident in the play of children as young as age 2 are metaphorically related actions, such as when a child uses a spoon to serve as a bed for a doll (Piaget, 1963). Moreover, 4-year-olds are likely to comment on perceptual similarities between objects, such as clouds looking like cotton, or pencils looking like rocket ships (Winner & Gardner, 1993).

Although these spontaneously generated examples indicate that very young children can draw metaphorical parallels between objects and words, it is not until later that they can correctly interpret more abstract, less perceptually bound metaphors presented out of context. In a comprehension experiment, Gentner and Stuart (1983) found that 5-year-old children are able to interpret metaphorical sentences in which the source and target are physically related, such as the color of cheeks and roses in "Her cheeks were roses." Even later, around age 7, children learn to draw similarities between targets and sources that are not perceptually related (e.g., "A mind is like a computer").

Comprehension studies of metaphorical knowledge often use metalinguistic tasks, such as those requiring children to explain a metaphor (see Nippold, 1988, and Winner & Gardner, 1993, for reviews). These tasks require that children not only interpret the relationship between target and source parts of the metaphor but that they also stand outside themselves and reflect on what they did. The tasks also tend to use decontextualized metaphors, in which the surrounding information, or context, has nothing to do with the particular relationship being drawn in the mataphor (Vosniadou, Ortony, Reynolds, & Wilson, 1984). So it is not surprising that the researchers using these sorts of tasks find that even teenagers are unable to complete them, unless they are able to assume a metalinguistic stance toward the material (Gardner, 1974).

So, Mary, Mary, quite contrary, how do your schemas grow? The question from the Mother Goose nursery rhyme was about gardens, and the answer had to do with silver bells and cockle shells and pretty maids all in a row. Judging from the literature reviewed in this section, the answer to the questions about how schemas grow will differ depending on the schema. Seven trends can be drawn from the literature and can be summarized as follows:

1. *From universal representations to language-specific ones.* This growth is characteristic of phonological prototypes that begin as innate language universals and in 6 months have already changed to reflect the characteristics of the specific input language.

2. *From comparatively simple to highly complex structures.* First-word narratives, while highly complex, do not yet contain episodic structure. These become narratives episodes, which later become narratives with episodes and internal responses.

3. *From wholes to parts.* The growth of all types of schemas proceeds from a schematic whole, with slots, to a filling in of the parts. This trajectory is also the basis of scaffolding in teaching, in which the instructor provides an overall form and the child fills it in with specific elements.

4. *From the top to the bottom, in top-down learning.* This metaphor has to do with learning being shaped by what is already known. Higher order conceptual structures influence the way lower order sensory and perceptual information are processed and then learned. For example, new experiences of events, such as birthday parties, are understood and remembered in accordance with an already-formed GER, a general schema for birthday parties that includes presents and birthday cakes.

5. *From the bottom to top in bottom-up learning.* This opposite of top-down learning involves old schemas being shaped into new ones by new experience. New schemas develop from old ones as a result of experiences that do not fit neatly into the old representations.

6. *From literal interpretation to inferencing.* Schemas, by their nature, are based on going beyond the information provided to a more general understanding. This ability to depart from the particulars and draw inferences grows over time.

7. *From direct representation to meta-representation.* Phonemes that develop and are used in a nonconscious way are examined consciously or metalinguistically in the course of learning the alphabetic principle. The meta-level representation also occurs for language meaning. For example, the nursery rhyme about Mary makes sense at first as a rhyme and as a poem about a girl and her garden. It entertains and charms children as they imagine pretty maids all in a row and enjoy the comparable rimes of *ary* in *Mary* and *contrary*, and *ow* in *grow* and *row*. Older children and adults reflecting on the poem might wonder who Mary is and why those maidens are in her garden; that is, what is beneath the surface of its cryptic references? (See Rooney Design, 2002, for two politically interpreted versions of this nursery rhyme.)

SCHEMAS: THEIR USE IN INTERMEDIATE AND UPPER GRADES

I have been discussing the literature related to various aspects of schema theory and to the earliest stages in schema development.

How does this information relate to older children, who have already begun reading and writing, and are now engaged in classroom activities in which they are reading to learn rather than learning to read?

When associated with middle- and upper-level classrooms or speech–language therapy situations, schema theory has taken on different contours and functions. One line of investigation has focused on schemas underlying the talk that goes on in school. Researchers have examined the regularities in school events, looking at how they are organized and how discourse is managed (e.g., Brice-Heath, 1983; Cazden, 1988; Mehan, 1979; Michaels, 1981; Panagos & Bliss, 1990; Ripich & Panagos, 1985; for a recent review, see Wilkinson & Silliman, 2000).

One favorite area of study, and a familiar event to both speech–language pathologists and teachers, is structured school lessons. Lessons are identifiable because of a turn-exchange pattern that begins with a teacher's question directed to the class, or a particular student in it, followed by a student response, which is then evaluated by the teacher for its quality or accuracy. This three-part exchange (IRE: Initiation, Response, Evaluation) qualifies as a schema. It is a patterned regularity that is abstract, and needs to be understood and represented conceptually by children in order for them to participate successfully in school lessons (including speech therapy sessions) (Mehan, 1979; Ripich & Panagos, 1985).

Other schema knowledge that is required for children in the middle or upper grades involves a variety of complex discourse genres needed for oral participation, language comprehension, reading, and writing. For example, students need to learn the format (schema) for writing and presenting a book report. Some teachers offer them a form to fill in, such as the following format provided to third-grade students (Bennett, Herold, & Vieille, 2000).

Paragraph 1: Type of book, title, name of author, names of characters, setting, problem, solution.
Paragraph 2: A summary of the story—tell what happened. Tell about the characters.

Try to write about the most important parts of the story.
Paragraph 3: Your recommendation. Write a paragraph telling why you would or would not recommend the book.

Included in this book review template are categories of story grammar (setting, problem, solution) that many children learned at their mother's knee during their preschool years. But in this assignment, the children need to know the names of the story parts and to talk about the story's parts rather than retell the story. Their book review requires them to assume a metalinguistic stance and to compose written text to describe the story elements and ascertain the main points or gist, a new skill that requires a manipulation (in this case, condensing) of what was previously known.

Similar requirements for schema knowledge are evidenced in fourth grade reading tests used in the National Assessment of Educational Progress (NAEP; National Center for Educational Statistics, 2001). For example, children are asked literal and inferential questions following their reading of an expository text about how people heated their houses and themselves in colonial times. The questions are based on their recall of different ways colonists warmed themselves (e.g., heated bricks, a metal bed warmer, animal skins, foot stoves, and a fireside hearth). These items fit together in schema fashion to create coherence for the text.

Students needed to have this overall structural conceptualization of the theme and its details in order to answer the NAEP questions in a satisfactory way. One child, for instance, answered the question about why the hearth was considered to be the center of the home in colonial times as follows: "Because a fireplace was fine. But the chimney was to large too" (National Center for Educational Statistics, 2001, section on student responses to question 5, on the Brick Story, grade 4). The child's answer had to do with the chimney being too large to be in the center of the home, but the fireplace being OK. This answer was an example of "no comprehension," because the child did not provide a reason why the fireplace was important in the home in colonial times—an idea that was part of the schema of the need for heat, upon which the story rested. (The child's answer also suggests that he does not have a schema relating a fireplace to its chimney.)

To sum up, schemas are very useful conceptual tools for teachers, speech–language pathologists, and their older students as they conduct the business of the curriculum. Just as for language understanding, schemas provide a conceptual structure for understanding all academic subjects. They provide the conceptual underpinning that allows students to follow the formats of lessons, to understand oral and written instructions, to abstract main ideas from texts, to determine their organizational structure, to draw inferences, and to spell and organize what they write. Finally, schemas underpin students' ability to reflect on what they have learned, so that they can use the knowledge elsewhere. Indeed, one could argue that schema understanding and use is at the heart of what it means to be educated.

SCHEMAS FOR CHILDREN WITH LANGUAGE-LEARNING DIFFICULTIES

Given their ubiquity and usefulness, one would predict that schemas would be central to research and education of children with communication difficulties. However, the research and clinical work has focused on only a few domains and only on children with certain types of communication disabilities.

One emphasis on schema learning has involved children's learning of story grammars. The students, most of whom have been diagnosed with specific SLI or language-learning disabilities (LLD), are assessed for their knowledge of story grammar elements. Teaching programs have been designed to provide them with the story grammar components that they have not yet acquired (e.g., Burns, 2002; Idol, 1987; Idol & Croll, 1987; Mind Wing Concepts, 2002).

A second focus on schemas in the disabilities literature has been in the field of reading comprehension. For example, re-searchers and educators have developed ways of teaching children to understand the overall structure of stories (Burns, 2002; Idol, 1987; Idol & Croll, 1987; Mind Wing Concepts, 2002), to extract themes from stories (Williams, 2002), and to understand schemas underlying expository text (Ogle, 1986; Westby & Velasquez, 2000).

What has been insufficiently examined in schema research is an in-depth exploration of how to make a schema-based curriculum accessible to students with communication disabilities. For example, the primary focus of inclusion research and practice has been on social inclusion and participation of the person with the disability (Beukelman & Mirenda, 1998). Educational programs have been designed to reduce interfering behaviors and improve the social skills of students with disabilities (Felton, 2001; Hunt & Goetz, 1997; Wolery, 1994). But there has been little mention in the disabilities literature of how specific teaching techniques, such as script learning, scaffolding, and script-based reading strategies, can foster schema acquisition and use by children with disabilities in regular classrooms.

SOME DILEMMAS RAISED BY SCHEMA THEORY AND SOME TENTATIVE SOLUTIONS

Schema theory brings with it certain dilemmas. Among the many are the following two: (1) that to view children's thinking as involving schemas can result in a passive, fragmented view of their abilities, and (2) that subscribers to schema theory have sometimes indulged in dichotomous thinking with divisive effects. These dilemmas are be discussed, along with some tentative solutions.

The Potential for a Passive, Fragmented View of Children's Thinking

The domains that have been cast within schema theory are sometimes treated separately and in static ways. Prototypes for phonemes have been studied mostly in relation to vowels. Such prototypes have not been applied to the alphabetic principle, phonics instruction, or to children's detection of rimes. Many of the studies of children's development of narrative schemas have emphasized the structural components of stories, neglecting the affective, social, or poetic aspects.

In some cases, schema theories have not yet been translated into clinical or educational procedures. Approaches for teaching children about object concepts tend to be based on classical models rather than on prototypical ones; that is, children are taught that objects have fixed features that are criterial (chairs have four legs, a back, a seat, and people sit in them) rather than that some objects are more chair-like than others, and that even a tree stump might be classified as a chair. Nor has there been much focus in curricula or language/literacy intervention on events or scripts. (See Constable, 1986; Culatta, 1994; and Sonnenmeier, 1994, for few notable exceptions.)

Another potential problem for schema theory applications is that they can be incorporated into a conduit, passive, copy model of learning. Scaffolding, or demonstrating the nature of schemas, can be carried out in a directive way, with teachers and speech–language pathologists presenting information for students to imitate or fill in. (See Silliman & Wilkinson, 1994, for more on this problem, one that they call "directive scaffolds.") For example, the following lively book review, written by a teenager for other teens, is interesting in part because it does not conform to a traditional schema (discussed earlier) for how to organize book reviews. (Spellings and punctuations are from the original.)

The Killer's Cousin—Nancy Werlin

Two lives lost. Two killers. Recently acquitted of murder, David Yaffle, clings to what is left of his life as he is abandoned by his family. Sent off to live in Cambridge, Massachusetts with his distant aunt, uncle and cousin, he is forced to live in the attic were just four years earlier his oldest cousin, Kathy, committed suicide.

Trying desperately to put his life back together he is surrounded with new faces. One of the romantic artist, Raina, who rents the first floor, then he meets Lily with her testing eyes and unfearing attitude, last he comes in contact with Frank, his skin head classmate. All the while his own guilt over Emily, his girlfriend's death is keeping him from moving on with his own life. To make matters worse his dead cousin is haunting the darkest corners of his mind and pleading with him to "Help Lily".

After a devastating fire in his uncle's house David finally realizes that he is not alone. That he's not betraying Emily by moving on with his life.

Nancy Werlin truly out did herself with this heart wrenching page turner. I would recommend this book to an older teen. *L. B.*

(St. Louis County Library, 2002, section on books reviewed by teens, for teens)

A number of clinical and educational approaches do not regard children's learning in these passive, fragmented ways. The following three examples present teaching schemas as active, flexible, dynamic entities that relate to one another.

1. *Participatory, experiential approaches to language and literacy.* Vivian Paley has written several books that give voices to the children in her kindergarten classroom through oral storytelling (1981, 1990, 2001). The stories are dictated by individual children to Paley and later acted out by all of the children in the class. Her emphasis is on the way children's stories are about their lives, their worries, and their thoughts about the world. Paley focuses on the profundity of children's stories and how they can provide a vehicle for living, learning, and interacting in the classroom.

2. *Transactional strategies instruction for reading comprehension (Pressley et al., 1992; Rosenblatt, 1938/1995).* Pressley and his colleagues have forwarded an instructional approach that they call "transactional," which means readers' transactions with the text, readers in transactions with one another about the text, and readers in transaction with teachers and other students about the text (Pressley, 2000). This socially and interactively based means of reading instruction involves teacher modeling and direct in-

struction, guided practice of strategies, and a view of reading that has led to instruction in which students are encouraged to go beyond the information provided in text.

3. *Concept-oriented reading instruction (Guthrie & Ozgungor, 2002).* This reading comprehension program involves children actively in creating core concepts related to various aspects of the curriculum. Activities are designed to involve students in (a) observing and personalizing information so that students ask their own questions and keep journals about the topic at hand; (b) searching and retrieving activities, during which students engage in a literature search for answers to the questions they have posed and write about what they found; (c) comprehending and integrating activities, in which students learn to extract the main ideas from texts and create summaries; and (d) communicating with others, so that students teach one another or children from other classes about their findings. (See Guthrie & Ozgungor, 2002, for specific examples of these activities created by a third-grade teacher and her students.)

Dichotomous Thinking

Schema theorists, like theorists from other camps, have sometimes drawn battle lines between schema theoretical and analytical approaches to language and literacy. The Land of the Schema is paradise, the Land of Whatever Else is purgatory, or worse. Those who do not live in the Land of the Schema, such as those who subscribe to a bottom-up analytical view of reality, are regarded as wrong-headed, deficient, boring, and deserving of their unfortunate fate.

The theory wars between schema theory and its natural enemies have been carried out in the literatures, on the conference floors, and within clinics and schools throughout the world. The conflicts take on different shapes, with battle lines drawn in different ways. Disagreements between speech–language pathologists of linguistic versus processing persuasions include different views of the role of conceptual structures such as schemas or linguistic rules. Disagreements between top-down and bottom-up views have to do with whether and

how much language information is contained in acoustic signals. Disagreements between whole-language and decoding or phonics approaches to reading include arguments about which units are most fundamental—whole words (schemas) or speech sounds and letters (elements). Disagreements between those who take a child-centered, cognitive approach and those who are more behaviorally inclined are often based in different views of the role of conceptual structures in children's learning.

There is some evidence in the recent literature that researchers in different camps are looking for a way to resolve their differences. A recent article exemplifies how schema theoretical approaches are being combined with more analytical, processing approaches to teach language and literacy to school-age children. Dahl, Scharer, and Lawson (1999) studied classroom approaches of first-grade teachers who were committed to a whole-language approach to teaching literacy. The teaching activities in eight first-grade classrooms were observed over a 6-month period. The authors selected "phonics transactions" as their unit of analysis:

> Because teachers and students worked together during instruction co-constructing knowledge, the unit of analysis was the phonics transaction. It was defined as teacher actions and teacher and student interactions imparting knowledge about specific phonics concepts, skills and strategies. (p. 315)

Dahl et al. (1999) found phonics transactions embedded in all of the whole-language activities. The activities were described, as were the phonics transactions within them. For example, for "language exploration," the researchers found the following two sorts of activities:

1. The teacher selected high-quality children's literature to read aloud to the class to notice language and discuss specific qualities of the author's words. Language features discussed included letter–sound relationships, such as initial consonants found in alphabet books and rhyming words in poetic texts.
2. Children created word collections and

discussed patterns they observed as they grouped words with the same letter–sound features (Dahl et al., 1999, Table 2, p. 333).

Dahl et al. not only carried out detailed qualitative analyses of what went on in these classrooms but they also evaluated whether the children's phonics abilities improved. They did, considerably.

The teachers and children in the Dahl et al. (1999) study have revealed a new approach that embeds phonics teaching in meaningful whole-language experiences. A warring stance should not be taken by proponents of schema theory. Nor should proponents of any theory promote their theory in ways that portray it as a wonderland and their competitors' theory as a land to be conquered. This is what Pressley and his colleagues (1998) have called a "balanced teaching approach."

I have raised but two of the many possible dilemmas associated with schema theory and its application to teaching language and literacy. To avoid treating schemas as fixed objects to be learned passively and in a fragmented way, I gave examples of literacy instruction that actively engages children, requiring that they not only become involved in texts, but that they also engage with their peers and teachers about what they read. To help solve the problem of dichotomous thinking, I described a program in which phonics instruction took place in the course of schema-based instruction—a blended approach.

But my concern about recommending a particular approach, such as the one involving blending, is that it, too, can be treated as doctrine. Although I am enthusiastic about the newly developing, balanced programs that include both nonschema and schema-based teachings, or ones that include schema teachings from different domains (phonological schemas along with narrative or event schemas), I do not feel that one should adopt such an approach wholesale. For example, such a blended approach requires that children frame-shift from a metalinguistic reality, in which they examine language from the outside, to an experiential reality, in which they live and experience

the meanings they get from the language. They need to shift from a frame in which they practice speaking or reading correctly, to one in which they speak to convey something or read to experience the action. This can be disconcerting for some children on some occasions. Teachers and speech–language pathologists have all experienced children's (or anyone's) annoyance at being asked to say or read a word again, or to stop and practice something, when what they want to do is continue with the event.

I have also argued in this chapter that even when working directly with sounds and letters, areas that are often seen as outside schema approaches, one can make use of the constructs from schema theory. Sounds and letters need to be organized into schemas and can be taught from a schema theoretical perspective. My recommendations are, then, that schema-based approaches to learning be taken seriously, that phonics and linguistic-based approaches be couched in schema theoretical constructs, and that, whenever possible, schemas having to do with phonology (oral language) and phonics (written language) be combined with teaching other schemas in a blended approach.

Finally, I suggest that the usual approach to teaching oral and written language be one that involves children in events where they experience the meaningful content of what they hear and read, or say and write. When that approach does not work, new teaching methods need to be devised, such as ones in which schemas of different domains (phonological vs. narrative) are separated. This selection of different approaches for different occasions requires that students, teachers, and clinicians be engaged in open, active reflection about the learning process, and that they all aim toward the creation of learning contexts that are empowering, engaging, relevant, and accessible to everyone. (See Duchan, 2004; Richie & Wilson, 2000; and Schon, 1983, for more on the role of reflective practices in teaching and learning.)

SCHEMAS: THEIR FUTURE

Despite the importance and pervasiveness of schemas in children's learning of language and literacy, one can see that the study of schemas is still in its infancy. More research is needed to examine further the role of schemas in children's thinking and their usefulness in supporting children's learning in the areas of language and literacy. The following future directions for research are recommended:

1. Schemas underlying objects, events, narratives, and metaphors, as well as other cognitive domains involved in meaning construction, should be given high priority in the study of children's language and literacy acquisition.
2. Individual differences in acquisition of schemas should be examined, with special attention given to students who have language and learning difficulties.
3. New theoretical models should be developed, grounded in experimental and qualitative research, to differentiate types and domains of schemas, their different dynamics, and how they work in combination.
4. Conceptual clarifications should be made between educational practices based on schema theoretical and other approaches, and how they might interrelate.
5. Additional educational practices should be developed in the areas of language and literacy to enhance children's flexible use of schemas in their everyday learning.
6. Researchers need to engage in self-reflection about their paradigms and research design. Because research results reflect the paradigms within which the research is carried out, it is important for researchers to examine their own biases as they make decisions about how to study the influence of schemas on children's learning. Studies of the belief systems of those engaged in research on language and literacy would help to reveal researchers' paradigms, and how those paradigms might be affecting the way they go about their studies.

CONCLUSIONS

I have been arguing that the role of schemas in children's learning has not been explored

to the extent that it should, and have invited researchers to continue their studies of schema theoretical foundations of children's learning. For example, in relation to learning to read and spell, I have suggested that schema theory could provide insights into children's acquisition of rime and could help to explain the irregularities in children's invented spellings, such as their use of letter names to represent sounds.

Furthermore, I have alluded to the usefulness of schemas in assessment, intervention, and educational practices. The error patterns of individual children can be assessed by determining the relationships between their errors, then deriving schema-based systematic theories to explain why some elements of related categories behave differently from others. I have pointed out, as have others, that the use of scaffolding and scripting to teach the structure of events, as well as narratives and expository genres, are approaches that are grounded in schema theoretical notions.

The tenor of my comments for future research was circumspect. I do not want to rely on the compilation of research findings for a final answer to the role of schema theory in children's language and literacy development. This is because research paradigms are also grounded in schemas, ones having to do with a composite of theories and schema-based approaches. Rather, I am asking that researchers, practitioners, and students explore the land they live and work in from a variety of perspectives, using a variety of means, and I am asking that all those engaged in such exploration make known to themselves and others their beliefs about reality and the nature of children's learning.

REFERENCES

Aitchison, J. (1987). *Words in the mind: An introduction to the mental lexicon.* Oxford, UK: Blackwell.

Applebee, A. (1978). *The child's concept of story.* Chicago: University of Chicago Press.

Aslin, R., Jusczyk, P., & Pisoni, D. (1997). Speech and auditory processing during infancy. In D. Kuhn & R. Siegler (Eds.), *Handbook of child psychology: Cognition, perception and language* (5th ed., pp. 147–198). New York: Wiley.

Bennett, S., Herold, C., & Vieille, M. (2000). How to

write a book report. Retrieved April 10, 2002, from *http://www.ga.k12.pa.us/academics/ls/3/bookreports/howtowritten.htm*

Beukelman, D., & Mirenda, P. (1998). *Augmentative and alternative communication: Management of severe communication disorders in children and adults* (2nd ed.). Baltimore: Brookes.

Bishop, D. (1997). *Uncommon understanding: Development and disorders of language comprehension in children*. East Sussex, UK: Psychology Press.

Bishop, D., & Adams, C. (1992). Comprehension problems in children with specific language impairment: Literal and inferential meaning. *Journal of Speech and Hearing Research, 12,* 114–129.

Botvin, G., & Sutton-Smith, B. (1977). The development of structural complexity in children's fantasy narratives. *Developmental Psychology, 13,* 377–388.

Brice-Heath, S. (1983). *Ways with words: Language, life, and work in communities and classrooms*. New York: Cambridge University Press.

Bruner, J. (1975). The ontogenesis of speech acts. *Journal of Child Language, 2,* 1–19.

Bruner, J., & Sherwood, V. (1976). Early rule structure: The case of peekaboo. In J. Bruner, A. Jolly & K. Sylva (Eds.), *Play: Its role in evolution and development*. New York: Penguin.

Burns, K. (2002). *Do you know your story grammar?* Retrieved on July 2, 2002 from *http://www.auburn.edu/~murraba/breakthroughs/burnsrl.html*

Cazden, C. (1988). *Classroom discourse: The language of teaching and learning*. Portsmouth, NH: Heinemann.

Clay, M. (1978). *Reading: The patterning of complex behavior*. Auckland, New Zealand: Heinemann.

Clay, M. (Ed.). (1982). *Observing young readers*. Portsmouth, NH: Heinemann.

Constable, C. (1986). The application of scripts in the organization of language intervention contexts. In K. Nelson (Ed.), *Event knowledge: Structure and function in development*. (pp. 205–230). Hillsdale, NJ: Erlbaum.

Culatta, B. (1994). Representational play and story enactments: Formats for language intervention. In J. Duchan & L. Hewitt, & R. Sonnenmeier (Eds.), *Pragmatics: From theory to practice* (pp. 105–119). Englewood Cliffs, NJ: Prentice-Hall.

Dahl, K., & Scharer, P., & Lawson, L. (1999). Phonics instruction and student achievement in whole language first grade classrooms. *Reading Research Quarterly, 34,* 312–341.

Duchan, J. (2004). *Frame work in language and literacy: How theory informs practice*. New York: Guilford Press.

Duchan, J., Bruder, G., & Hewitt, L. (1995). *Deixis in narrative: A cognitive science perspective*. Hillsdale, NJ: Erlbaum.

Erickson, K. (2000). All children are ready to learn: An emergent versus readiness perspective in early literacy assessment. *Seminars in Speech and Language, 21,* 193–203.

Felton, R. (2001). Case studies of students with several

reading disabilities [Special issue]. *Journal of Special Education, 35.*

Gardner, H. (1974). Metaphors and modalities: How children project polar adjectives onto diverse domains. *Child Development, 45,* 84–91.

Gee, J. (1999). *An introduction to discourse analysis: Theory and method*. New York: Routledge.

Gentner, D., & Stuart, P. (1983). *Metaphor as structure-mapping: What develops?* Cambridge, MA: Beranek & Newman.

Gentry, J. (1978). Early spelling strategies. *Elementary School Journal, 79,* 88–92.

Gernsbacher, M. (1990). *Language comprehension as structure building*. Hillsdale, NJ: Erlbaum.

Grieser, D., & Kuhl, P. (1989). Categorization of speech by infants: Support for speech–sound prototypes. *Developmental Psychology, 25,* 577–588.

Guthrie, J., & Ozgungor, S. (2002). Instructional contexts for reading engagement. In C. C. Block & M. Pressley (Eds.), *Comprehension instruction: Research-based best practices* (pp. 275–288). New York: Guilford Press.

Hunt, P., & Goetz, L. (1997). Research on inclusive education programs, practices, and outcomes for students with severe disabilities. *Journal of Special Education, 31,* 3–29.

Idol, L. (1987). Group story mapping: A comprehension strategy for both skilled and unskilled readers. *Journal of Learning Disabilities, 20,* 196–205.

Idol, L., & Croll, V. (1987). Story-mapping training as a means for improving reading comprehension. *Learning Disability Quarterly, 10,* 214–229.

Johnson, M. (1987). *The body in the mind: The bodily basis of meaning, imagination, and reason*. Chicago: University of Chicago Press.

Jusczyk, P. (1997). *The discovery of spoken language*. Cambridge, MA: MIT Press.

Kuhl, P. (1991). Human adults and human infants show a "perceptual magnet effect" for the prototypes of speech categories, monkeys do not. *Perception and Psychophysics, 50,* 93–107.

Labov, W., & Waletsky, J. (1967). Narrative analysis: Oral versions of personal experience. In J. Helm (Ed.), *Essays on the verbal and visual arts* (pp. 12–44). Seattle: University of Washington Press.

Lakoff, G. (1987). *Women, fire and dangerous things*. Chicago: University of Chicago Press.

Lakoff, G., & Johnson, M. (1980). *Metaphors we live by*. Chicago: University of Chicago Press.

Lakoff, G., & Johnson, M. (1999). *Philosophy in the flesh: The embodied mind and its challenge to western thought*. New York: Basic Books.

Mandler, J. (1979). Categorical and schematic organization in memory. In C. Puff (Ed.), *Memory organization and structure* (pp. 259–299). New York: Academic Press.

Mehan, H. (1979). *Learning lessons: Social organization in the classroom*. Cambridge, MA: Harvard University Press.

Michaels, S. (1981). "Sharing time": Children's narrative styles and differential access to literacy. *Language in Society, 10,* 423–442.

Minami, M., & McCabe, A. (1991). Haiku, as a discourse regulation device: A stanza analysis of Japanese children's personal narratives. *Language in Society, 20,* 577–599.

Mind Wing Concepts, Inc. (2002). *Story grammar marker.* Retrieved July 2, 2002, from *http://www.mindwingconcepts.com/index.html*

National Center for Educational Statistics. (2001). NAEP student responses. Retrieved April 10, 2002, from *http://nces.ed.gov/nationsreportcard/itmrls*

Nelson, K. (1986). *Event knowledge, structure, and function in development.* Hillsdale, NJ: Erlbaum.

Nelson, K., & Gruendel, J. (1981). Generalized event representations: Basic building blocks of cognitive development. In M. Lamb & A. Brown (Eds.), *Advances in developmental psychology* (pp. 131–158). Hillsdale, NJ: Erlbaum.

Nippold, M. (1988). *Later language development: Ages nine through nineteen.* Austin, TX: Pro-Ed.

Ogle, D. (1986). A teaching model that develops active reading of expository text. *Reading Teacher, 39,* 564–570.

Oshershon, D., & Smith, E. (1981). On the adequacy of prototype theory as a theory of concepts. *Cognition, 9,* 35–58.

Paley, V. (1981). *Wally's stories: Conversations in the kindergarten.* Cambridge, MA: Harvard University Press.

Paley, V. (1990). *The boy who would be a helicopter.* Cambridge, MA: Harvard University Press.

Paley, V. (2001). *In Mrs. Tully's room: A childcare portrait.* Cambridge, MA: Harvard University Press.

Panagos, J., & Bliss, L. (1990). Clinical presuppositions for speech thrapy lessons. *Journal of Childhood Communication Disorders, 13,* 19–28.

Peterson, C. (1990). The who, when, and where of early narratives. *Journal of Child Language, 17,* 433–455.

Piaget, J. (1963). *The origins of intelligence in children* (2nd ed.). New York: Norton.

Pressley, M. (1998). *Reading instruction that works: The case for balanced teaching.* New York: Guilford Press.

Pressley, M. (2000). What should comprehension instruction be the instruction of? In M. Kamil, P. Mosenthal, D. Pearson, & R. Barr (Eds.), *Handbook of reading research* (Vol. 3, pp. 545–561). Mahwah, NJ: Erlbaum.

Pressley, M., El-Dinary, P., Gaskins, J., Bergman, J., Almasi, J., & Brown, R. (1992). Beyond direct explanation: Transactional strategies instruction of reading comprehension strategies. *Elementary School Journal, 92,* 513–516.

Read, C. (1971). Preschool children's knowledge of English phonology. *Harvard Educational Review, 41,* 1–34.

Reddy, M. (1979). The conduit metaphor: A case of frame conflict in our language about language. In A. Ortony (Ed.), *Metaphor and thought* (pp. 164–201). New York: Cambridge University Press.

Reece, C., & Treiman, R. (2001). Children's spelling of syllabic /r/ and letter–name vowels: Broadening the study of spelling development. *Applied Psycholinguistics, 22,* 139–165.

Richgels, D. (2001). Invented spelling, phonemic awareness, and reading and writing instruction. In S. B. Neuman & D. K. Dickinson (Eds.), *Handbook of early literacy research* (pp. 142–155). New York: Guilford Press.

Richie, J., & Wilson, D. (2000). *Teacher narrative as critical inquiry: Rewriting the script.* New York: Teachers College Press.

Ripich, D., & Panagos, J. (1985). Accessing children's knowledge of sociolinguistic rules for speech therapy lessons. *Journal of Speech and Hearing Disorders, 50,* 335–344.

Rooney Design. (2002). A visual goose. Retrieved April 10, 2002, from *http://www.rooneydesign.com/marymary.html*

Rosch, E. (1978). Principles of categorization. In E. Rosch & B. Lloyd (Eds.), *Cognition and categorization* (pp. 27–48). Hillsdale, NJ: Erlbaum.

Rosch, E. (1981). Prototype classification and logical classification: The two systems. In E. Scholnick (Ed.), *New trends in cognitive representation: Challenges to Piaget's theory* (pp. 73–86). Hillsdale, NJ: Erlbaum.

Rosch, E., & Mervis, C. (1975). Family resemblances: Studies in the internal structure of categories. *Cognitive Psychology, 7,* 573–605.

Rosenblatt, L. (1995). *Literature as exploration* (5th ed.). New York: Modern Language Association of America. (Original work published in 1938)

Roth, F., & Spekman, N. (1986). Narrative discourse: Spontaneously generated stories of learning-disabled and normally achieving students. *Journal of Speech and Hearing Disorders, 51,* 8–23.

Rumelhart, D. (1980). Schemata: The building blocks of cognition. In R. Spiro, B. Bruce, & W. Brewer (Eds.), *Theoretical issues in reading and comprehension* (pp. 33–58). Hillsdale, NJ: Erlbaum.

St. Louis County Library. (2002). *Book review of* The Killer's Cousin. Retrieved April 12, 2002, from *http://www.slcl.lib.mo.us/teens/bkreviews/rev3.html*

Schon, D. (1983). *The reflective practitioner: How professionals think in action.* New York: Basic Books.

Samuel, A. (1982). Phonetic prototypes. *Perception and Psychophysics, 82,* 307–314.

Schank, R., & Abelson, R. (1977). *Scripts, plans, goals, and understanding.* Hilldsale, NJ: Erlbaum.

Seidman, S., Nelson, K., & Gruendel, J. (1986). Make believe scripts: The transformation of ERs in fantasy. In K. Nelson (Ed.), *Event knowledge: Structure and function in development* (pp. 161–187). Hillsdale, NJ: Erlbaum.

Silliman, E., & Wilkinson, L. (1994). Discourse scaffolds for classroom intervention. In G. Wallach & K. Butler (Eds.), *Language learning disabilities in school-age children and adolescents* (pp. 27–54). Boston: Allyn & Bacon.

Slackman, E., Hudson, J., & Fivush, R. (1986). Actions, actors, links and goals: The structure of children's event representations. In K. Nelson (Ed.), *Event knowledge: Structure and function in development* (pp. 47–69). Hillsdale, NJ: Erlbaum.

Sonnenmeier, R. (1994). Script-based language intervention: Learning to participate in life events. In J. Duchan, L. Hewitt, & R. Sonnenmeier (Eds.), *Pragmatics: From theory to practice* (pp. 134–148). Englewood Cliffs, NJ: Prentice-Hall.

Stein, N., & Glenn, C. R. (1979). An analysis of story comprehension in elementary school children. In R. Freedle (Ed.), *New directions in discourse processing* (Vol. 2, pp. 53–120). Norwood, NJ: Ablex.

Sussman, J., & Gekas, B. (1997). Phonetic category structure of [I]: Extent, best exemplars, and organization. *Journal of Speech, Language, and Hearing Research, 40,* 1406–1424.

Sutton-Smith, B. (1981). *The folkstories of children.* Philadelphia: University of Pennsylvania Press.

Teale, W., & Sulzby, E. (1986). *Emergent literacy: Writing and reading.* Norwood, NJ: Ablex.

Treiman, R. (1994). Use of consonant letter names in beginning spelling. *Developmental Psychology, 30,* 567–580.

Treiman, R., & Bourassa, D. (2000). The development of spelling skill. *Topics in Language Disorders, 20*(3), 1–18.

Varnhagen, C., McCallum, M., Burstow, M., Pawlik, L., & Poon, B. (1997). Is children's spelling naturally stagelike? *Reading and Writing: An Interdisciplinary Journal, 9,* 451–481.

Vosniadou, S., Ortony, A., Reynolds, R., & Wilson, P. (1984). Sources of difficulty in the young child's understanding of metaphorical language. *Child Development, 54,* 205–212.

Westby, C. (1988). Development of narrative language abilities. In G. Wallach & K. Butler (Eds.), *Language learning disabilities in school-age children* (pp. 103–127). San Diego: College Hill Press.

Westby, C., & Velasquez, D. (2000). Developing scientific literacy: A sociocultural approach. *Remedial and Special Education, 21,* 101–110.

Wilkinson, L., & Silliman, E. (2000). Classroom language and literacy learning. In M. Kamil, P. Mosenthal, D. Pearson, & R. Barr (Eds.), *Handbook of reading research* (Vol. 3, pp. 337–360). Mahwah, NJ: Erlbaum.

Williams, J. (2002). Using the theme scheme to improve story comprehension. In C. C. Block & M. Pressley (Eds.) *Comprehension instruction: Research-based best practices* (pp. 126–139). New York: Guilford Press.

Winner, E., & Gardner, H. (1993). Metaphor and irony: Two levels of understanding. In A. Ortony (Ed.), *Metaphor and thought* (2nd ed., pp. 425–443). New York: Cambridge University Press.

Wolery, M. (1994). Designing inclusive environs for young children with special needs. In M. Wolery & J. Wilbers (Eds.), *Including children with special needs in early childhood programs.* Washington, DC: National Association for the Education of Young Children.

19

A Language Perspective on Executive Functioning, Metacognition, and Self-Regulation in Reading

CAROL WESTBY

Skillful literacy in the 21st century involves more than reading the words on a page; it involves the ability to analyze critically and interpret what one reads, and to use the information gathered for effective problem solving. To do this, good readers must know why they are reading; they must be able to recognize if they are achieving their goal in reading, and if they are not, they must be able to implement strategies to remediate comprehension difficulties. Conscious knowledge of what one is expected to do, and strategies for doing it, is metacognitive knowledge—knowing about knowledge. Planning how to do the task and implementing the plan are often referred to as executive functioning, or self-regulation. This chapter presents (1) the nature of metacognition and executive functioning in the reading process, (2) the neurobiological development of self-regulation and socialization practices that influence this development, (3) strategies for evaluating self-regulation in reading, and (4) strategies for promoting self-regulation in reading. This chapter concludes with a theoretical language-intervention framework for conceptualizing deficits in executive functioning.

EFFECTIVE READING IS MORE THAN READING WORDS

To demonstrate how metacognitive knowledge and executive functioning are interrelated in the reading process, this chapter begins with four illustrations of this relationship. Several comic strip characters exemplify the use of metacognitive knowledge and executive functioning, or self-regulation, in the actual reading process. As a reader of *Peanuts* cartoons for years, I was concerned about Peppermint Patty, who never did well in school. She was confused about assignments, and she did poorly on tests, yet no one ever addressed her needs. I always felt that Peppermint Patty had potential, if only the teacher would take some additional time with her. In one cartoon, Peppermint Patty is sitting under a tree reading a book. Her friend, Marci, is nearby. Patty announces, "Nine in a row! That's a new record!" Marci responds, "What's a new record, sir?" Patty replies, "This is my summer reading program. I've read nine books in a row without understanding any of them!"

This example shows us something about Peppermint Patty's metacognition and executive functioning, or self-regulation. Patty had not understood what she had read, but she did have some strengths. She had been motivated to participate in a summer reading program. She had knowledge of the purpose of reading—to gain meaning. She had done some monitoring of her comprehension and realized that she had not understood what she read. These are extremely important aspects of metacognitive knowledge and executive function that many poor readers do not have. Despite her strengths, she lacks the self-regulatory skills to fix her comprehension difficulties.

Unlike Peppermint Patty, who has some strengths in metacognitive knowledge and motivation, Calvin exhibits deficits in metacognitive knowledge and motivation, as well as in self-regulation. He approaches his mother. "Mom, do we have a shoebox I can have? It's for a school project." His mother, searching in a closet, responds, "Here's one. What are you going to do with it?" Calvin explains, "I'm supposed to make a diorama. We're studying the different ecosystems and I'm going to make a desert scene." His mother comments, "That sounds interesting." Calvin continues, "I'll need some glue and paper and stuff, too. I'm going to build a cactus and a roadrunner." His mother asks, "When is it due?" Calvin announces, "It was due today, but I told the teacher I wasn't quite finished." Calvin seldom shows motivation for school tasks. He never has a plan for how to do assignments, and he seldom exhibits the ability to evaluate how well he has done.

Norman Drabble, a young-adult cartoon character, has limited metacognitive knowledge and self-regulation that affects his ability to be successful in college. Showing his brother, Patrick, a highlighter pen, he states, "If there's one thing every college student needs, it's a highlight pen! It saves time and energy! When I'm reading my textbooks, I highlight the important sentences. Then, when I review the chapter, I only have to read the highlights." Patrick, scanning through Norman's book, observes, "But you've highlighted every word in this book!" Norman responds, "I like to be on the safe side." Norman has a metacognitive awareness of a strategy to use in studying (highlighting), but he does not know how to use it. In contrast to Norman Drabble, Wayne Merlman, in another cartoon, has excellent metacognitive and executive function skills that he used when studying his social studies text. "Unable to find a Hi-Liter, Wayne Merlman used a black Magic Marker to cross out all the stuff he didn't want to read again." Wayne knew how to use the highlighting strategy effectively.

In comparison to Peppermint Patty, Calvin, and Norman Drabble, what do self-regulated readers do? They are intrinsically motivated; they read because of their interest or curiosity in learning, not because they will receive a reward (Guthrie & Knowles, 2001). Fully self-regulated readers know that the goal of reading is to get the meaning from the whole text. They orchestrate a variety of strategies as they read. In interviewing good comprehenders while they read, researchers have identified a variety of strategies and processes that they employ before, during, and after reading (Pressley, 2002; Pressley & Afflerbach, 1995). Before reading, good comprehenders make certain that they know the goal for reading the text. For example, are they to learn the material to discuss it, to recall it for a test, or to look for a specific piece of information? They often skim the text, or at least look through it, to get a sense of the length, organizational structure, where the important parts are, and if the text will meet their goal. They also activate prior knowledge that is likely to be related to the content of the text, and based on this prior knowledge, they make predictions of what will be covered in the text.

During reading, good comprehenders employ self-regulation. They generally read from the beginning to the end of a text, but they also may jump around, looking back for clarification on a point that was confusing, or looking ahead for information (self-regulating their reading). When good comprehenders encounter information that they consider important or relevant to their reading goals, they read more slowly. They engage in comprehension monitoring, noticing and fixing comprehension difficulties. They expect a text to be consistent, and when they encounter inconsistencies, they attempt to resolve them (Otero, 2002).

Using information in the text and their prior knowledge, good readers make inferences about characters in the text (their intents, goals, states of mind), the message the author intends to convey, or the cause–effect relationships between events or concepts. They monitor the hypotheses they made before they began reading to see if they are correct in their predictions. Good readers attempt to integrate parts of the text to get the main ideas. They evaluate the content and structure of the text, deciding if the text is interesting and if the arguments are credible. They monitor problems they encounter as they read, noting if the text is making sense to them, and if they are meeting their goals. If the text is not making sense, they adjust their strategies, reading more slowly, rereading parts, and asking questions of themselves and others. After reading, good comprehenders reflect on ideas in the text, constructing summaries and reasoning about the sensibility of the ideas.

How do good readers do what they do? What underlies their motivation and the metacognition and executive functioning they employ when they read?

METACOGNITION AND EXECUTIVE FUNCTIONING IN READING

The role of metacognition and executive processes in reading began to receive attention in the late 1970s. Flavell (1976) defined metacognition as "one's knowledge concerning one's own cognitive processes and products or anything related to them" (p. 232). Knowledge of cognition comprises (1) person variables, or knowledge about one's self and other's thinking; (2) task variables, or knowledge that different tasks have different demands; and (3) strategy variables, or knowledge of strategies for enhancing performance, including beliefs about what factors interact to affect the course or outcomes of a cognitive activity (Flavell, 1979). Brown (1980) was among the first to identify the executive, or self-regulatory, processes in reading as reader-controlled strategies.

These include selecting and studying the most important parts of text, monitoring to determine if comprehension is occurring, taking corrective actions when failures in comprehension are detected, selecting retrieval cues, and estimating readiness for tests. Self-regulation may be affected by patterns of arousal (anxiety, interest) and self-concept (self-esteem, self-efficacy).

Executive functions are proactive, largely future-oriented processes that enable anticipatory, voluntary control of actions (Denckla & Reader, 1983). Executive functioning includes working memory (the ability simultaneously to hold in mind and manipulate knowledge), planning, set maintenance, and organization. For example, students must remember the requirements of a literature assignment while searching for an appropriate book to use to for the assignment. They must plan to read enough pages each night to complete the book in sufficient time, they must maintain their motivation while reading and writing the review, and they must develop an organized format for their writing. At the highest level, executive functioning implies metacognition (knowing what one knows, what one needs to know) and self-regulation (generating and implementing strategies to acquire what is needed). Individuals with efficient executive functioning are able to self-regulate their behavior by setting realistic goals, monitoring their progress toward their goals, and appreciating when their goals are reached.

Components of Executive Functioning

Borkowski and Burke (1996) brought together the components of executive functions, metacognition, and self-regulation into a comprehensive developmental model encompassing affective factors. In this framework, executive functioning is the overarching structure with three components: (1) metacognitive knowledge, (2) motivational beliefs, and (3) self-regulation (Dickson, Collins, Simmons, & Kame'enui, 1998). Table 19.1 details the elements of these components of executive functioning and possible questions to ask to explore students' functioning in each area as related to the reading process.

TABLE 19.1. Components of Executive Functioning in Reading

Component	Type of Knowledge	Questions to Ask
Metacognitive knowledge	The self as learner	What do readers know about themselves? What information do they have related to the topic? Is the material easy or hard for them? Do they like it or not?
	The nature of the material to be learned.	Do students recognize the organizational structure of the text and the types of facts and the content that will appear?
	The task demands and the expected outcomes.	Students must understand what the product of the reading should be: Are students to retell the story? To answer a questions on a multiple-choice test or write a compare-and-contrast essay?
	How, when, and why one performs reading skills and strategies	Do the readers have strategies to help them comprehend? Can they make semantic maps of the material or use visual imagery? Do they know what they are and when to use them?
	Resources needed to perform reading tasks	What background knowledge must be activated? What resource materials might be needed to acquire or supplement the required background knowledge?
Motivational beliefs	One's general competency	Do students believe that they are, in general, competent and can handle academic activities? Do students look forward to the challenge of an activity or feel threatened by it?
	One's competency to perform specific reading tasks	Do students view reading as easy or hard? Do they think they can read literature assignments but not science assignments? Do they believe they can set a goal to achieve a task and accomplish the goal? Can they select reading materials appropriate to their skill level?
	One's ability to control/influence academic outcomes	How do students explain their successes or failures? Do they believe they have control over their performance? Do they attribute success to luck or hard work? Is failure interpreted as not working hard enough or not being smart enough, or is it due to a teacher who doesn't like them?
	Benefits of using a strategy	Research has shown that the majority of students can readily be trained to use a strategy, but few continue to employ it when they are no longer being externally monitored and reinforced in doing so. Do the students believe that employing a strategy is time-consuming and not worth the effort? Do they believe that they do better when they use particular strategies?

(*continued*)

TABLE 19.1. *Continued*

Component	Type of Knowledge	Questions to Ask
Self-regulation	Coordinating metacognitive knowledge	How do the students coordinate what they know about the task with the strategies they have available?
	Planning	How do students approach the task? What do they do first, second, next . . .?
	Monitoring one's reading behaviors and comprehension	Do students know when they understand and when they do not? Can they evaluate if they are accomplishing the task or their goal?
	Identifying causes of reading failure	When students have not understood, do they know why? Can they identify why they are having difficulty? Are they having difficulty reading the words? Is the vocabulary or the content unfamiliar?
	Remediating reading failures	What do students do when they do not comprehend? Do they reread? Do they ask someone else for assistance? Do they look for other resources?

Metacognitive knowledge includes information that students know about themselves as learners, the nature of the material they are to learn, the task demands, and expected outcomes. For example, students with metacognitive knowledge know if they find reading easy but math difficult. They recognize if the material they are to learn is supported by print, pictures, symbols, maps, graphs, or manipulatives such as math number blocks or science experiments, and they know if they understand how to use these materials. They understand the task demands, recognizing whether they must memorize information, use an algorithm, or critique what they read; they know what the final outcome will be or how it will be measured—whether they must pass a multiple-choice test, write an essay, or give an oral presentation to demonstrate their knowledge. Metacognitive knowledge also includes the skills and strategies students use when reading and whatever supports or resources they need to perform the tasks. Executive functioning is influenced by motivation factors such as positive self-esteem, an internal locus of control, and effort-related attributional beliefs about success and failure (Borkowski & Burke, 1996; Guthrie & Knowles, 2001). Students must believe they are capable of accomplishing the task, they must want to do the task for themselves not for another person, and they must believe that good performance depends on effort, not luck. Students must be motivated to use their metacognitive knowledge if they are to be self-regulated learners who use their knowledge to monitor their reading, identifying and correcting reading failures.

Figure 19.1 shows components in the process of self-regulation in reading. Metacognitive knowledge for each component of the process and motivation to employ the knowledge are essential to the use of self-regulatory executive functioning in reading comprehension. Students must evaluate what is required to do the task (e.g., identify the key points of the argument and supporting ideas) and their own competencies to accomplish the task (e.g., are they familiar with the topic and vocabulary words). Next, they must select a goal (e.g., provide a concise summary), select and implement a strategy or strategies to accomplish the goal, monitor progress toward the goal, evaluate

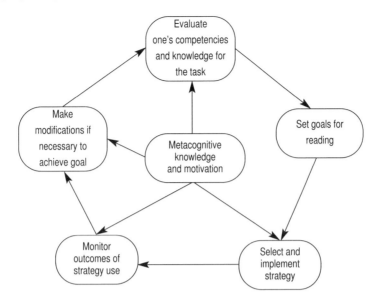

FIGURE 19.1. Self-regulated reading.

outcomes, and make modifications as necessary to accomplish the goal (McCombs, 2001).

Metacognitive and Metalinguistic Knowledge for Reading

If students are to employ executive functioning in the reading process, they must have metacognitive knowledge that represents conscious awareness of broad cognitive processes and metalinguistic knowledge, which is a specific type of metacognitive knowledge representing awareness of the structure and function of language. Their metacognitive and metalinguistic knowledge has three components: (1) declarative or factual knowledge about the cognitive and linguistic aspects of the texts they are to read, (2) procedural knowledge for how to use the declarative knowledge, and (3) conditional knowledge about when to use the declarative and procedural knowledge, and why it is important (Marzano, Hagerty, Valencia, & DiSteano, 1987; Paris, Cross, & Lipson, 1984; Schunk, 2001).

It is well established that students must have declarative knowledge of letter–sound relationships and procedural knowledge of to how employ this letter–sound knowledge quickly when reading, if they are to be fluent readers (Adams, 1990; Blachman, 1997; Lyon, 1999). Declarative and procedural letter–sound knowledge is not, however, sufficient to gain meaning from text (Armbruster, Lehr, & Osborn, 2001; Catts & Kamhi, 1999; RAND Reading Study Group, 2002). To comprehend texts, students must also have declarative knowledge of word structure and meaning, the syntactic structure of English, the discourse organization of different genres, schema or content knowledge on a wide variety of topics, and procedural and conditional knowledge of the strategies to employ to process each of these levels.

Word Knowledge

Students must know the meanings of words and have declarative knowledge of inflectional and derivational morphology (Moats, 2000). Inflectional morphemes show possession (the boy's), gender (alumna), or number (nations), if the word is a noun; tense (completed), voice (she *was* given), or mood (he *could have been* swimming), if the word is a verb; or comparison (eas*ier*, eas*iest*), if the word is an adjective. Derivational morphemes are generally prefixes and suffixes derived from Latin and

Greek that modify word meaning (e.g., prefixes such as *pre-, un-, dis-, mis-, ex-*; and suffixes such as *-able, -or, -ness, -ly*). (For further discussion of derivational morphology, see Carlisle, Chapter 15, this volume). Awareness of Latin roots of words can aid students in discovering meaning. For example, do they recognize and know meanings of roots such as *script, cept, struct, cred,* or *flex*? When students see words in print, they must employ procedural knowledge to isolate the roots, prefixes, and suffixes of words, retrieve the meanings of these elements, and integrate the meanings of the elements to determine the meaning of the words.

Awareness of semantic relationships among words also contributes to comprehension. For example, one might categorize vocabulary words about trees according to types of trees (*maple, oak, spruce*), parts of trees (*limbs, leaves, roots, bark*), things made of trees (*homes, boats, chairs*), and actions of trees (*blowing, bending, breaking*). One might learn words in clusters that share some conceptual basis, for example, occupations (*career, vocation, mayor, manager, teacher, employment*), time (*season, month, year, clock, earlier, later, afterward*), mental actions (*think, wonder, know, remember, plan, wisdom, belief*), and so on. Use of semantically related words in texts facilitates the cohesion of the texts for those who are aware of the relationships (Halliday & Hasan, 1976; see also McGregor, Chapter 14, this volume).

Structural Knowledge

Students must have declarative knowledge of the syntactic structures of English, including grammatical categories (nouns, verbs, adjectives, adverbs, etc.), increasing syntactic complexity (passive sentence structures, dependent clauses, participial and infinitive phrases), and cohesive elements (connectives, and pronominal and lexical reference) (Baker, 1985a). They must also have knowledge of the discourse structures or the superstructure organization for different genres (narrative and expository [descriptive, compare–contrast, cause–effect, argumentative, etc.]) and linguistic signals

for these patterns or relationships (Dickson, Simmons, & Kame'enui, 1998). (For elaboration, see Scott, Chapter 16, this volume.) They must then use their procedural knowledge to identify the organization of texts, and use this information to assist them in comprehending the relationships among elements of the texts.

Schema Knowledge

Students must have schema knowledge related to the material they are reading, and they must be able to relate the schema knowledge they possess from their previous experiences to the schema information presented in the texts. They must understand the types of relationships that can occur among objects, people, activities, events, and concepts. Schema knowledge is essential if students are to make appropriate inferences or "read between the lines." For example, the following passage makes little sense to someone who is unfamiliar with tennis.

> Kournikova out quickly, as usual. The only remarkable aspect of Wimbledon's opening day Monday was that the traditionally vexing grass surfaces of the All England Club were remarkably upset free. But following form meant that British tabloids had to bid an immediate ta-ta to their favorite slice of photographic cheesecake, as Ann Kournikova suffered her third consecutive first-round loss in a Grand Slam tournament. (*USA Today*, Tuesday, June 25, 2002, Section C, p. 1)

The word *tennis* is never stated in the entire article. Readers must recognize the name Kournikova as the name of a tennis star and Wimbledon as a major tennis tournament held in England. Although many tennis courts are made of clay or asphalt, the courts at Wimbledon are grass. The potentially greater variations in the ground of grass courts compared to clay or asphalt courts can result in greater unpredictability of the ball's path. This can be frustrating to players. On this Monday, however, there were no problems with the courts. Anna Kournikova is an attractive, young tennis player, who is frequently featured on the sports pages of British newspapers. This year, she lost early in the playoffs, so the newspapers had to say "good-bye" to her early. There are several schema-related reasons why students may fail to comprehend this or other passages: They may not have the schema knowledge for the topic, they might have the knowledge but fail to access it, or they may not realize that they must use their schema knowledge to "read between the lines." (For further elaboration on schema knowledge, see Duchan, Chapter 18, this volume.)

Theory of Mind and Strategy Knowledge

Finally, students must know when they know and when they do not know, know what it is that they need to know in order to comprehend, and know the usefulness of intervention strategies when they do not understand (Fitzgerald, 1983). They must possess the elements of a theory of mind. Students must realize the existence of mind, that is, that mental events exist. They must realize that there are distinct mental processes, such as knowing, remembering, forgetting, guessing, wishing, and so on. They must understand how these distinct mental processes are related (e.g., they can only remember or forget something that they once knew). They must know that certain variables can affect one's remembering and forgetting (e.g., it is more difficult to learn tasks that are longer or more complex) (Wellman, 1985). Awareness of these processes and variables influences the strategies students employ when reading.

Employing Conditional Knowledge

Employing metacognitive knowledge and executive functioning successfully to promote reading comprehension requires use of the conditional knowledge. Conditional knowledge takes students beyond the declarative language facts and procedural skills underlying reading. Using conditional knowledge, students determine when and why they should use specific declarative and procedural knowledge for a particular task; that is, they must recognize the conditions under which each type of declarative and procedural knowledge is best used (Paris,

Lipson, & Wixson, 1994). To employ conditional knowledge effectively, students must recognize their goals for reading. If students are to learn new vocabulary and concepts in scientific texts, they are likely to encounter a number of words with Latin roots and Greek suffixes; therefore, they should be prepared to use their knowledge about word structure. They may have to determine whether they will use a decoding strategy of sounding out each grapheme or a multisyllable decoding strategy that involves first identifying prefixes and suffixes. If students are expected to summarize a text, they must realize that identifying text structure is helpful to comprehension of a text because, by recognizing the structure, they will be able to identify the key elements of the text that will be important to include in a summary.

DEVELOPMENT OF SELF-REGULATION FOR READING

Just having metacognitive–metalinguistic knowledge of the reading process does not ensure that students will use this knowledge to self-regulate their reading behavior. For typically developing children in healthy environments where literacy is prominent, cognition, language, metacognition, and self-regulation develop together. In contrast, children with disabilities, children who are exposed to reduced types of language experiences because of poverty, and children from traumatic environments may frequently experience delays and disorders in development of metacognition and self-regulation (Diaz, 1991; Perry, 1997). Such children are likely to have smaller vocabularies (Hart & Risely, 1995) and to use language less frequently to direct their behavior, and to predict, reason, and talk about what others might be thinking and feeling (Tough, 1977).

Students must be motivated to use their cognitive and linguistic knowledge to comprehend and to have the self-regulatory skills for independent performance. Self-regulation is a developmental process. By early elementary school, children should be able to plan, guide, and monitor their behavior from within, and be flexible in changing circumstances. They remember what the teacher told them to do, gather the materials they need (book, paper, pencil), work on the assignment, know if they have finished the task, and recover if a fire drill disrupts the activity. The developmental path to this self-regulation begins in infancy and is influenced by both neurobiological development and environmental experiences (Diaz, Neal, & Amaya-Williams, 1990; Fuson, 1979; Luria, 1961).

Neurobiological Development of Self-Regulation

Neurophysiological Modulation

Healthy infants are able to modulate their arousal states through organized patterns of behavior that include reflex actions. They are able to modulate their sleep–wake cycles, and their heart and respiration rates. When highly aroused, such as after being handled during a physical examination, they are able to calm themselves. Children born prematurely or exposed *in utero* to drugs and alcohol are generally less able to modulate their own arousal states (Connor, Sampson, Bookstein, Barr, & Streissguth, 2000; Kodituwakku, Kalberg, & May, 2001). They require increased support from persons in the environment to facilitate their bodily regulation. Disruption of early neurophysiological modulation can put children at risk for later regulatory difficulties.

Sensorimotor Modulation

Toddlers are able to coordinate nonreflexive motor actions in response to environmental stimuli. They turn to what they hear and reach toward what they see or desire. Although children must have relatively intact sensorimotor systems for this modulation, they also require an environment that is responsive to their actions. Young children who live in abusive/neglectful environments are likely to have difficulty establishing sensorimotor modulation, because their actions have little effect on their environment (Coster & Cicchetti, 1993; Fox, Long, &

Langlois, 1988; Perry, 1997; Saarni, 1999). Crying may not get them food; reaching toward a desired object might result in a slap instead of getting the object. Children in such environments may learn that they cannot control themselves or their environment.

Control

Between ages 18 months and 3 years, children are able to begin, maintain, and stop actions in response to adults' directions. The source of the regulation at this stage is not within the child; rather, it is within the caregiving environment. Adults tell children what to do, and if children's receptive language skills are adequate, they are able to follow instructions. Adults can expect appropriate responses from children when they shout, "Don't touch the wires!", when they see a child approaching an outlet. Appropriate responses are also expected when adults announce, "Look what that the momma duck is doing," as they read a story to the child, or when they request, "Get a clean shirt," after the child has dribbled a cherry Popsicle on his or her clothes. Adult language serves as a mechanism for the external control of children's actions. For this to be the case, however, children must be able to hear and understand the language that is spoken.

Self-Control

By age 3 years, regulation is becoming internalized, and many children are able to comply with adults' commands and directives when the adult is not present. Children must have heard the rules for this internalization to occur, and they must have the receptive language skills to understand the rules. Just being physically stopped from performing an action would not be sufficient to enable the child to exercise self-control at a later time. Self-controlled behaviors occur in response to demands/expectations in the external environment and tend to be somewhat rigid. The situations must be similar to the ones in which children first experienced controlling statements, if they are to engage in self-control. Gradually, during the preschool years, children increasingly are able to comply with expectations of parents and teachers; they remember the rules that have been presented and can be heard to verbalize them (e.g., "You have to share"; "Keep your hands to yourself"; "Keep away from the street"). Preschool teachers may repeat the rules frequently during the day, but by elementary school, teachers expect students to exhibit self-control by remembering and complying with classroom rules, and by completing explicit assignments related to activities they have done in class (Westby, 1997).

Self-Regulation

By the late preschool/early elementary school years, children's behavior can be guided by a plan or goal formulated by the self rather than determined solely by demands of the environment. Children organize and adjust their behaviors according to changing goals. Children not only have internalized adults' commands and directives, but they also have taken over the regulating role of the adults. They can regulate their behavior in situations and for activities they have never before experienced. To self-regulate, children must be able to use language for a variety of functions. They must be able to predict what might happen and to reason about how to make it happen. In doing so, they have to reflect and report on past experiences, and to judge how they are similar or different from the present situation. When dealing with people, they must project into the thoughts and feelings of others and infer how these persons might respond. In supportive environments, children's ability to self-regulate increases during elementary school.

In the late elementary school years, teachers expect students to work relatively independently in developing projects in response to general assignments on a topic (Westby, 1997). Students self-regulate by generating thoughts, feelings, and actions that are planned and systematically adapted to affect their learning (Schunk & Ertmer, 2000). When this self-regulation is applied to academic tasks, students set goals for learning—attending to and concentrating on instruc-

tion; using effective strategies to organize, code, and rehearse information to be remembered; establishing a productive work environment, using resources effectively, monitoring performance, managing time effectively, and seeking assistance when needed. They hold positive beliefs about their abilities, value learning, and experience pride and satisfaction with their own efforts. They recognize factors that influence their learning and correctly anticipate outcomes of their actions.

Self-regulation has both qualitative and quantitative aspects. It involves which processes students use, how frequently they employ them, and how well they employ them. To self-regulate, students must have available both choice and control. They cannot self-regulate unless they have options for learning and are able to control those options. To provide students with options, teachers must gradually relinquish control by providing scaffolded activities that put increasing responsibility on students (Pearson & Gallagher, 1983).

Socialization of Self-Regulation for Reading

Parental Teaching Styles

Unlike growing taller as they mature, children do not spontaneously become self-regulated learners. They must be in environments in which they see self-regulated learners, and they must be scaffolded to develop these skills themselves. Development of self-regulation is related to parental teaching styles and child-rearing practices. Adult–child interactions that promote self-regulatory development emphasize the use of reasoning and verbal rationales ("That puzzle piece won't fit, because it's the wrong shape"), conceptual questioning ("How are these two alike?"), praise and encouragement, gradual relinquishment of parental control, and parents' use of direct relinquishing statements ("Now show Mom how to do it"). Children who experience these types of interactions are much more likely to develop an internal locus of control; that is, they see themselves as active, effective agents in their environment (Diaz et al., 1990). In contrast, children who remain dependent on others for guidance develop an external locus of control. They fail to develop a sense that they can be effective and that they are responsible for their own behavior and learning (Wilcox, 1982).

Parental styles in joint book-reading sessions can eventually lead young children to function independently and self-regulate their reading behaviors (Teale, 1981). Simply reading stories and talking about pictures in isolation with preschool children (e.g., "Let's count the strawberries. What color are the strawberries?") has minimal influence on their later reading comprehension. In contrast, nonimmediate talk about books—information that is not immediately available in the illustrations or text (e.g., "Why did the caterpillar have a stomachache?")—does contribute to children's reading comprehension at age 7 (De Temple, 2001; Wells, 1985). How does nonimmediate talk influence development of comprehension and self-regulatory strategies?

Language Distancing Strategies

Development of self-regulatory behaviors requires language distancing behaviors (Sigel, 1982). Distancing behaviors place a cognitive demand on children to separate themselves from the ongoing present. Parents foster children's representational thinking by using distancing strategies to create an environment in which children are stimulated to reconstruct past events, anticipate the future, or assume alternative perspectives on the present. Asking children to reflect on what they did yesterday or will do tomorrow, or asking, "Do you remember how you felt when . . ." facilitates development of distancing strategies. These types of requests require children to reconstruct prior events mentally. They are supported in imagining and picturing objects and events in their "mind's eye." Such thinking is critical in reading comprehension if children are to develop mental models for what is described in texts.

Researchers have documented relationships between the use of distancing language and academic performance (Blank,

1975; Sigel, Stinson, & Flaugher, 1991). Sigel et al. investigated the relationship between distancing strategies parents used with their 3½- to 7½-year-olds and the children's academic performance 5 years later. These researchers proposed three levels of distancing strategies. Level 1 strategies are low level, requiring only automatic, routine information, associations, or visual observations—children need only label, describe, or repeat a statement. Level 2 requires children to classify or relate dissimilar events. Although Level 2 demands transcend what is immediately observable, they are still tied to what can be seen or heard. For example, children may be required to sequence a set of events (e.g., report their experiences as the zoo), describe similarities and differences (e.g., in terms of color, size, shape, function), or categorize objects or ideas (e.g., animals, things to wear, places to go on vacation). Level 3 distancing strategies represent cognitive demands to engage in planning, causal inferencing, predicting outcomes, hypothetical reasoning, and evaluating consequences (e.g., "What do we need to take on our camping trip?"; "What will happen if we forget the tent?"; "Why isn't the camp stove working?"). The language used in Level 3 distancing strategies is the type that is essential for self-regulation. Reading requires the type of abstraction and transformation of information required by Level 3 demands. Students must employ Level 3 distancing strategies to "read between the lines," that is, to make causal inferences for events in a text, or to predict outcomes in a story or science experiment. Sigel et al. reported that the degree of language distancing used by parents with their preschool children positively correlated with children's subsequent academic achievement; scholastic areas such as math and reading, requiring the highest degree of representational competence, correlated most strongly with the high-distancing strategies (See also van Kleeck, Chapter 9, this volume).

Typically developing children from environments that provide experiences with distancing language develop the self-regulatory behaviors expected for academic success. Children from low socioeconomic status families with limited educational experiences and children with disabilities are more likely to exhibit self-regulatory deficiencies than are children from mainstream, middle-class backgrounds and children without disabilities. Two reasons may be lack of experiences with distancing language or difficulty with the abstraction required by distancing language.

There are four types of self-regulatory deficiencies (Fuson, 1979; Stone & Conca, 1993). Students with *comprehension deficiencies* may not comprehend the nature of a problem or task; thus, they cannot discover what verbal mediators to produce. Some students comprehend the task but have difficulty with *strategy selection* (Conca, 1989). They may rely on simpler, less efficient strategies than same-age peers. For example, if these students are trying to learn the names of animals in a biology lesson, they may simply attempt to memorize the list randomly, whereas same-age peers may organize the animal names into taxonomies (birds, reptiles, and mammals), then memorize the animal names within each taxonomy lists. Other students may have *production* or *execution deficiencies*. They may have correct strategies within their repertoires but fail to produce them spontaneously and appropriately (Ford, Pelham, & Ross, 1984; Swanson, 1983). For example, if reminded that they have learned a strategy (e.g., "Remember how we discussed some ways to identify themes in a story?"), they will use the strategy but will not think of it on their own. A *continued-use* deficiency occurs when children have been successfully instructed or trained to produce a strategy that is effective, but they fail to continue to employ the strategy when no longer constrained to do so. For example, students may be taught a strategy for reading multisyllable words (e.g., circle prefixes at beginnings of words, circle suffixes at ends of words, underline vowel sounds in the rest of the word, say the parts of the words, then say the parts fast) (Archer, Gleason, & Vachon, 2003). When they begin reading an assignment, they initially use the strategy as they encounter long words. As they continue reading a long assignment, however, they revert to guessing

the unfamiliar words based on initial and final sounds.

Importance of Language in Development of Self-Regulation

Educators and speech–language pathologists must recognize the critical role that language plays in the development of self-regulation. Genetic, neurological, or environmental events that disrupt language development are likely also to disrupt development of self-regulation. Therefore, children with histories of specific language impairment, persons who have experienced neurological insults (strokes, traumatic brain injuries), or children who have been raised in poverty or traumatic environments are at risk for exhibiting deficits in self-regulation (Fox et al., 1988). Children must have the capability to produce utterances to control their behaviors. To use conditional knowledge in deciding when and why they should use particular declarative and procedural knowledge, children must be able to produce a variety of complex clause structures, with connectives such as if–then ("If I am to produce a summary of this story, then I need to know the parts of a story"), when ("When I study my science words, I must use my knowledge of Greek suffixes to know how to pronounce the words"), or because ("I can skim this chapter instead of studying it, because I only have to list a major product for three countries"). Children with SLI are delayed in the development of these more complex sentence structures.

To understand and use metacognitive strategies, students must have a theory of mind and an understanding of words that relate to theory of mind or a landscape of consciousness (Bruner, 1986). This includes words referring to emotions, goals, and motivations, and words that refer to cognitive–metacognitive thinking processes (*think, guess, remember, forget, hypothesize, predict*). Students with autism spectrum disorder (ASD) tend to have difficulty learning words referring to emotions, goals, and motivations. Children from traumatic environments also tend to show delays or difficulties in comprehending and using such terms appropriately (Coster & Cicchetti, 1993; Saarni, 1999). Understanding characters' emotions and goals is critical for comprehension of narrative texts, and the ability to use words referring to thinking processes is essential for all metacognitive behavior.

EVALUATING SELF-REGULATION IN READING

The self-regulation strategies students use in reading have been evaluated by three procedures: (1) interviews, in which students are asked about the processes they use in reading, (2) think-aloud methods, in which students are given a reading task and asked to say aloud everything they think as they perform the task, and (3) error detection tasks, in which students must identify a contradiction or error in a text. Results of self-regulation studies in reading have shown two patterns. First, younger and poorer readers focus on decoding print rather than gaining meaning from texts; they have little awareness that they must attempt to make sense of texts. Second, younger and poorer readers do not seem to recognize when they do not understand (Gardner, 1987).

Interviews

A common assessment procedure is to ask students what they do in particular reading tasks. Students may be shown a text they are using in class and asked questions:

- What is the most important reason for reading this kind of material? Why does your teacher want you to read this?
- How good are you at reading this kind of material? How do you know?
- If the teacher told you to remember the information in this chapter, what would be the best way to do this? Have you ever tried to do _____?
- What is the hardest part of answering questions like the ones in this book? Does that make you do anything differently? (Wixson, Bosky, Yochum, & Alvermann, 1984, p. 348)

Or students may be given hypothetical situations that they are likely to have experienced and asked what they would do (Chamot & O'Malley, 1994, p. 77). For example:

- Your teacher is reading a story to the class. You don't understand all the words. Then your teacher asks you to predict an ending to the story. What do you do about the words you don't understand? How do you make up a good ending for the story?
- You have to read a story silently. You need to understand the plot and characters, then retell the story. What do you do to understand the plot and characters? How can you remember and retell the story?
- You have to read several pages in your science book. You need to understand and remember the important information. What do you do to understand the information as you read? What do you do to remember the information later on?

Several concerns have been raised about the data obtained from interviews. If an activity is automatic for a student, information about processes is out of the student's awareness, or the student may not remember what he or she did do in such a situation. In these cases, students may draw on what they think ideal readers do, or what teachers have told them to do, or they may give incomplete information. Even when students give apparently thorough responses, this may represent their metacognitive knowledge and not what they actually do to self-regulate their comprehension. Young students, those with language-learning disabilities, and second-language learners may not have the verbal fluency necessary to explain what they do when they read. Also, younger students and students with disabilities are likely to have difficulty responding to hypothetical or general questions about general events (Yussen, Mathews, & Hiebert, 1982).

Think-Alouds

Think-alouds are more specific than most interviews, but the purpose is the same.

Asking students to think aloud as they read provides valuable insight into the strategies they use as they attempt to comprehend texts. Students are given a text at their instructional level. An examiner asks students to stop at designated segments of the text and explain what they are thinking at that point. Ideally, the examiner models how to think aloud about a text.

Think-alouds have been used with readers from the upper elementary school grades through college. A variety of coding systems have been used in analyzing the processes readers employ (e.g., Cote, Goldman, & Saul, 1998; Leslie & Caldwell, 2001; Pressley & Afflerback, 1995). Think-aloud statements are generally coded according to statements that indicate understanding and lack of understanding of the text. Examples of statements that indicate comprehension include the following:

- *Restating, paraphrasing, or summarizing.* The student attempts to restate what the author has said, basically preserving the language of the author, or the student reports the gist of what the author is stating by summarizing the author's ideas.
- *Making new meaning.* The student makes an inference, draws a conclusion, or engages in reasoning.
- *Questioning that indicates understanding.* The student asks a question based on his or her understanding of the text, such as questioning the motivation of a character, applying text content to a similar situation, or projecting text content into a future point in time.
- *Noting understanding.* The student recognizes that he or she understands what was read.
- *Reporting prior knowledge.* The student reports a match with what was previously known, or indicates that prior knowledge was absent or in conflict with the text.
- *Identifying personally.* The student relates the text to personal experiences, makes a judgment of some sort on the basis of personal experiences, states interest or lack of it, or indicates like or dislike for a topic.

Examples of think-aloud statements that indicate a lack of understanding include the following:

- *Questioning content.* The student asks questions about character motivation or the applications of a concept that indicate his or her lack of understanding. The student also asks about the meaning of words or concepts.
- *Noting lack of understanding.* The student clearly states that he or she is confused about something.

Think-alouds avoid some of the criticisms associated with interviews. The task is a real rather than hypothetical activity. Retrieval of knowledge from memory is less of an issue than in interview tasks, because the distance between process and report is only a few seconds; knowledge-use discrepancies are unlikely because of the online nature of the task. There are at least three concerns, however. First, investigators may inadvertently cue readers about what to do by the way they present the task, or by positively reinforcing some of the statements the students make. Second, as with interviews, verbal fluency can affect the quality of the information obtained. A potentially serious third problem with think-alouds is the disruption and distortion that may occur when persons must read and simultaneously reflect on and report what they are doing as they are reading. The complexity of think-alouds places stress on working memory, because students must remember and reflect on what was read, while simultaneously organizing a verbal response to explain what they are doing to comprehend the text. Consequently, think-alouds are difficult for younger children and for those with language and learning disabilities who have more limited working memory capacities.

Error Detection

Error detection tasks have been employed to evaluate students' comprehension monitoring strategies (Baker, 1979; Gardner, 1987; Oakhill & Yuill, 1996; Otero, 2002; Zabrucky & Ratner, 1992). Researchers consider two aspects of comprehension monitoring—an evaluation, which involves noticing the comprehension problem, and regulation, which involves the process of repairing the problem once it has been detected (Zabrucky & Ratner, 1989). Readers are presented with texts to read that have some type of errors or inconsistencies. They are expected to notice and to fix comprehension difficulties so as to achieve consistency in the knowledge elements of a text (Otero, 2002). Errors or inconsistencies in texts can be of several types (Gardner, 1987):

- *Lexical:* A nonsense word or difficult vocabulary word is unknown (e.g., "It is so hot that most *brugens* would melt there").
- *External inconsistency:* An inconsistency between the readers' prior knowledge and text information (e.g., "They used sand from the trees to make many things"; or "Mother made me a peanut butter and ice-cream sandwich").
- *Internal inconsistency:* Inconsistencies between elements in the text (e.g., "The temperature on Venus is much higher than boiling water. Venus is about the same size as Earth. But it is much too cold for us to live there").

Tasks using internal inconsistencies are termed "contradiction paradigms," because texts are manipulated so that they contain contradictions.

Performance on these tasks depends on the type of instructions given, the types of errors inserted in the text, and the age and reading ability of the study participants. Yet neither children nor adults are very successful at identifying problems in the manipulated texts (Ehrlich, 1996). In some studies, students were asked, "Did the passage make sense?", or they were asked to rate the texts as easy or difficult to understand. In others, students were informed that the texts had errors or problems that they were to indicate by underlining them. Readers perform best when told explicitly that there are errors in the texts. They also find and correct more errors when told to find errors that would make the text difficult for someone other than themselves to understand (Gard-

ner, 1987). Younger and less able readers tend to employ a lexical standard of evaluation in evaluating errors, noting only words that they do not understand. They do improve on identifying other types of errors, however, if they are told the specific type of errors they are to look for (Baker, 1985a). Poor readers have particular difficulty detecting errors that violate internal consistency.

One must be cautious in interpreting results of error detection studies. Readers expect texts to make sense; consequently, even though they might notice an inconsistency, they may believe it is not a problem with the text, but with their inability to comprehend it. For example, children are less likely to report word-comprehension problems when nonsense words contain one rather than three syllables (Baker, 1985b). It may be that the children believed they should know the short words; consequently, they were reluctant to admit they did not. Readers may not detect external inconsistencies, because they lack knowledge about the content in a text; hence, they will accept something as fact that is actually an error. In other cases, a student may detect the inconsistency but lack the strategies for resolving it. Or readers may notice an inconsistency but use fix-up strategies to resolve the comprehension difficulty, such as modifying their mental model for the text so that they can accept the apparent inconsistency. In this case, they repair the contradiction themselves, without reporting the difficulty.

Issues in Evaluating Self-Regulation in Reading

All of the self-regulation evaluation tasks described—interviews, think-alouds, and error detection—require that students have the necessary oral-language skills to respond to the interview questions coherently and the ability to read well enough to talk about what they are doing as they read or to note errors as they read. In interviews and think-alouds, students with SLI may have difficulty formulating explanations about what they do when they read. Students with phonological deficits that affect the automaticity and fluency of their reading, and with syntactic, semantic, and inferencing deficits that affect their comprehension, will have difficulty with the think-alouds and error monitoring because of the demands placed on their working memory. If students are struggling with basic decoding strategies and comprehension, they will not have sufficient working memory available for self-regulation. Speech–language pathologists and educators will need to observe these students' reading behavior to develop hypotheses about the strategies they use when reading. A miscue analysis can provide insight into students' decoding strategies and use of semantic and syntactic cues to assist them in decoding. Students' responses to explicit and implicit questions about reading passages, such as those asked in the *Qualitative Reading Inventory* (Leslie & Caldwell, 2001), can be analyzed to determine which strategies the student is or is not using that contribute to errors in comprehension. One can note whether the errors are due to difficulty in making causal inferences, failure to link ideas across the passage (make relational inferences), excessive elaboration or overreliance on prior knowledge rather than information in the text, or difficulty in correctly parsing complex syntactic patterns (Dewitz & Dewitz, 2003). The speech–language pathologist or educator can then draw students' attention to the strategies they are using, or that they need to use, as a way to develop their metacognitive knowledge, which is essential if students are ultimately to self-regulate their own reading.

PROMOTING EXECUTIVE FUNCTIONING IN READING

Strategy instruction has become a common component in reading instruction. A variety of programs teach strategies to achieve specific goals or tasks, such as writing in different genres (Harris & Graham, 1996), memorizing, paraphrasing, or test taking (Deshler, Ellis, & Lenz, 1996). (See also the learning strategies curriculum described by Ehren, Deshler, & Lenz in Chapter 32, this volume). Just teaching strategies to students, however, does not ensure that they

will use the strategies. Educators must think about how they can promote students' independent, appropriate use of the strategies to facilitate monitoring their comprehension and learning; that is, the real question is how educators can assist students in becoming self-regulated readers. Students must understand the purpose of the reading activities, develop a metacognitive ability to reflect on the knowledge they have, and have the motivation to develop goals and procedural knowledge to implement strategies to achieve the goals.

Distancing Strategies to Promote Metacognition

Language distancing strategies promote metacognitive awareness that is a key underpinning for self-regulated reading. Demands or questions that foster these distancing behaviors in school can promote a depth of comprehension in reading. Raphael (1984, 1986) engaged children in noting the types of relationships between questions and answers that can be asked about texts. She proposed four types of question–answer relationships (QARs):

- *Right there,* in which the answer is explicitly stated in the text.
- *Think and search,* in which the answer is in the text but the words in the question and in the text are not the same, or the answer is not in just one location.
- *You and the author,* which involves students' thinking about what they have learned from the text and using what they already know to answer the question.
- *On my own,* in which the question is motivated by some information in the text, but the answer has to be generated from students' prior knowledge.

Responding to the four types of questions requires increased distancing from the explicit content of the text. The third and fourth questions require that readers reflect on their own knowledge. Following are examples of these questions asked about the book, *Passage to Freedom: The Sugihara Story* (Mochizuki, 1997). This picture book tells about the experiences of the Sugihara family in Lithuania at the beginning of the World War II. Mr. Sugihara was the Japanese ambassador to Lithuania. Jews fleeing the German military sought visas from Sugihara to leave the country. Sugihara's supervisors in Japan denied him the authority to issue visas, but he chose to do so anyway, putting himself and family in danger.

- *Right there:* Why was the Sugihara family living in Lithuania? (The author says they were there because Mr. Sugihara was the Japanese ambassador to Lithuania.)
- *Think and search:* In what ways did Hiroki's life change after the Polish Jews came to his house? (As one reads, one learns that Hiroki, Mr. Sugihara's son, can no longer play outside; he keeps the curtains drawn, and the family is running low on food.)
- *You and the author:* What is a visa? (One knows that the Jews outside the embassy want visas to leave the country, but a specific description or definition of a "visa" is not given; it must be inferred.) Why didn't Mrs. Sugihara help write the visas? (The author tells us that Mr. Sugihara does not want his wife to get into trouble, but we are not told what this trouble might be.)
- *On your own.* Can you think of someone else who has risked his or her own life to save other persons?

Beck, McKeown, Hamilton, and Kucan (1997) also proposed questions for students' use in questioning the authors (QtA) as a way to encourage reflection on the text content. A teacher may initiate a discussion by asking the following questions:

- What is the author trying to say here?
- What is the author's message?
- What is the author talking about?

Follow-up queries assist students in integrating and connecting ideas to construct meaning. They are encouraged to consider the ideas behind the author's words—to consider what the text means rather than what it says:

- What does the author mean here?
- Does the author explain this clearly?

Other queries relate information from different parts of a text or make connections with something that may be missing from the text:

- Does this make sense given what the author told us before?
- How does this connect to what the author told us here?

And, finally, queries help students figure out an author's reason for including particular information:

- Does the author tell us why?
- Why do you think the author tells us this now?

These questioning strategies arise from the teacher. Although these strategies can foster development of metacognitive awareness, by themselves, they will not lead students to self-regulation of the reading process. Educators need to employ strategies in which control of the process is gradually transferred from the educator to the student.

Instructional Strategies Promoting Self-Regulation

Three types of empirically validated strategies are found in the literature: reciprocal teaching, direct explanation, and transactional strategy instruction. Each is described briefly.

Reciprocal Teaching

Palincsar and Brown (1984) introduced reciprocal teaching as an instructional strategy in which educators scaffold students in metacognitive and self-regulatory behaviors valued in reading comprehension. This strategy involves a gradual release, from the teacher to the student, of responsibility for carrying out each part of the routine. This strategy has four shared goals: predicting, summarizing, questioning, and clarifying. The teacher assigns a paragraph for the students to read, then summarizes the paragraph and asks the students several questions about it. The teacher clarifies any mis-conceptions or difficult concepts, then asks the students to predict what will happen in the next paragraph. On the next cycle, the roles are reversed. A student summarizes the paragraph, asks questions of other students, and clarifies their misconceptions.

Direct Explanation Approach

Modeling and direct instruction of strate-gies, as run in reciprocal teaching, are im-portant but probably not sufficient for de-velopment of the self-regulation necessary for academic achievement. Students also need to be told explicitly the reasoning and mental processing involved in reading strategically (Williams, 2002). To address this need, Duffy and colleagues (1986) de-veloped the Direct Explanation approach to reading comprehension. Instead of focusing on teaching individual reading strategies, teachers help students to view reading as a problem-solving task that necessitates the use of strategic thinking, and to think strategically about solving reading-compre-hension problems. Teachers explain the rea-soning and mental processes that students are to use and demonstrate use of the strate-gies by thinking aloud. Students are moni-tored as they apply the strategies in the con-text of real reading. Teachers encourage transfer by explaining when and where the strategies can be used (Duffy, 2002).

Transactional Strategy Instruction

Transactional strategy instruction (TSI) in-cludes the elements of Direct Explanation but has a different role for the teacher. TSI focuses on the teacher's ability not only to provide explicit explanations but also to fa-cilitate discussions in which students collab-orate to form joint interpretations of texts and explicitly discuss the mental processes and cognitive strategies they are using (Williams, 2002). TSI is called "transaction-al" because of its emphasis on readers' in-teractions, or transactions, with texts and with one another (Pressley & Woloshyn, 1995; Pressley et al., 1992). TSI, a long-term process, goes on throughout the year. It involves direct explanations and teacher

modeling of strategies, followed by guided practice of the strategies. Educators explain to students the purpose of the strategies lessons (e.g., "Our objective is to take notes on important ideas"; "Before beginning, we must analyze the task"; Pressley & Woloshyn, 1995, p. 90) and how they will benefit from the strategies (e.g.,"Putting notes in your own words is a way to check your understanding"; "It's easier to remem-ber if you attach it to something you know"; Pressley & Woloshyn, 1995, p. 90). Educators emphasize that strategies are co-ordinated with one another before, during, and after reading, and that different strate-gies are appropriate at different points in a text, or with different types of texts.

The specific strategies that are taught in TSI classrooms vary, but, typically, students are explicitly taught the following strategies:

- Predicting upcoming content by relating prior knowledge to ideas already encoun-tered in the text, then, later, checking predictions.
- Constructing images (mental models) representing the ideas in the text.
- Slowing down, reading more carefully, rereading when unsure of one's compre-hension.
- Generating questions in response the text (e.g., QAR or QtA).
- Summarizing, which includes note taking on the important ideas.

Educators using TSI coach students to use the strategies as they complete assignments. They encourage students to use strategy terms and prompt them to think aloud as they apply strategies to texts. They cue stu-dents to choose a strategy they know at a particular point in the text. Educators may suggest a particular strategy or display cues on bulletin boards. They prompt students to evaluate the impact of strategy use on their reading and to explain the reasons they used a particular strategy. When they observe students using strategies, they praise them.

Learning Self-Regulation through Literature

Self-regulation is typically developed through experiences with others who model self-regulatory behavior and use language to scaffold self-regulatory experiences for children. Randi and Corno (2000) implemented an interesting approach to teaching self-regulation through literature to typically developing students in general education classes. They reasoned that, for generations, children have learned life's lessons through stories. They hypothesized that analyzing characters' self-regulation in narrations would be a means to bring self-regulated learning to a conscious level in students. They began their intervention using mythical quest literature, specifically, journey tales, which are "one hero stories." Journey tales represent rites of passage in which the hero undergoes a separation, initiation of a journey, and a return (Campbell, 1949). The hero encounters a situation in which he or she must leave traditional sources of support and draw on personal resources before returning home—in essence, the hero becomes self-regulated. The journey begins with a clear and predetermined goal (e.g., Jason searching for the golden fleece, or in a more modern story, Dorothy, in the *Wizard of Oz,* finding her way back to Kansas, or in a Native American legend, *Ahaiyute and Cloud Eater* [Hulpach, 1996], in which a young American Indian boy sets out on a journey to conquer the monster who is eating the clouds, which is why it hardly ever rains, and people and animals are dying of thirst). Many hero stories can potentially be used to teach self-regulation. To achieve a goal, the hero is challenged to his or her maximum potential and must achieve a series of subgoals. Gratification must be delayed. Personal costs of the pursuit stress the emotions. The hero must draw on strategies to manage self and task. The strategies are similar to strategies that have been identified in research on self-regulated learning, including knowledge/cognition of possible strategies, motivation to achieve the goal, and emotional control.

Using journey tales and other hero tales, teachers guide students to identify, label, and categorize the self-regulatory behaviors and strategies, such as persistence, resilience, and self-reliance. Students then discuss and apply these strategies to their own lives, for example, the goal of writing a book review, developing a project for a science fair, or earning the money necessary to go to the school prom in style. Ideally, a teacher selects a book and hero that appeal to the students. Currently, Harry Potter is a hero-like character who is popular with many older elementary and middle school students. Harry and his friends exhibit many aspects of self regulation. The examples of components of self-regulation in Table 19.2 are taken from *Harry Potter and the Goblet of Fire* (Rowling, 2000). Harry is a competitor in the Triwizard Tournament. He must accomplish three tasks: (1) get a golden egg from a dragon, (2) save a friend who has been taken underwater and held by Merpeople, and (3) get through a dark, obstacle-filled maze to find the goblet of fire. Harry's ultimate goal is to save the world from the evil wizard, Voldemort, who had killed his parents. Success with a journey/hero tale approach to developing self-regulation requires that students develop a theory of mind—that they develop the ability to perceive the events of the story through the eyes of the hero as a learner. Table 19.2 provides an example of the Harry's self-regulatory behaviors as he prepares for and wins the Triwizard Tournament and an example of a student preparing a project for a science fair. Harry's behavior serves as a model for students to use in their own activities and goals.

Necessity of Developing Executive Functioning in Reading

Speech–language pathologists and educators are now well aware of the need for students to develop phonological–phonemic awareness and phonics skills if they are to read the words of a text automatically. Both the National Reading Panel (2000) and the RAND Reading Study Group (2002), however, have also stressed the importance of comprehension. Comprehension in the 21st century requires executive functioning. Students must interpret text—analyzing and synthesizing ideas, reading between the lines, inferring ideas that are not stated explicitly, and integrating information interpreted from multiple texts to identify and solve problems (Morris & Tchudi, 1996). To accomplish this integration of ideas

TABLE 19.2. Literary and Student Examples of Self-Regulation

Metacognitive control
  Setting goals
    Literacy example: Harry wants to win the Triwizard Tournament. He needs to gather the information necessary to pass each of three tasks, and ultimately retrieve the goblet of fire.
    Student example: Develop a science project to enter in the 7th-grade science fair.
  Planning
    Literary example: Harry reads extensively to gain ideas for how to pass each task. He decides what he needs to complete the tasks and how he will get what he needs. He seeks the help of his friends, and he practices all the spells he thinks he might need.
    Student example: Read to gain ideas for the project. Decide on a project; determine the materials that are needed and how they can be obtained. Seek advice of science teacher. Mark on a calendar when each step of the project should be completed.
  Evaluating goals and progress
    Literary example: Harry monitors and evaluates the information he has to do the tasks. His friends give him feedback about how he is doing in preparing for each task.
    Student example: Monitor progress by checking off steps of project as completed. With teacher or parent, evaluate quality of project components. Are outcomes progressing as anticipated?

Motivation Control
  Focusing/positive thinking
    Literary example: Harry keeps reading in the library to find the information he needs—"One in the morning . . . two in the morning . . . the only way Harry could keep going was to tell himself, over and over again, next book . . . in the next one . . . the next one . . ." (p. 489).
    Student example: Imagine successfully completing a past assignment. Think about getting a ribbon at the science fair.
  Endurance and self-reliance
    Literacy example: Harry saves his friend Ron from the Merpeople who live under water; he has been under the water for some time. "Harry kicked his legs so hard and fast it felt as though his muscles were screaming in protest; his very brain felt waterlogged, he needed oxygen, he had to keep going, he could not stop—and then he felt his head break the surface of the lake" (p. 502).
    Student example: Part of project does not work as expected and must be repeated. Reward self for getting completing each step.

Emotion Control
  Literary example: Harry is filled with dread about the task, but has a "controlled panic. " He kept a "cool head."
  Student example: Choose an interesting topic so the task is not boring; take short breaks when frustrated with the task.

Control of the task situation
  Use of external resources
    Literary example: Harry uses his Firebolt broom to fly over the dragon. He uses gillyweed to breath under water.
    Student example: Use a computer program to analyze data and a graphics program to prepare display for science fair.
  Use of internal resources
    Literary example: Harry uses his good flying skills to get the golden dragon egg and escape the dragon's claws. He uses his intelligence to put together clues to figure out how to accomplish the tasks.
    Student example: Use knowledge of prefixes, suffixes, and word roots to comprehend words read in science texts; use knowledge of science of text structures to organize material for presentation on science fair poster.

(continued)

TABLE 19.2. *Continued*

Others in the task setting	
Requesting help from mentors	
Literary example:	Harry contacts his Uncle Sirius for information. He asks Hermione for help looking in books for information on how to deal with dragons; he asks her to teach him a summoning spell, so he can call his flying broom during the task.
Student example:	Ask librarian for assistance in finding resources on the topic. Ask parent or teacher to explain a concept you do not understand in reading materials.
Control others in the task setting	
Literary example:	Harry discovers that Krum, one of the four contestants in the tournament, is the using the crucio spell to stop the other contestants in maze from reaching their goal—the goblet of fire. Harry uses the stupefying spell on Krum to prevent him from harming Cedric, one of the other contestants.
Student example:	Ask brother to turn down TV, if it bothers you while reading.

across texts, students must understand the purpose of their reading. As they read, they must monitor (and self-regulate) to ensure that they are accomplishing their purpose. This monitoring–self-regulating is dependent on an adequate executive functioning system, which in turn requires an efficient working memory system that enables persons to engage in the act of reading while simultaneously monitoring, evaluating, self correcting, and interpreting.

Computer literacy, expected of all students in the 21st century, magnifies the demands on executive functioning and self-regulation in reading. Computers make use of hypertext, which is composed of blocks of text connected by electronic links that offer different pathways to users. Hypertext can be arranged and rearranged in a nonlinear manner. Readers create hypertext as they decide what threads or paths to follow. Unlike printed texts that require readers to read from left to right and top to bottom, hypertexts encourage readers to move rapidly from one text chunk to another nonsequentially. Ideally, hypertext readers must interpret and critically evaluate each piece of hypertext and link it in meaningful ways to other pieces of hypertext. Hypertexts provide less support for readers to construct frameworks essential for comprehension, because they do not possess the overall macrostructure organization and linguistic connectors between pieces that make relationships transparent. Readers must produce the structure and links themselves, while they are processing the information they are

reading. Consequently, computer literacy places high demands on working memory. Interventions that seek to promote the development of executive functioning in reading must attend to issues with working memory.

A LANGUAGE INTERVENTION FRAMEWORK FOR EXECUTIVE FUNCTIONING IN READING

Interventions to develop metacognitive and self-regulatory behaviors tend to focus on the teaching of specific declarative knowledge and procedural strategies. Little attention has been devoted to the possible underlying bases for metacognitive and self-regulatory deficits. Barkley (1997) proposed a theoretical model for executive functioning that can serve as a framework for developing research and interventions related to the self-regulation necessary for reading. In the model, inhibition is essential for self-regulation. Persons must be able to interrupt an ongoing pattern of behavior that shows signs of being ineffective (e.g., if students are reading the words but not comprehending, they must change what they are doing). They must also be able to protect periods of concentration from being disrupted by both outside and inside sources of interference. These aspects of behavioral inhibition provide the critical support for use of four components of executive function (nonverbal and verbal working memory, emotional control, and problem-solving) that are essential for management or self-regulation of behavior. These four functions are interactive and hierarchical, with a deficit in one executive function contributing to deficits in other executive functions. Table 19.3 outlines an intervention model that might be pursued in future research with students who have language and learning disabilities, and related difficulties in self-regulation. Included in the model are the four components of executive functioning, the results of deficits in each component, and the goals or interventions for deficits in each type of executive function.

Nonverbal Working Memory

The function of nonverbal working memory is to hold in mind events and information that will be used to control subsequent be-

havior. It represents nonverbal schemas or imagery for events, which are essential for developing mental models for texts that are read. Students with deficits in nonverbal working memory have difficulty holding events in mind; consequently, they have difficulty forming mental schemas or mental models that are essential for comprehension (Baddeley, 1986; Barkley, 1997). The use of nonverbal working memory to activate past sensory events allows for hindsight and forethought. With hindsight, an individual can evaluate what worked and did not work, and why. With forethought, an individual can predict what might happen and take action to make a positive event occur, or to avoid a negative event. Such prediction also enables students to predict what might occur in a text.

TABLE 19.3. Interventions to Facilitate Self-Regulation

Executive Function	Deficits	Goals/Interventions
Nonverbal working memory	Inability to remember events or information Poor schema formation Poor sense of time Limited self-awareness Deficits in anticipatory set/ hindsight and forethought	Develop nonverbal mental representations of actions and events/visual imagery. Support working memory with visual cues and schedules.
Internalization of self-directed speech (verbal working memory)	Reduced description and reflection Difficulty in self-questioning Deficient rule-governed behavior Delayed moral reasoning Impaired reading comprehension	Develop receptive language to comprehend instructions. Develop expressive language skills to describe sequence of actions and events. Increase range of language functions to include self-directing, reporting, reasoning, predicting, projecting, imagining. Develop and increase use of distancing language.
Emotional control (self-regulation of mood, motivation, and level of arousal)	Inability to regulate emotions Difficulty with self motivation Poor perspective taking Poor self-regulation of arousal and goal-directed action	Develop a vocabulary of emotions. Develop theory-of-mind skills projecting into thoughts and feelings of others. Provide social skills instruction. Use social stories.
Problem solving	Limited analysis and synthesis of tasks and behaviors	Develop self-determinism. Model problem-solving in realistic activities. Coach in problem-solving activities (i.e., scaffolding and questioning students during interactions).

The retention of a sequence of events in working memory provides the basis for the human sense of time, which in turn sensitizes persons to potential cause–effect relationships that are critical for comprehension of many types of texts (Langston & Trabasso, 1999). Because of a poor sense of time, students with nonverbal working memory deficits may forget important responsibilities, such as deadlines for assignments, or they may not adequately judge the time needed to complete assignments.

If students have poor nonverbal working memory, educators will need to provide external visual supports to reduce the load on working memory (Russell, 1997). Visual cues, including graphic organizers or outlines representing the structures of different text genres (Blachowicz & Ogle, 2001), visual schedules for steps in a task, or time lines for completion of components of an activity (Hodgdon, 1995), have been used with students with learning disabilities and ASD to facilitate comprehension and planning. Strategies to enhance visual imagery of nonverbal working memory can facilitate students' abilities to form mental models for texts (Armbruster et al., 2001; Gambrell & Koskinen, 2002). Students who are instructed in producing mental images are better at comprehension monitoring and integrating information across texts (Borduin, Borduin, & Manley, 1994).

Internalization of Language (Verbal Working Memory)

Language is used to code many of the schemas in nonverbal memory. It is used for self-talk that provides reflection, description, instruction, and questioning, which in turn facilitate problem solving, the development of rules to guide behavior, and moral reasoning. Without internalized language, or self-directed speech, one fails to develop appreciation of rule-governed behavior, and without this internalization, one lacks self-regulation. Persons with poor internalized language do not talk themselves through activities. They lack an "inner voice" or "conscience" that tells them right from wrong. When a parent or teacher leaves the room, the rules leave with them. Persons with deficits in internalized language depend on others to control their behavior by providing clear rules and immediate rewards when the rules are obeyed and punishments when they are not obeyed.

Deficits in internalization of language also result in reading comprehension problems, because readers may fail to monitor their comprehension. As a consequence, they fail to notice textual inconsistencies, particularly when the inconsistent pieces of information are separated in the texts. Such students may be distracted by detail when reading, failing to understand the main ideas of the text (Brock & Knapp, 1996; Cherkes-Julkowski & Stolzenberg, 1991; Tannock & Schachar, 1996). Even when students with executive dysfunctions do recognize their failure to comprehend, they may not possess, or use, appropriate strategies to repair their comprehension failure, because they have failed to internalize the strategies.

Verbal working memory is critical for self-regulation. Students cannot internalize language to control their behavior unless they understand the language directed to them, and have adequate vocabulary and syntactic skills that they can use to describe their own actions and experiences. Interventions should, therefore, develop students' receptive and expressive language skills, which includes increasing students' range of pragmatic language functions for directing, reporting, reasoning, and predicting (Tough, 1981). Students' language should not be limited to describing the immediate here and now. Educators should model and provide opportunities for students to use distancing language, as described earlier in the work of Sigel et al. (1991).

Emotional Control

The third component of executive functioning, emotional control, involves self-regulation of affect, motivation, and arousal. One must have internalized language to control one's emotions. Individuals with executive function deficits remain more dependent on external sources to provide their regulation and motivation. For example, such students work for tangible rewards rather than in response to interest or curiosity. They are less able to moderate their initial feelings, to motivate themselves in the absence of external consequences, and to arouse themselves in the service of future goals. Persons with deficits in this executive function may quickly become frustrated and angry. They fail to persist with a task they perceive as difficult or boring, and tasks that do not have quick and frequent rewards are perceived as difficult and boring. Even if they recognize that they are experiencing comprehension difficulties, they are unlikely to seek ways to remedy their difficulties.

Emotional control also necessitates a "theory of mind" (the ability to understand that others have beliefs, desires, and intentions that are different from one's own). Without an adequate theory of mind, persons are insensitive to the thoughts and feelings of others, and are likely to say whatever comes to mind, regardless of the consequences. Hence, they frequently make comments that alienate them from peers and family members. Deficits in emotional control as a result of an inadequate theory of mind also affect reading comprehension, because readers do not recognize the intentions and goals of characters. Hence, they are likely to miss the plots and themes of narratives they read.

Emotional control requires that individuals have an emotional vocabulary, and that they understand the relationships between events and emotions. They must be able to use their language to reflect on their own emotions, and they must have a sensitivity to the emotions of others. Activities should include developing emotional vocabulary, and interpreting thoughts and feelings of others. Possible activities might include developing "theory of mind" (i.e., projecting into the thoughts and feelings of others; Gray, 1995; Howlin, Baron-Cohen, & Hadwin, 1999) and social skills (Gajewski, Hirn, & Mayo, 1993, 1994, 1996), which can aid students in developing emotional control, as well as provide insight into the behaviors of persons in the texts they read.

Reconstitution or Problem Solving

Successful academic performance in middle and high school requires *dynamic literacy*

skills (Morris & Tchudi, 1996). Dynamic literacy involves cumulative acquisition and use of knowledge over time. Students must be able to compare and contrast the information provided in multiple texts on the same and similar topics, noting how the texts support or contradict one another. Students must integrate and act on the content gained from multiple texts for problem-raising and problem-solving matters. If one is to engage in creative problem solving, one must have some degree of behavioral inhibition, and be able to reflect on one's own behavior and regulate one's own arousal. In problem solving, individuals must be able to analyze behaviors and synthesize new behaviors; they must take apart and recombine behavioral sequences so as to create novel, complex, and organized response patterns that are goal-directed.

With limited reconstitution or problem-solving skills, persons do not readily generalize something learned in one context to a new situation. Persons with deficits in this executive function will have difficulty analyzing reading tasks, and selecting and implementing the appropriate strategies to facilitate comprehension. To facilitate students' problem-solving skills, educators must find challenging, motivating activities that are personally relevant to students. Then they coach or scaffold the students through the steps of planning ways to reach their goal and carrying out their plan.

CONCLUSIONS

Success in the 21st century requires higher levels of literacy than in past centuries; and higher levels for all persons, not just the elite. Successful achievement of these higher literacy levels requires that students be self-regulated learners—that they establish goals for reading, and appropriately and automatically apply their declarative, procedural, and conditional knowledge of language to the reading process. Students with histories of decoding and language-learning difficulties are likely to experience difficulties in becoming self-regulated readers, because they lack elements of declarative, procedural, and conditional knowledge and/or they cannot use the knowledge automatically. Without automaticity in use of these three types of knowledge, working memory is stressed, making it difficult for students to attend to comprehension monitoring while they attempt to decode or process information at word, sentence, or schema levels. Some students who appear to have learned effortlessly to read in the early grades may also be at risk for reading difficulties as the demands for developing and applying metacognitive knowledge in reading increase in late elementary and middle school. This is particularly true for students, such as those with attention-deficit/hyperactivity disorder (ADHD), Asperger syndrome, or high-functioning autism, who have well-documented disabilities in executive functioning (Barkley, 1997; Blakemore-Brown, 2002; Russell, 1997). Because these students may be fluent readers, their reading comprehension problems are not readily recognized, and the difficulties they exhibit in self-regulation (such as setting goals for a task and working toward those goals) are viewed as attentional or behavioral problems.

As students move through the education system, they become increasingly responsible for comprehension and integration of what they read, yet, traditionally, little explicit instruction has been provided in comprehension. If students are to be academically successful, they must develop a metacognitive awareness of themselves as learners, as well as of the nature of the material to be learned, expected task outcomes, and the strategies available to complete tasks. They must be motivated to do the tasks and must possess the self-regulatory skills that will enable them to plan how to accomplish the tasks and carry out the plan.

Teaching of metacognitive strategies in reading and writing has become increasingly popular. Some schools incorporate such instruction into reading or content courses, whereas others offer classes devoted exclusively to strategy instruction. Some of these strategies were developed for use with typically developing students in regular education classroom; others were specifically developed for students with disabilities. Regardless of the original purpose for strategy instruction, a number of principles related to facilitating development of self-regulatory behaviors are generally agreed upon.

Implications for Developing Self-Regulation

Students require explicit metacognitive instruction in self-regulating their comprehension processing and selection of strategies. Helping students become self-regulated comprehenders is a long-term process that requires commitment from many persons in students' lives. Targeting the development of self-regulation in students requires that speech–language pathologists and educators apply their understanding of the nature of metcognitive knowledge–executive functioning and the development of self-regulation as they implement strategy instruction. The following components should be part of instruction to facilitate self-regulation in reading:

- *Model self-regulation.* Self-regulation is learned by observing others regulate their own behavior. Speech–language pathologists and educators should make explicit their own self-regulation in reading activities. They should talk about why they choose to read particular materials, what they like and do not like about what they read, difficulties they encounter when reading, and what they do about these difficulties. They should also try to obtain a commitment from others in the child's environment to model and verbalize self-regulatory behaviors.
- *Teach students to set goals for reading.* Different reading goals require different strategies. One cannot self-regulate one's reading comprehension without an understanding of why one is reading.
- *Teach a few research-validated comprehension strategies well, rather than teaching a large number of strategies.* Analyze students' needs to determine what strategies to teach. No one method is a panacea for all students. Give clear and specific explanations of strategy use. Provide frequent descriptions and reexplanations of strategy reasoning.
- *Combine strategy instruction with content teaching so that students come to*

view strategies as part of assignments. This may mean teaching less content in order to focus on self-regulation strategies. Also, do not teach individual strategies in isolation from each other. Strategies may be introduced one at time, but students should be taught to use them as a coordinated set, so they can make judgments to choose the best strategy to meet the requirements of the task. Teach declarative, procedural, and conditional knowledge for each strategy.

- *Motivate students to use strategies and provide guided practice with strategy use, providing explicit, corrective feedback as required.* Show students how use of strategies improves their performance. Also, share personal experiences of effective strategy use with students.
- *Encourage students to monitor their comprehension.* Help them think about why they may be having difficulty comprehending. If students have automatic decoding, comprehension failure may be due to the text itself —if it is not clearly worded; or may be due to the student's lack of familiarity with the topic, vocabulary, or complex sentences; or to the failure to make necessary inferences. Strategy instruction should be geared to students' current levels of assessment knowledge and ability, and it should anticipate their next levels of competence. Speech–language pathologists and educators must become expert at identifying students' needs in relation to their developing ability to self-assess. This may be best accomplished through careful examination of students' reading processes and products. Through observation of student reading, the nature of development of students' self-assessment abilities can be better examined and understood. Observe if students read and attend to the text at hand while keeping track of the purpose for reading, and if their performances and responses reflect the mindfulness and attention to detail that are necessary for successful reading. The need for instruction that leads to able self-assessment is indicated if observations reveal that students do not realize when the reading process has gone astray, do not know how to correct an apparent difficulty, or are not monitoring reading in relation to the goal for teaching.
- *Stimulate students to reflect on their performance.* After reading, students can assess how well they met their goals. They can evaluate how well they selected comprehension strategies and review what they did well, what they might have done differently, and what they might change the next time they encounter a similar task.

A potential drawback of strategy-based instruction is that attention may become focused on the surface features of the strategies themselves rather than on reading for meaning (Beck, McKeown, Worthy, Sandora, & Kucan, 1996). Self-regulatory behavior must become automatic, just like decoding. Automaticity develops as learner's declarative knowledge becomes bundled into procedural knowledge that can be applied with ease. Strategy use must move from conscious and effortful to automatic and almost effortless as students move from relying on knowledge about the strategy to activating strategy use automatically. Students must realize that the goal is not to implement strategies, but to gain meaning from texts.

Implications for Research in Self-Regulation

Available efficacy data show that strategy instruction can improve self-regulatory reading behaviors in both typically developing children and children with disabilities, but many questions remain unanswered:

- When should children be taught self-regulating and comprehension-monitoring strategies? Are some strategies more foundational than others?
- Which type of strategy instruction is effective for which students, under what circumstances? Are some strategies more appropriate than others for readers of certain ages or abilities? What are the characteristics of readers who are most likely to benefit from strategy instruc-

tion? What specific strategies, and in which combination, are best for readers of different abilities?

- What is the best context in which to teach self-regulating strategies?
- Does instruction in self-regulation in one area improve performance in other areas? Does successful self-regulation in reading generalize across different text genres and content areas?
- What characteristics of speech–language pathologists and teachers influence successful instruction of self-regulation for reading? What are the most effective ways to prepare speech–language pathologists and educators to teach self-regulation strategies?
- What makes instruction in self-regulation work? In what ways does working memory influence self-regulation? How can deficits in working memory be assessed and treated?

Duffy (2002) maintains that research focus must not be on instructional techniques, but on thoughtful adaptive teaching. There is a need to abandon the search for foolproof techniques and concentrate on research that helps us develop professionals who possess the psychological mind-set to be adaptive to meet the needs of individual students.

REFERENCES

Adams, M. (1990). *Beginning to read: Thinking and learning about print*. Cambridge, MA: MIT Press.

Archer, A. L., Gleason, M. M., & Vachon, V. L. (2003). Decoding and fluency: Foundation skills for struggling older readers. *Language Disabilities Quarterly, 26*, 89–101.

Armbruster, B. B., Lehr, F., & Osborn, J. (2001). *Put reading first: The research building blocks for teaching children to read*. Washington, DC: U. S. Department of Education.

Baddeley, A. D. (1986). *Working memory*. Oxford, UK: Oxford University Press.

Baker, L. (1979). Comprehension monitoring: Identifying and coping with text confusions. *Journal of Reading Behavior, 11*, 365–374.

Baker, L. (1985a). How do we know when we don't understand?: Standards for evaluating text comprehension. In D. L. Forrest-Pressley, G. E. MacKinnon, & T. G. Waller (Eds.), *Metacognition, cognition, and human performance* (pp. 155–205). Orlando, FL: Academic Press.

Baker, L. (1985b, April). *When will children acknowledge failures of word comprehension?* Paper presented at the meeting of the Society for Research in Child Development,

Barkley, R. A. (1997). *ADHD and the nature of self-control*. New York: Guilford Press.

Baum, F. (2000). *The wizard of Oz*. New York: Henry Holt. (Original work published 1900).

Beck, I. L., McKeown, M. G., Hamilton, R. L., & Kucan, L. (1997). *Questioning the author: An approach for enhancing student engagement with text*. Newark, DE: International Reading Association.

Beck, I. L., McKeown, M. G., Worthy, J., Sandora, C. A., & Kucan, L. (1996). Questioning the author: A year-long implementation to engage students with text. *Elementary School Journal, 94*, 358–414.

Blachman, B. A. (Ed.). (1997). *Foundations of reading acquisition and dyslexia: Implications for early intervention*. Mahwah, NJ: Erlbaum.

Blachowicz, C., & Ogle, D. (2001). *Reading comprehension: Strategies for independent learners*. New York: Guilford Press.

Blakemore-Brown, L. (2002). *Reweaving the autistic tapestry: Autism, Asperger syndrome and ADHD*. Philadelphia: Jessica Kingsley.

Blank, M. (1975). Mastering the intangible through language. In D. Aaronson & R. W. Rieber (Eds.), *Developmental psycholinguistics and communication disorders* (pp. 44–58). New York: New York Academy of Sciences.

Borduin, B. J., Borduin, C. M., & Manley, C. M. (1994). The use of imagery training to improve reading comprehension of second graders. *Journal of Genetic Psychology, 155*, 115–118.

Borkowski, J. G., & Burke, J. E. (1996). Theories, models, and measurements of executive functioning. In G. R. Lyon & N. A. Krasnegor (Eds.), *Attention, memory, and executive function* (pp. 255–261). Baltimore: Brookes.

Brock, S. W., & Knapp, P. K. (1996). Reading comprehension abilities of children with attention-deficit/hyperactivity disorder. *Journal of Attention Disorders, 1*, 173–186.

Brown, A. L. (1980). Metacognitive development and reading. In R. J. Spiro, B. C. Bruce, & W. F. Brewer (Eds.), *Theoretical issues in reading comprehension* (pp. 453–481). Hillsdale, NJ: Erlbaum.

Bruner, J. (1986). *Actual minds, possible worlds*. Cambridge, MA: Harvard University Press.

Campbell, J. (1949). *The hero with a thousand faces*. Princeton, NJ: Princeton University Press.

Catts, H., & Kamhi, A. (Eds.). (1999), *Language and reading disabilities*. Needham, MA: Allyn & Bacon.

Chamot, A. U., & O'Malley, J. M. (1994). *The CALLA handbook: Implementing the cognitive academic learning approach*. Reading, MA: Addison-Wesley.

Cherkes-Julkowski, M. & Stolzenberg, J. (1991). Reading comprehension, extended processing and attention dysfunction. (ERIC Document Reproduction Service No. ED 340194)

Conca, L. (1989). Strategy choice by LD children with good and poor naming ability in a naturalistic memory situation. *Learning Disabilities Quarterly, 12,* 97–106.

Connor, P. D., Sampson, P. D., Bookstein, F. L., Barr, H. M., & Streissguth, A. P. (2000). Direct and indirect effects of prenatal alcohol damage on executive function. *Developmental Neuropsychology, 18,* 331–354.

Coster, W., & Cicchetti, D., (1993). Research on the communicative development of maltreated children: Clinical implications. *Topics in Language Disorders, 13*(4), 25–38.

Cote, N., Goldman, S. R., & Saul, E. U. (1998). Students making sense of informational text: Relations between processing and representation. *Discourse Processes, 25,* 1–53.

Denckla, M. B., & Reader, M. (1993). Education and psychological interventions. In R. Kurlan (Ed.), *Handbook of Tourette's syndrome and related tic and behavioral disorders* (pp. 431–451). New York: Marcel Dekker.

Deshler, D. D., Ellis, E. S., & Lenz, B. K. (1996). *Teaching adolescents with learning disabilities: Strategies and methods.* Denver: Love.

DeTemple, J. M. (2001). Parents and children reading books together. In D. K. Dickinson & P. O. Tabors (Eds.), *Beginning literacy with language* (pp. 31–51). Baltimore: Brookes.

Dewitz, P., & Dewitz, P. K. (2003). They can read the words, but they can't understand: Refining comprehension assessment. *Reading Teacher, 56*(5), 422–435.

Diaz, R. (1991). Maternal teaching in the zone of proximal development: A comparison of low- and high-risk dyads. *Merrill–Palmer Quarterly, 37,* 83–107.

Diaz, R., Neal, C. J., & Amaya-Williams, M. (1990). The social origins of self-regulation. In L. C. Moll (Ed.), *Vygotsky and education: Instructional implications and applications of sociohistorical psychology* (pp. 127–154). New York: Cambridge University Press.

Dickson, S. V., Collins, V. L., Simmons, D. C., & Kame'enui, E. J. (1998). Metacognitive strategies: Research bases. In D. C. Simmons & E. J. Kame'enui (Eds.), *What reading research tells us about children with diverse learning needs* (pp. 295–360). Mahwah, NJ: Erlbaum.

Dickson, S. V., Simmons, D. C., & Kame'enui, E. J. (1998). Text organization: Research bases. In *What reading research tells us about children with diverse learning needs* (pp. 239–277). Mahwah, NJ: Erlbaum.

Duffy, G. G. (2002). The case for direct explanation of strategies. In C. C. Block & M. Pressley (Eds.), *Comprehension instruction: Research-based best practices* (pp. 28–41). New York: Guildford Press.

Duffy, G. G., Roehler, L. R., Meloth, M. S., Vavrus, L. G., Book, C., Putnam, J., et al. (1986). The relationship between explicit verbal explanation during reading skill instruction and student awareness and achievement: A study of reading teacher effects. *Reading Research Quarterly, 21,* 237–252.

Ehrlich, M. F. (1996). Metacognitive monitoring in the processing of anaphoric devices in skilled and less skilled comprehenders. In C. Cornoldi & J. Oakhill (Eds.), *Reading comprehension difficulties* (pp. 221–249). Mahwah, NJ: Erlbaum.

Fitzgerald, J. (1983). Helping readers gain self-control over reading comprehension. *Reading Teacher, 37,* 249–253.

Flavell, J. H. (1976). Metacognitive aspects of problem solving, In L. B. Resnick (Ed.), *The nature of intelligence* (pp. 231–235). Hillsdale, NJ: Erlbaum.

Flavell, J. H. (1979). Metacognition and cognitive monitoring: A new area of cognitive-developmental inquiry. *American Psychologist, 34,* 906–911.

Ford, C. E., Pellham, W. E., & Ross, A. D. (1984). Select attention and rehearsal in the auditory short-term memory task performance of poor and normal readers. *Journal of Abnormal Child Psychology, 12,* 127–142.

Fox, L., Long, S., Langlois, A. (1988). Patterns of language comprehension deficit in abused and neglected children. *Journal of Speech and Hearing Disorders, 53,* 239–244.

Fuson, K. (1979). The development of self-regulating aspects of speech: A review. In G. Zivin (Ed.), *The development of self-regulation through private speech* (pp. 135–217). New York: Wiley.

Gajewski, N., Hirn, P., & Mayo, P. (1993) *Social Star Set 1: General interaction skills.* Eau Claire, WI: Thinking Publications.

Gajewski, N., Hirn, P., & Mayo, P. (1994). *Social Star Set 2: Peer interaction skills.* Eau Clare: Thinking Publications.

Gajewski, N., Hirn, P., & Mayo, P. (1996) *Social Star Set 3: Conflict resolution and community interaction skills.* Eau Claire, WI: Thinking Publications.

Gambrell, L. B. & Koskinen, P. S. (2002). Imagery: A strategy for enhancing comprehension. In C. C. Block & M. Pressley (Eds.), *Comprehension instruction: Research-based best practices* (pp. 305–318). New York: Guilford Press.

Gardner, R. (1987). *Metacognition and reading comprehension.* Norwood, NJ: Ablex.

Gray, C. A. (1995). Teaching children with autism to "read" social situations. In K. A. Quill (Ed.), *Teaching children with autism: Strategies to enhance communication and socialization* (pp. 219–241). New York: Delmar.

Guthrie, J. T., & Knowles, K. T. (2001). Promoting reading motivation. In L. Verhoeven & C. Snow (Eds.), *Literacy and motivation: Reading engagement in individuals and groups* (pp. 159–176). Mahwah, NJ: Erlbaum.

Halliday, M. A. K., & Hasan, R. (1976). *Cohesion in English.* London: Longman.

Harris, K. R., & Graham, S. (1996). *Making the writing process work: Strategies for composition and self-regulation.* Cambridge, MA: Brookline.

Hart, B., & Risley, T. (1995). *Meaningful differences in the everyday experience of young American children.* Baltimore: Brookes.

Hodgdon, L. A. (1995). *Visual strategies for improving communication.* Troy, MI: QuirkRoberts.

Howlin, P., Baron-Cohen, S., & Hadwin, J. (1999). *Teaching children with autism to mind-read: A practical guide.* New York: Wiley.

Hulpach, V. (1996). *Ahaiyute and the cloud eater.* San Diego: Harcourt Brace

Kodituwakku, P. W., Kalberg, W., & May, P. A. (2001). The effects of prenatal alcohol exposure on executive functioning. *Alcohol Research and Health, 25,* 192–198.

Langston, M., & Trabasso, T. (1999). Modeling causal integration and availability of information during comprehension of narrative texts. In H. van Oostendorp & S. R. Goldman (Eds.), *The construction of mental representation during reading* (pp. 29–69). Mawhah, NJ: Erlbaum.

Leslie, L., & Caldwell, J. (2001). *Qualitative Reading Inventory—3.* New York: Longman.

Luria, A. R. (1961). *The role of speech in the regulation of normal and abnormal behavior.* New York: Liveright.

Lyon, G. R. (1999). Reading development, reading disorders, and reading instruction: Research-based findings. *Newsletter of Division 1 Language Learning and Education, American Speech–Language–Hearing Association 6*(1), 8–16.

Marzano, R. J., Hagerty, P. A., Valencia, S. W., & DiSteano, P. P. (1987). *Reading diagnosis and instruction: Theory into practice.* Englewood Cliffs, NJ: Prentice-Hall.

McCombs, B. (2001). Self-regulated learning and academic achievement: A phenomenological view. In B. J. Zimmerman & D. H. Schunk (Eds.), *Self-regulated learning and academic achievement* (pp. 67–123). Austin, TX: Pro-Ed.

Moats, L. C. (2000). *Speech to print: Language essentials for teachers.* Baltimore: Brookes.

Mochizuki, K. (1997). *Passage to freedom: The Sugihara story.* New York: Lee & Low.

Morris, P. J., & Tchudi, S. (1996). *The new literacy: Moving beyond the 3Rs.* San Francisco: Jossey-Bass.

National Reading Panel. (2000). *Teaching children to read: An evidence-based assessment of scientific research literature on reading and its implications for reading instruction.* Washington, DC: National Institute of Child Health and Development.

Oakhill, J., & Yuill, N. (1996). Higher order factors in comprehension disability: Processes and remediation. In C. Cornoldi & J. Oakhill (Eds.), *Reading comprehension difficulties.* Mahwah, NJ: Erlbaum.

Otero, J. (2002). Noticing and fixing difficulties while understanding science texts. In J. Otero, J. A. Leon, & A. C. Graesser (Eds.), *The psychology of science text comprehension* (pp. 281–307). Mahwah, NJ: Erlbaum.

Palincsar, A. S., & Brown, A. L. (1984). Reciprocal teaching of comprehension fostering and monitoring activities. *Cognition and Instruction, 1,* 117–175.

Paris, S. G., Cross, D. R., & Lipson, M. Y. (1984). Informed strategies for learning: A program to improve children's reading awareness and comprehension. *Journal of Educational Psychology, 76,* 1239–1252.

Paris, S. G., Lipson, M. Y., & Wixson, K. K. (1994). Becoming a strategic reader. In R. B. Ruddell, M. R. Ruddell, & H. Singer (Eds.), *Theoretical models and processes of reading* (pp. 788–810). Newark, DE: International Reading Association.

Pearson, P. D., & Gallagher, M. D. (1983). The instruction of reading comprehension. *Contemporary Educational Psychology, 8,* 317–344.

Perry, B. (1997). Incubated in terror: Neurodevelopmental factors in the "cycle of violence." In J. D. Osofsky (Ed.), *Children in a violent society.* New York: Guilford Press.

Pressley, M. (2002). Metacognition and self-regulated comprehension. In A. E. Farstrup & S. J. Samuels (Ed.), *What research has to say about reading instruction* (pp. 291–309). Newark, DE: International Reading Association.

Pressley, M., & Afflerbach, P. (1995). *Verbal protocols of reading: The nature of constructively responsive reading.* Hillsdale, NJ: Erlbaum.

Pressley, M., El-Dinary, P. B., Gaskins, I., Shuder, T., Bergman, J., & Almasi, J. (1992). Beyond explanations: Transactional instruction of reading comprehension strategies. *Elementary School Journal, 92,* 513–555.

Pressley, M., & Woloshyn, V. (1995). *Cognitive strategy instruction that really improves children's academic performance.* Cambridge, MA: Brookline.

RAND Reading Study Group. (2002). *Reading for understanding: Toward and R&D program in reading comprehension.* Santa Monica, CA and Washington, DC: RAND Corporation.

Randi, J., & Corno, L. (2000). Teacher innovations in self-regulated learning. In M. Boekaerts, P. R. Pintrich, & M. Zeider (Eds.), *Handbook of self-regulation* (pp. 651–685). San Diego: Academic Press.

Raphael, T. E (1984). Teaching learners about sources of information for answering comprehension questions. *Journal of Reading, 27,* 303–311.

Raphael, T. E. (1986). Teaching question/answer relationships, revisited. *Reading Teacher, 39,* 516–522.

Russell, J. (1997). *Autism as an executive disorder.* New York: Oxford University Press.

Rowling, J. K. (2000). *Harry Potter and the goblet of fire.* New York: Scholastic.

Saarni, C. (1999). *The development of emotional competence.* New York: Guilford Press.

Schunk, D. H. (2001). Social cultural theory and self-regulated learning. In B. J. Zimmerman & D. H. Schunk (Eds.), *Self-regulated learning and academic achievement* (pp. 125–151). Austin, TX: Pro-Ed.

Schunk, D. H., & Ertmer, P. A. (2000). Self-regulation and academic learning: Self-Efficacy enhancing interventions. In M. Boekaerts, P. R. Pintrich, & M. Zeider (Eds.), *Handbook of self-regulation* (631–649). San Diego: Academic Press.

Sigel, I. E. (1982). The relationship between parental distancing strategies and the child's cognitive behavior. In L. M. Laosa & I. E. Sigel (Eds.), *Families as learning environments for children* (pp. 47–86). New York: Plenum Press.

Sigel, I. E., Stinson, E. T., & Flaugher, J. (1991). Socialization of representational competence in the family: The distancing paradigm. In L. Okagaki & R. K. Sternberg (Eds.), *Directors of development: Influences on the development of children's thinking* (pp. 121–144). Hillsdale, NJ: Erlbaum.

Stone, C. A., & Conca, L. (1993). The origin of strategy deficits in children with learning disabilities: A social constructivist perspective. In L. J. Meltzer (Ed.), *Strategy assessment and instruction for students with learning disabilities* (pp. 23–59). Austin: Pro-Ed.

Swanson, H. L. (1983). Relations among metamemory, rehearsal activity and word recall of learning disabled and non-disabled readers. *British Journal of Educational Psychology, 53,* 186–194.

Tannock, R., & Schachar, R. (1996). Executive dysfunction as an underlying mechanism of behavior and language problems in attention deficit hyperactivity disorder. In J. H. Beitchman, N. J. Cohen, M. M. Konstantareas, & R. Tannock (Eds.), *Language, learning, and behavior disorders: Developmental, biological, and clinical perspectives* (pp. 128–155). New York: Cambridge University Press.

Teale, W. H. (1981). Parents reading to their children: What we know and need to know. *Language Arts, 58,* 902–912.

Tough, J. (1977). *The development of meaning.* New York: Wiley.

Tough, J. (1981). *Talk for teaching and learning.* Portsmouth, NH: Heinemann.

Wellman, H. M. (1985). The origins of metacognition. In D. L. Forrest-Pressley, G. E. MacKinnon, & T. G. Waller (Eds.), *Metacognition, cognition, and human performance* (pp. 1–31). Orlando, FL: Academic Press.

Wells, G. (1985). Preschool literacy-related activities and success in school. In D. R. Olson, N. Torrance, & A. Hildyard (Eds.), *Literacy, language, and learning: The nature and consequences of reading and writing* (pp. 229–255). New York: Cambridge University Press.

Westby, C. E. (1997). There's more to passing than knowing the answers, *Language, Speech, Hearing Services in Schools, 28,* 274–287.

Wilcox, K. (1982). Differential socialization in the classroom: Implications for equal opportunity. In G. Spindler (Ed.), *Doing the ethnography of schooling* (pp. 268–309). New York: Holt, Rinehart & Winston.

Williams, J. P. (2002). Reading comprehension strategies and teacher preparation. In A. E. Farstrup & S. J. Samuels (Eds.), *What research has to say about reading instruction* (pp. 243–260). Newark, DE: International Reading Association.

Wixson, K., Bosky, M., Yochum, M., & Alvermann, D. (1984). An interview for assessing students' perceptions of classroom reading tasks. *Reading Teacher, 37,* 346–353.

Yussen, S. R., Mathews, S. R., & Hiebert, E. (1982). Metacognitive aspects of reading. In W. Ott & S. White (Eds.), *Reading expository material* (pp. 189–218). New York: Academic Press.

Zabrucky, K., & Ratner, H. H. (1989). Effects of reading ability on children's comprehension evaluation and regulation. *Journal of Reading Behavior, 21,* 69–83.

Zabrucky, K., & Ratner, H. H. (1992). Effects of passage type on comprehension monitoring and recall for good and poor readers. *Journal of Reading Behavior, 24,* 373–391.

IV

ADDRESSING THE NEEDS OF INDIVIDUALS WITH LANGUAGE AND LITERACY CHALLENGES

INTRODUCTION

This section considers both populations who are typically developing and those who are at risk for language and literacy challenges, including children, adolescents, and young adults with a language-learning disability. Unlike the previous sections, however, Part IV utilizes a consistent framework that capitalizes on developmental information to guide assessment and instruction/intervention in the areas of word recognition, reading comprehension, writing composition, and spelling. Within each of these four literacy domains, the reader first encounters developmental aspects of language and literacy. Four chapters (Ehri and Snowling, Chapter 20; Pressley, Duke, and Hilden, Chapter 23; Singer and Bashir, Chapter 26; Cassar and Treiman, Chapter 29) review the development of specific literacy skills and strategies with learners who are typical and atypical. These chapters set the context for the related chapters on assessment and instruction/intervention that follow.

The chapters focused on assessment issues related to each literacy domain. (Roth, Chapter 21; Carlisle and Rice, Chapter 24; Calfee and Wilson, Chapter 27; Apel, Masterson, and Niessen, Chapter 30) provide a theoretically and empirically grounded basis for assessing literacy, as well as the issues surrounding assessment practices. A common theme throughout these chapters is the need to definitively identify one's purpose for assessment and to consider how assessment should guide instructional and intervention practices.

The four instruction/intervention chapters (O'Connor and Bell, Chapter 22; Vaughn and Klingner, Chapter, 25; Wong and Berninger, Chapter 28; Bailet, Chapter 31) follow a logical progression from the two chapters preceding each of them. In this third group of chapters, instructional and intervention approaches that flow from the preceding information on development and assessment are presented. Readers are encouraged to use evidence-based practices, when available, to promote literacy acquisition for learners who are typical or atypical.

Following the set of four chapter triads, Ehren, Lenz, and Deshler (Chapter 32) complete the section with their focus on special considerations when working with adolescents and young adults. They make a strong case for the need to address literacy with older students in more sustained and intensive efforts than are presently underway and offer specific principles to guide such efforts.

429

Part IV mirrors the philosophy and goals of the *Handbook,* as well as the series itself, from a variety of perspectives. First, as the reader looks across the list of chapters, it is apparent that the authorship reflects integration of research and theory from across a variety of scientific disciplines. Thus, readers are provided empirically and theoretically based approaches that lead to productive learning outcomes in students with diverse needs. Second, the information contained in Part IV is timely and informative in its presentation and accessible to practitioners, academics, and students in the disciplines interested in students' language and literacy proficiency. Whether the reader is from the field of speech–language pathology, educational psychology, general education, or special education, the information contained in Part IV will suit his or her needs. Finally, the content of these chapters represents state-of-the-art knowledge that undoubtedly will guide those who strive to improve the personal, academic, social, and vocational lives of students who struggle with language and literacy.

WORD RECOGNITION

20

Developmental Variation
in Word Recognition

Linnea C. Ehri
Margaret J. Snowling

One of the great mysteries to challenge literacy researchers is how skilled readers are able to read and comprehend text so quickly. Several mental processes appear to contribute to the end result of apprehending meanings. Readers' eyes focus on squiggles on the page. They apply several types of knowledge held in memory: lexical knowledge about specific words, including their spellings, spoken forms, and meanings; knowledge about the conventions of the writing system, including grapheme–phoneme correspondences, spellings of morphemes, and other spelling regularities and patterns; and phonological knowledge about the constituent sounds and sound patterns in words. They apply this knowledge to convert the squiggles to familiar letters and words. They apply their syntactic knowledge about grammatical relations among words, word order, and phrase and clause markers to interrelate and integrate the words into sentences. They apply their semantic knowledge about word and sentence meanings, their knowledge of the world, and their memory of text already read to make sense of the succession of words, sentences, and paragraphs. They

continuously update their memory of the text as they process new information and integrate it with information from earlier sentences and paragraphs.

Although this description implies that the various processes occur sequentially, in actuality, these processes operate concurrently, in parallel with redundancies across the different processes, allowing readers to confirm and check their accuracy (Perfetti, 1985; Rumelhart, 1977). For example, during text reading, readers hold in memory the meaning of text they have already read. This causes them to expect specific words to appear in upcoming text. When they see spellings consistent with these expectations, they read the words more accurately or quickly. If the words recognized do not fit expectations, they implement repair strategies, such as rereading.

Skilled readers' attention and thought are focused on comprehension processes, while the mechanics of reading operate more or less automatically. This is possible because skilled readers can read most words automatically. Although three types of units are visible in text (i.e., letters, words, and sentences), the reader's eyes come to favor written words. The advantage of words over sentences is that words can be recognized in one glance. The advantage of words over letters is that written words correspond more reliably to spoken words than letters correspond to phonemes, at least in English. Many years ago, Cattell (1886), using a tachistoscope, found that readers could recognize a whole word as quickly as they could recognize a single letter, and in fact, they could name a word faster than a letter. This finding indicates that word recognition plays a fundamental role in explaining how reading skill is executed rapidly, and also how it is acquired.

The plan of this chapter is to summarize what is known about word reading processes and their development, based on theory and evidence. Then, the issue of developmental variation is considered. Of interest is whether the acquisition of word reading skill proceeds differently in students identified as atypical learners. Atypical learners include students diagnosed as dyslexic, students who are language impaired, and students with low cognitive ability (e.g.,with Down syndrome). Also "hyperlexia" is considered as a contrasting disorder.

WORD-READING SKILL AND ITS DEVELOPMENT

At the outset, it is important to note what "development" involves with regard to acquiring reading skill (Chall, 1983). Many factors influence the course of development, including the genetic, cognitive, and linguistic makeups of individual learners and the environments they experience. Most importantly, the reading instruction received formally in school, and the amount and quality of text reading practiced by the reader affect reading development, as do reciprocal interactions between characteristics of individuals and their experiences, such that each enhances the impact of the other (Stanovich, 1986, 2000). If acquisition falls short or fails for some students, environmental factors may be equally, if not more, responsible than factors within individual learners. This contrasts with other domains of development that may not be so dependent on envi-

ronmental causes, such as formal schooling. For example, factors influencing spoken-language development differ substantially from factors influencing reading acquisition (Liberman & Liberman, 1992).

For various reasons, some students acquire reading skill more rapidly or effectively than do others. In reviewing the course of development of word-reading skill, it is evident that there are several places where difficulties might arise and retard development. A question of interest in this chapter is whether specific, word-centered difficulties characterize and distinguish different groups of atypical learners from each other, as well as from normally developing readers.

Various Ways to Read Words

There are various ways that developing readers might read words (Ehri, 1991, 1994). The first three ways listed below enable readers to recognize new words they have seldom, if ever, read before. The fourth way portrays how familiar words are read.

Decoding

Words that are unfamiliar in print can be read by applying a decoding strategy, also called "word attack." Decoding involves identifying the sounds of individual letters, holding them in mind, and blending them into pronunciations that are recognized as real words. A more mature form of decoding that requires more alphabetic knowledge is to pronounce and blend familiar clusters of letters, such as phonograms (e.g., -ed, -ake, -ight), common affixes, syllables, and spelling patterns. In English, a decoding strategy works sometimes but not always. It is more effective when combined with other strategies.

Analogy

Another way to attack unfamiliar words is to read them by analogy, that is, by recognizing how the spellings of unfamiliar words are similar to words already known. To analogize, readers access the known word in memory, then adjust the pronunciation to accommodate the new word, for example, reading *fright* by analogy to *night* (Cunningham,

1976; Gaskins et al., 1988; Goswami, 1986; Marsh, Freidman, Welch, & Desberg, 1981). A natural breaking point in English syllables is between the onset and rime, that is, between the initial consonants and the vowel–consonant blend (i.e., *jump* divided into *j–ump*; *stamp* divided into *st–amp*) (Treiman, 1985). This enhances the ease of reading analogous words by their shared rimes.

Prediction

A third way to attack unknown words is to predict what the words might be. Various cues in text can be used, for example, initial letters in the words, the sentence context preceding the words, or pictures accompanying the text (Biemiller, 1970; Goodman, 1972, 1976; Tunmer & Chapman, 1998). Prediction, however, does not explain how most words in text are read, because most words, particularly content words, cannot be guessed very accurately (Gough & Walsh, 1991). Of course, if the words are not present in the reader's spoken vocabulary, guessing has no chance of yielding the correct word.

Memory/Sight

A very different way to read words is by sight, which involves using memory to read words that have been read before. Sight of the word activates its spelling, pronunciation, and meaning immediately in memory. When sight words are known well enough, readers can recognize their pronunciations and meanings automatically, without expending any attention or effort figuring out the word (Guttentag & Haith, 1978; LaBerge & Samuels, 1974). This property makes sight-word reading especially valuable for text reading, because it allows word reading processes to operate unobtrusively, while the reader's attention is focused on the meaning of print.

CLARIFICATION OF
SIGHT-WORD READING

It is important to clarify what sight-word reading involves, because research findings have challenged the commonsense view that sight words are learned by rote memorizing the visual forms of words (Ehri, 1980, 1987, 1992; Reitsma, 1983; Share, 1995, 1999). To account for sight-word learning, we must explain how readers are able to look at printed words they have read before and recognize those specific words, while bypassing thousands of other words also stored in memory, including words with very similar spellings or meanings. Moreover, we must explain how readers are able to store and remember new words easily after reading them only a few times. The kind of process at the heart of sight-word learning is a *connection-forming* process. Connections are formed that link the written forms of words to their pronunciations and meanings. This information is stored in memory in the reader's mental dictionary or lexicon.

What kinds of connections are formed to store sight words in memory? Ehri's (1980, 1987, 1992, 1998) work, as well as that of others, suggests that readers learn sight words by forming connections between graphemes in the spellings and phonemes in the pronunciations of individual words. The connections are formed out of readers' general knowledge of grapheme–phoneme correspondences. Graphemes are letter units symbolizing phonemes. Phonemes are the smallest units of "sound" in words. When readers look at the spelling of a particular word, pronounce it, and recognize its meaning, their graphophonemic knowledge is activated and forms connections between letters in that spelling and phonemes detectable in the word's pronunciation. These connections secure the sight word in memory, with its spelling, pronunciation, and meaning bonded together as a unit.

Figure 20.1 reveals the connections that might be activated to secure several different words in memory. Capital letters designate spellings, lowercase letters between slashes indicate phonemes, and lines linking letters to phonemes indicate connections. To secure sight words in memory in this way, readers must possess alphabetic knowledge, including letter shapes, how to segment pronunciations into phonemes, and which graphemes typically symbolize which phonemes (Ehri, 1997).

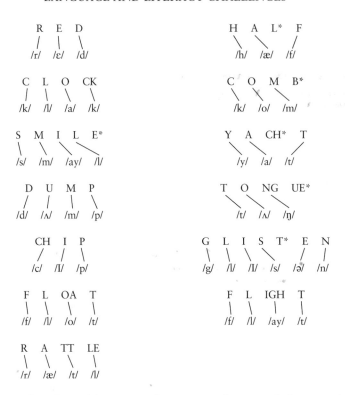

FIGURE 20.1. Connections formed in memory between graphemes and phonemes in specific words learned by sight. Capital letters indicate graphemes; lowercase letters between slashes indicate phonemes; lines indicate graphophonemic connections; asterisks indicate unpronounced letters.

The process of forming connections allows readers to remember how to read not only words containing conventional letter–sound correspondences but also words that have less regular spellings. Connections that might be formed to remember irregular words are included in Figure 20.1. Note that the same types of connections are evident. In fact, most of the letters in irregular words conform to grapheme–phoneme conventions. In remembering letters that do not correspond to phonemes, readers may remember them as extra visual forms. Or they may flag them as silent in memory. Or they may remember a special spelling pronunciation that includes the silent letter, for example, remembering *listen* as *lis–ten* or *chocolate* as *choc–o–late*. Or they may recognize them as part of a larger spelling pattern, for example, the *gh* in *-ight*.

As readers accumulate words in memory that share spelling patterns with other words, these spelling patterns become functional units that can be used to form connections. These patterns may be parts of words, for example, common vowel–consonant endings such as *-ight* or *-eak*, or they may be common words themselves, for example, *-it*, *-and*, or *-ate*, or bound morphemes such as *-ed* or *-ing*. This eases the task of retaining multisyllabic words in memory as sight words. For example, to remember how to read "interesting," readers can form connections between four written and spoken syllabic units, *in–ter–est–ing*, rather than 10 graphophonemic units.

Spellings of words are like maps that lay out their phonological and morphological forms visually. Skilled readers are able to compute these mapping relations very quickly when they read words. Knowledge of letter–sound relations provides a powerful mnemonic system that bonds the written forms of specific words to their pronunciations in memory. When readers acquire working knowledge of the alphabetic spelling system, they can build a lexicon of sight words easily as they encounter new words in their reading (Ehri, 1992). Others have proposed similar connectionist views of word recognition (Harm & Seidenberg, 1999; Perfetti, 1992; Rack, Hulme, Snowling, & Wightman, 1994; Share, 1995).

Reading Words in Text

In order for students to read and comprehend text, they must be able to read most of the words accurately. Conventional wisdom emerging from work by Betts (1954) and others specifies the levels of accuracy required. For texts that students can read independently, word accuracy levels are around 98%. For texts at a student's instructional level, word reading accuracy is around 95%. Texts become frustrating when accuracy drops to around 90%. In a longitudinal study by Juel (1988), children were tested on their ability to read core words drawn from basal texts they had read. The words were tested in isolation. Across grades 1–3, good readers read 91–97% of the words, whereas poor readers read only 71–83% of the words. Clearly, text reading was frustrating for the poor readers.

In addition to accuracy, students must learn to read text with sufficient speed and fluency. As portrayed earlier, multiple sources drawn from memory contribute to text reading. Readers' word reading accuracy and fluency are supported by their memory for the text already read, their background knowledge about the topic, their linguistic knowledge about how language is structured, their knowledge about the spelling system and decoding skill, and their lexicon of specific words. All of these sources create redundancy and help to maintain the reader's accuracy and fluency. This explains why students are able to read words faster in context than in isolation (Stanovich, 1981).

Although readers can read words in various ways, the way that is fastest and least intrusive to text reading is reading words from memory by sight. When sight words are

known well enough, readers recognize their pronunciations and meanings automatically (LaBerge & Samuels, 1974). They can read these words without expending any attention or effort decoding the words, because the words are present in memory and activated as soon as their spelling is seen. Studies of the Stroop phenomenon show that even when readers try to ignore familiar words, they cannot, because activation from memory occurs automatically. In a Stroop task, readers are directed to name the *color* of a string of words (e.g., the word *blue* written in yellow ink, the word *green* written in red ink, etc.) and to ignore the words that are the names of competing colors, or to name *drawings* of objects and to ignore competing words written on those objects (e.g., the word *chair* written on a picture of a table, or the word *cow* written on a drawing of a horse). In these tasks, readers find it impossible to ignore the words. This is evidenced by the fact that when words are present, readers take longer to name the colors or pictures than when nonwords or strings of letters are present (Guttentag & Haith, 1978). The explanation is that spellings of the familiar words are bonded to pronunciations and meanings in memory. Sight of the word's spelling activates the bonded unit very quickly and automatically, more quickly than the time it takes to retrieve the name of the color or picture from memory. The competing word, once activated, has to be suppressed in order to name the color or picture, so this creates a delay.

When readers read text, their attention is directed at constructing meaning and integrating it with meanings already apprehended. This process continues without interruption when words in the text can be recognized automatically by sight. However, comprehension is held up at least momentarily when words are decoded, read by analogy, or predicted, because the latter processes require attention and effort as readers recruit and apply knowledge about letter–sound correspondences, similarly spelled words, or word meaning expectations. This is why learning to read words by sight and building an extensive lexicon of sight words in memory are central in acquiring reading skill.

One of the hallmarks of skilled reading is the ability to read words accurately in or out of context (Stanovich, 1980). Poor readers have weaker context-free word reading skill, because they have poorly specified lexicons of sight words and lack adequate decoding skill (Rack, Snowling, & Olson, 1992). If readers cannot read a word by sight, and if they lack adequate decoding or analogizing skill, then the only source of help in reading the word comes from some of the letters plus the context (Nation & Snowling, 1998a). Stanovich has referred to this as "compensation," that is, reliance on context cues when the other sources fall short. Because context offers less precise cues than the spellings of words, their reading is less accurate.

Misreadings

Analyses of students' errors in reading words in text, also called "miscues" (Biemiller, 1970; Clay, 1967, 1968; Goodman, 1976), have provided insights about the information that readers use when they process words in text. Misreadings are more likely to occur when the words in text are unfamiliar in print or in speech. Evidence that readers use context when they read words is suggested by the high proportion of miscues that fit into the sentence being read and are consistent with its meaning. Evidence for the use of letter–sound cues is suggested by miscues that share letters with the words in print. Evidence that readers incorporate the words they read into sentence and text meanings is suggested by self-corrections. Misreadings that do not fit sentence and text meanings are more likely to be corrected than misreadings that fit the context. Miscues are more prevalent among beginning readers, among those having difficulty learning to read, and among readers given a text that is above their reading level.

Poor readers' miscues differ from those of good readers in several respects. Both produce about the same proportion of contextually acceptable errors (Biemiller, 1970), but poor readers produce fewer errors that preserve the letter–sound cues present in the printed words than do good readers. In Biemiller's study, the number of miscues that preserved initial letters revealed this

difference (i.e., misreading *kitty* as *puppy* vs. *kitten*). Also poor readers are less apt than good readers to self-correct their miscues (Biemiller, 1970; Clay, 1969).

The miscues evident in beginning readers differ depending on the type of instruction they receive. Children who receive synthetic phonics instruction in which they are taught to sound out and blend unfamiliar words may produce miscues that are nonsense words. This occurs when they attempt to convert spellings into recognizable pronunciations but their effort falls short, yielding a nonword (Carnine, Carnine, & Gersten, 1984; Cohen, 1974–1975). (We might note that because English consists of variable grapheme–phoneme correspondences, with one letter symbolizing more than one phoneme, this is not surprising.) In contrast, children who are taught in whole-word programs, or programs emphasizing the use of context to guess words, rarely produce nonsense words. Rather, their misreadings are other real words. Biemiller (1970) studied beginning readers who were receiving whole-word instruction. These students drew the words they produced as reading errors from the set of words they had already learned to read. They did not apply a decoding strategy.

Course of Development

Overview

Ehri (1995, 1999) has proposed and provided evidence for a phase theory portraying the acquisition of word reading skills for normally developing readers and for struggling readers (Ehri & McCormick, 1998). Four phases of word learning are distinguished, each characterized by the reader's understanding and use of the alphabetic system to read words. The four phases are (1) a *prealphabetic* phase; (2) a *partial-alphabetic* phase; (3) a *full-alphabetic* phase; (4) a *consolidated-alphabetic* phase. The concept of phase is preferred, because phase is a less stringent way to distinguish periods of development than the concept of stage. Each phase overlaps with the next phase, and mastery of one phase is not necessary to initiate movement to the next phase.

To provide an overview, the prealphabetic phase characterizes the period when pre-readers have little working knowledge of the alphabetic system. As a result, they remember how to read words by using salient, nonalphabetic visual cues. The partial-alphabetic phase characterizes the period when readers have rudimentary working knowledge of the alphabetic system but lack full knowledge, particularly vowel knowledge, so they read words using only partial letter–sound cues. As a result, the mental representations of words retained in memory remain fuzzy. The full-alphabetic phase characterizes the period when readers possess working knowledge of the major grapheme–phoneme units in the writing system and also phonemic segmentation skill. As a result, they can use full graphophonemic cues to decode new words, and they can retain full representations of sight words in memory. The consolidated-alphabetic phase characterizes the period when readers possess working knowledge of larger units involving graphosyllabic and subsyllabic spelling–sound patterns and morphographic patterns that they can use to decode new words and to retain sight words in memory.

It is important to note that each phase highlights the type of alphabetic knowledge that *predominates* in reading words. This means that, for example, children in the full-alphabetic phase may operate primarily with graphophonemic correspondences in reading words. However, they may also have acquired knowledge of some larger, consolidated units. As more of these are acquired and come to predominate, these readers move into the consolidated phase.

Typically, prealphabetic readers are found among preschoolers and kindergartners before they receive any reading instruction. Partial-alphabetic readers are common in kindergarten and early first grade, when letters are taught and initial reading instruction begins. Full-alphabetic readers are first graders who have acquired sufficient alphabetic knowledge to decode words. Consolidated alphabetic readers tend to be found in second grade and beyond. It is important to note that these phases are not tied to age or grade, but rather to readers' knowledge of the alphabetic system and its application to

read words. Even adolescents or adults may be found to function at the lowest phases if they lack working knowledge of the alphabetic system (Cardoso-Martins, Rodrigues, & Ehri, 2003). One step in assessing the difficulties of students who are struggling to acquire word reading skills is to determine their phase of development and the capabilities they lack and need to acquire through instruction and practice.

THE PREALPHABETIC PHASE

The first phase, called prealphabetic, is when letter–sound knowledge is not used to read words. As a result, prealphabetic readers have no ability to decode words or to analogize. They handle the task of reading words by memorizing their visual features or by guessing words from their context.

This phase has been called the "selective-cue" stage (Juel, 1991) because children attend to selected cues in remembering how to read words. It has been labeled the "paired-associate" stage (Gough & Hillinger, 1980) to denote that arbitrarily chosen associations are formed to link some feature of a written word to its spoken form or meaning. It has also been termed the "logographic" phase (Frith, 1985), because readers focus on nonalphabetic graphic features of words that have nothing to do with sounds in the words. Children at this phase have very limited knowledge of letters, and they do not understand that letters in written words map onto sounds in oral language.

The following word reading behaviors are in evidence during the prealphabetic phase of development (Ehri, 1987, 1991, 1994; Ehri & Wilce, 1985; Gough & Hillinger, 1980; Gough, Juel, & Roper-Schneider, 1983; Juel, Griffith, & Gough, 1985; Soderbergh, 1977):

1. Students may read words that they encounter frequently in their environment, for example, *stop, Burger King, Pepsi, milk.* However, when environmental cues such as logos and distinctive print are removed, and the word is presented by itself, children can no longer read the words (Mason, 1980). If a trick is played by showing children familiar words in their environment with one let-

ter altered, for example, changing the *P* to *X* on a can of *Xepsi,* children fail to detect the change and read the print as "Pepsi" (Masonheimer, Drum, & Ehri, 1984). This indicates that children "read the environment" rather than the print. They remember nonalphabetic visual cues rather than letters. This has been called "visual cue reading" (Ehri & Wilce, 1985).

2. Students have trouble learning to read words that are written without any context clues in the form of pictures or logos. With practice, they may learn some words, but the words are quickly forgotten (Mason, 1980). This is because the associations formed are arbitrary and hard to hold in memory. When students remember how to read words, they employ visual cues and rote learning. Bits of the word, such as its length or shape, or an irrelevant cue such as a thumbprint appearing next to the word, are selected rather than the sequence of letters (Gough et al., 1983; Seymour & Elder, 1986)

3. Students may select meaning-bearing cues in remembering how to read words, for example, remembering the word *look* because it has two "eyes" in the middle (Gough et al., 1983). This makes it easier to remember the word. However, because letters are not linked to sounds in memory, the letters do not constrain how the meaning is labeled. As a result, the student may read it as *see* rather than *look.* Another problem is that similarly spelled words such as *book, moon,* and *tool* may be mistaken as the same word. Because visual, meaning-bearing cues are absent in most words, this is not effective for building a sight vocabulary.

4. Connected text cannot be read independently. Readers may "pretend-read" text that they have heard several times and memorized. However, they are unable to read words that are singled out in the text or to do finger-point reading, that is, pointing to the words in the text as they read it. This exposes the prealphabetic nature of their reading (Ehri & Sweet, 1991; Morris, 1993).

5. The strategy of guessing from context cues may be used to read words. For example, prealphabetic students who are shown a picture of a Ford convertible with the word *wheels* printed beneath it will read the word as *car.* Letters exert little influence on the word that is guessed, because students lack knowledge of letter–sound relations.

The most telling sign that students are in the prealphabetic phase is their lack of letter knowledge. Children who know few letter names or sounds are shut off from reading words alphabetically, so by default, they process words as strictly visual forms. Another telling sign is lack of phonemic awareness, that is, lack of the ability to manipulate sounds in words, for example, identifying first or final sounds, or segmenting words into a sequence of sounds, or blending sounds to form words.

THE PARTIAL-ALPHABETIC PHASE

The second phase is called partial-alphabetic because students know at least some letters of the alphabet, usually their names, and can use them to remember how to read words by sight using partial-alphabetic cues. Also they can guess words using context and partial letter cues. However, they lack much ability to decode words and to read words by analogy, because both of these strategies require more working knowledge of the alphabetic system than they possess.

Mason (1980) called this the "visual recognition" stage, because children showed signs of detecting letters in words. This phase has also been labeled the "rudimentary-alphabetic" phase, because beginners can match some of the letters in words to sounds in their pronunciations (Ehri, 1991). The following capabilities characterize readers in the partial-alphabetic phase (Ehri, 1991, 1994; Ehri & Wilce, 1985, 1987a; Mason, 1980):

1. Students sample partial-letter cues in words combined with context cues to guess the identities of unfamiliar words (Stahl & Murray, 1998). For example, upon seeing a picture of a farm with a word beginning with *B* printed beneath the picture, students might read it as *barn.* This contrasts with the previous phase, where alphabet letters were ignored when words were guessed.

Words are often misread as other words having similar letters, for example, *man* for *men*, *this* for *that*, *horse* for *house*.

2. Students who read words backwards, for example, *was* for *saw*, are not seeing them backwards. Rather they have not acquired a strong left-to-right orientation in their word reading (Vellutino, 1979). One important achievement at this phase involves practicing the "reading direction" so that it becomes automatic.

3. Students who already know letter names are able to extract and learn easily those sounds contained in the names of the letters. This includes the long vowel sounds of *A*, *E*, *I*, *O*, and *U*, the consonant sounds found in *B*, *D*, *F*, *J*, *K*, *L*, *M*, *N*, *P*, *R*, *S*, *T*, *V*, *Z*, and the "soft" sounds of *C* (/s/) and *G* (/j/) (Ehri, 1983; Treiman, Sotak, & Bowman, 2001).

4. Students have a harder time learning letter–sound correspondences whose sounds are not present in the names of letters. This includes the hard sounds of *C* (i.e., /k/ as in *cat*) and *G* (i.e., /g/ as in *girl*) and the sounds of *H*, *W*, and *Y*, whose names are not informative about sounds and may even mislead. Because the name of *Y* begins with /w/, students who use letter names to infer letter–sounds commonly think that *Y* stands for /w/, and they invent spellings such as *wife* spelled YF, and *while* spelled YL (Henderson, 1981; Read, 1971; Treiman, 1993). Students at this phase also are not likely to know the digraphs *SH*, *WH*, *TH*, *CH*, *CK*, *NG*, or short vowel letter–sounds (i.e., the vowels in *at*, *Ed*, *it*, *odd*, and *up*). Until they are taught, students do not learn about the complexities of spelling long vowels with digraphs (e.g., b*oa*t, b*ea*d) or with silent *E* (e.g., g*ate*).

5. Partial-alphabetic phase readers' working knowledge of the alphabetic system is evident in their invented spellings of words when they are directed to write the sounds they hear. Their inventions are partial in that only some of the sounds are spelled, for example, *bumpy* spelled BMP.

6. Partial-phase students possess some phonemic awareness (PA). For example, they may be able to segment initial and final sounds in words, but they have difficulty distinguishing the two sounds in consonant blends such as *BL* or *ST*. One reason why the spellings they invent are only partial is that they are unable to distinguish all the phonemes in words.

7. Students can remember how to read words by sight more effectively in this phase than in the previous phase. This is because they have available some alphabetic knowledge and phonemic awareness to use in forming connections between letters and sounds in words (DeAbreu & Cardoso-Martins, 1998; Ehri & Wilce, 1985; Roberts, 2003; Treiman et al., 2001). However, because their knowledge of the system is limited, they process only partial letter–sound relations to form connections in learning sight words. For example, in remembering how to read *block*, they might link the initial and final letters *B* and *K* to sounds /b/ and /k/ in the pronunciation of the word. However, other letters and sounds in the word are overlooked. This causes a problem in that other similarly spelled words such as *book* and *black* may be mistaken for *block*. The use of partial graphophonemic cues to read words is called "phonetic cue reading" (Ehri & Wilce, 1985, 1987a, 1987b).

8. Neither decoding nor analogizing is available for reading unfamiliar words. Decoding is precluded by the lack of vowel knowledge and blending skill. Analogizing is not operable, because sight words are not represented in memory in sufficient detail to recognize that new words have similar spelling patterns to known words. Rather than read new words by analogy, the new words are often misread as the known words, because they share some of the same letters (Ehri & Robbins, 1992).

THE FULL-ALPHABETIC PHASE

The third phase is called "full-alphabetic" because readers possess extensive working knowledge of the graphophonemic system, and they can use this knowledge to analyze fully the connections between graphemes and phonemes in words (Ehri, 1991, 1992, 1999). This enables them to decode unfamiliar words and to store fully analyzed sight words in memory. This phase has also been called the "spelling–sound" stage

(Juel, 1991), the "cipher-reading" stage (Gough & Hillinger, 1980), and the "alphabetic" phase (Frith, 1985) to convey the point that learners acquire and use orderly relationships for transforming graphemes into phonemes to read words.

Readers at the full-alphabetic phase differ markedly from pre- and partial-alphabetic readers. The pre- and partial-phases occur inevitably among beginners who, because of insufficient knowledge of the alphabetic system, must grapple with word reading in less effective ways. The pre- and partial-alphabetic phases may emerge even without much instruction in how to read words. In contrast, for most students, the full-alphabetic phase requires systematic phonemic awareness and phonics instruction to establish the foundation for attaining mature word reading skill. Beginners who are taught to read words in writing systems whose spelling–sound correspondences are more regular than English, for example, German, and who receive systematic phonics instruction, may spend little, if any, time in the pre- and partial-alphabetic phases once they learn how letters symbolize sounds and how to use them to read (Wimmer, 1993, 1996; Wimmer & Goswami, 1994; Wimmer & Hummer, 1990). They may move quickly into the full-alphabetic phase.

The following characteristics portray students at the full-alphabetic phase (Ehri, 1991, 1994; Gough & Hillinger, 1980; Juel, 1991; Juel et al., 1985; Soderbergh, 1977):

1. Readers possess working knowledge of the major grapheme–phoneme correspondences, including vowels, and they possess phonemic awareness. This knowledge enables them to match graphemes in the conventional spellings of words to phonemes in pronunciations and to store these connections in memory for reading the words by sight. Because they possess fully represented sight words in memory, they can use them to read new words by analogy to known words. Because they know graphophonemic correspondences and how to blend, they can decode unfamiliar words. Also, this knowledge enables them to invent graphophonemically complete sound spellings of words and to remember correct

spellings of words more easily than was possible during the partial-alphabetic phase.

2. Early in this phase, word reading operations are executed slowly, sometimes more slowly than in the partial phase. Slow, nonfluent reading reflects the fact that readers have become "glued to print," that they consciously and deliberately sound out and blend letter–sound associations to read words (Chall, 1983). Painstaking decoding is a typically occurring, temporary aspect of reading development, often traceable to direct instruction in sequential decoding as a means of attacking unfamiliar words (e.g., Barr, 1974–1975; Carnine, 1977; Chall, 1983; Cohen, 1974–1975; Monaghan, 1983). As beginners practice decoding words, and as their knowledge of fully analyzed sight words grows, they speed up in applying this strategy. Decoding practice also familiarizes them with the most frequent sounds symbolized by letters and how these sounds are typically blended to form words.

3. One very important development at this phase is the sizable growth that occurs in students' sight vocabularies as a result of reading practice. Much of this practice involves reading words in the context of stories. As indicated earlier, students must possess working knowledge of the alphabetic system to be able to look at words in text and perform the matching operations that link graphemes to phonemes. Share (1995, 1999) describes this as a self-teaching mechanism in which students apply their decoding skill to read words, and this establishes the words in memory as sight words. Students who have practiced reading new words in this way, perhaps as few as four times (Reitsma, 1983), retain the new words in memory and can read them by sight. As a result, the learner's sight vocabulary increases steadily during the full-alphabetic phase.

4. At this phase, students become able to read unfamiliar words by analogy to familiar words they know by sight, for example, reading *beak* by analogy to *peak*. Goswami (1986, 1988) has shown that beginners can analogize early in their reading development, when the analogs are visibly present to prompt word reading. However, in order

for beginners to read new words by analogy to words stored in *memory,* they must have some decoding skill (Ehri & Robbins, 1992). This enables them to remember the sight words in sufficient letter detail to recognize that the new words resemble but are not identical to the known words, and to adapt their knowledge of known words in blending sounds to form new words. Although analogizing becomes possible at this phase, it is more common at the next phase as readers' knowledge of sight words grows (Leslie & Calhoun, 1995).

5. Text reading initially is slow and laborious even though students know most grapheme–phoneme relations. How laborious depends on the number of unfamiliar words in the text and how accessible the meaning of the text is. As indicated previously, text reading is easy and comfortable when accuracy levels are high, 98% and above. Text reading becomes frustrating when accuracy levels drop to 90%. If readers have to sound out and blend very many of the words, this increases the time and effort required.

Accuracy levels in reading words in text can be enhanced by having students read books that they have heard or read before. However, the problem is that if students rely mainly on their memory for the text and do not pay sufficient attention to letters in the print, this form of reading will contribute little to strengthening their text-reading fluency or their sight-word acquisition (Johnston, 2000). The alternative is to have students practice reading texts that they have not read before. The problem here is that texts must be found in which the words can by read by sight or by decoding, or by prediction, with at least 95% accuracy. It is especially hard to find such books for beginners with small sight vocabularies and slowly executed decoding skill. However, Hatcher (2000) describes a system of grading books for this purpose that allows teachers successfully to match book to learner.

Text-reading practice is essential for acquiring reading skill, particularly in English, which involves retaining the specific forms of words in memory to read them effectively

(Ehri, 1980, 1991, 1999; Hatcher, 1996; Share, 1999; Share & Stanovich, 1995). Students must be exposed to these words a sufficient number of times to learn how to read them. They must have the decoding and prediction skills to read the unfamiliar words accurately and to activate connection-forming processes that will retain the words in memory as sight words. Because each book they read contains only a few unfamiliar words, they need to read many books for their sight vocabularies to grow.

THE CONSOLIDATED-ALPHABETIC PHASE

The consolidated-alphabetic phase actually begins during the full-alphabetic phase. Its onset is characterized by the consolidation of grapheme–phoneme blends into larger units that recur in different words. This phase has also been referred to as the "orthographic" phase to indicate that the focus is on spelling patterns (Ehri, 1991; Frith, 1985). Word learning becomes more mature in several respects (Ehri, 1991, 1994; Juel, 1983; Treiman, Goswami, & Bruck, 1990).

1. The important alphabetic acquisition at this phase consists of working knowledge of sequences of letters that recur in different words and how they are pronounced as blended units. These consolidated units might include affixes, root words, onsets, rimes, and syllables. The patterns might be taught by linking them to their linguistic origins—Anglo-Saxon, Greek, and Latin—clarify the distinctions and regularities (Henry, 1989). The value of consolidated units is that they facilitate word decoding accuracy and speed (Juel, 1983) as well as sight-word learning (Ehri, 1995). Whereas full-alphabetic readers operate primarily with grapheme–phoneme relations, consolidated-alphabetic readers operate primarily with larger units, hence reducing the total number of units to be processed in words. In the example given earlier, the word *interesting* contains 10 graphophonemic units (including *ng,* symbolizing one phoneme) but only four graphosyllabic units. Among the first letter sequences that are likely to become consolidated are those that occur most frequently in children's texts. These in-

clude the morphemic suffixes -ed, -ing, -er, -est (Bryant, Nunes, & Bindman, 1997), as well as spelling patterns that recur in many words and are high-frequency words themselves, -it, -at, -in, -an, -and, -all.

There is evidence that words containing more familiar letter patterns are read more accurately by students than are words containing unfamiliar patterns, even when the words are constructed out of the same grapheme–phoneme correspondences (Treiman et al., 1990). Such effects are more apparent in advanced beginning readers than in novice beginners, indicating the contribution of a larger sight vocabulary to knowledge of common spelling patterns (Bowey & Hansen, 1994).

2. Students' sight vocabularies continue to grow rapidly during this phase. It is easier to store longer words in memory, because learners can form connections between familiar letter chunks. They are not limited to grapheme–phoneme connections only. Readers in the consolidated-alphabetic phase recognize sight words by remembering connections involving multiletter combinations, as well as single graphemes. When words are learned in this way, they are seldom confused with other words having similar spellings.

Multisyllabic words are retained in memory as sight words when readers fully analyze their constituent graphosyllabic units, for example, the four units in "in–ter–est–ing." In a study by Bhattacharya and Ehri (in press), adolescent readers who were reading behind grade level practiced reading 100 multisyllabic words by segmenting and pronouncing their graphosyllabic constituents. They were taught to fully analyze words by segmenting and matching written and spoken syllables. Each syllable had to contain only one vowel, but flexibility was allowed in the junctures between syllables (e.g., fin–ish or fi–nish). Control groups either practiced reading the words as wholes or received no treatment. On posttests, readers who benefited from the treatment (those reading at the third-grade-equivalent level) outperformed the control groups in reading unpracticed multisyllabic words and in decoding nonwords.

3. Students may learn the strategy of reading words by analogy. This helps them recognize spelling patterns that recur in different words and consolidate these letter sequences into units. Also, it helps them build neighborhoods of words organized in memory by spelling pattern (Laxon, Coltheart, & Keating, 1988).

4. To read unfamiliar words, decoding strategies are expanded to include hierarchical decoding, as well as sequential decoding. In hierarchical decoding, more complex understandings are acquired about the influence of graphemes in one part of the word on the sounds of graphemes in other parts of the word, for example, the influence of final -E on the preceding vowel (e.g., fine vs. fin), the influence of E and I on the preceding consonant G or C (e.g., wage vs. wag, cent vs. can't), the influence of double consonants on a preceding vowel (e.g., cutter vs. cuter, latter vs. later (Marsh et al., 1981; Venezky, 1970; Venezky & Johnson, 1973). Students acquire working knowledge of these relations. Teaching students explicitly stated rules may promote acquisition of working knowledge, but it is no guarantee (Beck, 1981). Evidence that students have acquired working knowledge is revealed in tasks requiring them to read real words they have never read before or nonwords containing the patterns, such as cibe or gatter.

WORD READING DEVELOPMENT IN ATYPICAL LEARNERS

Phase theory portrays the acquisition of word reading skills in normally developing readers and in struggling readers. However, different categories of struggling readers have been distinguished, and their course of development may not follow the same path. The purpose of the next section is to review evidence regarding reading development in atypical learners and to consider whether the variation in word reading that characterizes specific types of atypical learners is consistent with phase theory.

As we have seen from children learning to read in different languages, phase theory does not make specific predictions about the rate of reading development. Just as children learning to read in a regular language, such as German, may proceed to the full-alphabetic phase quickly (Wimmer & Hummer, 1990), children with low cognitive ability may be slow to proceed through the different phases of reading.

Reading is an example *par excellence* of a learned skill that involves developing connections in memory between visual symbols (letters and letter strings) and their verbal labels (pronunciations). Windfuhr and Snowling (2001) showed that the ability to learn mappings between visual symbols and verbal labels in a paired associate learning task made an independent contribution to reading ability, even after the contribution of phoneme awareness was controlled. It stands to reason, therefore, that children with general learning difficulties will be slow to learn letters and to consolidate sight words in memory. Notwithstanding this, an important question is whether the word-recognition skills of children who are atypical learners follow the same course of development as that of typically developing children or, alternatively, whether their word-recognition system is qualitatively different.

It turns out that this issue is difficult to resolve. Frith (1985) proposed that different forms of reading disability could be conceptualized as "arrest" at different phases of development. However, subsequent research has shown that "arrest" is seldom absolute given the natural tendency for development to right itself. For the same reasons, discrete disorders are rare in childhood, and more continuous variation tends to be the norm (Bishop, 1997). Therefore, a more reasonable question to ask is whether phase theory offers a productive framework for capturing the *predominant* difficulties associated with different developmental abnormalities. Furthermore, we can ask whether individual differences in the severity of a child's core difficulty, together with his or her reading experiences, modify the expression of the reading disability.

Table 20.1 presents a summary of the main characteristics of each phase of development, as reviewed above. We use these characterizations as a framework for discussing data from atypical learners who have reading difficulties. Before proceeding, it is perhaps important to note that, to date, the framework has rarely been used explicitly to investigate reading disorders. As a result, the empirical database does not always contain pertinent evidence. Second, phase theory focuses on the development of word-recognition skills. However, many reading disorders encompass problems of reading comprehension. We have relatively little to say about the latter, but we clarify when problems of reading comprehension are an important feature of the disorder we discuss.

Types of Atypical Learners

When given normal educational opportunities, the majority of children learn to read without difficulty. However, a significant number, perhaps as many as 10%, have difficulties that are not easily resolved without remediation. The most widely researched form of reading disability is dyslexia, a specific learning difficulty primarily affecting the ability to learn to read and spell, and associated with phonological processing difficulties (Snowling, 2000; Stanovich, 1994). Although many children with dyslexia have a history of slow or problematic speech and language development (Rutter & Yule, 1975; Scarborough, 1990), oral-language difficulties are primarily resolved in the school years and no longer give cause for concern.

Such a positive outcome is not the case for children with preschool speech–language impairment whose oral-language difficulties are deficient compared to their nonverbal ability at school entry (Bishop & Edmundson, 1987). Most children with persistent speech and language difficulties go on to have significant reading difficulties affecting both word recognition and reading comprehension (Catts, 1993; Catts, Fey, Zhang, & Tomblin, 1999; Stothard, Snowling, Bishop, Chipchase, & Kaplan, 1998). Although it is difficult to make comparisons among studies because of the different criteria used to select language-impaired children, it seems that word-level reading skills are better when children with language impairment learn to read in a transparent or

TABLE 20.1. A Summary of Word-Reading Characteristics That Predominate at Each of the Four Phases of Development According to Ehri's (1999) Theory

Prealphabetic	Partial alphabetic	Full alphabetic	Consolidated alphabetic
Limited if any letter knowledge	Most letter names and some GPCs known	Many GPCs[a] known	Consolidated blends of common GPCs, spelling patterns, and morphographic units known
Lack of phoneme awareness	Some phoneme awareness	Graphophonemic awareness[b]	Graphophonemic awareness[b]
Sight words read by remembering selective visual cues	Sight words read by remembering partial letter–sound cues	Sight words read by remembering GPC connections; expanding sight vocabulary; automatic word recognition	Sight words read by remembering GPC or larger unit connections; expanding sight vocabulary; automatic word recognition
Visual and semantic reading errors	Phonetic reading errors; words misread as other words sharing similar letters (e. g., *men–man*)	Relatively few errors reading familiar words	Relatively few errors reading familiar words
Cannot decode	Cannot decode	Can decode unfamiliar words; slow at outset	Can decode unfamiliar words proficiently
Cannot analogize	Cannot analogize	Some use of analogies	More frequent use of analogies
Words guessed from context	Words guessed from initial letters plus context		Context-free word reading skill
Words written nonphonetically	Partial phonetic spellings invented; weak memory for correct spellings	Phonetically accurate spellings invented; improved memory for correct spellings	Orthographic spellings invented; proficient memory for correct spellings

[a]GPCs refer to grapheme–phoneme (letter–sound) correspondences.
[b]Graphophonemic awareness refers to phoneme awareness conditioned by knowledge of the graphophonemic system, for example, segmenting words into the sounds symbolized by letters in a word's spelling.

regular orthography such as Spanish, Finnish, or German (Nauclér & Magnusson, 2000).

A third group of children who encounter problems learning to read are those with mental retardation, referred to as those with learning disabilities in the United Kingdom. Literacy skills in populations of children with low cognitive ability are under-researched. However, it is clear that low IQ per se is not a barrier to reading acqui-

sition (cf. Stanovich & Siegel, 1994). A growing number of studies have investigated the reading skills of children with Down syndrome (Boudreau, 2002; Cupples & Iacano, 2002; Laws & Gunn, 2002). The term "hyperlexia" refers to children who read at a level higher than that predicted from their mental age. Of interest is whether explanations for word reading ability apply to populations of cognitively challenged children in the same way that they do to populations of children whose IQ is in the normal range.

Dyslexia

Although the visual processing skills of readers with dyslexia continue to be debated (Cestnick & Coltheart, 1999), the consensus is that at the core in dyslexia is a phonological deficit (Morton & Frith, 1995). We cannot review here, for reasons of space, the extensive literature on the phonological skills of readers with dyslexia. Suffice it to say that studies have revealed robust impairments of phonological memory, phonological awareness, phonological learning, nonword repetition, and rapid automatized naming (see Snowling, 2000, for a review). The evidence is less clear regarding what might be considered "input phonological" processes, such as speech perception, in which studies have revealed large individual differences among children with dyslexia (Adlard & Hazan, 1997; Manis et al., 1997), or in spoken-word identification, in which findings are inconsistent (Griffiths & Snowling, 2002; Metsala, 1997).

For purposes of this discussion, a key issue is whether and to what extent children with dyslexia possess phoneme awareness, because this is necessary for transition to the alphabetic phases of development. Many studies point to problems of phonological awareness in children with dyslexia at the level of the rime and the phoneme (Bradley & Bryant, 1978; Manis, Custodio, & Szeszulski, 1993; Manis et al., 1997; Olson, Kliegel, Davidson, & Foltz, 1985; Scarborough, 1990). Moreover, as children with dyslexia develop, it seems that their difficulty with phoneme-level skills persists (Swan & Goswami, 1997), even into adulthood (Bruck, 1990; Pennington Orden, Smith, Green, & Haith, 1990). Clearly, this difficulty can be expected to place a major constraint on the development of word recognition. A second contributory factor to delayed reading, at least in the early years of schooling, is the poor letter knowledge shown by children who go on to become dyslexic (Gallagher, Frith, & Snowling, 2000; Scarborough, 1990). Taken together,

difficulties with phoneme awareness and with letter learning constitute a significant problem for the acquisition of the alphabetic principle (Byrne, 1998). This explains why the majority of children with dyslexia are slow to move from the prealphabetic to the partial-alphabetic phase.

A number of published case studies describe a very severe form of dyslexia in which children appear to read with only prealphabetic skills. These children are described as conforming to the pattern of performance observed in adults with an acquired form of "deep" dyslexia, whose reading is characterized by semantic and visual errors (Johnston, 1983; Siegel, 1985; Stuart & Howard, 1995). It should be noted, however that where data were provided, these children were below average in cognitive ability and perhaps not typical of the population of children with dyslexia.

DEVELOPMENTAL PHONOLOGICAL DYSLEXIA

A common pattern of reading observed among readers with dyslexia is the ability to read words more easily than matched nonwords (Rack et al., 1992; van IJzendoorn & Bus, 1994), coupled with a deficit in phoneme awareness. This reading pattern has been described as "developmental phonological dyslexia" (Castles & Coltheart, 1993; Manis, Seidenberg, Doi, McBride-Chang, & Petersen, 1996; Temple & Marshall, 1983). Children with developmental phonological dyslexia tend to make reading errors that deviate visually and phonetically from the written word, for example, reading *bowl* as *blow,* and *spade* as *space,* although some letter–sound correspondences may be preserved. They also make spelling errors that are typically "dysphonetic," (e.g., FISH → fin; TRAFFIC → tatin (Curtin, Manis, & Seidenberg, 2001; Snowling, Stackhouse, & Rack, 1986). When they store sight words in memory, they remember partial cues at the beginning or ends of words but lack knowledge about medial letters (Ehri & Saltmarsh, 1995). Hence, they are not terribly accurate and depend on sight-word memory supplemented by context for clarifying word identities when they read text. Because their alphabetic-knowledge and word-recognition systems are impaired, their ability to spell words either correctly or phonetically is limited. Because they show some use of alphabetic knowledge rather than a total absence, this places them in the partial-alphabetic phase.

Surprisingly little research has been directed at reading skills beyond the single-word level of children with dyslexia. Given their pattern of strengths and difficulties, with semantic and syntactic skills relatively intact despite phonological difficulties, it is likely that they attempt to use language skills outside of the phonological module to "bootstrap" their reading (e.g., Hulme & Snowling, 1992). Pursuing this hypothesis, Nation and Snowling (1998a) showed that children with dyslexia could make effective use of sentence context to read words that they could not read in isolation. In fact, they showed a contextual facilitation effect for both speed and accuracy that was greater than that shown by younger readers reading at the same overall level. This strategy is commonly observed among partial-alphabetic readers.

Even though transition to the alphabetic phase represents a considerable hurdle for children with dyslexia, development onward from this phase is possible. Snowling, Hulme, and Goulandris (1994) showed that JM, a young man with developmental phonological dyslexia, whom they had followed from the age of 8 to 15 years, demonstrated effective, automatic word-recognition skills typical of the consolidated-alphabetic phase, despite enduring deficits in nonword reading, phoneme awareness, and spelling. Similarly, Campbell and Butterworth (1985) described the case of RE, a young woman with reading and spelling levels commensurate with those of her undergraduate peers, despite impairments of phoneme awareness and nonword reading. It is likely that for these individuals, reading development proceeded by relying on a variety of compensatory strategies. JM had attended a specialist school for children with dyslexia, where he had benefited from multisensory teaching, and he had learned to use his good visual memory and semantic skills to build a sight vocabulary. RE had been taught to read on a word-by-word basis by her mother and also appeared to rely on visual skills. In a similar case described by Funnell and Davidson (1989), reading by analogy was a strategy that appeared to have been effective in the face of phonemic difficulties. It should be stressed that in all three cases, the use of compensatory visual strategies was a "lifeline" for the individuals concerned but visual reading was by no means an effective error-free strategy.

DEVELOPMENTAL SURFACE DYSLEXIA

A different profile of reading is seen in another group of children also labeled dyslexic. It is characterized by good nonword decoding coupled with poor sight-word reading, and, particularly for readers of English, a difficulty reading exception words that do not conform to grapheme–phoneme rules. In its pure form, this pattern is known as "developmental surface dyslexia" (Castles & Coltheart, 1993). People with surface dyslexia tend to read exception words as though they were regular, thereby making a large number of "regularizations" when they read, for example, reading *island* as IZLAND and *broad* as BRODE. Recent studies have suggested that pure surface dyslexia is relatively rare (Snowling, Goulandris, & Defty, 1998); more common is a "soft" subtype, in which exception word reading is relatively poorer than nonword reading (Manis et al., 1996; Stanovich, Siegel, & Gottardo, 1997). In comparison with children with developmental phonological dyslexia, the phoneme awareness skills of those with surface dyslexic profiles are relatively well developed, being less good than age expectations but in line with reading level. Consistent with this, their spelling errors are generally phonologically accurate (e.g., *grain* → GRANE; Curtin et al., 2001), but they betray incomplete knowledge of spelling–sound consistencies and orthographic conventions (Goulandris & Snowling, 1991). Thus, it would appear that children with developmental surface dyslexia have reached the full-alphabetic phase of reading development, but they do not possess extensive knowledge of higher order graphophonemic contingencies and spelling patterns, and their sight vocabulary is limited.

Consistent with this interpretation, though not well documented, the reading of children with surface dyslexia is slow and laborious, a feature that follows from their strong reliance on simple grapheme–phoneme correspondences. Interestingly, Hendriks and Kolk (1997) showed that, when placed under pressure of time, a group of children classified as surface dyslexic displayed reading errors characteristic of phonological dyslexia, suggesting that their word-decoding skill is slow to activate and, hence, quite fragile. A similar lack of reading fluency despite accurate decoding skills has been demonstrated for readers with dyslexia who are learning in a regular orthography, such as German (Wimmer, 1993). Such children are full-alphabetic readers who, as argued by Wimmer, Mayringer, and Landerl (1998), have problems in setting up the fully amalgamated orthographic representations of sight words in memory that are characteristic of the consolidated-alphabetic phase.

The causes of developmental surface dyslexia are not well understood. A number of single-case studies have suggested that the profile is associated with visual memory weaknesses (Goulandris & Snowling, 1991; Romani, Ward, & Olson, 1999), but the causal status of these visual difficulties is questionable (Hanley, Hastie, & Kay, 1992). An alternative hypothesis is that surface dyslexia and phonological dyslexia represent different manifestations of the same disorder, varying in severity, with surface dyslexia being the milder version (Griffiths & Snowling, 2002). Possibly consistent with this proposal is that behavior–genetic analyses have shown that the phonological subtype is more highly heritable than the surface dyslexia profile, which in turn appears to depend more on environmental factors such as low print exposure (Castles, Datta, Gayan, & Olson, 1999).

Put another way, it may be that children with surface dyslexia have developed the phoneme awareness and grapheme–phoneme skills of full-alphabetic readers, but because they do not read frequently and may even avoid reading, their sight vocabu-laries grow slowly, and their knowledge of exception words and irregular spellings remains poor. It may also be that their knowledge of the graphophonemic system is activated too slowly to secure fully represented sight words in memory when these words are read in text. Having a limited sight vocabulary of incompletely specified word spellings would be expected to impair movement into the consolidated-alphabetic phase. These possibilities need further study.

Children with Impairments of Speech and Language

The term "specific language impairment" (SLI) refers to children whose oral-language skills are below the level expected given their age and nonverbal ability. Although criteria for SLI are debated, it is common in practice to describe as language-impaired those children whose nonverbal IQ is in the normal range, while their performance on language tests is two standard deviations below the age norm. The population of children with SLI is heterogeneous (Rapin & Allen, 1987), making it difficult to form generalizations about their literacy skills.

An important distinction is usually drawn between children with speech problems and children with speech and language difficulty, the latter being more susceptible to reading failure than the former (Catts, 1993; Snowling, Bishop, & Stothard, 2000). Consistent with this are findings that reading and spelling skills are normal in children with peripheral articulation problems, such as cleft palate (Stackhouse, 1982). However, contrary to this view are the findings of Bird, Bishop, and Freeman (1995), who reported that children with expressive speech difficulties in the absence of language problems went on to have reading problems, if their speech difficulties had not resolved by school age. Beyond this critical age, the reading difficulties of children in this population appear to be like those of children with dyslexia, suggestive of a continuum of difficulty, with phonological deficits at the core.

Among children with speech–language impairments, children whose expressive phonology is disordered rather than merely slow to develop appear to have a particularly poor prognosis (Dodd, 1995). Stackhouse and Snowling (1992) described two such children with a diagnosis of verbal dyspraxia affecting the motor movements of speech. These children showed very limited knowledge of letter sounds and they lacked phonological awareness through to the teenage years. One of them, MC, had particularly poor speech production and was difficult to understand in spite of his good intelligence. Over half of his reading errors were visually based (e.g., *pint* → *paint*; *drug* → *drum*; *grill* → *glue*), and some appeared to be semantic in nature (e.g., *lime* → *lemon*). His spelling errors were quite bizarre due to problems not only with phoneme awareness but also with awareness of the syllabic structure of words (e.g., he spelled *bump* → BORR; *sack* → SATK; *instructed* → NISOKDER; *umbrella* → URMPT; *cigarette* → SICERK). MC's reading and spelling difficulties appear to be among the most severe reported in the literature. Stackhouse and Snowling (1992) argued that his output phonological deficits were a barrier to alphabetic reading, thus placing his reading and spelling skills within the prealphabetic phase.

Fortunately, not all children with SLI face such insurmountable reading difficulties. Bishop and Adams (1990) found that, at the age of 8 years, children with SLI, as a group, could read as accurately as normally developing children of the same nonverbal ability, and could decode and spell nonwords. In fact, although language impairment is a risk factor for dyslexia, only 6% of these children fulfilled criteria for specific reading difficulty at 8 years of age. Thus, the early reading development of this group appeared to follow a normal course.

However, a good start with reading does not preclude difficulties at a later phase of development. For this sample of children with SLI, the developmental picture deteriorated, and by the age of 15, the incidence of specific reading difficulties had increased to 24% (Snowling et al., 2000). One hypothesis derived from phase theory may explain the failure of literacy development to keep pace over time in children with SLI. These children may have difficulty proceeding to the consolidated-alphabetic phase as a result of a combination of factors involving poor vocabularies and limited acquisition of sight words, resulting in poorly developed knowledge of morphological and orthographic spelling patterns.

No direct data obtained from children with SLI that have a bearing on this hypothesis are available to our knowledge. However, some indirect findings are suggestive in studies of students having adequate decoding skill but poor comprehension. Nation and Snowling (1999) found that such "poor comprehenders" had poor vocabularies and restricted semantic knowledge, and showed a significant impairment relative to controls in the reading of low-frequency and irregular words (Nation & Snowling, 1998b). It is conceivable that some children with SLI might be impaired in their text comprehension as a result of the same word-based difficulties. This possibility awaits further study.

Children with Low Cognitive Ability

CHILDREN WITH DOWN SYNDROME

Down syndrome, a genetic disorder that occurs in about 1.5 per 1,000 births, is usually associated with trisomy of chromosome 21. Children with Down syndrome usually have Full Scale IQs in the range of 40–60, and they often have difficulties with language acquisition, including phonological problems, that are more severe than predicted by their nonverbal abilities. Although their lexical knowledge is relatively strong, their language problems encompass syntactic, conversational, and narrative difficulties. They also have severe phonological memory impairments (Laws, 1998).

Although the first published accounts of reading in children with Down syndrome appeared in the 1960s, the cognitive study of reading in this population was fueled by the controversial claims of Cossu and Marshall (1990), who reported the case study of TA, an Italian boy age 8 years, 11 months, with Down syndrome. TA's mental age was 4 years, 6 months, and he had an IQ of 57. His memory span was poor, with a digit span of 2, but he was considered to be a good reader. He attained a perfect score when reading words and nonwords that varied in word length and orthographic complexity, but his phonological awareness was poor, and he was not aware of phonemes. On the face of it, TA's profile would appear to be inconsistent with the predictions of phase theory.

On the basis of this case, Cossu and Marshall (1990) made the provocative proposal that phonological awareness is not a prerequisite of learning to read. In a second study, Cossu, Rossini, and Marshall (1993) bolstered their argument with data from 11 children with Down syndrome. These children, were age 11 years, 4 months on average, were compared with 10 younger, normal readers of similar reading skill, with a mean age of 7 years, 3 months. The children with Down syndrome did less well than the reading age-matched controls on tests of phoneme synthesis, oral spelling, phoneme counting, and phoneme deletion, even though they could read words and nonwords just as well.

The study by Cossu et al. (1993) had significant limitations. First, it is important to note that the report was of children learning to read in Italian, a highly transparent orthography that is much less difficult to decode than the opaque English orthography (Paulesu et al., 2001). Second, there was a discrepancy between the cognitive abilities of the two groups. The children with Down syndrome had a mean IQ of 44, whereas the control group had a mean IQ of 111. It follows that the metalinguistic tasks may have been beyond the cognitive capacity of the group with Down syndrome.

Different conclusions were drawn by Fowler (1995) in a study of English-speaking young adults with Down syndrome between the ages of 17 and 25 years, whose reading levels ranged from kindergarten to 12th grade (Fowler, Doherty, & Boyton, 1995). Fowler classified participants into one of four groups based on their decoding skills. *Novice readers* were able to decode 2 or fewer nonwords. *Emerging readers* and *developing readers* could decode between 3 and 10 nonwords and between 11 and 29 nonwords, respectively. *Skilled readers* showed even more advanced decoding skill,

although there were too few cases to properly evaluate this possibility. Each participant in Fowler's study was given tasks tapping phoneme awareness, verbal memory, and word naming from line drawings. Although performance was at or below the 6-year-level on phonological awareness tasks, a significant relationship between phonological skills and reading ability remained strong when general cognitive ability was controlled. Phonemic awareness accounted for 36% of the variance in word recognition and 49% of the variance in decoding nonwords. Furthermore, not a single individual in the group had the ability to read without possessing phoneme awareness. Thus, although the phonological skills of children with Down syndrome may not develop to the same degree as those of normal children, it is incorrect to suppose they do not possess these skills.

Similar findings have been reported by Cardoso-Martins and Frith (2001), who found that Portuguese-speaking persons with Down syndrome could detect phonemes as well as reading-age matched controls but had more difficulty in explicitly manipulating the phonological components of spoken words. Taken together, these findings suggest that the reading development of children with Down syndrome is along normal lines. For them, as for normally developing children, transition to the partial-alphabetic phase depends on possessing phoneme awareness.

However, a number of recent studies have suggested that the sequence of phonological development observed in normally developing children, favoring rhyming skills over phoneme skills, may be different for children with Down syndrome. Cardoso-Martins, Michalik, and Pollo (2002) studied a population of Brazilian children and adults with Down syndrome, 39 readers, and 30 nonreaders. The readers with Down syndrome found a rhyme-detection task significantly more difficult than two phoneme-detection tasks that involved matching initial or medial phonemes of words to a standard. A similar trend was seen in the nonreaders, although the majority of them were unable to complete the phonological awareness tasks.

In a similar vein, Gombert (2002) examined the performance of French-speaking readers with Down syndrome on phonological awareness tasks requiring judgments at the levels of the rime and phoneme. The performance of the group with Down syndrome was relatively poorer on tasks requiring rime judgement, rime oddity, and phoneme synthesis than on tasks requiring more explicit phonological awareness involving phoneme counting, phoneme deletion, and phoneme spelling. Finally, in three studies of English-speaking children with Down syndrome, Snowling, Hulme, and Mercer (2002) found that the group with Down syndrome performed only at chance level on tasks requiring rime awareness, while performance on initial phoneme detection was normal. Taken together, these findings indicate the presence of a rime impairment in persons with Down syndrome, despite relatively well-developed phoneme awareness skills. These results run counter to the widely accepted view that rime awareness is a necessary precursor of phoneme awareness.

It might be that impoverished educational opportunities distinguishing children with Down syndrome from normally developing children account for this difference. However, this explanation is rendered unlikely by the fact that the deficit was apparent in readers with Down syndrome speaking three different languages in countries providing very different educational experiences. It seems more likely that the rime deficit arises from the language impairment characterizing Down syndrome. The presence of phoneme-level abilities may be a consequence of learning to use letter–sound correspondences to read and spell (cf. Ehri, 1979, 1984; Morais, Cary, Alegria, & Bertelson, 1979). Longitudinal studies are needed to investigate this possibility. However, if this is the case, given their shaky foundation both in semantic and in phonological skills, then it is unlikely that children with Down syndrome are capable of proceeding to the consolidated-alphabetic phase. A deficiency in rime awareness would be expected to limit their ability to learn the spelling patterns in words sharing rimes. Moreover, impairments of syntactic skills (Boudreau, 2002) may limit their ability to use contextual cues to compensate in reading text. Thus, although children with Down syndrome are able to move into the partial and possibly the full phase of beginning reading, their capacity to acquire reading skill beyond this level appears to be severely limited.

HYPERLEXIA

The term "hyperlexia" is used to describe word-level reading skills that are more advanced than would be expected by the low cognitive ability of the readers. Many children with hyperlexia have an autism spectrum diagnosis; they learn to read before they receive any formal instruction and can be obsessive about reading, although their understanding of what they decode is extremely limited (Healy, 1982). Indeed, it is probably the case that the many hours they spend practicing accounts for the high levels of reading attainment they reach.

Much of the research on hyperlexia has involved case studies that, although informative about the general features of the syndrome, have not focused in any detail on the reading mechanisms that are involved (see Nation, 1999, for a review). An exception is a study by Frith and Snowling (1983), who reported that a group of children with autism, classified as "hyperlexic," could read words and nonwords as well as controls matched for reading age, and that they were sensitive to grammatical distinctions in text. However, the children with hyperlexia had more difficulty in pronouncing ambiguous words in context, such as *bow* and *lead,* and their comprehension of the details of what they read was poorer than that of younger reading- age-matched controls.

For present purposes, the important point to be made about hyperlexia is that this syndrome involves a dissociation between word-level reading and more general cognitive abilities. Unlike the majority of children of low cognitive ability, children with autism have exceptionally well-developed rote memory skills that depend on the storage and maintenance of phonological memory codes. Given this, it is not surprising that the phonemic and graphophonemic abilities of children with hyperlexia are well developed, just as they are for precocious readers (Stainthorp & Hughes, 1998). However, these capabilities have not, to our knowledge, been systematically explored in children with hyperlexia.

Whether or not these children have reached the consolidated-alphabetic phase is a moot point. Given the speed and automaticity with which they can recognize print, it is likely that they do have extensive knowledge of spelling patterns. However, it is at least plausible that the orthographic knowledge they possess is dissociated from meaning. This is suggested by the fact that when faced with a homograph, such as *lead*, an autistic child may show knowledge of both pronunciations ("led" and "leed") but be unable to pronounce the word correctly in context (Happé, 1997; Snowling & Frith, 1986).

VARIATION IN READING DIFFICULTIES AND PHASE THEORY: TAKING STOCK OF THE EVIDENCE AND CONSIDERATION OF INTERVENTION POSSIBILITIES

We have distinguished four phases of development to portray the course of learning to read words and have considered whether and how this framework might apply to atypical learners. It is apparent from the foregoing account that cases of clear developmental arrest within a particular phase have not been observed. In at least three of the four disorders considered, some children can be characterized as prealphabetic readers, whereas others may be able to function at the partial- or full-alphabetic phases. None of the children with word-level reading difficulties appears to have reached the consolidated-alphabetic phase, although more research on this point is needed. In contrast, for hyperlexia characterized by exceptional word-reading skill, it seems probable that children have reached the consolidated-alphabetic phase, albeit with limited reading comprehension. Evidence regarding their ability to spell words using orthographic patterns might shed additional light on this question.

The trajectories of word-reading development identified by phase theory appear to apply in the case of atypical readers. Also the different manifestations of reading disorders are consistent with the prerequisites required for transition between the phases. Among children with dyslexia, speech–language impairment, and Down syndrome, those who lacked phoneme awareness were unable to decode and had very limited sight vocabularies, whereas those with better developed phoneme awareness and grapheme–phoneme skills became partial- and perhaps full-alphabetic readers.

On the other hand, our analysis has highlighted a possible limitation of phase theory, in that it is silent with respect to the role of semantic skills in the development of sight-word reading (cf. Laing & Hulme, 1999). Phase theory explicitly acknowledges that children make use of context to read words, initially by guessing, and later by using partial cues. However, the ramifications of not being able to do so are not discussed. A growing body of evidence suggests that for children with language impairments, the use of a self-teaching device (Share, 1995) may be limited, with the result that orthographic knowledge fails to develop. This constraint is particularly significant for readers of English who have to learn a large number of variable grapheme–phoneme correspondences and exception words. The negative effects of poor vocabulary on the growth of orthographic skills may account for the relative slowing of the development of word recognition in the middle school years observed among children with SLI and among poor comprehenders. Its effects may be reduced in hyperlexia, in which extremely high levels of print exposure offer compensation. More research is needed regarding these possibilities.

Among children with "deep" dyslexia or severe speech disorders, the predominant characteristics reported across studies were those of the prealphabetic phase. This was also true of some children with Down syndrome. Children placed in the partial-alphabetic phase included those with developmental phonological dyslexia and expressive speech impairments, and some children with Down syndrome. Finally, the groups placed within the full-alphabetic phase included those with developmental surface dyslexia and the more advanced readers with SLI and Down syndrome who had decoding skill.

Various instructional activities are needed to foster the literacy skills of atypical learners. In selecting appropriate activities, the phase of learners must be considered: what learners know and can do, and what they need to learn to make progress toward the next phase. The information in Table 20.1 provides a framework for determining the knowledge which needs to be assessed to place learners in a phase, and the instructional objectives to move them to the next phase. It might be argued that the instructional activities appropriate for atypical learners at each phase of development are the same as those for any child. However, it needs to be borne in mind that atypical learners tend to have much poorer verbal memory and learning resources than normally developing children. The emphasis, therefore, needs to be on concrete instructions and multisensory learning to circumvent weaknesses, without extensive reliance on auditory processing.

The majority of children with learning disabilities have problems in moving to the full-alphabetic phase. A critical foundation skill to acquire is full phoneme awareness. There are now many phonological awareness training programs. However, the research consensus is that, for poor readers, training phonemes in isolation is much less effective than phoneme training linked to letters in print (Ehri et al., 2001; Hatcher, Hulme, & Ellis, 1994). It is therefore important that interventions involve text-level reading, not only to reinforce emerging phonics skill but also to encourage the strategic use of contextual cues and comprehension monitoring to promote decoding (Wise, Ring, & Olson, 1999).

Persistent problems for many atypical learners are the attainment of reading fluency and the development of accurate spelling skill. Many do not achieve proficiency in these skills (Hatcher, Snowling, & Griffiths, 2002). It is clear that in order to read fluently, the reader must abandon the laborious application of phonic reading strategies. The cause of this reading "style" is not well understood. It is generally believed that print exposure is limited in this group of readers, and that more reading practice may help to some extent. However, it is likely that more explicit teaching of larger blends of grapheme–phoneme units is required to discourage the overuse of inefficient word-attack strategies. Systematic spelling instruction is also needed by children in this phase of development to improve their knowledge of orthographic conventions.

In normal reading development, the transition from one phase to the next appears to follow a standard course. Most children require good teaching grounded in phonics to ensure safe passage to the full-alphabetic phase. In atypical learners, however, the journey is punctuated by obstacles, and different subskills may be out of synchrony with each other. However, with good remediation, attaining alphabetic reading skill is within reach for the majority.

REFERENCES

Adlard, A., & Hazan, V. (1997). Speech perception in children with specific reading difficulties (dyslexia). *Quarterly Journal of Experimental Psychology, 51*(1), 153–177.

Barr, R. (1974–1975). The effect of instruction on pupil reading strategies. *Reading Research Quarterly, 10*, 555–582.

Beck, I. (1981). Reading problems and instructional practices. In G. Mackinnon & T. Waller (Eds.), *Reading research: Advances in theory and practice* (Vol. 2, pp. 55–95). New York: Academic Press.

Betts, E. (1954). *Foundations of reading instruction* (3rd ed.). New York: American Book Company.

Bhattacharya, A., & Ehri, L. (in press). Syllable analysis helps disabled readers read and spell words. *Journal of Learning Disabilities.*

Biemiller, A. (1970). The development and use of graphic and contextual information as children learn to read. *Reading Research Quarterly, 6*, 75–96.

Bird, J., Bishop, D. V. M., & Freeman, N. H. (1995). Phonological awareness and literacy development in children with expressive phonological impairments. *Journal of Speech and Hearing Research, 38*, 446–462.

Bishop, D. V. M. (1997). *Uncommon understanding.* Hove, UK: Psychology Press.

Bishop, D. V. M., & Adams, C. (1990). A prospective study of the relationship between specific language impairment, phonological disorders and reading retardation. *Journal of Child Psychology and Psychiatry, 31*, 1027–1050.

Bishop, D. V. M., & Edmundson, A. (1987). Language-impaired four-year-olds: Distinguishing transient from persistent impairment. *Journal of Speech and Hearing Disorders, 52,* 156–173.

Boudreau, D. (2002). Literacy skills in children and adolescents with Down syndrome. *Reading and Writing, 15,* 497–525.

Bowey, J., & Hansen, J. (1994). The development of orthographic rimes as units of word recognition. *Journal of Experimental Child Psychology, 58,* 465–488.

Bradley, L., & Bryant, P. E. (1978). Difficulties in auditory organisation as a possible cause of reading backwardness. *Nature, 271,* 746–747.

Bruck, M. (1990). Word recognition skills of adults with childhood diagnoses of dyslexia. *Developmental Psychology, 26,* 439–454.

Bryant, P., Nunes, T., & Bindman, M. (1997). Children's understanding of the connection between grammar and spelling. Linguistic knowledge and learning to read and spell. In B. Blachman (Ed.), *Foundations of reading acquisition* (pp. 219–240). Mahwah, NJ: Erlbaum.

Byrne, B. (1998). *The foundation of literacy: The child's acquisition of the alphabetic principle.* Hove, UK: Psychology Press.

Campbell, R., & Butterworth, B. (1985). Phonological dyslexia and dysgraphia in a highly literate subject: A developmental case with associated deficits of phonemic processing and awareness. *Quarterly Journal of Experimental Psychology, 37A,* 435–475.

Cardoso-Martins, C., & Frith, U. (2001). Can individuals with Down syndrome acquire alphabetic literacy skills in the absence of phoneme awareness? *Reading and Writing, 14,* 361–375.

Cardoso-Martins, C., Michalick, M. F., & Pollo, T. C. (2002). Is sensitivity to rhyme a developmental precursor to sensitivity to phoneme?: Evidence from individuals with Down syndrome. *Reading and Writing, 15,* 439–454.

Cardoso-Martins, C., Rodrigues, L., & Ehri, L. (2003). Place of environmental print in reading development: Evidence from nonliterate adults. *Scientific Study of Reading, 7,* 335–355.

Carnine, D. (1977). Phonics versus look–say: Transfer to new words. *Reading Teacher, 30,* 636–640.

Carnine, L., Carnine, D., & Gersten, R. (1984). Analysis of oral reading errors made by economically disadvantaged students taught with a synthetic phonics approach. *Reading Research Quarterly, 19,* 343–356.

Castles, A., & Coltheart, M. (1993). Varieties of developmental dyslexia. *Cognition, 47,* 149–180.

Castles, A., Datta, H., Gayan, J., & Olson, R. K. (1999). Varieties of developmental reading disorder: Genetic and environmental influences. *Journal of Experimental Child Psychology, 72*(2), 73–94.

Cattell, J. (1886). The time it takes to see and name objects. *Mind, 11,* 63–65.

Catts, H. W. (1993). The relationship between speech–language and reading disabilities. *Journal of Speech and Hearing Research, 36,* 948–958.

Catts, H. W., Fey, M. E., Zhang, X., & Tomblin, J. B. (1999). Language basis of reading and reading disabilities: Evidence from a longitudinal investigation. *Scientific Studies of Reading, 3*(4), 331–361.

Cestnick, L., & Coltheart, M. (1999). The relationship between language-processing and visual-processing deficits in developmental dyslexia. *Cognition, 71,* 231–255.

Chall, J. (1983). *Stages of reading development.* New York: McGraw-Hill.

Clay, M. (1967). The reading behaviour of five-year-old children: A research report. *New Zealand Journal of Educational Studies, 2*(1), 11–31.

Clay, M. (1968). A syntactic analysis of reading errors. *Journal of Verbal Learning and Verbal Behavior, 7,* 434–438.

Clay, M. (1969). Reading errors and self-correction behavior. *British Journal of Educational Psychology, 39,* 47–56.

Cohen, A. (1974–1975). Oral reading errors of first grade children taught by a code-emphasis approach. *Reading Research Quarterly, 10,* 616–650.

Cossu, G., & Marshall, J. C. (1990). Are cognitive skills a prerequisite for learning to read and write? *Cognitive Neuropsychology, 7,* 21–40.

Cossu, G., Rossini, F., & Marshall, J. C. (1993). When reading is acquired but phonemic awareness is not: A study of literacy in Down's syndrome. *Cognition, 46,* 129–138.

Cunningham, P. (1976). Investigating a synthesized theory of mediated word identification. *Reading Research Quarterly, 11,* 127–143.

Cupples, L., & Iacano, T. (2002). The efficacy of "whole word" versus "analytic" reading instruction for children with Down syndrome. *Reading and Writing, 15,* 549–574.

Curtin, S, Manis, F. R., & Seidenberg, M. S. (2001). Parallels between the reading and spelling deficits of two groups of developmental dyslexics. *Reading and Writing, 14,* 515–547.

DeAbreu, M., & Cardoso-Martins, C. (1998). Alphabetic access route in beginning reading acquisition in Portuguese: The role of letter–name knowledge. *Reading and Writing, 10,* 85–104.

Dodd, B. (1995). *Differential diagnosis and treatment of children with speech disorder.* London: Whurr.

Ehri, L. (1979). Linguistic insight: Threshold of reading acquisition. In T. G. Waller & G. E. MacKinnon (Eds.), *Reading research: Advances in theory and practice* (Vol. 1, pp. 63–114). New York: Academic Press.

Ehri, L. (1980). The development of orthographic images. In U. Frith (Ed.), *Cognitive processes in spelling* (pp. 311–338). London: Academic Press.

Ehri. L. (1983). Summaries and a critique of five studies related to letter–name knowledge and learning to read. In L. Gentile, M. Kamil, & J. Blanchard (Eds.), *Reading research revisited* (pp. 131–153). Columbus, OH: Merrill.

Ehri, L. (1984) How orthography alters spoken language competencies in children learning to read and spell. In J. Downing & R. Valtin (Eds.), *Language awareness and learning to read* (pp. 119–147). New York: Springer-Verlag.

Ehri, L. (1987). Learning to read and spell words. *Journal of Reading Behavior, 19,* 5–31.

Ehri, L. (1991). Development of the ability to read words. In R. Barr, M. Kamil, P. Mosenthal, & P. Pearson (Eds.), *Handbook of reading research* (Vol. II, pp. 383–417). New York: Longman.

Ehri, L. (1992). Reconceptualizing the development of sight word reading and its relationship to recoding. In P. Gough, L. Ehri, & R. Treiman (Eds.), *Reading acquisition* (pp. 107–143). Hillsdale, NJ: Erlbaum.

Ehri, L. (1994). Development of the ability to read words: Update. In R. Ruddell, M. Ruddell, & H. Singer (Eds.), *Theoretical models and processes of reading* (4th ed., pp. 323–358). Newark, DE: International Reading Association.

Ehri, L. (1995). Phases of development in learning to read words by sight. *Journal of Research in Reading, 18,* 116–125.

Ehri, L. (1997). Sight word learning in normal readers and dyslexics. In B. Blachman (Ed.), *Foundations of reading acquisition* (pp. 163–189). Hillsdale, NJ: Erlbaum.

Ehri, L. (1998). Grapheme–phoneme knowledge is essential for learning to read words in English. In J. Metsala & L. Ehri (Eds.), *Word recognition in beginning literacy* (pp. 3–40). Mahwah, NJ: Erlbaum.

Ehri, L. (1999). Phases of development in learning to read words. In J. Oakhill & R. Beard (Eds.), *Reading development and the teaching of reading: A psychological perspective* (pp. 79–108). Oxford, UK: Blackwell.

Ehri, L., & McCormick, S. (1998). Phases of word learning: Implications for instruction with delayed and disabled readers. *Reading and Writing Quarterly, 14,* 135–163.

Ehri, L., Nunes, S., Willows, D., Schuster, B., Yaghoub-Zadeh, Z., & Shanahan, T. (2001). Phonemic awareness instruction helps children learn to read: Evidence from the National Reading Panel's meta-analysis. *Reading Research Quarterly, 36,* 250–287.

Ehri, L., & Robbins, C. (1992). Beginners need some decoding skill to read words by analogy. *Reading Research Quarterly, 27,* 12–26.

Ehri, L., & Saltmarsh, J. (1995). Beginning readers outperform older disabled readers in learning to read words by sight. *Reading and Writing: An Interdisciplinary Journal, 7,* 295–326.

Ehri, L., & Sweet, J. (1991). Fingerpoint reading of memorized text: What enables beginners to process the print? *Reading Research Quarterly, 26,* 442–462.

Ehri, L., & Wilce, L. (1985). Movement into reading: Is the first stage of printed word learning visual or phonetic? *Reading Research Quarterly, 20,* 163–179.

Ehri, L., & Wilce, L. (1987a). Cipher versus cue reading: An experiment in decoding acquisition. *Journal of Educational Psychology, 79,* 3–13.

Ehri, L. & Wilce, L. (1987b). Does learning to spell help beginners learn to read words? *Reading Research Quarterly, 22,* 47–65.

Fowler, A. (1995). Linguistic variability in persons

with Down syndrome. In L. Nadel & D. Rosenthal (Eds.), *Down syndrome: Living and learning.* New York: Wiley-Liss.

Fowler, A., Doherty, B., & Boynton, L. (1995). The basis of reading skill in young adults with Down syndrome. In L. Nadel & D. Rosenthal (Eds.), *Down syndrome: Living and learning.* New York: Wiley-Liss.

Frith, U., & Snowling, M. J. (1983). Reading for meaning and reading for sound in autistic and dyslexic children. *British Journal of Developmental Psychology, 1,* 329–342.

Frith, U. (1985). Beneath the surface of developmental dyslexia. In K. E. Patterson, J. C. Marshall, & M. Coltheart (Eds.), *Surface dyslexia: Neuropsychological and cognitive studies of phonological reading* (pp. 301–330). London: Erlbaum.

Funnell, E., & Davison, M. (1989). Lexical capture: A developmental disorder of reading and spelling. *Quarterly Journal of Experimental Psychology, 41A,* 471–488.

Gallagher, A., Frith, U., & Snowling, M. J. (2000). Precursors of literacy-delay among children at genetic risk of dyslexia. *Journal of Child Psychology and Psychiatry, 41*(2), 203–213.

Gaskins, I., Downer, M., Anderson, R., Cunningham, P., Gaskins, R., Schommer, M., et al. (1988). A metacognitive approach to phonics: Using what you know to decode what you don't know. *Remedial and Special Education, 9,* 36–41.

Gombert, J. E. (2002). Children with Down syndrome use phonological knowledge in reading. *Reading and Writing, 15,* 455–469.

Goodman, K. (1972). Orthography in a theory of reading instruction. *Elementary English, 49,* 1254–1261.

Goodman, K. (1976). Reading: A psycholinguistic guessing game. In H. Singer & R. Ruddell (Eds.), *Theoretical models and processes of reading* (2nd ed., pp. 497–508). Newark, DE: International Reading Association.

Goswami, U. (1986). Children's use of analogy in learning to read: A developmental study. *Journal of Experimental Child Psychology, 42,* 73–83.

Goswami, U. (1988). Orthographic analogies and reading development. *Quarterly Journal of Experimental Psychology, 40,* 239–268.

Gough, P., & Hillinger, M. (1980). Learning to read: An unnatural act. *Bulletin of the Orton Society, 30,* 179–196.

Gough, P., Juel, C., & Roper-Schneider, D. (1983). A two-stage model of initial reading acquisition. In J. A. Niles & L. A. Harris (Eds.), *Searches for meaning in reading/language processing and instruction* (pp. 207–211). Rochester, NY: National Reading Conference.

Gough, P., & Walsh, S. (1991). Chinese, Phoenicians, and the orthographic cipher of English. In S. Brady & D. Shankweiler (Eds.), *Phonological processes in literacy: A tribute to Isabelle Y. Liberman* (pp. 199–209). Hillsdale, NJ: Erlbaum.

Goulandris, N., & Snowling, M. J. (1991). Visual memory deficits: A plausible cause of developmental dyslexia?: Evidence from a single case study. *Cognitive Neuropsychology, 8*(2), 127–154.

Griffiths, Y. M., & Snowling, M. J. (2002). Predictors of exception word and nonword reading in dyslexic children: The severity hypothesis. *Journal of Educational Psychology, 94*, 34–43.

Guttentag, R., & Haith, M. (1978). Automatic processing as a function of age and reading ability. *Child Develoment, 49*, 707–716.

Hanley, J. R., Hastie, K., & Kay, J. (1992). Developmental surface dyslexia and dysgraphia: An orthographic processing impairment. *Quarterly Journal of Experimental Psychology, 44A*, 285–320.

Happé, F. G. E. (1997). Central coherence and theory of mind in autism: Reading homographs in context. *British Journal of Developmental Psychology, 15*, 1–12.

Harm, M. W., & Seidenberg, M. S. (1999). Reading acquisition, phonology, and dyslexia: Insights from connectionist models. *Psychological Review, 106*(3), 491–528.

Hatcher, P. J. (1996). Practising sound links in reading intervention with the school-age child. In M. Snowling & J. Stackhouse (Eds.), *Dyslexia, speech and language: A practitioner's handbook* (pp. 146–170). London: Whurr.

Hatcher, P. J. (2000). Predictors of reading recovery book levels. *Journal of Research in Reading, 23*(1), 67–77.

Hatcher, P. J., Hulme, C., & Ellis, A. W. (1994). Ameliorating early reading failure by integrating the teaching of reading and phonological skills: The phonological linkage hypothesis. *Child Development, 65*, 41–57.

Hatcher, J., Snowling, M. J., & Griffiths, Y. M. (2002). Cognitive assessment of dyslexic students in higher education. *British Journal of Educational Psychology, 72*, 119–133.

Healy, J. M. (1982) The enigma of hyperlexia. *Reading Research Quarterly, 7*, 319–318.

Henderson, E. (1981). *Learning to read and spell: The child's knowledge of words.* DeKalb: Northern Illinois University Press.

Hendriks, A., & Kolk, H. (1997). Strategic control in developmental dyslexia. *Cognitive Neuropsychology, 14*, 321–366.

Henry, M. (1989). Children's word structure knowledge: Implications for decoding and spelling instruction. *Reading and Writing: An Interdisciplinary Journal, 2*, 135–152.

Hulme, C., & Snowling, M. J. (1992). Deficits in output phonology: An explanation of reading failure? *Cognitive Neuropsychology, 9*, 47–72.

Johnston, F. (2000). Word learning in predictable text. *Journal of Educational Psychology, 92*, 248–255.

Johnston, R. S. (1983). Developmental deep dyslexia? *Cortex, 19*, 133–139.

Juel, C. (1983). The development and use of mediated word identification. *Reading Research Quarterly, 18*, 306–327.

Juel, C. (1988). Learning to read and write: A longitudinal study of fifty-four children from first through fourth grade. *Journal of Educational Psychology, 80*, 437–447.

Juel, C. (1991). Beginning reading. In R. Barr, M. Kamil, P. Mosenthal, & P. Pearson (Eds.), *Handbook of reading research* (Vol. II, pp. 759–788). New York: Longman.

Juel, C., Griffith, P., & Gough, P. (1985). Reading and spelling strategies of first-grade children. In J. Niles & R. Lalik (Eds.), *Issues in literacy: A research perspective* (pp. 306–309). Rochester, NY: National Reading Conference.

LaBerge, D., & Samuels, J. (1974). Toward a theory of automatic information processing in reading. *Cognitive Psychology, 6*, 293–323.

Laing, E., & Hulme, C. (1999). Phonological and semantic processes influence beginning readers' ability to learn to read words. *Journal of Experimental Child Psychology, 73*, 183–207.

Laws, G. (1998). The use of nonword repetition as a test of phonological memory in children with Down syndrome. *Journal of Child Psychology and Psychiatry, 39*, 1119–1130.

Laws, G., & Gunn, D. (2002). Relationships between reading, phonological skills and language development in individuals with Down syndrome: A five year follow up study. *Reading and Writing, 15*, 527–548.

Laxon, V., Coltheart, V., & Keating, C. (1988). Children find friendly words friendly too: Words with many orthographic neighbours are easier to read and spell. *British Journal of Educational Psychology, 58*, 103–119.

Leslie, L. & Calhoun, A. (1995). Factors affecting children's reading of rimes: Reading ability, word frequency, and rime-neighborhood size. *Journal of Educational Psychology, 87*, 576–586.

Liberman, I. & Liberman, A. (1992). Whole language versus code emphasis: Underlying assumptions and their implications for reading instruction. In P. Gough, L. Ehri, & R. Treiman (Eds.), *Reading acquisition* (pp. 343–366). Hillsdale, NJ: Erlbaum.

Manis, F. R., Custodio, R., & Szeszulski, P. A. (1993). Development of phonological and orthographic skill: A 2-year longitudinal study of dyslexic children. *Journal of Experimental Child Psychology, 56*, 64–86.

Manis, F. R., McBride-Chang, C., Seidenberg, M. S., Keating, P., Doi, L. M., Munson, B., & Petersen, A. (1997). Are speech perception deficits associated with developmental dyslexia? *Journal of Experimental Child Psychology, 66*, 211–235.

Manis, F. R., Seidenberg, M. S., Doi, L. M., McBride-Chang, C., & Petersen, A. (1996). On the bases of two subtypes of developmental dyslexia. *Cognition 58*, 157–195.

Marsh, G., Freidman, M., Welch, V., & Desberg, P. (1981). A cognitive-developmental theory of reading acquisition. In G. Mackinnon & T. G. Waller (Eds.), *Reading research: Advances in theory and practice* (Vol. 3, pp. 199–221). New York: Academic Press.

Mason, J. (1980). When do children learn to read: An exploration of four-year old children's letter and word reading competencies. *Reading Research Quarterly, 15*, 202–227.

Masonheimer, P., Drum, P., & Ehri, L. (1984). Does environmental print identification lead children into word reading? *Journal of Reading Behavior, 16*, 257–272.

Metsala, J. L. (1997). Spoken word recognition in reading disabled children. *Journal of Educational Psychology, 89*(1), 159–169.

Monaghan, J. (1983, April). *A four-year study of the acquisition of letter–sound correspondences.* Paper presented at the meeting of the American Educational Research Association, Montreal, Quebec.

Morais, J., Cary, L., Alegria, J., & Bertelson, P. (1979). Does awareness of speech as a sequence of phones arise spontaneously? *Cognition, 7*, 323–331.

Morris, D. (1993). The relationship between children's concept of word in text and phoneme awareness in learning to read: A longitudinal study. *Research in the Teaching of English, 27*, 133–154.

Morton, J., & Frith, U. (1995). Causal modelling: A structural approach to developmental psychopathology. In D. Cicchetti & D. J. Cohen (Eds.), *Manual of developmental psychopathology* (pp. 357–390). New York: Wiley.

Nation, K. (1999) Reading skills in hyperlexia: A developmental perspective. *Psychological Bulletin, 125*, 338–355.

Nation, K., & Snowling, M. J. (1998a). Individual differences in contextual facilitation: Evidence from dyslexia and poor reading comprehension. *Child Development, 69*(4), 996–1011.

Nation, K., & Snowling, M. J. (1998b). Semantic processing and the development of word recognition skills: Evidence from children with reading comprehension difficulties. *Journal of Memory and Language, 39*, 85–101.

Nation, K., & Snowling, M. J. (1999). Developmental differences in sensitivity to semantic relations among good and poor comprehenders: evidence from semantic priming. *Cognition, 70*(1) B1–B13.

Nauclér, K., & Magnusson, E. (2000). Language problems in poor readers. *Logopedics, Phoniatrics, Vocology, 25*, 12–21.

Olson, R. K., Kliegel, R., Davidson, B. J., & Foltz, G. (1985). Individual and developmental differences in reading disability. In G. E. MacKinnon & T. G. Waller (Eds.), *Reading research: Advances in theory and practice* (Vol. 4, pp. 1–64). New York: Academic Press.

Paulesu, E., Demonet, J. F., McCrory, E., Chanoine, V., Brunswick, N., Cappa, S. F., et al. (2001). Dyslexia: Cultural diversity and biological unity. *Science, 291*, 2165–2167.

Pennington, B. F., Orden, G. C. V., Smith, S. D., Green, P. A., & Haith, M. M. (1990). Phonological processing skills and deficits in adult dyslexics. *Child Development, 61*, 1753–1778.

Perfetti, C. (1985). Reading ability. New York: Oxford University Press.

Perfetti, C. (1992). The representation problem in reading acquisition. In P. Gough, L. Ehri, & R.

Treiman (Eds.), *Reading acquisition* (pp. 107–143). Hillsdale, NJ: Erlbaum.

Rack, J., Hulme, C., Snowling, M., & Wightman, J. (1994). The role of phonology in young children learning to read words: The direct-mapping hypothesis. *Journal of Experimental Child Psychology, 57*, 42–71.

Rack, J., Snowling, M., & Olson, R. (1992). The nonword reading deficit in developmental dyslexia: A review. *Reading Research Quarterly, 27*, 28–53.

Rapin, I., & Allen, D. (1987). Developmental dysphasia and autism in pre-school children: Characteristics and subtypes. In *First International Symposium on Specific Speech and Language Disorders in Children* (pp. 155–184). London: Association for All Speech Impaired Children.

Read, C. (1971). Pre-school children's knowledge of English phonology. *Harvard Educational Review, 41*, 1–34.

Reitsma, P. (1983). Printed word learning in beginning readers. *Journal of Experimental Child Psychology, 75*, 321–339.

Roberts, T. (2003). Effects of alphabet letter instruction on young children's word recognition. *Journal of Educational Psychology, 95*, 41–51.

Romani, C., Ward, J., & Olson, A. (1999). Developmental surface dysgraphia: What is the underlying cognitive impairment? *Quarterly Journal of Experimental Psychology, Section A: Human Experimental Psychology, 52*, 97–128.

Rumelhart, D. (1977). Toward an interactive model of reading. In S. Dornic (Ed.), *Attention and performance VI*. Hillsdale, NJ: Erlbaum.

Rutter, M., & Yule, W. (1975). The concept of specific reading retardation. *Journal of Child Psychology and Psychiatry, 16*, 181–197.

Scarborough, H. S. (1990). Very early language deficits in dyslexic children. *Child Development, 61*, 1728–1743.

Seymour, P., & Elder, L. (1986). Beginning reading without phonology. *Cognitive Neuropsychology, 3*, 1–36.

Share, D. (1995). Phonological recoding and self-teaching: Sine qua non of reading acquisition. *Cognition, 55*, 151–218.

Share, D. (1999). Phonological recoding and orthographic learning: A direct test of the self-teaching hypothesis. *Journal of Experimental Child Psychology, 72*, 95–129.

Share, D., & Stanovich, K. (1995). Cognitive processes in early reading development: Accommodating individual differences into a model of acquisition. *Issues in Education: Contributions from Educational Psychology, 1*, 1–57.

Siegel, L. S. (1985). Deep dyslexia in childhood? *Brain and Language, 26*, 16–27.

Snowling, M. J. (2000). *Dyslexia* (2nd ed.). Oxford: Blackwell.

Snowling, M., Bishop, D. V. M., & Stothard, S. E. (2000). Is preschool language-impairment a risk factor for dyslexia? *Journal of Child Psychology and Psychiatry, 41*, 587–600.

Snowling, M. J., & Frith, U. (1986). Comprehension in "hyperlexic" readers. *Journal of Experimental Child Psychology, 42,* 392–415.

Snowling, M. J., Goulandris, N., & Defty, N. (1998). Development and variation in developmental dyslexia. In C. Hulme & M. Joshi (Eds.), *Cognitive and linguistic bases of reading, writing and spelling* (pp. 201–217). Mahwah, NJ: Erlbaum.

Snowling, M. J., Hulme, C., & Goulandris, N. (1994). Word recognition in developmental dyslexia: A connectionist interpretation. *Quarterly Journal of Experimental Psychology, 47A,* 985–916.

Snowling, M. J. Hulme, C., & Mercer, R. C. (2002). Phonemes are easier than rimes for children with Down syndrome. *Reading and Writing, 15,* 471–495.

Snowling, M. J., Stackhouse, J., & Rack, J. (1986). Phonological dyslexia and dysgraphia: A developmental analysis. *Cognitive Neuropsychology, 3,* 309–339.

Soderbergh, R. (1977). *Reading in early childhood: A linguistic study of a preschool child's gradual acquisition of reading ability.* Washington, DC: Georgetown University Press.

Stackhouse, J. (1982). An investigation of reading and spelling performance in speech disordered children. *British Journal of Disorders of Communication, 17*(2), 53–60.

Stackhouse, J., & Snowling, M. J. (1992). Barriers to literacy development in two cases of developmental verbal dyspraxia. *Cognitive Neuropsychology, 9,* 273–299.

Stahl, S., & Murray, B. (1998). Issues involved in defining phonological awareness and its relation to early reading. In J. Metsala & L. Ehri (Eds.), *Word recognition in beginning literacy* (pp. 65–87). Mahwah, NJ: Erlbaum.

Stainthorp, R., & Hughes, D. (1998) Phonological sensitivity and reading: Evidence from precocious readers. *Journal of Research in Reading, 21,* 53–68.

Stanovich, K. E. (1980). Toward an interactive–compensatory model of individual differences in the development of reading fluency. *Reading Research Quarterly, 16,* 32–71.

Stanovich, K. E. (1981). Attentional and automatic context effects in reading. In A. Lesgold & C. Perfetti (Eds.), *Interactive processes in reading* (pp. 241–267). Hillsdale, NJ: Erlbaum.

Stanovich, K. E. (1986). Matthew effects in reading: Some consequences of individual differences in the acquisition of literacy. *Reading Research Quarterly, 21,* 360–406.

Stanovich, K. E. (1994). Does dyslexia exist? *Journal of Child Psychology and Psychiatry, 35*(4), 579–595.

Stanovich, K. E. (2000). *Progress in understanding reading.* New York: Guilford Press.

Stanovich, K. E., & Siegel, L. S. (1994). The phenotypic performance profile of reading-disabled children: A regression-based test of the phonological–core variable–difference model. *Journal of Educational Psychology, 86,* 24–53.

Stanovich, K. E., Siegel, L. S., & Gottardo, A. (1997). Progress in the search for dyslexia subtypes. In C. Hulme & M. Snowling (Eds.), *Dyslexia: Biology, cognition and intervention* (pp. 108–130). London: Whurr.

Stothard, S. E., Snowling, M. J., Bishop, D. V. M., Chipchase, B. B., & Kaplan, C. A. (1998). Language impaired preschoolers: A follow-up into adolescence. *Journal of Speech, Language, and Hearing Research, 41,* 407–418.

Stuart, M., & Howard, D. (1995). KJ: A developmental deep dyslexic. *Cognitive Neuropsychology, 12*(8), 793–824.

Swan, D., & Goswami, U. (1997). Phonological awareness deficits in developmental dyslexia and the phonological representations hypothesis. *Journal of Experimental Child Psychology, 60,* 334–353.

Temple, C., & Marshall, J. (1983). A case study of developmental phonological dyslexia. *British Journal of Psychology, 74,* 517–533.

Treiman, R. (1985). Onsets and rimes as units of spoken syllables: Evidence from children. *Journal of Experimental Psychology, 39,* 161–181.

Treiman, R. (1993). *Beginning to spell.* New York: Oxford University Press.

Treiman, R., Goswami, U., & Bruck, M. (1990). Not all nonwords are alike: Implications for reading development and theory. *Memory and Cognition, 18,* 559–567.

Treiman, R., Sotak, L., & Bowman, M. (2001). The roles of letter names and letter sounds in connecting print and speech. *Memory and Cognition, 29,* 860–873.

Tunmer, W., & Chapman, J. (1998). Language prediction skill, phonological recoding ability, and beginning reading. In C. Hulme & R. Joshi (Eds.), *Reading and spelling: Development and disorders* (pp. 33–67). Mahwah, NJ: Erlbaum.

van IJzendoorn, M. H., & Bus, A. G. (1994) Meta-analytic confirmation of the nonword reading deficit in developmental dyslexia. *Reading Research Quarterly, 29*(3) 267–275.

Vellutino, F. (1979). *Dyslexia: Theory and research.* Cambridge, MA: MIT Press.

Venezky, R. (1970). *The structure of English orthography.* The Hague: Mouton.

Venezky, R., & Johnson, D. (1973). Development of two letter–sound patterns in grades one through three. *Journal of Educational Psychology, 64,* 109–115.

Wimmer, H. (1993). Characteristics of developmental dyslexia in a regular writing system. *Applied Psycholinguistics, 14,* 1–33.

Wimmer, H. (1996). The nonword reading deficit in developmental dyslexia: Evidence from children learning to read German. *Journal of Experimental Child Psychology, 61,* 80–90.

Wimmer, H., & Goswami, U. (1994). The influence of orthographic consistency on reading development: Word recognition in English and German children. *Cognition, 51,* 91–103.

Wimmer, H., Mayringer, H., & Landerl, K. (1998).

Poor reading: A deficit in skill-automatization or a phonological deficit? *Scientific Studies of Reading,* 2(4), 321–340.

Wimmer, H., & Hummer, P. (1990). How German-speaking first graders read and spell: Doubts on the importance of the logographic stage. *Applied Psycholinguistics, 11,* 349–368.

Windfuhr, K., & Snowling, M. J. (2001). The relationship between paired associate learning and phonological skills in normally developing children. *Journal of Experimental Child Psychology, 80,* 160–173.

Wise, B. W., Ring, J., & Olson, R. (1999). Training phonological awareness with and without explicit attention to articulation. *Journal of Experimental Child Psychology, 72,* 271–304.

21

Word Recognition Assessment Frameworks

FROMA P. ROTH

To read effectively, students must link the printed representation of a word to its phonological counterpart and understand the meaning of individual words and printed text. In the "simple view" of reading, these two processes are termed "decoding" and "comprehension" (Gough & Tunmer, 1986). Decoding refers to word-level reading processes that transform print into words (including the reading of nonwords), and it is the assessment of these skills and strategies that constitutes the focus of this chapter. Word recognition is considered a basic, or lower level, reading process relative to reading comprehension, but it is not a unitary construct. Rather, it encompasses word identification and the fluent execution and coordination of word reading in connected written text. For this reason, the assessment of word recognition cannot be viewed as the examination of a single or isolated skill but must embrace broader contextual perspectives: (1) Fluent word reading is critical to reading comprehension development and proficiency (Ehri, 1987; Nation & Snowling, 1997; Perfetti, 1996; Robbins & Ehri, 1994); and (2) the dynamic reciprocity between oral language and reading development (Cooper,

Roth, Speece, & Schatschneider, 2002; Perfetti, Beck, Bell, & Hughes, 1987; Roth, Speece, & Cooper, 2002; Stanovich, 1986; Swank & Larivee, 1998; Torgesen, Wagner, & Rashotte, 1994). Moreover, the assessment of word recognition is not limited to young children but is germane across the age/developmental range to any student who has not acquired this essential building block of reading.

The primary aim of this chapter is to review traditional and alternative approaches to word recognition assessment through an examination of extant research, theoretical orientations, and assessment practices. To this end, the first sections address the importance of early identification, the interdisciplinary nature of the assessment process, contemporary hypotheses, and the developmental course of word recognition skill. Next, assessment guidelines are discussed, followed by a framework for assessment that examines both traditional and alternative approaches. The chapter closes with a brief discussion of current "best practices" and future directions for assessing word recognition processes of children and adolescents.

461

IMPORTANCE OF EARLY IDENTIFICATION

The majority of students with reading–learning disabilities evidence deficits in basic reading skills (i.e., word-level reading), and these problems are related to deficits in oral language and other aspects of emergent literacy (Catts, 1989, 1991; Scarborough, 1990; Wagner & Torgesen, 1987). According to Scarborough's data (2001), most students who have difficulty learning to read have trouble mastering the early word recognition "strands" of phonological awareness, letter identification, decoding, and sight-word reading. Moreover, longitudinal analyses indicate that 65–75% of children identified as having reading disabilities in early grades continue to read poorly throughout school-age years and into adulthood, whereas only about 5–10% of children who read adequately in the primary grades show reading difficulties in later grades (Scarborough, 1998). These data are particularly compelling, because they are based on a meta-analysis of 61 kindergarten prediction studies and clearly demonstrate that levels of reading achievement show considerable stability over time.

In addition to the knowledge strands discussed earlier, other emergent literacy skills significantly influence early reading development through their indirect association with various aspects of word recognition, and include oral language skills other than phonological awareness, home literacy experiences with print (Cooper et al., 2002; Reese & Cox, 1999; Senechal, 1997; Whitehurst, Epstein, Angell, Crone, & Fischel, 1994; Whitehurst & Lonigan, 1998), and spelling (Ehri, 1997; Goswami, 1988; Richgels, 1995).

Thus, children who enter school with weaker verbal abilities and emergent literacy knowledge are much more likely than their peers to experience difficulties in learning beginning reading skills (Aram & Hall, 1989; Bishop & Adams, 1990; Catts, Fey, & Tomblin, 1997; Catts, Fey, Zhang, & Tomblin, 1999; Scarborough & Dobrich, 1990; Stothard, Snowling, Bishop, Chipchase, & Kaplan, 1998). Furthermore, the cycle of reading failure frequently can be traced back to difficulty in acquiring fluent word reading skills. If these basic reading difficulties are not identified early and addressed effectively, Matthew Effects are a likely result. Taken from the biblical passage, "For every one that hath, shall be given, and he shall have abundance: but from him that not, shall be taken away even from which he hath" (Matthew XXXV: 29), Stanovich (1986) characterized the downward spiral of reading development as beginning with poor decoding skills and proceeding along the following path: unrewarding early experiences with print; less practice reading; less exposure to and experience with print; less involvement with reading-related activities; impeded development of automaticity and speed at the word recognition level; and hindrance in reading for meaning. In this view, reading comprehension is affected because cognitive resources that need to be allocated for higher level processes of reading are drained at the word recognition level. This cycle of failure not only has significant consequences for the reciprocity between lower and higher levels of reading, but also for the reciprocal, developmental connection between oral language and reading. Specifically, reading contributes to vocabulary growth, acquisition of general information, and knowledge of linguistic cohesion and complex and low-frequency syntactic structures (Stothard et al., 1998; Torgesen & Davis, 1996; Vellutino & Scanlon, 1991).

To ameliorate enduring and persistent problems, converging longitudinal and concurrent evidence indicate that word recognition assessment requires examination of several areas that contribute to the development of emergent and early literacy skills, including early phonological awareness (rhyming and alliteration), phonemic awareness and other aspects of phonological processing, recognition of environmental print, conventions of print, family/home literacy environment, knowledge of letter names, spelling, word and nonword reading, and word reading fluency. For older students, important additional areas of assessment may include morphological awareness and decoding of multisyllabic words and pseudowords.

WORD RECOGNITION ASSESSMENT: AN INTERDISCIPLINARY PROCESS

Because the assessment of word recognition skills crosses many developmental domains (e.g., oral language, written language, memory, motivation), several professionals play key roles. Speech–language pathologists (SLPs) are an integral part of the assessment process because of their knowledge of oral language and its subsystems, their understanding of speech and language processing in both normal and disordered populations, and their expertise in the diagnostic–prescriptive process (American Speech–Language–Hearing Association, 2001). The specific roles assumed by SLPs vary according to professional setting, service delivery models, administrative structure, policies and regulations, and clinician interests. An SLP may (1) provide direct assessment as a member of a diagnostic team evaluating students; (2) collaborate with teachers, other service providers, and parents throughout the assessment process (i.e., before, during, and after treatment); (3) disseminate information through professional staff development and other mechanisms about language–literacy connections and associated risk factors to promote early and appropriate referral and identification; (4) advocate for and educate school and district administrators to shape policy decisions regarding the increased early literacy risks for students with oral language difficulties and the importance of oral language proficiency for all children and adolescents; and (5) work in partnership with others to develop and test new screening and assessment methods that are language-based and literacy-sensitive (e.g., Catts, 1991; Justice, Invernizzi, & Meier, 2002). In short, to ensure credible early identification, accurate diagnosis, and appropriate remediation, a collaborative model of assessment is essential.

THEORETICAL CONSTRUCTS UNDERLYING AND CONTRIBUTING TO WORD RECOGNITION SKILL

Different theoretical perspectives have differential implications for assessment of the processes and products of word recognition skill. Two current, prevailing views are the core-deficit hypothesis (Liberman, Shankweiler, & Liberman, 1989; Shaywitz, Escobar, Shaywitz, Fletcher, & Makuch, 1992; Stanovich & Siegel, 1994) and the double-deficit hypothesis (Bowers, 1995; Bowers & Wolf, 1993; Felton & Brown, 1990).

Core-Deficit Hypothesis

Proponents of the core-deficit position posit that phonological processing skills underlie the development of word recognition. Phonological processes include phonological awareness (implicit awareness of the sound structure of words), phonological coding in lexical access (speed and accuracy necessary to store and retrieve phonological representations), and phonological coding in working memory (retaining and retrieving phonological information to decode words and read fluently). To learn to read, then, a student must recognize or have an awareness of words, be able to identify a specific word, translate the printed word into its corresponding sounds (phonological recoding), and match the word's meaning with a word in his or her mental lexicon (lexical access).

Advocates of the core-deficit position assert that children and some adolescents with reading problems have a specific impairment in the development of phonological awareness (particularly at the finer-grained level of phonemic awareness involving explicit knowledge of the structure of words) that interferes with the discovery of the alphabetic principle (knowledge of letter–sound correspondences necessary for accurate and rapid mapping between phonemes and graphemes) (Juel, Griffith, & Gough, 1986; Liberman & Shankweiler, 1985, 1991; Vellutino & Scanlon, 1991). This position is substantiated by an abundance of evidence showing that phonemic awareness and graphophonemic knowledge make significant and unique contributions to growth in reading skills, particularly word recognition (Adams, 1990; Burgess & Lonigan, 1998; Lonigan, Burgess, Anthony, & Barker, 1998). In particular, phonemic segmentation–elision tasks in kindergarten and first grade are the strongest correlates of beginning reading acquisition and successful response to explicit instruction (Foorman, Francis, Fletcher, Schatschneider, & Mehta, 1998; O'Connor, 2000; Perfetti et al., 1987; Roth et al., 2002; Torgesen & Davis, 1996; Torgesen, Morgan, & Davis, 1992).

The main implication of this position for the assessment of early reading is that phonological awareness is a prerequisite to word recognition and is thus a critical area to evaluate in any child who is at risk for or is having reading difficulty, particularly, but not limited to, the single-word level. Although the strong, direct relationship between phonological awareness and reading is undisputable, a cautionary note is warranted. Scarborough's (1998) close examination of the extant data showed that phonological awareness in kindergarten is actually a better predictor of future superior reading than of future reading problems, in that most of the variance in reading appears to be accounted for by the good readers. By inference, then, among the children entering kindergarten, few of those with strong phonological awareness skills will falter in learning to read, but many of those with weaker phonological awareness skills will go on to become good readers. Moreover, several studies have reported that other phonological processing skills are equivalent predictors of word reading (Felton & Brown, 1990; Felton & Wood, 1990).

Double-Deficit Hypothesis

The double deficit position focuses on the importance of another aspect of phonological processing—lexical access. It is based on the premise that the ability to access and retrieve phonologically coded information from memory rapidly makes an independent contribution to word reading, beyond that of phonemic awareness and graphophonemic knowledge (Bowers, 1995; Bowers & Wolf, 1993; Felton & Brown, 1990; Felton & Wood, 1990; Wolf & Bowers, 1999, 2000; Wolf, Bowers, & Biddle, 2000). Lexical retrieval is typically measured by naming tasks, which either require an individual to name a visual representa-

tion of a common word as quickly as possible before proceeding to the next item (confrontation naming, CN) or by serial naming, in which an individual is presented with a randomly repeated series of familiar pictured stimuli (e.g., objects, colors, letters) and asked to name the full array as quickly as possible (rapid automatized naming, RAN). The claim is that serial naming (RAN) relies heavily on nonphonological processes for word recognition, including attention, visual recognition, and information-processing speed. Children and adolescents with a "double-deficit" show reduced speed on naming tasks, which magnifies their word reading problems that arise from limited phonemic awareness. Thus, they are handicapped by poor decoding skills (due to reduced phonological sensitivity) and sight-word recognition (due to reduced ability to process information with the accuracy and rapidity necessary to store and retrieve orthographic sequences efficiently). Catts, Fey, Zhang, and Tomblin (1999), for example, reported that 29% of their second-grade "poor readers" demonstrated deficits in both areas, whereas 25% had phonological awareness deficits only, and 15% had RAN deficits only. The prediction of the double-deficit hypothesis is further borne out by evidence showing that students with a double-deficit are the most impaired word readers and accrue the least benefit from reading interventions (Allor, Fuchs, & Mathes, 2001; Bowers, 1995; Bowers & Wolf, 1993; Torgesen et al., 1994; Wolf & Bowers, 1999).

The primary implication of the double-deficit hypothesis for the assessment of beginning reading is that RAN must be considered as part of a comprehensive evaluation of word recognition because the most pronounced problem readers have deficits arising from both nonphonological and phonological processes that influence word reading development and proficiency.

Summary

Although phonemic awareness and RAN appear to contribute unique variance to word recognition, lively debate continues regarding the precise relationship between

these two aspects of phonological processing and the relative independence of their
roles in early reading development and disabilities. At the present time, it seems that
RAN may be more closely linked to reading
fluency, whereas phonemic sensitivity is
more directly connected to decoding. However, further evidence is needed to document the independence of RAN deficits in
students with reading disabilities by identifying youngsters who demonstrate deficits
on RAN tasks without concurrent deficits
in phonemic awareness. Moreover,
Schatschneider, Carlson, Francis, Foorman,
and Fletcher (2002) claim that the poor
scores RAN tasks displayed by children
with a double-deficit are actually a reflection of their lower scores on phonemic
awareness tasks, because these children are
likely to exhibit even lower phonological
awareness scores than children with deficits
only in phonological awareness.

The interrelationship among phonemic
awareness, RAN, and phonological coding
in working memory relative to early ability
also remains an open question (e.g., Torgesen & Wagner, 1998). Although not addressed specifically by either of the previously mentioned hypotheses, phonological
coding difficulties are strongly associated
with phonemic awareness deficits (Wagner,
Torgesen, Laughon, Simmons, & Rashotte,
1993) and early reading problems (Siegel,
1994; Torgesen & Wagner, 1998), and are
exhibited by children with language impairments (Montgomery, 1995). Phonological
coding relies on working memory processes
and requires the ability to encode, store,
and retrieve sounds encountered briefly. It
is most often measured by memory-span
tasks, which require the repetition of random series of digits, words, or letters.
Phonological coding problems place students at risk for acquiring the alphabetic
principle necessary to decode new words
(Torgesen & Wagner, 1998), presumably
because recovering phonological codes
from memory places immense demands on
working-memory capacity (Baddeley, 1986;
Gathercole & Adams, 1993). Thus, it is
clear that phonological sensitivity, RAN,
and phonological working memory are
each important candidate skills areas for a

comprehensive assessment of word recognition skills.

IMPLICATIONS OF WORD RECOGNITION DEVELOPMENT FOR ASSESSMENT

The developmental course of word recognition can be described as consisting of an
overlapping and reciprocal set of acquisitions: phonological awareness, phonemic
awareness, alphabetic principle, sight-word
reading, decoding, and fluency. Within this
basic sequence, researchers have put forth
various stagewise models to characterize the
developmental progression. Ehri (1991) and
Ehri and McCormick (1998), for example,
identify four stages in the acquisition of
real-word reading: (1) Phase 1 (prealphabetic; visual cue stage), the initial stage in
which children rely strictly on graphic features to recognize words; (2) Phase 2 (partial-alphabetic; phonetic cue stage), a transitional period in which children begin to
recognize words by processing letter–sound
relationships; (3) Phase 3 (full-alphabetic
stage), in which children recode spellings into pronunciations according to
grapheme–phoneme correspondence rules
and acquire the alphabetic principle; and (4)
Phase 4 (consolidated-alphabetic; orthographic stage), the final stage, in which a
young reader instantly analyzes words into
orthographic units without phonological
conversion.

Stahl, Kuhn, and Pickle's (1999) developmental model of reading was devised specifically to guide early reading assessment.
Based on Gough and Tunmer's (1986) simple view of reading, it contains a three-stage
strand for word recognition development
that incorporates the work of several reading development researchers, including
Chall (1983). First, in the *emergent literacy
stage,* children build concepts for learning
about print before formal literacy instruction begins and realize that print carries
meaning. This stage includes concepts of
word and word boundaries, directionality
of print, phoneme awareness, and alphabet
letters and sounds. Second, in the *accuracy
stage,* children master some basic sound–

symbol correspondences and some basic sight-word vocabulary. In the final stage, *automaticity,* children learn to read fluently, without having to decode each word; that is, word recognition is "transparent," allowing for rapid word identification and a shift in the child's attentional focus to the meaning of print rather than the print itself.

These models are particularly useful when applied to the developmental patterns of word recognition exhibited by children and adolescents with reading disabilities. Spear-Swerling and Sternberg (1994) describe four representative patterns: (1) non-alphabetic readers: those who have no knowledge of grapheme–phoneme correspondence rules (i.e., the alphabetic principle) and rely heavily on visual cues to word recognition; (2) compensatory readers: children with some, but very limited, knowledge of the alphabetic principle, who rely heavily on visual and other bootstrap strategies; (3) nonautomatic readers: students with decoding skills that are effortful rather than automatic, who read slowly and laboriously, "grunting and groaning" (Chall, 1983) their way through text. They may be able to provide a flawless oral reading of a passage but struggle over many words, reading dysfluently, and as a result, are unable to answer comprehension questions about the passage; and (4) delayed readers: those who have automatic word recognition skill but exhibit primary problems in higher level reading skills such as comprehension.

Taken together, the sensitivity of these models to developmental changes and their emphasis on the developmental nature of word recognition ability provide a solid foundation for practitioners who are responsible for assessment. The models also focus attention on the importance of the emergent literacy period during which typically developing children acquire essential linguistic and early metalinguistic skills that prepare them for beginning reading.

GUIDELINES FOR WORD RECOGNITION ASSESSMENT

The assessment of word recognition is guided by a number of factors that are motivated by developmental, theoretical, empirical, and clinical considerations.

1. The selection of assessment measures must be based on the age of the learner, as well as their developmental appropriateness for a given learner. For example, the growth of phonological awareness occurs along a continuum from rhyming and alliteration to blending to segmentation. Furthermore, within blending and segmentation, word-level tasks are easier than syllable-level tasks, which are easier than phoneme-level tasks. Along different lines, many tests use pseudowords (phonologically regular nonwords) to measure decoding accuracy, and there seems to be a developmental sequence in the acquisition of grapheme–phoneme conversion skill, which progresses from mastery of simple to complex spelling–sound correspondences (Ehri, 1991; Treiman, 1993). For example, the hard *c* in *cat* is mastered earlier than a soft *c* in *city* (Joshi, 1995; Joshi & Aaron, 1991). A similar developmental trend is seen for vowel–letter mappings (Joshi & Leong, 1993).

2. Different types of tasks require different levels of processing. In general, expressive tasks entail a more explicit grasp of information than do receptive tasks. A word recognition task, for instance, that requires a student to decode a written word aloud is more difficult than a receptive procedure that requires pointing to a target word from an array of printed words on a page. Similarly, rhyme detection is easier than generating a word that rhymes with a stimulus item provided by an examiner.

3. Determination of a word recognition deficit cannot be made on basis of a single measure. Reliance on a test battery that combines both traditional and alternative procedures is optimal, because the type and quality of information varies across approaches and individual measures (e.g., Justice et al., 2002). Also, some tests are very broad in scope, whereas others focus on a single or more limited array of skills. Furthermore, most commercially available tests are intended for use with children of kindergarten-age or older. Thus, the identification of preschool children at risk for word recognition problems often relies on the use of

qualitative measures, clinician–teacher observation, and professional judgment.

4. Consideration must be given to a student's cultural and linguistic background, because these variables directly influence the entire assessment process. Assessment tools, procedures, and interpretation criteria are inherently culturally bound, because they reflect the linguistic and social beliefs, values, and interaction styles of a society (Johnston & Rogers, 2001). In some cultures, emphasis is placed on what a youngster can accomplish independently, whereas others focus on what a learner can accomplish collaboratively (Barrs, Ellis, Hester, & Thomas, 1989). Furthermore, different cultures expect children to learn to read at different ages and demonstrate their literacy knowledge in different ways (e.g., macroskills—how literacy works, vs. microskills—specific letter, sound, and word knowledge) (Johnston, 1997). As a result, students who are English-language learners (ELLs) from linguistically diverse backgrounds may demonstrate depressed performance on word recognition measures that are not representative of their actual ability or potential (Gutièrrez-Clennen & Peña, 2002). The lack of reliable and valid instruments for these youngsters presents a significant challenge to professionals who are responsible for differentiating between language–learning disorders and language differences. For these learners, it is particularly important to use alternative assessment approaches, with the recognition that some procedures have high face validity without substantiated reliability, whereas others have high reliability but questionable validity (Peña, 1996).

5. The selection of norm-referenced measures must be made on the basis of their technical adequacy. Conventional psychometric indicators are reliability (consistency/stability of test results over repeated administrations), standard error of measurement (estimate of the accuracy of test results for a particular student, taking into account the degree of performance variability from administration to administration), and validity (extent to which a test measures the construct it purports to measure). For example, a test that claims to measure word reading accuracy using a multiple-choice format is actually assessing word recognition and is not a valid measure of decoding. Two additional concepts, essential to accurate identification, are sensitivity and selectivity (Fawcett & Nicolson, 2000). "Sensitivity" refers to how well a test identifies a problem, in this case, the degree to which a test differentiates between students who have or are at risk for word recognition problems and those who are not. An ideal test has a "hit rate" of 100% (true positives) and a "miss rate" of 0% (false negatives), identifying all students with a problem and none without a problem. In reality, a highly sensitive measure will correctly identify a significant percentage of those who are at risk but may also overidentify by incorrectly labeling a number of youngsters who are not at risk. "Specificity" refers to how accurately a measure identifies students who do not have a problem. A highly specific test will have a high hit rate of not identifying students who are not at risk (true negatives) and a low miss rate of failing to identify those who are at risk (false positives).

6. Assessment of certain skill areas, such as phonological awareness, frequently involves tasks that are unfamiliar to young children, and require sufficient demonstration and practice prior to test administration (Troia, Roth, & Graham, 1998). Otherwise, a valid appraisal of the child's abilities may not be obtained. A blending task, for example, may require a child to use blocks to designate each sound in the correct sequence to demonstrate one-to-one correspondence with individual sounds before synthesizing the sound into a word.

7. Evaluation of emergent and early reading skills is not limited to young or low-functioning children. Reading scores from the most recent National Assessment of Educational Progress (NAEP; U.S. Department of Education, 1999) indicate that 26% of eighth graders and 23% of 12th graders read below basic levels. Among such students, the grade equivalency reading levels range from as low as second grade to as high as sixth, with mixed profiles usually involving deficits in decoding and comprehension.

8. Finally, regardless of approach, all evaluation techniques are observations made under different conditions. To be a keen observer (and documenter) of word recognition behavior, a professional must have a solid understanding of language and literacy development, the independent and interdependent contributions of each domain to early reading development, and the range and characteristics of word recognition problems. Furthermore, a set of test scores remains meaningless without an individual who has the training and expertise to interpret the scores, form a composite profile of a student's relative strengths and weaknesses, and determine what the total results suggest about the remediation of the difficulties. Therefore, it is crucial to prioritize resources for professional development rather than investing only in testing devices themselves.

FRAMEWORK OF ASSESSMENT

From a philosophical perspective, it is important to differentiate between assessment and testing. "Assessment" refers to a spectrum of behaviors that includes observing, documenting, and interpreting performance (Johnston & Rogers, 2001). "Testing" is a component of assessment, in which behaviors are elicited and measured under controlled conditions, and tap a momentary level of functioning in time by sampling skills that are known or thought to be related to a given construct (in this case, word recognition). Unlike a static perspective of testing, assessment is viewed as an ongoing and dynamic process that is inextricably tied to intervention–instruction. As such, the professional must systematically and continually reassess both a student's progress and rate of progress to inform instruction and evaluate the effectiveness and appropriateness of the goals.

Within this framework are two general categories of word recognition assessment: traditional approaches and alternative approaches. These approaches have different purposes, strengths, limitations, and challenges. Even within each category, different tests measure different aspects of word

recognition abilities and strategies, so it is important to know what underlying skills each test is measuring and why a child may succeed or fail on a particular measure (Nation & Snowling, 1997).

Traditional assessment tools are frequently described as formal measures, in that they contain standardized procedures for test administration and scoring. Conversely, alternative approaches are classified as informal, because they more specifically address the importance of test individualization and utilize materials related to the curriculum (Salvia & Ysseldyke, 2001). Another distinction sometimes used to differentiate between traditional and alternative assessment procedures is that the goals of the former foster a discourse of disability, whereas the latter promotes a discourse of potential (Johnston & Rogers, 2001). For the topic of word recognition assessment, however, the framework of traditional–alternative more accurately captures the important conceptual distinctions and avoids the sometimes murky division between other dichotomies (e.g., criterion-referenced tests can be formal or informal).

Traditional Assessment Approaches

The overriding purpose of traditional testing is to identify and place students (i.e., diagnosis, eligibility) rather than to serve as a basis for ongoing instructional decision making and evaluating instructional effectiveness. Traditional tests most commonly include norm-referenced and criterion-referenced procedures. Norm-referenced tests are standardized measures that provide objective estimates of a student's word recognition abilities (e.g., an attained score on a word reading test) in comparison to students of the same age/grade and similar demographic characteristics. Criterion-referenced tests evaluate a student's performance relative to some predetermined set of objectives, based on knowledge about typical reading development. These measures are generally designed to provide more in-depth information about whether a learner has mastered a certain set of competencies in relation to predetermined mastery levels. Unlike norm-referenced procedures, criterion-referenced procedures describe rather than compare performance. Some criterion-referenced procedures are available in commercial form, whereas others are teacher–clinician developed and individualized to measure a particular student's mastery of specific skills.

Informal Reading Inventories (IRIs)

IRIs represent a category of traditional measures that are most often used by teachers and educational specialists to diagnose the nature and severity of a student's reading difficulty and to make recommendations for determining instructional reading level. They yield measures of both word reading accuracy and reading fluency. IRIs typically consist of a series of graded oral and/or silent reading passages with controlled vocabulary, which are followed by questions or requests for retellings. Most IRIs contain guided word lists to estimate a student's degree of mastery of word recognition skills to place a student at the appropriate passage level (O'Donnell & Wood, 1999). For orally read passages, the examiner records the number of errors (miscues) and the reading time. For the silent passages, the examiner records the time needed to read the passages and answer the questions. Word recognition accuracy is calculated by the percentage of miscues; word reading fluency is measured as the time needed to complete reading passages. A youngster's performance is generally rated as one of three levels: *independent:* the level at which a student can read without adult support; *instructional:* the level at which a student can read with adult guidance; and *frustration:* the level at which a student cannot read, even with outside assistance, and should not be targeted instructionally.

Of the variety of inventories available, some are published commercially, whereas others are developed by school districts, individual schools, or individual teachers. Some commercially available inventories suggest criteria for rating performances. For example, Richek, Caldwell, Jennings, and Lerner (1996) suggest 95–100%, 95–98%, and below 95%, respectively, for rating word recognition levels. Most use the same calculation for determining word recogni-

tion accuracy (total number of errors in a passage divided by the total number of words in a passage times 100) and word reading fluency (total number of words in a passage read per minute multiplied by 60 and divided by the number of seconds needed to read the selection to yield a words per minute reading rate). IRIs frequently include coding systems for miscue analyses, which generally consist of omissions, additions, substitutions, and reversals. Most provide guidelines for customary reading rates for different grade-level passages (Carver, 1990; Johns, 1993; Leslie & Caldwell, 1995), but these are quite broad (e.g., third grade: 85–139 words per minute).

Several advantages are associated with IRIs. Because the passages are graded and contain controlled vocabulary, they yield information that is instructionally useful and more representative of a student's word recognition abilities than the results of standardized tests. The miscue analyses move the level of assessment from one of identification to one of diagnosis, in which the examiner can determine the nature and dimensions of a student's word recognition problems (i.e., word reading and/or fluency) and the strategies the student uses to read, and determine the appropriate instructional level.

Limitations of Traditional Assessment

This approach to word recognition assessment frequently does not contribute diagnostically or instructionally useful information for several reasons:

1. It is frequently viewed as contrived, because the construct of reading is inconsistent with current research about reading and the current definition of skilled reading as an active and constructive process that is strategic, fluent, and motivated. Rather, reading is decontextualized and artificially parsed into a hierarchy of discrete measurable parts that do not capture the "interactive" aspect of literacy (e.g., between teacher and student, parent and child). Consequently, results may not reflect a student's actual word reading skill, because test items do not represent typical literacy activities in which the youngster engages.

2. Overreliance on these measures for placement and instructional decision making often exceeds what the tests can meaningfully assess. Administered once or twice per year, these instruments are not sensitive to documenting small gains, which is particularly important for learners who have or are at risk for reading difficulties. These students' progress tends to be slow and occur in small increments, and in areas not necessarily measured by the tests. As a result, this approach is often criticized for providing little direction for intervention planning and for informing ongoing instruction.

3. Certain pertinent developmental areas are not measured by available traditional test instruments (e.g., child's knowledge of story structure, home/family literacy, student's background knowledge).

4. Even the most well-normed tests are, by definition, based on group performance data, and are normed on children and adolescents performing at or near grade level. Thus, their predictive validity is reduced and sometimes misleading when applied to the scores of individual students and to populations of learners with special needs.

5. Their product (outcome) orientation does not permit identification of the strategies students are using to complete a task. Examiners must conduct post hoc item analyses to identify error patterns and to discover the processes underlying the behavioral products.

6. Available tests for screening and identifying children with literacy problems have a 50% error rate according to data from the National Association for the Education of Young Children (1991); that is, they frequently over- or under-identify students in need of further services.

7. Inadequate test validity may mislead interpretation of results. Some tests rely on multiple-choice response formats, so that the test is actually measuring recognition of words rather than reading production (Resnick & Resnick, 1992; Valencia, Hiebert, & Afflerbach, 1994). In the case of IRIs, their subjectivity often necessitates the sole reliance on clinical judgment for accurate interpretation. Finally, some tasks confound knowledge constructs. For example, a student's reading-rate accuracy on a passage may be confounded by a variety of factors, including background knowledge, reading comprehension level, and interest in subject matter.

Examples of Traditional Measures

Below is a small sample of norm- and criterion-based instruments that target different aspects and stages of word recognition skills that can be used to identify high-risk learners. These measures have demonstrated reliability and validity, are strongly predictive of future reading ability, and separate high and low performers.

Concepts of Print

TEST OF EARLY READING ABILITY–3 (TERA-3; REID, HRESKO & HAMMILL, 2001)

The TERA-3 is a norm-referenced test for children between 3 years, 6 months and 8 years, 6 months that contains a total of 80 items across three subtests that measure alphabetic knowledge and phonological sensitivity (e.g., letter-name identification, identification of initial and final sounds in printed words, identification of the number of syllables and sounds in printed words), conventions of print (e.g., correct orientation of a book, text genre, letter orientation, knowledge of punctuation), and meaning (e.g., logos; comprehension of words, sentences, and paragraphs; relational vocabulary). It is individually administered; administration takes approximately 30 minutes and is untimed.

EARLY LANGUAGE AND LITERACY CLASSROOM OBSERVATION (ELLCO) TOOLKIT (SMITH & DICKINSON, 2002)

The EELCO is a criterion-referenced measure for pre-K to third grade children that examines the role of environmental factors in early literacy and language development. Administered in classroooms, this tool consists of three parts: literacy environment checklist (15–20 minutes); classroom observation and teacher interviews (20–45 minutes); and literacy activities rating scale (10 minutes) for a total of 1–1½ hours.

TITLE RECOGNITION TEST (TRT) (CUNNINGHAM & STANOVICH, 1990)

The TRT is a criterion-referenced measure of print exposure for children beginning at third grade consisting of 39 items: 25 actual children's book titles and 14 foils for book names. Students place a checkmark next to the names of items recognized as actual books. It is a group/classroom-administered paper-and-pencil task; administration takes approximately 10 minutes and is untimed.

FAMILY/HOME LITERACY SURVEYS OR CHECKLISTS

Family/home literacy surveys or checklists may be administered to parents to determine availability of and access to literacy materials and activities in the home. The experimental questionnaires developed by Chaney (1994); Dickinson and DeTemple (1998); and Morrison McMahon-Griffith, Williamson, and Hardway (1993) provide items that address both literacy artifacts and experiences.

Phonological Processing

LINDAMOOD AUDITORY CONCEPTUALIZATION TEST—REVISED (LAC; LINDAMOOD & LINDAMOOD, 1979)

The LAC-R is a criterion-referenced test for children as young as kindergarten age. Children are asked to manipulate colored blocks in response to sound sequences given by examiner. It is individually administered; administration takes approximately 15–25 minutes and is untimed.

TEST OF PHONOLOGICAL AWARENESS— KINDERGARTEN (TOPA-K; TORGESEN & BRYANT, 1993)

This norm-referenced measure of phonemic sensitivity for 6- to 10-year-old children consists of items requiring students to indicate which of three words (represented by pictures) have the same first sound as target, and items that ask students to indicate which of four words (represented by pictures) begins with a different sound than the others. It is administered individually or in

small groups; administration takes approximately 6–10 minutes and is untimed.

YOPP–SINGER TEST OF PHONEME SEGMENTATION (YOPP, 1995)

This is a criterion-referenced measure for children in second half of kindergarten through first grade. Its 22 items require a child to separately articulate each phoneme in target words. It is individually administered; administration takes approximately 5–10 minutes and is untimed.

COMPREHENSIVE TEST OF PHONOLOGICAL PROCESSING (CTOPP; WAGNER, TORGESEN, & RASHOTTE, 1999)

The CTOPP is a norm-referenced test with a form for 5- to 6-year-olds and one for older children and adults. It assesses the three areas of phonological processing that underlie or are associated with early reading ability: phonological awareness, phonological memory, and rapid naming. It is individually administered; administration takes 30 minutes and is untimed.

PHONEME SEGMENTATION FLUENCY (FROM DYNAMIC INDICATORS OF BASIC EARLY LITERACY SKILLS [DIBELS]; GOOD & KAMINSKI, 2002)

This criterion-referenced procedure for children from the end of kindergarten through first grade has 18 forms, each of which consists of 10 words of two or three phonemes selected from the preprimer and primer levels of the Scribner basal reading series. DIBELS measures are sensitive to growth, and its multiple forms permit regular monitoring of a student's progress over time and response to instruction without compromising test integrity. It is individually administered and is timed.

RAPID LETTER NAMING (FROM DIBELS; GOOD & KAMINSKI, 2002)

This criterion-referenced measure for children from second half of kindergarten through first grade consists of 18 forms, with 104 randomly selected upper- and lowercase letters presented on one page. Children have 1 minute to name as many letters as possible in the order they appear on page. It is individually administered and is timed.

Spelling

NONWORD SPELLING (TORGESEN & DAVIS, 1996)

This criterion-referenced screening tool for children in the second half of kindergarten contains five nonwords (e.g., *feg, rit, mub, gof, pid*); children receive 1 point for each phoneme represented correctly in spelling. It is individually administered; administration takes 5 minutes and is untimed.

DEVELOPMENTAL STAGES OF SPELLING (GENTRY & GILLET, 1993)

This criterion-referenced procedure for invented spelling consisting of 10 dictation words for children to spell. A child's performance is placed in one of five developmental stages (precommunicative, semiphonetic, phonetic, transitional, conventional) based on the majority of the spelled words. It is administered individually or in small groups; administration takes 5–10 minutes or is untimed. (*Note.* Bear and Templeton's (1998) stages also can be used: prephonemic; semiphonemic; letter name; within-word pattern; syllable juncture, derivational constancy.)

Word-Level Reading

LETTER IDENTIFICATION SUBTEST OF THE WOODCOCK–JOHNSON PSYCHOEDUCATIONAL BATTERY— REVISED (WJ-R; WOODCOCK & JOHNSON, 1989)

The WJ-R is a norm-referenced test of single-word reading for children beginning at 5 years. Children read lists of words that gradually increase in length and complexity, while decreasing in frequency of occurrence in printed English. It is individually administered; administration takes approximately 5–10 minutes and is untimed.

WORD ATTACK SUBTEST OF THE WJ-R

In this norm-referenced measure of non-word reading, children are asked to sound out increasingly complex phonologically regular sound sequences. It is individually administered; administration takes 5–10 minutes or is untimed.

Word-Reading Fluency

GRAY ORAL READING TEST-FOURTH EDITION (WIEDERHOLT & BRYANT, 1992)

This norm-referenced measure is for children as young as 7 years. Children read aloud 13 increasingly difficult passages, each followed by comprehension questions. The test scores both accuracy and rate of reading, and has optional procedures for conducting qualitative miscue analyses.

TEST OF WORD READING EFFICIENCY (TOWRE; TORGESEN, WAGNER, & RASHOTTE, 1999)

This norm-referenced test of word reading accuracy and fluency for children 6 years and older consists of two cards, one containing real words and the other, nonwords. Children are given 45 seconds to read each card. It is individually administered; administration takes 5–10 minutes and is timed.

BASIC READING INVENTORY-EIGTH EDITION (JOHNS, 2001)

This criterion-referenced IRI for children from prekindergarten through grade 12 contains graded reading passages; reading rate is calculated as words correct per minute. It is individually administered and untimed.

Alternative Assessment Approaches

Alternative approaches to assessment place primary emphasis on optimizing student learning by linking the assessment process more directly to the curriculum and instruction (Calfee & Hiebert, 1991). Most are rooted in the constructivist theoretical orientation of emergent and early literacy which, by extension, views assessment as a process in which students are given consistent and repeated opportunities to demonstrate their knowledge in the context of their natural learning environments (Clay, 1985; Holdaway, 1979; Stanovich, 1994; Teale & Sulzby, 1986). Learners are active participants in the evaluation process rather than passive respondents. The main goal of alternative approaches is to align more directly the assessment process with pedagogical practices through continuous evaluation of the student's responsiveness to instruction. They are often considered more authentic or functional methods because, in contrast to traditional tests, they utilize curriculum content (or content-like) materials, resemble genuine literacy tasks found inside and outside of school, occur in or simulate the context of daily instructional environments, and are frequently administered by classroom teachers (Valencia, 1997; Valencia et al., 1994). The focus is on collecting meaningful and relevant information about a student's repertoire of reading skills and strategies, and how the student implements these in different contexts and when reading for different purposes (Clay, 1985; Valencia, 1997). Their structure and content allow for continuous refinement of instruction by monitoring student progress. As a result, the data have immediate utility for teachers and reveal patterns of student learning that are more meaningful to both educators and parents (Salinger, 2001).

Curriculum-Based Measurement (CBM)

A form of curriculum-based assessments, CBMs encompass formative systems of contextually based evaluation designed to (1) collect data on individual student progress in authentic learning environments and (2) provide information for teachers about instructional decisions that lead to more effective teaching (Deno, 1989, 1992). Developed in the 1970s, CBMs were originally conceived as a way to help teachers measure academic growth and improve the "fit" between instruction in basic skills (reading, writing, and mathematics) and student progress, using actual curriculum materials (Deno, 1998). They take a variety of forms but are most often either individually refer-

enced or criterion-referenced (particularly if local norms have been established). The underlying principles of CBMs have been extended to the assessment of other aspects of development, including language. For example, curriculum-based language assessments (CBLAs) have been developed that focus on whether students have the *language* skills to learn the curriculum, rather than on whether they are learning the curriculum *content* itself (Nelson, 1989).

Differences exist between these (and other) forms of curriculum-based procedures, but all embrace a common set of principles and are best used to complement one another as part of a comprehensive assessment of word recognition ability. Brief, frequent, samples of student performance are recommended, with simple, reliable administration and scoring procedures that are easy communicate. The materials are typically drawn from local curricula (Fuchs & Deno, 1994), and standardization of format (materials, time allowance for obtaining samples, scoring procedures) are deemed critical for permitting accurate comparisons of a student's performance over time (Pemberton, 2003). The basic, four-step process consists of (1) identifying behavioral objectives (condition, audience, behavior, and criteria) based on baseline performance; (2) creating a set of tasks (test items, timed probes, observations, running records, surveys, portfolios); (3) measuring student performance; and (4) graphing and evaluating results (Dyck, Pemberton, Woods & Sundbye, 1998; Pemberton, 2003). For example, a student may be asked to read aloud for 1 minute from a sample reading passage to measure growth in the number of words read aloud correctly, with the following behavioral objective: Given a passage from a third-grade storybook, the student will read at a rate of 120 words per minute, with no more than three errors in 5 minutes on three consecutive paragraphs in a 1-week period. Data are visually tracked and can be used immediately to modify instructional goals; the transparency of graphed results allows students to link efforts with progress and supports collaboration among professionals, between teachers and students, and between teachers and parents. Reliability and validity have been established for some CBM tasks demonstrating treatment efficacy, which is critical for accountability.

One type of CBM, the *running record,* is an informal procedure used mainly to identify and monitor a student's strategy use during reading. Passages are selected from the individual student's classroom materials (or recreational reading materials) and, therefore, do not necessarily contain controlled vocabulary. The emphasis is on determining the kinds of meaning cues (including semantic, syntactic, and visual) that the student is employing to understand written text.

Another specific approach to CBM, *portfolio assessment,* involves the systematic collection of a student's work in one or more subject areas to illustrate and document performance, progress, and achievement over a period of time in relation to specific instructional goals (DeFina, 1992; Pierce & O'Malley, 1992; Taylor, 1994). As described by Kratcoski (1998), portfolio assessment is a purposeful method of data gathering that is based on generating and testing hypotheses to discover why a student is experiencing problems (in this case, word recognition) in particular settings that are based on a student's actual use of behaviors. The accumulated information is then used to develop individualized instruction. In Kratcoski's model, hypotheses are generated in five areas, including curriculum (e.g., content material), teacher/instructional factors (e.g., how teacher is implementing instruction), environment (e.g., how the particular context is influencing student's performance), student skills (e.g., student's attainment of skills), and learner process (e.g., student's problem-solving strategies). The generated set of hypotheses guide formulation of predictions about a student's word recognition skills and how they can be modified in different contexts. Based on the hypotheses and predictions, decisions are made regarding the specific types of "artifacts" that should be sought for inclusion in the portfolio, such as language samples, observation notes, student interviews, test data, student work samples, and teacher interviews. The data compiled from the artifacts are collectively summarized and interpreted to identify patterns of performance, and relative strengths and weaknesses (i.e., confirm or reject hypotheses) to guide the development intervention goals. To be effective, goals must be stated in measurable terms with clear and objective evaluation criteria, so that change in student performance can be accurately documented over time and inform the next cycle of intervention. Students are encouraged to become active participants throughout the entire process through selection of materials to be included in the portfolio, self-evaluation of their strengths and weaknesses, and assessment of their own progress.

Portfolio assessment can contribute important and instructionally relevant information to the evaluation of numerous aspects of word recognition ability, including a student's knowledge of word boundaries, level of spelling development, vocabulary use, familiarity with conventions of print, letter and sound knowledge, knowledge of the alphabetic principle, and word and nonword reading. The use of multiple sampling procedures provides a more complete view of student capability. It also fosters collaboration among professionals (teachers, SLPs), parents, and students by tying assessment directly to educational decision making and long-term outcome. This emphasis provides a dynamic, flexible, and meaningful illustration of a student's growth over time rather than test scores that merely report change.

Dynamic Assessment

Dynamic assessment (DA) represents another form of alternative assessment. The term "dynamic" was originally used to contrast this approach with the summative and static nature of traditional norm-referenced tests, which focus attention on a child's performance at a particular moment in time (Feurstein, Rand, & Hoffman, 1979). DA views assessment as a formative and interactive process that provides "prescriptive" information about what learning conditions can bring about most improvement. Based on Vygotsky's (1986) theory of cognitive development, it maintains that a child's growth occurs in the "zone of proximal development"—the level of performance a child can attain independently and the level that can be attained with the assistance of an adult or more advanced language learner. The underlying assumption is that children initially depend on adults to acquire new information, but as knowledge becomes internalized, they gradually assume greater and greater responsibility for their own learning.

The primary purpose of DA is to estimate the "zone" by determining the amount of change that can be demonstrated during the assessment process with the adult examiner (Campione & Brown, 1987). The basic paradigm is test–teach–retest, in which the examiner first establishes a baseline level of performance and identifies deficient or emergent skills. Instruction is then given to modify the child's level of functioning in the targeted areas. Posttesting is administered, and gain scores serve as an indicator of child's degree of improvement (Budoff, 1987). Some researchers suggest supplementing gain scores with modifiability scores (e.g., Gutiérrez-Clennan, Brown, Robinson-Zañartu, & Conboy, 1998). These scores are operationalized as point-based rating scales that measure qualitative aspects of a child's performance, such as attention to task, self-regulation, and examiner effort. Peña and colleagues (Peña, 1996, 2000; Peña, Iglesias, & Lidz, 2001) report that children exhibit differences in modifiability scores despite lack of change in retest scores; that is, although they may not show quantitative improvement following instructional mediation, children evidence changes in the quality of their responses.

At this point in time, the most well-documented use of this qualitative approach to assessment is to distinguish between difference and disorder. According to Peña, Quinn, and Iglesias (1992), youngsters who benefit from a short period of guided teaching may be exhibiting culturally based differences, whereas those who do not may be at risk for disorder.

Challenges of Alternative Assessment Approaches

Among the main issues with this category of approaches are the following:

1. They are based on the assumption that SLPs and teachers will collect and analyze performance data in meaningful instructional contexts throughout the course of their daily interactions with students. This requires that professionals have a working knowledge of the curriculum and the language–literacy demands of curricular content. It also assumes a high level of knowledge about the benchmarks of early reading growth; which measures are the most sensitive underlying constructs/indicators of which benchmarks; how to collect, analyze, and interpret the data; and how to map results meaningfully onto underlying constructs to inform instruction and instructional modifications. To accomplish these goals, teachers and other professionals must be trained in the scientific method; otherwise, as Chen and Martin (1997) point out about portfolio assessment, data collection is likely to translate into a folder that simply contains sporadic samples of student work. Furthermore, the intensive training necessary to implement alternative approaches successfully is an obstacle to their adoption on a wide-scale basis (Haywood, Brown, & Wingenfeld, 1990).

2. Many of these tools are plagued by the "devil is in the details" problem of unclear criteria for acceptable performance, and how information is specifically to be used to modify instruction.

3. From a measurement perspective, the majority of these approaches are individually referenced and have not undergone sufficient research to demonstrate their reliability and validity. Many of these assessment systems are relatively new and are school-based, which may, in part, account for the lack of psychometric data. For example, scant empirical data exist that document the efficacy of portfolio assessment of word recognition. Even for descriptive evaluation purposes, reliability and validity of measurement are difficult to establish (with respect to test–retest and interrater reliability), and whether the changes observed are due to instruction. The degree to which these assessment systems are unique to a specific curriculum (classroom, school, district) also raises issues of their representativeness and generalizability.

4. Alternative approaches require an environment that is supportive of collaborative assessment (Glazer & Brown, 1993), and the time-consuming nature of the process. It is also difficult to manage successfully the frequent collection of systematic data required to ascertain meaningful evidence, without disrupting the course of normal classroom routines.

CONCLUSIONS

To serve our learners best, a comprehensive and accurate assessment of word recognition skills is carried out by a team of professionals that contribute their unique and shared disciplinary perspectives about language and literacy to attain a mutual goal. As a data-gathering process, the assessment of word recognition is best accomplished through the use of a combination of traditional and alternative measures that help to identify students with early reading problems, determine the specific nature of their problems, establish a baseline of emergent and early word reading skills, permit informed decisions about placement and instructional programming along a trajectory of word recognition learning, monitor progress to inform instruction, and evaluate the effectiveness of the instructional program through measurable changes in behavior in authentic learning environments. This holistic perspective is underscored by Whitehurst (2002), who notes that educational and clinical practice must combine scientifically informed research and "professional wisdom" to adapt to local settings and function effectively in areas for which research data are limited or unavailable. Ultimately, it is knowledge of the relative strengths and limitations associated with different forms of assessment that enables professionals to select procedures and interpret results in the most educationally meaningful and efficacious manner.

The philosophical shift toward alternative assessment is gaining support. However, traditional measurement procedures will likely remain a chief component of word recognition assessment for the foreseeable future despite inherent limitations. This situation is due, in part, to the current national climate of accountability. Federal, state, and district regulations mandate the use of high-stakes testing for classification and eligibility purposes, which is variously codified as learning standards or benchmarks of performance at different grade levels. Moreover, individualized education plans must contain a statement of a child's present level of educational performance in "objective measurable terms" (to the extent possible). Furthermore, the fact that tests are imperfect does not mean that they do not provide useful information, and is not sufficient justification for abandoning their use.

The adoption of alternative assessments on a large-scale basis will likely occur gradually over time, as they undergo further study to substantiate their psychometric integrity and generalizability, and as issues of widespread implementation and feasibility are addressed. As Shavelson, Baxter, and Pine (1992) commented, "We need to *ensure* that future [alternative] assessments capture high-level literacy outcomes and not simply assume that new or longer is better" (p. 27; italics added).

REFERENCES

Adams, M. J. (1990). *Beginning to read: Thinking and learning about print.* Cambridge, MA: MIT Press.

Allor, J. H., Fuchs, D., & Mathes, P. G. (2001). Do students with and without lexical retrieval weaknesses respond differently to instruction? *Journal of Learning Disabilities, 34,* 264–275.

American Speech–Language–Hearing Association. (2001). Roles and responsibilities of speech–language pathologists with respect to reading and writing in children and adolescents (position statement, executive summary of guidelines, technical report). *ASHA Supplement 21,* 17–28. Rockville, MD: Author.

Aram, D. M., & Hall, N. E. (1989). Longitudinal follow-up of children with preschool communication disorders: Treatment implications. *School Psychology Review, 18,* 487–501.

Baddeley, A. D. (1986). *Working memory.* Oxford, UK: Oxford University Press.

Barrs, M., Ellis, S., Hester, H., & Thomas, A. (1989). *The primary language record: Handbook for teachers.* London: Inner London Education Authority/ Centre for Language in Primary Education.

Bear, D., & Templeton, S. (1998). Explorations in spelling: Foundations for learning and teaching phonics, spelling, and vocabulary. *Reading Teacher, 52,* 222–242.

Bishop, D. V. M., & Adams, C. (1990). A prospective study of the relationship between specific language impairment, phonological disorders, and reading retardation. *Journal of Child Psychology and Psychiatry, 31,* 1027–1057.

Bowers, P. G. (1995). Tracing naming speed's unique contributions to reading disabilities over time. *Reading and Writing: An Interdisciplinary Journal, 7,* 189–216.

Bowers, P. G., & Wolf, M. (1993). Theoretical links among naming speed, precise timing mechanisms and orthographic skill in dyslexia. *Reading and Writing: An Interdisciplinary Journal, 5,* 69–85.

Budoff, M. (1987). Measures for assessing learning potential. In C. S. Lidz (Ed.), *Dynamic assessment: An interactional approach to evaluating learning potential* (pp. 173–195). New York: Guilford Press.

Burgess, S. R., & Lonigan, C. J. (1998). Bidirectional relations of phonological sensitivity and pre-reading abilities: Evidence from a preschool sample. *Journal of Experimental Psychology, 70,* 117–141.

Calfee, R., & Hiebert, E. H. (1991). Classroom assessment of reading. In R. Barr, M. L. Kamil, P. B. Mosenthal, & P. D. Pearson (Eds.), *Handbook of reading research* (Vol. 2, pp. 281–309). White Plains, NY: Longman.

Campione, J., & Brown, A. (1987). Linking dynamic assessment with school achievement. In C. S. Lidz (Ed.), *Dynamic assessment: An interactional approach to evaluating learning potential* (pp. 82–115). New York: Guilford Press.

Carver, R. B. (1990). *Reading rate: A review of research and theory.* San Diego: Academic Press.

Catts, H. W. (1989). Defining dyslexia as a developmental language disorder. *Annals of Dyslexia, 39,* 50–64.

Catts, H. W. (1991). Early identification of children with reading disabilities. *Topics in Language Disorders, 12,* 1–16.

Catts, H. W., Fey., M., & Tomblin, B. (1997, April). *The language basis for reading disabilities.* Paper presented at the meeting of the Society for the Scientific Study of Reading, Chicago, IL.

Catts, H. W., Fey, M., Zhang, X., & Tomblin, B. (1999). Language bases of reading and reading disabilities: Evidence from a longitudinal investigation. *Scientific Studies of Reading, 3,* 331–361.

Chall, J. S. (1983). *Stages of reading development.* New York: McGraw-Hill.

Chaney, C. (1994). Language development, metalinguistic awareness and emergent literacy skills in 3-year-old children in relation to social class. *Applied Psycholinguistics, 15,* 371–398.

Chen, Y., & Martin, M. A. (1997). Using performance assessment and portfolio assessment together in the elementary classroom. *Reading Improvement, 64,* 32–38.

Clay, M. M. (1985). *The early detection of reading difficulties* (3rd ed.). Auckland, New Zealand: Heinemann.

Cooper, D. H., Roth, F. P., Speece, D. L., & Schatschneider, C. (2002). The contribution of oral language skills to the development of phonological awareness. *Applied Psycholinguistics, 23,* 399–416.

Cunningham, A. E., & Stanovich, K. E. (1990). Assessing print exposure and orthographic processing skill in children: A quick measure of reading exposure. *Journal of Experimental Psychology, 82,* 733–740.

DeFina, A. A. (1992). *Portfolio assessment: Getting started.* New York: Scholastic Professional Books.

Deno, S. L. (1989). Curriculum-based measurement and special education services: A fundamental and direct relationship. In M. R. Shinn (Ed.), *Curriculum-based measurement: Assessing special children* (pp. 10–17). New York: Guilford Press.

Deno, S. L. (1992). The nature and development of curriculum-based measurement. *Preventing School Failure, 36,* 5–10.

Deno, S. L. (1998). Academic progress as incompatible behavior: Curriculum-based measurement (CBM) as intervention. *Beyond Behavior, 9,* 12–17.

Dickinson, D. K., & DeTemple, J. (1998). Putting parents in the picture: Maternal reports of preschoolers' literacy as a predictor of early reading. *Early Childhood Research Quarterly, 13,* 241–261.

Dyck, N., Pemberton, J. B., Woods, K., & Sundbye, N. (1998). *Creating inclusive schools.* Lawrence, KS: Curriculum Solutions, Inc.

Ehri, L. C. (1987). Learning to spell words. *Journal of Reading Behavior, 19,* 5–31.

Ehri, L. C. (1991). Developmental ability to read words. In R. Barr, M. L. Kamil, P. Mosenthal, & P. D. Pearson (Eds.), *Handbook of reading research* (Vol. 2, pp. 383–417). New York: Longman.

Ehri, L. C. (1997). Interactions in the development of reading and spelling: Stages, strategies, and exchange of knowledge. In C. Perfetti, L. Rieben, & M. Fayol (Eds.), *Learning to spell* (pp. 271–294). Hillsdale, NJ: Erlbaum.

Ehri, L. C., & McCormick, S. (1998). Phases of word learning: Implications for instruction with delayed and disabled readers. *Reading and Writing Quarterly, 14,* 135–164.

Fawcett, A. J., & Nicolson, R. I. (2000). Systematic screening and intervention for reading difficulty. In N. Badian (Ed.), *Prediction and prevention of reading failure* (pp. 57–85). Timonium, MD: York Press.

Felton, R. H., & Brown, I. S. (1990). Phonological processes as predictors of specific reading skills in children at risk for reading failure. *Reading and Writing: An Interdisciplinary Journal, 2,* 39–59.

Felton, R. H., & Wood, F. B. (1990). Cognitive deficits in reading disability and attention deficit disorder. In. J. K. Torgesen (Ed.), *Cognitive and behavioral characteristics of children with learning disabilities* (pp. 89–114). Austin, TX: PRO-ED.

Foorman, B. R., Francis, D. J., Fletcher, J. M., Schatschneider, C., & Mehta, P. (1998). The role of instruction in learning to read: Preventing reading failure in at-risk children. *Journal of Educational Psychology, 90,* 37–55.

Fuchs, D., & Deno, S. L. (1994). Must instructionally useful performance be based in the curriculum? *Exceptional Children, 61,* 15–24.

Fuerstein, R., Rand, Y., & Hoffman, M. B. (1979). *The dynamic assessment of retarded performers: The Learning Potential Assessment Device, theory, instruments, and techniques.* Baltimore: University Park Press.

Gathercole, S. E., & Adams, A. (1993). Phonological working memory in very young children. *Developmental Psychology, 29,* 770–778.

Gentry, J. R., & Gillet, J. (1993). *Teaching kids to spell.* Portsmouth, NH: Heinemann.

Glazer, S. M., & Brown, C. S. (1993). *Portfolios and beyond: Collaborative assessment in reading and writing.* Norwood, MA: Christopher-Gordon.

Good, R. H., & Kaminski, R. A. (2002). *Dynamic indicators of basic early literacy skills* (6th ed.). Eugene, OR: Institute for Development of Educational Achievement.

Goswami, U. (1988). Orthographic analogies and reading development. *Quarterly Journal of Experimental Psychology, 40A,* 239–268.

Gough, P. B., & Tunmer, W. E. (1986). Decoding, reading, and reading disability. *Remedial and Special Education, 7,* 6–10.

Gutièrrez-Clellen, V. F., Brown, S., Robinson-Zañartu, C., & Conboy, B. (1998). Modifiability. *Journal of Children's Communication Development, 19,* 31–43.

Gutièrrez-Clellen, V. F., & Peña, E. (2002). Dynamic assessment of diverse children: A tutorial. *Language, Speech and Hearing Services in Schools, 33,* 212–233.

Haywood, H. C., Brown, A. L., & Wingenfeld, S. (1990). Dynamic approaches to psychoeducational assessment. *School Psychology Review, 19,* 411–422.

Holdaway, D. (1979). *The foundations of literacy.* Sydney, Australia: Ashton Scholastic.

Johns, J. L. (2001). *Basic Reading Inventory* (8th ed.). Dubuque, IA: Kendall/Hunt.

Johns, J. L. (1993). *Informal reading inventories: An annotated reference guide.* DeKalb, IL: Communitech.

Johnston, P. H. (1997). *Knowing literacy: Constructive literacy assessment.* York, ME: Stenhouse.

Johnston, P. H., & Rogers, R. (2001). Early literacy assessment development: The case for "informed assessment." In S. B. Neuman & D. K. Dickinson (Eds.), *Handbook of early literacy research* (pp. 377–389). New York: Guilford Press.

Joshi, R. M. (1995). Assessing reading and spelling skills. *School Psychology Review, 24,* 361–375.

Joshi, R. M., & Aaron, P. G. (1991). Developmental reading spelling disabilities: Are these dissociable? In R. M. Joshi (Ed.), *Written language disorders* (pp. 1–24). Boston: Kluwer Academic.

Joshi, R. M., & Leong, C. K. (Eds.). (1993). *Reading disabilities: Diagnosis and component processes.* Boston: Kluwer Academic.

Juel, C., Griffith, P. L., & Gough, P. B. (1986). Acquisition of literacy: A longitudinal study of children in first and second grade. *Journal of Educational Psychology, 78,* 243–255.

Justice, L. M., Invernizzi, M. A., & Meier, J. D. (2002). Designing and implementing an early literacy screening protocol: Suggestions for the speech-language pathologist. *Language, Speech, and Hearing Services in Schools, 33,* 84–101.

Kratcoski, A. M. (1998). Guidelines for using portfolios in assessment and evaluation. *Language, Speech and Hearing Services in School, 29,* 3–10.

Leslie, L., & Caldwell, J. (1995). *The qualitative reading inventory* (2nd ed.). New York: HarperCollins.

Liberman, I. Y., & Shankweiler, D. (1985). Phonology and problems of learning to read and write. *Remedial and Special Education, 6,* 8–17.

Liberman, I. Y., & Shankweiler, D. (1991). Phonology and beginning reading: A tutorial. In L. Rieben & C. A. Perfetti (Eds.), *Learning to read: Basic research and its implications* (pp. 3–17). Hillsdale, NJ: Erlbaum.

Liberman, I. Y., Shankweiler, D., & Liberman, A. M. (1989). The alphabetic principle and learning to read. In D. Shankweiler & I. Y. Liberman (Eds.), *Phonology and reading disability: Solving the reading puzzle* (pp. 1–33). Ann Arbor: University of Michigan Press.

Lindamood, C. H., & Lindamood, P. C. (1979). *Lindamood Auditory Conceptualization Test—Revised.* Austin, TX: PRO-ED.

Lonigan, C., Burgess, S. R., Anthony, J. L., & Barker, T. A. (1998). Development of phonological sensitivity in 2-to 5-year-old children. *Journal of Educational Psychology, 90,* 294–311.

Montgomery, J. (1995). Examination of phonological working memory in specifically language-impaired children. *Applied Psycholinguistics, 16,* 355–378.

Morrison, F., McMahon-Griffith, E., Williamson, G. L., & Hardway, C. L. (1993). *Family literacy environment, learning-related social skills, and academic achievement.* Paper presented at the 2nd Annual Head Start Conference, Washington, DC.

Nation, K., & Snowling, M. (1997). Assessing reading difficulties: The validity and utility of current measures of reading skill. *British Journal of Educational Psychology, 67,* 359–370.

National Association for the Education of Young Children. (1991). Guidelines for the appropriate curriculum content and assessment in programs serving children ages 3 through 8: A position statement. *Young Children, 46,* 21–38.

Nelson, N. W. (1989). Curriculum-based language assessment and intervention. *Language, Speech, and Hearing Services in Schools, 20,* 170–184.

O'Connor, R. E. (2000). Increasing the intensity of intervention in kindergarten and first grade. *Learning Disabilities Research and Practice, 15,* 43–54.

O'Donnell, M. P., & Wood, M. (1999). *Becoming a reader: A developmental approach to reading instruction.* Boston: Allyn & Bacon.

Pemberton, J. B. (2003). Comunicating academic progress as an integrated part of assessment. *Teaching Exceptional Children, 35,* 16–20.

Peña, E. (1996). Dynamic assessment: The model and language applications. In K. Cole, P. Dale, & D. Thal (Eds.), *Assessment of communication and language* (pp. 281–307). Baltimore: Brookes.

Peña, E. (2000). Measurement of modifiability in children from culturally and linguistically diverse backgrounds. *Communication Disorders Quarterly, 21,* 87–97.

Peña, E., Iglesias, A., & Lidz, C. (2001). Reducing test bias through dynamic assessment of children's word learning ability. *American Journal of Speech–Language Pathology, 10,* 138–154.

Peña, E., Quinn, R., & Iglesias, A. (1992). The application of dynamic methods to language assessment: A non-biased procedure. *Journal of Special Education, 26,* 269–280.

Perfetti, C. A. (1996). Continuities in reading acquisition, reading skill, and reading disability. *Remedial and Special Education, 7,* 11–21.

Perfetti, C. A., Beck, I., Bell, L., & Hughes, C. (1987). Phonemic knowledge and learning to read are reciprocal: A longitudinal study. *Merrill–Palmer Quarterly, 33,* 283–319.

Pierce, L. V., & O'Malley, J. M. (1992). *Performance and portfolio assessment for language minority students (Program Information Guide Series No. 9).* (ERIC Document Reproduction Service No. ED346747)

Reese, E., & Cox, A. (1999). Quality of book reading affects children's emergent literacy. *Developmental Psychology, 35,* 20–28.

Reid, D. K., Hresko, W. P., & Hammill, D. D. (2001). *TERA-3: Test of Early Reading Ability.* Austin, TX: PRO-ED.

Resnick, D. L., & Resnick, L. B. (1992). Assessing the thinking curriculum: New tools for educational reform. In B. R. Gifford & C. O'Connor (Eds.), *Changing assessment: Alternative views of aptitude, achievement, and instruction* (pp. 37–75). Boston: Kluwer Academic.

Richek, M. A., Caldwell, J. S., Jennings, J. H., & Lerner, J. W. (1996). *Reading problems: Assessment and teachings strategies* (3rd ed.). Needham Heights, MA: Simon & Schuster.

Richgels, D. (1995). Invented spelling ability and printed word learning in kindergarten. *Reading Research Quarterly, 30,* 96–109.

Robbins, C., & Ehri, L. C. (1994). Reading storybooks to kindergarteners help them learn new vocabulary. *Journal of Educational Psychology, 86,* 54–64.

Roth, F. P., Speece, D. L., & Cooper, D. H. (2002). A longitudinal analysis of the connection between oral language and early reading. *Journal of Educational Research, 95,* 259–272.

Salinger, T. (2001). Assessing the literacy of young children: The case for multiple forms of evidence. In S. B. Neuman & D. K. Dickinson (Eds.), *Handbook of early literacy research* (pp. 390–418). New York: Guilford Press.

Salvia, J., & Ysseldyke, J. (2001). *Assessment* (8th ed.). Boston: Houghton Mifflin.

Scarborough, H. S. (1990). Very early language deficits in dyslexic children. *Child Development, 61,* 1728–1734.

Scarborough, H. S. (2001). Connecting early language and literacy to later reading (dis)abilities: Evidence, theory, and practice. In S. B. Neuman & D. K. Dickinson (Eds.), *Handbook of early literacy research* (pp. 97–110). New York: Guilford Press.

Scarborough, H. S. (1998). Early identification of children at risk for reading disabilities: Phonological awareness and some other predictors. In B. K. Shapiro, P. J. Accardo, & A. J. Capute (Eds.), *Specific reading disability: A view of the spectrum* (pp. 75–119). Baltimore: York Press.

Scarborough, H. S., & Dobrich, W. (1990). On the efficacy of reading to preschoolers. *Developmental Review, 14,* 245–302.

Schatschneider, C., Carlson, C. D., Francis, D. J., Foorman, B. R., & Fletcher, J. M. (2002). Relationship of rapid automatized naming and phonological awareness in early reading development: Implications for the double-deficit hypothesis. *Journal of Learning Disabilities, 35,* 245–256.

Senechal, M. (1997). The differential effect of storybook reading on preschoolers' acquisition of expressive and receptive vocabulary. *Journal of Child Language, 24,* 123–138.

Shavelson, R. J., Baxter, G. P., & Pine, J. (1992). Performance assessments: Political rhetoric and measurement reality. *Educational Researcher, 21,* 22–27.

Shaywitz, S. E., Escobar, M. D., Shaywitz, B. A., Fletcher, J. M., & Makuch, R. (1992). Evidence that dyslexia may represent the lower tail of a normal distribution of reading ability. *New England Journal of Medicine, 326,* 145–193.

Siegel, L. S. (1994). Working memory and reading: A life-span perspective. *International Journal of Behavioural Development, 17,* 109–124.

Smith, M. W., & Dickinson, D. K. (2002). *Early Language and Literacy Classroom Observation (ELLCO) Toolkit.* Baltimore, MD: Brookes.

Spear-Swerling, L., & Sternberg, R. J. (1994). The road not taken: An integrative theoretical model of reading disability. *Journal of Learning Disabilities, 27,* 91–103, 122.

Stahl, S A., Kuhn, M. R., & Pickle J. M. (1999). An educational model of assessment and targeted instruction for children with reading problems. *Advances in Reading–Language Research, 6,* 249–272.

Stanovich, K. E. (1986). Matthew Effects in reading: Some consequences of individual differences in the acquisition of literacy. *Reading Research Quarterly, 21,* 360–407.

Stanovich, K. E. (1994). Constructivism in reading education. *Journal of Special Education, 28,* 256–274.

Stanovich, K. E., & Siegel, L. S. (1994). Phenotypic performance profiles of children with reading disabilities: A regression-based test of the phonological core variable difference model. *Journal of Educational Psychology, 86,* 25–53.

Stothard, S. E., Snowling, M. J., Bishop, D. V. M., Chipchase, B. B., & Kaplan, C. A. (1998). Language-impaired preschoolers: A follow-up into adolescence. *Journal of Speech, Language, and Hearing Research, 41,* 407–418.

Swank, L. K., & Larivee, L. S. (1998). Phonology, metaphonology, and the development of literacy. In R. Paul (Ed.), *Exploring the speech–language connection* (pp. 253–297). Baltimore: Brookes.

Taylor, M. (1994). *Literacy portfolio assessment: A source for literacy workers.* (ERIC Document Reproduction Service No. ED372222).

Teale, W. H., & Sulzby, E. (Eds.). (1986). *Emergent literacy: Writing and reading.* Norwood, NJ: Ablex.

Torgesen, J. K., & Bryant, B. R. (1993). *Test of Phonological Awareness.* Austin, TX: PRO-ED.

Torgesen, J. K., & Davis, C. (1996). Individual difference variables that predict response to training in phonological awareness. *Journal of Experimental Child Psychology, 63,* 1–12.

Torgesen, J. K., Morgan, S., & Davis, C. (1992). The effects of two types of phonological awareness training on word learning in kindergarten children. *Journal of Educational Psychology, 84,* 364–370.

Torgesen, J. K., & Wagner, R. K. (1998). Alternative diagnostic approaches for specific developmental reading abilities. *Learning Disabilities Research and Practice, 13,* 220–232.

Torgesen, J. K., Wagner, R. K., & Rashotte, C. A. (1994). Longitudinal studies of phonological processing and reading. *Journal of Learning Disabilities, 27,* 276–286.

Torgesen, J. K., Wagner, R. K., & Rashotte, C. A. (1999). *Test of Word Reading Efficiency.* Austin, TX: PRO-ED.

Treiman, R. (1993). *Beginning to spell.* New York: Oxford University Press.

Troia, G. A., Roth, F. P., & Graham, S. (1998). An educator's guide to phonological awareness: Assessment measures and intervention activities. *Focus on Exceptional Children, 31,* 1–12.

U.S. Department of Education, Office of Educational Research and Improvement, National Center for Education Statistics. (1999). *NAEP 1998 Reading Report Card: National and state highlights* (NCES 1999-479). Washington, DC: Author.

Valencia, S. W. (1997). Authentic classroom assessment of early reading: Alternatives to standardized tests. *Preventing School Failure, 41*(2), 63–70.

Valencia, S. W., Hiebert, E. H., & Afflerbach, P. A. (Eds.). (1994). *Authentic reading assessment: Prac-* *tices and possibilities.* Newark, DE: International Reading Association.

Vellutino, F. R., & Scanlon, D. M. (1991). The preeminence of phonologically based skills in learning to read. In S. A. Brady & D. P. Shankweiler (Eds.), *Phonological processes in literacy: A tribute to Isabelle Y. Liberman* (pp. 237–252). Hillsdale, NJ: Erlbaum.

Vygotsky, L. S. (1986). *Thought and language.* Cambridge, MA: MIT Press.

Wagner, R. K., & Torgesen, J. K. (1987). The nature of phonological processes and its causal role in the acquisition of reading skills. *Psychological Bulletin, 101,* 192–221.

Wagner, R. K., Torgesen, J. K., Laughton, P. Simmons, K., & Rashotte, C. A. (1993). Development of young readers' phonological processing abilities. *Journal of Educational Psychology, 85,* 83–103.

Wagner, R. K., Torgesen, J. K., & Rashotte, C. A. (1999). *Comprehensive Test of Phonological Processing.* Austin, TX: PRO-ED.

Whitehurst, G. J. (2002). *Evidenced-based education.* Washington, DC: U. S. Department of Education.

Whitehurst, G. J., Epstein, J. N., Angell, A. C., Crone, D. A., & Fischel, J. E. (1994). Outcomes of an emergent literacy intervention in head start. *Journal of Educational Psychology, 86,* 542–555.

Whitehurst, G. J., & Lonigan, C. J. (1998). Child development and emergent literacy. *Child Development, 69,* 848–872.

Wiederholt, J. L., & Bryant, B. (1992). *Gray Oral Reading Test* (4th ed.). Austin, TX: PRO-ED.

Wolf, M., & Bowers, P. G. (1999). The double-deficit hypothesis for the developmental dyslexias. *Journal of Educational Psychology, 91,* 415–438.

Wolf, M., & Bowers, P. G. (2000). Naming speed deficits in developmental reading abilities: *Journal of Learning Disabilities, 33,* 322–324.

Wolf, M., Bowers, P. G., & Biddle, K. (2000). Naming speed processes, timing, and reading: A conceptual review. *Journal of Learning Disabilities, 33,* 387–407.

Woodcock, R., & Johnson, M. B. (1989). *Woodcock–Johnson Psychoeducational Battery—Revised.* Itasca, IL: Riverside.

Yopp, H. K. (1995). A test for assessing phonemic awareness in young children. *Reading Teacher, 49,* 20–29.

22

Teaching Students with Reading Disability to Read Words

ROLLANDA E. O'CONNOR
KATHRYN M. BELL

When children reach school age, it is often assumed that they will have the prerequisite skills needed to learn to read. Most students' basic language skills have been developed; they understand spoken language and are able to use language to communicate with others. It is from speech, and through speech, that most children come to understand written language as well. For some children, the connection between spoken language and the printed word is not an easy one to make; however, that connection may be the most important one they make in the first few years of school.

The recognition of words is by far the largest contributor to reading comprehension during the elementary years (Shankweiler et al., 1999). However, word recognition is also the greatest obstacle to effortless reading for students with learning disabilities (Rack, Snowling, & Olson, 1992; Spear-Swerling & Sternberg, 1994). Moreover, deficient skills in the phonological component of language and in mapping the alphabetic representation of words onto speech is the chief barrier to word recognition in learners who are still in the relatively early stages of reading (Shankweiler et al., 1999).

On average, good readers recognize over 80,000 distinct words (Nagy, Anderson, Schommer, Scott, & Stallman, 1989). They recognize these words instantly, without consciously working them out. For students with learning disability in reading (RD), the process of learning to recognize words can be long and arduous. They may persist in making the kinds of errors that good readers outgrow in first grade, such as confusing words that start with the same letter (e.g., *book* for *bag*). The laborious letter–sound by letter–sound decoding that marks good first-grade readers midway through the year may seem inappropriate in a fourth or eighth grader with RD, even though this decoding represents progress over the error-strewn "first sound and guess in context" approach on which too many poor readers rely (McCandliss, Beck, Sendak, & Perfetti, 2003).

The difficulty that students with RD have in reading words is compounded by the weakness of many preparation programs in teaching teachers to use the strategies that students will need to recognize words. Teachers of poor readers identify their lack of knowledge in teaching word recognition as a major instructional stumbling block (Bos, Mather, Silver-Pacuilla, & Narr, 2000;

McCutchen & Berninger, 1999), and reports from direct observations of classrooms reveal minimal instruction in word analysis (Juel & Minden-Cupp, 2000; Vaughn, Moody, & Schumm, 1998). Of 11 studies cited in the teacher education chapter of the National Reading Panel Report (2000), only one addressed instruction for word recognition. The good news is that when teachers change their instruction to reflect improved practices, student outcomes also improve (Darling-Hammond, 2000). When teachers use techniques that students have the knowledge and skills to understand and apply, students can make rapid gains, whether this instruction is offered as early intervention or after a diagnosis of RD has been made (Ehri & McCormick, 1998). In this chapter, we focus on instructional strategies for teaching students to recognize words in print, and on the evidence that supports particular approaches.

PHONOLOGICAL AWARENESS, PHONICS, AND THE ALPHABETIC PRINCIPLE

Understanding the relation between "phonological awareness," the ability to manipulate the sound system of our language (e.g., to hear that *make* and *shake* rhyme, or that *cat,* though a one-syllable word, has three smaller sounds within it), and students' ability to read and spell words they have not been taught has been called the greatest scientific breakthrough in reading in the 1980s (Vellutino, 1991). By the early 1990s, it had been established that children who could blend and segment the sounds of spoken words (i.e., phonological awareness at the level of individual phonemes, or "phonemic awareness") were more successful in the early stages of reading (Share, Jorm, Maclean, & Matthews, 1984). These findings led researchers to ask whether children who lacked phonemic awareness, but were taught these skills, would become better readers than those in control groups, who developed these skills at a later time, if at all (Ball & Blachman, 1991; Bradley & Bryant, 1983; Byrne & Fielding-Barnsley, 1993). Many kinds of activities promote children's ability

to hear and manipulate the sounds in spoken words, such as stretching spoken words (e.g., "Say *fat* as slowly as you can"), blending speech sounds together (e.g., "Say these sounds with me: Mmmiiike. Who is that?"), or combining phonemic awareness with letter–sound knowledge, such as in segment-to-spell (e.g., "Say all the sounds in *fat* [f–a–t]. Do you know a letter that says /fff/? Write it down") (O'Connor, Notari-Syverson, & Vadasy, 1998a). These instructional activities help students to link their knowledge of sounds in words with the sounds of alphabet letters, an understanding called the "alphabetic principle."

The early studies relevant to RD were designed to test the components of phonological awareness with the strongest effects on reading and spelling development. As examples, Ball and Blachman (1991) tested the effect of teaching letter sounds versus teaching a combination of segmenting alongside letter sounds; Torgesen, Morgan, and Davis (1992) tested the effect of one phonological skill versus a combination of blending and segmenting; O'Connor, Jenkins, and Slocum (1995) tested whether blending and segmenting alongside letter sounds was sufficient, or whether a broader array of phonological awareness (e.g., rhyming, phoneme identity, phoneme deletion) would be more helpful. The findings of these studies—all conducted with nonreaders in kindergarten—converged on the recommendation that blending, segmenting, and letter–sound knowledge were needed for nonreaders to begin to "decode," or to use their knowledge of the sounds of alphabet letters to "sound out" unknown words.

Several procedures have been used effectively to teach children to segment spoken words (i.e., to articulate all of the sounds). Most of these procedures begin with one-syllable words and aim to teach first sound, last sound, medial sound, or all of the sounds in sequence. Ball and Blachman's (1991) "Say-it-and-move-it" routine for teaching segmenting has been replicated in many studies. In this activity, children pronounce a one-syllable word, attempt to say the sounds in the word, and move blank markers into the rectangles on a three-box form to represent the sounds they hear. As children learn the sounds for letters, they can select a letter to move onto the rectangle to represent a phoneme, or select a blank marker, if they do not know a letter that could make the identified sound. With this kind of instruction, most children in kindergarten or first grade learn to segment spoken words in 10–20 fifteen-minute sessions.

Blending may be particularly difficult for students with RD, because many also have problems with articulation and short-term memory for sounds (Swanson & Alexander, 2000). To make blending less abstract, researchers have stretched the sounds in spoken words [fffaaat] and asked children to repeat the stretched form before they try to guess the identity of words (e.g., Lundberg, Frost, & Petersen, 1988; O'Connor et al., 1995; Williams, 1980). Once children have learned to collapse stretched forms into normal pronunciations, it becomes conceptually easier for them to blend isolated phonemes (spoken with pauses [f–a–t]), which more closely resembles what they will need to do in decoding printed words. For sounds that cannot be stretched, Warrick, Rubin, and Rowe-Walsh (1993), among others, suggest that teachers iterate the first sound to make it more salient [T–t–t–ooommm]. Stretching and iteration are also helpful to teach segmenting, and children are encouraged to say words in these "funny" ways.

Many of the studies in which researchers taught children to blend or segment phonemes began with stretched blending and segmenting, proceeded to onset-rime blending and segmenting (e.g., f–ish), and ended with completely isolated phoneme blending and segmenting. Research conducted by Goswami (1986) and Treiman and Zukowski (1988) found that onset-rime units were more accessible to young children, and instructional studies with students with disabilities (O'Connor et al., 1995) also found that onset-rime units were easier to perceive and easier for children to produce. Although onset-rime units could be useful as a stage in auditory blending and segmenting instruction, researchers who focus on real reading outcomes have found onset-rime to be a less effective instructional unit in reading than letter–sound by letter–sound decoding (Booth & Perfetti,

2002; Nation, Allen, & Hulme, 2001), and little evidence exists that children use rime patterns to recognize words during the beginning stages of reading.

As support accumulated for teaching phonemic awareness, researchers began testing the effects of whole-class instruction in phonemic awareness and letter sounds. Blachman, Ball, Black, and Tangel (1994) and O'Connor, Notari-Syverson, and Vadasy (1996) provided professional development to teachers, so that they could use these activities with their intact classes in urban areas with high proportions of students at risk for reading problems. Teachers used phonemic manipulation activities for brief lessons several times weekly, and incorporated alphabet letters alongside phonemic blending and segmenting. At the end of kindergarten, children with and without disabilities outperformed those in control classes. In follow-up studies at the end of first (O'Connor, Notari-Syverson, & Vadasy, 1998b) or second grade (Schneider, Roth, & Ennemoser, 2000), students with disabilities in treated classes continued to outperform those in control groups. However, children in the average and high-average range at the beginning of kindergarten no longer showed advantages from their kindergarten experience. The benefit of early instruction in phonemic awareness appears to be strongest for children with the lowest initial skill levels.

Evidence for how much phonemic awareness is helpful (and relatedly, when to stop teaching segmenting and shift attention to reading) comes from several sources, and the findings are remarkably consistent. By the end of kindergarten, children who can isolate two or more phonemes in a one-syllable word are unlikely to fall into the bottom 20% of readers at the end of first grade (O'Connor & Jenkins, 1999). Children who can identify three phonemes in one-syllable words early in first grade are likely to be good readers 1 year later and beyond (Good, Simmons, & Kame'enui, 2001). For children who do not achieve these milestones, it makes sense to offer specialized instruction to help them to do so. Strategies from the experimental studies have been collected in activity books for teachers (e.g., see Adams, Foorman, Lundberg, & Beeler, 1998, or O'Connor et al., 1998b). Teachers have shown such interest in this kind of instruction that Torgesen and Mathes (2000) have published a review of tests and instructional materials for teaching and assessing phonological awareness.

Summary

Regardless of the specific activities they use, most researchers in early reading agree on the importance of teaching students to blend and segment the sounds in spoken words, to associate the phonemes in words with the letter sounds of the alphabet, and to integrate phoneme awareness with letter knowledge for a firm grasp of the alphabetic principle. Activities in which children manipulate sounds in spoken words, and represent those sounds with alphabet letters, such as in "Say-it-and-move-it" or spelling, assist them in learning how sounds are captured with letters, and how phonemes contribute to the spellings of words. By the time letter sounds are added to instruction in phonemic awareness, it becomes difficult, if not impossible, to distinguish between instruction designed to teach the alphabetic principle and instruction in "phonics," which is using the sounds of alphabet letters and letter combinations to "decode," or to sound out, printed words. Many children without RD acquire these understandings through their interactions with books and print in the home and the environment, or through the informal activities led by teachers in kindergarten and first grade. These understandings are rarely acquired by students with RD in the primary grades, in the absence of specific instruction (Juel, 1988; Rack et al., 1992). Many of the recent efforts in early intervention have been designed to ensure that most students acquire the alphabetic principle as early as possible.

EARLY, INTENSIVE INTERVENTION TO DECREASE THE INCIDENCE AND SEVERITY OF READING DISABILITY

Prior to the last 8 years, most research programs of early intervention to decrease the severity of RDs were conducted through one-to-one instruction, as in Reading Recovery (RR; Clay, 1985). In RR, children from the bottom quartile of first grade achievement receive up to 16 weeks of individual tutoring by a highly trained teacher. Tutorial sessions include rereading stories from earlier lessons, learning letters, writing activities, reassembling sentence strips from stories, and reading new stories. In general, students eligible for special education are excluded from RR participation. Contrary to the rationale behind its widespread growth, independent analyses of the long-term benefits of RR for children at risk for RD (e.g., Center, Wheldahl, Freeman, Outhred, & McNaught, 1995; Chapman, Tunmer, & Prochnow, 2001; Hiebert, 1994; Shanahan & Barr, 1995) show little effect on the long-term trajectory of the poorest readers. Not only do few of these poor readers show average performance 2 years later but also several studies found no significant differences between children who received RR and control groups.

Researchers have suggested that the reason that poorest readers show ephemeral effects is that RR spends insufficient instructional time on decoding strategies for individual words, in particular, segmenting and letter sounds. The first prompt for word recognition that RR teachers are taught to use is "Does it make sense?" (Clay, 1985). But using the context as a word recognition strategy may be the least useful prompt during the earliest stages of reading (Perfetti, Goldman, & Hogaboam, 1979), because it encourages children to look at the first sound and guess—a dangerous and persistent strategy for older poor readers that inhibits their motivation to learn more effective and efficient procedures for recognizing words. Tunmer and Chapman (1998) argue that to get children reading as quickly as possible, RR overrelies on predictable books, in which guessing words often works. But most books are not predictable, and the likelihood of correct guesses for unknown words in a typical text is about 1 in 10 (Gough, 1983). Delaying systematic instruction in phoneme segmentation and letter sounds may also inhibit children's use of semantic and syntactic cues. To use these cues effectively, children need to be skilled in the alphabetic principle, so that they can verify their predictions by mapping their spoken word against the sequence of letter sounds in the printed word (Tunmer & Chapman, 1998). Researchers who redesigned RR lessons with focused and applied phonemic awareness instruction (Iversen & Tunmer, 1993) have found that the outcomes of RR could be improved with more emphasis on specific strategies for word recognition.

Over 25 years ago, Lindamood and Lindamood (1975/1984) developed Auditory Discrimination in Depth (ADD) to help students focus on mouth position as they articulate isolated phonemes. Students moved from articulation to decoding through segmenting words and identifying the phoneme type (e.g., the sounds for the letters *p* and *b* are "lip poppers"). In studies investigating whether treatments that focus on articulation, along with phoneme awareness and decoding, might be more effective than treatments without this focus (Brady, Fowler, Stone, & Winburg, 1994; Torgesen et al., 1999), reliable gains were found in word identification for children with low skills. Unfortunately, researchers were unable to determine whether these effects related to the articulation component or to much more time on phonemic decoding.

In another one-to-one tutoring program, Vellutino et al. (1996) selected first graders in the bottom 15th percentile in reading as participants to receive nearly 40 hours of daily one-to-one instruction that included phonemic blending and segmenting, word study, reading connected text, and writing. Overall, the intervention was successful, with many of these first graders improving to the reading level of their classroom peers within 15 weeks, but 26% of the students receiving this additional instruction showed very limited growth. As in most early intervention studies, it is unknown whether any of the students who showed good gains during the tutorials would have been labeled as having RD without this intervention.

Summary

These intensive interventions have several features in common. They were delivered one-to-one, which allowed teachers to be optimally attentive to children's current understanding of the reading and writing process. They took advantage of the 1:1 structure to pace instruction according to the child's rate of learning. The developers of most of these approaches assumed that reading requires a complex interplay of understandings and applications that include phoneme awareness, letter knowledge, sequential decoding, and application of new learning to reading running text. The expense of delivering individual instruction was another commonality across these programs, and even with the attention and expense, some students in each treatment failed to make good progress.

IMPROVING THE EFFECTS OF GENERAL CLASSROOM INSTRUCTION

Given the expense of the one-to-one treatments, several researchers have tested what could be gained through improved instruction on the part of general classroom teachers in first grade. Foorman, Francis, Fletcher, Schatschneider, and Mehta (1998) compared the effects of different reading approaches in first grade as delivered by classroom teachers. They found that explicit phonics instruction, combined with opportunities to apply their learning in reading connected text, produced the strongest reading gains. These gains were particularly apparent for the children who began with the lowest levels of phoneme awareness and word recognition. In an observational study, Juel and Minden-Cupp (2000) analyzed the instruction in four-first grade classrooms, along with the reading progress of the children. Children who had the lowest scores in the fall showed the strongest growth in classrooms with the most explicit phonics instruction during the first half of the year (e.g., focusing on consonant sounds, short and long vowel patterns in isolation, and spelling patterns). Early in the year, children blended and segmented sounds in spoken words alongside their printed versions. The teacher in the classroom with the strongest reading outcomes adjusted her instruction across reading groups during the year to re-flect the growing knowledge and skills of the children.

Similarly, Blachman, Tangel, Ball, Black, and McGraw (1999) extended their work in kindergartens by conducting multiyear investigations in which teachers learned to implement phonemic awareness in kinder-garten, explicit code-based instruction in first grade, and continuing code instruction in second grade for children who had not mastered first-grade content. The experi-mental programs included letter sounds, phoneme blending and segmenting, word study of decodable and sight words, read-ing connected text with a high proportion of decodable words, and spelling. Reading comprehension was also included as the children spent more time reading connected text. Effects of word recognition were significant across all grades. By second grade, some of the children who had been diagnosed with RD entered the average range for decoding skills; however, they still read more slowly than their nondisabled peers.

Where phonics is actively taught (e.g., teachers demonstrate the letter sounds, how to combine them into words, and how to analyze words into sounds), the instruction-al activities of the phonics program look quite a bit like phonemic awareness along-side letter sounds, as we mentioned earlier. The distinction is a fine one, and is perhaps less important than ensuring that by the end of first grade, children can not only sound out words and spell those that are decod-able but also read words efficiently in sto-ries and books.

Summary

In the successful approaches described in this section, teachers taught phonics along-side phonological awareness to the children who had not yet acquired these skills. Key here are the notions that what works for most children (some phonics instruction during first grade) may not be sufficient for children with RD. Children who have diffi-culty using known sound–symbol corre-spondences to decode words often lack the ability to segment spoken words into speech sounds, and without this level of phonemic awareness, "sounding out" makes no sense (McCandliss et al., 2003). It is important for teachers to understand that not all chil-dren need these structured approaches, and that children who begin first grade with strong reading skills tend to do well with a range of approaches. But most students with RD will need consistently clear, well-sequenced, systematic instruction that pro-ceeds in ways that encourage application of letter–sound correspondences to decoding words. This level of consistency and focus is rarely available in general classroom set-tings.

SYNTHETIC PHONICS APPROACHES FOR STUDENTS WITH READING DISABILITY

Awareness of the internal phonological structure of words is necessary in learning to read an alphabetic script such as English. It is impossible to teach all of the letter–sound correspondences that students will need to be able to sound out unknown words, but the usefulness of phonics in-struction may be that it prompts the student to look for the relationship between the let-ters in a printed word and the sounds ut-tered when saying the word. Children be-come aware of spoken words as sequences of somewhat separable speech units, while they attempt to represent speech with let-ters, as students do during phoneme aware-ness activities that are integrated with letter sounds, and during attempts to spell. It is this combination of developing phoneme awareness, basic letter–sound relationships, and phonological recoding (i.e., the connec-tions that link written words to their pro-nunciations) that enables a child to remem-ber an orthographic representation in memory. Unfortunately, most students diag-nosed with RD have less developed skills across all of these areas.

Among the features of decoding instruc-tion investigated with children with RD, how to move from letter sounds to decod-ing words has received considerable atten-tion. Most reading specialists agree that children need to learn to blend letter sounds, and that blending is especially difficult for students with RD. Fayne and Bryant (1981) investigated the relative efficacy of teaching various blending targets in words. They randomly assigned students with learning disabilities, ages 7–13 years, to small-group instruction in which teachers taught one of five potential ways of blending letter sounds in words: (1) initial bigrams with a final consonant (co–t); (2) onset-rime (c–ot); (3) three-letter sounds (c–o–t); (4) one day each of conditions 1 and 2; or (5) one day each of conditions 2 and 1. Students were assessed on their reading of words used during training, transfer words with the same initial bigrams used in training condition 1 (with different final consonants), transfer words with the same rime patterns used in condition 2 (with different onsets), transfer words with the same vowels as used in training, and words with other vowels. No significant differences were found on the words used in training across conditions, indicating that students learned their respective training sets, but significant differences were found on the transfer lists. Students who were taught to blend the initial bigrams read more of the transfer words correctly than any other group.

O'Connor and Padeliadu (2000) compared decoding instruction using Fayne and Bryant's (1981) technique with whole-word instruction using cumulative introduction. The researchers selected the poorest readers from first-grade classrooms, some of whom were already identified for special education, near the end of the school year. The researchers included equivalent amounts of letter–sound and spelling instruction in both treatment conditions. Following 10 instructional sessions, children were tested on trained and transfer word reading and spelling. On the immediate posttest, the groups differed on blending, which was only taught in the decoding treatment. Both groups made significant pre- to posttest gains on letter sounds, reading trained words, spelling, and on the transfer words that used taught letter sounds, with no significant differences between groups. On a delayed test 8–11 days later, children in the decoding treatment retained more of the

taught words and read more of the transfer words correctly.

Summary

These studies used a gradual blending approach whereby children first blended a consonant–vowel, then added a final consonant. Because blending relies on auditory memory, which may also be poor in some students with learning disabilities, strategies that reduce the short-term memory load may be especially important. With this strategy, most students learned to blend the sounds in one-syllable words within just a few instructional sessions. Two issues seem particularly relevant here. First, although these students with RD had experienced 2 to 4 years of reading instruction, most were unable to blend isolated speech sounds prior to direct instruction in blending. This point is important, because many studies of prereaders (not children with RD) have found that blending develops prior to segmenting (Perfetti, Beck, Bell, & Hughes, 1987). In O'Connor and Padeliadu's (2000) study, the segmenting skill of these very poor readers did not predict blending ability. Nevertheless, blending is the means most good readers use for reading words never before encountered (Share, 1995). Second, although children may learn to read words for the short term under many different instructional conditions, researchers may need to include delayed tests to assess the strength and maintenance of learning before assuming that treatment effects were equal.

Relatively little comparative research among phonics approaches and programs has been conducted, and existing studies suggest that the differences may be less important than the qualities of instruction: Instruction should be systematic, thorough, and include extensive opportunity to apply learned skills to new words, and to words in running text. The dearth of comparative research suggests at this time that doing something good in phonics instruction is more important than choosing a particular program. Stahl (1998) suggests that novelty may be key with older poor readers, because the variety of approaches in which these students have failed may make it more difficult and unlikely that they will engage in phonics instruction with the focus and interest it may take to be effective.

COMPUTER-ASSISTED INSTRUCTION

One way to provide novelty for students with RD, especially when they are severely behind their peers in reading skills, is through practice on computers. Barker and Torgesen (1995) have developed software for computer instruction in phoneme awareness. In Daisy Quest, children search for a friendly dragon. Synthetic and digitalized speech provide feedback as children categorize sounds, blend sounds together, and count phonemes. In an experimental test of effects with first-grade poor readers, 8 weeks of practice yielded significant effects in phoneme awareness and word recognition.

Wise, Ring, and Olson (2000) have conducted several experiments to test variations of Reading with ROSS (Reading with Orthographic and Speech Support), a computerized reading program in which students read stories on a computer screen and click on the words they cannot read independently. The researchers have tested levels of computer feedback for these unknown words, such as synthesized or digitalized reading of the whole word, syllable, rime, or phonemic segments. Recently, they have also combined teacher-led instruction in articulation of phonemes based on Lindamood and Lindamood's *Auditory Discrimination in Depth* (ADD) (1975/1984) with computer practice (Wise et al., 2000). Results have been generally positive, with lower skilled students benefiting most from the most intensive treatments.

Two programs have used voice recognition technology. Raskind and Higgins (1999) developed a writing program—DragonDictate—that captured students' words in print as they dictated sentences. When the software failed to distinguish a spoken word, choices appeared on the screen for students' selection. Mostow and Aist (1999) developed a Reading Tutor that "listens" to children read stories it displays on a computer screen, sentence by sentence. The Reading Tutor gives spoken and graphical help on a word or sentence when it detects a mistake, skip, or hesitation, when the student clicks for help, or preemptively, when the sentence contains a hard word. Assistance on an individual word varies depending on the structure of the missed word, and could include a rhyming hint, a vowel sound, or the spoken word, followed by the opportunity to reread the sentence. Both programs produced significant improvements, and both offered students considerable control over their learning. In DragonDictate, students constructed their own text. Students using the Reading Tutor can select the stories they most want to read, reread favorite stories to a degree beyond the patience of most listeners, and generally enjoy the experience.

Some researchers have suggested that the phonological impairments that have been well documented among students with RD stem from temporal processing deficits, in which children have difficulty perceiving rapidly changing auditory cues, such as those in the speech stream (Tallal, Sainburg, & Jernigan, 1991). Others have failed to find these differences (McAnally, Hansen, Cornelissen, & Stein, 1997). Fast ForWord (Tallal et al., 1991) is a computer-delivered program of acoustically modified speech, in which phonemes are stretched and stressed to make them easier to hear. Sounds are systematically adjusted toward normal speech, based on the progress of the child. Aside from developers of the program, the little research that has been conducted to test the effects of Fast ForWord (i.e., Hook, Macaruso, & Jones, 2001) suggests that gains in phonemic awareness and reading were not lasting. Fast ForWord may be as good as other programs for students with learning disabilities, but not better.

Summary

Across these studies, it is important to caution that technology by itself may not be key; rather, the teacher's choice and use of appropriate technology for individual students hold promise for students at risk for, or diagnosed with RD.

OLDER STUDENTS WITH READING DISABILITY

Older students with RD have struggled with reading for several years and may have incorporated faulty strategies into their repertoire of reading skills. Because of the prolonged difficulty they have experienced, motivating students to try again may need to be part of any new procedures. Despite these factors that adversely affect the older reader with RD, there are strengths that can be utilized to build better skills. Because of their exposure to and participation in school, these students already have at least rudimentary knowledge of the academic structure of school tasks, literacy, and language, and their comprehension—particularly of vocabulary words—is likely to be better than that of younger readers who read at similar levels. They may, then, be better able than younger readers to benefit from metacognitive reading and language strategies (Gaskins et al., 1988).

Simple phonics conventions are often transgressed in multisyllabic words, so instruction that includes affixes and common syllables is essential. Researchers have estimated that most of the conventions that children learn about syllabication come from repeatedly reading words in context. As students read, they begin to understand that a combination such as *dn* is more likely to signal a syllable break than is *dr*, which usually functions as a blend within a syllable (Cunningham, 1998). The frequency with which particular word parts are encountered influences the likelihood that readers will recognize or be able to decode a word correctly. But many students with RD seem to be caught in what Ehri and McCormick (1998) call the "partial-alphabetic stage." They have learned the consonant sounds and some variations on vowel sounds, but without anchoring this knowledge in ways that can be used to read words accurately. Because these students fail to process all letters within a word, they make frequent errors and substitutions of words with similar visual shapes or lengths. Without attending to all sounds within words, students cannot decode, nor can they analogize to known sight words (Ehri & Rob-

bins, 1992). They are denied access to self-teaching mechanisms by which good readers successfully decode the words they encounter in their reading so many times that they become part of their vocabulary of instantly recognized words (Share, 1995).

Nagy et al. (1989) estimated that four times as many multisyllabic words have affixes than root words alone, so knowledge of how word forms combine, along with recognition of morphologically related words (they estimate 88,533 distinct word families in printed school English), could enhance decoding and understanding the meanings of unfamiliar words encountered in print. Morphological connections among words may be more useful than orthographic similarities (e.g., rimes) in speeding the time it takes to recognize multisyllabic words.

Learning Styles

Before describing effective treatments to improve word recognition for older students, it is important to mention the studies that attempted to improve reading performance by matching modality strength or learning style to specific elements of instruction. Comprehensive reviews by researchers who assessed the effect of matching modality (e.g., Arter & Jenkins, 1979; Kavale & Forness, 1987) or matching learning styles to instruction (e.g., Good, Vollmer, Katz, & Chowdhri, 1993) have failed to show positive effects of such matching. The studies we review in this chapter also failed to find advantages to selecting different types of instructional methods for particular learners. For example, the students with double deficits (poor phonological processing and slow naming speed) learned to read words at a slower rate than did less impaired students; however, the most successful model overall—training in segmenting and letter sounds, and blending sounds in words—was also most successful for the students with double-deficits. Indeed, these studies suggest that our most powerful instructional models are particularly important for children with the most severe reading difficulties, who tend to make poor progress (when they make progress at all) in control conditions that mimic typical, general classroom reading instruction. Although what works for most students will not work for all, choosing a program because of a particular cognitive profile tends to be less effective than beginning with the approach that has produced the best evidence for positive effects, then adjusting the instruction for individual students who may need the mix "titrated" to respond optimally.

Reading Multisyllabic Words

Lenz and Hughes (1990) developed a word-recognition strategy for older students with RD that took advantage of word forms and affixes. The word-identification strategy (DISSECT) has seven steps: (1) *Discover the context, (2) *Isolate the word's prefix, (3) *Separate the word's suffix, (4) *Say the word's stem, (5) *Examine the word's stem, (6) *Check with another person to see if you are correct, (7) *Try to find the word in the dictionary. It was designed to provide a collection of flexible actions for students who lacked a strong decoding base. The step in part 4—Say the word's stem—was central to this strategy. This step introduced the rule of two's and three's to decode the base word, which often has more than one syllable, aside from the attached affixes. The researchers taught students that if a stem begins with a vowel, separate the first two letters; if a stem begins with a consonant, separate the first three letters, then say the syllable. After that, repeat the process until the whole stem has been decoded. Once the stem is recognized, the affixes are added back on to pronounce the whole word. The instructional routine included teacher modeling of the entire strategy, paraphrasing of each step by students, memorizing the steps, then several weeks of controlled practice and feedback on the individual steps and their combination. Accurate application of the strategy required 20 minutes at least three times per week over a 6-week period. Generalization probes after training demonstrated that students maintained use of the strategy after it was thoroughly learned. O'Connor et al. (2002) used an abbreviated version of DISSECT (BEST: *Break apart the affixes, *Examine the stem, *Say the parts,

*Try the whole thing in context), which was also successful in teaching older students with learning disabilities to decode multisyllabic words.

Several sources can provide the materials for teaching the commonly occurring word parts for strategies such as DISSECT and BEST. White, Sowell, and Yanagihara (1989) reanalyzed Carroll, Davies, and Richman's (1971) list of common words to derive the affixes that appeared in words most frequently. In their research, 20 prefixes accounted for 97% of all word prefixes, and 16 suffixes for 87% of words. Glass Analysis (Glass, 1973) provides lists of sequentially more difficult words containing common orthographic patterns (e.g., *rain, strain, detaining, container,* etc.), and Carnine, Silbert, and Kame'enui (1997) list orthographic patterns that are regularly pronounced over 75% of the time in single and multisyllabic words. These lists can help students to make use of the redundancies in printed English.

Another approach for older students with RD is word building. Although it has been recommended as an instructional strategy for many years (e.g., Cunningham, 1998), word building has recently been tested through a series of experiments conducted by McCandliss et al. (2003). In their first experiment, they identified the pattern of errors most common among their students with RD in the intermediate grades. These students accurately used the first grapheme in a word, followed by relatively worse decoding of the remaining vowels and consonants. They taught students to attend to the medial and final sounds by progressive minimal pairing of words that differed by only one grapheme. After 20 sessions, students not only read significantly more nonsense words than those in the control group but also generalized the patterns of words in the training set to real words that had not been taught.

Instructional Packages for Older Students

Several recent studies have developed effective instructional packages for students in the upper elementary and middle school grades who have failed to master the early skills of decoding and phonemic awareness. These programs are described here, and although the components will seem familiar, they consistently shatter the familiar adage that after the primary grades, decoding instruction is far less effective than it would have been earlier.

Some time ago, Williams (1980) developed a "starting over" approach for students ages 7–12 with RD. Her program began with auditory segmenting and blending, much like strategies now recommended in first grade. The program included letter sounds and a controlled sequence of blending activities that began with two- and three-letter words, and worked up to two-syllable decoding. Following a year of 20-minute sessions, students in treated classes outperformed control students in word identification and nonword reading, with an effect size of nearly one standard deviation.

Gaskins et al. (1988) developed an approach to word recognition at the Benchmark School that relied on learning the orthographic patterns of a collection of high-frequency key words, many of which were already in the sight vocabulary of older readers with RD. Taking advantage of the common invariant spelling patterns of these words, students gradually built their core of sight words in a read-by-analogy approach, in which they learned to analyze unknown words in light of familiar spelling patterns. Students used a metacognitive comparative process to break apart unknown words and sound them out, using larger decoding chunks than the letter-by-letter strategy common in developmental approaches.

Lovett and Steinbach (1997) tested the effects of this metacognitive strategy against systematic letter-by-letter decoding with students with RD in second through sixth grades. In the phonological awareness/direct instruction approach (PHAB), students learned letter–sound correspondences, blending sounds of letters in words, and segmenting, using lessons extracted from DISTAR Reading Mastery I (Engelmann & Bruner, 1988). In the metacognitive word instructional strategies training (WIST), students learned multiple approaches for recognizing words, beginning with decoding

and proceeding through analogizing to known words, breaking off affixes, and seeking known parts of words, based on the Benchmark program. Both of these approaches also included reading connected text, and both produced sizable effects in word identification and word attack. No age effects were found, suggesting that these strategies were as effective with older students as they were with poor readers in the primary grades.

Continuing this line of inquiry, Lovett et al. (2000) combined the two treatments in various orders to determine the most effective combination of PHAB and WIST. They labeled their winning combination PHAST (phonological and strategy training), and it began with phonological awareness, letter sounds, and decoding of short words, and proceeded through word-recognition strategy training in which students were taught to select among five procedures: letter-by-letter decoding, reading by analogy (based on Gaskins et al., 1988), seeking the part of the word you know, attempting variable pronunciations, and peeling off affixes in multisyllabic words. This experimental test was conducted in small groups of four, and the authors suggest that it may be effective in larger groups.

Practitioners should be aware, however, that in comparisons of the effects of group size on the academic behavior and outcomes for students with learning disabilities (Schumm, Moody, & Vaughn, 2000; Thurlow, Ysseldyke, Wotruba, & Algozzine, 1993) small groups and individual tutorial sessions were more consistently effective than larger group sizes. For example, Schumm et al. (2000) compared effects of group sizes of 1:1 versus 3:1 versus 10:1. Although they found no difference between the gains students made in 1:1 and 3:1 conditions, both small-group and individual instruction produced larger gains than groups of 10 students. Thus, little data exist to support teaching reading to students with learning disabilities in groups much larger than three.

Other researchers have developed one-to-one instruction focused on improving the word-recognition and general reading ability of students with RD across a range from third grade through middle school. Abbott and Berninger (1999) tested the effects of structural analysis instruction; Rashotte, MacPhee, and Torgesen (2001) tested adding a spelling component much like word building; Torgesen et al. (2001) replicated their earlier study of ADD (Lindamood & Lindamood, 1975/1984) with students in third through fifth grade; and O'Connor et al. (2002) compared the effects of using different levels of reading text (instructional or age/grade level), finding that students with RD who read text at their own instructional level made stronger gains in word recognition, fluency, and comprehension than those who used their classroom reading materials. In all of these studies, word-recognition instruction was embedded in a more complete package that included focus on phonemes within words, orthographic patterns, word analysis, spelling, and reading connected text. All found significant improvement in word recognition and other areas, and none found a significant age effect, which indicates that older students benefited as much as younger poor readers.

Corrective Reading (Engelmann et al., 1988) combines direct instruction in word-attack skills with practice reading stories written with decodable text that incorporates only the taught letter sounds and patterns. Students practice sounds in isolation, strategies for decoding words, reading word lists, and reading and rereading text until rate and accuracy benchmarks have been achieved. The results from experiments (Lloyd, Cullinan, Heins, & Epstein, 1980; Polloway, Epstein, Polloway, Patton, & Ball, 1986) found positive effects on word recognition, reading rate, and comprehension for students in the intermediate grades with learning disabilities.

Summary

Older students respond well to interventions in word recognition when they are of sufficient duration and intensity; however, little evidence exists regarding the long-term effects of these approaches. Strategies for decoding multisyllablic words were included in most of these treatments, along with

practice reading acquired words in connected text at a level commensurate with students' decoding skill. Although some of these strategies were metacognitive in nature, all required structured teaching in the early phases as students learned the steps and how to apply them to unfamiliar words. None were "quick fixes"; rather, the researchers used these strategies several times per week, over many weeks, before students could reliably use them independently.

READING WORDS QUICKLY

There is ample evidence that one of the major differences between good and poor readers is the amount of time they spend reading. For example, Allington (1977) found that the students who needed the most practice spent the least amount of time actually reading. Researchers have reported that good readers are exposed to anywhere from 2 to 10 times as many words as poor readers. Theoretically, students who recognize words effortlessly should be able to devote more attention to reading comprehension (Laberge & Samuels, 1974), and the relationship between rate of oral reading and reading comprehension is strong through the elementary years (Pinnell et al., 1995). Unfortunately, decoding practice, by itself, does not necessarily improve reading rate or fluency. Researchers have attempted to tease out the best ways to achieve automatic word recognition that is fast, effortless, requires minimal intention or deliberation, and does not interfere with other processes occurring at the same time. Studies in which students learned to recognize words quickly in lists have produced inconsistent findings for fluency in context. Fleischer, Jenkins, and Pany (1979) found no advantage in reading comprehension for teaching children to recognize words quickly out of context. In another instructional study, Levy, Abello, and Lysynchuk (1997) found that students' reading comprehension did not improve unless students recognized the words nearly as quickly in context as in lists. The range of reading speed among their participants led these researchers to suggest that most students with RD would need considerable practice before they were likely to generalize to improved reading in context.

How is this extensive practice to be achieved? One of the most promising approaches is repeated reading, in which students read a passage or page of text until improvement in rate of reading (usually a 25% increase or more) is achieved (Samuels, 1979). Herman (1985) found that repeated reading not only increased rate but also increased reading accuracy. Young, Bowers, and MacKinnon (1996) also found improvement in word recognition through repeated reading, but only when students were assisted with their errors during practice. This distinction is important, because some models of repeated reading have students rereading text independently or along with tape-recorded text. To improve accuracy along with rate, assistance from a more skilled reader—adult or peer—may be necessary.

In a recent review of the repeated reading literature, Meyer and Felton (1999) provided procedures for implementing the practice, along with the results teachers can expect to achieve. They provide guidelines for grade level (30–50 wpm in grade 1, 85–100 wpm for grade 2) that are consistent with the research that relates rate of reading across grades with passage of third-grade standardized tests (Good et al., 2001). The rate goals for repeated reading are generally higher than would be expected on unpracticed reading, particularly for students with learning disabilities. Many students achieve maximum oral reading fluency by fourth or fifth grade (upper limits are determined by the speed of speech, generally 150–200 wpm), and after these rates are attained, continuing fluency practice is not helpful. Students with RD do not generally reach these rates until much later, so fluency practice may be helpful until reading achievement reaches fourth-grade level or beyond. From reviews of two comprehensive approaches to building fluency, RAVE-O (Wolf & Bowers, 1999) and Great Leaps (Mercer & Campbell, 1998), Meyer and Felton (1999) recommended that poor readers practice building fluency for 10–20 minutes per day over a long duration, engage in reading aloud, and use text at an instructional level.

Summary

Fluency is not an end goal for students with RD; rather, students need to build sufficient fluency to enable efficient reading comprehension. For these older students, we lack evidence for how much fluency is sufficient.

ISSUES OF TRANSFER AND GENERALIZATION

The problem of generalization beyond taught words has plagued the intervention literature, but many of the studies reviewed here offer recommendations. Foremost is to teach students skills they will be able to use independently, which suggests much more than drill on high-frequency words. Students need to learn to blend sounds together, to decode letter sounds in sequence, and to segment all of the sounds in short words. Once they have acquired these very basic decoding skills, students can learn multistep strategies for reading longer words, and flexible use of multiple strategies for reading different kinds of words.

The level of reading material used for practice and word study may also affect the extent to which students transfer taught skills to new words and text (O'Connor et al., 2002). Students who are very far behind should read from instructional-level text. At their own instructional level, the redundancy of words from one passage to another is likely to be greater than in more difficult material, and such redundancy probably contributes to the transfer observed in studies of reading fluency. Teachers should understand that attaining meaningful increases in word recognition and fluency will require considerable practice.

EDUCATIONAL IMPLICATIONS AND DILEMMAS

Although many strategies are potentially useful for recognizing words, the most consistently useful strategy is decoding (Tunmer & Chapman, 1998). As many researchers have documented, phonological manipulation skills are central to learning to decode. The good news for teachers of students with learning disability is that many factors associated with disability need not interfere with students' responsiveness to good interventions. The strongest predictor of responsiveness to treatment is phoneme segmentation (Hatcher & Hulme, 1999), and segmentation is one of the easier skills to teach with strong instructional routines, even to older students who failed to acquire these awarenesses "on time" (O'Connor et al., 2002; Torgesen et al., 2001). Nevertheless, the goals of instruction will change as students move through phases of word recognition. To develop independent reading, students will need a thorough working knowledge of letter–sound correspondences, extensive practice applying these relations to real words, opportunities to analyze words for common spelling patterns, practice reading unknown words by analogizing to known words, and the practice necessary for building a large sight vocabulary, reading fluently, and understanding connected text.

At each level of word recognition, teachers need to select carefully the text students use to apply what they are learning. For older students with severe reading problems, text selection is a considerable challenge. The burgeoning industry of "high interest, low vocabulary" texts (e.g., fiction, nonfiction, rewritten classics, content area texts) provides a potentially helpful resource and a means to motivate students with materials that match interests, but these materials vary in quality and in usefulness, depending on students' current word-recognition ability.

Delivering the instruction we know students need provides additional hurdles for school systems typically short on personnel. Favorable findings from studies that have used adult volunteers (e.g., Baker, Gersten, & Keating, 2000; Invernizzi, Rosemary, Juel, & Richards, 1997; Vadasy, Jenkins, & Pool, 2000) and peer tutors (Fuchs, Fuchs, Mathes, & Simmons, 1997; Greenwood & Delquadri, 1995) offer potential solutions to supplement the instruction provided by

special education teachers. The approaches to early intervention advocated by Blachman et al. (1999), Foorman et al. (1998), and Jenkins and O'Connor (2002) offer other means to decrease the severity of RD. These approaches also bring with them some danger, however. All of these studies report a proportion of students who did not respond well enough to early intervention to become adequate readers. These students were eventually labeled as having RD despite strong and well-funded intervention efforts. Therefore, some resources should be held in reserve for the more intensive approaches that have been effective for older students with RD.

In practical terms, school-district personnel may need to rethink how services are provided to older students with RD, who appear to respond well when instruction is delivered one-to-one or in very small groups, several days per week, at their current reading level for a long period of time. It is unlikely that this kind of instruction can be delivered within the general education classroom or by special education teachers who may have as many students on their caseload as those of general education teachers. One of the most important questions facing school systems today is how to implement what we know works for students with RD, in a climate that shies away from intensive individual instruction.

REFERENCES

Abbott, S. P., & Berninger, V. W. (1999). It's never too late to remediate: Teaching word recognition to students with reading disabilities in Grades 4–7. *Annals of Dyslexia, 49,* 223–250.

Adams, M., Foorman, B., Lundberg, I., & Beeler, T. (1998). Phonemic awareness in young children. Baltimore: Brookes.

Allington, R. (1977). If they don't read much, how they ever gonna get good? *Journal of Reading, 21,* 57–61.

Arter, J., & Jenkins, J. R. (1979). Differential-diagnosis–prescriptive teaching: A critical appraisal. *Review of Educational Research, 49,* 517–555.

Baker, S., Gersten, R., & Keating, T. (2000). When less may be more: A 2-year longitudinal evaluation of a volunteer tutoring program requiring minimal training. *Reading Research Quarterly, 35,* 494–519.

Ball, E., & Blachman, B. (1991). Does phoneme awareness training in kindergarten make a difference in early word recognition and developmental spelling? *Reading Research Quarterly, 26,* 49–66.

Barker, T., & Torgesen, J. K. (1995). An evaluation of computer-assisted instruction in phonological awareness with below average readers. *Journal of Educational Computing Research, 13,* 89–103.

Blachman, B., Ball, E., Black, R., & Tangel, D. (1994). Kindergarten teachers develop phoneme awareness in low-income, inner-city classrooms: Does it make a difference? *Reading and Writing: An Interdisciplinary Journal, 6,* 1–18.

Blachman, B., Tangel, D., Ball, E., Black, R., & Mc-Graw, C. (1999). Developing phonological awareness and word recognition skills: A two-year intervention with low-income, inner-city children. *Reading and Writing: An Interdisciplinary Journal, 11,* 239–273.

Booth, J. R., & Perfetti, C. A. (2002). Onset and rime structure influences naming but not early word identification in children and adults. *Scientific Studies of Reading, 6,* 1–23.

Bos, C. S., Mather, N., Silver-Pacuilla, H., & Narr, R. (2000). Learning to teach literacy skills collaboratively. *Teaching Exceptional Children, 32,* 38–45.

Bradley, L., & Bryant, P. (1983). Categorizing sounds and learning to read: A causal connection. *Nature, 301,* 419–421.

Brady, S., Fowler, A., Stone, B., & Winburg, N. (1994). Training phonological awareness: A study with inner-city kindergarten children. *Annals of Dyslexia, 44,* 26–59.

Byrne, B., & Fielding-Barnsley, R. (1993). Evaluation of a program to teach phonemic awareness to young children. *Journal of Educational Psychology, 83,* 451–455.

Carnine, D., Silbert, J., & Kame'enui, E. (1997). *Direct instruction reading* (3rd ed.). New York: Merrill.

Carroll, J. B., Davies, P., & Richman, B. (1971). *Word frequency book.* New York: American Heritage.

Center, Y., Wheldahl, K., Freeman, L., Outhred, L., & McNaught, M. (1995). An evaluatin of reading recovery. *Reading Research Quarterly, 30,* 240–263.

Chapman, J. W., Tunmer, W. E., & Prochnow, J. E. (2001). Does success in the reading recovery program depend on developing proficiency in phonological-processing skills?: A longitudinal study in a whole language instructional context. *Scientific Studies of Reading, 5,* 141–176.

Clay, M. M. (1985). *The early detection of reading difficulties.* Portsmouth, NH: Heinemann.

Cunningham, P. M. (1998). The multisyllabic word dilemma: Helping students build meaning, spell, and read "big" words. *Reading and Writing Quarterly, 14,* 189–219.

Darling-Hammond, L. (2000). Teacher quality and student achievement: A review of state policy evidence. *Education and Policy Analysis Archives, 8*(1), 1–35. Available online at *http://epaa.asu.edu/epaa/v8n1/*

Ehri, L. C., & McCormick, S. (1998). Phases of word learning: Implications for instruction with delayed and disabled readers. *Reading and Writing Quarterly: Overcoming Learning Difficulties, 14,* 135–163.

Ehri, L. C., & Robbins, C. (1992). Beginners need some decoding skill to read by analogy. *Reading Research Quarterly, 27,* 12–26.

Engelmann, S., & Bruner, E. (1988). *Reading mastery I/II Fast cycle.* Chicago: Macmillan/McGraw-Hill.

Engelmann, S., Johnson, G., Carnine, L., Meyer, L., Becker, W., & Eisele, J. (1988). *Corrective reading decoding strategies.* Chicago: Macmillan/McGraw-Hill.

Fayne, H. R., & Bryant, N. D. (1981). Relative effects of various word synthesis strategies on the phonics achievement of learning disabled youngsters. *Journal of Educational Psychology, 73,* 616–623.

Fleischer, L. S., Jenkins, J. R., & Pany, D. (1979). Effects on poor readers' comprehension of training in rapid decoding. *Reading Research Quarterly, 14,* 30–48.

Foorman, B., Francis, D., Fletcher, J., Schatschneider, C., & Mehta, P. (1998). The role of instruction in learning to read: Preventing reading failure in at-risk children. *Journal of Educational Psychology, 90,* 37–55.

Fuchs, D., Fuchs, L. S., Mathes, P. G., & Simmons, D. C. (1997). Peer-assisted learning strategies: Making classrooms more responsive to diversity. *American Educational Research Journal, 34,* 174–206.

Gaskins, I. W., Downer, M. A., Anderson, R. C., Cunningham, P. M., Gaskins, R. W., Schommer, M., et al. (1988). A metacognitive approach to phonics: Using what you know to decode what you don't know. *Remedial and Special Education, 9,* 36–41, 66.

Glass, G. G. (1973). *Teaching decoding as separate from reading.* Garden City, NY: Adelphi University Press.

Good, R., Vollmer, M., Katz, L., & Chowdhri, S. (1993). Treatment utility of the Kaufman Assessment Battery for Children: Effects of matching instruction and students processing strength. *School Psychology Review, 22,* 8–26.

Good, R. H., Simmons, D. C., & Kameenui, E. J. (2001). The importance and decision-making utility of a continuum of fluency-based indicators of foundational reading skills for third-grade high-stakes outcomes. *Scientific Studies in Reading, 5,* 257–288.

Goswami, U. (1986). Children's use of analogy in learning to read: A developmental study. *Journal of Experimental Child Psychology, 42,* 73–83.

Gough, P. B. (1983). Context, form, and interaction. In K. Rayner (Ed.), *Eye movements in reading: Perceptual and language processes* (pp. 203–211). San Diego: Academic Press.

Greenwood, C. R., & Delquadri, J. (1995). Classwide peer tutoring and the prevention of school failure. *Preventing School Failure, 39,* 21–26.

Hatcher, P. J., & Hulme, C. (1999). Phonemes, rhymes, and intelligence as predictors of children's responsiveness to remedial reading instruction: Evidence from a longitudinal intervention study. *Journal of Experimental Child Psychology, 72,* 130–154.

Herman, P. (1985). The effect of repeated readings on reading rate, speech pauses, and word recognition accuracy. *Reading Research Quarterly, 20,* 553–565.

Hiebert, E. (1994). Reading Recovery in the United States: What difference does it make to an age cohort? *Educational Researcher, 23,* 15–25.

Hook, P. E., Macaruso, P., & Jones, S. (2001). Efficacy of Fast ForWord training on facilitating acquisition of reading skills bv children with reading difficulties: A longitudinal study. *Annals of Dyslexia, 51,* 75–96.

Invernizzi, M., Rosemary, C., Juel, C., & Richards, H. (1997). At-risk readers and community volunteers: A 3-year perspective. *Scientific Studies of Reading, 1,* 277–300.

Iversen, S., & Tunmer, W. E. (1993). Phonological processing skills and the reading recovery program. *Journal of Educational Psychology, 85,* 112–126.

Jenkins, J. R., & O'Connor, R. E. (2002). Early identification and intervention for young children with reading disabilities. In R. Bradley, L. Danielson, & D. Hallahan (Eds.), Identification of learning disabilities (pp. 99–149). Mahwah, NJ: Erlbaum.

Juel, C. (1988). Learning to read and write: A longitudinal study of 54 children from first through fourth grades. *Journal of Educational Psychology, 80,* 437–447.

Juel, C., & Minden-Cupp, C. (2000). Learning to read words: Linguistic units and instructional strategies. *Reading Research Quarterly, 35,* 458–492.

Kavale, K. A., & Forness, S. R. (1987). Substance over style: Assessing the efficacy of modality testing and teaching. *Exceptional Children, 54,* 228–239.

LaBerge, D., & Samuels, J. (1974). Toward a theory of automatic information processing in reading. *Cognitive Psychology, 6,* 293–323.

Lenz, B. K., & Hughes, C. A. (1990). A word identification strategy for adolescents with learning disabilities. *Journal of Learning Disabilities, 23,* 149–163.

Levy, B., Abello, B., & Lysynchuk, L. (1997). Transfer from word training to reading in context: Gains in reading fluency and comprehension. *Learning Disabilities Quarterly, 20,* 173–188.

Lindamood, C., & Lindamood, P. (1984). *The ADD program: Auditory discrimination in depth.* Austin, TX: Pro-Ed. (Original work published in 1975)

Lloyd, J., Cullinan, D., Heins, E., & Epstein, M. (1980). Direct instruction: Effects on oral and written language comprehension. *Learning Disabilities Quarterly, 3,* 70–76.

Lovett, M., Lacerenza, L., Borden, S., Frijiters, J., Steinbach, K., & De Palma, M. (2000). Components of effective remediation for developmental reading disability: Combining phonological and strategy-based instruction to improve outcomes. *Journal of Educational Psychology, 92,* 263–283.

Lovett, M. W., & Steinbach, K. A. (1997). The effectiveness of remedial programs for reading disabled children of different ages: Does the benefit decrease for older children? *Learning Disabilities Quarterly, 20,* 189–210.

Lundberg, I., Frost, J., & Petersen, O. (1988). Effects of an extensive program for teaching phonological awareness in preschool children. *Reading Research Quarterly, 23,* 263–284.

McAnnally, K. I., Hansen, P. C., Cornelissen, P. L., &

Stein, J. F. (1997). Effect of time and frequency manipulation on syllable perception in developmental dyslexics. *Journal of Speech and Hearing Research, 40,* 912–924.

McCandliss, B., Beck, I., Sendak, R., & Perfetti, C. (2003). Focusing attention on decoding for children with poor reading skills: Design and preliminary tests of the Word Building intervention. *Scientific Studies of Reading, 7,* 75–104.

McCutchen, D., & Berninger, V. (1999). Those who know, teach well: Helping teachers master literacy-related subject matter knowledge. *Learning Disabilities Research and Practice, 14,* 215–226.

Mercer, C., & Campbell, K. (1998). *Great Leaps reading program.* Micanopy, FL: Diarmuid, Inc.

Meyer, M. S., & Felton, R. H. (1999). Repeated reading to enhance fluency: Old approaches and new directions. *Annals of Dyslexia, 49,* 283–306.

Mostow, J., & Aist, G. (1999). Giving help and praise in a reading tutor with imperfect listening—because automated speech recognition means never being able to say you're certain. *CALICO Journal, 16,* 407–424.

Nagy, W., Anderson, R. C., Schommer, M., Scott, J., & Stallman, A. (1989). Morphological families in the internal lexicon. *Reading Research Quarterly, 24,* 262–282.

Nation, K., Allen, R., & Hulme, C. (2001). The limitations of orthographic analogy in early reading development: Performance on the clue-word task depends on phonological priming and elementary decoding skill, not the use of orthographic analogy. *Journal of Experimental Child Psychology, 80,* 75–94.

National Reading Panel Report. (2000). *Teaching children to read: An evidence-based assessment of the scientific research literature on reading and its implications for reading instruction.* Washington, DC: National Institute of Child Health and Human Development.

O'Connor, R. E., Bell, K. M., Harty, K. R., Larkin, L. K., Sackor, S., & Zigmond, N. (2002). Teaching reading to poor readers in the intermediate grades: A comparison of text difficulty. *Journal of Educational Psychology, 94,* 474–485.

O'Connor, R. E., & Jenkins, J. R. (1999). The prediction of reading disabilities in kindergarten and first grade. *Scientific Studies of Reading, 3,* 159–197.

O'Connor, R. E., Jenkins, J. R., & Slocum, T. A. (1995). Transfer among phonological tasks in kindergarten: Essential instructional content. *Journal of Educational Psychology, 87,* 202–217.

O'Connor, R. E., Notari-Syverson, N., & Vadasy, P. (1996). Ladders to literacy: The effects of teacher-led phonological activities for kindergarten children with and without disabilities. *Exceptional Children, 63,* 117–130.

O'Connor, R. E., Notari-Syverson, N., & Vadasy, P. (1998a). First-grade effects of teacher-led phonological activities in kindergarten for children with mild disabilities: A follow-up study. *Learning Disabilities Research and Practice, 13,* 43–52.

O'Connor, R. E., Notari-Syverson, N., & Vadasy, P.

(1998b). *Ladders to literacy: A kindergarten activity book*. Baltimore: Brookes.

O'Connor, R. E., & Padeliadu, S. (2000). Blending versus whole word approaches in first grade remedial reading: Short-term and delayed effects on reading and spelling words. *Reading and Writing: An Interdisciplinary Journal, 13*, 159–182.

Perfetti, C., Beck, I., Bell, L., & Hughes, C. (1987). Phonemic knowledge and learning to read are reciprocal: A longitudinal study of first grade children. *Merrill–Palmer Quarterly, 33*, 283–319.

Perfetti, C. A., Goldman, S. R., & Hogaboam, T. W. (1979). Reading skill and the identification of words in discourse context. *Memory and Cognition, 7*, 273–282.

Pinnell, G. S., Pikulski, J. J., Wixson, K. K., Campbell, J. R., Gough, P. B., & Beatty, A. S. (1995). *Listening to children read aloud*. Washington, DC: Office of Educational Research and Improvement, U.S. Department of Education.

Polloway, E., Epstein, M., Polloway, C., Patton, J., & Ball, D. (1986). Corrective Reading program: An analysis of effectiveness with learning disabled and mentally retarded students. *Remedial and Special Education, 7*, 41–47.

Rack, J., Snowling, M., & Olson, R. (1992). The nonword reading deficit in developmental dyslexia: A review. *Reading Research Quarterly, 27*, 29–53.

Rashotte, C. A., MacPhee, K., & Torgesen, J. K. (2001). The effectiveness of a group reading instruction program with poor readers in multiple grades. *Learning Disabilities Quarterly, 24*, 119–134.

Raskind, M. H., & Higgins, E. L. (1999). Speaking to read: The effects of speech recognition technology on the reading and spelling performance of children with learning disabilities. *Annals of Dyslexia, 49*, 251–281.

Samuels, S. J. (1979). The method of repeated readings. *Reading Teacher, 32*, 403–408.

Schneider, W., Roth, E., & Ennemoser, M. (2000). Training phonological skills and letter knowledge in children at risk for dyslexia: A comparison of three kindergarten intervention programs. *Journal of Educational Psychology, 92*, 284–295.

Schumm, J., Moody, S. W., & Vaughn, S. (2000). Grouping for reading instruction: Does one size fit all? *Journal of Learning Disabilities, 33*, 477–488.

Shanahan, T., & Barr, R. (1995). Reading Recovery: An independent evaluation of the effects of an early instructional intervention for at-risk learners. *Reading Research Quarterly, 30*, 958–996.

Shankweiler, D., Lundquist, E., Katz, L., Steubing, K., Fletcher, J., Brady, S., et al. (1999). Comprehension and decoding: Patterns of association in children with reading difficulties. *Scientific Studies of Reading, 3*, 69–94.

Share, D. (1995). Phonological recoding and self-teaching: Sine qua non of reading acquisition. *Cognition, 55*, 151–218.

Share, D., Jorm, A., Maclean, R., & Matthews, R. (1984). Sources of individual differences in reading acquisition. *Journal of Educational Psychology, 76*, 1309–1324.

Spear-Swerling, L. & Sternberg, R. (1994). The road not taken: An integrative theoretical model of reading disability. *Journal of Learning Disabilities, 27*, 91–103.

Stahl, S. A. (1998). Teaching children with reading problems to decoded: Phonics and "not-phonics" instruction. *Reading and Writing Quarterly: Overcoming Learning Difficulties, 14*, 165–188.

Swanson, H. L., & Alexander, J. E. (2000). Cognitive processes as predictors of word recognition and reading comprehension in learning-disabled and skilled readers. *Journal of Educational Psychology, 89*, 128–158.

Tallal, P., Sainburg, R. L., Jernigan, T. (1991). The neuropathology of developmental dysphasia: Behavioral, morphological, and physiological evidence for a pervasive temporal processing disorder. *Reading and Writing: An Interdisciplinary Journal, 3*, 363–377.

Thurlow, M. L., Ysseldyke, J. E., Wotruba, J. W., & Algozzine, B. (1993). Instruction in special education classrooms under varying student–teacher ratios. *Elementary School Journal, 93*, 305–320.

Torgesen, J. K., Alexander, A. W., Wagner, R. K., Rashotte, C. A., Voeller, K. K., & Conway, T. (2001). Intensive remedial instruction for children with severe reading disabilities: Immediate and long-term outcomes from two instructional approaches. *Journal of Learning Disabilities, 34*, 33–58, 78.

Torgesen, J. K., & Mathes, P. (2000). *A basic guide to understanding, assessing, and teaching phonological awareness*. Austin, TX: PRO-ED.

Torgesen, J. K., Morgan, S., & Davis, C. (1992). Effects of two types of phonological awareness training on word learning in kindergarten. *Journal of Educational Psychology, 84*, 364–370.

Torgesen, J. K., Wagner, R. K., Rashotte, C. A., Rose, E., Lindamood, P., & Conway, T. (1999). Preventing reading failure in young children with phonological processing disabilities: Group and individual responses to instruction. *Journal of Educational Psychology, 91*, 579–593.

Treiman, R., & Zukowski, A. (1988). Units of reading and spelling. *Journal of Memory and Language, 27*, 466–477.

Tunmer, W. E., & Chapman, J. W. (1998). Language prediction skill, phonological recoding ability, and reading. In C. Hulme & R. M. Joshi (Eds.), *Reading and spelling: Development and disorders* (pp. 33–67). Mahwah, NJ: Erlbaum.

Vadasy, P. F., Jenkins, J. R., & Pool, K. (2000). Effects of a first-grade tutoring program in phonological and early reading skills. *Journal of Learning Disabilities, 33*, 579–590.

Vaughn, S., Moody, S. W., & Schumm, J. S. (1998). Broken promises: Reading instruction in the resource room. *Exceptional Children, 64*, 211–225.

Vellutino, F. R. (1991). Introduction to three studies on reading acquisition: Convergent findings on theoretical foundations of code-oriented versus whole-language approaches to reading instruction. *Journal of Educational Psychology, 83*, 437–443.

Vellutino, F. R., Scanlon, D. M. Sipay, E., Small, S. Pratt, A. Chen, R., et al. (1996). Cognitive profiles of difficult-to-remediate and readily remediated poor readers: Early intervention as a vehicle for distinguishing between cognitive and experiental deficits as basic causes of specific reading disability. *Journal of Educational Psychology, 88,* 601–638.

Warrick, N., Rubin, H., & Rowe-Walsh, S. (1993). Phoneme awareness in language-delayed children: Comparative studies and intervention. *Annals of Dyslexia, 43,* 153–173.

White, T., Sowell, J., & Yanagihara, A. (1989). Teaching elementary students to use word-part cues. *Reading Teacher, 42,* 302–308.

Williams, J. (1980). Teaching decoding with an emphasis on phoneme analysis and phoneme blending. *Journal of Educational Psychology, 72,* 1–15.

Wise, B. W., Ring, J., & Olson, R. K. (2000). Individual differences in gains from computer-assisted remedial reading. *Journal of Experimental Child Psychology, 77,* 198–235.

Wolf, M., & Bowers, P. (1999). The double deficit hypothesis for the developmental dyslexias. *Journal of Educational Psychology, 91,* 415–438.

Young, A. R., Bowers, P. G., & MacKinnon, G. E. (1996). Effects of prosodic modeling and repeated reading on poor readers' fluency and comprehension. *Applied Psycholinguistics, 17,* 59–84.

Reading Comprehension

23

Difficulties with Reading Comprehension

NELL K. DUKE
MICHAEL PRESSLEY
KATHERINE HILDEN

A fourth grader, David, walks into your office with parents in tow. After a few niceties, David's parents explain what has brought them to you. David just doesn't seem to understand a lot of what he reads. He finishes a book and can hardly tell you what it was about; he struggles to follow written directions or to glean needed information from his textbooks; he just always seems to be missing something when text is involved.

David is experiencing difficulties with reading comprehension. Two questions, Why? and What can we do about it?, are at the forefront of his and his parents' minds. In this chapter, we discuss theory and research that bears on those two questions: Why do some students experience substantial difficulties with reading comprehension? What can we do to improve their reading comprehension? Before doing so, however, we begin with a brief discussion of students experiencing substantial difficulties with reading comprehension and how many such students there might be. We then devote the bulk of the chapter to discussing many different causes of comprehension difficulties. We propose a series of questions one should ask when a student like David walks into

one's office: For example, is he experiencing difficulties with word recognition and fluency? Does he have difficulties with oral language? Finally, we propose areas for future research and development.

WHO ARE THE READERS WITH SUBSTANTIAL DIFFICULTIES WITH READING COMPREHENSION?

For many of us, each time we open the IRS's instructions for completing the 1040 form, we experience difficulties with reading comprehension. This chapter does not deal with occasional or periodic difficulties with comprehension, but rather with comprehension difficulties that are persistent and pervasive. The student not only has difficulty understanding texts he or she is reading regularly, evidenced in grade-level academic assessments, but also other texts in other situations.

This chapter is based on a relatively broad definition of comprehension—that it is the "the process of simultaneously extracting and constructing meaning through interaction and involvement with written language" (RAND Reading Study Group, 2002, p. 11)—and as such includes difficulties with both literal and inferential comprehension. The focus is not on the ability to critique text or to apply text knowledge to accomplish a task (e.g., completing that IRS form). These are vitally important areas for research and practice, and it is likely that many readers have substantial difficulties with them, even if they have strong literal and inferential comprehension (in part because of inattention to these matters in many classrooms, and in part for other reasons). Discussion of these important topics, however, is simply beyond the scope of this chapter.

For many, "reading disability" means that the affected individual has difficulties with reading words (Lyon, 1996). In contrast, the definition of "reading disability" in this chapter includes those with comprehension difficulties above the word level (i.e., comprehension difficulties that are not caused simply by inability to read words). The decision to take this tack respects a distinction long recognized (Cromer, 1970; Oaken, Wiener, & Cromer, 1971; Steiner, Wiener, & Cromer, 1971), although frequently ignored, in recent discussions of reading disabilities (RD) that have focused so heavily on word-recognition problems.

Many who emphasize word-recognition processes seem to believe that comprehension is an almost automatic by-product of reading the words. Their simple view of reading (Gough, Hoover, & Peterson, 1996) is that if readers become fluent at word recognition and simply listen to themselves read, they will comprehend what is being read; that is, reading comprehension is word recognition and understanding oral language, the latter being an ability that is very much a part of the human endowment. Since Chomsky (1957), many have seen language comprehension abilities as innate, developing as oral language develops.

If reading is simply learning to recognize words and to comprehend oral language, then a direct deduction from the Chomskian perspective is that learning to recognize words is the main bottleneck in learning to read. Word recognition, in turn, depends greatly on learning letter–sound associations, then learning how to blend sounds mapped by letters and letter combinations to produce words (Adams, 1990). If there is a second bottleneck in reading development, according to the simple view, it is becoming fluent in word recognition, because sounding out words demands much cognitive capacity. As readers become more fluent, capacity that was required to sound out words is freed up, permitting comprehension of the words being read (LaBerge & Samuels, 1974). According to the simple view of reading, any subsequent bottlenecks in learning to read can only be explained by difficulties with oral-language comprehension stemming from oral-language impairment. The simple view of reading is very much a bottom-up view that meaning is constructed from individual words more than from any other factor.

In cognitive psychology, this bottom-up view is in contrast to an alternative view that understanding of text is constructed from the top-down, which means that comprehension depends on more than just the words. It depends largely on the reader's prior knowledge and processing of the words read relative to that prior knowledge. The emphasis is on readers' attempts to make sense of the words based on what they already know about the world (Goodman, 1967; Smith, 1971). This rich, prior knowledge has a massive effect on reading. Thus, based on the title of a text alone, readers often have strong expectations about content, making predictions about what will be in a text based on their prior knowledge (Anderson & Pearson, 1984), predictions that often are very conscious (Pressley & Afflerbach, 1995). As they read through texts, readers confirm predictions, update them, ask themselves questions, construct images representing ideas in the text, and consciously attempt to summarize what they have read (Pressley & Afflerbach, 1995). Good readers are very, very active as they go from the beginning to the end of the text.

Part of the reader's knowledge base is knowing what to look for in text, based on well-developed understandings of the structure of texts. Thus, good readers know what to expect in informational texts (Meyer, Brandt, & Bluth, 1980). Competent, mature readers also know the grammar of stories, that is, the parts of a story. Good readers expect stories first to present information about setting and characters, followed by a sequence of actions that includes problems faced by the characters and their attempts to resolve those problems. Eventually, there will be a resolution and an ending to the story. These expectations guide good readers' understanding and memory of stories (Mandler & Johnson, 1977; Stein & Glenn, 1979).

Good readers also make inferences as they read, ones permitted by their background knowledge. The most salient inferences that readers make, at least with narrative texts, are causal ones. Good readers pay more attention to causal relations than to other relations implied in texts (Magliano, 1999; Trabasso, van den Broek, & Suh, 1989). When a good reader reads, "One day, Jimmy saw his friend Tom riding a new bike. He wanted to buy a bike," he or she infers a causal relation—the desire to buy the new bike was set off by seeing Tom on a new bike. Later in the story, more causal inferences occur in reaction to this sequence: "Jimmy spoke to his mother. Jimmy's mother refused to get a bike for him. He was very sad." The good reader infers that the mother's refusal resulted in Jimmy's sadness. And so it goes, with the good reader emerging from a story with an understanding of how the various causes and effects go together to form a story. Of course, readers sometimes make many other types of inferences to increase the coherence of their understanding of text (Pressley & Afflerbach, 1995), for example, inferring the referents of pronouns ("she" refers to Dorothy and not the Wizard), the instruments used by protagonists (inferring that a gun was shot), and states of mind (that a protagonist who screamed at another person was emotionally distraught). Good readers do not generate inferences willy-nilly but as they are needed to make sense of ideas in text, with the result that their inferences generally are reasonable ones (Singer, 1994; van den Broek, 1994).

That good readers make associations and inferences that are well matched to ideas in text is a critical point. A mature reader's prior knowledge is vast. Moreover, the prior knowledge that could be related even to a tiny bit of text is vast. For example, consider this bit of text: "One day, Jimmy saw his friend Tom riding a new bike." Most readers know many Jimmies and Toms. There are also many ways to ride that might come to mind, from conventional bike riding, to doing so with training wheels, to doing a headstand on the handlebars. Also, an infinite number of images of bikes might be conjured by most youngsters, from classic Schwinns, to contemporary mountain bikes, to *tour de France*–style racing bikes. New bikes might be imagined in blue, green, black, or red! If a reader were to allow activation of prior knowledge to fire off willy-nilly, his or her head would be filled with an overwhelming amount of information, most of which would be irrelevant to the gist of the reading. Good readers make far fewer inferences than they are capable of making (Graesser, Singer, & Trabasso, 1994). Good readers focus on the associations and inferences that make the gist more sensible by filling in the gaps in text that permit them to understand the big ideas in the text. Just the research on reader inferences makes clear that a great deal of reading comprehension is driven by top-down processes. Readers relate to and elaborate specific points in the text relative to their vast prior knowledge that can be related to the text.

In contrast to emphasizing bottom-up or top-down processing, a third position is that reading is both bottom-up and top-down, that fluent word recognition and understanding of individual words matter as much as top-down processes, with the processing of individual words interacting with the reader's prior knowledge as the reader goes through a text (Rumelhart, 1977; Stanovich, 1980). It is this third position that makes the most sense to us; hence, both bottom-up and top-down contributions to RD account for specific disabilities in comprehension. That said, given the general lack of attention to top-down contributions to RD, this chapter focuses more on top-down than on bottom-up processes. This is a defensible approach given that a great deal has been learned about top-down processes in RD, including how to overcome them.

In making the case, studies that we have referenced differ substantially with respect to the students served. For example, there is very little research on those who are known to be adequate readers at the sound, letter, and word levels, but who experience comprehension difficulties (although, as discussed later, it is clear that such students exist). Thus, in many of the studies referenced in what follows, comprehension difficulties often are only one of several literacy-related problems faced by the students in the investigations. This situation provides many challenges with respect to assessment and intervention. Yet for many students, comprehension is just one of their reading problems; hence, dealing with research on readers whose only problem is comprehension would not be as informative as dealing with research on a broader array of readers.

HOW MANY STUDENTS HAVE SUBSTANTIAL DIFFICULTIES WITH READING COMPREHENSION?

How many students have RD in the sense that they have substantial difficulties with comprehension? The answer, of course, depends on where one draws the line for substantial difficulties with reading comprehension. For example, in the National Assessment of Educational Progress (NAEP; Donahue, Finnegan, Lutkus, Allen, & Campbell, 2001), one might say that scoring below the proficient category indicates substantial difficulties with comprehension, or one might say that only those who read at the basic level have such difficulties. Regardless of where the line is drawn by the NAEP, it is difficult to know whether the score reflects comprehension problems due to word-recognition or higher order difficulties. Such an assessment provides little or no insight about the proportion of students whose main problem is comprehension rather than lower order (i.e., sound-, letter-, or word-level difficulties). With a norm-referenced as opposed to a criterion-referenced test of reading comprehension achievement such as the NAEP, one might draw the line at the 20th percentile or lower, or at or below the 10th percentile.

Again, however, a low-percentile score could reflect comprehension difficulties due to word-recognition problems, or it could represent difficulties with abstracting and constructing meaning from text that the student can decode. So, based on these kinds of test scores, it is difficult to say how many students experience substantial difficulties with reading comprehension per se, that is, with comprehension not caused by difficulties at the word level.

At least some students have difficulties with comprehension that are not caused by difficulties at the word level. Consider the memorable example of students who can recognize words but still fail to comprehend what they read—a subset of students with autism spectrum disorders, who exhibit what has been called "hyperlexia."[1] As the label implies, these students often have extraordinary ability to recognize words; yet their comprehension of what they read is very weak! In other serious conditions, such as hydrocephalus, students also show this profile (Barnes, Faulkner, & Dennis, 2001). Such students are dramatic proof that word recognition does not suffice to ensure comprehension. But what about students who do not suffer from dramatic conditions such as autism or hydrocephaly? In fact, there are case studies of students, otherwise unimpaired, who can read words but not comprehend the text they are reading. Such cases have been documented through careful assessment by capable clinicians with expertise in reading (Dewitz & Dewitz, 2003). In research with a much larger number of students, Paris, Carpenter, Paris, and Hamilton (2002) found overall low correlations between students' fluent word recognition and their responses to comprehension questions about texts read, with the correlation declining with advancing age during the elementary grades (i.e., word recognition and comprehension were more strongly related at the primary level than in the middle and later elementary grades). Shankweiler et al. (1999) found higher correlations in their sample of students ages 7.5–9.5, but still found that 13.6% of students (27.8% of impaired readers) had what they termed "discordant profiles"—relatively high word recognition with poor comprehension or vice versa. Nation and Snowling (1998a) observed only moderate associations between word recognition and comprehension in the reading of 7- to 10-year-old students. When these same investigators (Nation & Snowling, 1998b) carefully assessed the decoding and comprehension skills of 8- to 10-year-old students, they had no difficulty identifying students who could sound out words but experienced problems with comprehension (see Yuill & Oakhill, 1991, for a review of earlier work in which such students were identified).

Buly and Valencia (2002) provided an especially analytical study. They studied fourth graders who had performed poorly on the reading portion of the Washington State Test. To do so, they administered other assessments that provided information about components of reading, including word-recognition skills isolated from comprehension. Eighteen percent of these students were "automatic word callers"—students who had strong word identification and poor comprehension. Several of the individual cases showcased by Buly and Valencia (2002) indicate clearly that some students can read words and still not comprehend well:

Tim . . . was very good at identifying words and applying phonics to nonsense words, with scores averaging 9th grade on the Woodcock Johnson Revised Letter–Word Identification and Word Attack tests. On the narrative passage from the state assessment, his total accuracy was 98%, an indication of his ability to independently and easily read the 4th-grade passage. His reading rate was among the highest of the students in the study—a rate of 174 words per minute. Although his standard score on the receptive vocabulary measure placed him in the average range (105), his comprehension scores on the Qualitative Reading Inventory—II [QRI-II] (Leslie & Caldwell, 1995) were low. He scored at the 2nd-grade level on the narrative passage and at a 3rd-grade level on the expository passage. . . . He could produce written responses to prompts and express his ideas in writing. When compared with all students across the state, Tim scored in the top level of proficiency on the state writing assessment of content, organization, ideas, and conventions. . . . However, [for written responses following reading], he scored only 5% of the total

points possible on open-ended response items and 48% of the total points possible on multiple-choice items. . . . He struggles to generate written responses and answer questions after reading. . . .

Marja's pattern is similar—above the mean for word identification and fluency, below for meaning. . . . She is a second language learner. Nevertheless, her word identification skills are strong. . . . For example, on the 4th-grade Washington state test narrative passage, Marja read with 98% accuracy and 99% acceptability, clearly demonstrating her strong decoding abilities. Her accuracy rates were similarly strong for the QRI-II passages she read. . . . Marja . . . read substantially faster than most of the students in the sample, averaging 107 words per minute. However, her comprehension performance was poor. . . . Her score of 74 [on the vocabulary assessment] was almost two standard deviations below the mean for students her age. . . . She appears to have a limited knowledge of word meanings, even when words were read aloud to her and when she only had to point to her responses. . . . It can take several years for a student to learn the complexities of a second language, and to develop a degree of cognitive ability and vocabulary in the second language that might be needed to read and understand new material. . . . (pp. 229–230)

Buly and Valencia have provided compelling quantitative and qualitative data substantiating that there are students who can read words well but cannot comprehend.

Catts and Hogan (2002) identified a group of students they call "late-emerging poor readers." These students showed no difficulties with word recognition or fluency in grades 2 or 4, and they fell within the normal range of reading comprehension in grade 2. But by grade 4, these students had poor comprehension. These students with normal word recognition and late-emerging poor comprehension accounted for about 3% of all the fourth graders in the sample and 19.5% of students with reading difficulties in grade 4.

Although the proportions and populations in the various studies have varied, they substantiate that students with normal word recognition and poor comprehension do exist, with this pattern probably becoming more prevalent in the middle elementary grades. Moreover, this pattern is evidenced by a nontrivial number of students, probably about 10–20% of struggling readers, roughly 2–4% of all readers.

This section has focused on students who can read words but experience comprehension problems. However, the absolutely critical role of word recognition and decoding in reading comprehension should not be dismissed. Indeed, as explained in the following section, a major conclusion is that, particularly in the primary grades, word-recognition difficulty is the most common cause of reading comprehension problems. The large proportion of students who experience both word-recognition and comprehension difficulties should also not be ignored. About 23% of the students failing the Washington State reading assessment evidenced this pattern (Buly & Valencia, 2002). Nonetheless, it is critical to attend to the students for whom difficulties with word recognition and decoding are not a major problem or the cause of difficulties with reading comprehension. Hence, the emphasis in this chapter is on those students.

WHAT CAUSES SUBSTANTIAL DIFFICULTIES WITH COMPREHENSION AND WHAT CAN WE DO ABOUT THEM?

As we have already implied, theory and research suggest that there is no single explanation of reading comprehension disability. Thus, when David walks into your office, you would not immediately know what was causing his comprehension difficulties. There are a number of different possible causes, and there is a very real possibility that multiple causes are at work simultaneously. This section presents a series of questions you might ask about David, or any student, experiencing difficulties with comprehension.

Is the Student Struggling with Word Recognition and Decoding?

This is the first question to ask, for it is often the most obvious symptom manifested by a student with an RD of any sort. (Yes, a whole host of correlated language problems are of-

ten apparent with careful diagnosis [see Scarborough, 2001], but the symptom that most often gets the student noticed as being "in trouble" with respect to reading is that he or she cannot read the words on pages that his or her classmates can read.) That the student has a word-recognition problem also is very easy to diagnose, using many standardized and informal assessments, typically, just to formalize the informal observations that would have led to concern in the first place. If the answer is "yes," the student is experiencing difficulties at the word level, one treatment conclusion is certain: There should be attempts to teach the student how to recognize words. It is not within the scope of this chapter to discuss effective word-recognition intervention, and readers are referred to O'Connor and Bell (Chapter 22, this volume) for a discussion of this topic. In any case, as instruction in word recognition proceeds, it often makes sense to consider supplementary instruction aimed at other reading competencies.

Is the Student Struggling with Fluency?

Sounding out words requires a great deal of conscious attention by the reader, with conscious attention being very limited for everyone. (Recall from cognitive psychology that normal adults can only remember 7 ± 2 pieces of information at a time [Miller, 1956]!) During reading, both word recognition and comprehension of words demand such conscious attention. The more that word recognition consumes consciousness, the less there is for comprehension (LaBerge & Samuels, 1974). As every primary grade teacher knows, struggling young readers manage to sound out the words, but it is so difficult that they do not notice at all what the words mean; hence, they recall little.

Again, Buly and Valencia's (2002) analysis was revealing with respect to students who lack fluency in word recognition. They found that 17% of the students who did poorly in the Washington State assessment had fluency as their principal difficulty, with concomitant problems in comprehension. One of their case study dysfluent students, Joey, could only read 70 words per minute in fourth-grade material, although he read the words correctly. José, another dysfluent reader, could only read 63 words per minute in a fourth-grade text. These rates are much slower than those of other fourth-grade readers.

There is a growing body of work on approaches to increasing reading fluency. Approaches that thus far appear to be effective include repeated reading, cross-age reading (i.e., having the struggling reader read to a younger student), partner reading, neurological impress (a form of echo reading), reading while listening, and oral recitation methods (Kuhn & Stahl, 2003; National Reading Panel, 2000). Most likely to be effective would be such a guided reading intervention by a practitioner who knows the tricks of the trade to motivate students to work hard during such sessions and to read additionally on their own (Kuhn, 2003; Kuhn & Stahl, 2003; Stahl, 2003), for instance, by involving students in tracking their progress and reading with peers. Also important is recognizing that fluency involves both automatic reading of individual words and reading with expression (i.e., prosody), and that such reading with expression and appropriate intonation both facilitates and reflects comprehension of what is being read (Kuhn & Stahl, 2003).

Does the Student Have Poor Short-Term or Working Memory?

Although, on average, normally functioning adults can hold 7 ± 2 pieces of information in mind at one time (Miller, 1956), not everyone can; plenty of evidence indicates that many students with RD seem to have less short-term memory (or working memory) capacity than same-age normally achieving readers (Swanson & Siegel, 2001). "Seem" is the appropriate word, because when a person has language disabilities, all language functioning consumes a great deal of capacity, which can make it seem that the learner has less capacity than agemates. There is dispute about what it means when a student with RD performs poorly on a verbal short-term memory task (Cornoldi, Corretti, & De Beni, 2001; Daneman, 2001; Hambrick, Wilhelm, & Engle, 2001; Torgesen, 2001; Vellutino, 2001; Wolters, 2001).

The suspicion that the underlying short-term capacity of students with RD might not be the culprit—but that inefficient language functioning is the problem—is supported when students with RD perform normally on short-term memory tasks that do not require verbal processing, but more poorly than agemates when the short-term memory task requires verbal processing (Nation, Adams, Bowyer-Crane, & Snowling, 1999).

If, in fact, students with RD do have less fundamental capacity for short-term memory (i.e., less of the neurological substrate that supports short-term processing), then it is challenging to imagine an instructional intervention that might improve the situation. More positively, researchers such as Nation et al. (1999) may be correct in their assumption that often at least part of what seems like a short-term memory problem is a problem in language functioning. If that is the case, then improving language functioning and efficiency might improve the situation. Other problems of oral-language functioning are discussed in the next section.

Does the Student Have Difficulties with Oral Language?

Although clearly not the same, oral-language and language functioning during reading have many parallels (Kucer, 2001). Therefore, it should not be surprising that difficulties in oral language would be associated with difficulties in written-language functioning. For a quarter of a century, it has been very clear that reading disabilities are often accompanied by other verbal disabilities that may be implicated causally with respect to the disability (Vellutino, 1979). In fact, the case for language problems during the preschool years predicting reading difficulties in the elementary years is simply overwhelming (Scarborough, 2001). Even so, there is a need for more information about the connection between early language difficulties and comprehension, despite some well-done and well-respected analyses linking speech and language disorders to reading comprehension problems (Catts, 1993; Catts, Fey, Tomblin, & Zhang, 2002; Catts, Fey, Zhang, &

Tomblin, 1999; Kamhi & Catts, 2002; Nation, 2001).

Still needed at this point, however, are more investigations of whether and when treating language disorders positively impacts reading comprehension. Without a doubt, the best-substantiated positive, language treatment–reading comprehension effect is that increasing phonemic awareness instruction has a small, positive effect on reading comprehension (National Reading Panel, 2000). If phonics instruction is considered treatment of a specific language disability (i.e., inability to map and blend letter–sound relationships), then the positive effect of phonics instruction on reading comprehension should probably be counted in the total (National Reading Panel, 2000). Unfortunately, the language impairments associated with risk for reading comprehension difficulties go well beyond phonological problems, including nearly all aspects of language functioning: morphology, syntax, semantics, and pragmatics (if one includes in pragmatics narrative discourse skills) (Kamhi & Catts, 2002; Menyuk & Chesnick, 1997; Roth, Speece, Cooper, & De La Paz, 1996).

Fortunately, there have been great advances in treating many language difficulties beginning in the preschool years (Fey, Windsor, & Warren, 1995). We join other researchers (e.g., Catts et al., 1999) in calling for longitudinal, experimental research evaluating the impact of a broad band of language interventions on subsequent reading comprehension.[2]

In the meantime, certainly, an assessment of a student with comprehension problems should include broadband assessment of oral-language skills, with many well-validated potential assessments to do so (Carlisle, 1989; Plake, Impara, Pale, & Spies, 2003). If there are clinically significant problems (i.e., that seem to impair the student's communication abilities), it makes sense to suggest that the language problems be treated using validated methods (Fey et al., 1995). Even if the language intervention does not impact reading, improving oral communication is a good thing to do in any case. As one treats a student for language difficulties, it makes sense to be attentive to whether there are concomitant improvements in reading comprehension.

Is the Student an English-Language Learner?

English-language learners (ELLs) are disproportionately likely to struggle with reading comprehension, including performance on standardized assessments (Garcia, 1991). There are a variety of possible explanations for apparent comprehension problems in such students. For example, sometimes student difficulties in responding orally, especially difficulties in pronunciation, cause teachers to underestimate a non-native speaker's comprehension (Moll & Diaz, 1985). Socioeconomic factors—that ELLs are disproportionately likely to be of low socioeconomic status (SES)—are probably relevant (Au, 2002). For example, low-SES students often receive lower quality instruction than more socioeconomically advantaged students (Au, 2002; Garcia, 2000). Once the student has learned to speak English, English proficiency often is not at the level of classmates, which can cause difficulties in understanding many of the subtleties of English that are used by authors (August & Hakuta, 1997).

What should an educator do when confronted with an ELL student who is struggling to understand text? There is one certain conclusion in the literature: It is indefensible to make much of a non-English speaker's scores on standardized tests of comprehension, if the tests were administered in English. Such scores simply are not interpretable (American Educational Research Association, 1999; Garcia, 1991). Indeed, given these problems of interpretation, one possibility that makes a lot of sense is to assess the student's competence to read in her or his first language; that is, if the student has been taught to read in the first language (Durgunoglu, 2002). It seems a safe assumption that if the student can comprehend when reading in the first language, then the problems of comprehension in the second language reflect unfamiliarity with the language rather than a fundamental inability to understand what is read.

Just as challenging as assessment is coming up with an intervention plan based on research evidence. Not much research exists on improving reading in second-language students, and very little on improving comprehension (Fitzgerald, 1995a, 1995b; Garcia, 2000; Weber, 1991). For example, a little bit of research evidence supports doing all possible to increase the student's oral-language skills in the second language (in this case, English), because learning to speak the second language sometimes positively impacts reading in the second language (e.g., Peregoy & Boyle, 1991; Verhoeven, 1990). What cannot be missed in reading this literature, however, is the emerging associations between elements of instruction generally associated with quality instruction in contemporary American schools and success in learning to read by ELL students. A strong focus on reading in English in primary grades instruction seems to promote learning to read in English (Fitzgerald, 1995b). The emphasis there is on reading, rather than on English, because there is evidence that learning to read in a first language substantially supports learning to read in a second (Garcia, 2000). As is the case with native-English speakers, there are clear associations between reading competence and use of comprehension strategies, such as predicting, seeking clarification when confused, questioning, and summarization (Jiménez, Garcia, & Pearson, 1996), with researchers sometimes reporting success in teaching ELL students to use such comprehension strategies as they read in their second language (Fung, Wilkinson, & Moore, 2003; Swicegood, 1990). It probably helps if the teacher is sensitive to when the second-language student is not comprehending, and adjusts instruction and demands to overcome confusion (Long, 2002). Second-language students benefit from interactive book reading in which adults engage the students in discussions about the story being read (Kim & Hall, 2002; Valdez-Menchaca & Whitehurst, 1992). Small-group, supplemental tutoring in reading that focuses on both word-level and comprehension skills improves the reading comprehension of ELL students in the primary grades (Linan-Thompson & Hickman-Davis, 2002; Linan-Thompson,

Vaughn, Hickman-Davis, & Kouzekanani, 2003). Flooding classrooms with books that ELL students can read increases comprehension (Koskinen et al., 2000). In short, an ELL student who is struggling with comprehension should be provided with an excellent, supportive, educational environment, where reading is taught by balancing the many elements of effective beginning reading instruction (Fitzgerald & Noblit, 2000; Pressley, 2002). The elements of instruction that work to improve native speakers' comprehension also seem to work with ELL students.

Does the Student Speak African American English?

African American students are also disproportionately likely to have difficulties with comprehension, again, at least as measured by standardized assessments (Donahue et al., 2001). As with ELL students, SES and SES-associated instructional factors play a role, but so might language. Most African American students use African American English (AAE), which varies from Standard American English (SAE) with respect to phonology, morphology, syntax, and semantics (Craig & Washington, Chapter 11, this volume). Such language differences may impact reading of SAE (Craig & Washington, Chapter 11, this volume; Labov, Baker, Bullock, Ross, & Brown, 1998; Wheldall & Joseph, 1985–1986). That said, studies investigating a link between use of AAE and reading comprehension specifically have not found one. This may be due to shortcomings in those studies (see discussion in Craig & Washington, Chapter 11, this volume), or because there really is no link.

Fortunately, whether or not there is any link between AAE use and increased likelihood of comprehension difficulties, the evidence is quite clear that the intense, balanced approach (i.e., balancing of skills instruction and more holistic reading and writing experiences) that works very well in general to promote literacy (Pressley, Allington, Wharton-McDonald, Block, & Morrow, 2001) also works very well for African American students who speak AAE (Craig & Washington, Chapter 11, this volume), as well as for students living in poverty (Knapp & Associates, 1995; Ladson-Billings, 1994). With respect to dialect in particular, it is possible and important to add fluency in SAE without subtracting AAE (Delpit, 1986; Perry & Delpit, 1998). Thus, for a student who may be having comprehension difficulties in part because of unfamiliarity with SAE, high-quality instruction that fosters Standard English is appropriate.

Does the Student Struggle with Particulars of Written Language?

As noted earlier, there are many parallels between oral and written language. However, they also differ in significant ways (Kucer, 2001). Oral language tends to be a more here-and-now language, more immediate, more person-to-person, and less permanent than written language. The receiver generally has more control over the processing of written text than of oral language. The reader can reread; the listener can recall what is said but typically cannot replay it. Written text is often more linear and carefully planned; whereas oral communication more often tends to be interactive, with the speaker and listener roles alternating, with planning usually in reaction to what has just been said and in anticipation of what to say next. Normally, getting the most out of an oral-language presentation requires intense attention and even explicit attempts to remember, whereas the opportunity to reread and review written text may permit more relaxed processing, because something missed the first time can be revisited.

Due in part to these pragmatic differences, the type of language typically used in speaking differs substantially from the type of language typically used in writing. Exceptions include spoken language that is more like written language, such as when reading aloud an academic paper, and written language that is more like spoken language, such as when dialogue is depicted in written text. Written-like language—what linguists call the "written language register"—differs lexically, syntactically, and in other respects from language in the oral register (Chafe & Danielewicz, 1986). Consider the following

language samples from a kindergartner who had been read to a great deal from birth. In the first sample, the child was asked to tell about her last birthday party; in the second sample, she was asked to pretend to read a wordless picture book:

Telling about a birthday party: Well . . . I had ten guests, . . . I don't remember all who they were, . . . but I remember one was Ola, . . . one was Sara and Kathy, . . . 'cause they are sisters. Older brother, . . . and . . . he also came, . . . he was tall, . . . and of course I had to invite my brother, . . . 'cause of course he was . . . right there in the house. A-n-d . . . let's see, . . . Ola, . . . and . . .

Pretending to read a wordless picture book: There once . . . was a brave knight, . . . and a beautiful lady. They went . . . on a trip . . . a dangerous trip. . . . They saw a castle. In the distance. They went to it. A mean . . . mean . . . mean hunter, . . . was following them, . . . through the bushes. At the entrance . . . of the little castle. As he creeped out of the bushes, . . . he thought what to do. As the drawbridge was opened, . . . they could easily get in, . . . and the question was. . . . how to trick them. . . . (Purcell-Gates, 1988, pp. 157–158)

There are marked differences between the language used in these two contexts. For example, in the wordless picture book sample (written register), the child uses pronominal adjectives, which are relatively rare in the oral register. She uses words, such as *drawbridge,* that are quite uncommon in speech (other than read aloud), and constructions, such as "there once was a brave knight," that are distinctly written in nature.

It seems reasonable to think that students who are not familiar with written-register language may experience reading, including comprehension, difficulties as a result (Purcell-Gates, 1995). That said, this is not a student characteristic that is likely to appear in isolation. For example, students who are unfamiliar with the written-language register may also be unfamiliar with the workings of print at the sound–letter level, which is also linked to comprehension difficulties. Specific features of the written-language register may also interact with other student difficulties. For example, students who have difficulties with syntactic processing may be especially stymied by the stacking of prepositional phrases (e.g., "through the bushes"; "At the entrance ... of the little castle") that is typical of the written register. Thus, in multiple ways, specific characteristics of written language may be contributing to a student's reading difficulties.

Just as there are differences *between* oral- and written-language registers, there are differences *among* oral- and written-language registers (Chafe & Danielewicz, 1986). For example, the way one speaks when talking casually with friends likely differs a great deal from the way one speaks in an academic seminar with colleagues. Similarly, the language of different genres of written text differs in substantial ways. Consider again the student's earlier reading of the wordless picture book. You would probably guess that the book would be classified as a fairy tale, and that this is by no means the first fairy tale book the student has encountered. The opening ("there once was a brave knight ..."), characters (brave knight, beautiful lady, mean hunter), setting (castle), problem ("and the question was ... how to trick them ...") are all characteristic of fictional narrative, in particular, fairy tale narrative, genres (Berman & Slobin, 1994). The language of other genres is decidedly different. Informational texts, for example, typically contain generic noun constructions and timeless verb constructions, as in "Princesses live in castles," as compared with narrative texts which often have specific nouns and timed verbs, as in "Princess Atalanta lived in a castle" (Duke & Kays, 1998).

Sometimes comprehension difficulties are linked to or are more prevalent in particular genres. For example, some students have more difficulty with persuasive and informational text than with narrative text (Hidi & Hildyard, 1983; Langer, 1985). Although it is difficult to know whether these difficulties are due to inherent differences in the level of challenge of each genre, or relative lack of exposure to or instruction with these genres (Duke, 2000; Kamberelis, 1998), genre is definitely a factor to consider in comprehension difficulties. This position is buttressed by work on text structure, one aspect of genre, documenting both that greater knowledge of text structure separates good from poor readers and that instruction in text structure improves comprehension (Dickson, Simmons, & Kameenui, 1998). Although work on other aspects of genre is at earlier stages (Purcell-Gates & Duke, 2001), it, too, may suggest the importance of considering genre knowledge in addressing comprehension difficulties.

A clear implication of work on both written-register and genre knowledge is that a student's reading comprehension must be assessed with multiple texts. Does the student have greater difficulty comprehending texts that are more written-like? Does the student have greater difficulty comprehending texts of certain genres? Indeed, many reading diagnosticians recommend assessing comprehension of different genres separately (Lipson & Wixson, 2002), and some assessment tools, such as many informal reading inventories, are designed to do that. Another clear implication is that extensive exposure to written text of a variety of genres, in particular those genres we want students to learn to comprehend, is critical (Duke, 2000; Purcell-Gates, McIntyre, & Freppon, 1995). Employing a variety of strategies to help students make sense of these texts, including modeling effective comprehension processes, explicitly teaching comprehension strategies, and perhaps explicitly teaching about the characteristics of written language and genres themselves is also in order.

Does the Student Think Actively the Way That Good Readers Think?

Comprehension Strategies

As discussed earlier in this chapter, good readers are very active as they read, using comprehension strategies from the beginning to the end of a text (predicting, questioning, imagining, clarifying, summarizing, making inferences, etc.). One of the most consistent findings in the instructional literature is that teaching students to use such comprehension strategies, in fact, improves their understanding and memory of text (Duke & Pearson, 2002; National Reading Panel, 2000; Pearson & Dole, 1987; Pressley, Johnson, Symons, McGoldrick, & Kurita, 1989); that is, elementary school students who do not necessarily use such comprehension strategies on their own, in any case, do so more following instruction. Indeed, a hallmark of poor comprehension is failure to produce the inferences when reading that other students produce, inferences that are essential to understanding text (Yuill & Oakhill, 1991).

One of the most certain conclusions that emerges from the literature on comprehension strategies instruction (Pressley, 2000) is that long-term teaching of a small repertoire of comprehension strategies (i.e., the ones good readers use—for example, prediction, questioning, imagining, clarifying, and summarizing), beginning with teacher explanations and modeling with gradual release of responsibility to the student (Pearson & Gallagher, 1983; Roehler & Duffy, 1984), is very effective in promoting students' reading comprehension. This conclusion holds for students with learning disabilities (LD) (Gersten, Fuchs, Williams, & Baker, 2001) as well as for students without LD (Pressley, El-Dinary, et al., 1992). This model of instruction is fundamentally used in one of the most widely disseminated comprehension strategies approaches employed with students with LD, the Strategic Instruction Model, developed by Donald Deshler, Jean Schumaker, and their colleagues at the University of Kansas Center for Research on Learning (Tralli, Colombo, Deshler, & Schumaker, 1996). For further discussion, see Ehren, Deshler & Lenz (Chapter 32, this volume).

Prior Knowledge

That active use of comprehension strategies improves comprehension should not undermine the point that conceptual knowledge matters very much in comprehension. What a reader gets out of a text depends on the prior knowledge the reader brings to the text, a point made especially clear by the research conducted at the University of Illinois Center for the Study of Reading during the 1970s and 1980s (Anderson & Pearson, 1984). When good readers make inferences as they read, as described earlier in this

chapter, such inferences almost always are driven by the reader's prior knowledge. And such inferences are often the result of deliberate strategic efforts that filter the ideas of text through the reader's prior knowledge. So predictions are really predictive inferences; they are made based on what the reader already knows about the topic of the text (e.g., "I bet this story about Mantle and Maris will talk a lot about their race for the home run record in 1961"). The images constructed by the reader are often based on prior knowledge, so that a reader experiencing Tolkien's *Hobbit* for the first time may construct very different images if he or she has seen the motion picture *Lord of the Rings*, and make very different imaginal inferences on the basis of the knowledge gained from the film (e.g., imagining Gandalf and Bilbo's interactions differently).

Thus, not having much prior conceptual knowledge that can be related to a text can be a problem that impairs comprehension (Anderson & Pearson, 1984). An obvious solution, when this is the case, is to do all possible to develop the student's conceptual knowledge. Suggestions include encouraging the student to read worthwhile books and watch worthwhile television, as well as encouraging parents to increase, as much as possible, experiences that can expand the student's understanding of the ideas that literate people know. Reading to students, taking them to libraries and museums, and talking with them about the news are all valuable in this regard.

Sometimes the problem is not that students do not have prior knowledge. They simply fail to relate it to the text being read. One way to encourage students to relate what they know already to the content they are reading is to encourage them to ask *why*-questions as they read (Pressley, Wood, et al., 1992). Why would ghosts come to visit Scrooge? Why does Scrooge say, "Humbug?" Why would Tiny Tim say, "God bless us, everyone!" When readers think about why the events and relationships specified in text are the way they are, they orient to knowledge related to the content of the text (Martin & Pressley, 1991). That *why*-questioning has large impact when students have prior knowledge they can relate to a text makes clear that students often fail to think about what is in text relative to information they already possess (Pressley, Wood, et al., 1992). That such *why*-questioning has small impact when students do not possess prior knowledge makes very clear that *why*-questioning effects depend on students' prior knowledge about the topic of the text (Woloshyn, Paivio, & Pressley, 1994; Woloshyn, Pressley, & Schneider, 1992). Teaching students with comprehension problems to ask themselves why the ideas in a text make sense has great potential for improving their comprehension dramatically.

Sometimes the problem is that the student uses prior knowledge that is tangential at best to the major messages of the text. For example, Williams (1993) asked junior high school students to read a story divided into three sections. After completing each section, the students summarized what was in the text. After reading the first two sections, they predicted what was in the next section. After reading the third section of the text, they stated the theme of the story. Normally achieving junior high readers recalled more of the story than did junior high students with LD. There was a trend toward the normal readers making more reasonable predictions than were made by the students with LD. The normally achieving readers were much more likely than the students with LD to state correctly the overall theme of the story. In fact, the students with LD distinguished themselves by offering predictions, summaries, or themes that were very much off the mark, often reflecting some tangential idea in the story that related to their own prior knowledge. More positively, Williams and her colleagues (Wilder & Williams, 2001; Williams, 1998; Williams, Brown, Silverstein, & deCani, 1994) have been able to demonstrate that students with LD can learn to abstract the theme if they are given careful and thorough instruction to make certain the knowledge they relate is centrally relevant to the story.

Is the Student Engaged in Reading?

Better readers read more and struggling comprehenders likely read less (National Reading Panel, 2000; Stanovich & Cunningham, 1992; Stanovich & West, 1989). Although such a correlational outcome cannot be interpreted causally with certainty, that lack of practice contributes to comprehension difficulties and practice reading contributes to improved comprehension are credible hypotheses. After all, repeated reading is implicated in the transition from reading words by sounding them out to reading them with automaticity (LaBerge & Samuels, 1974). Reading texts is a principle means of acquiring new vocabulary (Sternberg, 1987), and growth of vocabulary is an important determinant of text comprehension (National Reading Panel, 2000). Reading worthwhile texts can go far in building worthwhile world knowledge that can mediate comprehension of future reading (Anderson & Pearson, 1984). If practicing reading does not make for perfect reading, it certainly should make for better comprehension.

The only way that a student is going to read a great deal is if he or she decides to do so. Motivation to read is a key, but sadly, motivation to read declines as students progress through school, with the decline beginning during the primary grades (McKenna, Kear, & Ellsworth, 1995). What can be done to encourage more reading? There are a variety of approaches (Pressley et al., 2003). Simply providing students with more access to books and other reading materials through home reading programs, summer reading programs, and in-school reading programs seems to increase the amount of reading students do (Neuman, Celano, Greco, & Shue, 2001). Programs that offer external rewards for reading, such as pizza or prizes, have also been shown in some studies be effective (Gambrell, 1996). Particular teacher behaviors also foster development of internal motivation to read. One approach specifically designed to increase students' internal motivation to read—their engagement with reading—is Concept-Oriented Reading Instruction (CORI; Guthrie & McCann, 1997). In this approach, students read interesting, often self-selected, texts in science for the purpose of finding out things about the world around them. Their desire or need to find out is often driven by specific goals, such as answering questions they have raised or preparing a group presentation. Students involved in CORI develop higher intrinsic motivation and are more likely to apply comprehension strategies when they read, illustrating the link between motivation and comprehension (Guthrie et al., 1996).

Other Questions

Although the questions formulated to this point probably relate to the most common causes of or contributors to substantial difficulties with reading comprehension, this account is not exhaustive. For example, one study indicates that eye movement therapy can improve comprehension in some students with RD (Solan, Larson, Shelley-Tremblay, Ficarra, & Silverman, 2001), suggesting that faulty eye movement may be a cause of some students' difficulties. There is also some indication that self-regulatory or metacognitive issues beyond those addressed earlier may play a role for some learners (O'Shea & O'Shea, 1994). The good diagnostician is on the lookout for any possible cause or contributor to comprehension difficulty.

DIRECTIONS FOR FUTURE RESEARCH

It is striking how little research exists on the comprehension of students with RD. Much work needs to be done simply to determine what proportion of students struggle substantially with comprehension. As implied in the previous section, we suspect that poor comprehension has multiple causes, at least some of the time. For example, a student with word-recognition problems often will not use comprehension strategies and may have underdeveloped vocabulary and world knowledge. There is also much work ahead in the direction of Buly and Valencia's (2002) contribution, identifying the various ways that reading comprehension can go awry. Perhaps especially useful will be studies of students struggling with comprehension despite strength in word recognition and decoding. We suspect that this is a widespread,

though currently underrecognized phenomenon in research, policy, and practice.

The field would benefit from more research that examines brain activity during comprehension. Already, a number of neuroimaging studies have examined comprehension of text with one or a few sentences (Fiez, 2002). For example, Grossman et al. (2002) compared brain activity of seniors with good and poor sentence comprehension, finding substantially differing levels of activation. It may soon be possible to examine meaningfully reading of larger units of text as well. Research of this kind may help us understand more about causes of comprehension difficulties and effects of intervention.

A very different kind of research—on how highly effective teachers of comprehension do their work—also seems to be a promising direction for future work. Already, some research of this kind has examined effective teaching of reading–language arts in general (Bogner, Raphael, & Pressley, 2002; Dolezal, Welsh, Pressley, & Vincent, 2003; Morrow, Tracey, Woo, & Pressley, 1999; Pressley, Allington, Wharton-McDonald, Block, & Morrow, 2001; Pressley, Wharton-McDonald, Mistretta-Hampston, & Echevaria, 1998; Wharton-McDonald, Pressley, & Hampston, 1998). Although there also have been studies of teachers who teach comprehension strategies well (Pressley, El-Dinary, et al., 1992), we look forward to studies that analyze more completely the work of teachers who succeed in getting most of their students to be good comprehenders and, in particular, succeed in teaching initially poor comprehenders how to read with high comprehension. We suspect that such teachers succeed by articulating a number of instructional components, from attention to students' sound-, letter-, and word-level processing; vocabulary and strategies instruction; encouragement of massive reading; and motivating students to read and write whenever there is the opportunity.

SUMMARY

When a student does not comprehend text, there are a number of potential explanations. Often, the first possibility that comes to mind to reading professionals is that the student is still struggling with decoding, either not knowing how to do it well, or not making progress to the point of fluent word recognition. Alternatively, it may be that students' lack of oral-language skills interferes with their understanding of text; increasing evidence indicates that oral-language problems are associated with reading difficulties. A special case of comprehension not occurring because of language issues occurs with ELL students who do not know English. A related special case is the student whose dialect is mismatched to conventional written English, although there is dispute about the overall impact, if any, of AAE, at least, on comprehending written English texts. Finally, one of the best-supported conclusions in the reading literature is that reading comprehension depends greatly on students' thinking actively as they read—making predictions, asking questions, constructing images representing text, seeking clarifications when confused, summarizing, and so on. These comprehension strategies depend greatly on the students' having prior knowledge that can be related to ideas in text, for example, permitting credible predictive images and interpretive summaries. Finally, for both word-recognition and higher order comprehension skills to be honed, they must be practiced, which means that it is essential that students read extensively. A very reasonable hypothesis is that failing to read extensively undermines the development of comprehension skills.

Reading professionals face a real challenge in determining just what it is about a particular student that is undermining comprehension; that is, at present, there is no standard assessment regimen. Assessment should be thorough, in order to assess as many reading weaknesses and strengths as possible. Knowing what the student can and cannot do is essential in deciding on appropriate instruction. Be ready to accept the possibility that students who cannot comprehend have a variety of problems. Perhaps they are still struggling to sound out words or are not reading enough to develop fluency at the word level, not realizing that reading of a whole text is anything more than

reading the words, and lacking the vocabulary and other world knowledge to make sense of many of the ideas encountered in materials that are routinely read in the middle and upper elementary grades. Working on phonics skills is just a first step in a journey that will take years to complete. Many who have studied phonics seem to believe that facility in phonics is *the* gatekeeper to competency in reading comprehension (Rayner, Foorman, Perfetti, Pesetsky, & Seidenberg, 2001, 2002). We believe it is just one such competency.

As should be obvious at this point, our view is that experience matters, and that comprehension can be improved greatly by providing students with experiences that increase their word-recognition competencies, vocabulary, world knowledge, and comprehension skills. Although the particular emphasis placed on one or another of these areas should depend on the reader and the cause or causes of his or her difficulties, there is no one-to-one mapping; that is, comprehension difficulties with different underlying causes will often benefit from the same or similar instruction, such as the kinds of instruction we have referenced throughout this chapter.

The recommendations that we have made here are evidence-based, informed by decades of research of many different kinds, including experimental and quasi-experimental studies. Despite this rich research base, much, much more work needs to be done, and, as it is carried out, we expect new insights about comprehension processes and how to promote comprehension abilities in classrooms.

ACKNOWLEDGMENT

We wish to thank Nancy DeFrance for her assistance with this chapter.

NOTES

1. The term "hyperlexia" has been used in a variety of ways. Some researchers write of hyperlexia as occurring in students with autism spectrum disorders (Wahlberg, 2001); others use the term to refer to a broader population

of students with substantial cognitive, language, and social deficits combined with extraordinary word recognition (Nation, 1999; Snowling & Frith, 1986); still others seem to apply the term to any student with relative strength in word recognition and relative weakness in listening or reading comprehension (Catts, Fey, Tomblin, & Zhang, 2002; Gough & Tunmer, 1986). To avoid confusion, we do not use the term in the remainder of this chapter.

2. There may be considerable research attention in the future to the issue of whether improving language functioning via intervention impacts reading comprehension, especially interventions targeting listening comprehension. Recall the simple view of reading. According to that perspective, all difficulties in reading comprehension must stem from either difficulties with word recognition and/or oral language, in particular, listening comprehension (Gough & Tunmer, 1986). This is because in this view, reading is simply a process of decoding print, then listening to what has been said. Proponents of the simple view point to the impacts of phonemic awareness and phonics interventions on comprehension as supportive of their perspective (Gough et al., 1996). Their perspective would be much more completely informed if there were also experimental demonstrations that improvement of listening comprehension skills in students improves reading comprehension. If their perspective is correct, that should occur, with reading comprehension improvement in struggling readers most apparent when such students receive potent phonemic awareness, phonics, and listening-comprehension interventions.

REFERENCES

Adams, M. J. (1990). *Beginning to read.* Cambridge MA: Harvard University Press.

American Educational Research Association. (1999). *The standards for educational and psychological testing.* Washington DC: American Educational Research Association.

Anderson, R. C., & Pearson, P. D. (1984). A schema-theoretic view of basic processes in reading. In P. D. Pearson (Ed.), *Handbook of reading research* (pp. 255–291). New York: Longman.

Au, K. H. (2002). Multicultural factors and the effective instruction of students of diverse backgrounds. In A. E. Farstrup & S. J. Samuels (Eds.), *What research has to say about reading instruction* (3rd ed., pp. 392–413). Newark, DE: International Reading Association.

August, D., & Hakuta, K. (Eds.). (1997). *Improving schooling for language minority children: A research agenda.* Washington, DC: National Academy Press.

Barnes, M. A., Faulkner, H. J., & Dennis, M. (2001). Poor reading comprehension despite fast word decoding in children with hydrocephalus. *Brain and Language, 76,* 35–44.

Berman, R. A., & Slobin, D. I. (1994). *Relating events in narrative: A cross linguistic developmental study.* Hillsdale, NJ: Erlbaum.

Bogner, K., Raphael, L., & Pressley, M. (2002). How Grade 1 teachers motivate literacy activity by their students. *Scientific Studies of Reading, 6,* 135–165.

Buly, M. R., & Valencia, S. W. (2002). Below the bar: Profiles of students who fail state reading assessments. *Educational Evaluation and Policy Analysis, 24,* 219–239.

Carlisle, J. F. (1989). Diagnosing comprehension deficits through listening and reading. *Annals of Dyslexia, 39,* 159–176.

Catts, H. W. (1993). The relationship between speech–language impairments and reading disabilities. *Journal of Speech and Hearing Research, 36,* 948–958.

Catts, H. W., Fey, M. E., Tomblin, J. B., & Zhang, X. (2002). A longitudinal investigation of reading outcomes in children with language impairments. *Journal of Speech, Language, and Hearing Research, 45,* 1142–1157.

Catts, H. W., Fey, M. E., Zhang, X., & Tomblin, B. (1999). Language basis of reading and reading disabilities: Evidence from a longitudinal investigation. *Scientific Studies of Reading, 3,* 331–361.

Catts, H. W., & Hogan, T. P. (2002). *The fourth grade slump: Late emerging poor readers.* Poster presented at the Annual Meeting of the Society for the Scientific Study of Reading, Chicago, IL.

Chafe, W., & Danielewicz, J. (1986). Properties of spoken and written language. In R. Horowitz & S. J. Samuels (Eds.), *Comprehending oral and written language* (pp. 83–113). New York: Academic Press.

Chomsky, N. (1957). *Syntactic structures.* The Hague: Mouton.

Cornoldi, C., Corretti, B., & De Beni, R. (2001). How the pattern of deficits in groups of learning-disabled individuals help to understand the organization of working memory. *Issues in Education, 7,* 71–78.

Cromer, W. (1970). The difference model: A new explanation for some reading difficulties. *Journal of Educational Psychology, 61,* 471–483.

Daneman, M. (2001). Learning disabled individuals show deficits on working memory tasks: The question is why? *Issues in Education, 7,* 79–85.

Delpit, L. D. (1986). Skills and other dilemmas of a progressive black educator. *Harvard Educational Review, 56,* 379–385.

Dewitz, P., & Dewitz, P. K. (2003). They can read the words, but they can't understand: Refining comprehension assessment. *Reading Teacher, 56,* 422–435.

Dickson, S. V., Simmons, D. C., & Kameenui, E. J. (1998). Text organization: Research bases. In D. C. Simmons & E. J. Kameenui (Eds.), *What reading re-*

search tells us about children with diverse learning needs: Bases and basics (pp. 239–277). Mahwah, NJ: Erlbaum.

Dolezal, S. E., Welsh, L. M., Pressley, M., & Vincent, M. (2003). How grade–3 teachers motivate academic engagement in students. Elementary School Journal, 103, 239–267.

Donahue, P. L., Finnegan, R. J., Lutkus, A. D., Allen, N. L., & Campbell, J. R. (2001). The nation's report card: Fourth-grade reading 2000. Washington, DC: U. S. Department of Education, Center for Education Statistics.

Duke, N. K. (2000). 3.6 minutes per day: The scarcity of informational texts in first grade. Reading Research Quarterly, 35, 202–224.

Duke, N. K., & Kays, J. (1998). "Can I say 'Once upon a time'?": Kindergarten children developing knowledge of information book language. Early Childhood Research Quarterly, 13, 295–318.

Duke, N. K., & Pearson, P. D. (2002). Effective practices for developing reading comprehension. In A. E. Farstrup & S. J. Samuels (Eds.), What research has to say about reading instruction (3rd ed., pp. 205–242). Newark, DE: International Reading Association.

Durgunoglu, A. Y. (2002). Cross-linguistic transfer in literacy development and implications for language learners. Annals of Dyslexia, 52, 189–204.

Fey, M., Windsor, J., & Warren, S. (Eds.). (1995). Language interventions: Preschool through the elementary years (pp. 3–37). Baltimore: Brookes.

Fiez, J. (2002, June). Simple reading tasks and MRI. In C. Perfetti (Chair), Making inferences during reading: New directions from behavioral, computational, and cognitive neuroscience studies. Symposium presented at the Society for Scientific of Readings, Chicago, IL.

Fitzgerald, J. (1995a). English-as-second-language learners' cognitive reading processes: A review of research in the United States. Review of Educational Research, 65, 145–190.

Fitzgerald, J. (1995b). English-as-second-language reading instruction in the United States: A research review. Journal of Reading Behavior, 27, 115–152.

Fitzgerald, J., & Noblit, G. (2000). Balance in the making: Learning to read in an ethnically diverse first-grade classroom. Journal of Educational Psychology, 92, 3–22.

Fung, I. Y. Y., Wilkinson, I. A. G., & Moore, D. W. (2003). L1-assisted reciprocal teaching to improve ESL students' comprehension of English expository text. Learning and Instruction, 13, 1–31.

Gambrell, L. (1996). Creating classroom cultures that foster reading motivation. Reading Teacher, 50, 14–25.

Garcia, G. E. (1991). Factors influencing the English reading test performance of Spanish-speaking Hispanic children. Reading Research Quarterly, 26, 371–392.

Garcia, G. E. (2000). Bilingual children's reading. In M. L. Kamil, P. B. Mosenthal, P. D. Pearson, & R. Barr (Eds.), Handbook of reading research (Vol. 3, pp. 813–834). Mahwah NJ: Erlbaum.

Gersten, R., Fuchs, L. S., Williams, J. P., & Baker, S. (2001). Teaching reading comprehension strategies to students with learning disabilities: A review of research. Review of Educational Research, 71, 279–320.

Goodman, K. S. (1967). Reading: A psycholinguistic guessing game. Journal of Reading Specialist, 6, 126–135.

Gough, P. B., Hoover, W. A., & Peterson, C. L. (1996). Some observations on a simple view of reading. In C. Cornoldi, & J. Oakhill (Eds.), Reading comprehension difficulties (pp. 1–13). Mahwah, NJ: Erlbaum.

Gough, P. B., & Tunmer, W. E. (1986). Decoding, reading, and reading disability. Remedial and Special Education, 7, 6–10.

Graesser, A.C., Singer, M., & Trabasso, T. (1994). Constructing inferences during narrative text comprehension. Psychological Review, 101, 371–395.

Grossman, M., Cooke, A., DeVita, C., Chen, W., Moore, P., Detre, J., et al. (2002). Sentence processing strategies in healthy seniors with poor comprehension: An MRI study. Brain and Language, 80, 296–313.

Guthrie, J. T., & McCann, A. D. (1997). Characteristics of classrooms that promote motivations and strategies for learning. In J. T. Guthrie & A. Wigfield (Eds.), Reading engagement: Motivating readers through integrated curriculum (pp. 128–148). Newark, DE: International Reading Association.

Guthrie, J. T., Van Meter, P., McCann, A. D., Wigfield, A., Bennett, L., Poundstone, C. C., Rice, et al. (1996). Growth of literacy engagement: Changes in motivations and strategies during concept-oriented reading instruction. Reading Research Quarterly, 31, 306–332.

Hambrick, D. Z., Wilhelm, O., & Engle, R. W. (2001). The role of working memory in learning disabilities. Issues in Education, 7, 87–92.

Hidi, S. E., & Hildyard, A. (1983). The comparison of oral and written productions in two discourse types. Discourse Processes, 6, 91–105.

Jiménez, R. T., Garcia, G. E., & Pearson, P. D. (1996). The reading strategies of bilingual Latina/o students who are successful English readers: Opportunities and obstacles. Reading Research Quarterly, 31, 90–112.

Kamberelis, G. (1998). Relations between children's literacy diets and genre development: You write what you read. Literacy Teaching and Learning, 3, 7–53.

Kamhi, A. G., & Catts, H. W. (2002). The language basis of reading: Implications for classification and treatment of children with reading disabilities. In K. G. Butler & E. R. Silliman (Eds.), Speaking, reading, and writing in children with language learning disabilities in research and practice (pp. 45–72). Mahwah NJ: Erlbaum.

Kim, D., & Hall, J. K. (2002). The role of an interactive book reading program in the development of second language pragmatic competence. Modern Language Journal, 86, 332–348.

Knapp, M. S., & Associates (1995). *Teaching for meaning in high-poverty classrooms.* New York: Teachers College Press.

Koskinen, P. S., Blum, I. H., Bisson, S. A., Phillips, S. M., Creamer, T. S., & Baker, T. K. (2000). Book access, shared reading, and audio models: The effects of supporting the literacy learning of linguistically diverse students in school and at home. *Journal of Educational Psychology, 92,* 23–36.

Kucer, S. B. (2001). *Dimension of literacy: A conceptual base for teaching reading and writing in school settings.* Mahwah NJ: Erlbaum.

Kuhn, M. (2003). How can I help them pull it all together?: A guide to fluent reading instruction. In D. M. Barone & L. M. Morrow (Eds.), *Literacy and young children* (pp. 210–225). New York: Guilford Press.

Kuhn, M. R., & Stahl, S. (2003). Fluency: A review of developmental and remedial strategies. *Journal of Educational Psychology, 95,* 3–21.

LaBerge, D., & Samuels, S. J. (1974). Toward a theory of automatic information processing in reading. *Cognitive Psychology, 6,* 293–323.

Labov, W., Baker, B., Bullock, S., Ross, L., & Brown, M. (1998). *A graphemic–phonemic analysis of the reading errors of inner city children.* Unpublished manuscript, University of Pennsylvania. Available online at *http://www.ling.upenn.edu/~labov/papers/garec/garec.html*

Ladson-Billings, G. (1994). *The dreamkeepers: Successful teachers of African-American children.* San Francisco: Jossey-Bass.

Langer, J. (1985). The child's sense of genre: A study of performance on parallel reading and writing tasks. *Written Communication, 2,* 157–188.

Leslie, L., & Caldwell, J. (1995). *Qualitative Reading Inventory—II.* New York: Longman.

Linan-Thompson, S., & Hickman-Davis, P. (2002). Supplemental reading instruction for students at risk for reading disabilities: Improving reading 30 minutes at a time. *Learning Disabilities Research and Practice, 17,* 242–251.

Linan-Thompson, S., Vaughn, S., Hickman-Davis, P., & Kouzekanani, K. (2003). Effectiveness of supplemental reading instruction for second-grade English language learners with reading difficulties. *Elementary School Journal, 103,* 221–238.

Lipson, M. Y., & Wixson, K. K. (2002). *Assessment and instruction of reading and writing difficulties: An interactive approach* (3rd ed.). Needham Heights, MA: Allyn & Bacon.

Long, S. (2002). Tuning in to teacher-talk: A second language learner struggles to comprehend. *Reading Literacy and Language, 36,* 113–118.

Lyon, G. R. (1996). Learning disabilities. In E. J. Mash & R. A. Barkley (Eds.), *Child psychopathology* (pp. 390–435). New York: Guilford Press.

Magliano, J. P. (1999). Revealing inference processes during text comprehension. In S. R. Goldman, A. C. Graesser, & P. van den Broek (Eds.), *Narrative comprehension, causality, and coherence* (pp. 55–75). Mahwah NJ: Erlbaum.

Mandler, J. M., & Johnson, N. S. (1977). Remembrance of things parsed: Story structure and recall. *Cognitive Psychology, 9,* 111–151.

Martin, V. L., & Pressley, M. (1991). Elaborative interrogation effects depend on the nature of the question. *Journal of Educational Psychology, 83,* 113–119.

McKenna, M. C., Kear, D. J., & Ellsworth, R. A. (1995). Children's attitudes toward reading: A national survey. *Reading Research Quarterly, 30,* 934–956.

Menyuk, P., & Chesnick, M. (1997). Metalinguistic skills, oral language knowledge, and reading. *Topics in Language Disorders, 17,* 75–87.

Meyer, B. J. F., Brandt, D. H., & Bluth, G. J. (1980). Use of top-level structure in text: Key for reading comprehension of ninth-grade students. *Reading Research Quarterly, 16,* 72–103.

Miller, C. A. (1956). The magical number seven, plus or minus two: Some limits on our capacity for processing information. *Psychological Review, 63,* 81–97.

Moll, L. C., & Diaz, S. (1985). Ethnographic pedagogy: Promoting effective bilingual instruction. In E. Garcia & R. V. Padilla (Eds.), *Advances in bilingual education research* (pp. 127–149). Tucson: University of Arizona Press.

Morrow, L. M., Tracey, D. H., Woo, D. G., & Pressley, M. (1999). Characteristics of exemplary first-grade literacy instruction. *Reading Teacher, 52,* 462–476.

Nation, K. (1999). Reading skills in hyperlexia: A developmental perspective. *Psychological Bulletin, 125,* 338–355.

Nation, K. (2001). Reading and language in children: Exposing hidden deficits. *Psychologist, 14,* 238–242.

Nation, K., Adams, J. W., Bowyer-Crane, C. A., & Snowling, M. J. (1999). Working memory deficits in poor comprehenders reflect underlying language impairments. *Journal of Experimental Child Psychology, 73,* 139–158.

Nation, K., & Snowling, M. J. (1998a). Individual differences in contextual facilitation: Evidence from dyslexia and poor reading comprehension. *Child Development, 69,* 996–1011.

Nation, K., & Snowling, M. J. (1998b). Semantic processing and the development of word recognition skills: Evidence from children with reading comprehension difficulties. *Journal of Memory and Language, 39,* 85–101.

National Reading Panel. (2000). *Teaching children to read: An evidence-based assessment of the scientific research literature on reading and its implications for reading instruction: Reports of the subgroups.* Washington, DC: National Institute of Child Health and Development.

Neuman, S. B., Celano, D. C., Greco, A. N., & Shue, P. (2001). *Access for all: Closing the book gap for children in early education.* Newark, DE: International Reading Association.

O'Shea, L. J., & O'Shea, D. J. (1994). A component

analysis of metacognition in reading comprehension. The contributions of awareness and self-regulation. *International Journal of Disability, Development, and Education, 41,* 15–32.

Oaken, R., Wiener, M., & Cromer, W. (1971). Identification, organization, and reading comprehension in poor readers. *Journal of Educational Psychology, 62,* 71–78.

Paris, S. G., Carpenter, R. D., Paris, A. H., & Hamilton, E. E. (2002, November). *Spurious and genuine correlates of children's reading comprehension.* Paper presented at the Center for Improving Early Reading Achievement Comprehension Assessment Conference, Ypsilanti, MI.

Pearson, P. D., & Dole, J. A. (1987). Explicit comprehension instruction: A review of research and a new conceptualization of instruction. *Elementary School Journal, 88,* 151–165.

Pearson, P. D., & Gallagher, M. C. (1983). The instruction of reading comprehension. *Contemporary Educational Psychology, 8,* 317–334.

Peregoy, S. F., & Boyle, O. F. (1991). Second language oral proficiency characteristics of low, intermediate, and high second language readers. *Hispanic Journal of Behavioral Sciences, 13,* 35–47.

Perry, T., & Delpit, L. (Eds.). (1998). *The real ebonics debate: Power, language, and the education of African-American children.* Boston: Beacon Press.

Plake, B. S., Impara, J. C., Pale, B. S., & Spies, R. A. (2003). *The fifteenth mental measurements yearbook.* Lincoln, NE: Buros Institute.

Pressley, M. (2000). What should comprehension instruction be the instruction of? In M. Kamil, Mosenthal, P., Pearson, P. D., & Barr, R. (Eds.), *Handbook of reading research* (Vol. 3, pp. 545–561). Hillsdale, NJ: Erlbaum.

Pressley, M., & Afflerbach, P. (1995). *Verbal protocols of reading: The nature of constructively responsive reading.* Hillsdale, NJ: Erlbaum.

Pressley, M., Allington, R. L., Wharton-McDonald, R., Block, C. C., & Morrow, L. M. (2001). *Learning to read: Lessons from exemplary first-grade classrooms.* New York: Guilford Press.

Pressley, M., Dolezal, S. E., Raphael, L. M., Welsh, L. M., Roehrig, A. D., & Bogner, K. (2003). *Motivating primary-grade students.* New York: Guilford Press.

Pressley, M., El-Dinary, P. B., Gaskins, I., Schuder, T., Bergman, J. L., Almasi, J., et al. (1992). Beyond direct explanation: Transactional instruction of reading comprehension strategies. *Elementary School Journal, 92,* 511–554.

Pressley, M., Johnson, C. J., Symons, S., McGoldrick, J. A., & Kurita, J. A. (1989). Strategies that improve memory and comprehension of what is read. *Elementary School Journal, 90,* 3–32.

Pressley, M., Wharton-McDonald, R., Mistretta-Hampston, J., & Echevaria, M. (1998). Literacy instruction in ten fourth- and fifth-grade classrooms. *Scientific Studies of Reading, 2,* 159–194.

Pressley, M., Wood, E., Woloshyn, V. E., Martin, V., King, A., & Menke, D. (1992). Encouraging mindful use of prior knowledge: Attempting to construct explanatory answers facilitates learning. *Educational Psychologist, 27,* 91–110.

Purcell-Gates, V. (1988). Lexical and syntactic knowledge of written narrative held by well-read-to kindergartners and second graders. *Research in the Teaching of English, 22,* 128–160.

Purcell-Gates, V. (1995). *Other people's words: The cycle of low literacy.* Cambridge, MA: Harvard University Press.

Purcell-Gates, V., & Duke, N. K. (2001, August). *Explicit explanation/teaching of informational text genres: A model for research.* Paper presented at the Crossing Borders: Connecting Science and Literacy Conference, sponsored by the National Science Foundation, Baltimore, MD.

Purcell-Gates, V., McIntyre, E., & Freppon, P. (1995). Learning written storybook language in school: A comparison of low-SES children in skills-based and whole language classrooms. *American Educational Research Journal, 32,* 659–685.

RAND Reading Study Group. (2002). *Reading for understanding: Toward an R&D program in reading comprehension.* Santa Monica, CA: RAND.

Rayner, K., Foorman, B. R., Perfetti, C. A., Pesetsky, D., & Seidenberg, M. S. (2001). How psychological science informs the teaching of reading. *Psychological Science in the Public Interest, 2,* 31–74.

Rayner, K., Foorman, B. R., Perfetti, C. A., Pesetsky, D., & Seidenberg, M. S. (2002). *Scientific American, 286*(3), 84–91.

Roehler, L. R., & Duffy, G. G. (1984). Direct explanation of comprehension processes. In G. G. Duffy, L. R. Roehler, & J. Mason (Eds.), *Comprehension instruction: Perspectives and suggestions* (pp. 265–280). New York: Longman.

Roth, F. P., Speece, D. L., Cooper, D. H., & De La Paz, S. (1996). Unresolved mysteries: How do metalinguistic and narrative skills connect with early reading? *Journal of Special Education, 30,* 257–277.

Rumelhart, D.E. (1977). Toward an interactive model of reading. In S. Dornic (Ed.), *Attention and performance VI* (pp. 573–603). Hillsdale, NJ: Erlbaum.

Scarborough, H. (2001). Connecting early language and literacy to later reading (dis)abilities: Evidence, theory, and practice. In S. B. Neuman & D. K. Dickinson (Eds.), *Handbook of early literacy research* (pp. 97–110). New York: Guilford Press.

Shankweiler, D., Lundquist, E., Katz, L., Stuebing, K. K., Fletcher, J. M., Brady, S., et al. (1999). Comprehension and decoding: Patterns of association in children with reading difficulties. *Scientific Studies of Reading, 3,* 69–94.

Singer, M. (1994). Discourse inference processes. In M. A. Gernsbacher (Ed.), *Handbook of psycholinguistics* (pp. 479–509). San Diego: Academic Press.

Smith, F. (1971). *Understanding reading.* New York: Holt, Rinehart & Winston.

Snowling, M., & Frith, U. (1986). Comprehension in "hyperlexic" readers. *Journal of Experimental Psychology, 42,* 392–415.

Solan, H. A., Larson, S., Shelley-Tremblay, J., Ficarra,

A., & Silverman, M. (2001). The role of visual attention in cognitive control of oculomotor readiness in students with reading disabilities. *Journal of Learning Disabilities, 34,* 107–118.

Stahl, S. A. (2003). No more "madfaces": Motivation and fluency development with struggling readers. In D. M. Barone & L. M. Morrow (Eds.), *Literacy and young children* (pp. 195–209). New York: Guilford Press.

Stanovich, K. E. (1980). Toward an interactive–compensatory model of individual differences in the development of reading fluency. *Reading Research Quarterly, 16,* 32–71.

Stanovich, K. E., & Cunningham, A. E. (1992). Studying the consequences of literacy within a literate society: The cognitive correlates of print exposure. *Memory and Cognition, 20,* 51–68.

Stanovich, K. E., & West, R. F. (1989). Exposure to print and orthographic processing. *Reading Research Quarterly, 24,* 402–433.

Stein, N. L., & Glenn, C. G. (1979). An analysis of story comprehension in elementary school children. In R. O. Freedle (Eds.), *New directions in discourse processing* (Vol. 2). Norwood NJ: Ablex.

Steiner, R., Wiener, M., & Cromer, W. (1971). Comprehension training and identification for good and poor readers. *Journal of Educational Psychology, 62,* 506–513.

Sternberg, R. J. (1987). Most vocabulary is learned from context. In M. G. McKeown & M. E. Curtis (Eds.), *The nature of vocabulary acquisition* (pp. 89–105). Hillsdale, NJ: Erlbaum.

Swanson, H. L., & Siegel, L. (2001). Learning disabilities as a working memory deficit. *Issues in Education, 7,* 1–48.

Swicegood, M. A. (1990). The effects of metacognitive reading strategy training on the reading performance and student reading analysis strategies of third grade Spanish-dominant students. *Dissertation Abstracts International, 52,* 449A.

Torgesen, J. K. (2001). Learning disabilities as a working memory deficit: The important next questions. *Issues in Education, 7,* 93–102.

Trabasso, T., van den Broek, P., & Suh, S. (1989). Logical necessity and transitivity of causal relations in stories. *Discourse processes, 12,* 1–25.

Tralli, R., Colombo, B., Deshler, D. D., & Schumaker, J. B. (1996). The Strategies Intervention Model: A model for supported inclusion at the secondary level. *Remedial &Special Education, 17,* 204–216.

Valdez-Menchaca, M. C., & Whitehurst, G.J. (1992). Accelerating language development through picture book reading: A systematic extension to Mexican day care. *Developmental Psychology, 28,* 1106–1114.

van den Broek, P. (1994). Comprehension and memory of narrative texts: Inference and coherence. In M. A.

Gernsbacher (Ed.), *Handbook of psycholinguistics* (pp. 539–588). San Diego CA: Academic Press.

Vellutino, F. R. (1979). *Dyslexia: Theory and research.* Cambridge, MA: MIT Press.

Vellutino, F. R. (2001). Working memory deficit and learning disabilities: Reactions to Swanson and Siegel. *Issues in Education, 7,* 49–69.

Verhoeven, L. T. (1990). Acquisition of reading in a second language. *Reading Research Quarterly, 25,* 90–114.

Wahlberg, T. (2001). Language development and text comprehension in individuals with autism. *Advances in Special Education, 15,* 133–150.

Weber, R. M. (1991). Linguistic diversity and reading in American society. In R. Barr, M. L. Kamil, P. Mosenthal, & P. D. Pearson (Eds.), *Handbook of reading research* (Vol. 2), pp. 97–119). New York: Longman.

Wharton-McDonald, R., Pressley, M., & Hampston, J. M. (1998). Outstanding literacy instruction in first grade: Teacher practices and student achievement. *Elementary School Journal, 99,* 101–128.

Wheldall, K., & Joseph, R. (1985–1986). Young Black children's sentence comprehension skills: A comparison of performance in Standard English and Jamaican Creole. *First Language, 6,* 149–154.

Wilder, A. A., & Williams, J. P. (2001). Students with severe learning disabilities can learn higher order comprehension skills. *Journal of Educational Psychology, 93,* 268–278.

Williams, J. P. (1993). Comprehension of students with and without learning disabilities: Identification of narrative themes and idiosyncratic text representations. *Journal of Educational Psychology, 85,* 631–641.

Williams, J. P. (1998). Improving the comprehension of disabled readers. *Annals of Dyslexia, 48,* 213–238.

Williams, J. P., Brown, L. G., Silverstein, A. K., & deCani, J. S. (1994). An instructional program in comprehension of narrative themes for adolescents with learning disabilities. *Learning Disability Quarterly, 17,* 205–221.

Woloshyn, V. E., Paivio, A., & Pressley, M. (1994). Using elaborative interrogation to help students acquire information consistent with prior knowledge and information inconsistent with prior knowledge. *Journal of Educational Psychology, 86,* 79–89.

Woloshyn, V. E., Pressley, M., & Schneider, W. (1992). Elaborative interrogation and prior knowledge effects on learning of facts. *Journal of Educational Psychology, 84,* 115–124.

Wolters, G. (2001). Learning disability and working memory: A commentary. *Issues in Education, 7,* 103–106.

Yuill, N., & Oakhill. J. (1991). *Children's problems in text comprehension.* Cambridge, UK: Cambridge University Press.

24

Assessment of Reading Comprehension

JOANNE F. CARLISLE
MELINDA S. RICE

Because reading comprehension is a complex process, and because so many factors affect students' acquisition of comprehension skills, researchers and practitioners may approach the topic of assessment of reading comprehension with trepidation. In our current educational climate, a particular concern is the shockingly large percentage of students who are unable to demonstrate proficiency in text comprehension. For example, 68% of fourth graders were at or below "Basic" level on the reading assessment of the National Assessment of Educational Progress (National Center for Educational Statistics, 2000). These results have created a sense of urgency in our search for answers to the question of how best to assess students' reading comprehension.

Answers to this question are not easy to come by, in part because there are a number of different purposes and methods for assessing reading comprehension. Classroom teachers may approach comprehension assessment with the goals of identifying students' reading behaviors, determining their reading level, and documenting their progress (Caldwell, 2002), but they also are called upon to administer standardized tests of comprehension, devised for purposes

such as evaluating reading instruction or progress toward state or district curricular standards in reading. Similarly, educators are asked to play a role in identifying students with significant difficulties in reading comprehension even when the criteria for identifying students with reading disabilities are not clear-cut. In recent years, the increased role of policymakers and politicians in debates concerning the design and use of reading achievement measures has served to put pressure on educators to coordinate the different types of reading assessments that are given to students. Furthermore, they are often called on to interpret the results of different reading achievement measures for students and their parents. One point is clear: Because of the many ways that educators interface with reading comprehension assessment, they are in a good position to participate in debates about the nature, purposes, and value of different forms of reading comprehension assessment.

PURPOSES OF ASSESSMENT

Assessments are means of taking stock. Educational assessments are used to evaluate reading from a number of different perspectives. Some assessments of reading achievement are used to monitor students' learning and to fine-tune instructional programs. Educators usually choose, administer, and interpret the results of such assessments. Other assessments of reading are used to compare reading achievement in different classrooms, schools, districts, or states. Such assessments are usually designed by experts at the state level, or they are published tests used nationwide. District, state, and national educational agencies may use the results of such tests to set policies and to evaluate the effectiveness of schools. It is important to consider the purpose of a given reading assessment to avoid misinterpretation of the results or inappropriate uses of test results. This is true whether our interest is reading comprehension or any other area of school achievement.

In this chapter, we discuss four common purposes for reading assessments. One purpose is program evaluation and accountability. School administrators, as well as state and national educational agencies, are interested in making sure that teachers, schools, school districts, and states are successful in their efforts to teach students to read. A second purpose is identification of children with special needs in reading. This primarily involves determining whether a student who is having extreme difficulties learning to read qualifies for special education services, given federal, state, and local regulations concerning eligibility criteria. Such assessments must comply with established procedures and take into account the identification criteria for categories of exceptionality such as specific learning disabilities. A third purpose is identification of students at risk for significant learning problems, with the goal of providing appropriate services soon enough to forestall serious difficulties in acquiring literacy and concomitant social, emotional, and academic problems (Catts, Fey, Zhang, & Tomblin, 2001). Often considered a means of initiating preventive measures, identification of children at risk for reading disabilities can be carried out quite effectively as early as kindergarten (O'Connor & Jenkins, 1999). A fourth purpose is to monitor the progress of students in their classroom reading programs. Educators need this information to evaluate and modify reading instruction and learning activities for the whole class, and for individual students within the class.

Each of these purposes is aligned with specific views about appropriate assessment measures. The best known measures of reading comprehension are group-administered standardized tests. They provide a way to compare the performance of a given student to that of other students of the same age or grade level. Such tests are not developed to determine how much progress the student is making in the reading curriculum of his or her school. Curriculum-based measures, on the other hand, are one way to compare different students' response to instruction, given the content of the curriculum. These measures also provide a way to examine students' improvement in reading on a regular basis. However, they are not suitable for comparing students' reading in classrooms with the use of different instructional methods or materials. Informal measures of comprehension include informal reading inventories (published or teacher-made), analyses of students' oral reading accuracy and speed, or performance measures. In general, performance measures require students to use information or knowledge, whether this involves applications or simply explanations (Elliott, 1998). Performance measures vary on a dimension called "authenticity." Authentic measures reflect students' responses to reading and related activities in the context of their school courses. Authentic assessments might reflect students' interest in and feelings about books they have read, for example. Perhaps the most commonly used form of authentic reading assessment is the portfolio, which, when used to assess progress in reading, might include book reports a student has written, excerpts from a reading journal, and so on.

Experts generally agree that measures of reading comprehension should be valid and reliable, so that they can help us determine whether the students are learning what we hope and expect that they are learning. The same experts do not agree on the characteristics of tests that make them valid, however. For example, a common method for assessing passage comprehension involves asking students to read a short passage and then pick answers to multiple-choice questions. This activity may not reflect educators' views of what reading comprehension is all about. For instance, to teachers who expect students to read books in order to learn course content, the task could seem artificial. To them, it is important that readers understand and remember information from the text, but this task does not tap long-term memory. Rather, it indicates whether they can find answers to questions in the text, make inferences about information presented in the text, and the like.

Finding valid means of assessing comprehension of written texts has been a concern for decades. At present, no single measure appropriately assesses all aspects of reading comprehension about which educators and policymakers wish to know. Researchers continue to search for forms of assessment that reflect the dynamic nature of reading comprehension and engagement with natural texts and that are sensitive to developmental changes in comprehension capabilities. There is a need for assessments that reflect knowledge acquired from reading, engagement with reading, and application of information and ideas drawn from reading (Valencia & Wixson, 2000). There also is a need for assessments that tell us about the processes by which students construct meaning from texts, as well as provide insights into the outcomes of reading—what readers retain after reading and how they think about what they have read. Clearly, there are no simple solutions to the many challenges of designing effective assessments of reading comprehension. Because educators are responsible for selecting or designing classroom assessments, as well as interpreting the results of state assessments, they need to be well informed about current practices in the assessment of reading comprehension.

ASSESSMENT AT THE DISTRICT AND STATE LEVELS

In general, assessments designed and implemented at the district and state levels are used for broad purposes of educational planning and evaluation. Such assessments provide a way for administrators and policymakers to hold schools and teachers accountable for providing effective instruction in reading. Information about the performance of elementary students in reading, for example, would be gathered using a published, standardized reading achievement test or a reading test developed and mandated by the state. At the district level, the results might help the school administration evaluate organizational and educational matters, such as the effects of different reading programs, the way classes are constituted, or changes in demographics within the school district. The results of such reading tests are typically shared with parents, so that they have an opportunity to learn how their children perform in reading (and other areas) in comparison to other students in the same school or district.

Our current educational climate has fostered considerable interest in school reform—specifically, fostering changes in educational programs, instructional methods and materials, and assessment systems—in an effort to improve the reading achievement of all students, but particularly to improve the reading achievement of the least able students. School reform efforts often involve aligning curriculum, instruction, and assessment (Simmons, Kuykendall, King, Cornachione, & Kame'enui, 2000). Simmons et al. (2000) have recommended that, in formulating plans for assessment of reading, schools establish mechanisms for teachers to keep track of the performance of students on a regular basis, so that progress can be monitored and changes made in educational programs on a timely basis. Somewhat similarly, a study of effective schools found that students' reading achievement was significantly related to regular classroom assessment of pupil progress, home–school links, and collaborative efforts among teachers (Taylor, Pearson, Clark, & Walpole, 1999). School reform has made many teachers and administrators aware of the importance of coordinating assessment and instruction. Not surprisingly, current questions focus on the most useful types of reading assessments for purposes of improving schoolwide instruction.

Because a national goal is for every child to be able to read by the end of third grade, state agencies may choose to use the scores from the state achievement test to determine how successful schools and teachers are at meeting this goal. Most states have developed their own reading assessment instruments. According to Elliott, Erickson, Thurlow, and Shriner (2000), in 1995–1996, all but four states had a state assessment in place. Although the state instruments vary widely in content and tasks, they often attempt to link the assessment of reading to state standards for reading achievement. These standards articulate the goals of the reading or literacy curriculum at each grade level. State standards vary widely in specificity, content, and the extent to which they have been translated into particular systems of curriculum, instruction, and assessment (Wixson & Dutro, 1998). Because state standards and the assessment instruments have assumed such importance in determining how successfully schools teach students to read, it is a good idea for educators to be well informed about them. However, state reading tests are probably not going to tell educators all they want to know about their students' growth in reading. As noted earlier, such test scores provide a narrow window into the student's world of reading, as it were.

Prior to 1997, many states excused students with disabilities from participation in state assessments. However, with the reauthorization of the Individuals with Disabilities Education Act in 1997, special education funding was made contingent on the participation of students with disabilities in state assessments (Elliott et al., 2000). The law requires that an alternate assessment be developed for students who are judged unable to participate in the regular state assessment (Kleinert, Haig, Kearns & Kennedy, 2000; Ysseldyke & Olsen, 1999). In addition, schools must make decisions about providing appropriate accommodations for students with disabilities who do participate in the regular assessments. The term "accommodations" refers to adjustments in the conditions of taking the tests that make it possible for individuals with special needs to demonstrate their reading

skill and knowledge, including changes in the setting, timing, or method of taking a test. For example, a visually impaired student might take a comprehension test with a text published with large-print or in braille.

Policies concerning accommodations vary by state. The team that developed the student's Individualized Educational Program is usually given primary responsibility for making the decision about participation in testing and determination of accommodations (Thurlow, House, Scott, & Ysseldyke, 2000). However, states do not all allow the same accommodations. For example, in some states, test questions can be read aloud to the student (most often, in content-area courses), whereas in other states, no oral reading of the test questions is permitted.

Although it may seem unfair to require students with severe reading disabilities to take tests that require lots of reading, there are reasons why it is important to have information on state assessments about all children, regardless of their skill levels. Thurlow and her colleagues (2000) have explained some of the negative consequences of excluding students from the tests. One is that such exclusion results in students' not being required to follow the school's curriculum. Exclusion also leads to increases in retention, rate of referral to special education, and spurious comparisons across schools. Allington and McGill-Franzen (1992) recalculated data from high-achieving schools to include students who had been retained or placed in special education and found that the gains reported by such schools largely disappeared. Schools "look better" if they can exclude their poorest readers from the assessments, but to do so, they have to have a convincing reason, such as keeping students back a grade or placing them in more restrictive special education settings. Such actions may not be in the best interests of the students.

Accommodations can be thought of as falling into four categories (Thurlow et al., 2000). One is the *presentation format*. An example is using braille or large-print text for students who are visually impaired. A second, the *response format*, refers to the manner in which students respond. For example, they might be allowed to point to an answer or use a computer to respond. A third is the *setting of the test*. For example, a student might be allowed to take the test at home or in the resource room. The fourth is the *timing of the test*. For example, a student might be allowed extended time to take the test or be given additional breaks during the test. Students with reading disabilities are most likely to be given timing accommodations, particularly extended time to take the test.

A study of the effectiveness of accommodations (Fuchs et al., 2000) has shown that students with learning disabilities (LD) benefited from some accommodations more than others, but overall, they benefited more than students without LD who were given the same accommodations. Students with and without LD were given tests with and without accommodations of extended time, large print, or reading aloud. When performances on parallel tests were compared, the results showed that the accommodations gave a greater boost to students with LD than to students without LD. As a group, students with LD profited from reading aloud but not from extended time or large print. One concern raised by this study is that teachers' decisions about what were appropriate accommodations for their students did not correspond to the benefits the students derived from these accommodations. The results suggest that objective information (e.g., test scores) about students' special needs might provide a better basis for selecting accommodations.

Alternate forms of assessment are most needed for students with severe cognitive deficits or multiple disabilities, because these students cannot benefit sufficiently from the types of test accommodations described earlier (Ysseldyke & Olsen, 1999). Such students are typically not working toward a regular high school diploma. As a result, the content and the form of achievement tests are justifiably altered. Alternative assessments may involve observational assessments of the development of their life skills. An example in the area of reading might be assessment of functional reading skills (e.g., reading environmental signs). The option of alternate forms of assessment

is typically not appropriate for students with learning or reading disabilities.

ASSESSMENT FOR IDENTIFICATION OF A READING DISABILITY

The second purpose of assessment of reading is to identify those students who have sufficiently severe problems with reading that they qualify for special education services. Because our focus is on reading comprehension, a natural question to ask is whether there is such a thing as a specific disability in reading comprehension. There is, but students with specific problems with comprehension are less common than those who either have problems *only* with word reading or have combined problems with word reading and listening comprehension (Aaron, Joshi, & Williams, 1999). Put another way, only a small percentage of students found to have problems understanding what they read will have problems with reading comprehension *but not* decoding (Shankweiler et al., 1999). Many researchers consider deficits in phonological processes, which lead to poor skills in decoding, to be the defining characteristic of a reading disability (Stanovich, 1991; Torgesen & Wagner, 1998). We should also keep in mind that poor comprehension is often the result of decoding problems. If the student cannot read a text accurately and fluently, he or she will have trouble understanding it.

Patterns of Difficulties with Reading Comprehension

In order to devise appropriate educational programs, we need to distinguish three different patterns of severe reading problems. To do so, we need to use three types of measures: word reading (or, as some prefer, "decoding"), reading comprehension, and listening comprehension. Two of the patterns of students' performance on these tests involve word-reading problems that are or are not accompanied by language comprehension problems. In the flow chart of Figure 24.1, these patterns are shown at the far left and far right.

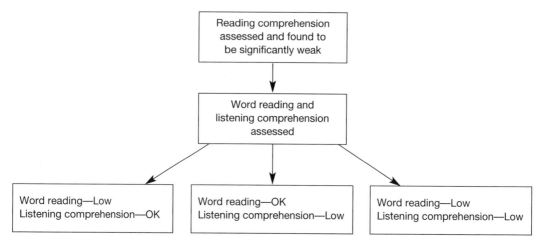

FIGURE 24.1. A process to identify patterns of difficulties in reading comprehension.

For both patterns, the students have significant word-reading problems, as well as very low reading comprehension scores. However, some of these students show language comprehension problems only when they read, not when they listen to passages of equivalent difficulty; that is, their comprehension problems in reading stem from their word-reading difficulties. The way to distinguish between students with language comprehension difficulties and those with specific reading comprehension problems is to assess both listening and reading comprehension (Carlisle, 1989; Carlisle & Felbinger, 1991). Students with language comprehension problems can be identified, because they perform significantly less well than their peers on a test of comprehension, both when passages are read aloud to them and when they read to themselves.

Comparing listening and reading comprehension is a fairly straightforward process when standardized tests are used, because both listening and reading measures will have been normed for the age group. If a test is standardized, it means that we can determine what is normal for students of different grades or ages. Thus, students who perform significantly below average on both tests of listening and reading comprehension would be likely to have general difficulties with language comprehension—difficulties that are not specific to reading.

However, if teachers compare listening and reading informally (e.g., using an Informal Reading Inventory), they need to interpret the results with an understanding of developmental expectations. Overviews of research on listening and reading comprehension, such as one written by Sticht and James (1984), are helpful resources for educators. In particular, it is important to understand developmental changes in reading and listening comprehension as they relate to assessment. First graders usually demonstrate better comprehension after listening than after reading a text, in large part because they are just learning to read words, and their small reading vocabulary places a limit on the difficulty level of text they can understand when reading on their own. By about fifth grade, however, students typically can understand passages they read and listen to that are equivalent in difficulty. This is because their word-reading skills are sufficiently automatic that they do not stand in the way of comprehension. By eighth grade, students often perform better on comprehension tests following reading than following listening. One reason is that the reader can proceed at his or her own pace in making sense of a difficult passage; the text is permanent and can be reread as needed in part or in its entirety. In contrast, texts presented for listening are delivered at a pace selected by the speaker and offer no opportunities to revisit the text in order to make sense of it.

Unlike the two patterns discussed so far, the third pattern that results in significant difficulties in reading comprehension involves students whose word reading is not significantly weak. Instead, their specific weakness is language comprehension and verbal reasoning. Their difficulties in understanding language are apparent following both reading and listening to passages. Of the three patterns, this one is the least common among school-age children. Most students with language comprehension problems have word reading problems as well (Aaron et al., 1999; Catts, Fey, Zhang, & Tomblin, 1999).

As Figure 24.1 shows, it is possible to identify students with these three patterns of reading difficulties using listening and reading discrepancy scores, and a word reading measure (Aaron, 1991; Spring & French, 1990). The flowchart also shows that the first step involves identifying students with significant weaknesses in reading comprehension. Once these students are given a word-reading and a listening comprehension test, the teacher (perhaps with the help of an educational consultant in the school) can determine which of the three patterns best represents the nature of the students' reading problems.

As noted earlier, one reason for determining the nature of reading comprehension problems is that this information is crucial in the design of an appropriate educational program for a student. Students with significant weaknesses in word reading will need an instructional program in letter–sound correspondences, phonics, decoding strategies, and the like. Students with both listening and reading comprehension weaknesses will need an instructional program in comprehension strategies, components of language (e.g., vocabulary, grammar), and the like. The students with weaknesses in both word reading and reading comprehension will, of course, need comprehensive programs that include both types of instruction. Finally, regardless of the pattern of strengths and weaknesses, students with reading comprehension problems benefit from exposure to literature and expository

texts, whether they listen to books on tape, or to a parent or classmate reading aloud. While they are receiving special instruction in reading, they should not be allowed to fall behind their peers in text comprehension because they are not gathering experience with written texts.

Some students with weaknesses in both listening and reading comprehension may have more significant problems with reading than with listening comprehension. Their oral-language comprehension is not so much weaker than that of their peers that they could be described as having a language disability. Primary among their traits is a difficulty in making inferences while reading (Cain & Oakhill, 1999; Oakhill & Yuill, 1996). Other aspects of verbal reasoning and metacognition may also be affected, so that these poor readers might particularly benefit from instruction in comprehension strategies and methods of comprehension monitoring.

Identification Criteria for Reading Disabilities

We have argued that we should attempt to identify different patterns of poor comprehension so that we can design appropriate educational programs. However, it is important to consider criteria that are used to determine whether students with these three patterns of poor comprehension qualify for special services in reading in today's schools. First, by "special services" we do not mean extra reading instruction and practice that takes place within the classroom or pullout programs designed to "jump-start" students who are having problems learning to read in first grade (e.g., Reading Recovery).

Students with severe reading problems are often several grade levels below their peers. Typically, their reading problems have been evident from the time they started to learn to read, and efforts to provide help in the classroom have not been adequate to solve the problem. Under these circumstances, students are referred for assessment to determine whether the reading problem is such that it fits the criteria for specific LD. A reading disability is regarded as one manifestation of a specific LD. Students with specific LD are eligible for special education services, which may include instruction in reading from a specialist.

The operational criteria for identifying a specific learning disability are part of federal law (U.S. Office of Education, 1977). These criteria specify that the student should be underachieving in one or more areas of language and academic functioning (e.g., oral expression, reading), that is, performing significantly below expectations for his or her age or grade level. There should also be a severe discrepancy between the student's learning potential (usually interpreted as intelligence) and his or her achievement in one or more of the above areas. There are exclusionary criteria as well; to qualify as having a specific learning disability, the student's learning problems cannot be primarily due to mental retardation, sensory impairment, emotional or behavioral disabilities, or cultural or economic disadvantage. For students with reading problems, underachievement is usually evident not only in significant problems on standardized tests but also in difficulties completing reading assignments in class. Students who are severely impaired in their reading ability are likely to be struggling academically in any of their courses that involve reading.

The most hotly debated aspect of the identification criteria is called the "discrepancy" requirement. The debate has focused on whether it is enough to identify reading disabilities on the basis of significant underachievement in reading, given grade-level expectations, or whether reading achievement must be significantly lower than intelligence (Siegel, 1992; Stanovich, 1991). Siegel (1992) has argued that IQ/achievement discrepancy should not be the basis for identification of students who need help with reading. She has shown that students with significant word-reading problems but different IQ levels have similar profiles in terms of phonological processes, working memory, and other reading-related characteristics. Whether students show significant discrepancies between reading and intelligence or not, her point is that all students with severe word-reading problems need considerable help learning to read.

An important point is that when a "discrepancy" system is used, on average, students are not identified as have a reading disability until age 10 (Fletcher et al., 1998). This is partly due to the lack of sensitivity of standardized measures. In the early elementary school years, students with reading problems often do not show the significant discrepancy needed to qualify for special education services. Several years may pass before their problems are severe, and they qualify for the LD label. The downside to late diagnosis of a severe reading problem is that the older the students, the harder it is to treat their reading problems effectively. Strag found that "when the diagnosis of dyslexia was made in the first two grades of school, nearly 82% of the students could be brought up to their normal classroom work, whereas only 46% of the dyslexic problems identified in the third grade were remediated and only 10 to 15% of those observed in grades five to seven could be helped when the diagnosis of learning problems was made at those grade levels" (in Fletcher et al., 1998, p. 197).

Finding a solution to the debate over the discrepancy requirement is extremely important, because the students who qualify as having specific LD will vary, depending on which of these systems is used (Fletcher et al., 1998; Torgesen & Wagner, 1998). If the criterion is very low achievement on reading tests, students who are very bright will not be identified as having a learning disability in reading, even if their reading level is much lower than would be expected, given their intelligence. If the criterion is a significant discrepancy between reading and IQ, students with mild problems in reading, relative to their IQ, will not qualify for special services in reading, even if their reading achievement is considerably below grade level. Both systems, used alone, have a number of theoretical and practical implications. For example, if the federal criteria for identifying reading disabilities specified significant underachievement in reading, without regard for IQ, then a large portion of the school-age population (about 16%) would be found to have specific LD and require special education services. This might seem to be an unnecessary inflation of the number of students who qualify for LD services. One suggestion for getting rid of the problematic use of IQ to establish a discrepancy is to identify specific reading disabilities by a significant discrepancy between listening and reading comprehension (e.g., Badian, 1999). However, this would mean that students who are weak in both listening and reading comprehension would not qualify for services in the LD category. Elimination of students with general problems in comprehension would not be a theoretically sound change.

Another implication concerns the belief that students with significant word-reading problems but different IQ levels respond differently to reading instruction (Torgesen & Wagner, 1998). To date, this issue has remained a difficult one on which to reach consensus. However, even if brighter students with significant reading problems do respond readily to special instruction, this factor probably should not dictate identification criteria. It seems unlikely that anyone wants to reserve the LD label for either those students whose problems are readily solved by special reading instruction or for those whose problems are particularly recalcitrant.

All educators, especially those concerned with identification of students with disabilities, should consider the implications of the two systems for identifying reading disabilities—underachievement and discrepancy from ability—and participate in the debate as they see fit. Because our focus is on reading comprehension, it is important to think about this debate with comprehension in mind. In the general population, intelligence is significantly related to reading comprehension. Not surprisingly, therefore, for many students with reading problems, we do not find a gap between verbal ability and reading comprehension. If such a gap were necessary for a student to receive special education services, there would be underidentification of children with severe comprehension problems. This might be particularly the case for students with language-learning problems, because they would be likely to perform at a similar below-average level on tests of verbal ability and reading comprehension.

ASSESSMENT TO IDENTIFY CHILDREN AT RISK FOR READING DISABILITIES

A third purpose for an assessment of reading is to identify those young children who are at risk for reading disabilities. There are several compelling arguments for carrying out such assessments. One is that it is far easier to prevent serious reading problems than to correct them once they are established. As early as first grade, students who struggle with reading are likely to lose interest in reading, to see themselves as less able students than their peers, and to begin to engage in avoidance behaviors (McKenna, Kear, & Ellsworth, 1995).

Assessment in kindergarten and first grade often does not entail designation of a reading disability or LD. Often the purpose is to identify children "at risk" for language and literacy problems. If we can identify those children with the beginning "symptoms" of difficulties in learning to read, we can take corrective measures early on. For example, we might want to identify children who are eligible for reading programs designed to catch and correct initial problems in learning to read (e.g., Reading Recovery). The focus of such assessments is not specifically comprehension. In fact, if comprehension is assessed at all, it is done with oral-language measures, sometimes focused on component skills, such as vocabulary knowledge. Even in first grade, children have very limited reading comprehension capabilities.

Two types of assessments designed to identify those students at risk for reading difficulties are in general usage. One type is screening tests to identify children who appear to lack the prerequisite capabilities to acquire word-reading skills. The other type is comprehensive screening batteries designed to identify children with a broader profile of language-learning problems that place them at risk for failure in learning to read. This would include potential problems with both word reading and comprehension.

An example of a kindergarten screening test is one developed by Muter, Hulme, and Snowling (in Muter, 2000), which is made up of measures of phonological awareness, a speech rate test (time repeating "buttercup") that serves as a measure of phonological memory, and a test of letter knowledge. Effective screening batteries are those that have good "hit" rates in prediction studies. This means that most of the children predicted to have reading problems 1 or 2 years later actually do so. A more detailed discussion of issues entailed in predicting reading achievement can be found in Chapter 4 of *Preventing Reading Difficulties in Young Children* by Snow, Burns, and Griffin (1998). A screening battery that effectively identifies children who are going to have trouble learning to read prevents the dual problems of providing unnecessary instruction for children who do not need it, and not providing instruction for children who really do need it, despite their performance on the screening test.

Because short screening batteries are efficient and practical for schools, researchers have worked to identify screening tests with a small number of measures that still are quite effective at identifying students who turn out to have serious difficulties in learning word reading a year or so later. O'Connor and Jenkins (1999) found that the time point of administration of the screening test affects the extent to which students' performances on the screening battery correctly predict reading disability. Their screening battery given at the start of first grade had greater predictive accuracy than the battery given in the spring in kindergarten, which in turn had greater predictive accuracy than a battery given in the fall of kindergarten. In addition, of the three best predictive measures, one changed over this time period. Letter naming and phonemic segmentation speed were strong predictors overall. Syllable deletion was useful when included in the early kindergarten battery but not in the late kindergarten battery; at this point, a task called sound repetition provided greater discrimination than did syllable deletion. At both screening points, three tasks identified most of the students who turned out to have significant word-reading problems at the end of grade 1. For example, in April, rapid letter naming, phoneme segmentation, and sound repetition identified all but one first grader who subsequently showed serious problems acquiring word-reading skill.

Some batteries assess a broader range of language-related capabilities. A compilation of the measures commonly used to predict reading difficulties at school entry can be found in Snow et al. (1998, p. 110); these measures include a variety of language and early literacy measures. The most common language measures are verbal memory for stories or sentences, receptive vocabulary, rapid serial naming, expressive language, and phonological awareness; the most common early literacy measures are reading readiness and letter identification. When researchers use multiple predictors, they typically use an index of early print skills (e.g., letter identification), phonological awareness, and IQ. However, with these measures, a number of children who will develop reading difficulties do not perform poorly enough to earn an at-risk designation. In all likelihood, adding language measures to the battery would improve the ability to identify children at risk for reading comprehension problems.

Other screening batteries have been developed with the purpose of identifying persistent reading problems (i.e., those that do not respond to common interventions in school). Badian (2000) found that, of the measures given to the students when they were in preschool, three were most effective at discriminating good and poor readers at grade 2—sentence memory, orthographic processing, and color naming. (Orthographic processing required the child to point to one of four stimuli that matched the item at the far left of the row; the items were made up of numbers, letter strings, and words; foils involved spatial and sequencing errors.) Overall, 92% of a first cohort and 87% of a second cohort were accurately identified as good or poor readers. Further analyses to identify the measures that discriminated students with persistent reading problems showed that, in grade 7, sentence memory, letter naming, and orthographic processing classified most of the students with enduring reading problems.

For teachers and clinicians working with children with possible speech and language disabilities, the more comprehensive screening batteries may provide more information about the various areas of language learning that would need to be addressed in children's school setting or in their language therapy (Catts et al., 2001). As Catts and his colleagues (1999) have pointed out, "Early recognition of these children's risks for future reading difficulties should result in broad-based language intervention programs that target literacy as well as oral language impairments" (p. 38). Comprehensive language instruction is important for such children; school programs offering instruction in phonological awareness and basic phonics will not be sufficient. They will help to access the code, but not the ideas and information on which children depend to improve their vocabulary, grammar, and ability to construct meaning while reading.

In thinking about the differences among early literacy screening batteries, educators might keep several principles in mind: (1) The more language traits measured, the wider the net cast to capture potentially struggling readers (but remember that the more comprehensive batteries take time and personnel to administer), and (2) the danger of screening in a narrow way is that students with problems not tapped by the screening battery will obviously not be identified as needing help. For example, although the three measures used by O'Connor and Jenkins (1999) do not take much time to administer, they identify only students who are likely to have word-reading problems.

Some educators resist recommendations to use preschool screening batteries, believing that too much testing is a waste of time. They prefer a "wait and watch" approach, in which they identify children at risk for reading difficulties by their slow progress in acquiring early literacy skills, such as alphabet and phonological awareness in kindergarten and first grade. As noted earlier, the danger of waiting until the end of first grade to identify children in need of more extended or intensive instruction is that it becomes difficult to offset the problems of initial reading failure. Quite a few early reading problems can be effectively addressed with timely intervention in kindergarten and first grade; however, some children's reading problems are persistent and require continued intervention (Vellutino, Scanlon, & Lyon, 2000).

Again, most screening instruments focus on oral language and initial indices of print awareness, not on reading comprehension. Screening instruments that are restricted to measures of phonological awareness and alphabet knowledge may predict early word-reading achievement, and this in turn indicates whether students can use written texts to access ideas and information; that is, students cannot understand texts they cannot read. However, screening instruments of this type fall short of helping us to identify the students who are already having trouble with comprehension (e.g., comprehension of stories that others read to them).

Recently, efforts have been made to find more satisfactory ways to assess emergent reading comprehension capabilities in kindergarten and first grade. One promising method is storybook retelling. In one project (Paris & Paris, 2001), kindergartners, first graders, and second graders were given tasks to assess their understanding of wordless storybooks. First, the students completed a "picture walk," which means that they talked about what they saw as they turned the pages of the storybook. Then they were asked to retell the story in the book. This measure of retelling was scored by using elements of story grammar, such as identification of the characters and the initiating event. Finally, children were asked comprehension questions that focused on their ability to infer causes of events or motives of characters (e.g., "why?" questions). Collectively, the three measures were sensitive to developmental changes in comprehension between kindergarten and second grade. Furthermore, they provided insights into the students' awareness of story structure and the depth of their understanding of the story told implicitly through the pictures. For students who are not able to read at all, or whose reading is at a primer level, storybook comprehension may be as valid a measure of reading comprehension as we can get.

ASSESSMENT FOR INSTRUCTION

A fourth purpose for assessing reading is to monitor students' progress in reading. The term "formative assessment" is appropriately used here, because the purpose is to collect data on students' progress toward particular short-term educational goals. Summative data collection, in contrast, involves assessment of students' progress toward long-term goals, as would be the case with most standardized tests of reading comprehension. In some cases, assessment of students' progress in the curriculum gives educators a way to monitor their response to instruction. With this information, they have the opportunity to fine-tune what and how they are teaching. In other cases, educators want to gather information about students' engagement in literacy activities (writing as well as reading) so that they have a picture of student learning that is richer and more naturalistic than the one provided by performance on standardized tests of reading. Approaches to assessment that serve these purposes include both quantitative and qualitative methods.

Curriculum-Based Measures

In terms of methods that provide quantitative measures of students' response to instruction in the classroom, curriculum-based measures (CBMs) have been shown to be valid and reliable tools for teachers. In general, CBMs employ tasks of measurable reading behaviors, such as oral reading accuracy and fluency. Passages are taken from the course readings, so that the teacher can assess performance on materials on which students are currently working (Espin & Foegen, 1996; Shin, Deno, & Espin, 2000). CBM measures can be administered to individuals or to groups. Even if CBM tasks measure isolated reading behaviors, performance on these measures tends to correspond with students' performance on more general tests of reading achievement. It is also related to learning and remembering content-area information (Espin & Deno, 1993; Espin & Foegen, 1996). For example, in a study of 10th-graders' performance on an oral reading measure, Espin and Deno (1993) found that performance was significantly related to students' grade point average and achievement test performance. A thought-provoking finding from this study

is that reading aloud was more strongly related to academic success for students at the lower than at the higher end of the grade-point distribution. This raises the possibility that an oral reading measure could be useful in estimating the comprehension of students with reading problems in content-area textbooks.

An oral reading CBM is typically carried out by asking the student to read aloud a passage at an appropriate level of difficulty (e.g., an excerpt from a book that student is reading in class). The educator records errors and marks the passage after 1 minute, and calculates the number of words read accurately in that time. One problem with this method is that oral reading lacks face validity as a test of comprehension. Educators do not get information about comprehension skills such as recalling main ideas. Therefore, oral reading measures are not seen as useful for evaluating and planning instruction in reading comprehension, in comparison to other measures of comprehension. However, oral reading measures can help educators make judgments about the extent to which students can work effectively in texts of different levels of difficulty. Whereas oral reading measures tend to correlate significantly with measures of comprehension, several other CBM measures may seem more closely related to reading comprehension (Fuchs, Fuchs, & Maxwell, 1988), including measures of oral or written recall (retelling the information in a passage) and a technique called the "maze task."

Oral and written recall measures, like oral reading measures, have been found to relate significantly to standardized reading achievement for students with disabilities (Fuchs et al., 1988). Recall measures show the amount of information the student retains after reading a passage; they also provide insights about how this information is organized in the student's memory. Scoring these measures may pose a challenge for educators. The most superficial way is to use a simple word count. The problem with this measure is that the number of words may not be a good reflection of the number of ideas from the passage included in the retelling. A second scoring method, counting the number of content words in the retelling, gives a better picture of the readers' grasp of information in the passage than does a single word count. A third method entails analysis of the idea units in the passage and use of this analysis as a template for scoring the ideas in students' written or oral retelling. The second and third methods require quite a bit of work on the educator's part, but the result may be a more detailed picture of the reader's comprehension and recall of the passage.

Another form of CBM, the maze task, is ostensibly more focused on word and passage comprehension (Shin et al., 2000). A maze task is constructed by deleting every seventh word in a passage and replacing it with three multiple-choice alternatives (one correct and two incorrect alternatives). Part of a sample maze passage, given in Shin et al. (p. 166), is as follows:

My mother always likes to go home. She was born on a nice (farm/big/soon) in a valley. Her father started (home/the/sat) farm before she was born. When (red/she/told) was a little girl they lived (to/fun/in) a very old log house on (call/date/the) farm.

Students are given 3 minutes to read the passage and select words among the alternatives, so speed of making decisions about correct words is a significant factor. The maze task has the advantage of being an efficiently administered measure of reading performance; it can be administered to groups, and it can be administered by computer. Recent studies have shown that the maze task is a valid tool for assessing reading growth in the classroom (Espin & Foegen, 1996).

In short, CBM measures are useful to monitor the progress of students in reading, and in content-area learning from reading. Information about students' progress in reading allows educators to make instructional adjustments that they might not have made, based on the test data they ordinarily have about their students' reading (e.g., standardized test scores). A study of special education teachers' use of students' CBM test results in mathematics showed that teachers did make instructional adjustments based on CBM data. In addition, students

whose instruction was adjusted because of their CBM performance made greater gains on global achievement tests than did peers whose instruction was not adjusted in this way (Stecker & Fuchs, 2000). It is possible that similar results would be found for teachers' use of CBM test results in reading.

Performance Assessments

Many educators prefer to assess students' progress by taking into account a broader range of their traits and of instructional variables than are measured by CBM or by traditional reading comprehension tests. They may want to use methods that are student-centered, focusing on students' motivation and interest. One form that such an assessment might take is a written response to a story that includes feelings and experiences inspired by the text. Alternatively, they may want to understand the reasoning processes that students use to arrive at an understanding of a text. One form that such an assessment might take is a verbal protocol, in which the student is asked to verbalize or "talk aloud" about his or her understanding of a text at points during the reading (Pressley & Afflerbach, 1995).

Measures of comprehension such as written responses or talk-aloud protocols are types of performance assessment. Performance assessment involves testing methods that require students to create an answer or a product that demonstrates their knowledge or skills (Elliott, 1998). Performance measures are considered authentic when they reflect the conditions under which students have constructed the meaning of the text, including group discussions, individual projects, or specific assignments the teacher has used to foster thinking about a given text. Authentic assessments are valued because they tap the natural uses of reading and provide indices of complex interactions with texts (Valencia, Hiebert, & Afflerbach, 1994). Other examples of authentic assessments include excerpts from students' reading journals, written responses to open-ended questions, and videotapes of plays read by students and acted out in class.

Performance measures differ from traditional tests in two ways. First, they are criterion-referenced, not norm-referenced. This means that the student is evaluated on criteria developed from an analysis of the content the test is covering. In contrast, norm-referenced measures evaluate a student's performance by comparing it to that of other students. Second, performance measures test knowledge of material that is taught in the classroom, whereas traditional comprehension tests sample knowledge in the content domain, regardless of the content of that particular course.

One popular type of authentic assessment is the portfolio, which may be assembled based on criteria set up ahead of time by the teacher, or it may include the students' choice of work products that they would like others to use to evaluate their reading and learning (Stowell & Tierney, 1995; Valencia et al., 1994). Portfolios are valuable because they reflect work done over a period of time. They may reveal changes in students' responses to instruction and may contain substantive indices of students' accomplishment.

Little has been written about the use of performance assessments specifically with students who are struggling to learn to read. In one study (Boerum, 2000), sixth graders with LD engaged in authentic learning experiences, reflection, goal-setting, and self-assessment. They also kept portfolios, so that they could document their growth as learners to an outside audience. The results suggest that when given the opportunity to engage in authentic learning experiences and assessment, students with LD can clarify their strengths and weaknesses as learners and begin to set reasonable goals for improvement.

Because portfolios provide an insight into students' learning in relation to their course work and personal experiences, reading experts have tried to find ways to determine whether they can be used as outcome measures or achievement tests, as well as measures of students' progress in the curriculum; that is, are they suitable for purposes of evaluation of instruction and learning within a given classroom and for purposes of comparing students' learning in different classrooms and schools? For portfolios to be useful across classrooms, there need to

be criteria for evaluating the contents of the portfolio that are systematic—a scoring rubric, for instance, that could be used reliably by different educators in different schools. Valencia and Wixson (2000) reported that despite efforts to find ways to evaluate students' reading portfolios, the scoring rubrics developed for this purpose are not as reliable and valid as they should be, if they are to be used to compare student performance in different classrooms or schools. Experts in measurement are finding statewide performance tests that require a variety of types of responses promising (Goldberg & Roswell, 2001), but there is much still to be learned about the usefulness of multimeasure tests for both teachers and policymakers.

The information gained from a portfolio might complement information gained from traditional achievement tests. Wiig (2000) has argued that we must find ways to identify students whose learning difficulties are due to neuropsychological deficits in language and literacy, in order to distinguish these students from others whose limited language and literacy development has other causes (e.g., limited motivation or opportunities to learn). Because different types of assessments have both limitations and advantages, she concluded that multidimensional and multiperspective assessments should be used. These might include not only traditional measures but also behavioral rating scales, portfolio assessments, and self-evaluations. She argued that only by using both formal and informal measures can the causes for low achievement in literacy and language be determined.

In some studies of reading instruction designed for diverse learners, assessment methods have included a variety of qualitative indices of growth and motivation, as well as test scores from a range of different literacy activities (e.g., written compositions, as well as oral reading performance) (Raphael, Brock, & Wallace, 1997). A comprehensive or multilayered approach helps us acquire a rich understanding of the experiences and progress of students who are struggling readers in different models of classroom reading instruction. Among other findings, such studies tend to suggest that attention to students' interest and involvement in evaluating their own literacy experiences may be valuable ways to gain information to aid them in learning.

COMMONLY ASKED QUESTIONS

Is There a Single Best Task to Rely on as a Measure of Reading Comprehension?

No, there is not. Different tasks yield different pictures of students' comprehension capabilities, because different tasks place different requirements on the reader. Tasks such as multiple-choice questions or the cloze procedure tend to be moderately correlated with one another, but the fact that they are not highly correlated suggests that they are measuring somewhat different reading behaviors or processes. Multiple-choice questions and cloze procedure tasks are typically used on standardized tests to assess understanding of short passages. Comprehension tests that use multiple-choice questions (e.g., Gates–MacGinitie Reading Test) are efficient to administer and score. They can help us understand students' ability to answer different kinds of questions (e.g., understanding of main ideas vs. details). However, because the passage is available for the student's use while answering questions, memory for passage information is not an issue. The test becomes one of interpretation of text, not the ability to construct a mental representation of the text while reading.

Somewhat different processing requirements are placed on students when the cloze procedure is used to assess reading comprehension. "Cloze" refers to omitting words systematically (e.g., every ninth word). On group tests, students are given several possible answers, and they pick the best word to complete the sentence. On tests that are administered individually, such as the Woodcock–Johnson III Tests of Achievement, Passage Comprehension subtest (Woodcock, McGrew, & Mather, 2001), the student tells the examiner the word that might best fill the empty slot in the sentence or passage. An excerpt from Salvia and Hughes (1990, p. 146), illustrates one form of a cloze test:

Jack and Jill climbed Goose Hill to get some water from the spring in the pine grove at the top. They each carried two _____ containers that clanked as _____ climbed. When they reached_____ grove and found the _____ they filled their pails _____ drank their fill. Then _____ back down.

Cloze tests tend to assess what we call "local" comprehension, which refers to sensitivity to the grammatical and semantic constraints on meaning. Like multiple-choice questions, cloze tests are not ideal if one wants to assess understanding and recall of ideas and information in natural passages.

Individualized tests of reading, particularly informal reading inventories (e.g., Qualitative Reading Inventory III; Leslie & Caldwell, 2000) may use retelling as a way to assess comprehension. When the student is asked to tell the examiner about what he or she read, the task is often called "free recall." Recently, revisions of some individually administered achievement batteries have included a subtest that uses free recall to assess comprehension (e.g., the Woodcock–Johnson Tests of Achievement). Free recall tasks require students to organize information that they have taken in while reading, in order to tell it to someone else. As a result, performance on free recall tasks reflects students' memory for passage information, expressive language capabilities, and metacognitive capabilities. Students with LD may perform relatively poorly, because such tasks require coordination of different processes. More specifically, although students with LD perform less well than their peers on various comprehension tasks, the gap between normally achieving and LD readers is more pronounced when the task is retelling (Carlisle, 1999). Even so, teachers may find recall a helpful way to monitor the progress their students are making in reading (Fuchs, Fuchs, & Hamlett, 1989).

Because students' retelling must somehow be analyzed for its content and structure, scoring free recall tests is more challenging than scoring multiple-choice question tests or cloze tests. Nonetheless, the richness of information that is likely to be gathered from retellings may be worth the time it takes to analyze students' retellings.

One other task used to assess reading comprehension is sentence verification. The sentence verification technique (SVT), developed by Royer, Kulhavy, Lee, and Peterson (1986), presents students with a series of sentences after they have read or listened to a passage. Students indicate whether a given sentence gives ideas and information that was in the passage. Those that give passage information are marked "old," and those that do not are marked "new." There are four sentence types: originals (sentences taken directly from the passage), paraphrases (lexical or word-order shifts that do not change the basic ideas), meaning changes (shifts of one or two words that change the meaning), and distractors (sentences with information not in the passage). The following excerpt adapted from Salvia and Hughes (1990, p. 143) shows sample SVT test items:

Excerpt from the passage:
Jack and Jill climbed Goose Hill to get some water from the spring in the pine grove at the top. They each carried two empty containers that clanked as they climbed. When they reached the grove and found the spring, they filled their pails and drank their fill. Then they headed back down . . .

Directions:
I want you to read each sentence below. Write old if there was a sentence in the passage that meant the same thing. Old sentences may use different words but they will mean the same thing. Write new if the information was not in the paragraph.

Test items:
_____ Jack and Jill went up the hill to bring back some water. (paraphrase)
_____ They filled their pails and drank their fill. (original)
_____The water was cool, and they were refrreshed. (distractor)
_____ It was hot and Jack decided to roll down the hill. (meaning change)

The SVT has been found to be a valid measure of students' understanding of short passages (typically 12–16 sentences). SVT tests are moderately strongly related to other types of comprehension tests, and they are sensitive to students' reading capabilities (Carlisle & Felbinger, 1991). One particular value is that the SVT offers a way to compare listening and reading comprehension (Royer et al., 1986). Because the passage is not present when students judge the test items after reading, as is also true after listening, performance in the two modalities can be directly compared. Another advantage is that the SVT is a good way to assess understanding of passage information without tapping expressive language capabilities. Finally, performances on the SVT are sensitive to students' memory for text information and understanding of text structures. Although sentence verification offers many advantages, it is not currently used in published tests of comprehension for group or individual administration.

There is one other task used to assess reading comprehension that does not place a requirement on expressive language. This involves selecting a picture from a set of four that best represents the meaning of a sentence or short passage, as in the comprehension subtest of the Peabody Individual Achievement Test (Markwardt, 2002). Like the SVT, picture selection does not require expressive language. It also does not require receptive language for processing the response options. However, one major limitation is that it can be used to assess only those sentences or passages that provide information that can be displayed in a single picture. It is very difficult to assess comprehension of abstract ideas or relations among ideas by use of pictorial representations.

To return to the question, different tasks are used to assess reading comprehension, because they provide different insights into students' reading processes and have different advantages and limitations as forms of measurement. When educators are given information about their students' performance in reading, an understanding of the nature of the test will help them to interpret the results. With the wide array of published tests and methods of assessing comprehension in mind, it is a good idea to build a professional library in schools that have resources such as books on reading assessment for teachers to use.

What Methods Might Teachers of Content-Area Courses Use to Assess Their Students' Ability To Read and Learn From the Textbook?

Methods used to assess reading and learning from texts should be selected on the basis of the goals and content of the instruction. No single method is ideal for all situations. One method to track changes in the ability to read and understand texts would be to use CBMs, including oral reading and a maze test, which were described earlier. More can be learned about the construction of such tests from Shin et al. (2000), Espin and Deno (1993), and Salvia and Hughes (1990). One advantage in using CBMs is that follow-up testing can be carried out after measures have been put in place to help students improve their comprehension of content-area textbooks.

Another solution would be use of performance assessment (e.g., free recall and written or oral reports). The tasks, content, or activities that make up the measure should reflect the curriculum and the goals and instructional methods of the teacher. For example, if a science teacher has taught students to use graphic organizers (e.g., concept maps) to aid in comprehension and recall of texts, he or she might ask students to read a selection in the textbook and make a concept map as a way to assess their learning "tools" in science.

Various options for carrying out performance assessment are currently being explored, because they offer more sensitive tools than are available through standardized tests for assessing the learning of students from culturally and linguistically different backgrounds and of students with learning disabilities (Elliott, 1998). "Hands-on" activities used for such assessments are more commonly found in studies of math and writing but can be used for reading as well. Comprehension assessment might include writing a sequel to a story, re-enacting a historical event, making a panorama that displays the setting and mood of a story, and so on. In designing a performance as-

sessment, the teacher needs to make decisions about not only the extent to which the test is an authentic measure of classroom learning but also reliable ways to score students' performance on such tests. Is it fair to give individual students scores on a measure that is based on a group project? Is it possible to assess reliably students' re-enactment of scenes from a Shakespeare play? Performance tests may not only help us gather insights into students' reactions to reading activities, but they may also offer many challenges in terms of devising sound and systematic methods of evaluation!

Are There Ways to Distinguish Students with Significant Learning Disabilities in the area of Reading Comprehension That Do Not Involve Standardized Tests?

It is difficult to determine whether a student's reading problems constitute a reading disability without norm-referenced measures of reading and related areas. However, Fuchs and Fuchs (1998) have suggested that teachers can use response to instruction as a way to make such a determination. They recommend using CBMs that have good technical characteristics (i.e., reliability and validity). With such instruments, teachers should be able to distinguish between ineffective teaching and unacceptable learning by one or more students in a class. The CBM tests, administered on a regular basis to all classes at a given grade level in a school or district, might show whether the growth rate of all students in a class is similar across teachers. The group mean and the amount of variation in each class would be important variables. Where there is a lot of variation in student response to instruction in a class, we would suspect that there are a few students with a slower rate of learning than is typical for that class. In contrast, when the class is making slow progress relative to other classes at that grade level, but with relatively little variation in the class, we might suspect a general lack of responsiveness on the part of the students.

Identifying students and classes that are making slow progress is, of course, the first step in taking corrective action. When students whose rate of learning is below that of the group are given special help, performance on subsequent CBMs should show whether these students responded to the classroom intervention. If they did not, it might be time to consider referral for a more thorough assessment of the students' learning capabilities. If, on the other hand, a student responds to the classroom intervention, it might be that his or her learning needs fall short of the severity and pervasiveness characteristic of learning disabilities or other categories of exceptionality. Teachers interested in this method of identifying students with significant comprehension problems would be well-advised to read about methods to implement a CBM that could be used for such purposes in a school system (e.g., Fuchs & Fuchs, 1998; Self, Benning, Marston, & Magnusson, 1991).

CONCLUDING REMARKS

Because educators are so involved in both assessment and instruction of reading comprehension, they can benefit from having a good understanding of purposes and methods of comprehension assessment. Many educational, philosophical, and even political factors are intertwined, and there are many stakeholders in the selection, use, and interpretation of reading achievement tests. This is a challenging area in the professional development of educators!

An altogether different aspect of the challenge of understanding comprehension assessment is the complexity of the process of comprehending written texts. Comprehension of written texts is a mental process, one that is not open to inspection or evaluation without asking the reader to do something with (or say something about) the information from the text. Various student characteristics and instructional factors affect students' developing comprehension capabilities. Too often, only student characteristics are considered in interpreting a weak performance on a test of reading comprehension (e.g., language development, word-recognition skills). It is important also to consider the kinds of texts students are asked to read, and the nature and extent of

the instruction they have received in comprehension strategies. In short, to make wise decisions about changes in reading instruction for individuals with reading problems and/or for schools with underachieving readers, educators would do well to assess the reading curriculum, methods of instruction and their alignment with methods of assessment, and the appropriateness and timely use of methods to address the needs of students who are experiencing significant problems with reading comprehension.

ACKNOWLEDGMENT

This chapter is adapted from Chapter 10, "Assessment of Reading Comprehension," in Carlisle and Rice (2002). Copyright 2002 by York Press. Adapted by permission.

REFERENCES

Aaron, P. G. (1991). Can reading disabilities be diagnosed without using intelligence tests? *Journal of Learning Disabilities, 24,* 178–186, 191.

Aaron, P. G., Joshi, M., & Williams, K. A. (1999). Not all reading disabilities are alike. *Journal of Learning Disabilities, 32,* 120–137.

Allington, R., & McGill-Franzen, A. (1992). Unintended effects of reform in New York. *Educational Policy, 6,* 397–414.

Badian, N. A. (1999). Reading disability defined as a discrepancy between listening and reading comprehension: A longitudinal study of stability, gender differences, and prevalence. *Journal of Learning Disabilities, 32,* 138–148.

Badian, N. A. (2000). Do preschool orthographic skills contribute to prediction of reading? In N. Badian (Ed.), *Prediction and prevention of reading failure* (pp. 31–56). Baltimore: York Press.

Boerum, L. J. (2000). Developing portfolios with learning disabled students. *Reading and Writing Quarterly, 16,* 211–238.

Cain, K., & Oakhill, J. V. (1999). Inference making ability and its relation to comprehension failure in young children. *Reading and Writing: An Interdisciplinary Journal, 11,* 489–503.

Caldwell, J. S. (2002). *Reading assessment: A primer for teachers and tutors.* New York: Guilford Press.

Carlisle, J. F. (1989). Diagnosing comprehension deficits through listening and reading. *Annals of Dyslexia, 39,* 159–176.

Carlisle, J. F. (1999). Free recall as a test of reading comprehension for students with learning disabilities. *Learning Disability Quarterly, 22,* 11–22.

Carlisle, J. F., & Felbinger, L. (1991). Profiles of listening and reading comprehension. *Journal of Educational Research, 84,* 345–354.

Carlisle, J. F., & Rice, M. S. (2002). *Improving reading comprehension: Research-based principles and practices.* Baltimore: York Press.

Catts, H. W., Fey, M. E., Zhang, X., & Tomblin, J. B. (1999). Language basis of reading and reading disabilities: Evidence from a longitudinal investigation. *Scientific Studies of Reading, 3,* 331–361.

Catts, H. W., Fey, M. E., Zhang, X., & Tomblin, J. B. (2001). Estimating the risk of future difficulties in kindergarten children: A research-based model and its clinical implementation. *Language, Speech, and Hearing Services in Schools, 32,* 38–50.

Elliott, J. L., Erickson, R. N., Thurlow, M. L., & Shriner, J. G. (2000). State-level accountability for the performance of students with disabilities. *Journal of Special Education, 34,* 39–47.

Elliott, S. N. (1998). Performance assessment of students' achievement: Research and practice. *Learning Disabilities Research and Practice, 13,* 233–241.

Espin, C. A., & Deno, S. L. (1993). Performance in reading from content-area texts as an indicator of achievement. *Remedial and Special Education, 14,* 47–59.

Espin, C. A., & Foegen, A. (1996). Validity of general outcome measures for predicting secondary students' performance on content-area tasks. *Exceptional Children, 62,* 497–514.

Fletcher, J. M., Francis, D. J., Shaywitz, S. E., Lyon, G. R., Foorman, B. R., Stuebing, K. K., et al.. (1998). Intelligent testing and the discrepancy model for children with learning disabilities. *Learning Disabilities Research and Practice, 13,* 186–203.

Fuchs, L. S., & Fuchs, D. (1998). Treatment validity: A unifying concept for reconceptualizing the identification of learning disabilities. *Learning Disabilities Research and Practice, 13,* 204–219.

Fuchs, L. S., Fuchs, D., Eaton, S. B., Hamlett, C., Binkley, E., & Crouch, R. (2000). Using objective data sources to enhance teacher judgments about test accommodations. *Exceptional Children, 67,* 67–81.

Fuchs, L. S., Fuchs, D., & Hamlett, C. L. (1989). Monitoring reading growth using student recalls: Effects of two teacher feedback systems. *Journal of Educational Research, 83,* 103–110.

Fuchs, L. S., Fuchs, D., & Maxwell, L. (1988). The validity of informal reading comprehension measures. *Remedial and Special Education, 9,* 20–28.

Goldberg, G. L., & Roswell, B. S. (2001). Are multiple measures meaningful?: Lessons from a statewide performance assessment. Applied Measurement in Education, 14, 125–150.

Kleinert, H. L., Haig, J., Kearns, J. F., & Kennedy, S. (2000). Alternate assessments: Lessons learned and roads to be taken. *Exceptional Children, 67,* 51–66.

Leslie, L., & Caldwell, J. (2000). *Qualitative Reading Inventory III.* New York: HarperCollins.

Markwardt, F. (2002). *Peabody Individual Achievement Test-R/NU.* Circle Pines, MN: American Guidance Service.

McKenna, M. C., Kear, D. J., & Ellsworth, R. A. (1995). Children's attitude toward reading: A national survey. *Reading Research Quarterly, 30,* 934–956.

Muter, V. (2000). Screening for early reading failure. In N. Badian (Ed.), *Prediction and prevention of reading failure* (pp. 1–29). Baltimore: York Press.

National Center for Educational Statistics. (2000). *National Assessment of Educational Progress.* Washington, DC: U.S. Department of Education.

Oakhill, J., & Yuill, N. (1996). Higher order factors in comprehension disability: Processes and remediation. In C. Cornoldi & J. Oakhill (Eds.), *Reading comprehension difficulties: Processes and intervention* (pp. 69–92). Mahwah, NJ: Erlbaum.

O'Connor, R. E., & Jenkins, J. R. (1999). Prediction of reading disabilities in kindergarten and first grade. *Scientific Studies of Reading, 3,* 159–197.

Paris, S., & Paris, A. (2001). Children's comprehension of narrative picture books. *Center for the Improvement of Early Reading Achievement* (Report No. 3-102). Ann Arbor: University of Michigan.

Pressley, M., & Afflerbach, P. (1995). *Verbal protocols of reading.* Hillsdale, NJ: Erlbaum.

Raphael, T. E., Brock, C. H., & Wallace, S. (1997). Encouraging quality peer talk with diverse students in mainstream classrooms: Learning from and with teachers. In J. R. Paratore & T. McCormick (Eds.), *Peer talk in the classroom: Learning from research* (pp. 176–206). Newark, DE: International Reading Association.

Royer, J., Kulhavy, R., Lee, S., & Peterson, S. (1986). The relationship between reading and listening comprehension. *Educational and Psychological Research, 6,* 299–314.

Salvia, J., & Hughes, C. (1990). *Curriculum-based assessment: Testing what is taught.* New York: Macmillan.

Self, H., Benning, A., Marston, D., & Magnusson, D. (1991). Cooperative teacher project: A model for students at risk. *Exceptional Children, 58,* 26–35.

Shankweiler, D., Lundquist, E., Katz, L., Steubing, K. K., Fletcher, J. M., Brady, S., et al. (1999). Comprehension and decoding: Patterns of association in children with reading difficulties. *Scientific Studies of Reading, 3,* 69–94.

Shin, J., Deno, S. L., & Espin, C. (2000). Technical adequacy of the maze task for curriculum-based measurement of reading growth. *Journal of Special Education, 34,* 164–172.

Siegel, L. S. (1992). An evaluation of the discrepancy definition of dyslexia. *Journal of Learning Disabilities, 25,* 618–629.

Simmons, D. C., Kuykendall, K., Cornachione, C., & Kame'enui, E. J. (2000). Implementation of a schoolwide reading improvement model: "No one ever told us it would be this hard!" *Learning Disabilities Research and Practice, 15,* 92–100.

Snow, C. E., Burns, S., & Griffin, P. (1998). *Preventing reading difficulties in young children.* Washington, DC: National Academy Press.

Spring, C., & French, L. (1990). Identifying children with specific reading disabilities from listening and reading discrepancy scores. *Journal of Learning Disabilities, 23,* 53–58.

Stanovich, K. E. (1991). Reading disability: Assessment issues. In H. L. Swanson (Ed.), *Handbook on the assessment of learning disabilities: Theory, research, and practice* (pp. 147–175). Austin, TX: Pro-Ed.

Stecker, P. M., & Fuchs, L. S. (2000). Effecting superior achievement using curriculum-based measurement: The importance of individual progress monitoring. *Learning Disabilities Research and Practice, 15,* 128–134.

Sticht, T. H., & James, H. J. (1984). Listening and reading. In P. D. Pearson (Ed.), *Handbook of reading research* (pp. 293–317). New York: Longman.

Stowell, L. P., & Tierney, R. J. (1995). Portfolios in the classroom: What happens when teachers and students negotiate assessment? In R. Allington & S. Walmsley (Eds.), *No quick fix: Rethinking literacy lessons in America's elementary schools* (pp. 78–94). New York: Teachers College Press.

Taylor, B. M., Pearson, P. D., Clark, K. F., & Walpole, S. (1999). Effective schools/accomplished teachers. *Reading Teacher, 53,* 156–159.

Thurlow, M. L., House, A. L., Scott, D. L., & Ysseldyke, J. F. (2000). Students with disabilities in large-scale assessments: State participation and accommodation policies. *Journal of Special Education, 34,* 154–163.

Torgesen, J. K., & Wagner, R. K. (1998). Alternative diagnostic approaches for specific developmental reading disabilities. *Learning Disabilities Research and Practice, 13,* 220–232.

United States Office of Education. (1977). Assistance to states for education of handicapped children: Procedures for evaluating specific learning disabilities. *Federal Register, 42,* G1082–G1085.

Valencia, S. W., Hiebert, E. H., & Afflerbach, P. P. (Eds.). (1994). *Authentic reading assessment: Practices and possibilities.* Newark, DE: International Reading Association.

Valencia, S. W., & Wixson, K. (2000). Policy-oriented research on literacy standards and assessment. In M. Kamil, P. B. Mosenthal, P. D. Pearson, & R. Barr (Eds.), *Handbook of Reading Research* (Vol. III, pp. 909–935). Mahwah, NJ: Erlbaum.

Vellutino, F., Scanlon, D. M., & Lyon, G. R. (2000). Differentiating between difficult-to-remediate and readily remediated poor readers: More evidence against the IQ-achievement discrepancy definition of reading disability. *Journal of Learning Disabilities, 33,* 223–238.

Wiig, E. H. (2000). Authentic and other assessments of language disabilities: When is fair fair? *Reading and Writing Quarterly, 16,* 179–210.

Wixson, K. K., & Dutro, E. (1998). *Standards for primary-grade reading: An analysis of state frameworks* (Center for the Improvement of Early Reading Achievement Report No. 2-001). Ann Arbor: University of Michigan.

Woodcock, R. W., McGrew, K. S., & Mather, N. (2001). *Woodcock–Johnson Tests of Achievement.* Itasca, IL: Riverside.

Ysseldyke, J., & Olsen, K. (1999). Putting alternate assessments into practice: What to measures and possible sources of data. *Exceptional Children, 65,* 175–185.

25

Teaching Reading Comprehension to Students with Learning Disabilities

Sharon Vaughn
Janette Klingner

In the last few years, the phonological awareness and decoding skills of students with reading disabilities have been identified as serious inhibitors to successful reading (Ball & Blachman, 1991; O'Connor & Jenkins, 1995; Vellutino & Scanlon, 1987). Although there is little question that this is true, students with learning disabilities (LD) have significant challenges understanding and learning from text even when they are able to decode adequately (Williams, 1998). Explicit and highly structured development of beginning reading skills is required, and so is highly structured instruction in reading comprehension (Gersten & Darch, 1986; Gersten, Fuchs, Williams, & Baker, 2001).

How likely is it that students with LD will receive structured instruction in reading comprehension? Durkin (1978–1979) conducted an observational study of reading comprehension instruction. She revealed that typical comprehension instruction followed a mentioning, practicing, and assessing procedure; that is, teachers would *mention* to students the skill that they wanted them to use, would give them opportunities to *practice* that skill through workbooks or skill sheets, and then would *assess* whether students used the skill successfully. Noticeably missing from this view of comprehension instruction is the instruction. In more than 4,000 minutes of reading instruction observed in fourth-grade classrooms, only 20 minutes of comprehension instruction was recorded. This study significantly influenced subsequent research in reading comprehension (Dole, Duffy, Roehler, & Pearson, 1991); however, observation studies revealed that this finding had little influence on classroom practice (Moody, Vaughn, Hughes, & Fischer, 2000; Pressley & El-Dinary, 1997; Schumm, Moody, & Vaughn, 2000; Vaughn, Moody, & Schumm, 1998).

Our purpose in this chapter is to review instructional practices used to improve the reading comprehension of students with LD. First, we address approaches employed before reading and during or after reading. Next, we discuss vocabulary instruction and expository text structure analysis, followed by a review of three multicomponent reading comprehension strategies: reciprocal teaching, transactional strategies instruction, and collaborative strategic reading.

INTERVENTION PRACTICES IN READING COMPREHENSION FOR STUDENTS WITH LEARNING DISABILITIES

The National Reading Panel (2000) conducted a meta-analysis of reading comprehension intervention strategies. Though not specific to students with reading and learning disabilities, based on 203 studies, the panel was able to identify intervention practices associated with improved outcomes in reading comprehension, including the following:

1. Teaching students to monitor their comprehension, and teaching procedures for adjusting when difficulties in understanding arise.
2. Using cooperative learning practices while implementing comprehension strategies in the context of reading.
3. Providing graphic and semantic organizers that assist students in writing or drawing relationships from the story.
4. Providing support for questioning strategies through (a) story structures that assist students in answering critical questions about the passage, (b) feedback to students regarding their answers to questions about the text, and (c) opportunities for students to ask and answer their own questions about the text.
5. Teaching students to write important ideas about what they have read and to summarize these ideas after they have read longer passages.
6. Combining multiple strategies for students to apply.

In a meta-analysis of intervention outcomes, Swanson (1999, 2001) identified the key components of effective reading comprehension instruction for students with LD. Direct instruction, strategy instruction, or a combination of both is associated with the highest effect sizes in reading comprehension for students with LD. Both direct instruction and strategy instruction have the following components in common: Assessment and evaluation of learning objectives, including orienting students to what they will be learning, and daily reviews of mater-

ial taught to ensure mastery. Another important component is teacher presentation of new material, which includes giving examples and demonstrating what students need to do. In this arena, (1) guided instruction, including asking questions to determine understanding and misunderstanding and providing feedback and correction, and (2) independent practice and review are essentials. For reading comprehension, the instructional components that contributed the most improved effect sizes were as follows:

1. Teacher and student questioning and interactive dialogue between teachers and students, and students and students.
2. Controlling task difficulty and scaffolding instruction.
3. Elaboration of steps or strategies and modeling by the teacher.
4. Small-group instruction.

Another significant component was the use of strategy cues to help students remember to use and apply what they learned.

PRACTICES BEFORE, DURING, AND AFTER READING

Students with LD are often the poorest readers in terms of both decoding, and of word reading, fluency, and comprehension. These students also demonstrate characteristics of inactive learners (Torgesen & Licht, 1983) who do not monitor their learning or use strategies effectively. They have not developed the metacognitive awareness to assess their understanding as they read, so that they know when comprehension has broken down (Flavell, 1981; Garner, 1992). Thus, many of the reading comprehension strategies associated with the highest effect sizes for students with LD are those that teach students strategies that prompt them to monitor and reflect before, during, and after reading. These strategies ask students to consider their background knowledge of the topic they are reading, to summarize key ideas, and to self-question while they read (e.g., Jenkins, Heliotis, Stein, & Haynes, 1987; Mastropieri, Scruggs, Bakken, & Whedon, 1996; Wong & Jones, 1982). Teaching stu-

Before Reading

Prior to reading, one of the most effective practices implemented by teachers is to activate, build, and use students' background knowledge to link to their reading. Teachers assist students in bridging what they know to what they are learning (Pearson, 1996). For many students with LD, this may mean building what they know through vocabulary and concept development (Anders & Bos, 1984; Snider, 1989). Some students will have had experiences that connect them to what they are reading. Others will need preteaching and discussion of key vocabulary and concepts to prepare them for reading and learning from text (Carnine, Silbert, & Kame'enui, 1997). Students are more motivated to read when they have a strong interest in a topic, and motivation is a key factor in fostering reading growth (Gambrell, 1996). Though helping students to connect their prior knowledge to what they are reading occurs primarily prior to reading, good teachers also assist students while they are reading, by verifying what students predicted and comparing what they identified as prior knowledge with what they are now learning. Graves, Juel, and Graves (2001) suggest the following activities prior to reading:

1. Set a purpose for reading.
2. Motivate students to read.
3. Preteach key vocabulary and concepts.
4. Link students background knowledge and experiences with the reading.
5. Relate the reading to students' lives.
6. Build student's knowledge of the text features.

Through "text preview," students learn to integrate prior knowledge with the text and are motivated to read for understanding (Graves, Prenn, & Cooke, 1985; Graves et al., 2001). If teachers use text preview with expository text, they may want to ensure that key vocabulary, concepts and important points are pretaught (Readence, Bean, & Baldwin, 1998). A text preview prepared by the teacher is an organized framework to assist students in bridging their experiences to the reading. Three sections comprise a text preview: (1) one that piques student's interest, (2) a brief description of the theme or story organization, and (3) questions to guide reading. A text preview should take approximately 5–10 minutes and include the following procedures: Cue the students to the new reading; discuss an interesting part of the story; connect to students' experiences and knowledge; and present the questions to guide reading. Though previewing takes time, it does assist students in understanding what they read (Chen & Graves, 1995; Dole, Valencia, Greer, & Wardrop, 1991).

During and after Reading

During reading, students need to monitor their understanding, to use "fix-up" strategies to assist with comprehension, and to consider linkages between what they are reading and learning, and previous knowledge and experiences. "Fix-up" strategies are techniques the reader employs to repair comprehension problems; for example, rereading difficult text. Practices that make sense during reading include (1) reminding students to monitor their understanding while they read, and to make notes of difficult words, concepts, or ideas; (2) asking students questions during reading to guide and focus their reading; (3) focusing students on aspects of the text that require inferences; (4) asking students to summarize the main idea of passages as they read; (5) encouraging students to consider predictions made prior to reading and to confirm, disconfirm, or extend them; (6) giving students opportunities to respond and extend what they have read; (7) allowing students to write questions about what they have read; and (8) asking students to summarize the key ideas about their reading (Becker &

McCormick, 1991; Gajria & Salvia, 1992; Malone & Mastropieiri, 1992; Mastropieri & Scruggs, 1997; Palincsar & Brown, 1984; Pressley, Brown, El-Dinary, & Afflerbach, 1995; Swanson, 1999).

After reading, students need to summarize the key ideas they have read and respond to the reading in various ways, including writing, drawing, and discussion. They also should identify confusing vocabulary or concepts and clarify meanings. Perhaps the most effective strategies for students with reading problems to learn to apply both during and after reading are questioning, determining the main idea, and summarizing (Gajria & Salvia, 1992; Jenkins et al., 1987; Malone & Mastropieri, 1992; Wong & Jones, 1982).

Questioning

Because questioning is the most prevalent way that teachers determine the comprehension of students, we address it in more detail. Teachers view questions as an essential feature for determining whether students truly understand and make connections with the text they read. Teachers who design questions that require students to draw conclusions, apply what they have learned, analyze what they have read, and synthesize and evaluate text are advancing their students' understanding and knowledge of reading. It is important for teachers both to ask good questions and to teach students to ask and answer good questions. The ReQuest procedure (Manzo & Manzo, 1993) can be used for this purpose:

1. *Silent reading.* The teacher and the student read the section of text independently and silently.
2. *Student questioning.* The teacher models how to answer questions, and to shape student questions. Students ask questions, and the teacher answers them.
3. *Teacher questioning.* The teacher models how to ask appropriate questions. Students answer questions, and the teacher assists by shaping their responses.
4. *Integration of the text.* The teacher repeats the procedure with the next section of text, this time integrating the previous

section of text with the newly read section. Questions and answers on both sections.
5. *Predictive questioning.* After students have read enough of the passage that they can make predictions about the rest of the text, the teacher asks them to stop and make predictions.
6. *Reading.* Students read to the end of the text to verify predictions, then discuss changes.

Another effective way for teachers to assist students in asking and answering worthwhile questions about what they read is the Questioning the Author strategy (Beck, McKeown, Sandora, Kucan, & Worthy, 1996). With Questioning the Author, the teacher has distinct goals and several queries that assist students in reaching those goals. For example, to initiate discussion, students are taught to ask, "What is the author trying to say?" To help students link information, the teacher asks, "How does that fit with what the author already told us?"

Another approach validated by the University of Kansas Center for Research on Learning is the Self-Questioning Strategy (Schumaker, Deshler, Nolan, & Alley, 1994). This instructional procedure teaches students how to generate questions about important information in a passage, predict the answers, search for the answers while reading, and talk to themselves about the answers by using the mnemonic, ASK IT: *A* (Step 1): Attend to the clues as you read; *S* (Step 2): Say some questions; *K* (Step 3): Keep predictions in mind; *I* (Step 4): Identify the answer; *T* (Step 5): Talk about the answers.

Determining the Main Idea and Summarizing

Williams (1988) indicated that constructing main ideas is essential for reading comprehension. It may be even more important for students with LD, because they rarely use comprehension strategies, even when the difficulty level of the reading passage increases (Simmons, Kame'enui, & Darch, 1988). Explicit and systematic instruction about the main idea is associated with improved outcomes in reading comprehension (Graves, 1986; Jenkins et al., 1987; Jitendra, Hoppes, & Xin, 2000; Wong & Jones, 1982). Furthermore, as stated previously, direct instruction plus strategy instruction is the best combination for providing powerful interventions for students with LD (Swanson, 1999, 2001; Swanson et al., 1999); thus, main idea instruction that addresses both direct instruction and strategy instruction is likely to yield the best outcomes.

Jitendra et al. (2000) combined strategy and direct instruction to improve main idea use for students with learning disabilities. They used the following information on a prompt card as a cue for the main idea: Does the paragraph tell what or who is the subject? Action is? Why—something happened? Where—something is or happened? When—something happened? How—something looks or is done? *Note:* Some paragraphs may contain a sentence or two that don't tell about the main idea!

Schumaker, Denton, and Deshler (1984) have developed and evaluated the effectiveness of the Paraphrasing Strategy in helping students with LD to comprehend text. Using the mnemonic RAP, first, students *R*ead the paragraph and think about what it means while reading; second, they *A*sk themselves, "What is the main idea and details of the paragraph?"; third, they *P*ut the main idea and supporting details into their own words.

Boyle and Weishaar (1997) examined the effects of student-generated and expert-generated cognitive organizers on the reading comprehension of high school students with LD, and focused on identifying and linking main ideas. Results indicated that the group that used student-generated cognitive organizers outperformed both the group using expert-generated cognitive organizers and the control group on comprehension measures. The group that used student-generated organizers followed the following strategy steps (TRAVEL): *T*—Topic: Write down the topic; *R*—Read: Read the paragraph; *A*—Ask: Ask what the main idea and three details are and write them down; *V*—Verify: Verify the main idea and linking details; *E*—

Examine: Examine the next paragraph and verify again; *L*—Link: When finished, link all of the main ideas.

Summarizing requires the student to generate multiple main ideas from across the reading, then combine them with supporting details to form a summary. Learning to summarize is an effective strategy for improving comprehension for students with learning disabilities (Gajria & Salvia, 1992; Nelson, Smith, & Dodd, 1992). One effective way to enhance summarizing skills is to teach students to retell key elements in a story by answering critical questions. Jenkins et al. (1987) improved the passage retelling and recall of students with LD by systematically teaching them to answer the questions about what they read: (1) Who is it about? (2) What's happening? Similarly, Malone and Mastropieri (1992) taught students to self-question while reading by asking (1) Who or what is the passage about? and (2) What is happening? Students with LD who participated in the training outperformed control students on recall of passage content.

Another approach to story retelling was offered by Bos (1987). The teacher first models retelling the story by identifying the key components: character, setting, problem, and resolution. For students who struggle with these components, teaching the components separately, then combining them can be an effective tool. Simple retelling includes the following steps:

1. Identify and retell the beginning, middle, and end of the story.
2. Describe the setting.
3. Identify the problem and resolution.

A more complete retelling includes the following steps:

1. Identify and retell events and facts in a sequence.
2. Make inferences to fill in missing information.
3. Identify and retell causes of actions or events and their effects.

The most complete retelling asks students to do the following:

1. Identify and retell a sequence of actions or events.
2. Make inferences to account for events or actions.
3. Offer an evaluation of the story.

According to Brown and Day (1983) there are five rules to consider when writing summaries:

1. Delete unimportant information.
2. Delete redundant information.
3. Identify the topic sentence.
4. Use a superordinate term for a list of terms or actions.
5. Develop a topic sentence when the author does not provide one.

VOCABULARY INSTRUCTION

Many students with LD have less extensive vocabularies than their peers without disabilities (Simmons & Kame'enui, 1998). Not only do students with LD typically know fewer words but also their understanding of concepts may lack depth. Many factors contribute to differential rates of vocabulary growth. Some of these students suffer from general language deficits that affect their vocabulary learning; others have problems with memory and/or recall (Swanson, 1987).

Numerous instructional methods designed to improve vocabulary learning have helped students with various types of learning difficulties. Students learn the majority of new words through *incidental* learning, while engaged in everyday experiences with oral and written language (Blachowicz & Fisher, 1996; Elley, 1988), with most of that learning occurring through reading as students get older (Anderson & Nagy, 1991; Baumann & Kame'enui, 1991). Many students with LD are less than their peers without disabilities likely to pick up words incidentally through listening and reading. Because of this, it is important to create opportunities for *intentional* learning to help improve their vocabulary acquisition. Intentional learning occurs when students are provided with systematic, explicit vocabulary instruction.

When focusing on vocabulary development with students, it is important to help students build an in-depth understanding of concepts, not just surface-level knowledge (Simmons & Kame'enui, 1998). Students must experience new concepts in a variety of learning situations. This helps students to develop a schema or conceptual framework that connects the new vocabulary term with prior knowledge. Multiple experiences with the same word enable students to expand their conceptual understanding of it. When students lack the background knowledge and experiences necessary to understand these terms, learning can be quite formidable. The focus of instruction should be on helping students make connections or associations between new words and previously learned information. It may be necessary to help them build the background knowledge needed to understand a concept. Whenever possible, new terms should be taught in categories rather than as isolated words. Meanings should be made explicit to students through demonstration, visual aids, discussion, and usage in varied contexts. In general, "less is more"—it is preferable to teach fewer words in depth rather than to teach many words superficially (Gersten & Jiménez, 1998). In this way, it is more likely the words will be retained.

According to Beck, McKeown, and Kucan (2002), words can be thought of according to a three-tier model. Words in Tier 1 are the most basic, such as *car, desk,* and *jump.* Words in Tier 2 are high-frequency, general words that make language use more mature. These are words such as *performed, benevolent,* and *capture.* Words in Tier 3 are low-frequency, more obscure, and may be used as technical terms or, infrequently, as adjectives. Technical words are specific to a particular subject, such as *photosynthesis.* Beck and colleagues suggest that teachers spend the majority of their time improving students' knowledge of Tier 2 words, and that they consider the following factors when selecting words for explicit instruction:

1. *Usefulness of the word.* Is the student likely to encounter this word again? Will learning this word help students in describing their own experiences?

2. *Relatedness of the word.* Does the word relate to what the class has been discussing or studying, or to a topic of interest to the student?
3. *Connection to text.* Does the word relate to the reading, or connect to big ideas in the reading?

Once vocabulary terms have been selected, many strategies can be used to provide explicit instruction in word meanings for students with LD.

Preteaching Word Meanings

Preteaching vocabulary helps students by not only providing them with background knowledge that can help them understand the topic they will be studying but also indicates what information is important and requires their attention while reading. Direct, explicit instruction in short segments can effectively increase students' understanding of new vocabulary (Bos & Anders, 1990; Echevarria & Graves, 1998). First, the teacher says the new term and writes it on the board. Students then say the word and write it on paper. Next, the teacher defines the word and uses pictures, demonstrations, and examples that are relevant to students to convey the meaning of the word.

Graphic Organizers

Graphic organizers can also be used to teach word meanings. They provide a visual or spatial framework for organizing the important conceptual relationships among new vocabulary words. Graphic organizers can be valuable learning tools for students who have difficulty understanding a concept, because they present key vocabulary terms, and indicate the relationships among the terms.

Semantic Map or Web

Semantic mapping is a process of diagramming related concepts from a reading passage or oral lesson (Heimlich & Pittelman, 1986). Webs can be completed as a pre- or postreading exercise. The technique can be used with the entire class to assist students in organizing and understanding the relationships among concepts, but it may be particularly helpful for students with comprehension-related learning difficulties. This teaching technique has also been used effectively with English-language learners (ELLs) with disabilities (Bos & Anders, 1992; Gallego, Duran, & Scanlon, 1990).

To construct a semantic map, use the following steps (adapted from Readence et al., 1998):

1. Select an important word or topic from the lecture or reading assignment (a semantic map can be constructed *before* or *after* the lesson or reading assignment).
2. Write the word on the chalkboard or overhead projector.
3. Ask students to say (or jot down) as many related words as they can think of from their own experiences, or from their reading of the text.
4. List these words on the chalkboard or overhead projector.
5. Organize the words into an octopus-like diagram.
6. Provide labels for the various categories. Elaborate by adding new categories or subcategories and related words as appropriate.

Perhaps the most important steps in this activity are the discussion and questioning activities that accompany the diagram.

Word Maps

Word maps are similar to semantic maps except that they are less elaborate and easier to complete (Blachowicz & Fisher, 1996). To create a word map, students think of a synonym, an antonym, an example, and a nonexample for a vocabulary word. These they arrange in boxes or circles, with the target word in the middle.

Semantic Feature Analysis

Semantic feature analysis is another strategy that helps students with disabilities understand concepts and word meanings (Bos & Anders, 1992). It is a process of categorizing important concepts from a reading passage by summarizing distinct ways in which related concepts are similar and different (see Figure 25.1). A semantic feature analysis can be completed in combination with a semantic map or as an activity by itself.

Readence et al. (1998) recommend the following steps for conducting a semantic feature analysis:

1. Select a category that consists of two or more items that are similar. Such categories might be things like kinds of animals, elements, foods, or famous historical characters.
2. List the category terms along the left side of the blackboard or overhead transparency. Try not to use a large number of items the first time the procedure is used.
3. List the features that will be used to describe the terms across the top of the blackboard or overhead transparency. Students may select the features, or the teacher may do it.
4. Students should be guided through the development of the feature chart as they indicate whether or not each category item possesses a given feature. A plus (+) shows that the category item has a feature. A minus (–) indicates that the category item does not have the feature. Every category item must have a plus or a minus for every feature; there should be no blank spots.
5. The final step is to have students make observations about the category items.

Give students an opportunity to make generalizations on their own.

Figuring Out the Meaning of Unknown Words While Reading

We all encounter unknown words while reading. Successful readers have developed many strategies for figuring out the meanings of words (Jiménez, García, & Pearson, 1995). These strategies are usually applied automatically and quickly, yet less proficient readers often struggle with unknown words and do not feel equipped to figure them out. Many students have been told to "just skip" the words they do not know (Klingner & Vaughn, 1996)—a technique that can leave them confused and frustrated. Yet even struggling readers can be assisted to learn strategies for determining the meanings of unknown words (Klingner, Vaughn, & Schumm, 1998).

Context Clues

The first step in helping students learn words in context is to teach them the ways in which content textbook authors provide definitions in context. There are three main types of context clues:

1. *Definition.* Key terms are often defined in the sentence in which they are introduced, although sometimes definitions

Trees						
	Broadleaf	Needleleaf	Cone-bearing	Fruit-bearing	Deciduous	Evergreen
Oak	+	–	–	+	+	–
Cypress	–	+	+	–	–	+
Maple	+	–	–	+	+	–
Holly	+	–	–	+	–	+
Pine	–	+	+	–	–	+
Spruce	–	+	+	–	–	+
Apple	+	–	–	+	+	–

FIGURE 25.1. Semantic feature analysis chart.

appear in previous or subsequent sentences; for example, "*Unemployment,* or the number of people without jobs, reached an all-time high."

2. *Description.* Although an explicit definition for the word is not provided, the word is described in such a way that a good guess can be made about its meaning; for example, "Many people lived crowded together in cheaply built *tenements.*"

3. *Contrast.* The word is compared with another word or concept, often its opposite; for example, "Many immigrants lived in *urban* areas while others chose to live in rural areas as farmers" (Readence et al., 1998).

Often, key vocabulary words are written in bold, underlined, or italicized to draw attention to their importance. Thus, students should be prompted to look for context clues when they see a word so highlighted.

Morphemic Analysis

Many of the long words that students encounter while reading can be broken into smaller parts. These word parts are called morphemes. Through this process, students can look for a prefix or suffix in the word and its root (e.g., *historian* = history + ian). Or they can look for smaller words they know (*landform* = land + form). High school students preparing for their college entrance tests are often taught to do this as a test-taking strategy. It is one way for the learner to become independent in vocabulary building.

References

External references provide a third source of information about unknown vocabulary words (Readence et al., 1998). These sources include glossaries, dictionaries, and thesauruses. Glossaries are typically the easiest form of external reference to use, because the meaning given will directly apply to its use in the book. Most textbooks include them (usually at the back of the book), and the definitions provided match those used in the book. When the textbook does not include a glossary, students might consult a dictionary. Yet dictionaries can be difficult to use and can lead to misunderstandings. Many students have not been taught how to use guide words and have trouble finding words. Also, most words have multiple definitions, and trying to determine the preferable one can be confusing. Increasingly, students are turning to thesauruses rather than dictionaries. Perhaps this is due, in part, to the inclusion of thesauruses with word-processing software.

EXPOSITORY TEXT STRUCTURE ANALYSIS

Text structure refers to the way the text is organized to guide readers in identifying key information and making connections among ideas. The ability to understand and make use of expository text structure is important for school success, yet it can be problematic for students with disabilities (Dickson, Simmons, & Kame'enui, 1995). According to Seidenberg (1989), students with LD demonstrate less awareness of the different expository text structures than their normally achieving peers. Because the structure of expository prose differs from that of narrative text, strategies that students have learned to implement with narrative prose do not necessarily transfer. When students have learned the various text structures typical of expository text, it becomes easier for them to identify the main idea and supporting evidence in a paragraph (Bakken, Mastropieri, & Scruggs, 1997).

The expository text structures found in science and social studies textbooks include a variety of formats, such as (1) enumeration, a list of facts concerning a single topic; (2) sequence, a series of events that occur over time; (3) compare–contrast, a focus on the similarities and differences between two or more topics; (4) classification, information organized according to categories; (5) generalization, one major idea contained within a few sentences; (6) problem–solution, the statement of a problem, followed by its solution; and (7) procedural description, the steps used to carry out a task (Weaver & Kintsch, 1991). Students must not only attend to the information in the text but also identify the type of text structure used to present it (Englert & Hiebert, 1984).

USING MULTICOMPONENT STRATEGY INSTRUCTION TO TEACH READING COMPREHENSION

In this section, we describe three comprehensive instructional approaches designed to teach students to be strategic readers who are proficient in applying strategies before, during, and after reading. All three approaches rely on peer discussion as a catalyst for improving comprehension.

Reciprocal Teaching

Developed by Palincsar and her colleagues (Palincsar, 1986; Palincsar & Brown, 1984; Palincsar, Brown, & Martin, 1987), reciprocal teaching was designed to improve comprehension for students who can decode but have difficulty comprehending text. Students are taught to use the four strategies of prediction, summarization, question generation, and clarification, and to apply these while discussing stories with the teacher and their peers. In comparison with traditional methods, reciprocal teaching has been found to be effective with a wide range of students for both narrative and expository texts: middle school students who were adequate decoders but poor comprehenders (e.g., Palincsar & Brown, 1984), middle school ELLs with LD, including low decoders (Klingner & Vaughn, 1996); high school students in remedial classes (Alfassi, 1998); average and above-average readers at various grade levels (Rosenshine & Meister, 1994); fourth graders (Lysynchuk, Pressley, & Vye, 1990); and fifth graders (King & Parent Johnson, 1999).

In related research, Marston, Deno, Kim, Diment, and Rogers (1995) compared six research-based teaching strategies, including reciprocal teaching, and found that student achievement was highest with the following three approaches: computer-assisted instruction, reciprocal teaching, and one of

two direct instruction conditions. Johnson-Glenberg (2000) trained third- through fifth-grade adequate decoders who were poor comprehenders for 10 weeks in either reciprocal teaching or a visualization program. The reciprocal teaching group excelled on several measures that depended on explicit, factual material, whereas the visualization group fared better on several visually mediated measures. Brand-Gruwal, Aarnoutse, and Van den Bos (1997) provided reciprocal teaching plus direct instruction in comprehension strategies to 9- to 11-year-olds who were poor in decoding, reading comprehension, and listening comprehension. Positive effects applied to strategic variables but not to general reading comprehension.

With reciprocal teaching, strategies are not learned and practiced in isolation, but in the context of reading. Students are introduced to all four strategies right from the beginning. Integral to reciprocal teaching is the scaffolding of instruction. Lessons are teacher-directed at first, with a great deal of modeling and prompting. As students develop proficiency applying the strategies, control is gradually turned over to them, and they lead discussions about text content. Students learn the following four strategies: predicting, clarifying, summarizing, and generating questions.

To implement reciprocal teaching, the teacher explains the purpose for learning comprehension strategies, telling students that the primary goal is for them to become better readers (more "strategic" and better comprehenders). Following this purpose-setting statement, the teacher models the entire process of reading a passage and applying the strategies, so that students are able to see "the big picture." On the second day, the teacher again models the entire process and provides students with the support necessary to implement the strategies and participate in a text-related discussion. On subsequent days, the teacher encourages students to take turns leading discussions in the role of "teacher," with the amount of support provided gradually decreasing as students become more proficient in leading discussions and applying the strategies. Explicit instruction in specific strategies may be provided as needed. By about the eighth day of reciprocal teaching, in their alternating roles as "teachers," students typically can implement the strategies with minimal assistance from the teacher.

Transactional Strategies Instruction

Pressley and colleagues developed a comprehensive, high-intensity, long-term approach to strategy implementation called "transactional strategies instruction." As with reciprocal teaching, in the transactional approach to strategy instruction, the teacher provides support and guidance to students as they apply strategies while interacting with the text and learning content. A long-term goal of instruction is the self-regulated use of strategies. The term "transactional" is used to emphasize that (1) meaning is determined through the interaction of prior knowledge and information conveyed through print; (2) one person's reaction is influenced by what other group members do, think, and say; and (3) the meaning that emerges is the product of group interactions (Pressley, Schuder, SAIL Faculty and Administration, Bergman, & El-Dinary, 1992; Pressley et al., 1995).

Pressley worked with colleagues to identify the characteristics of effective strategy instruction, and found the following common features:

1. Strategy instruction is long-term and integrated with ongoing instruction. Comprehension strategies are taught during language arts and applied in math, science, social studies, and other content areas.
2. Teachers make certain that students understand the connection between active, strategic thinking and academic success. Students learn when and where use of strategies pays off.
3. Effective strategy instruction does not emphasize the use of single strategies in isolation, but the flexible application of a repertoire of strategies.
4. Strategies are introduced one at a time and practiced with authentic texts. Teachers explain strategies and model their use. They scaffold students' efforts

to apply strategies by providing hints and additional explanations as needed.
5. Discussions of strategic processing occur everyday. Much of strategy instruction occurs in small groups, with students thinking aloud as they read and apply strategies. Ideal discussions are dynamic, with students reacting, interpreting, and offering alternative points of view.
6. Students learn that no two readers ever read a text in the same way. People's associations are unique, based on their own experiences and evaluations of text. Yet how one person reacts is influenced by what other participants in the group do and say. The meaning that emerges from a group is the product of the efforts of all the persons in that group.

The Students Achieving Independent Learning (SAIL) program represents an effective application of transactional strategies instruction (Bergman, 1992; Pressley et al., 1992). The SAIL program promotes extensive reading of children's literature and encourages students to set their own purposes and goals for reading. Through modeling, think-alouds, and coaching, students learn to use various strategies to monitor their comprehension and solve problems (as good readers do).

Pressley and colleagues have also written about the challenges in classrooms of implementing comprehensive strategy instruction programs (Pressley & El-Dinary, 1997; Pressley, Hogan, Wharton-McDonald, & Mistretta, 1996). They have identified the barriers that educators encounter in translating research-based strategy instruction models into workable, feasible, school-based interventions, noting that substantial progress has been made over the last several years.

Collaborative Strategic Reading

Influenced significantly by reciprocal teaching, collaborative strategic reading (CSR) teaches students to use comprehension strategies while working collaboratively with their peers in small groups (Klingner & Vaughn, 1999; Klingner, Vaughn, Dimino, Schumm, & Bryant, 2001). Initially, the teacher presents the strategies to the whole class using modeling, role playing, and teacher think-alouds. Students learn why, when, and how to apply the strategies. After students have developed proficiency using the strategies, they are then divided into heterogeneous groups. Each student performs a defined role as the groups implements the strategies collaboratively while learning from expository text.

The goals of CSR are to improve reading comprehension and to increase conceptual learning in ways that maximize students' involvement. CSR has yielded positive outcomes for students with LD and those at-risk for reading difficulties, as well as average- and high-achieving students (Bryant, Vaughn, Linan-Thompson, Ugel, & Hamff, 2000; Klingner et al., 1998), and ELLs (Klingner & Vaughn, 1996, 2000).

The four strategies that students learn as part of CSR are (1) "preview" (prior to reading a passage, to recall what they already know about the topic and to predict what the passage might be about); (2) "click and clunk" (to monitor comprehension during reading by identifying difficult words and concepts in the passage and using fix-up strategies when the text does not make sense); (3) "get the gist" (during reading, to restate the most important idea in a paragraph or section); and (4) wrap up (after reading, to summarize what has been learned and to generate questions "that a teacher might ask on a test").

As students develop proficiency with the strategies, they are divided into small groups of four or five students. Each student in a group performs a different role. The *leader* guides the group in the implementation of CSR by prompting peers when to apply each strategy. The *clunk expert* uses clunk cards to remind the group of the steps to follow when trying to figure out a difficult word or concept; these cards direct students to (1) reread the sentences before and after the clunk, looking for clues; (2) reread the sentence without the clunk, and think about what would make sense; (3) look for a prefix or suffix; (4) break the word into smaller parts and look for words that seem familiar. The *gist expert* helps peers come up with the most succinct and

accurate gist. The *announcer* calls on different group members to read or share an idea, and makes sure that only one person talks at a time, and that everyone has a turn. The *encourager* evaluates the group, gives feedback, and encourages all group members to participate and assist one another. The *time keeper* keeps track of how much time group members have to complete a section of the text they are reading. Roles are explicitly taught by the classroom teacher. Initially, students use cue cards with prompts that specify how to carry out the different roles. As students become confident in how to fulfill their roles, they are encouraged to set aside the cue cards, so that more natural discussions can take place. Students record their ideas in CSR Learning Logs and complete various follow-up activities (e.g., semantic maps and games to reinforce vocabulary).

CONCLUSIONS

As Mastropieri and Scruggs (1997) reported, students with LD can improve their reading comprehension if teachers (1) teach strategies that have been documented as effective in promoting reading comprehension; (2) design instruction that considers effective principles of direct instruction and strategy instruction; (3) provide modeling, support, guided instruction, practice, attributional feedback, and opportunities to practice across text types; and (4) monitor students' progress and make adjustments accordingly.

This chapter has provided a summary of the research on teaching reading comprehension to students with LD, including approaches designed to be used before, during, and after reading. Additional information about vocabulary instruction and expository text analysis was provided, along with descriptions of three specific, multicomponent approaches to reading instruction: reciprocal teaching, transactional strategies instruction, and collaborative strategic reading. This review of research-based approaches to teaching comprehension to students with LD yields several approaches to facilitate students understanding of text when they read.

ACKNOWLEDGMENT

Special thanks to Ae-Hwa Kim, who assisted in the preparation of this Chapter.

REFERENCES

Alfassi, M. (1998). Reading for meaning: The efficacy of reciprocal teaching in fostering reading comprehension in high school students in remedial classes. *American Educational Research Journal, 35*(2), 309–332.

Anders, P. L., & Bos, C. S. (1984). In the beginning: Vocabulary instruction in content classrooms. *Topics in Learning and Learning Disabilities, 3*(4), 53–65.

Anderson, R. C., & Nagy, W. E. (1991). Word meaning. In R. Barr, M. L. Kamil, P. B. Mosenthall, & P. D. Pearson (Eds.), *Handbook of reading research* (pp. 690–724). New York: Longman.

Bakken, J. P., Mastropieri, M. A., & Scruggs, T. E. (1997). Reading comprehension of expository science material and students with learning disabilities: A comparison of strategies. *Journal of Special Education, 31*, 300–324.

Ball, E. W., & Blachman, B. A. (1991). Does phoneme awareness training in kindergarten make a difference in early word recognition and developmental spelling? *Reading Research Quarterly, 26*(1), 49–66.

Baumann, J. F., & Kame'enui, E. J. (1991). Research on vocabulary instruction: Ode to Voltaire. In J. Flood, J. J. D. Lapp, & J. R. Squire (Eds.), *Handbook of research on teaching the English language arts* (pp. 604–632). New York: Macmillan.

Beck, I. L., McKeown, M. G., & Kucan, L. (2002). *Bringing words to life: Robust vocabulary instruction.* New York: Guilford Press.

Beck, I. L., McKeown, M. G., Sandora, C., Kucan, L., & Worthy, J. (1996). Questioning the author: A yearlong classroom implementation to engage students with text. *Elementary School Journal, 96*(4), 385–414.

Becker, E. Z., & McCormick, S. (1991). *A review of current research on reading instruction and the learning disabled student* (ERIC Document Reproduction Service No. ED342169).

Bergman, J. L. (1992). SAIL—a way to success and independence for low-achieving readers. *Reading Teacher, 45*, 598–602.

Blachowicz, C., & Fisher, P. (1996). *Teaching vocabulary in all classrooms.* Englewood Cliffs, NJ: Merrill.

Bos, C. S. (1987). *Promoting story comprehension using a story retelling strategy.* Paper presented at the Teachers Applying Whole Language Conference, Tucson, AZ.

Bos, C. S., & Anders, P. L. (1990). Effects of interactive vocabulary instruction on the vocabulary learning and reading comprehension of junior-high learning disabled students. *Learning Disability Quarterly, 13*, 31–42.

Bos, C. S., & Anders, P. L. (1992). A theory-driven interactive instructional model for text comprehension and content learning. In B. Y. L. Wong (Ed.), *Contemporary intervention research in learning disabilities: An international perspective* (pp. 81–95). New York: Springer-Verlag.

Boyle, J. R., & Weishaar, M. (1997). The effects of expert-generated versus student-generated cognitive organizers on the reading comprehension of students with learning disabilities. *Learning Disabilities Research and Practice, 12*(4), 228–235.

Brand-Gruwal, S., Aarnoutse, C. A. J., & Van den Bos, K. P. (1997). Improving text comprehension strategies in reading and listening settings. *Learning and Instruction, 8*(1), 63–81.

Brown, A. L., & Day, J. D. (1983). Macro rules for summarizing texts: The development of expertise. *Journal of Verbal Learning and Verbal Behavior, 22*(1), 1–14.

Bryant, D. P., Vaughn, S., Linan-Thompson, S., Ugel, N., & Hamff, A. (2000). Reading outcomes for students with and without learning disabilities in general education middle school content area classes. *Learning Disability Quarterly, 23*(3), 24–38.

Carnine, D. W., Silbert, J., & Kame'enui, E. J. (1997). *Direct instruction reading.* Upper Saddle River, NJ: Prentice-Hall.

Chen, H., & Graves, M. F. (1995). Effects of previewing and providing background knowledge on Taiwanese college students comprehension of American short stories. *TESOL Quarterly, 29*(4), 663–686.

Dickson, S. V., Simmons, D., & Kame'enui, E. J. (1995). Instruction in expository text: A focus on compare/contrast structure. *LD Forum, 20*(2), 8–15.

Dole, J. A., Duffy, G. G., Roehler, L. R., & Pearson, P. D. (1991). Moving from the old to the new: Research on reading comprehension instruction. *Review of Educational Research, 61*(2), 239–264.

Dole, J. A., Valencia, S. W., Greer, E. A., & Wardrop, J. L. (1991). Effects of two types of prereading instruction on the comprehension of narrative and expository text. *Reading Research Quarterly, 26*(2), 142–159.

Durkin, D. (1978–1979). What classroom observations reveal about reading comprehension instruction. *Reading Research Quarterly, 14*(4), 481–533.

Echevarria, J., & Graves, A. (1998). Curriculum adaptations. In *Sheltered content instruction: Teaching English-language learners with diverse abilities* (pp. 121–149). Needham Heights, MA: Allyn & Bacon.

Elley, W. B. (1988). Vocabulary acquisition from listening to stories. *Reading Research Quarterly, 24*, 174–187.

Englert, C. S., & Hiebert, E. H. (1984). Children's developing awareness of text structures in expository materials. *Journal of Educational Psychology, 76*, 65–75.

Flavell, J. H. (1981). Cognitive monitoring. In W. P. Dickson (Ed.), *Children's oral communication skills* (pp. 35–60). San Diego: Academic Press.

Gajria, M., & Salvia, J. (1992). The effects of summarization instruction on text comprehension of students with learning disabilities. *Exceptional Children, 58*(6), 508–516.

Gallego, M. A., Duran, G. Z., & Scanlon, D. J. (1990). Interactive teaching and learning: Facilitating learning disabled students' transition from novice to expert. In J. Zutell & S. McCormick (Eds.), *Literacy theory and research: Analyses from multiple paradigms* (pp. 311–319). Chicago: National Reading Conference.

Gambrell, L. B. (1996). Creating classroom cultures that foster reading motivation. *Reading Teacher, 50,* 14–25.

Garner, R. (1992). Metacognition and self-monitoring strategies. In S. J. Samuels & A. E. Farstrup (Eds.), *What research has to say about reading instruction* (2nd ed., pp. 236–252). Newark, DE: International Reading Association.

Gersten, R., & Darch, C. (1986). Direction-setting activities in reading comprehension: A comparison of two approaches. *Learning Disability Quarterly, 9,* 235–243.

Gersten, R., Fuchs, L., Williams, J. P., & Baker, S. (2001). Teaching reading comprehension strategies to students with learning disabilities. *Review of Educational Research, 71*(2), 279–320.

Gersten, R. M., & Jiménez, R. T. (1998). *Promoting learning for culturally and linguistically diverse students.* Belmont, CA: Wadsworth.

Graves, A. W. (1986). Effects of direct instruction and metacomprehension training on finding main ideas. *Learning Disabilities Research, 1,* 90–100.

Graves, M. F., Juel, C., & Graves, B. B. (2001). *Teaching reading in the 21st century* (2nd ed.). Boston: Allyn & Bacon.

Graves, M. F., Prenn, M., & Cooke, C. L. (1985). The coming attractions: Previewing short stories. *Journal of Reading, 28*(7), 594–598.

Heimlich, J. E., & Pittelman, S. D. (1986). *Semantic mapping: Classroom applications.* Newark, DE: International Reading Association.

Jenkins, J. R., Heliotis, J., Stein, M. L., & Haynes, M. (1987). Improving reading comprehension by using paragraph restatements. *Exceptional Children, 54,* 54–59.

Jiménez, R. T., García, G. E., & Pearson, P. D. (1995). Three children, two languages, strategic reading: Case studies in bilingual/monolingual reading. *American Educational Research Journal, 32,* 67–97.

Jitendra, A. K., Hoppes, M. K., & Xin, Y. P. (2000). Enhancing main idea comprehension for students with learning problems: The role of a summarization strategy and self-monitoring instruction. *Journal of Special Education, 34*(3), 127–139.

Johnson-Glenberg, M. C. (2000). Training reading comprehension in adequate decoders/poor comprehenders: Verbal versus visual strategies. *Journal of Educational Psychology, 92*(4), 772–782.

King, C. M., & Parent Johnson, L. M. (1999). Constructing meaning via reciprocal teaching. *Reading Research and Instruction, 38*(3), 169–186.

Klingner, J. K., & Vaughn, S. (1996). Reciprocal teaching of reading comprehension strategies for students with learning disabilities who use English as a second language. *Elementary School Journal, 96,* 275–293.

Klingner, J. K., & Vaughn, S. (1999). Promoting reading comprehension, content learning, and English acquisition through collaborative strategic reading (CSR). *Reading Teacher, 52,* 738–747.

Klingner, J. K., & Vaughn, S. (2000). The helping behaviors of fifth-graders while using collaborative strategic reading (CSR) during ESL content classes. *TESOL Quarterly, 34,* 69–98.

Klingner, J. K., Vaughn, S., Dimino, J., Schumm, J. S., & Bryant, D. P. (2001). *From clunk to click: Collaborative strategic reading.* Longmont, CO: Sopris West.

Klingner, J. K., Vaughn, S., & Schumm, J. S. (1998). Collaborative strategic reading during social studies in heterogeneous fourth-grade classrooms. *Elementary School Journal, 99,* 3–21.

Lysynchuk, L., Pressley, M., & Vye, N. (1990). Reciprocal teaching improves standardized reading-comprehension performance in poor comprehenders. *Elementary School Journal, 90*(5), 469–484.

Malone, L. D., & Mastropieri, M. (1992). Reading comprehension instruction: Summarization and self-monitoring training for students with learning disabilities. *Exceptional Children, 58*(3), 270–279.

Manzo, A. V., & Manzo, U. C. (1993). *Literacy disorders: Holistic diagnosis and remediation.* Fort Worth, TX: Harcourt Brace Jovanovich.

Marston, D., Deno, S. L., Kim, D., Diment, K., & Rogers, D. (1995). Comparison of reading intervention approaches for students with mild disabilities. *Exceptional Children, 62,* 20–37.

Mastropieri, M. A., & Scruggs, T. E. (1997). Best practices in promoting reading comprehension in students with learning disabilities. 1976 to 1996. *Remedial and Special Education, 18*(4), 197–214.

Mastropieri, M. A., Scruggs, T. E., Bakken, J. P., & Whedon, C. (1996). Reading comprehension: A synthesis of research in learning disabilities. *Advances in Learning and Behavioral Disabilities, 10B,* 201–227.

Moody, S. W., Vaughn, S., Hughes, M. T., & Fischer, M. (2000). Reading instruction in the resource room: Set up for failure. *Exceptional Children, 66*(3), 305–316.

National Reading Panel. (2000). *Teaching children to read: An evidence-based assessment of the scientific research literature on reading and its implications for reading instructions* (NIH Publication No. 00–4769). Washington, DC: National Institute of Child Health and Human Development.

Nelson, J. R., Smith, D. J., & Dodd, J. M. (1992). The effects of teaching a summary skills strategy to students identified as learning disabled on their comprehension of science text. *Education and Treatment of Children, 15*(3), 228–243.

O'Connor, R. E., & Jenkins, J. R. (1995). Improving the generalization of sound–symbol knowledge: Teaching spelling to kindergarten children with disabilities. *Journal of Special Education, 29*(3), 255–275.

Palincsar, A. S. (1986). The role of dialogue in providing scaffolded instruction. *Educational Psychologist, 21,* 73–98.

Palincsar, A. S., & Brown, A. L. (1984). The reciprocal teaching of comprehension-fostering and comprehension-monitoring activities. *Cognition and Instruction, 1,* 117–175.

Palincsar, A. S., Brown, A. L., & Martin, S. M. (1987). Peer interaction in reading comprehension instruction. *Educational Psychologist, 22,* 231–253.

Pearson, P. D. (1996). Reclaiming the center. In M. F. Graves, P. van den Broek, & B. M. Taylor (Eds.), *The first R: Every child's right to read* (pp. 259–274). New York: Teachers College Press.

Pressley, M., Brown, R., El-Dinary, P. B., & Afflerbach, P. (1995). The comprehension instruction that students need: Instruction fostering constructively responsive reading. *Learning Disabilities Research and Practice, 10,* 215–224.

Pressley, M., & El-Dinary, P. B. (1997). What we know about translating comprehension-strategies instruction research into practice. *Journal of Learning Disabilities, 30,* 486–488.

Pressley, M., Hogan, K., Wharton-McDonald, R., & Mistretta, J. (1996). The challenges of instructional scaffolding: The challenges of instruction that supports student thinking. *Learning Disabilities Research and Practice, 11,* 138–146.

Pressley, M., Schuder, T., SAIL Faculty and Administration, Berman, J. L., & El-Dinary, P. B. (1992). A researcher–educator collaborative interview study of transactional comprehension strategies instruction. *Journal of Educational Psychology, 84,* 231–246.

Readence, J. E., Bean, T. W., & Baldwin, R. S. (1998). *Content area literacy: An integrated approach* (6th ed.). Dubuque, IA: Kendall/Hunt.

Rosenshine, B., & Meister, C. (1994). Reciprocal teaching: A review of the research. *Review of Educational Research, 64,* 479–530.

Schumaker, J. B., Denton, P. H., & Deshler, D. D. (1984). *The paraphrasing strategy.* Lawrence: University of Kansas Press.

Schumaker, J. B., Deshler, D. D., Nolan, S. M., & Alley, G. R. (1994). *The self-questioning strategy.* Lawrence: University of Kansas Press.

Schumm, J. S., Moody, S. W., & Vaughn, S. R. (2000). Grouping for reading instruction: Does one size fit all? *Journal of Learning Disabilities, 33*(5), 477–488.

Seidenberg, P. L. (1989). Relating text-processing research to reading and writing instruction for learning disabled students. *Learning Disabilities Focus, 5,* 4–12.

Simmons, D.C., & Kame'enui, E.J. (1998). *What reading research tells us about children with diverse learning needs: Bases and basics.* Mahwah, NJ: Erlbaum.

Simmons, D. C., Kame'enui, E. J., & Darch, C. B. (1988). The effect of textual proximity on fourth- and fifth-grade LD students' metacognitive awareness and strategic comprehension behavior. *Learning Disability Quarterly, 11*(4), 380–395.

Snider, V. E. (1989). Reading comprehension performance of adolescents with learning disabilities. *Learning Disability Quarterly, 12*(2), 87–96.

Swanson, H. L. (1987). Information processing theory and learning disabilities: An overview. *Journal of Learning Disabilities, 20,* 3–7.

Swanson, H. L. (1999). Reading research for students with LD: A meta-analysis of intervention outcomes. *Journal of Learning Disabilities, 32*(6), 504–532.

Swanson, H. L. (2001). Reading intervention research outcomes and students with LD: What are the major instructional ingredients for successful outcomes? *Perspectives, 27*(2), 18–20.

Swanson, H. L., Hoskyn, M., & Lee, C. (1999). *Interventions for students with learning disabilities: A meta-analysis of treatment outcome.* New York: Guilford Press.

Torgesen, J. K., & Licht, B. (1983). The learning disabled child as an inactive learner: Restrospect and prospects. In J. D. McKinney & L. Feagans (Eds.), *Current topics in learning disabilities* (Vol. 1, pp. 3–32). Norwood, NJ: Ablex.

Vaughn, S., Moody, S., & Schumm, J. S. (1998). Broken promises: Reading instruction in the resource room. *Exceptional Children, 64*(2), 211–226.

Vellutino, F. R., & Scanlon, D. M. (1987). Phonological coding, phonological awareness, and reading ability: Evidence from a longitudinal and experimental study. *Merrill–Palmer Quarterly, 33*(3), 321–363.

Weaver, C.A., III, & Kintsch, W. (1991). Expository text. In R. Barr, M. L. Kamil, P. Mosenthal, & P. D. Pearson (Eds.), *Handbook of reading research* (Vol. 2, pp. 230–244). White Plains, NY: Longman.

Williams, J. P. (1988). Identifying main ideas: A basic aspect of reading comprehension. *Topics in Language Disorders, 8*(3), 1–13.

Williams, J. P. (1998). Improving the comprehension of disabled readers. *Annals of Dyslexia, 48,* 213–218.

Wong, B. Y. L., & Jones, W. (1982). Increasing metacomprehension in learning disabled and normally achieving students through self-questing training. *Learning Disability Quarterly, 5,* 228–240.

WRITING COMPOSITION

26

Developmental Variations in Writing Composition Skills

BONNIE D. SINGER
ANTHONY S. BASHIR

Writing is a deliberate, generative task that requires the recruitment and integration of a range of different neurodevelopmental abilities. Because writing is intentional action, it is under the control of executive and self-regulatory processes. The demands of writing are staggering. It requires the coordination and accommodation of graphomotor and cognitive–linguistic abilities, as well as knowledge of social, rhetorical, and text production conventions. Writing is influenced by the writer's world knowledge, motivation, beliefs, and attitudes. Although it is not surprising that some students struggle extensively with writing, it is more surprising that others *do not*.

For all students, writing is effective and efficient to the degree that the writer is able to integrate requisite processes in a smooth and fluid manner to achieve desired text outcomes. Some students do this with relative ease. Others struggle. For the individual with language-learning disabilities (LLD),[1] writing is an arduous process. Singer and Bashir (2004), summarizing the cumulative research on students with LLD, note:

They have difficulty reading their assignments and knowing how to complete their work. They struggle with planning, organizing, and revising their writing. Their texts are short and poorly structured. Their use of language is problematic in terms of syntax, vocabulary diversity and cohesion, and they make frequent errors in spelling and writing mechanics. They have difficulty making transitions from one step in the writing process to the next. Lacking an inner voice to mediate their written language production, they often present as overwhelmed by the multiple demands of expository writing and appear to have difficulty allocating sufficient cognitive resources to meet various writing demands (e.g., knowing where to begin, how to stay on and develop a topic, how to represent their ideas with language, etc.). As a result, they are ineffective and inefficient writers.

A model of writing is presented in this chapter that is intended to clarify and explain the variations and difficulties seen in the production of written language. This model is based on our current understanding of the processes typical writers engage during the composing process (Bereiter &

Scardamalia, 1987; Berninger & Swanson, 1994; Hayes, 2000; Hayes & Flower, 1980). Extending earlier models, the model presented here is useful for understanding how various factors comprise and constrain the writing process of typically developing students and those with LLD.

In this chapter, an overview of the principles that inform the model is offered and followed by a review of research findings that support the inclusion of specific aspects of the model. Finally, the implications of the

model for understanding variations in writing development are explored.

A MODEL OF TEXT PRODUCTION

The model presented in Figure 26.1 proposes that the underlying challenge that students encounter with writing is one of managing and coordinating *multiple* processes *simultaneously*, not simply managing *one* writing skill or cognitive, linguistic, or mo-

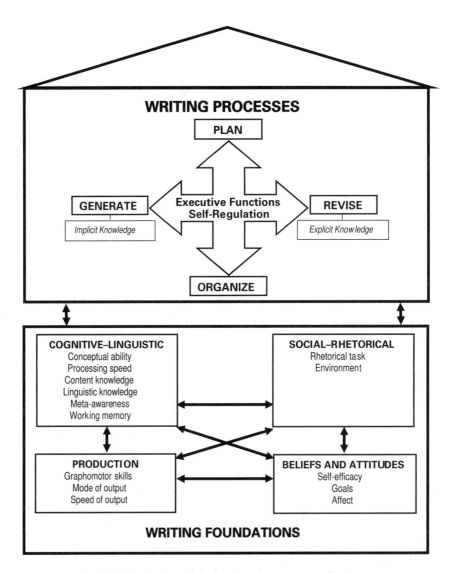

FIGURE 26.1. A model of written language production.

toric process at a time (Flower & Hayes, 1980; Singer & Bashir, 2004). By acknowledging the basic processes that must be recruited for composing and the numerous variables that control and constrain those processes, we can begin to understand why writers might struggle one day and generate text with ease the next.

Writing can be viewed metaphorically in a number of ways. Some may view composing through the metaphor of uncovering; others may view it through the metaphor of painting. The model presented is based on the metaphor of construction; hence, the model's visual presentation as a building (see Figure 26.1). In accordance with this metaphor, written texts are envisioned as discourse structures that are intentionally, purposefully, and skillfully built by writers to represent meaning according to the conventions of a social community. Similar to architectural plans, texts have underlying structures that are influenced by patterns of thought and are specific to various discourse genres (Englert & Raphael, 1988; Stein & Glenn, 1979). Text structures are built with the writer's tools—words that are chained in sentences that vary in syntactic form and are tied together meaningfully via cohesive devices.

For texts to be built, writers must recruit and coordinate a set of cognitive and linguistic processes. In this model, written language comprises two components: writing processes and writing foundations. These two components are represented in the model within the building itself. To encode text onto a page, writers employ four writing processes (*planning, organizing, generating,* and *revising*) to represent their thoughts and ideas with language. These four processes are directed by *executive functions* and *self-regulatory* processes, and are supported and constrained by a number of foundational variables that are conceptualized within four functional domains: *cognitive–linguistic, social–rhetorical, text production,* and *beliefs and attitudes.* If any of these domains are underdeveloped, the foundation is weakened, thereby weakening the integrity of the building structure itself—the composing process.

The model also has built-in "circuitry" (interactive feedback and feedforward sys-

tems) that allows the components in the building to communicate with one another. The functional domains within the foundation interact with each other and with the building's writing processes, which also interact with each other. As a result, foundation variables differentially influence the act of writing. However, when foundation variables and/or executive and self-regulatory skills are not well developed, they may constrain other skills and the composing processes profoundly, because writers recruit the writing processes and foundation variables synergistically as they sit to write. A "dysfunction at the junctions" occurs in the face of such asynergy (Levine, 2003). Sometimes mild delays or deficits in the development of a particular skill or process can have far-reaching effects on composing, because multiple processes must be coordinated rapidly and precisely.

For the developing writer, intraindividual variations occur within component skills and processes. Attempts to recruit developmental domains that are not developing in synchrony yield wide variability in performance and sometimes compromise the composing process. Consistent with developmental trajectories outlined by Berninger and Swanson (1994), the model presented here represents all of the composing processes and foundations necessary for writing. It represents a "best case scenario" when it comes to writing. The reader is cautioned to consider the developmental literature carefully to appreciate when and how foundation skills and composing processes emerge and develop in young writers. With that overview in mind, let us now turn to each portion of the model to examine it more closely.

WRITING PROCESSES

Drawing on prior models (Hayes, 2000; Hayes & Flower, 1980), the upper portion of the model presented here details the processes involved in composing text. These consist of planning, organizing, generating, and revising processes. When composing, writers need to conceive of and access the ideas they wish to convey (*plan*); consider how to structure those ideas so as to convey their meanings (*organize*); encode such ideas into linear strings of words, phrases, and clauses to express those meanings (*generate*); and reconsider and recast those linguistic structures so that they convey what the writer intended according to the writing conventions of the culture (*revise*). Hence, these four processes are central to the composing process itself.

The work of Hayes and Flower (1980), Hayes (2000), Bereiter and Scardamalia (1987) and the extensive work of Berninger and her colleagues (Berninger, & Abbott, 1993; Berninger, Cartwright, Yates, Swanson, & Abbott, 1994; Berninger & Swanson, 1994; Berninger et al., 1992) on typically developing writers suggest that cognitive processes dedicated to composition are recursively, rather than linearly, enlisted in the pursuit of text production. Planning, generating, organizing, and revising are coordinated processes, and writers shift among them actively and frequently during all stages of text development. Writers may plan an idea, consider how to encode it linguistically, and actively shape its form within a specific text structure as they are writing, such that they make last minute changes to words, sentences, and paragraphs as their pens hit the page or fingers hit the keyboard (Scardamalia, Bereiter, & Goelman, 1982). Similarly, they may plan an idea and immediately reject it, determining that it does not support their textual goals. As a result, writing is a messy process.

The recursive coordination of planning, organizing, generating, and revising processes is revealed in the text in Figure 26.2. This text was created by a high school student with LLD, who was instructed to show every move she made in developing a piece. Rather than mask the actions she took by erasing or taking time to formulate ideas in her mind before committing them to paper, she wrote what she thought as she thought it and showed how she changed her mind, rethought, reorganized, restated, and changed her mind some more. The result looks more like a cognitive–linguistic wrestling match than a smooth flow of ideation. The think-aloud protocols of Hayes and Flower (1980) reflect verbally what this student showed us visually about the nature of the writing processes involved in composing.

What controls the writer's recursive moves among basic composing processes? Previous models (Hayes, 2000; Hayes & Flower, 1980) have left unclear what mechanisms control and coordinate the cognitive processes of composing. In this model, the recursive moves among planning, organizing, generating, and revising processes are overseen and managed by executive function and self-regulation processes. These are the "bosses" of the house, and they work together to control the moment-to-moment coordination and shifting among the four composing processes. When executive and self-regulatory processes are impaired or poorly developed, the coordination of the composing processes is not managed efficiently or effectively. This affects the writer's process and product, as well as the degree to which the writer is able to compensate for variables constraining those processes (e.g., cognitive–linguistic or graphomotor weaknesses).

For the sake of clarity in the sections that follow, we review developmental variations in the component processes of writing separately. However, the reader is cautioned to keep in mind that there is some overlap between such processes and that they are not recruited in any particular order when one sits to write.

Planning

For something to be written, writers must have something they want to communicate. In this model, the process of *planning* is considered to involve the retrieval of preverbal representations (Collins & Gentner, 1980; i.e., conceptual information that is represented in nonlinguistic form). In other words, planning involves idea generation and retrieval (Berninger & Swanson, 1994). Having an idea of what to convey in writing, the writer then engages the *generating* processes to transcribe this onto the page. As such, planning is a necessary but insufficient process where writing is concerned. Planning is an internal process that is distinct from generating. As a result, it is difficult to isolate and to examine empirically.

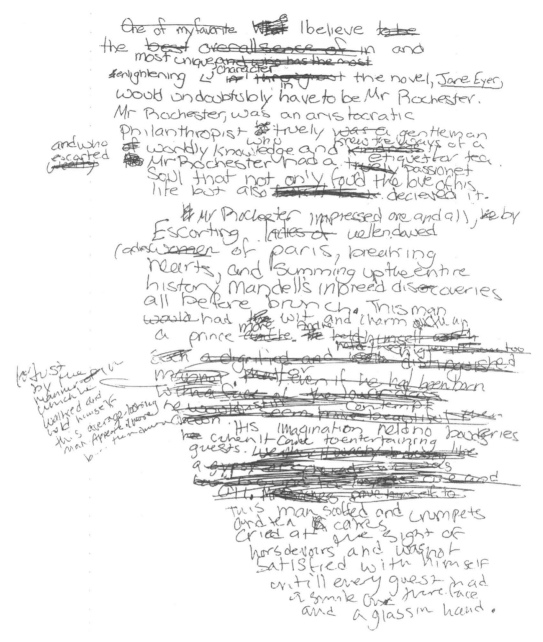

FIGURE 26.2. Text produced by a high school student with LLD that reflects the active and recursive dance between planning, organizing, generating, and revising processes.

Planning encompasses processes related to goal attainment that might be visible or invisible to an observer. Research shows that visible plans created by intermediate-grade children (i.e., explicit plans made prior to generating text) do not necessarily control the text that is later generated (Whitaker, Berninger, Johnston, & Swanson, 1994). However, junior high students' advanced plans do seem to influence text production (Berninger, Whitaker, Feng, Swanson, & Abbott, 1996). Thus, research shows that the influence of advanced planning on the composing process is not generally seen until the junior high grades for typically developing children. Yet such research does not account for the instructional methods used for teaching writing within classrooms. With the increasingly popular use of direct instruction and graphic organizers as tools for advanced planning within schools today, the influence of explicit plans on text generation may be evident earlier in development (see, e.g., Englert, 2004).

Students with LLD fail to engage advanced planning processes when they write both narrative and expository text (McAlister, Nelson, & Bahr, 1999; Zipprich, 1995). Even when engaged in structured interventions that use explicit planning and organizing strategies, students with LLD may fail to use such strategies, because they have little understanding of their purpose (McAlister et al., 1999). Indeed, MacArthur and Graham (1987) note that students with LLD average less than 1 minute of time planning prior to writing, unless they are explicitly taught *how* to plan. Though we know that students with LLD do little advanced planning prior to writing, unless they receive direct instruction and support (Troia, Graham, & Harris, 1999; Zipprich, 1995), we know comparatively little about the nature of their online planning abilities.

Organizing

Writing taxes problem solving, which Hayes (2000) defines as "an activity of putting together a sequence of steps to reach a goal" (p. 31). *Organization* processes are engaged when the writer decides how to structure and sequence the ideational content of a text. Organizing processes are interwoven with *planning* and *generating* processes; students enlist organizing processes when they implicitly and/or explicitly plan how to attain their goals for a text and generate language reflecting what they know about the topic (i.e., content-specific knowledge). The ability to organize thoughts and ideas draws heavily on one's knowledge of text schema and genre, as well as temporal–sequential processing and visual–spatial abilities.

"In effective writing a meaningful organization of information takes its logic from the writer's higher level plan to do something" (Flower & Hayes, 1980, p. 49). This involves not only planning and generating the content of a text, but also considering how to organize that content so that it achieves the writer's composition goals and has the desired effect on the reader. An internalized understanding of the organizational patterns and principles underlying different kinds of text is acquired through reading. Able writers have a sense of how to sequence their ideas in patterns familiar to their culture and to the genre in which they are writing (Westby, 1994).

In addition to drawing on cultural frameworks for expressing ideas, organization draws on visual–spatial processing. Although there is a paucity of research on the contribution of visual-spatial processing to text production, case studies (e.g., Singer & Bashir, 1999) and clinical experience suggest that visual–spatial abilities influence organization at the discourse level. The ability to organize text seems distinctly influenced by the writer's ability to conceive of the visual–spatial "skeleton" that typifies different genres of text. Thus, though they may have very strong semantic and syntactic abilities and extensive content-specific knowledge, students whose visual–spatial skills are not well developed often have difficulty with writing, because they cannot "see" how to organize their ideas so that they make sense to a reader. Though we are aware of no formal research that examines this hypothesis, extensive clinical experience suggests that students with nonverbal learning disorders are uniquely influenced by such difficulties (Rourke, 2003), and that influence is seen in both oral and written discourse formulation. Students with LLD also show vulnerabilities in this area.

Students with LLD struggle with organizing ideas for writing. Left to their own devices, they persist in using a "knowledge telling" approach to composition (Englert & Thomas, 1987), one that typically developing writers use in the early elementary school grades (Bereiter & Scardamalia, 1987). This approach is characterized by a retrieve-and-write strategy. Students write whatever comes to mind in whatever order it comes to mind. Thus, they string ideas together associatively instead of actively shaping them according to the text structure dictated by the genre and/or writing task. Even when they have brainstormed ideas prior to writing, students with LLD do not apply logical and well-defined schemas for organizing the information when composing (Englert, Raphael, Anderson, Gregg, & Anthony, 1989) As a result, their writing is often poorly organized and incoherent.

Generating

The *generating* process encompasses two general functions (Berninger & Swanson, 1994). The first is *text generation,* which involves turning ideas that are generated in the planning process into language representations within working memory, so that they can be expressed in writing. Drawing on phonologic, morpho-syntactic, and semantic knowledge, the writer formulates knowledge and ideas into linguistic units. Knowledge of cohesion, coherence, and discourse are recruited as the writer strings meaningful linguistic units together to convey meaning. The *generating* process in the proposed model involves implicit representation and encoding of ideas into written language. In the representational process, the writer draws on knowledge of language meaning, structure, spelling, writing mechanics, and text structure. The writer accesses and uses automatic, or intuitive, knowledge about language—that which is learned through participation in his or her culture and community—when putting ideas onto the page. Thus, text that is generated may or may not be grammatically intact, meaningful, well organized, coherent, or cohesive, yet it reflects the writer's automatic formulation of ideas into language.

The notion of implicit (automatic) versus explicit (reflective) encoding of language distinguishes the *generating* process from the *revising* process. Revising taps *explicit* linguistic knowledge. Changes to word choice, sentence structure, spelling, punctuation, and so on are brought about by one's explicit (or metalinguistic) knowledge of language meaning, form, and use. During online production of text, writers recruit both implicit and explicit linguistic knowledge. They encode ideas implicitly, then reflect on the degree to which they have accurately represented their intentions and, when necessary, explicitly use their knowledge of language to reformulate, clarify, or elaborate. Thus, the recursive recruitment of composing processes is required for writers to generate sentence and text patterns and mindfully be aware of the need for changes to that automatic production as they compose.

Scant research documents the text generation abilities of typically developing children. In a large-scale study, Berninger, Mizokawa, Bragg, Cartwright, and Yates (1994) found evidence for both inter- and intraindividual variation in children's text generation skills. Specifically, they found that children possess different levels of ability across word, sentence, and textual levels of written language. Accordingly, one cannot predict a child's text generation ability at one language level based on demonstrated ability at another level.

The second aspect of *generating* a text is *transcription,* which involves encoding verbal mental representations into written symbols (Berninger & Swanson, 1994). Recruiting knowledge of spelling, writing mechanics, and writing conventions, writers transcribe formulated ideas onto paper (by handwriting or typing).

In the early primary grades especially, text generation and writing quality are most constrained by a child's handwriting fluency (Berninger & Swanson, 1994). Because children who have not yet mastered handwriting must direct attention to letter formation, they do not generate much text. By the intermediate grades, when handwriting is automatized for most children, its constraint on text generation is minimized and texts become longer. With age, text length and quality become increasingly related (Berninger & Swanson, 1994). Gregg, Coleman, Stennett, and Davis (2002) report a high correlation between written verbosity (measured as text length) and text quality in college-age writers, suggesting that fluent language generating processes are associated with quality writing.

Students with LLD are known to have difficulty formulating language to represent their ideas (Lahey & Bloom, 1994). Problems within one or more linguistic domain (i.e., phonology, semantics, morpho-syntactics, pragmatics, discourse) render their oral language generation processes deficient as compared to their typically developing peers. The result is that they have trouble finding and pronouncing words to convey their thoughts accurately (German & Simon, 1991), stringing words together to form grammatical utterances (Wiig & Semel, 1975), and sequencing utterances to form meaningful and coherent discourse units (Lahey, 1988). Such difficulties also plague these students when they sit to write; they struggle with every aspect of written language production (Gillam & Johnston, 1992; Johnson, 1987; Johnson & Grant, 1989; Scott, 1994; Singer, 1997; Singer & Bashir, 2004).

For students with LLD, text generation difficulties are confounded by the simultaneous demands for text generation and transcription, for encoding ideas onto paper demands both language and graphomotor control—both of which can be problematic (Graham, 1990). For example, the work of Englert, Raphael, Anderson et al. (1988) suggests that students with LLD may have dissociated text generation and text transcription abilities. Text generation abilities may be better developed than transcription abilities. Consequently, some students can formulate more text orally than they can transcribe in print.

Text generation can break down for students with LLD in a number of ways, because they cannot devote sufficient cognitive resources to the numerous skills and processes that must be recruited for writing (Singer & Bashir, 2004). When component skills and processes (e.g., language formulation, handwriting, spelling) are not automatic, greater cognitive resources must be allocated to manage them (Lahey & Bloom, 1994). This places a burden on working memory (Berninger, 1994).

Revising

Revision involves making changes to text so that it conveys the writer's intended meaning and adheres to the linguistic and discourse conventions of a community. As such, it requires the writer to draw explicitly on knowledge of language at the subword, word, sentence, and discourse levels. In typically developing writers, Hayes (2000) proposes that revision is controlled by a task schema, or a set of condition–action rules that mutually activate each other. The task schema can include text improvement goals, any number of different revision activities (e.g., read to evaluate, problem solve, edit), plans for what to attend to or to avoid in the revising process, templates and quality criteria, and strategies for fixing problems. Hayes notes that the failure to revise may occur because the writer may present with an inadequate revision schema or revision processes. In addition, the writer may fail to detect problems when reading, or may lack the necessary working memory to coordinate the revision processes. Furthermore, the writer may detect problems in the text but may lose focus before being able to fix them.

Berninger and Swanson (1994) make a distinction between online revision (revisions performed in the act of transcribing text) and posttranslation revision (changes to text made after the text is produced in its entirety). Most research on writing has examined students' facility with posttranslation revision. Typically developing writers in the early elementary school grades tend to make changes to mechanics and word choices when revising their texts (Butterfield, Hacker, & Plumb, 1994). Older children are able to make revisions to text that improve composition quality, and this skill typically emerges in the intermediate grades. Berninger, Whitaker, Feng, Swanson, and Abbott (1996) and Whitaker et al. (1994) reported that revisions made by intermediate-grade children showed improvements at the text level but not at the sentence or word levels. However, junior high school students' revisions showed improvements at all three levels (i.e., word, sentence, and text). Thus, with age, writers are able to attend to, make judgments about, and change increasingly finer aspects of text.

When asked to revise their texts, students with LLD most often look only for spelling, capitalization, and punctuation errors

(MacArthur & Graham, 1987). Considering notions put forth by Hayes (2000), these students may well demonstrate an inadequate revision task schema. To complicate matters, students with LLD often present with concomitant reading disabilities (Kamhi & Catts, 1999). As a result, they struggle with the foundation skill of revision: reading comprehension. Students with LLD struggle not only to decode and to comprehend their own writing but also to comprehend and evaluate what they read in terms of its meaning, form, style, clarity, organization, and effect on the reader. These skills tax metalinguistic, metatextual, metapragmatic, metacognitive and social-cognitive domains (Espin & Sindelar, 1988; McAlister et al., 1999; McNamara, Carter, McIntosh, & Gerken, 1998; Windsor, 1999). As well, many have limited working memory capacity, which impedes their ability to hold global goals and subgoals for their text in mind, while they read to evaluate whether they achieved those goals (McCutchen, 1994; Swanson & Berninger, 1994). Given the numerous skills and processes that must be recruited to support revision, it is not surprising that students struggle with it to the degree that they often do.

Executive Functions and Self-Regulation

The term "executive functions" subsumes a number of neurodevelopmental abilities that are generally assessed with the use of neuropsychological measures. These include attentional processes (selective, sustained, and divided attention; span of attention; and ability to shift attention), inhibition, maintenance of cognitive set, and anticipatory processes (working memory, planning, organization) (Denckla & Reader, 1993). Research shows that development of such processes extends well into adulthood, with noticeable advances around the age of 10, in midadolescence, and in the late 20s (Denckla, 1998; Denckla & Reader, 1993).

Despite differences in terminology, professionals generally agree that intentional and deliberate behaviors must be planned, organized, and monitored, and that such processes enlist various attentional as well

as working memory systems. Within the presented model, we use the term "executive functions" to refer to these cognitive and behavioral control mechanisms.

Denckla and Reader (1993) argue that executive functions serve a cognitive "command and control" function over "all contexts and content domains" (p. 443). As such, executive functions influence *all* aspects of behavioral, linguistic, and cognitive functioning. In the face of a compromised executive system, then, all of these systems are affected. Language has a central role in guiding planning, organizing, and self-monitoring processes (Singer & Bashir, 1999; Vygotsky, 1962; Wertsch, 1998). Therefore, executive functions are intertwined with language functioning.

"Self-regulation" refers to behaviors that are used to guide, monitor, and direct the success of one's performance (Bandura, 1986). Zimmerman (2002) notes that "self-regulation is not a mental ability or an academic performance skill; rather it is the self-directed process by which learners transform their mental abilities into academic skills" (p. 65). He goes on to say that self-regulation is not a single trait that students possess or lack. Rather, it involves the selective use of processes that are adapted to a learning task. The component skills that comprise self-regulation include (1) goal setting, (2) adopting strategies for attaining goals, (3) monitoring performance for signs of progress, (4) restructuring physical and social contexts to make them compatible with goal attainment, (5) effective time management, (6) self-evaluation of one's methods, (7) attributing causation to performance outcomes, and (8) adapting future methods (Zimmerman, 2002). Thus, students appropriate self-regulated behaviors before, during, and after executing a goal-oriented behavior. When engaged in a task such as writing, self-regulated learners self-monitor, self-evaluate, and make behavioral adjustments to their performance (Zimmerman, 1989).

In some fields, the terms "executive functions" and "self-regulation" are used synonymously. We make a distinction between these two terms, while recognizing the ways in which they overlap. Both are considered "meta" constructs that are involved with the orchestration, flow, and regulation of behavior and thinking (Singer & Bashir, 1999). Writing requires both executive and self-regulatory control.

Within any task, several factors influence the degree to which one enlists executive and self-regulatory controls, which are essential to intentional action (e.g., writing a story, debating, performing a science experiment). These include (1) the degree to which the task at hand is novel, thereby taxing problem-solving processes of planning, organizing, and self-monitoring; (2) the degree to which the student can manage the task's working memory demands; (3) the extent to which the student possesses sufficient content knowledge and experience with performing similar tasks; (4) the student's motivation, interest, and related affect; and (5) the amount of relevant prior instruction that has been provided (Torgesen, 1994).

In the face of novel and challenging tasks, students recruit executive and self-regulatory control processes. According to Vygotsky (1962), human beings use "inner speech" to mediate and regulate their problem solving and behavior. They talk themselves through difficult tasks, planning and evaluating their options, and they talk to themselves as they appropriate various strategies to assist their performance. Language, then, becomes a central tool not only for communication with others but also for communication with one's self, and cognition is inextricably intertwined with language. This, then, poses a problem for students with LLD, for they vary considerably when it comes to using language to regulate their thinking and behavior. Children who have executive function deficits in addition to LLD may have difficulty compensating for their LLD, because compensations for that language disorder must be initiated, coordinated, and monitored by the executive system, which is also impaired (Denckla, 1998).

The range of language production difficulties seen in students with LLD are not solely explained by language factors alone. Students with LLD who have additional weaknesses with executive functions also may fail to apply compensatory linguistic strategies, because they lack the metacognitive and ex-ecutive controls necessary for (1) recognizing when strategies would benefit their oral and/or written communication, (2) identifying which strategies they need to recruit, and/or (3) monitoring the effectiveness of using a strategy. Similarly, students who have LLD and executive dysfunction may fail to show the range of language that they do have (Singer & Bashir, 1999). This is seen in contexts where they must plan and organize complex thoughts and put them into words while monitoring the integrity of their production within a social context. This can leave them "at a loss for words." Therefore, talking and writing may be sparse.

Because writing is intentional action, it is an executive challenge for all students. It requires intentional behavior and monitoring. Yet not all types of writing tax executive functions and self-regulation processes equally; different kinds of writing require greater or lesser amounts of executive and self-regulatory control (Singer & Bashir, 1999). Hooper, Swartz, Wakely, de Kruif, and Montgomery (2002) report that measures of executive functions tapping initiation, set shifting, and sustained attention distinguish good and poor writers. These researchers failed to find a unique contribution of executive function measures to writing variance, however. This may be due to the nature of their writing task. Fourth- and fifth-grade students in this study were given a story starter and asked to complete a narrative within 15 minutes. At this point in their development, fourth- and fifth-grade students may well have internalized strategies for writing narratives. The task may not have been complex enough to tax the executive function and problem-solving skills of students at this age level given that the narrative genre is the focus of most writing curricula in the primary grades. Had the authors elicited expository text from these students, they may well have found a measurable influence of executive functions.

WRITING FOUNDATIONS

The production of written text is influenced by many variables, including a writer's knowledge, and numerous skills and abilities. The presented model suggests that, for any writer, these form the foundation on which the four writing processes rest and function synergistically. When writing foundations are strong, they support well-developed composing processes. However, consistent with a limited resource allocation model (Lahey & Bloom, 1994), the greater the number and severity of foundation weaknesses, the more heavily the writer's resources are strained. Precious cognitive energies must be devoted to managing them. Thus, the writing processes are constrained by both demands of the writing task and, given the breadth of the writer's knowledge base and integrity of the many variables that influence the writing processes, the writer's capacity to meet those demands.

Within the proposed model, four general domains are conceptualized that constrain the writing processes: *cognitive–linguistic, social–rhetorical, production,* and *beliefs and attitudes*. These form the foundation on which writers draw to construct meaning in print. Next, we consider the multiple variables that comprise each domain and that are known to influence the writing processes, as evidenced by text that is actually produced or by observable behaviors. Each is examined from the perspective of how it constrains both the writing process and the written product.

Cognitive–Linguistic Foundations

A number of foundation variables are considered to fall under the general category of cognitive–linguistic constraints. These consist of *conceptual ability, processing speed, prior content knowledge, linguistic knowledge, meta-abilities,* and *working memory.*

It is well known that general *conceptual ability* affects a range of talents, including the ability to write (Loban, 1963). Verbal conceptual ability, as measured by Verbal IQ, accounts for the greatest amount of variance in text generation and quality in typically developing intermediate and junior high students (Berninger, Abbott, Abbott, Graham, & Richards, 2002; Berninger & Swanson, 1994; Berninger et al., 1992).

In addition to conceptual ability, *processing speed* also influences and constrains the

writer. Evidence of this comes primarily from studies of students with LLD. Torgesen (1994), citing evidence that students with LLD process verbal information more slowly than nondisabled peers, suggests that slow or inefficient lower level processes might account for reduced higher level metacognitive processing. Montgomery (2002) reports that children with language disorders are slower than same age peers on language comprehension tasks that tax both storage and processing aspects of verbal working memory, though their accuracy matches that of younger children. Citing evidence from studies of oral language processing, he notes that slowed processing speed affects their performance on verbal working memory tasks.

Currently, the way in which processing speed influences written language for students with LLD is not well understood. However, given its influence on working memory, which is known to constrain written language generation and revising processes, we presume that students exhibiting slower processing speed will struggle with these writing processes.

Prior content knowledge also influences the writing processes. A student cannot write unless he or she has something to say—some knowledge, insight, or understanding to convey to a remote reader. Thus, writers must tap what they know—their fund of knowledge stored in long-term memory. Flower and Hayes (1980) note that "knowledge is a resource, not a constraint. However, it becomes a constraint on the process when it is not in an acceptable form" (p. 34). They add that "much of the work of writing can be the task of transforming incoherent thought and loosely related pockets of information into a highly conceptualized and precisely related network" (p. 34). For typical writers, this work can be arduous. The think-aloud protocols of Flower and Hayes (1980) and Hayes and Flower (1980) clearly show that typical writers exert much energy trying to retrieve knowledge and to conceptualize what they think and understand about a topic, so that they can represent that knowledge linguistically. In so doing, they enlist language—specifically, language related to the topic and their ideas about the topic.

McCutchen (1986, 1987) asserts that prior content knowledge influences what children write and interacts with linguistic knowledge to influence the way in which they convey that knowledge. For example, she found that children who had extensive knowledge about football wrote longer and more coherent essays than children whose topic knowledge of football was comparatively sparse. Moreover, prior knowledge influenced the content of their essays. Children in the high-knowledge group provided elaborated details about specific plays, whereas children in the low-knowledge group wrote about the general goals of the game (e.g., scoring points). Overall, her results reveal that "differences in topic knowledge affect *what* gets said, but knowledge of a different sort affects *how* it gets said" (McCutchen, 1986, p. 442). Thus, the marriage of prior knowledge and linguistic knowledge influences text production.

Linguistic and discourse knowledge improve with age and experience with text (McCutchen, 1986). This is evident in measures of sentence-to-sentence connections, or local coherence. Thus, children who have extensive linguistic knowledge can mask (to some degree) their impoverished content knowledge, because they can express what little they know with sophisticated sentence structures that coalesce within coherent and cohesive text. However, the reverse is not necessarily so. Extensive content knowledge may not compensate for reduced linguistic knowledge when it comes to composing. Knowing a lot about topic does not ensure that one will be able to convey that knowledge within sentences and discourse that are structured well.

Clinical experience suggests that students with LLD are often literally at a loss for words in the face of academic writing tasks. This occurs in part because they lack sufficient knowledge of academic content to support the reflection or analysis that academic writing requires, and in part because they struggle to acquire content vocabulary at a rate commensurate with their peers. Here, we see the effects of oral language and reading difficulties on knowledge acquisition. Students who read and are read to become better readers with larger vocabularies (Stanovich, 1986), which in turn makes them better writers. Students who struggle with language and reading tend to avoid it. This yields less exposure to texts, impoverished print literacy, and a limited fund of knowledge about the world and our culture—knowledge that most students encounter and acquire through reading. Depending on the demands of a writing task, students with LLD may have insufficient prior knowledge to draw on in support of the composing process. Having little to say, they may not write much.

Linguistic knowledge refers to all stored knowledge about the content (semantics), form (syntax and morphology), and use (pragmatics and discourse) of oral and written language. In the proposed model, reading and spelling ability, as well as knowledge of writing conventions (i.e., capitalization and punctuation rules), are included within this category because these domains are rooted in linguistic processes (MacArthur, 2001; Moats, 1995). In typically developing children, different domains of language knowledge are dedicated to different aspects of composing. For example, Berninger and Swanson (1994) report that in the intermediate grades, word- and subword-level skills play a role in spelling; however, language skills at the word, sentence, and text levels play a role in text composition. Furthermore, in the elementary grades, one's fluency with language (measured by text length) is correlated with composition quality, and the strength of this correlation increases in the intermediate and junior high school grades.

Students with LLD, by definition, have reduced knowledge and flexibility with language. They may struggle with one or more domains of semantics, syntax, morphology, phonology, and/or pragmatics. As well, they may lack the metalinguistic ability to reflect on any of those domains (Kamhi, 1985, 1987). Problems with all of these aspects of language are apparent in both their oral and written language.

Language deficits are revealed in writing at the subword, word, and/or sentence levels. At the subword level, spelling is a long-term problem for students with LLD (Moats, 1995). They also have difficulty learning and applying conventions of capitalization and punctuation (MacArthur, 1999; Poplin, Gray, Larsen, Banikowski, & Mehring, 1980). At the word level, difficulty with acquiring and retrieving content-specific vocabulary (McGregor, Newman, Reilly, & Capone, 2002) affects their ability to represent what they know and understand in school-sponsored writing. Also, written syntax and morphology remain especially problematic for students with LLD well into the school years (Gillam & Johnston, 1992, Rubin, Patterson, & Kantor, 1991; Scott & Windsor, 2000; Singer, 1997; Windsor, Scott, & Street, 2000). Even when their spoken syntax is relatively error-free, their writing can be riddled with agrammatic sentence structures (Singer, 1997).

Ample research indicates that, compared to typically developing students, students with LLD have impoverished mental representations of text and discourse schemas (Barenbaum, Newcomer, & Nodine, 1987; Englert & Thomas, 1987; Thomas, Englert, & Gregg, 1987; Wong, Wong, & Blenkinsop, 1989). Thomas et al. (1987) found that students with LLD in grades 3, 4, 6, and 7 are more likely than their peers matched for age, IQ, and reading ability to terminate text early and to add egocentric points of view and irrelevant information in written texts. Their findings suggest that students with LLD have difficulty retrieving and using schemas from memory that might sustain their thinking in a generative way. Moreover, difficulty with higher order control and management of text structure impedes their writing proficiency. Accordingly, their writing is disorganized and fails to include text elements that characterize different genres. No doubt, this is fueled by deficits in reading that limit their exposure to different kinds of text and, by extension, their insight into how text is structured and how to reveal that knowledge through language.

Meta-abilities (i.e., metalinguistic and metacognitive insight) also constrain the writing process. Writing activates metalinguistic knowledge that is not activated in spontaneous speech (Gombert, 1993). We know little about when and how typical children acquire metacognitive and metalinguistic control over their writing. Develop-

ing writers must gain a solid footing in text generation processes before they are able to step back from text and judge the integrity of its form and meaning. It is yet unclear how this burdens the cognitive system at various levels of writing. Although findings across studies are varied, the general pattern is that typically developing students in the primary grades (1–3) have little metacognitive and metalinguistic control over writing. This appears to develop in the intermediate grades (McCutchen, 1988; Whitaker et al., 1994). Typically developing, intermediate-grade children show greater ability to generate text than to make judgments about and revise it. Moreover, they show intraindividual differences in their revision skill across word, sentence, and text levels (Whitaker et al., 1994).

Studies of students with LLD generally show that, whereas they have some metacognition about writing, their development of metacognition is qualitatively delayed and similar to younger typical peers, revealing preoccupations with lower level writing skills (e.g., handwriting neatness, spelling, punctuation) rather than an understanding of what writing involves and the nature of their writing problems (McAlister et al., 1999; Wong et al., 1989). Englert, Raphael, Fear, and Anderson (1988) report that students with LLD differ from low- and high-achieving writers in their metacognitive knowledge of the writing process and how to organize ideas. Moreover, their metacognitive knowledge was correlated with their expository writing performance. Accordingly, students who have greater metacognitive insights about writing tend to produce better text.

Working memory is yet another constraint on the writing process. The central role that working memory plays in all facets of text production, including text generation processes, is becoming increasingly apparent (Berninger & Swanson, 1994; Hayes, 2000; McCutchen, 1994). Working memory entails the memory processes involved with holding in mind information that is retrieved from long-term memory, until it can be translated into language with which writer is comfortable and then committed to the page (Baddeley, 1986; Scardamalia et al., 1982). It is the "buffer" between long-term storage and generating text. Butterfield (1994) proposes that all writing processes (e.g., planning, generating, revising, and monitoring) take place in working memory. Thus, variations in working memory capacity and efficiency affect all aspects of writing.

Berninger (1994) notes that working memory is capacity-limited, meaning that one can hold only a limited amount of information in mind while processing it actively. It is also a mechanism for coordinating (in real time) both automatic (e.g., handwriting) and nonautomatic (i.e., strategic, conceptual) processes. Therefore, it is capacity-limited *and* temporally constrained. As a result, planning, generating, and revising processes compete for working memory resources (Berninger & Swanson, 1994; McCutchen, 1994), and executive and self-regulatory resources assist with the synergistic coordination of automatic and nonautomatic composing processes (Berninger, 1994).

The limits of working memory constrain the text production ability of young writers more than older writers. Work by McCutchen (1994) reveals that young writers are prone to losing the anchor of their topic when composing. As such, they frequently produce sentences that are not related to the topic. However, older and more skilled writers perform better than less skilled writers on tasks of working memory. By sixth and eighth grade, over half of sentences produced by typically developing children are linked with linguistic markers that cohere ideas (e.g., lexical repetition, pronominal reference) to preceding sentences. This does not suggest that skilled writers have larger working memory capacity; rather, their efficiency of processing allows them to divert cognitive resources to storage, access, and retrieval. The writer coordinates planning, generating, and revising processes in working memory in the moment-to-moment act of composing. Writers who are more efficient at translating ideas into language have greater resources for online planning and reviewing, which support fluent text production (McCutchen, 1994).

When writing, students with LLD must retrieve words and ideas (a vulnerable skill in and of itself), and they must hold them in mind long enough to get them written down, while simultaneously directing processing resources to control all of the "nonautomated activities" of writing (Hayes, 2000, p. 15). Many students' working memory capacity is not sufficient to allow for such parallel processing. As such, they either forget what they were writing before they get it written down, or they forgo attention to nonautomated processes. The result of the former option is they often do not write very much. The result of the latter option is the production of text riddled with problematic spelling, punctuation, word choice, and grammar (Berninger & Swanson, 1994; Daiute, 1981).

Social–Rhetorical Foundations

Another set of foundational variables that influence the composing process can be conceptualized as *social–rhetorical* in nature. These consist of the *rhetorical task* at hand, and the social and physical *environment*.

The *rhetorical task* of writing supports and constrains the composing process. Writing is a speech act (Flower & Hayes, 1980). However, because written text is preserved across space, preserved through time, capable of being edited and revised, separated from the recipient, and used for different purposes than oral language (Olsen, 1981), it cannot operate just like speech written down. It is characterized by its own unique conventions that compensate for the absent reader. This allows the text to stand alone. Summarizing the distinctions between spoken and written language, Olsen and Torrance (1981, p. 253) note:

> Text is explicit while the child's speech is somewhat elliptical; speech occurs in the context of non-linguistic activity while text provides its own context; speech is primarily rhetorical or interpersonally biased while text is primarily truth-functionally biased; speech hesitates at every point to adjust itself to the requirements of the listener while text is fixed and the child is required to come around to the requirements of the text; speech is an elaboration of previously shared meanings, while text specifies a set of meanings which are somewhat foreign and often incongruent with the world view of the child.

As Olsen (1981) notes, "What is 'said' and what is 'meant' are more or less conflated in ordinary oral language, but they come to be differentiated during the school years" (p. 105). Writing places an emphasis on the latter, which "gives rise to the explicit, logical prose" that typifies the literate language of school (p. 108). Within oral exchanges, then, interpersonal functions predominate. Speakers and listeners focus less on what is said than on what is meant and make use of contextual cues to resolve ambiguities. In written exchanges, where such contextual clues are absent, logical and ideational functions predominate. A reader cannot ask a text what it means (Olsen, 1977). Thus, the writer's task in acquiring literate competence is to say what he or she means—to make text an "adequate and autonomous" representation of the writer's intended meaning (Olsen & Torrance, 1981, p. 248). Such is the rhetorical task of writing.

Rather than having unique characteristics, speaking and writing vary along several dimensions in accordance with rhetorical demands (Biber, 1987; Chafe & Tannen, 1987). Typical writers make lexical, syntactic, and textual structure choices based on their purpose(s) for writing and their awareness of their unseen reader(s). Collectively, these choices contribute to an author's writing style and the tone of a text. Spoken and written language vary in the degree to which they embody "spoken" versus "written" rhetorical characteristics (Biber, 1987; Chafe & Danielewicz, 1987; Scott, 1994). The degree to which spoken language may be "writtenlike" or written language may be "spokenlike" is influenced by the communication context and purpose and the subject matter being spoken or written about (Chafe & Danielewicz, 1987, p. 84). Thus, all spoken and written language can be placed on a "spoken" to "written" continuum.

In the early grades, students' written syntax mirrors their spoken (stylistically "oral") syntax and is characterized by simple clauses strung together in a linear fashion (Perera, 1984). Similarly, children use casual vocabulary that is commonly used in speaking (such as "Hey!" and "OK") in writing. As such, their texts read like speech written down (Temple, Nathan, Temple, & Burris, 1993). Around the fourth grade, development in syntax brings about the use of embedded clauses in writing, which allows writers to translate their thoughts more densely through sentences that are structured hierarchically (Perera, 1984). As a result, written syntax begins to diverge from spoken syntax and takes on a more formal and "literate" style. Exposure to a wide range of text through reading supports the development of vocabulary and the use of low-frequency words in writing that more commonly appear in text than in speaking. As well, children gain familiarity with and insights about different text structures through reading. Increased linguistic and textual knowledge arms young writers with options for meeting the rhetorical demands of a range of writing tasks.

Decisions about rhetorical style in writing are made based on the purpose(s) for writing and the effect the writer wishes to have on the reader. The rhetorical task, then, encompasses a writer's goals and subgoals for a text and dictates both *what* gets written and *how* it gets written. Flower and Hayes (1980) note that three types of plans are used by good writers in the act of composing: *plans to do* (plans for performing a speech act and for responding to the rhetorical task), *plans to say* (plans for the content to include in the text), and *composing plans* (internal speech used by the writer to guide and self-regulate the writing process). Good writers use all three types of plans recursively in the face of a written rhetorical task. Poor writers focus on plans to say, without revisiting the rhetorical problem or how to go about the composing process.

Much literature now points to the difficulty students with LLD have with managing various written rhetorical demands. Studies reveal they have difficulty producing narratives and all expository genres (e.g., descriptive, enumerative, informative, persuasive, compare–contrast, summary) (Barenbaum et al., 1987; Thomas et al., 1987). A good deal of research shows that they tend to persist in the use of an "oral" style of writing when their nondisabled peers have begun to adopt the more "literate" forms and conventions of schooled writing (Englert & Thomas, 1987). Clinical experience suggests that many students struggle with understanding the rhetorical demands of their writing assignments. Although this may in part be due to concomitant reading comprehension difficulties, it is not at all uncommon for a student with LLD to read (or listen to) an assignment and immediately ask, "What do I have to do?" The student with LLD commonly struggles with identifying the nature of a written task, establishing rhetorical goals and subgoals for a text, and making conscious choices about linguistic words, structures, and style based on the nature of the rhetorical task.

Social and physical *environments* also support and constrain the composing process. Because writing is a communicative act, it is bound by social and interactive constraints. Learning to write requires learning to communicate with an unseen reader and sustaining a monologue without social input. This requires that one transcend dependence on a conversational partner (Bereiter & Scardamalia, 1987), whose role is to provide external prompts that support the development of shared meaning.

It remains unclear when and how typically developing students and those with LLD move from open (i.e., dialogic) to closed (i.e., monologic) discourse schemas when writing, though we know this transition happens through the elementary school years (Bereiter & Scardamalia, 1987). It is known, however, that both show significant increases in text length and composition quality when they are provided with conversational inputs in the form of prompts to say (write) more (Bereiter & Scardamalia, 1987; Graham, 1990).

In addition to being influenced by the social environment, composing can also be influenced by the physical environment. Some students prefer to write to music; others need background noise, and still others prefer absolute quiet. In typical learners, awareness of what distracts them improves from ages 5 to 20. With increased awareness, students employ greater control over their learning environment to ensure their performance success (Pressley, Borkowski, & Schneider, 1987). When environmental factors are inconsistent with one's prefer-

ences, the writing process can be seriously derailed. This may have to do with factors that promote engagement and involvement with writing (Reed, Schallert, & Deithloff, 2002).

A written text itself can constitute a physical environment that influences the writer and the composing process. As text is produced, it shapes the writing environment, such that writers consider what they have already written before adding more (Hayes, 2000; Hayes & Flower, 1980). Thus, the text produced so far is a key ingredient in the environment that constrains self-regulated composing.

The mode of output, that is, whether students use technology to compose or write by hand, is yet an additional environmental factor that can constrain the composing process. Different modes of output differentially support different composing processes. Typically developing writers do more advanced planning when handwriting than they do when using a computer (Haas, 1989), and they make more revisions when writing with a computer or dictating than when handwriting (MacArthur, 2001).

Production Foundations

An additional set of variables that influence and constrain the writing process can be conceptualized under the umbrella of text *production*. The literature points to three variables that support or bog down the composing processes: *graphomotor skills* (those processes responsible for transcribing ideas onto a page by hand), *mode of output* (whether text is produced with a pencil or pen, by keyboard, or via dictation), and *speed of output* (the degree to which the writer is able to transcribe text fluently and automatically within a chosen mode of output). Sometimes one of these variables has a strong influence on the composing process, yet more often, we see text production constrained by their interaction. Sometimes attempts to bypass these constraints introduce additional constraints on the writer.

Graphomotor skills are those fine motor skills involved with encoding graphemes on paper. For typically developing children, handwriting automaticity constrains the composing process, presumably because writers whose handwriting is not fluent and automatic must devote attention to this "low-level" factor while they compose, which leaves them with fewer cognitive resources to devote to text generation. Automaticity of handwriting contributes strongly to composition quality in the early grades, when children are learning to handwrite (grades 1–3), and it continues to contribute to composition length and quality in the intermediate and junior high school grades (Berninger & Swanson, 1994). But in the intermediate grades, handwriting is largely automatized for typically developing children, so the degree to which it constrains text generation is minimized. Throughout the elementary and junior high school years, girls tend to write more than boys, which is likely due to their stronger graphomotor integration abilities supporting automatized handwriting (Berninger & Swanson, 1994).

What is generally most striking about the text produced by students with LLD is that there is not much of it. Stories written by children with LLD are reported to be one-third to one-half the length of those produced by their nondisabled peers (Mykelbust, 1975). They contain fewer words, sentences, and propositions than stories written by nondisabled peers (Barenbaum et al., 1987). The paucity of output can be explained, at least in part, by a difficulty getting print onto the page. This interferes with both the quality and quantity of text they produce (Graham, 1990).

Graphomotor difficulties, seen as slow and effortful output with inconsistent letter formation and spacing, are believed to affect all other composing processes. The effort and conscious control required to move ideas from students' minds through their hands to the page is great enough to usurp resources otherwise devoted to higher level cognitive processes such as planning and meaning making (Graham, 1990; Lahey & Bloom, 1994).

The difficulty that students with LLD exhibit with handwriting has led many educators to explore other *modes of output* as a means for bypassing graphomotor difficulties. For example, students might be encouraged to dictate their texts to an adult who will transcribe for them, or they may use a keyboard to type ideas into a computer. Although well intentioned, these alternate avenues for text production do not always prove effective because each can introduce additional constraints on the writer and the composing process.

First, dictated texts may surpass handwritten texts in terms of length and quality for some students (Graham, 1990; MacArthur, 2001). However, dictation can be an equally or even more problematic mode of output for some students, especially those who struggle with language and/or working memory. Because they have less time for formulation when speaking than they do when writing, students with reduced oral language formulation abilities sometimes have greater difficulty dictating texts (Singer & Bashir, 1999). This causes them to produce text orally that is disorganized, poorly formed, or incoherent. Thus, dictation bypasses handwriting difficulties and introduces additional problems that impede text production.

Second, students with language and/or memory limitations may experience difficulty with dictation because it places a heavy burden on working memory, which is known to influence oral language formulation (MacArthur, 1999, 2001; Singer & Bashir, 2004). When dictating, students encode ideas verbally and must then wait for their scribe to write them down. This may leave them vulnerable to forgetting what they were planning to say before they are able to formulate all of their ideas about a topic. Alternately, it may afford them extra time to formulate their next thought. Indeed, Graham (1990) compared text production via dictation, slow dictation (i.e., dictation matched to the speed of students' handwriting), and handwriting by students with LLD. He found that essays produced in dictation and slow dictation modes were of higher quality those that were handwritten, revealing that text transcription interferes with composing quality. No difference in length was found between normally dictated and handwritten texts. However, slowly dictated essays were twice as long as normally dictated essays, suggesting that students used the pause time available in the slow dictation condition to formulate ideas. Yet students using slow dictation seemed to forget high-level textual plans, because almost 43% of text units offered were nonfunctional (i.e., repetitive). These findings suggest that working memory limits the dictation ability of some students.

Finally, written language differs from spoken language with respect to syntactic and semantic form (Perera, 1986; Scott & Windsor, 2000; Singer, 1997) as well as text structure (Scott & Klutzenbaker, 1989). Unless students are adept at "talking like a book," their dictated texts may read like conversation rather than written prose. In an effort to shape language into forms more consistent with written conventions, scribes may inadvertently recast what students actually say, transforming sentence structures so that they capture students' intended meaning.

Aside from dictation, computer technology is increasingly being used as an alternate mode of output for text transcription. Despite its apparent promise for students with both language and handwriting problems, word processing has not been found to be the "magic bullet" that many have hoped it would be. Some studies show increased text length and/or quality when students compose via word processor versus handwriting (Outhred, 1989), and others show the opposite pattern (Outhred, 1989; Shaw, 1994; Zhang, Brooks, Frields, & Redelfts, 1995). What is not well accounted for in these studies is the degree to which students are fluent and automatic at typing. Though no formal research has explored the influence of typing speed and writing quality, given the known connection between handwriting speed and writing quality, slow typing speed likely burdens working memory (MacArthur, 1999), thereby affecting writing quality.

Some teachers have suggested that students with poor fine motor functioning should be allowed to use a keyboard for all writing activities so as to foster keyboarding fluency at an early age. This, too, has its consequences. Berninger (personal communication, June 24, 2002) notes that encouraging keyboard rather than pencil use at an early age may have detrimental effects on the acquisition of mental orthographic representations, which may in turn affect reading and spelling ability (Apel, 2002).

The degree to which one is able to transcribe thoughts into text rapidly, automatically, and fluidly in *any* mode, then, influences developing writers considerably. Children in the early elementary school grades are highly constrained by graphomotor difficulties because they are in the process of acquiring fluency with handwriting; this is evident in their short and laboriously produced texts. When handwriting fails to become automatic, as is often the case for students with LLD (Graham, 1990), the effects of transcription difficulty are far-reaching into the school years. Fewer cognitive resources are available for managing other composing processes when extensive resources must be allocated to managing transcription through the pen, the keyboard, or the mouth. Consequently, the writer is less able to attend directly to such variables as language form and meaning, spelling, text and discourse structure, and reader awareness—variables that take cognitive precedence in typically developing upper elementary and early middle school writers (Berninger, Cartwright et al., 1994). Thus, early in their academic careers, writers with LLD who struggle with text production soon fall behind their same-age peers due to the constraints that transcription processes place on their ability to plan, organize, generate, and revise text.

Beliefs and Attitudes Foundations

The final set of variables within the model that supports and constrains the writing process can be conceptualized under the umbrella of *beliefs and attitudes*. These include *self-efficacy, affect,* and *writer's goals*.

Self-efficacy for writing, or the writer's perceived capacity to meet the desired standards of a writing task, is linked to the regulation of affect and one's interest and involvement in writing (Reed et al., 2002; Zimmerman & Risemberg, 1997). An important aspect of self-efficacy is the notion of agency, or the link between the *self* and the *means* to a desired outcome (Paris & Byrnes, 1989). Self-efficacy for writing is a judgment of whether one possesses the skills and abilities to meet (or exceed) the demands of a writing task. Students' self-efficacy beliefs are shaped by several factors, including their (1) attention to task outcomes, (2) attribution of outcomes to their own performance, (3) understanding of trade-offs between competence and task difficulty, and (4) differentiation between competence and performance, with an understanding of causal notions of effort and ability (Pressley et al., 1987). Feedback suggesting competence or poor performance fuels either an increase or decrease in self-efficacy. This, in turn, affects the student's "mind-set" for future writing. Self-efficacy, then, becomes predictive of one's interest in writing, motivation to write, and feelings about one's self as a writer.

Self-efficacy is shaped by both external and internal feedback. Reviewing the literature on typically developing children, Paris and Byrnes (1989) note that self-efficacy is largely influenced by academic grades through grade 4. But by fifth or sixth grade, students determine their abilities by comparing their performance to that of their peers and to internal and external standards. It is also at this time that they learn to distinguish domain-specific areas of strength and weakness (e.g., relative ability or disability in math versus writing), and they show preferences for academic tasks they believe themselves to be capable of accomplishing well, for these preserve their self-esteem (Paris & Byrnes, 1989).

Research on self-efficacy reveals its relationship to effort and affective states. Through second grade, children generally believe that effort can compensate for innate ability and, moreover, that practice and effort together bring forth greater ability (Paris & Byrnes, 1989). By age 10, effort and ability become distinguished. Students come to view trying hard as an indicator of low ability. They value success that requires little effort more than success that requires high effort, and they view failure that requires high effort as a "devastating indication of poor ability" (Paris & Byrnes, 1989, p. 186).

With writing, students who understand that their performance outcomes are at least in part influenced by effort generally persist with writing tasks and use strategies longer than those who believe their performance is due to innate ability (Pressley et al., 1987). Students who see themselves as having low ability are more prone to giving up prematurely with a task. Moreover, students who believe they have solid writing abilities set higher writing goals and persist longer with writing than those whose self-efficacy for writing is low (Zimmerman, 1995). Thus, self-efficacy becomes intricately intertwined with self-regulation.

An emerging literature on students with LLD shows that their sense of self-efficacy and their actual performance with writing are asynchronous. Studies show that students with LLD have elevated self-efficacy ratings in comparison to their peers and to their parents and teachers, but their performance on language tasks is below that of their peers (Graham & Harris, 1989a, 1989b; Graham, Schwartz, & MacArthur, 1993; Klassen, 2002; Sawyer, Graham, & Harris, 1992; Stone & May, 2002). Klassen (2002) notes that overconfidence in one's ability to perform a task can reflect either erroneous task analysis or reduced metacognition; the work of Stone and May (2002), as well as that of Kruger and Dunning (1999), suggests the latter. It also has been hypothesized that asynchronous self-efficacy/performance ratings may serve to protect a fragile sense of self-worth resulting from chronic academic struggle.

Students' self-efficacy for writing is strongly related to their *affect* about writing, which also can constrain the composing process. When students attribute success to their ability and/or effort, they feel pride. Conversely, they feel shame or guilt when they attribute poor performance to low effort and/or ability (Weiner, 1986).

Bandura (1989) notes that "gross miscalculations (between efficacy judgments and performance) can create problems" (p. 1177). We speculate that such miscalculations may affect the writing process differentially. Underconfidence in one's ability may lead a student to dislike writing, which may in turn stall planning and/or generating processes and result in little or no output. Conversely, overconfidence in one's ability may lead to a feeling of detachment or indifference, which may in turn interfere with organizing and/or revising processes. Students may assume that the text they generate is perfect and, therefore, may not monitor and evaluate their written product closely.

Self-efficacy beliefs and associated affective states influence and are influenced by *goals*. Because writing is a communicative act, writers produce text for some purpose. Hence, they establish goals for their texts, which may include having a desired effect on a reader (e.g., to inform, persuade, explain) or achieving a standard of literate performance (e.g., use interesting vocabulary, vary sentence structures, write a specified number of words or sentences).

Good adult writers develop high-level goals and subgoals for their texts and continue to develop these as they write (Flower & Hayes, 1981). Global textual goals influence word choices and sentence construction, and they are constrained by the rhetorical task. Young writers do not develop high-level goals for their texts. Rather, they retrieve information from memory and write it down in the order in which it comes to mind (Bereiter & Scardamalia, 1987). Thus, the language generation processes of young writers are encapsulated and beyond the reach of metacognitive control (McCutchen, 1988).

Students can be taught to set goals for their writing. Moreover, goal setting has positive effects on composition quality for students with LLD. Sawyer et al. (1992) note that students with LLD who received explicit writing instruction that included goal-setting and self-monitoring strategies displayed higher schematic structure than students who did not learn these techniques. As well, students with LLD who set specific process goals for revising made better revisions than students who set a general outcome goal to improve their text (Graham, MacArthur, & Schwartz, 1995). Research by Zimmerman and Kintsantas (1999) shows that goal setting, along with self-recording of accuracy, results in high performance on writing tasks. Furthermore, students perform best when they shift from setting process goals based on a model to setting outcome goals after attaining automaticity with targeted writing skills. In all, the findings suggest that setting performance goals and shifting the nature of those goals based on performance yield high reports of self-efficacy, feelings of satisfaction, and greater intrinsic motivation to pursue the skill further.

Students with LLD tend to show a reduced interest in writing, which likely stems from their repeated failure with the task. Chronic failure with writing mirrors chronic failure with reading (e.g., Torgesen, 1994; see also Stanovich, 1986). It creates a repeating, self-defeating cycle, wherein unsuccessful output causes the student to attribute failure to poor innate ability, which reduces self-efficacy and results in task avoidance. This can result in a reduced opportunity to acquire a broad repertoire of writing skills and strategies, leading to further failure, reduced self-efficacy, task avoidance, and so on.

CONCLUDING THOUGHTS

A model of writing has been proposed that contains two components: writing processes and writing foundations. The writing processes consist of four synergistic processes (*planning, generating, organizing,* and *revising*) under the direction of executive function and self-regulatory processes. These writing processes rest on four foundational components (*cognitive–linguistic, social–rhetorical, production,* and *beliefs and attitudes*). All components of the model are connected through feedback and feedforward mechanisms. Inefficient or ineffective processing within any one aspect affects all others, thereby "contaminating" the accuracy and efficiency of functioning and one or more of the composing processes. Support for the model comes from the research on the development of writing and studies that document the difficulties that students with LLD have when they write. The model extends earlier models of writing, in that it accounts for the unique composing difficulties demonstrated by students with LLD.

The model suggests that there are many reasons why writing can be problematic for any student. Consequently, it provides a framework for identifying potential subtypes of written language difficulties. Further research will illuminate the need for changes in the model and also help educators better focus their assessment, instruction, and intervention efforts for all students.

NOTE

1. The majority of reported studies of writing in children with "learning disabilities" have not specified subjects' linguistic functioning (Singer, 1997). Even when subjects are identified as having language-based learning disabilities, the aspects of language that are problematic (e.g., semantic, syntactic, or pragmatic domains of language) typically are not specified. Consequently, we know only a little about the patterns of written language difficulty demonstrated by students with *language*-learning disabilities. Whereas subjects with learning disabilities within the studies reviewed in this chapter exhibit difficulty with written *language,* for the purposes of this chapter, we refer to these students as having LLD.

REFERENCES

Apel, K. (2002, March). *Spelling it out for SLPs: Spelling development, assessment and intervention.* Paper presented at the California meeting of the Speech–Language–Hearing Association, Los Angeles.

Baddeley, A. D. (1986). *Working memory.* London: Oxford University Press.

Bandura, A. (1986). *Social foundations of thought and action: A social cognitive theory.* Englewood Cliffs, NJ: Prentice-Hall.

Bandura, A. (1989). Human agency in social cognitive theory. *American Psychologist, 44,* 1175–1184.

Barenbaum, E., Newcomer, P. L., & Nodine, B. (1987). Children's ability to write stories as a function of variation in task, age and developmental level. *Learning Disabilities Quarterly, 10,* 175–188.

Bereiter, C., & Scardamalia, M. (1987). *The psychology of written composition.* Hillsdale, NJ: Erlbaum.

Berninger, V. W. (1994). Coordination transcription and text generation in working memory during composing: Automatic and constructive processes. *Learning Disability Quarterly, 22,* 99–112.

Berninger, V. W., & Abbott, R. D. (1993). Structural equation modeling of relationships among developmental skills and writing skills in primary- and inter-

mediate-grade writers. *Journal of Educational Psychology, 85*(3), 478–508.

Berninger, V. W., Abbott, R. D., Abbott, S., Graham, S., & Richards, T. (2002). Writing and reading: Connections between language by hand and language by eye. *Journal of Learning Disabilities, 35,* 39–56.

Berninger, V. W., Cartwright, A. C., Yates, C. M., Swanson, H. L., & Abbott, R. (1994). Developmental skills related to writing and reading in the intermediate grades. *Reading and Writing: An Interdisciplinary Journal, 6,* 161–196.

Berninger, V. W., Mizokawa, D. T., Bragg, R., Cartwright, A., & Yates, C. (1994). Intraindividual differences in levels of written language. *Reading and Writing Quarterly: Overcoming Learning Difuclties, 10,* 259–275.

Berninger, V. W., & Swanson, H. L. (1994). Modifying Hayes and Flower's model of skilled writing to explain beginning and developing writing. In E. C. Butterfield (Ed.), *Children's writing: Toward a process theory of the development of skilled writing* (pp. 57–81). Greenwich, CT: JAI Press.

Berninger, V. W., Whitaker, D., Feng, Y., Swanson, H. L., & Abbott, R. (1996). Assessment of planning, translation, and revising in junior high students. *Journal of School Psychology, 34,* 23–52.

Berninger, V. W., Yates, C., Cartwright, A., Rutberg, J., Remy, E., & Abbott, R. (1992). Lower level developmental skills in beginning writing. *Reading and Writing: An Interdisciplinary Journal, 4,* 257–280.

Biber, D. (1987). *Textual relations in speech and writing.* Cambridge, UK: Cambridge University Press.

Butterfield, E. C. (1994). Diverse data about writing processes and their theoretical implications. In *Children's writing: Toward a process theory of the development of skilled writing* (pp. 199–208). Greenwich, CT: JAI Press.

Butterfield, E. C., Hacker, D. J., & Plumb, C. (1994). Topic knowledge, linguistic knowledge, and revision skill as determinants of text revision. In E. C. Butterfield (Ed.), *Children's writing: Toward a process theory of the development of skilled writing* (pp. 83–141). Greenwich, CT: JAI Press.

Chafe, W., & Danielewicz, J. (1987). Properties of spoken and written language. In R. Horowitz & S. J. Samuels (Eds.), *Comprehending oral and written language* (pp. 83–13). San Diego: Academic Press.

Chafe, W., & Tannen, D. (1987). The relation between spoken and written language. *Annual Review of Anthropology, 16,* 383–407.

Collins, A., & Gentner, D. (1980). A framework for a cognitive theory of writing. In L. Gregg & E. Steinberg (Eds.), *Cognitive processes in writing* (pp. 51–72). Hillsdale, NJ: Erlbaum.

Daiute, C. (1981). Psycholinguistic foundations of the writing process. *Research in the Teaching of English, 15*(1), 5–22.

Denckla, M. (1998, November). *Understanding the role of executive functions in language, academics, and daily life.* Paper presented at American International College. Springfield, MA.

Denckla, M., & Reader, M. J. (1993). Education and psychosocial interventions: Executive dysfunction and its consequences. In R. Kurban (Ed.), *Handbook of Tourette's syndrome and related tic and behavioral disorders.* Rochester, NY: Marcel Dekker.

Englert, C. S. (2004). The role of dialogue in constructing effective literacy settings for students with language and learning disabilities. In E. Silliman & L. Wilkinson (Eds.), *Language and literacy learning.* New York: Guilford Press.

Englert, C. S., & Raphael, T. (1988). Constructing well-formed prose: Process, structure, and metacognitive control. *Exceptional Children, 54*(6), 513–521.

Englert, C. S., Raphael, T. E., Anderson, L. M., Anthony, H. M., Fear, K. L., & Gregg, S. L. (1988). A case for writing intervention: Strategies for writing informational text. *Learning Disabilities Focus, 3*(2), 98–113.

Englert, C. S., Raphael, T. E., Anderson, L. M., Gregg, S. L., & Anthony, H. M. (1989). Exposition: Reading, writing and the metacognitive knowledge of learning disabled students. *Learning Disabilities Research, 5*(1), 5–24.

Englert, C. S., Raphael, T. E., Fear, K. L., & Anderson, L. M. (1988). Students' metacognitive knowledge about how to write informational texts. *Learning Disability Quarterly, 11*, 18–46.

Englert, C. S., & Thomas, C. C. (1987). Sensitivity to text structure in reading and writing: A comparison of learning disabled and non-learning disabled students. *Learning Disability Quarterly, 11*, 18–46.

Espin, C. A., & Sindelar, P. T. (1988). Auditory feedback and writing: Learning disabled and nondisabled students. *Exceptional Children, 55*(1), 45–51.

Flower, L. S., & Hayes, J. R. (1980). The dynamics of composing: Making plans and juggling constraints. In L. W. Gregg & E. R. Steinberg (Eds.), *Cognitive processes in writing* (pp. 31–50). Hillsdale, NJ: Erlbaum.

Flower, L. S., & Hayes, J. R. (1981). A cognitive process theory of writing. *College Composition and Communication, 32*, 365–387.

German, D., & Simon, E. (1991). Analysis of children's word finding skills in discourse. *Journal of Speech and Hearing Research, 34*(2), 309–316.

Gillam, R. B., & Johnston, J. R. (1992). Spoken and written language relationships in language/learning-impaired and normally achieving school-age children. *Journal of Speech, Language, and Hearing Research, 35*(6), 1303–1315.

Gombert, J. E. (1993). Metacognition, metalanguage and matapragmatics. *International Journal of Psychology, 28*(5), 571–580.

Graham, S. (1990). The role of production factors in learning disabled students' compositions. *Journal of Educational Research, 82*, 781–791.

Graham, S., & Harris, K. (1989a). Components analysis of cognitive strategy instruction: Effects on learning disabled students' compositions and self-efficacy. *Journal of Educational Psychology, 81*, 353–361.

Graham, S., & Harris, K. (1989b). Improving learning disabled students' skills at composing essays: Self-instructional strategy training. *Exceptional Children, 56*, 201–214.

Graham, S., MacArthur, C., & Schwartz, S. (1995). Effects of goal setting and procedural facilitation on the revising behavior and writing performance of students with writing and learning problems. *Journal of Educational Psychology, 98*, 230–240.

Graham, S., Schwartz, S., & MacArthur, C. (1993). Learning disabled and normally achieving students' knowledge of writing and the composing process, attitudes toward writing, and self-efficacy for students with and without learning disabilities. *Journal of Learning Disabilities, 26*, 237–249.

Gregg, N., Coleman, C., Stennett, R., & Davis, M. (2002). Discourse complexity of college writers with and without learning disabilities. *Journal of Learning Disabilities, 35*(1), 23–40.

Haas, C. (1989). Does the medium make a difference?: Two studies of writing with pen and paper with computers. *Human–Computer Interaction, 4*(2), 149–169.

Hayes, J. R. (2000). A new framework for understanding cognition and affect in writing. In R. Indrisano & J. R. Squire (Eds.), *Perspectives on writing: Research, theory, and practice* (pp. 6–44). Newark, DE: International Reading Association.

Hayes, J. R., & Flower, L. S. (1980). Identifying the organization of the writing process. In L. W. Gregg, & E. R. Steinberg (Eds.), *Cognitive processes in writing* (pp. 3–30). Hillsdale, NJ: Erlbaum.

Hooper, S. R., Swartz, C. W., Wakely, M. B., de Kruif, R. E. L., & Montgomery, J. W. (2002). Executive functions in elementary school children with and without problems in written expression. *Journal of Learning Disabilities, 35*(1), 57–68.

Johnson, D. (1987). Disorders of written language. In D. Johnson & J. Blalock (Eds.), *Adults with learning disabilities: Clinical studies* (pp. 173–203). New York: Grune & Stratton.

Johnson, D., & Grant, J. O. (1989). Written narratives of normal and learning disabled children. *Annals of Dyslexia, 39*, 140–159.

Kamhi, A. (1985). Metalinguistic awareness in normal and language-disordered children. *Language, Speech, and Hearing Services in Schools, 16*, 199–210.

Kamhi, A. (1987). Metalinguistic abilities in language impaired children. *Topics in Language Disorders, 7*(2), 1–12.

Kamhi, A., & Catts, H. (1999). Language and reading: Convergence and divergence. In *Language and reading disabilities* (pp. 1–24). Needham Heights, MA: Allyn & Bacon.

Kruger, J., & Dunning, D. (1999). Unskilled and unaware of it: How difficulties in recognizing one's own incompetence lead to inflated self-assessments. *Journal of Personality and Social Psychology, 77*, 1121–1134.

Klassen, R. (2002). A question of calibration: A review of the self-efficacy beliefs of students with learning disabilities. *Learning Disability Quarterly, 25*, 88–102.

Lahey, M. (1988). *Language disorders and language development*. New York: Macmillan.

Lahey, M., & Bloom, L. (1994). Variability and Language Learning Disabilities. In G. P. Wallach & K. G. Butler, (Eds.), *Language learning disabilities in school-age children and adolescents: Some principles and applications* (pp. 354–372). Needham Heights, MA: Allyn & Bacon.

Levine, M. D. (2003, April). *Educating all kinds of minds: A nonlabeling approach to understanding differences in learning*. Seminar sponsored by Educare Consulting Group, Burlington, MA.

Loban, W. (1963). *The language of elementary school children* (Research Report No. 1). Urbana, IL: National Council of Teachers of English.

McAlister, K. M., Nelson, N. W., & Bahr, C. M. (1999). Perceptions of students with language and learning disabilities about writing process instruction. *Learning Disabilities Research and Practice, 14*(3), 159–172.

MacArthur, C. (1999). Overcoming barriers to writing: Computer support for basic writing skills. *Reading and Writing Quarterly, 15*(2), 169–193.

MacArthur, C. (2001, November). *Integrating technology with writing instruction*. Paper presented at the 19th Annual Learning Differences Conference, Harvard University, Cambridge, MA.

MacArthur, C., & Graham, S. (1987). Learning disabled students' composing under three methods of text production: Handwriting, word processing, and dictation. *Journal of Special Education, 21*(3), 22–42.

McCutchen, D. (1986). Domain knowledge and linguistic knowledge in the development of writing ability. *Journal of Memory and Language, 25,* 431–444.

McCutchen, D. (1987). Children's discourse skill: Form and modality requirements of schooled writing. *Discourse Processes, 10,* 267–286.

McCutchen, D. (1988). Functional automaticity in children's writing: A problem of metacognitive control. *Written Communication, 5*(3), 306–324.

McCutchen, D. (1994). The magical number three, plus or minus two: Working memory in writing. In E. C. Butterfield (Ed.), *Children's writing: Toward a process theory of the the development of skilled writing* (pp. 1–30). Greenwich, CT: JAI Press.

McGregor, K. K., Newman, R. M., Reilly, R. M., & Capone, N. C. (2002). Semantic representation and naming in children with language impairment. *Journal of Speech, Language, and Hearing Research, 45*(5), 998–1015.

McNamara, M., Carter, A., McIntosh, B., & Gerken, L. (1998). Sensitivity to grammatical morphemes in children with specific language impairment. *Journal of Speech, Language, and Hearing Research, 41*(5), 1147–1157.

Moats, L. C. (1995). *Spelling: Development, disability and instruction*. Baltimore: York Press.

Montgomery, J. (2002). Understanding the language difficulties of children with specific language impairments: Does working memory matter? *American Journal of Speech–Language Pathology, 11,* 77–91.

Mykelbust, H. (1975). *Progress in learning disabilities* (Vol. 3). New York: Grune & Stratton.

Olsen, D. (1977). Oral and written language and the cognitive processes of children. *Journal of Communication, 27*(3), 10–26.

Olsen, D. (1981). Writing: The divorce of the author from text. In B. M. Kroll & R. J. Vann (Eds.), *Exploring speaking–writing relationships* (pp. 99–110). Urbana, IL: National Council of Teachers of English.

Olsen, D., & Torrance, N. (1981). Learning to meet the requirements of written text: Language development in the school years. In C. H. Frederiksen & J. F. Dominic (Eds.), *Writing: The nature, development and teaching of written communication: Vol. 2. Writing: Process, development and communication* (pp. 285–255). Hillside, NJ: Erlbaum.

Outhred, L. (1989). Word processing: Its impact on children's writing. *Journal of Learning Disabilities, 22*(4), 262–264.

Paris, S. G., & Byrnes, J. P. (1989). The constructivist approach to self-regulation and learning in the classroom. In B. J. Zimmerman & D. H. Schunk (Eds.), *Self-regulated learning and academic achievement: Theory, research and practice* (pp. 169–200). New York: Springer-Verlag.

Perera, K. (1984). *Children's writing and reading: Analysing classroom language*. Oxford, UK: Blackwell.

Perera, K. (1986). Grammatical differentiation between speech an writing in children aged 8 to 12. In A. Wilkinson (Ed.), *The writing of writing* (pp. 90–108). Philadelphia: Open University Press.

Poplin, M., Gray, R., Larsen, S., Banikowski, A., & Mehring, T. (1980). A comparison of components of written expression abilities in learning disabled and non-disabled children at three grade levels. *Learning Disability Quarterly, 3,* 46–53.

Pressley, M., Borkowski, J. G., & Schneider, W. (1987). Cognitive strategies: Good strategy users coordinate metacognition and knowledge. *Annals of Child Development, 4,* 89–129.

Reed, J. H., Shallert, D. L., & Deithloff, L. F. (2002). Investigating the interface between self-regulation and involvement processes. *Educational Psychologist, 37*(1), 53–57.

Rourke, B. (2003, April). *Differential diagnosis of nonverbal learning disabilities*. Paper presented at the Norman Howard School, Rochester, NY.

Rubin, H., Patterson, P., & Kantor, M. (1991). Morphological development and writing ability in childen and adults. *Language, Speech, and Hearing Services in Schools, 22*(4), 228–235.

Sawyer, R. J., Graham, S., & Harris, K. (1992). Direct teaching, strategy instruction, and strategy instruction with explicit self-regulation: Effects on composition skills and self-efficacy of students with learning disabilities. *Journal of Educational Psychology, 84,* 340–352.

Scardamalia, M., Bereiter, C., & Goelman, H. (1982). The role of production factors in writing ability. In M. Nystrand (Ed.), *What writers know: The lan-*

guage process, and structure of written discourse (pp. 173–210). Orlando, FL: Academic Press.

Scott, C. (1994). A discourse continuum for school-age students: Impact of modality and genre. In G. P. Wallach & K. G. Butler (Eds.), *Language learning disabilities in school-age children and adolescents: Some principles and applications* (pp. 219–252). New York: Macmillan.

Scott, C., & Klutzenbaker, K. (1989, November). *Comparing spoken and written summaries: Text structure and surface form.* Paper presented at the Annual Convention of the American Speech, Language, and Hearing Association, St. Louis, MO.

Scott, C., & Windsor, J. (2000). General language performance measures in spoken and written discourse produced by school-age children with and without language learning disabilities. *Journal of Speech, Language, and Hearing Research, 43*(2), 324–339.

Shaw, E. L. (1994). Comparison of spontaneous and word processed compositions in elementary classrooms: A three-year study. *Journal of Computing in Education, 5*(3–4), 319–327.

Singer, B. D. (1997). *Parallels between spoken and written syntax in children with language-learning disabilities.* Unpublished doctoral dissertation, Emerson College, Boston, MA.

Singer, B. D., & Bashir, A. S. (1999). What are executive functions and self-regulation, and what do they have to do with language learning disabilities? *Language, Speech and Hearing Services in Schools, 30,* 265–273.

Singer, B. D., & Bashir, A. S. (2004). EmPOWER: A strategy for teaching students with language learning disabilities how to write expository text. In E. Silliman & L. Wilkinson (Eds.), *Language and literacy learning.* New York: Guilford Press.

Stanovich, K. E. (1986). Matthew effects in reading: Some consequences of individual differences in the acquisition of literacy. *Reading Research Quarterly, 86,* 360–406.

Stein, N. L., & Glenn, C. G. (1979). An analysis of story comprehension in elementary school children. In R. O. Freedle (Ed.), *New directions in discourse processing* (pp. 53–120). Norwood, NJ: Ablex.

Stone, C. A., & May, A. L. (2002). The accuracy of academic self-evaluations in adolescents with learning disabilities. *Journal of Learning Disabilities, 35*(4), 370–383.

Swanson, H. L., & Berninger, V. W. (1994). Working memory as a source of individual differences in children's writing. In E. C. Butterfield (Ed.), *Children's writing: Toward a process theory of the development of skilled writing* (pp. 31–56). Greenwich, CT: JAI Press.

Temple, C., Nathan, R., Temple, F., & Burris, N. (1993). *The beginnings of writing.* Boston: Allyn & Bacon.

Thomas, C. C. Englert, C. S., & Gregg, S. (1987). An analysis of error and strategies in the expository writing of learning disabled students. *Remedial and Special Education, 8*(1), 21–30, 46.

Torgesen, J. (1994). Issues in the assessment of execu-

tive function. In G. R. Lyon (Ed.), *Frames of reference for the assessment of learning disabilities: New views on measurement issues* (pp. 143–162). Baltimore: Brookes.

Troia, G., Graham, S., & Harris, K. (1999). Teaching students with learning disabilities to mindfully plan when writing. *Exceptional Children, 65*(1), 235–252.

Vygotsky, L. (1962). *Thought and language.* Cambridge, MA: MIT Press.

Weiner, B. (1986). *An attributional theory of motivation and emotions.* New York: Springer-Verlag.

Wertsch, J. V. (1998). *Mind as action.* New York: Oxford University Press.

Westby, C. (1994). The effects of culture on genre, structure, and style of oral and written texts. In G. P. Wallach & K. G. Butler (Eds.), *Language learning disabilities in school-age children and adolescents: Some principles and applications* (pp. 180–218). New York: Macmillan.

Whitaker, D., Berninger, V. W., Johnston, J., & Swanson, L. H. (1994). Intraindividual differences in levels of language in the intermediate grades: Implications for the translating process. *Learning and Individual Differences, 6,* 107–130.

Wiig, E., & Semel, E. M. (1975). Productive language abilities in learning disabled adolescents. *Journal of Learning Disabilities, 6,* 457–586.

Windsor, J. (1999). Effects of semantic inconsistency on sentence grammaticality judgements for children with and without language-learning disabilities. *Language Testing, 16*(3), 293–313.

Windsor, J., Scott, C. M., & Street, C. K. (2000). Verb and noun morphology in the spoken and written language of children with language learning disabilities. *Journal of Speech, Language, and Hearing Research, 43*(6), 1322–1336.

Wong, B. Y. L., Wong, R., & Blenkinsop, J. (1989). Cognitive and metacognitive aspects f learning disabled adolescents' composing problems. *Learning Disabilities Quarterly, 12,* 300–322.

Zhang, Y., Brooks, D., Frields, T., & Redelfs, M. (1995). Quality of writing by elementary students with learning disabilities. *Journal of Research on Computing in Education, 27*(4), 483–499.

Zimmerman, B. J. (1989). A social cognitive view of self-regulated academic learning. *Journal of Educational Psychology, 81,* 329–339.

Zimmerman, B. J. (2002). Becoming a self-regulated learner: An overview. *Theory Into Practice, 41*(2), 64–70.

Zimmerman, B. J., & Kintsantas, A. (1999). Acquiring writing revision skill: Shifting from process to outcome self-regulatory goals. *Journal of Educational Psychology, 91*(2), 241–250.

Zimmerman, B. J., & Risemberg, R. (1997). Becoming a self-regulated writer: A social cognitive perspective. *Contemporary Educational Psychology, 22,* 73–101.

Zipprich, M. (1995). Teaching web making as a guided planning tool to improve student narrative writing. *Remedial and Special Education, 16*(1), 3–17.

27

A Classroom-Based Writing Assessment Framework

ROBERT C. CALFEE
KATHLEEN M. WILSON

As children move through the grades, a critical time in their written language development spans third through ninth grades, as they move from informal journaling to more serious writing (e.g., book reports, essays, and synthetic reports) (Nelson & Calfee, 1998). It is also the time when large-scale writing assessments begin to appear in classrooms (Calfee, 2002). Simmons and Carroll (2003), speaking specifically of the adolescent years, bemoan the situation: "The problem of valid, communicable, consistent, and, above all, positive approaches to the judgment of student writing is one that has bedeviled honest, thoughtful teachers since the Lyceum" (p. 381). National assessments point to writing as a problematic area for many students (Persky, Daane, & Jin, 2003). The 2002 National Assessment of Educational Progress (NAEP) results show slight improvements over the 1998 scores in grades 4 and 8, along with slight declines in grade 12. In general, however, the performance levels are rather low. For instance, in 2002 at grades 4 and 8, one in seven students scored Below Basic, whereas one in four students in grade 12 fell into this bottom category. Only 28% of fourth graders

and 31% of eighth graders performed at or above the Proficient level, which dropped to 24% at grade 12. As students move through the grades, they encounter an increased demand for writing not only in English classes but also across the curriculum in science and social studies. Facility in writing is important in its own right, but it is equally critical as a means for students to demonstrate their understanding in various academic areas.

Although most students find it a challenge to produce formal text, some experience greater difficulty than others. Students with academic problems are typically characterized as having "reading disabilities," but Lerner's perspective may be more appropriate. She concluded that "poor facility in expressing thoughts through written language is probably the most prevalent disability of the communication skills" (Lerner, 1976, p. 20; also see Hooper, Swartz, Wakely, de Kruif, & Montgomery, 2002). In fact, literacy-related problems encompass the entire domain of formal linguistic language competence—speaking, listening, reading, *and* writing. Students with written composition problems perform poorly on psycholinguistic assessments ranging from phonology through metalinguistics, semantics, discourse, and both oral- and written-language perception and production (Berninger, 2000; Vellutino, 1979).

What are the reasons for these problems with formal language, and what are effective ways to assess students' skill and knowledge in order to remedy any difficulties? This chapter focuses on one facet of these questions—writing assessment in the middle years from third through ninth grade. The proposal is to embed assessment of student writing within a coherent framework that encompasses both oral-language and text comprehension, and to link curriculum, instruction, and assessment within this framework.

Writing instruction in today's classrooms often takes shape as stand-alone assignments. Students compose a work without clear purpose or support. The paper is then returned with a grade and red marks indicating mechanical errors. "Instruction" is a matter of assignments. A principal goal in this chapter is to present a different exemplar for writing assessment. The framework relies on scaffolded instruction incorporating explicit rhetorical structures connected to carefully designed writing prompts, in which substantive content is the basis for preparing students to read and write complex texts in a strategic and self-regulated manner across a range of domains and tasks. The model provides a seamless transition between instruction and assessment. The purpose is not "writing to write" in response to an on-demand prompt, but authentic writing to demonstrate academic competence, with resources and feedback supporting the best product a student can write. In this framework, formative assessment guides students along the way, leading toward summative assessment that evaluates students' final accomplishments, often in the form of externally mandated district or state tests. The strategy addresses the broad range of endemic problems described by Berninger (1996): limited instruction, weak oral-language skills, cognitive deficits, limited cultural experiences, and low motivation. The situation is exacerbated by significant shifts in the importance of writing in the academic curriculum in the midelementary grades. Of the items on the previous list, instruction offers the most promising locus for designing assessment that in turn serves as the fundamental guide to instruction.

An essential feature of the model is the "read–write connection" (Flower et al., 1990; Nelson & Calfee, 1998; Nystrand, 1986; Sperling, 1996; Sperling & Freedman, 2001; Tierney & Shanahan, 1996), which blends text-based strategies and structures for both reading and writing instruction and assessment. Including the study of a background "source" passage as a key element in a writing assignment makes sense for several reasons. First, it provides students with a common base of content knowledge, with words and ideas as substantive starting points for composing; rarely do "real" authors start out "cold turkey." Second, explicit engagement in a background passage heightens students' awareness of rhetorical structures (Cope & Kalantzis, 1993; Spivey & King, 1989) that offer the foundation for basic tasks such as summarization and paraphrasing, as well as more complex operations such as expansion and transformation of a concept. When reading and writing are taught in tandem, students benefit from clearer thinking and more effective communication skills. The process begins by constructing networked images that can be molded and refined; first comes substance, followed by style, structure, and conventions.

More than exposure to resources and guidance about process is needed in order for novices to develop competence in writing, however. They need to be actively engaged in strategic thinking about text (Wong, 1994). Metacognition emerges from explicit teacher modeling with think-alouds, demonstrating how to identify and utilize specific rhetorical structures (Hayes, 1996). These strategies promote transfer by encouraging students to make their thinking public in low-risk contexts (Calfee, 1998). As students' skills in utilizing a variety of text structures and strategies increases, their motivation for writing is also enhanced. Research shows that the reciprocality between skill and will is a critical combination for learning (Paris & Cross, 1983). Assessments that do not deal with motivation are especially problematic for students who experience difficulty with academic writing. The approach to writing assessment in this chapter responds to the challenges of valid evaluation of students with special needs. The perspective is different from the approaches found in various handbooks, where the emphasis is typically on portfolios, rating scales, and so on (e.g., Dyson & Freedman, 2003; Goodman, 2003). Nor does it rely primarily on accommodations, such as additional time, task clarification, and so on (Thurlow, Elliott, & Ysseldyke, 2002). The underlying rationale for the argument in this chapter is that assessment of student compositions is most valid when resources, scaffolding, and explicit feedback are provided, so that all students fully understand the task and the criteria. This approach to classroom assessment seems appropriate for all students but is essential for students with special needs in the middle grades. It supports both growth in academic competence required in the later years of schooling, as well as competence in handling large-scale on-demand testing.

The remainder of the chapter lays out a road map for writing assessment that connects reading and writing, and blends assessment with instruction. The chapter is organized in four sections. In the first section, we describe the variety of commercially produced, standardized writing assessments that are presently available, providing a sketch of current practice. In the second, we present the CORE model as a conceptual framework for the read–write connection, a model that meshes constructivist concepts with classroom instruction and assessment. In the third, we describe CLAS-Plus, a practical embodiment of the preceding ideas, springing from a large-scale assessment introduced in California a decade ago. In the final section, we discuss issues related to the technical integrity of formative, classroom-based assessments.

STANDARDIZED WRITING ASSESSMENTS

Commercially produced, standardized instruments provide one measurement option for teachers and language specialists (Table 27.1). The offerings appear rather limited in number and diagnostic breadth. The Woodcock–Johnson III Test of Achievement (Woodcock, McGrew, & Mather, 2001), for instance, contains subtests of basic writing skills, with checklists to score written sentences for skills such as punctuation, spelling, vocabulary, and ideas. In most instruments that require writing of extended text, students compose in the familiar narrative style. Although this is appropriate in the primary grades, in the later grades, students are expected to create expositions (e.g., book reports, inquiry reports in social studies, laboratory reports in science, and essay answers on tests). Expository writing requires students to employ skills that can be particularly challenging for students with language disorders. For example, they need to demonstrate familiarity with complex rhetorical structures, facility with general and technical vocabulary that they can use with precision around specific topics, a solid working knowledge of how to apply grammatical rules and writing conventions in simple and complex sentences, and correct spelling of morphologically complex words. Commercial tests seldom cover these areas in any depth, nor with resources adequate to scaffold writing.

THE READING–WRITING CONNECTION

The formulation of the read–write connection (RWC) in this section springs from the CORE model developed by Calfee (Calfee & Patrick, 1995; Miller & Calfee, 2004): Connect with background experience and purpose; Organize using graphic and rhetorical structures; Reflect to capture ideas essential for transfer (Vygotsky, 1978); and Extend to transfer learning to novel situations. Figure 27.1 displays the CORE model as applied to writing assessment. The elements form a circle without arrows, indicating the dynamic interplay of the components. Although there is a natural flow through the four components, the design does not imply a strict sequence; however, for convenience of presentation, the compo-

TABLE 27.1. **Standardized Writing Assessments**

Title	Authors Publisher (publication date)	Age/grade level	Administration	Format
Diagnostic Achievement Test for Adolescents (DATA), 2nd Ed.	Newcomer & Bryant PRO-ED (1993)	Gr. 7–12	Individual	Three picture prompts to write narrative text.
Test of Early Written Language (TEWL-2), 2nd Ed.	Hresko, Herron, & Peak PRO-ED (1996)	Ages 3 years, 0 months– 10 years, 11 months	Individual	Picture prompt to write narrative text.
Test of Written Expression (TOWE)	McGhee, Bryant, Larsen, & Rivera PRO-ED (1995)	Ages 6 years, 6 months– 14 years, 11 months	Individual or group	Two subtests: 1. 76-item series on writing skills 2. Student hears or reads a narrative that creates a situation and is asked to complete it.
Test of Written Language (TOWL-3) 3rd Ed.	Hammill & Larsen PRO-ED (1988)	Ages 7 years, 6 months– 17 years, 11 months	Individual or group	Essay writing (narrative) from picture prompt. Skills subtest also available.
Test of Written Spelling (TWS-4), 4th ed.	Larsen, Hammill, & Moats (1999)	Grades 1–12	Individual or group	Words are given orally with illustrative sentences.
Woodcock–Johnson III Test of Achievement (WJ-III)	Woodcock, McGrew, & Mather, Riverside (2001)	Grades 1–12	Individual	Subtests: 1. Spelling, orally presented works 2. Writing Fluency, writing single sentences quickly 3. Writing Samples, handwriting and writing from a prompt 4. Editing, spelling, punctuation, and capitalization
Writing Process Test	Warden & Hutchinson PRO-ED (1991–1992)	Ages 8–19	Individual or group	Assesses process and product. Student asked to plan, write, and revise original composition (optional).
Written Language Assessment	Grill & Kirwin Academic Therapy Publications (1989)	Ages 8–18	Individual or group	Two picture prompts available, or one prompt without picture. Writing samples: expressive, instructive, and creative writing.

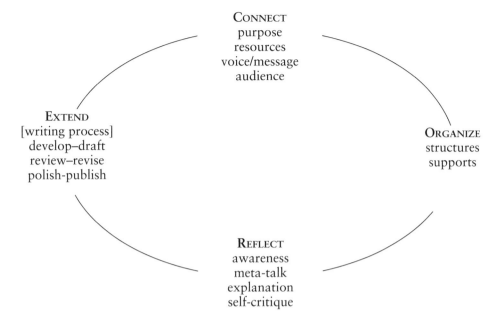

FIGURE 27.1. The CORE model for the read–write connection.

nents are presented as lesson segments. The following material elaborates the four concepts, which are then applied to formative writing assessment.

The *Connect* element sets the stage for thinking about the particulars of a task and gives the teacher an opportunity to gauge students' prior knowledge of the topic. This part of the process also serves to establish an understanding of the purposes and goals of the writing task. What will students accomplish through their work? What are the audiences for the final product? The aim is to move from the "assignment" mode familiar to most of us (including teachers) toward a communicative sense of presentation, toward creation of a product that influences how others think or act, that entertains or alarms, that moves beyond grades and red marks. Another important aspect of this element is establishing links to resources needed for the task, including not only collective experience but also relevant text sources, a broad category in today's Internet world. *Connecting* begins the writing project but then threads throughout the entire process, especially for the novice.

During the *Organize* segment, the aim is to guide students in exploring what they

know (i.e., their prior knowledge and experience) and what they need to find out. Because the CORE model is grounded in the concept of social cognition, collaborative learning activities are incorporated in the exploration, which proceeds most effectively by having students interact in small- or whole-group configurations while constructing graphic structures (e.g., a matrix or weave, a T chart, or web) that publicly organize information and support thinking. A trip to the library or a web-based search may assist in locating additional information and completing the organizer. The teacher's role is supportively directive, pointing toward resources and structuring the information. By emphasizing strategies for choosing an appropriate visual structure and discussing reasons for making particular choices, the teacher guides students to become self-regulated writers, capable of implementing similar strategies and graphic structures. During the assessment, the teacher has the opportunity to observe how students use the structures and strategies for the task at hand.

Throughout the project, the teacher initiates activities and discourse that promote explicit *Reflection* around both process and product. Students practice meta-talk—talking about thinking during the construction of the project, in which they justify and explain their thinking. The teacher's role is to orchestrate supportive critique of self and others.

In the fourth element of the model, students *Extend* learning as they synthesize the various activities to move toward completion of the final product. This element incorporates the key facets of the writing process (Hayes, 2000; Hayes & Flower, 1980). Students develop initial drafts in response to the writing task. They review their texts in response to self-criticism, along with peer comments and suggestions (DiPardo & Freedman, 1988). They and their peers participate in applying the assessment criteria. Self-evaluation along the way leads students to view their writing from the reader's perspective. Although assessment is the nominal goal of the project, students may polish their drafts for publication (e.g., a school newspaper, an argument for a change in locker policy, a class anthology of poems). A moment's thought reveals the essential dynamism of the model. The initial connection must contain an image of the final product; as students work toward the final polishing, a review of the original goals—which are likely to have altered along the way—becomes a reflective exercise. These reflections, when shared publicly, give the teacher an additional opportunity to assess the growth in students' thinking about the writing process as it moves from a first draft to one that is rich and complex.

This perspective on assessment may appear radical at first glance, because it stretches the bounds of authenticity (Wiggins, 1993). Yet one can certainly find examples that resonate with the basic concepts, generally when the instructional investment is substantial and the aim is to optimize student potential. Advanced placement and dissertation defenses come to mind as illustrative of the concept. Cold-turkey, on-demand writing assessment is more properly placed at the end of a learning process that begins with substantial scaffolding, including engagement in a rich array of resources and models, within a classroom environment that promotes cooperative activities and relies on instructional processes that support engagement in meaningful tasks (Sperling & Freedman, 2001).

The CORE model is designed to scaffold *all students* in their production of text. This model is especially supportive for students with language and literacy problems, because it gives them experience with an integrated activity. This aspect is important because so much instructional practice for today's students consists of remedial work focused on piecemeal low-level writing skills. When confronted with a large-scale assignment, students become stymied and do not know where to begin. For struggling writers, the task becomes a simplified question-and-answer activity; they write the first thing that comes to mind (Graham & Harris, 1994). Students with language and literacy challenges typically compose short texts with familiar words and little sense of audience, rhetorical demands, or text organization (Graham, 1990; Graham & Harris, 1994; Scardamalia & Bereiter, 1986). Teachers who follow the remedial model (and students subjected to it) are unlikely to experience writing as development from novice to expert status.

The model described here is based on a paradigm in which student writers routinely deliberate about purpose, audience, organization, and rhetorical stance. By connecting reading and writing, the teacher supports students in the creation of fully developed texts by helping them draw on and extend their background knowledge and generate topic interest. It is through scaffolded practice with this strategy that students, particularly struggling writers, make progress on the continuum from novice to expert writer, including the task of handling high-stakes, large-scale assessments.

In what ways should instruction and assessment differ for students with language and literacy problems? All students find cognitively complex tasks more interesting and challenging than simplistic ones. Meece and Miller (1999) studied the reading and writing task preferences of third graders of low, average, and high achievement. They found that students preferred high-challenge tasks—collaborating with peers in reading and writing multiple paragraphs over several days—to low-challenge tasks performed individually—underlining answers or writing single words or phrases. This finding held for students from *all* reading–writing achievement levels in classrooms that routinely featured high-challenge tasks, as well as classrooms that seldom employed complex tasks. In addition, when students perceive themselves as optimally challenged (i.e., they think they can manage the task, if they put out their best effort) and self-efficacious for a particular task, they are more likely to develop situational or topic interest (Hidi & Krapp, 1992; Schiefele, 1999) and to adopt volitional strategies that keep them on task (Corno, 1993). The assessment framework described in the next section incorporates this combination of principles.

CLAS-PLUS: AN RWC CLASSROOM-BASED ASSESSMENT MODEL

This section presents a concrete "activity structure" offering a practical foundation for classroom writing assessment, an activity that has its roots in a rather remarkable experiment in large-scale assessment. California is earthquake territory in more than one way. The state's assessment programs have gone through enormous changes during the past two decades, from the respected California Assessment Program (CAP) of the 1980s to the current reliance on norm-referenced tests, a collage of standards-based multiple-choice items, and a sprinkling of on-demand writing tasks. Midway through these events, the California Learning Assessment System (CLAS) appeared briefly in the mid-1990s as a large-scale strategy quite different from previous practices (Underwood, 1999). Although CLAS was short-lived, its positive features engaged classroom teachers throughout the state, who saw in the activity a foundation for linking curriculum, instruction, and assessment.

The Process

CLAS consisted of three basic elements: (1) Students read and responded to a text; (2) they discussed their reactions to the text and writing plans in small groups; and (3) they wrote individual essays. The tasks were standardized. The teacher passed out materials and managed the process. Students were told that they were "taking a test," which defined purpose and audience.

CLAS-Plus augments the original CLAS model in several ways in order to enhance the validity of the assessment. The teacher, rather than acting as a "test-giver," becomes the orchestrator of a scaffolded, dynamic assessment that supports the social construction of knowledge by students as they participate in prereading and -writing activities. The teacher introduces the task to the entire class, then structures small-group discussions with prompts and visual organizers. Students then study short, interesting, well-structured texts studded with brief "thinking" questions in the text margins. The "composing" then moves to small-group activities and, finally, to individual productions—the "real" assessments.

CLAS-Plus adds several features to the original design, employing CORE to guide students from an initial fully scaffolded reading–writing assessment toward assignments in which they are increasingly self-reliant (Figure 27.2). The basic design applies to a wide range of subject matter and classroom settings but is particularly appropriate for expository writing, including research papers in science and social studies classes.

The enhancements serve to guide and model the reading–writing process for the novice. Thus, rather than assuming that students can activate prior experience on their own, the teacher begins with a whole-class webbing activity, which remains on the wall throughout the process. Purpose and audience are made explicit in a variety of ways. CLAS texts were chosen for interest, but within the constraints of large-scale standardization; CLAS-Plus texts are not constrained, and can be selected to mesh with local events and conditions. To encourage interactive reading, CLAS provided a blank margin for comments, a reasonable idea. But for most students, the idea of writing while reading is unfortunately rather alien. In CLAS-Plus, marginal miniprompts elicit on-the-fly reactions. Postreading responses are guided by graphic organizers, along with in-

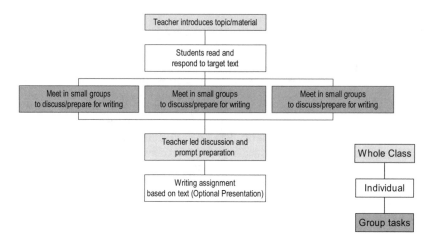

FIGURE 27.2. The CLAS-Plus model of assessment.

struction in summarization and analysis. The teacher orchestrates small-group discussions through a variety of cooperative-learning techniques. Finally, the preparation of the final essay is shaped by the elements of process writing, including the use of graphic organizers and vocabulary strategies. The technique, like other dynamic assessment methods, blurs the boundaries between assessment and instruction (for comprehensive reviews of dynamic assessment, see Grigorenko & Sternberg, 1998; Lidz & Elliott, 2000). The approach may seem to offer students "too much help," but as a formative strategy designed for classroom purposes, the advantages can be substantial; the teacher is able to discover the upper limits of individual performance, along with the conditions under which individual students can and cannot succeed.

The Scoring Rubrics

The process just described generates a product. Assessment also entails judgments about the quality of the result for feedback, for grading, and for program evaluation. In writing assessments, these judgments are typically defined by rubrics, the analytical dimensions that delineate both growth and accomplishment, how much a student is learning, and the degree to which the student is meeting a standard (Calfee, 1997). Holistic rubrics, the equivalent of a grade,

are frequently used in large-scale assessment for efficiency; they often serve classroom assessment for the same reasons. Middle school teachers handling five to seven classes of 30–40 students cannot be expected to read and grade individual papers on a regular basis. The typical practice, understandably, is to skim the draft, scribble a few red marks, and record a grade (Sperling, 1998). This technique offers limited feedback for students and can discourage those in need of supportive guidance. The CLAS-Plus system employs analytical dimensions that are understandable to students as well as to teachers, and that can be explicitly incorporated in the writing process.

Evaluation by self and peers is the ultimate solution to workload issues. Learning to evaluate one's own work is a desirable outcome of effective schooling for reasons both cognitive and motivational. Many students experiencing difficulty with reading–writing tasks have not learned what matters; they know neither the rules of the game nor the tricks of the trade. Small-group interactions provide the context in CLAS-Plus assessments for peer evaluations that can reveal both rules and tricks. Orchestrating these activities requires adaptive teaching skills, but the payoff can be long-lasting. In this scenario, classroom assessment becomes the occasion to inform the teacher and to enlighten the student. Students (and teachers) certainly know about grades but have less experience with rubrics. An important feature of CLAS-Plus is to make the rubric concept and procedures available to all the participants.

In large-scale assessment, schools, districts, and states often rely on the six-trait rubric as an alternative to holistic scoring: Ideas, Organization, Voice, Word Choice, Sentence Fluency, and Conventions (Spandel, 2001). CLAS-Plus relies on four elements that parallel the six-trait system, with modifications designed to make the dimensions more transparent: Length, Coherence, Vocabulary, and Grammar/mechanics/ spelling (see Table 27.2). Length may seem somewhat quaint, but students frequently often ask, "How long?", and length is a consistent correlate of holistic ratings. Coherence and Vocabulary correspond to the Ideas–Organization and Word Choice entries, respectively. *Voice* has an intuitive appeal, but can be difficult to explain to students. Conventions encompass the surface features that are essential to an effective final product.

Each scale is described as concretely as

TABLE 27.2. Rubric Dimensions for CLAS-Plus Design

Score	Length	Coherence	Vocabulary	Grammar/mechanics/ spelling
6	3+ pages	Clearly elaborated main topic. Support with appropriate details, descriptions, and examples. Clear shifts in topic and smooth transitions.	Substantial use of complex Latin words. Lexical variety and precision in dealing with topic.	Few errors in grammar, punctuation, or spelling. Variety in sentence structures. Correct spelling of complex words.
5	1–2 pages	Main topic is clearly stated, unwavering. Some support for selected points. Linkages are provided but transitions are not always clear.	Some evidence of complex but familiar Latin words. Limited variety and reliance on relatively common words (national).	Some variation in sentence structure, including phrases and clauses. Command of long–short vowels, but other vowel errors (e.g., vowel digraphs).
4	3/4 page	Topic is clear with digressions. Information and examples are plentiful but list-like.	Substantial number of familiar polysyllabic words (*interesting, understand*). Noticeable precision (*friendly* for *nice*).	Sentence completeness and variety, with few run-ons and fragments. Few errors in punctuation. Short vowels accurate, with emergence of long–short contrast.
3	4 sentences —½ page	Addresses the topic, but with little description, elaboration, or support.	1- to 2-syllable words, but mostly familiar and little variety or precision.	Simple repetitive sentences, fragments, and run-ons. Consonants generally correct, with vowel omissions and substitutions, but readable.
2	2–3 sentences	States the topic minimally, and wanders off topic. Little support.	Frequent one-syllable and basic sight words.	Many fragments–run-ons. Consonants generally correct, but omission of most vowels.
1	1 sentence or less	Unrelated or unintelligible.	Most words difficult to interpret.	Generally unintelligible.

possible in the CLAS-Plus model. *Vocabulary* and *Spelling,* for instance, make explicit reference to identifiable word patterns. Students tend to adopt a conservative strategy when writing a lengthy report, foregoing complex words because of concerns about misspelling, even when the words are available in the target text or on a wall chart. The CLAS-Plus rubrics encourage and reward risky explorations in the vocabulary arena.

CLAS-Plus in Action

Day 1

The following description, which emphasizes the CORE model as a guiding framework, portrays the activities of a CLAS-Plus assessment in a middle school classroom from a large, urban school district serving mainly middle- and low-SES families in Southern California. The example takes place in a grade 8 English class over 2 days. It is January, and during the fall, the class had studied societal influences on individual behavior as a theme uniting the social studies and English curricula. A secondary aim of the assessment project is to capture students' abilities to synthesize and apply previous learning. The primary writing assessment goal is to determine students' strengths and weaknesses in various composition domains, in order to set the stage for instruction during the remainder of the school year, and to prepare the students for upcoming state tests, which include a stand-alone "argue–persuade" writing assignment.

Many in the class are low achievers with little writing experience, so the exercise incorporates substantial teacher guidance. As the task becomes more routine later in the year, students can assume greater independence, with the teacher alert to the need to provide scaffolding to handle variations in task difficulty and student needs. As is often the case, the elementary grades provided these students with little experience in structured expository writing, but they will soon enter high school, where the expectations call for both competence and independence.

A typical CLAS-Plus assessment is administered during two consecutive, 50-minute class periods. The first day's activities scaffold the students' thinking in preparation for writing by (1) *connecting* prior knowledge and experience to the topic, while adding to their knowledge base through text-related *reading and note-taking*; (2) *organizing* the information in response to the writing prompt; and (3) *reflecting* on both the products of their preparatory work and the processes they are employing along the way. When they encounter externally mandated writing tests, students have limited time and resources, but they will need to initiate the same prewriting activities to complete a composition of high quality.

PREREADING: CONNECTIONS
AND ORGANIZATION

The teacher begins with a prereading activity designed to stimulate interest and engagement, while assisting students to make *connections* with prior knowledge and experience. In this example, adapted from an actual assessment event, the teacher, Ms. Hansen, first sets the purpose of the activity: "Today and tomorrow you'll be doing a reading–writing assignment like the ones we did before vacation. Remember we were talking about how the way individuals behave affects the whole society." She then poses the question that will be the basis for the writing prompt: "Our world is filled with violence. Every night on the news we witness evidence of this fact. What causes violence? Take a few minutes to jot down ideas that come to mind." Students had learned during the fall to jot down words or phrases, and that spelling did not matter when they were brainstorming. By allowing students time to record their ideas in "word-splash" fashion, the teacher begins with a strategy that activates working memory. After a few moments for these initial notes, the students pair up to discuss the lists. They are encouraged to add items to their notes from those shared by their partners, along with new ideas from the discussion. During this initial brainstorming, students are generating rich collections of words and ideas, along with explanations for their choices.

Following the pair-share activity, Ms. Hansen asks the student teams to present their ideas to the class, while she records the main points on a large piece of paper. At this point, the brainstormed list typically lacks any obvious organization. She asks students to examine the information for patterns and leads the class through the construction of a topical web on chart paper (a transparency or the chalkboard does as well for some purposes, but the chart paper can remain in sight on the wall).

The students begin by offering subheadings or categories for the web. As they propose categories, Ms. Hansen asks them to *reflect,* to tell why they have suggested a subheading, making public their thinking. Such modeling benefits struggling writers as they learn about organizational strategies and engage in metacognitive thinking. Once several categories have been put in place, the process moves along as the teacher assigns items from the brainstorm that relate to the subheadings, a step that students must also justify along the way. This part of the task can be done by student pairs or in small groups. In the latter instance, the teacher's role transitions from directing the whole-class exchanges to serving as small-group facilitator, with increased control passing to students, allowing greater opportunities for the teacher to observe.

As students' interests and prior knowledge begin to take shape, Ms. Hansen reminds the class of the purposes of the activities and refines the assignment:

"Today and tomorrow you will be talking and reading about what some people believe causes violence. You will share your thoughts and learn ideas from others. Tomorrow you will write an opinion essay—like a newspaper editorial—where you say what you think causes violence. You will present the arguments that support your opinion and debate arguments against your opinion. At the end of the year, you can look back at this essay to see how you've developed as a writer."

READING: THE READ–WRITE CONNECTION

In the next step, students read the text chosen to support and stimulate their thinking on the topic, in this instance, an expository article from *Time* magazine (Corliss, 1999), chosen by Ms. Hansen for contemporaneous interest value and writing quality. After distributing the text, Ms. Hansen points out the marginal questions designed to guide and stimulate students' thinking as they read through the text. Ms. Hansen also directs them to underline or circle key words and phrases. Depending on the skill level of her students, she may suggest or model specific strategies: how to identify a key idea, or to study the lead sentence in each paragraph. Ms. Hansen pairs students with decoding problems with more able readers, instructing them to take turns reading the passage quietly to each other and then discuss the meaning. After completing the text, students individually summarize the main points, either by note taking or a more formal summary. In this instance, the students had limited experience with the CLAS-Plus protocol, and the responses were informal rather than scripted.

POSTREADING: NARROWING THE RWC FOCUS

At this point Ms. Hansen returns to the web to incorporate and *organize* the newly acquired information. She directs the class in expanding the web based on what they have learned from the article.

The next activity formally introduces students to the writing prompt, in order to shape their thoughts about how to respond to it. Studying the prompt is especially critical for struggling writers, who are often unclear about the task demands. Here is the prompt:

"Many people believe that violence in the movies and on television triggers violent behavior in young people. Do you believe this? Or, do you believe that other factors are involved? Is violence learned? Or, are people naturally violent."

Through leading questions, Ms. Hansen helps the students approach the prompt as a reading comprehension task. She focuses attention on key words and phrases (e.g., "factors"), asking students to rephrase in their own words.

To provide an explicit organization for responding to this prompt, Ms. Hansen sketches the matrix in Table 27.3. She first lays out an empty "weave" or matrix, writing the topic in the upper left corner. She then turns to the students to identify factors in the passage that the author discusses as the causes of violence. The first response is "movies and television," which she records in the first row.

She then asks the students to think about building an argument around this entry: What might they say to convince the audience about the claim? These responses go into the second column. Several students offer opposing views, which go under the third heading. Ms. Hansen records the emerging arguments and counterarguments, encouraging students to revisit the text, while also encouraging spontaneous comments based on individual views and experiences. The matrix takes shape as a collective construction. Additions to the graphic continue throughout the process, but once a substantial amount of information has been gathered, Ms. Hansen leads the discussion toward *reflection*. She raises questions about the processes they employed, as well as the products (e.g., the graphic organizers) they are constructing, in order to evoke explicit justification for the prewriting activities. Rendering "thinking about process" public promotes students' independent use of these kinds of prewriting activities in the future. It also gives Ms. Hansen a means to determine where individual students fall on the continuum of independent and self-regulated writing. She models by summarizing the information and setting the stage for the upcoming writing activity:

"Tomorrow each of you will use this information to write a persuasive essay about the effect of television and movies on violence. This spring you have to take the state test, which has a persuasive essay; tomorrow's work is the first step in getting ready for the state test."

Day 2: Pulling the Pieces Together

The second day, the *Extend* phase, begins with a brief review of the previous day's work. Ms. Hansen also reminds the students of the essay format: a series of related paragraphs that include an introduction, body, and conclusion. She encourages them to look over their prewriting notes, to jot reminders for themselves before beginning the actual essay, and to proofread their essays before submitting them for the evaluation. She also reminds students about the writing rubrics (Table 27.2), which have been posted since the beginning of the school year and emphasized when evaluating previous writing assignments. She has engaged in think-alouds since the beginning of the school year to illustrate her reasoning processes for samples of written compositions. The students have practiced self-assessments and used the rubrics for peer assessments. Through these activities, they have built an understanding of the surface indicators—Length and Grammar/mechanics/spelling—and are beginning to grasp the less transparent, deeper components of Coherence and Vocabulary.

The students then begin their individual essays, which may seem to be the start of the "real" assessment. In fact, students' activities and discussion during the preceding activities provide the basis for significant judgments about their capacities, understanding, and motivation, including the metacognitive elements of the process. Although one might develop a checklist to document these observations, qualitative

TABLE 27.3. Matrix Developed to Support Essays on Causes of Violence

Causes of violence	Supporting statements	Arguments against
Movies, television, and websites	Glamorizing violent actions; steady diet of violence	Movies don't actually kill people
Dysfunctional families	Morals not emphasized; violence in the home	

notes are equally appropriate in most instances. During the composition, students have access to the individual notes from the previous day, as well as the collective resources posted on the walls. But as preparation for large-scale tests, Ms. Hansen instructs the students to work on their own in this stage of the process. She helps with time management along the way, with reminders to save several minutes for proofreading at the end.

Because this assessment serves for significant instructional decisions for the class and individuals, Ms. Hansen scores the essays later in the day, using the rubrics in Table 27.2. Length is concrete and relatively straightforward. Coherence might seem more difficult, but the matrix provides the basis for fairly "quick reads." Ms. Hansen "ticks" significant vocabulary along the way, with special attention to complex words (many of which are available on the walls) and unusual usages. She also marks mistakes in grammar and spelling, although these are not her main priorities in this particular assessment.

Later in the week, Ms. Hansen discusses the results with the class, using samples from individual compositions to illustrate particular strengths and areas for improvement, emphasizing general trends rather than focusing on individuals. The aim is to promote further discussion about both process and product; the "report back" is a further extension of the assessment activity. She will discuss individual results with specific students later as time allows.

TECHNICAL INTEGRITY

CLAS-Plus, although it has origins in large-scale summative testing, is intended to serve as a model for classroom-based formative assessment. The technical characteristics of external tests build on a half-century tradition of methodologies; the situation for classroom assessments is much less rigorous (Farnan & Dahl, 2003; Ruth & Murphy, 1988; Stiggins, 2000). To be sure, technical standards have been recently proposed for classroom assessments (Joint Committee on Standards for Educational Evaluation,

2002), but these have yet to see significant implementation. In addition, teachers generally receive little preparation in test design and interpretation; therefore, they rely on tradition more than on technology. The CLAS-Plus model provides a foundation for teachers to develop reading–writing assessments incorporating significant technical features that support trustworthiness. This focus differs from the typical psychometric approach, which starts with psychometric reliability. Rather, this chapter emphasizes the creation of tests that are valid and allow immediate application.

Several technical considerations warrant attention during the construction and implementation of writing assessments. Of paramount importance are the *selection of the topic and target text,* and the relation of these choices to the ultimate writing task. These decisions are particularly critical in guiding novices. For adolescents, interest and personal involvement establish engagement in the project. Reading and writing are hard work; for those students who have the most to learn, the work must appear doable and worthwhile. In adolescence, youngsters' attention centers around themselves and their peers; they possess incredible energy, and the key is to harness and direct that drive in the service of academic outcomes (Deci & Ryan, 1985; Deci, Vallerand, Pelletier, & Ryan, 1991). Once skills are developed and routines established, the stage is set for more esoteric and demanding topics and texts. Text design is also a key consideration, including coherent structure and rhetorical clarity. Sources that serve well are newspapers and magazines—not just the substitutes published for children, but the real things. Library books and website locations are also good sources.

A second element of technical significance is the *creation of effective prompts.* Students can be easily misled by abbreviated instructions that seem obvious to adults. Research on this topic is sparse, and this chapter relies on two leads: (1) examining student work products, and (2) asking youngsters to think aloud about prompts. To illustrate how a prompt can distract, consider that text-based writing prompts often ask writers to draw on their experience as well as the target text: "Give your opinion about the effect of television violence, using what you have just read and movies that you have seen recently." Students tend to rely on the richest and most accessible information—their personal experiences. The result is that they may ignore the text as a resource, leading judges to rate the essay as "unacceptable," no matter how coherent, absorbing, and well crafted.

Several issues bear on *reliability and validity* in classroom-based assessments. Technical reliability is of paramount importance in large-scale assessments, with validity usually taking second place. This relation needs to be reversed in classroom practice. "Reliability" refers to the consistency of the measures available from a test. If the purpose of Ms. Hansen's exercise were to give students a "writing grade," then, ideally, students should line up about the same on all the rubrics, which would allow her to average the rubric scores. An alternative approach would be to administer two or three assessments early in the year and average these scores for the grade. Ms. Hansen's goal was quite different—to identify areas of strength and weakness in the various domains identified by the rubrics for the class as a whole and for individual students. Here, the validity of the indicators is critically important. Do the indicators mean what they are supposed to mean? Suppose, for example, that most students write only a few lines in response to the exercise. If the prompt had been administered as a stand-alone writing assignment, one might imagine several reasons for the performance: (1) a lack of ideas, (2) a lack of interest; or (3) a lack of understanding. The scaffolding provided in the CLAS-Plus model tends to eliminate these and other explanations that are irrelevant to the purpose of the assessment and provide little in the way of instructional guidance. These abbreviated responses do not call for "failing" the class, but for discussing the matter to understand the origins of the students' responses.

Teachers generally focus on assessing what they think needs to be learned. CLAS-Plus strategies address this issue in two ways. First, the overall design, including the sequence of tasks and the scoring rubrics, emphasizes validity—the creation of an essay built around a basic structure and incorporating elements from target sources. The reliance on externalization of the process (marginal jottings, small-group discourse and notes, explicit prewriting) provides numerous opportunities for the teacher to observe and direct students' thinking along the way. Of course, the design works only when the teacher spends time observing and directing. Second, the repetition of procedures within and between CLAS-Plus tasks provides the basis for judging "consistency," another name for reliability, but using techniques quite different from those found in most psychometric textbooks. Although one can estimate reliability from CLAS-Plus data using conventional procedures, more important is the teacher's attention to departures from expected patterns—the student who experiences a sudden slump, a topic that leaves the boys yawning, or a prompt that misdirects the entire class. In these instances, the lack of consistency does not mean that the teacher should discard the project; rather, he or she should investigate the sources of variability to generate leads for improving future actions.

A final comment on technical integrity addresses the significant challenge in this age of accountability of *linking externally mandated and classroom-based assessments* of student achievements (Shepard, 2001), of making the connection between formative and summative assessment. In many curriculum areas, this connection requires a serious stretch, mostly because of the difficulty of tapping student knowledge and skill by means of multiple-choice tests. The result is that test preparation often comes down to test-taking strategies. In the writing domain, the formative–summative connection appears arguably closer, and instructional support for large-scale testing can be designed in ways that address important academic outcomes. To be sure, externally mandated writing assignments vary greatly (Hillocks, 2002), but all rely on standardized conditions in which students have limited time and resources, cannot ask for clarification or support, and generally lack a clear and meaningful purpose and audience. The CLAS-Plus model offers the potential to bridge this gap, first, by providing students with experience in authentic writing, then arranging situations that foster explicit links to the standardized setting, where students have to manufacture a sense of audience, purpose, and motivation. These links may resemble test preparation in some respects, but they also serve valuable purposes in their own right.

Repeated practice with CLAS-Plus assessments allows students to *routinize efficient patterns of thinking* that allow them to plan, organize, and execute responses in settings where the supports are minimal. The teacher's role in orchestrating this development is critical, especially for students with special needs. The key is to view the school year as a developmental continuum. CLAS-Plus assessments will look quite different in the fall than in the spring. At first, a project may take several days to complete, depending on the amount of scaffolding that the teacher needs to provide as students explore the various activities. As the year progresses, skills and strategies become routinized, and scaffolding can be withdrawn. But task complexity and difficulty should also be increased, which will call for a different type of support. Success for all students in challenging activities such as those exemplified by CLAS-Plus requires a high level of professional knowledge and skill from teachers—including the capacity to build a classroom community in which students support one another's growth toward expertise. The goal for both teachers and students is the capacity to communicate effectively in a variety of settings, which means that they have mastered the ability to consider topic, purpose, audience, and structure whenever confronted with the need to compose, whether it be for school or for the many facets of life beyond school.

CONCLUSIONS

The CLAS-Plus assessment approach offers teachers of students experiencing difficulty with language and literacy a comprehensive perspective on students' writing as they traverse the continuum from novice toward expert. The 2-day assessments represent a sub-stantial time investment, but the activities also offer insight and provide practice with significant feedback about genuine academic content. The process allows the teacher to monitor the thinking processes that undergird the written products. The opportunities to scaffold student performance allow the teacher to establish the limits of individual potential in an ideal situation. By examining students' interactions during the prewriting activities, their prewriting products, and the final essays, using the analytic rubrics as lenses, the teacher is well informed by assessments that can effectively guide future instruction. The strategy provides a framework that can be adapted in a wide variety of ways to address curriculum requirements and to meet individual needs; it serves as an example, rather than an answer, to the challenges of classroom-based writing assessment.

REFERENCES

Berninger, V. W. (1996). *Reading and writing acquisition: A developmental neuropsychological perspective.* New York: Westview Press.
Berninger, V. W. (2000). Development of language by hand and its connections to language by ear, mouth, and eye. *Topics in Language Disorders, 23,* 65–84.
Calfee, R. C. (1997). Assessing development and learning over time. In J. Flood, S. B. Heath, & D. Lapp (Eds.), *Handbook for literacy educators: Research on teaching the communicative and visual arts* (pp. 144–166). New York: Macmillan.
Calfee, R. C. (1998). Leading middle grade students from reading to writing: Conceptual and practical aspects. In N. Nelson & R. C. Calfee (Eds.), *The reading–writing connection: 97th yearbook of the National Society for the Study of Education, Part II* (pp. 203–228). Chicago: University of Chicago Press.
Calfee, R. C. (2002). Writing assessment in large-scale contexts. In B. Guzzetti (Ed.), *Literacy in America: An encyclopedia of history, theory, and practice.* Santa Barbara, CA: ABC-CLIO.
Calfee, R. C., & Patrick, C. L. (1995). *Teach our children well: Bringing K–12 education into the 21st century.* Stanford, CA: Stanford Alumni Association.
Cope, B., & Kalantzis, M. (Eds.). (1993). *The powers of literacy: A genre approach to teaching writing.* London: Falmer Press.
Corliss, R. (1999, May 3). Bang, you're dead!: Revenge fantasies are proliferating in movies and on TV. But should a they be blamed for Littleton? *Time,* pp. 49–50.

Corno, L. (1993). The best-laid plans: Modern conceptions of volition and educational research. *Educational Researcher, 22,* 14–22.

Deci, E. L., & Ryan, R. M. (1985). *Intrinsic motivation and self-determination in human behavior.* New York: Plenum Press.

Deci, E. L., Vallerand, R. J., Pelletier, L G., & Ryan, R. M. (1991). Motivation and education: The self-determination perspective. *Educational Psychologist, 26,* 325–347.

DiPardo, A., & Freedman, S. W. (1988). Peer response groups in the writing classroom: Theoretic foundations and new directions. *Review of Educational Research, 58*(2), 119–149.

Dyson, A. H., & Freedman, S. W. (2003). Writing. In J. Flood, D. Lapp, J. R. Squire, & J. M. Jensen (Eds.), *Handbook of research on teaching the English language arts* (2nd ed., pp. 967–992). Mahwah, NJ: Erlbaum.

Farnan, N., & Dahl, K. (2003). Children's writing: Research and practice. In J. Flood, D. Lapp, J. R. Squire, & J. M. Jensen (Eds.), *Handbook of research on teaching the English language arts* (2nd ed., pp. 993–1007. Mahwah, NJ: Erlbaum.

Flower, L. S., Stein, V., Ackerman, J. M., Kantz, P., McCormick, K., & Peck, W. (1990). *Reading to write: Exploring a cognitive and social process.* New York: Oxford University Press.

Goodman, Y. M. (2003). Informal methods of evaluation. In J. Flood, D. Lapp, J. R. Squire, & J. M. Jensen (Eds.), *Handbook of research on teaching the English Language arts* (2nd ed., pp. 600–607). Mahwah, NJ: Erlbaum.

Graham, S. (1990). The role of production factors in learning disabled students' compositions. *Journal of Educational Psychology, 82,* 781–791.

Graham, S., & Harris, K. (1994). The role and development of self-regulation in the writing process. In D. H. Schunk & B. J. Zimmerman (Eds.), *Self-regulation of learning and performance: Issues and educational applications* (pp. 203–228). Hillsdale, NJ: Erlbaum.

Grigorenko, E. L., & Sternberg, R. J. (1998). Dynamic testing. *Psychological Review, 124,* 75–111.

Grill, J. J., & Kirwin, M. M. (1989). *Written language assessment.* Novato, CA: Academic Therapy.

Hammil, D. D., & Larsen, S. C. (1988). *Test of Written Language* (3rd ed.). Austin, TX: PRO-ED.

Hayes, J. R. (1996). A new framework for understanding cognition and affect in writing. In C. M. Levy & S. Ransdell (Eds.), *The science of writing: Theories, methods, individual differences, and applications* (pp. 1–27). Mahwah NJ: Erlbaum.

Hayes, J. R. (2000). A new framework for understanding cognition and affect in writing. In R. Indrisano & J. R. Squire (Eds.), *Perspectives on writing: Research, theory, and practice* (pp. 6–44). Newark, DE: International Reading Association.

Hayes, J. R., & Flower, L. S. (1980). Identifying the organization of writing processes. In L. Gregg & E. R. Steinberg (Eds.), *Cognitive processes in writing* (pp. 176–240). Hillsdale, NJ: Erlbaum.

Hidi, S. D., & Krapp, A. (1992). Situational interest and its impact on reading and expository writing. In K. A. Renninger, S. Hidi, & A. Krapp (Eds.), *The role of interest in learning and development* (pp. 215–238). Hillsdale, NJ: Erlbaum.

Hillocks, G., Jr. (2002). *The testing trap: How state writing assessments control learning.* New York: Teachers College Press.

Hooper, S. R., Swartz, C. W., Wakely, M. B., de Kruif, R. E. L., & Montgomery, J. W. (2002). Executive functions in elementary school children with and without problems in written expression. *Journal of Learning Disabilities, 35,* 57–68.

Hresko, W. P., Herron, S. R., & Peak, P.K. (1996). *Test of early written language* (2nd ed.). Austin, TX: PRO-ED.

Joint Committee on Standards for Educational Evaluation. (2002). *Student evaluation standards.* Thousand Oaks, CA: Corwin Press.

Larsen, S. C., Hammill, D. D., & Moats, L. (1999). *Test of Written Spelling* (4th ed.). Austin, TX: PRO-ED.

Lerner, J. W. (1976). *Children with learning disabilities: Theories, diagnosis, teaching strategies.* Boston: Houghton Mifflin.

Lidz, C. C., & Elliott, J. G. (Eds.). (2000). *Dynamic assessment: Prevailing models and applications.* Greenwich, CT: JAI Press.

McGhee, R., Bryant, B. R., Larsen, S. C., & Rivera, D. M. (1995). *Test of Written Expression.* Austin, TX: PRO-ED.

Meece, J. L., & Miller S. D. (1999). Changes in elementary school children's achievement goals for reading and writing: Results of a longitudinal and an intervention study. *Scientific Studies of Reading, 3,* 207–229.

Miller, R. G., & Calfee, R. C. (2004). Building a better reading-writing assessment: Bridging cognitive theory, instruction, and assessment. *English Leadership Quarterly, 26*(3), 6–13.

Nelson, N., & Calfee, R. C. (1998). The reading–writing connection viewed historically. In *The reading–writing connection: 97th yearbook for the National Society for the Study of Education—Part II),* (pp. 1–52). Chicago: National Society for the Study of Education.

Newcomer, P. L., & Bryant, B. R. (1993). *Diagnostic Achievement Test for Adolescents* (2nd ed.). Austin, TX: PRO-ED.

Nystrand, M. (1986). *The structure of written communication: Studies in reciprocity between writers and readers.* Orlando, FL: Academic Press.

Paris, S., & Cross, R. D. (1983). Ordinary learning: Pragmatic connections among children's beliefs, motives, and actions. In J. Bisanz, G. L. Bisanz, & R. Kail (Eds.), *Learning in children: Progress in cognitive development research* (pp. 137–169). New York: Springer-Verlag.

Persky, H. R., Daane, M. C., & Jin Y. (2003). *The nation's report card: Writing 2002.* Washington, DC: U.S. Department of Education, Institute of Education Sciences, National Center for Education Statistics.

Ruth, L., & Murphy, S. (1988). *Designing writing tasks for the assessment of writing*. Norwood, NJ: Ablex.

Scardamalia, M., & Bereiter, C. (1986). Written composition. In M. Wittrock (Ed.), *Handbook of research on teaching* (3rd ed., pp 778–803). New York: Macmillan.

Schiefele, U. (1999). Interest and learning from text. *Scientific Studies of Reading, 3*, 257–279.

Shepard, L. A. (2001). The role of classroom assessment in teaching and learning. In V. Richardson (Ed.), *Handbook of research on teaching* (4th ed., pp. 1066–1121). Washington, DC: American Educational Research Association.

Simmons, J., & Carroll, P. S. (2003). Today's middle grades: Different structures, students, and classrooms. In J. Flood, D. Lapp, J. R. Squire, & J. M. Jensen (Eds.), *Handbook of research on teaching the English language arts* (2nd ed., pp. 357–392). Mahwah, NJ: Erlbaum

Spandel, V. (2001). *Creating writers through 6-trait writing assessment and instruction*. New York: Addison-Wesley/Longman.

Sperling, M. (1996). Revisiting the reading–writing connection: Challenges for research on writing and writing instruction. *Review of Educational Research, 66*(1), 53–86.

Sperling, M. (1998). Teachers as readers of student writing. In N. Nelson & R. C. Calfee (Eds.), *The reading–writing connection: 97th yearbook of the National Society for the Study of Education* (pp. 131–152). Chicago: University of Chicago Press.

Sperling M., & Freedman, S. W. (2001). Research on writing. In V. Richardson (Ed.), *Handbook of research on teaching* (4th ed., pp. 370–389). Washington, DC: American Educational Research Association.

Spivey, N. N., & King, J. R. (1989). Readers as writers composing from sources. In R. B. Ruddell, M. R. Ruddell, & H. Singer (Eds.), *Theoretical models and processes of reading* (4th ed., pp. 668–694). Newark, DE: International Reading Association.

Stiggins, R. J. (2000). *Student-centered classroom assessment* (3rd ed.). New York: Prentice-Hall.

Thurlow, M. L., Elliott, J. L., & Ysseldyke, J. E. (2002). *Testing students with disabilities: Practical strategies for complying with district and state requirements* (2nd ed.). Arlington, VA: Council for Exceptional Children.

Tierney, R. J., & Shanahan, T. (1996). Research on the reading–writing relation: Interactions, transactions, and outcomes. In R. Barr, M. L. Kamil, P. Mosenthal, & P. D. Pearson (Eds.), *Handbook of reading research* (Vol. 2, pp. 246–280). Mahwah NJ: Erlbaum.

Underwood, T. (1999). *The portfolio project: A study of assessment, instruction, and middle school reform*. Urbana, IL: National Council of Teachers of English.

Vellutino, F. R. (1979). *Dyslexia: theory and research*. Cambridge, MA: MIT Press.

Vygotsky, L. S. (1978). *Mind in society*. Cambridge, MA: Harvard University Press.

Warden, R., & Hutchinson, T. A. (1991–1992). *Writing Process Test*. Austin, TX: PRO-ED.

Wiggins, G. (1993). *Assessing student performance: Exploring the purpose and limits of testing*. San Francisco: Jossey-Bass.

Wong, B. Y. L. (1994). Instructional parameters promoting transfer of learned strategies in students with learning disabilities. *Learning Disabilities Quarterly, 20*(17), 110–120.

Woodcock, R. W., McGrew, K. S., & Mather, N. (2001). *Woodcock–Johnson III Test of Achievement*. Chicago: Riverside.

28

Cognitive Processes of Teachers in Implementing Composition Research in Elementary, Middle, and High School Classrooms

BERNICE Y. L. WONG
VIRGINIA W. BERNINGER

PARADIGM SHIFTS IN WRITING INSTRUCTION AND RESEARCH

Four paradigm shifts dramatically changed research on written composition and instructional practice in writing during the last two decades of the 20th century. The first shift broadened the developmental lens beyond a narrow focus on high school and college writers to include emerging writers in early childhood and developing writers in elementary school (Berninger, 2000; Graves, 1983; Hillocks, 1986). The second shift redirected exclusive concern with pedagogy to additional concern with the cognitive processes inside the writer's mind during composing (Hayes & Flower, 1980). The third shift replaced a preoccupation about the writing product with greater interest in the process leading to the product (Hillocks, 1986). Increasingly, school writing involves more than a student's handing in a written assignment that is graded, with no further revision of the product. The fourth shift redefined writing as a social activity rather than as a purely individual activity (Englert,

1992). Not only do writers compose for an audience, but also they benefit from constructing and revising their compositions in a social context in which teachers and peers provide feedback throughout the process. Written communication is also used to perform social acts (Britton, 1978).

These four paradigm shifts are the result of two separate research traditions that initially developed separately but subsequently were integrated. We begin this chapter by briefly discussing both of these traditions—process-writing instruction (Calkins, 1986; Graves, 1983) and the cognitive processes of the writer (Hayes & Flower, 1980). The first relied on naturalistic observation, and the second employed "think-alouds" as research tools (Humes, 1983).

We then introduce the idea that teachers, like writers, must plan, translate, and review and revise their instruction in writing. In discussing the cognitive processes of the teacher, we emphasize the contribution of research to composition instruction. Scientifically supported instructional practices require an intervening step between research and practice. We call this translation process the "implementation step." It is sometimes referred to as reduction of research to practice. During implementation, knowledge based on research is packaged for delivery in one's own school and classroom. The same research-generated knowledge may be packaged uniquely in different school settings and with different groups of students. The effectiveness of implementation can be assessed by using program evaluation techniques, which draw on some of the same but not identical tools as research methodology.

We begin with the translating processes of the teacher in applying research to practice, because instruction itself is most salient to teachers. We discuss *pedagogical principles* for accomplishing this translation process. We then turn to the planning processes of the teacher in designing instruction in composition. Although planning is less observable, it is crucial to instructional process. We discuss *instructional-design principles* that teachers may draw on in planning and designing their own instructional programs. Clearly, there is more than one way to implement research findings effectively in the classroom, but effective implementation requires advance planning. The instructional-design principles are supported by research, and teachers may draw on them in the planning process.

Finally, we turn teachers to the reviewing and revising processes in evaluating the effectiveness of instruction and modifying it, if necessary. We call these *evaluation/modification principles*. Teachers can rely on these in gathering empirical evidence to evaluate whether intervention is effective for individual children, and to decide whether instruction should be modified because children are not making reasonable progress toward instructional goals.

The instructional-design principles and the evaluation/modification principles are organized within a developmental framework because, for the student, learning to write is a long journey. It takes years to master the craft (Kellogg, 1994), and both apprentices and mentors need to be patient in perfecting the process. This framework covers three broad stages of development:

(1) emerging and conventional beginning writing in the primary grades, (2) developing writing in the upper elementary school and junior high years, and (3) increasingly skilled writing in the high school years.

In discussing the research on instructional practices in composition at each developmental level, we draw on four programmatic lines of research on composition instruction at Simon Fraser University, the University of Maryland, Michigan State University, and the University of Washington. The Simon Fraser group specializes in middle school and high school writers; the Michigan State University group specializes in early to upper-grade elementary school students; the University of Maryland group specializes mainly, but not exclusively, in upper elementary and middle school students; and the University of Washington group specializes in the first four grades for the purposes of early intervention and prevention of later written expression problems. These research programs have been in operation for over a decade, have integrated the process instruction and cognitive processes of the writer traditions, and have studied students who struggled in learning to write English (e.g., at-risk writers in the lower grades, low achievers in the later grades, students with learning disabilities, and/or students whose first language is not English).

Process Writing as an Instructional Approach

Graves (1983) originated the process approach to writing instruction in North America, and Calkins (1986) actively promoted this instructional approach to composition. Concurrently in New Zealand, Clay (1982, 1985) developed integrated reading–writing instruction, which shares much in common with process writing and has been adapted for use in North American schools. Hallmark instructional components of process writing include the following: (1) authentic writing assignments for real-world purposes; (2) teacher conferencing with students to discuss their writing in progress; (3) Author's Chair for students to share their writing with peers, who offer feedback to improve the writing in progress; (4) multiple drafts; (5) publication of students' final products; and (6) authentic assessment, for example, with portfolios containing writing samples that are inspected for improvement over time. In addition, process writing mirrors the processes in which professional writers engage: planning, independently composing multiple drafts, and reviewing and revising many times based on feedback from peers and editors along the way.

Since Graves's (1983) and Calkins's (1986) pioneering efforts, the process writing movement has gained considerable popularity among teachers. Based on a teacher survey included in the National Assessment of Educational Progress (NAEP), Applebee (2000) reported that 51% of teachers use the process approach. Despite its popularity, little controlled research has examined its effectiveness in general education classrooms compared to an alternative approach. However, for an empirical study showing that integrated reading–writing instruction is as effective as explicit instruction of reading and writing for first graders in the regular educational program, see Traweek and Berninger (1997). Most of the experimental research on the process instructional approach has been done with special populations of struggling writers. Although many teachers are familiar with the process approach to writing instruction, many are not familiar with the research on the cognitive processes of the writer, or with the benefits of teaching these cognitive processes explicitly.

Cognitive Processes of the Writer

Teachers used to assume that composing involved three sequential processes—planning, drafting, and revising. Hayes and Flowers (1980) studied college students thinking aloud as they composed, and what they discovered dispelled this instructional myth. These processes interacted recursively, not sequentially, throughout the composition process. Their resulting model of the cognitive processes in writing has been the most influential model of the composing process, resulting in changes in instructional prac-

tices, as well as stimulating considerable research on composition (e.g., Alamargot & Chanquay, 2001; Butterfield, 1994). Like writing, models of writing are also revised, and as research driven by the original model generated new research understandings (e.g., on working memory; McCutchen, 1994, 1996; Swanson & Berninger, 1996), Hayes revised his original model (1996, 2000). The revised model (Figure 28.1) has two major components: task environment and the individual. The task environment comprises (1) the social environment, which in turn subsumes the audience and collaborators; and (2) the physical environment, which subsumes the text produced thus far and the composing medium (e.g., the computer). The individual component comprises (1) motivation/affect, (2) working memory, (3) long-term memory, and (4) cognitive processes, which essentially refer to the revision processes. Revision, which is the meaning-based changes in text, should not be equated with editing, that is, detecting spelling errors or changing surface features such as capitalization and punctuation (Fitzgerald, 1987).

Like Baddeley's working memory model (Baddeley, 1979; Gathercole & Baddeley, 1993), Hayes's revised model of writing has a working memory component with a central executive that (1) coordinates the phonological loop and visual–spatial sketchpad storing verbal or nonverbal information, respectively; (2) retrieves information from long-term memory; and (3) allocates resources for managing tasks not fully automated that require decision making or problem solving. Hayes also added a semantic memory component because of its role in text production. Moreover, he put decision making under the cognitive processes of reflection, instead of being part of the executive processes of working memory. Of greatest relevance to teaching composition, Hayes realized, based on extensive research with expert and nonexpert adult writers (Hayes, Flower, Schriver, Stratman, & Carey, 1987), that reading text for comprehension and reading text to evaluate it for purposes of revision involve different processes. In reading to comprehend text, the reader integrates multiple sources of knowledge to construct meaning. These

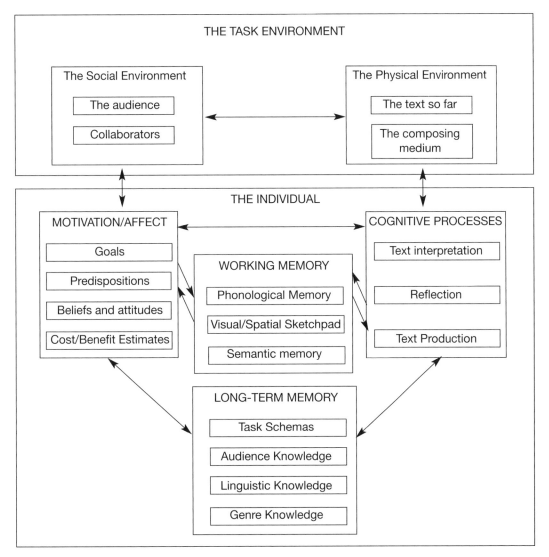

FIGURE 28.1. The general organization of Hayes's new model of writing. Copyright 1996 by Lawrence Erlbaum Associates. Reprinted by permission.

knowledge sources include (1) decoding words; (2) activating knowledge of grammar, semantics, schemas, and genre conventions; (3) identifying gist; and (4) inferring the writer's intentions and points of view. In reading to revise a text, readers actively detect and diagnose text problems that lead to differential levels of revision, for example, to revise a text locally in a selected portion compared to wholesale revision of an entire text, or at least a large part of it. It follows that revision draws on a specialized form of reading that involves three cognitive processes—text interpretation, reflection (which includes planning), and text production to remedy detected problems in text. Developing writers revise better when they read text from the perspective of the reader than when they revise after receiving feedback on a prior version, with or without an opportunity to evaluate the prior version (Holliway & McCutchen, in press).

COGNITIVE PROCESSES OF THE TEACHER IN COMPOSITION INSTRUCTION

Pedagogical Principles

From this model of the cognitive processes of the writer, Wong and colleagues (Wong, Butler, Ficzere, & Kuperis, 1996, 1997; Wong, Butler, Ficzere, Kuperis, & Corden, 1994) have derived and field-tested seven pedagogical principles that can be used in a process writing instructional program. The first is based on the working memory component of Hayes's model. The second is based on the reading component of revision in Hayes's model. The third is based on writing-specific knowledge stored in the long-term memory component. The fourth is based on the motivational/affect component that interacts with the cognitive component. The fifth is related to the social environment in which composing takes place. The sixth and seventh are related to the physical environment in which composing takes place. Taken together, cognitively oriented pedagogical principles may assist teachers in translating both of the previously discussed research traditions in composition into instructional practice.

First Pedagogical Principle

Because working memory is a limited resource, use procedural facilitators (e.g., Graham, MacArthur, & Schwartz, 1995; Montague, Graves, & Leavell, 1991; Scardamalia & Bereiter, 1983) *to bypass its limitations while composing.* For example, procedural facilitators may make it easier to store verbal information in the phonological loop and/or nonverbal information in the nonverbal visual–spatial sketchpad. For young children, procedural facilitation may consist of letting children tape-record their plans as they think aloud, or their text generation as they compose orally, thereby eliminating the additional concurrent task of transcribing those plans and thoughts into writing (Flood & Lapp, 2000). At a subsequent time, the tape can be replayed and text generation can continue, or the tape-recorded text can be transcribed. For

children in the intermediate grades, procedural facilitation can take the form of think–plan sheets (Englert, 1992) that reduce load on both the phonological loop and visual–spatial sketch pad by encouraging children to write their ideas in external memory on a sheet with graphic organizers. For adolescents in high school, procedural facilitation may be achieved by collaborative planning before individual, independent writing: Two minds working together may bypass the limitations of one working memory system by combining their mental resources. Students discuss and complete the plan sheet jointly, for example, for an opinion essay (see Figure 28.2).

Second Pedagogical Principle

Help students understand the relationship between reading and writing, and teach a specific kind of reading related to reviewing and revising writing. Just because a student can comprehend text, it does not mean that he or she will be able to read his or her own text critically, detect problems (such as ambiguities in text), then repair the problem. Teachers have four opportunities for teaching reading–writing connections.

The first occurs in the context of teacher–student conferencing about the student's writing. The teacher focuses the student on an ambiguous sentence through interactive dialogue to help the student realize that the teacher cannot understand it. The teacher may say, "Do you see as you reread the sentence now, how it is not clear to the reader, me, or to Bob, your classmate? That's why you are going to revise it, to make it clear to me and to Bob." She then helps the student revise the sentence with suitable clarification or elaboration. A conceivable script for making the reading–writing relationship clear may include the following: "You see how your rereading leads to rewriting that sentence? After we talked about clarity in your writing, and went over that sentence and talked about whether it says clearly what you wanted, you read it over and realized it wasn't clear enough. So we fixed it. It's your reading that sentence carefully for clarity that did the trick. It made you revise and improve your writ-

Topic: _____

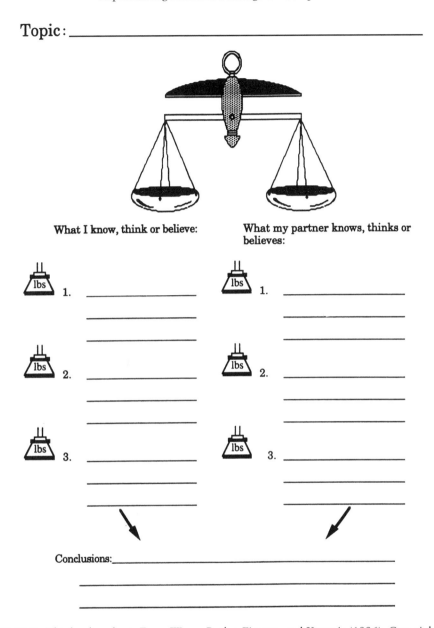

ing!" Both younger and older writers can often revise text successfully, if someone helps them detect where text is not comprehensible (Beal, 1996).

The second opportunity occurs when students have to do research to write a paper, for example, in social studies. Students have to read relevant materials (Hayes, 1996) to hone up on knowledge of topic before they can write informative papers. Teaching explicit strategies for reading sourcebooks helps developing writers to obtain accurate and relevant information that is correctly attributed to the author *and* to create novel and informative schemas for organizing the information in the source material. Instead of having all students consult different source materials, teachers may provide the same source materials for all students, then closely monitor how different students use the same source material. Teachers can then give students feedback on the reports they write that differentiates between quality of the content in the written report, based on the source material, and on quality of presentation, based on students' writing about that source material. In this way, students begin to learn how reading and writing about source material differ but are interrelated.

The third opportunity occurs when students have to read to understand or define the writing task (Hayes, 1996). Despite having the requisite knowledge gleaned from reading, many students have done poorly on a writing task or test simply because they misread or misunderstood the instructions. Specific terms in the writing assignment may stymie students and lead them astray. For example, in a test, the university student is told, "Draw the implications of the research on metacognition and writing for teachers." The particular student does not understand the word *implications* and summarizes the research findings without discussing their implications for teaching. Teachers should drive home the point that reading is closely aligned to writing in defining the task, whether on tests or other written assignments.

The fourth opportunity occurs when teachers increase students' awareness of audience for the goal of improving clarity in writing. In writing instruction, teachers routinely conference with students or use peer conferencing to teach revising and editing. It is during such conferencing that teachers can actively foster student authors' awareness of the audience as readers of their writing. To achieve this goal, Wong and her associates (1994, 1996, 1997) use the following dialogue script with individual students:

"It's all clear in your head what you're saying here (in this sentence). But it's not clear to me, because I'm not in your head space. I can't take an X-ray of what's in your head. So when you write, you have to make it clear enough for me to understand what you're saying. You have to remember I can't get inside your head, OK?"

Wong and her associates emphasize to students the value of their ideas and avoid any criticism of their ideas. Rather, they emphasize the importance of clearly communicating those ideas to the audience—readers who have direct access to those ideas only through the writer's written language.

Third Pedagogical Principle

Teach well-honed schemas for paragraph structure and genre-specific text structures to facilitate the text-generation component of composing. Students who understand paragraph structure realize the organizational role of a main-idea or topic sentence around which the other sentences in the paragraph cluster. Students need to understand the role of the main idea in paragraphs in source material they read and in the paragraphs they construct (Aulls, 1978; Wong et al., 1996). They also need to understand that some paragraphs contain more than one main idea, and how discourse devices organize those ideas. Examples of paragraphs containing more than one main idea can often be found in social studies texts. When teachers introduce reading expository text structure, for example, around fourth grade, they should teach strategies for identifying the main idea(s) and structure of paragraphs.

Similarly, students benefit from explicit instruction on specific genres of text, each of which has its own discourse structure (e.g., Crowhurst, 1987). For example, deep knowledge of the differences between narrative and expository texts allows students to activate schemas to use in their own writing (Wong, 1997). Different kinds of narratives exist, for example, mysteries, horror stories, action adventures, and so on. Different kinds of expository schemas also exist, including informative essays that report, describe, express an opinion, or compare and contrast (see Figure 28.3), and persuasive essays that present and defend arguments.

Name _____   Date _____

COMPARE / CONTRAST PLAN

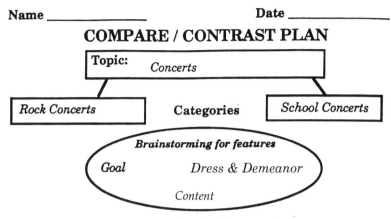

Topic: *Concerts*

Rock Concerts   Categories   *School Concerts*

Brainstorming for features

Goal   *Dress & Demeanor*

Content

Thesis sentence (see prompt for help)

In this essay, I am going to compare and contrast rock concerts and school concert.
I have chosen to write on three features: Goal, Content, and Dress and Demeanor.

Features (Themes)	**Ideas** (Details)	Sim	Dif
1. *Goal*	a. *both provide entertainment*	√	
	b. *rock concerts (pay); school concerts (free)*		√
	c.		
2. *Content*	a. *different types of music*		√
	b. *rock concerts idols, school concerts none*		√
	c. *both concerts need practice & rehearsals*	√	
3. *Dress & Demeanor*	a. *correct attire important for rock concerts; not for school concerts*		√
	b. *rowdy audience in rock concerts, not so in school concerts*		√
	c.		

Conclusion: (see prompt for help)

After comparing and contrasting _rock concerts_ **and**
school concerts **, I think I prefer** _school concerts_ **because**

they are free, have my kind of music and they don't allow rowdy behaviors!

FIGURE 28.3. Compare–contrast plan. From Wong, Butler, Ficzere, and Kuperis (1997). Copyright 1997 by PRO-ED. Reprinted by permission.

In general, narrative discourse structure is learned earlier than expository structure (Kellogg, 1994). Persuasive expository essays have a complex discourse structure that is typically the hardest to learn: Take a position, present the counterargument(s), provide evidence for and against the positions, and reach a conclusion, with the goal of convincing the audience that this is the best position. Writers may use discourse schemas at the planning, text-generating, and reviewing and revising stages of composing.

Just as certain technical terms and phrases assist students in solving math word problems, certain words and phrases associated with a specific genre assist writers in reading source material and in generating text. They prepare the reader for what comes next. For example, the following phrases are relevant to opinion and persuasive essays: "From my point of view," "In my opinion," "I disagree with . . ." The following words and phrases are relevant to compare and contrast essays: "in common," *Similarly,* "in contrast to," and *whereas.* These genre-specific terms and phrases should be explicitly modeled by the teacher in think- alouds and can also be provided for students on the prompt cards they use when writing independently (Wong et al., 1994, 1997).

Fourth Pedagogical Principle

Motivate students to write by teaching (1) self-regulation strategies (Harris & Graham, 1996) *and (2) self-efficacy in writing* (Graham, Schwartz, & MacArthur, 1993; Wong et al., 1996). Self-regulation, which is the ability to manage a task independently, guides the writing process by helping the writer to set and attain goals (Harris & Graham, 1992), energize and channel thoughts and actions (Harris & Graham, 1992), and stay focused on writing and ward off distractions (Kuhl, 1985). Graham and Harris (1992) developed a model called self-regulated strategy development (SRSD), which they use to enable students to

> master higher level cognitive processes in composing; develop autonomous, reflective, self-regulated use of effective writing strategies; increase knowledge about the characteristics of good writing; and form positive attitudes about writing and their capabilities as writers. (Graham, Harris, MacArthur, & Schwartz, 1998, p. 401)

Within this model, children are scaffolded in learning self-regulation skills that guide their effective use of writing strategies and help them coordinate the subprocesses in the writing process. Teachers can enhance the self-efficacy, which is one's sense of competence, of poor writers by regularly showing them records of their teacher-assigned scores on specific writing goals on

at least two occasions (e.g., first and second drafts) (Wong et al., 1996). Each score is based on a scale of 0 to 5, allowing room for improvement, and is graphed. Even poor writers improve with practice, and this improvement enhances their self-efficacy, that is, their belief in their ability to write. Success in writing motivates students to work hard toward further improvement.

Fifth Pedagogical Principle

Create an optimal social environment for the composing process. Student writers need to interact with both teachers and classmates as they plan, and to offer and receive feedback on first drafts and revised drafts (what they liked, what was unclear, etc.). Five instructional practices optimize social interactions among writers. First, students should be given writing assignments that are meaningful to them. These assignments should be kept in portfolios (Valencia, 1998) that can be read and reread by authors and peers. Second, students should, to the extent possible, be given choice in writing (topics and genres), because choice promotes interest and autonomy (Gambrell & Morrow, 1996). Autonomous writers interact more comfortably with others. Third, Author's Chair gives authors the floor to read aloud their writings, which can be enjoyed as aural texts in public, social settings, as well written texts in private. Fourth, collaborative planning in which pairs of students co-construct plans leads to meaningful writing goals (Wong et al., 1994, 1996, 1997). Fifth, teachers can model writing, discuss their own writing problems and how they work on them, and share their own writing with students to demonstrate that they value writing as a mode of social communication.

Sixth Pedagogical Principle

Adapt writing instruction to the physical environment in which writing naturally occurs, which includes the physical tools used to generate text. Students currently attending school in North America do not know a world without the computer, which is increasingly the tool on which they complete writing assignments. A third grader in Berninger's longitudinal study of writing observed that writing is something you do when the computer is not working. It is easy to confuse the tool (pencil) and the process if a distinction is not made in instruction between the process of composing and the tools used to support it, which may include a keyboard as well as a pen or pencil. However, computers are not a bypass strategy for handwriting, unless keyboarding skills are taught and practiced until students are reasonably accurate and automatic (Wong et al., 1994, 1996, 1997).

Seventh Pedagogical Principle

Organize the classroom for an optimal physical layout for large-group, small-group, and independent activities. Teachers require specialized knowledge and skills, including good classroom management strategies, for dealing with the enormous diversity typically found in any classroom (Wong, 1989). Flood and Lapp (2000) interviewed teachers in a multiethnic, multiracial, and multilingual elementary school with 1,000 students. Teachers reported the most frustration with how to group and manage a diverse class during process writing instruction. Flood and Lapp then devised and tested the Center–Activity–Rotation System (CARS) model in the same school. Seven activity centers were established: a Writing Center, a Resource Center, a Listening Center, a Viewing Center, a Conference Center, a Computer Center, and a Teacher-Sharing Center. At the Writing Center, children write on a variety of topics, using different genres. Children are encouraged to interact in this center and consult with each other on spelling, word choice, and stylistic issues. At the Resource Center, children consult written source materials, including encyclopedias, newspapers, magazines, or books. They can read source material collaboratively or independently. At the Listening Center, children listen to tapes of source material relevant to their writing. They also tape-record their writings and listen to them for the purpose of self-assessment. They also read their writings to each other. At the Viewing Center, children look at videos,

films, and DVDs, which also serve as source material for their writing. At the Conference Center, children conference with peers. They rotate with one another in this center, so that they receive feedback from all students. The Computer Center gives them access to the Internet, another source of material for their writing. In the Teacher-Sharing Center, the teacher pulls from one activity center a small, homogeneous group whose members require instruction on the same writing skill. When she finishes with the member of one small group, those students return to the activity center, and she pulls another small group for individualized instruction. Students are given a weekly rotation plan, so that they know how to rotate through the centers.

To these pedagogical principles used by Wong and colleagues, we add three more that are based on the research of the Lesley College (Boston) group and the University of Kansas Center for Research on Learning (n.d.).

Eighth Pedagogical Principle

Teach metalinguistic awareness of the difference between the oral and literate language styles or registrars and strategies for achieving the oral-literate shift (Singer, 1995). Although younger normal writers used as many cohesive ties as older normal writers, those of the younger writers tend to reflect the oral rather than literate registrar (Singer, 1995). Writing development requires a shift from the oral to the literate registrar. One way to help students achieve this shift is by providing models of good writing by age peers that reflect the literate (written discourse constructed for a nonpresent audience) rather than the oral register (conversational talk written down) (Singer, 1995).

Ninth Pedagogical Principle

Provide verbal self-prompting cues or questions to guide each subprocess in writing (Singer & Bashir, 2004). Effective composition instruction integrates teaching of linguistic strategies with teaching of metacognitive strategies for executive control of the writing process (Singer & Bashir, 1999). To accomplish this integration, Singer and Bashir (2004) modified Englert and Raphael's (1988) POWER (Plan, Organize, Work, Evaluate, and Rework) model for writing instruction to include a systematic set of verbal prompts for mediating and managing each of the writing subprocesses.

Tenth Pedagogical Principle

Implement strategy instruction for low-achieving writers in the context of a systems model that includes a partnership between general education and special education. In the strategic instructional model developed by Deschler and colleagues (e.g., Schumaker, Deschler, & McKnight, in press), the general education program teaches content in a way students can understand, and the special education program teaches strategies for facilitating learning to learn independently when in the general education classroom. Such strategies include sentence writing strategies (Schmidt, Deschler, Schumaker, & Alley, 1989; Schumaker & Sheldon, 1985) and paragraph writing strategies (Schmidt et al., 1989).

Instructional-Design Principles

Implementing instructional research of others into one's own classroom requires considerable planning and forethought. Instructional research typically compares the effectiveness of one or more discrete methods. However, effective instruction in the classroom involves the integration of multiple instructional components rather than a single method. Teachers need to plan how to integrate or package those components within the school day. They also need to plan how to apply research findings to individual students, who are not all alike in their instructional needs. On the one hand, instructional research may be based on students who meet well-defined criteria, whereas instruction in the classroom is aimed at all students, who may exhibit more diversity than research samples considering the normal variation typically found among writers at the same grade level (Berninger & Abbott, 2001). On the other

hand, much instructional research on low-achieving students in writing does not adequately describe the profile of language skills of the students, so teachers do not know how or whether to generalize the results to their own students (Singer & Bashir, 2004).

We propose that instructional-design principles, based on research, can be used to guide the planning process for applying research to practice. Some of the research-supported instructional-design principles we recommend cut across developmental level of writers; these are discussed in this section. Others that are developmentally specific are discussed later in the chapter. All require general knowledge of teaching strategies and domain-specific knowledge about genres of writing for effective implementation (Wong, 1994).

First Instructional-Design Principle

Give careful consideration to the timing of the instructional components. Timing instructional components within the same lesson, so that they are close in time, is necessary to ensure that, in working memory, which has temporal and not just spatial capacity limitations, connections form between all the components of the writing system, so that they function in concert (Berninger, 1998, 1999; Berninger & Richards, 2002). On the one hand, too much repetition of low-level skills in the same session leads to habituation and wasted practice that does not lead to learning. On the other hand, some amount of practice is needed to automatize low-level transcription skills (handwriting, keyboarding, spelling) in order to free up working memory resources for the high-level composing skills (Berninger, 1998; Berninger & Richards, 2002; McCutchen, 1994, 1996). Teaching these skills at different times of the day fragments the writing process for novice writers. If students cannot coordinate all the necessary components of the emerging functional writing system, they do not begin to think of themselves as writers. See Berninger (1998) and Berninger and Richards (2002) for specific suggestions on how to time instructional components within lessons. That is why, within the primary-grade classroom, composing should always follow instruction in transcription (handwriting or spelling, the tools of composing).

Within the intermediate-grade classroom, timing of instructional components across lessons over the short run (e.g., a week or two) becomes important, because students are increasingly given assignments that cannot be completed within one session. Many students need more than practice in completing multistep assignments that require more than one session. They need to be taught strategies for setting goals, making plans, and executing plans to complete the longer written assignments in a timely and competent manner. These strategies might include locating source material, reading source material, taking notes based on the source material, using notes to generate a written report, learning strategies for organizing material within a paragraph (main idea and supporting detail), and developing text-level schemas for tying together multiple paragraphs. The point is that students need to be taught explicitly to engage in multiple steps organized across time (sessions and maybe even weeks). See Harris and Graham (1996) for specific strategies for achieving across-session writing goals.

Within the regular high school curriculum, or the modified high school curriculum for students with learning differences, timing of instructional components across lessons throughout the semester or entire academic year becomes important, because students in high school are given many long-range assignments that may require more steps and time to complete than in the earlier grades. In addition, they are often given written tests on which successful performance depends on the notes they took during class lectures or other activities. They need explicit instruction in how to integrate note taking with instructor talk, which places great demands on temporally sensitive working memory (e.g., how to select the relevant ideas to record in writing). Furthermore, they need explicit instruction in how to integrate these notes with text reading in studying for tests, another activity that requires sustained mental activity involving multiple components over time. See

Wong et al. (1994, 1996, 1997) for specific suggestions on how to time instructional components across lessons within a week, and across weeks, in a semester.

Second Instructional-Design Principle

Provide explicit instruction within an interactive dialogue mode of instruction (Englert, 1992; Wong, Wong, Darlington, & Jones, 1991; Wong et al., 1994, 1996, 1997). Explicit instruction is not the same as direct instruction, which is a systematic program of scripted instruction that is implemented in invariant ways across classrooms. Explicit instruction means that teachers structure learning activities so that students (1) gain conscious access to information already in their implicit, unconscious memory system, or (2) create precise representations of new information in short- and long-term memory (Berninger & Richards, 2002). Inservice teachers are more likely than preservice teachers to recognize the importance of explicit literacy instruction (Mather, Bos, & Babur, 2001). Hillocks's (1986) meta-analysis showed that combining explicit, teacher-directed instruction in writing and free-writing activities is more effective than either method alone in improving composition. Interactive dialogues are also not the same as Socratic dialogues, which are based only on logical deduction using information already in long-term memory. In contrast, interactive dialogues, which have been shown to be effective (Wong et al., 1991), employ two kinds of explicit instructional components to create new, high-order knowledge: (1) teacher modeling by thinking aloud about some point he or she is trying to make about writing, and (2) teacher–student dialogues to clarify, in response to student input, the point the teacher is making (Wong et al., 1996). Interactive dialogues may also involve student–student interchange as a pair of students constructs plans collaboratively using think–plan sheets, role plays contrasting view points, or revises collaboratively, with students alternating in the role of critic to call attention to ambiguities in the other's writing (Wong et al., 1996, 1997).

For interactive dialogue to achieve its instructional goals, the teacher has to have all the activities and instructional materials well planned in advance. Having a well-conceived plan to guide but not dictate the learning process allows the teacher to respond flexibly to students, who often respond to instruction in unpredictable ways, without losing sight of what the instructional goals are and, when necessary, redirecting the dialogue.

Third Instructional-Design Principle

Design writing activities so that children succeed but move along their zone of proximal development (Vygotsky, 1978). On the one hand, unless writing tasks are within reach, emerging and developing writers might become discouraged and avoid writing, thereby eliminating opportunities for further growth. On the other hand, unless writing tasks are cognitively engaging and challenging, student writers may not be sufficiently invested in them to grow as writers. The instructional goal is to cheer the writer on to a higher level of writing achievement, but one that is within reach. The tool for moving writers along their proximal zone is called "scaffolding" (see Wong, 1998, for a special issue on this important topic). For empirical evidence that children grow more in writing when instruction is aimed at the zone of proximal development, rather than at a writing skill within easy reach, see Berninger, Vaughan, et al. (2002). Knowing individual students' zones of proximal development requires regular collection of assessment data (see next section), and planning daily and weekly instruction on the basis of how individual students are progressing.

Fourth Instructional-Design Principle

Design writing activities so that students develop self-efficacy as writers, that is, the belief that they can communicate effectively with others through written language (Graham et al., 1993; Wong et al., 1996). One bridge to self-efficacy is to help writers increase the amount they write, in order to convince them that they can succeed at writing. Another bridge to *self*-efficacy is through *others*. Without the opportunity to share with others, writers will not gain a

sense that they can use written language to communicate with others. A third bridge to self-efficacy is to coordinate temporally all necessary components, so that the writing system is functional and the writer begins to think of him- or herself as a writer. Thus, the writing instructor must plan ways to incorporate all three bridges to self-efficacy in the writing program.

Fifth Instructional-Design Principle

Teach for transfer—both near transfer to taught knowledge/skills over time and far transfer to generalize knowledge/skills to novel contexts (Wong, 1994). For example, spelling should be taught in a weekly, systematic spelling program, but it should also be taught in the context of composing, in which spelling is used for functional communication. Personal spelling dictionaries are one way spelling can be integrated with composition instruction (e.g., Berninger et al., 1998). Self-regulated strategy instruction (Harris & Graham, 1996) is ideally suited to teaching for far transfer and generalization across settings and tasks. Achieving the goals of near and far transfer requires careful planning of not only the instructional activities but also the evaluation activities (see next section).

Sixth Instructional-Design Principle

Evaluate specific writing skills on a daily basis, so that writers receive feedback as to what they are doing well and what they need to try to improve. Specify the skill, and use a scale that allows room for improvement (e.g., 1 to 5). Have students graph the scores they received for each target skill, so that they have a visible record of their progress and of the skills on which they still need to improve (see Wong et al., 1994, 1996, 1997). Teachers must plan both the kind of feedback to provide (related to the instructional goals) and the way in which it will be provided.

Seventh Instructional-Design Principle

Be patient and do not expect instant mastery of writing skills. Becoming a good writer takes time and evolves over a long time period (Kellogg, 1994). If students do not make reasonable progress, based on inspection of daily performance records reviewed on a daily, weekly, and monthly basis, brainstorm and evaluate alternative approaches, but do not get discouraged if students do not show instant improvement. Both teachers' and parents' expectations for what is good writing need to be developmentally appropriate, based on what is typical of other normally developing writers of the same age or grade. Emerging and developing writing should not be gauged against skilled writing; nor should it be assumed that immature writers (for age or grade) will improve solely on the basis of maturation: Explicit, scaffolded instruction is needed to move students along their zone of proximal development. Such instruction requires considerable preplanning, as well as patience in understanding that the best instructional plans do not result in immediate mastery of a skill.

Eighth Instructional-Design Principle

Do not expect computers alone to transform poor writers into good writers. Wong's (2001) review of the literature led to the conclusion that improvement in composition requires a combination of instruction in word processing, instruction in writing strategies, and a process approach to writing instruction; Berninger and Amtmann (2003) reached a similar conclusion based on their review of the literature. The University of Maryland Group (e.g., MacArthur & Graham, 1987) contributed much of the research supporting this conclusion. The added value of computers over and above pencil or pen should be evaluated for both the secretary and author roles in writing, and may be specific to revision rather than to the other cognitive processes in writing (Kellogg, 1994). Even if writing is computer-assisted, teachers still need to plan how they will explicitly teach all the processes of composing.

Evaluation/Modification Principles

Teachers must also monitor and evaluate how students respond to implemented teaching plans and modify the instructional program when students do not respond to it or make reasonable progress in writing. Contemporary instructional practice often relies on the "teachable moment" to change writing behavior; that is, as a teacher circulates and monitors, she notes problems individual students are facing and provides individually tailored instruction and feedback as to how each child is doing. Skillful use of teachable moments requires considerable teacher knowledge for knowing when and how to provide such individually tailored instruction. Teachers also make instructional decisions based on student performance over longer stretches of time than the momentary daily performance. This kind of decision making involves more than monitoring and feedback. It may require modification of the instructional plan. For example, if a student is not showing progress in the regular writing program that seems to be working well for other students, how might the program be modified and adapted to that student? Modifications might include any of the following: (1) adding missing components, (2) eliminating components that are not working, (3) adding additional practice or supplementary instruction, or (4) changing the way a skill is taught or practiced. What information should teachers take into account in brainstorming alternative instructional approaches that might be more effective? Unfortunately, teachers receive little preservice or inservice education on how to make such decisions.

The first step is to monitor on daily, weekly, and monthly bases how children are responding to instruction. The second step is to diagnose why a child who is not responding well to instruction may be having difficulty, that is, to identify the process(es) that are not developing normally. The third step is to decide, when necessary, on the basis of the results from the first two steps, how to modify the instructional program to meet the identified difficulty, and how to evaluate whether the modification is working. If the modification is not found to be effective, brainstorming additional approaches to modifying the instructional program should follow.

Next, for each of three developmental levels—the primary grades, the middle school grades, and the high school grade, we offer instructional-design principles based on research that might guide the teacher in planning instruction and setting instructional goals, and we discuss issues in instructional decision making during the evaluation/modification processes in writing instruction.

DEVELOPMENTAL FRAMEWORK

Beginning Writing in the Primary Grades

Instructional-Design Principles

EMERGING WRITING PHASE (PREKINDERGARTEN TO KINDERGARTEN)

One instructional goal is to help children gain the insight that talk can be represented in writing. Toward this end, invented spelling (Chomsky, 1979) is encouraged that helps children develop orthographic awareness that letters in written words represent sound segments (phonemes) in spoken words. (Orthographic awareness develops in tandem with phonological awareness of the component phonemes in spoken words.) Because letter names often contain a phoneme associated with a letter, children often discover many of the letter–phoneme correspondences on their own (Treiman, 1993). Thus, teachers who encourage emerging writers to use invented spelling are fostering orthographic and phonological awareness. A second instructional goal is to help children develop a willingness to use the written communication channel to express their thoughts, that is, to discover that writing can be used to communicate with others, just as talking can. A third instructional goal is to show children the links between writing and listening, talking, and reading. For further discussion of the contributions of listening, talking, and reading to emerging writing, see Berninger (2000). For further discussion of instructional issues in early literacy, see Englert, Raphael, and Mariage (1994). The following example illustrates how teachers can draw on children's listening, talking, and reading to develop writing in the early literacy classroom that integrates reading–writing instruction.

Every day, the teacher models the process of composing by thinking aloud her plans for writing, then, based on those plans, generates text for children, who watch the unfolding written text appear on the chalkboard. From time to time, the teacher pauses and asks children for assistance in spelling words. To do so, children consult a small card held in their hands, which has pictured words and letters that correspond to the first sound (phoneme) in each of the pictured words. First, they sound out the word, phoneme by phoneme; then, they look at their cards for a letter that could spell each of those sounds. Next, the teacher reviews the "What I think I can Say, and What I can say I can Write" strategy. She encourages children to talk out loud about what they would like to write about, and to generate text orally. Then she models for them how to say each word, sound by sound (phoneme by phoneme), and to look for the letters that go with each sound on the little card that each child has at his or her desk or work station. She models how the children can use this process to generate their own talk written down. What follows is a buzz of talk as children generate text orally and segment spoken words into sound units that can be converted into alphabet letters. When the session for composing is over, children then take turns reading what they have written to their classmates. From time to time, children also choose their favorite compositions, copy them over in their best handwriting, and illustrate them. These are shared with classmates, who read them to themselves and tell the authors what they liked about them. At the end of the year, each child publishes a book of his or her best writing, and these books are shared with teachers and the rest of the school in a book fair. For further discussion of this integrated reading–writing approach based on Clay (1982, 1985) but adapted by Katahira, see Traweek and Berninger (1997), Berninger (1998) and Berninger and Richards (2002).

CONVENTIONAL WRITING PHASE (FIRST TO THIRD GRADE)

The primary instructional goals are to develop accurate and automatic transcription (handwriting and spelling), fluent text generation (Berninger et al., 1992), and to transfer these low-level skills to growth in higher level composing (Berninger et al., 1997, 1998). Based on their research with primary-grade students, the University of Washington and the University of Maryland groups have developed a model of beginning writing, which they call the simple view of writing (Berninger & Amtmann, 2003; Berninger, Vaughan, et al., 2002). The foundational components are (a) *transcription* (handwriting or letter production, and spelling or word production) at one corner of the base of the writing triangle, and (b) *emerging executive functions* (for planning, monitoring, and revising) at the other corner of the base. Together, these two corner components support a third component—text generation, the main writing goal of the beginning writer, in a memory environment (the interior of the triangle that draws on short-term, working, and long-term memory processes). Text generation occurs at the word, sentence, and text levels. The instructional-design principles for developing conventional writing in beginning writers are derived from this simple view of writing model.

DEVELOPING THE TRANSCRIPTION COMPONENT

Numbered arrows provide instructional cues for developing the complex eye–motor–hand programs for letter writing. In addition to copying letters from such visual models, children need practice in writing letters from memory (after covering up the model letter, or from dictation), so that they create mental procedures for representing letters in memory and retrieve them from memory. Naming letters while learning to write them provides an additional memory retrieval cue. Practicing each letter once a day (rather than mindless, repeated copying of a few letters) avoids habituation, during which learning does not occur, but allows children to automatize the basic unit of written text production. For further discussion of these research-supported instructional-design principles, see Berninger et al. (1997) and Berninger (1998). Automatic

production of letters is necessary but not sufficient. Children must also spell words. Because written English is based on the alphabetic principle, correspondences between phonemes and spelling units should be taught explicitly. In English, predictable correspondences often involve two letters rather than a single letter (Venezky, 1970, 1999). The correspondences for letter(s) to phoneme used in reading are not identical to the correspondences for phoneme to letters used in spelling, and should be taught explicitly in the phoneme-to-letter(s) direction for spelling (see Berninger, 1998; Berninger et al., 1998).

DEVELOPING THE EXECUTIVE FUNCTION COMPONENT AND TEACHING FOR TRANSFER

Beginning writers have immature self-regulation functions; therefore, they require considerable other-regulation in the form of explicit teacher modeling and scaffolding (guided assistance) (Berninger & Richards, 2002). Providing composition prompts helps children plan a topic (what to write about) and typically results in longer compositions for at-risk writers than does free writing in journals. Beginning writers engage in little spontaneous revision. One way we have found to effectively encourage beginning writers to revise is to give them pencils without erasers and instruct them to cross out if they want to make a change. We emphasize that the first written production does not have to be perfect, and that it is perfectly normal to make changes as one writes. To teach for far transfer from transcription to text generation, explicit instruction in handwriting or spelling is always followed in the same session with an independent composing activity, followed by authors reading their compositions to peers (Berninger et al., 1997, 1998). Repeated practice in writing specific words in dictated sentences and explicit instruction in the syllable types of written English also helps at-risk spellers once they have had some instruction in alphabetic principle for going from spoken to written words (Berninger et al., 2000). Struggling beginning writers at the conventional stage also benefit from integrated reading–writing instruction (Abbott, Reed, Abbott, & Berninger, 1997).

DEVELOPING THE TEXT GENERATION COMPONENT

Teacher prompts to keep writing are effective when the child stops prematurely. For example, the teacher might say, "What else can you think of?," "Try to write one more thing," What happened next?" Beginning writers also benefit from explicit strategies for managing the text-generation process (see Harris & Graham, 1996). The PWRR strategy (Plan, Write, Review, and Revise; Berninger, Abbott, Whitaker, Sylvester, & Nolen, 1995) increased length and quality of composing and decreased writing resistance of the taught group versus control group of at-risk writers (at the transition from third to fourth grade, when writing requirements increase dramatically). Children in that study also benefited from teacher modeling of the planning, translating, and reviewing/revising processes, then providing guided assistance as children planned, translated, and reviewed and revised. Beginning writers also benefit from explicit instruction in planning and generating specific text structures. Englert and colleagues (e.g., Englert, Raphael, Anderson, Anthony, & Stevens, 1991; Englert, Stewart, & Hiebart, 1988) developed and validated Think–Plan–Write sheets that can be used to teach expository as well as narrative text structures to beginning writers. As teachers scaffold the process of text generation, they should consider the normal developmental progression of text structure for each genre (see Berninger, Fuller, & Whitaker, 1996). For example, if the child is spontaneously producing wheel structures, the next goal in the zone of proximal development should be to write webs (topic in the central hub) with elaboration on spokes of the wheel rather than to expect full-blown narrative or expository structure. Compared to controls, at-risk writers in third grade benefited from explicit cueing at the word-, sentence-, and text-levels as they learned to compose persuasive essays, demonstrating the benefits of combining explicit instruction in discourse genre and instruction aimed at all levels of language (Berninger, Vaughan, et al., 2002).

Evaluation/Modification Principles

For the first step of evaluating progress, beginning writers like to see visible records of their progress. For example, they might color-in a rung of a Writing Rocket for each composition they complete (see Berninger, 1998). They might also graph on a daily basis the number of words written. Teachers can then monitor the length of their compositions. Beginning writers also enjoy rereading their compositions kept in a Writing Portfolio that teachers can review to evaluate according to developmentally appropriate criteria whether children are making reasonable progress in their writing (Valencia, 1998). For the second step of diagnosing why a child might not be responding well to instruction, teachers should try to tease apart whether the underlying problem is related to problems in handwriting legibility, automaticity of letter production, and/or spelling (all of which interfere with development of composition in beginning writers; see Berninger & Amtmann, 2003, for review). Alternatively, some children have trouble finding ideas to write about, or finding the language to express their ideas. Their bottleneck is not in transcription but in text generation, as evidence by the diagnostic procedure of asking them to generate a text orally, without writing it down. If children cannot do that even when transcription requirements are removed, they need instructional activities designed to promote idea generation and oral expression of their ideas. For the third step, depending on where the bottleneck is found in the second step, the teacher decides how to modify the instructional program to meet the identified difficulty, and how to evaluate whether the modification is working. A general principle is that during the primary grades, early intervention to remediate handwriting and spelling problems is still possible; teachers should not expect that simply having the children use computer keyboards to bypass these problems is a sufficient solution.

Developing Writing in the Upper Elementary and Middle School Grades

Instructional-Design Principles

DEVELOPING THE TEXT GENERATION COMPONENT

By the middle of elementary school, many, but not all, children have sufficient transcription skills and benefit by focus on text generation and executive function components. Hillocks's (1984, 1986) meta-analyses showed that instruction in sentence syntax, the main focus of much composition training in an earlier era, does not generalize to improved quality of compositions. Explicit instruction aimed at the discourse level (content, organization, clarity, etc.) is also required. In three empirical studies (e.g., Whitaker, Berninger, Johnston, & Swanson, 1994) we found intraindividual differences in how well the word, sentence, and discourse levels of composing were developed in individual intermediate-grade writers. Word-level skill (vocabulary choice) did not predict sentence-level skill (syntax) or discourse-level skill (quality of content and organization), and sentence-level skill did not predict discourse-level skill. Therefore, instruction aimed at all levels of language—word, sentence, and discourse—in written text will address the less developed levels of language for all students, who vary considerably in which levels are less developed. For text generation at the discourse level, explicit instruction in the text structure for the specific genre of writing is necessary (Englert, Raphael, Fear, & Anderson, 1988; Englert, Stewart, & Hiebart, 1988; Graham & Harris, 1992; Harris & Graham, 1992; Wong, 1997).

DEVELOPING THE SELF-REGULATION COMPONENT

Developing writers continue to need explicit instruction in the planning (e.g., De la Paz & Graham, 1997; Graham & Harris, 1996) and reviewing/revising (e.g., Graham, 1997) components of composing. Graphic organizers for planning and reviewing/revising (Calfee & Patrick, 1995) are effective in teaching these executive functions for regulating the composing process (Berninger, Fuller, & Abbott, 2001; Berninger, Vaughan, et al., 2002). Visual–spatial graphical displays assist developing writers in planning their ideas, translating their ideas into written language, and reviewing and revising their compositions to improve them. This integration of visual–spatial and linguistic representations in composing is consistent with the revised Hayes (1996, 2000) model of composing.

At this stage of writing development, students still benefit from teacher-provided prompts, because they are not fully self-regulated writers. In addition to the general prompts discussed for beginning writers (e.g., to write one more thing), developing writers benefit from more specific prompts based on the 21 algorithms normally developing writers use to write the next sentence in text, for example, to add a physical description, to explain how a character is feeling, to add a qualifying statement, or to add an example to illustrate a point (see Berninger et al., 1996).

At this developmental stage, writers also benefit from self-regulated strategy development (SRSD), which has been found to be more effective than a control treatment (Sawyer, Graham, & Harris, 1992) and to transfer across settings and teachers (Sexton, Harris, & Graham, 1998). For example, teaching goal setting and a strategy for refuting counterarguments was effective in improving the quality of composing in seventh and eighth graders (Page-Voth & Graham, 1999). If dictation is used as a procedural facilitator in the fifth through seventh grades, then explicit planning in advance planning is also necessary (De la Paz & Graham, 1997). Although writers generally find it easier to repair spelling, capitalization, and punctuation, a revision strategy for coordinating specific elements of text led to more frequent revising and more meaning-based changes to text in fifth and sixth graders (De la Paz et al., 1998). Table 9.6 in Berninger and Richards (2002) summarizes the validated strategies, organized by developmental stage, from research of the Michigan State, University of Maryland, and Simon Fraser groups. Writers at this stage have a tendency to use a strategy of telling what they know instead of transforming what they know for the audience reading their text (Scardamalia & Bereiter, 1989). More research is needed on how interactive dialogues and SRSD may improve authors' ability to use knowledge-transforming strategies at this and subsequent stages of writing development.

DEVELOPING COORDINATED SKILLS IN FUNCTIONAL SYSTEMS

As with beginning writing, developing writing continues to draw on reading–writing connections (Fitzgerald & Shanahan, 2000; Nelson & Calfee, 1998). Research on the most effective ways to teach *reading–writing connections* is only in its infancy (e.g., Berninger, Abbott, Abbott, Graham, & Richards, 2001). At this developmental stage, teachers should also explicitly teach strategies for listening to teachers talk and taking notes that are read later when studying for tests and for reading source material to write reports. Teachers should also explicitly teach strategies for long-term management of multistep writing activities.

In many states, students take their first high-stakes test in writing during the intermediate grades. Some schools are experimenting with extended-day models to provide students at risk for passing these writing assessments extra practice and supplementary assistance. In one empirical evaluation of an extended-day model, writing clubs were offered before or after school. The curriculum integrated word play; explicit instruction in handwriting, spelling, and the cognitive processes of composing; graphic organizers for planning, writing, and reviewing/revising; instruction aimed at all levels of language; and writers' publication in a monthly newspaper. Students in the clubs outperformed matched control groups in quality of composing on the state-administered high-stakes test and an experimenter-administered standardized test of writing (Berninger, Fulton, & Abbott, 2001). This example serves as a reminder that changing student performance outcomes in writing depends on integrating many research-supported instructional components in an instructional program de-

signed for a particular school setting and purpose.

Evaluation/Modification Principles

For the first step, students should graph daily their performance for specified writing goals (number of illegible letters and words, and misspelled words in daily compositions; paragraph organization—presence of a topic sentence, number of supporting details, logical coherence of the paragraph, etc.). In addition, writing portfolios should be kept and jointly reviewed by students and teachers to evaluate improvement on specific writing goals (Valencia, 1998). For the second step, teachers need to evaluate how the writing process may be breaking down for students who are not showing reasonable progress. At this developmental stage, teachers should try to tease apart whether the bottleneck is in insufficiently developed transcription skills, problems in generating ideas, problems in word choice, problems in written sentence construction (including syntax), problems in organization of paragraphs or overall discourse, or problems in repairing only surface features and not text meaning during revision. The third step depends on the outcome of the teacher's second-step analysis. See Berninger (1998) for planning forms for such modifications, if necessary.

Increasingly Skilled Writing in High School

Instructional-Design Principles

First, teachers should develop an organization plan across multiple sessions within a week and across weeks that meshes with the organization of the high school into periods per day and week, and across weeks for grading periods (see Wong et al., 1991, 1994, 1996, 1997). For example, in working with high school students in modified language arts blocks who have problems with writing, Wong and colleagues use a prewriting phase to train students to achieve prerequisite accuracy and speed criteria in keyboarding (e.g., 15–30 words per minute), so that the students can use a computer for the subsequent composing activities. This prewriting phase usually lasts 1 or 2 months, in which three 50-minute periods per week are devoted to keyboard training. Automaticity in keyboarding (Bowers, 2001) is as critical to writing development as is automaticity in letter production. Phase I sessions focus on planning and last 1 or 2 months (three 50-minute periods per week); explicit instruction in planning is provided, and students practice planning with multiple writing topics, mostly yoked to assignments in the regular classroom, but also including some free choice topics to promote writer's autonomy. Phase II sessions focus on composing with computer word-processing programs and written plans generated in prior sessions and continue for the same number of weeks as Phase I, generally 1 week per writing topic. Phase III sessions focus on reading first drafts and revising them, with input from teachers and other peers, and continue the same number of weeks as Phases I and II, generally 1 week per writing topic. Adolescents are able to work on the same assignments over longer stretches of time than during middle childhood, when assignments may be structured to cycle through the Phase I planning, Phase II composing, and Phase III reviewing and revising in three consecutive sessions for the same topic (Berninger, Vaughan, et al., 2002).

Second, teachers should structure each session to include multiple instructional components (see Wong et al., 1991, 1994, 1996, 1997). For example, each Phase I session may consist of 25 minutes of explicit teacher-modeling of the planning process, with the teacher thinking aloud as she plans for a specific writing topic and discourse genre (e.g., opinion or compare and contrast essay) and leading interactive student dialogues in which she engages students in discussion to clarify what the planning process entails. For the last 25 minutes, writers engage in student–student interactive dialogues in which they mutually generate ideas and complete a written Think–Plan Sheet relevant to the topic and discourse genre at hand. Each Phase II session consists of 50 minutes of composing at the computer, with the author using teacher-designed prompt cards for the discourse genre

being practiced, and the teacher circulating among student authors to provide individual scaffolding. Two copies of the composition are produced at the end of each session, one for the teacher to evaluate and provide written feedback to the student, and the other for the student to use in Phase III reviewing and revising. For the first 25 minutes of each Phase III revising session, the teacher reads a Phase II composition aloud, hums when she comes to an unclear portion of text, and engages students in interactive dialogue to brainstorm how to make that text clearer. For the last 25 minutes, students work in the same pairs as in Phase I for that topic and genre, and highlight the portions of each other's compositions that are unclear. Then they alternate in roles of critic and editor to provide constructive feedback for making the text clear.

Third, although adolescents who are poor writers are likely to have problems with lower order skills (e.g., spelling, capitalization, and punctuation) (Houck & Billingsley, 1989) and higher order cognitive and metacognitive processes (e.g., planning, text generation, self-monitoring, reading to detect problems in text, and revising) (Graham, 1997; Graham et al., 1998), in order to motivate them to write, it is best to focus first on high-level skills and defer work on lower order skills until the end of the revision phase (see Wong, 2000). Strategy instruction aimed at learning to learn is developmentally appropriate for adolescents (Alley & Deschler, 1979; Schumaker et al., in press).

Fourth, teach explicit planning, composing, and reviewing/revising strategies for specific discourse genre (Wong, 1997; e.g., opinion essays, Wong et al., 1996; compare and contrast essays, Wong et al., 1997). The teacher should model, by thinking aloud, explicit strategies for planning. For example, for planning an essay on the "scariest event in my life," the strategy might include searching long-term memory, reliving the event in one's mind's eye, and rekindling emotions associated with the event. In modeling the planning process, teachers should emphasize the relevance of planning to real-life situations (e.g., planning to attend a rock concert). This linking of the planning process to other activities may enhance its far transfer to other writing activities and other life situations. Learning to plan ahead is an important developmental goal for adolescents in general. Role playing may used during planning to model opposing points of view for writing both sides of an argument in an opinion (persuasive) essay. Teachers should use interactive dialogue to teach planning and revision. Interactive dialogue enhances cognitive engagement in the writing process and also provides feedback from the perspective of audience. Student pairs also should engage in interactive dialogues during planning and revision. Think–Plan Sheets can be used for student–student interactive dialogue during the planning phase (see Wong, 2000, Fig. 1, for opinion essays, and Fig. 2, for compare and contrast essays) and Read–Think–Plan Sheets can be used during the revision phase. During composing, students can use teacher-designed prompt cards with vocabulary and phrases specific to different kinds of discourse genre (see Wong et al., 1997, for examples), and teachers can circulate to provide individually tailored scaffolding.

Fifth, continue to provide explicit instruction in reading–writing connections, especially for note taking during lectures and for specific kinds of reports, use of notes in studying for written tests, strategies for writing on essay tests, and specific kinds of report writing.

Evaluation/Modification Principles

For the first step, at the end of each composing session, teachers evaluate specific target writing skills (clarity—lack of ambiguity, appropriateness to topic, thematic salience, organization of ideas, etc.) on a scale of 1 to 5; students graph scores for draft 1 and draft 2 to see a visible record of improvement and to target skills that need additional work. In addition, teachers periodically rate students' attitudes toward writing, metacognitions about writing, and writers' self-efficacy (see Wong et al., 1996, for questionnaires), and *students complete self-monitoring checklists* (see Wong, 1997) at the end of the Phase I planning unit, the Phase II composing unit, and the Phase III

revising unit. For the second step, teachers note which students are not responding well to the explicit, systematic program of writing instruction, then troubleshoot to determine which of the processes are problematic for an individual student. At the high school level, the most important processes to include in this analysis of student response are planning, reading/revising, self-monitoring, self-regulation, and executive control processes in general (see Hooper, Swartz, de Kruif, & Montgomery, 2002). For the third step, teachers brainstorm and problem-solve how to adapt instruction to meet the problems of individual students. This instructional decision making draws on the cognitive processes of the teacher, who reflects on how each student responds to instruction, and modifies instruction if necessary.

CONCLUDING REMARKS

Readers may wonder why this chapter in a handbook on language and literacy has not focused on language processes. The reason is that, in recent years, cognitive paradigms have dominated research on teaching composition to children and youth. Nevertheless, some research specific to language processes in children's compositions has appeared in the literature. For example, McCutchen (1986, 1987) conducted in-depth developmental analyses of local and cohesive discourse ties in text, and the resulting psychological coherence. Berninger and colleagues studied levels of language in planning, generating, and reviewing/revising text at the word, sentence, and text levels (e.g., Whitaker et al., 1994), the relationship between the current sentence and prior text (Berninger et al., 1996), and the developmental stages in narrative and expository text structures (Berninger et al., 1996). Clearly, more research is needed on the language processes in composing.

Considerable progress has been made in understanding the cognitive processes in writing and in articulating cognitive principles of instruction, but much work remains to implement this knowledge more widely in teaching practice. More research is needed on teachers' cognitive processes in planning implementations, translating research findings, and evaluating/revising student performance related to composition. The next frontiers in research on the cognitive processes in writing should focus on writing to learn, the reading–writing connections, and the role of imagination in composing. Just as children first learn to read and then read to learn (Chall, 1979), children first learn to write and then write to learn (Klein, 1999). According to Klein, writing is used to learn in four ways: (1) to generate new knowledge, (2) to consider the implications of existing knowledge, (3) to construct new organization schemes for existing knowledge, and (4) to problem-solve for domain-specific content and goals. Reading–writing connections are complex and need to be studied for different developmental levels, student characteristics, and writing goals. Cognitive approaches to writing have emphasized the role of memory—reactivating the past—rather than imagination—envisioning the future that does not yet exist. We know little about the source of ideas. It is unlikely that idea generation is merely a matter of revisiting representations in memory (Berninger, 1999). According to Kellogg (1994), the unique cognitive activity in writing is its meaning making, which relies on two states of consciousness. The first, the semiconscious dream state, draws on a creative flow (the stream of thought) and is vulnerable temporally to interruptions. The second, a conscious, directed thinking state, has spatial capacity limitations (the amount of mental activity that can be the object of conscious attention). Whereas the first thrives on mental play, the latter requires mental work (hence, the term "working memory") (Berninger & Richards, 2002). The challenge of future research is to develop and validate instructional approaches that simultaneously foster both mental play and mental work in beginning, developing, and increasingly skilled writers.

ACKNOWLEDGMENTS

Preparation of this chapter was supported by Grant No. 639110 from the Social Sciences and Research Council of Canada to Bernice Y. L. Wong and by Grant No. HD 25858-11 from the National Institute of Child Health and Human Development to Virginia W. Berninger.

REFERENCES

Abbott, S., Reed, L., Abbott, R., & Berninger, V. (1997). Year-long balanced reading/writing tutorial: A design experiment used for dynamic assessment. *Learning Disabilities Quarterly, 20,* 249–263.

Alamargot, D., & Chanquay, L. (2001). *Through the models of writing.* Dordrecht, The Netherlands: Kluwer Academic.

Alley, G., & Deschler, D. (1979). *Teaching the learning-disabled adolescent: Strategies and methods.* Denver, CO: Love.

Applebee, N. A. (2000). Alternate models of writing development. In R. Indrisano, & J. R. Squire (Eds.), *Perspectives on writing* (pp. 90–111). Newark, DE: International Reading Association.

Aulls, M. W. (1978). *Developmental and remedial reading in the middle grades.* Boston: Allyn & Bacon.

Baddeley, A. D. (1979). Working memory and reading. In P. Kolers, M. Wrolstad, & H. Bouma (Eds.), *Processing visible language* (pp. 355–370). New York: Plenum Press.

Beal, C. (1996). The role of comprehension monitoring in children's revision. *Educational Psychology Review, 8,* 219–238.

Berninger, V. (1998). *Process assessment of the learner: Guides for reading and writing intervention.* San Antonio, TX: Psychological Corporation.

Berninger, V. (1999). Coordinating transcription and text generation in working memory during composing: Automatized and constructive processes. *Learning Disability Quarterly, 22,* 99–112.

Berninger, V. (2000). Development of language by hand and its connections to language by ear, mouth, and eye. *Topics in Language Disorders, 20,* 65–84.

Berninger, V., & Abbott, R. (2001). Developmental and individual variability in reading and writing acquisition: A developmental neuropsychological perspective. In D. Molfese & U. Kirk (Eds.), *Developmental variability in language and learning* (pp. 275–308). Hillsdale, NJ: Erlbaum.

Berninger, V., Abbott, R., Abbott, S., Graham, S., & Richards, T. (2001). Writing and reading: Connections between language by hand and language by eye. *Journal of Learning Disabilities 35,* 39–56.

Berninger, V., Abbott, R., Whitaker, D., Sylvester, L., & Nolen, S. (1995). Integrating low-level skills and high-level skills in treatment protocols for writing disabilities. *Learning Disability Quarterly, 18,* 293–309.

Berninger, V., & Amtmann, D. (2003). Preventing written expression disabilities through early and continuing assessment and intervention for handwriting and/or spelling problems: Research into practice. In H. L. Swanson, K. R. Harris, & S. Graham (Eds.), *Handbook of learning disabilities* (pp. 345–363). New York: Guilford Press.

Berninger, V., Fuller, F., & Whitaker, D. (1996). A process approach to writing development across the life span. *Educational Psychology Review, 8,* 193–218.

Berninger, V., Fulton, C., & Abbott, R. (2001, December). *Second-grade reading clubs and fourth-grade writing clubs: Empirical evaluation of extended learning for students at-risk for passing WASL.* Seattle: Washington Educational Research Association.

Berninger, V., & Richards, T. (2002). *Brain literacy for educators and psychologists.* New York: Academic Press.

Berninger, V., Vaughan, K., Abbott, R., Abbott, S., Brooks, A., Rogan, L., et al. (1997). Treatment of handwriting fluency problems in beginning writing: Transfer from handwriting to composition. *Journal of Educational Psychology, 89,* 652–666.

Berninger, V., Vaughan, K., Abbott, R., Begay, K., Byrd, K., Curtin, G., et al. (2002). Teaching spelling and composition alone and together: Implications for the simple view of writing. *Journal of Educational Psychology, 94,* 291–304.

Berninger, V., Vaughan, K., Abbott, R., Brooks, A., Abbott, S., Reed, E., et al. (1998). Early intervention for spelling problems: Teaching spelling units of varying size within a multiple connections framework. *Journal of Educational Psychology, 90,* 587–605.

Berninger, V., Vaughan, K., Abbott, R., Brooks, A., Begay, K., Curtin, G., Byrd, K., & Graham, S. (2000). Language-based spelling instruction: Teaching children to make multiple connections between spoken and written words. *Learning Disability Quarterly, 23,* 117–135.

Berninger, V., Yates, C., Cartwright, A., Rutberg, J., Remy, E., & Abbott, R. (1992). Lower-level developmental skills in beginning writing. *Reading and Writing: An Interdisciplinary Journal, 4,* 257–280.

Bowers, P. (2001). Exploration of basis for rapid naming's relationship to reading. In M. Wolf (Ed.), *Dyslexia, fluency, and the brain* (pp. 41–63). Timonium, MD: York Press.

Britton, J. (1978). The composing processes and the functions of writing. In C. Cooper & D. Odell (Eds.), *Research on composing: Points of departure* (pp. 13–28). Urbana, IL: National Council of Teachers of English.

Butterfield, E. (1994). *Children's writing: Toward a process theory of development of skilled writing* (pp. 57–81). Greenwich, CT: JAI Press.

Calfee, R., & Patrick, C. (1995). *Teach our children well: Bringing K–12 education into the 21st century.* Stanford, CA: Stanford Alumni Association.

Calkins, L. (1986). *The art of teaching writing.* Portsmouth, NH: Heinemann.

Chall, J. (1979). The great debate: Ten years later with a modest proposal for reading stages. In L. Resnick, & P. Weaver (Eds.), *Theory and practice of early reading* (Vol. 1, pp. 22–25). Hillsdale, NJ: Erlbaum.

Chomsky, C. (1979). Reading, writing, and phonology. *Harvard Educational Review, 40,* 287–309.

Clay, M. (1982). Research update: Leaning and teaching writing: A developmental perspective. *Language Arts, 59,* 65–70.

Clay, M. (1985). *The early detection of reading difficulties* (3rd ed.). Auckland, NZ: Heinemann.

Crowhurst, M (1987). Cohesion in argument and narration at three grade levels. *Research in the Teaching of English, 21,* 185–230.

De la Paz, S., & Graham, S. (1997). Effects of dictation and advanced planning instruction on the composing of students with writing and learning problems. *Journal of Educational Psychology, 89,* 203–222.

De la Paz, S., Swanson, P., & Graham, S. (1998). The contribution of executive control to the revising by students with writing and learning difficulties. *Journal of Educational Psychology, 90,* 448–460.

Englert, C. S. (1992). Writing instruction from a sociocultural perspective: The holistic, dialogue, and social enterprise of writing. *Journal of Learning Disabilities, 25,* 153–172.

Englert, C., & Raphael, T. (1988). Constructing well formed prose: Process, structure, and metacognitive knowledge. *Exceptional Children, 54,* 513–521.

Englert, C. S., Raphael, T., Anderson, L., Anthony, H., & Stevens, D. (1991). Making strategies and self-talk visible: Writing instruction in regular and special education classrooms. *American Educational Research Journal, 28,* 337–372.

Englert, S., Raphael, T., Fear, K., & Anderson, L. (1988). Students' metacognitive knowledge about how to write informational tests. *Learning Disability Quarterly, 11,* 18–46.

Englert, C. S., Raphael, T., & Mariage, T. (1994). Developing a school-based discourse for literacy learning: A principled search for understanding. *Learning Disability Quarterly, 17,* 2–32.

Englert, C., S., Stewart, S., & Hiebart, E. (1988). Young writers' use of text structure in expository text generation. *Journal of Educational Psychology, 8,* 143–151.

Fitzgerald, J. (1987). Research on revision in writing. Review of Educational Research, 57, 481–506.

Fitzgerald, J., & Shanahan, T. (2000). Reading and writing relations and their development. *Educational Psychologist, 35,* 39–50.

Flood, J., & Lapp, D. (2000). Teaching writing in urban schools: Cognitive processes, curriculum resources, and the missing links—management and grouping. In R. Indrisano & J. R. Squire (Eds.), *Perspectives on writing* (pp. 233–250). Newark, DE: International Reading Association.

Gambrell, L. B., & Morrow, L. M. (1996). Creating motivating contexts for literacy learning. In L. Baker, P. Afflenbach, & D. Reinking (Eds.), *Developing engaged readers in home and school communities* (pp. 115–136). Hillsdale, NJ: Erlbaum.

Gathercole, S. E., & Baddeley, A. D. (1993). *Working memory and language.* Hove, UK: Erlbaum.

Graham, S. (1997). Executive control in the revising of students with learning and writing difficulties. *Journal of Educational Psychology, 89,* 223–234.

Graham, S., & Harris, K. R. (1992). Self-instructional strategy development: Programmatic research in writing. In B. Y. L. Wong (Ed.), *Contemporary intervention research in learning disabilities: An international perspective* (pp. 47–64). New York: Springer-Verlag.

Graham, S., Harris, K. R., MacArthur, C., & Schwartz, S. (1998). Writing instruction. In B. Y. L. Wong (Ed.), *Learning about learning disabilities* (2nd ed., pp. 391–423). San Diego: Academic Press.

Graham, S., MacArthur, C., & Schwartz, S. (1995). Effects of goal setting and procedural facilitation on the revising behavior and writing performances of students with writing and learning problems. *Journal of Educational Psychology, 87,* 230–240.

Graham, S., Schwartz, S. & McArthur, C. (1993). Knowledge of writing and the composing process, attitude "toward" writing, and self-efficacy for students with and without learning disabilities. *Journal of Learning Disabilities, 26,* 237–249.

Graves, D. (1983). *Writing: Teachers and children at work.* Exeter, NH: Heinemann.

Harris, K. R., & Graham, S. (1992). Self-regulated strategy development: A part of the writing process. In M. Pressley, K. R. Harris, & J. T. Guthrie (Eds.), *Promoting academic competence and literacy in school* (pp. 277–309). San Diego: Academic Press.

Harris, K. R., & Graham, S. (1996). *Making the writing process work: Strategies for composition and self-regulation.* Cambridge, MA: Brookline.

Hayes, J. R. (1996). A new framework for understanding cognition and affect in writing. In C. M. Levy & S. Randall (Eds.), *The science of writing: Theories, methods, individual differences, and applications* (pp. 1–27). Mahwah, NJ: Erlbaum.

Hayes, J. R. (2000). A new framework for understanding cognition and affect in writing. In R. Indrisano & J. R. Squire (Eds.), *Perspectives on writing* (pp. 6–44). Newark, DE: International Reading Association.

Hayes, J. R., & Flower, L. S. (1980). Identifying the organization of writing processes. In L. W. Gregg & E. R. Steinberg (Eds.), *Cognitive processes in writing* (pp. 3–30). Hillsdale, NJ: Erlbaum.

Hayes, J. R., Flower, L. S., Schriver, K. A., Stratman, J., & Carey, L. (1987). Cognitive processes in revision. In S. Rosenberg (Ed.), *Advances in applied psycholinguistics: Vol. 2. Reading, writing, and language processes* (pp. 176–240). New York: Cambridge University Press.

Hillocks, G. (1984). What works in teaching composition: A metaanalysis of experimental treatment studies. *American Journal of Education,* 133–170.

Hillocks, G. (1986). *Research on written composition: New directions for teaching.* Urbana, IL: National Conference on Research in English.

Holliway, D., & McCutchen, D. (in press). Audience perspective in young writers' composing and revising: Reading as the reader. In L. Allal, L. Chanquay, P. Langy, & Y. Rouiller (Eds.), *Revision of written language: Cognitive and instructional processes.* New York: Kluwer Academic.

Hooper, S., Swartz, C., de Kruif, R., & Montgomery, J. (2002). Executive functions in elementary school children with and without problems in written expression. *Journal of Learning Disabilities, 35,* 57–68.

Houck, C., & Billingsley, B. (1989). Written expression of students with and without learning disabilities: Differences across the grades. *Journal of Learning Disabilities, 22,* 561–568.

Humes, A. (1983). Research on the composing process. *Review of Educational Research, 53,* 201–216.

Kellogg, R. (1994). *The psychology of writing.* New York: Oxford University Press.

Klein, P. (1999). Reopening inquiry into cognitive processes in writing-to-learn. *Educational Psychology Review, 11,* 203–270.

Kuhl, J. (1985). Volitional mediators of cognition-behavior consistency: Self-regulatory processes and action versus state orientation. In J. Kuhl & J. Beckmann (Eds.), *Action control: From cognition to behavior* (pp. 101–128). New York: Springer.

MacArthur, C., & Graham, S. (1987). Learning disabled students' composing with three methods: Handwriting, dictation, and word processing. *Journal of Special Education, 21,* 2–42.

Mather, N., Bos, C., & Babur, N. (2001). Perceptions and knowledge of preservice and inservice teachers about early literacy instruction. *Journal of Learning Disabilities, 4,* 471–482.

McCutchen, D. (1986). Domain knowledge and linguistic knowledge in the development of writing ability. *Journal of Memory and Language, 25,* 431–444.

McCutchen, D. (1987). Children's discourse skill: Form and modality requirements of schooled writing. *Discourse Processes, 10,* 267–286.

McCutchen, D. (1994). The magical number three, plus or minus two: Working memory in writing. In J. S. Carlson (Series Ed.) & E. Butterfield (Vol. Ed.), *Children's writing: Toward a process theory of development of skilled writing* (pp. 57–81). Greenwich, CT: JAI Press.

McCutchen, D. (1996). A capacity theory of writing: Working memory in composition. *Educational Psychology Review, 8,* 299–325.

Montague, M., Graves, A., & Leavell, A. (1991). Planning, procedural facilitation, and narrative composition of junior high students with learning disabilities. *Learning Disabilities Research and Practice, 6,* 219–224.

Nelson, N., & Calfee, R. (Eds.). (1998). The reading–writing connection viewed historically. In *Ninety-seventh yearbook of the National Society for the Study of Education* (Part II, pp. 1–52). Chicago: NSSE.

Page-Voth, V., & Graham, S. (1999). Effects of goal setting and strategy use on writing performance and self-efficacy of students with writing and learning problems. *Journal of Educational Psychology, 91,* 230–240.

Sawyer, R., Graham, S., & Harris, K. (1992). Direct teaching, strategy instruction, and strategy instruction with explicit self-regulation: Effects on the composition skills and self-efficacy of students with learning disabilities. *Journal of Educational Psychology, 84,* 340–352.

Scardamalia, M., & Bereiter, C. (1983). The development of evaluative, diagnostic, and remedial capabilities in children's composing. In M. Martlew (Ed.), *The psychology of written language: Development and educational perspectives* (pp. 67–95). London: Wiley.

Scardamalia, M., & Bereiter, C. (1989). Knowledge telling and knowledge transforming in written composition. In S. Rosenberg (Ed.), *Advances in applied psycholinguistics: Vol. 2: Reading, writing, and language learning* (pp. 142–175). Cambridge, UK: Cambridge, University Press.

Schmidt, J., Deschler, D., Schumaker, J., & Alley, G. (1989). Effects of generalization instruction on the written language performance of adolescents with learning disabilities in the mainstream classroom. *Reading, Writing, and Learning Disabilities, 4,* 291–309.

Schumaker, J., Deschler, D., & McKnight, P. (in press). Ensuring success in the secondary general education curriculum through the use of teaching routines. In G. Stover, M. Shinn, & H. Walker (Eds.), *Interventions for achievement and behavior problems.* Washington, DC: National Association of School Psychologists.

Schumaker, J., & Sheldon, J. (1985). *The Sentence Writing Strategy: Instructor's manual.* Lawrence: University of Kansas Center for Research on Learning.

Sexton, M., Harris, K., & Graham, S. (1998). Self-regulated strategy development and the writing process: Effects on essay writing and attributions. *Exceptional Children, 64,* 295–311.

Singer, B. (1995). Written language development and disorders: Selected principles, patterns, and intervention possibilities. *Topics in Language Disorders, 16,* 83–93.

Singer, B., & Bashir, A. (1999). What are executive functions and self regulation and what do they have to do with language-learning disorders? *Language, Speech, and Hearing Services in Schools, 30,* 265–273.

Singer, B., & Bashir, A. (2004). An approach to helping students with language disabilities learn to write. In E. R. Silliman & L. C. Wilkinson (Eds.), *Language and literacy learning.* New York: Guilford Press.

Swanson, H. L., & Berninger, V. (1996). Individual differences in children's working memory and writing skills. *Journal of Experimental Child Psychology, 63,* 358–385.

Traweek, D., & Berninger, V. (1997). Comparison of beginning literacy programs: Alternative paths to the same learning outcome. *Learning Disability Quarterly, 20,* 160–168.

Treiman, R. (1993). *Beginning to spell.* Cambridge, UK: Cambridge University Press.

University of Kansas Center for Research on Learning. (n. d.). *The expression strand: Fundamentals in the sentence writing strategy, proficiency in the sentence writing strategy, and paragraph writing strategy.* Lawrence, KS: Edge Enterprises.

Valencia, S. (1998). *Literacy portfolios in action.* Fort Worth, TX: Harcourt Brace.

Venezky, R. (1970). *The structure of English orthography.* The Hague: Mouton.

Venezky, R. (1999). *The American way of spelling.* New York: Guilford Press.

Vygotsky, L. (1978). *Mind and society.* Cambridge, MA: Harvard University Press.

Whitaker, D., Berninger, V., Johnston, J., & Swanson, L. (1994). Intraindividual differences in levels of language in intermediate grade writers: Implications for the translating process. *Learning and Individual Differences, 6,* 107–130.

Wong, B. Y. L. (1989). Critical knowledge and skills required in effective teaching and management of individual differences in the general education classroom. *Teacher Education and Special Education, 12,* 161–163.

Wong, B. Y. L. (1994). Instructional parameters promoting transfer of learned strategies in students with learning disabilities. *Learning Disability Quarterly, 17,* 110–120.

Wong, B. Y. L. (1997). Research on genre-specific strategies for enhancing writing in adolescents with learning disabilities. *Learning Disability Quarterly, 20,* 140–159.

Wong, B. Y. L. (1998). Analyses of instrinsic and extrinsic problems in use of the scaffolding metaphor in learning disabilities intervention research: An introduction. *Journal of Learning Disabilities, 31,* 340–343.

Wong, B. Y. L. (2000). Writing strategies for instruction for expository essays for adolescents with and without learning disabilities. *Topics in Language Disorders, 20,* 29–44.

Wong, B. Y. L. (2001). Pointers for literacy instruction from educational technology and research on writing instruction. *Elementary School Journal, 101,* 359–369.

Wong, B. Y. L., Butler, D. L., Ficzere, S. A., & Kuperis, S. (1996). Teaching adolescents with learning disabilities and low achievers to plan, write, and revise opinion essays. *Journal of Learning Disabilities, 29,* 197–212.

Wong, B. Y. L., Butler, D. L., Ficzere, S. A., & Kuperis, S. (1997). Teaching adolescents with learning disabilities and low achievers to plan, write, and revise compare- and contrast- essays. *Learning Disabilities Research and Practice, 12,* 2–15.

Wong, B. Y. L., Butler, D. L., Ficzere, S. A., Kuperis, S., & Corden, M. (1994). Teaching problem learners revision skills and sensitivity to audience through two instructional modes: Student–teacher versus student–student interactive dialogues. *Learning Disabilities Research and Practice, 9,* 78–90.

Wong, B. Y. L., Wong, R., Darlington, D., & Jones, W. (1991). Interactive teaching: An effective way to teach revision skills to adolescents with learning disabilities. *Learning Disabilities Research and Practice, 6,* 117–127.

SPELLING

29

Developmental Variations in Spelling

Comparing Typical and Poor Spellers

MARIE CASSAR
REBECCA TREIMAN

Most children acquire basic reading and writing skills during the first few years of elementary school. For some children, however, even the smallest advance toward learning to read and write requires extraordinary effort. Such children are often labeled delayed, disabled, or dyslexic. Many researchers (Brady, 1997; Frith, 1985; Goswami & Bryant, 1990; Liberman, Rubin, Duques, & Carlisle, 1985; Stanovich, 1992) suggest that deficits in phonological skill underlie these children's difficulties. In this chapter, we focus on children with dyslexia and beginning spelling development using this phonological deficit hypothesis as a framework. We begin with a short discussion of typical beginners' spelling development and the importance of phonological skills. We then consider studies that compare the phonological skills of children with dyslexia and typical children in tasks other than spelling. Studies that have compared children with dyslexia and typical children's spellings of real words and nonwords are then reviewed. That discussion leads to a consideration of orthographic knowledge

and its influence on spelling skill. The importance of interactions between phonological and orthographic skills for typical word-knowledge development is considered next. The chapter concludes with a discussion about possible inefficiencies in the interaction of phonological and orthographic skills for children with dyslexia.

Studies that have examined the spelling of children with poor reading and spelling skills often compare such children to younger children with similar levels of spelling or reading skill. We focus on studies that compare such skill-matched groups, because they are more informative than studies that compare same-age groups of children. In skill-matched comparisons, researchers can identify the similarities and differences between the skills of poor readers and spellers, and those of typical children. Age-matched comparisons primarily confirm the skill differences between children with dyslexia and their same-age peers; they do not show whether and how the pattern of performance for children with dyslexia differs from that of typical children. Indeed, Bryant and Impey (1986) argued for skill-matched rather than age-matched comparisons when stating that "if the causes of a child's reading difficulties are to be traced back to his or her peculiar reading patterns . . . then these patterns must be different from those of other children whose progress in reading is quite normal" (p. 123).

SPELLING DEVELOPMENT

To become a good speller, one must learn how the English writing system codes spoken words. Although the English system represents aspects of language in addition to phonology (see Kessler & Treiman, 2003), it is in large part an alphabetic code for the phonemes or individual sounds in words. Therefore, phonemic awareness is a critical foundation for skilled spelling and reading. Phonemic awareness includes skills such as isolating and manipulating the separate speech sounds represented by the writing system. In this chapter, we use the terms "phonemic awareness" and "phonological skill" to refer to children's skill with English phonology.

Many studies have demonstrated a strong link between phonemic awareness and early performance in reading and spelling. For example, Juel, Griffith, and Gough (1986) found that beginning first graders' ability to manipulate phonemes in words (e.g., segmenting, deleting, blending, and substituting phonemes in real words) predicted their reading and spelling achievement at the end of the first and second grades. A link between children's phoneme segmentation ability at age 4 and their spelling achievement at ages 5 and 6 was also found by Muter, Hulme, Snowling, and Taylor (1998). Moreover, Byrne and Fielding-Barnsley (1989) demonstrated through a series of training experiments that preliterate children need some understanding that words are composed of identifiable, segmentable sounds, before they can use letter–sound associations to decode unknown words. Stated another way, young children must possess some phonological skill in order to grasp the alphabetic principle. As we will see, phonological skills play an important role in learning to spell.

Ehri (1997) discussed three processes by which words may be spelled—by memory, by analogy, or by invention. Spelling a word by memory requires that the speller already know the word's spelling. Spelling a word by analogy requires the speller to recognize the phonological similarity between the target word and other known words. The parts of the known spelling that represent the similarity between the words are transferred to the new spelling. Finally, spelling by invention requires that spellers analyze words into phonemes and apply alphabetic knowledge of phoneme–grapheme correspondences to create spellings. Children who are just beginning to read and write have little knowledge of words' spellings. They cannot spell many words using memory or analogy and must often rely on invention. Therefore, an understanding of how typical children invent spellings provides a foundation for studies of poor readers and writers. It allows us to determine whether the writing of children with dyslexia is appropriate for their level of development, even if it is inappropriate for their age. The following description of invented spellings introduces some of the characteristics of young children's writing, as well as the components of word knowledge.

Many researchers (e.g., Durrell, 1980; Ehri, 1983, 1986; Gentry, 1982; Henderson, 1985; Treiman & Kessler, 2003) have argued that children's knowledge of letter names plays an important role early in spelling acquisition. The connection between letters and their names is thought to provide a foundation for knowledge about grapheme–phoneme correspondences, or alphabetic knowledge. Most children in literate societies can identify a number of letters of the alphabet before they begin formal schooling. For example, Worden and Boettcher (1990) found that U.S. 4-year-olds correctly named about 14 of the 26 letters, and 5-year-olds correctly named about 22. Letter–name knowledge, however, does not automatically elucidate the links between letters and their sounds. When Worden and Boettcher asked children about the sounds associated with the letters, the 4-year-olds were successful on about six letters and the 5-year-olds on about 8.

Although knowledge of letter names does not guarantee knowledge of letter sounds, it is useful for the majority of English letters. Consider Treiman's (1994) findings with preschoolers who attempted to spell syllables such as /gɑr/, /zɛf/ and /tib/.[1] Preschoolers who knew the letter names produced many single-letter spellings. The single letter that they used was often the consonant letter suggested by the letter name in the spoken syllable. For example, these preschoolers often spelled /gɑr/ as R, /zɛf/ as F, and /tib/ as T. (Children's spellings are in capital letters here and throughout the chapter.) Although spellings such as R for /gɑr/ appear very primitive, children who produce such spellings may appreciate that certain aspects of conventional print, such as the r in car and the p in pizza, make sense given words' phonological forms. Letter–name knowledge may thus help children take their first steps toward understanding that writing is connected to speech.

As children advance, they continue to employ their letter–name knowledge by using letters to represent the sounds of the letter's name. For instance, they may spell car as CR, using r to represent the entire /ɑr/ sequence. Letter–name spellings are more common for some consonant letters than others. For example, Treiman (1993, 1994) found that kindergartners and first graders used letter–name spellings most often for r, next most often for l, and least frequently for other consonant letters such as m, n, f, s, t, p, and k. Letter–name errors occur on vowels when children transcribe long vowels with the single vowel suggested by the letter name rather than with the appropriate final e or vowel digraph. Thus, children make errors such as HOM for home, BOT for boat, and AWA for away (Bissex, 1980; Gentry, 1982; Henderson, 1985; Read, 1986; Treiman, 1993).

According to the stage theories that are often used to describe spelling development (Ehri, 1983, 1986, 1997; Gentry, 1982; Henderson, 1985), letter–name spellings appear when children are at the partial-alphabetic and alphabetic stages of development. These stages are also sometimes called the semiphonetic and phonetic stages, respectively. Children at these spelling stages are most often found in kindergarten, first, and second grade. Their spellings suggest that they understand that writing represents the sounds in words. However, the children's spelling attempts are often inaccurate, because their phonological skill is still rudimentary and their knowledge of the alphabetic system incomplete.

As well as producing letter–name spellings, young children at the partial-alphabetic and alphabetic stages commonly produce other kinds of errors. For example, children have problems with initial and final consonant clusters, as in sled and jump. Children sometimes write these words as SED and JUP, respectively, symbolizing only the first consonant of an initial cluster or the last consonant of a final cluster. Children also often fail to represent reduced vowels in spelling, omitting the second vowel in carrot. In addition, children often leave out the vowel when spelling words with a syllabic r or l, as in SPIDR for spider and LITL for little. These spellers represent the past tense ending -ed with d, t, or vowel + d according to its sound, as in PED for pinned, STAPT for stepped, and PLATID for planted (Bissex, 1980; Ehri, 1986; Gentry, 1982; Henderson, 1985; Read, 1986; Reece & Treiman, 2001; Treiman, 1993).

Errors such as these become less common as children progress, partially as a result of children's increased exposure to print. Through experiences with printed words, as in reading, children begin to develop orthographic knowledge. "Orthographic knowledge" refers to an understanding of the conventions of the writing system, including knowledge about spaces between words, acceptable and unacceptable letter sequences, and the various representations for certain phonemes, depending on such factors as their position in a word. This knowledge, in addition to phonology, then influences spelling.

Orthographic knowledge begins with very simple observations. For example, a child who spells car as CR may note that printed words in books usually contain a vowel letter. Such observations may lead the child to include vowels in words, but in the wrong place (Treiman, 1994). Consider the spelling GRE for the nonword /gɑr/. A young child's belief that /ɑr/ is an indivisible phonological unit suggests that the unit be spelled with single *r*; the child's orthographic knowledge suggests that the word contain a vowel. The child solves this conflict by placing an *e*, which occurs as a silent letter in words such as *came* and *give*, at the end of the spelling (see Reece & Treiman, 2001). Thus, even early in the development of spelling, children notice what words look like and use this information when constructing their own spellings.

Young children also use morphological relations among words, to some extent, to guide their spelling. Although we focus on children's use of phonology in this chapter, it is important to discuss briefly the influence of morphology on children's spelling. Nunes, Bryant, and Bindman (1997) proposed that children's morphological spelling strategies may develop in stages. These researchers examined how children's use of the past tense spelling *-ed* changed over time. On three separate occasions over a 20-month period, the researchers asked children, ages 6.5–8.5 years at session 1, to spell regular verbs, irregular verbs, and nonverbs. They found that beginning spellers primarily relied on a phonetic spelling strategy, such as spelling *kissed* as KIST. As their spelling skills developed, the children began to use the *-ed* spelling. However, interestingly, they used the *-ed* spelling for /t/ and /d/ in regular verbs, irregular verbs, and nonverbs. For example, children spelled *kissed, slept,* and *soft* as KISSED, SLEPED, and SOFED. The children apparently realized that *-ed* sometimes spells /t/ and /d/, without understanding the spelling's connection with past-tense verbs. As the young spellers advanced further, they began to limit their generalization of the *-ed* spelling to regular and irregular verbs, apparently, as they began to understand the grammatical basis for the spelling. Nunes, Bryant, and Bindman suggest that young spellers' initial use of a phonetic spelling strategy provides opportunities for acquiring the new morphological strategy.

We also have obtained results suggesting that young children's awareness of morphology aids their spelling. In one study, we considered how the addition of the past-tense morpheme sometimes creates a final cluster, as in *rained*. Earlier, we described how children often have difficulties spelling final consonant clusters. In our study, we reasoned that if children relied only on phonology to spell, omissions of consonants in final clusters should be equally likely for two-morpheme words, such as *rained*, and one-morpheme words, such as *brand*. However, we (Treiman & Cassar, 1996) found that children in kindergarten, first, and second grade made fewer errors on consonant clusters in two-morpheme than in one-morpheme words. For example, children were less likely to spell *rained* as RAD than to spell *brand* as BRAD. The children did not use morphology to the full extent possible, however, because they left out the *n* when spelling *rained* more often then when spelling *rain*. In a different set of studies, Treiman, Cassar, and Zukowski (1994) found that children in kindergarten, first, and second grade were able to use morphology to aid their spelling of flaps in two-morpheme words such as *dirty* and *waited*. However, as in the study just mentioned, the children were more likely to spell correctly the root words, such as *dirt* and *wait*, than the two-morpheme words. Thus, young spellers sometimes use morphology to override their phonological strategies, but phonology plays an important role.

To summarize, the typical errors of young spellers reveal their developing phonological skills. As children gain experience with printed words, their orthographic and morphological knowledge begins to have a larger influence on their spelling choices. Children's spelling performance, phonological skill, and alphabetic knowledge thus improve in concert. If phonological skill is poor, or if it does not interact appropriately with other types of knowledge, then improvement may be extremely slow. Given the importance of phonology, in the next section, we consider studies that have directly examined the phonological skills of poor and typical readers, and spellers using tasks other than spelling.

Phonological Skill

Children who struggle at learning to read and write often have poor phonological skills. For example, Bradley and Bryant

(1978) asked poorly reading 10-year-olds and typical 6-year-olds of the same reading level to identify the word with the odd sound from lists of spoken words. The children heard words such as *weed, need, deed,* and *peel,* and were to identify *peel* as the odd word. The poor readers had more difficulty than the typical children identifying the odd words. The poor readers also had more difficulty with another phonological task, producing rhymes for words. Olson (1985) reported that older poor readers were worse than younger children of the same reading level at choosing nonwords that sound like familiar words. For example, the nonword *kake* sounds like a word, but *dake* does not. Siegel and Ryan (1988) found that poor readers were worse than their reading-level-matched peers at reading and spelling nonwords and choosing spellings for orally presented nonwords. Finally, Bruck (1992) found that children with dyslexia between the ages of 8 and 16 years performed more poorly than age-matched and reading-level-matched controls on six tasks tapping phonological skill—syllable counting, phoneme counting with nondigraph stimuli, phoneme counting with digraph stimuli, syllable onset deletion, phoneme deletion with nondigraph stimuli, and phoneme deletion with digraph stimuli. Digraphs are spellings that use two letters to represent one sound, as with *ph* for /f/ in *graph*. Bruck further reported that adults with dyslexia performed more poorly than reading-level-matched typical children on phoneme deletion and phoneme counting.

In each of these studies, the phonological skills of children with reading disabilities were inferior to those of younger typical children with the same level of reading ability. Other research aimed at uncovering subtypes of reading disabilities provides further evidence that phonological difficulties are a primary characteristic of children with reading problems. Morris et al. (1998) gave 234 children ages 7–9 years multiple measures of verbal and nonverbal skills. These measures fell into eight skill categories—phonological awareness, verbal short-term memory, rapid naming, lexical vocabulary, speech production, visuospatial skill, visual attention, and nonverbal short-term memory.

The researchers formed subgroups based on the children's strengths and weaknesses across the measures. Morris et al. had expected to uncover three disability subtypes—phonological awareness impaired, phonological–verbal–short-term memory impaired, and general cognitive impaired. However, three statistical clustering procedures revealed that 183 of the children consistently fell into seven rather than three deficit subtypes. Six of the seven subtypes were characterized by poor phonological skills. Slow picture naming, poor visual block pattern repetition, and poor word and nonword repetition characterized the seventh subtype, the rate deficit group. Morris et al. suggested, based on their results, that developmental dyslexia involves "a core problem in the development of phonological awareness skills" (p. 368). They argued that the variety of subtypes reflects the influence of phonological deficits on other skills, such as short-term memory.

Although the phonological skills of poor readers often appear inadequate given their ability to read real words, their skill may be commensurate with their performance on other tasks. Instead of comparing children with poor reading skills only to younger children matched on real-word reading, Metsala (1999) also matched groups for their ability to pronounce nonwords. This task of "sounding out" novel items likely relies more on phonological skill and knowledge of grapheme–phoneme correspondences than does real-word reading. Factors other than phonological skill, for example, rote memory and experience with print, contribute importantly to real-word reading skill. To measure phonological awareness, Metsala asked the children to delete the first or last phonemes from real words and say the remaining word. For example, the children were asked to say *crew* without the /k/. The children with poor reading skill, ages 6–14 years, performed significantly worse than the real-word reading-matched children on this task. However, there was no difference between the performance of the poor readers and the nonword reading-matched group. These findings, together with those described earlier, suggest that poor readers possess poorer phonological skills than typical children with similar levels of word-reading skill. The new finding is that poor readers may demonstrate phonological skills equal to those of typical children with similar levels of skill in nonword reading. In other words, poor readers' phonological awareness may be appropriate for their (low) level of phonological decoding skill. Another task that may track phonological skill is spelling. It may be that the phonological skills of children with poor reading and spelling skills are also commensurate with their level of spelling development.

As mentioned earlier, learning to spell requires an ability to segment spoken words into phonemes. Therefore, poor phonological skill should be linked to poor spelling ability. Phonological skill may actually relate more closely to spelling than to reading. Perin (1983) found that individuals who were good readers but poor spellers, and those who were poor at both reading and spelling, were worse than individuals with good reading and spelling skills at creating Spoonerisms, such as *Jon Dohnson* for *Don Johnson,* and counting phonemes in real and nonsense words. As mentioned earlier, children can apparently develop some real-word reading skill independent of phonology. Spelling, in contrast, may show minimal development in the absence of good phonological skills. Consistent with this view, longitudinal studies of children with poor reading skill show that their spelling typically lags behind their reading (Rourke & Orr, 1977; Rutter, Tizard, Yule, Graham, & Whitmore, 1976). In the studies discussed earlier, the children with poor reading skill had poorer phonological skills than reading-matched children. Given the link between spelling and phonological skill, it is likely that the children with poor reading skill were poorer spellers than the reading-matched children. Such a difference between reading skill and phonological and spelling skills may be especially likely in studies involving poor readers with more advanced reading skills.

The close relationship between phonological skill and spelling suggests that spelling-level-matched comparisons should find similar levels of phonological skill in children with dyslexia and younger spelling-level-matched typical children, even if reading-level-matched studies do not; that is, if spelling relies primarily on phonology, then children with dyslexia should possess a level of phonological skill that is commensurate with their spelling ability. Supporting this notion, Cassar, Treiman, Moats, Pollo, and Kessler (2003) found that children with dyslexia between the ages of 8 and 15, and typical younger children, all with second-grade spelling skills, performed similarly on a phoneme counting task. The nonwords in the phoneme counting task contained either a phonological sequence that is a letter name, as in /dɑr/ or /vɛl/, or an initial or final consonant cluster, as in /blop/ or /fɪmp/. The children with dyslexia and the younger children counted the same numbers of phonemes and made the same types of errors on these nonwords. The children with dyslexia and the younger children differed only on one measure. The children with dyslexia were more likely to count the *r* letter–name sequence than the *l* letter–name sequence as one phoneme. The younger children made the *r* and *l* errors equally often. In general, however, the children with dyslexia and the younger children were very similar in their level of phoneme segmentation skill and the nature of their errors.

Other studies using a spelling-level-matched design do not support the idea that poor spellers' phonological skills are commensurate with their spelling ability. Rohl and Tunmer (1988) used a spelling-level-matched design to compare typical second and third graders, and poorly spelling fifth graders on their ability to count phonemes in nonwords. The older poor spellers performed significantly worse than the younger children. This result, in contrast to the one described earlier, suggests that poor spellers' phonological skills are even poorer than expected given their level of spelling performance.

Bruck and Treiman (1990) found mixed results when testing children with dyslexia who spelled at the second-grade level. The children with dyslexia were on average 10 years of age. In some cases, the children with dyslexia had more difficulty manipulating phonemes in nonwords than spelling-level-matched typical children, and in other cases they did not. The children with dyslexia performed significantly worse than the typical children when asked to recognize a phoneme in the second position of a consonant cluster. For instance, the children with dyslexia had more difficulty than the typical children saying that /gli/ contained /l/. However, the children with dyslexia and the typical children performed similarly on word-initial targets, such as the /s/ in /spoi/ and /saip/, and second-phoneme targets in syllables without consonant clusters, such as the /l/ in /əli/. The children made very few errors on these items, however, which may explain the lack of differences. The children with dyslexia were significantly worse than the typical children at deleting the initial sound of a consonant cluster and stating the remaining nonword. For example, the children with dyslexia had more difficulty removing the /s/ from /staib/ to respond /taib/.

Bruck and Treiman concluded that their children with dyslexia generally had poorer phonological skills than the younger typical children with similar spelling levels. However, they noted that the phonological difficulties experienced by the children with dyslexia were qualitatively similar to those experienced by typical children. This is an important point. Both groups of children made the same types of mistakes in the phoneme recognition and deletion tasks; the children with dyslexia made more of them in some cases but not others.

The similar errors made by poor and typical spellers in the spelling-level-matched studies suggest that the phonological skills of children with dyslexia develop along the same lines as those of typical children. Both groups encounter difficulties with consonant clusters and other phonological features. The higher error rates of the children with dyslexia in some of the studies reveal the slowness of this development. This brings us to a discussion of the phonological and orthographic quality of the spellings of children with dyslexia, and how they compare with the spellings of typical children.

Comparing Poor and Typical Spellers' Word Spellings

A number of researchers have compared the spellings of children with dyslexia and typi-

cal children matched for level of spelling skill. These researchers analyzed the children's spellings of words and nonwords, examining the types of errors produced by the two groups and the frequency of the errors. Such analyses should help reveal whether the spellings of children with dyslexia differ from those of typical children. Researchers have also examined the children's misspellings more generally for phonological and orthographic accuracy. It is possible that, because of their phonological weaknesses, children with dyslexia rely more on an orthographic than on a phonological strategy when spelling. If so, the spellings of children with dyslexia should be higher in orthographic quality than those of typical children. However, the results that we review suggest that the spellings of children with dyslexia and typical children are very similar, at least at the early skill levels that have been the focus of most research.

Nelson (1980) compared the real-word spellings of children with second-grade spelling abilities. The children with dyslexia were on average age 11 years, and the typical children were on average age 7 years. Three types of spelling errors were examined—letter order errors, phonetically implausible spellings, and orthographically illegal spellings. A spelling contained a letter order error if the word's letters were all present but out of order, as in YSA for *say*. A phonetically implausible error omitted, added, or substituted a phoneme, as in OOTS for *its*. Finally, an orthographically illegal spelling contained a letter group that does not occur in that position or order in English, as in CKAK for *cake*. Nelson found no significant differences between the spellings of the children with dyslexia and the typical children on any of the measures, suggesting that the spellings of children with dyslexia at this level are quite similar to those of younger typical children.

Moats (1983) conducted a similar study of real-word spelling using an error classification scheme based on typical errors made by typical beginning spellers. The children studied by Moats, like those studied by Nelson (1980), spelled at a second-grade level. Moats compared her children with dyslexia and typical children on serial order errors and phonetic accuracy. Spellings containing letter order confusions, letter duplications, or insertions were considered serial order errors, as in SRTUK for *struck*. A number of spelling patterns were examined to measure phonetic accuracy. For example, Moats investigated long-vowel letter-name spellings such as MAK for *make* and the use of *r* and *l* syllabically, as in LITTL for *little*. In addition, Moats classified spelling errors as either conventional or preconventional. The conventional scoring criteria considered whether an error conformed to English spelling–sound rules. The preconventional scoring criteria considered whether an error followed patterns frequently found with typical beginning spellers, which were discussed earlier. For example, LODE for *load* was a conventional error and the letter-name spelling LOD was a preconventional error. Moats found that the spellings of the children with dyslexia and the typical children were indistinguishable on each measure. These results suggest that the spelling errors of children with dyslexia performing at a second-grade level are similar in nature and quantity to those of typical younger children. Moats did not formally compare the orthographic accuracy of the spellings produced by the two groups further than the measure of serial order errors. However, she noted that the children with dyslexia appeared to be "better informed about spelling conventions" (p. 132) than the typical children. For example, the children with dyslexia were more likely to include vowels in syllabic endings, as when spelling *tiger*, and to double consonants when adding a suffix, as in *bigger*.

Lennox and Siegel (1996) examined children with dyslexia and typical children's misspelling of words from a standardized spelling test. The children in their study spelled at the second-grade level, as in the studies previously described. Lennox and Siegel scored the errors for constrained phonological accuracy, unconstrained phonological accuracy, and visual overlap with the intended word. The constrained phonological accuracy measure considered whether the spellings for the phonemes in a word were acceptable given the other letters in the word. The unconstrained phonologi-

cal accuracy measure considered whether the spelling contained an acceptable representation of each phoneme regardless of its acceptability in that letter context. For example, RECH for *reach* was acceptable using the unconstrained measure but not acceptable using the constrained measure. REECH or RECHE would be acceptable using the constrained measure. The visual overlap measure was based on whether the error spelling contained the correct letters and bigrams, considering letter order, for the target word. The children with dyslexia and the typical children produced similar percentages of spelling errors that were accurate using the constrained scoring measure and the visual overlap measure. However, the children with dyslexia produced fewer errors than the typical children that were accurate using the unconstrained phonological measure. In this study, then, there was some evidence that children with dyslexia were poorer than younger typical children at representing the phonological forms of words at the same overall level of spelling development. However, the ability of children with dyslexia to represent the orthographic forms of words was similar to that of the younger children.

Cassar et al. (2003) also compared the phonological and orthographic accuracy of real-word spellings produced by children with dyslexia and typical children. As in the preceding studies, the children with dyslexia and the typical children performed at a second-grade spelling level. The children with dyslexia were on average 11 years of age. The words selected for the spelling test contained many of the patterns that typical beginning spellers find challenging. For example, children were asked to spell words containing letter names, as in *jar* and *enter*, ong vowels, as in *money* and *people*, reduced vowels, as in *correct* and *heaven*, and initial and final consonant clusters, as in *spider* and *bump*. The children's spellings were analyzed for the typicality of errors for each spelling pattern. Examples of typical errors are JR, NTR (letter names), MUNE, PEPL (long vowels), KRET, HEVN (reduced vowels), and SIDR and BUP (consonant clusters). The spellings were also analyzed for phonological and orthographic accuracy more generally. Four scoring systems were used—phonologically correct–constrained, phonologically correct–unconstrained, phonological skeleton, and orthographic acceptability. The phonologically correct–constrained and phonologically correct–unconstrained measures were essentially the same as Lennox and Siegel's (1996) constrained phonological accuracy and unconstrained phonological accuracy measures, respectively. The measure of orthographic acceptability was similar to Nelson's (1980) measure of orthographically legal versus illegal spellings. The phonological skeleton scoring system assessed whether a spelling preserved the word's pattern of consonants and vowels. For example, HEVIN preserves the phonological structure of *heaven* even though it is incorrect. The children with dyslexia produced spellings that were statistically indistinguishable from those of the typical children on all measures. Even a measure of letter reversals, which have long been considered a common characteristic of dyslexia, and one that makes the errors of children with dyslexia qualitatively different from those of typical children (e.g., Vernon, 1957), showed similar results for the two groups. These results suggest that for children with dyslexia performing at the second-grade level, spelling errors are similar in both quality and quantity to those of younger, normally progressing typical children.

Bourassa and Treiman (2003) also compared children with dyslexia and younger typical children who performed at a second-grade level on a standardized spelling test. The two groups' spellings were statistically equivalent on a composite measure of phonological and orthographic sophistication, on representation of the phonological skeleton of the target items, and on orthographic legality. The children with dyslexia did not show more variability than the typical children, the same finding reported by Cassar et al. (2003). Again, the conclusion is that low-performing children with dyslexia produce spellings that are similar to those of typical beginners.

Pennington et al. (1986) also compared the spellings of individuals with dyslexia to those of nondyslexic individuals. Their dyslexics, in contrast to those in the studies described so far, were adults. The adults with dyslexia, who averaged 33 years in age, were compared with age-matched typical adults and younger, spelling-matched children. The adults with dyslexia and the children spelled at a sixth-grade level. Pennington and colleagues found no differences between the adults with dyslexia and the children on measures of phonological spelling accuracy. The spellings of both the adults with dyslexia and the children were less phonologically accurate than the spellings of the typical adults. Pennington et al. also found no differences among the three groups on a measure of simple orthographic accuracy. This measure required a spelling to contain the correct initial and final letters, and no illegal letter sequences. On a measure tapping complex aspects of orthographic knowledge, however, Pennington et al. found group differences. This measure examined spellings for patterns such as vowel clusters, as in court*eou*s and bel*ie*ve, and double consonants, as in i*ll*ogical and necessity. The adults with dyslexia appeared to have less sophisticated knowledge of complex patterns than their age-matched peers but somewhat better knowledge than the spelling-level-matched children. This result differs from those of the previously described studies that found dyslexic and nondyslexic children to be similar on orthographic measures. One possible explanation for the difference stems from the idea that Pennington et al.'s adults with dyslexia had more experience with print and more opportunities to increase their orthographic knowledge than did the children with dyslexia in the studies described earlier. As the skills of spellers with dyslexia advance, their orthographic knowledge may surpass their phonological skill.

The spelling comparison studies demonstrate that the phonological accuracy of real-word spellings produced by children with dyslexia is often similar to that of younger children with the same level of spelling skill. Also, the types of errors made by low-performing children with dyslexia are similar to those made by typically developing children who are just learning to spell. A few studies suggest that the orthographic quality of the spellings is higher in children with dyslexia than in younger control children. Most studies, especially those examining children with dyslexia who have lower levels of spelling skill, do not find such differences. However, it may be premature to draw conclusions from data on real words only. The children with dyslexia, being older than the children with whom they are compared, may have had more experience with the words on which they were tested than the younger children. This may account for their occasionally higher levels of orthographic skill.

Another approach to uncovering whether children with dyslexia rely more on orthographic spelling strategies than do typical children is to compare their spellings of regular and irregular words. Bruck (1988) reasoned that if children with dyslexia do not use phonological strategies to spell words, regularity should not affect their performance. She compared the spellings produced by children with dyslexia and younger, spelling-matched typical children for five types of words that varied in sound-to-spelling regularity. The words included highly regular words (e.g., *sharp*), less regular words containing sounds with more than one legal spelling (e.g., *real* and *feel*), exceptions (e.g., *touch, such*), words with strange or rare spelling patterns (e.g., *busy*), and nonwords that were similar to the highly regular and less regular words (e.g., /lArp/, /bil/). The children with dyslexia were affected by regularity, as were the control children. Both the children with dyslexia and the typical children made fewest errors on highly regular words and fewer errors on less regular words than on exception and strange words. The children with dyslexia produced significantly fewer phonetically accurate misspellings of the real words than the younger children. This latter finding does not agree with the results of the studies reviewed earlier in which children with dyslexia and typical children produced similar rates of phonetically accurate spelling errors (Bourassa & Treiman, 2003; Cassar et al., 2003; Moats, 1983; Nelson, 1980). Bruck concluded that children with dyslexia use phonology to spell words and nonwords, but that they do so less efficiently than typical children. Although children with dyslexia do not totally bypass phonol-

ogy when they spell, it is possible that they rely less on phonology and more on other strategies than do typical children.

Another way to assess the relative use of orthographic and phonological spelling strategies by children with dyslexia is to compare their spellings of nonwords to those of younger spelling-matched children. Children have not been exposed to the nonwords prior to an experiment, and their novelty should encourage children to use a phonological spelling strategy, if they are able to do so. A few of the studies already discussed included comparisons of nonword spelling by older children with dyslexia and younger spelling-level-matched typical children. Bruck (1988), mentioned above, found that children with dyslexia and typical children spelled nonwords similarly. Bourassa and Treiman (2003) found that children with dyslexia and younger typical children performed similarly on nonwords, as well as words.

Bruck and Treiman (1990) and Cassar et al. (2003) asked their children with dyslexia and younger typical children to spell nonwords, as well as segment them, in phoneme counting tasks (the results of which were reported earlier). Recall that Bruck and Treiman's (1990) nonwords contained initial consonant clusters, as in /spoi/ and /staib/. Both children with dyslexia and typical children more often failed to spell the second consonants than the first consonants of initial clusters. Omission rates were higher for the children with dyslexia than for the typical children. This pattern of group differences in spelling was the same as that observed in the phoneme recognition task. In other words, the children's spellings of the initial consonant cluster nonwords closely mirrored their phonological skill. Cassar et al. (2003) included letter names, long vowels, reduced vowels, and initial and final consonant clusters in the nonwords that their children with dyslexia and typical children spelled. In this study, the only difference between the groups' nonword spellings was that the children with dyslexia were somewhat less likely than the typical children to omit the first consonants of final clusters. The groups' nonword spellings did not differ on any of the other spelling patterns or on general measures of phonological and orthographic accuracy. Like Bruck and Treiman (1990), Cassar et al. (2003) found that both groups' spellings of the nonwords generally followed their phoneme counting performance. The one exception was that the children with dyslexia were much more likely to spell the /ɑr/ letter–name sequence appropriately, with a vowel letter and a consonant letter, than to count two phonemes for this sequence. That the children with dyslexia performed particularly poorly when counting the phonemes in /ɑr/ suggests that something other than phonological skill supported their spelling in this case. One possible explanation is that the children with dyslexia consider /ɑr/ as a single sound that is spelled with two letters, a digraph. This subtle difference may suggest that orthography and phonology interact differently in children with dyslexia than in normally progressing children. We have more to say about this possibility later.

To summarize, children with dyslexia produce spelling errors that are very similar to those of younger children with the same level of spelling skill. Even when children with dyslexia make more errors (Bruck, 1988; Bruck & Treiman, 1990; Lennox & Siegel, 1996), their errors are similar in nature to those of typical children. Children with dyslexia are influenced by phonology when spelling, just as are typical children. The similar orthographic accuracy of the spellings produced by children with dyslexia and typical children does not support the idea that children with dyslexia rely more on orthographic strategies than on phonological strategies when spelling. However, children with dyslexia may begin to rely disproportionately on orthographic knowledge as their spelling skills advance. Children with dyslexia may also possess more orthographic knowledge than is revealed in their spellings. In the next section, we consider the orthographic knowledge of children with dyslexia and typical children on tasks designed to assess this knowledge directly.

Orthographic Skill

As stated earlier, the phonological difficulties of individuals with dyslexia suggest that they may rely heavily on orthographic knowledge to support their spelling. The studies reviewed in the previous section found few differences in the orthographic accuracy of spellings produced by children with dyslexia and typical children. However, both orthography and phonology undoubtedly influence spelling choices, and spelling is not a pure measure of orthographic knowledge. In this section, we consider research that assessed the orthographic knowledge of children with dyslexia and typical children using spelling recognition and spelling choice tasks. The studies reviewed employed reading-level, as well as spelling-level, matched comparisons. The results of these studies are mixed. In some cases, children with dyslexia perform better than typical children on orthographic tasks. In other studies, children with dyslexia and typical children are indistinguishable.

Olson (1985) asked children to choose the real words in pairs, such as *rain* (word) and *rane* (pseudohomonym). Olson argued that this pseudohomonym choice task taps orthographic knowledge, because the phonological forms of the items in each pair are alike. Seventh graders with reading disabilities and younger, reading-level-matched children performed equally well on the pseudohomonym choice task. However, these same children with reading disabilities demonstrated poorer phonological skill than the typical readers when reading nonwords. That the children with reading disabilities had better orthographic than phonological skill supports the idea that they rely more on orthographic than on phonological knowledge when reading.

The findings of Manis, Custodio, and Szeszulski (1993) also support the idea that children with dyslexia rely heavily on orthographic skills for reading. These researchers measured orthographic processing using two tasks. In the first task, the child heard a word, saw its spelling, and judged whether the spelling was correct. The spelling was either correct (e.g., *street*) or phonetically plausible but incorrect (e.g., *streat*). In the second task, the child heard a sentence using a homonym, saw a spelling for the homonym, and stated whether the spelling was correct. For instance, a child heard

"Monday is the first day of the week" and saw either *week* or *weak*. These two tasks require orthographic rather than phonological skill, because both spellings are phonologically acceptable. The children with dyslexia completed the tasks on two occasions spaced 2 years apart. At the time of first test, the children with dyslexia averaged 12 years of age and read at a fourth-grade level. By the second test, the children read at a sixth-grade level. The performance of the children with dyslexia was compared to that of separate groups of reading-matched typical children for each test. The performance of the children with dyslexia on the orthographic tasks, while not as good as that of the nondyslexic children, improved over the 2 years. The word-identification skills of the children with dyslexia also improved. However, the children with dyslexia made no progress over the same period in their ability to pronounce certain types of nonsense words, delete phonemes from nonwords, and spell irregular words. Manis et al. concluded that the increasing orthographic skill of the children with dyslexia contributed to their improvements in word identification.

The studies by Olson (1985) and Manis et al. (1993) assessed children's ability to distinguish conventional spellings of real words from phonetically plausible alternatives. These tasks tapped children's knowledge about the orthographic forms of the specific words that were tested. Orthographic knowledge, however, includes more than knowledge about the spellings of specific words. As we stated earlier, orthographic knowledge includes an understanding of writing conventions, acceptable letter sequences, and variations for representing phonemes. The studies we describe next assessed these broader aspects of orthographic knowledge.

Siegel, Share, and Geva (1995), instead of tapping word-specific knowledge by using real words, examined children's more general knowledge of acceptable letter patterns. Children with dyslexia and younger typical children matched for reading level were asked to select the item that looked more like a word from pairs of nonwords such as *clid–cdil*. The groups each contained similar

numbers of children reading at first-through eighth-grade levels. As a group, the children with dyslexia performed significantly better than the typical children. Siegel et al. also found that the children with dyslexia were significantly worse than the typical children on nonword reading. Comparisons for the children at each specific reading level were not reported. The researchers suggested, on the basis of the results, that children with dyslexia rely more on orthographic than on phonological knowledge when reading.

Stanovich, Siegel, and Gottardo (1997) asked children with reading disabilities and typical children with second-grade reading levels to complete the same orthographic choice task used by Siegel et al. (1995). The average age of the children with reading disabilities in this study was 9 years. The study, designed to explore possible reading disability subtypes, also included phonological tasks. The results suggested that the children with reading disabilities experienced phonological difficulties of various degrees. However, the children with reading disabilities and reading-level-matched typical children performed nearly identically on the word-likeness task. This result differs from that of Siegel et al., who found that dyslexic children performed better than typical children on the orthographic choice task. The different results may reflect the fact that Siegel et al. examined the combined performances of first- through eighth-grade readers. The children studied by Stanovich et al. (1997), in contrast, were all reading at the second grade level. Taken together, the findings support our earlier suggestion that children with dyslexia begin to show superiority on orthographic tasks when they achieve more advanced reading levels.

Cassar et al. (2003) also examined what children with dyslexia and typical children know about acceptable letter patterns. The children, all with second-grade spelling levels, were asked to choose the "made-up word" that they thought looked most like a real word from pairs of nonwords. Each pair contrasted a spelling containing a common letter sequence with a spelling containing an uncommon or illegal sequence. The nonword pairs contrasted common and uncommon consonant doublets, as in *jull* and *jukk*, common and uncommon vowel doublets, as in *geed* and *gaad*, common and illegal word–initial consonant clusters, as in *skad* and *mkad*, common and illegal word–final consonant clusters, as in *pilt* and *pibk*, and word-final and word–initial consonant doublets, as in *pess* and *ppes*. On each type of pair, the children with dyslexia and the typical children chose the common item significantly more often than expected by chance. Performance of the children with dyslexia was slightly better than that of the typical children, but the group differences were not statistically significant.

Thus, children with dyslexia possess orthographic knowledge about words and letter patterns that is at least commensurate with their level of reading and spelling skill. As we saw earlier, some of the spelling comparison studies suggest that children with dyslexia rely more heavily on this information than do normally progressing children. However, the majority of the spelling data suggest that the relative use of phonological and orthographic strategies is similar in children with dyslexia and typical children.

Interactions between Phonological and Orthographic Knowledge

In addition to considering children's orthographic and phonological strategies separately, we must consider how the two types of knowledge interact. Although children with dyslexia appear to have orthographic skills commensurate with their reading and spelling skills, their phonological skills have often been found to lag behind. This evidence can be taken to suggest that their orthographic knowledge does not interact with phonological knowledge in the same way that it does in normally progressing children. Exposure to word spellings when reading helps typical children learn about the separate sounds in words (e.g., Thompson, Fletcher-Flinn, & Cottrell, 1999). Knowledge about word spellings can even cause children to overestimate sounds for words in phoneme counting tasks. This occurs when knowledge of spellings containing silent letters leads children to count extra phonemes for words, a phenomenon

referred to as "overshoot errors." For example, Ehri and Wilce (1980) demonstrated that 9-year-olds judge a word such as *pitch* to contain more phonemes than a word such as *rich*, even though the *tch* in *pitch* and the *ch* in *rich* correspond to the same phoneme. Ehri and Wilce also examined the effect of spelling on phoneme counting performance with nonwords. One group of children learned nonword spellings that contained "extra" letters, as in *zitch* for /zɪtʃ/. Another group of children learned spellings for the same nonwords that did not contain extra letters, as in *zich* for /zɪtʃ/. The children who had learned the extra letter spellings tended to make overshoot errors on the nonwords. Tunmer and Nesdale (1982) also found that even 6-year-olds in first grade sometimes made overshoot errors when segmenting nonwords containing digraphs. Both Tunmer and Nesdale and Ehri and Wilce (1980) concluded that children's segmentation is influenced by their spelling knowledge, and that this can lead to errors in certain cases.

Are children with dyslexia, like typical children, influenced by spelling when counting phonemes and performing other phonological tasks? Landerl, Frith, and Wimmer (1996) examined the phoneme counting performance of children with dyslexia and younger, spelling-level-matched typical children on three types of words—phonologically transparent words, such as *ham* and *hot*, digraph words, such as *roof* and *bath*, and silent-letter words, such as *lamb* and *half*. The typical children were much more likely than the children with dyslexia to make overshoot errors on words with digraphs and silent letters; that is, the phonological performance of the children with dyslexia was less influenced by their knowledge of spelling.

Results similar to those of Landerl et al. (1996) have been found with nonwords. In the reading-level-matched study discussed earlier, Bruck (1992) included digraph and nondigraph nonwords in the phoneme counting task. The nondigraph nonwords were most naturally spelled without digraphs, as with /tɪsk/. The digraph nonwords contained phonemes that were conventionally spelled with two letters, as with the vowel of /lim/. The children with dyslexia were less likely than the typical children to make overshoot errors on the digraph nonwords.

The results of Bruck (1992) and Landerl et al. (1996) suggest that the performance of children with dyslexia on phonological tasks is not influenced by orthographic knowledge to the same extent as that in typical children. We suggested earlier that children's experience with print gradually leads them from phonetic spellings to mature, conventional spellings. As this occurs, typical children's conceptions of spoken words are shaped by their knowledge of the words' spellings. This causes errors in certain cases, as when counting phonemes in words that are spelled with digraphs, but it usually helps children divide words into smaller units. If the phonological systems of children with dyslexia are less influenced by print learning, then their phonological skills would often appear underdeveloped in spite of their adequate orthographic skills. This is the result we have seen in a number of the studies reviewed here.

Interactions between phonological and orthographic skills are a critical feature of several theories about children's developing word knowledge. In the next section, we discuss these views about how phonological and orthographic skills interact throughout development to serve reading and spelling skill.

THEORIES OF WORD KNOWLEDGE DEVELOPMENT

The theories discussed in this section describe how children develop mental representations for words. Mature word representations are proposed to contain the phonological information for a word linked to its orthographic information. One important feature of the theories is the interaction of phonological and orthographic knowledge during development. As children learn about the orthographic forms for words, this knowledge influences their phonological representations. The inefficient interaction between knowledge bases may provide an explanation for disabled speller's poor phonological skill.

Ehri (1997) proposes that the word representations that serve reading and spelling develop in four phases. The first phase is a logographic, or visual cue phase, in which a child relies on salient graphic features to recognize a word. For example, a child may "read" a fast-food logo or traffic sign based on the colors of the letters and the background but does not yet know that the letters are related to the words' pronunciations (also see Frith, 1986). When children begin to learn about the names and sounds of letters, they enter the second phase. In this partial-alphabetic phase, children begin to form connections between the letters they see in words and the sounds they detect in pronunciations. However, children have only rudimentary knowledge about the letter–sound relations. For example, a child in this second phase might guess "dog" and then "dad" when confronted with *door*, only able to use letter–sound relationships for the word's first letter. These children employ letter–name strategies when spelling and have difficulty representing all of a word's sounds with letters, as discussed in the earlier section on spelling development. Ehri suggests that, as phonemic segmentation and reading skills develop, all the letters in words become linked to phonemes. At this point, learners are in the third phase, the full-alphabetic level. Children now create more complete word spellings. Finally, at the consolidated-alphabetic level, children develop full visual–phonological representations of word spellings. These representations link individual letters with their sounds and also link groups of letters with groups of phonemes (e.g., eam with /im/). Ehri proposes that spellings and pronunciations merge such that the "orthographic image" of a word influences how a child judges its phonemic structure. This merger usually helps children to make accurate phonological judgments, but it can lead to overshoot errors on digraphs, as discussed earlier.

Perfetti's (1992, 1997) notions add to Ehri's (1997) by further specifying how representations of words change with development. Perfetti's description begins when a word exists in the learner's spoken vocabulary. The existing pronunciation may change or become elaborated as the written form is learned. According to Perfetti, two principles characterize the development of word representations—precision and redundancy. A precise or fully specified representation contains all the letters in the printed word, together with their exact phonemic values. Before it becomes fully specified, a word's representation contains variables. Some letters are well specified, such as initial letters, and others are variable or indistinct, such as vowels. The lesser precision of vowel representations in English reflects the complex phoneme–grapheme mappings for vowels. As word representations become better specified, the information within the representation becomes more redundant. Mappings are created between letters and phonemes, between larger orthographic and phonemic strings, and between the complete spelling and the pronunciation. This redundancy leads to a strong and memorable bond between the word's spelling and its sound. The phonological and orthographic representations merge into a single representation and are no longer separate entities.

Ehri (1997) and Perfetti (1992, 1997) stress the interactions between phonology and orthography that occur in the development of reading and writing. They suggest that phonological and orthographic knowledge do not develop in isolation. Each supports and interacts with the other. For Ehri and Perfetti, phonological and orthographic information combine into unitary word representations. The theorists suggest that one knowledge base cannot develop properly if the other is inadequate.

The evidence reviewed in this chapter suggests that children with dyslexia have phonological skills that are weak, whereas their orthographic skills are adequate for their level of literacy development. As the preceding theories predict, this imbalance in skills retards the progress of children with dyslexia in both reading and spelling. Why does the imbalance exist? The theories suggest that improvements in one type of knowledge should result in improvements in the other. An imbalance in the two types of skills suggests a problem with the interaction of the knowledge bases. Some evidence

for such a problem was presented earlier in the contrast between the spellings and phoneme counting for /ɑr/ produced by children with dyslexia (Cassar et al., 2003) and their phoneme counting for words and nonwords with silent letters and digraphs (Landerl et al., 1996; Bruck, 1992). If the information about word spellings that children with dyslexia encounter has little effect on their representations of the words' sounds, then the development of phonological skills may be delayed.

CONCLUSIONS

Because the majority of studies comparing children with dyslexia and typical children have focused on children at early stages of spelling development, our conclusions must be limited to this group. Children with dyslexia, we have seen, are slow to develop phonological skills. Nevertheless, the linguistic stumbling blocks encountered by children with dyslexia are much the same as those encountered by typical children, and children with dyslexia appear to employ strategies based on sound when they try to spell. As a result, children with dyslexia produce misspellings that are very similar to those of younger typical children. Despite these similarities, the time and effort expended by the children with dyslexia to acquire their spelling ability is much greater than the time and effort expended by typical children. One possible explanation for this difference is that orthographic and phonological knowledge do not support one another in children with dyslexia to the same extent that they do in typical children; that is, the interaction between the two types of knowledge may be weak. It may be possible to bridge this gap by explicitly teaching children with dyslexia to break spellings apart and to break pronunciations apart. Children with dyslexia should benefit from the explicit pairing of visual and verbal word components. Such teaching may help to ensure that what children with dyslexia learn about orthography affects their knowledge of phonology and vice versa, allowing each type of skill to support the other.

NOTE

1. Key to notation: /i/ as in *bee*, /ai/ as in *buy*, /o/ as in *toe*, /ɑ/ as in *father*, /ɛ/ as in *bed*, /ɪ/ as in *bit*, /oi/ as in *boy*, /ə/ as in *sofa*, /b/ as in *bib*, /d/ as in *did*, /f/ as in *fluff*, /g/ as in *gag*, /k/ as in *kick*, /l/ as in *lull*, /m/ as in *mime*, /p/ as in *pup*, /r/ as in *roar*, /s/ as in *sassy*, /ʃ/ as in *show*, /tʃ/ as in *church*, /v/ as in *verve*, /z/ as in *zoo*.

REFERENCES

Bissex, G. L. (1980). *Gnys at wrk*. Cambridge, MA: Harvard University Press.

Bourassa, D., & Treiman, R. (2003). Spelling in dyslexic children: Analyses from the Treiman–Bourassa Early Spelling Test. *Scientific Studies of Reading, 7,* 309–333.

Bradley, L., & Bryant, P. E. (1978). Difficulties in auditory organization as a possible cause of reading backwardness. *Nature, 271,* 746–747.

Brady, S. A. (1997). Ability to encode phonological representations: An underlying difficulty of poor readers. In B. A. Blachman (Ed.), *Foundations of reading acquisition and dyslexia: Implications for early intervention* (pp. 21–47). Mahwah, NJ: Erlbaum.

Bruck, M. (1988). The word recognition and spelling of dyslexic children. *Reading Research Quarterly, 23,* 51–69.

Bruck, M. (1992). Persistence of dyslexics' phonological awareness deficits. *Developmental Psychology, 28,* 874–886.

Bruck, M., & Treiman, R. (1990). Phonological awareness and spelling in normal children and dyslexics: The case of initial consonant clusters. *Journal of Experimental Child Psychology, 50,* 156–178.

Bryant, P., & Impey, L. (1986). The similarities between normal readers and developmental and acquired dyslexics. *Cognition, 24,* 121–137.

Byrne, B., & Fielding-Barnsley, R. (1989). Phonemic awareness and letter knowledge in the child's acquisition of the alphabetic principle. *Journal of Educational Psychology, 81,* 313–321.

Cassar, M., Treiman, R., Moats, L., Pollo, T. C., & Kessler, B. (2003). *How do the spellings of children with dyslexia compare with those of typical children?* Manuscript submitted for publication.

Durrell, D. D. (1980). Letter–name values in reading and spelling. *Reading Research Quarterly, 16,* 159–163.

Ehri, L. C. (1983). A critique of five studies related to letter–name knowledge and learning to read. In L. M. Gentile, M. L. Kamil, & J. Blanchard (Eds.), *Reading research revisited* (pp. 143–153). Columbus, OH: Merrill.

Ehri, L. C. (1986). Sources of difficulty in learning to spell and read. *Advances in Developmental and Behavioral Pediatrics, 7,* 121–195.

Ehri, L. C. (1997). Learning to read and learning to spell are one and the same, almost. In C. A. Perfetti, L. Rieben, & M. Fayol (Eds.), *Learning to spell: Research, theory, and practice across languages* (pp. 237–269). Mahwah, NJ: Erlbaum.

Ehri, L. C., & Wilce, L. S. (1980). The influence of orthography on reader's conceptualization of the phonemic structure of words. *Applied Psycholinguistics, 1,* 371–385.

Frith, U. (1985). Beneath the surface of developmental dyslexia. In K. E. Patterson, J. C. Marshall, & M. Coltheart (Eds.), *Surface dyslexia: Neuropsychological and cognitive studies of phonological reading* (pp. 301–330). Hillsdale, NJ: Erlbaum.

Frith, U. (1986). A developmental framework for developmental dyslexia. *Annals of Dyslexia, 36,* 69–81.

Gentry, J. R. (1982, November). An analysis of developmental spelling in GNYS AT WRK. *Reading Teacher,* pp. 192–200.

Goswami, U., & Bryant, P. E. (1990). *Phonological skills and learning to read*. London: Erlbaum.

Henderson, E. (1985). *Teaching spelling*. Boston: Houghton Mifflin.

Juel, C., Griffith, P. L., & Gough, P. B. (1986). Acquisition of literacy: A longitudinal study of children in first and second grade. *Journal of Educational Psychology, 78,* 243–255.

Kessler, B., & Treiman, R. (2003). Is English spelling chaotic?: Misconceptions concerning its irregularity. *Reading Psychology, 24,* 267.

Landerl, K., Frith, U., & Wimmer, H. (1996). Intrusion of orthographic knowledge on phoneme awareness: Strong in normal readers, weak in dyslexic readers. *Applied Psycholinguistics, 17,* 1–14.

Lennox, C., & Siegel, L. S. (1996). The development of phonological rules and visual strategies in average and poor spellers. *Journal of Experimental Child Psychology, 62,* 60–83.

Liberman, I. Y., Rubin, H., Duques, S., & Carlisle, J. (1985). Linguistic abilities and spelling proficiency in kindergartners and adult poor spellers. In D. B. Gray & J. F. Kavanagh (Eds.), *Biobehavioral measures of dyslexia* (pp. 163–176). Parkton, MD: York Press.

Manis, F. R., Custodio, R., & Szeszulski, P. A. (1993). Development of phonological and orthographic skill: A 2-year longitudinal study of dyslexic children. *Journal of Experimental Child Psychology, 56,* 64–86.

Metsala, J. L. (1999). The development of phonemic awareness in reading-disabled children. *Applied Psycholinguistics, 20,* 149–158.

Moats, L. C. (1983). A comparison of the spelling errors of older dyslexic and second-grade normal children. *Annals of Dyslexia, 33,* 121–140.

Morris, R. D., Stuebing, K. K., Fletcher, J. M., Shaywitz, S. E., Lyon, G. R., Shankweiler, D. P., et al. (1998). Subtypes of reading disability: Variability around a phonological core. *Journal of Educational Psychology, 90,* 347–373.

Muter, V., Hulme, C., Snowling, M., & Taylor, S. (1998). Segmentation, not rhyming, predicts early progress in learning to read. *Journal of Experimental Child Psychology, 71,* 3–27.

Nelson, H. E. (1980). Analysis of spelling errors in normal and dyslexic children. In U. Frith (Ed.), *Cognitive processes in spelling* (pp. 475–493). London: Academic Press.

Nunes, T., Bryant, P., & Bindman, M. (1997). Morphological spelling strategies: Developmental stages and processes. *Developmental Psychology, 33,* 637–649.

Olson, R. K. (1985). Disabled reading processes and cognitive profiles. In D. B. Gray & J. F. Kavanagh (Eds.), *Biobehavioral measures of dyslexia* (pp. 215–243). Baltimore: York Press.

Pennington, B. F., McCabe, L. L., Smith, S. D., Lefly, D. L., Bookman, M. O., Kimberling, W. J., et al. (1986). Spelling errors in adults with a form of familial dyslexia. *Child Development, 57,* 1001–1013.

Perfetti, C. A. (1992). The representation problem in reading acquisition. In P. B. Gough, L. C. Ehri, & R. Treiman (Eds.), *Reading acquisition* (pp. 145–174). Hillsdale, NJ: Erlbaum.

Perfetti, C. A. (1997). The psycholinguistics of spelling and reading. In C. A. Perfetti, L. Rieben, & M. Fayol (Eds.), *Learning to spell: Research, theory, and practice across languages* (pp. 21–38). Mahwah, NJ: Erlbaum.

Perin, D. (1983). Phonemic segmentation and spelling. *British Journal of Psychology, 74,* 129–144.

Read, C. (1986). *Children's creative spelling.* London: Routledge & Kegan Paul.

Reece, C., & Treiman, R. (2001). Children's spelling of syllabic /r/ and letter–name vowels: Broadening the study of spelling development. *Applied Psycholinguistics, 22,* 139–165.

Rohl, M., & Tunmer, W. E. (1988). Phonemic segmentation skill and spelling acquisition. *Applied Psycholinguistics, 9,* 335–350.

Rourke, B. P., & Orr, R. R. (1977). Prediction of the reading and spelling performances of normal and retarded readers: A four-year follow up. *Journal of Abnormal Child Psychology, 5,* 9–20.

Rutter, M., Tizard, J., Yule, W., Graham, P., & Whitmore, K. (1976). Research report: Isle of Wight studies, 1964–1974. *Psychological Medicine, 6,* 313–332.

Siegel, L. S., & Ryan, E. B. (1988). Development of grammatical-sensitivity, phonological, and short-term memory skills in normally achieving and learning disabled children. *Developmental Psychology, 24,* 28–37.

Siegel, L. S., Share, D., & Geva, E. (1995). Evidence for superior orthographic skills in dyslexics. *Psychological Science, 6,* 250–254.

Stanovich, K. E. (1992). Speculations on the causes and consequences of individual differences in early reading acquisition. In P. B. Gough, L. Ehri, & R. Treiman (Eds.), *Reading acquisition* (pp. 307–342). Hillsdale, NJ: Erlbaum.

Stanovich, K. E., Siegel, L. S., & Gottardo, A. (1997). Converging evidence for phonological and surface subtypes of reading disability. *Journal of Educational Psychology, 89,* 114–127.

Thompson, G. B., Fletcher-Flinn, C. M., & Cottrell, D. S. (1999). Learning correspondences between letters and phonemes without explicit instruction. *Applied Psycholinguistics, 20,* 21–50.

Treiman, R. (1993). *Beginning to spell: A study of first grade children.* New York: Oxford University Press.

Treiman, R. (1994). Use of consonant letter names in beginning spelling. *Developmental Psychology, 30,* 567–580.

Treiman, R., & Cassar, M. (1996). Effects of morphology on children's spelling of final consonant clusters. *Journal of Experimental Child Psychology, 63,* 141–170.

Treiman, R., Cassar, M., & Zukowski, A. (1994). What types of linguistic information do children use in spelling?: The case of flaps. *Child Development, 65,* 1310–1329.

Treiman, R., & Kessler, B. (2003). The role of letter names in the acquisition of literacy. In R. Kail (Ed.), *Advances in child development and behavior* (Vol. 31, pp. 105–135). San Diego: Academic Press.

Tunmer, W. E., & Nesdale, A. R. (1982). The effects of digraphs and pseudowords on phonemic segmentation in young children. *Applied Psycholinguistics, 3,* 299–311.

Vernon, M. D. (1957). *Backwardness in reading: A study of its nature and origin.* Cambridge, UK: Cambridge University Press.

Worden, P. E., & Boettcher, W. (1990). Young children's acquisition of alphabet knowledge. *Journal of Reading Behavior, 22,* 277–295.

30

Spelling Assessment Frameworks

KENN APEL
JULIE J. MASTERSON
NICOLE L. NIESSEN

Spelling often is an afterthought. Whether as a content area to be taught in classrooms or as an area for assessment, spelling frequently takes a backseat to other academic areas and domains of literacy. It is not surprising, then, that research on spelling assessment procedures, and the rationale for how and why spelling is assessed and analyzed, is minimal. The paucity of information for spelling assessment and analysis is likely due to two basic issues: confusions or misconceptions about what spelling is and what it can tell us about a student's linguistic knowledge, and a poor understanding of how spelling develops and what knowledge bases serve as its foundations.

Our purpose in this chapter, a brief review of these two issues, then serves as the basis for suggested spelling assessment procedures. Embedded within this discussion is the purpose of assessment, the kinds of data that should be collected during the assessment process, and the information that can be obtained about a student's linguistic system through detailed analyses of his or her spellings.

SPELLING AS A LANGUAGE SKILL

Perhaps one of the most common myths or misconceptions about spelling is that it is a visual–spatial skill (Bailet, Chapter 31, this volume; Kamhi & Hinton, 2000). Equally erroneous is the myth that individuals are destined, or "wired," ultimately to become part of a simple dichotomy: (1) good spellers, or (2) poor spellers. This belief seems to be held by general society and, unfortunately, some educators. Frequently, students and adults are heard to say, "I'm just not a good speller," as if to imply that they have no control over their spelling abilities, and that their spelling proficiency can never change. With these myths and misconceptions, then, one would not be expected to assess spelling beyond simple measures to determine whether a student can or cannot spell at age or grade level. Indeed, this is precisely the type of assessment that commonly occurs. Contrary to this stance, however, spelling research and developmental theory of the last few decades have provided definitive data that should reshape common practices. Theory and research confirm the linguistic nature of spelling: Specific language components serve as the foundation of spelling abilities, and the nature of spelling development falls within the linguistic domain.

Language Components Underlying Spelling

Spelling is a complex, language-based skill (Apel & Masterson, 2001; Bailet, 2001; Kamhi & Hinton, 2000). Recent research indicates that several linguistic knowledge sources provide the foundation for spelling abilities (Bourassa & Treiman, 2001; Masterson & Crede, 1999). These linguistic foundations include knowledge and awareness of phonology, orthography, semantics, and morphology, as well as clear and concise mental orthographic images (Apel & Masterson, 2001; Masterson & Crede, 1999; Wasowicz, Apel, & Masterson, 2003). Individuals must be able to access and apply these linguistic sources as they write to be successful spellers.

"Phonological awareness" refers to the ability to identify explicitly, reflect on, and manipulate the sound structures of a language (Apel, Masterson, & Hart, in press; Kelman & Apel, in press). It involves the ability to segment, blend, and manipulate syllables and sounds in words. "Phonemic awareness," an aspect of phonological awareness that focuses on manipulation at the phoneme (sound) level, has consistently been shown to be a strong predictor of early childhood spelling abilities (Ehri, 2000; Nation & Hulme, 1997). Intact phonemic awareness skills allow a speller to identify the number of sounds within a word, which serves as the basis for the number of graphemes that will be used to spell a word. Phonemic awareness, coupled with orthographic knowledge for phoneme–grapheme correspondence (i.e., the alphabetic principle), often leads to the construction of words whose spellings are not automatically known (Cassar & Treiman, Chapter 29, this volume).

"Orthographic knowledge" involves understanding how to translate spoken language into written form (Masterson & Apel, 2000; Masterson & Crede, 1999). Knowl-

edge of English orthography takes several forms (Treiman & Bourassa, 2000). Orthographic knowledge includes an understanding of phoneme–grapheme correspondences (e.g., knowing that the sound /k/ can be represented by letters *k*, *c*, *cc*, *ch*, or *qu*), knowledge of rules for acceptable sequences of letters (e.g., a *qd* letter combination does not exist in the English language), and orthotactics, an understanding of positional constraints on spelling patterns (e.g., the digraph *ck* never appears in the word-initial position but can be found in the word-final position) (Masterson & Apel, 2000). Additionally, orthographic knowledge includes comprehension of orthographic patterns and rules, such as those for transcribing long and short vowels or *r*-controlled vowels (Scott, 2000; Treiman & Bourassa, 2000).

For spelling assessment, "semantics" refers to the use of vocabulary knowledge to spell words. A speller's ability to understand, accurately store, and recall spellings for homophones is contingent on adequate appreciation for word meanings. Homophones are words that sound alike but have different meanings and spellings. Examples include *witch* and *which*; *their, they're*, and *there*; and *fair* and *fare*. Individuals who do not use their semantic knowledge are likely to confuse the spelling of homophones (Wasowicz et al., 2003).

"Morphological awareness" refers to the awareness of morphemes, the smallest units of language that carry meaning (i.e., prefixes, suffixes, roots, and base words). Using their knowledge of the morphological component of language, spellers recognize and mark (1) the presence of an additional morpheme (e.g., dog<u>s</u>), (2) the correct and consistent spelling of a morpheme, regardless of its pronunciation (e.g., regular past tense is always spelled with an *-ed*, such as in *pick<u>ed</u>*, *begg<u>ed</u>*, and *chatt<u>ed</u>*); and (3) how base words may be modified when an additional morpheme is attached (e.g., *stop* becomes *stop<u>ped</u>* with the addition of the regular past-tense marker). Morphological awareness also helps spellers understand relationships between base words or roots (e.g., *play, love, busy, vis*) and related inflected or derived words (e.g., *playing, lovely, business; visual, vision*). A reliance on morphological relationships among words for spelling aids reading comprehension for many English words, because many words are spelled based on meaning rather than sound (e.g., *Canada/Canadian*; *sign/signature*).

"Mental orthographic images" (MOIs) are the images of words, syllables, and morphemes that spellers store in memory over time (Apel & Masterson, 2001; Wasowicz et al., 2003). Typically, spellers develop these MOIs (also known as "visual orthographic images" or "mental graphemic representations") through repeated attempts at decoding words or word parts (Glenn & Hurley, 1993; Treiman & Bourassa, 2000). With repeated exposure to written language, and as decoding abilities improve, the number and clarity of MOIs increase in memory; thus, spelling becomes more fluent and automatic (Ehri & Wilce, 1982). Although the other linguistic components of spelling (i.e., phonological and morphological awareness, orthographic and semantic knowledge) frequently allow individuals to spell words correctly, at times, these components are insufficient to formulate completely a correct spelling. Spellers, then, need to rely on clear MOIs to spell some words, or parts of words, correctly.

The linguistic components that underlie spelling also underlie reading abilities (Ehri, 2000). Thus, spelling and reading are intimately linked and intertwined in development. Both linguistic skills follow a similar course of acquisition and rely on individuals' phonological and morphological awareness, orthographic and semantic knowledge, and MOIs. It is not surprising, then, that development in one skill often leads to further acquisition of skills in the other. For example, in spelling intervention, researchers have found that learning to spell enhances word-level reading abilities (e.g., Apel & Masterson, 2001; Kelman & Apel, in press; Treiman, 1998). In such studies, clinically significant gains in reading decoding have occurred as a result of spelling instruction.

Theories of Spelling Development

Individuals utilize all of the different language factors underlying spelling across the developmental period (Bourassa & Treiman, 2001); however, researchers of spelling development differ somewhat in their views on how and when these foundational linguistic components influence spelling. Some scholars argue for a stage theory of development (e.g., Bear, Invernizzi, Templeton, & Johnston, 2000; Bear & Templeton, 1998; Henderson, 1990; Templeton & Morris, 1999). According to the stage theory of spelling development, some types of information are used at one stage and not at others. In the first stage (prephonetic stage), children spell by scribbling. There is minimal attention provided to specific letter shapes and the relationship between sounds and letters. As children become cognizant of letter names and how they are written, they use this knowledge to make attempts at spellings that begin to approximate the English language. However, in this semiphonetic stage, children often use one letter to represent a whole word, with the one letter chosen based on how the name of the letter sounds, rather than the sound the letter creates. In the third stage, the phonetic stage, children rely more on their knowledge of phoneme–grapheme correspondences as they spell. In this stage, spellings often contain multiple-letter combinations. In the fourth stage (within-word stage), children demonstrate an understanding for the orthographic rules or patterns of English orthography, such as marking long vowels with two vowel letters.

According to stage theory, it is not until the final two stages (syllable juncture and derivational constancy stages) that children in the third or fourth grades begin to rely on their understanding of inflectional and derivational morphology. Inflectional morphemes are suffixes added to base words that serve to provide information about time or quantity, without changing the meaning or class of the word (e.g., *walk–walked*). Derivational morphemes are prefixes, suffixes, or other derived forms that change the meaning and/or the word class of base words (e.g., *art–artist*). In these latter stages, children demonstrate in their spellings knowledge of the rules for modifications made at syllable boundaries to spell multisyllabic words.

Recently, stage theory has been called into question (Bourassa & Treiman, 2001; Sawyer, Wade, & Kim, 1999). Based on research suggesting that children utilize the multiple linguistic factors *throughout* the process of learning to spell (e.g., Lyster, 2002; Reece & Treiman, 2001; Treiman & Bourassa, 2000), other authors (Apel et al., in press; Kelman & Apel, in press; Brea-Spahn, Masterson, Apel, & Goldstein, 2003) have proposed a *repertoire theory* of spelling development. Based on the work of Sulzby (1996) and research findings on the early use of multiple strategies for spelling (e.g., Hughes & Searle, 1997; Rittle-Johnson & Siegler, 1999; Sawyer et al., 1999), a repertoire theory of spelling development suggests that children use multiple strategies and a variety of linguistic knowledge sources (phonologic, orthographic, semantic, morphologic) as they develop their spelling abilities. For example, across several studies, Treiman and her colleagues (Reece & Treiman, 2001; Treiman & Cassar, 1996; Treiman, Cassar, & Zukowski, 1994) have shown how children apply orthographic and morphological knowledge to their spellings in kindergarten and first grade, a finding that seems to conflict with the stage theory of spelling development.

A repertoire theory of spelling development suggests that children use a range of linguistic knowledge as they develop their spelling skills, with the degree to which they use each factor varying across time (Apel et al., in press; Brea-Spahn et al., 2003). During the pre-spelling (or emergent literacy) period, children rely very little on phonological, orthographic, and morphological knowledge, but they may use mental orthographic images in their early writings of logos. The literature has shown that children rely on visual cues in early reading experiences (Neuman, Copple, & Bredekamp, 2000). In the early phase of spelling (preschool to first grade), children may rely more heavily on their phonemic awareness and orthographic knowledge to spell, yet have access to and use their morphological knowledge and MOIs to spell some words. In the intermediate phase of spelling (first through third grade), children rely largely on their orthographic knowledge and mor-

phological awareness but make use of their phonemic awareness when they spell complex, multimorphemic words. During this phase, and the subsequent advanced phase of spelling, spellers use MOIs more frequently as they become better readers. Increased exposure to and practice with words lead to stronger, clearer MOIs, which then are used for both spelling and reading. In the advanced phase of reading, morphological awareness may be used frequently, as children are required to spell more complex inflected and derived words. Children still utilize their phonemic awareness and orthographic knowledge, however, when spelling less familiar words.

The repertoire theory of spelling suggests that from kindergarten through adulthood, spellers access and utilize the various linguistic factors underlying spelling across time. This theory also supports what, at times, appear to be uneven or inconsistent spelling abilities. For example, as children develop their spelling knowledge, they may learn certain spelling patterns (e.g., doubling of consonants) in certain contexts (e.g., doubling consonants at the end of words, such as tall) before others (e.g., doubling consonants when adding an inflectional morpheme, such as hopping). By second grade, most children seem to understand, and represent in their spellings, the need for one or more graphemes to represent the phonemes they hear in a word. However, older students may misspell more complex words, omitting graphemes for phonemes present in a word. This latter example likely occurs because students are grappling with the demands of more complex inflected or derived word forms and writing them within more mature written compositions. The task, then, exceeds the capabilities of the student, and a skill that appeared automatic and learned at an earlier stage is recognized as being vulnerable to the linguistic contexts and demands of writing.

Spelling assessment practices are influenced by an appreciation of the linguistic nature of spelling, the interrelationship of spelling and reading, and the theory of spelling development to which one subscribes. These beliefs and understandings often guide the goal of assessment, as well as how data are collected and analyzed.

SPELLING ASSESSMENT

Spelling assessment occurs less often than other content or literacy skills assessed in the classroom. Even when spelling is assessed more globally through writing assessments, it often is considered to be a "convention" or "mechanic." Additionally, when spelling assessment is conducted, the manner in which data are collected and analyzed varies greatly. Typically, spelling is assessed in one context and scored as correct or incorrect. Thus, valuable information that might lead to more efficient instruction is lost.

Goals of Assessment

Carlisle and Rice (Chapter 24, this volume) list several goals of assessment. Evaluators may conduct an assessment of a particular curriculum or program to determine accountability for instructional practices. For example, in the area of reading, local, state, and federal agencies often demand that students' skills be assessed to determine how well schools and school districts are preparing their students to be literate citizens. Interestingly, the current focus on reading assessment associated with the No Child Left Behind legislation and the Reading First federal funding program (Learning First Alliance, 2002) has not resulted in a comparable focus on the assessment of spelling. Given the reciprocal and interactive relationship of reading and spelling, this is surprising. Indeed, some global assessments of students' literacy abilities relegate spelling abilities to a "miscellaneous" level of interest. This lack of appreciation for the linguistic nature of spelling is illustrated in Figure 30.1, which shows the results from a sixth-grade student's performance on a standardized, commonly used, national-level spelling test. Examination of the graph shows that reading performance is given as a composite and subdivided into general reading and vocabulary. Similarly, a language composite score, as well as individual scores, separates language and language mechanics. The student's "total score" is based on performance

in reading, language, and mathematics. Performance in "other areas" is not included in the total score, but is depicted on the right side of the graph. Spelling, last of all, is one of the "other areas"! On this test, spelling was not included as a language mechanic. This lack of attention to spelling only serves to perpetuate the myth that spelling is a splinter skill that holds little importance in the academic, vocational, or social worlds of the individual.

Carlisle and Rice (Chapter 24, this volume) state two additional goals of assessment: to identify children with special needs in a certain skill, or those who may be at risk for deficits in that skill. The first of these two goals allows evaluators to qualify a child with special needs for services, so that appropriate remediation may occur, whereas the second enables educators to provide early, preventive instruction to minimize or negate the need for more intensive services at a later date. Interestingly, whereas these goals seem to be frequently addressed for children who are struggling with the reading process, much less attention is given to similar goals for spelling. Again, this is likely due to a misunderstanding and underappreciation of the linguistic basis of spelling, and the important and complementary role it plays in reading development. Clinical experience suggests that many school-based professionals are discouraged or denied the ability to assess spelling, because administrators do not judge spelling to be a skill for which children qualify for services. Thus, in many contexts, spelling assessment as a means to identify students who are at risk, or who present with spelling deficiencies, is infrequently employed.

A final goal of assessment discussed by Carlisle and Rice (Chapter 24, this volume) is to monitor student progress and to evaluate and adapt instructional procedures and tasks to meet the needs of a classroom of children or an individual child. Perhaps the most common form of spelling assessment based on this goal is the "Friday Spelling Test." In most classrooms around the nation, students from first through fifth grade (and perhaps into middle school) are provided a spelling list on Monday and assessed on their retention of those spellings on Friday (Johnston, 2001; Scott, 2000).

National Percentiles

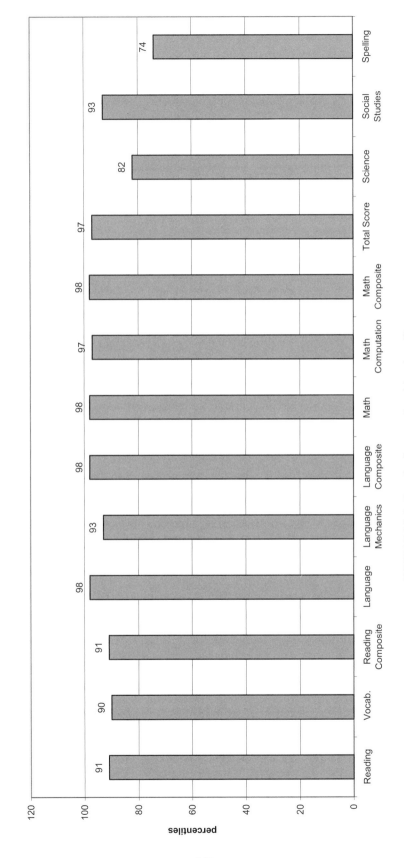

FIGURE 30.1. Results from national-level spelling test.

Ostensibly, these tests measure students' progress on memorizing a list of often unrelated words. Unfortunately, even though students may score well on a Friday Spelling Test, perhaps teachers' most common lament is that students show little retention of the correct spelling of those words in subsequent weeks (Gill & Scharer, 1996; Johnston, 2001). In actuality, then, these weekly measures do not conform to their purported objective, which is to determine student progress and the appropriateness of the instructional procedures, because changes in students' spelling skills and/or instructional activities do not occur on a task that primarily measures short-term, rote memorization skills (Johnston, 2001).

The Friday Spelling Test is not the only type of testing, however, that fits with Carlisle and Rice's (Chapter 24, this volume) notion of assessment for the purposes of evaluating student progress and adapting instructional practices. There is an alternative that is potentially more effective. Taken to its utmost, this goal of assessment can be viewed as a "prescriptive approach" to assessment (Wasowicz et al., 2003). This approach to spelling assessment is a hypothesis-driven method that allows the evaluator to determine the language component(s) a student is or is not using to spell. This approach, then, examines misspellings and generates hypotheses, based on specific data and probes, to develop appropriate treatment goals for systematic and effective remediation. Prescriptive assessment leads to explicit instruction that targets specific deficits or needs, providing more focused time for intensive instruction and practice. It is through initial and ongoing prescriptive assessments that evaluators can determine whether students are progressing in their spelling skills (Abbot, 2000; Berninger & Amtmann, 2003). Prescriptive assessment also ensures the use of appropriate tasks and learning strategies that lead to increased spelling abilities.

Spelling instruction based on a prescriptive approach to spelling assessment appears to lead to specific and timely advances in spelling abilities (see Apel & Masterson, 2001; Apel et al., in press; Butyniec-Thomas & Woloshyn, 1997; Kelman & Apel, in press). Additionally, when the goal of assessment is prescriptive in nature, the other goals discussed (accountability for programs, identification of students who are at risk or have specific disabilities) are addressed as well. The manner in which the data are collected and analyzed, however, may or may not correspond to a prescriptive assessment approach to spelling.

Data Collection

As Moats has suggested (1995), prescriptive spelling assessment procedures should sample a broad range of orthographic patterns and rules, phoneme to grapheme–digraph relationships, and morphological inflections and derivations. The number of stimuli should allow for detailed measurement of abilities across a wide range of developmental levels and linguistic components (Berninger & Amtmann, 2003; Templeton, 2003). The procedures also should provide a means to measure competence and performance. The method in which data are collected may or may not meet these basic criteria. The three most common methods for collecting data regarding a student's spelling performance are norm-referenced tests, writing samples, and word inventories (Masterson & Apel, 2000). Each of these methods is described next.

Norm-Referenced Measures

Some evaluators may use standardized, norm-referenced tests to assess spelling. Measures such as the Test of Written Spelling–4 (Larsen, Hammill, & Moats, 1999), the Test of Written Language (Hammill & Larsen, 1996), and the Wide Range Achievement Test–3 (Wilkinson, 1995) permit an evaluator to compare students' spelling skills to that of their peers, and determine whether the target students are within the typical range of abilities. On these measures, a raw score is calculated from each test or subtest, then converted to derived scores, such as a standard score/quotient, percentile, and age and grade equivalency. Descriptions of these tests exist elsewhere (Bain, Bailet, & Moats,

1991; Salvia & Ysseldyke, 1995). Although reviewers concluded that these tests met the minimal standards of the American Psychological Association for technical adequacy, the tests are not able to sample the entire domain of English orthographic patterns sufficiently (Moats, 1994). Thus, data collected with the use of norm-referenced tests, while valuable in identifying students who have special spelling needs, do not address the goal of prescriptive assessment; that is, they provide little information about students' spelling performance or competence.

Writing Samples

Students' writing samples are perhaps the best measure of their spelling performance (Westwood, 1999). As Singer and Bashir (Chapter 26, this volume) state, spelling is one of several cognitive-linguistic foundational component skills and processes that support and constrain the writing process. When engaged in writing composition, students must balance the demands of spelling along with other skills and processes (e.g., affect, graphomotor skills, content knowledge) to complete the task successfully. Thus, spelling is affected by, and may affect, myriad components of the writing task. Spelling data collected from a writing sample, then, represent an authentic illustration of how students spell when all aspects of written composition are engaged.

There are potential dangers to the use of writing samples as the *only* means of assessing spelling abilities. Students with spelling deficits often avoid attempts to spell words that they do not know how to spell (Masterson & Scott, 1997). A selection and avoidance phenomenon occurs, in which students often select simple, one- to two-syllable, uninflected words for their written composition, avoiding more complex, multimorphemic words that require a blended strategy of considering phonology, orthography, semantics, and morphology (Masterson & Scott, 1997). Unless the evaluator dictates the specific words to be used in the writing task, students have control over the vocabulary used. Thus, students' selection and avoidance strategies may disguise or overestimate their spelling abilities.

The writing task itself also may influence spelling performance in written composition, as well as comparisons among writing samples. Singer and Bashir (Chapter 26, this volume) point out that students' knowledge of content, genre structure, and language style, among other variables, may cause their spelling abilities to deteriorate. Comparisons within or across students' writing samples may not be valid measures, because the constraints and demands of the writing tasks may vary within and across groups of students.

A final concern about writing tasks as a means to assess students' spelling skills is the length of the sample (Berninger & Amtmann, 2003). Currently, no data suggest what comprises a representative sample of a student's written composition. The domain of spelling patterns in the English language is quite large, and several exemplars of each pattern should be collected to obtain a representative sample of a student's spelling ability. Masterson and Apel (2000) have suggested a minimum of 50–100 words as a basis for later data analysis. For some students, particularly those with spelling and other literacy-related deficits, this may require several writing samples (Berninger & Amtmann, 2003). Clinical experiences suggest that collecting a week's worth of writing samples from typically developing elementary school students' results in small samples of writing (Crider, Brashears, & Masterson, 2002; Keller & Masterson, 1999). It may be that evaluators need to determine the specific sample length desired (e.g., 100 different words in connected writing), then collect successive samples over time, until the desired sample length is obtained. The aforementioned cautions, however, still operate during this data collection method. Thus, it appears best that evaluators consider obtaining students' spellings from connected writing samples *and* dictated word inventories. In this way, both performance and competence are measured.

Word Inventories

The use of word inventories to obtain adequate samples of students' spelling abilities is not new (Masterson & Apel, 2000). Typically, an inventory is administered by pronouncing aloud the target word, using it in a sentence, and repeating it. Students then are required to spell the target word, either through handwriting (e.g., Bear et al., 2000; Schlagal, 1992) or via keyboarding (e.g., Masterson, Apel, & Wasowicz, 2002).

Various authors have constructed word inventories based on grade-level expectations (e.g., Schlagal, 1992), word-frequency lists (e.g., Graham, Harris, & Loynachan, 1993), stage theory (Bear et al., 2000; Ganske, 2000), or repertoire theory (Masterson et al., 2002). Within these inventories, words are chosen based on specific features that capture the authors' view of the demands of the classroom curricula or how spelling develops. For those constructed inventories based on spelling development theory, data are collected in a manner that facilitates placement of students at a stage of development (Bear et al., 2000; Ganske, 2000) or determination of the underlying linguistic components that students are or are not using to spell (Masterson et al., 2002).

Like other word inventories, those of Bear et al. (2000) and Ganske (2000) provide a means to establish the stage at which students are spelling. Bear at al. (2000) provide a series of elementary, upper level, and content-specific inventories consisting of 25 words each. Ganske's Developmental Spelling Analysis inventory also provides a 20-word screening tool to determine the appropriate inventory to administer. For all of these word inventories, the authors provide feature analysis sheets and forms to allow evaluators to determine the primary developmental stage at which students are spelling. Tables 30.1 and 30.2 list the features used to assign an individual to a spelling stage in the procedures of Bear et al. (2000) and Ganske (2000).

The word inventories of Masterson et al. (2002) are administered via a multimedia CD-ROM computer program, Spelling Performance Evaluation for Language and Learning (SPELL). Similar to Ganske's (2000) screening inventory, Masterson et al.'s program uses a Selector Module containing 40 words to determine which of four levels from a Main Test Module should be administered. Depending on the Main Test Module administered, students spell from 82 to 184 additional words. The number of patterns assessed also varies according to the module selected for the student. Levels 1–4 focus on 29, 52, 59, and 65 orthographic patterns, respectively. A list of examples of specific patterns assessed at each level appears in Table 30.3. Accuracy for each spelling pattern and feature assessed is calculated and documented via sophisticated

TABLE 30.1. Features Used to Assign an Individual to a Spelling Stage in *Words Their Way* (Bear et al., 2000).

Feature	Emergent	Letter name–alphabetic	Within-word pattern	Syllables and affixes	Derivational relations
Initial and final consonants	×	×			
Short vowels		×			
Digraphs and blends		×	×		
Long-vowel patterns			×		
Other vowel patterns			×		
Syllable juncture, consonant doubling, inflected endings, prefixes, suffixes				×	
Base and roots					×

TABLE 30.2. Features Used to Assign an Individual to a Spelling Stage in *Word Journeys* (Ganske, 2000)

Feature	Letter-name stage	Within-word stage	Syllable-juncture stage	Derivational constancy stage
Initial and final consonants	×			
Initial consonant blends and digraphs	×			
Short vowels	×			
Affricates	×			
Final consonant blends and digraphs	×			
Long vowels (-*VCe*)		×		
R-controlled vowels		×		
Other common long vowels		×		
Complex consonants		×		
Abstract vowels		×		
Doubling and *e*-drop with -*ed* and -*ing*			×	
Other syllable juncture doubling			×	
Long-vowel patterns in stressed syllables			×	
R-controlled vowels in stressed syllables			×	
Unstressed-syllable vowel patterns			×	
Silent and sounded consonants				×
Consonant changes				×
Vowel changes				×
Latin-derived suffixes				×
Assimilated prefixes				×

computerized algorithms. Depending on the students' level of performance on these inventories, additional supplemental modules are administered, measuring linguistic foundational skills such as phonemic segmentation, phonemic discrimination, and morphological awareness. Unlike the stage theory–oriented inventories of Bear et al. (2000) and Ganske (2000), the repertoire theory–oriented inventories used in Masterson et al. (2000) are designed to determine what linguistic component(s) underlie the spelling errors exhibited in students' writing at all points in development.

Using the results of these word inventories, or those of others (e.g., Schlagal, 1992), coupled with the results of connected writing samples, specific procedures and tasks to increase students' abilities in a developmentally appropriate manner can be

TABLE 30.3. Orthographic Structures Assessed at the Different Developmental Assessment Levels Included in SPELL (Masterson et al., 2002)

Orthographic structure	Level 1	Level 2	Level 3	Level 4
Consonants	*b, d, p, t, v, z, r, l, g, h, w, y, qu,* hard *c* and *k*	soft *c*, soft *g*, flapped *tt*, *dd*, *t*, *d*		/sh, ch, zh/ spelled as *c*(i), *t*(i), *s*(i)
Consonant diagraphs	*ng, wh, sh, th*			
Short vowels	All short vowels			
Long vowels	Long vowels spelled as *vCe*, and digraphs	Long vowels in multisyllabic words		
Within-word doubling		All in Level 2		
Nasal clusters		All in Level 2		
Liquid clusters		All in Level 2		
S clusters and abutting consonants		All in Level 2		
Vocalic *r*, *l*		All in Level 2		
Silent *e* and silent consonants		All in Level 2		
Unstressed vowels (schwas)			Schwa in two- and three-syllable words	Schwa in four-plus-syllable words
Inflected words			All in Level 3	
Derived words				All in Level 4

developed and implemented. Thus, these procedures allow evaluators to address the goal of prescriptive assessment: evaluating students' progress and adapting instructional practices. The manner in which the data are analyzed, however, may lead to differences in instructional practices.

Data Analysis

Undoubtedly, data analysis is, or should be, most influenced by the evaluator's theory of spelling development. When consistency between theory and practice occurs, accountability, efficacy, flexibility, and creativity of services provided are likely outcomes (Apel,

1999). For spelling assessment, one's theory of spelling development influences greatly the analysis procedures applied to the data collected. The analysis procedures described here for the stage and repertoire theories can be applied to both writing samples and word inventories. For ease of description and reference, and because of the inherent difficulties associated with writing samples, these examples are related to common, readily available word inventories.

Analysis Based on Stage Theory

Spelling analysis grounded in stage theory often requires four general steps (e.g., Bear et al., 2000; Ganske, 2000). In the first step after data collection, the evaluator determines the number of correctly spelled words or features within a word. Based on this number, authors of stage theory–based word inventories provide scoring procedures for assigning a stage level (e.g., emergent or alphabetic stage, within-word stage) to characterize the speller's overall abilities. Next, an analysis of the features expected for the assigned stage level is conducted. Features of words analyzed may include the use of initial consonants, digraphs, doubling of consonants, inflectional morphemes, and so on. The analysis procedures of Bear et al. (2000) and Ganske (2000) also provide error and/or feature guides to help evaluators determine which errors in spelling represent students struggles with certain orthographic features. Next, graded sublevels within major stage levels (e.g., early or novice within-word stage level) assignments are made. Finally, authors of stage theory–based word inventories often suggest goals and activities for spelling instruction based on students' assigned developmental spelling stage. Examples of specific data analysis procedures can be found in Bear et al. (2000) and Ganske (2000).

Data analysis based on stage theory is not straightforward. As authors who support this approach recognize, boundaries between stages are not always clear (Bear et al., 2000). Students do not typically exhibit spelling errors that are consistent with just one developmental stage. Additionally, such analyses often are based on a small number of words, which may not be a representative sample of a student's spelling competence. Finally, although a stage theory–based analysis procedure allows evaluators to assign a developmental level to students' spelling abilities, it does not provide information for the language component(s) that students are or are not using. This analysis, then, does not provide evaluators with an understanding of specific linguistic factors that are deficient or unknown to students. Because students use the various language components to spell across time (Bourassa & Treiman, 2001), spelling analyses based on a repertoire theory of spelling development not only determine appropriate

spelling instructional goals and tasks but also identify weaknesses in language skills that serve as the foundation for spelling development.

Analysis Based on Repertoire Theory

Masterson and Apel (2000) were the first to suggest a hypothesis-driven spelling analysis approach consistent with repertoire theory. In their description of spelling analysis, the authors proposed the Spelling Assessment Flowchart (SAF) as a visual representation of the hypothesis and problem-solving algorithms needed to determine the underlying language deficiencies in students' spelling errors. Since that time, Masterson, Apel, and Wasowicz (2003) have updated and further developed the SAF as part of the SPELL program discussed earlier. Additionally, others have provided similar plans based on assessment of multiple sources of linguistic knowledge (e.g., Berninger & Amtmann, 2003). The SPELL program elicits and analyzes initial data, then conducts any necessary supplemental language probes (described later) automatically, using algorithms based on artificial intelligence principles. However, the analysis procedure can be conducted by human computation. Figure 30.2 provides a schematic of the revised flowchart depicting how error patterns are examined to determine possible underlying deficits in the linguistic foundational skills of spelling (Masterson et al., 2003). The reader is encouraged to follow this schematic as the hypothesis-driven analysis approach is detailed below.

After examiners obtain a sufficient sample of a student's spelling, a prescriptive spelling assessment approach requires that they explore spelling accuracies for the specific orthographic structures (e.g., consonants, short vowels, consonant clusters) that are developmentally appropriate for the student. Structures that are misspelled more than 40% of the time are identified for further analysis. Orthographic structures that are infrequently misspelled (i.e., less than 40% of the time) are more appropriately addressed by facilitating and encouraging the student's consistent application of spelling knowledge and by devel-

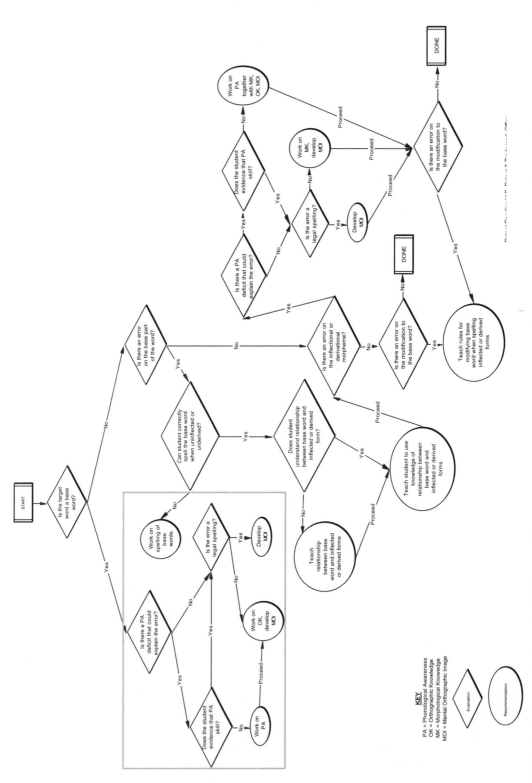

FIGURE 30.2. Flowchart for hypothesis-driven spelling analysis. From Masterson, Apel, and Wasowicz (2003). Copyright 2003 by Learning By Design, Inc. Reprinted by permission.

oping the student's self-monitoring and proofing of his or her own written work in authentic writing tasks.

Next, the evaluator attempts to identify a pattern, or consistent trend, in the misspellings that occur for each target orthographic structure. Initially, an evaluator looks at the misspellings in base words (i.e., words without affixes) to begin searching for the underlying cause(s) of those misspellings. Misspelled base words are chosen first for analysis, because spelling accuracy for base words develops before accuracy for inflected or derived words (Henderson, 1990).

Looking at a pattern of errors, the evaluator determines whether a phonemic awareness deficit might be leading to errors in spelling. In this case, if a student is consistently omitting graphemes for phonemes present in a word, then the evaluator hypothesizes that the student is lacking in, or not using, the requisite phonemic segmentation skills necessary to represent each sound in a word. For example, the evaluator may note a consistent pattern of deleting an *n* or *m* grapheme within nasal clusters (e.g., DAP for *damp* or SAD for *sand*). The student's phonemic awareness abilities are assessed for the particular phonemic awareness skill in question. In the case of nasal deletion, the evaluator would present a series of phonemic segmentation probes involving *n* or *m* cluster words, and ask the student to segment the words into their individual phonemes. If the student performs poorly on the task, the evaluator hypothesizes that the student does not have the phonemic awareness skills required to represent certain sounds in a word. An instructional objective is set to facilitate the student's phonemic awareness skills in this area, so that, with improved abilities, all sounds in words will be represented by one or more graphemes. Once this skill is developed, the evaluator will need to determine whether specific orthographic patterns and/or MOI objectives are required.

If the error patterns occurring on base words do not suggest a phonemic awareness deficit, the evaluator should determine whether the misspellings represent "legal" spellings (Bruck & Waters, 1988; Kamhi & Hinton, 2000). Legal misspellings are those errors that, although not spelled correctly, follow specific and allowable English spelling patterns or rules. For example, word spellings such as SPEACH, PEECH, and TEECH are incorrect spellings of *speech, peach,* and *teach,* respectively; however, the errors (in this case, the vowels) represent allowable orthographic patterns in the English language. If a student spelled those same words as SPACH, PACH, and TACH, respectively, the errors would not be considered legal misspellings, because the *a* never represents the phoneme /i/ in the English language. If the pattern of misspellings represents legal misspellings, as in the former example, then the evaluator's analysis leads to an instructional objective of developing adequate MOIs for these types of words. If, however, the pattern of misspelled words is considered to violate English orthographic rules or patterns, as in the case of the latter example, the evaluator develops an instructional objective to increase the student's knowledge of the orthographic pattern and, if needed later, appropriate MOIs.

Once the evaluator determines that a student is adequately spelling base words correctly, it is prudent to examine words that are inflected or derived forms of base words. When a pattern of errors is recognized, the evaluator first must determine whether the spelling errors occur on the base part of the word. For example, it may be that a student spells words such as *magician, friendly,* and *hoped,* as MAJICIAN, FRENDLY, and HOEPED, respectively. In cases such as this, the evaluator must determine whether the student can spell correctly the base words of these inflected and derived words when they occur by themselves, or without the extra morpheme(s). A follow-up word inventory that included the base forms of these words (i.e., *magic, friend, hope*) would be administered to determine whether the student can spell these words. If results of this follow-up assessment reveal incorrect spelling for the target base words, the evaluator then begins the hypothesis-driven analysis approach described earlier for base words.

If the results of the follow-up assessment suggest adequate spelling of base words, the evaluator should probe the student's understanding of the relationship between base words and their inflected and/or derived forms. Such a follow-up might take the form of a task similar to Carlisle's morphological cloze procedure tasks (1987, 1988). In these tasks, the student is asked to spell a base word (e.g., *magic*), then to spell an inflected or derived form of the base word that completes a sentence (e.g., "Houdini was a great _____"). The order can be reversed, so that a student spells an inflected or derived word (e.g., *business*) and completes the sentence with the corresponding base word (e.g., "My work keeps me very _____"). The results of this probe determine whether the evaluator's objective is to increase the student's understanding of the relationship between base words and their inflectional or derivational forms, or to encourage the student to use his or her existing knowledge of base words and their inflectional and derivational forms when spelling.

Students' error patterns on inflected and derived words may occur on the inflectional or derivational unit of the word. In this condition, a different set of problem-solving algorithms is employed. Take, for example, the situation in which a student spells words such as *bats, walked,* and *teacher,* as BAT, WALK, and TEACH, respectively. This pattern of errors occurs on the inflectional and derivational units of the words. With such a pattern, the evaluator should determine whether the errors (omissions, in this case) may be resulting from a deficit in or misuse of phonemic awareness skills. Consistent with the repertoire theory of spelling development, students who appear to have adequate phonemic awareness skills when spelling base words may not have the phonemic awareness skills required when spelling more advanced, complex vocabulary. Similar to the probe used to analyze base words, the evaluator assesses the student's phonemic awareness skills using a phonemic segmentation task based on the specified errors. If the student fails the probe, an objective is set to develop phonemic awareness of these errors patterns in concert with the orthographic patterns and morphological knowledge of inflections and derivations for these particular patterns.

It may be that a student's error patterns on inflected and derived units of a word do not suggest a phonemic awareness deficit, such as when a student spells *matches* and *walked* as MATCHEZ and WALKT, respectively. The evaluator must question whether these errors are legal spellings according to English orthography. In the aforementioned examples, the error pattern does not represent a legal spelling for the plural or past-tense morpheme. Certainly the sounds /z/ and /t/ can be spelled with a *z* and *t*, respectively; however, the morphological principles, and not simple sound–letter relationships, must govern this type of spelling. Consequently, these errors would be considered deficits in morphological awareness, and instruction would focus on the student's learning the correct spellings for the plural (i.e., *s* or *es*) and past (i.e., *ed*) morphemes.

In some cases, the error that affects the spelling of the morpheme could be considered legal. For example, the morpheme that turns a verb into a noun can be spelled with either an *er* (e.g., *teach–teacher*) or an *or* (e.g., *sail–sailor*). If the findings of the analysis suggest that the student is using legal but incorrect patterns to spell inflectional and derivational units of words, then developing clear MOIs for those types of words becomes an instructional objective.

At times, it may be that a student's error patterns for inflected and derived forms are not on the base form of the inflected or derived forms, nor are they on the inflectional or derivational units of the words. Rather, the error patterns represent errors on the modification of the base word when the inflectional or derivational units are attached to the base form (e.g., BABYES for *babies* and HOPING for *hopping*). When an error occurs on the modification of a base word, the evaluator establishes an instructional objective for the student to learn how base words are modified when spelling inflected or derived forms.

The hypothesis-driven heuristics just described represent a repertoire theory of spelling development. As represented through the different arms of the flowchart, the evaluator attempts to identify the possible linguistic component(s) that lead to the spelling error patterns observed. It is important to recognize that misspelled words may contain several error patterns, resulting in multiple examples of spelling error patterns (Berninger & Amtmann, 2003; Masterson et al., 2002). Additionally, though presented as a means to determine instructional objectives, the same assessment process may be conducted to measure ongoing progress in development (Abbott, 2000).

CONCLUSIONS

Our purpose in this chapter has been to illustrate how systematic the process of spelling is. Contrary to notions that spelling is capricious and illogical, the linguistic skill of spelling is quite logical and predictable (Berninger & Amtmann, 2003). Certainly, an individual's spellings offer hard evidence of the knowledge sources that are used in spelling. However, spellings also may offer credible insight into the types of knowledge the individual is using in reading. We often refer to spelling as a "window into the literacy mind" of a student. Such an important skill should receive high priority and focus on both assessment and instruction, and not be viewed as merely an afterthought or a mechanic. It is likely that such a focus will result in gains in all components of an individual's performance in literacy.

REFERENCES

Abbott, M. (2000). Identifying reliable generalizations for spelling words: The importance of multilevel analysis. *Elementary School Journal, 101,* 233–245.

Apel, K. (1999). Checks and balances: Keeping the science in our profession. *Language, Speech, and Hearing Services in Schools, 30,* 98–107.

Apel, K., & Masterson, J. J. (2001). Theory-guided spelling assessment and intervention: A case study. *Language, Speech, and Hearing Services in Schools, 32,* 182–195.

Apel, K., Masterson, J. J., & Hart, P. (in press). Integration of language components in spelling: Instruction that maximizes students' learning. In E. R. Silliman & L. C. Wilkinson (Eds.), *Language and literacy learning in the schools.* New York: Guilford Press.

Bailet, L. L. (2001). Development and disorders of spelling in the beginning school years. In A. M. Bain, L. L. Bailet, & L. C. Moats (Eds.), *Written language disorders: Theory into practice* (2nd ed., pp. 1–41). Austin, TX: PRO-ED.

Bain, A., Bailet, L., & Moats, L. (1991). *Written language disorders: Theory into practice.* Austin, TX: PRO-ED.

Bear, D., Invernizzi, M., Templeton, S., & Johnston, F. (2000). *Words their way: Word study for phonics, vocabulary, and spelling instruction* (2nd. ed.). Upper Saddle River, NJ: Prentice-Hall.

Bear, D. R., & Templeton, S. (1998). Explorations in developmental spelling: Foundations for learning and teaching phonics, spelling, and vocabulary. *Reading Teacher, 52,* 222–242.

Berninger, V. W., & Amtmann, D. (2003). Preventing written expression disabilities through early and continuing assessment and intervention for handwriting and/or spelling problems: Research into practice. In H. L Swanson, K. R. Harris, & S. Graham (Eds.), *Handbook of learning disabilities* (pp. 354–363). New York: Guilford Press.

Bourassa, D. C., & Treiman, R. (2001). Spelling development and disability: The importance of linguistic factors. *Language, Speech, and Hearing Services in Schools, 32,* 172–181.

Brea-Spahn, M., Masterson, J. J., Apel, K., & Goldstein, B. (2003). El deletreo en inglés y en español: Desarrollo, evaluación, e intervención [Spelling in English and Spanish: Development, assessment, and intervention]. *Revista Chilena de Fonoaudiologia, 4*(2), 17–30.

Bruck, M., & Waters, G. (1988). An analysis of the spelling errors of children who differ in their reading and spelling skills. *Applied Psycholinguistics, 9,* 77–92.

Butyniec-Thomas, J., & Woloshyn, V. E. (1997). The effects of explicit strategy and whole-language instruction on students' spelling ability. *Journal of Experimental Education, 65,* 293–302.

Carlisle, J. F. (1987). The use of morphological knowledge in spelling derived forms by learning-disabled and normal students. *Annals of Dyslexia, 9,* 247–266.

Carlisle, J. F. (1988). Knowledge of derivational morphology and spelling ability in fourth, sixth, and eighth graders. *Applied Psycholinguistics, 9,* 247–266.

Crider, K., Brashears, A., & Masterson, J. (2002). *Longitudinal study of students' spelling skills: Year 1.* Poster presented at the Annual Convention of the Missouri Speech–Language–Hearing Association, Osage Beach.

Ehri, L., & Wilce, L. (1982). Recognition of spellings printed in lower and mixed case: Evidence for orthographic images. *Journal of Reading Behavior, 14,* 219–230.

Ehri, L. C. (2000). Learning to read and learning to spell: Two sides of a coin. *Topics in Language Disorders, 20*(3), 19–36.

Ganske, K. (2000). *Word journeys.* New York: Guilford Press.

Gill, C. H., & Scharer, P. L. (1996). Why do they get it on Friday and misspell it on Monday? *Language Arts, 73,* 89–96.

Glenn, P., & Hurley, S. (1993). Preventing spelling disabilities. *Child Language Teaching and Therapy, 9,* 1–12.

Graham, S., Harris, K. R., & Loynachan, C. (1993). The basic vocabulary list. *Journal of Educational Research, 86,* 363–369.

Hammill, D. D., & Larsen, S. C. (1996). *Test of Written Language* (4th ed.). Austin, TX: PRO-ED.

Henderson, E. (1990). *Teaching spelling.* Boston: Houghton Mifflin.

Hughes, M., & Searle, D. (1997). *The violent E and other tricky sounds: Learning to spell from kindergarten through grade 6.* York, ME: Stenhouse.

Johnston, F. R. (2001). Exploring classroom teachers' spelling practices and beliefs. *Reading Research and Instruction, 40,* 143–156.

Kamhi, A. G., & Hinton, L. N. (2000). Explaining individual differences in spelling ability. *Topics in Language Disorders, 20*(3), 37–49.

Keller, K., & Masterson, J. (1999). *The effects of clinician directed treatment versus independent access to technology-based tools on spelling.* Poster presented at the Annual Convention of the Missouri Speech–Language–Hearing Association, St. Louis.

Kelman, M. K., & Apel, K. (in press). The effects of a multiple linguistic prescriptive approach to spelling instruction: A case study. *Communication Disorders Quarterly.*

Larsen, S. C., Hammill, D. D., & Moats, L. C. (1999). *Test of Written Spelling* (4th ed.). Austin, TX: PRO-ED.

Learning First Alliance. (2002). *Major changes to ESEA in the No Child Left Behind Act.* Washington, DC: Author.

Lyster, S. H. (2002). The effects of morphological versus phonological awareness training in kindergarten on reading development. *Reading and Writing: An Interdisciplinary Journal, 15,* 261–294.

Masterson, J. J., & Apel, K. (2000). Spelling assessment: Charting a path to optimal intervention. *Topics in Language Disorders, 20*(3), 50–65.

Masterson, J. J., Apel, K., & Wasowicz, J. (2002). *SPELL: Spelling Performance Evaluation for Language and Literacy.* Evanston, IL: Learning By Design.

Masterson, J. J., Apel, K., & Wasowicz, J. (2003). *SPELL model of assessment* (Technical Publication No. 03-1). Evanston, IL: Learning By Design.

Masterson, J. J., & Crede, L. A. (1999). Learning to spell: Implications for assessment and intervention. *Language, Speech, and Hearing Services in Schools, 30,* 243–254.

Masterson, J. J., & Scott, C. (1997, November). *Improving spelling skills in children with and without language disorders.* Seminar presented at the annual convention of the American Speech–Language–Hearing Association, Boston, MA.

Moats, L. (1994). Assessment of spelling in learning disabilities research. In G. R. Lyon (Ed.), *Frames of reference for the assessment of learning disabilities* (pp. 333–350). Baltimore: Brookes.

Moats, L. (1995). *Spelling: Development, disability, and instruction.* Baltimore: York Press.

Nation, K., & Hulme, C. (1997). Phonemic segmentation, not onset-rime segmentation, predicts early reading and spelling skills. *Reading Research Quarterly, 32,* 154–167.

Neuman, S., Copple, C., & Bredekamp, S. (2000). *Learning to read and write: Developmentally appropriate practices for young children.* Washington, DC: National Association for the Education of Young Children.

Reece, C., & Treiman, R. (2001). Children's spelling of syllabic /r/ and letter-name vowels: Broadening the study of spelling development. *Applied Psycholinguistics, 22,* 139–165.

Rittle-Johnson, B., & Siegler, R. S. (1999). Learning to spell: Variability, choice, and change in children's strategy use. *Child Development, 70,* 332–348.

Salvia, J., & Ysseldyke, J. (1995). *Assessment.* Boston: Houghton Mifflin.

Sawyer, D. J., Wade, S., & Kim, J. K. (1999). Spelling errors as a window on variations in phonological deficits among students with dyslexia. *Annals of Dyslexia, 49,* 137–159.

Schlagal, R. (1992). Patterns of orthographic development into the intermediate grades. In S. Templeton & D. Bear (Eds.), *Development of orthographic knowledge and the foundations of literacy: A memorial Fetschrift for Edmund H. Henderson* (pp. 31–52). Hillsdale, NJ: Erlbaum.

Scott, C. M. (2000). Principles and methods of spelling instruction: Applications for poor spellers. *Topics in Language Disorders, 20*(3), 66–82.

Sulzby, E. (1996). Roles of oral and written language as children approach literacy. In C. Pontecorvo, M. Orsolini, B. Burge, & L. B. Resnick (Eds.), *Children's early text construction* (pp. 25–46). Mahwah, NJ: Erlbaum.

Templeton, S. (2003). Spelling: Best ideas = best practices. *Voices from the Middle, 10*(4), 48–49.

Templeton, S., & Morris, D. (1999). Questions teachers ask about spelling. *Reading Research Quarterly, 34,* 102–112.

Treiman, R. (1998). Beginning to spell in English. In C. Hulme & R. M. Joshi (Eds.), *Reading and spelling: Development and disorders* (pp. 371–194). Mahwah, NJ: Erlbaum.

Treiman, R., & Bourassa, D. C. (2000). The development of spelling skills. *Topics in Language Disorders, 20*(3), 1–18.

Treiman, R., & Cassar, M. (1996). Effects of morphology on children's spelling of final consonant clusters. *Journal of Experimental Psychology, 63,* 141–170.

Treiman, R., Cassar, M., & Zukowski, A. (1994). What types of linguistic information do children use in spelling?: The case of flaps. *Child Development, 65,* 1310–1329.

Wasowicz, J., Apel, K., & Masterson, J. J. (2003). Spelling assessment: Applying research in school-based practice. *Perspectives on School-Based Issues Newsletter, 4*(1), 3–7.

Westwood, P. (1999). Spelling approaches to teaching and assessment. Melbourne, Australia: ACER Press.

Wilkinson, G. S. (1995). *The Wide Range Achievement Test–3.* Wilmington, DE: Jastak Associates.

31

Spelling Instructional and Intervention Frameworks

LAURA L. BAILET

A small proportion of students learn to spell with little effort, whereas for most, learning to spell is a lengthy process that requires deliberate instruction and practice. For students with spelling disabilities, it is essential that teachers understand the linguistic principles that underlie the English spelling system. In addition, careful selection of spelling words and instructional activities, appropriate pacing, distributed practice, and direct instruction in problem solving, self-monitoring, and error correction are essential for sustainable gains in spelling proficiency. Nearly all students can improve their spelling with extended, direct instruction based on sound linguistic principles that typically incorporate specialized techniques. This chapter reviews current research-based spelling instructional strategies, with emphasis on teaching students with learning disabilities (LD).

HISTORICAL OVERVIEW

Spelling instruction historically was a core subject in U.S. education and was closely connected to reading instruction until the early 1900s (Venezky, 1980). Many educators in the 1700s and 1800s were convinced that spelling was the foundation for reading and therefore primary in terms of instructional focus (Venezky, 1980). As the 20th century progressed, however, interest in spelling instruction declined, and for the most part, spelling came to be viewed as a minor subject entirely separate from reading. Whereas this practice most likely hinders spelling and reading development to some extent in typically developing children, it contributes significantly to the reading and spelling problems of students with language-based LD (Ehri, 2000). Fortunately, during the past 25 years or so, a number of researchers have become interested in spelling development and disorders, and in particular have been investigating interconnections between spelling and other language processes (i.e., oral language and reading). Results from this research make it clear that, to be maximally effective, spelling instruction must be understood by students and teachers alike within the broader context of global language competency.

Given the history of spelling instruction during the 20th century, it is not surprising that too little research on best teaching practices for spelling exists as yet, progress within the past 25 years notwithstanding. Many of the available studies have significant methodological problems or limited generalizability. Intervention research and associated instructional recommendations also reflect the controversies, conflicts, and politics of the broader issue of language arts instruction, particularly whole-language reading and writing process approaches versus more discrete, skills-oriented language instruction (Graham, 2000). Proponents of an implicit spelling approach assume that children will learn to spell simply by engaging in interesting reading and writing activities. Although some studies have shown that young children can progress in their spelling without explicit instruction, advancing to a higher level of spelling proficiency is unlikely without it. Other studies have demonstrated that children make the best progress in spelling when given explicit spelling instruction versus reading instruction alone (O'Connor & Jenkins, 1995; Uhry & Shepherd, 1993). Several studies have assessed the relative benefits of direct spelling instruction versus various other forms of writing activities, with mixed results (Clark, 1988; Gettinger, 1993). For students with LD, sustained progress generally is negligible without long-term, explicit spelling instruction (MacArthur, Graham, Schwartz, & Schafer, 1995; McIntyre, 1995).

WEEKLY SPELLING TESTS

Perhaps some of the resistance among educators to explicit spelling instruction reflects fundamental problems with the content and instructional activities in basal spelling series, and a lack of teacher training in how to teach spelling effectively and why this is beneficial across the language arts curriculum. Wide variability exists in the type and source of words chosen for weekly spelling tests. Basal series publishers do not consistently describe how word lists are selected or base their selection on current linguistic spelling principles and developmental research in spelling (Moats, 1995; Scott, 2000). Teachers often devise their own spelling lists based on high-frequency words or words from other parts of the curriculum (Scott, 2000),

which may or may not be developmentally appropriate for the class as a whole or for individual students. A fundamental problem, as noted by Kamhi and Hinton (2000), is that "most people still believe that spelling is primarily a visually-based skill" (p. 48). Helping students grasp the many linguistic principles of our language through long-term, direct spelling instruction can enhance word recognition, reading comprehension, and vocabulary knowledge, along with spelling and written-expression ability (Ehri, 2000). Embedding focused spelling practice within a comprehensive language arts curriculum will enhance its effectiveness, relevance and interest to both students and teachers (Allal, 1997; Graham, Harris, & Loynachan, 1994; Scott, 2000).

Invernizzi, Abouzeid, and Gill (1994) described a method for identifying the proper spelling instructional level for individual students, emphasizing that the instructional focus should be on those words and patterns for which the child demonstrates emerging skills. Graham et al. (1994) suggested creating word lists with words that occur most frequently in children's writing, and they have published such lists through grade 3 (Scott, 2000). The McGuffey Qualitative Inventory of Word Knowledge (Schlagal, 1992) provides graded word lists that can be administered to groups of students to identify individual instructional levels. The inventory, for grades 1–8, is included in the appendix of *Words Their Way* (Bear, Invernizzi, Templeton, & Johnson, 2000), along with more advanced spelling inventories. Words were selected to include key features that reflect different spelling stages and are thus guideposts for instruction (Masterson & Apel, 2000). *Spellmaster* (Greenbaum, 1987) provides more detailed criterion-referenced tests to individualize spelling instruction within classrooms, through diagnostic assessment of spelling rules, patterns, homonyms, and irregular words (Moats, 1995).

RESEARCH FOR STUDENTS WITH LEARNING DISABILITIES

Spelling disability is a defining characteristic of dyslexia; thus, it often co-occurs with reading disability. It also may occur as an isolated disability, in which case reading and math skills are generally satisfactory (Frith, 1980), although recent research suggests these cases are rare and may actually reflect a mild, compensated form of dyslexia (Bruck & Waters, 1988; Ehri, 2000; Newman, Fields, & Wright, 1993). In some cases, spelling and math disability occur together, as described in several studies by Rourke and his colleagues (e.g., Rourke & Strang, 1983). However, most children with significant spelling disability also will have some degree of reading disability, particularly during the elementary school grades. For these children, underlying deficits in phonological processing often contribute significantly to their reading and spelling problems. Spelling disability also often co-occurs with handwriting disability and/or a broader written-expression disability. Finally, I have observed in my clinical practice that children with attention-deficit/hyperactivity disorder (ADHD) often display spelling difficulty, particularly with more advanced spelling skills that involve conditional rules and letter sequences that include silent or ambiguous letters. Moats (1995) also described a similar case. Of course, dyslexia and ADHD have high comorbidity, and this combination of deficits may have its most severe, long-term academic impact on spelling and written expression.

Spelling intervention studies with students with spelling disability are sparse, and most of the available research has been conducted with younger students. Several researchers have demonstrated the benefits of direct instruction in phonological processing for later reading and spelling outcomes (Bradley & Bryant, 1985; Fox & Routh, 1976, 1984; O'Connor, Notari-Syverson, & Vadasy, 1996; Rubin & Eberhardt, 1996). Students with LD tend to need more individualized, intensive training in these skills than typically developing learners in order for gains in reading and spelling achievement to become evident (O'Connor et al., 1996).

However, progress in phonological processing skills and reading is likely to exceed progress in spelling, and the gap between reading and spelling skills in students with dyslexia may widen over time (Moats,

1995). Torgesen and colleagues (2001) recently reported an intervention study of 60 children with severe reading disabilities. Subjects received two individual, 50-minute sessions per day for 8 weeks, incorporating instruction in phonemic awareness and phonemic decoding skills. Whereas significant gains were reported in word recognition and reading comprehension, and were maintained over time, spelling skills improved to a far lesser extent and generally were not maintained over time.

McNaughton, Hughes, and Clark (1994) reviewed 27 published studies on spelling instruction for students with LD. They identified several instructional practices for which empirical support existed, including the following:

1. Limiting the number of new words introduced daily.
2. Including peer-assisted and student-directed instruction.
3. Instructing students to name letters aloud as they practice spelling.
4. Incorporating instruction in morphemic analysis.
5. Providing immediate error imitation and correction.
6. Using motivating reinforcers.
7. Providing periodic review and retesting.

Fulk and Stormont-Spurgin (1995) also reviewed studies of spelling interventions for students with disabilities. They noted empirical support for many of these same principles, as well as multisensory techniques, analogy training, and direct instruction in study strategies and self-monitoring techniques. Scott (2000) emphasized the importance of four types of spelling activities that are supported by research: memorizing words, word analysis and sorting, authentic reading and writing activities, and instruction in the strategic self-monitoring of spelling.

SPELLING INSTRUCTIONAL GUIDELINES

The following section on spelling instructional guidelines is designed to address a diverse age range, as well as a broad spectrum encompassing both typically developing spellers and children with significant spelling disability. Although some interventions have wide applicability to most learners, more specific interventions should be selected based on in-depth assessment of learner characteristics, as described in other chapters within this text.

Words can be grouped for instruction in many ways. Several sources provide comprehensive methods for organizing spelling instruction (e.g., Bear et al., 2000; Henry, 1988; Moats, 1995). For purposes of this chapter, the following categories have been selected for emphasis:

1. The basic alphabetic principle and code (e.g., sound–letter correspondences).
2. Unique, high-frequency "sight" words that must be memorized.
3. Predictable orthographic rules.
4. Homophones.
5. Syllable spelling patterns within multisyllabic words.
6. Morphophonemic principles for spelling.

These components of the spelling system are generally written in developmental order. However, teachers may find themselves teaching examples from each level throughout the entire process of spelling instruction, particularly for students with LD. What we often see in the misspellings of students with language-based LD is that their errors may span several developmental stages, even the primitive letter-name stage, well into the late elementary school grades and beyond. Kamhi and Hinton (2000) noted that poor spellers may follow a different developmental pattern as they learn to spell, often relying excessively on visual memory due to persistent deficits in phonological processing. We now have the linguistic knowledge to understand the basis for most spelling errors and to predict which phoneme–grapheme, orthographic, and morphophonemic patterns are most likely to cause difficulty (Masterson & Apel, 2000).

Each of these aspects of our spelling system overlaps with all the other aspects, and maturing spellers must learn over time to integrate and apply all aspects in the most accurate and efficient way. Only the most basic phoneme–grapheme patterns can be applied in an almost reflexive way. The student must sound out most words, then make some decisions about the precise letter sequence to select, because so many phonemes can be represented by more than one grapheme pattern, and many orthographic and morphophonemic rules affect the precise spelling (Kamhi & Hinton, 2000; Moats, 1995; Treiman & Bourassa, 2000).

Teaching Basic Phoneme–Grapheme Correspondence and Orthographic Patterns

Mastering the basic alphabetic principle of the English spelling system is the first essential task for a young speller. Studies of invented spelling in young children prior to or at the beginning stage of literacy instruction have identified predictable, rule-based representational patterns (Beers, 1980; Beers & Henderson, 1977; Chomsky, 1979; Marsh, Friedman, Welch, & Desberg, 1980; Read, 1975). Children often are able to sort out for themselves the simplest of phoneme–grapheme correspondences, matching up some sounds with their corresponding letter names. Reliance on articulation features of words plays a predominant role in how young children try to spell. Use of a single letter to represent an entire syllable is common when the letter name is the same as or close to that syllable (e.g., CAN-D for *candy*). The opportunity to invent one's own spelling increases active processing of letter sounds and ways to best represent them in writing (Treiman & Bourassa, 2000).

The kindergarten writing sample in Figure 31.1 provides an illustration of many common patterns seen in the writing of normally developing young spellers. Justin displays consistent use of the letter-name strategy in using *r* for *er* (e.g., NAVR, AMR, WRR, AVR) and a lack of knowledge about orthographic rules that mark vowels as long (e.g., NIT, GIS). He also shows a typical pattern of substitution of *a* for the short-*e* sound (e.g., DAD for *dead*, AND for *end*), a common variation of the letter-name strategy. On the other hand, he shows correct spelling for many words and

Once a pot a time there was a nit named Justin. And he wod navr di. He wod cill the bad gis. And it was hrd but not for him. And the bad gis thrid to cill him but tay codint. He had to mac amr. Tay wrr dad. And Justin livd fr avr. The and.

FIGURE 31.1. Kindergartner's story: *Justin the Knight.*

consistency in his misspellings (e.g., CILL for *kill*, GIS for *guys*), suggesting that he already is applying patterning and structure to his spelling attempts. Time and ongoing instruction in reading, spelling, and written expression should enable him to develop expanded spelling knowledge without difficulty.

Individual or group practice in phonological processing skills is strongly recommended in the early school grades as well. Many studies have documented the beneficial effect of phonological processing instruction on reading and spelling development, both for normally developing children and those with LD (e.g., Mann, Tobin, & Wilson, 1987; Tangel & Blachman, 1995; Treiman & Bourassa, 2000; Vellutino & Scanlon, 1987). *Phonemic Awareness in Young Children* (Adams, Foorman, Lundberg, & Beeler, 1998) describes many classroom, group-based activities to develop phonological awareness skills in young children. Snider (1995) and Moats (1995) also described several activities for this purpose. These activities are brief and involve readily available materials. They should be used in conjunction with general activities to promote oral-language development and literacy readiness.

For students with phonological processing deficits, direct instruction in these skills provides an essential building block for subsequent reading and spelling instruction. For those with the most severe phonological processing deficits, a more intensive program to develop these skills is recommended. Key components of this type of training in phonological awareness include a focus on articulation of each phoneme, the use of manipulative materials (e.g., chips or blocks) to represent phonemes, and explicit instruction and practice in hearing, saying, counting, and comparing phonemes within

words. Pictures typically are used initially, with printed words introduced as students begin reading. Examples include the Elkonin (1973), Ball and Blachman (1991) and Lindamood and Lindamood (1998) methods.

It is emphasized that phonological processing tasks focus primarily on specialized listening skills, thus comprising only one piece of a comprehensive language arts curriculum. Simultaneous with this type of instruction, children should receive explicit practice in reading and spelling skills. Instruction in each of these areas is mutually supportive and enables the child to develop increasingly varied and sophisticated spelling strategies (Treiman & Bourassa, 2000).

Bear et al. (2000) and Moats (1995) provide detailed scope and sequence charts for introducing all the major phoneme–grapheme correspondences, orthographic rules, and spelling patterns associated with multisyllable words, prefixes, and suffixes. Although no particular instructional sequence has been empirically validated in its entirety, it is critical to follow a sequence that begins with the easiest patterns in terms of linguistic properties and orthographic complexities, and eventually works through the most challenging patterns in a structured fashion.

Formal spelling instruction generally should begin with introduction of a few consonants and short vowels, along with a few high-frequency sight words. The consonants selected initially should be those whose letter names are most similar to their sounds (e.g., *b, p, t, s*). The consonants *h, w,* and *y* should not be among the first ones taught, because their sounds do not match their names (Ehri, 2000). Beginning spellers often substitute *y* for *w* if they are relying on a letter-name strategy for this reason (e.g., YOT for *want*). Similarly, phonemes represented by more than one grapheme (e.g., /k/ can be represented by *c* or *k*), and graphemes that correspond to more than one phoneme or involve multiple letters (e.g., *gh, th, sh*) should be introduced only after simpler phoneme–grapheme correspondences have been mastered. Teachers should always keep in mind that any increase in linguistic complexity increases the chance of spelling errors and the concomitant need for direct instruction and extended practice.

Initial, focused practice with one short vowel and several consonants is recommended for all children, and is essential for those with spelling disabilities. In this way, the teacher reduces the complexity of new material and can better ensure a higher rate of response accuracy, which in turn motivates the child to progress to the next skill. For each pattern, as many examples as possible should be presented. *The New Reading Teacher's Book of Lists* (Fry, Fountoukidis, & Polk, 1985), *Spellmaster* (Greenbaum, 1987), *Teaching Spelling* (Henderson, 1990), and *Words Their Way* (Bear et al., 2000) provide lists of words for spelling patterns, simplifying lesson preparation.

Paradoxically, research suggests that, from the beginning of spelling instruction, it is important to include some words that are less predictable using basic phoneme–grapheme correspondence patterns. Berninger, Vaughan, et al. (1998) found that words with moderate to minimum predictability added unique variance to training outcomes in second-grade students with LD. Including less predictable words in spelling lessons early on may emphasize the need to seek spelling patterns, simultaneous with recognition that some words may not precisely fit the pattern of focus (Scott, 2000). For each student, the key is to find the proper balance between reducing linguistic and orthographic complexity within a lesson, yet maintaining the student's active processing to improve long-term problem solving and spelling retention.

An alphabetic phonics method may be preferable, in which students and teacher sound out each phoneme, matching it to the corresponding grapheme (e.g., *b-a-t, bat*).

Some studies have shown that emphasis on the articulation features of phonemes enhances learning (Alexander, Andersen, Heilman, Voeller, & Torgesen, 1991; Torgesen & Morgan, 1992). This fits well with phonological awareness activities. However, for children who struggle with this approach, an analytical phonics approach may be used. With this method, whole words are presented that follow a phonics pattern (e.g., *bat, cat, mat, pat*), but the student does not articulate each phoneme, instead saying only the whole word. Achieving a high accuracy rate on fundamental phoneme–grapheme correspondences is critical, because they form the foundation for subsequent spelling growth (see Chapter 20 by Ehri and Snowling, this volume).

Consonant blends, digraphs, and double-vowel patterns are particularly challenging for students with LD and may require extra emphasis and practice. Liquids (e.g., /l/ and /r/) and nasals (e.g., /m/, /n/, and /ng/) are especially problematic for students with LD, particularly when they follow a vowel (Moats, 1995; Scott, 2000). Schwa or unaccented vowels are another source of frequent spelling errors, such that word groups or patterns should be emphasized in instruction (Ehri, 2000; Moats, 1995; Scott, 2000).

When teaching specific spelling patterns, teachers should incorporate a variety of activities that are linked with phonological awareness, reading, and vocabulary building activities. Particularly for students with spelling disabilities, multisensory strategies may be needed. Some of the earliest instructional techniques for teaching students with LD were multisensory, for example, the Orton–Gillingham (Gillingham & Stillman, 1960) and Fernald (1943) teaching methods. More recent, empirically based examples include Graham and Freeman's Five-Step Study Strategy (1986) and Berninger, Abbott, et al.'s Eight-Step Method (1998). In general, such methods emphasize simultaneously seeing, saying, and writing or tracing each letter, and checking response accuracy. These methods may enhance attention and activate multiple parts of the brain, thereby increasing the likelihood that true learning and retention will occur. Some empirical data support the use of multisensory teaching techniques versus unisensory approaches (Bradley & Bryant, 1985; Fulk & Stormont-Spurgin, 1995; Hulme, Monk, & Ives, 1987; Thomson, 1991). Once a foundation is built, spelling instruction may proceed at a somewhat faster pace, although for students with significant LD, this type of multisensory approach may be needed long-term, particularly for words with unique spellings that must be memorized.

Word-Sorting Activities

Word-sorting activities should be introduced early on in spelling instruction. These activities may take many forms and be devised for individuals or groups (Bear et al., 2000; Fresch & Wheaton, 1997; Schlagal & Schlagal, 1992). For young children, or those with significant LD, the teacher can write individual words on cards for students to sort into categories (e.g., *-ar* words vs. *-or* words). In my experience, the physical manipulation of word cards facilitates learning, even for adults with LD. Alternatively, students might be asked to assist the teacher in sorting words into two or more categories by writing them in columns on the chalkboard or overhead projector. This type of activity requires active mental processing and encourages students to look for patterns across words (Scott, 2000). Graham (1999) found that the knowledge gained from word-classification activities enhances generalization to the spelling of unknown words. Scott (2000) provides a table listing examples of various word-sort targets (p. 74).

Teaching Individual Words

Mastery of high-frequency sight words with unique, idiosyncratic spellings is a major challenge for students with spelling disabilities. Fernald (1943) demonstrated that students with spelling disabilities may need up to 40 opportunities to write a word correctly before achieving long-term mastery (Moats, 1995). The reasons for this are numerous. One factor may be that these words often lack concrete meaning and instead serve primarily a grammatical function (*of, for*) or have a meaning that is relative to other words within a given sentence (*there, where, here*) (Scott, 2000). A second factor is that many of these words are derived from Old and Middle English and have idiosyncratic spellings. Some are homophones (e.g., *there, their, they're; here, hear*) that require accurate semantic associations, along with spelling recall. For these reasons, such words almost always require an explicit instructional focus that may need to involve the multisensory techniques previously described.

Research has demonstrated that for poor spellers, when learning sight words, the number of words to be learned should be reduced, and known words should be removed from the study list (Scott, 2000). Research generally supports the study of about three to five new words per day, with no more than six to 12 new words per week (Fulk & Stormont-Spurgin, 1995; Graham & Voth, 1990; Moats, 1995). In addition to the multisensory methods cited, contingent modeling methods also may be beneficial (Gordon, Vaughn, & Schumm, 1993; Nulman & Gerber, 1984). With these methods, the teacher gives immediate feedback as to whether a student's spelling is correct or incorrect. If it is incorrect, the teacher imitates the misspelling, then presents the correct spelling. The student then says and writes the correct spelling. Johnson and Myklebust (1967) described a similar technique that, although not empirically validated, incorporates contingent modeling principles, as follows:

1. Write the word on a card and present it to the student(s) for reading, spelling, and discussion.
2. Present several subsequent cards with the word misspelled in various ways, asking the student(s) each time to say whether the spelling is correct or incorrect, and to say what the error is for the incorrect spellings.
3. Present 10 or more cards for each word, with occasional cards having the correct spelling.
4. Ask the student(s) to write the word from memory.
   Example: *where, were, hwere, wheer, where, wehre, where, weer, hwere, where.*

Berninger, Abbott, et al. (1998) found that for low predictability words, spelling practice using the computer facilitates mastery. Similar techniques are useful for teaching homophone pairs (e.g., *their, there, they're*). In addition, having students develop mnemonic strategies often facilitates recall (e.g., You *hear* with an *ear*). Visually highlighting the letters that differ in each homophone pair can improve recall. However, such words can only be learned through many exposures within a meaningful context, such that this aspect of spelling instruction must be closely linked to reading and language activities. Including reading and written-expression activities in each spelling lesson, along with focused spelling instruction, is supported by recent spelling research (Berninger, Vaughan, et al., 1998; Masterson & Scott, 1997).

Instruction in Advanced Spelling Skills

One deficiency of spelling instruction, including some remedial spelling programs, is that explicit instruction often ends after the basic phoneme–grapheme and orthographic patterns have been presented at the single-syllable level (Henry, 1988). Many students, and essentially all students with spelling disabilities, need continued focused instruction and practice in applying phoneme–grapheme and orthographic principles at the multisyllabic word level, and integrating those skills with more advanced spelling knowledge related to morphological and morphophonemic principles (Allal, 1997; Scott, 2000). Direct spelling instruction in the basic syllable patterns within multisyllabic words, and linkages to phoneme–grapheme correspondence patterns learned at the single-syllable level, will improve both spelling and reading vocabulary skills. Using individual syllable cards to sort into syllable patterns and engage in word-building activities is helpful in reinforcing pattern recognition and providing varied practice activities that keep students actively engaged in the learning process. Patterns that require explicit instruction (Bear et al., 2000; Moats, 1995) include the following:

1. Closed syllable (e.g., *velvet, fantastic*), in which the word consists of two or more vowel–consonant (VC) or consonant–vowel–consonant (CVC) syllables with short vowels.
2. Open syllable (e.g., *vibrant, locate*), in which the first syllable has a long vowel.
3. Various syllable accent patterns.
4. Spelling patterns for final syllables (*-le, -el, -or, -ar, -er*, etc.).

For such words, the student must learn to apply conditional rules, analyze several aspects of the word, and recall which pattern the word fits, to spell correctly. Older students with spelling disabilities often show major deficiencies at this level due to the increased complexities of the spelling patterns, lack of systematic instruction, and persistent, fundamental deficits in phonological analysis (Moats, 1995; Scott, 2000). Many teaching materials contain lists of words that follow specific syllable patterns and activities to develop spelling skills at this level, such as *Megawords* (Johnson & Bayrd, 1983), *Solving Language Difficulties* (Steere, Peck, & Kahn, 1971), and *Syllable Plus* (Stoner, 1985).

Instruction in syllable patterns can be linked to instruction in recognizing and spelling base words, prefixes, and suffixes. This aspect of reading and spelling is often referred to as "structural analysis." Systematic practice with common base words, prefixes, and suffixes is needed, because this is the level at which morphophonemic rules come into play, and patterns can be complex. For initial dictation spelling activities, either dictating the base word first, followed by the derived or inflected form, or having the student say or write the base word first, facilitates spelling of the longer word (Bailet, 1990).

Three rules that are a perennial source of difficulty for students with spelling disabilities are the "double, drop and change" rules that affect spelling with several suffixes (e.g., *-ed, -ing, -er, -est, -ly*), as follows:

1. For base words ending in a single consonant preceded by a single vowel, the final consonant must be doubled before adding a suffix that starts with a vowel (e.g., *rub–rubbed*).
2. For base words that end with a silent *e*, the *e* must be dropped before adding a

suffix that starts with a vowel (e.g., *tape–taped–taping*).

3. For words ending in *y*, the *y* must be changed to *i* before adding some suffixes (e.g., *reply–replied; happy–happily*).

Each of these rules has several components that require sequential decision making. Instruction in these rules generally begins in second or third grade but may need to be reviewed in later years because of their complexity. Practice should include many examples of words for which the rule applies. Students also should be challenged to identify words for which the rule does not apply, and describe the differences in the patterns.

Working with prefixes (e.g., *pre-, dis-, re-, un-*) and derivational suffixes, such as *-tion, -able,* and *-ous,* requires introduction of more advanced linguistic concepts. These patterns generally are introduced in the later elementary grades and require ongoing instruction, often into the high school years, for students with spelling disabilities. Spelling work at this level, although challenging, can be interesting and fun for older students, particularly those with advanced oral vocabulary and verbal-reasoning skills. Information on word origins and meanings facilitates spelling, improves vocabulary knowledge and reading comprehension, and provides variety in remedial spelling lessons. Understanding the linguistic dimensions along which inflected and derived word forms vary enables the spelling teacher to predict patterns that will be more or less difficult. Carlisle (1987), Carlisle and Nomanbhoy (1993), and Bear et al. (2000) noted that shifts in the pronunciation or spelling of the base word, or both, increase the complexity of inflected and derived words. The semantic link between the base word and the inflected or derived form in this case is opaque (e.g., *relate–relative*), versus the simpler, transparent pattern, in which neither the base-word spelling nor pronunciation changes when the suffix is added (e.g., *quick–quickly*) (Masterson & Apel, 2000).

As was recommended for teaching basic phoneme–grapheme correspondence patterns, extended practice with one pattern at the structural analysis level is important until a high rate of correct spelling is achieved. Additional patterns should then be intro-duced, one at a time, gradually combining two or more patterns into one spelling activity as student proficiency increases. Henry (1988) and Moats (1995) describe detailed lesson plans for a spelling unit at this level of word complexity.

Students with spelling disabilities almost by definition have difficulty with long-term retention of word images. For this reason, specific patterns and unique, challenging words need to be restudied periodically, particularly as new and potentially confusing patterns are introduced. As Scott (2000) noted, this requires teachers to maintain detailed records, and incorporate distributed practice and periodic review into the spelling curriculum. It is tremendously important to remember that children's minds and knowledge bases are continually evolving. Spelling principles and methods that did not work with a particular student at a young age may be beneficial a year or two later. Particularly in adolescence, when students gain increased abstract and integrative thinking capabilities, focused spelling instruction may make a significant difference in academic performance. In years past, formal spelling instruction and remedial spelling intervention were typically abandoned after elementary school, at the very point when they might have made the biggest impact. If students can see the relevance of such instruction to reading comprehension and written-expression skills, they are more likely to put forth the necessary effort to progress. The challenge falls to the teacher to keep lessons focused, interesting, varied, and embedded within broader language activities that benefit students across multiple aspects of the school curriculum.

Spelling Instruction for Students with Handwriting Difficulty

For students who have not yet become automatic in their handwriting, spelling instruction and practice can proceed in a number of interesting ways. Young children may enjoy spelling with stamp sets, plastic alphabet letters, or alphabet-letter cards placed in a spelling pocket. These alternatives to handwriting offer the added advantage of physical manipulation, as previously described. Plastic letters or letter cards help children grasp spelling patterns, because they can literally remove and exchange the beginning, middle, or ending letter and note the new word that results.

For spelling activities that involve handwriting, an alphabet strip can be placed on the child's desk until all letters have been learned. Searching on an alphabet chart attached to the top of the classroom wall is time-consuming and frustrating for students with handwriting and spelling difficulties. As such, it is likely to increase frustration and decrease perseverance for essential spelling activities. Older students with severe dysgraphia may need to practice spelling by typing on a computer or AlphaSmart keyboard. Typing instruction and training in the use of the computer or keyboard need to be included in the instructional plan in such cases (Bain, 2001).

The underlying principle here is that spelling practice should not always be complicated by handwriting struggles. Each should receive separate, although complementary, instructional focus. Students, particularly those who are young and/or who have LD, are more likely to progress in a skill if only one challenge is presented at a time. The teacher must determine the skill to teach in a particular activity, then design instruction to minimize other, simultaneous cognitive and physical demands, at least during the initial learning phase.

As the student progresses in handwriting skill, spelling instruction should incorporate handwriting. Some research evidence suggests that the motor act of handwriting facilitates learning and retention of letter sequences for later spelling recall. However, this is most likely to occur if the proper motor patterns for writing each letter are solidly established first, although explicit instruction in letter writing itself may contribute to letter knowledge, which in turn promotes spelling acquisition (Berninger, Abbott, et al., 1998).

Berninger, Abbott, et al. (1998) reported results from a study assessing the impact of using a pencil versus a computer response mode on spelling accuracy in young children with either isolated spelling disability or combined spelling and handwriting disability. They found that their poor spellers performed better with a pencil for highly predictable sound–spelling correspondences, whereas poor spellers performed better with the computer when spelling words with lower sound–spelling predictability. They hypothesized that for more challenging words, using the computer allowed the students to devote more mental energy to spelling, rather than having to attend simultaneously to the motor demands of handwriting. Therefore, these data support the need to reduce simultaneous mental demands on students when they are initially learning a new skill or confronting a more advanced level of a familiar skill. The data also suggest that both traditional handwriting and use of a computer can play beneficial roles in supporting spelling instruction.

Spelling Disability in the Context of Written Expression

Not surprisingly, poor spellers typically make more spelling errors in expressive writing than in dictation spelling activities. The reason for this is that expressive writing requires the application of multiple cognitive and linguistic skills. Most writers try to apply these multiple skills simultaneously, making themselves more vulnerable to errors in spelling, handwriting, grammar, punctuation, capitalization, and formulation. Spelling instruction should incorporate expressive writing activities, along with dictation spelling practice. Ideally, these writing activities should follow a natural progression from highly structured to completely unstructured. Berninger, Vaughan, et al. (1998) and Masterson and Scott (1997) recommend that there be some text-level spelling activity in every lesson. This might include finding examples of a particular spelling pattern in a reading passage, or writing a story using words from one or more designated patterns. Scott (2000) also suggested using e-mail and Internet searches as extension activities. A sample instructional sequence might include the following activities (not necessarily within one lesson):

1. Focused practice with a single spelling pattern, including single-word dictation activities.

2. A word search within a reading passage to find words following one or more designated patterns.
3. Single-word dictation activities, including two or three patterns that have been previously practiced separately.
4. Sentence dictation activities in which the words or patterns of interest are embedded. Sentence complexity should be adjusted to students' spelling and reading level.
5. Written sentence formulation by the student, including target words.
6. Written paragraph formulation by the student, including target words.

Without explicit instruction and practice in using newly mastered spelling words in their writing, students are likely to lapse into using more familiar and easier words. We often see expressive writing that is far below students' cognitive and oral-language levels, because they are trying, either consciously or subconsciously, to use only those words they feel comfortable spelling. With focused practice, teachers can expand students' repertoire of words with which they feel competent. Explicit practice using targeted spelling words in expressive writing also increases teaching opportunities to address morphophonemic spelling principles and to discuss word meanings. Students can practice changing word forms in structured activities (e.g., "Sue is *related* to John"; "Sue and John are *relatives*") and then be guided in editing their own writing samples using these morphophonemic principles.

Students should be encouraged and instructed in using computers for writing from an early age. Computer technology and software to support all aspects of the writing process, at all levels of writing sophistication, have expanded dramatically within the last decade (Meyer, Murray, & Pisha, 2001). Use of a computer is essential for students with handwriting and spelling disabilities, because it can alleviate much of the stress associated with writing and result in better writing products. However, the computer is a supplement, not a substitute for a teacher. A carefully planned, teacher-directed instructional sequence integrated within the language arts curriculum is essen-tial for students with spelling disabilities to take full advantage of computer technology for writing purposes.

Problem-Solving, Self-Monitoring, and Error Correction Strategies

Several LD researchers have emphasized the importance of teaching students explicit strategies for finding and correcting their own spelling mistakes (Gerber & Hall, 1989; Graham, 1999; Berninger, Abbott, et al., 1998). As summarized by Scott (2000), some of the strategies identified as improving outcomes include the following:

1. Self-questioning and self-guidance.
2. Locating the specific letter or part of the word where the error has occurred.
3. Using word analogies to generate alternative spellings.
4. Using peer editors.
5. Using multiple error-detection strategies.
6. Using computer spell-check programs effectively.

Teachers should consistently look for opportunities to make spelling patterns and potential pitfalls explicit for their students, to model aloud their own strategic problem-solving strategies, and to provide guided practice to help students learn these skills.

Because students with LD need to expend considerable mental energy on spelling during expressive writing activities and are thus vulnerable to multiple types of writing errors, it is important to teach explicit editing and proofreading strategies. Research-based instruction from a writing process approach is beneficial in this regard, with emphasis on the prewriting, drafting, revising, and editing components of written expression (Gould, 2001). Students with LD, however, need an explicit, multistep sequence for the editing and proofreading phases, and guided practice in its application. It is critical to teach error-correction strategies, beyond error detection. MacArthur, Graham, Haynes, and De la Paz (1996) demonstrated that students with LD detected many more errors than they were able to correct, even when using spell-check programs (Scott, 2000).

The InSPECT method (McNaughton & Hughes, 1999) is one comprehensive approach for finding and correcting spelling errors. Students with LD often need an individualized, written guide for proofreading. An example for the student described in the second case example at the end of this chapter might be as follows:

1. Check for spacing errors between and within words.
2. Check for misspellings of words ending in *-ed* and *-s* (plural).
3. Check for misspellings of words with *-le*.

This type of guide needs to be tailored to each student's instructional level and particular spelling challenges. As Gould (2001) notes, it is important to emphasize steady progress in error correction, rather than perfection. Students should be taught strategies to correct as many errors as possible independently through self-monitoring, spell-check programs, and dictionaries, and to recognize when to seek assistance from peers and adults (Graham, 1999).

Table 31.1 provides a summary of the main principles of spelling instruction described in this chapter.

CASE EXAMPLES

Two clinical cases are presented here to illustrate some of the instructional principles previously described. The first is a girl diagnosed with severe dyslexia characterized by significant deficits in phonological processing, reading, and spelling. Her intellectual level was average to high-average, and her math skills were average. She was in seventh grade at the time of the evaluation from which these spelling errors were taken. One can see in Table 31.2 that some of her error patterns are identical to those made by the normally developing kindergarten speller described earlier (e.g., SOCR, MIT, EADVATR, COD, HAD). In addition, she shows significant difficulty spelling words with both beginning and ending consonant blends (e.g., BALID, FAD, LEP), and makes errors in basic sound–symbol correspondences. Some of her errors appear extreme,

TABLE 31.1. Key Principles of Spelling Instruction

1. Become familiar with basic linguistic terms, principles, rules, and patterns that relate to English spelling.
2. Become familiar with developmental spelling trends and spelling patterns that tend to be challenging for most students.
3. Provide writing opportunities for young children to engage in invented spelling.
4. Provide direct instruction in phonological awareness skills.
5. Begin formal spelling instruction by teaching the simplest phoneme–grapheme patterns, using phonemes and graphemes with the lowest degree of linguistic complexity.
6. Provide as many examples as possible of each spelling pattern presented.
7. Teach spelling rules in an explicit manner, and encourage students to actively search for positive examples (e.g., those that follow the rule) and negative examples (e.g., those that do not).
8. Emphasize aspects of the word that you are trying to teach, by changing the color or font, exaggerating phoneme or syllable pronunciation, or stating the base word within a longer word that the student has to write.
9. Introduce examples that do not precisely fit the pattern early in instruction, to encourage active mental processing.
10. Begin with spelling activities that have the highest degree of structure (i.e., dictation tasks with one spelling pattern) and gradually progress to activities with less structure (i.e., written expression tasks using target words from one or more patterns).
11. Incorporate manipulative activities through the use of individual alphabet-letter cards or syllable cards for word-sorting and word-building activities.
12. Introduce only a few sight words each day and practice each for several consecutive days.
13. Use multisensory techniques and mnemonic devices, particularly for words with unique spellings.
14. Incorporate text-level activities, either reading or writing, in each spelling lesson.
15. Provide immediate correction of errors, when possible.
16. Provide frequent review and periodic retesting of previously mastered words.
17. Provide direct instruction in multiple types of proofreading, error detection, and correction strategies.
18. Provide frequent positive feedback for effort and progress.

TABLE 31.2. Spelling Responses of a 13-Year-Old Girl with Dyslexia

Target word	Written response
adventure	EADVATR
cough	COUT
lamp	LEP
might	MIT
soccer	SOCR
could	COD
over	OFR
head	HAD
vacation	VECSI
bottom	BADA
blind	BALID
fold	FAD
walking	WOKING
toward	TOD
a chair	ATRW

such as VECSI for *vacation*. It is important to remember that error analysis is most appropriate with words for which the child has some level of word knowledge. For words above that level, the student is forced to guess under frustrating conditions, such that meaningful diagnostic patterns cannot be ascertained (Moats, 1995; Morris, Nelson, & Perney, 1986; Schlagal, 1992).

This child's misspellings also vividly illustrate that students with spelling disabilities are not exactly like typically developing younger spellers, although some similar patterns are present. She has persistent, severe deficits in analyzing the phonological structure of words, pairing individual phonemes to the appropriate grapheme, and sequencing them accurately. Without intensive effort to remediate these fundamental deficits, she will have little hope of mastering more complex orthographic and morphophonemic patterns (Bailet, 2001). Many of her misspellings are of particular interest, because they violate basic English orthographic rules and are hence considered "orthographically illegal." For example, she writes OFIV and OFV for *over,* and DIV for *dive;* in English spelling, words never end in *v.* Typically developing young spellers learn very quickly through general reading and writing activities which patterns look like English and which do not, whereas children with severe spelling disabilities are slower in

developing that basic visual–linguistic sensitivity.

Instructional priorities might include intensive instruction in phonological awareness, sequencing, and blending skills, and a review of basic phoneme–grapheme correspondence patterns. She would also benefit from explicit instruction in spelling words with consonant blends, particularly those involving the liquid and nasal consonant sounds. Efforts to increase her visual sensitivity to letter sequences that are orthographically illegal in English might improve her ability to self-monitor for spelling errors in her own writing. Word-sorting, word-search, and simple written-expression activities, such as e-mail, would allow her to practice specific spelling skills within a meaningful context that encourages active mental processing.

The misspellings in Table 31.3 are those of a 10-year-old boy diagnosed with spelling disability. He was known to have intellectual skills in the superior to very superior range, whereas his reading skills were average, and phonological processing skills were low-average to average. He had struggled with reading skills in the early elementary school grades but was progressing well in reading at the time this writing sample was obtained. Thus, he displayed a mild

TABLE 31.3. Spelling Responses of a 10-Year-Old Boy with Spelling Disability

Dictated word	Written response
in	IN
he	HE
six	SIX
green	GRENE
are	ARE
was	WHAS
under	UNDIR
house	HOUS
rain	RANE
table	TABIL
when	WIN
cooked	COOKTE
sixteen	SIXTENO
floor	FLOUR
second	SECIND
early	ERLEY
rewards	REWORDES

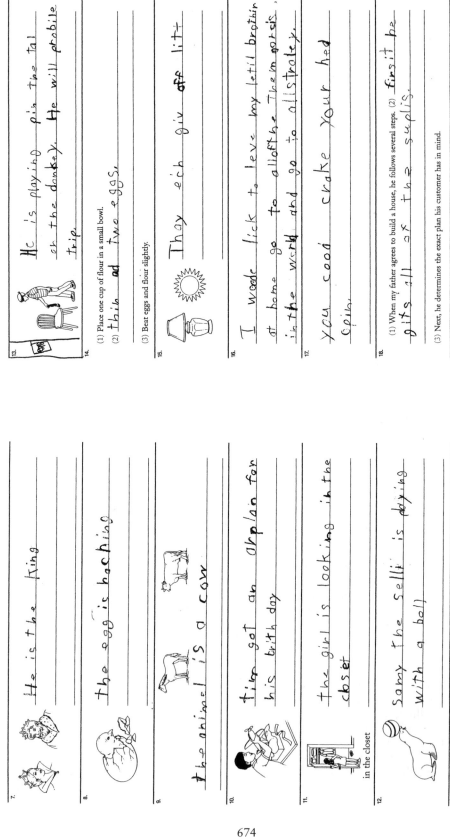

FIGURE 31.2. Written responses of a 10-year-old boy with spelling disability: Woodcock–Johnson III Tests of Achievement (Woodcock, McGrew, & Mather, 2001) Writing Samples subtest.

residual dyslexia pattern. Children like this boy, if given appropriate intervention, often make reasonable progress in reading but continue to display significant spelling disability.

His errors for the most part represent accurately the sound structure of the dictated words. He needs explicit instruction in basic orthographic spelling rules for English, such as the consonant *-le* syllable pattern in *table,* and in double-vowel patterns (e.g., *ai, ee, oo, ea*). He also made errors on words with inflectional suffixes *-ed* and *-s,* and would benefit from review and practice in this skill. Analysis of his spelling errors in a written expression task also revealed confusion regarding short- and long-vowel spelling patterns, as well as additional examples of his difficulty with double-vowel patterns and spelling rules related to inflectional suffixes (see Figure 31.2).

His writing also reflects difficulty with word boundaries. In Item 16, note the words *all of the,* written as one word. On another page within this test, he wrote BRITH DAY for *birthday.* Children with spelling disabilities often display difficulty representing word units accurately within sentences and benefit from focused practice for words and phrases they misrepresent.

Instructional priorities might include word-sorting activities to improve his ability to spell words with long-vowel patterns (e.g., *ee* vs. *ea* vs. *eCe* patterns), word searches in written text, and sentence or paragraph writing that includes multiple words of a designated pattern. He also needs instruction in spelling principles for inflectional suffixes *-ed* and *-s* plural, as well as the *-le* ending syllable pattern.

CONCLUSIONS

Spelling disability should be viewed as a chronic condition that, in most cases, is treatable but not curable. Remediating to the extent possible, then managing the spelling disability should be our focus, such that it does not ultimately derail the pursuit of higher educational or occupational goals. We cannot hope to eliminate all spelling errors in anyone's writing, much less all those

of students with LD. Both students and teachers experience unnecessary frustration and a sense of failure unless reasonable, explicit goals are established. Perhaps our most important goals as spelling teachers are (1) to provide students with enough focused practice and explicit knowledge of spelling principles and patterns that they feel confident in trying to spell many different words in their writing assignments, and (2) to teach students when and how to tap a variety of strategies and resources for spelling-error detection and correction. We must consider spelling within the broader context of student learning and performance, and recognize that it is only one component among many that deserve our focus. The worst outcome occurs when students so restrict their writing, due to low spelling ability and confidence, that their teachers never know the richness of their thoughts, and the students never discover the sense of accomplishment that comes through writing one's thoughts well. Fortunately, increasingly effective teaching methods and materials are emerging as a result of recent research efforts and the consequent evolution of knowledge related to the linguistic and developmental principles that guide how children learn to spell.

REFERENCES

Adams, M. J., Foorman, B. R., Lundberg, I., & Beeler, T. (1998). *Phonemic awareness in young children.* Baltimore: Brookes.

Alexander, A. W., Anderson, H. G., Heilman, P. C., Voeller, K. S., & Torgesen, J. K. (1991). Phonological awareness training and remediation of analytic decoding deficits in a group of severe dyslexics. *Annals of Dyslexia, 41,* 193–206.

Allal, L. (1997). Learning to spell in the classroom. In C. Perfetti, L. Rieben, & M. Fayol (Eds.), *Learning to spell: Research, theory, and practice across languages* (pp. 129–150). Mahwah, NJ: Erlbaum.

Bailet, L. L. (1990). Spelling rule usage among students with learning disabilities and normally achieving students. *Journal of Learning Disabilities, 23*(2), 121–128.

Bailet, L. L. (2001). Development and disorders of spelling in the beginning school years. In A. M. Bain, L. L. Bailet, & L. C. Moats (Eds.), *Written language disorders: Theory into practice* (2nd ed., pp. 1–41). Austin, TX: PRO-ED.

Bain, A. M. (2001). Handwriting disorders. In A. M.

Bain, L. L. Bailet, & L. C. Moats (Eds.), *Written language disorders: Theory into practice* (2nd ed., pp. 77–101). Austin, TX: PRO-ED.

Ball, E. W., & Blachman, B. A. (1991). Does phoneme awareness training in kindergarten make a difference in early word recognition and spelling development? *Reading Research Quarterly, 26,* 46–66.

Bear, D., Invernizzi, M., Templeton, S., & Johnson, F. (2000). *Words their way* (2nd ed.). Columbus, OH: Merrill.

Beers, J. W. (1980). Developmental strategies of spelling competence in primary school children. In E. H. Henderson & J. W. Beers (Eds.), *Developmental and cognitive aspects of learning to spell: A reflection of word knowledge* (pp. 35–45). Newark, DE: International Reading Association.

Beers, J. W., & Henderson, E. (1977). A study of developing orthographic concepts among first graders. *Research in the Teaching of English, 11*(2), 133–148.

Berninger, V., Abbot, R., Rogan, L., Reed, E., Abbott, S., Brooks, A., et al. (1998). Teaching spelling to children with specific learning disabilities: The mind's ear and eye beat the computer or pencil. *Learning Disability Quarterly, 21,* 106–122.

Berninger, V., Vaughan, K., Abbot, R., Brooks, A., Abbott, S., Rogan, L., et al. (1998). Early intervention for spelling problems: Teaching functional spelling units of varying size with a multiple-connections framework. *Journal of Educational Psychology, 90,* 587–605.

Bradley, L., & Bryant, P. E. (1985). *Rhyme and reason in reading and spelling* (International Academy of Research in Learning Disabilities Monographs No. 1). Ann Arbor: University of Michigan Press.

Bruck, M., & Waters, G. (1988). An analysis of the spelling errors of children who differ in their reading and spelling skills. *Applied Psycholinguistics, 9,* 77–92.

Carlisle, J. F. (1987). The use of morphological knowledge in spelling derived forms by learning-disabled and normal students. *Annals of Dyslexia, 9,* 247–266.

Carlisle, J. F., & Nomanbhoy, D. M. (1993). Phonological and morphological awareness in first graders. *Applied Psycholinguistics, 14,* 177–195.

Chomsky, C. (1979). Approaching reading through invented spelling. In L. B. Resnick & P. A. Weaver (Eds.), *Theory and practice of early reading* (Vol. 2, pp. 43–66). Hillsdale, NJ: Erlbaum.

Clark, D. B. (1988). *Theory and practice of remedial instruction.* Parkton, MD: York Press.

Ehri, L. C. (2000). Learning to read and learning to spell: Two sides of a coin. *Topics in Language Disorders, 20*(3), 19–36.

Elkonin, D. B. (1973). U.S.S.R. In J. Downing (Ed.), *Comparative reading* (pp. 551–579). New York: Macmillan.

Fernald, G. (1943). *Remedial techniques in basic school subjects.* New York: McGraw-Hill.

Fox, B., & Routh, D. K. (1976). Phonemic analysis and synthesis as word-attack skills. *Journal of Educational Psychology, 68,* 70–74.

Fox, B., & Routh, D. K. (1984). Phonemic analysis and synthesis as word attack skills: Revisited. *Journal of Educational Psychology, 76*(6), 1059–1067.

Fresch, J., & Wheaton, A. (1997). Sort, search, and discover: Spelling in the child-centered classroom. *Reading Teacher, 51,* 20–31.

Frith, U. (1980). Unexpected spelling problems. In U. Frith (Ed.), *Cognitive processes in spelling* (pp. 495–515). London: Academic Press.

Fry, E., Fountoukidis, D. L., & Polk, J. K. (1985). *The new reading teacher's book of lists.* Englewood Cliffs, NJ: Prentice-Hall.

Fulk, B. M., & Stormont-Spurgin, M. (1995). Spelling interventions for students with disabilities: A review. *Journal of Special Education, 28*(4), 488–513.

Gerber, M., & Hall, R. (1989). Cognitive-behavioral training in spelling for learning handicapped students. *Learning Disability Quarterly, 12,* 159–171.

Gettinger, M. (1993). Effects of invented spelling and direct instruction on spelling performance of second-grade boys. *Journal of Applied Behavior Analysis, 26,* 281–291.

Gillingham, A., & Stillman, B. (1960). *Remedial training for children with specific disability in reading, spelling and penmanship.* Cambridge, MA: Educators Publishing Service.

Gordon, J., Vaughn, S., & Schumm, J. (1993). Spelling interventions: A review of literature and implications for instruction for students with learning disabilities. *Learning Disabilities Practice, 8,* 175–181.

Gould, B. W. (2001). Curricular strategies for written expression. In A. M. Bain, L. L. Bailet, & L. C. Moats (Eds.), *Written language disorders: Theory into practice* (2nd ed., pp. 185–220). Austin, TX: PRO-ED.

Graham, S. (1999). Handwriting and spelling instruction for students with learning disabilities: A review. *Learning Disability Quarterly, 22,* 78–98.

Graham, S. (2000). Should the natural learning approach replace spelling instruction? *Journal of Educational Psychology, 92*(2), 235–247.

Graham, S., & Freeman, S. (1986). Strategy training and teacher- vs. student-controlled study conditions: Effects on LD students' performance. *Learning Disability Quarterly, 9,* 15–22.

Graham, S., Harris, K., & Loynachan, C. (1994). The spelling for writing list. *Journal of Learning Disabilities, 27,* 210–214.

Graham, S., & Voth, V. (1990). Spelling instruction: Making modifications for students with learning disabilities. *Academic Therapy, 25,* 447–457.

Greenbaum, C. R. (1987). *Spellmaster.* Austin, TX: PRO-ED.

Henderson, E. (1990). *Teaching spelling.* Boston: Houghton Mifflin.

Henry, M. K. (1988). Beyond phonics: Integrated decoding and spelling instruction based on word origin and structure. *Annals of Dyslexia, 38,* 258–275.

Hulme, C., Monk, A., & Ives, S. (1987). Some experimental studies of multisensory teaching: The effects of manual tracing on children's paired-associate learning. *British Journal of Developmental Psychology, 5,* 299–307.

Invernizzi, M., Abouzeid, M., & Gill, J. T. (1994). Using students' invented spellings as a guide for spelling instruction that emphasizes word study. *Elementary School Journal, 95,* 155–167.

Johnson, D. J., & Myklebust, H. R. (1967). *Learning disabilities: Educational principles and practices.* New York: Grune & Stratton.

Johnson, K., & Bayrd, P. (1983). *Megawords.* Cambridge, MA: Educators Publishing Service.

Kamhi, A. G., & Hinton, L. N. (2000). Explaining individual differences in spelling ability. *Topics in Language Disorders, 20*(3), 37–49.

Lindamood, C. H., & Lindamood, P. (1998). *The Lindamood Phoneme Sequencing Program for reading, spelling, and speech.* Austin, TX: PRO-ED.

MacArthur, C., Graham, S., Haynes, J., & De La Paz, S. (1996). Spelling checkers and students with learning disabilities: Performance comparisons and impact of spelling. *Journal of Special Education, 30,* 35–57.

MacArthur, C., Graham, S., Schwartz, S., & Schafer, W. (1995). Evaluation of a writing instruction model that integrated a process approach, strategy instruction, and word processing. *Learning Disability Quarterly, 18,* 278–291.

Mann, V. A., Tobin, P., & Wilson, R. (1987). Measuring phonological awarenesss through the invented spellings of kindergarten children. *Merrill–Palmer Quarterly, 33*(3), 365–389.

Marsh, G., Friedman, M., Welch, V., & Desberg, P. (1980). The development of strategies in spelling. In U. Frith (Ed.), *Cognitive processes in spelling* (pp. 339–353). London: Academic Press.

Masterson, J. J., & Apel, K. (2000). Spelling assessment: Charting a path to optimal intervention. *Topics in Language Disorders, 20*(3), 50–65.

Masterson, J. J., & Scott, C. (1997, November). *Improving the spelling skills of children with and without language disorders.* A seminar presented at the Annual Meeting of the American Speech–Language–Hearing Association, Boston, MA.

McIntyre, E. (1995). Teaching and learning writing skills in a low-SES, urban primary classroom. *Journal of Reading Behavior, 27,* 213–242.

McNaughton, D., & Hughes, C. A. (1999). *InSPECT: A strategy for finding and correcting spelling errors.* Lawrence, KS: Edge Enterprises.

McNaughton, D., Hughes, C. A., & Clark, K. (1994). Spelling instruction for students with learning disabilities: Implications for research and practice. *Learning Disability Quarterly, 17,* 169–185.

Meyer, A., Murray, E., & Pisha, B. (2001). More than words: Learning to write in the digital world. In A. M. Bain, L. L. Bailet, & L. C. Moats (Eds.), *Written language disorders: Theory into practice* (2nd ed., pp. 137–184) Austin, TX: PRO- ED.

Moats, L. C. (1995). *Spelling development, disability, and instruction.* Baltimore: York Press.

Morris, D., Nelson, L. J., & Perney, J. (1986). Exploring the concept of "spelling instructional level"

through the analysis of error-types. *Elementary School Journal, 87,* 181–200.

Newman, S., Fields, H., & Wright, S. (1993). A developmental study of specific spelling disability. *British Journal of Educational Psychology, 63,* 287–296.

Nulman, J., & Gerber, M. (1984). Improving spelling performance by imitating a child's errors. *Journal of Learning Disabilities, 17,* 328–331.

O'Connor, R., & Jenkins, J. (1995). Improving the generalization of sound/symbol knowledge: Teaching spelling to kindergarten children with disabilities. *Journal of Special Education, 29,* 255–275.

O'Connor, R. E., Notari-Syverson, A., & Vadasy, P. F. (1996). Ladders to literacy: The effects of teacher-led phonological activities for kindergarten children with and without disabilities. *Exceptional Children, 63*(1), 117–130.

Read, C. (1975). Lessons to be learned from the preschool orthographer. In E. Lenneberg & E. Lenneberg (Eds.), *Foundations of language development* (Vol. 2, pp. 329–346). New York: Academic Press.

Rourke, B. P., & Strang, J. D. (1983). Subtypes of reading and arithmetical disabilities: A neuropsychological analysis. In M. Rutter (Ed.), *Developmental neuropsychiatry* (pp. 473–488). New York: Guilford Press.

Rubin, H., & Eberhardt, N. (1996). Facilitating invented spelling through language analysis instruction: An integrated model. *Reading and Writing: An Interdisciplinary Journal, 8,* 27–43.

Schlagal, R. C. (1992). Patterns of orthographic development in the middle grades. In S. Templeton & D. Bear (Eds.), *Development of orthographic knowledge and the foundations of literacy.* Hillsdale, NJ: Erlbaum.

Schlagal, R. C., & Schlagal, J. (1992). The integrated character of spelling: Teaching strategies for multiple purposes. *Language Arts, 69,* 418–424.

Scott, C. M. (2000). Principles and methods of spelling instruction: Applications for poor spellers. *Topics in Language Disorders, 20*(3), 66–82.

Snider, V. E. (1995). A primer on phonemic awareness: What it is, why it's important, and how to teach it. *School Psychology Review, 24*(3), 443–455.

Steere, A., Peck, C. Z., & Kahn, L. (1971). *Solving language difficulties.* Cambridge, MA: Educators Publishing Service.

Stoner, J. (1985). *Syllable Plus.* Cambridge, MA: Educators Publishing Service.

Tangel, D. M., & Blachman, B. A. (1995). Effect of phoneme awareness instruction on the invented spelling of first grade children: A one year follow-up. *Journal of Reading Behavior, 27,* 153–185.

Thomson, M. (1991). The teaching of spelling using techniques of simultaneous oral spelling and visual inspection. In M. Snowling & M. Thomson (Eds.), *Dyslexia: Integrating theory and practice* (pp. 244–250). London: Whurr.

Torgesen, J. K., Alexander, A. W., Wagner, R. K., Rashotte, C. A., Voeller, K. K. S., & Conway, T. (2001). Intensive remedial instruction for children with severe reading disabilities: Immediate and long-term outcomes from two instructional approaches. *Journal of Learning Disabilities, 34,* 33–58, 78.

Torgesen, J. K., & Morgan, S. (1992). The effects of two types of phonological awareness training on word learning in kindergarten children. *Journal of Experimental Psychology, 84,* 364–370.

Treiman, R., & Bourassa, D. C. (2000). The development of spelling skill. *Topics in Language Disorders, 20*(3), 1–18.

Uhry, J. K., & Shepherd, M. J. (1993). Segmentation /spelling instruction as part of a first-grade reading program: Effects on several measures of reading. *Reading Research Quarterly, 28,* 219–233.

Vellutino, F. R., & Scanlon, D. M. (1987). Phonological coding, phonological awareness and reading ability: Evidence from a longitudinal and experimental study. *Merrill–Palmer Quarterly, 33*(3), 321–363.

Venezky, R. L. (1980). From Webster to Rice to Roosevelt. In U. Frith (Ed.), *Cognitive processes in spelling* (pp. 9–30). London: Academic Press.

Woodcock, R. W., McGrew, K. S., & Mather, N. (2001). *Woodcock–Johnson III Tests of Achievement.* Itasca, IL: Riverside.

SPECIAL CONSIDERATIONS WITH ADOLESCENTS AND YOUNG ADULTS

32

Enhancing Literacy Proficiency with Adolescents and Young Adults

Barbara J. Ehren
B. Keith Lenz
Donald D. Deshler

The challenge to prepare adolescents and young adults for the complex world that awaits them includes the task of helping them to develop the literacy skills and strategies they will need for their future. The enormity and importance of this task are captured by the International Reading Association (IRA) Commission on Adolescent Literacy in its position statement:

> Adolescents entering the adult world in the 21st century will read and write more than at any other time in human history. They will need advanced levels of literacy to perform their jobs, run their households, act as citizens, and conduct their personal lives. They will need literacy to cope with the flood of information they will find everywhere they turn. They will need literacy to feed their imaginations so they can create the world of the future. (Moore, Bean, Birdyshaw, & Rycik, 1999, p. 3)

Given the advanced literacy levels needed to be productive citizens, it is crucial to our democratic society that our adolescents and young adults be prepared for what lies ahead of them. In this chapter, we consider the status and direction of that important mission. First, we discuss how well our adolescents and young adults are doing with literacy. Next, we explore the consequences of limited literacy proficiency. Last, we present key principles that should be considered in addressing the literacy needs of adolescents and young adults, principles that dispel prevailing myths. Although concern for the literacy challenges of youth with learning disabilities (LD) is central to this chapter, we wish to make the case that the venue of adolescent and young adult literacy warrants a more global view of struggling readers and writers, including those with LD.

THE CURRENT PICTURE

By all indications, large numbers of adolescents in our country are not in a position to read and write at levels to meet the demands of the 21st century (Hock & Deshler, 2003). Several sources of data support this conclusion. In the area of reading on the National

Assessment of Education Progress (NAEP), adolescents continue to read at levels that indicate limited growth in reading proficiency. Of note are the data regarding students' reading at Basic and Proficient levels. Reading at the Basic level on the NAEP means partial mastery of prerequisite knowledge and skills that are fundamental for proficient work at a grade, not good enough for an educated citizenry. The Proficient level represents solid academic performance, with students demonstrating subject matter knowledge, application of knowledge to real-world situations, and analytical skills appropriate to the subject matter (Grigg, Daane, Ying, & Campbell, 2003).

Although eighth graders have made improvements over the years, many are not performing at acceptable levels. In 2002, 75% were performing at or above the Basic level. This level of performance was higher than in all previous assessment years but still indicates that one-fourth of our 13-year-olds are not even reading at a Basic level. Thirty-three percent of eighth graders performed at or above the Proficient level, meaning that 67% are not reading as well as they need to. Although this performance was higher in 2002 than in 1992, there was no significant change from the 1998 test.

For 12th graders, the picture is more dismal, with lower results in 2002 than in 1998 and 1992. The percentage of 12th graders performing at or above Basic level was 74%, with 36% at or above Proficient level. This means that 26% of our 17-year-olds getting ready to face either postsecondary education or employment do not even have the reading fundamentals they need, whereas 64% of them who are not reading proficiently are not equipped to meet the high literacy expectations of their future.

The NAEP data for 12th graders may actually underestimate the problem, because many poor readers drop out of school before 12th grade. It should also be noted that the data on 8th and 12th graders are in contrast to the generally upward trend with readers in 4th grade, who are showing improvement at all levels. This disparity may be attributed to a greater emphasis on improved reading in younger students at na-

tional, state, and local levels. It is also distressing to note that as our nation struggles to address the performance of specific populations of students, no changes have been noted in the gap between white and black students, and white and Hispanic students at grades 8 and 12 since 1992 (Grigg et al., 2003).

In the area of writing, the percentage of eighth graders at or above the Basic level (85%) and at or about the Proficient level (31%) showed a slight increase in 2002. However, these data mean that 15% of our 13-year-olds do not demonstrate a fundamental ability to communicate in writing, which may include the following: a general understanding of the writing task at hand; awareness of the audience; inclusion of supporting details in an organized way; sufficiently accurate grammar, spelling, punctuation, and capitalization to communicate to a reader, with errors sometimes interfering with meaning. The 69% who are not proficient writers may lack the following qualities: understanding of both the writing task and the audience; use of organizational techniques, such as sequencing or a clearly marked beginning and ending; use of details and some elaboration to support and develop the main idea of the piece; precise language and some variety in sentence structure; analytical, evaluative, or creative thinking; sufficiently accurate grammar, spelling, punctuation, and capitalization to communicate to a reader, with minor errors that do not get in the way of meaning.

For the 12th grade, the percentage of students at or above the Proficient level rose slightly in 2002, but the percentage at the Basic level declined from 1998 to 2002, with 74% of our students now writing at a basic level. This finding means that 26% of our 17-year-olds have difficulty in the following areas: producing an effective response within the time allowed that shows an understanding of both the writing task and the audience; analytical, evaluative, or creative thinking; providing details that support and develop the central idea of the piece; clear organization, making use of techniques such as consistency in topic or theme, sequencing, and a clear introduction and conclusion; grammar, spelling, punctuation, and capitalization that is accurate enough to communicate to a reader, with few errors that do not get in the way of meaning. Seventy-six percent are not performing at the Proficient level, where they should be able to produce an effectively organized and fully developed response within the time allowed that includes analytical, evaluative, or creative thinking; details that support and develop the main idea of the piece; and use of precise language and variety in sentence structure to engage the audience (Persky, Daane, & Jin, 2003).

Because competition in the world marketplace is one of the driving forces behind our country's concern that our young people meet rigorous standards, including literacy, it is important also to look at their performance from an international perspective. When our 15-year-olds were compared to peers from other countries on the Programme for International Student Assessment (PISA), they performed at the international average in reading literacy. However, 18% of American students scored at the lowest level and did not progress beyond proficiency in the simplest of reading tasks (Organisation for Economic Co-Operation and Development [OECD], 2003).

Our adolescents with limited literacy proficiency, upon entering postsecondary education or the workforce, will continue to struggle unless something is done to improve their abilities. Although many would argue that postsecondary education is becoming increasingly important for career development (Perin, 2002), various studies have found that between 30 and 90% of students entering community college need remedial reading, writing, or mathematics courses, with approximately 41% actually enrolling in such courses (National Center for Educational Statistics, 1996; Perin, 2002; Roueche & Roueche, 1999). According to Saxon and Boylan (n.d.), academically underprepared students have represented a major population in American community colleges for decades. They also speculate that the number of students needing remediation will increase in the future, reasoning that because ethnic minority groups are the largest growing population in community colleges, and this population is already overrepresented in remedial programs, more of these students in community colleges will increase the need for remedial programs. More to the point, students of poverty, regardless of their ethnic background, will be underprepared to deal with the requirements of college, which include literacy (Lavin & Hyllegard, 1996; McCabe & Day, 1998).

CONSEQUENCES OF LITERACY FAILURE

When adolescents and young adults are not literacy-proficient, the short- and long-term consequences can be severe. For example, low achievement in literacy correlates with high rates of school dropout, poverty, and underemployment (Snow, Burns, & Griffin, 1998; Wagner, 2000). Literacy difficulties encountered by adolescents and young adults bode ill for their success in school, in the community, and in employment settings, among other arenas. School-related problems include academic failure and school dropout. Impact on the community may include poverty, diminished civic participation, and increased crime. In addition to unemployment and underemployment, other problems exist related to a poorly prepared workforce.

School-Related Problems

Students who cannot read and write face enormous challenges in the day-to-day participation in classroom activities. As students progress through the grades, more and more instruction relies on their ability to read and comprehend text, and to demonstrate their competence through written responses. The situation is even more problematic for the majority of students with LD, who are ill-prepared to succeed in school (Swanson & Deshler, 2003). Further, these students demonstrate a host of performance and adjustment problems, including higher rates of absenteeism, lower grade-point averages, higher course failure rates, more prevalent feelings of poor self-esteem (Wagner, Blackorby, & Hebbeler, 1993), and higher rates of inappropriate social behaviors (Schumaker, 1992) than the student population at large.

Students who struggle in school because of literacy problems are at risk for dropping out. Although myriad factors contribute to the dropout dilemma, included among them are low levels of literacy (Denti & Guerin, 1999; Hock & Deshler, 2003; Kaestle, Campbell, Finn, Johnson, & Mikulecky, 2001). Overall, a little over 10% of the 34.6 million 16- through 24-year-olds in the United States have dropped out of school (Kaufman, Alt, & Chapman, 2001). The rate is higher for students with LD. According to data from the National Longitudinal Transition Study (SRI International, 1993), 38% of students with disabilities who left school did so by dropping out, 30% enrolled in high school but did not finish, and 8% dropped out before entering high school.

Community Impact

According to the Laubach Literacy Action Group (2000), one out of five adults lacks the literacy skills needed to fulfill his or her potential. This lack limits these individuals' roles as parents and as members of their communities. Adult illiteracy has devastating personal costs, including fear, social isolation, and loss of self-esteem; affects family life; and reduces economic productivity. For example, 18- to 23-year-olds least proficient in the basic skills of reading and mathematics are more likely to be living in poverty and not enrolled in any type of schooling (U. S. Department of Labor, 1997; William T. Grant Foundation, 1989).

In the United States, civic participation requires sophisticated reading comprehension, expressive writing, oral language, and computational skills (Boylan, 1999). Without the necessary literacy skills and strategies, young Americans enter adulthood without the tools for participating in our democracy. Not only do they lose a vital part of the richness of being an American, but also America loses valuable human resources.

According to Hock and Deshler (2003), poor literacy skills may lead to a series of emotional difficulties that propel adolescents toward criminal behavior. They cite frustration, embarrassment, loss of self-esteem, a sense of hopelessness, and a longing for a "way out." The National Center on Education, Disability, and Juvenile Justice (2002) reports that whereas illiteracy and poor academic performance are not direct causes of delinquency, empirical studies consistently demonstrate a strong link between marginal literacy skills and the likelihood of involvement in the juvenile justice system. Whether one is inclined to suspect literacy problems as a causative factor or not, the fact remains that 85% of all incarcerated juveniles are marginally literate or illiterate and have experienced school failure and grade retention (Center on Crime, Communities, and Culture, 1997). Most incarcerated youth lag two or more years behind their age peers in basic academic skills, and have higher rates of grade retention, absenteeism, and suspension or expulsion, whereas higher levels of literacy are associated with lower rates of juvenile delinquency, rearrest, and recidivism (National Center on Education, Disability, and Juvenile Justice, 2002).

Employment Issues

Young adults leaving school without the needed literacy skills are not prepared to enter the workforce. In fact, the U. S. Department of Labor estimates that 43% of persons in today's workforce have not graduated from high school, and 60% of unemployed workers lack the basic skills necessary to be trained for high-tech jobs in today's economy (U. S. Department of Labor, 1997). Unfortunately, a substantial fraction of our nation's labor force displays quite limited proficiencies in the three areas of literacy assessed on the National Adult Literacy Survey (Sum, 1999): prose literacy, document literacy, and quantitative literacy. Data from the private sector confirm the impact of limited literacy on performance in the workforce; 55% of American companies expressed dissatisfaction with their workers' written communication skills (National Association of Manufacturers, 1997).

Further, our ability to compete in the world marketplace will diminish, if we cannot address the literacy needs of our youth.

According to the OECD (2003), countries with high-average performance in literacy are likely to have a considerable economic and social advantage. Another factor relates to losses in business and industry attributable to basic skill deficiencies in workers. Low productivity, errors, and accidents related to literacy deficiencies cost hundreds of millions of dollars annually (Center for Workplace Preparation, 2001).

THE NEED FOR INCREASED EFFORTS

Given the dire consequences of low levels of literacy for our society, it is logical to assume that American education is proceeding full tilt at addressing the literacy problems of adolescents and young adults. Unfortunately, that is not the case. "Over the last decade, researchers and policymakers have all but abandoned attention to secondary remediation to focus on preventing the need for it" (Peterson, Caverly, Nicholson, O'Neal, & Cusenbary, 2000, p. 1). At the service-delivery level in many high schools, the only intervention for struggling readers and writers is found in special education, with those not eligible for these services receiving no help. Poor achievement in reading, writing, and speaking is often ignored as students are taught in less than rigorous classes and passed from grade to grade (Hock & Deshler, 2003).

So far, our nation's attention has focused on literacy programs for preschool, elementary, and middle school grades. For example the Reading First Initiative, established as part of the No Child Left Behind Act of 2001 (2002), has provided nearly $5 billion in federal funding over several years to establish reading instruction programs for children in kindergarten through third grade. A corresponding commitment has been made to preschool children through the Early Reading First Initiative. No one would argue that young children must get off to a good start in reading and that effective programming early on will result in fewer problems for older students.

However, it is a serious mistake to assume that a good start is sufficient for producing confi-

dent readers. The ability to comprehend a variety of texts, to use sophisticated comprehension and study strategies, to read critically, and to develop a lifelong desire to read are not acquired entirely during the early years. A good start is critical, but not sufficient. (International Reading Association, 2001, p. 1)

The same claims can be made about the need for continued writing instruction, as the demands for more complex composition increase through the grades (Kellogg, 1994). So, from the perspective of normal growth and development, educators should routinely be prepared to address literacy proficiency with adolescents and young adults.

Further, despite early literacy efforts, there are bound to be some students, especially those with LD, for whom acquiring even the basic reading skills will continue to be problematic. Such students will require intervention in secondary schools and beyond. These students may need work in word recognition and fluency, as well as comprehension. Other students may have adequate word recognition and fluency but have specific problems in constructing meaning from text (Catts & Kamhi, 1999; Pressley, Duke, & Hilden, Chapter 23, this volume; Stothard & Hulme, 1992) and may need more explicit instruction in comprehension strategies to meet more complex text demands than is typically provided in secondary courses. In short, given the complex and demanding literacy needs for the future, adolescent literacy warrants serious and continuing attention (Moje, Young, Readence, & Moore, 2000).

The two equally important missions, then, for educators are (1) to help all students acquire the multimedia literacy they need to manipulate the complex information they encounter as they progress through the grades and (2) to provide added assistance to struggling students who do not read and write at levels commensurate with their peers or with the demands of their educational settings. These students are likely to include students with LD, students of poverty, and those for whom English is a second language. The focus of this chapter, as indicated, is on providing assistance to youth struggling with literacy.

KEY PRINCIPLES IN ASSISTING STRUGGLING STUDENTS

Considering the many myths surrounding literacy relative to older students, it may be helpful to acknowledge the attitudes, beliefs, and misinformation that have contributed to the current status, and to counter them with positive action principles. What follows are key principles that should be addressed in programming for struggling readers and writers. These principles dispel specific myths.

Learner and Setting Characteristics

• *Myth: The tacit assumption that instruction that works with young children will be equally effective for older students.*

Nobody who has been around adolescents and young adults would argue that they are just like younger children, only bigger! However, the assumption is often made that the approaches that work with young children should be used with older students. Although important ground has been broken in research on emergent literacy, it remains to be seen whether the instruction that appears appropriate for young emergent readers and writers is applicable to older students at beginning literacy levels.

Evidence does exist that a large number of students who have experienced traditional basic skills instruction, as defined by commercial basal reading programs, move into secondary schools many years behind their peers (Curtis, 2002). For example, in one of the first major studies on the skill status of adolescents, Deshler, Warner, Schumaker, and Alley (1983) studied about 300 students classified as having LD and 300 students classified as low-achieving, but without LD. Deshler et al. reported a clear trend in the achievement levels of these students from 7th to 12th grade. In reading, and writing, the average performance began at about the high third to fourth grade level for seventh graders and plateaued at about the fifth- to sixth-grade level for students in the upper grades. The students in the study who were low achieving and did not have LD received very little or no additional reading instruction, and the additional services beyond the regular curriculum provided to students with LD emphasized basic skills remediation.

Research has not been conducted to determine whether a continued adherence to a basic skills regimen could address these skill deficits. However, the work of Deshler and his colleagues (1983) suggests that covert efforts to weave traditional reading programs into the traditional secondary environment will be unsuccessful. On the one hand, current and ongoing problems in the status of adolescent literacy in secondary schools (see the NAEP and PISA data discussed previously) would indicate that, for the most part, progress and thinking about how to address this achievement gap has not changed over the past 20 years. On the other hand, Klenk and Kibby (2000) have called for abandonment of a remedial orientation to improve student reading performance and the adoption of a "mediational process" orientation in its place.

• *Key Principle: The uniqueness of learner and setting characteristics for adolescents and young adults should be acknowledged in designing appropriate assessment and instructional approaches.*

Learner Characteristics

Young adolescents in the middle school years, teenagers in high school, and young adults in postsecondary educational or employment settings have different characteristics and needs (Deshler & Putnam, 1996). The myriad background experiences, cultures, and values that drive their attitudes, beliefs, and learning behaviors must be considered for learning to take place. The fact that their priorities include the need for social interaction and establishing a personal identity (Peterson et al., 2000) also should factor into the literacy learning experiences provided. For example, a growing desire for independence can become an important building block for literacy learning partnerships between students and teachers. A partnership approach would prompt the design of different kinds of learning experiences than are typically provided, at least at the secondary level. Instead of providing intervention *to* students, educators would plan and implement intervention *with* students, engaging them actively in these processes.

Teenagers in this day and age face unprecedented challenges that often distract them from learning (Whitmire, 2000). For many older students who have family responsibilities or have to hold jobs, school may not be a priority. Students affected by the growing violence encountered in schools may approach school with a certain uneasiness for fear of bullying and intimidation tactics by certain groups or gangs. In general, students tend to be more worldly at earlier ages, owing largely to their exposure to information from a variety of sources, including the Internet. As they get older, they have little patience for "just because" learning tasks for which they see little application (Ehren, 2002a).

O'Connor and Bell (Chapter 22, this volume) point out that older students with reading disabilities who have struggled with reading for several years may have incorporated faulty strategies into their repertoire of reading. In addition, adolescents and young adults with long-standing problems in reading are likely to suffer Matthew Effects, as Stanovich (1986) noted. These "Matthew Effects," mean that "the rich get richer and the poor get poorer"; that is, good readers, armed with proficient skills and strategies, acquire an increasingly stronger language base with which to be even more successful readers, while poor readers suffer further negative consequences of not being able to process text. As a result, they may be missing the higher level knowledge and skills that are required for reading more complex material; for example, vocabulary knowledge, knowledge of more complex language structures, and background knowledge—all of which are foundational for later school success.

However, they also have strengths that can be utilized to build better skills. For example, older students are likely to have at least rudimentary knowledge of the academic structure of school tasks, literacy, and language. They also are likely to have better comprehension, especially of vocabulary words, than younger readers who read at similar levels (O'Connor & Bell, Chapter 22, this volume).

Considering these characteristics, programs to address our youth's literacy needs will have to be palatable to them, respectful of their age and experience, and viewed by them as relevant to their personal, social, academic, or vocational success. The huge gaps in their literacy skills and strategies, which widen with continued difficulties, will have to be addressed within the constraints of the increased demands on their time and increased complexity of learning situations. Educators would be well-advised to capture their attention, cast reading and writing as forms of communication to serve specific purposes, and provide clear messages about how specific skill work that may need to be done relates to their goals.

Setting Characteristics

Middle schools, high schools, and postsecondary institutions have unique features that warrant consideration. In general, though, as students move through secondary and postsecondary settings, important shifts occur in demands placed on them. Learning tasks become larger and more complex. Educators in these settings are more likely to focus on curriculum expectations than on problems of individuals, especially in this era of standards-based education and accountability. The expectation of adult behavior increases with a corresponding requirement for independent learning. Students should be encouraged to participate actively in decision making about their programs, which, for students with LD would mean contributing in a significant way to the development of their individualized education programs (IEPs). For others, it would mean setting and reaching goals outside of an IEP process. As students mature into independent adults, they will have to learn to take responsibility for their own literacy progress (Ehren, 2002a).

The physical and organizational structures of secondary and postsecondary schools are different from those of elementary school settings. They are often located on sprawling campuses characterized by a high activity level, in which many events occur simultaneously. Students have to change classes and travel to different parts of the campus quickly. Instruction is departmentalized, requiring students to interact with many different teachers with a variety of teaching routines and requirements (Ehren, 2002a).

The instructional demands of these settings further complicate learning. Success is related to a student's ability to acquire, manipulate, store, and use large amounts of information from sources that often do not take into consideration the learning inefficiencies evidenced by students with disabilities (Lenz, Bulgren, & Kissam, 1995). Beginning in high school, students are expected to gain information from textbooks that are often both poorly organized and written, on the average, at the 11th-grade reading level (Putnam, 1988). Students are also required to gain large amounts of information from classroom lectures that often lack explicit organization, appropriate instruction on prerequisite vocabulary, and sufficient repetition of key information (Lenz, Alley, & Schumaker, 1987).

Literacy programs need to fit within the organizational framework and standard operating principles of these settings. For example, the one-on-one tutorial approach, sometimes used in elementary schools during the school day, may be disruptive to the operation of a typical middle or high school, and may also be met with resistance from youth who would prefer not to be singled out. A setting-sensitive alternative might be a before- or after-school tutorial program.

Language and Literacy Development

• *Myth: Underlying language ability has little to do with literacy achievement for older students.*
It was not very long ago that reading was considered to be primarily a visual process. However, in the 1970s, as reading failure based on visual aspects failed to account for the types of problems students have with reading, the language-processing aspects received greater attention (Kavanaugh & Mattingly, 1972; Scarborough, 1998; Vellutino, 1977). However, because of the nature of their professional preparation, most

secondary and postsecondary educators are often not cognizant of the language basis of reading (and writing as well). It is more common for primary-grade teachers to understand the importance of oral language in the development of written language, but as students get older, the connection among the language processes of listening, speaking, reading, and writing frequently disappears from consideration by teachers.

A mistaken notion interfering with a comprehensive view of literacy needs with adolescents and young adults is that, by the time children enter school, they have developed the language base that will serve them for the rest of their lives. We now know that language ability continues to grow tremendously all through the school years, even into adulthood (McGhee-Bidlack, 1991; Nippold, 1995; Nippold, Schwarz, & Undlin, 1992; Nippold, Uhden, & Schwarz, 1997). This myth is probably related to a misunderstanding of the complexity of language itself. Educators typically expect students' vocabularies to expand over the years, but they do not always consider that syntactic, semantic, pragmatic, metalinguistic, and metacognitive areas continue to develop as well, and that it is this growth than enables students to develop the skills and strategies that are essential for them to be able to meet curriculum demands (Ehren, 2002a). A result of this view is that secondary educators do not typically conceptualize literacy failure as language-related.

Another misconception about language processes is that the development of listening, speaking, reading, and writing is linear; that is, children first learn to listen, then to speak, to read, and finally, to write. What we now realize is that all of the language processes are interrelated in the way they develop and in the way they are used by human beings (Berninger, 2000). Although, in a broad sense, typical children do develop a basic command of spoken language before they learn to read and write it, the development in many ways is reciprocal, especially as children get older; that is, the development of skills in one mode facilitates and enhances the development in the other modes (Cooper, Roth, Speece, & Schatschneider, 2002; Perfetti, Beck, Bell, &

Hughes, 1987; Roth, Speece, & Cooper, 2002; Stanovich, 1986; Stothard, Snowling, Bishop, Chipchase, & Kaplan, 1998; Swank & Larivee, 1998; Torgesen & Davis, 1996; Torgesen, Wagner, & Rashotte, 1994; Vellutino, Scanlon, Small, & Tanzman, 1991; Vellutino & Scanlon, 1991). For example, Curtis (2002) suggests that the language production involved in note taking and summarizing may assist students in making explicit connections that they might not otherwise have noticed.

• *Key Principle: The language underpinnings of listening, speaking, reading, and writing, and the interrelationships among these processes, are important factors in addressing literacy.*

As Snow et al. (1998) point out, language problems may play a causal role in reading disabilities and may also be a consequence of them. According to Catts and Kamhi (1999), "The fact that language deficits are both a cause and consequence of reading disabilities ensures that language problems will be a major component of almost all cases of reading disabilities" (p. 116). A causal relationship should not be surprising given the nature of reading as a language process. The same case can be made for writing (Berninger, 2000). That early language problems persist into adolescence and adulthood, albeit with changing symptomatology, has been well established (Aram & Nation, 1980; Bashir, 1989; Bashir & Scavuzzo, 1992; Stothard et al., 1998). These connections should alert educators to the need for addressing the language underpinnings of literacy with older students who are struggling.

The negative language consequences of reading disabilities also must be considered by educators. Poor readers do not read as much as good readers and have less opportunity to acquire linguistic knowledge from reading (Stanovich, 1986; Guthrie, Wigfield, Metsala, & Cox, 1999). So, with students with reading disabilities, it is reasonable to suspect that Matthew Effects, previously described, will create further language problems for them as they struggle with learning to read. For one thing, as they get older and continue to struggle with written language, they ultimately wind up with deficits in knowledge and use of higher level vocabulary, advanced grammar, and text-level structures (Cain & Oakhill, 1998; Stothard et al., 1998).

The reciprocal and multiple relationships among spoken- and written-language processes point to the need to integrate them in instruction. However, especially for those who struggle, it is often the case that reading goals are addressed in isolation, with other language processes minimized. Further, the language correlates of literacy problems, whether they be cause or consequence, beckon the active involvement of speech–language pathologists (SLPs) well-versed in language, in assessment, and intervention efforts (American Speech–Language–Hearing Association, 2001; Ehren, 1994, 2002a, 2002b). Unfortunately, it is not typical for SLPs to have a presence in secondary and postsecondary settings, a practice that needs to change (Ehren, 2002a, 2002b; Ehren & Lenz, 1989).

The Definition of Literacy

• *Myth: Basic skills in print reading should be the focal point of literacy efforts.*

In the previous section, the case has been made for integrating listening, speaking, reading, and writing in instruction given the reciprocity of these language processes. Although the major argument proffered there countered the myth that reading and writing are discrete processes, unrelated to core-language abilities, a related myth is that it is sufficient to address basic skills in reading (and print reading at that) and the rest will take care of itself. The result of this myth can be seen in remedial reading programs for adolescents and young adults that ignore reading beyond basic skills, students' difficulties with writing, and multimedia literacy.

• *Key Principle: The definitions that guide research and programming efforts should attend to skills and strategies that go beyond basics and include multiple literacies across language processes.*

The many definitions for literacy that are relevant for older populations typically assume multiple levels and kinds of literacy that bear on real-life situations and are sensitive to skills needed in school-based, as well as out-of-school contexts (Wagner, 2000). The major world conference held in Jomtien in 2000 (Mellor & Skilbeck, 2001) broadened the worldview of literacy, with discussions centered around basic learning competencies (BLCs) that focus not only on reading, writing and arithmetic, but also on knowledge, problem solving, and life skills. BLCs are meant to support independent functioning and coping with practical problems, or choices of adults as parents, workers, and/or citizens. The definitions of literacy that reflect this view refer both to formal, school-based skills and to the ability to manage functional tasks and demands (Wagner, 2000).

Consistent with this view, the National Literacy Act of 1991 (1992) defines "literacy" as "an individual's ability to read, write, and speak in English and compute and solve problems at levels of proficiency necessary to function on the job and in society, to achieve one's goals, and to develop one's knowledge and potential" (Section 3). The 1992 and 2003 National Assessments of Adult Literacy use the following definition of "literacy": "using printed and written information to function in society, to achieve one's goals, and to develop one's knowledge and potential" (Kirsch, Jungeblut, Jenkins, & Kolstad, 2002, p. 2). This definition would involve ability to locate and use information from texts that include editorials, news stories, poems, and fiction, as well as information contained in job applications, payroll forms, transportation schedules, maps, tables, and graphs.

Another dimension of moving beyond basic skills is the need to ensure that older students have the comprehension and composition skills and strategies they need to deal with complex learning demands in school. What is needed is what Langer (1999) terms "high literacy," which includes not only basic reading and writing skills but also the ability to use language, content, and reasoning in ways that are appropriate for particular situations and disciplines. In essence, high literacy involves students' abilities to engage in thoughtful reading, writing, and discussion about content in the classroom.

To promote high literacy, educators have

to think beyond the teaching of word-level skills to adolescents and young adults, who struggle with reading and writing, and include an emphasis on comprehension and composition. Given that many adolescents and young adults have difficulty making inferences even when they can decode fluently (Peterson et al., 2000), addressing word recognition alone will be insufficient to help such students acquire the high-literacy skills and strategies they need. Likewise, focus on vocabulary and spelling, although important, will not address the complex text-manipulation needs of older students.

A related factor is that well-structured, or considerate, text can help build fluency but does not help a struggling reader move beyond literal levels of understanding (McNamara & Kintsch, 1996; McNamara, Kintsch, Songer, & Nintsch, 1996; Peterson et al, 2000). Therefore, students need opportunities to engage with more complicated text, along with support in how to use background knowledge and text structure to determine relationships among ideas and draw conclusions (Peterson et al., 2000). They also need to be taught to manipulate the variety of texts that occur across disciplines. Although discipline-specific texts share some similarities, they can differ in substantive ways (Grossman & Stodolsky, 1995). In this regard, those who are low performing, will benefit from the teaching of reading and writing strategies to help them deal with demanding and varied texts (Graham, Harris, & Troia, 2000; Wong, 2000).

Further, as educators look to solving "reading" problems, they will be advised to consider a point that has been made previously: The language processes of listening, speaking, reading and writing are integrally and reciprocally related, and need to be addressed in relation to each other. In particular, with regard to written language, writing instruction and intervention need to be part and parcel of literacy efforts. It is inconsistent with current understanding of the development of written language processes to segregate reading instruction as if it were distinct from manipulation of language in the process of written expression.

Alvermann's (2001) exhortation to consider multimedia literacy also applies here.

She argues that our young people deal with an array of texts, including textbooks, digital texts, and hypertexts, and that young people find their own reasons for becoming literate that go beyond the reading of academic texts. Further, different texts and social contexts require different reading skills. Therefore, she makes a case for including multiple literacies in instruction that extend beyond formal school situations.

Instructional Practices

• *Myth: It is fruitless to spend time and money on adolescent and young adults, because they have passed the point at which instruction can make a real difference.*

It is likely that pessimism about what can be accomplished with older students is at the heart of limited efforts with adolescent and young adult literacy. In fact, it is not uncommon for secondary educators to say that adolescents have missed the boat, and to opine that literacy problems should have been taken care of in elementary schools. As discussed previously, early intervention is certainly an important component in prevention of later problems, but the likelihood that all adolescent literacy problems will be eliminated with such efforts is slim. Regardless of the reasons for the current state of affairs, educators cannot dismiss the large number of adolescents and young adults who cannot read and write well.

It is also possible that pessimism relates to a lack of awareness of what can and has been accomplished with older students in effective programs, or to a lack of success using the same methods used with younger students. Another factor may be that educators succumb to the temptation to give up with older students out of the frustration that both teachers and students encounter with widening gaps in performance. There are no quick fixes for the long-standing problems of adolescents and young adults, and the sustained and intensive efforts needed can surely be daunting for all concerned. However, it is unconscionable for educators to give up on a whole generation of young Americans, especially given that evidence exists that intervention with them can be effective.

• *Key Principle: Evidence-based prac-*

tices can and should be used in instructional programs, with an optimistic view that the literacy needs of adolescents and young adults can be met.

As Allen (1995) has suggested in the title of her book, *It's Never Too Late* to help adolescents become literate. A number of different attempts to do so have been successful. Explicit instruction for word recognition has been found to be effective with struggling secondary readers (Gaskins, Cuncelli, & Satlow, 1992; Lenz & Hughes, 1990; Lewkowicz, 1985; Meyer, 1982). In an analysis of research on adolescent reading, Curtis (2002) notes that significant improvements can result in adolescents' performance on standardized reading measures, with programs focusing on knowledge and application of symbol–sound relationships. As O'Connor and Bell (Chapter 22, this volume) observe, older students respond well to interventions in word recognition when they are of sufficient duration and intensity. In the research studies they reviewed, effective treatment frequently included structured teaching several times per week over many weeks, decoding of multisyllabic words, and practice reading words in connected text.

Research also demonstrates that reading fluency can be improved in secondary level struggling readers (Chall, 1996), with instruction that emphasizes reading practice with different kinds of texts (Snow et al., 1998). Vocabulary instruction improves adolescents' comprehension, with the following factors as key features of successful programs: students' active process of new word meanings, and application of new vocabulary knowledge (Curtis, 2002)

Importantly, higher order, strategic processing is responsive to instruction in adolescents, as noted by many researchers. We know that methods that encourage active construction of meaning from text enhance comprehension (Graesser, Millis, & Zwan, 1997). Successful reading comprehension involves using a variety of reading strategies before, during, and after the reading of a passage (Pearson & Fielding, 1991; Pressley, Symons, Snyder, & Cariglia-Bull, 1989). Some of these strategies include activating prior knowledge, predicting, paraphrasing, summarizing, self-questioning, visualizing, and using graphic organizers to organize and remember what is read. Other types of strategies enable readers to monitor their understanding of what they are reading, and to use multiple comprehension strategies as they are needed (Paris, Lipson, & Wixson, 1994).

Over the past 25 years, Deshler and colleagues, at the University of Kansas, Center for Research on Learning, have developed and validated a series of reading and writing strategies (e.g., Word Identification, Paraphrasing, Self-Questioning, Visual Imagery, Proficiency in Sentence Writing, Paragraph Writing, Theme Writing), among other types of learning strategies, specifically with struggling adolescents. These learning strategies, part of the Strategic Instruction Model (SIM), employ an eight-stage instruction model (Ellis, Deshler, Lenz, Schumaker, & Clark, 1991) and require intensive, explicit instruction (Fisher, Schumaker, & Deshler, 2002). These strategies have been empirically validated with small groups of students with LD and low-achieving students. Studies have demonstrated that adolescents and young adults can make significant gains in strategic reading and writing (Fisher et al., 2002; Lenz & Hughes, 1990; Scanlon, Deshler, & Schumaker, 1996; Schumaker & Deshler, 1992; Schumaker, Deshler, Alley, Warner, & Denton, 1982; Seybert, 1998; Wedel, Deshler, & Schumaker, 1988).

The principles employed in SIM are consistent with principles outlined by others as essential for teaching strategies to struggling students. Characteristics of strategic instruction include teaching students how, when, and why to use strategies; modeling; guided practice; independent practice in different texts and contexts; systematic feedback; and shifting responsibility for learning from the teacher to learner (Borkowski, Weyhing, & Carr, 1988; Dickson, Collins, Simmons, & Kameenui, 1998; Gersten, Fuchs, Williams, & Baker; 1999; Graham & Harris, 1989; Mastropieri & Scruggs, 1997; Peterson et al., 2000). Further, in the teaching of strategies, it is essential to attend specifically to generalization as part of the overall instructional approach, not as an afterthought at the end of instruction (Ellis, Lenz, & Sabornie, 1987a, 1987b).

The reciprocal teaching (RT) model has also been validated for use with adolescents. Students learn about specific cognitive strategies and how to self-regulate their use by generating questions as they read, predicting what will happen next, summarizing what has been read, and clarifying difficult material. An ongoing dialogue between students and teacher throughout the reading process involves joint construction of meaning and scaffolded instruction (Palinscar & Brown, 1984). RT significantly increased students' ability to use reading strategies and to attain higher scores on standardized comprehension measures.

Another approach that has been successful with a range of students, including adolescents, is Collaborative Strategic Reading (CSR; Vaughn, Klingner, & Bryant, 2001). In this approach, four reading comprehension strategies are taught to a class as a whole, with the teacher describing the strategy, modeling its use, role-playing the implementation of the strategy, and calling on students to demonstrate implementation of the strategy. The students then apply the strategy regularly with expository text. The four strategies are previewing and predicting (Preview), monitoring for understanding and vocabulary knowledge (Click and Clunk), finding the main idea (Get the Gist), and self-questioning and passage understanding (Wrap-Up).

Motivation

- *Myth: Little can be done for students who are not motivated to engage in literacy activities.*

Adolescents with literacy problems often lack the motivation, commitment, or belief that more instruction will make a difference in their performance. As a consequence, they expend little effort to improve their situation (Alvermann, 2001). This problem does not go unnoticed by secondary educators, who frequently bemoan the lack of motivation of struggling adolescents to read and write. From what we know about the importance of frequent encounters with print and other media, the reluctance on the part of students to read and write is a serious detriment to their developing literacy proficiency (Dickson et al., 1998). Guthrie and Davis (2003) point out, however, that the factors involved include not only personal attributes of the students but also instructional attributes and practices of teachers. As an example, McCombs and Barton (1998) found that school and classroom cultures can significantly support or undermine the development of positive literacy identities in adolescents. Cultures that have a positive impact are characterized by connections, interaction, and responsiveness, which lead to student engagement and reflection (Collins, 1991; Davidson & Koppenhaver, 1993; Krogness, 1995; Moore et al., 1999; Schunk & Zimmerman, 1997; Wilhelm, 1995).

• *Key Principle: Motivation is a variable to be addressed in research and program design.*

Motivation involves a complex set of issues. Many experts cast motivation as a metacognitive component, because they believe it may mediate students' use of and benefit from metacognitive knowledge and self-regulation processes (Borkowski, 1992; Johnston & Winograd, 1985). It may be the force that propels students to develop metacognitive knowledge and use it to control, or self-regulate, reading behavior. It is predicated on self-efficacy, the belief in one's own competence to perform specific reading tasks. Students have to believe that they are able to control or influence academic outcomes (Alvermann, 2001; Wigfield, Eccles, & Rodriquez, 1998). Included in self-efficacy are beliefs in the following: competence to perform specific reading tasks, ability to control or influence academic outcomes, the causes and extent of academic success and failure, and the benefits of using a strategy (Dickson et al., 1998). Students who do not attribute reading success and failure to use or nonuse of effective strategies may not be motivated to expend effort to use appropriate strategies. Of special concern are students with LD, who have different attributional patterns from those of average achievers. They are more likely to attribute success to external forces (such as good luck or an easy test) and failure to internal forces (such as not being smart enough), whereas average achievers

tend to attribute success to personal effort and failure to external causes (Borkowski et al., 1988). When students fail to learn, they lose their enthusiasm and develop negative self-perceptions and attitudes about reading (Paris & Oka, 1989). Anxiety and low self-efficacy perceptions can undermine students' use of metacognitive control processes and can inhibit their setting long-term goals (Miranda, Villaescusa, & Vidal-Abarca, 1997).

The complex nature of this problem makes it of paramount importance for educators to accept responsibility for working on the motivation component, rather than assuming that motivation is a prerequisite to literacy intervention over which they have little control. Teachers need to think about sustained, engaged reading as a teaching goal (Guthrie & Ozgungor, 2002). Although it is a challenge to engage the struggling reader, a number of instructional practices have demonstrated effectiveness (Meltzer, n.d.):

1. Classroom goals set by the teacher influence the students' goals (e.g., if learning is a primary aim of the teacher, the students will internalize that value).
2. Support for learner autonomy and control increases intrinsic motivation.
3. Teacher involvement can show students that the teacher knows them and knows what they need to learn.
4. Setting short-term goals and tasks increases self-efficacy and is crucial for low learners.
5. High effort fosters a sense of control and accomplishment (e.g., "I succeeded because I worked at it").
6. Making connections to students' lives makes engagement meaningful.

Shared Responsibility

• *Myth: Literacy is not the job of secondary and postsecondary educators.*

Perhaps the greatest challenge in improving literacy in older students is the lack of serious effort on the part of secondary and postsecondary educators to take on this mission. They do not typically see literacy as their role. Further, they are not usually prepared to teach listening, speaking, reading, and writing as part of their teacher education programs. Their priorities and expertise tend to lie with teaching their respective academic disciplines, and they often do not see the connection between subject-area achievement and the literacy access skills and strategies to promote content mastery. They often express the opinion that literacy should have been taught by elementary-level teachers.

• *Key Principle: All educators in secondary and postsecondary settings need to share responsibility for the literacy acquisition of all the learners in that setting, including typically developing students, students with LD, students of poverty, and students for whom English is a second language.*

Although there may be reasons for educators to be less than enthusiastic about accepting the responsibility to improve the literacy lot of adolescents and young adults, "all hands on deck" are needed to address the complex problems involved. Professionals and other stakeholders will have to join forces and share the responsibility for helping all students become literate. Although additional staff may be needed in some settings to provide the intervention required, increased resources in the form of resource personnel will not exonerate secondary and postsecondary classroom teachers who do not do their share. From what we know about the problems of transfer of learning with struggling students (Ellis et al., 1987a, 1987b), literacy gaps will not decrease without a collaborative effort at a site base.

To assist with this challenge, the University of Kansas Center for Research in Learning has developed a Content Literacy Continuum (Lenz & Ehren, 1999) to provide a framework for shared responsibility in secondary schools. The Content Literacy Continuum involves five levels of literacy support that should be in place in every secondary school. These five levels in this continuum emphasize that it is important to infuse literacy instruction throughout the secondary school curriculum, and that a host of secondary educators with different types of expertise will be required to address successfully the broad array of needs presented by adolescents. Additionally, be-

cause the problems of adolescents with literacy problems are so significant, intervention outside of the school day may be warranted. Hence, secondary schools should consider the important function that before- and after-school tutoring programs serve to support services across the Content Literacy Continuum.

Level 1: Ensuring Mastery of Critical Content in All Subject Area Classes

Adolescents with poor literacy skills typically have great difficulty understanding most of the curriculum taught by their subject-matter teachers during class; thus, they do not acquire the core knowledge expected. Background knowledge suffers, and the cycle of Matthew Effects continues to affect reading adversely. It is important that all subject matter teachers use teaching aids and devices that will help students better understand and remember the content they are teaching. The use of tools such as graphic organizers, prompted outlines, structured reviews, guided discussions, and other instructional tactics that modify and enhance the curriculum content in ways that promote its understanding and mastery have been shown to enhance performance greatly. These modifications represent a teacher's first response to meeting the needs of struggling readers and writers within content instruction. Although Level 1 interventions are designed to help those students with limited levels of literacy, they also must be designed in such a way that their use benefits *all* of the students in an academically diverse class.

An example of this is the use of a "unit organizer" to help students understand the potentially confusing and complex subject matter covered in a unit of instruction. This organizer displays the main topics, and the relationship of these topics to each other and to other units being studied in the course. By carefully configuring the unit organizer to display core concepts and important vocabulary, then having students regularly use this organizer for studying material from the unit, teachers improve outcomes of students with literacy problems on unit tests considerably (Lenz, 1994).

Level 2: Weaving Learning Strategies within Rigorous General Education Classes

When Level 1 interventions are insufficient to impact the performance of students with literacy problems in a classroom, teachers must consider instructional methods at the next point on the intervention continuum, Level 2. Here, teachers incorporate instruction on selected reading and writing strategies into their classes. On an ongoing basis, while teaching subject-matter material, teachers look for opportunities to point out to students particular strategies that help them manipulate the information being taught. It is not enough, however, for teachers merely to tell students about a strategy that would be helpful for them to use. It is important that they explain how to use the strategy, model its use, then require students to use the strategy in relation to their content assignments. In short, the purpose is to teach the students "how to learn" the subject-matter material. Teachers can incorporate into their subject-matter classes strategies for acquiring, remembering, and expressing course information.

By teaching students strategies that are directly relevant to the demands of their course, teachers are shifting the instructional emphasis, in part, from just learning course content to acquiring the underlying processes to enable students to independently understand and remember the content. An example of how a general education teacher might incorporate learning strategy instruction into ongoing class activities is as follows: At the beginning of an academic year, a history teacher might explain to the class that being able to read and paraphrase written historical information is important, because paraphrasing is required to write reports, answer questions, and discuss information in class. The teacher would then share the specific steps involved in paraphrasing content reading materials and model how actually to paraphrase historical information to complete different types of learning tasks. Class activities and assignments would, in turn, be structured to require students to paraphrase text and use the paraphrased information. The teacher would expect students to use the newly learned strategy in a host of naturally occur-

ring situations within the course, and would provide feedback on students' work.

Level 3: Supporting Mastery of Learning Strategies for Targeted Students

Some students who lack literacy have great difficulty mastering literacy strategies within the classroom, as presented in Level 2. The instructional conditions are not conducive to their learning (i.e., the large numbers of students, little time for individual feedback, limited opportunity to ask questions for clarification), Level 3 interventions may be necessary. In these interventions, students with literacy problems receive specialized, intensive instruction from someone other than the subject-matter teacher (e.g., a special education teacher, a study-skills teacher, a resource room teacher). Continuing with the example cited earlier for Level 2 interventions, if the history teacher notices that some student(s) in the class are struggling to master paraphrasing, support personnel (e.g., the special education teacher) would be asked to provide much more explicit, intensive, and systematic instruction in the strategy. An explicit instructional sequence would be followed to ensure student understanding of each step of the strategy, provide sufficient opportunities to practice in materials that are at the appropriate instructional reading levels, provide elaborated feedback after each practice attempt, and teach students to generalize the strategy to a broad array of learning tasks and materials. Such intensive instruction would be provided until the student gained the necessary confidence and mastered the strategy at a level of fluency.

Level 4: Developing Intensive Instructional Options for Students Who Lack Foundational Skills

In nearly every secondary school, there is a small group of students that cannot respond adequately to the intensive strategy instruction provided in Level 3 interventions. For these students, teachers need to consider interventions at Levels 4 and 5 on the continuum. Although the number of students who require interventions at these levels is relatively small in most school systems, educators need to be aware that these students exist and require a type of instruction that is often not available to them. Many of these students may have severe LD and specific, underlying language disorders in linguistic, metalinguistic, and metacognitive areas. They may also be English as a second language (ESL) learners, or students who have had prolonged histories of moving from one school to another. As a result, they may lack many of the foundational skills required for advanced literacy.

Students assigned to Level 4 interventions learn content literacy skills and strategies through specialized, direct, and intensive instruction in listening, speaking, reading, and writing. Reading specialists and special education teachers work together at this level to develop intensive and coordinated instructional experiences designed to address severe literacy deficits. For example, they may implement an intensive reading program for those students who are reading at the first-through third-grade levels. These professionals may also assist content teachers in making appropriate modifications in content instruction to accommodate severe literacy deficits.

Level 5: Developing Intensive Clinical Options for Language Intervention

In Level 5 interventions, students with underlying language disorders learn the linguistic, metalinguistic, and metacognitive underpinnings they need to acquire the necessary content skills and strategies. Generally, at this level, speech–language pathologists deliver small-group, curriculum-relevant language therapy (Ehren, 2002a) in collaboration with other support personnel teaching literacy. They assist content teachers in making appropriate modifications in content instruction to accommodate severe language disorders.

Before and After-School Supports

Adolescents with literacy problems often need additional support and opportunities to practice learning newly literacy skills and strategies. Before- and after-school tutoring programs can be an effective component to

an overall literacy program. When tutoring programs are designed to teach students specific strategies in how to learn, as well as content skills, student outcomes increase. An example of this is the research-based Strategic Tutoring program (Hock, Schumaker, & Deshler, 1995, 2001) that teaches adolescents core-literacy skills needed to complete school assignments, as well as the associated learning strategies that helps students learn independently and stay abreast of class assignments. In order to be effective, before- and after-school tutoring programs must be research-based and well organized, with the major goal being the improvement of students' overall literacy proficiency.

CONCLUSIONS

We have made the case that it is essential to our democracy that adolescents and young adults be prepared to meet the advanced literacy requirements their future will require, but that, by all indications, they lack the necessary levels of proficiency. This status places our youth at great risk for academic failure, school dropout, and a host of other problems, such as poverty, diminished civic participation, and criminal behavior. Further, as they enter the workforce poorly prepared, they are likely to experience unemployment and underemployment, among other problems.

Complicating the picture are prevailing myths that, if not dispelled, will thwart progress in addressing literacy successfully with these populations of struggling students. We suggest six key principles that dispel these myths and should be considered in addressing their literacy needs:

1. The uniqueness of learner and setting characteristics for adolescents and young adults should be acknowledged in designing appropriate assessment and instructional approaches.
2. The language underpinnings of listening, speaking, reading, and writing, and the interrelationships among these processes, are important factors in addressing literacy.

3. The definitions that guide research and programming efforts should attend to skills and strategies that go beyond basics and include multiple literacies across language processes.
4. Evidence-based practices can and should be used in instructional programs, with an optimistic view that the literacy needs of adolescents and young adults can be met.
5. Motivation is a variable to be addressed in research and program design.
6. All educators in secondary and postsecondary settings need to share responsibility for the literacy acquisition of all the learners in that setting, including typically developing students, students LD, students of poverty, and students for whom English is a second language.

In *Every Child a Graduate*, the Alliance for Excellent Education (2002) makes the case that now is the time to extend our national commitment to raising the literacy levels of America's children beyond the early grades. They call for an expansion of the Reading First program by adding an Adolescent Literacy initiative to its mission, including increased funding for diagnostic assessments, research-based curricula, release time for teachers to participate in professional development, and literacy specialists to train all teachers in Title I middle and high schools. Such an initiative would certainly provide a major impetus for improving the status of adolescent and young adult literacy. However, money is not the only capital needed. It is our hope that stakeholders will ponder the ideas presented and take appropriate action within their spheres of influence in ways that are currently feasible to them to alter the course of literacy proficiency for adolescents and young adults, especially those who struggle.

REFERENCES

Allen, J. (1995). *It's never too late: Leading adolescents to lifelong literacy.* Portsmouth, NH: Heinemann.

Alliance for Excellent Education. (2002). *Every child a graduate: A framework for an excellent education for all middle and high school students.* Washington, DC: Author.

American Speech–Language–Hearing Association. (2001). *Roles and responsibilities of speech–language pathologists with respect to reading and writing in children and adolescents (position statement and guidelines).* Rockville, MD: Author.

Alvermann, D. E. (2001). *Effective literacy instruction for adolescents.* Chicago: National Reading Conference.

Aram, D. M., & Nation, J. E. (1980). Preschool language disorders and subsequent language and academic difficulties. *Journal of Communication Disorders, 13,* 159–170.

Bashir, A. S. (1989). Language intervention and the curriculum. *Seminars in Speech and Language, 10*(3), 181–191.

Bashir, A. S., & Scavuzzo, A. (1992). Children with language disorders: Natural history and academic success. *Journal of Learning Disabilities, 25*(1), 53–65.

Berninger, V. (2000). Development of language by hand and its connections with language by ear, mouth and eye. *Topics in Language Disorders, 20*(4), 65–84.

Borkowski, J. G. (1992). Metacognitive theory: A framework for teaching literacy, writing, and math skills. *Journal of Learning Disabilities, 25*(4), 253–257.

Borkowski, J. G., Weyhing, T. M., & Carr, M. (1988). Effects of attributional retraining on strategy-based reading comprehension in learning-disabled students. *Journal of Educational Psychology, 80,* 46–53.

Boylan, H. R. (1999). Developmental education: Demographics, outcomes, and activities. *Journal of Developmental Education, 23*(2), 2–10.

Cain, K., & Oakhill, J. (1998). Comprehension skill and inference-making ability: Issues and causality. In C. Hulme & R. M. Joshi (Eds.), *Reading and spelling: Development and disorders* (pp. 329–342). London: Erlbaum.

Catts, H. W., & Kamhi, A. G. (1999). *Language and reading disabilities.* Boston: Allyn & Bacon.

Center for Workplace Preparation. (2001). *Effects of low literacy skills on business productivity.* Washington, DC: Author.

Center on Crime, Communities, and Culture. (1997). *Education as crime prevention* (Occasional Paper Series No. 2). New York: Author.

Chall, J. S. (1996). *Stages of reading development.* New York: McGraw-Hill.

Collins, C. (1991). Reading instruction that increases thinking abilities. *Journal of Reading, 34,* 510–516.

Cooper, D. H., Roth, F. P., Speece, D. L., & Schatschneider, C. (2002). The contribution of oral language skills to the development of phonological awareness. *Applied Psycholinguistics, 23,* 399–416.

Curtis, M. E. (May, 2002). *Adolescent reading: A synthesis of research.* The Partnership for Reading. Retrieved August 23, 2002, from *http://216.26.160.105/conf/nichd/synthesis.asp.*

Davidson, J., & Koppenhaver, D. (1993). *Adolescent*

literacy: What works and why (2nd ed.). New York: Garland.

Denti, L. G., & Guerin, G. (1999). Dropout prevention: A case for enhanced early literacy efforts. *Clearing House, 72*(4), 231–235.

Deshler, D. D., & Putman, M. L. (1996). Learning disabilities in adolescents: A perspective. In D. D. Deshler, E. S. Ellis & B. K. Lenz (Eds.) *Teaching adolescents with learning disabilities: Strategies and methods* (2nd ed., pp. 1–7). Denver, CO: Love.

Deshler, D. D., Warner, M., Schumaker, J., & Alley, G. (1983). The learning strategies intervention model: Key components and current status. In J. D. McKinney & L. Feagans (Eds.), *Current topics in learning disabilities* (Vol. 1, pp. 54–71). Norwood, NJ: Ablex.

Dickson, S. V., Collins, V. L., Simmons, D. C., & Kameenui, E. J. (1998). Metacognitive strategies: Research bases. In D. C. Simmons & E. J. Kameenui (Eds.), *What reading research tells us about children with diverse learning needs: Bases and basics* (pp. 295–360). Mahwah, NJ: Erlbaum.

Ehren, B. J. (1994). New directions for meeting the academic needs of adolescents with language learning disabilities. In G. P. Wallach & K. G. Butler (Eds.), *Language learning disabilities in school-age children and adolescents* (pp. 393–417). New York: Merrill.

Ehren, B. J. (2002a). Speech–language pathologists contributing significantly to the academic success of high school students: A vision for professional growth. *Topics in Language Disorders, 22*(2), 60–80.

Ehren, B. J. (April, 2002b). Getting in the adolescent literacy game. *ASHA Leader,* pp. 4–5, 10. Rockville, MD: American Speech–Language–Hearing Association.

Ehren, B. J., & Lenz, B. K. (1989). Adolescents with language disorders: Special considerations in providing academically relevant language intervention. *Seminars in Speech and Language, 10*(3), 192–294.

Ellis, E. S., Deshler, D. D., Lenz, B. K., Schumaker, J. B., & Clark, F. L. (1991). An instructional model for teaching learning strategies. *Focus on Exceptional Children, 23*(6), 1–24.

Ellis, E. S., Lenz, B. K., & Sabornie, E. J. (1987a). Generalization and adaptation of learning strategies to natural environment: Part 1. Critical agents. *Remedial and Special Education, 8*(1), 6–20.

Ellis, E. S., Lenz, B. K., & Sabornie, E. J. (1987b). Generalization and adaptation of learning strategies to natural environment: Part 2. Research into practice. *Remedial and Special Education, 8*(2), 6–23.

Fisher, J. B., Schumaker, J. B., & Deshler, D. D. (2002). Improving the reading comprehension of at risk adolescents. In C. C. Block & M. Pressley (Eds.), *Comprehension instruction: Research-based best practices* (pp. 351–364). New York: Guilford Press.

Gaskins, I., Cuncelli, E., & Satlow, E. (1992). Implementing an across-the-curriculum strategies program: Reaction to change. In J. Pressley, K. Harris,

& J. Guthrie (Eds.), *Promoting academic competence and literacy in school* (pp. 411–426). Boston: Academic Press.

Gersten, R., Fuchs, L. S., Williams, J. P., & Baker, S. (1999). *Reading comprehension instruction for students with learning disabilities: A research synthesis* (report). Washington, DC: U. S. Department of Education.

Graesser, A. C., Millis, K. K., & Zwan, R. A. (1997). Discourse comprehension. *Annual Review of Psychology, 48,* 163–189.

Graham, S., & Harris, K. R. (1989). Components analysis of cognitive strategy instruction: Effects on learning disabled students' compositions and self-efficacy. *Journal of Educational Psychology, 81,* 353–361.

Graham, S., Harris, K., & Troia, G. (2000). Self-regulated strategy development revisited: Teaching writing strategies to struggling writers. *Topics in Language Disorders, 20*(4), 1–14.

Grossman, P. L., & Stodolsky, S. S. (1995). Content as context: The role of school subjects in secondary school teaching. *Educational Researcher, 24*(8), 5–11.

Guthrie, J. T., & Davis, M. H. (2003). Motivating struggling readers in middle school through an engagement model of classroom practice. *Reading and Writing Quarterly, 19,* 59–85.

Guthrie, J. T., & Ozgungor, S. (2002). Instructional contexts for reading engagement. In C. C. Block & M. Pressley (Eds.), *Comprehension instruction: Research-based practices* (pp. 275–288). New York: Guilford Press.

Guthrie, J. T., Wigfield, A., Metsala, J. L., & Cox, K. E. (1999). Motivational and cognitive predictors of text comprehension and reading amount. *Scientific Studies of Reading, 3*(3), 231–256.

Grigg, W. S., Daane, M. C., Ying, J., & Campbell, J. R. (2003). *The nation's report card: Reading 2002.* Washington, DC: U.S. Department of Education, Institute of Education Sciences. National Center for Education Statistics.

Hock, M. F., & Deshler, D. D. (2003). Don't forget the adolescents. *Principal Leadership, 4*(30), 50–57.

Hock, M. F., Schumaker, J. B., & Deshler, D. D. (1995). Training strategic tutors to enhance learner independence. *Journal of Developmental Education, 19*(1), 18–26.

Hock, M. F., Schumaker, J. B., & Deshler, D. D. (2001). The case for strategic tutoring. *Educational Leadership, 58*(7), 50–52.

International Reading Association. (2001). *Supporting young adolescents' literacy learning: A joint position paper of the International Reading Association and National Middle School Association.* Newark, DE: Author.

Johnston, P. H., & Winograd, P. N. (1985). Passive failure in reading. *Journal of Reading Behavior, 17*(4), 279–301.

Kaestle, C. F., Campbell, A., Finn, J. D., Johnson, S. T., & Mikulecky, L. H. (2001). *Adult literacy and education in America: Four studies based on the Na-*

tional Adult Literacy Survey. Washington, DC: U.S. Department of Education, National Center for Education Statistics.

Kaufman, P., Alt, M. N., & Chapman, C. (2001). *Dropout rates in the United States: 2000.* Washington, DC: U.S. Department of Education, National Center for Education Statistics.

Kavanaugh, J. F., & Mattingly, I. G. (Eds.). (1972). *Language by ear and eye: The relationships between speech and reading.* Cambridge, MA: MIT Press.

Kellogg, R. (1994). *The psychology of writing.* New York: Oxford University Press.

Kirsch, I. S., Jungeblut, A., Jenkins, L., & Kolstad, A. (2002). *Adult literacy in America: A first look at the findings of the National Adult Literacy Survey* (3rd ed.). Washington, DC: U.S. Department of Education, National Center for Education Statistics.

Klenk, L., & Kibby, M. W. (2000). Re-mediating reading difficulties: Appraising the past, reconciling the present, constructing the future. In M. L. Kamil, P. B. Mosenthal, P. D. Pearson, & R. Barr (Eds.), *Handbook of reading research* (Vol. 3, pp. 667–690). Mahwah, NJ: Erlbaum.

Krogness, M. M. (1995). *Just teach me, Mrs. K.: Talking, reading, and writing with resistant adolescent learners.* Portsmouth, NH: Heinemann.

Langer, J. A. (1999). *Beating the odds: Teaching middle and high school students to read and write well* (Research Report No. 12014). Albany: National Research Center on English Learning and Achievement, State University of New York.

Laubach Literacy Action Group. (2000). [untitled pamphlet]. Syracuse, NY: Laubach Literacy International.

Lavin, D., & Hyllegard, D. (1996). *Changing the odds: Open admissions and the life changes of the disadvantaged.* New Haven, CT: Yale University Press.

Lenz, B. K. (with Bulgren, J. A., Schumaker, J. B., Deshler, D. D., & Boudah, D. J.) (1994). *The unit organizer routine.* Lawrence, KS: Edge Enterprises.

Lenz, B. K., Alley, G. R., & Schumaker, J. B. (1987). Activating the inactive learner: Advance organizers in the secondary content classroom. *Learning Disability Quarterly, 10*(1), 53–67.

Lenz, K. B., Bulgren, J., & Kissam, B. (1995). *Pedagogies for academic diversity in secondary schools: Smarter planning* (Monograph). Lawrence: University of Kansas, Center for Research on Learning.

Lenz, B. K., & Ehren, B. J. (1999). Strategic content literacy initiative: Focusing on reading in secondary schools. *Stratenotes, 8*(1), 1–6.

Lenz, B. K., & Hughes, C. A. (1990). A word identification strategy for adolescents with learning disabilities. *Journal of Learning Disabilities, 23*(3), 149–158, 163.

Lewkowicz, N. K. (1985). Attacking longer words: Don't begin at the beginning. *Journal of Reading, 29*(3), 226–237.

Mastropieri, M. A., & Scruggs, T. E. (1997). Best practices in promoting reading comprehension in students with learning disabilities: 1976 to 1996. *Remedial and Special Education, 18*(4), 197–213.

McCabe, R. H., & Day, P. R., Jr. (Eds.). (1998). *Developmental education: A twenty-first century social and economic imperative.* Mission Viejo, CA: League for Innovation in the Community College, The College Board.

McCombs, B. L., & Barton, M. L. (1998). Motivating secondary school students to read their textbooks. *NASSP Bulletin, 82*(6), 24–33.

McGhee-Bidlack, B. (1991). The development of noun definitions: A metalinguistic analysis. *Journal of Child Language, 18*, 417–434.

McNamara, D. S., Kintsch, E., Songer, N. B., & Kintsch, W. (1996). Are good texts always better?: Interactions of text coherence, background knowledge, and levels of understanding in learning from text. *Cognition and Instruction, 14*(1), 1–43.

McNamara, D. S., & Kintsch, W. (1996). Learning from texts: Effects of prior knowledge and text coherence. *Discourse Processes, 22*(3), 247–288.

Mellor, W., & Skilbeck, M. (2001). *Education for All 2000 assessment: Global synthesis.* Paris, France: United Nations Educational, Scientific and Cultural Organization.

Meltzer, J. (n.d.). *Adolescent literacy resources: Linking research and practice.* Providence, RI: Education Alliance at Brown University.

Meyer, L. A. (1982). The relative effects of word-analysis and word-study correction procedures with poor readers during word attack training. *Reading Research Quarterly, 17*(4), 544–555.

Miranda, A., Villaescusa, M. I., & Vidal-Abarca, E. (1997). Is attribution retraining necessary?: Use of self-regulation procedures for enhancing the reading comprehension strategies of children with learning disabilities. *Journal of Learning Disabilities, 30*(5), 503–512.

Moje, E. B., Young, J. P., Readence, J. E., & Moore, D. W. (2000). Reinventing adolescent literacy for new times: Perennial and millennial issues. *Journal of Adolescent and Adult Literacy, 43*(5), 400–410.

Moore, D. W., Bean, T. W., Birdyshaw, D., & Rycik, J. A. (1999). *Adolescent literacy: A position statement for the Commission on Adolescent Literacy of the International Reading Association.* Newark, DE: International Reading Association.

National Association of Manufacturers. (1997). *The skilled workforce shortage: A growing challenge to the future competitiveness of American manufacturing.* Washington, DC: Author.

National Center on Education, Disability, and Juvenile Justice. (2002). *Juvenile correctional education programs: The case for quality education in juvenile correctional facilities.* Retrieved on June 1, 2003, from *http://www.edjj.org/education*

National Center for Educational Statistics. (1996). *Remedial education at higher education institutions in fall 1995* (Report No. NCES 97-584). Washington, DC: Author.

National Literacy Act of 1991, Pub. L. No. 102-73, 20 USC 1211 (1992).

Nippold, M. A. (1995). Language norms in school-age

children and adolescents: An introduction. *Language, Speech, and Hearing Services in Schools, 26*(4), 307–308.

Nippold, M. A., Schwarz, I. E., & Undlin, R. A. (1992). Use and understanding of adverbial conjuncts: A developmental study of adolescents and young adults. *Journal of Speech and Hearing Research, 35*, 108–118.

Nippold, M. A., Uhden, L. D., & Schwarz, I. E. (1997). Proverb explanation through the lifespan: A developmental study of adolescents and adults. *Journal of Speech, Language and Hearing Research, 40*, 245–253.

No Child Left Behind Act of 2001, Pub. L. No. 107-110, 20 USC 6301 (2002).

Organization for Economic Co-Operation and Development. (2003). *Literacy skills for the world of tomorrow—further results from PISA 2000*. Paris, France: Author.

Palincsar, A. S., & Brown, A. L. (1984). Reciprocal teaching of comprehension-fostering and comprehension-monitoring activities. *Cognition and Instruction, 2*, 117–175.

Paris, S., Lipson, M., & Wixson, K. (1994). Becoming a strategic reader. In R B. Ruddell, M. R. Ruddell, & H. Singer (Eds.), *Theoretical models and processes of reading* (pp. 788–810). Newark, DE: International Reading Association.

Paris, S., & Oka, E. (1989). Strategies for comprehending text and coping with reading difficulties. *Learning Disability Quarterly, 12*, 32–42.

Pearson, P. D., & Fielding, L. (1991). Comprehension instruction. In R. Barr, M. L. Kamil, P. B. Mosenthal, & P. D. Pearson (Eds.), *Handbook of reading research* (Vol. 2, pp. 951–983). White Plains, NY: Longman.

Perfetti, C. A., Beck, I., Bell, L., & Hughes, C. (1987). Phonemic knowledge and learning to read are reciprocal: A longitudinal study. *Merrill–Palmer Quarterly, 33*, 283–319.

Perin, D. (2002). *Literacy education after high school* (ERIC Document No. ED467689). New York: ERIC Clearinghouse on Urban Education.

Persky, H. R., Daane, M. C., & Jin, Y. (2003). *The nation's report card: Writing 2002*. Washington, DC: U.S. Department of Education, Institute of Education Sciences. National Center for Education Statistics.

Peterson, C. L., Caverly, D. C., Nicholson, S. A., O'Neal, S., & Cusenbary, S. (2000). *Building reading proficiency at the secondary level: A guide to resources*. Austin, TX: Southwest Educational Development Laboratory.

Pressley, M., Symons, S., Snyder, B. L., & Cariglia-Bull, T. (1989). Strategy instruction research comes of age. *Learning Disabilities Quarterly, 86*, 360–406.

Putnam, M. L. (1988). *An investigation of the curricular demands in secondary mainstream classrooms containing students with mild handicaps*. Unpublished dissertation, University of Kansas, Lawrence.

Roth, F. P., Speece, D. L., & Cooper, D. H. (2002). A longitudinal analysis of the connection between oral language and early reading. *Journal of Educational Research, 95*, 259–272.

Roueche, J. E., & Roueche, S. D. (1999). *High stakes, high performance: Making remedial education work*. Washington, DC: Community College Press.

Saxon, D. P., & Boylan, H. R. (n.d.). *Characteristics of community college remedial students*. Retrieved on August 5, 2003, from *http://www.ced.appstate.edu/centers/ncde/reserve_reading/student_characteristics.htm*

Scanlon, D., Deshler, D. D., & Schumaker, J. B. (1996). Can a strategy be taught and learned in secondary inclusive classrooms? *Learning Disabilities Research and Practice, 11*, 41–57.

Scarborough, H. S. (1998). Early identification of children at risk for reading disabilities: Phonological awareness and some other predictors. In B. K. Shapiro, P. J. Accord, & A. J. Capute (Eds.), *Specific reading disability: A view of the spectrum* (pp. 75–119). Baltimore: York Press.

Schumaker, J. B. (1992). Social performance of individuals with learning disabilities. *School Psychology Review, 21*(3), 387–399.

Schumaker, J. B., & Deshler, D. D. (1992). Validation of learning strategy learning interventions for students with learning disabilities: Results of a programmatic research effort. In B. Y. L. Wong (Ed.), *Contemporary research with students with learning disabilities: An international perspective* (pp. 22–46). New York: Springer-Verlag.

Schumaker, J. B., Deshler, D. D., Alley, G. R., Warner, M. M., & Denton, P. H. (1982). Multipass: A learning strategy for improving reading comprehension. *Learning Disability Quarterly, 5*(3), 295–304.

Schunk D. H., & Zimmerman, B. J. (1997). Developing self-efficacious readers and writers: The role of social and self-regulatory processes. In J. T. Guthrie & A. Wigfield (Eds.), *Reading for engagement: Motivating readers through integrated instruction* (pp. 34–50). Newark, DE: International Reading Association.

Seybert L. (1998). *The development and evaluation of a model of intensive reading strategies instruction for teachers in inclusive, secondary classrooms*. Unpublished dissertation, University of Kansas, Lawrence.

Snow, C. E., Burns, M. S., & Griffin, P. (1998). *Preventing reading difficulties in young children*. Washington, DC: National Research Council.

SRI International. (1993). *National Longitudinal Transition Study for Special Education Students*. Menlo Park, CA: Author.

Stanovich, K. E. (1986). Matthew Effects in reading: Some consequences of individual differences in the acquisition of literacy. *Reading Research Quarterly, 21*(4), 360–364

Stothard, S., & Hulme, C. (1992). Reading comprehension difficulties in children: The role of language comprehension and working memory skills. *Reading and Writing: An Interdisciplinary Journal, 4*, 245–256.

Stothard, S. E., Snowling, M. J., Bishop, D. V. M., Chipchase, B. B., & Kaplan, C. A. (1998). Language-impaired preschoolers: A follow-up into adolescence. *Journal of Speech, Language, and Hearing Research, 41,* 407–418.

Sum, A. (1999). *Literacy in the labor force: Results from the National Adult Literacy Survey.* Washington, DC: U.S. Department of Education, National Center for Education Statistics

Swank, L. K., & Larivee, L. S. (1998). Phonology, metaphonology, and the development of literacy. In R. Paul (Ed.), *Exploring the speech–language connection.* Baltimore: Brookes.

Swanson, H. L., & Deshler, D. D. (2003). Instructing adolescents with learning disabilities: Converting a meta-analysis to practice. *Journal of Learning Disabilities, 36*(2), 124–135.

Torgesen, J. K., & Davis, C. (1996). Individual difference variables that predict response to training in phonological awareness. *Journal of Experimental Child Psychology, 63,* 1–12.

Torgesen, J. K., Wagner, R. K., & Rashotte, C. A. (1994). Longitudinal studies of phonological processing and reading. *Journal of Learning Disabilities, 27,* 276–286.

U.S. Department of Labor. (1997). *Profile of the working poor.* Washington, DC: U.S. Bureau of Justice Statistics.

Vaughn, S., Klingner, J. K., & Bryant, D. P. (2001). Collaborative strategic reading as a means to enhance peer-mediated instruction for reading comprehension and content area learning. *Remedial and Special Education, 22*(2), 66–74.

Vellutino, F. R. (1977). Alternative conceptualizations of dyslexia: Evidence in support of a verbal deficit hypothesis. *Harvard Educational Review, 47*(3), 334–354.

Vellutino, F. R., & Scanlon, D. M. (1991). The preeminence of phonologically based skills in learning to read. In S. A. Brady & D. P. Shankweiler (Eds.), *Phonological processes in literacy: A tribute to Isabelle Y. Liberman* (pp. 237–252). Hillsdale, NJ: Erlbaum.

Vellutino, F. R., Scanlon, D. M., Small, S., & Tanzman, M. S. (1991). The linguistic bases of reading ability: Converting written to oral language. *Text, 11,* 99–133.

Wagner, D. A. (2000). *EFA 2000 thematic study on literacy and adult education: For presentation at the World Education Forum, Dakar.* Philadelphia: International Literacy Institute.

Wagner, M., Blackorby, J., & Hebbeler, K. (1993). *Beyond the report card: The multiple dimensions of secondary school performance of students with disabilities.* A report from the National Longitudinal Study of Special Education Students. Menlo Park, CA: Stanford Research Institute International.

Wedel, M., Deshler, D. D., & Schumaker, J. B. (1988). *The effects of teaching at-risk students a vocabulary learning strategy in the general education classroom* (Research Report No. 73). Lawrence: University of Kansas, Center for Research on Learning.

Whitmire, K. A. (2000). Adolescence as a developmental phase: A tutorial. *Topics in Language Disorders, 20*(2), 1–14.

William T. Grant Foundation. (1989). *The forgotten half: Non-college youth in America.* Washington, DC: Author.

Wigfield, A., Eccles, J. S., & Rodriguez, D. (1998). The development of children's motivation in schools contexts. *Review of Research in Education, 23,* 73–118.

Wilhelm, J. D. (1995). *"You gotta BE the book": Teaching engaged and reflective reading with adolescents.* New York: Teachers College Press.

Wong, B. Y. L. (2000). Writing strategies for instruction for expository essays for adolescents with and without learning disabilities. *Topics in Language Disorders, 20,* 29–44.

Author Index

Subject Index

f indicates a figure; n, a note; t, a table.